State Rankings 2016

A Statistical View of America

Editors

**Kathleen O'Leary Morgan
and
Scott Morgan**

For information:

CQ Press
An Imprint of SAGE Publications, Inc.
2455 Teller Road
Thousand Oaks, California 91320
E-mail: order@sagepub.com

SAGE Publications Ltd.
1 Oliver's Yard
55 City Road
London, EC1Y 1SP
United Kingdom

SAGE Publications India Pvt. Ltd.
B 1/I 1 Mohan Cooperative Industrial Area
Mathura Road, New Delhi 110 044
India

SAGE Publications Asia-Pacific Pte. Ltd.
3 Church Street
#10-04 Samsung Hub
Singapore 049483

Acquisitions Editor: Andrew Boney
Assistant Editor: Diana Aleman
Production Editor: Tracy Buyan
Cover Designer: Michael Dubowe
Marketing Manager: Carmel Schrire

Copyright © 2016 by CQ Press, an imprint of SAGE. CQ Press is a registered trademark of Congressional Quarterly Inc.

All rights reserved. No part of this book may be reproduced or utilized in any form or by any means, electronic or mechanical, including photocopying, recording, or by any information storage and retrieval system, without permission in writing from the publisher.

Printed in the United States of America.

ISBN 978-1-5063-3371-7 (cloth)
ISBN 978-1-5063-3370-0 (paper)
ISSN 1057-3623

16 17 18 19 20 10 9 8 7 6 5 4 3 2 1

Contents

Detailed Table of Contents	vi
Introduction and Methodology	xiv
About the Editors	xv
The 2016 State Rankings	xvi
Date Each State Admitted to Statehood	xvii
State Fast Facts	xviii

Subject Rankings

Agriculture	1
Crime and Law Enforcement	27
Defense	67
Economy	83
Education	115
Employment and Labor	167
Energy and Environment	209
Geography	239
Government Finances: Federal	257
Government Finances: State and Local	293
Health	375
Households and Housing	419
Population	449
Social Welfare	517
Transportation	557

Sources	597
Index	600

Detailed Table of Contents

I. AGRICULTURE
Number of Farms in 2014 3
Land in Farms in 2014 4
Average Number of Acres per Farm in 2014 5
Average per-Acre Value of Farmland in 2015 6
Percent Change in Average per-Acre Value of Farmland:
    2014 to 2015 7
Net Farm Income in 2014 8
Net Farm Income per Operation in 2014 9
Net Farm Income per Acre in 2014 10
Farm Income: Cash Receipts from Commodities in 2014 .. 11
Farm Income: Crops in 2014 12
Farm Income: Livestock in 2014 13
Farm Income: Government Payments in 2014 14
Acres Planted in 2015 15
Acres Harvested in 2015 16
Acres Harvested: Corn in 2015 17
Acres Harvested: Soybeans in 2015 18
Acres Harvested: Wheat in 2015 19
Cattle on Farms in 2016 20
Milk Cows on Farms in 2014 21
Milk Production in 2014 22
Milk Production per Milk Cow in 2014 23
Hogs and Pigs on Farms in 2015 24
Chickens in 2014 25
Eggs Produced in 2014 26

II. CRIME AND LAW ENFORCEMENT
Crimes in 2014 29
Crime Rate in 2014 30
Percent Change in Crime Rate: 2013 to 2014 31
Violent Crimes in 2014 32
Violent Crime Rate in 2014 33
Percent Change in Violent Crime Rate: 2013 to 2014 34
Murders in 2014 35
Murder Rate in 2014 36
Percent of Murders Involving Firearms in 2014 37
Rapes in 2014 38
Rape Rate in 2014 39
Rapes (Revised Definition) in 2014 40
Rape Rate (Revised Definition) in 2014 41
Robberies in 2014 42
Robbery Rate in 2014 43
Aggravated Assaults in 2014 44
Aggravated Assault Rate in 2014 45
Property Crimes in 2014 46
Property Crime Rate in 2014 47
Percent Change in Property Crime Rate: 2013 to 2014 ... 48
Burglaries in 2014 49
Burglary Rate in 2014 50
Larceny-Thefts in 2014 51
Larceny-Theft Rate in 2014 52
Motor Vehicle Thefts in 2014 53
Motor Vehicle Theft Rate in 2014 54
Rate of Consumer Fraud Complaints in 2014 55
Rate of Identity Theft Complaints in 2014 56
Reported Arrest Rate in 2014 57
Reported Juvenile Arrest Rate in 2014 58
Prisoners in State Correctional Institutions: Year End
    2014 59
State Prisoner Imprisonment Rate in 2014 60
Percent Change in Number of State Prisoners: 2013 to
    2014 61
Prisoners under Sentence of Death in 2013 62
Rate of State and Local Police Officers in 2014 63
Per Capita State and Local Government Expenditures for
    Police Protection in 2013 64
Per Capita State and Local Government Expenditures for
    Corrections in 2013 65
Per Capita State and Local Government Expenditures for
    Judicial and Legal Services in 2013 66

III. DEFENSE
Homeland Security Grants in 2015 69
Per Capita Homeland Security Grants in 2015 70
U.S. Department of Defense Expenditures in 2013 71
Per Capita U.S. Department of Defense Expenditures in
    2013 72
U.S. Department of Defense Procurement Contract
    Awards in 2013 73
Per Capita U.S. Department of Defense Procurement
    Contract Awards in 2013 74

U.S. Department of Defense Grants in 2013 75
Per Capita U.S. Department of Defense Grants in 2013.... 76
U.S. Active Duty Military Personnel Stationed in the
    United States in 2014............................ 77
U.S. Selected Reserve Personnel Stationed in the
    United States in 2014............................ 78
Veterans in 2014 79
Percent of Adult Population Who Are Veterans in 2014.... 80
U.S. Military Fatalities in Iraq and Afghanistan as of
    February 1, 2016 81
Rate of U.S. Military Fatalities in Iraq and Afghanistan
    as of February 1, 2016 82

IV. ECONOMY

Gross Domestic Product in 2014 85
Percent Change in Gross Domestic Product: 2010 to 2014
    (Adjusted to Constant 2009 Dollars) 86
Average Annual Change in Gross Domestic Product:
    2010 to 2014 (Adjusted to Constant 2009 Dollars) 87
Per Capita Gross Domestic Product in 2014............. 88
Percent Change in Per Capita Gross Domestic Product:
    2010 to 2014 (Adjusted to Constant 2009 Dollars) 89
State Exports in 2014 90
Per Capita State Exports in 2014 91
State Imports in 2014 92
Per Capita State Imports in 2014 93
Personal Income in 2014............................. 94
Change in Personal Income: 2013 to 2014.............. 95
Per Capita Personal Income in 2014................... 96
Change in Per Capita Personal Income: 2013 to 2014 97
Disposable Personal Income in 2014 98
Per Capita Disposable Personal Income in 2014 99
Median Household Income in 2014 100
Regional Price Parities in 2013...................... 101
Real Personal Income in 2013 102
Percent Change in Real Personal Income: 2012 to 2013 .. 103
Per Capita Real Personal Income in 2013.............. 104
Percent Change in Per Capita Real Personal Income:
    2012 to 2013.................................. 105
Personal Consumption Expenditures in 2014........... 106
Per Capita Personal Consumption Expenditures in
    2014 107
Percent Change in Personal Consumption Expenditures:
    2013 to 2014................................... 108
Percent Change in Per Capita Personal Consumption
    Expenditures: 2013 to 2014 109
Bankruptcy Filings in 2015.......................... 110
Personal Bankruptcy Rate in 2015 111
Percent Change in Personal Bankruptcy Rate: 2014 to
    2015 112
2016 State Business Tax Climate Index 113
Fortune 500 Companies in 2015..................... 114

V. EDUCATION

Estimated Percent of School-Age Population in Public
    Schools in 2014 117
Regular Public Elementary and Secondary School
    Districts in 2013................................ 118
Private Elementary and Secondary Schools in 2012 119

Private Elementary and Secondary School Enrollment
    in 2012 120
Public Elementary and Secondary Schools in 2014 121
Enrollment in Public Elementary and Secondary Schools
    in 2014 122
Public Elementary and Secondary School Teachers
    in 2014 123
Pupil-Teacher Ratio in Public Elementary and Secondary
    Schools in 2014 124
Estimated Average Salary of Public School Teachers
    in 2015 (National Education Association) 125
Average Teacher's Salary as a Percent of Average
    Annual Pay in 2014 126
Percent of Public School Fourth Graders Proficient or
    Better in Reading in 2015 127
Percent of Public School Eighth Graders Proficient or
    Better in Reading in 2015 128
Percent of Public School Fourth Graders Proficient or
    Better in Mathematics in 2015.................... 129
Percent of Public School Eighth Graders Proficient or
    Better in Mathematics in 2015.................... 130
Percent of Population Graduated from High School
    in 2014 131
Public High School Graduates in 2013................. 132
Adjusted Cohort Graduation Rate for Public High
    Schools in 2013 133
Public High School Dropout Rate in 2012 134
ACT Average Composite Score in 2015................ 135
Education Expenditures by State and Local Governments
    in 2013 136
Per Capita State and Local Government Expenditures for
    Education in 2013 137
Expenditures for Education as a Percent of All State and
    Local Government Expenditures in 2013 138
State and Local Government Expenditures for Elementary
    and Secondary Education in 2013 139
Per Capita State and Local Government Expenditures for
    Elementary and Secondary Education in 2013 140
Expenditures for Elementary and Secondary Education
    as a Percent of All State and Local Government
    Expenditures in 2013 141
Estimated Per Pupil Public Elementary and Secondary
    School Current Expenditures in 2015 142
Higher Education Expenditures by State and Local
    Governments in 2013........................... 143
Per Capita State and Local Government Expenditures for
    Higher Education in 2013 144
Expenditures for Higher Education as a Percent of All
    State and Local Government Expenditures in 2013.... 145
Average Faculty Salary at Institutions of Higher
    Education in 2014 146
Average Student Costs at Public Institutions of Higher
    Education in 2014 147
Average Student Costs at Private Institutions of Higher
    Education in 2014 148
Average College Graduate Debt: Class of 2014 149
Percent of College Graduates with Debt: Class of 2014... 150
Institutions of Higher Education in 2014 151
Enrollment in Institutions of Higher Education in 2013... 152

Enrollment Rate in Institutions of Higher Education
in 2013 153
Enrollment in Public Institutions of Higher Education
in 2013 154
Enrollment in Private Institutions of Higher Education
in 2013 155
Percent of Population with a Bachelor's Degree or More
in 2014 156
Percent of Population Who Have Completed an Advanced
Degree in 2014............................. 157
Public Libraries and Branches in 2012................ 158
Rate of Public Libraries and Branches in 2012 159
Rate of Books in Public Libraries in 2012 160
Rate of Electronic Books in Public Libraries in 2012 161
Internet Terminals in Public Libraries in 2012 162
Rate of Internet Terminals in Public Libraries in 2012.... 163
Per Capita State Art Agencies' Legislative Appropriations
in 2016 164
Federal Allocations for Head Start Program in 2014 165
Head Start Program Enrollment in 2014............... 166

VI. EMPLOYMENT AND LABOR

Average Annual Pay in 2014......................... 169
Percent Change in Average Annual Pay: 2013 to 2014 ... 170
Median Earnings of Male Full-Time Workers in 2014.... 171
Median Earnings of Female Full-Time Workers in 2014 .. 172
State Minimum Wage Rates in 2016................... 173
Average Hourly Earnings of Production Workers on
Manufacturing Payrolls in 2015.................. 174
Average Weekly Earnings of Production Workers on
Manufacturing Payrolls in 2015.................. 175
Average Work Week of Production Workers on
Manufacturing Payrolls in 2015.................. 176
Average Weekly Unemployment Benefit in 2015........ 177
Workers' Compensation Benefit Payments in 2013 178
Workers' Compensation Benefit Payment per Covered
Worker in 2013............................. 179
Percent Change in Workers' Compensation Benefit
Payments: 2012 to 2013....................... 180
Civilian Labor Force in 2015 181
Employed Civilian Labor Force in 2015 182
Employment to Population Ratio in 2015.............. 183
Unemployed Civilian Labor Force in 2015 184
Unemployment Rate in 2015 185
Women in Civilian Labor Force in 2014 186
Percent of Women in the Civilian Labor Force in 2014... 187
Percent of Civilian Labor Force Comprised of Women
in 2014 188
Job Growth: 2014 to 2015.......................... 189
Employees on Nonfarm Payrolls in 2015.............. 190
Employees in Construction in 2015 191
Percent of Nonfarm Employees in Construction in 2015.. 192
Employees in Education and Health Services in 2015.... 193
Percent of Nonfarm Employees in Education and Health
Services in 2015............................. 194
Employees in Financial Activities in 2015............. 195
Percent of Nonfarm Employees in Financial Activities
in 2015 196

Employees in Government in 2015................... 197
Percent of Nonfarm Employees in Government in 2015 .. 198
Employees in Leisure and Hospitality in 2015.......... 199
Percent of Nonfarm Employees in Leisure and Hospitality
in 2015 200
Employees in Manufacturing in 2015................. 201
Percent of Nonfarm Employees in Manufacturing
in 2015 202
Employees in Mining and Logging in 2015 203
Percent of Nonfarm Employees in Mining and Logging
in 2015 204
Employees in Professional and Business Services
in 2015 205
Percent of Nonfarm Employees in Professional and
Business Services in 2015 206
Employees in Trade, Transportation, and Public Utilities
in 2015 207
Percent of Nonfarm Employees in Trade, Transportation,
and Public Utilities in 2015 208

VII. ENERGY AND ENVIRONMENT

Energy Consumption in 2013 211
Per Capita Energy Consumption in 2013 212
Energy Prices in 2013............................ 213
Energy Expenditures in 2013 214
Per Capita Energy Expenditures in 2013 215
Average Monthly Electric Bill for Industrial Customers
in 2014 216
Average Monthly Electric Bill for Commercial Customers
in 2014 217
Average Monthly Electric Bill for Residential Customers
in 2014 218
Electricity Generated through Renewable Sources
in 2014 219
Percent of Electricity Generated through Renewable
Sources in 2014 220
Average Price of Natural Gas Delivered to Industrial
Customers in 2014........................... 221
Average Price of Natural Gas Delivered to Commercial
Customers in 2014........................... 222
Average Price of Natural Gas Delivered to Residential
Customers in 2014........................... 223
Natural Gas Consumption in 2014 224
Coal Mines in 2013............................... 225
Coal Production in 2013........................... 226
Gasoline Used in 2014 227
Per Capita Gasoline Used in 2014 228
Daily Production of Crude Oil in 2014................ 229
Fossil Fuel Emissions in 2013 230
Per Capita Fossil Fuel Emissions in 2013.............. 231
Percent Change in Fossil Fuel Emissions: 2009 to 2013 .. 232
Toxic Releases: Total Pollution Released in 2014 233
Toxic Releases: Total Air Emissions in 2014 234
Toxic Releases: Total Surface Water Discharges in 2014.. 235
Hazardous Waste Sites on the National Priority List
in 2016 236
Hazardous Waste Sites on the National Priority List per
10,000 Square Miles in 2016 237

Hazardous Waste Sites Deleted from the National
   Priorities List as of 2016 238

VIII. GEOGRAPHY

Total Area of States in Square Miles in 2010 241
Land Area of States in Square Miles in 2010 242
Water Area of States in Square Miles in 2010 243
Highest Point of Elevation in Feet 244
Lowest Point of Elevation in Feet..................... 245
Approximate Mean Elevation in Feet................... 246
Normal Daily Mean Temperature 247
Percent of Days That Are Sunny....................... 248
Average Wind Speed (MPH)........................... 249
Hazardous Weather Fatalities in 2014 250
Tornadoes in 2015.................................. 251
Fatalities Caused by Tornadoes: 2008 to 2015 252
Cost of Damage from Hazardous Weather in 2014 253
National Park Service Land in 2014.................... 254
Recreation Visits to National Park Service Areas in 2014.. 255
Percent Change in National Park Service Recreation
   Visits: 2013 to 2014 256

IX. GOVERNMENT FINANCES: FEDERAL

Internal Revenue Service Gross Collections in 2014 259
Per Capita Internal Revenue Service Gross Collections
   in 2014 260
Federal Individual Income Tax Collections in 2014...... 261
Average Revenue Collection per Federal Individual
   Income Tax Return in 2014 262
Adjusted Gross Income in 2013 263
Per Capita Adjusted Gross Income in 2013 264
Federal Business Income Tax Collections in 2014....... 265
Average Revenue Collection per Federal Business
   Income Tax Return in 2014 266
Federal Tax Returns Filed in 2014 267
Percent of Federal Returns Filed Electronically in 2014 .. 268
Federal Individual Income Tax Returns Filed in 2014 ... 269
Percent of Federal Individual Income Tax Returns Filed
   Electronically in 2014 270
Federal Business Income Tax Returns Filed in 2014 271
Federal Tax Refunds in 2014 272
Value of Federal Tax Refunds in 2014 273
Average Value of Federal Tax Refunds in 2014 274
Value of Federal Individual Income Tax Refunds
   in 2014 275
Average Value of Federal Individual Income Tax
   Refunds in 2014.................................. 276
Value of Federal Business Income Tax Refunds in 2014 .. 277
Average Value of Federal Business Income Tax Refunds
   in 2014 278
Federal Government Expenditures in 2014 279
Per Capita Federal Government Expenditures in 2014.... 280
Federal Government Contract Awards in 2014.......... 281
Per Capita Expenditures for Federal Government Contract
   Awards in 2014.................................. 282
Federal Government Assistance in 2014................ 283
Per Capita Federal Government Assistance in 2014...... 284
Federal Government Grants in 2014................... 285

Per Capita Expenditures for Federal Government Grants
   in 2014 286
Federal Government Loans in 2014 287
Per Capita Federal Government Loans in 2014 288
Federal Government "Other Financial Assistance"
   in 2014 289
Per Capita Federal Government "Other Financial
   Assistance" in 2014 290
Federal Civilian Employees in 2014.................... 291
Rate of Federal Civilian Employees in 2014 292

X. GOVERNMENT FINANCES: STATE AND LOCAL

State and Local Government Total Revenue in 2013 295
Per Capita State and Local Government Revenue
   in 2013 296
State and Local Government Revenue from the Federal
   Government in 2013.............................. 297
Per Capita State and Local Government Revenue from
   the Federal Government in 2013 298
Percent of State and Local Government Revenue from
   the Federal Government in 2013 299
State and Local Government Own Source Revenue
   in 2013 300
Per Capita State and Local Government Own Source
   Revenue in 2013................................. 301
State and Local Government Tax Revenue in 2013 302
Per Capita State and Local Government Tax Revenue
   in 2013 303
Percent of State and Local Government Revenue from
   Taxes in 2013 304
State and Local Government Tax Revenue as a Percent
   of Personal Income in 2013 305
State and Local Government General Sales Tax Revenue
   in 2013 306
Per Capita State and Local Government General Sales
   Tax Revenue in 2013 307
State and Local Government Property Tax Revenue
   in 2013 308
Per Capita State and Local Government Property Tax
   Revenue in 2013................................. 309
State and Local Government Property Tax as a Percent of
   State and Local Government Total Revenue in 2013... 310
State and Local Government Property Tax Revenue as a
   Percent of State and Local Government Own Source
   Revenue in 2013................................. 311
State and Local Tax Burden as a Percent of Income
   in 2012 312
State and Local Government Total Expenditures
   in 2013 313
Per Capita State and Local Government Total
   Expenditures in 2013 314
State and Local Government Direct General
   Expenditures in 2013 315
Per Capita State and Local Government Direct General
   Expenditures in 2013 316
State and Local Government Debt Outstanding in 2013 .. 317
Per Capita State and Local Government Debt
   Outstanding in 2013.............................. 318

State and Local Government Full-Time Equivalent
    Employees in 2014. 319
Rate of State and Local Government Full-Time Equivalent
    Employees in 2014. 320
Average Annual Earnings of Full-Time State and Local
    Government Employees in 2014 321
State Government Total Revenue in 2013 322
Per Capita State Government Total Revenue in 2013. 323
State Government Intergovernmental Revenue in 2013. . . 324
Per Capita State Government Intergovernmental Revenue
    in 2013 325
State Government Own Source Revenue in 2013. 326
Per Capita State Government Own Source Revenue
    in 2013 327
Per Capita Profits of State Lotteries in 2014. 328
Projected vs. Actual State Tax Collections in 2015 329
State Government Tax Revenue in 2014. 330
Per Capita State Government Tax Revenue in 2014. 331
State Government Tax Revenue as a Percent of Personal
    Income in 2014. 332
State Government Individual Income Tax Revenue
    in 2014 333
Per Capita State Government Individual Income Tax
    Revenue in 2014. 334
State Government Corporation Net Income Tax Revenue
    in 2014 335
Per Capita State Government Corporation Net Income
    Tax Revenue in 2014 336
State Government General Sales Tax Revenue in 2014 . . . 337
Per Capita State Government General Sales Tax Revenue
    in 2014 338
State Government Motor Fuels Sales Tax Revenue
    in 2014 339
Per Capita State Government Motor Fuel Sales Tax
    Revenue in 2014. 340
State Tax Rates on Gasoline in 2016 341
State Government Motor Vehicle and Operators' License
    Tax Revenue in 2014 342
Per Capita State Government Motor Vehicle and
    Operators' License Tax Revenue in 2014. 343
State Government Tobacco Product Sales Tax Revenue
    in 2014 344
Per Capita State Government Tobacco Sales Tax Revenue
    in 2014 345
State Tax on a Pack of Cigarettes in 2016 346
State Government Alcoholic Beverage Sales Tax Revenue
    in 2014 347
Per Capita State Government Alcoholic Beverage Sales
    Tax Revenue in 2014 348
State Government Total Expenditures in 2013. 349
Per Capita State Government Total Expenditures in 2013. . 350
State Government Direct General Expenditures in 2013 . . 351
Per Capita State Government Direct General Expenditures
    in 2013 352
State Government Debt Outstanding in 2013. 353
Per Capita State Government Debt Outstanding in 2013. . 354
State Government Full-Time Equivalent Employees
    in 2014 355

Rate of State Government Full-Time Equivalent
    Employees in 2014. 356
Average Annual Earnings of Full-Time State Government
    Employees in 2014. 357
Local Government Total Revenue in 2013. 358
Per Capita Local Government Total Revenue in 2013 359
Local Government Revenue from the Federal
    Government in 2013. 360
Per Capita Local Government Revenue from the Federal
    Government in 2013. 361
Local Government Own Source Revenue in 2013 362
Per Capita Local Government Own Source Revenue
    in 2013 363
Local Government Tax Revenue in 2013 364
Per Capita Local Government Tax Revenue in 2013 365
Local Government Total Expenditures in 2013 366
Per Capita Local Government Total Expenditures
    in 2013 367
Local Government Direct General Expenditures
    in 2013 368
Per Capita Local Government Direct General
    Expenditures in 2013 369
Local Government Debt Outstanding in 2013 370
Per Capita Local Government Debt Outstanding
    in 2013 371
Local Government Full-Time Equivalent Employees
    in 2014 372
Rate of Local Government Full-Time Equivalent
    Employees in 2014. 373
Average Annual Earnings of Full-Time Local
    Government Employees in 2014 374

XI. HEALTH

Average Annual Single Coverage Health Insurance
    Premium per Enrolled Employee in 2014 377
Average Annual Family Coverage Health Insurance
    Premium per Enrolled Employee in 2014 378
Percent of Private-Sector Establishments That Offer
    Health Insurance: 2014 379
Persons Not Covered by Health Insurance in 2014 380
Percent of Population Not Covered by Health Insurance
    in 2014 381
Percent of Population Lacking Access to Primary Care
    in 2013 382
Physicians in 2013 383
Rate of Physicians in 2013 384
Rate of Registered Nurses in 2014 385
Rate of Dentists in 2016 386
Community Hospitals in 2014 387
Rate of Community Hospitals in 2014 388
Births in 2014 389
Birth Rate in 2014. 390
Births of Low Birthweight as a Percent of All Births
    in 2014 391
Births to Teenage Mothers as a Percent of All Births
    in 2013 392
Births to Unmarried Women as a Percent of All Births
    in 2014 393

Percent of Women Receiving Late or No Prenatal Care
   in 2013 394
Reported Legal Abortions in 2012 395
Reported Legal Abortions per 1,000 Live Births in 2012. . 396
Infant Deaths in 2013 397
Infant Mortality Rate in 2013 398
Deaths in 2013 399
Age-Adjusted Death Rate in 2013 400
Estimated Deaths by Cancer in 2015 401
Estimated Death Rate by Cancer in 2015 402
Estimated New Cancer Cases in 2015 403
Estimated Rate of New Cancer Cases in 2015 404
Deaths by Accidents in 2013 405
Age-Adjusted Death Rate by Accidents in 2013 ... 406
Deaths by Cerebrovascular Diseases in 2013 407
Age-Adjusted Death Rate by Cerebrovascular Diseases
   in 2013 408
Deaths by Diseases of the Heart in 2013 409
Age-Adjusted Death Rate by Diseases of the Heart
   in 2013 410
Deaths by Suicide in 2013 411
Age-Adjusted Death Rate by Suicide in 2013 412
Deaths by AIDS in 2013 413
Age-Adjusted Death Rate by AIDS in 2013 414
Adult Per Capita Alcohol Consumption in 2013 ... 415
Percent of Adults Who Smoke: 2013 416
Percent of Adults Overweight or Obese: 2013 417
Percent of Children Aged 19 to 35 Months Fully
   Immunized in 2014 418

XII. HOUSEHOLDS AND HOUSING

Households in 2014 421
Persons per Household in 2014 422
Percent of Households with One Person in 2014 ... 423
Percent of Households Headed by Married Couples
   in 2014 424
Percent of Households Headed by Single Mothers
   in 2014 425
Percent of Households Headed by Single Fathers
   in 2014 426
Same-Sex Couple Households in 2014 427
Percent of Same-Sex Household Couples Who Are
   Married: 2014 428
Housing Units in 2014 429
Housing Units per Square Mile in 2014 430
Percent of Housing Units That Are Owner-Occupied
   in 2014 431
New Housing Units Authorized in 2015 432
Value of New Housing Units Authorized in 2015 ... 433
Average Value of New Housing Units in 2015 434
Median Value of Owner-Occupied Housing in 2014 ... 435
Percent Change in House Prices: 2014 to 2015 436
Percent Change in House Prices: 2011 to 2015 437
Percent of Owner-Occupied Housing Units with a
   Mortgage in 2014 438
Median Monthly Mortgage Payment in 2014 439
Percent of Home Owners Spending 30% or More of
   Household Income on Housing Costs in 2014 ... 440

Median Annual Real Estate Taxes in 2014 441
Homeownership Rate in 2014 442
Percent of Housing Units That Are Renter-Occupied
   in 2014 443
Median Monthly Rental Payment in 2014 444
Percent of Renters Spending 30% or More of Household
   Income on Rent and Utilities in 2014 445
State and Local Government Expenditures for Housing
   and Community Development in 2013 446
Per Capita State and Local Government Expenditures for
   Housing and Community Development in 2013 ... 447
State & Local Government Spending for Housing and
   Community Development as a Percent of All State and
   Local Government Expenditures in 2013 448

XIII. POPULATION

Population in 2015 451
Population in 2014 452
Numerical Population Change: 2014 to 2015 453
Percent Change in Population: 2014 to 2015 454
Population in 2010 Census 455
Projected State Population in 2030 456
Population per Square Mile in 2015 457
Male Population in 2014 458
Female Population in 2014 459
Male to Female Ratio in 2014 460
White Population in 2014 461
Percent of Population White in 2014 462
Black Population in 2014 463
Percent of Population Black in 2014 464
Hispanic Population in 2014 465
Percent of Population Hispanic in 2014 466
Asian Population in 2014 467
Percent of Population Asian in 2014 468
American Indian Population in 2014 469
Percent of Population American Indian in 2014 ... 470
Native Hawaiian or Other Pacific Islander Population
   in 2014 471
Percent of Population Native Hawaiian or Other Pacific
   Islander in 2014 472
Non-Hispanic White Population in 2014 473
Percent of Population Non-Hispanic White in 2014 ... 474
Multiple Race Population in 2014 475
Percent of Population Multiple Races in 2014 476
Median Age in 2014 477
Population under 5 Years Old in 2014 478
Percent of Population under 5 Years Old in 2014 ... 479
Population 5 to 17 Years Old in 2014 480
Percent of Population 5 to 17 Years Old in 2014 ... 481
Population 18 Years Old and Older in 2014 482
Percent of Population 18 Years Old and Older in 2014 ... 483
Population 18 to 24 Years Old in 2014 484
Percent of Population 18 to 24 Years Old in 2014 ... 485
Population 25 to 44 Years Old in 2014 486
Percent of Population 25 to 44 Years Old in 2014 ... 487
Population 45 to 64 Years Old in 2014 488
Percent of Population 45 to 64 Years Old in 2014 ... 489
Population 65 Years Old and Older in 2014 490

Percent of Population 65 Years Old and Older in 2014 ... 491
Population 85 Years Old and Older in 2014 492
Percent of Population 85 Years Old and Older in 2014 ... 493
Percent of Native Population Born in Their State of
    Residence in 2014 494
Domestic Migration of Population: 2014 to 2015 495
Net International Migration: 2014 to 2015............. 496
Percent of Population Foreign Born in 2014 497
Percent of Population Speaking a Language Other Than
    English at Home in 2014 498
Percent of Population Speaking Spanish at Home
    in 2014 499
Marriage Rate for Men in 2014 500
Estimated Median Age of Men at First Marriage
    in 2014 501
Marriage Rate for Women in 2014 502
Estimated Median Age of Women at First Marriage
    in 2014 503
Ratio of Unmarried Men to Unmarried Women in 2014 .. 504
Divorce Rate for Men in 2014 505
Divorce Rate for Women in 2014..................... 506
Average Family Size in 2014 507
Seats in the U.S. House of Representatives in 2016...... 508
Estimated Population per U.S. House Seat in 2016 509
State Legislators in 2015............................ 510
Population per State Legislator in 2015 511
Registered Voters in 2014........................... 512
Percent of Eligible Voters Reported Registered in 2014... 513
Persons Voting in 2014 514
Percent of Eligible Population Reported Voting in 2014 .. 515
Percent of Registered Population Reported Voting
    in 2014 516

XIV. SOCIAL WELFARE

Poverty Rate in 2014............................... 519
Percent of Senior Citizens Living in Poverty in 2014 520
Percent of Children Living in Poverty in 2014.......... 521
Percent of Families Living in Poverty in 2014.......... 522
Percent of Female-Headed Families with Children Living
    in Poverty in 2014 523
State and Local Government Expenditures for Public
    Welfare Programs in 2013 524
Per Capita State and Local Government Expenditures for
    Public Welfare Programs in 2013.................. 525
State and Local Government Spending for Public
    Welfare Programs as a Percent of All State and Local
    Government Expenditures in 2013................. 526
Social Security (OASDI) Payments in 2013............ 527
Per Capita Social Security (OASDI) Payments in 2013... 528
Social Security (OASDI) Monthly Payments in 2013 529
Social Security (OASDI) Beneficiaries in 2013 530
Average Monthly Social Security (OASDI) Payment
    in 2013 531
Social Security Supplemental Security Income
    Beneficiaries in 2013 532
Average Monthly Social Security Supplemental Security
    Income Payment in 2013 533
Medicare Enrollees in 2014 534

Percent of Population Enrolled in Medicare in 2014 535
Medicare Program Payments in 2012................. 536
Medicare Program Payments per Enrollee in 2012 537
Medicaid Enrollment in 2013 538
Percent of Population Enrolled in Medicaid in 2013 539
Estimated Medicaid Expenditures in 2015............. 540
Percent Change in Medicaid Expenditures: 2014 to
    2015 541
Percent of Population Receiving Public Aid in 2013 542
Recipients of Temporary Assistance to Needy Families
    (TANF) Payments in 2015....................... 543
Percent Change in TANF Recipients: 2014 to 2015...... 544
TANF Work Participation Rates in 2013 545
Average Monthly TANF Assistance per Family in 2013 .. 546
Percent of Households with Food Insecurity in 2014..... 547
Supplemental Nutrition Assistance Program Benefits
    in 2015 548
Monthly Supplemental Nutrition Assistance Program
    Recipients in 2015 549
Average Monthly Supplemental Nutrition Assistance
    Program Benefit per Recipient in 2015 550
Percent of Population Receiving Supplemental Nutrition
    Assistance Program Benefits in 2015................ 551
Percent of Households Receiving Supplemental Nutrition
    Assistance Program Benefits in 2015................ 552
Average Monthly Participants in Women, Infants, and
    Children (WIC) Special Nutrition Program in 2015 ... 553
Average Monthly Benefit per Participant in Women,
    Infants, and Children (WIC) Special Nutrition Program
    in 2015 554
Percent of Public Elementary and Secondary School
    Students Eligible for Free or Reduced-Price Meals
    in 2014 555
Child Support Collections in 2014 556

XV. TRANSPORTATION

Federal Highway Funding in 2013 559
Per Capita Federal Highway Funding in 2013 560
Public Road and Street Mileage in 2013................ 561
Percent of Public Road and Street Mileage Federally
    Funded in 2013................................. 562
Interstate Highway Mileage in 2013.................. 563
Rural Road and Street Mileage in 2013 564
Urban Road and Street Mileage in 2013................ 565
Percent of Roadways in Mediocre or Poor Condition
    in 2013 566
Bridges in 2014.................................... 567
Deficient Bridges in 2014 568
Deficient Bridges as a Percent of Total Bridges in 2014 .. 569
Vehicle-Miles of Travel in 2013 570
Highway Fatalities in 2013.......................... 571
Highway Fatality Rate in 2013....................... 572
Percent of Traffic Fatalities That Were Speeding-Related
    in 2013 573
Percent of Vehicles Involved in Fatal Crashes That Were
    Large Trucks in 2013 574
Lives Saved by Child Restraints, Seat Belts, Air Bags,
    and Motorcycle Helmets in 2013.................. 575

Safety Belt Usage Rate in 2014 576
Percent of Passenger Car Occupant Fatalities Where
   Victim Used a Seat Belt in 2013 577
Fatalities in Alcohol-Related Crashes in 2013 578
Fatalities in Alcohol-Related Crashes as a Percent of
   All Highway Fatalities in 2013 579
Percent of Fatal Traffic Accidents Involving Older
   Drivers in 2013................................ 580
Percent of Highway Fatalities Who Were Young Drivers
   in 2013 581
Licensed Drivers in 2013 582
Licensed Drivers per 1,000 Driving Age Population
   in 2013 583
Motor Vehicle Registrations in 2013 584
Motor Vehicles per Driving Age Population in 2013 585
Average Travel Time to Work in 2014 586
Percent of Commuters Who Drive to Work Alone
   in 2014 587
Percent of Commuters Who Drive to Work in Carpools
   in 2014 588
Percent of Commuters Who Travel to Work by Public
   Transportation in 2014......................... 589
Annual Miles per Vehicle in 2013.................... 590
Average Miles per Gallon in 2013 591
Airports in 2013 592
Inland Waterway Mileage in 2013 593
Percent of Recreational Boating Accidents Involving
   Alcohol in 2014 594
Railroad Accidents and Incidents in 2014 595
Railroad Mileage Operated in 2012 596

Introduction and Methodology

State Rankings 2016 provides an easily accessible collection of data in a broad range of quality of life factors in the United States. In this latest 2016 edition, *State Rankings* compares data from the fifty states and the District of Columbia in 566 tables in the following fifteen different livability categories: agriculture, crime and law enforcement, defense, economy, education, employment and labor, energy and environment, geography, federal government finances, state and local government finances, health, households and housing, population, social welfare, and transportation.

Purpose of This Book

State Rankings 2016 translates complicated and often convoluted statistics into meaningful, easy-to-understand information. Too often there is an abundance of data but far too little information putting those data into context. This book allows researchers, legislators, policy analysts, journalists, and the general public to access information in a manner that not only provides basic facts about a state's quality of life but also gives a meaningful framework by comparing individual states against the rest of the country.

These data and rankings can be used in a variety of ways, by a variety of audiences, including the following examples:

- Policy makers can use the data to help identify areas warranting further study.
- Journalists can easily find impartial state information that puts stories into context.
- The general public can see how a particular state is faring compared to other states.
- Librarians can use the data as a quick reference to assist patrons in research and offer the sources and websites included as a starting point for finding other related data.

The comparison rankings in *State Rankings 2016* provide an annual snapshot of how the states are doing in the fifteen livability categories mentioned above. There are two principle approaches to using these rankings. The first is to examine how a state is doing compared to all other states via the comparison rankings in this book. The second approach is to compare a state to itself over a given period of time. Both approaches are important to achieving a good understanding of how and whether a state is making progress. It is important to keep in mind that the rankings are not a definitive determination of which state is the "best." However, since so many issues are surrounded by emotions, tracking them by the numbers can help bring the discussion back to a more balanced, unbiased review that in the end leads to better decisions.

Data and Limitations

The data featured in *State Rankings 2016* were chosen specifically by the editors from a variety of government and private sector sources. The statistics presented are intended to cover a broad array of quality-of-life subject areas, giving users of the book a solid collection of state information. Nonetheless, the statistics are not inclusive of all the possible data that might be available. The statistics in the book are the latest available from the sources. In a few cases, we have retained tables that have not been updated for several years because we believe our readers will find the data relevant, even if updates are not available. In other cases, we replaced obsolete data with new tables. Long-time users should note in particular that we have updated Government Finances: Federal with new government spending data from the OMB's USASpending.gov, but differences in methodology make those data difficult to compare with past editions.

Previous editions of the book have used the term *most livable* when describing states with the highest livability ranking. This term is no longer being used because it is purely descriptive—at no time do we attempt to explain *why* a particular state is ranking higher or lower in livability factors than others or against the national average. This explanation—currently sought by social science researchers—is beyond the scope of this book. While our selection of factors clearly affects the rankings, we believe the rankings provide a solid measurement of how the fifty states and Washington, D.C., are faring with regard to quality of life in the United States. Researchers, practitioners, and others can confidently use the data to understand livability issues and guide policy decisions.

Methodology

The comparison rankings for *State Rankings 2016* are determined using the same methodology as we have used for the past twenty-plus years. The editors used the previously mentioned fifteen livability categories to select forty-three quality of life factors from a broad range of economic, educational, health-oriented, public safety, and environmental statistics. Overall comparison rankings were determined by averaging each state's ranking for each category. The scale is one to fifty, the higher the number, the higher the state is in the rankings (i.e., 50 is the best score to receive). Data used are for the most recent year for which comparable numbers are available from most states. All factors are given equal weight.

While the 566 tables provided in *State Rankings 2016* are ranked highest to lowest without any subjective determination as to whether a subject is "positive" or "negative," for the state comparison rankings, the editors do make a subjective determination as to whether something is "positive" or "negative." Twenty-five of the forty-three factors were determined to be negative, and the remaining eighteen were viewed as positive.

The reason for this division between positive and negative is that if a state ranks first in crime rate (i.e., it has the highest crime rate), its comparison ranking is reduced. Whereas if a state ranks first in per-capita personal income (i.e., it has the highest income), its comparison ranking is increased. To account for this, we subtract the rankings for the positive factors from 51 so that a state with the highest ranking in a positive factor ends up with a 50 for that factor (remember, high numbers are best).

Once we have chosen the factors and divided them into positive and negative groupings, we simply average the ranking for each state in all forty-three factors. If a state is missing data for a given factor, its standing is based on the average ranking for the remaining factors. The book uses the latest available data for each livability factor.

As an example, Maine ranks 46th in crime rate (negative factor), 42nd in personal bankruptcy rate (negative factor), and ranks 9th in percent of population graduated from high school (positive factor). The 46th and 42nd rankings go straight into the comparison formula, whereas the number nine ranking in percent of population graduated from high school is first subtracted from 51 with the resulting 42 going into the ranking. For these three factors for Maine, we would average 46, 42, and 42 with the result being 41. If these three factors were the only ones we used, then the resulting average of 41 would be the figure we would use to compare Maine to the other forty-nine states. However, for the *State Rankings* comparison rankings, an additional forty factors are added into the calculations before the final results are determined.

Designed with the researcher in mind, the numbers shown in *State Rankings* require no additional calculations to convert them from millions, thousands, and so on. All states are ranked on a high-to-low basis, with any ties among the states listed alphabetically for a given ranking. Negative numbers are shown in parentheses. For tables displaying national totals (as opposed to rates, per capita, etc.), a separate column is included that shows what percent of the national total each individual state's total represents. This column is headed by "% of USA." This percentage figure is particularly interesting when compared with a state's population in a given year. Rates may be per 10,000 persons, per 100,000 persons, or per some other denominator; these are clearly explained by the text following the national rate and, if necessary, the footnotes.

To further assist readers, source information and footnotes clearly are shown at the bottom of each page, while national totals, rates, and percentages are prominently displayed at the top of each table. Every other line is shaded in gray for easier reading. Numerous information-finding tools are provided: a thorough table of contents, table listings at the beginning of each chapter, and a detailed index. In addition, a roster of sources with addresses, phone numbers, and websites is found in the back of the book.

About the Editors

Kathleen O'Leary Morgan and Scott Morgan founded Morgan Quitno Press in 1990. They edited more than 2,700 annual state and city statistical reference publications before selling the titles to CQ Press in 2007. They also edited a monthly journal, *State Statistical Trends,* for six years. They have continued to edit a number of the publications continued by CQ Press, as well as an ever-growing online database.

Kathleen received a BS and a master's in Public Administration from the University of Kansas. She served in a number of media and legislative positions within the U.S. Department of Transportation, where she also served as deputy director of congressional affairs.

Scott received both a BS and a law degree from the University of Kansas. He previously worked on the staffs of two U.S. senators as well as the Senate Judiciary Committee. He represented the Senate on the Federal Election Commission and served as Chief Counsel for Senator Bob Dole's presidential campaign in 1988. He was Chief Counsel for Governor Mike Hayden in Kansas until 1990.

The 2016 State Rankings

ALPHA ORDER

RANK	STATE	AVG	15 RANK	CHANGE
47	Alabama	18.53	49	2
26	Alaska	25.33	26	0
40	Arizona	21.28	37	-3
42	Arkansas	20.81	47	5
23	California	25.60	23	0
10	Colorado	30.72	6	-4
12	Connecticut	30.02	10	-2
29	Delaware	25.00	23	-6
38	Florida	21.93	38	0
41	Georgia	20.84	40	-1
19	Hawaii	27.00	32	13
20	Idaho	26.53	16	-4
31	Illinois	24.21	21	-10
36	Indiana	22.86	35	-1
3	Iowa	32.16	4	1
14	Kansas	28.49	13	-1
43	Kentucky	20.56	48	5
49	Louisiana	16.98	42	-7
15	Maine	27.84	15	0
20	Maryland	26.53	25	5
4	Massachusetts	31.81	8	4
25	Michigan	25.58	26	1
2	Minnesota	33.07	3	1
50	Mississippi	14.47	50	0
33	Missouri	23.63	29	-4
28	Montana	25.12	20	-8
4	Nebraska	31.81	5	1
39	Nevada	21.30	41	2
1	New Hampshire	34.19	1	0
11	New Jersey	30.58	17	6
46	New Mexico	18.98	43	-3
30	New York	24.42	30	0
37	North Carolina	22.26	36	-1
4	North Dakota	31.81	2	-2
35	Ohio	23.12	34	-1
34	Oklahoma	23.21	39	5
22	Oregon	25.74	22	0
32	Pennsylvania	23.81	33	1
23	Rhode Island	25.60	30	7
44	South Carolina	19.88	45	1
13	South Dakota	29.53	14	1
45	Tennessee	19.67	43	-2
27	Texas	25.28	28	1
9	Utah	31.19	9	0
8	Vermont	31.35	7	-1
18	Virginia	27.30	18	0
16	Washington	27.44	19	3
48	West Virginia	17.70	46	-2
17	Wisconsin	27.33	12	-5
7	Wyoming	31.67	11	4

RANK ORDER

RANK	STATE	AVG	15 RANK	CHANGE
1	New Hampshire	34.19	1	0
2	Minnesota	33.07	3	1
3	Iowa	32.16	4	1
4	Massachusetts	31.81	8	4
4	Nebraska	31.81	5	1
4	North Dakota	31.81	2	-2
7	Wyoming	31.67	11	4
8	Vermont	31.35	7	-1
9	Utah	31.19	9	0
10	Colorado	30.72	6	-4
11	New Jersey	30.58	17	6
12	Connecticut	30.02	10	-2
13	South Dakota	29.53	14	1
14	Kansas	28.49	13	-1
15	Maine	27.84	15	0
16	Washington	27.44	19	3
17	Wisconsin	27.33	12	-5
18	Virginia	27.30	18	0
19	Hawaii	27.00	32	13
20	Idaho	26.53	16	-4
20	Maryland	26.53	25	5
22	Oregon	25.74	22	0
23	California	25.60	23	0
23	Rhode Island	25.60	30	7
25	Michigan	25.58	26	1
26	Alaska	25.33	26	0
27	Texas	25.28	28	1
28	Montana	25.12	20	-8
29	Delaware	25.00	23	-6
30	New York	24.42	30	0
31	Illinois	24.21	21	-10
32	Pennsylvania	23.81	33	1
33	Missouri	23.63	29	-4
34	Oklahoma	23.21	39	5
35	Ohio	23.12	34	-1
36	Indiana	22.86	35	-1
37	North Carolina	22.26	36	-1
38	Florida	21.93	38	0
39	Nevada	21.30	41	2
40	Arizona	21.28	37	-3
41	Georgia	20.84	40	-1
42	Arkansas	20.81	47	5
43	Kentucky	20.56	48	5
44	South Carolina	19.88	45	1
45	Tennessee	19.67	43	-2
46	New Mexico	18.98	43	-3
47	Alabama	18.53	49	2
48	West Virginia	17.70	46	-2
49	Louisiana	16.98	42	-7
50	Mississippi	14.47	50	0

Date Each State Admitted to Statehood*

ALPHA ORDER

RANK	STATE	DATE OF ADMISSION
22	Alabama	December 14, 1819
49	Alaska	January 3, 1959
48	Arizona	February 14, 1912
25	Arkansas	June 15, 1836
31	California	September 9, 1850
38	Colorado	August 1, 1876
5	Connecticut	January 9, 1788
1	Delaware	December 7, 1787
27	Florida	March 3, 1845
4	Georgia	January 2, 1788
50	Hawaii	August 21, 1959
43	Idaho	July 3, 1890
21	Illinois	December 3, 1818
19	Indiana	December 11, 1816
29	Iowa	December 28, 1846
34	Kansas	January 29, 1861
15	Kentucky	June 1, 1792
18	Louisiana	April 30, 1812
23	Maine	March 15, 1820
7	Maryland	April 28, 1788
6	Massachusetts	February 6, 1788
26	Michigan	January 26, 1837
32	Minnesota	May 11, 1858
20	Mississippi	December 10, 1817
24	Missouri	August 10, 1821
41	Montana	November 8, 1889
37	Nebraska	March 1, 1867
36	Nevada	October 31, 1864
9	New Hampshire	June 21, 1788
3	New Jersey	December 18, 1787
47	New Mexico	January 6, 1912
11	New York	July 26, 1788
12	North Carolina	November 21, 1789
39	North Dakota	November 2, 1889
17	Ohio	March 1, 1803
46	Oklahoma	November 16, 1907
33	Oregon	February 14, 1859
2	Pennsylvania	December 12, 1787
13	Rhode Island	May 29, 1790
8	South Carolina	May 23, 1788
39	South Dakota	November 2, 1889
16	Tennessee	June 1, 1796
28	Texas	December 29, 1845
45	Utah	January 4, 1896
14	Vermont	March 4, 1791
10	Virginia	June 26, 1788
42	Washington	November 11, 1889
35	West Virginia	June 20, 1863
30	Wisconsin	May 29, 1848
44	Wyoming	July 10, 1890

RANK ORDER

RANK	STATE	DATE OF ADMISSION
1	Delaware	December 7, 1787
2	Pennsylvania	December 12, 1787
3	New Jersey	December 18, 1787
4	Georgia	January 2, 1788
5	Connecticut	January 9, 1788
6	Massachusetts	February 6, 1788
7	Maryland	April 28, 1788
8	South Carolina	May 23, 1788
9	New Hampshire	June 21, 1788
10	Virginia	June 26, 1788
11	New York	July 26, 1788
12	North Carolina	November 21, 1789
13	Rhode Island	May 29, 1790
14	Vermont	March 4, 1791
15	Kentucky	June 1, 1792
16	Tennessee	June 1, 1796
17	Ohio	March 1, 1803
18	Louisiana	April 30, 1812
19	Indiana	December 11, 1816
20	Mississippi	December 10, 1817
21	Illinois	December 3, 1818
22	Alabama	December 14, 1819
23	Maine	March 15, 1820
24	Missouri	August 10, 1821
25	Arkansas	June 15, 1836
26	Michigan	January 26, 1837
27	Florida	March 3, 1845
28	Texas	December 29, 1845
29	Iowa	December 28, 1846
30	Wisconsin	May 29, 1848
31	California	September 9, 1850
32	Minnesota	May 11, 1858
33	Oregon	February 14, 1859
34	Kansas	January 29, 1861
35	West Virginia	June 20, 1863
36	Nevada	October 31, 1864
37	Nebraska	March 1, 1867
38	Colorado	August 1, 1876
39	North Dakota	November 2, 1889
39	South Dakota	November 2, 1889
41	Montana	November 8, 1889
42	Washington	November 11, 1889
43	Idaho	July 3, 1890
44	Wyoming	July 10, 1890
45	Utah	January 4, 1896
46	Oklahoma	November 16, 1907
47	New Mexico	January 6, 1912
48	Arizona	February 14, 1912
49	Alaska	January 3, 1959
50	Hawaii	August 21, 1959

Source: U.S. Bureau of the Census
  "1980 Census of Population" (vol. 1, part A, PC80-1-A)
*First thirteen states show date of ratification of Constitution.

STATE FAST FACTS

STATE	NICKNAME	CAPITAL	POPULATION*	AREA**
Alabama	Heart of Dixie	Montgomery	4,858,979	52,420
Alaska	The Last Frontier	Juneau	738,432	665,384
Arizona	Grand Canyon State	Phoenix	6,828,065	113,990
Arkansas	The Natural State	Little Rock	2,978,204	53,179
California	Golden State	Sacramento	39,144,818	163,695
Colorado	Centennial State	Denver	5,456,574	104,094
Connecticut	Constitution State	Hartford	3,590,886	5,543
Delaware	First State	Dover	945,934	2,489
Florida	Sunshine State	Tallahassee	20,271,272	65,758
Georgia	Peach State	Atlanta	10,214,860	59,425
Hawaii	Aloha State	Honolulu	1,431,603	10,932
Idaho	Gem State	Boise	1,654,930	83,569
Illinois	Land of Lincoln	Springfield	12,859,995	57,914
Indiana	Hoosier State	Indianapolis	6,619,680	36,420
Iowa	Hawkeye State	Des Moines	3,123,899	56,273
Kansas	Sunflower State	Topeka	2,911,641	82,278
Kentucky	Bluegrass State	Frankfort	4,425,092	40,408
Louisiana	Pelican State	Baton Rouge	4,670,724	52,378
Maine	Pine Tree State	Augusta	1,329,328	35,380
Maryland	Free State	Annapolis	6,006,401	12,406
Massachusetts	Bay State	Boston	6,794,422	10,554
Michigan	Great Lake State	Lansing	9,922,576	96,714
Minnesota	North Star State	St. Paul	5,489,594	86,936
Mississippi	Magnolia State	Jackson	2,992,333	48,432
Missouri	Show Me State	Jefferson City	6,083,672	69,707
Montana	Treasure State	Helena	1,032,949	147,040
Nebraska	Cornhusker State	Lincoln	1,896,190	77,348
Nevada	Silver State	Carson City	2,890,845	110,572
New Hampshire	Granite State	Concord	1,330,608	9,349
New Jersey	Garden State	Trenton	8,958,013	8,723
New Mexico	Land of Enchantment	Santa Fe	2,085,109	121,590
New York	Empire State	Albany	19,795,791	54,555
North Carolina	Tar Heel State	Raleigh	10,042,802	53,819
North Dakota	Peace Garden State	Bismarck	756,927	70,698
Ohio	Buckeye State	Columbus	11,613,423	44,826
Oklahoma	Sooner State	Oklahoma City	3,911,338	69,899
Oregon	Beaver State	Salem	4,028,977	98,379
Pennsylvania	Keystone State	Harrisburg	12,802,503	46,054
Rhode Island	Ocean State	Providence	1,056,298	1,545
South Carolina	Palmetto State	Columbia	4,896,146	32,020
South Dakota	Mount Rushmore State	Pierre	858,469	77,116
Tennessee	Volunteer State	Nashville	6,600,299	42,144
Texas	Lone Star State	Austin	27,469,114	268,596
Utah	Beehive State	Salt Lake City	2,995,919	84,897
Vermont	Green Mountain State	Montpelier	626,042	9,616
Virginia	Old Dominion	Richmond	8,382,993	42,775
Washington	Evergreen State	Olympia	7,170,351	71,298
West Virginia	Mountain State	Charleston	1,844,128	24,230
Wisconsin	Badger State	Madison	5,771,337	65,496
Wyoming	Equality State	Cheyenne	586,107	97,813

*U.S. Bureau of the Census, "Population Estimates" (December 2015, http://www.census.gov/popest/data/index.html)
**Total of land and water area in square miles.

STATE FAST FACTS

STATE SONG	STATE FLOWER	STATE TREE	STATE BIRD
Alabama	Camellia	Southern Pine	Yellowhammer
Alaska's Flag	Forget-Me-Not	Sitka Spruce	Willow Ptarmigan
Arizona	Saguaro Cactus Blossom	Palo Verde	Cactus Wren
Arkansas	Apple Blossom	Pine	Mockingbird
I Love You, California	Golden Poppy	California Redwood	California Valley Quail
Where the Columbines Grow	Rocky Mountain Columbine	Colorado Blue Spruce	Lark Bunting
Yankee Doodle Dandy	Mountain Laurel	White Oak	American Robin
Our Delaware	Peach Blossom	American Holly	Blue Hen Chicken
Swanee River	Orange Blossom	Sabal Palmetto Palm	Mockingbird
Georgia On My Mind	Cherokee Rose	Live Oak	Brown Thrasher
Hawaii Ponoi	Yellow Hibiscus	Candlenut	Nene
Here We Have Idaho	Syringa	White Pine	Mountain Bluebird
Illinois	Purple Violet	White Oak	Cardinal
On the Banks of the Wabash, Far Away	Peony	Tulip Poplar	Cardinal
The Song of Iowa	Wild Rose	Oak	Eastern Goldfinch
Home on the Range	Sunflower	Cottonwood	Western Meadowlark
My Old Kentucky Home	Goldenrod	Tulip Tree	Cardinal
Give Me Louisiana	Magnolia	Cypress	Eastern Brown Pelican
State of Maine Song	White Pine Cone and Tassel	Eastern White Pine	Chickadee
Maryland, My Maryland	Black-eyed Susan	White Oak	Baltimore Oriole
All Hail to Massachusetts	Mayflower	American Elm	Chickadee
Michigan, My Michigan	Apple Blossom	White Pine	Robin
Hail! Minnesota	Pink and White Lady's Slipper	Red Pine	Common Loon
Go, Mississippi!	Magnolia	Magnolia	Mockingbird
Missouri Waltz	Hawthorn	Dogwood	Bluebird
Montana	Bitterroot	Ponderosa Pine	Western Meadowlark
Beautiful Nebraska	Goldenrod	Cottonwood	Western Meadowlark
Home Means Nevada	Sagebrush	Single-Leaf Pinon	Mountain Bluebird
Old New Hampshire	Purple Lilac	White Birch	Purple Finch
Ode to New Jersey	Purple Violet	Red Oak	Eastern Goldfinch
O Fair New Mexico	Yucca	Pinon	Roadrunner
I Love New York	Rose	Sugar Maple	Bluebird
The Old North State	Dogwood	Pine	Cardinal
North Dakota Hymn	Wild Prairie Rose	American Elm	Western Meadowlark
Beautiful Ohio	Scarlet Carnation	Buckeye	Cardinal
Oklahoma!	Mistletoe	Redbud	Scissortailed Flycatcher
Oregon, My Oregon	Oregon Grape	Douglas Fir	Western Meadowlark
Hail! Pennsylvania	Mountain Laurel	Hemlock	Ruffed Grouse
Rhode Island	Violet	Red Maple	Rhode Island Red
Carolina	Yellow Jessamine	Palmetto	Carolina Wren
Hail, South Dakota	Pasque Flower	Black Hills Spruce	Ringnecked Pheasant
The Tennessee Waltz	Iris	Tulip Poplar	Mockingbird
Texas, Our Texas	Bluebonnet	Pecan	Mockingbird
Utah, We Love Thee	Sego Lily	Blue Spruce	Seagull
Hail, Vermont	Red Clover	Sugar Maple	Hermit Thrush
Carry Me Back to Old Virginia	Dogwood	Dogwood	Cardinal
Washington, My Home	Western Rhododendron	Western Hemlock	Willow Goldfinch
The West Virginia Hills; This Is My West Virginia; and West Virginia, My Home, Sweet Home	Big Rhododendron	Sugar Maple	Cardinal
On Wisconsin!	Wood Violet	Sugar Maple	Robin
Wyoming	Indian Paintbrush	Cottonwood	Meadowlark

I. Agriculture

Number of Farms in 2014 3
Land in Farms in 2014 4
Average Number of Acres per Farm in 2014 5
Average per-Acre Value of Farmland in 2015 6
Percent Change in Average per-Acre Value of Farmland:
    2014 to 2015 7
Net Farm Income in 2014 8
Net Farm Income per Operation in 2014 9
Net Farm Income per Acre in 2014 10
Farm Income: Cash Receipts from Commodities in 2014 .. 11
Farm Income: Crops in 2014 12
Farm Income: Livestock in 2014 13
Farm Income: Government Payments in 2014 14

Acres Planted in 2015 15
Acres Harvested in 2015 16
Acres Harvested: Corn in 2015 17
Acres Harvested: Soybeans in 2015 18
Acres Harvested: Wheat in 2015 19
Cattle on Farms in 2016 20
Milk Cows on Farms in 2014 21
Milk Production in 2014 22
Milk Production per Milk Cow in 2014 23
Hogs and Pigs on Farms in 2015 24
Chickens in 2014 25
Eggs Produced in 2014 26

Number of Farms in 2014

National Total = 2,084,000 Farms*

ALPHA ORDER

RANK	STATE	FARMS	% of USA
21	Alabama	43,400	2.1%
50	Alaska	760	0.0%
36	Arizona	19,600	0.9%
20	Arkansas	44,000	2.1%
5	California	76,400	3.7%
26	Colorado	35,000	1.7%
45	Connecticut	6,000	0.3%
48	Delaware	2,500	0.1%
18	Florida	47,600	2.3%
22	Georgia	41,100	2.0%
44	Hawaii	7,000	0.3%
33	Idaho	24,400	1.2%
7	Illinois	74,500	3.6%
14	Indiana	58,200	2.8%
3	Iowa	88,000	4.2%
12	Kansas	61,000	2.9%
5	Kentucky	76,400	3.7%
31	Louisiana	27,200	1.3%
41	Maine	8,200	0.4%
38	Maryland	12,300	0.6%
42	Massachusetts	7,800	0.4%
15	Michigan	51,600	2.5%
9	Minnesota	74,000	3.6%
23	Mississippi	37,100	1.8%
2	Missouri	97,700	4.7%
30	Montana	27,800	1.3%
17	Nebraska	49,100	2.4%
47	Nevada	4,200	0.2%
46	New Hampshire	4,400	0.2%
40	New Jersey	9,100	0.4%
32	New Mexico	24,700	1.2%
25	New York	35,500	1.7%
16	North Carolina	49,500	2.4%
29	North Dakota	30,300	1.5%
7	Ohio	74,500	3.6%
4	Oklahoma	79,600	3.8%
27	Oregon	34,600	1.7%
13	Pennsylvania	58,800	2.8%
49	Rhode Island	1,240	0.1%
33	South Carolina	24,400	1.2%
28	South Dakota	31,700	1.5%
11	Tennessee	67,300	3.2%
1	Texas	245,500	11.8%
37	Utah	18,100	0.9%
43	Vermont	7,300	0.4%
19	Virginia	45,900	2.2%
24	Washington	36,700	1.8%
35	West Virginia	21,300	1.0%
10	Wisconsin	69,000	3.3%
39	Wyoming	11,700	0.6%

RANK ORDER

RANK	STATE	FARMS	% of USA
1	Texas	245,500	11.8%
2	Missouri	97,700	4.7%
3	Iowa	88,000	4.2%
4	Oklahoma	79,600	3.8%
5	California	76,400	3.7%
5	Kentucky	76,400	3.7%
7	Illinois	74,500	3.6%
7	Ohio	74,500	3.6%
9	Minnesota	74,000	3.6%
10	Wisconsin	69,000	3.3%
11	Tennessee	67,300	3.2%
12	Kansas	61,000	2.9%
13	Pennsylvania	58,800	2.8%
14	Indiana	58,200	2.8%
15	Michigan	51,600	2.5%
16	North Carolina	49,500	2.4%
17	Nebraska	49,100	2.4%
18	Florida	47,600	2.3%
19	Virginia	45,900	2.2%
20	Arkansas	44,000	2.1%
21	Alabama	43,400	2.1%
22	Georgia	41,100	2.0%
23	Mississippi	37,100	1.8%
24	Washington	36,700	1.8%
25	New York	35,500	1.7%
26	Colorado	35,000	1.7%
27	Oregon	34,600	1.7%
28	South Dakota	31,700	1.5%
29	North Dakota	30,300	1.5%
30	Montana	27,800	1.3%
31	Louisiana	27,200	1.3%
32	New Mexico	24,700	1.2%
33	Idaho	24,400	1.2%
33	South Carolina	24,400	1.2%
35	West Virginia	21,300	1.0%
36	Arizona	19,600	0.9%
37	Utah	18,100	0.9%
38	Maryland	12,300	0.6%
39	Wyoming	11,700	0.6%
40	New Jersey	9,100	0.4%
41	Maine	8,200	0.4%
42	Massachusetts	7,800	0.4%
43	Vermont	7,300	0.4%
44	Hawaii	7,000	0.3%
45	Connecticut	6,000	0.3%
46	New Hampshire	4,400	0.2%
47	Nevada	4,200	0.2%
48	Delaware	2,500	0.1%
49	Rhode Island	1,240	0.1%
50	Alaska	760	0.0%
	District of Columbia	0	0.0%

Source: U.S. Department of Agriculture, National Agricultural Statistics Service
"Farms and Land in Farms" (http://usda.mannlib.cornell.edu/MannUsda/viewDocumentInfo.do?documentID=1259)
*A farm is any establishment from which $1,000 or more of agricultural products were sold or would normally be sold during the year. This includes places with five or more horses, except horses in boarding stables or racetracks.

Land in Farms in 2014

National Total = 913,000,000 Acres*

ALPHA ORDER

RANK	STATE	ACRES	% of USA
31	Alabama	8,900,000	1.0%
44	Alaska	830,000	0.1%
14	Arizona	26,000,000	2.8%
22	Arkansas	13,800,000	1.5%
16	California	25,500,000	2.8%
9	Colorado	31,800,000	3.5%
49	Connecticut	440,000	0.0%
47	Delaware	500,000	0.1%
29	Florida	9,500,000	1.0%
30	Georgia	9,400,000	1.0%
43	Hawaii	1,120,000	0.1%
24	Idaho	11,800,000	1.3%
13	Illinois	26,900,000	2.9%
18	Indiana	14,700,000	1.6%
10	Iowa	30,500,000	3.3%
3	Kansas	46,000,000	5.0%
23	Kentucky	13,000,000	1.4%
34	Louisiana	7,800,000	0.9%
41	Maine	1,450,000	0.2%
40	Maryland	2,030,000	0.2%
46	Massachusetts	520,000	0.1%
28	Michigan	9,950,000	1.1%
15	Minnesota	25,900,000	2.8%
26	Mississippi	10,900,000	1.2%
12	Missouri	28,300,000	3.1%
2	Montana	59,700,000	6.5%
4	Nebraska	45,200,000	5.0%
37	Nevada	5,950,000	0.7%
48	New Hampshire	470,000	0.1%
45	New Jersey	720,000	0.1%
6	New Mexico	43,200,000	4.7%
36	New York	7,180,000	0.8%
32	North Carolina	8,400,000	0.9%
7	North Dakota	39,300,000	4.3%
21	Ohio	14,000,000	1.5%
8	Oklahoma	34,300,000	3.8%
17	Oregon	16,400,000	1.8%
35	Pennsylvania	7,720,000	0.8%
50	Rhode Island	70,000	0.0%
38	South Carolina	5,000,000	0.5%
5	South Dakota	43,300,000	4.7%
26	Tennessee	10,900,000	1.2%
1	Texas	130,000,000	14.2%
25	Utah	11,000,000	1.2%
42	Vermont	1,250,000	0.1%
33	Virginia	8,200,000	0.9%
18	Washington	14,700,000	1.6%
39	West Virginia	3,600,000	0.4%
20	Wisconsin	14,500,000	1.6%
11	Wyoming	30,400,000	3.3%

RANK ORDER

RANK	STATE	ACRES	% of USA
1	Texas	130,000,000	14.2%
2	Montana	59,700,000	6.5%
3	Kansas	46,000,000	5.0%
4	Nebraska	45,200,000	5.0%
5	South Dakota	43,300,000	4.7%
6	New Mexico	43,200,000	4.7%
7	North Dakota	39,300,000	4.3%
8	Oklahoma	34,300,000	3.8%
9	Colorado	31,800,000	3.5%
10	Iowa	30,500,000	3.3%
11	Wyoming	30,400,000	3.3%
12	Missouri	28,300,000	3.1%
13	Illinois	26,900,000	2.9%
14	Arizona	26,000,000	2.8%
15	Minnesota	25,900,000	2.8%
16	California	25,500,000	2.8%
17	Oregon	16,400,000	1.8%
18	Indiana	14,700,000	1.6%
18	Washington	14,700,000	1.6%
20	Wisconsin	14,500,000	1.6%
21	Ohio	14,000,000	1.5%
22	Arkansas	13,800,000	1.5%
23	Kentucky	13,000,000	1.4%
24	Idaho	11,800,000	1.3%
25	Utah	11,000,000	1.2%
26	Mississippi	10,900,000	1.2%
26	Tennessee	10,900,000	1.2%
28	Michigan	9,950,000	1.1%
29	Florida	9,500,000	1.0%
30	Georgia	9,400,000	1.0%
31	Alabama	8,900,000	1.0%
32	North Carolina	8,400,000	0.9%
33	Virginia	8,200,000	0.9%
34	Louisiana	7,800,000	0.9%
35	Pennsylvania	7,720,000	0.8%
36	New York	7,180,000	0.8%
37	Nevada	5,950,000	0.7%
38	South Carolina	5,000,000	0.5%
39	West Virginia	3,600,000	0.4%
40	Maryland	2,030,000	0.2%
41	Maine	1,450,000	0.2%
42	Vermont	1,250,000	0.1%
43	Hawaii	1,120,000	0.1%
44	Alaska	830,000	0.1%
45	New Jersey	720,000	0.1%
46	Massachusetts	520,000	0.1%
47	Delaware	500,000	0.1%
48	New Hampshire	470,000	0.1%
49	Connecticut	440,000	0.0%
50	Rhode Island	70,000	0.0%
	District of Columbia	0	0.0%

Source: U.S. Department of Agriculture, National Agricultural Statistics Service
"Farms and Land in Farms" (http://usda.mannlib.cornell.edu/MannUsda/viewDocumentInfo.do?documentID=1259)
*A farm is any establishment from which $1,000 or more of agricultural products were sold or would normally be sold during the year. This includes places with five or more horses, except horses in boarding stables or racetracks.

Average Number of Acres per Farm in 2014

National Average = 438 Acres*

ALPHA ORDER

RANK	STATE	ACRES
29	Alabama	205
8	Alaska	1,092
6	Arizona	1,327
22	Arkansas	314
21	California	334
10	Colorado	909
48	Connecticut	73
32	Delaware	200
32	Florida	200
27	Georgia	229
44	Hawaii	160
14	Idaho	484
18	Illinois	361
26	Indiana	253
20	Iowa	347
11	Kansas	754
39	Kentucky	170
25	Louisiana	287
37	Maine	177
42	Maryland	165
49	Massachusetts	67
34	Michigan	193
19	Minnesota	350
23	Mississippi	294
24	Missouri	290
2	Montana	2,147
9	Nebraska	921
4	Nevada	1,417
46	New Hampshire	107
47	New Jersey	79
3	New Mexico	1,749
31	New York	202
39	North Carolina	170
7	North Dakota	1,297
35	Ohio	188
16	Oklahoma	431
15	Oregon	474
45	Pennsylvania	131
50	Rhode Island	56
29	South Carolina	205
5	South Dakota	1,366
43	Tennessee	162
13	Texas	530
12	Utah	608
38	Vermont	171
36	Virginia	179
17	Washington	401
41	West Virginia	169
28	Wisconsin	210
1	Wyoming	2,598

RANK ORDER

RANK	STATE	ACRES
1	Wyoming	2,598
2	Montana	2,147
3	New Mexico	1,749
4	Nevada	1,417
5	South Dakota	1,366
6	Arizona	1,327
7	North Dakota	1,297
8	Alaska	1,092
9	Nebraska	921
10	Colorado	909
11	Kansas	754
12	Utah	608
13	Texas	530
14	Idaho	484
15	Oregon	474
16	Oklahoma	431
17	Washington	401
18	Illinois	361
19	Minnesota	350
20	Iowa	347
21	California	334
22	Arkansas	314
23	Mississippi	294
24	Missouri	290
25	Louisiana	287
26	Indiana	253
27	Georgia	229
28	Wisconsin	210
29	Alabama	205
29	South Carolina	205
31	New York	202
32	Delaware	200
32	Florida	200
34	Michigan	193
35	Ohio	188
36	Virginia	179
37	Maine	177
38	Vermont	171
39	Kentucky	170
39	North Carolina	170
41	West Virginia	169
42	Maryland	165
43	Tennessee	162
44	Hawaii	160
45	Pennsylvania	131
46	New Hampshire	107
47	New Jersey	79
48	Connecticut	73
49	Massachusetts	67
50	Rhode Island	56
	District of Columbia**	NA

Source: U.S. Department of Agriculture, National Agricultural Statistics Service
"Farms and Land in Farms" (http://usda.mannlib.cornell.edu/MannUsda/viewDocumentInfo.do?documentID=1259)
*A farm is any establishment from which $1,000 or more of agricultural products were sold or would normally be sold during the year. This includes places with five or more horses, except horses in boarding stables or racetracks.

Average per-Acre Value of Farmland in 2015

National Average = $3,020 per Acre*

ALPHA ORDER

RANK	STATE	PER-ACRE VALUE
32	Alabama	$2,630
NA	Alaska**	NA
20	Arizona	3,780
26	Arkansas	3,050
7	California	7,700
44	Colorado	1,440
3	Connecticut	11,300
5	Delaware	8,180
13	Florida	5,400
24	Georgia	3,270
NA	Hawaii**	NA
34	Idaho	2,470
8	Illinois	7,500
9	Indiana	7,150
6	Iowa	8,000
40	Kansas	2,030
25	Kentucky	3,250
30	Louisiana	2,800
38	Maine	2,090
10	Maryland	7,000
4	Massachusetts	10,400
14	Michigan	4,900
15	Minnesota	4,700
35	Mississippi	2,420
22	Missouri	3,350
46	Montana	890
26	Nebraska	3,050
45	Nevada	1,130
19	New Hampshire	4,280
2	New Jersey	13,000
48	New Mexico	510
29	New York	3,000
17	North Carolina	4,500
42	North Dakota	1,920
11	Ohio	5,750
43	Oklahoma	1,730
37	Oregon	2,120
12	Pennsylvania	5,500
1	Rhode Island	13,800
28	South Carolina	3,010
36	South Dakota	2,320
21	Tennessee	3,650
41	Texas	1,940
39	Utah	2,050
23	Vermont	3,300
18	Virginia	4,320
31	Washington	2,700
33	West Virginia	2,600
15	Wisconsin	4,700
47	Wyoming	660

RANK ORDER

RANK	STATE	PER-ACRE VALUE
1	Rhode Island	$13,800
2	New Jersey	13,000
3	Connecticut	11,300
4	Massachusetts	10,400
5	Delaware	8,180
6	Iowa	8,000
7	California	7,700
8	Illinois	7,500
9	Indiana	7,150
10	Maryland	7,000
11	Ohio	5,750
12	Pennsylvania	5,500
13	Florida	5,400
14	Michigan	4,900
15	Minnesota	4,700
15	Wisconsin	4,700
17	North Carolina	4,500
18	Virginia	4,320
19	New Hampshire	4,280
20	Arizona	3,780
21	Tennessee	3,650
22	Missouri	3,350
23	Vermont	3,300
24	Georgia	3,270
25	Kentucky	3,250
26	Arkansas	3,050
26	Nebraska	3,050
28	South Carolina	3,010
29	New York	3,000
30	Louisiana	2,800
31	Washington	2,700
32	Alabama	2,630
33	West Virginia	2,600
34	Idaho	2,470
35	Mississippi	2,420
36	South Dakota	2,320
37	Oregon	2,120
38	Maine	2,090
39	Utah	2,050
40	Kansas	2,030
41	Texas	1,940
42	North Dakota	1,920
43	Oklahoma	1,730
44	Colorado	1,440
45	Nevada	1,130
46	Montana	890
47	Wyoming	660
48	New Mexico	510
NA	Alaska**	NA
NA	Hawaii**	NA
	District of Columbia**	NA

Source: U.S. Department of Agriculture, National Agricultural Statistics Service
"Land Values and Cash Rents" (http://usda.mannlib.cornell.edu/MannUsda/viewDocumentInfo.do?documentID=1446)
*Value of farmland and buildings in nominal dollars.
**Not applicable or available.

Percent Change in Average per-Acre Value of Farmland: 2014 to 2015

National Percent Change = 2.4% Increase*

ALPHA ORDER

RANK	STATE	PERCENT CHANGE
28	Alabama	1.2
NA	Alaska**	NA
30	Arizona	1.1
6	Arkansas	7.0
9	California	5.5
8	Colorado	6.7
32	Connecticut	0.9
35	Delaware	0.0
22	Florida	2.9
42	Georgia	(0.9)
NA	Hawaii**	NA
14	Idaho	4.7
41	Illinois	(0.3)
22	Indiana	2.9
48	Iowa	(5.9)
43	Kansas	(1.0)
21	Kentucky	3.2
11	Louisiana	4.9
34	Maine	0.5
26	Maryland	1.4
35	Massachusetts	0.0
16	Michigan	4.3
44	Minnesota	(1.1)
19	Mississippi	3.4
4	Missouri	8.1
18	Montana	3.5
47	Nebraska	(2.2)
15	Nevada	4.6
35	New Hampshire	0.0
24	New Jersey	1.6
46	New Mexico	(1.9)
2	New York	11.1
40	North Carolina	(0.2)
9	North Dakota	5.5
17	Ohio	3.6
3	Oklahoma	9.5
19	Oregon	3.4
45	Pennsylvania	(1.8)
33	Rhode Island	0.7
35	South Carolina	0.0
1	South Dakota	12.1
26	Tennessee	1.4
11	Texas	4.9
31	Utah	1.0
28	Vermont	1.2
35	Virginia	0.0
5	Washington	8.0
24	West Virginia	1.6
7	Wisconsin	6.8
13	Wyoming	4.8

RANK ORDER

RANK	STATE	PERCENT CHANGE
1	South Dakota	12.1
2	New York	11.1
3	Oklahoma	9.5
4	Missouri	8.1
5	Washington	8.0
6	Arkansas	7.0
7	Wisconsin	6.8
8	Colorado	6.7
9	California	5.5
9	North Dakota	5.5
11	Louisiana	4.9
11	Texas	4.9
13	Wyoming	4.8
14	Idaho	4.7
15	Nevada	4.6
16	Michigan	4.3
17	Ohio	3.6
18	Montana	3.5
19	Mississippi	3.4
19	Oregon	3.4
21	Kentucky	3.2
22	Florida	2.9
22	Indiana	2.9
24	New Jersey	1.6
24	West Virginia	1.6
26	Maryland	1.4
26	Tennessee	1.4
28	Alabama	1.2
28	Vermont	1.2
30	Arizona	1.1
31	Utah	1.0
32	Connecticut	0.9
33	Rhode Island	0.7
34	Maine	0.5
35	Delaware	0.0
35	Massachusetts	0.0
35	New Hampshire	0.0
35	South Carolina	0.0
35	Virginia	0.0
40	North Carolina	(0.2)
41	Illinois	(0.3)
42	Georgia	(0.9)
43	Kansas	(1.0)
44	Minnesota	(1.1)
45	Pennsylvania	(1.8)
46	New Mexico	(1.9)
47	Nebraska	(2.2)
48	Iowa	(5.9)
NA	Alaska**	NA
NA	Hawaii**	NA
	District of Columbia**	NA

Source: U.S. Department of Agriculture, National Agricultural Statistics Service
"Land Values and Cash Rents" (http://usda.mannlib.cornell.edu/MannUsda/viewDocumentInfo.do?documentID=1446)
*Value of farmland and buildings in nominal dollars.
**Not applicable or available.

Net Farm Income in 2014

National Total = $90,361,197,000*

ALPHA ORDER

RANK	STATE	FARM INCOME	% of USA
20	Alabama	$1,775,078,000	2.0%
50	Alaska	(26,363,000)	0.0%
30	Arizona	755,346,000	0.8%
15	Arkansas	2,155,944,000	2.4%
1	California	15,087,007,000	16.7%
26	Colorado	1,136,707,000	1.3%
44	Connecticut	107,027,000	0.1%
35	Delaware	572,560,000	0.6%
16	Florida	2,129,574,000	2.4%
14	Georgia	2,345,896,000	2.6%
45	Hawaii	79,636,000	0.1%
18	Idaho	1,990,807,000	2.2%
10	Illinois	2,773,924,000	3.1%
8	Indiana	2,881,122,000	3.2%
3	Iowa	5,084,952,000	5.6%
13	Kansas	2,535,325,000	2.8%
21	Kentucky	1,768,261,000	2.0%
27	Louisiana	881,393,000	1.0%
41	Maine	202,865,000	0.2%
34	Maryland	590,940,000	0.7%
49	Massachusetts	4,199,000	0.0%
32	Michigan	724,013,000	0.8%
7	Minnesota	2,931,765,000	3.2%
24	Mississippi	1,535,174,000	1.7%
6	Missouri	3,476,354,000	3.8%
33	Montana	720,289,000	0.8%
2	Nebraska	6,020,174,000	6.7%
42	Nevada	173,489,000	0.2%
47	New Hampshire	41,733,000	0.0%
43	New Jersey	167,039,000	0.2%
25	New Mexico	1,167,106,000	1.3%
22	New York	1,717,587,000	1.9%
5	North Carolina	3,917,675,000	4.3%
39	North Dakota	295,918,000	0.3%
23	Ohio	1,702,588,000	1.9%
9	Oklahoma	2,798,053,000	3.1%
28	Oregon	789,651,000	0.9%
12	Pennsylvania	2,693,403,000	3.0%
48	Rhode Island	10,813,000	0.0%
40	South Carolina	275,897,000	0.3%
17	South Dakota	2,048,919,000	2.3%
31	Tennessee	739,830,000	0.8%
4	Texas	4,235,144,000	4.7%
36	Utah	549,728,000	0.6%
37	Vermont	327,876,000	0.4%
29	Virginia	770,956,000	0.9%
19	Washington	1,929,024,000	2.1%
46	West Virginia	58,077,000	0.1%
11	Wisconsin	2,746,524,000	3.0%
38	Wyoming	322,691,000	0.4%

RANK ORDER

RANK	STATE	FARM INCOME	% of USA
1	California	$15,087,007,000	16.7%
2	Nebraska	6,020,174,000	6.7%
3	Iowa	5,084,952,000	5.6%
4	Texas	4,235,144,000	4.7%
5	North Carolina	3,917,675,000	4.3%
6	Missouri	3,476,354,000	3.8%
7	Minnesota	2,931,765,000	3.2%
8	Indiana	2,881,122,000	3.2%
9	Oklahoma	2,798,053,000	3.1%
10	Illinois	2,773,924,000	3.1%
11	Wisconsin	2,746,524,000	3.0%
12	Pennsylvania	2,693,403,000	3.0%
13	Kansas	2,535,325,000	2.8%
14	Georgia	2,345,896,000	2.6%
15	Arkansas	2,155,944,000	2.4%
16	Florida	2,129,574,000	2.4%
17	South Dakota	2,048,919,000	2.3%
18	Idaho	1,990,807,000	2.2%
19	Washington	1,929,024,000	2.1%
20	Alabama	1,775,078,000	2.0%
21	Kentucky	1,768,261,000	2.0%
22	New York	1,717,587,000	1.9%
23	Ohio	1,702,588,000	1.9%
24	Mississippi	1,535,174,000	1.7%
25	New Mexico	1,167,106,000	1.3%
26	Colorado	1,136,707,000	1.3%
27	Louisiana	881,393,000	1.0%
28	Oregon	789,651,000	0.9%
29	Virginia	770,956,000	0.9%
30	Arizona	755,346,000	0.8%
31	Tennessee	739,830,000	0.8%
32	Michigan	724,013,000	0.8%
33	Montana	720,289,000	0.8%
34	Maryland	590,940,000	0.7%
35	Delaware	572,560,000	0.6%
36	Utah	549,728,000	0.6%
37	Vermont	327,876,000	0.4%
38	Wyoming	322,691,000	0.4%
39	North Dakota	295,918,000	0.3%
40	South Carolina	275,897,000	0.3%
41	Maine	202,865,000	0.2%
42	Nevada	173,489,000	0.2%
43	New Jersey	167,039,000	0.2%
44	Connecticut	107,027,000	0.1%
45	Hawaii	79,636,000	0.1%
46	West Virginia	58,077,000	0.1%
47	New Hampshire	41,733,000	0.0%
48	Rhode Island	10,813,000	0.0%
49	Massachusetts	4,199,000	0.0%
50	Alaska	(26,363,000)	0.0%
	District of Columbia	0	0.0%

Source: U.S. Department of Agriculture, Economic Research Service
"Farm Sector Financial Indicators, State Rankings"
(http://www.ers.usda.gov/data-products/farm-income-and-wealth-statistics.aspx)

*Net farm income is a measure of the net value of production in a given year. It is determined by subtracting total production expenses from gross farm income.

Net Farm Income per Operation in 2014

National Average = $43,362 per Operation*

ALPHA ORDER

RANK	STATE	PER OPERATION
21	Alabama	$40,795
50	Alaska	(34,944)
24	Arizona	38,483
11	Arkansas	48,984
2	California	197,728
28	Colorado	32,724
38	Connecticut	17,739
1	Delaware	229,000
17	Florida	44,800
8	Georgia	57,250
42	Hawaii	11,360
4	Idaho	81,796
25	Illinois	37,183
10	Indiana	49,588
7	Iowa	57,949
18	Kansas	41,470
34	Kentucky	23,120
29	Louisiana	32,431
33	Maine	24,780
13	Maryland	48,015
49	Massachusetts	536
41	Michigan	14,089
23	Minnesota	39,550
19	Mississippi	41,454
26	Missouri	35,670
32	Montana	25,764
3	Nebraska	122,493
20	Nevada	41,093
46	New Hampshire	9,523
37	New Jersey	18,328
14	New Mexico	47,223
12	New York	48,278
5	North Carolina	79,220
45	North Dakota	10,376
35	Ohio	22,936
27	Oklahoma	35,342
36	Oregon	22,752
15	Pennsylvania	45,719
47	Rhode Island	8,624
43	South Carolina	11,275
6	South Dakota	64,202
44	Tennessee	11,016
39	Texas	17,490
30	Utah	30,400
16	Vermont	44,802
40	Virginia	16,826
9	Washington	52,531
48	West Virginia	2,704
22	Wisconsin	39,690
31	Wyoming	28,578

RANK ORDER

RANK	STATE	PER OPERATION
1	Delaware	$229,000
2	California	197,728
3	Nebraska	122,493
4	Idaho	81,796
5	North Carolina	79,220
6	South Dakota	64,202
7	Iowa	57,949
8	Georgia	57,250
9	Washington	52,531
10	Indiana	49,588
11	Arkansas	48,984
12	New York	48,278
13	Maryland	48,015
14	New Mexico	47,223
15	Pennsylvania	45,719
16	Vermont	44,802
17	Florida	44,800
18	Kansas	41,470
19	Mississippi	41,454
20	Nevada	41,093
21	Alabama	40,795
22	Wisconsin	39,690
23	Minnesota	39,550
24	Arizona	38,483
25	Illinois	37,183
26	Missouri	35,670
27	Oklahoma	35,342
28	Colorado	32,724
29	Louisiana	32,431
30	Utah	30,400
31	Wyoming	28,578
32	Montana	25,764
33	Maine	24,780
34	Kentucky	23,120
35	Ohio	22,936
36	Oregon	22,752
37	New Jersey	18,328
38	Connecticut	17,739
39	Texas	17,490
40	Virginia	16,826
41	Michigan	14,089
42	Hawaii	11,360
43	South Carolina	11,275
44	Tennessee	11,016
45	North Dakota	10,376
46	New Hampshire	9,523
47	Rhode Island	8,624
48	West Virginia	2,704
49	Massachusetts	536
50	Alaska	(34,944)

District of Columbia** NA

Source: CQ Press using data from U.S. Department of Agriculture, Economic Research Service
"Farm Sector Financial Indicators, State Rankings"
(http://www.ers.usda.gov/data-products/farm-income-and-wealth-statistics.aspx)
*Calculated by multiplying average acres per farm by average net farm income per acre.
**Not applicable.

Net Farm Income per Acre in 2014

National Average = $99 per Acre*

ALPHA ORDER

RANK	STATE	PER ACRE
12	Alabama	$199
50	Alaska	(32)
42	Arizona	29
17	Arkansas	156
2	California	592
40	Colorado	36
8	Connecticut	243
1	Delaware	1,145
11	Florida	224
7	Georgia	250
33	Hawaii	71
15	Idaho	169
28	Illinois	103
13	Indiana	196
16	Iowa	167
35	Kansas	55
21	Kentucky	136
26	Louisiana	113
20	Maine	140
5	Maryland	291
48	Massachusetts	8
32	Michigan	73
26	Minnesota	113
19	Mississippi	141
24	Missouri	123
46	Montana	12
22	Nebraska	133
42	Nevada	29
30	New Hampshire	89
10	New Jersey	232
44	New Mexico	27
9	New York	239
3	North Carolina	466
48	North Dakota	8
25	Ohio	122
31	Oklahoma	82
38	Oregon	48
4	Pennsylvania	349
18	Rhode Island	154
35	South Carolina	55
39	South Dakota	47
34	Tennessee	68
41	Texas	33
37	Utah	50
6	Vermont	262
29	Virginia	94
23	Washington	131
45	West Virginia	16
14	Wisconsin	189
47	Wyoming	11

RANK ORDER

RANK	STATE	PER ACRE
1	Delaware	$1,145
2	California	592
3	North Carolina	466
4	Pennsylvania	349
5	Maryland	291
6	Vermont	262
7	Georgia	250
8	Connecticut	243
9	New York	239
10	New Jersey	232
11	Florida	224
12	Alabama	199
13	Indiana	196
14	Wisconsin	189
15	Idaho	169
16	Iowa	167
17	Arkansas	156
18	Rhode Island	154
19	Mississippi	141
20	Maine	140
21	Kentucky	136
22	Nebraska	133
23	Washington	131
24	Missouri	123
25	Ohio	122
26	Louisiana	113
26	Minnesota	113
28	Illinois	103
29	Virginia	94
30	New Hampshire	89
31	Oklahoma	82
32	Michigan	73
33	Hawaii	71
34	Tennessee	68
35	Kansas	55
35	South Carolina	55
37	Utah	50
38	Oregon	48
39	South Dakota	47
40	Colorado	36
41	Texas	33
42	Arizona	29
42	Nevada	29
44	New Mexico	27
45	West Virginia	16
46	Montana	12
47	Wyoming	11
48	Massachusetts	8
48	North Dakota	8
50	Alaska	(32)
	District of Columbia**	NA

Source: CQ Press using data from U.S. Department of Agriculture, Economic Research Service
"Farm Sector Financial Indicators, State Rankings"
(http://www.ers.usda.gov/data-products/farm-income-and-wealth-statistics.aspx)
*Net farm income is a measure of the net value of production in a given year. It is determined by subtracting total production expenses from gross farm income.
**Not applicable.

Farm Income: Cash Receipts from Commodities in 2014

National Total = $421,940,522,000*

ALPHA ORDER

RANK	STATE	FARM INCOME	% of USA
26	Alabama	$6,435,292,000	1.5%
50	Alaska	31,873,000	0.0%
30	Arizona	4,358,900,000	1.0%
13	Arkansas	10,272,270,000	2.4%
1	California	53,492,081,000	12.7%
22	Colorado	7,583,529,000	1.8%
46	Connecticut	629,826,000	0.1%
39	Delaware	1,479,878,000	0.4%
20	Florida	8,462,653,000	2.0%
16	Georgia	9,966,228,000	2.4%
45	Hawaii	718,052,000	0.2%
17	Idaho	8,768,017,000	2.1%
5	Illinois	19,295,188,000	4.6%
9	Indiana	12,979,830,000	3.1%
2	Iowa	30,957,029,000	7.3%
7	Kansas	16,502,935,000	3.9%
25	Kentucky	6,525,551,000	1.5%
33	Louisiana	3,946,424,000	0.9%
44	Maine	831,338,000	0.2%
36	Maryland	2,430,859,000	0.6%
47	Massachusetts	458,309,000	0.1%
19	Michigan	8,586,668,000	2.0%
6	Minnesota	18,827,590,000	4.5%
24	Mississippi	6,573,317,000	1.6%
11	Missouri	10,944,283,000	2.6%
29	Montana	4,625,782,000	1.1%
3	Nebraska	24,942,122,000	5.9%
42	Nevada	867,739,000	0.2%
48	New Hampshire	249,964,000	0.1%
40	New Jersey	1,023,281,000	0.2%
34	New Mexico	3,659,649,000	0.9%
27	New York	6,359,513,000	1.5%
8	North Carolina	13,006,621,000	3.1%
18	North Dakota	8,668,091,000	2.1%
15	Ohio	10,031,778,000	2.4%
23	Oklahoma	7,518,444,000	1.8%
28	Oregon	5,237,783,000	1.2%
21	Pennsylvania	8,294,977,000	2.0%
49	Rhode Island	75,213,000	0.0%
35	South Carolina	2,674,502,000	0.6%
12	South Dakota	10,872,820,000	2.6%
31	Tennessee	4,237,471,000	1.0%
4	Texas	24,734,963,000	5.9%
37	Utah	2,378,261,000	0.6%
41	Vermont	992,220,000	0.2%
32	Virginia	4,176,569,000	1.0%
14	Washington	10,117,439,000	2.4%
43	West Virginia	832,767,000	0.2%
10	Wisconsin	12,828,621,000	3.0%
38	Wyoming	1,834,506,000	0.4%

RANK ORDER

RANK	STATE	FARM INCOME	% of USA
1	California	$53,492,081,000	12.7%
2	Iowa	30,957,029,000	7.3%
3	Nebraska	24,942,122,000	5.9%
4	Texas	24,734,963,000	5.9%
5	Illinois	19,295,188,000	4.6%
6	Minnesota	18,827,590,000	4.5%
7	Kansas	16,502,935,000	3.9%
8	North Carolina	13,006,621,000	3.1%
9	Indiana	12,979,830,000	3.1%
10	Wisconsin	12,828,621,000	3.0%
11	Missouri	10,944,283,000	2.6%
12	South Dakota	10,872,820,000	2.6%
13	Arkansas	10,272,270,000	2.4%
14	Washington	10,117,439,000	2.4%
15	Ohio	10,031,778,000	2.4%
16	Georgia	9,966,228,000	2.4%
17	Idaho	8,768,017,000	2.1%
18	North Dakota	8,668,091,000	2.1%
19	Michigan	8,586,668,000	2.0%
20	Florida	8,462,653,000	2.0%
21	Pennsylvania	8,294,977,000	2.0%
22	Colorado	7,583,529,000	1.8%
23	Oklahoma	7,518,444,000	1.8%
24	Mississippi	6,573,317,000	1.6%
25	Kentucky	6,525,551,000	1.5%
26	Alabama	6,435,292,000	1.5%
27	New York	6,359,513,000	1.5%
28	Oregon	5,237,783,000	1.2%
29	Montana	4,625,782,000	1.1%
30	Arizona	4,358,900,000	1.0%
31	Tennessee	4,237,471,000	1.0%
32	Virginia	4,176,569,000	1.0%
33	Louisiana	3,946,424,000	0.9%
34	New Mexico	3,659,649,000	0.9%
35	South Carolina	2,674,502,000	0.6%
36	Maryland	2,430,859,000	0.6%
37	Utah	2,378,261,000	0.6%
38	Wyoming	1,834,506,000	0.4%
39	Delaware	1,479,878,000	0.4%
40	New Jersey	1,023,281,000	0.2%
41	Vermont	992,220,000	0.2%
42	Nevada	867,739,000	0.2%
43	West Virginia	832,767,000	0.2%
44	Maine	831,338,000	0.2%
45	Hawaii	718,052,000	0.2%
46	Connecticut	629,826,000	0.1%
47	Massachusetts	458,309,000	0.1%
48	New Hampshire	249,964,000	0.1%
49	Rhode Island	75,213,000	0.0%
50	Alaska	31,873,000	0.0%
	District of Columbia	0	0.0%

Source: U.S. Department of Agriculture, Economic Research Service
"Farm Sector Financial Indicators, State Rankings" (www.ers.usda.gov/data-products/farm-income-and-wealth-statistics.aspx)
*Commodities include crops and livestock.

Farm Income: Crops in 2014

National Total = $209,729,724,000

ALPHA ORDER

RANK	STATE	FARM INCOME	% of USA
33	Alabama	$1,271,877,000	0.6%
50	Alaska	26,098,000	0.0%
30	Arizona	1,974,032,000	0.9%
16	Arkansas	4,525,199,000	2.2%
1	California	38,174,656,000	18.2%
28	Colorado	2,341,744,000	1.1%
42	Connecticut	382,158,000	0.2%
43	Delaware	318,346,000	0.2%
11	Florida	6,080,192,000	2.9%
20	Georgia	3,298,956,000	1.6%
38	Hawaii	567,838,000	0.3%
21	Idaho	3,296,962,000	1.6%
2	Illinois	16,090,514,000	7.7%
6	Indiana	8,692,950,000	4.1%
3	Iowa	14,082,016,000	6.7%
12	Kansas	6,036,735,000	2.9%
22	Kentucky	2,861,021,000	1.4%
24	Louisiana	2,604,323,000	1.2%
40	Maine	426,551,000	0.2%
35	Maryland	961,833,000	0.5%
44	Massachusetts	314,284,000	0.1%
15	Michigan	4,632,634,000	2.2%
5	Minnesota	9,978,349,000	4.8%
23	Mississippi	2,788,185,000	1.3%
14	Missouri	5,684,492,000	2.7%
27	Montana	2,360,439,000	1.1%
4	Nebraska	10,410,964,000	5.0%
45	Nevada	264,928,000	0.1%
48	New Hampshire	106,134,000	0.1%
36	New Jersey	890,512,000	0.4%
37	New Mexico	700,514,000	0.3%
29	New York	2,101,024,000	1.0%
17	North Carolina	4,155,979,000	2.0%
8	North Dakota	7,054,719,000	3.4%
13	Ohio	5,926,642,000	2.8%
32	Oklahoma	1,291,107,000	0.6%
19	Oregon	3,334,806,000	1.6%
25	Pennsylvania	2,603,743,000	1.2%
49	Rhode Island	49,200,000	0.0%
34	South Carolina	1,080,368,000	0.5%
10	South Dakota	6,227,770,000	3.0%
26	Tennessee	2,417,961,000	1.2%
7	Texas	7,704,689,000	3.7%
39	Utah	535,153,000	0.3%
46	Vermont	178,621,000	0.1%
31	Virginia	1,346,922,000	0.6%
9	Washington	6,960,705,000	3.3%
47	West Virginia	150,101,000	0.1%
18	Wisconsin	3,422,538,000	1.6%
41	Wyoming	400,734,000	0.2%

RANK ORDER

RANK	STATE	FARM INCOME	% of USA
1	California	$38,174,656,000	18.2%
2	Illinois	16,090,514,000	7.7%
3	Iowa	14,082,016,000	6.7%
4	Nebraska	10,410,964,000	5.0%
5	Minnesota	9,978,349,000	4.8%
6	Indiana	8,692,950,000	4.1%
7	Texas	7,704,689,000	3.7%
8	North Dakota	7,054,719,000	3.4%
9	Washington	6,960,705,000	3.3%
10	South Dakota	6,227,770,000	3.0%
11	Florida	6,080,192,000	2.9%
12	Kansas	6,036,735,000	2.9%
13	Ohio	5,926,642,000	2.8%
14	Missouri	5,684,492,000	2.7%
15	Michigan	4,632,634,000	2.2%
16	Arkansas	4,525,199,000	2.2%
17	North Carolina	4,155,979,000	2.0%
18	Wisconsin	3,422,538,000	1.6%
19	Oregon	3,334,806,000	1.6%
20	Georgia	3,298,956,000	1.6%
21	Idaho	3,296,962,000	1.6%
22	Kentucky	2,861,021,000	1.4%
23	Mississippi	2,788,185,000	1.3%
24	Louisiana	2,604,323,000	1.2%
25	Pennsylvania	2,603,743,000	1.2%
26	Tennessee	2,417,961,000	1.2%
27	Montana	2,360,439,000	1.1%
28	Colorado	2,341,744,000	1.1%
29	New York	2,101,024,000	1.0%
30	Arizona	1,974,032,000	0.9%
31	Virginia	1,346,922,000	0.6%
32	Oklahoma	1,291,107,000	0.6%
33	Alabama	1,271,877,000	0.6%
34	South Carolina	1,080,368,000	0.5%
35	Maryland	961,833,000	0.5%
36	New Jersey	890,512,000	0.4%
37	New Mexico	700,514,000	0.3%
38	Hawaii	567,838,000	0.3%
39	Utah	535,153,000	0.3%
40	Maine	426,551,000	0.2%
41	Wyoming	400,734,000	0.2%
42	Connecticut	382,158,000	0.2%
43	Delaware	318,346,000	0.2%
44	Massachusetts	314,284,000	0.1%
45	Nevada	264,928,000	0.1%
46	Vermont	178,621,000	0.1%
47	West Virginia	150,101,000	0.1%
48	New Hampshire	106,134,000	0.1%
49	Rhode Island	49,200,000	0.0%
50	Alaska	26,098,000	0.0%
	District of Columbia	0	0.0%

Source: U.S. Department of Agriculture, Economic Research Service
"Farm Sector Financial Indicators, State Rankings" (www.ers.usda.gov/data-products/farm-income-and-wealth-statistics.aspx)

Farm Income: Livestock in 2014

National Total = $212,210,798,000*

ALPHA ORDER

RANK	STATE	FARM INCOME	% of USA
16	Alabama	$5,163,415,000	2.4%
50	Alaska	5,775,000	0.0%
28	Arizona	2,384,868,000	1.1%
11	Arkansas	5,747,071,000	2.7%
3	California	15,317,425,000	7.2%
15	Colorado	5,241,785,000	2.5%
44	Connecticut	247,668,000	0.1%
39	Delaware	1,161,532,000	0.5%
29	Florida	2,382,461,000	1.1%
9	Georgia	6,667,272,000	3.1%
45	Hawaii	150,214,000	0.1%
13	Idaho	5,471,055,000	2.6%
24	Illinois	3,204,674,000	1.5%
18	Indiana	4,286,880,000	2.0%
2	Iowa	16,875,013,000	8.0%
5	Kansas	10,466,200,000	4.9%
23	Kentucky	3,664,530,000	1.7%
38	Louisiana	1,342,101,000	0.6%
43	Maine	404,787,000	0.2%
36	Maryland	1,469,026,000	0.7%
46	Massachusetts	144,025,000	0.1%
21	Michigan	3,954,034,000	1.9%
8	Minnesota	8,849,241,000	4.2%
22	Mississippi	3,785,132,000	1.8%
14	Missouri	5,259,791,000	2.5%
30	Montana	2,265,343,000	1.1%
4	Nebraska	14,531,158,000	6.8%
42	Nevada	602,811,000	0.3%
47	New Hampshire	143,830,000	0.1%
48	New Jersey	132,769,000	0.1%
26	New Mexico	2,959,135,000	1.4%
19	New York	4,258,489,000	2.0%
7	North Carolina	8,850,642,000	4.2%
34	North Dakota	1,613,372,000	0.8%
20	Ohio	4,105,136,000	1.9%
10	Oklahoma	6,227,337,000	2.9%
31	Oregon	1,902,977,000	0.9%
12	Pennsylvania	5,691,234,000	2.7%
49	Rhode Island	26,013,000	0.0%
35	South Carolina	1,594,134,000	0.8%
17	South Dakota	4,645,050,000	2.2%
33	Tennessee	1,819,510,000	0.9%
1	Texas	17,030,274,000	8.0%
32	Utah	1,843,108,000	0.9%
40	Vermont	813,599,000	0.4%
27	Virginia	2,829,647,000	1.3%
25	Washington	3,156,734,000	1.5%
41	West Virginia	682,666,000	0.3%
6	Wisconsin	9,406,083,000	4.4%
37	Wyoming	1,433,772,000	0.7%

RANK ORDER

RANK	STATE	FARM INCOME	% of USA
1	Texas	$17,030,274,000	8.0%
2	Iowa	16,875,013,000	8.0%
3	California	15,317,425,000	7.2%
4	Nebraska	14,531,158,000	6.8%
5	Kansas	10,466,200,000	4.9%
6	Wisconsin	9,406,083,000	4.4%
7	North Carolina	8,850,642,000	4.2%
8	Minnesota	8,849,241,000	4.2%
9	Georgia	6,667,272,000	3.1%
10	Oklahoma	6,227,337,000	2.9%
11	Arkansas	5,747,071,000	2.7%
12	Pennsylvania	5,691,234,000	2.7%
13	Idaho	5,471,055,000	2.6%
14	Missouri	5,259,791,000	2.5%
15	Colorado	5,241,785,000	2.5%
16	Alabama	5,163,415,000	2.4%
17	South Dakota	4,645,050,000	2.2%
18	Indiana	4,286,880,000	2.0%
19	New York	4,258,489,000	2.0%
20	Ohio	4,105,136,000	1.9%
21	Michigan	3,954,034,000	1.9%
22	Mississippi	3,785,132,000	1.8%
23	Kentucky	3,664,530,000	1.7%
24	Illinois	3,204,674,000	1.5%
25	Washington	3,156,734,000	1.5%
26	New Mexico	2,959,135,000	1.4%
27	Virginia	2,829,647,000	1.3%
28	Arizona	2,384,868,000	1.1%
29	Florida	2,382,461,000	1.1%
30	Montana	2,265,343,000	1.1%
31	Oregon	1,902,977,000	0.9%
32	Utah	1,843,108,000	0.9%
33	Tennessee	1,819,510,000	0.9%
34	North Dakota	1,613,372,000	0.8%
35	South Carolina	1,594,134,000	0.8%
36	Maryland	1,469,026,000	0.7%
37	Wyoming	1,433,772,000	0.7%
38	Louisiana	1,342,101,000	0.6%
39	Delaware	1,161,532,000	0.5%
40	Vermont	813,599,000	0.4%
41	West Virginia	682,666,000	0.3%
42	Nevada	602,811,000	0.3%
43	Maine	404,787,000	0.2%
44	Connecticut	247,668,000	0.1%
45	Hawaii	150,214,000	0.1%
46	Massachusetts	144,025,000	0.1%
47	New Hampshire	143,830,000	0.1%
48	New Jersey	132,769,000	0.1%
49	Rhode Island	26,013,000	0.0%
50	Alaska	5,775,000	0.0%
	District of Columbia	0	0.0%

Source: U.S. Department of Agriculture, Economic Research Service
"Farm Sector Financial Indicators, State Rankings" (www.ers.usda.gov/data-products/farm-income-and-wealth-statistics.aspx)
*Includes livestock products.

Farm Income: Government Payments in 2014

National Total = $9,766,845,000*

ALPHA ORDER

RANK	STATE	FARM INCOME	% of USA
24	Alabama	$118,423,000	1.2%
43	Alaska	10,043,000	0.1%
34	Arizona	68,953,000	0.7%
9	Arkansas	329,557,000	3.4%
13	California	246,649,000	2.5%
10	Colorado	285,927,000	2.9%
49	Connecticut	5,735,000	0.1%
46	Delaware	7,514,000	0.1%
31	Florida	82,580,000	0.8%
11	Georgia	266,245,000	2.7%
40	Hawaii	24,665,000	0.3%
30	Idaho	82,968,000	0.8%
17	Illinois	188,620,000	1.9%
27	Indiana	106,856,000	1.1%
7	Iowa	450,438,000	4.6%
4	Kansas	665,466,000	6.8%
14	Kentucky	238,153,000	2.4%
21	Louisiana	135,621,000	1.4%
41	Maine	14,574,000	0.1%
39	Maryland	26,895,000	0.3%
47	Massachusetts	6,741,000	0.1%
35	Michigan	60,578,000	0.6%
12	Minnesota	261,397,000	2.7%
18	Mississippi	177,257,000	1.8%
5	Missouri	510,195,000	5.2%
19	Montana	158,925,000	1.6%
3	Nebraska	697,637,000	7.1%
37	Nevada	43,179,000	0.4%
45	New Hampshire	8,125,000	0.1%
48	New Jersey	6,578,000	0.1%
15	New Mexico	228,578,000	2.3%
38	New York	27,479,000	0.3%
8	North Carolina	346,093,000	3.5%
16	North Dakota	217,242,000	2.2%
33	Ohio	78,137,000	0.8%
2	Oklahoma	1,013,243,000	10.4%
25	Oregon	115,899,000	1.2%
36	Pennsylvania	53,306,000	0.5%
50	Rhode Island	1,896,000	0.0%
26	South Carolina	108,675,000	1.1%
6	South Dakota	458,833,000	4.7%
23	Tennessee	121,302,000	1.2%
1	Texas	1,150,629,000	11.8%
32	Utah	78,842,000	0.8%
44	Vermont	8,846,000	0.1%
29	Virginia	86,013,000	0.9%
22	Washington	122,506,000	1.3%
42	West Virginia	14,418,000	0.1%
28	Wisconsin	92,142,000	0.9%
20	Wyoming	156,277,000	1.6%

RANK ORDER

RANK	STATE	FARM INCOME	% of USA
1	Texas	$1,150,629,000	11.8%
2	Oklahoma	1,013,243,000	10.4%
3	Nebraska	697,637,000	7.1%
4	Kansas	665,466,000	6.8%
5	Missouri	510,195,000	5.2%
6	South Dakota	458,833,000	4.7%
7	Iowa	450,438,000	4.6%
8	North Carolina	346,093,000	3.5%
9	Arkansas	329,557,000	3.4%
10	Colorado	285,927,000	2.9%
11	Georgia	266,245,000	2.7%
12	Minnesota	261,397,000	2.7%
13	California	246,649,000	2.5%
14	Kentucky	238,153,000	2.4%
15	New Mexico	228,578,000	2.3%
16	North Dakota	217,242,000	2.2%
17	Illinois	188,620,000	1.9%
18	Mississippi	177,257,000	1.8%
19	Montana	158,925,000	1.6%
20	Wyoming	156,277,000	1.6%
21	Louisiana	135,621,000	1.4%
22	Washington	122,506,000	1.3%
23	Tennessee	121,302,000	1.2%
24	Alabama	118,423,000	1.2%
25	Oregon	115,899,000	1.2%
26	South Carolina	108,675,000	1.1%
27	Indiana	106,856,000	1.1%
28	Wisconsin	92,142,000	0.9%
29	Virginia	86,013,000	0.9%
30	Idaho	82,968,000	0.8%
31	Florida	82,580,000	0.8%
32	Utah	78,842,000	0.8%
33	Ohio	78,137,000	0.8%
34	Arizona	68,953,000	0.7%
35	Michigan	60,578,000	0.6%
36	Pennsylvania	53,306,000	0.5%
37	Nevada	43,179,000	0.4%
38	New York	27,479,000	0.3%
39	Maryland	26,895,000	0.3%
40	Hawaii	24,665,000	0.3%
41	Maine	14,574,000	0.1%
42	West Virginia	14,418,000	0.1%
43	Alaska	10,043,000	0.1%
44	Vermont	8,846,000	0.1%
45	New Hampshire	8,125,000	0.1%
46	Delaware	7,514,000	0.1%
47	Massachusetts	6,741,000	0.1%
48	New Jersey	6,578,000	0.1%
49	Connecticut	5,735,000	0.1%
50	Rhode Island	1,896,000	0.0%
	District of Columbia	0	0.0%

Source: U.S. Department of Agriculture, Economic Research Service
"Farm Sector Financial Indicators, State Rankings" (www.ers.usda.gov/data-products/farm-income-and-wealth-statistics.aspx)
*Government payments made directly to farmers in cash.

Acres Planted in 2015

National Total = 318,512,000 Acres*

ALPHA ORDER

RANK	STATE	ACRES	% of USA
30	Alabama	2,320,000	0.7%
NA	Alaska**	NA	NA
38	Arizona	715,000	0.2%
15	Arkansas	7,112,000	2.2%
27	California	2,987,000	0.9%
18	Colorado	5,987,000	1.9%
46	Connecticut	79,000	0.0%
40	Delaware	461,000	0.1%
35	Florida	1,158,000	0.4%
23	Georgia	3,694,000	1.2%
48	Hawaii	19,000	0.0%
22	Idaho	4,109,000	1.3%
4	Illinois	22,616,000	7.1%
10	Indiana	12,065,000	3.8%
1	Iowa	24,655,000	7.7%
3	Kansas	23,320,000	7.3%
17	Kentucky	6,243,000	2.0%
26	Louisiana	3,392,000	1.1%
43	Maine	260,000	0.1%
33	Maryland	1,582,000	0.5%
45	Massachusetts	112,000	0.0%
16	Michigan	6,419,000	2.0%
6	Minnesota	20,015,000	6.3%
21	Mississippi	4,274,000	1.3%
9	Missouri	12,081,000	3.8%
13	Montana	9,331,000	2.9%
7	Nebraska	19,653,000	6.2%
41	Nevada	334,000	0.1%
47	New Hampshire	63,000	0.0%
42	New Jersey	314,000	0.1%
36	New Mexico	975,000	0.3%
28	New York	2,839,000	0.9%
20	North Carolina	4,751,000	1.5%
2	North Dakota	23,710,000	7.4%
12	Ohio	9,974,000	3.1%
11	Oklahoma	10,116,000	3.2%
31	Oregon	2,106,000	0.7%
25	Pennsylvania	3,568,000	1.1%
49	Rhode Island	9,000	0.0%
32	South Carolina	1,624,000	0.5%
8	South Dakota	18,100,000	5.7%
19	Tennessee	4,926,000	1.5%
5	Texas	21,603,000	6.8%
37	Utah	902,000	0.3%
44	Vermont	237,000	0.1%
29	Virginia	2,705,000	0.8%
24	Washington	3,645,000	1.1%
39	West Virginia	676,000	0.2%
14	Wisconsin	7,999,000	2.5%
34	Wyoming	1,497,000	0.5%

RANK ORDER

RANK	STATE	ACRES	% of USA
1	Iowa	24,655,000	7.7%
2	North Dakota	23,710,000	7.4%
3	Kansas	23,320,000	7.3%
4	Illinois	22,616,000	7.1%
5	Texas	21,603,000	6.8%
6	Minnesota	20,015,000	6.3%
7	Nebraska	19,653,000	6.2%
8	South Dakota	18,100,000	5.7%
9	Missouri	12,081,000	3.8%
10	Indiana	12,065,000	3.8%
11	Oklahoma	10,116,000	3.2%
12	Ohio	9,974,000	3.1%
13	Montana	9,331,000	2.9%
14	Wisconsin	7,999,000	2.5%
15	Arkansas	7,112,000	2.2%
16	Michigan	6,419,000	2.0%
17	Kentucky	6,243,000	2.0%
18	Colorado	5,987,000	1.9%
19	Tennessee	4,926,000	1.5%
20	North Carolina	4,751,000	1.5%
21	Mississippi	4,274,000	1.3%
22	Idaho	4,109,000	1.3%
23	Georgia	3,694,000	1.2%
24	Washington	3,645,000	1.1%
25	Pennsylvania	3,568,000	1.1%
26	Louisiana	3,392,000	1.1%
27	California	2,987,000	0.9%
28	New York	2,839,000	0.9%
29	Virginia	2,705,000	0.8%
30	Alabama	2,320,000	0.7%
31	Oregon	2,106,000	0.7%
32	South Carolina	1,624,000	0.5%
33	Maryland	1,582,000	0.5%
34	Wyoming	1,497,000	0.5%
35	Florida	1,158,000	0.4%
36	New Mexico	975,000	0.3%
37	Utah	902,000	0.3%
38	Arizona	715,000	0.2%
39	West Virginia	676,000	0.2%
40	Delaware	461,000	0.1%
41	Nevada	334,000	0.1%
42	New Jersey	314,000	0.1%
43	Maine	260,000	0.1%
44	Vermont	237,000	0.1%
45	Massachusetts	112,000	0.0%
46	Connecticut	79,000	0.0%
47	New Hampshire	63,000	0.0%
48	Hawaii	19,000	0.0%
49	Rhode Island	9,000	0.0%
NA	Alaska**	NA	NA
	District of Columbia**	NA	NA

Source: U.S. Department of Agriculture, National Agricultural Statistics Service
"Crop Production: 2015 Summary" (January 2016)
(http://usda.mannlib.cornell.edu/MannUsda/viewDocumentInfo.do?documentID=1047)
*Estimated totals.
**No acreage or not available.

Acres Harvested in 2015

National Total = 304,532,000 Acres*

ALPHA ORDER

RANK	STATE	ACRES	% of USA
30	Alabama	2,224,000	0.7%
NA	Alaska**	NA	NA
38	Arizona	704,000	0.2%
15	Arkansas	6,923,000	2.3%
29	California	2,568,000	0.8%
18	Colorado	5,611,000	1.8%
46	Connecticut	74,000	0.0%
40	Delaware	442,000	0.1%
35	Florida	1,130,000	0.4%
25	Georgia	3,367,000	1.1%
48	Hawaii	19,000	0.0%
22	Idaho	3,944,000	1.3%
4	Illinois	22,388,000	7.4%
9	Indiana	11,895,000	3.9%
1	Iowa	24,422,000	8.0%
3	Kansas	22,557,000	7.4%
17	Kentucky	6,073,000	2.0%
26	Louisiana	3,320,000	1.1%
43	Maine	254,000	0.1%
32	Maryland	1,462,000	0.5%
45	Massachusetts	109,000	0.0%
16	Michigan	6,319,000	2.1%
5	Minnesota	19,701,000	6.5%
21	Mississippi	4,193,000	1.4%
10	Missouri	11,751,000	3.9%
12	Montana	8,917,000	2.9%
6	Nebraska	19,175,000	6.3%
41	Nevada	330,000	0.1%
47	New Hampshire	62,000	0.0%
42	New Jersey	304,000	0.1%
37	New Mexico	768,000	0.3%
27	New York	2,782,000	0.9%
20	North Carolina	4,584,000	1.5%
2	North Dakota	23,308,000	7.7%
11	Ohio	9,843,000	3.2%
13	Oklahoma	8,336,000	2.7%
31	Oregon	2,059,000	0.7%
24	Pennsylvania	3,488,000	1.1%
49	Rhode Island	9,000	0.0%
34	South Carolina	1,367,000	0.4%
8	South Dakota	17,253,000	5.7%
19	Tennessee	4,811,000	1.6%
7	Texas	18,194,000	6.0%
36	Utah	864,000	0.3%
44	Vermont	233,000	0.1%
28	Virginia	2,581,000	0.8%
23	Washington	3,553,000	1.2%
39	West Virginia	669,000	0.2%
14	Wisconsin	7,840,000	2.6%
33	Wyoming	1,454,000	0.5%

RANK ORDER

RANK	STATE	ACRES	% of USA
1	Iowa	24,422,000	8.0%
2	North Dakota	23,308,000	7.7%
3	Kansas	22,557,000	7.4%
4	Illinois	22,388,000	7.4%
5	Minnesota	19,701,000	6.5%
6	Nebraska	19,175,000	6.3%
7	Texas	18,194,000	6.0%
8	South Dakota	17,253,000	5.7%
9	Indiana	11,895,000	3.9%
10	Missouri	11,751,000	3.9%
11	Ohio	9,843,000	3.2%
12	Montana	8,917,000	2.9%
13	Oklahoma	8,336,000	2.7%
14	Wisconsin	7,840,000	2.6%
15	Arkansas	6,923,000	2.3%
16	Michigan	6,319,000	2.1%
17	Kentucky	6,073,000	2.0%
18	Colorado	5,611,000	1.8%
19	Tennessee	4,811,000	1.6%
20	North Carolina	4,584,000	1.5%
21	Mississippi	4,193,000	1.4%
22	Idaho	3,944,000	1.3%
23	Washington	3,553,000	1.2%
24	Pennsylvania	3,488,000	1.1%
25	Georgia	3,367,000	1.1%
26	Louisiana	3,320,000	1.1%
27	New York	2,782,000	0.9%
28	Virginia	2,581,000	0.8%
29	California	2,568,000	0.8%
30	Alabama	2,224,000	0.7%
31	Oregon	2,059,000	0.7%
32	Maryland	1,462,000	0.5%
33	Wyoming	1,454,000	0.5%
34	South Carolina	1,367,000	0.4%
35	Florida	1,130,000	0.4%
36	Utah	864,000	0.3%
37	New Mexico	768,000	0.3%
38	Arizona	704,000	0.2%
39	West Virginia	669,000	0.2%
40	Delaware	442,000	0.1%
41	Nevada	330,000	0.1%
42	New Jersey	304,000	0.1%
43	Maine	254,000	0.1%
44	Vermont	233,000	0.1%
45	Massachusetts	109,000	0.0%
46	Connecticut	74,000	0.0%
47	New Hampshire	62,000	0.0%
48	Hawaii	19,000	0.0%
49	Rhode Island	9,000	0.0%
NA	Alaska**	NA	NA
	District of Columbia**	NA	NA

Source: U.S. Department of Agriculture, National Agricultural Statistics Service
"Crop Production: 2015 Summary" (January 2016)
(http://usda.mannlib.cornell.edu/MannUsda/viewDocumentInfo.do?documentID=1047)
*Estimated totals.
**No acreage or not available.

Acres Harvested: Corn in 2015

National Total = 80,749,000 Acres*

ALPHA ORDER

RANK	STATE	ACRES	% of USA
28	Alabama	245,000	0.3%
NA	Alaska**	NA	NA
39	Arizona	34,000	0.0%
21	Arkansas	445,000	0.6%
33	California	60,000	0.1%
15	Colorado	950,000	1.2%
NA	Connecticut**	NA	NA
29	Delaware	164,000	0.2%
35	Florida	50,000	0.1%
25	Georgia	285,000	0.4%
NA	Hawaii**	NA	NA
32	Idaho	70,000	0.1%
2	Illinois	11,500,000	14.2%
5	Indiana	5,480,000	6.8%
1	Iowa	13,050,000	16.2%
7	Kansas	3,920,000	4.9%
14	Kentucky	1,310,000	1.6%
22	Louisiana	390,000	0.5%
NA	Maine**	NA	NA
23	Maryland	380,000	0.5%
NA	Massachusetts**	NA	NA
12	Michigan	2,070,000	2.6%
4	Minnesota	7,600,000	9.4%
20	Mississippi	490,000	0.6%
9	Missouri	3,080,000	3.8%
35	Montana	50,000	0.1%
3	Nebraska	9,150,000	11.3%
NA	Nevada**	NA	NA
NA	New Hampshire**	NA	NA
31	New Jersey	72,000	0.1%
37	New Mexico	40,000	0.0%
19	New York	590,000	0.7%
17	North Carolina	730,000	0.9%
11	North Dakota	2,560,000	3.2%
8	Ohio	3,260,000	4.0%
26	Oklahoma	280,000	0.3%
40	Oregon	30,000	0.0%
16	Pennsylvania	940,000	1.2%
NA	Rhode Island**	NA	NA
27	South Carolina	260,000	0.3%
6	South Dakota	5,030,000	6.2%
17	Tennessee	730,000	0.9%
13	Texas	1,970,000	2.4%
41	Utah	15,000	0.0%
NA	Vermont**	NA	NA
24	Virginia	300,000	0.4%
30	Washington	75,000	0.1%
38	West Virginia	35,000	0.0%
10	Wisconsin	3,000,000	3.7%
34	Wyoming	59,000	0.1%

RANK ORDER

RANK	STATE	ACRES	% of USA
1	Iowa	13,050,000	16.2%
2	Illinois	11,500,000	14.2%
3	Nebraska	9,150,000	11.3%
4	Minnesota	7,600,000	9.4%
5	Indiana	5,480,000	6.8%
6	South Dakota	5,030,000	6.2%
7	Kansas	3,920,000	4.9%
8	Ohio	3,260,000	4.0%
9	Missouri	3,080,000	3.8%
10	Wisconsin	3,000,000	3.7%
11	North Dakota	2,560,000	3.2%
12	Michigan	2,070,000	2.6%
13	Texas	1,970,000	2.4%
14	Kentucky	1,310,000	1.6%
15	Colorado	950,000	1.2%
16	Pennsylvania	940,000	1.2%
17	North Carolina	730,000	0.9%
17	Tennessee	730,000	0.9%
19	New York	590,000	0.7%
20	Mississippi	490,000	0.6%
21	Arkansas	445,000	0.6%
22	Louisiana	390,000	0.5%
23	Maryland	380,000	0.5%
24	Virginia	300,000	0.4%
25	Georgia	285,000	0.4%
26	Oklahoma	280,000	0.3%
27	South Carolina	260,000	0.3%
28	Alabama	245,000	0.3%
29	Delaware	164,000	0.2%
30	Washington	75,000	0.1%
31	New Jersey	72,000	0.1%
32	Idaho	70,000	0.1%
33	California	60,000	0.1%
34	Wyoming	59,000	0.1%
35	Florida	50,000	0.1%
35	Montana	50,000	0.1%
37	New Mexico	40,000	0.0%
38	West Virginia	35,000	0.0%
39	Arizona	34,000	0.0%
40	Oregon	30,000	0.0%
41	Utah	15,000	0.0%
NA	Alaska**	NA	NA
NA	Connecticut**	NA	NA
NA	Hawaii**	NA	NA
NA	Maine**	NA	NA
NA	Massachusetts**	NA	NA
NA	Nevada**	NA	NA
NA	New Hampshire**	NA	NA
NA	Rhode Island**	NA	NA
NA	Vermont**	NA	NA
	District of Columbia**	NA	NA

Source: U.S. Department of Agriculture, National Agricultural Statistics Service
"Crop Production: 2015 Summary" (January 2016)
(http://usda.mannlib.cornell.edu/MannUsda/viewDocumentInfo.do?documentID=1047)
*Estimated totals. Acres harvested for grain.
**No acreage or not available.

Acres Harvested: Soybeans in 2015

National Total = 81,849,000 Acres*

ALPHA ORDER

RANK	STATE	ACRES	% of USA
22	Alabama	490,000	0.6%
NA	Alaska**	NA	NA
NA	Arizona**	NA	NA
11	Arkansas	3,170,000	3.9%
NA	California**	NA	NA
NA	Colorado**	NA	NA
NA	Connecticut**	NA	NA
27	Delaware	173,000	0.2%
30	Florida	31,000	0.0%
25	Georgia	315,000	0.4%
NA	Hawaii**	NA	NA
NA	Idaho**	NA	NA
2	Illinois	9,720,000	11.9%
5	Indiana	5,500,000	6.7%
1	Iowa	9,800,000	12.0%
10	Kansas	3,860,000	4.7%
15	Kentucky	1,810,000	2.2%
18	Louisiana	1,395,000	1.7%
NA	Maine**	NA	NA
21	Maryland	515,000	0.6%
NA	Massachusetts**	NA	NA
13	Michigan	2,020,000	2.5%
3	Minnesota	7,550,000	9.2%
12	Mississippi	2,270,000	2.8%
9	Missouri	4,480,000	5.5%
NA	Montana**	NA	NA
6	Nebraska	5,270,000	6.4%
NA	Nevada**	NA	NA
NA	New Hampshire**	NA	NA
29	New Jersey	103,000	0.1%
NA	New Mexico**	NA	NA
26	New York	301,000	0.4%
16	North Carolina	1,790,000	2.2%
4	North Dakota	5,720,000	7.0%
8	Ohio	4,740,000	5.8%
24	Oklahoma	375,000	0.5%
NA	Oregon**	NA	NA
20	Pennsylvania	575,000	0.7%
NA	Rhode Island**	NA	NA
23	South Carolina	405,000	0.5%
7	South Dakota	5,120,000	6.3%
17	Tennessee	1,720,000	2.1%
28	Texas	115,000	0.1%
NA	Utah**	NA	NA
NA	Vermont**	NA	NA
19	Virginia	620,000	0.8%
NA	Washington**	NA	NA
31	West Virginia	26,000	0.0%
14	Wisconsin	1,870,000	2.3%
NA	Wyoming**	NA	NA

RANK ORDER

RANK	STATE	ACRES	% of USA
1	Iowa	9,800,000	12.0%
2	Illinois	9,720,000	11.9%
3	Minnesota	7,550,000	9.2%
4	North Dakota	5,720,000	7.0%
5	Indiana	5,500,000	6.7%
6	Nebraska	5,270,000	6.4%
7	South Dakota	5,120,000	6.3%
8	Ohio	4,740,000	5.8%
9	Missouri	4,480,000	5.5%
10	Kansas	3,860,000	4.7%
11	Arkansas	3,170,000	3.9%
12	Mississippi	2,270,000	2.8%
13	Michigan	2,020,000	2.5%
14	Wisconsin	1,870,000	2.3%
15	Kentucky	1,810,000	2.2%
16	North Carolina	1,790,000	2.2%
17	Tennessee	1,720,000	2.1%
18	Louisiana	1,395,000	1.7%
19	Virginia	620,000	0.8%
20	Pennsylvania	575,000	0.7%
21	Maryland	515,000	0.6%
22	Alabama	490,000	0.6%
23	South Carolina	405,000	0.5%
24	Oklahoma	375,000	0.5%
25	Georgia	315,000	0.4%
26	New York	301,000	0.4%
27	Delaware	173,000	0.2%
28	Texas	115,000	0.1%
29	New Jersey	103,000	0.1%
30	Florida	31,000	0.0%
31	West Virginia	26,000	0.0%
NA	Alaska**	NA	NA
NA	Arizona**	NA	NA
NA	California**	NA	NA
NA	Colorado**	NA	NA
NA	Connecticut**	NA	NA
NA	Hawaii**	NA	NA
NA	Idaho**	NA	NA
NA	Maine**	NA	NA
NA	Massachusetts**	NA	NA
NA	Montana**	NA	NA
NA	Nevada**	NA	NA
NA	New Hampshire**	NA	NA
NA	New Mexico**	NA	NA
NA	Oregon**	NA	NA
NA	Rhode Island**	NA	NA
NA	Utah**	NA	NA
NA	Vermont**	NA	NA
NA	Washington**	NA	NA
NA	Wyoming**	NA	NA
	District of Columbia**	NA	NA

Source: U.S. Department of Agriculture, National Agricultural Statistics Service
   "Crop Production: 2015 Summary" (January 2016)
      (http://usda.mannlib.cornell.edu/MannUsda/viewDocumentInfo.do?documentID=1047)
*Estimated totals.
**No acreage or not available.

Acres Harvested: Wheat in 2015

National Total = 47,094,000 Acres*

ALPHA ORDER

RANK	STATE	ACRES	% of USA
23	Alabama	220,000	0.5%
NA	Alaska**	NA	NA
31	Arizona	142,000	0.3%
22	Arkansas	240,000	0.5%
24	California	210,000	0.4%
8	Colorado	2,147,000	4.6%
NA	Connecticut**	NA	NA
37	Delaware	65,000	0.1%
39	Florida	15,000	0.0%
30	Georgia	145,000	0.3%
NA	Hawaii**	NA	NA
11	Idaho	1,135,000	2.4%
15	Illinois	520,000	1.1%
21	Indiana	260,000	0.6%
39	Iowa	15,000	0.0%
1	Kansas	8,700,000	18.5%
18	Kentucky	440,000	0.9%
36	Louisiana	92,000	0.2%
NA	Maine**	NA	NA
20	Maryland	270,000	0.6%
NA	Massachusetts**	NA	NA
17	Michigan	475,000	1.0%
9	Minnesota	1,473,000	3.1%
33	Mississippi	120,000	0.3%
13	Missouri	610,000	1.3%
3	Montana	5,265,000	11.2%
10	Nebraska	1,210,000	2.6%
41	Nevada	8,000	0.0%
NA	New Hampshire**	NA	NA
38	New Jersey	20,000	0.0%
27	New Mexico	190,000	0.4%
35	New York	110,000	0.2%
14	North Carolina	570,000	1.2%
2	North Dakota	7,915,000	16.8%
16	Ohio	480,000	1.0%
4	Oklahoma	3,800,000	8.1%
12	Oregon	828,000	1.8%
28	Pennsylvania	175,000	0.4%
NA	Rhode Island**	NA	NA
29	South Carolina	160,000	0.3%
6	South Dakota	2,236,000	4.7%
19	Tennessee	395,000	0.8%
5	Texas	3,550,000	7.5%
34	Utah	119,000	0.3%
NA	Vermont**	NA	NA
24	Virginia	210,000	0.4%
7	Washington	2,215,000	4.7%
42	West Virginia	4,000	0.0%
24	Wisconsin	210,000	0.4%
32	Wyoming	130,000	0.3%

RANK ORDER

RANK	STATE	ACRES	% of USA
1	Kansas	8,700,000	18.5%
2	North Dakota	7,915,000	16.8%
3	Montana	5,265,000	11.2%
4	Oklahoma	3,800,000	8.1%
5	Texas	3,550,000	7.5%
6	South Dakota	2,236,000	4.7%
7	Washington	2,215,000	4.7%
8	Colorado	2,147,000	4.6%
9	Minnesota	1,473,000	3.1%
10	Nebraska	1,210,000	2.6%
11	Idaho	1,135,000	2.4%
12	Oregon	828,000	1.8%
13	Missouri	610,000	1.3%
14	North Carolina	570,000	1.2%
15	Illinois	520,000	1.1%
16	Ohio	480,000	1.0%
17	Michigan	475,000	1.0%
18	Kentucky	440,000	0.9%
19	Tennessee	395,000	0.8%
20	Maryland	270,000	0.6%
21	Indiana	260,000	0.6%
22	Arkansas	240,000	0.5%
23	Alabama	220,000	0.5%
24	California	210,000	0.4%
24	Virginia	210,000	0.4%
24	Wisconsin	210,000	0.4%
27	New Mexico	190,000	0.4%
28	Pennsylvania	175,000	0.4%
29	South Carolina	160,000	0.3%
30	Georgia	145,000	0.3%
31	Arizona	142,000	0.3%
32	Wyoming	130,000	0.3%
33	Mississippi	120,000	0.3%
34	Utah	119,000	0.3%
35	New York	110,000	0.2%
36	Louisiana	92,000	0.2%
37	Delaware	65,000	0.1%
38	New Jersey	20,000	0.0%
39	Florida	15,000	0.0%
39	Iowa	15,000	0.0%
41	Nevada	8,000	0.0%
42	West Virginia	4,000	0.0%
NA	Alaska**	NA	NA
NA	Connecticut**	NA	NA
NA	Hawaii**	NA	NA
NA	Maine**	NA	NA
NA	Massachusetts**	NA	NA
NA	New Hampshire**	NA	NA
NA	Rhode Island**	NA	NA
NA	Vermont**	NA	NA
	District of Columbia**	NA	NA

Source: U.S. Department of Agriculture, National Agricultural Statistics Service
"Crop Production: 2015 Summary" (January 2016)
(http://usda.mannlib.cornell.edu/MannUsda/viewDocumentInfo.do?documentID=1047)
*Estimated totals.
**No acreage or not available.

Cattle on Farms in 2016

National Total = 91,988,000 Cattle*

ALPHA ORDER

RANK	STATE	CATTLE	% of USA
25	Alabama	1,250,000	1.4%
49	Alaska	11,000	0.0%
32	Arizona	900,000	1.0%
16	Arkansas	1,700,000	1.8%
4	California	5,200,000	5.7%
10	Colorado	2,700,000	2.9%
44	Connecticut	49,000	0.1%
48	Delaware	16,000	0.0%
18	Florida	1,690,000	1.8%
30	Georgia	1,100,000	1.2%
42	Hawaii	140,000	0.2%
13	Idaho	2,400,000	2.6%
27	Illinois	1,180,000	1.3%
33	Indiana	890,000	1.0%
7	Iowa	3,950,000	4.3%
3	Kansas	6,250,000	6.8%
14	Kentucky	2,170,000	2.4%
36	Louisiana	780,000	0.8%
43	Maine	81,000	0.1%
41	Maryland	190,000	0.2%
45	Massachusetts	38,000	0.0%
28	Michigan	1,150,000	1.3%
12	Minnesota	2,420,000	2.6%
31	Mississippi	940,000	1.0%
6	Missouri	4,100,000	4.5%
11	Montana	2,650,000	2.9%
2	Nebraska	6,450,000	7.0%
37	Nevada	435,000	0.5%
46	New Hampshire	35,000	0.0%
47	New Jersey	28,000	0.0%
22	New Mexico	1,380,000	1.5%
21	New York	1,460,000	1.6%
35	North Carolina	800,000	0.9%
16	North Dakota	1,700,000	1.8%
26	Ohio	1,240,000	1.3%
5	Oklahoma	4,850,000	5.3%
23	Oregon	1,320,000	1.4%
19	Pennsylvania	1,600,000	1.7%
50	Rhode Island	5,000	0.0%
39	South Carolina	340,000	0.4%
7	South Dakota	3,950,000	4.3%
15	Tennessee	1,830,000	2.0%
1	Texas	11,700,000	12.7%
34	Utah	830,000	0.9%
40	Vermont	260,000	0.3%
20	Virginia	1,480,000	1.6%
28	Washington	1,150,000	1.3%
38	West Virginia	390,000	0.4%
9	Wisconsin	3,500,000	3.8%
24	Wyoming	1,310,000	1.4%

RANK ORDER

RANK	STATE	CATTLE	% of USA
1	Texas	11,700,000	12.7%
2	Nebraska	6,450,000	7.0%
3	Kansas	6,250,000	6.8%
4	California	5,200,000	5.7%
5	Oklahoma	4,850,000	5.3%
6	Missouri	4,100,000	4.5%
7	Iowa	3,950,000	4.3%
7	South Dakota	3,950,000	4.3%
9	Wisconsin	3,500,000	3.8%
10	Colorado	2,700,000	2.9%
11	Montana	2,650,000	2.9%
12	Minnesota	2,420,000	2.6%
13	Idaho	2,400,000	2.6%
14	Kentucky	2,170,000	2.4%
15	Tennessee	1,830,000	2.0%
16	Arkansas	1,700,000	1.8%
16	North Dakota	1,700,000	1.8%
18	Florida	1,690,000	1.8%
19	Pennsylvania	1,600,000	1.7%
20	Virginia	1,480,000	1.6%
21	New York	1,460,000	1.6%
22	New Mexico	1,380,000	1.5%
23	Oregon	1,320,000	1.4%
24	Wyoming	1,310,000	1.4%
25	Alabama	1,250,000	1.4%
26	Ohio	1,240,000	1.3%
27	Illinois	1,180,000	1.3%
28	Michigan	1,150,000	1.3%
28	Washington	1,150,000	1.3%
30	Georgia	1,100,000	1.2%
31	Mississippi	940,000	1.0%
32	Arizona	900,000	1.0%
33	Indiana	890,000	1.0%
34	Utah	830,000	0.9%
35	North Carolina	800,000	0.9%
36	Louisiana	780,000	0.8%
37	Nevada	435,000	0.5%
38	West Virginia	390,000	0.4%
39	South Carolina	340,000	0.4%
40	Vermont	260,000	0.3%
41	Maryland	190,000	0.2%
42	Hawaii	140,000	0.2%
43	Maine	81,000	0.1%
44	Connecticut	49,000	0.1%
45	Massachusetts	38,000	0.0%
46	New Hampshire	35,000	0.0%
47	New Jersey	28,000	0.0%
48	Delaware	16,000	0.0%
49	Alaska	11,000	0.0%
50	Rhode Island	5,000	0.0%
	District of Columbia	0	0.0%

Source: U.S. Department of Agriculture, National Agricultural Statistics Service
"Cattle" (http://usda.mannlib.cornell.edu/MannUsda/viewDocumentInfo.do?documentID=1017)
*As of January 1, 2016.

Milk Cows on Farms in 2014

National Total = 9,257,000 Milk Cows*

ALPHA ORDER

RANK	STATE	MILK COWS	% of USA
43	Alabama	8,000	0.1%
50	Alaska	300	0.0%
13	Arizona	193,000	2.1%
44	Arkansas	7,000	0.1%
1	California	1,780,000	19.2%
15	Colorado	144,000	1.6%
34	Connecticut	19,000	0.2%
47	Delaware	4,800	0.1%
19	Florida	123,000	1.3%
25	Georgia	81,000	0.9%
48	Hawaii	2,200	0.0%
4	Idaho	575,000	6.2%
22	Illinois	94,000	1.0%
14	Indiana	178,000	1.9%
12	Iowa	207,000	2.2%
16	Kansas	141,000	1.5%
26	Kentucky	63,000	0.7%
37	Louisiana	15,000	0.2%
32	Maine	30,000	0.3%
28	Maryland	50,000	0.5%
40	Massachusetts	13,000	0.1%
8	Michigan	390,000	4.2%
7	Minnesota	460,000	5.0%
40	Mississippi	13,000	0.1%
24	Missouri	89,000	1.0%
38	Montana	14,000	0.2%
27	Nebraska	54,000	0.6%
33	Nevada	29,000	0.3%
38	New Hampshire	14,000	0.2%
44	New Jersey	7,000	0.1%
9	New Mexico	323,000	3.5%
3	New York	615,000	6.6%
29	North Carolina	46,000	0.5%
35	North Dakota	16,000	0.2%
11	Ohio	267,000	2.9%
31	Oklahoma	40,000	0.4%
18	Oregon	124,000	1.3%
5	Pennsylvania	530,000	5.7%
49	Rhode Island	900	0.0%
35	South Carolina	16,000	0.2%
20	South Dakota	97,000	1.0%
29	Tennessee	46,000	0.5%
6	Texas	463,000	5.0%
21	Utah	95,000	1.0%
17	Vermont	132,000	1.4%
23	Virginia	93,000	1.0%
10	Washington	273,000	2.9%
42	West Virginia	9,000	0.1%
2	Wisconsin	1,271,000	13.7%
46	Wyoming	6,000	0.1%

RANK ORDER

RANK	STATE	MILK COWS	% of USA
1	California	1,780,000	19.2%
2	Wisconsin	1,271,000	13.7%
3	New York	615,000	6.6%
4	Idaho	575,000	6.2%
5	Pennsylvania	530,000	5.7%
6	Texas	463,000	5.0%
7	Minnesota	460,000	5.0%
8	Michigan	390,000	4.2%
9	New Mexico	323,000	3.5%
10	Washington	273,000	2.9%
11	Ohio	267,000	2.9%
12	Iowa	207,000	2.2%
13	Arizona	193,000	2.1%
14	Indiana	178,000	1.9%
15	Colorado	144,000	1.6%
16	Kansas	141,000	1.5%
17	Vermont	132,000	1.4%
18	Oregon	124,000	1.3%
19	Florida	123,000	1.3%
20	South Dakota	97,000	1.0%
21	Utah	95,000	1.0%
22	Illinois	94,000	1.0%
23	Virginia	93,000	1.0%
24	Missouri	89,000	1.0%
25	Georgia	81,000	0.9%
26	Kentucky	63,000	0.7%
27	Nebraska	54,000	0.6%
28	Maryland	50,000	0.5%
29	North Carolina	46,000	0.5%
29	Tennessee	46,000	0.5%
31	Oklahoma	40,000	0.4%
32	Maine	30,000	0.3%
33	Nevada	29,000	0.3%
34	Connecticut	19,000	0.2%
35	North Dakota	16,000	0.2%
35	South Carolina	16,000	0.2%
37	Louisiana	15,000	0.2%
38	Montana	14,000	0.2%
38	New Hampshire	14,000	0.2%
40	Massachusetts	13,000	0.1%
40	Mississippi	13,000	0.1%
42	West Virginia	9,000	0.1%
43	Alabama	8,000	0.1%
44	Arkansas	7,000	0.1%
44	New Jersey	7,000	0.1%
46	Wyoming	6,000	0.1%
47	Delaware	4,800	0.1%
48	Hawaii	2,200	0.0%
49	Rhode Island	900	0.0%
50	Alaska	300	0.0%
	District of Columbia	0	0.0%

Source: U.S. Department of Agriculture, National Agricultural Statistics Service
"Milk Production, Disposition and Income: 2014 Summary" (April 2015)
(http://usda.mannlib.cornell.edu/MannUsda/viewDocumentInfo.do?documentID=1105)
*Average number during year. Excludes heifers not yet fresh.

Milk Production in 2014

National Total = 206,046,000,000 Pounds of Milk*

ALPHA ORDER					RANK ORDER			
RANK	STATE	POUNDS	% of USA		RANK	STATE	POUNDS	% of USA
45	Alabama	109,000,000	0.1%		1	California	42,337,000,000	20.5%
50	Alaska	3,500,000	0.0%		2	Wisconsin	27,795,000,000	13.5%
12	Arizona	4,699,000,000	2.3%		3	Idaho	13,873,000,000	6.7%
47	Arkansas	96,000,000	0.0%		4	New York	13,733,000,000	6.7%
1	California	42,337,000,000	20.5%		5	Pennsylvania	10,683,000,000	5.2%
15	Colorado	3,593,000,000	1.7%		6	Texas	10,310,000,000	5.0%
34	Connecticut	383,000,000	0.2%		7	Michigan	9,609,000,000	4.7%
46	Delaware	96,700,000	0.0%		8	Minnesota	9,127,000,000	4.4%
19	Florida	2,507,000,000	1.2%		9	New Mexico	8,105,000,000	3.9%
24	Georgia	1,684,000,000	0.8%		10	Washington	6,584,000,000	3.2%
48	Hawaii	29,900,000	0.0%		11	Ohio	5,425,000,000	2.6%
3	Idaho	13,873,000,000	6.7%		12	Arizona	4,699,000,000	2.3%
22	Illinois	1,850,000,000	0.9%		13	Iowa	4,646,000,000	2.3%
14	Indiana	3,892,000,000	1.9%		14	Indiana	3,892,000,000	1.9%
13	Iowa	4,646,000,000	2.3%		15	Colorado	3,593,000,000	1.7%
16	Kansas	3,111,000,000	1.5%		16	Kansas	3,111,000,000	1.5%
27	Kentucky	1,002,000,000	0.5%		17	Vermont	2,666,000,000	1.3%
40	Louisiana	204,000,000	0.1%		18	Oregon	2,555,000,000	1.2%
33	Maine	600,000,000	0.3%		19	Florida	2,507,000,000	1.2%
28	Maryland	987,000,000	0.5%		20	Utah	2,182,000,000	1.1%
39	Massachusetts	233,000,000	0.1%		21	South Dakota	2,109,000,000	1.0%
7	Michigan	9,609,000,000	4.7%		22	Illinois	1,850,000,000	0.9%
8	Minnesota	9,127,000,000	4.4%		23	Virginia	1,780,000,000	0.9%
41	Mississippi	188,000,000	0.1%		24	Georgia	1,684,000,000	0.8%
25	Missouri	1,383,000,000	0.7%		25	Missouri	1,383,000,000	0.7%
36	Montana	301,000,000	0.1%		26	Nebraska	1,195,000,000	0.6%
26	Nebraska	1,195,000,000	0.6%		27	Kentucky	1,002,000,000	0.5%
32	Nevada	690,000,000	0.3%		28	Maryland	987,000,000	0.5%
37	New Hampshire	282,000,000	0.1%		29	North Carolina	961,000,000	0.5%
44	New Jersey	127,000,000	0.1%		30	Tennessee	750,000,000	0.4%
9	New Mexico	8,105,000,000	3.9%		31	Oklahoma	697,000,000	0.3%
4	New York	13,733,000,000	6.7%		32	Nevada	690,000,000	0.3%
29	North Carolina	961,000,000	0.5%		33	Maine	600,000,000	0.3%
35	North Dakota	324,000,000	0.2%		34	Connecticut	383,000,000	0.2%
11	Ohio	5,425,000,000	2.6%		35	North Dakota	324,000,000	0.2%
31	Oklahoma	697,000,000	0.3%		36	Montana	301,000,000	0.1%
18	Oregon	2,555,000,000	1.2%		37	New Hampshire	282,000,000	0.1%
5	Pennsylvania	10,683,000,000	5.2%		38	South Carolina	262,000,000	0.1%
49	Rhode Island	17,100,000	0.0%		39	Massachusetts	233,000,000	0.1%
38	South Carolina	262,000,000	0.1%		40	Louisiana	204,000,000	0.1%
21	South Dakota	2,109,000,000	1.0%		41	Mississippi	188,000,000	0.1%
30	Tennessee	750,000,000	0.4%		42	West Virginia	140,000,000	0.1%
6	Texas	10,310,000,000	5.0%		43	Wyoming	129,500,000	0.1%
20	Utah	2,182,000,000	1.1%		44	New Jersey	127,000,000	0.1%
17	Vermont	2,666,000,000	1.3%		45	Alabama	109,000,000	0.1%
23	Virginia	1,780,000,000	0.9%		46	Delaware	96,700,000	0.0%
10	Washington	6,584,000,000	3.2%		47	Arkansas	96,000,000	0.0%
42	West Virginia	140,000,000	0.1%		48	Hawaii	29,900,000	0.0%
2	Wisconsin	27,795,000,000	13.5%		49	Rhode Island	17,100,000	0.0%
43	Wyoming	129,500,000	0.1%		50	Alaska	3,500,000	0.0%
						District of Columbia	0	0.0%

Source: U.S. Department of Agriculture, National Agricultural Statistics Service
"Milk Production, Disposition and Income: 2014 Summary" (April 2015)
(http://usda.mannlib.cornell.edu/MannUsda/viewDocumentInfo.do?documentID=1105)
*Excludes milk suckled by calves.

Milk Production per Milk Cow in 2014

National Average = 22,258 Pounds of Milk per Cow*

ALPHA ORDER

RANK	STATE	POUNDS
47	Alabama	13,625
50	Alaska	11,667
4	Arizona	24,347
46	Arkansas	13,714
8	California	23,785
2	Colorado	24,951
27	Connecticut	20,158
29	Delaware	20,146
23	Florida	20,382
21	Georgia	20,790
49	Hawaii	13,591
5	Idaho	24,127
34	Illinois	19,681
16	Indiana	21,865
10	Iowa	22,444
14	Kansas	22,064
42	Kentucky	15,905
48	Louisiana	13,600
31	Maine	20,000
33	Maryland	19,740
38	Massachusetts	17,923
3	Michigan	24,638
32	Minnesota	19,841
45	Mississippi	14,462
44	Missouri	15,539
19	Montana	21,500
13	Nebraska	22,130
7	Nevada	23,793
30	New Hampshire	20,143
37	New Jersey	18,143
1	New Mexico	25,093
11	New York	22,330
20	North Carolina	20,891
25	North Dakota	20,250
24	Ohio	20,318
39	Oklahoma	17,425
22	Oregon	20,605
28	Pennsylvania	20,157
36	Rhode Island	19,000
40	South Carolina	16,375
17	South Dakota	21,742
41	Tennessee	16,304
12	Texas	22,268
9	Utah	22,968
26	Vermont	20,197
35	Virginia	19,140
6	Washington	24,117
43	West Virginia	15,556
15	Wisconsin	21,869
18	Wyoming	21,583

RANK ORDER

RANK	STATE	POUNDS
1	New Mexico	25,093
2	Colorado	24,951
3	Michigan	24,638
4	Arizona	24,347
5	Idaho	24,127
6	Washington	24,117
7	Nevada	23,793
8	California	23,785
9	Utah	22,968
10	Iowa	22,444
11	New York	22,330
12	Texas	22,268
13	Nebraska	22,130
14	Kansas	22,064
15	Wisconsin	21,869
16	Indiana	21,865
17	South Dakota	21,742
18	Wyoming	21,583
19	Montana	21,500
20	North Carolina	20,891
21	Georgia	20,790
22	Oregon	20,605
23	Florida	20,382
24	Ohio	20,318
25	North Dakota	20,250
26	Vermont	20,197
27	Connecticut	20,158
28	Pennsylvania	20,157
29	Delaware	20,146
30	New Hampshire	20,143
31	Maine	20,000
32	Minnesota	19,841
33	Maryland	19,740
34	Illinois	19,681
35	Virginia	19,140
36	Rhode Island	19,000
37	New Jersey	18,143
38	Massachusetts	17,923
39	Oklahoma	17,425
40	South Carolina	16,375
41	Tennessee	16,304
42	Kentucky	15,905
43	West Virginia	15,556
44	Missouri	15,539
45	Mississippi	14,462
46	Arkansas	13,714
47	Alabama	13,625
48	Louisiana	13,600
49	Hawaii	13,591
50	Alaska	11,667
	District of Columbia**	NA

Source: U.S. Department of Agriculture, National Agricultural Statistics Service
"Milk Production, Disposition and Income: 2014 Summary" (April 2015)
(http://usda.mannlib.cornell.edu/MannUsda/viewDocumentInfo.do?documentID=1105)
*Excludes milk suckled by calves.
**Not applicable.

Hogs and Pigs on Farms in 2015

National Total = 68,299,300 Hogs and Pigs*

ALPHA ORDER

RANK	STATE	HOGS AND PIGS	% of USA
29	Alabama	100,000	0.1%
47	Alaska	1,400	0.0%
27	Arizona	132,000	0.2%
24	Arkansas	166,000	0.2%
30	California	95,000	0.1%
15	Colorado	700,000	1.0%
44	Connecticut	2,500	0.0%
43	Delaware	3,000	0.0%
33	Florida	16,000	0.0%
25	Georgia	160,000	0.2%
37	Hawaii	9,000	0.0%
NA	Idaho**	NA	NA
4	Illinois	5,050,000	7.4%
5	Indiana	3,750,000	5.5%
1	Iowa	20,800,000	30.5%
10	Kansas	1,930,000	2.8%
18	Kentucky	415,000	0.6%
38	Louisiana	8,000	0.0%
40	Maine	4,500	0.0%
32	Maryland	21,000	0.0%
35	Massachusetts	11,000	0.0%
13	Michigan	1,110,000	1.6%
3	Minnesota	7,950,000	11.6%
17	Mississippi	515,000	0.8%
7	Missouri	3,000,000	4.4%
23	Montana	175,000	0.3%
6	Nebraska	3,300,000	4.8%
48	Nevada	1,000	0.0%
42	New Hampshire	3,900	0.0%
34	New Jersey	12,000	0.0%
45	New Mexico	1,500	0.0%
31	New York	76,000	0.1%
2	North Carolina	8,800,000	12.9%
26	North Dakota	138,000	0.2%
8	Ohio	2,470,000	3.6%
9	Oklahoma	2,100,000	3.1%
36	Oregon	10,000	0.0%
12	Pennsylvania	1,160,000	1.7%
45	Rhode Island	1,500	0.0%
21	South Carolina	235,000	0.3%
11	South Dakota	1,360,000	2.0%
22	Tennessee	220,000	0.3%
14	Texas	860,000	1.3%
16	Utah	670,000	1.0%
41	Vermont	4,000	0.0%
20	Virginia	270,000	0.4%
NA	Washington**	NA	NA
39	West Virginia	5,000	0.0%
19	Wisconsin	320,000	0.5%
28	Wyoming	105,000	0.2%

RANK ORDER

RANK	STATE	HOGS AND PIGS	% of USA
1	Iowa	20,800,000	30.5%
2	North Carolina	8,800,000	12.9%
3	Minnesota	7,950,000	11.6%
4	Illinois	5,050,000	7.4%
5	Indiana	3,750,000	5.5%
6	Nebraska	3,300,000	4.8%
7	Missouri	3,000,000	4.4%
8	Ohio	2,470,000	3.6%
9	Oklahoma	2,100,000	3.1%
10	Kansas	1,930,000	2.8%
11	South Dakota	1,360,000	2.0%
12	Pennsylvania	1,160,000	1.7%
13	Michigan	1,110,000	1.6%
14	Texas	860,000	1.3%
15	Colorado	700,000	1.0%
16	Utah	670,000	1.0%
17	Mississippi	515,000	0.8%
18	Kentucky	415,000	0.6%
19	Wisconsin	320,000	0.5%
20	Virginia	270,000	0.4%
21	South Carolina	235,000	0.3%
22	Tennessee	220,000	0.3%
23	Montana	175,000	0.3%
24	Arkansas	166,000	0.2%
25	Georgia	160,000	0.2%
26	North Dakota	138,000	0.2%
27	Arizona	132,000	0.2%
28	Wyoming	105,000	0.2%
29	Alabama	100,000	0.1%
30	California	95,000	0.1%
31	New York	76,000	0.1%
32	Maryland	21,000	0.0%
33	Florida	16,000	0.0%
34	New Jersey	12,000	0.0%
35	Massachusetts	11,000	0.0%
36	Oregon	10,000	0.0%
37	Hawaii	9,000	0.0%
38	Louisiana	8,000	0.0%
39	West Virginia	5,000	0.0%
40	Maine	4,500	0.0%
41	Vermont	4,000	0.0%
42	New Hampshire	3,900	0.0%
43	Delaware	3,000	0.0%
44	Connecticut	2,500	0.0%
45	New Mexico	1,500	0.0%
45	Rhode Island	1,500	0.0%
47	Alaska	1,400	0.0%
48	Nevada	1,000	0.0%
NA	Idaho**	NA	NA
NA	Washington**	NA	NA
	District of Columbia	0	0.0%

Source: U.S. Department of Agriculture, National Agricultural Statistics Service
"Quarterly Hogs and Pigs" (http://usda.mannlib.cornell.edu/MannUsda/viewDocumentInfo.do?documentID=1086)
*As of December 1, 2015.
**Not available. Figures for Idaho and Washington withheld to avoid disclosing data for individual operations. The two states combined had 52,000 hogs and pigs.

Chickens in 2014

National Total = 8,544,100,000 Chickens*

ALPHA ORDER

RANK	STATE	CHICKENS	% of USA
2	Alabama	1,061,500,000	12.4%
NA	Alaska***	NA	NA
NA	Arizona***	NA	NA
3	Arkansas	969,800,000	11.4%
NA	California**	NA	NA
NA	Colorado***	NA	NA
NA	Connecticut***	NA	NA
11	Delaware	244,100,000	2.9%
18	Florida	66,700,000	0.8%
1	Georgia	1,324,200,000	15.5%
NA	Hawaii***	NA	NA
NA	Idaho***	NA	NA
NA	Illinois**	NA	NA
NA	Indiana**	NA	NA
NA	Iowa**	NA	NA
NA	Kansas***	NA	NA
7	Kentucky	308,000,000	3.6%
NA	Louisiana**	NA	NA
NA	Maine***	NA	NA
9	Maryland	287,800,000	3.4%
NA	Massachusetts***	NA	NA
NA	Michigan**	NA	NA
20	Minnesota	46,800,000	0.5%
5	Mississippi	727,200,000	8.5%
8	Missouri	288,500,000	3.4%
NA	Montana***	NA	NA
NA	Nebraska**	NA	NA
NA	Nevada***	NA	NA
NA	New Hampshire***	NA	NA
NA	New Jersey***	NA	NA
NA	New Mexico***	NA	NA
NA	New York**	NA	NA
4	North Carolina	795,200,000	9.3%
NA	North Dakota***	NA	NA
17	Ohio	75,600,000	0.9%
13	Oklahoma	205,300,000	2.4%
NA	Oregon**	NA	NA
14	Pennsylvania	181,300,000	2.1%
NA	Rhode Island***	NA	NA
12	South Carolina	232,500,000	2.7%
NA	South Dakota***	NA	NA
15	Tennessee	180,600,000	2.1%
6	Texas	591,800,000	6.9%
NA	Utah***	NA	NA
NA	Vermont***	NA	NA
10	Virginia	262,000,000	3.1%
NA	Washington**	NA	NA
16	West Virginia	95,300,000	1.1%
19	Wisconsin	53,400,000	0.6%
NA	Wyoming***	NA	NA

RANK ORDER

RANK	STATE	CHICKENS	% of USA
1	Georgia	1,324,200,000	15.5%
2	Alabama	1,061,500,000	12.4%
3	Arkansas	969,800,000	11.4%
4	North Carolina	795,200,000	9.3%
5	Mississippi	727,200,000	8.5%
6	Texas	591,800,000	6.9%
7	Kentucky	308,000,000	3.6%
8	Missouri	288,500,000	3.4%
9	Maryland	287,800,000	3.4%
10	Virginia	262,000,000	3.1%
11	Delaware	244,100,000	2.9%
12	South Carolina	232,500,000	2.7%
13	Oklahoma	205,300,000	2.4%
14	Pennsylvania	181,300,000	2.1%
15	Tennessee	180,600,000	2.1%
16	West Virginia	95,300,000	1.1%
17	Ohio	75,600,000	0.9%
18	Florida	66,700,000	0.8%
19	Wisconsin	53,400,000	0.6%
20	Minnesota	46,800,000	0.5%
NA	Alaska***	NA	NA
NA	Arizona***	NA	NA
NA	California**	NA	NA
NA	Colorado***	NA	NA
NA	Connecticut***	NA	NA
NA	Hawaii***	NA	NA
NA	Idaho***	NA	NA
NA	Illinois**	NA	NA
NA	Indiana**	NA	NA
NA	Iowa**	NA	NA
NA	Kansas***	NA	NA
NA	Louisiana**	NA	NA
NA	Maine***	NA	NA
NA	Massachusetts***	NA	NA
NA	Michigan**	NA	NA
NA	Montana***	NA	NA
NA	Nebraska**	NA	NA
NA	Nevada***	NA	NA
NA	New Hampshire***	NA	NA
NA	New Jersey***	NA	NA
NA	New Mexico***	NA	NA
NA	New York**	NA	NA
NA	North Dakota***	NA	NA
NA	Oregon**	NA	NA
NA	Rhode Island***	NA	NA
NA	South Dakota***	NA	NA
NA	Utah***	NA	NA
NA	Vermont***	NA	NA
NA	Washington**	NA	NA
NA	Wyoming***	NA	NA
	District of Columbia***	NA	NA

Source: U.S. Department of Agriculture, National Agricultural Statistics Service
"Poultry - Production and Value: 2014 Summary" (April 2015)
(http://usda.mannlib.cornell.edu/MannUsda/viewDocumentInfo.do?documentID=1130)

*Broilers. Total includes numbers for states not shown separately but excludes states producing less than 500,000 birds. **These states produced a combined total of 546,500,000 chickens. They are combined to avoid disclosing individual operations. National total does not include chickens used for egg production. ***Produces fewer than 500,000 chickens or are not available.

Eggs Produced in 2014

National Total = 99,768,000,000 Eggs*

ALPHA ORDER

RANK	STATE	EGGS	% of USA
15	Alabama	2,148,000,000	2.2%
NA	Alaska**	NA	NA
NA	Arizona**	NA	NA
11	Arkansas	2,962,000,000	3.0%
7	California	4,551,000,000	4.6%
18	Colorado	1,450,000,000	1.5%
31	Connecticut	669,000,000	0.7%
NA	Delaware**	NA	NA
14	Florida	2,390,000,000	2.4%
6	Georgia	4,723,000,000	4.7%
NA	Hawaii**	NA	NA
NA	Idaho**	NA	NA
20	Illinois	1,409,000,000	1.4%
3	Indiana	7,747,000,000	7.8%
1	Iowa	16,449,000,000	16.5%
NA	Kansas**	NA	NA
22	Kentucky	1,219,000,000	1.2%
32	Louisiana	541,000,000	0.5%
25	Maine	989,000,000	1.0%
26	Maryland	785,000,000	0.8%
36	Massachusetts	44,000,000	0.0%
8	Michigan	3,867,000,000	3.9%
10	Minnesota	3,071,000,000	3.1%
21	Mississippi	1,351,000,000	1.4%
13	Missouri	2,407,000,000	2.4%
35	Montana	143,000,000	0.1%
12	Nebraska	2,860,000,000	2.9%
NA	Nevada**	NA	NA
NA	New Hampshire**	NA	NA
NA	New Jersey**	NA	NA
NA	New Mexico**	NA	NA
17	New York	1,493,000,000	1.5%
9	North Carolina	3,381,000,000	3.4%
NA	North Dakota**	NA	NA
2	Ohio	8,731,000,000	8.8%
30	Oklahoma	712,000,000	0.7%
29	Oregon	727,000,000	0.7%
4	Pennsylvania	7,570,000,000	7.6%
NA	Rhode Island**	NA	NA
24	South Carolina	1,117,000,000	1.1%
28	South Dakota	752,000,000	0.8%
33	Tennessee	341,000,000	0.3%
5	Texas	5,109,000,000	5.1%
23	Utah	1,180,000,000	1.2%
37	Vermont	36,000,000	0.0%
27	Virginia	765,000,000	0.8%
16	Washington	1,950,000,000	2.0%
34	West Virginia	270,000,000	0.3%
19	Wisconsin	1,449,000,000	1.5%
NA	Wyoming**	NA	NA

RANK ORDER

RANK	STATE	EGGS	% of USA
1	Iowa	16,449,000,000	16.5%
2	Ohio	8,731,000,000	8.8%
3	Indiana	7,747,000,000	7.8%
4	Pennsylvania	7,570,000,000	7.6%
5	Texas	5,109,000,000	5.1%
6	Georgia	4,723,000,000	4.7%
7	California	4,551,000,000	4.6%
8	Michigan	3,867,000,000	3.9%
9	North Carolina	3,381,000,000	3.4%
10	Minnesota	3,071,000,000	3.1%
11	Arkansas	2,962,000,000	3.0%
12	Nebraska	2,860,000,000	2.9%
13	Missouri	2,407,000,000	2.4%
14	Florida	2,390,000,000	2.4%
15	Alabama	2,148,000,000	2.2%
16	Washington	1,950,000,000	2.0%
17	New York	1,493,000,000	1.5%
18	Colorado	1,450,000,000	1.5%
19	Wisconsin	1,449,000,000	1.5%
20	Illinois	1,409,000,000	1.4%
21	Mississippi	1,351,000,000	1.4%
22	Kentucky	1,219,000,000	1.2%
23	Utah	1,180,000,000	1.2%
24	South Carolina	1,117,000,000	1.1%
25	Maine	989,000,000	1.0%
26	Maryland	785,000,000	0.8%
27	Virginia	765,000,000	0.8%
28	South Dakota	752,000,000	0.8%
29	Oregon	727,000,000	0.7%
30	Oklahoma	712,000,000	0.7%
31	Connecticut	669,000,000	0.7%
32	Louisiana	541,000,000	0.5%
33	Tennessee	341,000,000	0.3%
34	West Virginia	270,000,000	0.3%
35	Montana	143,000,000	0.1%
36	Massachusetts	44,000,000	0.0%
37	Vermont	36,000,000	0.0%
NA	Alaska**	NA	NA
NA	Arizona**	NA	NA
NA	Delaware**	NA	NA
NA	Hawaii**	NA	NA
NA	Idaho**	NA	NA
NA	Kansas**	NA	NA
NA	Nevada**	NA	NA
NA	New Hampshire**	NA	NA
NA	New Jersey**	NA	NA
NA	New Mexico**	NA	NA
NA	North Dakota**	NA	NA
NA	Rhode Island**	NA	NA
NA	Wyoming**	NA	NA
	District of Columbia	0	0.0%

Source: U.S. Department of Agriculture, National Agricultural Statistics Service
"Poultry - Production and Value: 2014 Summary" (April 2015)
(http://usda.mannlib.cornell.edu/MannUsda/viewDocumentInfo.do?documentID=1130)
*Includes hatching and market (table) eggs. **These states produced a combined 2,410,000,000 eggs. They are combined to avoid disclosing individual operations.

II. Crime and Law Enforcement

Crimes in 2014 29
Crime Rate in 2014 30
Percent Change in Crime Rate: 2013 to 2014 31
Violent Crimes in 2014 32
Violent Crime Rate in 2014 33
Percent Change in Violent Crime Rate: 2013 to 2014 34
Murders in 2014 35
Murder Rate in 2014 36
Percent of Murders Involving Firearms in 2014 37
Rapes in 2014 38
Rape Rate in 2014 39
Rapes (Revised Definition) in 2014 40
Rape Rate (Revised Definition) in 2014 41
Robberies in 2014 42
Robbery Rate in 2014 43
Aggravated Assaults in 2014 44
Aggravated Assault Rate in 2014 45
Property Crimes in 2014 46
Property Crime Rate in 2014 47
Percent Change in Property Crime Rate: 2013 to 2014 48
Burglaries in 2014 49
Burglary Rate in 2014 50
Larceny-Thefts in 2014 51
Larceny-Theft Rate in 2014 52
Motor Vehicle Thefts in 2014 53
Motor Vehicle Theft Rate in 2014 54
Rate of Consumer Fraud Complaints in 2014 55
Rate of Identity Theft Complaints in 2014 56
Reported Arrest Rate in 2014 57
Reported Juvenile Arrest Rate in 2014 58
Prisoners in State Correctional Institutions: Year End
    2014 59
State Prisoner Imprisonment Rate in 2014 60
Percent Change in Number of State Prisoners: 2013 to
    2014 61
Prisoners under Sentence of Death in 2013 62
Rate of State and Local Police Officers in 2014 63
Per Capita State and Local Government Expenditures for
    Police Protection in 2013 64
Per Capita State and Local Government Expenditures for
    Corrections in 2013 65
Per Capita State and Local Government Expenditures for
    Judicial and Legal Services in 2013 66

I. Arrests:

Important Note Regarding Arrest Numbers

The state arrest numbers reported by the FBI and shown on page 57 are only from those law enforcement agencies that submitted complete arrests reports for 12 months in 2014. The arrest rates were calculated by the editors using population totals provided by the FBI for those jurisdictions reporting. Reports from law enforcement agencies in Alabama, Hawaii, Illinois, and the District of Columbia were insufficient to calculate rates. Reports from Mississippi, New York, and Oregon represented less than 60 percent of their state population. Rates for these states should be interpreted with caution.

V. Juveniles:

Important Note Regarding Juvenile Arrest Rates

The juvenile arrest rates shown on page 58 were calculated by the editors as follows:

The state arrest numbers reported by the FBI are only from those law enforcement agencies that submitted complete arrests reports for 12 months in 2014. Included in the FBI report are population totals of these reporting jurisdictions by state. Using these FBI population figures, we first determined what percentage the FBI numbers represented of each state's total resident population. Next, using 2014 Census state estimates for 10- to 17-year-olds, we multiplied the percentages derived from the FBI population figures into the Census Bureau's total juvenile population counts. The resulting juvenile population is the base that was used to determine juvenile arrests per 100,000 juvenile population. The national rate was calculated in the same manner.

Reports from law enforcement agencies in Alabama, Hawaii, Illinois, and the District of Columbia were insufficient to calculate rates. Reports from Mississippi, New York, and Oregon represented less than 60 percent of their state population. Rates for these states should be interpreted with caution.

Crimes in 2014

National Total = 9,443,212 Crimes*

ALPHA ORDER

RANK	STATE	CRIMES	% of USA
21	Alabama	174,252	1.8%
46	Alaska	24,802	0.3%
12	Arizona	241,242	2.6%
28	Arkansas	112,680	1.2%
1	California	1,097,772	11.6%
22	Colorado	151,146	1.6%
35	Connecticut	77,381	0.8%
41	Delaware	32,339	0.3%
3	Florida	784,455	8.3%
5	Georgia	368,524	3.9%
38	Hawaii	46,846	0.5%
40	Idaho	33,643	0.4%
8	Illinois	313,970	3.3%
15	Indiana	198,304	2.1%
36	Iowa	73,253	0.8%
33	Kansas	89,218	0.9%
29	Kentucky	107,949	1.1%
17	Louisiana	184,375	2.0%
44	Maine	27,996	0.3%
20	Maryland	176,045	1.9%
23	Massachusetts	151,115	1.6%
11	Michigan	242,671	2.6%
24	Minnesota	137,333	1.5%
30	Mississippi	95,506	1.0%
14	Missouri	202,420	2.1%
42	Montana	28,514	0.3%
37	Nebraska	52,512	0.6%
31	Nevada	92,221	1.0%
43	New Hampshire	28,507	0.3%
18	New Jersey	178,018	1.9%
34	New Mexico	85,932	0.9%
4	New York	413,165	4.4%
7	North Carolina	317,784	3.4%
48	North Dakota	17,483	0.2%
6	Ohio	356,613	3.8%
26	Oklahoma	131,226	1.4%
27	Oregon	123,123	1.3%
9	Pennsylvania	286,140	3.0%
45	Rhode Island	25,140	0.3%
16	South Carolina	190,681	2.0%
47	South Dakota	18,631	0.2%
13	Tennessee	239,625	2.5%
2	Texas	920,191	9.7%
32	Utah	90,548	1.0%
50	Vermont	10,162	0.1%
19	Virginia	176,182	1.9%
10	Washington	281,318	3.0%
39	West Virginia	43,016	0.5%
25	Wisconsin	136,446	1.4%
49	Wyoming	12,571	0.1%

RANK ORDER

RANK	STATE	CRIMES	% of USA
1	California	1,097,772	11.6%
2	Texas	920,191	9.7%
3	Florida	784,455	8.3%
4	New York	413,165	4.4%
5	Georgia	368,524	3.9%
6	Ohio	356,613	3.8%
7	North Carolina	317,784	3.4%
8	Illinois	313,970	3.3%
9	Pennsylvania	286,140	3.0%
10	Washington	281,318	3.0%
11	Michigan	242,671	2.6%
12	Arizona	241,242	2.6%
13	Tennessee	239,625	2.5%
14	Missouri	202,420	2.1%
15	Indiana	198,304	2.1%
16	South Carolina	190,681	2.0%
17	Louisiana	184,375	2.0%
18	New Jersey	178,018	1.9%
19	Virginia	176,182	1.9%
20	Maryland	176,045	1.9%
21	Alabama	174,252	1.8%
22	Colorado	151,146	1.6%
23	Massachusetts	151,115	1.6%
24	Minnesota	137,333	1.5%
25	Wisconsin	136,446	1.4%
26	Oklahoma	131,226	1.4%
27	Oregon	123,123	1.3%
28	Arkansas	112,680	1.2%
29	Kentucky	107,949	1.1%
30	Mississippi	95,506	1.0%
31	Nevada	92,221	1.0%
32	Utah	90,548	1.0%
33	Kansas	89,218	0.9%
34	New Mexico	85,932	0.9%
35	Connecticut	77,381	0.8%
36	Iowa	73,253	0.8%
37	Nebraska	52,512	0.6%
38	Hawaii	46,846	0.5%
39	West Virginia	43,016	0.5%
40	Idaho	33,643	0.4%
41	Delaware	32,339	0.3%
42	Montana	28,514	0.3%
43	New Hampshire	28,507	0.3%
44	Maine	27,996	0.3%
45	Rhode Island	25,140	0.3%
46	Alaska	24,802	0.3%
47	South Dakota	18,631	0.2%
48	North Dakota	17,483	0.2%
49	Wyoming	12,571	0.1%
50	Vermont	10,162	0.1%
	District of Columbia	42,226	0.4%

Source: CQ Press using reported data from the Federal Bureau of Investigation
"Crime in the United States 2014" (Uniform Crime Reports, September 28, 2015, http://www.fbi.gov/about-us/cjis/ucr/)
*Includes murder, rape (legacy definition), robbery, aggravated assault, burglary, larceny-theft, and motor vehicle theft.

Crime Rate in 2014

National Rate = 2,961.7 Crimes per 100,000 Population*

ALPHA ORDER

RANK	STATE	RATE
9	Alabama	3,593.2
14	Alaska	3,366.5
10	Arizona	3,583.7
6	Arkansas	3,798.5
26	California	2,829.2
27	Colorado	2,822.0
43	Connecticut	2,151.5
11	Delaware	3,456.4
5	Florida	3,943.3
8	Georgia	3,649.7
16	Hawaii	3,300.0
48	Idaho	2,058.4
33	Illinois	2,437.6
24	Indiana	3,006.0
37	Iowa	2,357.5
23	Kansas	3,072.2
32	Kentucky	2,445.9
3	Louisiana	3,965.3
46	Maine	2,104.9
25	Maryland	2,945.6
39	Massachusetts	2,240.3
31	Michigan	2,448.8
30	Minnesota	2,516.6
19	Mississippi	3,189.9
15	Missouri	3,338.2
29	Montana	2,785.7
28	Nebraska	2,791.0
17	Nevada	3,248.2
44	New Hampshire	2,148.6
49	New Jersey	1,991.8
1	New Mexico	4,120.3
47	New York	2,092.3
18	North Carolina	3,195.7
36	North Dakota	2,364.3
22	Ohio	3,075.8
13	Oklahoma	3,383.7
20	Oregon	3,101.0
40	Pennsylvania	2,237.6
34	Rhode Island	2,382.6
4	South Carolina	3,945.8
41	South Dakota	2,183.7
7	Tennessee	3,658.8
12	Texas	3,413.7
21	Utah	3,076.9
50	Vermont	1,621.9
45	Virginia	2,116.0
2	Washington	3,983.9
38	West Virginia	2,324.8
35	Wisconsin	2,369.9
42	Wyoming	2,152.0

RANK ORDER

RANK	STATE	RATE
1	New Mexico	4,120.3
2	Washington	3,983.9
3	Louisiana	3,965.3
4	South Carolina	3,945.8
5	Florida	3,943.3
6	Arkansas	3,798.5
7	Tennessee	3,658.8
8	Georgia	3,649.7
9	Alabama	3,593.2
10	Arizona	3,583.7
11	Delaware	3,456.4
12	Texas	3,413.7
13	Oklahoma	3,383.7
14	Alaska	3,366.5
15	Missouri	3,338.2
16	Hawaii	3,300.0
17	Nevada	3,248.2
18	North Carolina	3,195.7
19	Mississippi	3,189.9
20	Oregon	3,101.0
21	Utah	3,076.9
22	Ohio	3,075.8
23	Kansas	3,072.2
24	Indiana	3,006.0
25	Maryland	2,945.6
26	California	2,829.2
27	Colorado	2,822.0
28	Nebraska	2,791.0
29	Montana	2,785.7
30	Minnesota	2,516.6
31	Michigan	2,448.8
32	Kentucky	2,445.9
33	Illinois	2,437.6
34	Rhode Island	2,382.6
35	Wisconsin	2,369.9
36	North Dakota	2,364.3
37	Iowa	2,357.5
38	West Virginia	2,324.8
39	Massachusetts	2,240.3
40	Pennsylvania	2,237.6
41	South Dakota	2,183.7
42	Wyoming	2,152.0
43	Connecticut	2,151.5
44	New Hampshire	2,148.6
45	Virginia	2,116.0
46	Maine	2,104.9
47	New York	2,092.3
48	Idaho	2,058.4
49	New Jersey	1,991.8
50	Vermont	1,621.9
	District of Columbia	6,408.6

Source: CQ Press using reported data from the Federal Bureau of Investigation
"Crime in the United States 2014" (Uniform Crime Reports, September 28, 2015, http://www.fbi.gov/about-us/cjis/ucr/)
*Includes murder, rape (legacy definition), robbery, aggravated assault, burglary, larceny-theft, and motor vehicle theft.

Percent Change in Crime Rate: 2013 to 2014

National Percent Change = 5.1% Decrease*

ALPHA ORDER

RANK	STATE	PERCENT CHANGE
21	Alabama	(5.4)
9	Alaska	(3.3)
23	Arizona	(5.5)
32	Arkansas	(6.6)
39	California	(8.0)
16	Colorado	(4.7)
18	Connecticut	(5.0)
31	Delaware	(6.2)
1	Florida	10.0
10	Georgia	(3.4)
14	Hawaii	(4.5)
5	Idaho	(1.2)
44	Illinois	(10.1)
27	Indiana	(6.0)
13	Iowa	(4.3)
37	Kansas	(7.4)
25	Kentucky	(5.9)
7	Louisiana	(2.7)
49	Maine	(12.8)
30	Maryland	(6.1)
41	Massachusetts	(8.7)
48	Michigan	(11.9)
19	Minnesota	(5.1)
2	Mississippi	6.9
35	Missouri	(7.0)
6	Montana	(2.6)
11	Nebraska	(3.5)
24	Nevada	(5.7)
46	New Hampshire	(11.5)
40	New Jersey	(8.3)
19	New Mexico	(5.1)
27	New York	(6.0)
38	North Carolina	(7.6)
3	North Dakota	(0.1)
16	Ohio	(4.7)
43	Oklahoma	(9.9)
42	Oregon	(9.6)
36	Pennsylvania	(7.3)
47	Rhode Island	(11.6)
25	South Carolina	(5.9)
8	South Dakota	(2.9)
15	Tennessee	(4.6)
34	Texas	(6.8)
21	Utah	(5.4)
50	Vermont	(31.2)
32	Virginia	(6.6)
4	Washington	(0.7)
27	West Virginia	(6.0)
12	Wisconsin	(4.2)
45	Wyoming	(10.2)

RANK ORDER

RANK	STATE	PERCENT CHANGE
1	Florida	10.0
2	Mississippi	6.9
3	North Dakota	(0.1)
4	Washington	(0.7)
5	Idaho	(1.2)
6	Montana	(2.6)
7	Louisiana	(2.7)
8	South Dakota	(2.9)
9	Alaska	(3.3)
10	Georgia	(3.4)
11	Nebraska	(3.5)
12	Wisconsin	(4.2)
13	Iowa	(4.3)
14	Hawaii	(4.5)
15	Tennessee	(4.6)
16	Colorado	(4.7)
16	Ohio	(4.7)
18	Connecticut	(5.0)
19	Minnesota	(5.1)
19	New Mexico	(5.1)
21	Alabama	(5.4)
21	Utah	(5.4)
23	Arizona	(5.5)
24	Nevada	(5.7)
25	Kentucky	(5.9)
25	South Carolina	(5.9)
27	Indiana	(6.0)
27	New York	(6.0)
27	West Virginia	(6.0)
30	Maryland	(6.1)
31	Delaware	(6.2)
32	Arkansas	(6.6)
32	Virginia	(6.6)
34	Texas	(6.8)
35	Missouri	(7.0)
36	Pennsylvania	(7.3)
37	Kansas	(7.4)
38	North Carolina	(7.6)
39	California	(8.0)
40	New Jersey	(8.3)
41	Massachusetts	(8.7)
42	Oregon	(9.6)
43	Oklahoma	(9.9)
44	Illinois	(10.1)
45	Wyoming	(10.2)
46	New Hampshire	(11.5)
47	Rhode Island	(11.6)
48	Michigan	(11.9)
49	Maine	(12.8)
50	Vermont	(31.2)

| | District of Columbia | 6.2 |

Source: CQ Press using reported data from the Federal Bureau of Investigation
"Crime in the United States 2014" (Uniform Crime Reports, September 28, 2015, http://www.fbi.gov/about-us/cjis/ucr/)
*Includes murder, rape (legacy definition), robbery, aggravated assault, burglary, larceny-theft, and motor vehicle theft.

Violent Crimes in 2014

National Total = 1,165,383 Violent Crimes*

ALPHA ORDER

RANK	STATE	CRIMES	% of USA
20	Alabama	20,158	1.7%
39	Alaska	4,468	0.4%
14	Arizona	26,002	2.2%
27	Arkansas	13,662	1.2%
1	California	150,580	12.9%
24	Colorado	15,636	1.3%
33	Connecticut	8,311	0.7%
40	Delaware	4,439	0.4%
3	Florida	105,009	9.0%
9	Georgia	37,208	3.2%
41	Hawaii	3,549	0.3%
42	Idaho	3,327	0.3%
5	Illinois	46,585	4.0%
17	Indiana	23,528	2.0%
34	Iowa	8,197	0.7%
30	Kansas	9,787	0.8%
32	Kentucky	8,783	0.8%
16	Louisiana	23,551	2.0%
48	Maine	1,575	0.1%
12	Maryland	26,186	2.2%
15	Massachusetts	25,848	2.2%
6	Michigan	40,124	3.4%
29	Minnesota	11,956	1.0%
35	Mississippi	8,044	0.7%
13	Missouri	26,183	2.2%
43	Montana	3,202	0.3%
38	Nebraska	5,033	0.4%
22	Nevada	17,683	1.5%
45	New Hampshire	2,466	0.2%
19	New Jersey	23,025	2.0%
28	New Mexico	12,055	1.0%
4	New York	73,883	6.3%
10	North Carolina	32,087	2.8%
47	North Dakota	1,878	0.2%
11	Ohio	32,085	2.8%
26	Oklahoma	15,244	1.3%
31	Oregon	8,818	0.8%
8	Pennsylvania	39,124	3.4%
46	Rhode Island	2,205	0.2%
18	South Carolina	23,464	2.0%
44	South Dakota	2,729	0.2%
7	Tennessee	39,178	3.4%
2	Texas	106,257	9.1%
36	Utah	5,837	0.5%
50	Vermont	611	0.1%
25	Virginia	15,462	1.3%
21	Washington	19,612	1.7%
37	West Virginia	5,368	0.5%
23	Wisconsin	16,208	1.4%
49	Wyoming	1,094	0.1%

RANK ORDER

RANK	STATE	CRIMES	% of USA
1	California	150,580	12.9%
2	Texas	106,257	9.1%
3	Florida	105,009	9.0%
4	New York	73,883	6.3%
5	Illinois	46,585	4.0%
6	Michigan	40,124	3.4%
7	Tennessee	39,178	3.4%
8	Pennsylvania	39,124	3.4%
9	Georgia	37,208	3.2%
10	North Carolina	32,087	2.8%
11	Ohio	32,085	2.8%
12	Maryland	26,186	2.2%
13	Missouri	26,183	2.2%
14	Arizona	26,002	2.2%
15	Massachusetts	25,848	2.2%
16	Louisiana	23,551	2.0%
17	Indiana	23,528	2.0%
18	South Carolina	23,464	2.0%
19	New Jersey	23,025	2.0%
20	Alabama	20,158	1.7%
21	Washington	19,612	1.7%
22	Nevada	17,683	1.5%
23	Wisconsin	16,208	1.4%
24	Colorado	15,636	1.3%
25	Virginia	15,462	1.3%
26	Oklahoma	15,244	1.3%
27	Arkansas	13,662	1.2%
28	New Mexico	12,055	1.0%
29	Minnesota	11,956	1.0%
30	Kansas	9,787	0.8%
31	Oregon	8,818	0.8%
32	Kentucky	8,783	0.8%
33	Connecticut	8,311	0.7%
34	Iowa	8,197	0.7%
35	Mississippi	8,044	0.7%
36	Utah	5,837	0.5%
37	West Virginia	5,368	0.5%
38	Nebraska	5,033	0.4%
39	Alaska	4,468	0.4%
40	Delaware	4,439	0.4%
41	Hawaii	3,549	0.3%
42	Idaho	3,327	0.3%
43	Montana	3,202	0.3%
44	South Dakota	2,729	0.2%
45	New Hampshire	2,466	0.2%
46	Rhode Island	2,205	0.2%
47	North Dakota	1,878	0.2%
48	Maine	1,575	0.1%
49	Wyoming	1,094	0.1%
50	Vermont	611	0.1%
	District of Columbia	8,079	0.7%

Source: Reported data from the Federal Bureau of Investigation
"Crime in the United States 2014" (Uniform Crime Reports, September 28, 2015, http://www.fbi.gov/about-us/cjis/ucr/)
*Violent crimes are offenses of murder, rape (legacy definition), robbery, and aggravated assault.

Violent Crime Rate in 2014

National Rate = 365.6 Violent Crimes per 100,000 Population*

ALPHA ORDER

RANK	STATE	RATE
12	Alabama	415.6
2	Alaska	606.5
17	Arizona	386.2
9	Arkansas	460.5
16	California	388.1
28	Colorado	291.9
39	Connecticut	231.1
8	Delaware	474.4
5	Florida	527.8
20	Georgia	368.5
38	Hawaii	250.0
43	Idaho	203.6
21	Illinois	361.7
22	Indiana	356.6
35	Iowa	263.7
23	Kansas	337.0
44	Kentucky	199.0
6	Louisiana	506.5
49	Maine	118.5
10	Maryland	438.1
18	Massachusetts	383.2
13	Michigan	404.9
41	Minnesota	219.1
33	Mississippi	268.7
11	Missouri	431.7
26	Montana	312.8
34	Nebraska	267.5
1	Nevada	622.8
47	New Hampshire	185.9
36	New Jersey	257.7
4	New Mexico	578.0
19	New York	374.1
24	North Carolina	322.6
37	North Dakota	254.0
32	Ohio	276.7
15	Oklahoma	393.0
40	Oregon	222.0
27	Pennsylvania	305.9
42	Rhode Island	209.0
7	South Carolina	485.5
25	South Dakota	319.8
3	Tennessee	598.2
14	Texas	394.3
45	Utah	198.4
50	Vermont	97.5
48	Virginia	185.7
31	Washington	277.8
29	West Virginia	290.1
30	Wisconsin	281.6
46	Wyoming	187.3

RANK ORDER

RANK	STATE	RATE
1	Nevada	622.8
2	Alaska	606.5
3	Tennessee	598.2
4	New Mexico	578.0
5	Florida	527.8
6	Louisiana	506.5
7	South Carolina	485.5
8	Delaware	474.4
9	Arkansas	460.5
10	Maryland	438.1
11	Missouri	431.7
12	Alabama	415.6
13	Michigan	404.9
14	Texas	394.3
15	Oklahoma	393.0
16	California	388.1
17	Arizona	386.2
18	Massachusetts	383.2
19	New York	374.1
20	Georgia	368.5
21	Illinois	361.7
22	Indiana	356.6
23	Kansas	337.0
24	North Carolina	322.6
25	South Dakota	319.8
26	Montana	312.8
27	Pennsylvania	305.9
28	Colorado	291.9
29	West Virginia	290.1
30	Wisconsin	281.6
31	Washington	277.8
32	Ohio	276.7
33	Mississippi	268.7
34	Nebraska	267.5
35	Iowa	263.7
36	New Jersey	257.7
37	North Dakota	254.0
38	Hawaii	250.0
39	Connecticut	231.1
40	Oregon	222.0
41	Minnesota	219.1
42	Rhode Island	209.0
43	Idaho	203.6
44	Kentucky	199.0
45	Utah	198.4
46	Wyoming	187.3
47	New Hampshire	185.9
48	Virginia	185.7
49	Maine	118.5
50	Vermont	97.5
	District of Columbia	1,226.1

Source: Reported data from the Federal Bureau of Investigation
"Crime in the United States 2014" (Uniform Crime Reports, September 28, 2015, http://www.fbi.gov/about-us/cjis/ucr/)
*Violent crimes are offenses of murder, rape (legacy definition), robbery, and aggravated assault.

Percent Change in Violent Crime Rate: 2013 to 2014

National Percent Change = 5.7% Decrease*

ALPHA ORDER

RANK	STATE	PERCENT CHANGE
30	Alabama	(7.7)
11	Alaska	0.4
37	Arizona	(9.9)
15	Arkansas	(1.9)
34	California	(8.4)
23	Colorado	(5.0)
49	Connecticut	(18.5)
45	Delaware	(13.8)
2	Florida	8.4
16	Georgia	(3.0)
8	Hawaii	2.9
16	Idaho	(3.0)
42	Illinois	(13.1)
3	Indiana	3.4
12	Iowa	(0.7)
25	Kansas	(5.5)
41	Kentucky	(11.5)
10	Louisiana	2.1
19	Maine	(3.2)
32	Maryland	(8.2)
26	Massachusetts	(5.8)
39	Michigan	(11.0)
24	Minnesota	(5.1)
6	Mississippi	3.3
21	Missouri	(4.3)
1	Montana	12.2
3	Nebraska	3.4
9	Nevada	2.3
44	New Hampshire	(13.5)
40	New Jersey	(11.2)
6	New Mexico	3.3
31	New York	(7.9)
35	North Carolina	(8.7)
3	North Dakota	3.4
32	Ohio	(8.2)
47	Oklahoma	(17.2)
38	Oregon	(10.2)
46	Pennsylvania	(14.0)
48	Rhode Island	(17.4)
43	South Carolina	(13.4)
14	South Dakota	(1.2)
27	Tennessee	(6.3)
20	Texas	(3.5)
22	Utah	(4.6)
50	Vermont	(31.5)
16	Virginia	(3.0)
28	Washington	(6.8)
36	West Virginia	(9.4)
13	Wisconsin	(0.8)
29	Wyoming	(7.0)

RANK ORDER

RANK	STATE	PERCENT CHANGE
1	Montana	12.2
2	Florida	8.4
3	Indiana	3.4
3	Nebraska	3.4
3	North Dakota	3.4
6	Mississippi	3.3
6	New Mexico	3.3
8	Hawaii	2.9
9	Nevada	2.3
10	Louisiana	2.1
11	Alaska	0.4
12	Iowa	(0.7)
13	Wisconsin	(0.8)
14	South Dakota	(1.2)
15	Arkansas	(1.9)
16	Georgia	(3.0)
16	Idaho	(3.0)
16	Virginia	(3.0)
19	Maine	(3.2)
20	Texas	(3.5)
21	Missouri	(4.3)
22	Utah	(4.6)
23	Colorado	(5.0)
24	Minnesota	(5.1)
25	Kansas	(5.5)
26	Massachusetts	(5.8)
27	Tennessee	(6.3)
28	Washington	(6.8)
29	Wyoming	(7.0)
30	Alabama	(7.7)
31	New York	(7.9)
32	Maryland	(8.2)
32	Ohio	(8.2)
34	California	(8.4)
35	North Carolina	(8.7)
36	West Virginia	(9.4)
37	Arizona	(9.9)
38	Oregon	(10.2)
39	Michigan	(11.0)
40	New Jersey	(11.2)
41	Kentucky	(11.5)
42	Illinois	(13.1)
43	South Carolina	(13.4)
44	New Hampshire	(13.5)
45	Delaware	(13.8)
46	Pennsylvania	(14.0)
47	Oklahoma	(17.2)
48	Rhode Island	(17.4)
49	Connecticut	(18.5)
50	Vermont	(31.5)
	District of Columbia	(1.3)

Source: Reported data from the Federal Bureau of Investigation
"Crime in the United States 2014" (Uniform Crime Reports, September 28, 2015, http://www.fbi.gov/about-us/cjis/ucr/)
*Violent crimes are offenses of murder, rape (legacy definition), robbery, and aggravated assault.

Murders in 2014

National Total = 14,249 Murders*

ALPHA ORDER

RANK	STATE	MURDERS	% of USA
20	Alabama	276	1.9%
40	Alaska	41	0.3%
18	Arizona	319	2.2%
25	Arkansas	165	1.2%
1	California	1,699	11.9%
28	Colorado	151	1.1%
33	Connecticut	86	0.6%
38	Delaware	54	0.4%
3	Florida	1,149	8.1%
7	Georgia	580	4.1%
43	Hawaii	26	0.2%
42	Idaho	32	0.2%
4	Illinois	685	4.8%
17	Indiana	330	2.3%
37	Iowa	60	0.4%
31	Kansas	91	0.6%
27	Kentucky	160	1.1%
10	Louisiana	477	3.3%
46	Maine	21	0.1%
14	Maryland	365	2.6%
29	Massachusetts	132	0.9%
8	Michigan	535	3.8%
32	Minnesota	88	0.6%
21	Mississippi	258	1.8%
12	Missouri	403	2.8%
41	Montana	37	0.3%
38	Nebraska	54	0.4%
24	Nevada	170	1.2%
49	New Hampshire	12	0.1%
15	New Jersey	349	2.4%
30	New Mexico	101	0.7%
5	New York	617	4.3%
9	North Carolina	510	3.6%
45	North Dakota	22	0.2%
11	Ohio	464	3.3%
22	Oklahoma	175	1.2%
34	Oregon	81	0.6%
6	Pennsylvania	614	4.3%
44	Rhode Island	25	0.2%
19	South Carolina	311	2.2%
47	South Dakota	20	0.1%
13	Tennessee	371	2.6%
2	Texas	1,184	8.3%
36	Utah	67	0.5%
50	Vermont	10	0.1%
16	Virginia	338	2.4%
23	Washington	174	1.2%
35	West Virginia	74	0.5%
25	Wisconsin	165	1.2%
48	Wyoming	16	0.1%

RANK ORDER

RANK	STATE	MURDERS	% of USA
1	California	1,699	11.9%
2	Texas	1,184	8.3%
3	Florida	1,149	8.1%
4	Illinois	685	4.8%
5	New York	617	4.3%
6	Pennsylvania	614	4.3%
7	Georgia	580	4.1%
8	Michigan	535	3.8%
9	North Carolina	510	3.6%
10	Louisiana	477	3.3%
11	Ohio	464	3.3%
12	Missouri	403	2.8%
13	Tennessee	371	2.6%
14	Maryland	365	2.6%
15	New Jersey	349	2.4%
16	Virginia	338	2.4%
17	Indiana	330	2.3%
18	Arizona	319	2.2%
19	South Carolina	311	2.2%
20	Alabama	276	1.9%
21	Mississippi	258	1.8%
22	Oklahoma	175	1.2%
23	Washington	174	1.2%
24	Nevada	170	1.2%
25	Arkansas	165	1.2%
25	Wisconsin	165	1.2%
27	Kentucky	160	1.1%
28	Colorado	151	1.1%
29	Massachusetts	132	0.9%
30	New Mexico	101	0.7%
31	Kansas	91	0.6%
32	Minnesota	88	0.6%
33	Connecticut	86	0.6%
34	Oregon	81	0.6%
35	West Virginia	74	0.5%
36	Utah	67	0.5%
37	Iowa	60	0.4%
38	Delaware	54	0.4%
38	Nebraska	54	0.4%
40	Alaska	41	0.3%
41	Montana	37	0.3%
42	Idaho	32	0.2%
43	Hawaii	26	0.2%
44	Rhode Island	25	0.2%
45	North Dakota	22	0.2%
46	Maine	21	0.1%
47	South Dakota	20	0.1%
48	Wyoming	16	0.1%
49	New Hampshire	12	0.1%
50	Vermont	10	0.1%
	District of Columbia	105	0.7%

Source: Reported data from the Federal Bureau of Investigation
"Crime in the United States 2014" (Uniform Crime Reports, September 28, 2015, http://www.fbi.gov/about-us/cjis/ucr/)
*Includes nonnegligent manslaughter.

Murder Rate in 2014

National Rate = 4.5 Murders per 100,000 Population*

ALPHA ORDER

RANK	STATE	RATE
9	Alabama	5.7
12	Alaska	5.6
20	Arizona	4.7
12	Arkansas	5.6
22	California	4.4
35	Colorado	2.8
38	Connecticut	2.4
7	Delaware	5.8
7	Florida	5.8
9	Georgia	5.7
46	Hawaii	1.8
42	Idaho	2.0
15	Illinois	5.3
17	Indiana	5.0
45	Iowa	1.9
30	Kansas	3.1
28	Kentucky	3.6
1	Louisiana	10.3
47	Maine	1.6
5	Maryland	6.1
42	Massachusetts	2.0
14	Michigan	5.4
47	Minnesota	1.6
2	Mississippi	8.6
3	Missouri	6.6
28	Montana	3.6
33	Nebraska	2.9
6	Nevada	6.0
50	New Hampshire	0.9
27	New Jersey	3.9
18	New Mexico	4.8
30	New York	3.1
16	North Carolina	5.1
32	North Dakota	3.0
25	Ohio	4.0
21	Oklahoma	4.5
42	Oregon	2.0
18	Pennsylvania	4.8
38	Rhode Island	2.4
4	South Carolina	6.4
40	South Dakota	2.3
9	Tennessee	5.7
22	Texas	4.4
40	Utah	2.3
47	Vermont	1.6
24	Virginia	4.1
37	Washington	2.5
25	West Virginia	4.0
33	Wisconsin	2.9
36	Wyoming	2.7

RANK ORDER

RANK	STATE	RATE
1	Louisiana	10.3
2	Mississippi	8.6
3	Missouri	6.6
4	South Carolina	6.4
5	Maryland	6.1
6	Nevada	6.0
7	Delaware	5.8
7	Florida	5.8
9	Alabama	5.7
9	Georgia	5.7
9	Tennessee	5.7
12	Alaska	5.6
12	Arkansas	5.6
14	Michigan	5.4
15	Illinois	5.3
16	North Carolina	5.1
17	Indiana	5.0
18	New Mexico	4.8
18	Pennsylvania	4.8
20	Arizona	4.7
21	Oklahoma	4.5
22	California	4.4
22	Texas	4.4
24	Virginia	4.1
25	Ohio	4.0
25	West Virginia	4.0
27	New Jersey	3.9
28	Kentucky	3.6
28	Montana	3.6
30	Kansas	3.1
30	New York	3.1
32	North Dakota	3.0
33	Nebraska	2.9
33	Wisconsin	2.9
35	Colorado	2.8
36	Wyoming	2.7
37	Washington	2.5
38	Connecticut	2.4
38	Rhode Island	2.4
40	South Dakota	2.3
40	Utah	2.3
42	Idaho	2.0
42	Massachusetts	2.0
42	Oregon	2.0
45	Iowa	1.9
46	Hawaii	1.8
47	Maine	1.6
47	Minnesota	1.6
47	Vermont	1.6
50	New Hampshire	0.9
	District of Columbia	15.9

Source: Reported data from the Federal Bureau of Investigation
"Crime in the United States 2014" (Uniform Crime Reports, September 28, 2015, http://www.fbi.gov/about-us/cjis/ucr/)
*Includes nonnegligent manslaughter.

Percent of Murders Involving Firearms in 2014

National Percent = 67.9% of Murders*

ALPHA ORDER

RANK	STATE	PERCENT
NA	Alabama***	NA
37	Alaska	53.7
31	Arizona	59.3
11	Arkansas	72.1
14	California	68.9
29	Colorado	61.1
28	Connecticut	61.4
10	Delaware	72.2
NA	Florida***	NA
4	Georgia	77.0
NA	Hawaii***	NA
40	Idaho	50.0
1	Illinois**	86.7
7	Indiana	74.2
42	Iowa	49.1
23	Kansas	62.9
13	Kentucky	70.0
2	Louisiana	78.4
46	Maine	28.6
17	Maryland	67.3
26	Massachusetts	61.8
20	Michigan	64.4
39	Minnesota	51.2
5	Mississippi	75.8
3	Missouri	78.1
22	Montana	63.0
24	Nebraska	62.7
34	Nevada	55.6
40	New Hampshire	50.0
11	New Jersey	72.1
35	New Mexico	55.2
33	New York	56.1
15	North Carolina	67.8
44	North Dakota	42.9
21	Ohio	63.5
25	Oklahoma	62.3
38	Oregon	53.4
6	Pennsylvania	74.4
43	Rhode Island	48.0
9	South Carolina	72.8
45	South Dakota	40.0
19	Tennessee	66.5
18	Texas	67.0
32	Utah	59.0
30	Vermont	60.0
16	Virginia	67.7
36	Washington	54.7
47	West Virginia	25.8
8	Wisconsin	74.1
27	Wyoming	61.5

RANK ORDER

RANK	STATE	PERCENT
1	Illinois**	86.7
2	Louisiana	78.4
3	Missouri	78.1
4	Georgia	77.0
5	Mississippi	75.8
6	Pennsylvania	74.4
7	Indiana	74.2
8	Wisconsin	74.1
9	South Carolina	72.8
10	Delaware	72.2
11	Arkansas	72.1
11	New Jersey	72.1
13	Kentucky	70.0
14	California	68.9
15	North Carolina	67.8
16	Virginia	67.7
17	Maryland	67.3
18	Texas	67.0
19	Tennessee	66.5
20	Michigan	64.4
21	Ohio	63.5
22	Montana	63.0
23	Kansas	62.9
24	Nebraska	62.7
25	Oklahoma	62.3
26	Massachusetts	61.8
27	Wyoming	61.5
28	Connecticut	61.4
29	Colorado	61.1
30	Vermont	60.0
31	Arizona	59.3
32	Utah	59.0
33	New York	56.1
34	Nevada	55.6
35	New Mexico	55.2
36	Washington	54.7
37	Alaska	53.7
38	Oregon	53.4
39	Minnesota	51.2
40	Idaho	50.0
40	New Hampshire	50.0
42	Iowa	49.1
43	Rhode Island	48.0
44	North Dakota	42.9
45	South Dakota	40.0
46	Maine	28.6
47	West Virginia	25.8
NA	Alabama***	NA
NA	Florida***	NA
NA	Hawaii***	NA
	District of Columbia	69.5

Source: CQ Press using reported data from the Federal Bureau of Investigation
"Crime in the United States 2014" (Uniform Crime Reports, September 28, 2015, http://www.fbi.gov/about-us/cjis/ucr/)
*Of the 11,930 murders in 2014 for which supplemental data were received by the F.B.I. There were an additional 2,319 murders for which the type of murder weapon was not reported to the F.B.I. Includes nonnegligent manslaughter. National and state percents based on reporting jurisdictions only. **Illinois's percent is for Chicago and Rockford only.
***Not available.

Rapes in 2014

National Total = 84,041 Rapes*

ALPHA ORDER

RANK	STATE	RAPES	% of USA
20	Alabama	1,436	1.7%
38	Alaska	555	0.7%
9	Arizona	2,464	2.9%
23	Arkansas	1,182	1.4%
1	California	8,398	10.0%
12	Colorado	2,121	2.5%
37	Connecticut	571	0.7%
48	Delaware	249	0.3%
3	Florida	6,051	7.2%
11	Georgia	2,159	2.6%
44	Hawaii	314	0.4%
39	Idaho	468	0.6%
7	Illinois	3,081	3.7%
17	Indiana	1,615	1.9%
34	Iowa	828	1.0%
26	Kansas	1,075	1.3%
33	Kentucky	883	1.1%
30	Louisiana	992	1.2%
43	Maine	360	0.4%
25	Maryland	1,144	1.4%
16	Massachusetts	1,629	1.9%
5	Michigan	4,049	4.8%
19	Minnesota	1,452	1.7%
35	Mississippi	764	0.9%
15	Missouri	1,706	2.0%
41	Montana	430	0.5%
36	Nebraska	620	0.7%
29	Nevada	995	1.2%
40	New Hampshire	458	0.5%
31	New Jersey	953	1.1%
27	New Mexico	1,071	1.3%
6	New York	3,918	4.7%
14	North Carolina	1,740	2.1%
46	North Dakota	276	0.3%
4	Ohio	4,097	4.9%
22	Oklahoma	1,277	1.5%
28	Oregon	1,052	1.3%
8	Pennsylvania	2,787	3.3%
47	Rhode Island	253	0.3%
18	South Carolina	1,480	1.8%
42	South Dakota	413	0.5%
13	Tennessee	1,861	2.2%
2	Texas	8,236	9.8%
32	Utah	945	1.1%
50	Vermont	99	0.1%
21	Virginia	1,432	1.7%
10	Washington	2,171	2.6%
45	West Virginia	285	0.3%
24	Wisconsin	1,168	1.4%
49	Wyoming	126	0.1%

RANK ORDER

RANK	STATE	RAPES	% of USA
1	California	8,398	10.0%
2	Texas	8,236	9.8%
3	Florida	6,051	7.2%
4	Ohio	4,097	4.9%
5	Michigan	4,049	4.8%
6	New York	3,918	4.7%
7	Illinois	3,081	3.7%
8	Pennsylvania	2,787	3.3%
9	Arizona	2,464	2.9%
10	Washington	2,171	2.6%
11	Georgia	2,159	2.6%
12	Colorado	2,121	2.5%
13	Tennessee	1,861	2.2%
14	North Carolina	1,740	2.1%
15	Missouri	1,706	2.0%
16	Massachusetts	1,629	1.9%
17	Indiana	1,615	1.9%
18	South Carolina	1,480	1.8%
19	Minnesota	1,452	1.7%
20	Alabama	1,436	1.7%
21	Virginia	1,432	1.7%
22	Oklahoma	1,277	1.5%
23	Arkansas	1,182	1.4%
24	Wisconsin	1,168	1.4%
25	Maryland	1,144	1.4%
26	Kansas	1,075	1.3%
27	New Mexico	1,071	1.3%
28	Oregon	1,052	1.3%
29	Nevada	995	1.2%
30	Louisiana	992	1.2%
31	New Jersey	953	1.1%
32	Utah	945	1.1%
33	Kentucky	883	1.1%
34	Iowa	828	1.0%
35	Mississippi	764	0.9%
36	Nebraska	620	0.7%
37	Connecticut	571	0.7%
38	Alaska	555	0.7%
39	Idaho	468	0.6%
40	New Hampshire	458	0.5%
41	Montana	430	0.5%
42	South Dakota	413	0.5%
43	Maine	360	0.4%
44	Hawaii	314	0.4%
45	West Virginia	285	0.3%
46	North Dakota	276	0.3%
47	Rhode Island	253	0.3%
48	Delaware	249	0.3%
49	Wyoming	126	0.1%
50	Vermont	99	0.1%
	District of Columbia	352	0.4%

Source: Reported data from the Federal Bureau of Investigation
"Crime in the United States 2014" (Uniform Crime Reports, September 28, 2015, http://www.fbi.gov/about-us/cjis/ucr/)
*Although the definition of rape was revised in 2013 the FBI continues to release estimates based on the legacy definition for comparison purposes to previous years. The legacy definition used for these figures is "Forcible rape is the carnal knowledge of a female forcibly and against her will. Assaults or attempts to commit rape by force or threat of force are included. However, statutory rape without force and other sex offenses are excluded."

Rape Rate in 2014

National Rate = 26.4 Rapes per 100,000 Population*

ALPHA ORDER

RANK	STATE	RATE
21	Alabama	29.6
1	Alaska	75.3
10	Arizona	36.6
6	Arkansas	39.8
37	California	21.6
7	Colorado	39.6
47	Connecticut	15.9
26	Delaware	26.6
20	Florida	30.4
39	Georgia	21.4
35	Hawaii	22.1
22	Idaho	28.6
34	Illinois	23.9
31	Indiana	24.5
26	Iowa	26.6
9	Kansas	37.0
42	Kentucky	20.0
40	Louisiana	21.3
25	Maine	27.1
44	Maryland	19.1
32	Massachusetts	24.1
5	Michigan	40.9
26	Minnesota	26.6
30	Mississippi	25.5
24	Missouri	28.1
4	Montana	42.0
14	Nebraska	33.0
12	Nevada	35.0
13	New Hampshire	34.5
50	New Jersey	10.7
2	New Mexico	51.4
43	New York	19.8
45	North Carolina	17.5
8	North Dakota	37.3
11	Ohio	35.3
15	Oklahoma	32.9
29	Oregon	26.5
36	Pennsylvania	21.8
33	Rhode Island	24.0
18	South Carolina	30.6
3	South Dakota	48.4
23	Tennessee	28.4
18	Texas	30.6
16	Utah	32.1
48	Vermont	15.8
46	Virginia	17.2
17	Washington	30.7
49	West Virginia	15.4
41	Wisconsin	20.3
37	Wyoming	21.6

RANK ORDER

RANK	STATE	RATE
1	Alaska	75.3
2	New Mexico	51.4
3	South Dakota	48.4
4	Montana	42.0
5	Michigan	40.9
6	Arkansas	39.8
7	Colorado	39.6
8	North Dakota	37.3
9	Kansas	37.0
10	Arizona	36.6
11	Ohio	35.3
12	Nevada	35.0
13	New Hampshire	34.5
14	Nebraska	33.0
15	Oklahoma	32.9
16	Utah	32.1
17	Washington	30.7
18	South Carolina	30.6
18	Texas	30.6
20	Florida	30.4
21	Alabama	29.6
22	Idaho	28.6
23	Tennessee	28.4
24	Missouri	28.1
25	Maine	27.1
26	Delaware	26.6
26	Iowa	26.6
26	Minnesota	26.6
29	Oregon	26.5
30	Mississippi	25.5
31	Indiana	24.5
32	Massachusetts	24.1
33	Rhode Island	24.0
34	Illinois	23.9
35	Hawaii	22.1
36	Pennsylvania	21.8
37	California	21.6
37	Wyoming	21.6
39	Georgia	21.4
40	Louisiana	21.3
41	Wisconsin	20.3
42	Kentucky	20.0
43	New York	19.8
44	Maryland	19.1
45	North Carolina	17.5
46	Virginia	17.2
47	Connecticut	15.9
48	Vermont	15.8
49	West Virginia	15.4
50	New Jersey	10.7
	District of Columbia	53.4

Source: Reported data from the Federal Bureau of Investigation
"Crime in the United States 2014" (Uniform Crime Reports, September 28, 2015, http://www.fbi.gov/about-us/cjis/ucr/)
*Although the definition of rape was revised in 2013 the FBI continues to release estimates based on the legacy definition for comparison purposes to previous years. The legacy definition used for these figures is "Forcible rape is the carnal knowledge of a female forcibly and against her will. Assaults or attempts to commit rape by force or threat of force are included. However, statutory rape without force and other sex offenses are excluded."

Rapes (Revised Definition) in 2014

National Total = 116,645 Rapes*

ALPHA ORDER					RANK ORDER			
RANK	STATE	RAPES	% of USA		RANK	STATE	RAPES	% of USA
20	Alabama	2,005	1.7%		1	California	11,527	9.9%
38	Alaska	771	0.7%		2	Texas	11,393	9.8%
9	Arizona	3,378	2.9%		3	Florida	8,563	7.3%
23	Arkansas	1,763	1.5%		4	Michigan	6,273	5.4%
1	California	11,527	9.9%		5	New York	5,433	4.7%
11	Colorado	3,039	2.6%		6	Ohio	5,042	4.3%
37	Connecticut	782	0.7%		7	Illinois	4,159	3.6%
46	Delaware	386	0.3%		8	Pennsylvania	3,827	3.3%
3	Florida	8,563	7.3%		9	Arizona	3,378	2.9%
10	Georgia	3,048	2.6%		10	Georgia	3,048	2.6%
45	Hawaii	445	0.4%		11	Colorado	3,039	2.6%
39	Idaho	609	0.5%		12	Washington	2,695	2.3%
7	Illinois	4,159	3.6%		13	Tennessee	2,531	2.2%
17	Indiana	2,186	1.9%		14	North Carolina	2,420	2.1%
34	Iowa	1,128	1.0%		15	Missouri	2,379	2.0%
30	Kansas	1,411	1.2%		16	Virginia	2,310	2.0%
29	Kentucky	1,440	1.2%		17	Indiana	2,186	1.9%
31	Louisiana	1,375	1.2%		18	Massachusetts	2,180	1.9%
43	Maine	485	0.4%		19	South Carolina	2,068	1.8%
25	Maryland	1,619	1.4%		20	Alabama	2,005	1.7%
18	Massachusetts	2,180	1.9%		21	Minnesota	2,001	1.7%
4	Michigan	6,273	5.4%		22	Oklahoma	1,777	1.5%
21	Minnesota	2,001	1.7%		23	Arkansas	1,763	1.5%
35	Mississippi	1,058	0.9%		24	Wisconsin	1,674	1.4%
15	Missouri	2,379	2.0%		25	Maryland	1,619	1.4%
41	Montana	541	0.5%		26	New Mexico	1,475	1.3%
36	Nebraska	862	0.7%		27	Oregon	1,458	1.2%
32	Nevada	1,357	1.2%		28	Utah	1,454	1.2%
40	New Hampshire	594	0.5%		29	Kentucky	1,440	1.2%
33	New Jersey	1,274	1.1%		30	Kansas	1,411	1.2%
26	New Mexico	1,475	1.3%		31	Louisiana	1,375	1.2%
5	New York	5,433	4.7%		32	Nevada	1,357	1.2%
14	North Carolina	2,420	2.1%		33	New Jersey	1,274	1.1%
48	North Dakota	358	0.3%		34	Iowa	1,128	1.0%
6	Ohio	5,042	4.3%		35	Mississippi	1,058	0.9%
22	Oklahoma	1,777	1.5%		36	Nebraska	862	0.7%
27	Oregon	1,458	1.2%		37	Connecticut	782	0.7%
8	Pennsylvania	3,827	3.3%		38	Alaska	771	0.7%
47	Rhode Island	361	0.3%		39	Idaho	609	0.5%
19	South Carolina	2,068	1.8%		40	New Hampshire	594	0.5%
44	South Dakota	470	0.4%		41	Montana	541	0.5%
13	Tennessee	2,531	2.2%		42	West Virginia	505	0.4%
2	Texas	11,393	9.8%		43	Maine	485	0.4%
28	Utah	1,454	1.2%		44	South Dakota	470	0.4%
50	Vermont	110	0.1%		45	Hawaii	445	0.4%
16	Virginia	2,310	2.0%		46	Delaware	386	0.3%
12	Washington	2,695	2.3%		47	Rhode Island	361	0.3%
42	West Virginia	505	0.4%		48	North Dakota	358	0.3%
24	Wisconsin	1,674	1.4%		49	Wyoming	174	0.1%
49	Wyoming	174	0.1%		50	Vermont	110	0.1%
						District of Columbia	472	0.4%

Source: Reported data from the Federal Bureau of Investigation
"Crime in the United States 2014" (Uniform Crime Reports, September 28, 2015, http://www.fbi.gov/about-us/cjis/ucr/)
*The definition of rape was revised in 2013 to "Penetration, no matter how slight, of the vagina or anus with any body part or object, or oral penetration by a sex organ of another person, without the consent of the victim. Attempts or assaults to commit rape are also included; however, statutory rape and incest are excluded." This revised definition includes both male and female victims and drops "forcible" from the title.

Rape Rate (Revised Definition) in 2014

National Rate = 36.6 Rapes per 100,000 Population*

ALPHA ORDER

RANK	STATE	RATE
20	Alabama	41.3
1	Alaska	104.7
8	Arizona	50.2
4	Arkansas	59.4
40	California	29.7
5	Colorado	56.7
48	Connecticut	21.7
20	Delaware	41.3
17	Florida	43.0
37	Georgia	30.2
36	Hawaii	31.3
25	Idaho	37.3
34	Illinois	32.3
32	Indiana	33.1
29	Iowa	36.3
10	Kansas	48.6
33	Kentucky	32.6
41	Louisiana	29.6
28	Maine	36.5
46	Maryland	27.1
34	Massachusetts	32.3
3	Michigan	63.3
26	Minnesota	36.7
30	Mississippi	35.3
22	Missouri	39.2
7	Montana	52.9
13	Nebraska	45.8
12	Nevada	47.8
15	New Hampshire	44.8
50	New Jersey	14.3
2	New Mexico	70.7
44	New York	27.5
47	North Carolina	24.3
11	North Dakota	48.4
16	Ohio	43.5
13	Oklahoma	45.8
26	Oregon	36.7
38	Pennsylvania	29.9
31	Rhode Island	34.2
18	South Carolina	42.8
6	South Dakota	55.1
23	Tennessee	38.6
19	Texas	42.3
9	Utah	49.4
49	Vermont	17.6
43	Virginia	27.7
24	Washington	38.2
45	West Virginia	27.3
42	Wisconsin	29.1
39	Wyoming	29.8

RANK ORDER

RANK	STATE	RATE
1	Alaska	104.7
2	New Mexico	70.7
3	Michigan	63.3
4	Arkansas	59.4
5	Colorado	56.7
6	South Dakota	55.1
7	Montana	52.9
8	Arizona	50.2
9	Utah	49.4
10	Kansas	48.6
11	North Dakota	48.4
12	Nevada	47.8
13	Nebraska	45.8
13	Oklahoma	45.8
15	New Hampshire	44.8
16	Ohio	43.5
17	Florida	43.0
18	South Carolina	42.8
19	Texas	42.3
20	Alabama	41.3
20	Delaware	41.3
22	Missouri	39.2
23	Tennessee	38.6
24	Washington	38.2
25	Idaho	37.3
26	Minnesota	36.7
26	Oregon	36.7
28	Maine	36.5
29	Iowa	36.3
30	Mississippi	35.3
31	Rhode Island	34.2
32	Indiana	33.1
33	Kentucky	32.6
34	Illinois	32.3
34	Massachusetts	32.3
36	Hawaii	31.3
37	Georgia	30.2
38	Pennsylvania	29.9
39	Wyoming	29.8
40	California	29.7
41	Louisiana	29.6
42	Wisconsin	29.1
43	Virginia	27.7
44	New York	27.5
45	West Virginia	27.3
46	Maryland	27.1
47	North Carolina	24.3
48	Connecticut	21.7
49	Vermont	17.6
50	New Jersey	14.3
	District of Columbia	71.6

Source: Reported data from the Federal Bureau of Investigation
"Crime in the United States 2014" (Uniform Crime Reports, September 28, 2015, http://www.fbi.gov/about-us/cjis/ucr/)
*The definition of rape was revised in 2013 to "Penetration, no matter how slight, of the vagina or anus with any body part or object, or oral penetration by a sex organ of another person, without the consent of the victim. Attempts or assaults to commit rape are also included; however, statutory rape and incest are excluded." This revised definition includes both male and female victims and drops "forcible" from the title.

Robberies in 2014

National Total = 325,802 Robberies*

ALPHA ORDER

RANK	STATE	ROBBERIES	% of USA
22	Alabama	4,701	1.4%
41	Alaska	629	0.2%
15	Arizona	6,249	1.9%
33	Arkansas	2,050	0.6%
1	California	48,680	14.9%
29	Colorado	3,039	0.9%
27	Connecticut	3,159	1.0%
36	Delaware	1,269	0.4%
3	Florida	24,914	7.6%
8	Georgia	12,417	3.8%
37	Hawaii	1,107	0.3%
45	Idaho	204	0.1%
5	Illinois	15,299	4.7%
14	Indiana	6,897	2.1%
38	Iowa	1,045	0.3%
34	Kansas	1,362	0.4%
26	Kentucky	3,336	1.0%
18	Louisiana	5,695	1.7%
44	Maine	304	0.1%
10	Maryland	9,544	2.9%
16	Massachusetts	6,036	1.9%
12	Michigan	8,021	2.5%
25	Minnesota	3,687	1.1%
30	Mississippi	2,430	0.7%
20	Missouri	5,592	1.7%
46	Montana	203	0.1%
39	Nebraska	1,043	0.3%
17	Nevada	5,954	1.8%
42	New Hampshire	537	0.2%
9	New Jersey	10,498	3.2%
32	New Mexico	2,086	0.6%
4	New York	24,045	7.4%
11	North Carolina	8,416	2.6%
48	North Dakota	173	0.1%
7	Ohio	12,753	3.9%
28	Oklahoma	3,048	0.9%
31	Oregon	2,093	0.6%
6	Pennsylvania	13,534	4.2%
43	Rhode Island	529	0.2%
24	South Carolina	3,997	1.2%
47	South Dakota	200	0.1%
13	Tennessee	7,265	2.2%
2	Texas	31,181	9.6%
35	Utah	1,312	0.4%
49	Vermont	70	0.0%
23	Virginia	4,292	1.3%
19	Washington	5,640	1.7%
40	West Virginia	651	0.2%
21	Wisconsin	5,066	1.6%
50	Wyoming	53	0.0%

RANK ORDER

RANK	STATE	ROBBERIES	% of USA
1	California	48,680	14.9%
2	Texas	31,181	9.6%
3	Florida	24,914	7.6%
4	New York	24,045	7.4%
5	Illinois	15,299	4.7%
6	Pennsylvania	13,534	4.2%
7	Ohio	12,753	3.9%
8	Georgia	12,417	3.8%
9	New Jersey	10,498	3.2%
10	Maryland	9,544	2.9%
11	North Carolina	8,416	2.6%
12	Michigan	8,021	2.5%
13	Tennessee	7,265	2.2%
14	Indiana	6,897	2.1%
15	Arizona	6,249	1.9%
16	Massachusetts	6,036	1.9%
17	Nevada	5,954	1.8%
18	Louisiana	5,695	1.7%
19	Washington	5,640	1.7%
20	Missouri	5,592	1.7%
21	Wisconsin	5,066	1.6%
22	Alabama	4,701	1.4%
23	Virginia	4,292	1.3%
24	South Carolina	3,997	1.2%
25	Minnesota	3,687	1.1%
26	Kentucky	3,336	1.0%
27	Connecticut	3,159	1.0%
28	Oklahoma	3,048	0.9%
29	Colorado	3,039	0.9%
30	Mississippi	2,430	0.7%
31	Oregon	2,093	0.6%
32	New Mexico	2,086	0.6%
33	Arkansas	2,050	0.6%
34	Kansas	1,362	0.4%
35	Utah	1,312	0.4%
36	Delaware	1,269	0.4%
37	Hawaii	1,107	0.3%
38	Iowa	1,045	0.3%
39	Nebraska	1,043	0.3%
40	West Virginia	651	0.2%
41	Alaska	629	0.2%
42	New Hampshire	537	0.2%
43	Rhode Island	529	0.2%
44	Maine	304	0.1%
45	Idaho	204	0.1%
46	Montana	203	0.1%
47	South Dakota	200	0.1%
48	North Dakota	173	0.1%
49	Vermont	70	0.0%
50	Wyoming	53	0.0%
	District of Columbia	3,497	1.1%

Source: Reported data from the Federal Bureau of Investigation
"Crime in the United States 2014" (Uniform Crime Reports, September 28, 2015, http://www.fbi.gov/about-us/cjis/ucr/)
*Robbery is the taking or attempting to take anything of value by force or threat of force.

Robbery Rate in 2014

National Rate = 102.2 Robberies per 100,000 Population*

ALPHA ORDER

RANK	STATE	RATE
17	Alabama	96.9
23	Alaska	85.4
18	Arizona	92.8
32	Arkansas	69.1
4	California	125.5
34	Colorado	56.7
22	Connecticut	87.8
3	Delaware	135.6
5	Florida	125.2
6	Georgia	123.0
30	Hawaii	78.0
48	Idaho	12.5
9	Illinois	118.8
15	Indiana	104.5
43	Iowa	33.6
39	Kansas	46.9
31	Kentucky	75.6
7	Louisiana	122.5
46	Maine	22.9
2	Maryland	159.7
20	Massachusetts	89.5
27	Michigan	80.9
33	Minnesota	67.6
26	Mississippi	81.2
19	Missouri	92.2
47	Montana	19.8
35	Nebraska	55.4
1	Nevada	209.7
41	New Hampshire	40.5
10	New Jersey	117.5
16	New Mexico	100.0
8	New York	121.8
24	North Carolina	84.6
44	North Dakota	23.4
13	Ohio	110.0
29	Oklahoma	78.6
36	Oregon	52.7
14	Pennsylvania	105.8
38	Rhode Island	50.1
25	South Carolina	82.7
44	South Dakota	23.4
12	Tennessee	110.9
11	Texas	115.7
40	Utah	44.6
49	Vermont	11.2
37	Virginia	51.5
28	Washington	79.9
42	West Virginia	35.2
21	Wisconsin	88.0
50	Wyoming	9.1

RANK ORDER

RANK	STATE	RATE
1	Nevada	209.7
2	Maryland	159.7
3	Delaware	135.6
4	California	125.5
5	Florida	125.2
6	Georgia	123.0
7	Louisiana	122.5
8	New York	121.8
9	Illinois	118.8
10	New Jersey	117.5
11	Texas	115.7
12	Tennessee	110.9
13	Ohio	110.0
14	Pennsylvania	105.8
15	Indiana	104.5
16	New Mexico	100.0
17	Alabama	96.9
18	Arizona	92.8
19	Missouri	92.2
20	Massachusetts	89.5
21	Wisconsin	88.0
22	Connecticut	87.8
23	Alaska	85.4
24	North Carolina	84.6
25	South Carolina	82.7
26	Mississippi	81.2
27	Michigan	80.9
28	Washington	79.9
29	Oklahoma	78.6
30	Hawaii	78.0
31	Kentucky	75.6
32	Arkansas	69.1
33	Minnesota	67.6
34	Colorado	56.7
35	Nebraska	55.4
36	Oregon	52.7
37	Virginia	51.5
38	Rhode Island	50.1
39	Kansas	46.9
40	Utah	44.6
41	New Hampshire	40.5
42	West Virginia	35.2
43	Iowa	33.6
44	North Dakota	23.4
44	South Dakota	23.4
46	Maine	22.9
47	Montana	19.8
48	Idaho	12.5
49	Vermont	11.2
50	Wyoming	9.1
	District of Columbia	530.7

Source: Reported data from the Federal Bureau of Investigation
"Crime in the United States 2014" (Uniform Crime Reports, September 28, 2015, http://www.fbi.gov/about-us/cjis/ucr/)
*Robbery is the taking or attempting to take anything of value by force or threat of force.

Aggravated Assaults in 2014

National Total = 741,291 Aggravated Assaults*

ALPHA ORDER				RANK ORDER			
RANK	STATE	ASSAULTS	% of USA	RANK	STATE	ASSAULTS	% of USA
19	Alabama	13,745	1.9%	1	California	91,803	12.4%
39	Alaska	3,243	0.4%	2	Florida	72,895	9.8%
14	Arizona	16,970	2.3%	3	Texas	65,656	8.9%
25	Arkansas	10,265	1.4%	4	New York	45,303	6.1%
1	California	91,803	12.4%	5	Tennessee	29,681	4.0%
24	Colorado	10,325	1.4%	6	Illinois	27,520	3.7%
34	Connecticut	4,495	0.6%	7	Michigan	27,519	3.7%
40	Delaware	2,867	0.4%	8	Pennsylvania	22,189	3.0%
2	Florida	72,895	9.8%	9	Georgia	22,052	3.0%
9	Georgia	22,052	3.0%	10	North Carolina	21,421	2.9%
43	Hawaii	2,102	0.3%	11	Missouri	18,482	2.5%
41	Idaho	2,623	0.4%	12	Massachusetts	18,051	2.4%
6	Illinois	27,520	3.7%	13	South Carolina	17,676	2.4%
18	Indiana	14,686	2.0%	14	Arizona	16,970	2.3%
31	Iowa	6,264	0.8%	15	Louisiana	16,387	2.2%
29	Kansas	7,259	1.0%	16	Maryland	15,133	2.0%
35	Kentucky	4,404	0.6%	17	Ohio	14,771	2.0%
15	Louisiana	16,387	2.2%	18	Indiana	14,686	2.0%
49	Maine	890	0.1%	19	Alabama	13,745	1.9%
16	Maryland	15,133	2.0%	20	Washington	11,627	1.6%
12	Massachusetts	18,051	2.4%	21	New Jersey	11,225	1.5%
7	Michigan	27,519	3.7%	22	Oklahoma	10,744	1.4%
30	Minnesota	6,729	0.9%	23	Nevada	10,564	1.4%
33	Mississippi	4,592	0.6%	24	Colorado	10,325	1.4%
11	Missouri	18,482	2.5%	25	Arkansas	10,265	1.4%
42	Montana	2,532	0.3%	26	Wisconsin	9,809	1.3%
38	Nebraska	3,316	0.4%	27	Virginia	9,400	1.3%
23	Nevada	10,564	1.4%	28	New Mexico	8,797	1.2%
45	New Hampshire	1,459	0.2%	29	Kansas	7,259	1.0%
21	New Jersey	11,225	1.5%	30	Minnesota	6,729	0.9%
28	New Mexico	8,797	1.2%	31	Iowa	6,264	0.8%
4	New York	45,303	6.1%	32	Oregon	5,592	0.8%
10	North Carolina	21,421	2.9%	33	Mississippi	4,592	0.6%
46	North Dakota	1,407	0.2%	34	Connecticut	4,495	0.6%
17	Ohio	14,771	2.0%	35	Kentucky	4,404	0.6%
22	Oklahoma	10,744	1.4%	36	West Virginia	4,358	0.6%
32	Oregon	5,592	0.8%	37	Utah	3,513	0.5%
8	Pennsylvania	22,189	3.0%	38	Nebraska	3,316	0.4%
47	Rhode Island	1,398	0.2%	39	Alaska	3,243	0.4%
13	South Carolina	17,676	2.4%	40	Delaware	2,867	0.4%
44	South Dakota	2,096	0.3%	41	Idaho	2,623	0.4%
5	Tennessee	29,681	4.0%	42	Montana	2,532	0.3%
3	Texas	65,656	8.9%	43	Hawaii	2,102	0.3%
37	Utah	3,513	0.5%	44	South Dakota	2,096	0.3%
50	Vermont	432	0.1%	45	New Hampshire	1,459	0.2%
27	Virginia	9,400	1.3%	46	North Dakota	1,407	0.2%
20	Washington	11,627	1.6%	47	Rhode Island	1,398	0.2%
36	West Virginia	4,358	0.6%	48	Wyoming	899	0.1%
26	Wisconsin	9,809	1.3%	49	Maine	890	0.1%
48	Wyoming	899	0.1%	50	Vermont	432	0.1%
					District of Columbia	4,125	0.6%

Source: Reported data from the Federal Bureau of Investigation
"Crime in the United States 2014" (Uniform Crime Reports, September 28, 2015, http://www.fbi.gov/about-us/cjis/ucr/)
*Aggravated assault is an attack for the purpose of inflicting severe bodily injury.

Aggravated Assault Rate in 2014

National Rate = 232.5 Aggravated Assaults per 100,000 Population*

ALPHA ORDER

RANK	STATE	RATE
11	Alabama	283.4
2	Alaska	440.2
16	Arizona	252.1
8	Arkansas	346.0
21	California	236.6
29	Colorado	192.8
43	Connecticut	125.0
9	Delaware	306.4
5	Florida	366.4
25	Georgia	218.4
38	Hawaii	148.1
35	Idaho	160.5
27	Illinois	213.7
24	Indiana	222.6
28	Iowa	201.6
17	Kansas	250.0
48	Kentucky	99.8
7	Louisiana	352.4
50	Maine	66.9
15	Maryland	253.2
14	Massachusetts	267.6
12	Michigan	277.7
44	Minnesota	123.3
37	Mississippi	153.4
10	Missouri	304.8
18	Montana	247.4
31	Nebraska	176.2
4	Nevada	372.1
47	New Hampshire	110.0
42	New Jersey	125.6
3	New Mexico	421.8
23	New York	229.4
26	North Carolina	215.4
30	North Dakota	190.3
41	Ohio	127.4
13	Oklahoma	277.0
39	Oregon	140.8
32	Pennsylvania	173.5
40	Rhode Island	132.5
6	South Carolina	365.8
19	South Dakota	245.7
1	Tennessee	453.2
20	Texas	243.6
45	Utah	119.4
49	Vermont	68.9
46	Virginia	112.9
34	Washington	164.7
22	West Virginia	235.5
33	Wisconsin	170.4
36	Wyoming	153.9

RANK ORDER

RANK	STATE	RATE
1	Tennessee	453.2
2	Alaska	440.2
3	New Mexico	421.8
4	Nevada	372.1
5	Florida	366.4
6	South Carolina	365.8
7	Louisiana	352.4
8	Arkansas	346.0
9	Delaware	306.4
10	Missouri	304.8
11	Alabama	283.4
12	Michigan	277.7
13	Oklahoma	277.0
14	Massachusetts	267.6
15	Maryland	253.2
16	Arizona	252.1
17	Kansas	250.0
18	Montana	247.4
19	South Dakota	245.7
20	Texas	243.6
21	California	236.6
22	West Virginia	235.5
23	New York	229.4
24	Indiana	222.6
25	Georgia	218.4
26	North Carolina	215.4
27	Illinois	213.7
28	Iowa	201.6
29	Colorado	192.8
30	North Dakota	190.3
31	Nebraska	176.2
32	Pennsylvania	173.5
33	Wisconsin	170.4
34	Washington	164.7
35	Idaho	160.5
36	Wyoming	153.9
37	Mississippi	153.4
38	Hawaii	148.1
39	Oregon	140.8
40	Rhode Island	132.5
41	Ohio	127.4
42	New Jersey	125.6
43	Connecticut	125.0
44	Minnesota	123.3
45	Utah	119.4
46	Virginia	112.9
47	New Hampshire	110.0
48	Kentucky	99.8
49	Vermont	68.9
50	Maine	66.9
	District of Columbia	626.1

Source: Reported data from the Federal Bureau of Investigation
"Crime in the United States 2014" (Uniform Crime Reports, September 28, 2015, http://www.fbi.gov/about-us/cjis/ucr/)
*Aggravated assault is an attack for the purpose of inflicting severe bodily injury.

Property Crimes in 2014

National Total = 8,277,829 Property Crimes*

ALPHA ORDER

RANK	STATE	CRIMES	% of USA
20	Alabama	154,094	1.9%
46	Alaska	20,334	0.2%
11	Arizona	215,240	2.6%
29	Arkansas	99,018	1.2%
1	California	947,192	11.4%
22	Colorado	135,510	1.6%
35	Connecticut	69,070	0.8%
41	Delaware	27,900	0.3%
3	Florida	679,446	8.2%
5	Georgia	331,316	4.0%
38	Hawaii	43,297	0.5%
40	Idaho	30,316	0.4%
8	Illinois	267,385	3.2%
15	Indiana	174,776	2.1%
36	Iowa	65,056	0.8%
32	Kansas	79,431	1.0%
28	Kentucky	99,166	1.2%
17	Louisiana	160,824	1.9%
42	Maine	26,421	0.3%
21	Maryland	149,859	1.8%
24	Massachusetts	125,267	1.5%
12	Michigan	202,547	2.4%
23	Minnesota	125,377	1.5%
30	Mississippi	87,462	1.1%
14	Missouri	176,237	2.1%
44	Montana	25,312	0.3%
37	Nebraska	47,479	0.6%
33	Nevada	74,538	0.9%
43	New Hampshire	26,041	0.3%
19	New Jersey	154,993	1.9%
34	New Mexico	73,877	0.9%
4	New York	339,282	4.1%
7	North Carolina	285,697	3.5%
48	North Dakota	15,605	0.2%
6	Ohio	324,528	3.9%
26	Oklahoma	115,982	1.4%
27	Oregon	114,305	1.4%
10	Pennsylvania	247,016	3.0%
45	Rhode Island	22,935	0.3%
16	South Carolina	167,217	2.0%
47	South Dakota	15,902	0.2%
13	Tennessee	200,447	2.4%
2	Texas	813,934	9.8%
31	Utah	84,711	1.0%
50	Vermont	9,551	0.1%
18	Virginia	160,720	1.9%
9	Washington	261,706	3.2%
39	West Virginia	37,648	0.5%
25	Wisconsin	120,238	1.5%
49	Wyoming	11,477	0.1%

RANK ORDER

RANK	STATE	CRIMES	% of USA
1	California	947,192	11.4%
2	Texas	813,934	9.8%
3	Florida	679,446	8.2%
4	New York	339,282	4.1%
5	Georgia	331,316	4.0%
6	Ohio	324,528	3.9%
7	North Carolina	285,697	3.5%
8	Illinois	267,385	3.2%
9	Washington	261,706	3.2%
10	Pennsylvania	247,016	3.0%
11	Arizona	215,240	2.6%
12	Michigan	202,547	2.4%
13	Tennessee	200,447	2.4%
14	Missouri	176,237	2.1%
15	Indiana	174,776	2.1%
16	South Carolina	167,217	2.0%
17	Louisiana	160,824	1.9%
18	Virginia	160,720	1.9%
19	New Jersey	154,993	1.9%
20	Alabama	154,094	1.9%
21	Maryland	149,859	1.8%
22	Colorado	135,510	1.6%
23	Minnesota	125,377	1.5%
24	Massachusetts	125,267	1.5%
25	Wisconsin	120,238	1.5%
26	Oklahoma	115,982	1.4%
27	Oregon	114,305	1.4%
28	Kentucky	99,166	1.2%
29	Arkansas	99,018	1.2%
30	Mississippi	87,462	1.1%
31	Utah	84,711	1.0%
32	Kansas	79,431	1.0%
33	Nevada	74,538	0.9%
34	New Mexico	73,877	0.9%
35	Connecticut	69,070	0.8%
36	Iowa	65,056	0.8%
37	Nebraska	47,479	0.6%
38	Hawaii	43,297	0.5%
39	West Virginia	37,648	0.5%
40	Idaho	30,316	0.4%
41	Delaware	27,900	0.3%
42	Maine	26,421	0.3%
43	New Hampshire	26,041	0.3%
44	Montana	25,312	0.3%
45	Rhode Island	22,935	0.3%
46	Alaska	20,334	0.2%
47	South Dakota	15,902	0.2%
48	North Dakota	15,605	0.2%
49	Wyoming	11,477	0.1%
50	Vermont	9,551	0.1%
	District of Columbia	34,147	0.4%

Source: Reported data from the Federal Bureau of Investigation
"Crime in the United States 2014" (Uniform Crime Reports, September 28, 2015, http://www.fbi.gov/about-us/cjis/ucr/)
*Property crimes are offenses of burglary, larceny-theft, and motor vehicle theft.

Property Crime Rate in 2014

National Rate = 2,596.1 Property Crimes per 100,000 Population*

ALPHA ORDER

RANK	STATE	RATE
9	Alabama	3,177.6
21	Alaska	2,760.0
8	Arizona	3,197.5
6	Arkansas	3,338.0
29	California	2,441.1
25	Colorado	2,530.1
44	Connecticut	1,920.4
14	Delaware	2,982.0
5	Florida	3,415.5
7	Georgia	3,281.2
11	Hawaii	3,050.0
47	Idaho	1,854.8
36	Illinois	2,075.9
23	Indiana	2,649.4
34	Iowa	2,093.8
22	Kansas	2,735.2
31	Kentucky	2,246.9
4	Louisiana	3,458.8
39	Maine	1,986.4
27	Maryland	2,507.5
46	Massachusetts	1,857.1
37	Michigan	2,043.9
30	Minnesota	2,297.5
15	Mississippi	2,921.2
16	Missouri	2,906.5
28	Montana	2,472.9
26	Nebraska	2,523.5
24	Nevada	2,625.4
41	New Hampshire	1,962.7
48	New Jersey	1,734.1
2	New Mexico	3,542.3
49	New York	1,718.2
19	North Carolina	2,873.1
33	North Dakota	2,110.3
20	Ohio	2,799.1
13	Oklahoma	2,990.7
17	Oregon	2,879.0
42	Pennsylvania	1,931.7
32	Rhode Island	2,173.6
3	South Carolina	3,460.3
45	South Dakota	1,863.9
10	Tennessee	3,060.6
12	Texas	3,019.4
18	Utah	2,878.5
50	Vermont	1,524.4
43	Virginia	1,930.3
1	Washington	3,706.1
38	West Virginia	2,034.7
35	Wisconsin	2,088.3
40	Wyoming	1,964.7

RANK ORDER

RANK	STATE	RATE
1	Washington	3,706.1
2	New Mexico	3,542.3
3	South Carolina	3,460.3
4	Louisiana	3,458.8
5	Florida	3,415.5
6	Arkansas	3,338.0
7	Georgia	3,281.2
8	Arizona	3,197.5
9	Alabama	3,177.6
10	Tennessee	3,060.6
11	Hawaii	3,050.0
12	Texas	3,019.4
13	Oklahoma	2,990.7
14	Delaware	2,982.0
15	Mississippi	2,921.2
16	Missouri	2,906.5
17	Oregon	2,879.0
18	Utah	2,878.5
19	North Carolina	2,873.1
20	Ohio	2,799.1
21	Alaska	2,760.0
22	Kansas	2,735.2
23	Indiana	2,649.4
24	Nevada	2,625.4
25	Colorado	2,530.1
26	Nebraska	2,523.5
27	Maryland	2,507.5
28	Montana	2,472.9
29	California	2,441.1
30	Minnesota	2,297.5
31	Kentucky	2,246.9
32	Rhode Island	2,173.6
33	North Dakota	2,110.3
34	Iowa	2,093.8
35	Wisconsin	2,088.3
36	Illinois	2,075.9
37	Michigan	2,043.9
38	West Virginia	2,034.7
39	Maine	1,986.4
40	Wyoming	1,964.7
41	New Hampshire	1,962.7
42	Pennsylvania	1,931.7
43	Virginia	1,930.3
44	Connecticut	1,920.4
45	South Dakota	1,863.9
46	Massachusetts	1,857.1
47	Idaho	1,854.8
48	New Jersey	1,734.1
49	New York	1,718.2
50	Vermont	1,524.4
	District of Columbia	5,182.5

Source: Reported data from the Federal Bureau of Investigation
 "Crime in the United States 2014" (Uniform Crime Reports, September 28, 2015, http://www.fbi.gov/about-us/cjis/ucr/)
*Property crimes are offenses of burglary, larceny-theft, and motor vehicle theft.

Percent Change in Property Crime Rate: 2013 to 2014

National Percent Change = 5.0% Decrease*

ALPHA ORDER

RANK	STATE	PERCENT CHANGE
22	Alabama	(5.1)
10	Alaska	(4.1)
20	Arizona	(5.0)
33	Arkansas	(7.2)
40	California	(7.9)
16	Colorado	(4.7)
6	Connecticut	(3.0)
19	Delaware	(4.9)
1	Florida	10.3
9	Georgia	(3.5)
22	Hawaii	(5.1)
5	Idaho	(1.0)
43	Illinois	(9.6)
32	Indiana	(7.1)
18	Iowa	(4.8)
38	Kansas	(7.6)
24	Kentucky	(5.4)
8	Louisiana	(3.4)
49	Maine	(13.3)
28	Maryland	(5.7)
42	Massachusetts	(9.2)
48	Michigan	(12.1)
20	Minnesota	(5.0)
2	Mississippi	7.2
35	Missouri	(7.4)
12	Montana	(4.2)
10	Nebraska	(4.1)
35	Nevada	(7.4)
47	New Hampshire	(11.3)
39	New Jersey	(7.8)
30	New Mexico	(6.4)
27	New York	(5.6)
35	North Carolina	(7.4)
4	North Dakota	(0.5)
13	Ohio	(4.3)
41	Oklahoma	(8.8)
43	Oregon	(9.6)
29	Pennsylvania	(6.2)
46	Rhode Island	(11.1)
16	South Carolina	(4.7)
7	South Dakota	(3.2)
13	Tennessee	(4.3)
33	Texas	(7.2)
24	Utah	(5.4)
50	Vermont	(31.2)
31	Virginia	(6.9)
3	Washington	(0.3)
26	West Virginia	(5.5)
15	Wisconsin	(4.6)
45	Wyoming	(10.5)

RANK ORDER

RANK	STATE	PERCENT CHANGE
1	Florida	10.3
2	Mississippi	7.2
3	Washington	(0.3)
4	North Dakota	(0.5)
5	Idaho	(1.0)
6	Connecticut	(3.0)
7	South Dakota	(3.2)
8	Louisiana	(3.4)
9	Georgia	(3.5)
10	Alaska	(4.1)
10	Nebraska	(4.1)
12	Montana	(4.2)
13	Ohio	(4.3)
13	Tennessee	(4.3)
15	Wisconsin	(4.6)
16	Colorado	(4.7)
16	South Carolina	(4.7)
18	Iowa	(4.8)
19	Delaware	(4.9)
20	Arizona	(5.0)
20	Minnesota	(5.0)
22	Alabama	(5.1)
22	Hawaii	(5.1)
24	Kentucky	(5.4)
24	Utah	(5.4)
26	West Virginia	(5.5)
27	New York	(5.6)
28	Maryland	(5.7)
29	Pennsylvania	(6.2)
30	New Mexico	(6.4)
31	Virginia	(6.9)
32	Indiana	(7.1)
33	Arkansas	(7.2)
33	Texas	(7.2)
35	Missouri	(7.4)
35	Nevada	(7.4)
35	North Carolina	(7.4)
38	Kansas	(7.6)
39	New Jersey	(7.8)
40	California	(7.9)
41	Oklahoma	(8.8)
42	Massachusetts	(9.2)
43	Illinois	(9.6)
43	Oregon	(9.6)
45	Wyoming	(10.5)
46	Rhode Island	(11.1)
47	New Hampshire	(11.3)
48	Michigan	(12.1)
49	Maine	(13.3)
50	Vermont	(31.2)
	District of Columbia	8.2

Source: Reported data from the Federal Bureau of Investigation
"Crime in the United States 2014" (Uniform Crime Reports, September 28, 2015, http://www.fbi.gov/about-us/cjis/ucr/)
*Property crimes are offenses of burglary, larceny-theft, and motor vehicle theft.

Burglaries in 2014

National Total = 1,729,806 Burglaries*

ALPHA ORDER

RANK	STATE	BURGLARIES	% of USA
14	Alabama	39,715	2.3%
46	Alaska	3,150	0.2%
13	Arizona	43,562	2.5%
23	Arkansas	24,790	1.4%
1	California	202,670	11.7%
25	Colorado	23,472	1.4%
35	Connecticut	11,955	0.7%
41	Delaware	5,768	0.3%
3	Florida	143,220	8.3%
6	Georgia	76,428	4.4%
39	Hawaii	7,778	0.4%
40	Idaho	6,428	0.4%
9	Illinois	50,008	2.9%
16	Indiana	36,893	2.1%
34	Iowa	14,428	0.8%
33	Kansas	15,828	0.9%
26	Kentucky	23,244	1.3%
15	Louisiana	38,337	2.2%
42	Maine	5,030	0.3%
21	Maryland	28,012	1.6%
22	Massachusetts	24,964	1.4%
12	Michigan	44,184	2.6%
30	Minnesota	20,773	1.2%
24	Mississippi	24,352	1.4%
18	Missouri	35,258	2.0%
45	Montana	3,595	0.2%
38	Nebraska	7,950	0.5%
28	Nevada	21,927	1.3%
44	New Hampshire	4,162	0.2%
19	New Jersey	31,710	1.8%
31	New Mexico	18,505	1.1%
8	New York	50,781	2.9%
4	North Carolina	79,373	4.6%
48	North Dakota	2,707	0.2%
5	Ohio	78,845	4.6%
20	Oklahoma	29,508	1.7%
32	Oregon	17,230	1.0%
11	Pennsylvania	45,720	2.6%
43	Rhode Island	4,823	0.3%
17	South Carolina	36,721	2.1%
47	South Dakota	2,818	0.2%
10	Tennessee	46,642	2.7%
2	Texas	169,234	9.8%
36	Utah	11,518	0.7%
49	Vermont	2,034	0.1%
27	Virginia	23,122	1.3%
7	Washington	55,290	3.2%
37	West Virginia	8,973	0.5%
29	Wisconsin	21,216	1.2%
50	Wyoming	1,689	0.1%

RANK ORDER

RANK	STATE	BURGLARIES	% of USA
1	California	202,670	11.7%
2	Texas	169,234	9.8%
3	Florida	143,220	8.3%
4	North Carolina	79,373	4.6%
5	Ohio	78,845	4.6%
6	Georgia	76,428	4.4%
7	Washington	55,290	3.2%
8	New York	50,781	2.9%
9	Illinois	50,008	2.9%
10	Tennessee	46,642	2.7%
11	Pennsylvania	45,720	2.6%
12	Michigan	44,184	2.6%
13	Arizona	43,562	2.5%
14	Alabama	39,715	2.3%
15	Louisiana	38,337	2.2%
16	Indiana	36,893	2.1%
17	South Carolina	36,721	2.1%
18	Missouri	35,258	2.0%
19	New Jersey	31,710	1.8%
20	Oklahoma	29,508	1.7%
21	Maryland	28,012	1.6%
22	Massachusetts	24,964	1.4%
23	Arkansas	24,790	1.4%
24	Mississippi	24,352	1.4%
25	Colorado	23,472	1.4%
26	Kentucky	23,244	1.3%
27	Virginia	23,122	1.3%
28	Nevada	21,927	1.3%
29	Wisconsin	21,216	1.2%
30	Minnesota	20,773	1.2%
31	New Mexico	18,505	1.1%
32	Oregon	17,230	1.0%
33	Kansas	15,828	0.9%
34	Iowa	14,428	0.8%
35	Connecticut	11,955	0.7%
36	Utah	11,518	0.7%
37	West Virginia	8,973	0.5%
38	Nebraska	7,950	0.5%
39	Hawaii	7,778	0.4%
40	Idaho	6,428	0.4%
41	Delaware	5,768	0.3%
42	Maine	5,030	0.3%
43	Rhode Island	4,823	0.3%
44	New Hampshire	4,162	0.2%
45	Montana	3,595	0.2%
46	Alaska	3,150	0.2%
47	South Dakota	2,818	0.2%
48	North Dakota	2,707	0.2%
49	Vermont	2,034	0.1%
50	Wyoming	1,689	0.1%
	District of Columbia	3,466	0.2%

Source: Reported data from the Federal Bureau of Investigation
"Crime in the United States 2014" (Uniform Crime Reports, September 28, 2015, http://www.fbi.gov/about-us/cjis/ucr/)
*Burglary is the unlawful entry of a structure to commit a felony or theft. Attempts are included.

Burglary Rate in 2014

National Rate = 542.5 Burglaries per 100,000 Population*

ALPHA ORDER

RANK	STATE	RATE
4	Alabama	819.0
31	Alaska	427.6
15	Arizona	647.1
2	Arkansas	835.7
23	California	522.3
29	Colorado	438.2
44	Connecticut	332.4
17	Delaware	616.5
12	Florida	719.9
11	Georgia	756.9
20	Hawaii	547.9
33	Idaho	393.3
35	Illinois	388.2
19	Indiana	559.3
26	Iowa	464.4
21	Kansas	545.0
22	Kentucky	526.7
3	Louisiana	824.5
37	Maine	378.2
25	Maryland	468.7
38	Massachusetts	370.1
28	Michigan	445.9
36	Minnesota	380.7
5	Mississippi	813.3
18	Missouri	581.5
43	Montana	351.2
32	Nebraska	422.5
8	Nevada	772.3
47	New Hampshire	313.7
42	New Jersey	354.8
1	New Mexico	887.3
50	New York	257.2
6	North Carolina	798.2
40	North Dakota	366.1
14	Ohio	680.0
9	Oklahoma	760.9
30	Oregon	434.0
41	Pennsylvania	357.5
27	Rhode Island	457.1
10	South Carolina	759.9
45	South Dakota	330.3
13	Tennessee	712.2
16	Texas	627.8
34	Utah	391.4
46	Vermont	324.6
49	Virginia	277.7
7	Washington	783.0
24	West Virginia	484.9
39	Wisconsin	368.5
48	Wyoming	289.1

RANK ORDER

RANK	STATE	RATE
1	New Mexico	887.3
2	Arkansas	835.7
3	Louisiana	824.5
4	Alabama	819.0
5	Mississippi	813.3
6	North Carolina	798.2
7	Washington	783.0
8	Nevada	772.3
9	Oklahoma	760.9
10	South Carolina	759.9
11	Georgia	756.9
12	Florida	719.9
13	Tennessee	712.2
14	Ohio	680.0
15	Arizona	647.1
16	Texas	627.8
17	Delaware	616.5
18	Missouri	581.5
19	Indiana	559.3
20	Hawaii	547.9
21	Kansas	545.0
22	Kentucky	526.7
23	California	522.3
24	West Virginia	484.9
25	Maryland	468.7
26	Iowa	464.4
27	Rhode Island	457.1
28	Michigan	445.9
29	Colorado	438.2
30	Oregon	434.0
31	Alaska	427.6
32	Nebraska	422.5
33	Idaho	393.3
34	Utah	391.4
35	Illinois	388.2
36	Minnesota	380.7
37	Maine	378.2
38	Massachusetts	370.1
39	Wisconsin	368.5
40	North Dakota	366.1
41	Pennsylvania	357.5
42	New Jersey	354.8
43	Montana	351.2
44	Connecticut	332.4
45	South Dakota	330.3
46	Vermont	324.6
47	New Hampshire	313.7
48	Wyoming	289.1
49	Virginia	277.7
50	New York	257.2
	District of Columbia	526.0

Source: Reported data from the Federal Bureau of Investigation
"Crime in the United States 2014" (Uniform Crime Reports, September 28, 2015, http://www.fbi.gov/about-us/cjis/ucr/)
*Burglary is the unlawful entry of a structure to commit a felony or theft. Attempts are included.

Larceny-Thefts in 2014

National Total = 5,858,496 Larceny-Thefts*

ALPHA ORDER

RANK	STATE	THEFTS	% of USA
21	Alabama	104,238	1.8%
46	Alaska	15,445	0.3%
11	Arizona	154,091	2.6%
29	Arkansas	68,627	1.2%
1	California	592,670	10.1%
22	Colorado	99,464	1.7%
33	Connecticut	51,005	0.9%
42	Delaware	20,865	0.4%
3	Florida	493,647	8.4%
5	Georgia	228,034	3.9%
38	Hawaii	31,640	0.5%
40	Idaho	22,227	0.4%
7	Illinois	199,926	3.4%
16	Indiana	124,022	2.1%
35	Iowa	46,477	0.8%
32	Kansas	56,697	1.0%
28	Kentucky	69,604	1.2%
18	Louisiana	112,596	1.9%
43	Maine	20,592	0.4%
20	Maryland	108,745	1.9%
24	Massachusetts	92,043	1.6%
13	Michigan	137,206	2.3%
23	Minnesota	96,237	1.6%
31	Mississippi	58,591	1.0%
15	Missouri	124,622	2.1%
44	Montana	19,674	0.3%
37	Nebraska	35,074	0.6%
36	Nevada	42,426	0.7%
41	New Hampshire	21,022	0.4%
19	New Jersey	111,578	1.9%
34	New Mexico	49,082	0.8%
4	New York	272,765	4.7%
8	North Carolina	192,694	3.3%
48	North Dakota	11,384	0.2%
6	Ohio	227,668	3.9%
27	Oklahoma	75,891	1.3%
26	Oregon	87,526	1.5%
9	Pennsylvania	188,256	3.2%
45	Rhode Island	16,279	0.3%
17	South Carolina	117,594	2.0%
47	South Dakota	12,077	0.2%
12	Tennessee	141,206	2.4%
2	Texas	576,154	9.8%
30	Utah	65,895	1.1%
50	Vermont	7,273	0.1%
14	Virginia	129,933	2.2%
10	Washington	175,769	3.0%
39	West Virginia	26,779	0.5%
25	Wisconsin	89,103	1.5%
49	Wyoming	9,185	0.2%

RANK ORDER

RANK	STATE	THEFTS	% of USA
1	California	592,670	10.1%
2	Texas	576,154	9.8%
3	Florida	493,647	8.4%
4	New York	272,765	4.7%
5	Georgia	228,034	3.9%
6	Ohio	227,668	3.9%
7	Illinois	199,926	3.4%
8	North Carolina	192,694	3.3%
9	Pennsylvania	188,256	3.2%
10	Washington	175,769	3.0%
11	Arizona	154,091	2.6%
12	Tennessee	141,206	2.4%
13	Michigan	137,206	2.3%
14	Virginia	129,933	2.2%
15	Missouri	124,622	2.1%
16	Indiana	124,022	2.1%
17	South Carolina	117,594	2.0%
18	Louisiana	112,596	1.9%
19	New Jersey	111,578	1.9%
20	Maryland	108,745	1.9%
21	Alabama	104,238	1.8%
22	Colorado	99,464	1.7%
23	Minnesota	96,237	1.6%
24	Massachusetts	92,043	1.6%
25	Wisconsin	89,103	1.5%
26	Oregon	87,526	1.5%
27	Oklahoma	75,891	1.3%
28	Kentucky	69,604	1.2%
29	Arkansas	68,627	1.2%
30	Utah	65,895	1.1%
31	Mississippi	58,591	1.0%
32	Kansas	56,697	1.0%
33	Connecticut	51,005	0.9%
34	New Mexico	49,082	0.8%
35	Iowa	46,477	0.8%
36	Nevada	42,426	0.7%
37	Nebraska	35,074	0.6%
38	Hawaii	31,640	0.5%
39	West Virginia	26,779	0.5%
40	Idaho	22,227	0.4%
41	New Hampshire	21,022	0.4%
42	Delaware	20,865	0.4%
43	Maine	20,592	0.4%
44	Montana	19,674	0.3%
45	Rhode Island	16,279	0.3%
46	Alaska	15,445	0.3%
47	South Dakota	12,077	0.2%
48	North Dakota	11,384	0.2%
49	Wyoming	9,185	0.2%
50	Vermont	7,273	0.1%
	District of Columbia	26,898	0.5%

Source: Reported data from the Federal Bureau of Investigation "Crime in the United States 2014" (Uniform Crime Reports, September 28, 2015, http://www.fbi.gov/about-us/cjis/ucr/)

*Larceny-theft is the unlawful taking of property without use of force, violence, or fraud. Attempts are included. Motor vehicle thefts are excluded.

Larceny-Theft Rate in 2014

National Rate = 1,837.3 Larceny-Thefts per 100,000 Population*

ALPHA ORDER

RANK	STATE	RATE
14	Alabama	2,149.5
16	Alaska	2,096.4
7	Arizona	2,289.1
6	Arkansas	2,313.5
38	California	1,527.4
26	Colorado	1,857.1
43	Connecticut	1,418.1
10	Delaware	2,230.1
2	Florida	2,481.5
8	Georgia	2,258.4
11	Hawaii	2,228.9
48	Idaho	1,359.9
33	Illinois	1,552.2
24	Indiana	1,880.0
39	Iowa	1,495.8
21	Kansas	1,952.4
30	Kentucky	1,577.1
4	Louisiana	2,421.6
34	Maine	1,548.2
27	Maryland	1,819.6
47	Massachusetts	1,364.5
45	Michigan	1,384.5
28	Minnesota	1,763.5
19	Mississippi	1,956.9
17	Missouri	2,055.3
23	Montana	1,922.1
25	Nebraska	1,864.1
40	Nevada	1,494.3
29	New Hampshire	1,584.4
49	New Jersey	1,248.3
5	New Mexico	2,353.4
46	New York	1,381.4
22	North Carolina	1,937.8
37	North Dakota	1,539.5
18	Ohio	1,963.6
19	Oklahoma	1,956.9
12	Oregon	2,204.6
41	Pennsylvania	1,472.2
36	Rhode Island	1,542.8
3	South Carolina	2,433.4
44	South Dakota	1,415.5
13	Tennessee	2,156.0
15	Texas	2,137.3
9	Utah	2,239.1
50	Vermont	1,160.8
32	Virginia	1,560.5
1	Washington	2,489.1
42	West Virginia	1,447.3
35	Wisconsin	1,547.6
31	Wyoming	1,572.4

RANK ORDER

RANK	STATE	RATE
1	Washington	2,489.1
2	Florida	2,481.5
3	South Carolina	2,433.4
4	Louisiana	2,421.6
5	New Mexico	2,353.4
6	Arkansas	2,313.5
7	Arizona	2,289.1
8	Georgia	2,258.4
9	Utah	2,239.1
10	Delaware	2,230.1
11	Hawaii	2,228.9
12	Oregon	2,204.6
13	Tennessee	2,156.0
14	Alabama	2,149.5
15	Texas	2,137.3
16	Alaska	2,096.4
17	Missouri	2,055.3
18	Ohio	1,963.6
19	Mississippi	1,956.9
19	Oklahoma	1,956.9
21	Kansas	1,952.4
22	North Carolina	1,937.8
23	Montana	1,922.1
24	Indiana	1,880.0
25	Nebraska	1,864.1
26	Colorado	1,857.1
27	Maryland	1,819.6
28	Minnesota	1,763.5
29	New Hampshire	1,584.4
30	Kentucky	1,577.1
31	Wyoming	1,572.4
32	Virginia	1,560.5
33	Illinois	1,552.2
34	Maine	1,548.2
35	Wisconsin	1,547.6
36	Rhode Island	1,542.8
37	North Dakota	1,539.5
38	California	1,527.4
39	Iowa	1,495.8
40	Nevada	1,494.3
41	Pennsylvania	1,472.2
42	West Virginia	1,447.3
43	Connecticut	1,418.1
44	South Dakota	1,415.5
45	Michigan	1,384.5
46	New York	1,381.4
47	Massachusetts	1,364.5
48	Idaho	1,359.9
49	New Jersey	1,248.3
50	Vermont	1,160.8
	District of Columbia	4,082.3

Source: Reported data from the Federal Bureau of Investigation
"Crime in the United States 2014" (Uniform Crime Reports, September 28, 2015, http://www.fbi.gov/about-us/cjis/ucr/)
*Larceny-theft is the unlawful taking of property without use of force, violence, or fraud. Attempts are included. Motor vehicle thefts are excluded.

Motor Vehicle Thefts in 2014

National Total = 689,527 Motor Vehicle Thefts*

ALPHA ORDER

RANK	STATE	THEFTS	% of USA
22	Alabama	10,141	1.5%
42	Alaska	1,739	0.3%
8	Arizona	17,587	2.6%
34	Arkansas	5,601	0.8%
1	California	151,852	22.0%
18	Colorado	12,574	1.8%
33	Connecticut	6,110	0.9%
45	Delaware	1,267	0.2%
3	Florida	42,579	6.2%
5	Georgia	26,854	3.9%
38	Hawaii	3,879	0.6%
43	Idaho	1,661	0.2%
9	Illinois	17,451	2.5%
12	Indiana	13,861	2.0%
37	Iowa	4,151	0.6%
30	Kansas	6,906	1.0%
31	Kentucky	6,318	0.9%
24	Louisiana	9,891	1.4%
48	Maine	799	0.1%
14	Maryland	13,102	1.9%
27	Massachusetts	8,260	1.2%
6	Michigan	21,157	3.1%
26	Minnesota	8,367	1.2%
35	Mississippi	4,519	0.7%
10	Missouri	16,357	2.4%
39	Montana	2,043	0.3%
36	Nebraska	4,455	0.6%
21	Nevada	10,185	1.5%
47	New Hampshire	857	0.1%
19	New Jersey	11,705	1.7%
32	New Mexico	6,290	0.9%
11	New York	15,736	2.3%
13	North Carolina	13,630	2.0%
44	North Dakota	1,514	0.2%
7	Ohio	18,015	2.6%
20	Oklahoma	10,583	1.5%
25	Oregon	9,549	1.4%
15	Pennsylvania	13,040	1.9%
41	Rhode Island	1,833	0.3%
16	South Carolina	12,902	1.9%
46	South Dakota	1,007	0.1%
17	Tennessee	12,599	1.8%
2	Texas	68,546	9.9%
29	Utah	7,298	1.1%
50	Vermont	244	0.0%
28	Virginia	7,665	1.1%
4	Washington	30,647	4.4%
40	West Virginia	1,896	0.3%
23	Wisconsin	9,919	1.4%
49	Wyoming	603	0.1%

RANK ORDER

RANK	STATE	THEFTS	% of USA
1	California	151,852	22.0%
2	Texas	68,546	9.9%
3	Florida	42,579	6.2%
4	Washington	30,647	4.4%
5	Georgia	26,854	3.9%
6	Michigan	21,157	3.1%
7	Ohio	18,015	2.6%
8	Arizona	17,587	2.6%
9	Illinois	17,451	2.5%
10	Missouri	16,357	2.4%
11	New York	15,736	2.3%
12	Indiana	13,861	2.0%
13	North Carolina	13,630	2.0%
14	Maryland	13,102	1.9%
15	Pennsylvania	13,040	1.9%
16	South Carolina	12,902	1.9%
17	Tennessee	12,599	1.8%
18	Colorado	12,574	1.8%
19	New Jersey	11,705	1.7%
20	Oklahoma	10,583	1.5%
21	Nevada	10,185	1.5%
22	Alabama	10,141	1.5%
23	Wisconsin	9,919	1.4%
24	Louisiana	9,891	1.4%
25	Oregon	9,549	1.4%
26	Minnesota	8,367	1.2%
27	Massachusetts	8,260	1.2%
28	Virginia	7,665	1.1%
29	Utah	7,298	1.1%
30	Kansas	6,906	1.0%
31	Kentucky	6,318	0.9%
32	New Mexico	6,290	0.9%
33	Connecticut	6,110	0.9%
34	Arkansas	5,601	0.8%
35	Mississippi	4,519	0.7%
36	Nebraska	4,455	0.6%
37	Iowa	4,151	0.6%
38	Hawaii	3,879	0.6%
39	Montana	2,043	0.3%
40	West Virginia	1,896	0.3%
41	Rhode Island	1,833	0.3%
42	Alaska	1,739	0.3%
43	Idaho	1,661	0.2%
44	North Dakota	1,514	0.2%
45	Delaware	1,267	0.2%
46	South Dakota	1,007	0.1%
47	New Hampshire	857	0.1%
48	Maine	799	0.1%
49	Wyoming	603	0.1%
50	Vermont	244	0.0%
	District of Columbia	3,783	0.5%

Source: Reported data from the Federal Bureau of Investigation
"Crime in the United States 2014" (Uniform Crime Reports, September 28, 2015, http://www.fbi.gov/about-us/cjis/ucr/)
*Includes the theft or attempted theft of a self-propelled vehicle. Excludes motorboats, construction equipment, airplanes, and farming equipment.

Motor Vehicle Theft Rate in 2014

National Rate = 216.2 Motor Vehicle Thefts per 100,000 Population*

ALPHA ORDER

RANK	STATE	RATE
23	Alabama	209.1
16	Alaska	236.0
10	Arizona	261.3
27	Arkansas	188.8
2	California	391.3
17	Colorado	234.8
30	Connecticut	169.9
37	Delaware	135.4
19	Florida	214.0
9	Georgia	266.0
5	Hawaii	273.3
45	Idaho	101.6
36	Illinois	135.5
22	Indiana	210.1
38	Iowa	133.6
14	Kansas	237.8
34	Kentucky	143.2
21	Louisiana	212.7
49	Maine	60.1
18	Maryland	219.2
40	Massachusetts	122.5
20	Michigan	213.5
32	Minnesota	153.3
33	Mississippi	150.9
7	Missouri	269.8
25	Montana	199.6
15	Nebraska	236.8
3	Nevada	358.7
48	New Hampshire	64.6
39	New Jersey	131.0
4	New Mexico	301.6
47	New York	79.7
35	North Carolina	137.1
24	North Dakota	204.7
31	Ohio	155.4
6	Oklahoma	272.9
13	Oregon	240.5
44	Pennsylvania	102.0
28	Rhode Island	173.7
8	South Carolina	267.0
41	South Dakota	118.0
26	Tennessee	192.4
11	Texas	254.3
12	Utah	248.0
50	Vermont	38.9
46	Virginia	92.1
1	Washington	434.0
43	West Virginia	102.5
29	Wisconsin	172.3
42	Wyoming	103.2

RANK ORDER

RANK	STATE	RATE
1	Washington	434.0
2	California	391.3
3	Nevada	358.7
4	New Mexico	301.6
5	Hawaii	273.3
6	Oklahoma	272.9
7	Missouri	269.8
8	South Carolina	267.0
9	Georgia	266.0
10	Arizona	261.3
11	Texas	254.3
12	Utah	248.0
13	Oregon	240.5
14	Kansas	237.8
15	Nebraska	236.8
16	Alaska	236.0
17	Colorado	234.8
18	Maryland	219.2
19	Florida	214.0
20	Michigan	213.5
21	Louisiana	212.7
22	Indiana	210.1
23	Alabama	209.1
24	North Dakota	204.7
25	Montana	199.6
26	Tennessee	192.4
27	Arkansas	188.8
28	Rhode Island	173.7
29	Wisconsin	172.3
30	Connecticut	169.9
31	Ohio	155.4
32	Minnesota	153.3
33	Mississippi	150.9
34	Kentucky	143.2
35	North Carolina	137.1
36	Illinois	135.5
37	Delaware	135.4
38	Iowa	133.6
39	New Jersey	131.0
40	Massachusetts	122.5
41	South Dakota	118.0
42	Wyoming	103.2
43	West Virginia	102.5
44	Pennsylvania	102.0
45	Idaho	101.6
46	Virginia	92.1
47	New York	79.7
48	New Hampshire	64.6
49	Maine	60.1
50	Vermont	38.9
	District of Columbia	574.1

Source: Reported data from the Federal Bureau of Investigation
"Crime in the United States 2014" (Uniform Crime Reports, September 28, 2015, http://www.fbi.gov/about-us/cjis/ucr/)
*Includes the theft or attempted theft of a self-propelled vehicle. Excludes motorboats, construction equipment, airplanes, and farming equipment.

Rate of Consumer Fraud Complaints in 2014

National Rate = 705.7 Complaints per 100,000 Population*

ALPHA ORDER

RANK	STATE	RATE
13	Alabama	574.2
45	Alaska	408.7
16	Arizona	562.1
32	Arkansas	465.2
8	California	644.6
10	Colorado	598.6
24	Connecticut	509.1
4	Delaware	769.2
1	Florida	1,007.3
2	Georgia	777.7
43	Hawaii	419.6
34	Idaho	456.8
30	Illinois	473.9
33	Indiana	464.7
48	Iowa	365.4
40	Kansas	432.8
35	Kentucky	451.1
19	Louisiana	538.9
37	Maine	444.3
6	Maryland	675.5
17	Massachusetts	554.8
5	Michigan	749.2
41	Minnesota	423.0
38	Mississippi	443.4
21	Missouri	516.3
36	Montana	444.5
44	Nebraska	414.9
3	Nevada	773.2
15	New Hampshire	562.6
9	New Jersey	598.9
28	New Mexico	506.1
22	New York	514.0
26	North Carolina	507.9
50	North Dakota	334.4
27	Ohio	506.3
39	Oklahoma	436.5
29	Oregon	505.5
18	Pennsylvania	544.7
12	Rhode Island	589.4
20	South Carolina	534.2
49	South Dakota	348.6
14	Tennessee	570.2
7	Texas	647.2
46	Utah	389.8
47	Vermont	389.7
11	Virginia	594.9
23	Washington	511.6
31	West Virginia	466.6
42	Wisconsin	422.4
25	Wyoming	508.1

RANK ORDER

RANK	STATE	RATE
1	Florida	1,007.3
2	Georgia	777.7
3	Nevada	773.2
4	Delaware	769.2
5	Michigan	749.2
6	Maryland	675.5
7	Texas	647.2
8	California	644.6
9	New Jersey	598.9
10	Colorado	598.6
11	Virginia	594.9
12	Rhode Island	589.4
13	Alabama	574.2
14	Tennessee	570.2
15	New Hampshire	562.6
16	Arizona	562.1
17	Massachusetts	554.8
18	Pennsylvania	544.7
19	Louisiana	538.9
20	South Carolina	534.2
21	Missouri	516.3
22	New York	514.0
23	Washington	511.6
24	Connecticut	509.1
25	Wyoming	508.1
26	North Carolina	507.9
27	Ohio	506.3
28	New Mexico	506.1
29	Oregon	505.5
30	Illinois	473.9
31	West Virginia	466.6
32	Arkansas	465.2
33	Indiana	464.7
34	Idaho	456.8
35	Kentucky	451.1
36	Montana	444.5
37	Maine	444.3
38	Mississippi	443.4
39	Oklahoma	436.5
40	Kansas	432.8
41	Minnesota	423.0
42	Wisconsin	422.4
43	Hawaii	419.6
44	Nebraska	414.9
45	Alaska	408.7
46	Utah	389.8
47	Vermont	389.7
48	Iowa	365.4
49	South Dakota	348.6
50	North Dakota	334.4
	District of Columbia	1,002.4

Source: Federal Trade Commission, Consumer Sentinel
"Consumer Sentinel Network Data Book for January - December 2014" (February 2015, http://www.ftc.gov/sentinel/)
*National rate includes complaints not shown by state. Rates include "other" complaints but do not include identity theft or "Do Not Call" registry complaints.

Rate of Identity Theft Complaints in 2014

National Rate = 104.3 Complaints per 100,000 Population*

ALPHA ORDER

RANK	STATE	RATE
22	Alabama	77.7
29	Alaska	73.6
9	Arizona	96.0
15	Arkansas	83.6
7	California	100.5
13	Colorado	85.5
14	Connecticut	85.4
21	Delaware	78.1
1	Florida	186.3
5	Georgia	112.7
49	Hawaii	40.9
39	Idaho	58.9
12	Illinois	95.6
33	Indiana	68.2
47	Iowa	48.5
35	Kansas	65.2
43	Kentucky	53.4
27	Louisiana	73.8
44	Maine	52.1
10	Maryland	95.9
25	Massachusetts	75.8
6	Michigan	104.3
38	Minnesota	59.2
18	Mississippi	80.5
4	Missouri	118.7
40	Montana	57.2
46	Nebraska	48.6
8	Nevada	100.2
41	New Hampshire	54.7
19	New Jersey	79.9
23	New Mexico	77.2
17	New York	80.8
27	North Carolina	73.8
48	North Dakota	43.1
20	Ohio	79.0
32	Oklahoma	68.5
3	Oregon	124.6
16	Pennsylvania	81.7
34	Rhode Island	66.2
30	South Carolina	73.3
50	South Dakota	36.3
24	Tennessee	76.2
10	Texas	95.9
42	Utah	53.9
36	Vermont	64.2
31	Virginia	71.1
2	Washington	154.8
37	West Virginia	61.4
26	Wisconsin	74.4
45	Wyoming	49.1

RANK ORDER

RANK	STATE	RATE
1	Florida	186.3
2	Washington	154.8
3	Oregon	124.6
4	Missouri	118.7
5	Georgia	112.7
6	Michigan	104.3
7	California	100.5
8	Nevada	100.2
9	Arizona	96.0
10	Maryland	95.9
10	Texas	95.9
12	Illinois	95.6
13	Colorado	85.5
14	Connecticut	85.4
15	Arkansas	83.6
16	Pennsylvania	81.7
17	New York	80.8
18	Mississippi	80.5
19	New Jersey	79.9
20	Ohio	79.0
21	Delaware	78.1
22	Alabama	77.7
23	New Mexico	77.2
24	Tennessee	76.2
25	Massachusetts	75.8
26	Wisconsin	74.4
27	Louisiana	73.8
27	North Carolina	73.8
29	Alaska	73.6
30	South Carolina	73.3
31	Virginia	71.1
32	Oklahoma	68.5
33	Indiana	68.2
34	Rhode Island	66.2
35	Kansas	65.2
36	Vermont	64.2
37	West Virginia	61.4
38	Minnesota	59.2
39	Idaho	58.9
40	Montana	57.2
41	New Hampshire	54.7
42	Utah	53.9
43	Kentucky	53.4
44	Maine	52.1
45	Wyoming	49.1
46	Nebraska	48.6
47	Iowa	48.5
48	North Dakota	43.1
49	Hawaii	40.9
50	South Dakota	36.3
	District of Columbia	142.8

Source: Federal Trade Commission, Consumer Sentinel
"Consumer Sentinel Network Data Book for January - December 2014" (February 2015, http://www.ftc.gov/sentinel/)
*National rate includes complaints not shown by state. Rates do not include consumer fraud or "Do Not Call" registry complaints.

Reported Arrest Rate in 2014

National Rate = 3,576.6 Reported Arrests per 100,000 Population*

ALPHA ORDER

RANK	STATE	RATE
NA	Alabama**	NA
3	Alaska	5,528.1
17	Arizona	4,147.6
9	Arkansas	4,553.9
36	California	3,143.6
8	Colorado	4,619.3
38	Connecticut	2,999.2
21	Delaware	3,940.5
11	Florida	4,363.6
30	Georgia	3,506.9
NA	Hawaii**	NA
25	Idaho	3,610.9
NA	Illinois**	NA
39	Indiana	2,974.7
27	Iowa	3,574.2
31	Kansas	3,482.0
20	Kentucky	4,101.8
15	Louisiana	4,268.7
26	Maine	3,601.0
16	Maryland	4,218.5
46	Massachusetts	2,076.3
45	Michigan	2,614.8
43	Minnesota	2,770.2
1	Mississippi	5,845.0
10	Missouri	4,513.4
37	Montana	3,014.2
12	Nebraska	4,360.1
13	Nevada	4,328.4
22	New Hampshire	3,791.6
28	New Jersey	3,561.5
6	New Mexico	5,018.5
44	New York***	2,618.1
19	North Carolina	4,109.7
14	North Dakota	4,310.6
41	Ohio	2,861.7
33	Oklahoma	3,245.5
29	Oregon	3,525.3
32	Pennsylvania	3,340.4
40	Rhode Island	2,885.5
23	South Carolina	3,757.7
7	South Dakota	4,644.1
2	Tennessee	5,598.1
34	Texas	3,189.5
18	Utah	4,142.3
47	Vermont	2,043.8
24	Virginia	3,651.0
42	Washington	2,830.2
35	West Virginia	3,144.6
5	Wisconsin	5,063.1
4	Wyoming	5,512.2

RANK ORDER

RANK	STATE	RATE
1	Mississippi	5,845.0
2	Tennessee	5,598.1
3	Alaska	5,528.1
4	Wyoming	5,512.2
5	Wisconsin	5,063.1
6	New Mexico	5,018.5
7	South Dakota	4,644.1
8	Colorado	4,619.3
9	Arkansas	4,553.9
10	Missouri	4,513.4
11	Florida	4,363.6
12	Nebraska	4,360.1
13	Nevada	4,328.4
14	North Dakota	4,310.6
15	Louisiana	4,268.7
16	Maryland	4,218.5
17	Arizona	4,147.6
18	Utah	4,142.3
19	North Carolina	4,109.7
20	Kentucky	4,101.8
21	Delaware	3,940.5
22	New Hampshire	3,791.6
23	South Carolina	3,757.7
24	Virginia	3,651.0
25	Idaho	3,610.9
26	Maine	3,601.0
27	Iowa	3,574.2
28	New Jersey	3,561.5
29	Oregon	3,525.3
30	Georgia	3,506.9
31	Kansas	3,482.0
32	Pennsylvania	3,340.4
33	Oklahoma	3,245.5
34	Texas	3,189.5
35	West Virginia	3,144.6
36	California	3,143.6
37	Montana	3,014.2
38	Connecticut	2,999.2
39	Indiana	2,974.7
40	Rhode Island	2,885.5
41	Ohio	2,861.7
42	Washington	2,830.2
43	Minnesota	2,770.2
44	New York***	2,618.1
45	Michigan	2,614.8
46	Massachusetts	2,076.3
47	Vermont	2,043.8
NA	Alabama**	NA
NA	Hawaii**	NA
NA	Illinois**	NA
	District of Columbia**	NA

Source: CQ Press using reported data from the Federal Bureau of Investigation
"Crime in the United States 2014" (Uniform Crime Reports, September 28, 2015, http://www.fbi.gov/about-us/cjis/ucr/)
*By law enforcement agencies submitting complete reports to the F.B.I. for 12 months in 2014. These rates based on population estimates for areas under the jurisdiction of those agencies reporting. Arrest rate based on the F.B.I. estimate of total arrests is 3,514.4 reported and unreported arrests per 100,000 population.
**Not available. ***New York's figure does not include New York City.

Reported Juvenile Arrest Rate in 2014

National Rate = 3,157.8 Reported Arrests per 100,000 Juvenile Population*

ALPHA ORDER

RANK	STATE	RATE
NA	Alabama**	NA
19	Alaska	3,643.2
16	Arizona	3,809.3
32	Arkansas	2,818.1
42	California	2,051.3
7	Colorado	4,927.2
35	Connecticut	2,497.6
9	Delaware	4,564.9
20	Florida	3,624.5
31	Georgia	2,900.4
NA	Hawaii**	NA
12	Idaho	4,167.7
NA	Illinois**	NA
28	Indiana	2,976.4
10	Iowa	4,395.5
38	Kansas	2,388.4
44	Kentucky	1,436.3
13	Louisiana	4,107.4
25	Maine	3,120.9
18	Maryland	3,672.9
45	Massachusetts	1,426.1
43	Michigan	1,867.6
14	Minnesota	3,973.1
24	Mississippi	3,463.1
17	Missouri	3,688.9
6	Montana	5,050.6
3	Nebraska	6,448.8
22	Nevada	3,563.1
23	New Hampshire	3,554.3
39	New Jersey	2,375.0
27	New Mexico	3,025.6
40	New York***	2,311.4
30	North Carolina	2,908.9
4	North Dakota	5,553.2
33	Ohio	2,771.0
34	Oklahoma	2,747.1
21	Oregon	3,595.0
8	Pennsylvania	4,730.2
29	Rhode Island	2,925.0
26	South Carolina	3,120.6
5	South Dakota	5,303.6
15	Tennessee	3,935.6
41	Texas	2,289.4
11	Utah	4,349.3
46	Vermont	1,292.6
36	Virginia	2,449.1
37	Washington	2,425.8
47	West Virginia	961.3
1	Wisconsin	8,958.0
2	Wyoming	6,617.9

RANK ORDER

RANK	STATE	RATE
1	Wisconsin	8,958.0
2	Wyoming	6,617.9
3	Nebraska	6,448.8
4	North Dakota	5,553.2
5	South Dakota	5,303.6
6	Montana	5,050.6
7	Colorado	4,927.2
8	Pennsylvania	4,730.2
9	Delaware	4,564.9
10	Iowa	4,395.5
11	Utah	4,349.3
12	Idaho	4,167.7
13	Louisiana	4,107.4
14	Minnesota	3,973.1
15	Tennessee	3,935.6
16	Arizona	3,809.3
17	Missouri	3,688.9
18	Maryland	3,672.9
19	Alaska	3,643.2
20	Florida	3,624.5
21	Oregon	3,595.0
22	Nevada	3,563.1
23	New Hampshire	3,554.3
24	Mississippi	3,463.1
25	Maine	3,120.9
26	South Carolina	3,120.6
27	New Mexico	3,025.6
28	Indiana	2,976.4
29	Rhode Island	2,925.0
30	North Carolina	2,908.9
31	Georgia	2,900.4
32	Arkansas	2,818.1
33	Ohio	2,771.0
34	Oklahoma	2,747.1
35	Connecticut	2,497.6
36	Virginia	2,449.1
37	Washington	2,425.8
38	Kansas	2,388.4
39	New Jersey	2,375.0
40	New York***	2,311.4
41	Texas	2,289.4
42	California	2,051.3
43	Michigan	1,867.6
44	Kentucky	1,436.3
45	Massachusetts	1,426.1
46	Vermont	1,292.6
47	West Virginia	961.3
NA	Alabama**	NA
NA	Hawaii**	NA
NA	Illinois**	NA
	District of Columbia**	NA

Source: CQ Press using reported data from the Federal Bureau of Investigation
"Crime in the United States 2014" (Uniform Crime Reports, September 28, 2015, http://www.fbi.gov/about-us/cjis/ucr/)
*By law enforcement agencies submitting complete reports to the F.B.I. for 12 months in 2014. Arrests of youths 17 years and younger divided into population of 10 to 17 year olds.
**Not available.
***New York's figure does not include New York City.

Prisoners in State Correctional Institutions: Year End 2014

National Total = 1,350,958 State Prisoners*

ALPHA ORDER

RANK	STATE	PRISONERS	% of USA
15	Alabama	31,771	2.4%
42	Alaska	5,216	0.4%
10	Arizona	42,259	3.1%
27	Arkansas	17,874	1.3%
2	California	136,088	10.1%
24	Colorado	20,646	1.5%
28	Connecticut	16,636	1.2%
38	Delaware	6,955	0.5%
3	Florida	102,870	7.6%
4	Georgia	52,949	3.9%
40	Hawaii	5,866	0.4%
35	Idaho	8,117	0.6%
8	Illinois	48,278	3.6%
16	Indiana	29,271	2.2%
34	Iowa	8,838	0.7%
33	Kansas	9,663	0.7%
20	Kentucky	21,657	1.6%
11	Louisiana	38,030	2.8%
48	Maine	2,242	0.2%
23	Maryland	21,011	1.6%
31	Massachusetts	10,713	0.8%
9	Michigan	43,390	3.2%
32	Minnesota	10,637	0.8%
25	Mississippi	18,793	1.4%
14	Missouri	31,942	2.4%
43	Montana	3,699	0.3%
41	Nebraska	5,441	0.4%
30	Nevada	12,537	0.9%
46	New Hampshire	2,963	0.2%
21	New Jersey	21,590	1.6%
37	New Mexico	7,021	0.5%
5	New York	52,518	3.9%
13	North Carolina	37,096	2.7%
50	North Dakota	1,718	0.1%
6	Ohio	51,519	3.8%
18	Oklahoma	27,650	2.0%
29	Oregon	15,075	1.1%
7	Pennsylvania	50,694	3.8%
45	Rhode Island	3,359	0.2%
22	South Carolina	21,401	1.6%
44	South Dakota	3,608	0.3%
17	Tennessee	28,769	2.1%
1	Texas	166,043	12.3%
36	Utah	7,026	0.5%
49	Vermont	1,979	0.1%
12	Virginia	37,544	2.8%
26	Washington	18,120	1.3%
39	West Virginia	6,896	0.5%
19	Wisconsin	22,597	1.7%
47	Wyoming	2,383	0.2%

RANK ORDER

RANK	STATE	PRISONERS	% of USA
1	Texas	166,043	12.3%
2	California	136,088	10.1%
3	Florida	102,870	7.6%
4	Georgia	52,949	3.9%
5	New York	52,518	3.9%
6	Ohio	51,519	3.8%
7	Pennsylvania	50,694	3.8%
8	Illinois	48,278	3.6%
9	Michigan	43,390	3.2%
10	Arizona	42,259	3.1%
11	Louisiana	38,030	2.8%
12	Virginia	37,544	2.8%
13	North Carolina	37,096	2.7%
14	Missouri	31,942	2.4%
15	Alabama	31,771	2.4%
16	Indiana	29,271	2.2%
17	Tennessee	28,769	2.1%
18	Oklahoma	27,650	2.0%
19	Wisconsin	22,597	1.7%
20	Kentucky	21,657	1.6%
21	New Jersey	21,590	1.6%
22	South Carolina	21,401	1.6%
23	Maryland	21,011	1.6%
24	Colorado	20,646	1.5%
25	Mississippi	18,793	1.4%
26	Washington	18,120	1.3%
27	Arkansas	17,874	1.3%
28	Connecticut	16,636	1.2%
29	Oregon	15,075	1.1%
30	Nevada	12,537	0.9%
31	Massachusetts	10,713	0.8%
32	Minnesota	10,637	0.8%
33	Kansas	9,663	0.7%
34	Iowa	8,838	0.7%
35	Idaho	8,117	0.6%
36	Utah	7,026	0.5%
37	New Mexico	7,021	0.5%
38	Delaware	6,955	0.5%
39	West Virginia	6,896	0.5%
40	Hawaii	5,866	0.4%
41	Nebraska	5,441	0.4%
42	Alaska	5,216	0.4%
43	Montana	3,699	0.3%
44	South Dakota	3,608	0.3%
45	Rhode Island	3,359	0.2%
46	New Hampshire	2,963	0.2%
47	Wyoming	2,383	0.2%
48	Maine	2,242	0.2%
49	Vermont	1,979	0.1%
50	North Dakota	1,718	0.1%
	District of Columbia**	NA	NA

Source: U.S. Department of Justice, Bureau of Justice Statistics
"Prisoners in 2014" (September 2015, NCJ 248955, http://bjs.ojp.usdoj.gov/)
*As of December 31, 2014. Totals reflect all prisoners, including those sentenced to a year or less and those unsentenced.
National total does not include 210,567 prisoners under federal jurisdiction. State and federal prisoners combined total 1,561,525.
**Responsibility for sentenced felons in D.C. was transferred to the Federal Bureau of Prisons in 2001.

State Prisoner Imprisonment Rate in 2014

National Rate = 412 State Prisoners per 100,000 Population*

ALPHA ORDER

RANK	STATE	RATE
3	Alabama	633
27	Alaska	374
6	Arizona	593
4	Arkansas	599
32	California	349
24	Colorado	383
35	Connecticut	326
16	Delaware	440
10	Florida	513
9	Georgia	517
40	Hawaii	257
11	Idaho	489
26	Illinois	375
15	Indiana	442
38	Iowa	282
36	Kansas	322
12	Kentucky	474
1	Louisiana	816
50	Maine	153
33	Maryland	346
48	Massachusetts	188
17	Michigan	437
47	Minnesota	194
5	Mississippi	597
8	Missouri	526
30	Montana	360
37	Nebraska	283
19	Nevada	434
45	New Hampshire	219
42	New Jersey	241
34	New Mexico	329
39	New York	265
31	North Carolina	358
46	North Dakota	214
14	Ohio	444
2	Oklahoma	700
25	Oregon	378
23	Pennsylvania	394
49	Rhode Island	178
20	South Carolina	429
21	South Dakota	421
17	Tennessee	437
7	Texas	584
44	Utah	237
42	Vermont	241
13	Virginia	449
41	Washington	254
28	West Virginia	372
29	Wisconsin	371
22	Wyoming	408

RANK ORDER

RANK	STATE	RATE
1	Louisiana	816
2	Oklahoma	700
3	Alabama	633
4	Arkansas	599
5	Mississippi	597
6	Arizona	593
7	Texas	584
8	Missouri	526
9	Georgia	517
10	Florida	513
11	Idaho	489
12	Kentucky	474
13	Virginia	449
14	Ohio	444
15	Indiana	442
16	Delaware	440
17	Michigan	437
17	Tennessee	437
19	Nevada	434
20	South Carolina	429
21	South Dakota	421
22	Wyoming	408
23	Pennsylvania	394
24	Colorado	383
25	Oregon	378
26	Illinois	375
27	Alaska	374
28	West Virginia	372
29	Wisconsin	371
30	Montana	360
31	North Carolina	358
32	California	349
33	Maryland	346
34	New Mexico	329
35	Connecticut	326
36	Kansas	322
37	Nebraska	283
38	Iowa	282
39	New York	265
40	Hawaii	257
41	Washington	254
42	New Jersey	241
42	Vermont	241
44	Utah	237
45	New Hampshire	219
46	North Dakota	214
47	Minnesota	194
48	Massachusetts	188
49	Rhode Island	178
50	Maine	153
	District of Columbia**	NA

Source: U.S. Department of Justice, Bureau of Justice Statistics "Prisoners in 2014" (September 2015, NCJ 248955, http://bjs.ojp.usdoj.gov/)

*Figures as of December 31, 2014. Includes only inmates sentenced to more than one year. Does not include federal imprisonment rate of 60 prisoners per 100,000 population. State and federal combined imprisonment rate is 471 prisoners per 100,000 population.

**Responsibility for sentenced felons in D.C. was transferred to the Federal Bureau of Prisons in 2001.

Percent Change in Number of State Prisoners: 2013 to 2014

National Percent Change = 0.7% Decrease*

ALPHA ORDER

RANK	STATE	PERCENT CHANGE
34	Alabama	(1.9)
NA	Alaska**	NA
9	Arizona	2.6
4	Arkansas	3.7
21	California	0.1
13	Colorado	1.3
NA	Connecticut**	NA
25	Delaware	(0.7)
23	Florida	(0.2)
36	Georgia	(2.0)
3	Hawaii	4.2
31	Idaho	(1.5)
27	Illinois	(0.8)
38	Indiana	(2.1)
10	Iowa	1.6
NA	Kansas**	NA
8	Kentucky	3.0
42	Louisiana	(3.2)
6	Maine	3.2
31	Maryland	(1.5)
39	Massachusetts	(2.2)
27	Michigan	(0.8)
5	Minnesota	3.4
45	Mississippi	(14.5)
13	Missouri	1.3
10	Montana	1.6
2	Nebraska	8.3
NA	Nevada**	NA
33	New Hampshire	(1.8)
43	New Jersey	(3.8)
13	New Mexico	1.3
34	New York	(1.9)
19	North Carolina	0.5
1	North Dakota	9.0
24	Ohio	(0.4)
20	Oklahoma	0.4
40	Oregon	(2.8)
30	Pennsylvania	(1.4)
22	Rhode Island	(0.1)
41	South Carolina	(3.0)
36	South Dakota	(2.0)
17	Tennessee	0.9
29	Texas	(1.3)
25	Utah	(0.7)
44	Vermont	(4.8)
12	Virginia	1.5
18	Washington	0.8
16	West Virginia	1.1
NA	Wisconsin**	NA
6	Wyoming	3.2

RANK ORDER

RANK	STATE	PERCENT CHANGE
1	North Dakota	9.0
2	Nebraska	8.3
3	Hawaii	4.2
4	Arkansas	3.7
5	Minnesota	3.4
6	Maine	3.2
6	Wyoming	3.2
8	Kentucky	3.0
9	Arizona	2.6
10	Iowa	1.6
10	Montana	1.6
12	Virginia	1.5
13	Colorado	1.3
13	Missouri	1.3
13	New Mexico	1.3
16	West Virginia	1.1
17	Tennessee	0.9
18	Washington	0.8
19	North Carolina	0.5
20	Oklahoma	0.4
21	California	0.1
22	Rhode Island	(0.1)
23	Florida	(0.2)
24	Ohio	(0.4)
25	Delaware	(0.7)
25	Utah	(0.7)
27	Illinois	(0.8)
27	Michigan	(0.8)
29	Texas	(1.3)
30	Pennsylvania	(1.4)
31	Idaho	(1.5)
31	Maryland	(1.5)
33	New Hampshire	(1.8)
34	Alabama	(1.9)
34	New York	(1.9)
36	Georgia	(2.0)
36	South Dakota	(2.0)
38	Indiana	(2.1)
39	Massachusetts	(2.2)
40	Oregon	(2.8)
41	South Carolina	(3.0)
42	Louisiana	(3.2)
43	New Jersey	(3.8)
44	Vermont	(4.8)
45	Mississippi	(14.5)
NA	Alaska**	NA
NA	Connecticut**	NA
NA	Kansas**	NA
NA	Nevada**	NA
NA	Wisconsin**	NA
	District of Columbia***	NA

Source: U.S. Department of Justice, Bureau of Justice Statistics
"Prisoners in 2014" (September 2015, NCJ 248955, http://bjs.ojp.usdoj.gov/)
*From December 31, 2013 to December 31, 2014. Includes inmates sentenced to more than one year and those sentenced to a year or less or with no sentence. The percent change in number of prisoners under federal jurisdiction during the same period was an 2.5% decrease. The combined state and federal increase was 1.0%. **Not available.
***Responsibility for sentenced felons in D.C. was transferred to the Federal Bureau of Prisons in 2001.

Prisoners under Sentence of Death in 2013

National Total = 2,923 State Prisoners*

ALPHA ORDER

RANK	STATE	PRISONERS	% of USA
4	Alabama	190	6.5%
NA	Alaska**	NA	NA
8	Arizona	122	4.2%
17	Arkansas	37	1.3%
1	California	735	25.1%
30	Colorado	3	0.1%
24	Connecticut	10	0.3%
20	Delaware	17	0.6%
2	Florida	398	13.6%
10	Georgia	82	2.8%
NA	Hawaii**	NA	NA
22	Idaho	12	0.4%
NA	Illinois**	NA	NA
21	Indiana	14	0.5%
NA	Iowa**	NA	NA
25	Kansas	9	0.3%
19	Kentucky	33	1.1%
9	Louisiana	84	2.9%
NA	Maine**	NA	NA
29	Maryland	5	0.2%
NA	Massachusetts**	NA	NA
NA	Michigan**	NA	NA
NA	Minnesota**	NA	NA
13	Mississippi	50	1.7%
15	Missouri	45	1.5%
32	Montana	2	0.1%
23	Nebraska	11	0.4%
11	Nevada	81	2.8%
34	New Hampshire	1	0.0%
NA	New Jersey**	NA	NA
32	New Mexico	2	0.1%
36	New York	0	0.0%
6	North Carolina	151	5.2%
NA	North Dakota**	NA	NA
7	Ohio	136	4.7%
14	Oklahoma	48	1.6%
18	Oregon	34	1.2%
4	Pennsylvania	190	6.5%
NA	Rhode Island**	NA	NA
15	South Carolina	45	1.5%
30	South Dakota	3	0.1%
12	Tennessee	75	2.6%
3	Texas	273	9.3%
27	Utah	8	0.3%
NA	Vermont**	NA	NA
28	Virginia	7	0.2%
25	Washington	9	0.3%
NA	West Virginia**	NA	NA
NA	Wisconsin**	NA	NA
34	Wyoming	1	0.0%

RANK ORDER

RANK	STATE	PRISONERS	% of USA
1	California	735	25.1%
2	Florida	398	13.6%
3	Texas	273	9.3%
4	Alabama	190	6.5%
4	Pennsylvania	190	6.5%
6	North Carolina	151	5.2%
7	Ohio	136	4.7%
8	Arizona	122	4.2%
9	Louisiana	84	2.9%
10	Georgia	82	2.8%
11	Nevada	81	2.8%
12	Tennessee	75	2.6%
13	Mississippi	50	1.7%
14	Oklahoma	48	1.6%
15	Missouri	45	1.5%
15	South Carolina	45	1.5%
17	Arkansas	37	1.3%
18	Oregon	34	1.2%
19	Kentucky	33	1.1%
20	Delaware	17	0.6%
21	Indiana	14	0.5%
22	Idaho	12	0.4%
23	Nebraska	11	0.4%
24	Connecticut	10	0.3%
25	Kansas	9	0.3%
25	Washington	9	0.3%
27	Utah	8	0.3%
28	Virginia	7	0.2%
29	Maryland	5	0.2%
30	Colorado	3	0.1%
30	South Dakota	3	0.1%
32	Montana	2	0.1%
32	New Mexico	2	0.1%
34	New Hampshire	1	0.0%
34	Wyoming	1	0.0%
36	New York	0	0.0%
NA	Alaska**	NA	NA
NA	Hawaii**	NA	NA
NA	Illinois**	NA	NA
NA	Iowa**	NA	NA
NA	Maine**	NA	NA
NA	Massachusetts**	NA	NA
NA	Michigan**	NA	NA
NA	Minnesota**	NA	NA
NA	New Jersey**	NA	NA
NA	North Dakota**	NA	NA
NA	Rhode Island**	NA	NA
NA	Vermont**	NA	NA
NA	West Virginia**	NA	NA
NA	Wisconsin**	NA	NA
	District of Columbia**	NA	NA

Source: U.S. Department of Justice, Bureau of Justice Statistics
"Capital Punishment 2013" (Bulletin, December 2014, NCJ 248448, http://bjs.ojp.usdoj.gov/)
*As of December 31, 2013. Does not include 56 federal prisoners under sentence of death. There were 39 executions in 2013.
**No death penalty as of December 31, 2013.

Rate of State and Local Police Officers in 2014

National Rate = 22 Officers per 10,000 Population*

ALPHA ORDER

RANK	STATE	RATE
10	Alabama	23
46	Alaska	16
21	Arizona	21
21	Arkansas	21
35	California	18
29	Colorado	20
12	Connecticut	22
21	Delaware	21
21	Florida	21
12	Georgia	22
12	Hawaii	22
38	Idaho	17
4	Illinois	26
35	Indiana	18
38	Iowa	17
12	Kansas	22
38	Kentucky	17
2	Louisiana	28
38	Maine	17
7	Maryland	24
7	Massachusetts	24
38	Michigan	17
46	Minnesota	16
7	Mississippi	24
12	Missouri	22
38	Montana	17
29	Nebraska	20
38	Nevada	17
12	New Hampshire	22
2	New Jersey	28
12	New Mexico	22
1	New York	37
12	North Carolina	22
33	North Dakota	19
29	Ohio	20
29	Oklahoma	20
48	Oregon	15
21	Pennsylvania	21
12	Rhode Island	22
10	South Carolina	23
33	South Dakota	19
4	Tennessee	26
21	Texas	21
48	Utah	15
38	Vermont	17
21	Virginia	21
50	Washington	14
35	West Virginia	18
21	Wisconsin	21
6	Wyoming	25

RANK ORDER

RANK	STATE	RATE
1	New York	37
2	Louisiana	28
2	New Jersey	28
4	Illinois	26
4	Tennessee	26
6	Wyoming	25
7	Maryland	24
7	Massachusetts	24
7	Mississippi	24
10	Alabama	23
10	South Carolina	23
12	Connecticut	22
12	Georgia	22
12	Hawaii	22
12	Kansas	22
12	Missouri	22
12	New Hampshire	22
12	New Mexico	22
12	North Carolina	22
12	Rhode Island	22
21	Arizona	21
21	Arkansas	21
21	Delaware	21
21	Florida	21
21	Pennsylvania	21
21	Texas	21
21	Virginia	21
21	Wisconsin	21
29	Colorado	20
29	Nebraska	20
29	Ohio	20
29	Oklahoma	20
33	North Dakota	19
33	South Dakota	19
35	California	18
35	Indiana	18
35	West Virginia	18
38	Idaho	17
38	Iowa	17
38	Kentucky	17
38	Maine	17
38	Michigan	17
38	Montana	17
38	Nevada	17
38	Vermont	17
46	Alaska	16
46	Minnesota	16
48	Oregon	15
48	Utah	15
50	Washington	14
	District of Columbia	60

Source: CQ Press using data from U.S. Bureau of the Census, Governments Division
"Government Employment and Payroll" (http://www.census.gov/govs/apes/index.html)
*Full-time equivalent as of March 2014. Does not include employees of police departments who are not officers.

Per Capita State and Local Government Expenditures for Police Protection in 2013
National Per Capita = $320*

ALPHA ORDER

RANK	STATE	PER CAPITA
35	Alabama	$251
1	Alaska	507
15	Arizona	323
44	Arkansas	217
3	California	423
14	Colorado	325
18	Connecticut	319
10	Delaware	353
9	Florida	374
39	Georgia	237
28	Hawaii	275
33	Idaho	253
7	Illinois	390
49	Indiana	181
43	Iowa	222
28	Kansas	275
50	Kentucky	158
12	Louisiana	339
48	Maine	192
4	Maryland	403
13	Massachusetts	332
31	Michigan	259
17	Minnesota	320
39	Mississippi	237
25	Missouri	286
27	Montana	279
45	Nebraska	214
5	Nevada	392
22	New Hampshire	297
8	New Jersey	378
19	New Mexico	309
2	New York	473
21	North Carolina	303
37	North Dakota	243
23	Ohio	294
36	Oklahoma	249
24	Oregon	293
30	Pennsylvania	271
11	Rhode Island	346
41	South Carolina	231
46	South Dakota	207
26	Tennessee	281
33	Texas	253
42	Utah	229
20	Vermont	305
32	Virginia	258
38	Washington	240
47	West Virginia	195
15	Wisconsin	323
6	Wyoming	391

RANK ORDER

RANK	STATE	PER CAPITA
1	Alaska	$507
2	New York	473
3	California	423
4	Maryland	403
5	Nevada	392
6	Wyoming	391
7	Illinois	390
8	New Jersey	378
9	Florida	374
10	Delaware	353
11	Rhode Island	346
12	Louisiana	339
13	Massachusetts	332
14	Colorado	325
15	Arizona	323
15	Wisconsin	323
17	Minnesota	320
18	Connecticut	319
19	New Mexico	309
20	Vermont	305
21	North Carolina	303
22	New Hampshire	297
23	Ohio	294
24	Oregon	293
25	Missouri	286
26	Tennessee	281
27	Montana	279
28	Hawaii	275
28	Kansas	275
30	Pennsylvania	271
31	Michigan	259
32	Virginia	258
33	Idaho	253
33	Texas	253
35	Alabama	251
36	Oklahoma	249
37	North Dakota	243
38	Washington	240
39	Georgia	237
39	Mississippi	237
41	South Carolina	231
42	Utah	229
43	Iowa	222
44	Arkansas	217
45	Nebraska	214
46	South Dakota	207
47	West Virginia	195
48	Maine	192
49	Indiana	181
50	Kentucky	158
	District of Columbia	862

Source: CQ Press using data from U.S. Bureau of the Census, Governments Division
"2013 State and Local Government Finances" (http://www.census.gov/govs/local/)
*Direct general expenditures.

Per Capita State and Local Government Expenditures for Corrections in 2013

National Per Capita = $232*

ALPHA ORDER

RANK	STATE	PER CAPITA
47	Alabama	$144
1	Alaska	461
21	Arizona	216
30	Arkansas	186
3	California	343
18	Colorado	224
31	Connecticut	183
6	Delaware	305
23	Florida	201
17	Georgia	229
48	Hawaii	143
24	Idaho	199
41	Illinois	157
43	Indiana	153
44	Iowa	152
33	Kansas	179
37	Kentucky	171
5	Louisiana	309
48	Maine	143
7	Maryland	298
39	Massachusetts	163
13	Michigan	252
39	Minnesota	163
35	Mississippi	177
46	Missouri	145
15	Montana	237
25	Nebraska	196
14	Nevada	248
50	New Hampshire	139
16	New Jersey	236
8	New Mexico	296
4	New York	323
36	North Carolina	174
31	North Dakota	183
42	Ohio	156
28	Oklahoma	188
9	Oregon	271
10	Pennsylvania	270
26	Rhode Island	193
45	South Carolina	151
26	South Dakota	193
38	Tennessee	166
20	Texas	221
34	Utah	178
21	Vermont	216
10	Virginia	270
18	Washington	224
28	West Virginia	188
12	Wisconsin	259
2	Wyoming	370

RANK ORDER

RANK	STATE	PER CAPITA
1	Alaska	$461
2	Wyoming	370
3	California	343
4	New York	323
5	Louisiana	309
6	Delaware	305
7	Maryland	298
8	New Mexico	296
9	Oregon	271
10	Pennsylvania	270
10	Virginia	270
12	Wisconsin	259
13	Michigan	252
14	Nevada	248
15	Montana	237
16	New Jersey	236
17	Georgia	229
18	Colorado	224
18	Washington	224
20	Texas	221
21	Arizona	216
21	Vermont	216
23	Florida	201
24	Idaho	199
25	Nebraska	196
26	Rhode Island	193
26	South Dakota	193
28	Oklahoma	188
28	West Virginia	188
30	Arkansas	186
31	Connecticut	183
31	North Dakota	183
33	Kansas	179
34	Utah	178
35	Mississippi	177
36	North Carolina	174
37	Kentucky	171
38	Tennessee	166
39	Massachusetts	163
39	Minnesota	163
41	Illinois	157
42	Ohio	156
43	Indiana	153
44	Iowa	152
45	South Carolina	151
46	Missouri	145
47	Alabama	144
48	Hawaii	143
48	Maine	143
50	New Hampshire	139
	District of Columbia	386

Source: CQ Press using data from U.S. Bureau of the Census, Governments Division
"2013 State and Local Government Finances" (http://www.census.gov/govs/local/)
*Direct general expenditures.

Per Capita State and Local Government Expenditures for Judicial and Legal Services in 2013
National Per Capita = $135*

ALPHA ORDER

RANK	STATE	PER CAPITA
44	Alabama	$84
1	Alaska	332
12	Arizona	149
49	Arkansas	68
3	California	212
19	Colorado	130
6	Connecticut	196
2	Delaware	224
31	Florida	112
33	Georgia	109
6	Hawaii	196
21	Idaho	126
30	Illinois	113
46	Indiana	78
31	Iowa	112
34	Kansas	107
28	Kentucky	117
8	Louisiana	171
48	Maine	70
17	Maryland	138
14	Massachusetts	145
27	Michigan	118
25	Minnesota	123
43	Mississippi	85
45	Missouri	80
16	Montana	144
42	Nebraska	87
9	Nevada	166
35	New Hampshire	104
9	New Jersey	166
11	New Mexico	158
5	New York	202
47	North Carolina	76
25	North Dakota	123
12	Ohio	149
41	Oklahoma	94
14	Oregon	145
18	Pennsylvania	137
21	Rhode Island	126
50	South Carolina	66
37	South Dakota	101
39	Tennessee	100
40	Texas	98
20	Utah	128
29	Vermont	114
37	Virginia	101
21	Washington	126
24	West Virginia	125
35	Wisconsin	104
4	Wyoming	203

RANK ORDER

RANK	STATE	PER CAPITA
1	Alaska	$332
2	Delaware	224
3	California	212
4	Wyoming	203
5	New York	202
6	Connecticut	196
6	Hawaii	196
8	Louisiana	171
9	Nevada	166
9	New Jersey	166
11	New Mexico	158
12	Arizona	149
12	Ohio	149
14	Massachusetts	145
14	Oregon	145
16	Montana	144
17	Maryland	138
18	Pennsylvania	137
19	Colorado	130
20	Utah	128
21	Idaho	126
21	Rhode Island	126
21	Washington	126
24	West Virginia	125
25	Minnesota	123
25	North Dakota	123
27	Michigan	118
28	Kentucky	117
29	Vermont	114
30	Illinois	113
31	Florida	112
31	Iowa	112
33	Georgia	109
34	Kansas	107
35	New Hampshire	104
35	Wisconsin	104
37	South Dakota	101
37	Virginia	101
39	Tennessee	100
40	Texas	98
41	Oklahoma	94
42	Nebraska	87
43	Mississippi	85
44	Alabama	84
45	Missouri	80
46	Indiana	78
47	North Carolina	76
48	Maine	70
49	Arkansas	68
50	South Carolina	66
	District of Columbia	177

Source: CQ Press using data from U.S. Bureau of the Census, Governments Division "2013 State and Local Government Finances" (http://www.census.gov/govs/local/)

*Direct general expenditures. Includes courts, prosecution and legal services, and public defense.

III. Defense

Homeland Security Grants in 2015.................... 69
Per Capita Homeland Security Grants in 2015........... 70
U.S. Department of Defense Expenditures in 2013....... 71
Per Capita U.S. Department of Defense Expenditures in 2013... 72
U.S. Department of Defense Procurement Contract Awards in 2013................................. 73
Per Capita U.S. Department of Defense Procurement Contract Awards in 2013........................ 74
U.S. Department of Defense Grants in 2013............ 75
Per Capita U.S. Department of Defense Grants in 2013.... 76
U.S. Active Duty Military Personnel Stationed in the United States in 2014............................ 77
U.S. Selected Reserve Personnel Stationed in the United States in 2014............................ 78
Veterans in 2014.................................. 79
Percent of Adult Population Who Are Veterans in 2014.... 80
U.S. Military Fatalities in Iraq and Afghanistan as of February 1, 2016................................ 81
Rate of U.S. Military Fatalities in Iraq and Afghanistan as of February 1, 2016........................... 82

Homeland Security Grants in 2015

National Total = $989,000,000*

ALPHA ORDER

RANK	STATE	GRANTS	% of USA
29	Alabama	$3,734,500	0.4%
29	Alaska	3,734,500	0.4%
13	Arizona	10,068,000	1.0%
29	Arkansas	3,734,500	0.4%
2	California	183,452,500	18.5%
18	Colorado	6,979,000	0.7%
23	Connecticut	3,978,000	0.4%
29	Delaware	3,734,500	0.4%
8	Florida	19,540,500	2.0%
9	Georgia	12,307,000	1.2%
21	Hawaii	6,734,500	0.7%
29	Idaho	3,734,500	0.4%
3	Illinois	85,908,500	8.7%
23	Indiana	3,978,000	0.4%
29	Iowa	3,734,500	0.4%
29	Kansas	3,734,500	0.4%
23	Kentucky	3,978,000	0.4%
23	Louisiana	3,978,000	0.4%
29	Maine	3,734,500	0.4%
12	Maryland	11,653,500	1.2%
7	Massachusetts	23,645,000	2.4%
10	Michigan	12,158,000	1.2%
14	Minnesota	9,478,000	1.0%
29	Mississippi	3,734,500	0.4%
19	Missouri	6,978,000	0.7%
29	Montana	3,734,500	0.4%
29	Nebraska	3,734,500	0.4%
21	Nevada	6,734,500	0.7%
29	New Hampshire	3,734,500	0.4%
6	New Jersey	29,154,000	2.9%
29	New Mexico	3,734,500	0.4%
1	New York	257,875,000	26.1%
15	North Carolina	8,489,000	0.9%
29	North Dakota	3,734,500	0.4%
16	Ohio	7,698,000	0.8%
29	Oklahoma	3,734,500	0.4%
20	Oregon	6,837,000	0.7%
5	Pennsylvania	31,554,500	3.2%
29	Rhode Island	3,734,500	0.4%
29	South Carolina	3,734,500	0.4%
29	South Dakota	3,734,500	0.4%
23	Tennessee	3,978,000	0.4%
4	Texas	60,998,000	6.2%
29	Utah	3,734,500	0.4%
29	Vermont	3,734,500	0.4%
17	Virginia	7,445,500	0.8%
11	Washington	11,993,000	1.2%
29	West Virginia	3,734,500	0.4%
23	Wisconsin	3,978,000	0.4%
29	Wyoming	3,734,500	0.4%

RANK ORDER

RANK	STATE	GRANTS	% of USA
1	New York	$257,875,000	26.1%
2	California	183,452,500	18.5%
3	Illinois	85,908,500	8.7%
4	Texas	60,998,000	6.2%
5	Pennsylvania	31,554,500	3.2%
6	New Jersey	29,154,000	2.9%
7	Massachusetts	23,645,000	2.4%
8	Florida	19,540,500	2.0%
9	Georgia	12,307,000	1.2%
10	Michigan	12,158,000	1.2%
11	Washington	11,993,000	1.2%
12	Maryland	11,653,500	1.2%
13	Arizona	10,068,000	1.0%
14	Minnesota	9,478,000	1.0%
15	North Carolina	8,489,000	0.9%
16	Ohio	7,698,000	0.8%
17	Virginia	7,445,500	0.8%
18	Colorado	6,979,000	0.7%
19	Missouri	6,978,000	0.7%
20	Oregon	6,837,000	0.7%
21	Hawaii	6,734,500	0.7%
21	Nevada	6,734,500	0.7%
23	Connecticut	3,978,000	0.4%
23	Indiana	3,978,000	0.4%
23	Kentucky	3,978,000	0.4%
23	Louisiana	3,978,000	0.4%
23	Tennessee	3,978,000	0.4%
23	Wisconsin	3,978,000	0.4%
29	Alabama	3,734,500	0.4%
29	Alaska	3,734,500	0.4%
29	Arkansas	3,734,500	0.4%
29	Delaware	3,734,500	0.4%
29	Idaho	3,734,500	0.4%
29	Iowa	3,734,500	0.4%
29	Kansas	3,734,500	0.4%
29	Maine	3,734,500	0.4%
29	Mississippi	3,734,500	0.4%
29	Montana	3,734,500	0.4%
29	Nebraska	3,734,500	0.4%
29	New Hampshire	3,734,500	0.4%
29	New Mexico	3,734,500	0.4%
29	North Dakota	3,734,500	0.4%
29	Oklahoma	3,734,500	0.4%
29	Rhode Island	3,734,500	0.4%
29	South Carolina	3,734,500	0.4%
29	South Dakota	3,734,500	0.4%
29	Utah	3,734,500	0.4%
29	Vermont	3,734,500	0.4%
29	West Virginia	3,734,500	0.4%
29	Wyoming	3,734,500	0.4%
	District of Columbia	58,141,500	5.9%

Source: CQ Press using data from U.S. Department of Homeland Security
"FY 2015 Homeland Security Grant Program (HSGP)" (https://www.fema.gov/media-library/assets/documents/103698)
*For fiscal year 2015. National total includes $7,150,000 in grants to U.S. territories. The Homeland Security Grant Program (HSGP) includes three sub-grant programs: State Homeland Security Program (SHSP), Urban Area Security Initiative (UASI), and Operation Stonegarden (OPSG). Law Enforcement Terrorism Prevention Activities (LETPA) allocations are a 25 percent subset of the SHSP and UASI allocations.

Per Capita Homeland Security Grants in 2015

National Per Capita = $3.05*

ALPHA ORDER

RANK	STATE	PER CAPITA
45	Alabama	$0.77
5	Alaska	5.06
28	Arizona	1.47
31	Arkansas	1.25
8	California	4.69
29	Colorado	1.28
38	Connecticut	1.11
10	Delaware	3.95
39	Florida	0.96
35	Georgia	1.20
7	Hawaii	4.70
19	Idaho	2.26
2	Illinois	6.68
49	Indiana	0.60
35	Iowa	1.20
29	Kansas	1.28
41	Kentucky	0.90
43	Louisiana	0.85
15	Maine	2.81
23	Maryland	1.94
13	Massachusetts	3.48
34	Michigan	1.23
25	Minnesota	1.73
31	Mississippi	1.25
37	Missouri	1.15
11	Montana	3.62
22	Nebraska	1.97
18	Nevada	2.33
15	New Hampshire	2.81
14	New Jersey	3.25
24	New Mexico	1.79
1	New York	13.03
43	North Carolina	0.85
6	North Dakota	4.93
48	Ohio	0.66
40	Oklahoma	0.95
26	Oregon	1.70
17	Pennsylvania	2.46
12	Rhode Island	3.54
46	South Carolina	0.76
9	South Dakota	4.35
49	Tennessee	0.60
20	Texas	2.22
31	Utah	1.25
4	Vermont	5.97
42	Virginia	0.89
27	Washington	1.67
21	West Virginia	2.03
47	Wisconsin	0.69
3	Wyoming	6.37

RANK ORDER

RANK	STATE	PER CAPITA
1	New York	$13.03
2	Illinois	6.68
3	Wyoming	6.37
4	Vermont	5.97
5	Alaska	5.06
6	North Dakota	4.93
7	Hawaii	4.70
8	California	4.69
9	South Dakota	4.35
10	Delaware	3.95
11	Montana	3.62
12	Rhode Island	3.54
13	Massachusetts	3.48
14	New Jersey	3.25
15	Maine	2.81
15	New Hampshire	2.81
17	Pennsylvania	2.46
18	Nevada	2.33
19	Idaho	2.26
20	Texas	2.22
21	West Virginia	2.03
22	Nebraska	1.97
23	Maryland	1.94
24	New Mexico	1.79
25	Minnesota	1.73
26	Oregon	1.70
27	Washington	1.67
28	Arizona	1.47
29	Colorado	1.28
29	Kansas	1.28
31	Arkansas	1.25
31	Mississippi	1.25
31	Utah	1.25
34	Michigan	1.23
35	Georgia	1.20
35	Iowa	1.20
37	Missouri	1.15
38	Connecticut	1.11
39	Florida	0.96
40	Oklahoma	0.95
41	Kentucky	0.90
42	Virginia	0.89
43	Louisiana	0.85
43	North Carolina	0.85
45	Alabama	0.77
46	South Carolina	0.76
47	Wisconsin	0.69
48	Ohio	0.66
49	Indiana	0.60
49	Tennessee	0.60
	District of Columbia	86.49

Source: CQ Press using data from U.S. Department of Homeland Security
"FY 2015 Homeland Security Grant Program (HSGP)" (https://www.fema.gov/media-library/assets/documents/103698)
*For fiscal year 2015. National per capita does not include grants to U.S. territories. The Homeland Security Grant Program (HSGP) includes three sub-grant programs: State Homeland Security Program (SHSP), Urban Area Security Initiative (UASI), and Operation Stonegarden (OPSG). Law Enforcement Terrorism Prevention Activities (LETPA) allocations are a 25 percent subset of the SHSP and UASI allocations.

U.S. Department of Defense Expenditures in 2013

National Total = $314,000,000,000*

ALPHA ORDER

RANK	STATE	EXPENDITURES	% of USA
12	Alabama	$7,865,894,000	2.5%
35	Alaska	1,322,859,000	0.4%
5	Arizona	11,367,362,000	3.6%
42	Arkansas	513,869,000	0.2%
1	California	34,549,290,000	11.0%
18	Colorado	4,508,007,000	1.4%
9	Connecticut	10,116,829,000	3.2%
48	Delaware	201,179,000	0.1%
7	Florida	10,665,368,000	3.4%
15	Georgia	5,541,720,000	1.8%
30	Hawaii	1,743,712,000	0.6%
43	Idaho	403,706,000	0.1%
20	Illinois	3,363,506,000	1.1%
25	Indiana	2,208,906,000	0.7%
38	Iowa	1,112,502,000	0.4%
34	Kansas	1,356,716,000	0.4%
14	Kentucky	5,890,616,000	1.9%
28	Louisiana	1,974,860,000	0.6%
27	Maine	1,979,734,000	0.6%
4	Maryland	12,107,066,000	3.9%
6	Massachusetts	10,940,279,000	3.5%
21	Michigan	2,946,583,000	0.9%
26	Minnesota	2,040,914,000	0.6%
19	Mississippi	4,250,832,000	1.4%
10	Missouri	8,101,438,000	2.6%
49	Montana	193,622,000	0.1%
40	Nebraska	637,163,000	0.2%
29	Nevada	1,938,682,000	0.6%
31	New Hampshire	1,524,106,000	0.5%
16	New Jersey	5,176,256,000	1.6%
37	New Mexico	1,208,516,000	0.4%
13	New York	7,480,069,000	2.4%
22	North Carolina	2,939,914,000	0.9%
46	North Dakota	217,242,000	0.1%
17	Ohio	4,530,471,000	1.4%
32	Oklahoma	1,476,367,000	0.5%
41	Oregon	563,964,000	0.2%
8	Pennsylvania	10,188,518,000	3.2%
39	Rhode Island	712,767,000	0.2%
23	South Carolina	2,654,135,000	0.8%
44	South Dakota	348,729,000	0.1%
36	Tennessee	1,226,197,000	0.4%
3	Texas	32,573,714,000	10.4%
33	Utah	1,464,380,000	0.5%
45	Vermont	248,489,000	0.1%
2	Virginia	33,672,719,000	10.7%
11	Washington	7,957,394,000	2.5%
47	West Virginia	213,600,000	0.1%
24	Wisconsin	2,420,836,000	0.8%
50	Wyoming	120,045,000	0.0%

RANK ORDER

RANK	STATE	EXPENDITURES	% of USA
1	California	$34,549,290,000	11.0%
2	Virginia	33,672,719,000	10.7%
3	Texas	32,573,714,000	10.4%
4	Maryland	12,107,066,000	3.9%
5	Arizona	11,367,362,000	3.6%
6	Massachusetts	10,940,279,000	3.5%
7	Florida	10,665,368,000	3.4%
8	Pennsylvania	10,188,518,000	3.2%
9	Connecticut	10,116,829,000	3.2%
10	Missouri	8,101,438,000	2.6%
11	Washington	7,957,394,000	2.5%
12	Alabama	7,865,894,000	2.5%
13	New York	7,480,069,000	2.4%
14	Kentucky	5,890,616,000	1.9%
15	Georgia	5,541,720,000	1.8%
16	New Jersey	5,176,256,000	1.6%
17	Ohio	4,530,471,000	1.4%
18	Colorado	4,508,007,000	1.4%
19	Mississippi	4,250,832,000	1.4%
20	Illinois	3,363,506,000	1.1%
21	Michigan	2,946,583,000	0.9%
22	North Carolina	2,939,914,000	0.9%
23	South Carolina	2,654,135,000	0.8%
24	Wisconsin	2,420,836,000	0.8%
25	Indiana	2,208,906,000	0.7%
26	Minnesota	2,040,914,000	0.6%
27	Maine	1,979,734,000	0.6%
28	Louisiana	1,974,860,000	0.6%
29	Nevada	1,938,682,000	0.6%
30	Hawaii	1,743,712,000	0.6%
31	New Hampshire	1,524,106,000	0.5%
32	Oklahoma	1,476,367,000	0.5%
33	Utah	1,464,380,000	0.5%
34	Kansas	1,356,716,000	0.4%
35	Alaska	1,322,859,000	0.4%
36	Tennessee	1,226,197,000	0.4%
37	New Mexico	1,208,516,000	0.4%
38	Iowa	1,112,502,000	0.4%
39	Rhode Island	712,767,000	0.2%
40	Nebraska	637,163,000	0.2%
41	Oregon	563,964,000	0.2%
42	Arkansas	513,869,000	0.2%
43	Idaho	403,706,000	0.1%
44	South Dakota	348,729,000	0.1%
45	Vermont	248,489,000	0.1%
46	North Dakota	217,242,000	0.1%
47	West Virginia	213,600,000	0.1%
48	Delaware	201,179,000	0.1%
49	Montana	193,622,000	0.1%
50	Wyoming	120,045,000	0.0%
	District of Columbia	4,008,021,000	1.3%

Source: U.S. Office of Management and Budget, USAspending.gov
"Prime Award Spending Data Summary" (http://www.usaspending.gov/, as of February 4, 2015)
*Total includes $821,373,000 in U.S. territories and $40,408,963,000 in expenditures not distributed by state. Expenditures allocated based on place of performance of a contract. Includes Contracts, Grants, Direct Payments, Insurance, and "Other."
This source replaces a previous data series, "Atlas/Data Abstract for the United States", and definitions may differ.

Per Capita U.S. Department of Defense Expenditures in 2013

National Per Capita = $862*

ALPHA ORDER

RANK	STATE	PER CAPITA
7	Alabama	$1,627
4	Alaska	1,794
5	Arizona	1,713
48	Arkansas	174
16	California	899
17	Colorado	855
2	Connecticut	2,811
44	Delaware	217
25	Florida	544
24	Georgia	554
12	Hawaii	1,238
43	Idaho	250
42	Illinois	261
38	Indiana	336
36	Iowa	360
27	Kansas	469
11	Kentucky	1,339
28	Louisiana	427
8	Maine	1,490
3	Maryland	2,039
6	Massachusetts	1,631
41	Michigan	298
35	Minnesota	376
9	Mississippi	1,421
10	Missouri	1,340
46	Montana	191
37	Nebraska	341
19	Nevada	694
14	New Hampshire	1,152
21	New Jersey	581
22	New Mexico	579
34	New York	380
40	North Carolina	299
39	North Dakota	300
32	Ohio	392
33	Oklahoma	383
49	Oregon	144
18	Pennsylvania	797
20	Rhode Island	677
23	South Carolina	556
30	South Dakota	412
47	Tennessee	189
13	Texas	1,229
26	Utah	504
31	Vermont	396
1	Virginia	4,072
15	Washington	1,141
50	West Virginia	115
29	Wisconsin	422
45	Wyoming	206

RANK ORDER

RANK	STATE	PER CAPITA
1	Virginia	$4,072
2	Connecticut	2,811
3	Maryland	2,039
4	Alaska	1,794
5	Arizona	1,713
6	Massachusetts	1,631
7	Alabama	1,627
8	Maine	1,490
9	Mississippi	1,421
10	Missouri	1,340
11	Kentucky	1,339
12	Hawaii	1,238
13	Texas	1,229
14	New Hampshire	1,152
15	Washington	1,141
16	California	899
17	Colorado	855
18	Pennsylvania	797
19	Nevada	694
20	Rhode Island	677
21	New Jersey	581
22	New Mexico	579
23	South Carolina	556
24	Georgia	554
25	Florida	544
26	Utah	504
27	Kansas	469
28	Louisiana	427
29	Wisconsin	422
30	South Dakota	412
31	Vermont	396
32	Ohio	392
33	Oklahoma	383
34	New York	380
35	Minnesota	376
36	Iowa	360
37	Nebraska	341
38	Indiana	336
39	North Dakota	300
40	North Carolina	299
41	Michigan	298
42	Illinois	261
43	Idaho	250
44	Delaware	217
45	Wyoming	206
46	Montana	191
47	Tennessee	189
48	Arkansas	174
49	Oregon	144
50	West Virginia	115
	District of Columbia	6,175

Source: CQ Press using data from U.S. Office of Management and Budget, USAspending.gov
"Prime Award Spending Data Summary" (http://www.usaspending.gov/, as of February 4, 2015)
*National per capita excludes expenditures and population for territories and undistributed amounts. Expenditures allocated based on place of performance of a contract. Includes Contracts, Grants, Direct Payments, Insurance, and "Other." This source replaces a previous data series, "Atlas/Data Abstract for the United States", and definitions may differ.

U.S. Department of Defense Procurement Contract Awards in 2013

National Total = $308,600,000,000*

ALPHA ORDER

RANK	STATE	EXPENDITURES	% of USA
11	Alabama	$7,816,198,000	2.5%
34	Alaska	1,284,520,000	0.4%
5	Arizona	11,251,610,000	3.6%
42	Arkansas	451,954,000	0.1%
1	California	33,992,128,000	11.0%
17	Colorado	4,431,160,000	1.4%
8	Connecticut	10,036,108,000	3.3%
48	Delaware	174,824,000	0.1%
7	Florida	10,495,435,000	3.4%
15	Georgia	5,452,173,000	1.8%
30	Hawaii	1,656,993,000	0.5%
43	Idaho	353,525,000	0.1%
20	Illinois	3,221,987,000	1.0%
25	Indiana	2,137,623,000	0.7%
38	Iowa	1,061,727,000	0.3%
35	Kansas	1,274,089,000	0.4%
14	Kentucky	5,845,383,000	1.9%
29	Louisiana	1,899,475,000	0.6%
27	Maine	1,960,220,000	0.6%
4	Maryland	11,641,738,000	3.8%
6	Massachusetts	10,631,821,000	3.4%
21	Michigan	2,862,838,000	0.9%
26	Minnesota	1,976,960,000	0.6%
19	Mississippi	4,164,453,000	1.3%
10	Missouri	8,047,786,000	2.6%
49	Montana	155,403,000	0.1%
40	Nebraska	611,414,000	0.2%
28	Nevada	1,919,709,000	0.6%
31	New Hampshire	1,481,195,000	0.5%
16	New Jersey	5,106,706,000	1.7%
36	New Mexico	1,170,167,000	0.4%
13	New York	7,259,501,000	2.4%
22	North Carolina	2,775,647,000	0.9%
47	North Dakota	190,904,000	0.1%
18	Ohio	4,395,830,000	1.4%
33	Oklahoma	1,393,404,000	0.5%
41	Oregon	508,472,000	0.2%
9	Pennsylvania	9,964,084,000	3.2%
39	Rhode Island	679,384,000	0.2%
23	South Carolina	2,607,835,000	0.8%
44	South Dakota	341,574,000	0.1%
37	Tennessee	1,162,255,000	0.4%
3	Texas	32,328,694,000	10.5%
32	Utah	1,416,197,000	0.5%
45	Vermont	222,621,000	0.1%
2	Virginia	33,470,741,000	10.8%
12	Washington	7,709,814,000	2.5%
46	West Virginia	206,974,000	0.1%
24	Wisconsin	2,348,033,000	0.8%
50	Wyoming	94,027,000	0.0%

RANK ORDER

RANK	STATE	EXPENDITURES	% of USA
1	California	$33,992,128,000	11.0%
2	Virginia	33,470,741,000	10.8%
3	Texas	32,328,694,000	10.5%
4	Maryland	11,641,738,000	3.8%
5	Arizona	11,251,610,000	3.6%
6	Massachusetts	10,631,821,000	3.4%
7	Florida	10,495,435,000	3.4%
8	Connecticut	10,036,108,000	3.3%
9	Pennsylvania	9,964,084,000	3.2%
10	Missouri	8,047,786,000	2.6%
11	Alabama	7,816,198,000	2.5%
12	Washington	7,709,814,000	2.5%
13	New York	7,259,501,000	2.4%
14	Kentucky	5,845,383,000	1.9%
15	Georgia	5,452,173,000	1.8%
16	New Jersey	5,106,706,000	1.7%
17	Colorado	4,431,160,000	1.4%
18	Ohio	4,395,830,000	1.4%
19	Mississippi	4,164,453,000	1.3%
20	Illinois	3,221,987,000	1.0%
21	Michigan	2,862,838,000	0.9%
22	North Carolina	2,775,647,000	0.9%
23	South Carolina	2,607,835,000	0.8%
24	Wisconsin	2,348,033,000	0.8%
25	Indiana	2,137,623,000	0.7%
26	Minnesota	1,976,960,000	0.6%
27	Maine	1,960,220,000	0.6%
28	Nevada	1,919,709,000	0.6%
29	Louisiana	1,899,475,000	0.6%
30	Hawaii	1,656,993,000	0.5%
31	New Hampshire	1,481,195,000	0.5%
32	Utah	1,416,197,000	0.5%
33	Oklahoma	1,393,404,000	0.5%
34	Alaska	1,284,520,000	0.4%
35	Kansas	1,274,089,000	0.4%
36	New Mexico	1,170,167,000	0.4%
37	Tennessee	1,162,255,000	0.4%
38	Iowa	1,061,727,000	0.3%
39	Rhode Island	679,384,000	0.2%
40	Nebraska	611,414,000	0.2%
41	Oregon	508,472,000	0.2%
42	Arkansas	451,954,000	0.1%
43	Idaho	353,525,000	0.1%
44	South Dakota	341,574,000	0.1%
45	Vermont	222,621,000	0.1%
46	West Virginia	206,974,000	0.1%
47	North Dakota	190,904,000	0.1%
48	Delaware	174,824,000	0.1%
49	Montana	155,403,000	0.1%
50	Wyoming	94,027,000	0.0%
	District of Columbia	3,873,214,000	1.3%

Source: U.S. Office of Management and Budget, USAspending.gov
"Prime Award Spending Data Summary" (http://www.usaspending.gov/, as of February 4, 2015)
*Total includes $785,691,000 in U.S. territories and $40,297,782,000 in expenditures not distributed by state. Expenditures allocated based on place of performance of a contract. Includes funds awarded to a non-federal entity for a defined public or private purpose in which services are not rendered to the federal government. This source replaces a previous data series, "Atlas/Data Abstract for the United States", and definitions may differ.

Per Capita U.S. Department of Defense Procurement Contract Awards in 2013

National Per Capita = $845*

ALPHA ORDER

RANK	STATE	PER CAPITA
6	Alabama	$1,617
4	Alaska	1,742
5	Arizona	1,696
47	Arkansas	153
16	California	884
17	Colorado	840
2	Connecticut	2,788
44	Delaware	189
25	Florida	535
23	Georgia	546
13	Hawaii	1,176
43	Idaho	219
42	Illinois	250
38	Indiana	325
36	Iowa	343
27	Kansas	440
11	Kentucky	1,329
28	Louisiana	410
8	Maine	1,475
3	Maryland	1,960
7	Massachusetts	1,585
39	Michigan	289
33	Minnesota	365
9	Mississippi	1,392
10	Missouri	1,331
47	Montana	153
37	Nebraska	327
19	Nevada	688
14	New Hampshire	1,120
21	New Jersey	573
22	New Mexico	561
32	New York	369
40	North Carolina	282
41	North Dakota	264
31	Ohio	380
34	Oklahoma	362
49	Oregon	129
18	Pennsylvania	780
20	Rhode Island	645
23	South Carolina	546
30	South Dakota	404
45	Tennessee	179
12	Texas	1,220
26	Utah	488
35	Vermont	355
1	Virginia	4,047
15	Washington	1,106
50	West Virginia	112
29	Wisconsin	409
46	Wyoming	161

RANK ORDER

RANK	STATE	PER CAPITA
1	Virginia	$4,047
2	Connecticut	2,788
3	Maryland	1,960
4	Alaska	1,742
5	Arizona	1,696
6	Alabama	1,617
7	Massachusetts	1,585
8	Maine	1,475
9	Mississippi	1,392
10	Missouri	1,331
11	Kentucky	1,329
12	Texas	1,220
13	Hawaii	1,176
14	New Hampshire	1,120
15	Washington	1,106
16	California	884
17	Colorado	840
18	Pennsylvania	780
19	Nevada	688
20	Rhode Island	645
21	New Jersey	573
22	New Mexico	561
23	Georgia	546
23	South Carolina	546
25	Florida	535
26	Utah	488
27	Kansas	440
28	Louisiana	410
29	Wisconsin	409
30	South Dakota	404
31	Ohio	380
32	New York	369
33	Minnesota	365
34	Oklahoma	362
35	Vermont	355
36	Iowa	343
37	Nebraska	327
38	Indiana	325
39	Michigan	289
40	North Carolina	282
41	North Dakota	264
42	Illinois	250
43	Idaho	219
44	Delaware	189
45	Tennessee	179
46	Wyoming	161
47	Arkansas	153
47	Montana	153
49	Oregon	129
50	West Virginia	112
	District of Columbia	5,967

Source: CQ Press using data from U.S. Office of Management and Budget, USAspending.gov
"Prime Award Spending Data Summary" (http://www.usaspending.gov/, as of February 4, 2015)
*National per capita excludes expenditures and population for territories and undistributed amounts. Expenditures allocated based on place of performance of a contract. Includes funds awarded to a non-federal entity for a defined public or private purpose in which services are not rendered to the federal government. This source replaces a previous data series, "Atlas/Data Abstract for the United States", and definitions may differ.

U.S. Department of Defense Grants in 2013

National Total = $5,800,000,000*

ALPHA ORDER

RANK	STATE	EXPENDITURES	% of USA
32	Alabama	$49,696,000	0.9%
38	Alaska	38,338,000	0.7%
13	Arizona	115,752,000	2.0%
28	Arkansas	61,915,000	1.1%
1	California	549,092,000	9.5%
21	Colorado	76,847,000	1.3%
20	Connecticut	80,721,000	1.4%
42	Delaware	26,356,000	0.5%
9	Florida	168,353,000	2.9%
14	Georgia	89,547,000	1.5%
15	Hawaii	86,719,000	1.5%
36	Idaho	44,016,000	0.8%
11	Illinois	141,520,000	2.4%
24	Indiana	71,283,000	1.2%
31	Iowa	50,775,000	0.9%
19	Kansas	82,627,000	1.4%
35	Kentucky	45,233,000	0.8%
22	Louisiana	75,385,000	1.3%
47	Maine	19,514,000	0.3%
2	Maryland	465,327,000	8.0%
3	Massachusetts	307,706,000	5.3%
17	Michigan	83,744,000	1.4%
26	Minnesota	63,954,000	1.1%
16	Mississippi	86,379,000	1.5%
30	Missouri	53,653,000	0.9%
40	Montana	34,003,000	0.6%
46	Nebraska	25,748,000	0.4%
48	Nevada	18,973,000	0.3%
37	New Hampshire	42,911,000	0.7%
25	New Jersey	69,550,000	1.2%
39	New Mexico	36,442,000	0.6%
7	New York	215,102,000	3.7%
10	North Carolina	141,909,000	2.4%
43	North Dakota	26,338,000	0.5%
12	Ohio	129,974,000	2.2%
18	Oklahoma	82,964,000	1.4%
29	Oregon	55,493,000	1.0%
6	Pennsylvania	224,263,000	3.9%
41	Rhode Island	33,382,000	0.6%
34	South Carolina	46,301,000	0.8%
49	South Dakota	7,154,000	0.1%
27	Tennessee	63,943,000	1.1%
5	Texas	245,019,000	4.2%
33	Utah	48,183,000	0.8%
45	Vermont	25,868,000	0.4%
8	Virginia	200,383,000	3.5%
4	Washington	246,178,000	4.2%
50	West Virginia	6,626,000	0.1%
23	Wisconsin	72,803,000	1.3%
44	Wyoming	26,018,000	0.4%

RANK ORDER

RANK	STATE	EXPENDITURES	% of USA
1	California	$549,092,000	9.5%
2	Maryland	465,327,000	8.0%
3	Massachusetts	307,706,000	5.3%
4	Washington	246,178,000	4.2%
5	Texas	245,019,000	4.2%
6	Pennsylvania	224,263,000	3.9%
7	New York	215,102,000	3.7%
8	Virginia	200,383,000	3.5%
9	Florida	168,353,000	2.9%
10	North Carolina	141,909,000	2.4%
11	Illinois	141,520,000	2.4%
12	Ohio	129,974,000	2.2%
13	Arizona	115,752,000	2.0%
14	Georgia	89,547,000	1.5%
15	Hawaii	86,719,000	1.5%
16	Mississippi	86,379,000	1.5%
17	Michigan	83,744,000	1.4%
18	Oklahoma	82,964,000	1.4%
19	Kansas	82,627,000	1.4%
20	Connecticut	80,721,000	1.4%
21	Colorado	76,847,000	1.3%
22	Louisiana	75,385,000	1.3%
23	Wisconsin	72,803,000	1.3%
24	Indiana	71,283,000	1.2%
25	New Jersey	69,550,000	1.2%
26	Minnesota	63,954,000	1.1%
27	Tennessee	63,943,000	1.1%
28	Arkansas	61,915,000	1.1%
29	Oregon	55,493,000	1.0%
30	Missouri	53,653,000	0.9%
31	Iowa	50,775,000	0.9%
32	Alabama	49,696,000	0.9%
33	Utah	48,183,000	0.8%
34	South Carolina	46,301,000	0.8%
35	Kentucky	45,233,000	0.8%
36	Idaho	44,016,000	0.8%
37	New Hampshire	42,911,000	0.7%
38	Alaska	38,338,000	0.7%
39	New Mexico	36,442,000	0.6%
40	Montana	34,003,000	0.6%
41	Rhode Island	33,382,000	0.6%
42	Delaware	26,356,000	0.5%
43	North Dakota	26,338,000	0.5%
44	Wyoming	26,018,000	0.4%
45	Vermont	25,868,000	0.4%
46	Nebraska	25,748,000	0.4%
47	Maine	19,514,000	0.3%
48	Nevada	18,973,000	0.3%
49	South Dakota	7,154,000	0.1%
50	West Virginia	6,626,000	0.1%
	District of Columbia	134,807,000	2.3%

Source: U.S. Office of Management and Budget, USAspending.gov
"Prime Award Spending Data Summary" (http://www.usaspending.gov/, as of February 4, 2015)
*Total includes $35,682,000 in U.S. territories and $569,531,000 in expenditures not distributed by state. Expenditures allocated based on place of performance of a contract. Includes funds awarded to a non-federal entity for a defined public or private purpose in which services are not rendered to the federal government. This source replaces a previous data series, "Atlas/Data Abstract for the United States", and definitions may differ.

Per Capita U.S. Department of Defense Grants in 2013

National Per Capita = $16*

ALPHA ORDER

RANK	STATE	PER CAPITA
38	Alabama	$10
3	Alaska	52
21	Arizona	17
19	Arkansas	21
28	California	14
26	Colorado	15
17	Connecticut	22
14	Delaware	28
42	Florida	9
42	Georgia	9
2	Hawaii	62
15	Idaho	27
34	Illinois	11
34	Indiana	11
24	Iowa	16
12	Kansas	29
38	Kentucky	10
24	Louisiana	16
26	Maine	15
1	Maryland	78
4	Massachusetts	46
46	Michigan	8
33	Minnesota	12
12	Mississippi	29
42	Missouri	9
9	Montana	34
28	Nebraska	14
49	Nevada	7
10	New Hampshire	32
46	New Jersey	8
21	New Mexico	17
34	New York	11
28	North Carolina	14
7	North Dakota	36
34	Ohio	11
17	Oklahoma	22
28	Oregon	14
20	Pennsylvania	18
10	Rhode Island	32
38	South Carolina	10
46	South Dakota	8
38	Tennessee	10
42	Texas	9
21	Utah	17
6	Vermont	41
16	Virginia	24
8	Washington	35
50	West Virginia	4
32	Wisconsin	13
5	Wyoming	45

RANK ORDER

RANK	STATE	PER CAPITA
1	Maryland	$78
2	Hawaii	62
3	Alaska	52
4	Massachusetts	46
5	Wyoming	45
6	Vermont	41
7	North Dakota	36
8	Washington	35
9	Montana	34
10	New Hampshire	32
10	Rhode Island	32
12	Kansas	29
12	Mississippi	29
14	Delaware	28
15	Idaho	27
16	Virginia	24
17	Connecticut	22
17	Oklahoma	22
19	Arkansas	21
20	Pennsylvania	18
21	Arizona	17
21	New Mexico	17
21	Utah	17
24	Iowa	16
24	Louisiana	16
26	Colorado	15
26	Maine	15
28	California	14
28	Nebraska	14
28	North Carolina	14
28	Oregon	14
32	Wisconsin	13
33	Minnesota	12
34	Illinois	11
34	Indiana	11
34	New York	11
34	Ohio	11
38	Alabama	10
38	Kentucky	10
38	South Carolina	10
38	Tennessee	10
42	Florida	9
42	Georgia	9
42	Missouri	9
42	Texas	9
46	Michigan	8
46	New Jersey	8
46	South Dakota	8
49	Nevada	7
50	West Virginia	4
	District of Columbia	208

Source: CQ Press using data from U.S. Office of Management and Budget, USAspending.gov
"Prime Award Spending Data Summary" (http://www.usaspending.gov/, as of February 4, 2015)
*National per capita excludes expenditures and population for territories and undistributed amounts. Expenditures allocated based on place of performance of a contract. Includes funds awarded to a non-federal entity for a defined public or private purpose in which services are not rendered to the federal government. This source replaces a previous data series, "Atlas/Data Abstract for the United States", and definitions may differ.

U.S. Active Duty Military Personnel Stationed in the United States in 2014

National Total = 1,149,159 Personnel*

ALPHA ORDER

RANK	STATE	PERSONNEL	% of USA
24	Alabama	7,875	0.7%
18	Alaska	19,608	1.7%
16	Arizona	19,792	1.7%
30	Arkansas	4,998	0.4%
1	California	155,051	13.5%
9	Colorado	37,731	3.3%
27	Connecticut	6,139	0.5%
32	Delaware	3,426	0.3%
6	Florida	60,095	5.2%
5	Georgia	69,322	6.0%
8	Hawaii	49,519	4.3%
33	Idaho	3,369	0.3%
15	Illinois	19,797	1.7%
43	Indiana	815	0.1%
49	Iowa	222	0.0%
13	Kansas	24,886	2.2%
11	Kentucky	35,901	3.1%
19	Louisiana	14,953	1.3%
48	Maine	241	0.0%
12	Maryland	28,100	2.4%
40	Massachusetts	1,969	0.2%
42	Michigan	1,101	0.1%
45	Minnesota	466	0.0%
22	Mississippi	11,322	1.0%
20	Missouri	14,179	1.2%
35	Montana	3,255	0.3%
29	Nebraska	5,964	0.5%
23	Nevada	10,902	0.9%
41	New Hampshire	1,185	0.1%
28	New Jersey	6,005	0.5%
21	New Mexico	12,111	1.1%
14	New York	22,263	1.9%
4	North Carolina	100,867	8.8%
25	North Dakota	6,901	0.6%
26	Ohio	6,516	0.6%
17	Oklahoma	19,643	1.7%
46	Oregon	408	0.0%
38	Pennsylvania	2,266	0.2%
34	Rhode Island	3,316	0.3%
10	South Carolina	36,670	3.2%
36	South Dakota	3,233	0.3%
39	Tennessee	1,987	0.2%
3	Texas	117,623	10.2%
31	Utah	3,749	0.3%
50	Vermont	116	0.0%
2	Virginia	122,884	10.7%
7	Washington	57,926	5.0%
47	West Virginia	275	0.0%
44	Wisconsin	534	0.0%
37	Wyoming	2,930	0.3%

RANK ORDER

RANK	STATE	PERSONNEL	% of USA
1	California	155,051	13.5%
2	Virginia	122,884	10.7%
3	Texas	117,623	10.2%
4	North Carolina	100,867	8.8%
5	Georgia	69,322	6.0%
6	Florida	60,095	5.2%
7	Washington	57,926	5.0%
8	Hawaii	49,519	4.3%
9	Colorado	37,731	3.3%
10	South Carolina	36,670	3.2%
11	Kentucky	35,901	3.1%
12	Maryland	28,100	2.4%
13	Kansas	24,886	2.2%
14	New York	22,263	1.9%
15	Illinois	19,797	1.7%
16	Arizona	19,792	1.7%
17	Oklahoma	19,643	1.7%
18	Alaska	19,608	1.7%
19	Louisiana	14,953	1.3%
20	Missouri	14,179	1.2%
21	New Mexico	12,111	1.1%
22	Mississippi	11,322	1.0%
23	Nevada	10,902	0.9%
24	Alabama	7,875	0.7%
25	North Dakota	6,901	0.6%
26	Ohio	6,516	0.6%
27	Connecticut	6,139	0.5%
28	New Jersey	6,005	0.5%
29	Nebraska	5,964	0.5%
30	Arkansas	4,998	0.4%
31	Utah	3,749	0.3%
32	Delaware	3,426	0.3%
33	Idaho	3,369	0.3%
34	Rhode Island	3,316	0.3%
35	Montana	3,255	0.3%
36	South Dakota	3,233	0.3%
37	Wyoming	2,930	0.3%
38	Pennsylvania	2,266	0.2%
39	Tennessee	1,987	0.2%
40	Massachusetts	1,969	0.2%
41	New Hampshire	1,185	0.1%
42	Michigan	1,101	0.1%
43	Indiana	815	0.1%
44	Wisconsin	534	0.0%
45	Minnesota	466	0.0%
46	Oregon	408	0.0%
47	West Virginia	275	0.0%
48	Maine	241	0.0%
49	Iowa	222	0.0%
50	Vermont	116	0.0%
	District of Columbia	8,475	0.7%

Source: U.S. Department of Defense
"Demographics 2014" (http://www.militaryonesource.mil/footer?content_id=279104)
*Includes 278 not shown by state. Numbers reflect where the personnel are stationed.

U.S. Selected Reserve Personnel Stationed in the United States in 2014

National Total = 805,845 Personnel*

ALPHA ORDER					RANK ORDER			
RANK	STATE	PERSONNEL	% of USA		RANK	STATE	PERSONNEL	% of USA
11	Alabama	20,829	2.6%		1	California	58,348	7.2%
42	Alaska	4,956	0.6%		2	Texas	53,057	6.6%
25	Arizona	14,215	1.8%		3	Florida	36,488	4.5%
29	Arkansas	12,484	1.5%		4	Pennsylvania	31,936	4.0%
1	California	58,348	7.2%		5	New York	30,257	3.8%
27	Colorado	13,469	1.7%		6	Ohio	28,227	3.5%
37	Connecticut	6,794	0.8%		7	Georgia	27,340	3.4%
40	Delaware	5,260	0.7%		8	Virginia	26,414	3.3%
3	Florida	36,488	4.5%		9	Illinois	24,526	3.0%
7	Georgia	27,340	3.4%		10	North Carolina	23,230	2.9%
34	Hawaii	9,377	1.2%		11	Alabama	20,829	2.6%
39	Idaho	5,659	0.7%		12	Louisiana	20,212	2.5%
9	Illinois	24,526	3.0%		13	Indiana	19,885	2.5%
13	Indiana	19,885	2.5%		14	Tennessee	19,535	2.4%
31	Iowa	11,514	1.4%		15	Missouri	19,518	2.4%
32	Kansas	11,262	1.4%		16	Washington	19,027	2.4%
28	Kentucky	13,211	1.6%		17	Minnesota	18,852	2.3%
12	Louisiana	20,212	2.5%		18	South Carolina	18,657	2.3%
49	Maine	4,124	0.5%		19	Maryland	18,136	2.3%
19	Maryland	18,136	2.3%		20	New Jersey	17,396	2.2%
22	Massachusetts	15,977	2.0%		21	Mississippi	16,833	2.1%
23	Michigan	15,813	2.0%		22	Massachusetts	15,977	2.0%
17	Minnesota	18,852	2.3%		23	Michigan	15,813	2.0%
21	Mississippi	16,833	2.1%		24	Wisconsin	14,993	1.9%
15	Missouri	19,518	2.4%		25	Arizona	14,215	1.8%
44	Montana	4,667	0.6%		26	Oklahoma	13,914	1.7%
38	Nebraska	6,494	0.8%		27	Colorado	13,469	1.7%
36	Nevada	7,620	0.9%		28	Kentucky	13,211	1.6%
48	New Hampshire	4,161	0.5%		29	Arkansas	12,484	1.5%
20	New Jersey	17,396	2.2%		30	Utah	12,039	1.5%
41	New Mexico	5,126	0.6%		31	Iowa	11,514	1.4%
5	New York	30,257	3.8%		32	Kansas	11,262	1.4%
10	North Carolina	23,230	2.9%		33	Oregon	10,135	1.3%
46	North Dakota	4,598	0.6%		34	Hawaii	9,377	1.2%
6	Ohio	28,227	3.5%		35	West Virginia	8,490	1.1%
26	Oklahoma	13,914	1.7%		36	Nevada	7,620	0.9%
33	Oregon	10,135	1.3%		37	Connecticut	6,794	0.8%
4	Pennsylvania	31,936	4.0%		38	Nebraska	6,494	0.8%
45	Rhode Island	4,636	0.6%		39	Idaho	5,659	0.7%
18	South Carolina	18,657	2.3%		40	Delaware	5,260	0.7%
43	South Dakota	4,803	0.6%		41	New Mexico	5,126	0.6%
14	Tennessee	19,535	2.4%		42	Alaska	4,956	0.6%
2	Texas	53,057	6.6%		43	South Dakota	4,803	0.6%
30	Utah	12,039	1.5%		44	Montana	4,667	0.6%
47	Vermont	4,241	0.5%		45	Rhode Island	4,636	0.6%
8	Virginia	26,414	3.3%		46	North Dakota	4,598	0.6%
16	Washington	19,027	2.4%		47	Vermont	4,241	0.5%
35	West Virginia	8,490	1.1%		48	New Hampshire	4,161	0.5%
24	Wisconsin	14,993	1.9%		49	Maine	4,124	0.5%
50	Wyoming	2,971	0.4%		50	Wyoming	2,971	0.4%
						District of Columbia	4,139	0.5%

Source: U.S. Department of Defense
"Demographics 2014" (http://www.militaryonesource.mil/footer?content_id=279104)
*Numbers reflect where the personnel are stationed.

Veterans in 2014

National Total = 21,999,108 Veterans*

ALPHA ORDER

RANK	STATE	VETERANS	% of USA
21	Alabama	413,618	1.9%
45	Alaska	73,397	0.3%
13	Arizona	532,206	2.4%
29	Arkansas	249,274	1.1%
1	California	1,851,470	8.4%
22	Colorado	413,271	1.9%
34	Connecticut	213,420	1.0%
44	Delaware	78,099	0.4%
3	Florida	1,583,697	7.2%
9	Georgia	752,882	3.4%
41	Hawaii	121,007	0.6%
39	Idaho	132,395	0.6%
10	Illinois	721,575	3.3%
16	Indiana	476,283	2.2%
30	Iowa	231,655	1.1%
32	Kansas	221,206	1.0%
27	Kentucky	330,599	1.5%
28	Louisiana	330,145	1.5%
40	Maine	127,234	0.6%
17	Maryland	437,762	2.0%
23	Massachusetts	379,772	1.7%
11	Michigan	658,469	3.0%
24	Minnesota	369,149	1.7%
33	Mississippi	220,389	1.0%
15	Missouri	494,346	2.2%
43	Montana	99,646	0.5%
38	Nebraska	143,375	0.7%
31	Nevada	228,027	1.0%
42	New Hampshire	113,660	0.5%
18	New Jersey	428,396	1.9%
35	New Mexico	171,528	0.8%
5	New York	892,221	4.1%
8	North Carolina	775,020	3.5%
48	North Dakota	57,395	0.3%
6	Ohio	866,481	3.9%
25	Oklahoma	337,571	1.5%
26	Oregon	331,632	1.5%
4	Pennsylvania	939,069	4.3%
47	Rhode Island	71,966	0.3%
19	South Carolina	417,554	1.9%
46	South Dakota	72,030	0.3%
14	Tennessee	506,340	2.3%
2	Texas	1,680,418	7.6%
37	Utah	151,719	0.7%
50	Vermont	48,602	0.2%
7	Virginia	781,388	3.6%
12	Washington	603,623	2.7%
36	West Virginia	167,355	0.8%
20	Wisconsin	413,723	1.9%
49	Wyoming	49,708	0.2%

RANK ORDER

RANK	STATE	VETERANS	% of USA
1	California	1,851,470	8.4%
2	Texas	1,680,418	7.6%
3	Florida	1,583,697	7.2%
4	Pennsylvania	939,069	4.3%
5	New York	892,221	4.1%
6	Ohio	866,481	3.9%
7	Virginia	781,388	3.6%
8	North Carolina	775,020	3.5%
9	Georgia	752,882	3.4%
10	Illinois	721,575	3.3%
11	Michigan	658,469	3.0%
12	Washington	603,623	2.7%
13	Arizona	532,206	2.4%
14	Tennessee	506,340	2.3%
15	Missouri	494,346	2.2%
16	Indiana	476,283	2.2%
17	Maryland	437,762	2.0%
18	New Jersey	428,396	1.9%
19	South Carolina	417,554	1.9%
20	Wisconsin	413,723	1.9%
21	Alabama	413,618	1.9%
22	Colorado	413,271	1.9%
23	Massachusetts	379,772	1.7%
24	Minnesota	369,149	1.7%
25	Oklahoma	337,571	1.5%
26	Oregon	331,632	1.5%
27	Kentucky	330,599	1.5%
28	Louisiana	330,145	1.5%
29	Arkansas	249,274	1.1%
30	Iowa	231,655	1.1%
31	Nevada	228,027	1.0%
32	Kansas	221,206	1.0%
33	Mississippi	220,389	1.0%
34	Connecticut	213,420	1.0%
35	New Mexico	171,528	0.8%
36	West Virginia	167,355	0.8%
37	Utah	151,719	0.7%
38	Nebraska	143,375	0.7%
39	Idaho	132,395	0.6%
40	Maine	127,234	0.6%
41	Hawaii	121,007	0.6%
42	New Hampshire	113,660	0.5%
43	Montana	99,646	0.5%
44	Delaware	78,099	0.4%
45	Alaska	73,397	0.3%
46	South Dakota	72,030	0.3%
47	Rhode Island	71,966	0.3%
48	North Dakota	57,395	0.3%
49	Wyoming	49,708	0.2%
50	Vermont	48,602	0.2%
	District of Columbia	29,825	0.1%

Source: U.S. Department of Veteran Affairs
"Veteran Data and Information" (http://www.va.gov/vetdata/Veteran_Population.asp)
*Estimates based on 2014 data. Includes 207,515 veterans in U.S. territories or other countries.

Percent of Adult Population Who Are Veterans in 2014

National Percent = 9.0%*

ALPHA ORDER

RANK	STATE	PERCENT
12	Alabama	11.1
1	Alaska	13.4
20	Arizona	10.6
12	Arkansas	11.1
48	California	6.3
22	Colorado	10.3
44	Connecticut	7.6
16	Delaware	10.8
23	Florida	10.2
29	Georgia	10.0
14	Hawaii	11.0
9	Idaho	11.2
46	Illinois	7.3
34	Indiana	9.6
30	Iowa	9.8
23	Kansas	10.2
30	Kentucky	9.8
37	Louisiana	9.4
4	Maine	11.9
36	Maryland	9.5
47	Massachusetts	7.2
42	Michigan	8.6
40	Minnesota	8.9
30	Mississippi	9.8
20	Missouri	10.6
2	Montana	12.6
23	Nebraska	10.2
19	Nevada	10.7
16	New Hampshire	10.8
49	New Jersey	6.2
15	New Mexico	10.9
50	New York	5.8
23	North Carolina	10.2
23	North Dakota	10.2
33	Ohio	9.7
5	Oklahoma	11.6
16	Oregon	10.8
38	Pennsylvania	9.3
42	Rhode Island	8.6
7	South Carolina	11.3
7	South Dakota	11.3
28	Tennessee	10.1
41	Texas	8.7
44	Utah	7.6
34	Vermont	9.6
3	Virginia	12.2
9	Washington	11.2
6	West Virginia	11.4
38	Wisconsin	9.3
9	Wyoming	11.2

RANK ORDER

RANK	STATE	PERCENT
1	Alaska	13.4
2	Montana	12.6
3	Virginia	12.2
4	Maine	11.9
5	Oklahoma	11.6
6	West Virginia	11.4
7	South Carolina	11.3
7	South Dakota	11.3
9	Idaho	11.2
9	Washington	11.2
9	Wyoming	11.2
12	Alabama	11.1
12	Arkansas	11.1
14	Hawaii	11.0
15	New Mexico	10.9
16	Delaware	10.8
16	New Hampshire	10.8
16	Oregon	10.8
19	Nevada	10.7
20	Arizona	10.6
20	Missouri	10.6
22	Colorado	10.3
23	Florida	10.2
23	Kansas	10.2
23	Nebraska	10.2
23	North Carolina	10.2
23	North Dakota	10.2
28	Tennessee	10.1
29	Georgia	10.0
30	Iowa	9.8
30	Kentucky	9.8
30	Mississippi	9.8
33	Ohio	9.7
34	Indiana	9.6
34	Vermont	9.6
36	Maryland	9.5
37	Louisiana	9.4
38	Pennsylvania	9.3
38	Wisconsin	9.3
40	Minnesota	8.9
41	Texas	8.7
42	Michigan	8.6
42	Rhode Island	8.6
44	Connecticut	7.6
44	Utah	7.6
46	Illinois	7.3
47	Massachusetts	7.2
48	California	6.3
49	New Jersey	6.2
50	New York	5.8
	District of Columbia	5.6

Source: CQ Press using data from U.S. Department of Veteran Affairs
"Veteran Data and Information" (http://www.va.gov/vetdata/Veteran_Population.asp)
*Estimates based on 2014 data. National figures does not include veterans in U.S. territories or other countries. Percent calculated with population 18 years old and older in 2013.

U.S. Military Fatalities in Iraq and Afghanistan as of February 1, 2016

National Total = 6,863 Fatalities*

ALPHA ORDER

RANK	STATE	FATALITIES	% of USA
25	Alabama	105	1.5%
46	Alaska	23	0.3%
13	Arizona	153	2.2%
29	Arkansas	89	1.3%
1	California	736	10.7%
26	Colorado	104	1.5%
38	Connecticut	47	0.7%
49	Delaware	19	0.3%
3	Florida	347	5.1%
9	Georgia	218	3.2%
43	Hawaii	36	0.5%
36	Idaho	50	0.7%
7	Illinois	251	3.7%
12	Indiana	156	2.3%
32	Iowa	73	1.1%
31	Kansas	75	1.1%
23	Kentucky	113	1.6%
20	Louisiana	125	1.8%
36	Maine	50	0.7%
22	Maryland	118	1.7%
17	Massachusetts	127	1.9%
8	Michigan	226	3.3%
27	Minnesota	97	1.4%
30	Mississippi	80	1.2%
15	Missouri	144	2.1%
40	Montana	40	0.6%
33	Nebraska	61	0.9%
35	Nevada	54	0.8%
40	New Hampshire	40	0.6%
21	New Jersey	124	1.8%
34	New Mexico	57	0.8%
4	New York	297	4.3%
11	North Carolina	187	2.7%
48	North Dakota	20	0.3%
6	Ohio	279	4.1%
18	Oklahoma	126	1.8%
24	Oregon	109	1.6%
5	Pennsylvania	292	4.3%
50	Rhode Island	17	0.2%
28	South Carolina	96	1.4%
45	South Dakota	24	0.3%
16	Tennessee	140	2.0%
2	Texas	606	8.8%
38	Utah	47	0.7%
44	Vermont	26	0.4%
10	Virginia	199	2.9%
14	Washington	148	2.2%
40	West Virginia	40	0.6%
18	Wisconsin	126	1.8%
47	Wyoming	22	0.3%

RANK ORDER

RANK	STATE	FATALITIES	% of USA
1	California	736	10.7%
2	Texas	606	8.8%
3	Florida	347	5.1%
4	New York	297	4.3%
5	Pennsylvania	292	4.3%
6	Ohio	279	4.1%
7	Illinois	251	3.7%
8	Michigan	226	3.3%
9	Georgia	218	3.2%
10	Virginia	199	2.9%
11	North Carolina	187	2.7%
12	Indiana	156	2.3%
13	Arizona	153	2.2%
14	Washington	148	2.2%
15	Missouri	144	2.1%
16	Tennessee	140	2.0%
17	Massachusetts	127	1.9%
18	Oklahoma	126	1.8%
18	Wisconsin	126	1.8%
20	Louisiana	125	1.8%
21	New Jersey	124	1.8%
22	Maryland	118	1.7%
23	Kentucky	113	1.6%
24	Oregon	109	1.6%
25	Alabama	105	1.5%
26	Colorado	104	1.5%
27	Minnesota	97	1.4%
28	South Carolina	96	1.4%
29	Arkansas	89	1.3%
30	Mississippi	80	1.2%
31	Kansas	75	1.1%
32	Iowa	73	1.1%
33	Nebraska	61	0.9%
34	New Mexico	57	0.8%
35	Nevada	54	0.8%
36	Idaho	50	0.7%
36	Maine	50	0.7%
38	Connecticut	47	0.7%
38	Utah	47	0.7%
40	Montana	40	0.6%
40	New Hampshire	40	0.6%
40	West Virginia	40	0.6%
43	Hawaii	36	0.5%
44	Vermont	26	0.4%
45	South Dakota	24	0.3%
46	Alaska	23	0.3%
47	Wyoming	22	0.3%
48	North Dakota	20	0.3%
49	Delaware	19	0.3%
50	Rhode Island	17	0.2%
	District of Columbia	10	0.1%

Source: U.S. Department of Defense, Defense Casualty Analysis System
"U.S. Military Casualties" (https://www.dmdc.osd.mil/dcas/pages/report_sum_all.xhtml)
*Total includes 114 deaths of soldiers from U.S. territories. Total does not include deaths of United Kingdom soldiers or other coalition nations. Includes 5,364 combat and 1,466 noncombat deaths. Includes 4,484 deaths in Iraq, 2,366 deaths in Afghanistan, and 13 deaths fighting Islamic State in Syria and Iraq.

Rate of U.S. Military Fatalities in Iraq and Afghanistan as of February 1, 2016

National Rate = 2.1 Fatalities per 100,000 Population*

ALPHA ORDER

RANK	STATE	RATE
27	Alabama	2.2
7	Alaska	3.1
27	Arizona	2.2
8	Arkansas	3.0
39	California	1.9
39	Colorado	1.9
50	Connecticut	1.3
35	Delaware	2.0
45	Florida	1.7
32	Georgia	2.1
19	Hawaii	2.5
8	Idaho	3.0
35	Illinois	2.0
20	Indiana	2.4
24	Iowa	2.3
16	Kansas	2.6
16	Kentucky	2.6
12	Louisiana	2.7
3	Maine	3.8
35	Maryland	2.0
39	Massachusetts	1.9
24	Michigan	2.3
44	Minnesota	1.8
12	Mississippi	2.7
20	Missouri	2.4
2	Montana	3.9
5	Nebraska	3.2
39	Nevada	1.9
8	New Hampshire	3.0
49	New Jersey	1.4
12	New Mexico	2.7
48	New York	1.5
39	North Carolina	1.9
16	North Dakota	2.6
20	Ohio	2.4
5	Oklahoma	3.2
12	Oregon	2.7
24	Pennsylvania	2.3
46	Rhode Island	1.6
35	South Carolina	2.0
11	South Dakota	2.8
32	Tennessee	2.1
27	Texas	2.2
46	Utah	1.6
1	Vermont	4.2
20	Virginia	2.4
32	Washington	2.1
27	West Virginia	2.2
27	Wisconsin	2.2
3	Wyoming	3.8

RANK ORDER

RANK	STATE	RATE
1	Vermont	4.2
2	Montana	3.9
3	Maine	3.8
3	Wyoming	3.8
5	Nebraska	3.2
5	Oklahoma	3.2
7	Alaska	3.1
8	Arkansas	3.0
8	Idaho	3.0
8	New Hampshire	3.0
11	South Dakota	2.8
12	Louisiana	2.7
12	Mississippi	2.7
12	New Mexico	2.7
12	Oregon	2.7
16	Kansas	2.6
16	Kentucky	2.6
16	North Dakota	2.6
19	Hawaii	2.5
20	Indiana	2.4
20	Missouri	2.4
20	Ohio	2.4
20	Virginia	2.4
24	Iowa	2.3
24	Michigan	2.3
24	Pennsylvania	2.3
27	Alabama	2.2
27	Arizona	2.2
27	Texas	2.2
27	West Virginia	2.2
27	Wisconsin	2.2
32	Georgia	2.1
32	Tennessee	2.1
32	Washington	2.1
35	Delaware	2.0
35	Illinois	2.0
35	Maryland	2.0
35	South Carolina	2.0
39	California	1.9
39	Colorado	1.9
39	Massachusetts	1.9
39	Nevada	1.9
39	North Carolina	1.9
44	Minnesota	1.8
45	Florida	1.7
46	Rhode Island	1.6
46	Utah	1.6
48	New York	1.5
49	New Jersey	1.4
50	Connecticut	1.3
	District of Columbia	1.5

Source: CQ Press using data from U.S. Department of Defense, Defense Casualty Analysis System
"U.S. Military Casualties" (https://www.dmdc.osd.mil/dcas/pages/report_sum_all.xhtml)
*National rate does not include deaths of soldiers from U.S. territories. Includes combat and noncombat deaths. Calculated with 2015 population estimates.

IV. Economy

Gross Domestic Product in 2014 85
Percent Change in Gross Domestic Product: 2010 to 2014
   (Adjusted to Constant 2009 Dollars) 86
Average Annual Change in Gross Domestic Product:
   2010 to 2014 (Adjusted to Constant 2009 Dollars) 87
Per Capita Gross Domestic Product in 2014............ 88
Percent Change in Per Capita Gross Domestic Product:
   2010 to 2014 (Adjusted to Constant 2009 Dollars) 89
State Exports in 2014 90
Per Capita State Exports in 2014 91
State Imports in 2014 92
Per Capita State Imports in 2014 93
Personal Income in 2014............................ 94
Change in Personal Income: 2013 to 2014.............. 95
Per Capita Personal Income in 2014................... 96
Change in Per Capita Personal Income: 2013 to 2014 97
Disposable Personal Income in 2014 98
Per Capita Disposable Personal Income in 2014 99
Median Household Income in 2014 100

Regional Price Parities in 2013...................... 101
Real Personal Income in 2013 102
Percent Change in Real Personal Income: 2012 to 2013 .. 103
Per Capita Real Personal Income in 2013............. 104
Percent Change in Per Capita Real Personal Income:
   2012 to 2013................................. 105
Personal Consumption Expenditures in 2014........... 106
Per Capita Personal Consumption Expenditures in
   2014 107
Percent Change in Personal Consumption Expenditures:
   2013 to 2014................................. 108
Percent Change in Per Capita Personal Consumption
   Expenditures: 2013 to 2014 109
Bankruptcy Filings in 2015......................... 110
Personal Bankruptcy Rate in 2015 111
Percent Change in Personal Bankruptcy Rate: 2014 to
   2015 112
2016 State Business Tax Climate Index 113
Fortune 500 Companies in 2015..................... 114

Gross Domestic Product in 2014

National Total = $17,232,618,000,000*

ALPHA ORDER

RANK	STATE	G.D.P.	% of USA
26	Alabama	$200,414,000,000	1.2%
43	Alaska	56,647,000,000	0.3%
21	Arizona	286,554,000,000	1.7%
34	Arkansas	120,035,000,000	0.7%
1	California	2,305,921,000,000	13.4%
18	Colorado	305,871,000,000	1.8%
24	Connecticut	250,569,000,000	1.5%
41	Delaware	63,404,000,000	0.4%
4	Florida	838,939,000,000	4.9%
10	Georgia	474,696,000,000	2.8%
38	Hawaii	76,171,000,000	0.4%
42	Idaho	63,235,000,000	0.4%
5	Illinois	736,285,000,000	4.3%
16	Indiana	318,085,000,000	1.8%
30	Iowa	169,707,000,000	1.0%
31	Kansas	144,407,000,000	0.8%
28	Kentucky	187,788,000,000	1.1%
23	Louisiana	251,672,000,000	1.5%
46	Maine	54,324,000,000	0.3%
15	Maryland	346,857,000,000	2.0%
12	Massachusetts	455,732,000,000	2.6%
13	Michigan	448,243,000,000	2.6%
17	Minnesota	317,237,000,000	1.8%
36	Mississippi	104,753,000,000	0.6%
22	Missouri	279,835,000,000	1.6%
48	Montana	44,135,000,000	0.3%
35	Nebraska	111,007,000,000	0.6%
33	Nevada	135,038,000,000	0.8%
40	New Hampshire	70,358,000,000	0.4%
8	New Jersey	551,828,000,000	3.2%
37	New Mexico	91,885,000,000	0.5%
3	New York	1,395,488,000,000	8.1%
9	North Carolina	481,876,000,000	2.8%
44	North Dakota	55,978,000,000	0.3%
7	Ohio	576,056,000,000	3.3%
29	Oklahoma	183,174,000,000	1.1%
25	Oregon	212,807,000,000	1.2%
6	Pennsylvania	658,290,000,000	3.8%
45	Rhode Island	54,492,000,000	0.3%
27	South Carolina	189,278,000,000	1.1%
47	South Dakota	46,169,000,000	0.3%
19	Tennessee	297,159,000,000	1.7%
2	Texas	1,641,044,000,000	9.5%
32	Utah	140,031,000,000	0.8%
50	Vermont	29,312,000,000	0.2%
11	Virginia	462,861,000,000	2.7%
14	Washington	422,877,000,000	2.5%
39	West Virginia	74,296,000,000	0.4%
20	Wisconsin	289,616,000,000	1.7%
49	Wyoming	43,800,000,000	0.3%

RANK ORDER

RANK	STATE	G.D.P.	% of USA
1	California	$2,305,921,000,000	13.4%
2	Texas	1,641,044,000,000	9.5%
3	New York	1,395,488,000,000	8.1%
4	Florida	838,939,000,000	4.9%
5	Illinois	736,285,000,000	4.3%
6	Pennsylvania	658,290,000,000	3.8%
7	Ohio	576,056,000,000	3.3%
8	New Jersey	551,828,000,000	3.2%
9	North Carolina	481,876,000,000	2.8%
10	Georgia	474,696,000,000	2.8%
11	Virginia	462,861,000,000	2.7%
12	Massachusetts	455,732,000,000	2.6%
13	Michigan	448,243,000,000	2.6%
14	Washington	422,877,000,000	2.5%
15	Maryland	346,857,000,000	2.0%
16	Indiana	318,085,000,000	1.8%
17	Minnesota	317,237,000,000	1.8%
18	Colorado	305,871,000,000	1.8%
19	Tennessee	297,159,000,000	1.7%
20	Wisconsin	289,616,000,000	1.7%
21	Arizona	286,554,000,000	1.7%
22	Missouri	279,835,000,000	1.6%
23	Louisiana	251,672,000,000	1.5%
24	Connecticut	250,569,000,000	1.5%
25	Oregon	212,807,000,000	1.2%
26	Alabama	200,414,000,000	1.2%
27	South Carolina	189,278,000,000	1.1%
28	Kentucky	187,788,000,000	1.1%
29	Oklahoma	183,174,000,000	1.1%
30	Iowa	169,707,000,000	1.0%
31	Kansas	144,407,000,000	0.8%
32	Utah	140,031,000,000	0.8%
33	Nevada	135,038,000,000	0.8%
34	Arkansas	120,035,000,000	0.7%
35	Nebraska	111,007,000,000	0.6%
36	Mississippi	104,753,000,000	0.6%
37	New Mexico	91,885,000,000	0.5%
38	Hawaii	76,171,000,000	0.4%
39	West Virginia	74,296,000,000	0.4%
40	New Hampshire	70,358,000,000	0.4%
41	Delaware	63,404,000,000	0.4%
42	Idaho	63,235,000,000	0.4%
43	Alaska	56,647,000,000	0.3%
44	North Dakota	55,978,000,000	0.3%
45	Rhode Island	54,492,000,000	0.3%
46	Maine	54,324,000,000	0.3%
47	South Dakota	46,169,000,000	0.3%
48	Montana	44,135,000,000	0.3%
49	Wyoming	43,800,000,000	0.3%
50	Vermont	29,312,000,000	0.2%
	District of Columbia	116,378,000,000	0.7%

Source: U.S. Department of Commerce, Bureau of Economic Analysis
"Gross Domestic Product Data" (http://www.bea.gov/iTable/index_regional.cfm)
*G.D.P. is the market value of goods and services produced by the labor and property located in a state. It is the state counterpart to the nation's Gross Domestic Product. This was formerly known as Gross State Product (G.S.P.).

Percent Change in Gross Domestic Product: 2010 to 2014
(Adjusted to Constant 2009 Dollars)
National Percent Change = 7.0% Increase*

ALPHA ORDER

RANK	STATE	PERCENT CHANGE
24	Alabama	5.3
47	Alaska	0.4
15	Arizona	7.3
20	Arkansas	5.9
9	California	8.7
4	Colorado	10.4
48	Connecticut	0.0
44	Delaware	0.9
18	Florida	6.3
17	Georgia	7.0
31	Hawaii	4.2
28	Idaho	4.8
35	Illinois	3.6
36	Indiana	3.3
7	Iowa	9.1
34	Kansas	3.7
27	Kentucky	4.9
50	Louisiana	(2.8)
49	Maine	(2.3)
38	Maryland	2.8
19	Massachusetts	6.1
13	Michigan	7.9
14	Minnesota	7.7
43	Mississippi	1.1
46	Missouri	0.5
11	Montana	8.1
5	Nebraska	9.6
29	Nevada	4.5
31	New Hampshire	4.2
37	New Jersey	3.2
41	New Mexico	2.1
23	New York	5.5
24	North Carolina	5.3
1	North Dakota	44.1
16	Ohio	7.2
3	Oklahoma	11.4
22	Oregon	5.6
30	Pennsylvania	4.3
40	Rhode Island	2.5
20	South Carolina	5.9
8	South Dakota	8.8
10	Tennessee	8.5
2	Texas	21.1
6	Utah	9.4
38	Vermont	2.8
42	Virginia	1.6
12	Washington	8.0
33	West Virginia	4.0
24	Wisconsin	5.3
45	Wyoming	0.8

RANK ORDER

RANK	STATE	PERCENT CHANGE
1	North Dakota	44.1
2	Texas	21.1
3	Oklahoma	11.4
4	Colorado	10.4
5	Nebraska	9.6
6	Utah	9.4
7	Iowa	9.1
8	South Dakota	8.8
9	California	8.7
10	Tennessee	8.5
11	Montana	8.1
12	Washington	8.0
13	Michigan	7.9
14	Minnesota	7.7
15	Arizona	7.3
16	Ohio	7.2
17	Georgia	7.0
18	Florida	6.3
19	Massachusetts	6.1
20	Arkansas	5.9
20	South Carolina	5.9
22	Oregon	5.6
23	New York	5.5
24	Alabama	5.3
24	North Carolina	5.3
24	Wisconsin	5.3
27	Kentucky	4.9
28	Idaho	4.8
29	Nevada	4.5
30	Pennsylvania	4.3
31	Hawaii	4.2
31	New Hampshire	4.2
33	West Virginia	4.0
34	Kansas	3.7
35	Illinois	3.6
36	Indiana	3.3
37	New Jersey	3.2
38	Maryland	2.8
38	Vermont	2.8
40	Rhode Island	2.5
41	New Mexico	2.1
42	Virginia	1.6
43	Mississippi	1.1
44	Delaware	0.9
45	Wyoming	0.8
46	Missouri	0.5
47	Alaska	0.4
48	Connecticut	0.0
49	Maine	(2.3)
50	Louisiana	(2.8)

District of Columbia   3.7

Source: CQ Press using data from U.S. Department of Commerce, Bureau of Economic Analysis
"Gross Domestic Product Data" (http://www.bea.gov/iTable/index_regional.cfm)

*G.D.P. is the market value of goods and services produced by the labor and property located in a state. It is the state counterpart to the nation's Gross Domestic Product. This was formerly known as Gross State Product (G.S.P.). Adjusted for inflation using chained 2009 dollars.

Average Annual Change in Gross Domestic Product: 2010 to 2014
(Adjusted to Constant 2009 Dollars)
National Annual Percent Change = 1.4% Increase*

ALPHA ORDER

RANK	STATE	PERCENT CHANGE
24	Alabama	1.0
46	Alaska	0.1
15	Arizona	1.4
21	Arkansas	1.1
8	California	1.7
4	Colorado	2.0
48	Connecticut	0.0
43	Delaware	0.2
18	Florida	1.2
15	Georgia	1.4
30	Hawaii	0.8
28	Idaho	0.9
34	Illinois	0.7
36	Indiana	0.6
5	Iowa	1.8
34	Kansas	0.7
24	Kentucky	1.0
50	Louisiana	(0.6)
49	Maine	(0.5)
39	Maryland	0.5
18	Massachusetts	1.2
12	Michigan	1.5
12	Minnesota	1.5
43	Mississippi	0.2
46	Missouri	0.1
10	Montana	1.6
5	Nebraska	1.8
28	Nevada	0.9
30	New Hampshire	0.8
36	New Jersey	0.6
41	New Mexico	0.4
21	New York	1.1
24	North Carolina	1.0
1	North Dakota	7.6
15	Ohio	1.4
3	Oklahoma	2.2
21	Oregon	1.1
30	Pennsylvania	0.8
39	Rhode Island	0.5
18	South Carolina	1.2
8	South Dakota	1.7
10	Tennessee	1.6
2	Texas	3.9
5	Utah	1.8
36	Vermont	0.6
42	Virginia	0.3
12	Washington	1.5
30	West Virginia	0.8
24	Wisconsin	1.0
43	Wyoming	0.2

RANK ORDER

RANK	STATE	PERCENT CHANGE
1	North Dakota	7.6
2	Texas	3.9
3	Oklahoma	2.2
4	Colorado	2.0
5	Iowa	1.8
5	Nebraska	1.8
5	Utah	1.8
8	California	1.7
8	South Dakota	1.7
10	Montana	1.6
10	Tennessee	1.6
12	Michigan	1.5
12	Minnesota	1.5
12	Washington	1.5
15	Arizona	1.4
15	Georgia	1.4
15	Ohio	1.4
18	Florida	1.2
18	Massachusetts	1.2
18	South Carolina	1.2
21	Arkansas	1.1
21	New York	1.1
21	Oregon	1.1
24	Alabama	1.0
24	Kentucky	1.0
24	North Carolina	1.0
24	Wisconsin	1.0
28	Idaho	0.9
28	Nevada	0.9
30	Hawaii	0.8
30	New Hampshire	0.8
30	Pennsylvania	0.8
30	West Virginia	0.8
34	Illinois	0.7
34	Kansas	0.7
36	Indiana	0.6
36	New Jersey	0.6
36	Vermont	0.6
39	Maryland	0.5
39	Rhode Island	0.5
41	New Mexico	0.4
42	Virginia	0.3
43	Delaware	0.2
43	Mississippi	0.2
43	Wyoming	0.2
46	Alaska	0.1
46	Missouri	0.1
48	Connecticut	0.0
49	Maine	(0.5)
50	Louisiana	(0.6)
	District of Columbia	0.7

Source: CQ Press using data from U.S. Department of Commerce, Bureau of Economic Analysis
"Gross Domestic Product Data" (http://www.bea.gov/iTable/index_regional.cfm)
*G.D.P. is the market value of goods and services produced by the labor and property located in a state. It is the state counterpart to the nation's Gross Domestic Product. This was formerly known as Gross State Product (G.S.P.). Adjusted for inflation using chained 2009 dollars.

Per Capita Gross Domestic Product in 2014

National Per Capita = $54,036*

ALPHA ORDER

RANK	STATE	PER CAPITA
44	Alabama	$41,353
1	Alaska	76,857
41	Arizona	42,586
46	Arkansas	40,459
11	California	59,443
16	Colorado	57,112
5	Connecticut	69,704
6	Delaware	67,742
43	Florida	42,146
34	Georgia	47,013
21	Hawaii	53,632
49	Idaho	38,680
15	Illinois	57,155
30	Indiana	48,210
18	Iowa	54,577
27	Kansas	49,753
42	Kentucky	42,557
19	Louisiana	54,135
45	Maine	40,837
14	Maryland	58,048
7	Massachusetts	67,465
38	Michigan	45,203
13	Minnesota	58,133
50	Mississippi	34,994
36	Missouri	46,148
40	Montana	43,132
12	Nebraska	58,953
31	Nevada	47,577
23	New Hampshire	52,981
8	New Jersey	61,734
39	New Mexico	44,058
4	New York	70,662
29	North Carolina	48,477
2	North Dakota	75,642
28	Ohio	49,673
33	Oklahoma	47,215
22	Oregon	53,588
25	Pennsylvania	51,454
24	Rhode Island	51,656
48	South Carolina	39,195
20	South Dakota	54,106
37	Tennessee	45,383
9	Texas	60,827
32	Utah	47,557
35	Vermont	46,767
17	Virginia	55,578
10	Washington	59,871
47	West Virginia	40,187
26	Wisconsin	50,286
3	Wyoming	74,961

RANK ORDER

RANK	STATE	PER CAPITA
1	Alaska	$76,857
2	North Dakota	75,642
3	Wyoming	74,961
4	New York	70,662
5	Connecticut	69,704
6	Delaware	67,742
7	Massachusetts	67,465
8	New Jersey	61,734
9	Texas	60,827
10	Washington	59,871
11	California	59,443
12	Nebraska	58,953
13	Minnesota	58,133
14	Maryland	58,048
15	Illinois	57,155
16	Colorado	57,112
17	Virginia	55,578
18	Iowa	54,577
19	Louisiana	54,135
20	South Dakota	54,106
21	Hawaii	53,632
22	Oregon	53,588
23	New Hampshire	52,981
24	Rhode Island	51,656
25	Pennsylvania	51,454
26	Wisconsin	50,286
27	Kansas	49,753
28	Ohio	49,673
29	North Carolina	48,477
30	Indiana	48,210
31	Nevada	47,577
32	Utah	47,557
33	Oklahoma	47,215
34	Georgia	47,013
35	Vermont	46,767
36	Missouri	46,148
37	Tennessee	45,383
38	Michigan	45,203
39	New Mexico	44,058
40	Montana	43,132
41	Arizona	42,586
42	Kentucky	42,557
43	Florida	42,146
44	Alabama	41,353
45	Maine	40,837
46	Arkansas	40,459
47	West Virginia	40,187
48	South Carolina	39,195
49	Idaho	38,680
50	Mississippi	34,994
	District of Columbia	176,374

Source: CQ Press using data from U.S. Department of Commerce, Bureau of Economic Analysis
"Gross Domestic Product Data" (http://www.bea.gov/iTable/index_regional.cfm)
*G.D.P. is the market value of goods and services produced by the labor and property located in a state. It is the state counterpart to the nation's Gross Domestic Product. This was formerly known as Gross State Product (G.S.P.).

Percent Change in Per Capita Gross Domestic Product: 2010 to 2014
(Adjusted to Constant 2009 Dollars)
National Percent Change = 3.9% Increase*

ALPHA ORDER

RANK	STATE	PERCENT CHANGE
17	Alabama	3.9
48	Alaska	(2.7)
29	Arizona	2.2
12	Arkansas	4.3
10	California	4.6
14	Colorado	4.1
41	Connecticut	(0.5)
49	Delaware	(3.0)
37	Florida	0.7
26	Georgia	2.9
40	Hawaii	0.1
37	Idaho	0.7
22	Illinois	3.3
32	Indiana	1.6
5	Iowa	7.1
30	Kansas	2.1
20	Kentucky	3.4
50	Louisiana	(5.0)
46	Maine	(2.5)
41	Maryland	(0.5)
23	Massachusetts	3.2
4	Michigan	7.6
9	Minnesota	4.8
39	Mississippi	0.4
44	Missouri	(0.6)
10	Montana	4.6
7	Nebraska	6.6
41	Nevada	(0.5)
20	New Hampshire	3.4
32	New Jersey	1.6
36	New Mexico	1.1
18	New York	3.6
35	North Carolina	1.2
1	North Dakota	31.4
6	Ohio	6.7
3	Oklahoma	8.0
30	Oregon	2.1
18	Pennsylvania	3.6
28	Rhode Island	2.3
32	South Carolina	1.6
14	South Dakota	4.1
8	Tennessee	5.3
2	Texas	13.4
24	Utah	3.1
27	Vermont	2.7
45	Virginia	(2.0)
24	Washington	3.1
13	West Virginia	4.2
14	Wisconsin	4.1
47	Wyoming	(2.6)

RANK ORDER

RANK	STATE	PERCENT CHANGE
1	North Dakota	31.4
2	Texas	13.4
3	Oklahoma	8.0
4	Michigan	7.6
5	Iowa	7.1
6	Ohio	6.7
7	Nebraska	6.6
8	Tennessee	5.3
9	Minnesota	4.8
10	California	4.6
10	Montana	4.6
12	Arkansas	4.3
13	West Virginia	4.2
14	Colorado	4.1
14	South Dakota	4.1
14	Wisconsin	4.1
17	Alabama	3.9
18	New York	3.6
18	Pennsylvania	3.6
20	Kentucky	3.4
20	New Hampshire	3.4
22	Illinois	3.3
23	Massachusetts	3.2
24	Utah	3.1
24	Washington	3.1
26	Georgia	2.9
27	Vermont	2.7
28	Rhode Island	2.3
29	Arizona	2.2
30	Kansas	2.1
30	Oregon	2.1
32	Indiana	1.6
32	New Jersey	1.6
32	South Carolina	1.6
35	North Carolina	1.2
36	New Mexico	1.1
37	Florida	0.7
37	Idaho	0.7
39	Mississippi	0.4
40	Hawaii	0.1
41	Connecticut	(0.5)
41	Maryland	(0.5)
41	Nevada	(0.5)
44	Missouri	(0.6)
45	Virginia	(2.0)
46	Maine	(2.5)
47	Wyoming	(2.6)
48	Alaska	(2.7)
49	Delaware	(3.0)
50	Louisiana	(5.0)
	District of Columbia	(4.7)

Source: CQ Press using data from U.S. Department of Commerce, Bureau of Economic Analysis
"Gross Domestic Product Data" (http://www.bea.gov/iTable/index_regional.cfm)
*G.D.P. is the market value of goods and services produced by the labor and property located in a state. It is the state counterpart to the nation's Gross Domestic Product. This was formerly known as Gross State Product (G.S.P.). Adjusted for inflation using chained 2009 dollars.

State Exports in 2014

National Total = $1,623,442,910,000*

ALPHA ORDER

RANK	STATE	EXPORTS	% of USA
23	Alabama	$19,517,560,000	1.2%
40	Alaska	5,153,120,000	0.3%
21	Arizona	21,123,580,000	1.3%
36	Arkansas	6,856,920,000	0.4%
2	California	174,128,620,000	10.7%
32	Colorado	8,367,660,000	0.5%
25	Connecticut	15,941,190,000	1.0%
38	Delaware	5,292,470,000	0.3%
7	Florida	58,637,060,000	3.6%
11	Georgia	39,365,290,000	2.4%
50	Hawaii	1,452,110,000	0.1%
41	Idaho	5,135,520,000	0.3%
5	Illinois	68,182,150,000	4.2%
13	Indiana	35,452,470,000	2.2%
26	Iowa	15,100,590,000	0.9%
30	Kansas	12,003,560,000	0.7%
17	Kentucky	27,541,230,000	1.7%
6	Louisiana	65,085,100,000	4.0%
45	Maine	2,751,870,000	0.2%
29	Maryland	12,241,250,000	0.8%
18	Massachusetts	27,363,930,000	1.7%
8	Michigan	55,751,140,000	3.4%
20	Minnesota	21,371,630,000	1.3%
31	Mississippi	11,414,180,000	0.7%
27	Missouri	14,141,190,000	0.9%
49	Montana	1,529,390,000	0.1%
33	Nebraska	7,863,220,000	0.5%
34	Nevada	7,701,390,000	0.5%
42	New Hampshire	4,424,340,000	0.3%
12	New Jersey	36,836,020,000	2.3%
43	New Mexico	3,788,920,000	0.2%
4	New York	86,006,570,000	5.3%
15	North Carolina	31,290,510,000	1.9%
39	North Dakota	5,289,470,000	0.3%
9	Ohio	52,129,530,000	3.2%
37	Oklahoma	6,299,740,000	0.4%
22	Oregon	20,919,800,000	1.3%
10	Pennsylvania	40,226,860,000	2.5%
46	Rhode Island	2,393,840,000	0.1%
16	South Carolina	29,703,980,000	1.8%
48	South Dakota	1,590,080,000	0.1%
14	Tennessee	32,956,890,000	2.0%
1	Texas	289,023,270,000	17.8%
28	Utah	12,265,690,000	0.8%
44	Vermont	3,642,580,000	0.2%
24	Virginia	19,194,380,000	1.2%
3	Washington	90,645,900,000	5.6%
35	West Virginia	7,496,040,000	0.5%
19	Wisconsin	23,432,550,000	1.4%
47	Wyoming	1,757,150,000	0.1%

RANK ORDER

RANK	STATE	EXPORTS	% of USA
1	Texas	$289,023,270,000	17.8%
2	California	174,128,620,000	10.7%
3	Washington	90,645,900,000	5.6%
4	New York	86,006,570,000	5.3%
5	Illinois	68,182,150,000	4.2%
6	Louisiana	65,085,100,000	4.0%
7	Florida	58,637,060,000	3.6%
8	Michigan	55,751,140,000	3.4%
9	Ohio	52,129,530,000	3.2%
10	Pennsylvania	40,226,860,000	2.5%
11	Georgia	39,365,290,000	2.4%
12	New Jersey	36,836,020,000	2.3%
13	Indiana	35,452,470,000	2.2%
14	Tennessee	32,956,890,000	2.0%
15	North Carolina	31,290,510,000	1.9%
16	South Carolina	29,703,980,000	1.8%
17	Kentucky	27,541,230,000	1.7%
18	Massachusetts	27,363,930,000	1.7%
19	Wisconsin	23,432,550,000	1.4%
20	Minnesota	21,371,630,000	1.3%
21	Arizona	21,123,580,000	1.3%
22	Oregon	20,919,800,000	1.3%
23	Alabama	19,517,560,000	1.2%
24	Virginia	19,194,380,000	1.2%
25	Connecticut	15,941,190,000	1.0%
26	Iowa	15,100,590,000	0.9%
27	Missouri	14,141,190,000	0.9%
28	Utah	12,265,690,000	0.8%
29	Maryland	12,241,250,000	0.8%
30	Kansas	12,003,560,000	0.7%
31	Mississippi	11,414,180,000	0.7%
32	Colorado	8,367,660,000	0.5%
33	Nebraska	7,863,220,000	0.5%
34	Nevada	7,701,390,000	0.5%
35	West Virginia	7,496,040,000	0.5%
36	Arkansas	6,856,920,000	0.4%
37	Oklahoma	6,299,740,000	0.4%
38	Delaware	5,292,470,000	0.3%
39	North Dakota	5,289,470,000	0.3%
40	Alaska	5,153,120,000	0.3%
41	Idaho	5,135,520,000	0.3%
42	New Hampshire	4,424,340,000	0.3%
43	New Mexico	3,788,920,000	0.2%
44	Vermont	3,642,580,000	0.2%
45	Maine	2,751,870,000	0.2%
46	Rhode Island	2,393,840,000	0.1%
47	Wyoming	1,757,150,000	0.1%
48	South Dakota	1,590,080,000	0.1%
49	Montana	1,529,390,000	0.1%
50	Hawaii	1,452,110,000	0.1%
	District of Columbia	935,630,000	0.1%

Source: U.S. Bureau of the Census
"State Trade Data" (http://www.census.gov/foreign-trade/statistics/state/)
*Based on the state from which the merchandise starts its journey to the port of export; that is, the data reflect the transportation origin of exports. Total includes exports from Puerto Rico, Virgin Islands, and exports with unidentified origin.

Per Capita State Exports in 2014

National Per Capita = $ 4,856*

ALPHA ORDER

RANK	STATE	PER CAPITA
27	Alabama	$4,027
5	Alaska	6,992
35	Arizona	3,139
40	Arkansas	2,311
17	California	4,489
48	Colorado	1,562
18	Connecticut	4,435
9	Delaware	5,655
37	Florida	2,946
29	Georgia	3,899
50	Hawaii	1,022
34	Idaho	3,141
12	Illinois	5,293
11	Indiana	5,373
15	Iowa	4,856
22	Kansas	4,136
6	Kentucky	6,241
1	Louisiana	14,000
43	Maine	2,069
44	Maryland	2,049
26	Massachusetts	4,051
10	Michigan	5,622
28	Minnesota	3,916
30	Mississippi	3,813
39	Missouri	2,332
49	Montana	1,495
20	Nebraska	4,176
38	Nevada	2,713
31	New Hampshire	3,332
23	New Jersey	4,121
46	New Mexico	1,817
19	New York	4,355
32	North Carolina	3,148
4	North Dakota	7,148
16	Ohio	4,495
47	Oklahoma	1,624
13	Oregon	5,268
33	Pennsylvania	3,144
42	Rhode Island	2,269
7	South Carolina	6,151
45	South Dakota	1,863
14	Tennessee	5,033
3	Texas	10,713
21	Utah	4,166
8	Vermont	5,812
41	Virginia	2,305
2	Washington	12,834
25	West Virginia	4,055
24	Wisconsin	4,069
36	Wyoming	3,007

RANK ORDER

RANK	STATE	PER CAPITA
1	Louisiana	$14,000
2	Washington	12,834
3	Texas	10,713
4	North Dakota	7,148
5	Alaska	6,992
6	Kentucky	6,241
7	South Carolina	6,151
8	Vermont	5,812
9	Delaware	5,655
10	Michigan	5,622
11	Indiana	5,373
12	Illinois	5,293
13	Oregon	5,268
14	Tennessee	5,033
15	Iowa	4,856
16	Ohio	4,495
17	California	4,489
18	Connecticut	4,435
19	New York	4,355
20	Nebraska	4,176
21	Utah	4,166
22	Kansas	4,136
23	New Jersey	4,121
24	Wisconsin	4,069
25	West Virginia	4,055
26	Massachusetts	4,051
27	Alabama	4,027
28	Minnesota	3,916
29	Georgia	3,899
30	Mississippi	3,813
31	New Hampshire	3,332
32	North Carolina	3,148
33	Pennsylvania	3,144
34	Idaho	3,141
35	Arizona	3,139
36	Wyoming	3,007
37	Florida	2,946
38	Nevada	2,713
39	Missouri	2,332
40	Arkansas	2,311
41	Virginia	2,305
42	Rhode Island	2,269
43	Maine	2,069
44	Maryland	2,049
45	South Dakota	1,863
46	New Mexico	1,817
47	Oklahoma	1,624
48	Colorado	1,562
49	Montana	1,495
50	Hawaii	1,022
	District of Columbia	1,418

Source: CQ Press using data from U.S. Bureau of the Census
   "State Trade Data" (http://www.census.gov/foreign-trade/statistics/state/)
*Based on the state from which the merchandise starts its journey to the port of export; that is, the data reflect the transportation origin of exports. Total includes exports from Puerto Rico, Virgin Islands, and exports with unidentified origin.

State Imports in 2014

National Total = $2,345,187,080,000*

ALPHA ORDER

RANK	STATE	IMPORTS	% of USA
24	Alabama	$22,210,870,000	0.9%
48	Alaska	2,007,720,000	0.1%
25	Arizona	19,714,910,000	0.8%
38	Arkansas	7,600,040,000	0.3%
1	California	403,451,560,000	17.2%
28	Colorado	14,255,430,000	0.6%
22	Connecticut	23,924,240,000	1.0%
34	Delaware	10,745,290,000	0.5%
9	Florida	71,785,100,000	3.1%
7	Georgia	83,743,100,000	3.6%
41	Hawaii	5,327,960,000	0.2%
40	Idaho	5,690,510,000	0.2%
3	Illinois	139,726,550,000	6.0%
15	Indiana	48,726,900,000	2.1%
35	Iowa	10,019,160,000	0.4%
31	Kansas	11,637,160,000	0.5%
16	Kentucky	39,174,610,000	1.7%
12	Louisiana	57,693,020,000	2.5%
44	Maine	3,871,680,000	0.2%
20	Maryland	30,154,450,000	1.3%
19	Massachusetts	34,179,640,000	1.5%
6	Michigan	122,533,870,000	5.2%
18	Minnesota	34,580,600,000	1.5%
27	Mississippi	17,240,250,000	0.7%
26	Missouri	18,264,510,000	0.8%
39	Montana	6,236,390,000	0.3%
43	Nebraska	4,050,700,000	0.2%
37	Nevada	7,852,420,000	0.3%
32	New Hampshire	11,220,900,000	0.5%
5	New Jersey	126,323,370,000	5.4%
47	New Mexico	2,236,310,000	0.1%
4	New York	133,759,000,000	5.7%
13	North Carolina	52,998,970,000	2.3%
45	North Dakota	3,830,740,000	0.2%
10	Ohio	70,105,720,000	3.0%
30	Oklahoma	13,508,950,000	0.6%
29	Oregon	13,806,430,000	0.6%
8	Pennsylvania	83,171,190,000	3.5%
36	Rhode Island	8,354,110,000	0.4%
17	South Carolina	37,719,090,000	1.6%
50	South Dakota	1,041,850,000	0.0%
11	Tennessee	69,755,530,000	3.0%
2	Texas	302,072,650,000	12.9%
33	Utah	11,103,180,000	0.5%
42	Vermont	4,737,200,000	0.2%
21	Virginia	24,279,960,000	1.0%
14	Washington	52,040,880,000	2.2%
46	West Virginia	3,811,820,000	0.2%
23	Wisconsin	23,515,180,000	1.0%
49	Wyoming	1,902,840,000	0.1%

RANK ORDER

RANK	STATE	IMPORTS	% of USA
1	California	$403,451,560,000	17.2%
2	Texas	302,072,650,000	12.9%
3	Illinois	139,726,550,000	6.0%
4	New York	133,759,000,000	5.7%
5	New Jersey	126,323,370,000	5.4%
6	Michigan	122,533,870,000	5.2%
7	Georgia	83,743,100,000	3.6%
8	Pennsylvania	83,171,190,000	3.5%
9	Florida	71,785,100,000	3.1%
10	Ohio	70,105,720,000	3.0%
11	Tennessee	69,755,530,000	3.0%
12	Louisiana	57,693,020,000	2.5%
13	North Carolina	52,998,970,000	2.3%
14	Washington	52,040,880,000	2.2%
15	Indiana	48,726,900,000	2.1%
16	Kentucky	39,174,610,000	1.7%
17	South Carolina	37,719,090,000	1.6%
18	Minnesota	34,580,600,000	1.5%
19	Massachusetts	34,179,640,000	1.5%
20	Maryland	30,154,450,000	1.3%
21	Virginia	24,279,960,000	1.0%
22	Connecticut	23,924,240,000	1.0%
23	Wisconsin	23,515,180,000	1.0%
24	Alabama	22,210,870,000	0.9%
25	Arizona	19,714,910,000	0.8%
26	Missouri	18,264,510,000	0.8%
27	Mississippi	17,240,250,000	0.7%
28	Colorado	14,255,430,000	0.6%
29	Oregon	13,806,430,000	0.6%
30	Oklahoma	13,508,950,000	0.6%
31	Kansas	11,637,160,000	0.5%
32	New Hampshire	11,220,900,000	0.5%
33	Utah	11,103,180,000	0.5%
34	Delaware	10,745,290,000	0.5%
35	Iowa	10,019,160,000	0.4%
36	Rhode Island	8,354,110,000	0.4%
37	Nevada	7,852,420,000	0.3%
38	Arkansas	7,600,040,000	0.3%
39	Montana	6,236,390,000	0.3%
40	Idaho	5,690,510,000	0.2%
41	Hawaii	5,327,960,000	0.2%
42	Vermont	4,737,200,000	0.2%
43	Nebraska	4,050,700,000	0.2%
44	Maine	3,871,680,000	0.2%
45	North Dakota	3,830,740,000	0.2%
46	West Virginia	3,811,820,000	0.2%
47	New Mexico	2,236,310,000	0.1%
48	Alaska	2,007,720,000	0.1%
49	Wyoming	1,902,840,000	0.1%
50	South Dakota	1,041,850,000	0.0%
	District of Columbia	1,116,650,000	0.0%

Source: U.S. Bureau of the Census
"State Trade Data" (http://www.census.gov/foreign-trade/statistics/state/)
*Based on where the merchandise is destined, as known at the time of entry summary filing. If the contents of the shipment are destined to more than one state, territory, or possession, or if the entry summary represents a consolidated shipment, the state of destination is that with the greatest aggregate value.

Per Capita State Imports in 2014

National Per Capita = $7,240*

ALPHA ORDER

RANK	STATE	PER CAPITA
28	Alabama	$4,583
44	Alaska	2,724
40	Arizona	2,930
46	Arkansas	2,562
8	California	10,400
45	Colorado	2,662
18	Connecticut	6,655
4	Delaware	11,480
33	Florida	3,606
11	Georgia	8,294
32	Hawaii	3,751
35	Idaho	3,481
6	Illinois	10,846
15	Indiana	7,385
38	Iowa	3,222
30	Kansas	4,009
9	Kentucky	8,878
2	Louisiana	12,410
42	Maine	2,910
27	Maryland	5,046
26	Massachusetts	5,060
3	Michigan	12,357
20	Minnesota	6,337
23	Mississippi	5,759
39	Missouri	3,012
21	Montana	6,095
47	Nebraska	2,151
43	Nevada	2,767
10	New Hampshire	8,449
1	New Jersey	14,132
50	New Mexico	1,072
17	New York	6,773
24	North Carolina	5,332
25	North Dakota	5,176
22	Ohio	6,045
34	Oklahoma	3,482
36	Oregon	3,477
19	Pennsylvania	6,501
12	Rhode Island	7,919
13	South Carolina	7,811
49	South Dakota	1,221
7	Tennessee	10,653
5	Texas	11,197
31	Utah	3,771
14	Vermont	7,558
41	Virginia	2,915
16	Washington	7,368
48	West Virginia	2,062
29	Wisconsin	4,083
37	Wyoming	3,257

RANK ORDER

RANK	STATE	PER CAPITA
1	New Jersey	$14,132
2	Louisiana	12,410
3	Michigan	12,357
4	Delaware	11,480
5	Texas	11,197
6	Illinois	10,846
7	Tennessee	10,653
8	California	10,400
9	Kentucky	8,878
10	New Hampshire	8,449
11	Georgia	8,294
12	Rhode Island	7,919
13	South Carolina	7,811
14	Vermont	7,558
15	Indiana	7,385
16	Washington	7,368
17	New York	6,773
18	Connecticut	6,655
19	Pennsylvania	6,501
20	Minnesota	6,337
21	Montana	6,095
22	Ohio	6,045
23	Mississippi	5,759
24	North Carolina	5,332
25	North Dakota	5,176
26	Massachusetts	5,060
27	Maryland	5,046
28	Alabama	4,583
29	Wisconsin	4,083
30	Kansas	4,009
31	Utah	3,771
32	Hawaii	3,751
33	Florida	3,606
34	Oklahoma	3,482
35	Idaho	3,481
36	Oregon	3,477
37	Wyoming	3,257
38	Iowa	3,222
39	Missouri	3,012
40	Arizona	2,930
41	Virginia	2,915
42	Maine	2,910
43	Nevada	2,767
44	Alaska	2,724
45	Colorado	2,662
46	Arkansas	2,562
47	Nebraska	2,151
48	West Virginia	2,062
49	South Dakota	1,221
50	New Mexico	1,072
	District of Columbia	1,692

Source: CQ Press using data from U.S. Bureau of the Census
 "State Trade Data" (http://www.census.gov/foreign-trade/statistics/state/)
*Based on where the merchandise is destined, as known at the time of entry summary filing. If the contents of the shipment are destined to more than one state, territory, or possession, or if the entry summary represents a consolidated shipment, the state of destination is that with the greatest aggregate value.

Personal Income in 2014

National Total = $14,683,147,000,000*

ALPHA ORDER

RANK	STATE	INCOME	% of USA
25	Alabama	$181,908,767,000	1.2%
47	Alaska	39,792,685,000	0.3%
20	Arizona	255,092,928,000	1.7%
33	Arkansas	112,076,107,000	0.8%
1	California	1,939,527,656,000	13.2%
18	Colorado	261,735,447,000	1.8%
23	Connecticut	233,293,455,000	1.6%
44	Delaware	43,391,982,000	0.3%
4	Florida	850,177,746,000	5.8%
12	Georgia	393,593,652,000	2.7%
40	Hawaii	65,347,949,000	0.4%
41	Idaho	60,040,758,000	0.4%
5	Illinois	613,671,539,000	4.2%
19	Indiana	261,092,396,000	1.8%
30	Iowa	139,624,515,000	1.0%
31	Kansas	130,364,095,000	0.9%
28	Kentucky	165,044,051,000	1.1%
24	Louisiana	195,426,167,000	1.3%
42	Maine	54,195,046,000	0.4%
15	Maryland	323,778,035,000	2.2%
11	Massachusetts	396,205,941,000	2.7%
10	Michigan	403,726,369,000	2.7%
16	Minnesota	267,389,243,000	1.8%
35	Mississippi	103,090,592,000	0.7%
22	Missouri	252,482,438,000	1.7%
46	Montana	40,843,525,000	0.3%
36	Nebraska	89,478,670,000	0.6%
32	Nevada	115,671,839,000	0.8%
38	New Hampshire	70,020,358,000	0.5%
7	New Jersey	515,020,298,000	3.5%
37	New Mexico	77,356,150,000	0.5%
3	New York	1,098,102,853,000	7.5%
13	North Carolina	389,512,571,000	2.7%
45	North Dakota	41,264,895,000	0.3%
8	Ohio	489,694,974,000	3.3%
27	Oklahoma	169,227,826,000	1.2%
29	Oregon	163,652,836,000	1.1%
6	Pennsylvania	609,679,210,000	4.2%
43	Rhode Island	51,026,876,000	0.3%
26	South Carolina	177,242,275,000	1.2%
48	South Dakota	38,631,202,000	0.3%
17	Tennessee	264,965,180,000	1.8%
2	Texas	1,231,084,591,000	8.4%
34	Utah	110,841,885,000	0.8%
50	Vermont	29,090,044,000	0.2%
9	Virginia	419,184,911,000	2.9%
14	Washington	350,321,729,000	2.4%
39	West Virginia	66,856,850,000	0.5%
21	Wisconsin	254,404,802,000	1.7%
49	Wyoming	31,885,231,000	0.2%

RANK ORDER

RANK	STATE	INCOME	% of USA
1	California	$1,939,527,656,000	13.2%
2	Texas	1,231,084,591,000	8.4%
3	New York	1,098,102,853,000	7.5%
4	Florida	850,177,746,000	5.8%
5	Illinois	613,671,539,000	4.2%
6	Pennsylvania	609,679,210,000	4.2%
7	New Jersey	515,020,298,000	3.5%
8	Ohio	489,694,974,000	3.3%
9	Virginia	419,184,911,000	2.9%
10	Michigan	403,726,369,000	2.7%
11	Massachusetts	396,205,941,000	2.7%
12	Georgia	393,593,652,000	2.7%
13	North Carolina	389,512,571,000	2.7%
14	Washington	350,321,729,000	2.4%
15	Maryland	323,778,035,000	2.2%
16	Minnesota	267,389,243,000	1.8%
17	Tennessee	264,965,180,000	1.8%
18	Colorado	261,735,447,000	1.8%
19	Indiana	261,092,396,000	1.8%
20	Arizona	255,092,928,000	1.7%
21	Wisconsin	254,404,802,000	1.7%
22	Missouri	252,482,438,000	1.7%
23	Connecticut	233,293,455,000	1.6%
24	Louisiana	195,426,167,000	1.3%
25	Alabama	181,908,767,000	1.2%
26	South Carolina	177,242,275,000	1.2%
27	Oklahoma	169,227,826,000	1.2%
28	Kentucky	165,044,051,000	1.1%
29	Oregon	163,652,836,000	1.1%
30	Iowa	139,624,515,000	1.0%
31	Kansas	130,364,095,000	0.9%
32	Nevada	115,671,839,000	0.8%
33	Arkansas	112,076,107,000	0.8%
34	Utah	110,841,885,000	0.8%
35	Mississippi	103,090,592,000	0.7%
36	Nebraska	89,478,670,000	0.6%
37	New Mexico	77,356,150,000	0.5%
38	New Hampshire	70,020,358,000	0.5%
39	West Virginia	66,856,850,000	0.5%
40	Hawaii	65,347,949,000	0.4%
41	Idaho	60,040,758,000	0.4%
42	Maine	54,195,046,000	0.4%
43	Rhode Island	51,026,876,000	0.3%
44	Delaware	43,391,982,000	0.3%
45	North Dakota	41,264,895,000	0.3%
46	Montana	40,843,525,000	0.3%
47	Alaska	39,792,685,000	0.3%
48	South Dakota	38,631,202,000	0.3%
49	Wyoming	31,885,231,000	0.2%
50	Vermont	29,090,044,000	0.2%
	District of Columbia	46,015,860,000	0.3%

Source: U.S. Department of Commerce, Bureau of Economic Analysis
"Annual State Personal Income" (http://www.bea.gov/iTable/index_regional.cfm)
*The national total shown here is the sum of the state estimates. It differs from the national income and product accounts (NIPA) estimate of personal income because it omits the earnings of federal civilian and military personnel stationed abroad and of U.S. residents employed abroad temporarily by private U.S. firms.

Change in Personal Income: 2013 to 2014

National Percent Change = 4.4% Increase*

ALPHA ORDER

RANK	STATE	PERCENT CHANGE
28	Alabama	4.0
7	Alaska	5.3
14	Arizona	4.7
34	Arkansas	3.7
11	California	4.9
1	Colorado	6.2
23	Connecticut	4.4
21	Delaware	4.6
9	Florida	5.0
14	Georgia	4.7
14	Hawaii	4.7
23	Idaho	4.4
47	Illinois	2.4
31	Indiana	3.8
44	Iowa	3.2
50	Kansas	1.6
26	Kentucky	4.3
43	Louisiana	3.4
45	Maine	3.1
31	Maryland	3.8
23	Massachusetts	4.4
27	Michigan	4.1
28	Minnesota	4.0
47	Mississippi	2.4
37	Missouri	3.6
39	Montana	3.5
39	Nebraska	3.5
5	Nevada	5.6
12	New Hampshire	4.8
14	New Jersey	4.7
8	New Mexico	5.1
28	New York	4.0
14	North Carolina	4.7
12	North Dakota	4.8
31	Ohio	3.8
14	Oklahoma	4.7
4	Oregon	5.7
37	Pennsylvania	3.6
9	Rhode Island	5.0
14	South Carolina	4.7
49	South Dakota	2.0
34	Tennessee	3.7
2	Texas	6.0
22	Utah	4.5
39	Vermont	3.5
39	Virginia	3.5
3	Washington	5.8
46	West Virginia	2.6
34	Wisconsin	3.7
5	Wyoming	5.6

RANK ORDER

RANK	STATE	PERCENT CHANGE
1	Colorado	6.2
2	Texas	6.0
3	Washington	5.8
4	Oregon	5.7
5	Nevada	5.6
5	Wyoming	5.6
7	Alaska	5.3
8	New Mexico	5.1
9	Florida	5.0
9	Rhode Island	5.0
11	California	4.9
12	New Hampshire	4.8
12	North Dakota	4.8
14	Arizona	4.7
14	Georgia	4.7
14	Hawaii	4.7
14	New Jersey	4.7
14	North Carolina	4.7
14	Oklahoma	4.7
14	South Carolina	4.7
21	Delaware	4.6
22	Utah	4.5
23	Connecticut	4.4
23	Idaho	4.4
23	Massachusetts	4.4
26	Kentucky	4.3
27	Michigan	4.1
28	Alabama	4.0
28	Minnesota	4.0
28	New York	4.0
31	Indiana	3.8
31	Maryland	3.8
31	Ohio	3.8
34	Arkansas	3.7
34	Tennessee	3.7
34	Wisconsin	3.7
37	Missouri	3.6
37	Pennsylvania	3.6
39	Montana	3.5
39	Nebraska	3.5
39	Vermont	3.5
39	Virginia	3.5
43	Louisiana	3.4
44	Iowa	3.2
45	Maine	3.1
46	West Virginia	2.6
47	Illinois	2.4
47	Mississippi	2.4
49	South Dakota	2.0
50	Kansas	1.6
	District of Columbia	3.3

Source: U.S. Department of Commerce, Bureau of Economic Analysis
"Annual State Personal Income" (http://www.bea.gov/iTable/index_regional.cfm)
*Based on revised 2013 figures.

Per Capita Personal Income in 2014

National Per Capita = $46,049*

ALPHA ORDER

RANK	STATE	PER CAPITA
44	Alabama	$37,512
8	Alaska	54,012
41	Arizona	37,895
42	Arkansas	37,782
11	California	49,985
14	Colorado	48,869
1	Connecticut	64,864
20	Delaware	46,378
28	Florida	42,737
40	Georgia	38,980
21	Hawaii	46,034
47	Idaho	36,734
17	Illinois	47,643
38	Indiana	39,578
24	Iowa	44,937
25	Kansas	44,891
45	Kentucky	37,396
30	Louisiana	42,030
33	Maine	40,745
7	Maryland	54,176
2	Massachusetts	58,737
35	Michigan	40,740
13	Minnesota	48,998
50	Mississippi	34,431
31	Missouri	41,639
37	Montana	39,903
18	Nebraska	47,557
34	Nevada	40,742
9	New Hampshire	52,773
3	New Jersey	57,620
46	New Mexico	37,091
5	New York	55,611
39	North Carolina	39,171
4	North Dakota	55,802
29	Ohio	42,236
27	Oklahoma	43,637
32	Oregon	41,220
16	Pennsylvania	47,679
15	Rhode Island	48,359
48	South Carolina	36,677
23	South Dakota	45,279
36	Tennessee	40,457
22	Texas	45,669
43	Utah	37,664
19	Vermont	46,428
10	Virginia	50,345
12	Washington	49,610
49	West Virginia	36,132
26	Wisconsin	44,186
6	Wyoming	54,584

RANK ORDER

RANK	STATE	PER CAPITA
1	Connecticut	$64,864
2	Massachusetts	58,737
3	New Jersey	57,620
4	North Dakota	55,802
5	New York	55,611
6	Wyoming	54,584
7	Maryland	54,176
8	Alaska	54,012
9	New Hampshire	52,773
10	Virginia	50,345
11	California	49,985
12	Washington	49,610
13	Minnesota	48,998
14	Colorado	48,869
15	Rhode Island	48,359
16	Pennsylvania	47,679
17	Illinois	47,643
18	Nebraska	47,557
19	Vermont	46,428
20	Delaware	46,378
21	Hawaii	46,034
22	Texas	45,669
23	South Dakota	45,279
24	Iowa	44,937
25	Kansas	44,891
26	Wisconsin	44,186
27	Oklahoma	43,637
28	Florida	42,737
29	Ohio	42,236
30	Louisiana	42,030
31	Missouri	41,639
32	Oregon	41,220
33	Maine	40,745
34	Nevada	40,742
35	Michigan	40,740
36	Tennessee	40,457
37	Montana	39,903
38	Indiana	39,578
39	North Carolina	39,171
40	Georgia	38,980
41	Arizona	37,895
42	Arkansas	37,782
43	Utah	37,664
44	Alabama	37,512
45	Kentucky	37,396
46	New Mexico	37,091
47	Idaho	36,734
48	South Carolina	36,677
49	West Virginia	36,132
50	Mississippi	34,431
	District of Columbia	69,838

Source: U.S. Department of Commerce, Bureau of Economic Analysis
"Annual State Personal Income" (http://www.bea.gov/iTable/index_regional.cfm)
*The national figure is based on the sum of the state estimates. It differs from the national income and product accounts (NIPA) estimate of personal income because it omits the earnings of federal civilian and military personnel stationed abroad and of U.S. residents employed abroad temporarily by private U.S. firms.

Change in Per Capita Personal Income: 2013 to 2014

National Percent Change = 3.6% Increase*

ALPHA ORDER

RANK	STATE	PERCENT CHANGE
19	Alabama	3.7
1	Alaska	5.4
34	Arizona	3.2
28	Arkansas	3.4
14	California	3.9
6	Colorado	4.5
8	Connecticut	4.4
25	Delaware	3.5
25	Florida	3.5
19	Georgia	3.7
14	Hawaii	3.9
35	Idaho	3.1
47	Illinois	2.5
28	Indiana	3.4
44	Iowa	2.7
49	Kansas	1.3
12	Kentucky	4.0
38	Louisiana	3.0
38	Maine	3.0
35	Maryland	3.1
14	Massachusetts	3.9
14	Michigan	3.9
32	Minnesota	3.3
48	Mississippi	2.4
32	Missouri	3.3
45	Montana	2.6
41	Nebraska	2.8
14	Nevada	3.9
8	New Hampshire	4.4
8	New Jersey	4.4
3	New Mexico	5.2
19	New York	3.7
19	North Carolina	3.7
45	North Dakota	2.6
23	Ohio	3.6
12	Oklahoma	4.0
5	Oregon	4.6
23	Pennsylvania	3.6
4	Rhode Island	4.8
28	South Carolina	3.4
50	South Dakota	1.1
40	Tennessee	2.9
11	Texas	4.3
35	Utah	3.1
25	Vermont	3.5
41	Virginia	2.8
6	Washington	4.5
41	West Virginia	2.8
28	Wisconsin	3.4
1	Wyoming	5.4

RANK ORDER

RANK	STATE	PERCENT CHANGE
1	Alaska	5.4
1	Wyoming	5.4
3	New Mexico	5.2
4	Rhode Island	4.8
5	Oregon	4.6
6	Colorado	4.5
6	Washington	4.5
8	Connecticut	4.4
8	New Hampshire	4.4
8	New Jersey	4.4
11	Texas	4.3
12	Kentucky	4.0
12	Oklahoma	4.0
14	California	3.9
14	Hawaii	3.9
14	Massachusetts	3.9
14	Michigan	3.9
14	Nevada	3.9
19	Alabama	3.7
19	Georgia	3.7
19	New York	3.7
19	North Carolina	3.7
23	Ohio	3.6
23	Pennsylvania	3.6
25	Delaware	3.5
25	Florida	3.5
25	Vermont	3.5
28	Arkansas	3.4
28	Indiana	3.4
28	South Carolina	3.4
28	Wisconsin	3.4
32	Minnesota	3.3
32	Missouri	3.3
34	Arizona	3.2
35	Idaho	3.1
35	Maryland	3.1
35	Utah	3.1
38	Louisiana	3.0
38	Maine	3.0
40	Tennessee	2.9
41	Nebraska	2.8
41	Virginia	2.8
41	West Virginia	2.8
44	Iowa	2.7
45	Montana	2.6
45	North Dakota	2.6
47	Illinois	2.5
48	Mississippi	2.4
49	Kansas	1.3
50	South Dakota	1.1
	District of Columbia	1.8

Source: U.S. Department of Commerce, Bureau of Economic Analysis
"Annual State Personal Income" (http://www.bea.gov/iTable/index_regional.cfm)
*Based on revised 2013 figures.

Disposable Personal Income in 2014

National Total = $12,904,591,000,000*

ALPHA ORDER

RANK	STATE	INCOME	% of USA
25	Alabama	$165,006,231,000	1.3%
47	Alaska	36,224,859,000	0.3%
19	Arizona	229,824,065,000	1.8%
33	Arkansas	101,260,141,000	0.8%
1	California	1,668,232,072,000	12.9%
20	Colorado	229,183,071,000	1.8%
23	Connecticut	194,902,674,000	1.5%
44	Delaware	38,594,635,000	0.3%
4	Florida	761,637,987,000	5.9%
11	Georgia	350,256,353,000	2.7%
40	Hawaii	58,640,307,000	0.5%
41	Idaho	54,179,635,000	0.4%
6	Illinois	532,411,849,000	4.1%
17	Indiana	233,486,127,000	1.8%
30	Iowa	125,021,007,000	1.0%
31	Kansas	116,191,322,000	0.9%
28	Kentucky	148,207,019,000	1.1%
24	Louisiana	176,526,975,000	1.4%
42	Maine	48,576,806,000	0.4%
15	Maryland	280,295,336,000	2.2%
13	Massachusetts	334,046,624,000	2.6%
10	Michigan	358,235,401,000	2.8%
18	Minnesota	231,113,016,000	1.8%
35	Mississippi	94,594,478,000	0.7%
21	Missouri	225,575,377,000	1.7%
45	Montana	36,341,355,000	0.3%
36	Nebraska	80,084,267,000	0.6%
32	Nevada	103,475,955,000	0.8%
38	New Hampshire	62,959,410,000	0.5%
7	New Jersey	444,987,688,000	3.4%
37	New Mexico	70,353,945,000	0.5%
3	New York	913,574,416,000	7.1%
12	North Carolina	347,313,157,000	2.7%
46	North Dakota	36,233,538,000	0.3%
8	Ohio	435,449,391,000	3.4%
27	Oklahoma	152,679,278,000	1.2%
29	Oregon	142,751,984,000	1.1%
5	Pennsylvania	538,783,439,000	4.2%
43	Rhode Island	45,277,513,000	0.4%
26	South Carolina	159,751,111,000	1.2%
48	South Dakota	35,105,349,000	0.3%
16	Tennessee	243,182,099,000	1.9%
2	Texas	1,104,922,033,000	8.6%
34	Utah	98,839,925,000	0.8%
50	Vermont	26,060,296,000	0.2%
9	Virginia	367,534,237,000	2.8%
14	Washington	313,619,742,000	2.4%
39	West Virginia	60,480,629,000	0.5%
22	Wisconsin	225,144,409,000	1.7%
49	Wyoming	28,193,376,000	0.2%

RANK ORDER

RANK	STATE	INCOME	% of USA
1	California	$1,668,232,072,000	12.9%
2	Texas	1,104,922,033,000	8.6%
3	New York	913,574,416,000	7.1%
4	Florida	761,637,987,000	5.9%
5	Pennsylvania	538,783,439,000	4.2%
6	Illinois	532,411,849,000	4.1%
7	New Jersey	444,987,688,000	3.4%
8	Ohio	435,449,391,000	3.4%
9	Virginia	367,534,237,000	2.8%
10	Michigan	358,235,401,000	2.8%
11	Georgia	350,256,353,000	2.7%
12	North Carolina	347,313,157,000	2.7%
13	Massachusetts	334,046,624,000	2.6%
14	Washington	313,619,742,000	2.4%
15	Maryland	280,295,336,000	2.2%
16	Tennessee	243,182,099,000	1.9%
17	Indiana	233,486,127,000	1.8%
18	Minnesota	231,113,016,000	1.8%
19	Arizona	229,824,065,000	1.8%
20	Colorado	229,183,071,000	1.8%
21	Missouri	225,575,377,000	1.7%
22	Wisconsin	225,144,409,000	1.7%
23	Connecticut	194,902,674,000	1.5%
24	Louisiana	176,526,975,000	1.4%
25	Alabama	165,006,231,000	1.3%
26	South Carolina	159,751,111,000	1.2%
27	Oklahoma	152,679,278,000	1.2%
28	Kentucky	148,207,019,000	1.1%
29	Oregon	142,751,984,000	1.1%
30	Iowa	125,021,007,000	1.0%
31	Kansas	116,191,322,000	0.9%
32	Nevada	103,475,955,000	0.8%
33	Arkansas	101,260,141,000	0.8%
34	Utah	98,839,925,000	0.8%
35	Mississippi	94,594,478,000	0.7%
36	Nebraska	80,084,267,000	0.6%
37	New Mexico	70,353,945,000	0.5%
38	New Hampshire	62,959,410,000	0.5%
39	West Virginia	60,480,629,000	0.5%
40	Hawaii	58,640,307,000	0.5%
41	Idaho	54,179,635,000	0.4%
42	Maine	48,576,806,000	0.4%
43	Rhode Island	45,277,513,000	0.4%
44	Delaware	38,594,635,000	0.3%
45	Montana	36,341,355,000	0.3%
46	North Dakota	36,233,538,000	0.3%
47	Alaska	36,224,859,000	0.3%
48	South Dakota	35,105,349,000	0.3%
49	Wyoming	28,193,376,000	0.2%
50	Vermont	26,060,296,000	0.2%
	District of Columbia	39,269,091,000	0.3%

Source: U.S. Department of Commerce, Bureau of Economic Analysis
"Annual State Personal Income" (http://www.bea.gov/iTable/index_regional.cfm)
*Disposable personal income is personal income less personal tax and nontax payments. It is the income available to persons for spending or saving.

Per Capita Disposable Personal Income in 2014

National Per Capita = $40,471*

ALPHA ORDER

RANK	STATE	PER CAPITA
43	Alabama	$34,026
4	Alaska	49,170
41	Arizona	34,142
42	Arkansas	34,136
12	California	42,993
14	Colorado	42,791
1	Connecticut	54,190
21	Delaware	41,251
28	Florida	38,286
40	Georgia	34,688
20	Hawaii	41,309
47	Idaho	33,148
19	Illinois	41,334
38	Indiana	35,394
24	Iowa	40,237
25	Kansas	40,010
46	Kentucky	33,581
29	Louisiana	37,965
33	Maine	36,521
8	Maryland	46,900
3	Massachusetts	49,522
35	Michigan	36,149
16	Minnesota	42,350
50	Mississippi	31,594
31	Missouri	37,202
37	Montana	35,504
15	Nebraska	42,564
34	Nevada	36,447
7	New Hampshire	47,452
2	New Jersey	49,785
44	New Mexico	33,734
9	New York	46,266
39	North Carolina	34,927
5	North Dakota	48,999
30	Ohio	37,558
26	Oklahoma	39,370
36	Oregon	35,956
17	Pennsylvania	42,135
13	Rhode Island	42,910
48	South Carolina	33,058
22	South Dakota	41,147
32	Tennessee	37,131
23	Texas	40,988
45	Utah	33,586
18	Vermont	41,593
11	Virginia	44,141
10	Washington	44,412
49	West Virginia	32,686
27	Wisconsin	39,104
6	Wyoming	48,264

RANK ORDER

RANK	STATE	PER CAPITA
1	Connecticut	$54,190
2	New Jersey	49,785
3	Massachusetts	49,522
4	Alaska	49,170
5	North Dakota	48,999
6	Wyoming	48,264
7	New Hampshire	47,452
8	Maryland	46,900
9	New York	46,266
10	Washington	44,412
11	Virginia	44,141
12	California	42,993
13	Rhode Island	42,910
14	Colorado	42,791
15	Nebraska	42,564
16	Minnesota	42,350
17	Pennsylvania	42,135
18	Vermont	41,593
19	Illinois	41,334
20	Hawaii	41,309
21	Delaware	41,251
22	South Dakota	41,147
23	Texas	40,988
24	Iowa	40,237
25	Kansas	40,010
26	Oklahoma	39,370
27	Wisconsin	39,104
28	Florida	38,286
29	Louisiana	37,965
30	Ohio	37,558
31	Missouri	37,202
32	Tennessee	37,131
33	Maine	36,521
34	Nevada	36,447
35	Michigan	36,149
36	Oregon	35,956
37	Montana	35,504
38	Indiana	35,394
39	North Carolina	34,927
40	Georgia	34,688
41	Arizona	34,142
42	Arkansas	34,136
43	Alabama	34,026
44	New Mexico	33,734
45	Utah	33,586
46	Kentucky	33,581
47	Idaho	33,148
48	South Carolina	33,058
49	West Virginia	32,686
50	Mississippi	31,594
	District of Columbia	59,599

Source: U.S. Department of Commerce, Bureau of Economic Analysis
"Annual State Personal Income" (http://www.bea.gov/iTable/index_regional.cfm)
*Disposable personal income is personal income less personal tax and nontax payments. It is the income available to persons for spending or saving.

Median Household Income in 2014

National Median = $53,657*

ALPHA ORDER

RANK	STATE	INCOME
48	Alabama	$42,278
5	Alaska	67,629
37	Arizona	49,254
44	Arkansas	44,922
14	California	60,487
11	Colorado	60,940
4	Connecticut	70,161
20	Delaware	57,522
42	Florida	46,140
36	Georgia	49,555
3	Hawaii	71,223
29	Idaho	53,438
25	Illinois	54,916
38	Indiana	48,060
19	Iowa	57,810
28	Kansas	53,444
46	Kentucky	42,786
47	Louisiana	42,406
32	Maine	51,710
1	Maryland	76,165
10	Massachusetts	63,151
31	Michigan	52,005
6	Minnesota	67,244
50	Mississippi	35,521
22	Missouri	56,630
33	Montana	51,102
21	Nebraska	56,870
34	Nevada	49,875
2	New Hampshire	73,397
8	New Jersey	65,243
41	New Mexico	46,686
26	New York	54,310
40	North Carolina	46,784
12	North Dakota	60,730
35	Ohio	49,644
39	Oklahoma	47,199
16	Oregon	58,875
24	Pennsylvania	55,173
17	Rhode Island	58,633
43	South Carolina	44,929
30	South Dakota	53,053
45	Tennessee	43,716
27	Texas	53,875
9	Utah	63,383
13	Vermont	60,708
7	Virginia	66,155
15	Washington	59,068
49	West Virginia	39,552
18	Wisconsin	58,080
23	Wyoming	55,690

RANK ORDER

RANK	STATE	INCOME
1	Maryland	$76,165
2	New Hampshire	73,397
3	Hawaii	71,223
4	Connecticut	70,161
5	Alaska	67,629
6	Minnesota	67,244
7	Virginia	66,155
8	New Jersey	65,243
9	Utah	63,383
10	Massachusetts	63,151
11	Colorado	60,940
12	North Dakota	60,730
13	Vermont	60,708
14	California	60,487
15	Washington	59,068
16	Oregon	58,875
17	Rhode Island	58,633
18	Wisconsin	58,080
19	Iowa	57,810
20	Delaware	57,522
21	Nebraska	56,870
22	Missouri	56,630
23	Wyoming	55,690
24	Pennsylvania	55,173
25	Illinois	54,916
26	New York	54,310
27	Texas	53,875
28	Kansas	53,444
29	Idaho	53,438
30	South Dakota	53,053
31	Michigan	52,005
32	Maine	51,710
33	Montana	51,102
34	Nevada	49,875
35	Ohio	49,644
36	Georgia	49,555
37	Arizona	49,254
38	Indiana	48,060
39	Oklahoma	47,199
40	North Carolina	46,784
41	New Mexico	46,686
42	Florida	46,140
43	South Carolina	44,929
44	Arkansas	44,922
45	Tennessee	43,716
46	Kentucky	42,786
47	Louisiana	42,406
48	Alabama	42,278
49	West Virginia	39,552
50	Mississippi	35,521
	District of Columbia	68,277

Source: U.S. Bureau of the Census
"Median Household Income by State" (http://www.census.gov/hhes/www/income/data/historical/household/index.html)
*This is a one-year figure. Census has discontinued three-year averages that had been used previously.

Regional Price Parities in 2013

National Index = 100.0*

ALPHA ORDER

RANK	STATE	RATIO
47	Alabama	87.7
8	Alaska	106.0
24	Arizona	97.1
49	Arkansas	87.5
4	California	112.3
12	Colorado	102.2
6	Connecticut	108.5
13	Delaware	101.4
16	Florida	98.8
32	Georgia	91.9
1	Hawaii	116.2
31	Idaho	92.8
14	Illinois	101.0
34	Indiana	91.4
41	Iowa	90.3
37	Kansas	90.8
45	Kentucky	89.1
36	Louisiana	91.2
21	Maine	97.7
5	Maryland	110.9
7	Massachusetts	107.3
29	Michigan	94.2
22	Minnesota	97.6
50	Mississippi	86.8
44	Missouri	89.2
28	Montana	94.4
39	Nebraska	90.5
19	Nevada	98.2
9	New Hampshire	105.9
3	New Jersey	114.5
27	New Mexico	95.0
2	New York	115.3
33	North Carolina	91.7
34	North Dakota	91.4
43	Ohio	89.6
42	Oklahoma	89.9
17	Oregon	98.7
18	Pennsylvania	98.6
20	Rhode Island	98.1
39	South Carolina	90.5
48	South Dakota	87.6
38	Tennessee	90.6
25	Texas	96.7
23	Utah	97.2
15	Vermont	100.2
11	Virginia	103.0
10	Washington	103.2
46	West Virginia	88.4
30	Wisconsin	92.9
26	Wyoming	95.8

RANK ORDER

RANK	STATE	RATIO
1	Hawaii	116.2
2	New York	115.3
3	New Jersey	114.5
4	California	112.3
5	Maryland	110.9
6	Connecticut	108.5
7	Massachusetts	107.3
8	Alaska	106.0
9	New Hampshire	105.9
10	Washington	103.2
11	Virginia	103.0
12	Colorado	102.2
13	Delaware	101.4
14	Illinois	101.0
15	Vermont	100.2
16	Florida	98.8
17	Oregon	98.7
18	Pennsylvania	98.6
19	Nevada	98.2
20	Rhode Island	98.1
21	Maine	97.7
22	Minnesota	97.6
23	Utah	97.2
24	Arizona	97.1
25	Texas	96.7
26	Wyoming	95.8
27	New Mexico	95.0
28	Montana	94.4
29	Michigan	94.2
30	Wisconsin	92.9
31	Idaho	92.8
32	Georgia	91.9
33	North Carolina	91.7
34	Indiana	91.4
34	North Dakota	91.4
36	Louisiana	91.2
37	Kansas	90.8
38	Tennessee	90.6
39	Nebraska	90.5
39	South Carolina	90.5
41	Iowa	90.3
42	Oklahoma	89.9
43	Ohio	89.6
44	Missouri	89.2
45	Kentucky	89.1
46	West Virginia	88.4
47	Alabama	87.7
48	South Dakota	87.6
49	Arkansas	87.5
50	Mississippi	86.8
	District of Columbia	117.7

Source: U.S. Department of Commerce, Bureau of Economic Analysis
"Annual State Personal Income" (http://www.bea.gov/iTable/index_regional.cfm)
*Regional Price Parities (RPPs) are regional price levels expressed as a percentage of the overall national price level for a given year. The price levels are determined by the average prices paid by consumers for the mix of goods and services consumed in each region. Taking the ratio of RPPs shows the difference in price levels across regions.

Real Personal Income in 2013

National Total = $13,184,554,113,000*

ALPHA ORDER

RANK	STATE	INCOME	% of USA
24	Alabama	$187,517,626,000	1.4%
48	Alaska	32,429,791,000	0.2%
21	Arizona	235,490,298,000	1.8%
32	Arkansas	115,766,494,000	0.9%
1	California	1,542,356,065,000	11.7%
22	Colorado	225,413,638,000	1.7%
25	Connecticut	187,450,675,000	1.4%
47	Delaware	38,142,645,000	0.3%
4	Florida	765,662,472,000	5.8%
10	Georgia	383,845,007,000	2.9%
42	Hawaii	50,920,320,000	0.4%
40	Idaho	58,585,580,000	0.4%
5	Illinois	558,625,515,000	4.2%
17	Indiana	258,873,242,000	2.0%
30	Iowa	142,921,809,000	1.1%
31	Kansas	132,020,530,000	1.0%
28	Kentucky	166,652,123,000	1.3%
23	Louisiana	194,936,628,000	1.5%
41	Maine	51,878,337,000	0.4%
15	Maryland	268,458,618,000	2.0%
13	Massachusetts	332,924,669,000	2.5%
11	Michigan	382,627,163,000	2.9%
20	Minnesota	246,002,342,000	1.9%
33	Mississippi	109,003,058,000	0.8%
18	Missouri	256,882,341,000	1.9%
45	Montana	39,484,369,000	0.3%
36	Nebraska	90,810,494,000	0.7%
34	Nevada	103,986,788,000	0.8%
39	New Hampshire	59,479,260,000	0.5%
8	New Jersey	401,477,360,000	3.0%
37	New Mexico	73,596,391,000	0.6%
3	New York	865,577,991,000	6.6%
9	North Carolina	387,428,663,000	2.9%
46	North Dakota	39,251,948,000	0.3%
7	Ohio	494,615,489,000	3.8%
27	Oklahoma	167,221,838,000	1.3%
29	Oregon	147,960,615,000	1.1%
6	Pennsylvania	558,402,021,000	4.2%
43	Rhode Island	46,971,426,000	0.4%
26	South Carolina	176,382,605,000	1.3%
44	South Dakota	41,389,656,000	0.3%
16	Tennessee	264,633,668,000	2.0%
2	Texas	1,118,895,839,000	8.5%
35	Utah	101,940,402,000	0.8%
50	Vermont	26,529,618,000	0.2%
12	Virginia	365,385,611,000	2.8%
14	Washington	300,529,266,000	2.3%
38	West Virginia	69,485,436,000	0.5%
19	Wisconsin	249,190,238,000	1.9%
49	Wyoming	29,954,660,000	0.2%

RANK ORDER

RANK	STATE	INCOME	% of USA
1	California	$1,542,356,065,000	11.7%
2	Texas	1,118,895,839,000	8.5%
3	New York	865,577,991,000	6.6%
4	Florida	765,662,472,000	5.8%
5	Illinois	558,625,515,000	4.2%
6	Pennsylvania	558,402,021,000	4.2%
7	Ohio	494,615,489,000	3.8%
8	New Jersey	401,477,360,000	3.0%
9	North Carolina	387,428,663,000	2.9%
10	Georgia	383,845,007,000	2.9%
11	Michigan	382,627,163,000	2.9%
12	Virginia	365,385,611,000	2.8%
13	Massachusetts	332,924,669,000	2.5%
14	Washington	300,529,266,000	2.3%
15	Maryland	268,458,618,000	2.0%
16	Tennessee	264,633,668,000	2.0%
17	Indiana	258,873,242,000	2.0%
18	Missouri	256,882,341,000	1.9%
19	Wisconsin	249,190,238,000	1.9%
20	Minnesota	246,002,342,000	1.9%
21	Arizona	235,490,298,000	1.8%
22	Colorado	225,413,638,000	1.7%
23	Louisiana	194,936,628,000	1.5%
24	Alabama	187,517,626,000	1.4%
25	Connecticut	187,450,675,000	1.4%
26	South Carolina	176,382,605,000	1.3%
27	Oklahoma	167,221,838,000	1.3%
28	Kentucky	166,652,123,000	1.3%
29	Oregon	147,960,615,000	1.1%
30	Iowa	142,921,809,000	1.1%
31	Kansas	132,020,530,000	1.0%
32	Arkansas	115,766,494,000	0.9%
33	Mississippi	109,003,058,000	0.8%
34	Nevada	103,986,788,000	0.8%
35	Utah	101,940,402,000	0.8%
36	Nebraska	90,810,494,000	0.7%
37	New Mexico	73,596,391,000	0.6%
38	West Virginia	69,485,436,000	0.5%
39	New Hampshire	59,479,260,000	0.5%
40	Idaho	58,585,580,000	0.4%
41	Maine	51,878,337,000	0.4%
42	Hawaii	50,920,320,000	0.4%
43	Rhode Island	46,971,426,000	0.4%
44	South Dakota	41,389,656,000	0.3%
45	Montana	39,484,369,000	0.3%
46	North Dakota	39,251,948,000	0.3%
47	Delaware	38,142,645,000	0.3%
48	Alaska	32,429,791,000	0.2%
49	Wyoming	29,954,660,000	0.2%
50	Vermont	26,529,618,000	0.2%
	District of Columbia	38,585,472,000	0.3%

Source: U.S. Department of Commerce, Bureau of Economic Analysis
"Annual State Personal Income" (http://www.bea.gov/iTable/index_regional.cfm)
*Real personal income is personal income at Regional Price Parities (RPPs) divided by the national Personal Consumption Expenditure price index (a measure of U.S. inflation). RPPs are regional price levels expressed as a percentage of the overall national price level for a given year. The price levels are determined by the average prices paid by consumers for the mix of goods and services consumed in each region. Taking the ratio of RPPs shows the difference in price levels across regions.

Percent Change in Real Personal Income: 2012 to 2013

National Percent Change = 0.8% Increase*

ALPHA ORDER

RANK	STATE	PERCENT CHANGE
18	Alabama	1.0
34	Alaska	0.2
9	Arizona	1.6
38	Arkansas	0.0
3	California	2.2
18	Colorado	1.0
35	Connecticut	0.1
8	Delaware	1.7
15	Florida	1.1
13	Georgia	1.2
5	Hawaii	2.0
1	Idaho	3.5
25	Illinois	0.7
33	Indiana	0.4
29	Iowa	0.6
15	Kansas	1.1
44	Kentucky	(0.2)
23	Louisiana	0.9
7	Maine	1.9
47	Maryland	(0.3)
41	Massachusetts	(0.1)
31	Michigan	0.5
44	Minnesota	(0.2)
41	Mississippi	(0.1)
31	Missouri	0.5
44	Montana	(0.2)
3	Nebraska	2.2
29	Nevada	0.6
25	New Hampshire	0.7
38	New Jersey	0.0
49	New Mexico	(0.6)
48	New York	(0.4)
35	North Carolina	0.1
50	North Dakota	(4.4)
25	Ohio	0.7
25	Oklahoma	0.7
18	Oregon	1.0
35	Pennsylvania	0.1
18	Rhode Island	1.0
9	South Carolina	1.6
5	South Dakota	2.0
18	Tennessee	1.0
12	Texas	1.3
2	Utah	2.3
9	Vermont	1.6
38	Virginia	0.0
13	Washington	1.2
41	West Virginia	(0.1)
15	Wisconsin	1.1
24	Wyoming	0.8

RANK ORDER

RANK	STATE	PERCENT CHANGE
1	Idaho	3.5
2	Utah	2.3
3	California	2.2
3	Nebraska	2.2
5	Hawaii	2.0
5	South Dakota	2.0
7	Maine	1.9
8	Delaware	1.7
9	Arizona	1.6
9	South Carolina	1.6
9	Vermont	1.6
12	Texas	1.3
13	Georgia	1.2
13	Washington	1.2
15	Florida	1.1
15	Kansas	1.1
15	Wisconsin	1.1
18	Alabama	1.0
18	Colorado	1.0
18	Oregon	1.0
18	Rhode Island	1.0
18	Tennessee	1.0
23	Louisiana	0.9
24	Wyoming	0.8
25	Illinois	0.7
25	New Hampshire	0.7
25	Ohio	0.7
25	Oklahoma	0.7
29	Iowa	0.6
29	Nevada	0.6
31	Michigan	0.5
31	Missouri	0.5
33	Indiana	0.4
34	Alaska	0.2
35	Connecticut	0.1
35	North Carolina	0.1
35	Pennsylvania	0.1
38	Arkansas	0.0
38	New Jersey	0.0
38	Virginia	0.0
41	Massachusetts	(0.1)
41	Mississippi	(0.1)
41	West Virginia	(0.1)
44	Kentucky	(0.2)
44	Minnesota	(0.2)
44	Montana	(0.2)
47	Maryland	(0.3)
48	New York	(0.4)
49	New Mexico	(0.6)
50	North Dakota	(4.4)
	District of Columbia	0.3

Source: U.S. Department of Commerce, Bureau of Economic Analysis
"Annual State Personal Income" (http://www.bea.gov/iTable/index_regional.cfm)

*Real personal income is personal income at Regional Price Parities (RPPs) divided by the national Personal Consumption Expenditure price index (a measure of U.S. inflation). RPPs are regional price levels expressed as a percentage of the overall national price level for a given year. The price levels are determined by the average prices paid by consumers for the mix of goods and services consumed in each region. Taking the ratio of RPPs shows the difference in price levels across regions.

Per Capita Real Personal Income in 2013

National Per Capita = $41,706*

ALPHA ORDER

RANK	STATE	PER CAPITA
37	Alabama	$38,794
15	Alaska	44,114
48	Arizona	35,537
34	Arkansas	39,119
30	California	40,236
22	Colorado	42,786
2	Connecticut	52,126
28	Delaware	41,202
33	Florida	39,159
39	Georgia	38,415
47	Hawaii	36,267
46	Idaho	36,340
20	Illinois	43,364
31	Indiana	39,397
7	Iowa	46,247
8	Kansas	45,619
40	Kentucky	37,916
27	Louisiana	42,144
35	Maine	39,056
10	Maryland	45,280
4	Massachusetts	49,744
38	Michigan	38,666
9	Minnesota	45,385
45	Mississippi	36,441
24	Missouri	42,501
36	Montana	38,895
6	Nebraska	48,600
43	Nevada	37,269
12	New Hampshire	44,942
11	New Jersey	45,113
49	New Mexico	35,293
16	New York	44,047
32	North Carolina	39,341
1	North Dakota	54,261
23	Ohio	42,747
18	Oklahoma	43,428
41	Oregon	37,648
17	Pennsylvania	43,715
13	Rhode Island	44,670
44	South Carolina	36,940
5	South Dakota	48,989
29	Tennessee	40,738
26	Texas	42,305
50	Utah	35,141
25	Vermont	42,337
14	Virginia	44,233
21	Washington	43,109
42	West Virginia	37,473
19	Wisconsin	43,392
3	Wyoming	51,410

RANK ORDER

RANK	STATE	PER CAPITA
1	North Dakota	$54,261
2	Connecticut	52,126
3	Wyoming	51,410
4	Massachusetts	49,744
5	South Dakota	48,989
6	Nebraska	48,600
7	Iowa	46,247
8	Kansas	45,619
9	Minnesota	45,385
10	Maryland	45,280
11	New Jersey	45,113
12	New Hampshire	44,942
13	Rhode Island	44,670
14	Virginia	44,233
15	Alaska	44,114
16	New York	44,047
17	Pennsylvania	43,715
18	Oklahoma	43,428
19	Wisconsin	43,392
20	Illinois	43,364
21	Washington	43,109
22	Colorado	42,786
23	Ohio	42,747
24	Missouri	42,501
25	Vermont	42,337
26	Texas	42,305
27	Louisiana	42,144
28	Delaware	41,202
29	Tennessee	40,738
30	California	40,236
31	Indiana	39,397
32	North Carolina	39,341
33	Florida	39,159
34	Arkansas	39,119
35	Maine	39,056
36	Montana	38,895
37	Alabama	38,794
38	Michigan	38,666
39	Georgia	38,415
40	Kentucky	37,916
41	Oregon	37,648
42	West Virginia	37,473
43	Nevada	37,269
44	South Carolina	36,940
45	Mississippi	36,441
46	Idaho	36,340
47	Hawaii	36,267
48	Arizona	35,537
49	New Mexico	35,293
50	Utah	35,141
	District of Columbia	59,688

Source: U.S. Department of Commerce, Bureau of Economic Analysis
"Annual State Personal Income" (http://www.bea.gov/iTable/index_regional.cfm)
*Real personal income is personal income at Regional Price Parities (RPPs) divided by the national Personal Consumption Expenditure price index (a measure of U.S. inflation). RPPs are regional price levels expressed as a percentage of the overall national price level for a given year. The price levels are determined by the average prices paid by consumers for the mix of goods and services consumed in each region. Taking the ratio of RPPs shows the difference in price levels across regions.

Percent Change in Per Capita Real Personal Income: 2012 to 2013

National Percent Change = 0.1% Increase*

ALPHA ORDER

RANK	STATE	PERCENT CHANGE
11	Alabama	0.7
38	Alaska	(0.5)
18	Arizona	0.4
34	Arkansas	(0.3)
5	California	1.3
38	Colorado	(0.5)
27	Connecticut	0.0
7	Delaware	0.8
30	Florida	(0.1)
18	Georgia	0.4
6	Hawaii	0.9
1	Idaho	2.4
14	Illinois	0.6
30	Indiana	(0.1)
25	Iowa	0.1
7	Kansas	0.8
40	Kentucky	(0.6)
18	Louisiana	0.4
2	Maine	1.9
48	Maryland	(1.0)
44	Massachusetts	(0.8)
18	Michigan	0.4
45	Minnesota	(0.9)
34	Mississippi	(0.3)
23	Missouri	0.2
49	Montana	(1.2)
4	Nebraska	1.4
41	Nevada	(0.7)
14	New Hampshire	0.6
34	New Jersey	(0.3)
41	New Mexico	(0.7)
41	New York	(0.7)
45	North Carolina	(0.9)
50	North Dakota	(7.3)
14	Ohio	0.6
32	Oklahoma	(0.2)
23	Oregon	0.2
27	Pennsylvania	0.0
7	Rhode Island	0.8
17	South Carolina	0.5
11	South Dakota	0.7
22	Tennessee	0.3
32	Texas	(0.2)
11	Utah	0.7
3	Vermont	1.5
45	Virginia	(0.9)
25	Washington	0.1
27	West Virginia	0.0
7	Wisconsin	0.8
34	Wyoming	(0.3)

RANK ORDER

RANK	STATE	PERCENT CHANGE
1	Idaho	2.4
2	Maine	1.9
3	Vermont	1.5
4	Nebraska	1.4
5	California	1.3
6	Hawaii	0.9
7	Delaware	0.8
7	Kansas	0.8
7	Rhode Island	0.8
7	Wisconsin	0.8
11	Alabama	0.7
11	South Dakota	0.7
11	Utah	0.7
14	Illinois	0.6
14	New Hampshire	0.6
14	Ohio	0.6
17	South Carolina	0.5
18	Arizona	0.4
18	Georgia	0.4
18	Louisiana	0.4
18	Michigan	0.4
22	Tennessee	0.3
23	Missouri	0.2
23	Oregon	0.2
25	Iowa	0.1
25	Washington	0.1
27	Connecticut	0.0
27	Pennsylvania	0.0
27	West Virginia	0.0
30	Florida	(0.1)
30	Indiana	(0.1)
32	Oklahoma	(0.2)
32	Texas	(0.2)
34	Arkansas	(0.3)
34	Mississippi	(0.3)
34	New Jersey	(0.3)
34	Wyoming	(0.3)
38	Alaska	(0.5)
38	Colorado	(0.5)
40	Kentucky	(0.6)
41	Nevada	(0.7)
41	New Mexico	(0.7)
41	New York	(0.7)
44	Massachusetts	(0.8)
45	Minnesota	(0.9)
45	North Carolina	(0.9)
45	Virginia	(0.9)
48	Maryland	(1.0)
49	Montana	(1.2)
50	North Dakota	(7.3)
	District of Columbia	(1.8)

Source: U.S. Department of Commerce, Bureau of Economic Analysis
"Annual State Personal Income" (http://www.bea.gov/iTable/index_regional.cfm)
*Real personal income is personal income at Regional Price Parities (RPPs) divided by the national Personal Consumption Expenditure price index (a measure of U.S. inflation). RPPs are regional price levels expressed as a percentage of the overall national price level for a given year. The price levels are determined by the average prices paid by consumers for the mix of goods and services consumed in each region. Taking the ratio of RPPs shows the difference in price levels across regions.

Personal Consumption Expenditures in 2014

National Total = $11,860,250,000,000*

ALPHA ORDER

RANK	STATE	EXPENDITURES	% of USA
26	Alabama	$147,879,000,000	1.2%
47	Alaska	34,059,000,000	0.3%
16	Arizona	228,423,000,000	1.9%
35	Arkansas	87,300,000,000	0.7%
1	California	1,482,477,000,000	12.5%
21	Colorado	210,037,000,000	1.8%
23	Connecticut	164,885,000,000	1.4%
45	Delaware	39,016,000,000	0.3%
4	Florida	724,066,000,000	6.1%
10	Georgia	331,348,000,000	2.8%
40	Hawaii	58,232,000,000	0.5%
42	Idaho	53,206,000,000	0.4%
5	Illinois	496,313,000,000	4.2%
18	Indiana	222,696,000,000	1.9%
30	Iowa	109,551,000,000	0.9%
31	Kansas	100,659,000,000	0.8%
28	Kentucky	140,240,000,000	1.2%
25	Louisiana	153,342,000,000	1.3%
41	Maine	54,730,000,000	0.5%
15	Maryland	247,780,000,000	2.1%
11	Massachusetts	323,916,000,000	2.7%
9	Michigan	358,916,000,000	3.0%
17	Minnesota	222,922,000,000	1.9%
34	Mississippi	87,985,000,000	0.7%
19	Missouri	212,542,000,000	1.8%
44	Montana	39,426,000,000	0.3%
37	Nebraska	69,346,000,000	0.6%
32	Nevada	97,860,000,000	0.8%
38	New Hampshire	61,874,000,000	0.5%
8	New Jersey	406,652,000,000	3.4%
36	New Mexico	70,790,000,000	0.6%
3	New York	863,447,000,000	7.3%
13	North Carolina	318,760,000,000	2.7%
46	North Dakota	35,302,000,000	0.3%
7	Ohio	409,653,000,000	3.5%
29	Oklahoma	125,131,000,000	1.1%
27	Oregon	145,973,000,000	1.2%
6	Pennsylvania	493,704,000,000	4.2%
43	Rhode Island	41,969,000,000	0.4%
24	South Carolina	155,991,000,000	1.3%
48	South Dakota	31,481,000,000	0.3%
20	Tennessee	211,871,000,000	1.8%
2	Texas	929,576,000,000	7.8%
33	Utah	95,369,000,000	0.8%
49	Vermont	28,050,000,000	0.2%
12	Virginia	323,164,000,000	2.7%
14	Washington	284,456,000,000	2.4%
39	West Virginia	59,785,000,000	0.5%
22	Wisconsin	208,940,000,000	1.8%
50	Wyoming	22,826,000,000	0.2%

RANK ORDER

RANK	STATE	EXPENDITURES	% of USA
1	California	$1,482,477,000,000	12.5%
2	Texas	929,576,000,000	7.8%
3	New York	863,447,000,000	7.3%
4	Florida	724,066,000,000	6.1%
5	Illinois	496,313,000,000	4.2%
6	Pennsylvania	493,704,000,000	4.2%
7	Ohio	409,653,000,000	3.5%
8	New Jersey	406,652,000,000	3.4%
9	Michigan	358,916,000,000	3.0%
10	Georgia	331,348,000,000	2.8%
11	Massachusetts	323,916,000,000	2.7%
12	Virginia	323,164,000,000	2.7%
13	North Carolina	318,760,000,000	2.7%
14	Washington	284,456,000,000	2.4%
15	Maryland	247,780,000,000	2.1%
16	Arizona	228,423,000,000	1.9%
17	Minnesota	222,922,000,000	1.9%
18	Indiana	222,696,000,000	1.9%
19	Missouri	212,542,000,000	1.8%
20	Tennessee	211,871,000,000	1.8%
21	Colorado	210,037,000,000	1.8%
22	Wisconsin	208,940,000,000	1.8%
23	Connecticut	164,885,000,000	1.4%
24	South Carolina	155,991,000,000	1.3%
25	Louisiana	153,342,000,000	1.3%
26	Alabama	147,879,000,000	1.2%
27	Oregon	145,973,000,000	1.2%
28	Kentucky	140,240,000,000	1.2%
29	Oklahoma	125,131,000,000	1.1%
30	Iowa	109,551,000,000	0.9%
31	Kansas	100,659,000,000	0.8%
32	Nevada	97,860,000,000	0.8%
33	Utah	95,369,000,000	0.8%
34	Mississippi	87,985,000,000	0.7%
35	Arkansas	87,300,000,000	0.7%
36	New Mexico	70,790,000,000	0.6%
37	Nebraska	69,346,000,000	0.6%
38	New Hampshire	61,874,000,000	0.5%
39	West Virginia	59,785,000,000	0.5%
40	Hawaii	58,232,000,000	0.5%
41	Maine	54,730,000,000	0.5%
42	Idaho	53,206,000,000	0.4%
43	Rhode Island	41,969,000,000	0.4%
44	Montana	39,426,000,000	0.3%
45	Delaware	39,016,000,000	0.3%
46	North Dakota	35,302,000,000	0.3%
47	Alaska	34,059,000,000	0.3%
48	South Dakota	31,481,000,000	0.3%
49	Vermont	28,050,000,000	0.2%
50	Wyoming	22,826,000,000	0.2%
	District of Columbia	36,332,000,000	0.3%

Source: U.S. Department of Commerce, Bureau of Economic Analysis
"Personal Consumption Expenditures by State" (http://www.bea.gov/iTable/index_regional.cfm)
*PCE by state is the state counterpart of the Nation's personal consumption expenditures (PCE). PCE represents the goods and services purchased by or on behalf of households, plus the purchases of nonprofit institutions serving households. For each state and for the District of Columbia, personal consumption expenditures are those expenditures made by or on behalf of residents. These expenditures include expenditures on activities outside of the state.

Per Capita Personal Consumption Expenditures in 2014

National Per Capita = $37,196*

ALPHA ORDER

RANK	STATE	PER CAPITA
48	Alabama	$30,494
4	Alaska	46,229
36	Arizona	33,934
49	Arkansas	29,430
22	California	38,206
16	Colorado	39,216
5	Connecticut	45,844
9	Delaware	41,701
26	Florida	36,397
39	Georgia	32,815
12	Hawaii	41,021
40	Idaho	32,553
20	Illinois	38,532
37	Indiana	33,758
30	Iowa	35,258
32	Kansas	34,662
47	Kentucky	31,775
38	Louisiana	32,979
11	Maine	41,148
10	Maryland	41,460
1	Massachusetts	48,020
28	Michigan	36,218
13	Minnesota	40,849
50	Mississippi	29,386
31	Missouri	35,052
21	Montana	38,518
24	Nebraska	36,857
34	Nevada	34,469
3	New Hampshire	46,633
6	New Jersey	45,496
35	New Mexico	33,943
8	New York	43,727
46	North Carolina	32,056
2	North Dakota	47,739
29	Ohio	35,333
45	Oklahoma	32,266
25	Oregon	36,767
19	Pennsylvania	38,609
15	Rhode Island	39,774
44	South Carolina	32,280
23	South Dakota	36,899
42	Tennessee	32,350
33	Texas	34,484
41	Utah	32,406
7	Vermont	44,768
18	Virginia	38,813
14	Washington	40,282
43	West Virginia	32,311
27	Wisconsin	36,290
17	Wyoming	39,076

RANK ORDER

RANK	STATE	PER CAPITA
1	Massachusetts	$48,020
2	North Dakota	47,739
3	New Hampshire	46,633
4	Alaska	46,229
5	Connecticut	45,844
6	New Jersey	45,496
7	Vermont	44,768
8	New York	43,727
9	Delaware	41,701
10	Maryland	41,460
11	Maine	41,148
12	Hawaii	41,021
13	Minnesota	40,849
14	Washington	40,282
15	Rhode Island	39,774
16	Colorado	39,216
17	Wyoming	39,076
18	Virginia	38,813
19	Pennsylvania	38,609
20	Illinois	38,532
21	Montana	38,518
22	California	38,206
23	South Dakota	36,899
24	Nebraska	36,857
25	Oregon	36,767
26	Florida	36,397
27	Wisconsin	36,290
28	Michigan	36,218
29	Ohio	35,333
30	Iowa	35,258
31	Missouri	35,052
32	Kansas	34,662
33	Texas	34,484
34	Nevada	34,469
35	New Mexico	33,943
36	Arizona	33,934
37	Indiana	33,758
38	Louisiana	32,979
39	Georgia	32,815
40	Idaho	32,553
41	Utah	32,406
42	Tennessee	32,350
43	West Virginia	32,311
44	South Carolina	32,280
45	Oklahoma	32,266
46	North Carolina	32,056
47	Kentucky	31,775
48	Alabama	30,494
49	Arkansas	29,430
50	Mississippi	29,386
	District of Columbia	55,141

Source: U.S. Department of Commerce, Bureau of Economic Analysis
"Personal Consumption Expenditures by State" (http://www.bea.gov/iTable/index_regional.cfm)
*PCE by state is the state counterpart of the Nation's personal consumption expenditures (PCE). PCE represents the goods and services purchased by or on behalf of households, plus the purchases of nonprofit institutions serving households. For each state and for the District of Columbia, personal consumption expenditures are those expenditures made by or on behalf of residents. These expenditures include expenditures on activities outside of the state.

Percent Change in Personal Consumption Expenditures: 2013 to 2014

National Percent Change = 4.2% Increase*

ALPHA ORDER

RANK	STATE	PERCENT CHANGE
46	Alabama	2.8
39	Alaska	3.3
10	Arizona	4.5
46	Arkansas	2.8
13	California	4.4
2	Colorado	5.7
25	Connecticut	3.7
15	Delaware	4.3
7	Florida	4.9
13	Georgia	4.4
10	Hawaii	4.5
15	Idaho	4.3
29	Illinois	3.6
43	Indiana	3.1
25	Iowa	3.7
29	Kansas	3.6
48	Kentucky	2.4
39	Louisiana	3.3
33	Maine	3.5
33	Maryland	3.5
10	Massachusetts	4.5
22	Michigan	3.9
20	Minnesota	4.0
45	Mississippi	2.9
49	Missouri	2.3
8	Montana	4.8
25	Nebraska	3.7
19	Nevada	4.1
18	New Hampshire	4.2
29	New Jersey	3.6
33	New Mexico	3.5
6	New York	5.0
15	North Carolina	4.3
1	North Dakota	7.4
36	Ohio	3.4
25	Oklahoma	3.7
4	Oregon	5.3
43	Pennsylvania	3.1
36	Rhode Island	3.4
36	South Carolina	3.4
22	South Dakota	3.9
29	Tennessee	3.6
2	Texas	5.7
4	Utah	5.3
22	Vermont	3.9
39	Virginia	3.3
8	Washington	4.8
50	West Virginia	2.1
39	Wisconsin	3.3
20	Wyoming	4.0

RANK ORDER

RANK	STATE	PERCENT CHANGE
1	North Dakota	7.4
2	Colorado	5.7
2	Texas	5.7
4	Oregon	5.3
4	Utah	5.3
6	New York	5.0
7	Florida	4.9
8	Montana	4.8
8	Washington	4.8
10	Arizona	4.5
10	Hawaii	4.5
10	Massachusetts	4.5
13	California	4.4
13	Georgia	4.4
15	Delaware	4.3
15	Idaho	4.3
15	North Carolina	4.3
18	New Hampshire	4.2
19	Nevada	4.1
20	Minnesota	4.0
20	Wyoming	4.0
22	Michigan	3.9
22	South Dakota	3.9
22	Vermont	3.9
25	Connecticut	3.7
25	Iowa	3.7
25	Nebraska	3.7
25	Oklahoma	3.7
29	Illinois	3.6
29	Kansas	3.6
29	New Jersey	3.6
29	Tennessee	3.6
33	Maine	3.5
33	Maryland	3.5
33	New Mexico	3.5
36	Ohio	3.4
36	Rhode Island	3.4
36	South Carolina	3.4
39	Alaska	3.3
39	Louisiana	3.3
39	Virginia	3.3
39	Wisconsin	3.3
43	Indiana	3.1
43	Pennsylvania	3.1
45	Mississippi	2.9
46	Alabama	2.8
46	Arkansas	2.8
48	Kentucky	2.4
49	Missouri	2.3
50	West Virginia	2.1
	District of Columbia	5.1

Source: U.S. Department of Commerce, Bureau of Economic Analysis
"Personal Consumption Expenditures by State" (http://www.bea.gov/iTable/index_regional.cfm)
*PCE by state is the state counterpart of the Nation's personal consumption expenditures (PCE). PCE represents the goods and services purchased by or on behalf of households, plus the purchases of nonprofit institutions serving households. For each state and for the District of Columbia, personal consumption expenditures are those expenditures made by or on behalf of residents. These expenditures include expenditures on activities outside of the state.

Percent Change in Per Capita Personal Consumption Expenditures: 2013 to 2014
National Percent Change = 3.4% Increase*

ALPHA ORDER

RANK	STATE	PERCENT CHANGE
45	Alabama	2.4
23	Alaska	3.3
33	Arizona	3.0
43	Arkansas	2.6
18	California	3.4
4	Colorado	4.0
11	Connecticut	3.8
27	Delaware	3.2
18	Florida	3.4
18	Georgia	3.4
11	Hawaii	3.8
36	Idaho	2.9
15	Illinois	3.7
42	Indiana	2.7
27	Iowa	3.2
23	Kansas	3.3
48	Kentucky	2.1
36	Louisiana	2.9
18	Maine	3.4
39	Maryland	2.8
5	Massachusetts	3.9
11	Michigan	3.8
18	Minnesota	3.4
39	Mississippi	2.8
50	Missouri	2.0
5	Montana	3.9
31	Nebraska	3.1
45	Nevada	2.4
5	New Hampshire	3.9
23	New Jersey	3.3
16	New Mexico	3.6
2	New York	4.8
23	North Carolina	3.3
1	North Dakota	5.2
27	Ohio	3.2
33	Oklahoma	3.0
3	Oregon	4.2
33	Pennsylvania	3.0
27	Rhode Island	3.2
48	South Carolina	2.1
36	South Dakota	2.9
39	Tennessee	2.8
5	Texas	3.9
11	Utah	3.8
5	Vermont	3.9
43	Virginia	2.6
17	Washington	3.5
47	West Virginia	2.3
31	Wisconsin	3.1
5	Wyoming	3.9

RANK ORDER

RANK	STATE	PERCENT CHANGE
1	North Dakota	5.2
2	New York	4.8
3	Oregon	4.2
4	Colorado	4.0
5	Massachusetts	3.9
5	Montana	3.9
5	New Hampshire	3.9
5	Texas	3.9
5	Vermont	3.9
5	Wyoming	3.9
11	Connecticut	3.8
11	Hawaii	3.8
11	Michigan	3.8
11	Utah	3.8
15	Illinois	3.7
16	New Mexico	3.6
17	Washington	3.5
18	California	3.4
18	Florida	3.4
18	Georgia	3.4
18	Maine	3.4
18	Minnesota	3.4
23	Alaska	3.3
23	Kansas	3.3
23	New Jersey	3.3
23	North Carolina	3.3
27	Delaware	3.2
27	Iowa	3.2
27	Ohio	3.2
27	Rhode Island	3.2
31	Nebraska	3.1
31	Wisconsin	3.1
33	Arizona	3.0
33	Oklahoma	3.0
33	Pennsylvania	3.0
36	Idaho	2.9
36	Louisiana	2.9
36	South Dakota	2.9
39	Maryland	2.8
39	Mississippi	2.8
39	Tennessee	2.8
42	Indiana	2.7
43	Arkansas	2.6
43	Virginia	2.6
45	Alabama	2.4
45	Nevada	2.4
47	West Virginia	2.3
48	Kentucky	2.1
48	South Carolina	2.1
50	Missouri	2.0
	District of Columbia	3.6

Source: U.S. Department of Commerce, Bureau of Economic Analysis
"Personal Consumption Expenditures by State" (http://www.bea.gov/iTable/index_regional.cfm)
*PCE by state is the state counterpart of the Nation's personal consumption expenditures (PCE). PCE represents the goods and services purchased by or on behalf of households, plus the purchases of nonprofit institutions serving households. For each state and for the District of Columbia, personal consumption expenditures are those expenditures made by or on behalf of residents. These expenditures include expenditures on activities outside of the state.

Bankruptcy Filings in 2015

National Total = 860,182 Bankruptcies*

ALPHA ORDER

RANK	STATE	BANKRUPTCIES	% of USA
12	Alabama	25,505	3.0%
50	Alaska	426	0.0%
19	Arizona	17,448	2.0%
28	Arkansas	10,259	1.2%
1	California	86,949	10.1%
22	Colorado	15,389	1.8%
34	Connecticut	6,486	0.8%
40	Delaware	2,699	0.3%
2	Florida	59,050	6.9%
4	Georgia	51,240	6.0%
44	Hawaii	1,593	0.2%
37	Idaho	4,162	0.5%
3	Illinois	57,974	6.7%
10	Indiana	27,303	3.2%
35	Iowa	4,563	0.5%
33	Kansas	6,998	0.8%
21	Kentucky	15,688	1.8%
23	Louisiana	13,954	1.6%
43	Maine	1,930	0.2%
18	Maryland	18,521	2.2%
30	Massachusetts	9,280	1.1%
8	Michigan	33,322	3.9%
26	Minnesota	10,976	1.3%
27	Mississippi	10,863	1.3%
15	Missouri	19,557	2.3%
45	Montana	1,310	0.2%
36	Nebraska	4,244	0.5%
29	Nevada	9,902	1.2%
42	New Hampshire	2,211	0.3%
11	New Jersey	25,652	3.0%
38	New Mexico	3,508	0.4%
9	New York	30,682	3.6%
20	North Carolina	15,894	1.8%
49	North Dakota	592	0.1%
5	Ohio	39,309	4.6%
31	Oklahoma	9,195	1.1%
25	Oregon	11,134	1.3%
14	Pennsylvania	22,516	2.6%
41	Rhode Island	2,611	0.3%
32	South Carolina	7,080	0.8%
46	South Dakota	1,110	0.1%
6	Tennessee	36,644	4.3%
7	Texas	34,308	4.0%
24	Utah	12,520	1.5%
48	Vermont	664	0.1%
13	Virginia	23,218	2.7%
17	Washington	19,017	2.2%
39	West Virginia	3,241	0.4%
16	Wisconsin	19,149	2.2%
47	Wyoming	921	0.1%

RANK ORDER

RANK	STATE	BANKRUPTCIES	% of USA
1	California	86,949	10.1%
2	Florida	59,050	6.9%
3	Illinois	57,974	6.7%
4	Georgia	51,240	6.0%
5	Ohio	39,309	4.6%
6	Tennessee	36,644	4.3%
7	Texas	34,308	4.0%
8	Michigan	33,322	3.9%
9	New York	30,682	3.6%
10	Indiana	27,303	3.2%
11	New Jersey	25,652	3.0%
12	Alabama	25,505	3.0%
13	Virginia	23,218	2.7%
14	Pennsylvania	22,516	2.6%
15	Missouri	19,557	2.3%
16	Wisconsin	19,149	2.2%
17	Washington	19,017	2.2%
18	Maryland	18,521	2.2%
19	Arizona	17,448	2.0%
20	North Carolina	15,894	1.8%
21	Kentucky	15,688	1.8%
22	Colorado	15,389	1.8%
23	Louisiana	13,954	1.6%
24	Utah	12,520	1.5%
25	Oregon	11,134	1.3%
26	Minnesota	10,976	1.3%
27	Mississippi	10,863	1.3%
28	Arkansas	10,259	1.2%
29	Nevada	9,902	1.2%
30	Massachusetts	9,280	1.1%
31	Oklahoma	9,195	1.1%
32	South Carolina	7,080	0.8%
33	Kansas	6,998	0.8%
34	Connecticut	6,486	0.8%
35	Iowa	4,563	0.5%
36	Nebraska	4,244	0.5%
37	Idaho	4,162	0.5%
38	New Mexico	3,508	0.4%
39	West Virginia	3,241	0.4%
40	Delaware	2,699	0.3%
41	Rhode Island	2,611	0.3%
42	New Hampshire	2,211	0.3%
43	Maine	1,930	0.2%
44	Hawaii	1,593	0.2%
45	Montana	1,310	0.2%
46	South Dakota	1,110	0.1%
47	Wyoming	921	0.1%
48	Vermont	664	0.1%
49	North Dakota	592	0.1%
50	Alaska	426	0.0%
	District of Columbia	723	0.1%

Source: CQ Press using data from Administrative Office of the U.S. Courts
"Table F-2, U.S. Bankruptcy Courts" (http://www.uscourts.gov/Statistics/BankruptcyStatistics.aspx)
*For 12 months through September 2015. Includes business (24,985) and non-business (835,197) filings. Includes all chapters of bankruptcy. National total includes 10,692 bankruptcies in U.S. territories.

Personal Bankruptcy Rate in 2015

National Rate = 259 Personal Bankruptcies per 100,000 Population*

ALPHA ORDER

RANK	STATE	RATE
2	Alabama	519
50	Alaska	52
23	Arizona	251
9	Arkansas	338
30	California	216
18	Colorado	279
32	Connecticut	174
28	Delaware	229
17	Florida	286
3	Georgia	498
47	Hawaii	107
24	Idaho	246
4	Illinois	440
6	Indiana	408
41	Iowa	141
26	Kansas	235
8	Kentucky	349
16	Louisiana	293
42	Maine	136
15	Maryland	302
43	Massachusetts	131
12	Michigan	329
31	Minnesota	194
7	Mississippi	356
14	Missouri	317
45	Montana	122
29	Nebraska	221
10	Nevada	335
36	New Hampshire	156
18	New Jersey	279
35	New Mexico	161
39	New York	147
37	North Carolina	155
49	North Dakota	76
11	Ohio	333
27	Oklahoma	231
20	Oregon	275
33	Pennsylvania	170
25	Rhode Island	239
40	South Carolina	143
44	South Dakota	125
1	Tennessee	553
46	Texas	120
5	Utah	418
48	Vermont	100
21	Virginia	270
22	Washington	263
33	West Virginia	170
13	Wisconsin	326
38	Wyoming	152

RANK ORDER

RANK	STATE	RATE
1	Tennessee	553
2	Alabama	519
3	Georgia	498
4	Illinois	440
5	Utah	418
6	Indiana	408
7	Mississippi	356
8	Kentucky	349
9	Arkansas	338
10	Nevada	335
11	Ohio	333
12	Michigan	329
13	Wisconsin	326
14	Missouri	317
15	Maryland	302
16	Louisiana	293
17	Florida	286
18	Colorado	279
18	New Jersey	279
20	Oregon	275
21	Virginia	270
22	Washington	263
23	Arizona	251
24	Idaho	246
25	Rhode Island	239
26	Kansas	235
27	Oklahoma	231
28	Delaware	229
29	Nebraska	221
30	California	216
31	Minnesota	194
32	Connecticut	174
33	Pennsylvania	170
33	West Virginia	170
35	New Mexico	161
36	New Hampshire	156
37	North Carolina	155
38	Wyoming	152
39	New York	147
40	South Carolina	143
41	Iowa	141
42	Maine	136
43	Massachusetts	131
44	South Dakota	125
45	Montana	122
46	Texas	120
47	Hawaii	107
48	Vermont	100
49	North Dakota	76
50	Alaska	52
	District of Columbia	102

Source: CQ Press using data from Administrative Office of the U.S. Courts
"Table F-2, U.S. Bankruptcy Courts" (http://www.uscourts.gov/Statistics/BankruptcyStatistics.aspx)
*For 12 months through September 2015. National rate does not include bankruptcies or population in U.S. territories. Includes all nonbusiness bankruptcies.

Percent Change in Personal Bankruptcy Rate: 2014 to 2015

National Percent Change = 11.3% Decrease*

ALPHA ORDER

RANK	STATE	PERCENT CHANGE
1	Alabama	0.0
9	Alaska	(7.1)
45	Arizona	(17.7)
18	Arkansas	(9.6)
50	California	(21.5)
47	Colorado	(18.2)
8	Connecticut	(7.0)
28	Delaware	(10.9)
44	Florida	(17.6)
3	Georgia	(5.0)
36	Hawaii	(13.7)
45	Idaho	(17.7)
5	Illinois	(6.4)
15	Indiana	(9.3)
38	Iowa	(14.5)
18	Kansas	(9.6)
25	Kentucky	(10.7)
23	Louisiana	(10.1)
29	Maine	(11.1)
34	Maryland	(13.0)
39	Massachusetts	(14.9)
21	Michigan	(9.9)
37	Minnesota	(14.2)
2	Mississippi	(4.8)
21	Missouri	(9.9)
49	Montana	(19.7)
31	Nebraska	(12.0)
42	Nevada	(16.9)
43	New Hampshire	(17.5)
12	New Jersey	(8.2)
31	New Mexico	(12.0)
15	New York	(9.3)
10	North Carolina	(7.2)
48	North Dakota	(19.1)
11	Ohio	(7.5)
20	Oklahoma	(9.8)
33	Oregon	(12.7)
13	Pennsylvania	(8.6)
41	Rhode Island	(16.7)
6	South Carolina	(6.5)
25	South Dakota	(10.7)
15	Tennessee	(9.3)
14	Texas	(9.1)
25	Utah	(10.7)
34	Vermont	(13.0)
7	Virginia	(6.9)
40	Washington	(15.2)
3	West Virginia	(5.0)
30	Wisconsin	(11.7)
23	Wyoming	(10.1)

RANK ORDER

RANK	STATE	PERCENT CHANGE
1	Alabama	0.0
2	Mississippi	(4.8)
3	Georgia	(5.0)
3	West Virginia	(5.0)
5	Illinois	(6.4)
6	South Carolina	(6.5)
7	Virginia	(6.9)
8	Connecticut	(7.0)
9	Alaska	(7.1)
10	North Carolina	(7.2)
11	Ohio	(7.5)
12	New Jersey	(8.2)
13	Pennsylvania	(8.6)
14	Texas	(9.1)
15	Indiana	(9.3)
15	New York	(9.3)
15	Tennessee	(9.3)
18	Arkansas	(9.6)
18	Kansas	(9.6)
20	Oklahoma	(9.8)
21	Michigan	(9.9)
21	Missouri	(9.9)
23	Louisiana	(10.1)
23	Wyoming	(10.1)
25	Kentucky	(10.7)
25	South Dakota	(10.7)
25	Utah	(10.7)
28	Delaware	(10.9)
29	Maine	(11.1)
30	Wisconsin	(11.7)
31	Nebraska	(12.0)
31	New Mexico	(12.0)
33	Oregon	(12.7)
34	Maryland	(13.0)
34	Vermont	(13.0)
36	Hawaii	(13.7)
37	Minnesota	(14.2)
38	Iowa	(14.5)
39	Massachusetts	(14.9)
40	Washington	(15.2)
41	Rhode Island	(16.7)
42	Nevada	(16.9)
43	New Hampshire	(17.5)
44	Florida	(17.6)
45	Arizona	(17.7)
45	Idaho	(17.7)
47	Colorado	(18.2)
48	North Dakota	(19.1)
49	Montana	(19.7)
50	California	(21.5)
	District of Columbia	(6.4)

Source: CQ Press using data from Administrative Office of the U.S. Courts
"Table F-2, U.S. Bankruptcy Courts" (http://www.uscourts.gov/Statistics/BankruptcyStatistics.aspx)
*Twelve months ending in September 2014 to 12 months ending in September 2015. National rate does not include bankruptcies or population in U.S. territories. Includes all nonbusiness bankruptcies.

2016 State Business Tax Climate Index

National Average Score = 5.20*

ALPHA ORDER

RANK	STATE	SCORE
29	Alabama	5.00
3	Alaska	7.34
24	Arizona	5.18
38	Arkansas	4.61
48	California	3.75
18	Colorado	5.33
44	Connecticut	4.33
14	Delaware	5.58
4	Florida	6.92
39	Georgia	4.58
31	Hawaii	4.97
19	Idaho	5.27
23	Illinois	5.18
8	Indiana	5.95
40	Iowa	4.47
22	Kansas	5.22
28	Kentucky	5.02
37	Louisiana	4.70
34	Maine	4.85
41	Maryland	4.46
25	Massachusetts	5.11
13	Michigan	5.63
47	Minnesota	4.03
20	Mississippi	5.24
17	Missouri	5.39
6	Montana	6.19
27	Nebraska	5.08
5	Nevada	6.66
7	New Hampshire	6.07
50	New Jersey	3.36
35	New Mexico	4.75
49	New York	3.61
15	North Carolina	5.57
26	North Dakota	5.08
42	Ohio	4.43
33	Oklahoma	4.86
11	Oregon	5.80
32	Pennsylvania	4.91
45	Rhode Island	4.26
36	South Carolina	4.74
2	South Dakota	7.42
16	Tennessee	5.46
10	Texas	5.82
9	Utah	5.91
46	Vermont	4.10
30	Virginia	4.99
12	Washington	5.78
21	West Virginia	5.24
43	Wisconsin	4.43
1	Wyoming	7.54

RANK ORDER

RANK	STATE	SCORE
1	Wyoming	7.54
2	South Dakota	7.42
3	Alaska	7.34
4	Florida	6.92
5	Nevada	6.66
6	Montana	6.19
7	New Hampshire	6.07
8	Indiana	5.95
9	Utah	5.91
10	Texas	5.82
11	Oregon	5.80
12	Washington	5.78
13	Michigan	5.63
14	Delaware	5.58
15	North Carolina	5.57
16	Tennessee	5.46
17	Missouri	5.39
18	Colorado	5.33
19	Idaho	5.27
20	Mississippi	5.24
21	West Virginia	5.24
22	Kansas	5.22
23	Illinois	5.18
24	Arizona	5.18
25	Massachusetts	5.11
26	North Dakota	5.08
27	Nebraska	5.08
28	Kentucky	5.02
29	Alabama	5.00
30	Virginia	4.99
31	Hawaii	4.97
32	Pennsylvania	4.91
33	Oklahoma	4.86
34	Maine	4.85
35	New Mexico	4.75
36	South Carolina	4.74
37	Louisiana	4.70
38	Arkansas	4.61
39	Georgia	4.58
40	Iowa	4.47
41	Maryland	4.46
42	Ohio	4.43
43	Wisconsin	4.43
44	Connecticut	4.33
45	Rhode Island	4.26
46	Vermont	4.10
47	Minnesota	4.03
48	California	3.75
49	New York	3.61
50	New Jersey	3.36
	District of Columbia	4.43

Source: The Tax Foundation
"State Business Tax Climate Index" (November 2015, http://taxfoundation.org/article/2016-state-business-tax-climate-index)
*This index looks at levels of taxation and complexity of compliance to compare the states on how "business friendly" each state is compared to the others. The scale for each factor considered is one to ten, with ten being the "best." Rankings are based on unrounded scores and reflect those of The Tax Foundation.

Fortune 500 Companies in 2015

National Total = 500 Companies*

ALPHA ORDER

RANK	STATE	COMPANIES	% of USA
35	Alabama	1	0.2%
39	Alaska	0	0.0%
23	Arizona	5	1.0%
21	Arkansas	7	1.4%
3	California	53	10.6%
19	Colorado	9	1.8%
11	Connecticut	17	3.4%
32	Delaware	2	0.4%
13	Florida	15	3.0%
6	Georgia	20	4.0%
39	Hawaii	0	0.0%
35	Idaho	1	0.2%
4	Illinois	34	6.8%
22	Indiana	6	1.2%
32	Iowa	2	0.4%
29	Kansas	3	0.6%
23	Kentucky	5	1.0%
32	Louisiana	2	0.4%
39	Maine	0	0.0%
27	Maryland	4	0.8%
15	Massachusetts	12	2.4%
6	Michigan	20	4.0%
11	Minnesota	17	3.4%
39	Mississippi	0	0.0%
17	Missouri	10	2.0%
39	Montana	0	0.0%
23	Nebraska	5	1.0%
27	Nevada	4	0.8%
39	New Hampshire	0	0.0%
8	New Jersey	19	3.8%
39	New Mexico	0	0.0%
1	New York	55	11.0%
14	North Carolina	14	2.8%
39	North Dakota	0	0.0%
5	Ohio	23	4.6%
23	Oklahoma	5	1.0%
29	Oregon	3	0.6%
10	Pennsylvania	18	3.6%
29	Rhode Island	3	0.6%
35	South Carolina	1	0.2%
39	South Dakota	0	0.0%
16	Tennessee	11	2.2%
2	Texas	54	10.8%
35	Utah	1	0.2%
39	Vermont	0	0.0%
8	Virginia	19	3.8%
17	Washington	10	2.0%
39	West Virginia	0	0.0%
20	Wisconsin	8	1.6%
39	Wyoming	0	0.0%

RANK ORDER

RANK	STATE	COMPANIES	% of USA
1	New York	55	11.0%
2	Texas	54	10.8%
3	California	53	10.6%
4	Illinois	34	6.8%
5	Ohio	23	4.6%
6	Georgia	20	4.0%
6	Michigan	20	4.0%
8	New Jersey	19	3.8%
8	Virginia	19	3.8%
10	Pennsylvania	18	3.6%
11	Connecticut	17	3.4%
11	Minnesota	17	3.4%
13	Florida	15	3.0%
14	North Carolina	14	2.8%
15	Massachusetts	12	2.4%
16	Tennessee	11	2.2%
17	Missouri	10	2.0%
17	Washington	10	2.0%
19	Colorado	9	1.8%
20	Wisconsin	8	1.6%
21	Arkansas	7	1.4%
22	Indiana	6	1.2%
23	Arizona	5	1.0%
23	Kentucky	5	1.0%
23	Nebraska	5	1.0%
23	Oklahoma	5	1.0%
27	Maryland	4	0.8%
27	Nevada	4	0.8%
29	Kansas	3	0.6%
29	Oregon	3	0.6%
29	Rhode Island	3	0.6%
32	Delaware	2	0.4%
32	Iowa	2	0.4%
32	Louisiana	2	0.4%
35	Alabama	1	0.2%
35	Idaho	1	0.2%
35	South Carolina	1	0.2%
35	Utah	1	0.2%
39	Alaska	0	0.0%
39	Hawaii	0	0.0%
39	Maine	0	0.0%
39	Mississippi	0	0.0%
39	Montana	0	0.0%
39	New Hampshire	0	0.0%
39	New Mexico	0	0.0%
39	North Dakota	0	0.0%
39	South Dakota	0	0.0%
39	Vermont	0	0.0%
39	West Virginia	0	0.0%
39	Wyoming	0	0.0%
	District of Columbia	2	0.4%

Source: Fortune magazine
   "Fortune 500" (June 15, 2015)
*By state where each company's headquarters is located.

V. Education

Estimated Percent of School-Age Population in Public
 Schools in 2014 117
Regular Public Elementary and Secondary School
 Districts in 2013............................... 118
Private Elementary and Secondary Schools in 2012 119
Private Elementary and Secondary School Enrollment
 in 2012 120
Public Elementary and Secondary Schools in 2014 121
Enrollment in Public Elementary and Secondary Schools
 in 2014 122
Public Elementary and Secondary School Teachers
 in 2014 123
Pupil-Teacher Ratio in Public Elementary and Secondary
 Schools in 2014 124
Estimated Average Salary of Public School Teachers
 in 2015 (National Education Association)........... 125
Average Teacher's Salary as a Percent of Average
 Annual Pay in 2014 126
Percent of Public School Fourth Graders Proficient or
 Better in Reading in 2015 127
Percent of Public School Eighth Graders Proficient or
 Better in Reading in 2015 128
Percent of Public School Fourth Graders Proficient or
 Better in Mathematics in 2015.................... 129
Percent of Public School Eighth Graders Proficient or
 Better in Mathematics in 2015.................... 130
Percent of Population Graduated from High School
 in 2014 131
Public High School Graduates in 2013................ 132
Adjusted Cohort Graduation Rate for Public High
 Schools in 2013 133
Public High School Dropout Rate in 2012 134
ACT Average Composite Score in 2015............... 135
Education Expenditures by State and Local Governments
 in 2013 136
Per Capita State and Local Government Expenditures for
 Education in 2013 137
Expenditures for Education as a Percent of All State and
 Local Government Expenditures in 2013 138
State and Local Government Expenditures for Elementary
 and Secondary Education in 2013 139
Per Capita State and Local Government Expenditures for
 Elementary and Secondary Education in 2013 140
Expenditures for Elementary and Secondary Education
 as a Percent of All State and Local Government
 Expenditures in 2013 141
Estimated Per Pupil Public Elementary and Secondary
 School Current Expenditures in 2015 142
Higher Education Expenditures by State and Local
 Governments in 2013........................... 143
Per Capita State and Local Government Expenditures for
 Higher Education in 2013 144
Expenditures for Higher Education as a Percent of All
 State and Local Government Expenditures in 2013.... 145
Average Faculty Salary at Institutions of Higher
 Education in 2014 146
Average Student Costs at Public Institutions of Higher
 Education in 2014 147
Average Student Costs at Private Institutions of Higher
 Education in 2014 148
Average College Graduate Debt: Class of 2014......... 149
Percent of College Graduates with Debt: Class of 2014... 150
Institutions of Higher Education in 2014 151
Enrollment in Institutions of Higher Education in 2013... 152
Enrollment Rate in Institutions of Higher Education
 in 2013 153
Enrollment in Public Institutions of Higher Education
 in 2013 154
Enrollment in Private Institutions of Higher Education
 in 2013 155
Percent of Population with a Bachelor's Degree or More
 in 2014 156
Percent of Population Who Have Completed an Advanced
 Degree in 2014................................ 157

(Continued)

(Continued)

Public Libraries and Branches in 2012 158
Rate of Public Libraries and Branches in 2012 159
Rate of Books in Public Libraries in 2012 160
Rate of Electronic Books in Public Libraries in 2012 161
Internet Terminals in Public Libraries in 2012 162
Rate of Internet Terminals in Public Libraries in 2012. . . . 163
Per Capita State Art Agencies' Legislative Appropriations
  in 2016 164
Federal Allocations for Head Start Program in 2014 165
Head Start Program Enrollment in 2014. 166

Estimated Percent of School-Age Population in Public Schools in 2014

National Percent = 93.2%*

ALPHA ORDER

RANK	STATE	PERCENT
29	Alabama	91.8
3	Alaska	99.3
24	Arizona	92.6
8	Arkansas	95.1
8	California	95.1
6	Colorado	96.2
21	Connecticut	93.2
42	Delaware	89.0
31	Florida	91.6
14	Georgia	94.2
50	Hawaii	86.1
19	Idaho	93.5
16	Illinois	94.0
39	Indiana	90.1
11	Iowa	94.8
8	Kansas	95.1
27	Kentucky	92.0
45	Louisiana	88.4
12	Maine	94.7
47	Maryland	88.3
20	Massachusetts	93.3
18	Michigan	93.7
34	Minnesota	91.2
30	Mississippi	91.7
38	Missouri	90.2
48	Montana	88.0
33	Nebraska	91.5
23	Nevada	92.8
27	New Hampshire	92.0
24	New Jersey	92.6
22	New Mexico	93.0
41	New York	89.8
36	North Carolina	91.1
43	North Dakota	88.5
43	Ohio	88.5
4	Oklahoma	99.2
13	Oregon	94.3
45	Pennsylvania	88.4
40	Rhode Island	89.9
17	South Carolina	93.9
49	South Dakota	87.4
37	Tennessee	90.8
2	Texas	99.9
7	Utah	95.9
5	Vermont	97.3
15	Virginia	94.1
31	Washington	91.6
1	West Virginia	101.2
34	Wisconsin	91.2
24	Wyoming	92.6

RANK ORDER

RANK	STATE	PERCENT
1	West Virginia	101.2
2	Texas	99.9
3	Alaska	99.3
4	Oklahoma	99.2
5	Vermont	97.3
6	Colorado	96.2
7	Utah	95.9
8	Arkansas	95.1
8	California	95.1
8	Kansas	95.1
11	Iowa	94.8
12	Maine	94.7
13	Oregon	94.3
14	Georgia	94.2
15	Virginia	94.1
16	Illinois	94.0
17	South Carolina	93.9
18	Michigan	93.7
19	Idaho	93.5
20	Massachusetts	93.3
21	Connecticut	93.2
22	New Mexico	93.0
23	Nevada	92.8
24	Arizona	92.6
24	New Jersey	92.6
24	Wyoming	92.6
27	Kentucky	92.0
27	New Hampshire	92.0
29	Alabama	91.8
30	Mississippi	91.7
31	Florida	91.6
31	Washington	91.6
33	Nebraska	91.5
34	Minnesota	91.2
34	Wisconsin	91.2
36	North Carolina	91.1
37	Tennessee	90.8
38	Missouri	90.2
39	Indiana	90.1
40	Rhode Island	89.9
41	New York	89.8
42	Delaware	89.0
43	North Dakota	88.5
43	Ohio	88.5
45	Louisiana	88.4
45	Pennsylvania	88.4
47	Maryland	88.3
48	Montana	88.0
49	South Dakota	87.4
50	Hawaii	86.1

| | District of Columbia | 107.9 |

Source: CQ Press using data from U.S. Department of Education, National Center for Education Statistics
"Common Core of Data (CCD) Database" (http://nces.ed.gov/ccd/)
*Estimate based on 2014 Census population estimates for 5- to 17-year-olds compared to estimated 2013-2014 school year public school student membership. Student membership figures include counts for pre-kindergarten programs. Figures higher than 100 percent reflect using different sources for population and for student membership.

Regular Public Elementary and Secondary School Districts in 2013

National Total = 13,515 Districts*

ALPHA ORDER

RANK	STATE	DISTRICTS	% of USA
34	Alabama	135	1.0%
43	Alaska	53	0.4%
23	Arizona	223	1.7%
20	Arkansas	238	1.8%
2	California	948	7.0%
26	Colorado	178	1.3%
30	Connecticut	169	1.3%
48	Delaware	19	0.1%
41	Florida	67	0.5%
24	Georgia	180	1.3%
50	Hawaii	1	0.0%
36	Idaho	116	0.9%
3	Illinois	863	6.4%
16	Indiana	297	2.2%
13	Iowa	348	2.6%
15	Kansas	309	2.3%
29	Kentucky	174	1.3%
40	Louisiana	70	0.5%
22	Maine	231	1.7%
47	Maryland	24	0.2%
21	Massachusetts	237	1.8%
7	Michigan	550	4.1%
14	Minnesota	336	2.5%
31	Mississippi	151	1.1%
8	Missouri	521	3.9%
12	Montana	410	3.0%
19	Nebraska	249	1.8%
49	Nevada	17	0.1%
26	New Hampshire	178	1.3%
6	New Jersey	601	4.4%
38	New Mexico	89	0.7%
4	New York	696	5.1%
37	North Carolina	115	0.9%
28	North Dakota	177	1.3%
5	Ohio	616	4.6%
8	Oklahoma	521	3.9%
24	Oregon	180	1.3%
10	Pennsylvania	500	3.7%
46	Rhode Island	32	0.2%
39	South Carolina	84	0.6%
31	South Dakota	151	1.1%
33	Tennessee	141	1.0%
1	Texas	1,029	7.6%
45	Utah	41	0.3%
18	Vermont	294	2.2%
35	Virginia	134	1.0%
17	Washington	295	2.2%
42	West Virginia	55	0.4%
11	Wisconsin	423	3.1%
44	Wyoming	48	0.4%

RANK ORDER

RANK	STATE	DISTRICTS	% of USA
1	Texas	1,029	7.6%
2	California	948	7.0%
3	Illinois	863	6.4%
4	New York	696	5.1%
5	Ohio	616	4.6%
6	New Jersey	601	4.4%
7	Michigan	550	4.1%
8	Missouri	521	3.9%
8	Oklahoma	521	3.9%
10	Pennsylvania	500	3.7%
11	Wisconsin	423	3.1%
12	Montana	410	3.0%
13	Iowa	348	2.6%
14	Minnesota	336	2.5%
15	Kansas	309	2.3%
16	Indiana	297	2.2%
17	Washington	295	2.2%
18	Vermont	294	2.2%
19	Nebraska	249	1.8%
20	Arkansas	238	1.8%
21	Massachusetts	237	1.8%
22	Maine	231	1.7%
23	Arizona	223	1.7%
24	Georgia	180	1.3%
24	Oregon	180	1.3%
26	Colorado	178	1.3%
26	New Hampshire	178	1.3%
28	North Dakota	177	1.3%
29	Kentucky	174	1.3%
30	Connecticut	169	1.3%
31	Mississippi	151	1.1%
31	South Dakota	151	1.1%
33	Tennessee	141	1.0%
34	Alabama	135	1.0%
35	Virginia	134	1.0%
36	Idaho	116	0.9%
37	North Carolina	115	0.9%
38	New Mexico	89	0.7%
39	South Carolina	84	0.6%
40	Louisiana	70	0.5%
41	Florida	67	0.5%
42	West Virginia	55	0.4%
43	Alaska	53	0.4%
44	Wyoming	48	0.4%
45	Utah	41	0.3%
46	Rhode Island	32	0.2%
47	Maryland	24	0.2%
48	Delaware	19	0.1%
49	Nevada	17	0.1%
50	Hawaii	1	0.0%
	District of Columbia	1	0.0%

Source: U.S. Department of Education, National Center for Education Statistics
"Digest of Education Statistics 2014" (http://nces.ed.gov/programs/digest/index.asp)
*For school year 2012-2013. Regular school districts are agencies responsible for providing free public education for school-age children residing within their jurisdiction. Included in these figures are districts that reported having no students. This can occur when a small district has no pupils or contracts with another district to educate the students under its jurisdiction.

Private Elementary and Secondary Schools in 2012

National Total = 30,861 Schools*

ALPHA ORDER

RANK	STATE	SCHOOLS	% of USA
25	Alabama	402	1.3%
48	Alaska	51	0.2%
28	Arizona	341	1.1%
32	Arkansas	234	0.8%
1	California	3,479	11.3%
22	Colorado	414	1.3%
23	Connecticut	406	1.3%
42	Delaware	124	0.4%
4	Florida	1,880	6.1%
16	Georgia	710	2.3%
41	Hawaii	134	0.4%
42	Idaho	124	0.4%
5	Illinois	1,572	5.1%
9	Indiana	969	3.1%
30	Iowa	300	1.0%
24	Kansas**	404	1.3%
29	Kentucky	329	1.1%
26	Louisiana	394	1.3%
38	Maine	157	0.5%
15	Maryland	736	2.4%
12	Massachusetts	803	2.6%
13	Michigan	791	2.6%
20	Minnesota	504	1.6%
34	Mississippi	221	0.7%
8	Missouri**	1,270	4.1%
46	Montana	111	0.4%
33	Nebraska	222	0.7%
38	Nevada	157	0.5%
31	New Hampshire	278	0.9%
7	New Jersey	1,289	4.2%
36	New Mexico	174	0.6%
3	New York	1,931	6.3%
17	North Carolina	642	2.1%
49	North Dakota	46	0.1%
10	Ohio	968	3.1%
35	Oklahoma	181	0.6%
21	Oregon	432	1.4%
2	Pennsylvania	2,325	7.5%
40	Rhode Island	144	0.5%
27	South Carolina	378	1.2%
47	South Dakota	74	0.2%
19	Tennessee	512	1.7%
6	Texas	1,502	4.9%
37	Utah	160	0.5%
45	Vermont	114	0.4%
14	Virginia	755	2.4%
18	Washington	633	2.1%
42	West Virginia	124	0.4%
11	Wisconsin	844	2.7%
50	Wyoming	38	0.1%

RANK ORDER

RANK	STATE	SCHOOLS	% of USA
1	California	3,479	11.3%
2	Pennsylvania	2,325	7.5%
3	New York	1,931	6.3%
4	Florida	1,880	6.1%
5	Illinois	1,572	5.1%
6	Texas	1,502	4.9%
7	New Jersey	1,289	4.2%
8	Missouri**	1,270	4.1%
9	Indiana	969	3.1%
10	Ohio	968	3.1%
11	Wisconsin	844	2.7%
12	Massachusetts	803	2.6%
13	Michigan	791	2.6%
14	Virginia	755	2.4%
15	Maryland	736	2.4%
16	Georgia	710	2.3%
17	North Carolina	642	2.1%
18	Washington	633	2.1%
19	Tennessee	512	1.7%
20	Minnesota	504	1.6%
21	Oregon	432	1.4%
22	Colorado	414	1.3%
23	Connecticut	406	1.3%
24	Kansas**	404	1.3%
25	Alabama	402	1.3%
26	Louisiana	394	1.3%
27	South Carolina	378	1.2%
28	Arizona	341	1.1%
29	Kentucky	329	1.1%
30	Iowa	300	1.0%
31	New Hampshire	278	0.9%
32	Arkansas	234	0.8%
33	Nebraska	222	0.7%
34	Mississippi	221	0.7%
35	Oklahoma	181	0.6%
36	New Mexico	174	0.6%
37	Utah	160	0.5%
38	Maine	157	0.5%
38	Nevada	157	0.5%
40	Rhode Island	144	0.5%
41	Hawaii	134	0.4%
42	Delaware	124	0.4%
42	Idaho	124	0.4%
42	West Virginia	124	0.4%
45	Vermont	114	0.4%
46	Montana	111	0.4%
47	South Dakota	74	0.2%
48	Alaska	51	0.2%
49	North Dakota	46	0.1%
50	Wyoming	38	0.1%
	District of Columbia	79	0.3%

Source: U.S. Department of Education, National Center for Education Statistics
"Characteristics of Private Schools in the United States" (http://nces.ed.gov/pubsearch/pubsinfo.asp?pubid=2013316)
*For school year 2011-2012. Includes private schools that provide instruction for one or more grades kindergarten through 12 (or comparable ungraded levels).
**Interpret data for these states with caution.

Private Elementary and Secondary School Enrollment in 2012

National Total = 4,494,845 Students*

ALPHA ORDER

RANK	STATE	STUDENTS	% of USA
22	Alabama	67,479	1.5%
49	Alaska	4,087	0.1%
29	Arizona	43,134	1.0%
35	Arkansas	25,164	0.6%
1	California	523,088	11.6%
27	Colorado	45,697	1.0%
24	Connecticut	58,399	1.3%
37	Delaware	21,667	0.5%
3	Florida	284,238	6.3%
9	Georgia	120,488	2.7%
33	Hawaii	33,994	0.8%
44	Idaho	11,262	0.3%
5	Illinois	226,265	5.0%
16	Indiana	111,872	2.5%
25	Iowa	58,180	1.3%
31	Kansas	39,016	0.9%
23	Kentucky	60,590	1.3%
14	Louisiana	112,645	2.5%
41	Maine	17,011	0.4%
10	Maryland	117,657	2.6%
13	Massachusetts	112,684	2.5%
11	Michigan	116,461	2.6%
21	Minnesota	76,693	1.7%
28	Mississippi	45,419	1.0%
12	Missouri	115,553	2.6%
46	Montana	8,561	0.2%
32	Nebraska	36,163	0.8%
39	Nevada	20,396	0.5%
38	New Hampshire	21,264	0.5%
8	New Jersey	166,508	3.7%
40	New Mexico	19,360	0.4%
2	New York	430,293	9.6%
17	North Carolina	106,661	2.4%
48	North Dakota	6,535	0.1%
7	Ohio	190,810	4.2%
34	Oklahoma	30,063	0.7%
30	Oregon	42,694	0.9%
4	Pennsylvania	240,993	5.4%
36	Rhode Island	22,539	0.5%
26	South Carolina	47,259	1.1%
45	South Dakota	10,266	0.2%
19	Tennessee	81,499	1.8%
6	Texas	223,469	5.0%
42	Utah	15,498	0.3%
47	Vermont	8,323	0.2%
18	Virginia	98,439	2.2%
20	Washington	77,279	1.7%
43	West Virginia	11,890	0.3%
15	Wisconsin	112,025	2.5%
50	Wyoming	1,947	0.0%

RANK ORDER

RANK	STATE	STUDENTS	% of USA
1	California	523,088	11.6%
2	New York	430,293	9.6%
3	Florida	284,238	6.3%
4	Pennsylvania	240,993	5.4%
5	Illinois	226,265	5.0%
6	Texas	223,469	5.0%
7	Ohio	190,810	4.2%
8	New Jersey	166,508	3.7%
9	Georgia	120,488	2.7%
10	Maryland	117,657	2.6%
11	Michigan	116,461	2.6%
12	Missouri	115,553	2.6%
13	Massachusetts	112,684	2.5%
14	Louisiana	112,645	2.5%
15	Wisconsin	112,025	2.5%
16	Indiana	111,872	2.5%
17	North Carolina	106,661	2.4%
18	Virginia	98,439	2.2%
19	Tennessee	81,499	1.8%
20	Washington	77,279	1.7%
21	Minnesota	76,693	1.7%
22	Alabama	67,479	1.5%
23	Kentucky	60,590	1.3%
24	Connecticut	58,399	1.3%
25	Iowa	58,180	1.3%
26	South Carolina	47,259	1.1%
27	Colorado	45,697	1.0%
28	Mississippi	45,419	1.0%
29	Arizona	43,134	1.0%
30	Oregon	42,694	0.9%
31	Kansas	39,016	0.9%
32	Nebraska	36,163	0.8%
33	Hawaii	33,994	0.8%
34	Oklahoma	30,063	0.7%
35	Arkansas	25,164	0.6%
36	Rhode Island	22,539	0.5%
37	Delaware	21,667	0.5%
38	New Hampshire	21,264	0.5%
39	Nevada	20,396	0.5%
40	New Mexico	19,360	0.4%
41	Maine	17,011	0.4%
42	Utah	15,498	0.3%
43	West Virginia	11,890	0.3%
44	Idaho	11,262	0.3%
45	South Dakota	10,266	0.2%
46	Montana	8,561	0.2%
47	Vermont	8,323	0.2%
48	North Dakota	6,535	0.1%
49	Alaska	4,087	0.1%
50	Wyoming	1,947	0.0%
	District of Columbia	15,368	0.3%

Source: U.S. Department of Education, National Center for Education Statistics
"Characteristics of Private Schools in the United States" (http://nces.ed.gov/pubsearch/pubsinfo.asp?pubid=2013316)
*For school year 2011-2012. Includes private schools that provide instruction for one or more grades kindergarten through 12 (or comparable ungraded levels).

Public Elementary and Secondary Schools in 2014

National Total = 98,271 Schools*

ALPHA ORDER

RANK	STATE	SCHOOLS	% of USA
23	Alabama	1,637	1.7%
44	Alaska	507	0.5%
15	Arizona	2,252	2.3%
32	Arkansas	1,112	1.1%
1	California	10,276	10.5%
21	Colorado	1,832	1.9%
31	Connecticut	1,152	1.2%
50	Delaware	219	0.2%
4	Florida	4,295	4.4%
14	Georgia	2,379	2.4%
49	Hawaii	288	0.3%
39	Idaho	706	0.7%
5	Illinois	4,204	4.3%
18	Indiana	1,928	2.0%
27	Iowa	1,382	1.4%
28	Kansas	1,346	1.4%
24	Kentucky	1,565	1.6%
26	Louisiana	1,412	1.4%
42	Maine	619	0.6%
25	Maryland	1,442	1.5%
19	Massachusetts	1,865	1.9%
7	Michigan	3,538	3.6%
11	Minnesota	2,414	2.5%
34	Mississippi	1,066	1.1%
12	Missouri	2,410	2.5%
37	Montana	824	0.8%
33	Nebraska	1,102	1.1%
41	Nevada	653	0.7%
45	New Hampshire	482	0.5%
10	New Jersey	2,508	2.6%
36	New Mexico	880	0.9%
3	New York	4,801	4.9%
9	North Carolina	2,588	2.6%
43	North Dakota	512	0.5%
6	Ohio	3,656	3.7%
22	Oklahoma	1,789	1.8%
29	Oregon	1,246	1.3%
8	Pennsylvania	3,068	3.1%
48	Rhode Island	304	0.3%
30	South Carolina	1,243	1.3%
40	South Dakota	699	0.7%
20	Tennessee	1,855	1.9%
2	Texas	8,748	8.9%
35	Utah	1,006	1.0%
47	Vermont	316	0.3%
17	Virginia	2,166	2.2%
13	Washington	2,381	2.4%
38	West Virginia	758	0.8%
16	Wisconsin	2,249	2.3%
46	Wyoming	366	0.4%

RANK ORDER

RANK	STATE	SCHOOLS	% of USA
1	California	10,276	10.5%
2	Texas	8,748	8.9%
3	New York	4,801	4.9%
4	Florida	4,295	4.4%
5	Illinois	4,204	4.3%
6	Ohio	3,656	3.7%
7	Michigan	3,538	3.6%
8	Pennsylvania	3,068	3.1%
9	North Carolina	2,588	2.6%
10	New Jersey	2,508	2.6%
11	Minnesota	2,414	2.5%
12	Missouri	2,410	2.5%
13	Washington	2,381	2.4%
14	Georgia	2,379	2.4%
15	Arizona	2,252	2.3%
16	Wisconsin	2,249	2.3%
17	Virginia	2,166	2.2%
18	Indiana	1,928	2.0%
19	Massachusetts	1,865	1.9%
20	Tennessee	1,855	1.9%
21	Colorado	1,832	1.9%
22	Oklahoma	1,789	1.8%
23	Alabama	1,637	1.7%
24	Kentucky	1,565	1.6%
25	Maryland	1,442	1.5%
26	Louisiana	1,412	1.4%
27	Iowa	1,382	1.4%
28	Kansas	1,346	1.4%
29	Oregon	1,246	1.3%
30	South Carolina	1,243	1.3%
31	Connecticut	1,152	1.2%
32	Arkansas	1,112	1.1%
33	Nebraska	1,102	1.1%
34	Mississippi	1,066	1.1%
35	Utah	1,006	1.0%
36	New Mexico	880	0.9%
37	Montana	824	0.8%
38	West Virginia	758	0.8%
39	Idaho	706	0.7%
40	South Dakota	699	0.7%
41	Nevada	653	0.7%
42	Maine	619	0.6%
43	North Dakota	512	0.5%
44	Alaska	507	0.5%
45	New Hampshire	482	0.5%
46	Wyoming	366	0.4%
47	Vermont	316	0.3%
48	Rhode Island	304	0.3%
49	Hawaii	288	0.3%
50	Delaware	219	0.2%
	District of Columbia	225	0.2%

Source: U.S. Department of Education, National Center for Education Statistics
"Selected Statistics From the Public Elementary and Secondary Education Universe: School Year 2013-14"
(https://nces.ed.gov/pubsearch/pubsinfo.asp?pubid=2015151)
*For school year 2013-2014.

Enrollment in Public Elementary and Secondary Schools in 2014

National Total = 50,044,522 Students*

ALPHA ORDER

RANK	STATE	STUDENTS	% of USA
23	Alabama	746,204	1.5%
46	Alaska	130,944	0.3%
13	Arizona	1,102,445	2.2%
34	Arkansas	489,979	1.0%
1	California	6,312,623	12.6%
19	Colorado	876,999	1.8%
30	Connecticut	546,200	1.1%
45	Delaware	131,687	0.3%
4	Florida	2,720,744	5.4%
8	Georgia	1,723,909	3.4%
40	Hawaii	186,825	0.4%
38	Idaho	296,476	0.6%
5	Illinois	2,066,990	4.1%
15	Indiana	1,047,385	2.1%
31	Iowa	502,964	1.0%
32	Kansas	496,440	1.0%
27	Kentucky	677,389	1.4%
25	Louisiana	711,491	1.4%
42	Maine	183,995	0.4%
21	Maryland	866,169	1.7%
17	Massachusetts	955,739	1.9%
9	Michigan	1,548,841	3.1%
22	Minnesota	850,973	1.7%
33	Mississippi	492,586	1.0%
18	Missouri	918,288	1.8%
43	Montana	144,129	0.3%
37	Nebraska	307,677	0.6%
35	Nevada	451,831	0.9%
41	New Hampshire	186,310	0.4%
11	New Jersey	1,370,295	2.7%
36	New Mexico	339,244	0.7%
3	New York	2,732,770	5.5%
10	North Carolina	1,530,857	3.1%
48	North Dakota	103,947	0.2%
7	Ohio	1,724,111	3.4%
26	Oklahoma	681,848	1.4%
29	Oregon	593,000	1.2%
6	Pennsylvania	1,755,236	3.5%
44	Rhode Island	142,008	0.3%
24	South Carolina	745,657	1.5%
47	South Dakota	130,890	0.3%
16	Tennessee	993,556	2.0%
2	Texas	5,153,702	10.3%
28	Utah	625,461	1.2%
50	Vermont	88,690	0.2%
12	Virginia	1,273,825	2.5%
14	Washington	1,058,936	2.1%
39	West Virginia	280,958	0.6%
20	Wisconsin	874,414	1.7%
49	Wyoming	92,732	0.2%

RANK ORDER

RANK	STATE	STUDENTS	% of USA
1	California	6,312,623	12.6%
2	Texas	5,153,702	10.3%
3	New York	2,732,770	5.5%
4	Florida	2,720,744	5.4%
5	Illinois	2,066,990	4.1%
6	Pennsylvania	1,755,236	3.5%
7	Ohio	1,724,111	3.4%
8	Georgia	1,723,909	3.4%
9	Michigan	1,548,841	3.1%
10	North Carolina	1,530,857	3.1%
11	New Jersey	1,370,295	2.7%
12	Virginia	1,273,825	2.5%
13	Arizona	1,102,445	2.2%
14	Washington	1,058,936	2.1%
15	Indiana	1,047,385	2.1%
16	Tennessee	993,556	2.0%
17	Massachusetts	955,739	1.9%
18	Missouri	918,288	1.8%
19	Colorado	876,999	1.8%
20	Wisconsin	874,414	1.7%
21	Maryland	866,169	1.7%
22	Minnesota	850,973	1.7%
23	Alabama	746,204	1.5%
24	South Carolina	745,657	1.5%
25	Louisiana	711,491	1.4%
26	Oklahoma	681,848	1.4%
27	Kentucky	677,389	1.4%
28	Utah	625,461	1.2%
29	Oregon	593,000	1.2%
30	Connecticut	546,200	1.1%
31	Iowa	502,964	1.0%
32	Kansas	496,440	1.0%
33	Mississippi	492,586	1.0%
34	Arkansas	489,979	1.0%
35	Nevada	451,831	0.9%
36	New Mexico	339,244	0.7%
37	Nebraska	307,677	0.6%
38	Idaho	296,476	0.6%
39	West Virginia	280,958	0.6%
40	Hawaii	186,825	0.4%
41	New Hampshire	186,310	0.4%
42	Maine	183,995	0.4%
43	Montana	144,129	0.3%
44	Rhode Island	142,008	0.3%
45	Delaware	131,687	0.3%
46	Alaska	130,944	0.3%
47	South Dakota	130,890	0.3%
48	North Dakota	103,947	0.2%
49	Wyoming	92,732	0.2%
50	Vermont	88,690	0.2%
	District of Columbia	78,153	0.2%

Source: U.S. Department of Education, National Center for Education Statistics
"Common Core of Data (CCD) Database" (http://nces.ed.gov/ccd/)
*For school year 2013-2014.

Public Elementary and Secondary School Teachers in 2014

National Total = 3,113,764 Teachers*

ALPHA ORDER				RANK ORDER			
RANK	STATE	TEACHERS	% of USA	RANK	STATE	TEACHERS	% of USA
24	Alabama	47,162	1.5%	1	Texas	334,580	10.7%
49	Alaska	7,898	0.3%	2	California	259,506	8.3%
22	Arizona	48,359	1.6%	3	New York	206,693	6.6%
31	Arkansas	34,933	1.1%	4	Florida	177,853	5.7%
2	California	259,506	8.3%	5	Illinois	136,355	4.4%
21	Colorado	50,157	1.6%	6	Pennsylvania	121,330	3.9%
26	Connecticut	43,443	1.4%	7	New Jersey	114,581	3.7%
46	Delaware	9,388	0.3%	8	Georgia	109,441	3.5%
4	Florida	177,853	5.7%	9	Ohio	106,010	3.4%
8	Georgia	109,441	3.5%	10	North Carolina	99,327	3.2%
42	Hawaii	11,781	0.4%	11	Virginia	90,098	2.9%
40	Idaho	15,002	0.5%	12	Michigan	85,786	2.8%
5	Illinois	136,355	4.4%	13	Massachusetts	70,490	2.3%
16	Indiana	59,823	1.9%	14	Missouri	66,651	2.1%
30	Iowa	35,397	1.1%	15	Tennessee	65,847	2.1%
29	Kansas	38,153	1.2%	16	Indiana	59,823	1.9%
28	Kentucky	41,820	1.3%	17	Maryland	58,611	1.9%
25	Louisiana	46,437	1.5%	18	Wisconsin	57,980	1.9%
39	Maine	15,452	0.5%	19	Washington	54,867	1.8%
17	Maryland	58,611	1.9%	20	Minnesota	54,413	1.7%
13	Massachusetts	70,490	2.3%	21	Colorado	50,157	1.6%
12	Michigan	85,786	2.8%	22	Arizona	48,359	1.6%
20	Minnesota	54,413	1.7%	23	South Carolina	48,151	1.5%
32	Mississippi	32,292	1.0%	24	Alabama	47,162	1.5%
14	Missouri	66,651	2.1%	25	Louisiana	46,437	1.5%
43	Montana	10,310	0.3%	26	Connecticut	43,443	1.4%
35	Nebraska	22,401	0.7%	27	Oklahoma	41,983	1.3%
37	Nevada	21,921	0.7%	28	Kentucky	41,820	1.3%
41	New Hampshire	14,826	0.5%	29	Kansas	38,153	1.2%
7	New Jersey	114,581	3.7%	30	Iowa	35,397	1.1%
36	New Mexico	22,239	0.7%	31	Arkansas	34,933	1.1%
3	New York	206,693	6.6%	32	Mississippi	32,292	1.0%
10	North Carolina	99,327	3.2%	33	Utah	27,247	0.9%
47	North Dakota	8,805	0.3%	34	Oregon	26,733	0.9%
9	Ohio	106,010	3.4%	35	Nebraska	22,401	0.7%
27	Oklahoma	41,983	1.3%	36	New Mexico	22,239	0.7%
34	Oregon	26,733	0.9%	37	Nevada	21,921	0.7%
6	Pennsylvania	121,330	3.9%	38	West Virginia	19,978	0.6%
44	Rhode Island	9,824	0.3%	39	Maine	15,452	0.5%
23	South Carolina	48,151	1.5%	40	Idaho	15,002	0.5%
45	South Dakota	9,510	0.3%	41	New Hampshire	14,826	0.5%
15	Tennessee	65,847	2.1%	42	Hawaii	11,781	0.4%
1	Texas	334,580	10.7%	43	Montana	10,310	0.3%
33	Utah	27,247	0.9%	44	Rhode Island	9,824	0.3%
48	Vermont	8,375	0.3%	45	South Dakota	9,510	0.3%
11	Virginia	90,098	2.9%	46	Delaware	9,388	0.3%
19	Washington	54,867	1.8%	47	North Dakota	8,805	0.3%
38	West Virginia	19,978	0.6%	48	Vermont	8,375	0.3%
18	Wisconsin	57,980	1.9%	49	Alaska	7,898	0.3%
50	Wyoming	7,555	0.2%	50	Wyoming	7,555	0.2%
					District of Columbia	5,991	0.2%

Source: U.S. Department of Education, National Center for Education Statistics
    "Common Core of Data (CCD) Database" (http://nces.ed.gov/ccd/)
*For school year 2013-2014. Counts are full-time equivalent figures.

Pupil-Teacher Ratio in Public Elementary and Secondary Schools in 2014

National Ratio = 16.1 Pupils Per Teacher*

ALPHA ORDER

RANK	STATE	RATIO
16	Alabama	15.8
11	Alaska	16.6
3	Arizona	22.8
35	Arkansas	14.0
1	California	24.3
9	Colorado	17.5
44	Connecticut	12.6
35	Delaware	14.0
22	Florida	15.3
16	Georgia	15.8
15	Hawaii	15.9
6	Idaho	19.8
26	Illinois	15.2
9	Indiana	17.5
32	Iowa	14.2
43	Kansas	13.0
13	Kentucky	16.2
22	Louisiana	15.3
48	Maine	11.9
29	Maryland	14.8
41	Massachusetts	13.6
8	Michigan	18.1
18	Minnesota	15.6
22	Mississippi	15.3
38	Missouri	13.8
35	Montana	14.0
40	Nebraska	13.7
5	Nevada	20.6
44	New Hampshire	12.6
47	New Jersey	12.0
22	New Mexico	15.3
42	New York	13.2
20	North Carolina	15.4
49	North Dakota	11.8
12	Ohio	16.3
13	Oklahoma	16.2
4	Oregon	22.2
30	Pennsylvania	14.5
30	Rhode Island	14.5
19	South Carolina	15.5
38	South Dakota	13.8
27	Tennessee	15.1
20	Texas	15.4
2	Utah	23.0
50	Vermont	10.6
33	Virginia	14.1
7	Washington	19.3
33	West Virginia	14.1
27	Wisconsin	15.1
46	Wyoming	12.3

RANK ORDER

RANK	STATE	RATIO
1	California	24.3
2	Utah	23.0
3	Arizona	22.8
4	Oregon	22.2
5	Nevada	20.6
6	Idaho	19.8
7	Washington	19.3
8	Michigan	18.1
9	Colorado	17.5
9	Indiana	17.5
11	Alaska	16.6
12	Ohio	16.3
13	Kentucky	16.2
13	Oklahoma	16.2
15	Hawaii	15.9
16	Alabama	15.8
16	Georgia	15.8
18	Minnesota	15.6
19	South Carolina	15.5
20	North Carolina	15.4
20	Texas	15.4
22	Florida	15.3
22	Louisiana	15.3
22	Mississippi	15.3
22	New Mexico	15.3
26	Illinois	15.2
27	Tennessee	15.1
27	Wisconsin	15.1
29	Maryland	14.8
30	Pennsylvania	14.5
30	Rhode Island	14.5
32	Iowa	14.2
33	Virginia	14.1
33	West Virginia	14.1
35	Arkansas	14.0
35	Delaware	14.0
35	Montana	14.0
38	Missouri	13.8
38	South Dakota	13.8
40	Nebraska	13.7
41	Massachusetts	13.6
42	New York	13.2
43	Kansas	13.0
44	Connecticut	12.6
44	New Hampshire	12.6
46	Wyoming	12.3
47	New Jersey	12.0
48	Maine	11.9
49	North Dakota	11.8
50	Vermont	10.6
	District of Columbia	13.0

Source: U.S. Department of Education, National Center for Education Statistics
"Common Core of Data (CCD) Database" (http://nces.ed.gov/ccd/)
*For school year 2013-2014. Based on full-time equivalency counts of teachers.

Estimated Average Salary of Public School Teachers in 2015
(National Education Association)
National Average = $57,379*

ALPHA ORDER

RANK	STATE	SALARY
34	Alabama	$49,497
6	Alaska	66,755
46	Arizona	45,406
39	Arkansas	48,017
3	California	72,535
33	Colorado	49,828
4	Connecticut	71,709
13	Delaware	59,195
35	Florida	48,992
23	Georgia	53,382
17	Hawaii	57,189
47	Idaho	45,218
11	Illinois	61,083
29	Indiana	50,502
24	Iowa	52,862
36	Kansas	48,990
25	Kentucky	51,093
40	Louisiana	47,886
32	Maine	50,017
8	Maryland	64,845
2	Massachusetts	74,805
10	Michigan	62,778
19	Minnesota	56,670
49	Mississippi	42,564
42	Missouri	47,394
26	Montana	50,999
30	Nebraska	50,318
18	Nevada	56,703
14	New Hampshire	58,554
5	New Jersey	69,038
43	New Mexico	46,003
1	New York	77,628
41	North Carolina	47,783
31	North Dakota	50,025
20	Ohio	56,172
48	Oklahoma	44,628
12	Oregon	59,811
9	Pennsylvania	64,717
7	Rhode Island	65,918
37	South Carolina	48,709
50	South Dakota	40,661
38	Tennessee	48,503
28	Texas	50,576
44	Utah	45,848
16	Vermont	57,642
27	Virginia	50,620
22	Washington	53,714
45	West Virginia	45,647
21	Wisconsin	54,535
15	Wyoming	57,715

RANK ORDER

RANK	STATE	SALARY
1	New York	$77,628
2	Massachusetts	74,805
3	California	72,535
4	Connecticut	71,709
5	New Jersey	69,038
6	Alaska	66,755
7	Rhode Island	65,918
8	Maryland	64,845
9	Pennsylvania	64,717
10	Michigan	62,778
11	Illinois	61,083
12	Oregon	59,811
13	Delaware	59,195
14	New Hampshire	58,554
15	Wyoming	57,715
16	Vermont	57,642
17	Hawaii	57,189
18	Nevada	56,703
19	Minnesota	56,670
20	Ohio	56,172
21	Wisconsin	54,535
22	Washington	53,714
23	Georgia	53,382
24	Iowa	52,862
25	Kentucky	51,093
26	Montana	50,999
27	Virginia	50,620
28	Texas	50,576
29	Indiana	50,502
30	Nebraska	50,318
31	North Dakota	50,025
32	Maine	50,017
33	Colorado	49,828
34	Alabama	49,497
35	Florida	48,992
36	Kansas	48,990
37	South Carolina	48,709
38	Tennessee	48,503
39	Arkansas	48,017
40	Louisiana	47,886
41	North Carolina	47,783
42	Missouri	47,394
43	New Mexico	46,003
44	Utah	45,848
45	West Virginia	45,647
46	Arizona	45,406
47	Idaho	45,218
48	Oklahoma	44,628
49	Mississippi	42,564
50	South Dakota	40,661
	District of Columbia	75,490

Source: National Education Association, Washington, D.C.
"Rankings and Estimates" (Copyright © 2015, NEA, used with permission, http://www.nea.org/home/44479.htm)
*Estimates for school year 2014-2015 for classroom teachers.

Average Teacher's Salary as a Percent of Average Annual Pay in 2014

National Average = 111.0% of Average Annual Pay*

ALPHA ORDER

RANK	STATE	PERCENT
27	Alabama	113.4
9	Alaska	124.2
47	Arizona	96.7
18	Arkansas	119.2
14	California	121.9
49	Colorado	94.3
31	Connecticut	111.3
31	Delaware	111.3
36	Florida	108.0
33	Georgia	110.4
8	Hawaii	125.5
21	Idaho	118.1
30	Illinois	112.0
20	Indiana	118.4
11	Iowa	123.3
26	Kansas	113.8
16	Kentucky	121.2
38	Louisiana	106.9
13	Maine	122.7
23	Maryland	116.8
24	Massachusetts	115.4
4	Michigan	128.8
36	Minnesota	108.0
25	Mississippi	114.2
41	Missouri	106.4
3	Montana	129.8
16	Nebraska	121.2
7	Nevada	125.8
29	New Hampshire	113.0
28	New Jersey	113.3
35	New Mexico	109.4
22	New York	116.9
43	North Carolina	103.1
45	North Dakota	97.0
15	Ohio	121.8
44	Oklahoma	101.9
5	Oregon	127.3
6	Pennsylvania	127.0
1	Rhode Island	132.5
19	South Carolina	119.1
42	South Dakota	104.3
40	Tennessee	106.5
50	Texas	94.2
39	Utah	106.6
2	Vermont	132.0
48	Virginia	94.9
45	Washington	97.0
34	West Virginia	110.1
10	Wisconsin	123.5
12	Wyoming	122.9

RANK ORDER

RANK	STATE	PERCENT
1	Rhode Island	132.5
2	Vermont	132.0
3	Montana	129.8
4	Michigan	128.8
5	Oregon	127.3
6	Pennsylvania	127.0
7	Nevada	125.8
8	Hawaii	125.5
9	Alaska	124.2
10	Wisconsin	123.5
11	Iowa	123.3
12	Wyoming	122.9
13	Maine	122.7
14	California	121.9
15	Ohio	121.8
16	Kentucky	121.2
16	Nebraska	121.2
18	Arkansas	119.2
19	South Carolina	119.1
20	Indiana	118.4
21	Idaho	118.1
22	New York	116.9
23	Maryland	116.8
24	Massachusetts	115.4
25	Mississippi	114.2
26	Kansas	113.8
27	Alabama	113.4
28	New Jersey	113.3
29	New Hampshire	113.0
30	Illinois	112.0
31	Connecticut	111.3
31	Delaware	111.3
33	Georgia	110.4
34	West Virginia	110.1
35	New Mexico	109.4
36	Florida	108.0
36	Minnesota	108.0
38	Louisiana	106.9
39	Utah	106.6
40	Tennessee	106.5
41	Missouri	106.4
42	South Dakota	104.3
43	North Carolina	103.1
44	Oklahoma	101.9
45	North Dakota	97.0
45	Washington	97.0
47	Arizona	96.7
48	Virginia	94.9
49	Colorado	94.3
50	Texas	94.2
	District of Columbia	86.5

Source: CQ Press using data from National Education Association, Washington, D.C.
 "Rankings and Estimates" (Copyright © 2015, NEA, used with permission, http://www.nea.org/home/32073.htm)
 "Quarterly Census of Employment and Wages" (http://www.bls.gov/cew/home.htm)
*Average of public elementary and secondary teacher salary for school years 2013-2014 and 2014-2015 compared to each state's 2014 average annual pay for all workers covered by federal unemployment.

Percent of Public School Fourth Graders Proficient or Better in Reading in 2015
National Percent = 35%*

ALPHA ORDER

RANK	STATE	PERCENT
43	Alabama	29
40	Alaska	30
40	Arizona	30
38	Arkansas	32
48	California	28
15	Colorado	39
4	Connecticut	43
21	Delaware	37
15	Florida	39
33	Georgia	34
43	Hawaii	29
26	Idaho	36
30	Illinois	35
9	Indiana	40
18	Iowa	38
30	Kansas	35
9	Kentucky	40
43	Louisiana	29
26	Maine	36
21	Maryland	37
1	Massachusetts	50
43	Michigan	29
15	Minnesota	39
49	Mississippi	26
26	Missouri	36
21	Montana	37
9	Nebraska	40
43	Nevada	29
2	New Hampshire	46
4	New Jersey	43
50	New Mexico	23
26	New York	36
18	North Carolina	38
21	North Dakota	37
18	Ohio	38
35	Oklahoma	33
33	Oregon	34
7	Pennsylvania	41
9	Rhode Island	40
35	South Carolina	33
30	South Dakota	35
35	Tennessee	33
39	Texas	31
9	Utah	40
3	Vermont	45
4	Virginia	43
9	Washington	40
40	West Virginia	30
21	Wisconsin	37
7	Wyoming	41

RANK ORDER

RANK	STATE	PERCENT
1	Massachusetts	50
2	New Hampshire	46
3	Vermont	45
4	Connecticut	43
4	New Jersey	43
4	Virginia	43
7	Pennsylvania	41
7	Wyoming	41
9	Indiana	40
9	Kentucky	40
9	Nebraska	40
9	Rhode Island	40
9	Utah	40
9	Washington	40
15	Colorado	39
15	Florida	39
15	Minnesota	39
18	Iowa	38
18	North Carolina	38
18	Ohio	38
21	Delaware	37
21	Maryland	37
21	Montana	37
21	North Dakota	37
21	Wisconsin	37
26	Idaho	36
26	Maine	36
26	Missouri	36
26	New York	36
30	Illinois	35
30	Kansas	35
30	South Dakota	35
33	Georgia	34
33	Oregon	34
35	Oklahoma	33
35	South Carolina	33
35	Tennessee	33
38	Arkansas	32
39	Texas	31
40	Alaska	30
40	Arizona	30
40	West Virginia	30
43	Alabama	29
43	Hawaii	29
43	Louisiana	29
43	Michigan	29
43	Nevada	29
48	California	28
49	Mississippi	26
50	New Mexico	23
	District of Columbia	27

Source: U.S. Department of Education, National Center for Education Statistics
"The Nation's Report Card: Reading 2015" (http://nces.ed.gov/nationsreportcard/)
*There are four achievement levels: Below Basic, Basic, Proficient, and Advanced. Proficient represents solid academic mastery for 4th graders. Students reaching this level have demonstrated competency over challenging subject matter, including subject matter knowledge, application of such knowledge to real-world situations, and analytical skills appropriate to the subject matter.

Percent of Public School Eighth Graders Proficient or Better in Reading in 2015
National Percent = 33%*

ALPHA ORDER

RANK	STATE	PERCENT
46	Alabama	26
33	Alaska	31
33	Arizona	31
43	Arkansas	27
40	California	28
9	Colorado	38
4	Connecticut	43
33	Delaware	31
36	Florida	30
36	Georgia	30
46	Hawaii	26
12	Idaho	37
25	Illinois	35
12	Indiana	37
17	Iowa	36
25	Kansas	35
17	Kentucky	36
48	Louisiana	23
17	Maine	36
12	Maryland	37
1	Massachusetts	46
32	Michigan	32
6	Minnesota	40
49	Mississippi	20
17	Missouri	36
12	Montana	37
9	Nebraska	38
43	Nevada	27
2	New Hampshire	45
5	New Jersey	41
49	New Mexico	20
30	New York	33
36	North Carolina	30
28	North Dakota	34
17	Ohio	36
39	Oklahoma	29
17	Oregon	36
7	Pennsylvania	39
25	Rhode Island	35
40	South Carolina	28
28	South Dakota	34
30	Tennessee	33
40	Texas	28
9	Utah	38
3	Vermont	44
17	Virginia	36
12	Washington	37
43	West Virginia	27
7	Wisconsin	39
17	Wyoming	36

RANK ORDER

RANK	STATE	PERCENT
1	Massachusetts	46
2	New Hampshire	45
3	Vermont	44
4	Connecticut	43
5	New Jersey	41
6	Minnesota	40
7	Pennsylvania	39
7	Wisconsin	39
9	Colorado	38
9	Nebraska	38
9	Utah	38
12	Idaho	37
12	Indiana	37
12	Maryland	37
12	Montana	37
12	Washington	37
17	Iowa	36
17	Kentucky	36
17	Maine	36
17	Missouri	36
17	Ohio	36
17	Oregon	36
17	Virginia	36
17	Wyoming	36
25	Illinois	35
25	Kansas	35
25	Rhode Island	35
28	North Dakota	34
28	South Dakota	34
30	New York	33
30	Tennessee	33
32	Michigan	32
33	Alaska	31
33	Arizona	31
33	Delaware	31
36	Florida	30
36	Georgia	30
36	North Carolina	30
39	Oklahoma	29
40	California	28
40	South Carolina	28
40	Texas	28
43	Arkansas	27
43	Nevada	27
43	West Virginia	27
46	Alabama	26
46	Hawaii	26
48	Louisiana	23
49	Mississippi	20
49	New Mexico	20
	District of Columbia	19

Source: U.S. Department of Education, National Center for Education Statistics
"The Nation's Report Card: Reading 2015" (http://nces.ed.gov/nationsreportcard/)
*There are four achievement levels: Below Basic, Basic, Proficient, and Advanced. Proficient represents solid academic mastery for 8th graders. Students reaching this level have demonstrated competency over challenging subject matter, including subject matter knowledge, application of such knowledge to real-world situations, and analytical skills appropriate to the subject matter.

Percent of Public School Fourth Graders Proficient or Better in Mathematics in 2015
National Percent = 39%*

ALPHA ORDER

RANK	STATE	PERCENT
50	Alabama	26
39	Alaska	35
29	Arizona	38
44	Arkansas	32
48	California	29
18	Colorado	43
21	Connecticut	41
33	Delaware	37
20	Florida	42
39	Georgia	35
29	Hawaii	38
29	Idaho	38
33	Illinois	37
4	Indiana	50
14	Iowa	44
21	Kansas	41
25	Kentucky	40
46	Louisiana	30
21	Maine	41
25	Maryland	40
1	Massachusetts	54
42	Michigan	34
2	Minnesota	53
46	Mississippi	30
29	Missouri	38
21	Montana	41
9	Nebraska	46
44	Nevada	32
3	New Hampshire	51
6	New Jersey	47
49	New Mexico	27
39	New York	35
14	North Carolina	44
10	North Dakota	45
10	Ohio	45
33	Oklahoma	37
33	Oregon	37
10	Pennsylvania	45
33	Rhode Island	37
38	South Carolina	36
25	South Dakota	40
25	Tennessee	40
14	Texas	44
14	Utah	44
18	Vermont	43
6	Virginia	47
6	Washington	47
43	West Virginia	33
10	Wisconsin	45
5	Wyoming	48

RANK ORDER

RANK	STATE	PERCENT
1	Massachusetts	54
2	Minnesota	53
3	New Hampshire	51
4	Indiana	50
5	Wyoming	48
6	New Jersey	47
6	Virginia	47
6	Washington	47
9	Nebraska	46
10	North Dakota	45
10	Ohio	45
10	Pennsylvania	45
10	Wisconsin	45
14	Iowa	44
14	North Carolina	44
14	Texas	44
14	Utah	44
18	Colorado	43
18	Vermont	43
20	Florida	42
21	Connecticut	41
21	Kansas	41
21	Maine	41
21	Montana	41
25	Kentucky	40
25	Maryland	40
25	South Dakota	40
25	Tennessee	40
29	Arizona	38
29	Hawaii	38
29	Idaho	38
29	Missouri	38
33	Delaware	37
33	Illinois	37
33	Oklahoma	37
33	Oregon	37
33	Rhode Island	37
38	South Carolina	36
39	Alaska	35
39	Georgia	35
39	New York	35
42	Michigan	34
43	West Virginia	33
44	Arkansas	32
44	Nevada	32
46	Louisiana	30
46	Mississippi	30
48	California	29
49	New Mexico	27
50	Alabama	26
	District of Columbia	31

Source: U.S. Department of Education, National Center for Education Statistics
"The Nation's Report Card: Mathematics 2015" (http://nces.ed.gov/nationsreportcard/)

*There are four achievement levels: Below Basic, Basic, Proficient, and Advanced. Proficient represents solid academic mastery for 4th graders. Students reaching this level have demonstrated competency over challenging subject matter, including subject matter knowledge, application of such knowledge to real-world situations, and analytical skills appropriate to the subject matter.

Percent of Public School Eighth Graders Proficient or Better in Mathematics in 2015
National Percent = 32%*

ALPHA ORDER

RANK	STATE	PERCENT
50	Alabama	17
28	Alaska	32
18	Arizona	35
44	Arkansas	25
40	California	27
14	Colorado	37
16	Connecticut	36
34	Delaware	30
41	Florida	26
38	Georgia	28
34	Hawaii	30
23	Idaho	34
28	Illinois	32
7	Indiana	39
14	Iowa	37
26	Kansas	33
38	Kentucky	28
49	Louisiana	18
18	Maine	35
18	Maryland	35
1	Massachusetts	51
36	Michigan	29
2	Minnesota	48
46	Mississippi	22
32	Missouri	31
7	Montana	39
11	Nebraska	38
41	Nevada	26
3	New Hampshire	46
3	New Jersey	46
47	New Mexico	21
32	New York	31
26	North Carolina	33
7	North Dakota	39
18	Ohio	35
45	Oklahoma	23
23	Oregon	34
16	Pennsylvania	36
28	Rhode Island	32
41	South Carolina	26
23	South Dakota	34
36	Tennessee	29
28	Texas	32
11	Utah	38
5	Vermont	42
11	Virginia	38
7	Washington	39
47	West Virginia	21
6	Wisconsin	41
18	Wyoming	35

RANK ORDER

RANK	STATE	PERCENT
1	Massachusetts	51
2	Minnesota	48
3	New Hampshire	46
3	New Jersey	46
5	Vermont	42
6	Wisconsin	41
7	Indiana	39
7	Montana	39
7	North Dakota	39
7	Washington	39
11	Nebraska	38
11	Utah	38
11	Virginia	38
14	Colorado	37
14	Iowa	37
16	Connecticut	36
16	Pennsylvania	36
18	Arizona	35
18	Maine	35
18	Maryland	35
18	Ohio	35
18	Wyoming	35
23	Idaho	34
23	Oregon	34
23	South Dakota	34
26	Kansas	33
26	North Carolina	33
28	Alaska	32
28	Illinois	32
28	Rhode Island	32
28	Texas	32
32	Missouri	31
32	New York	31
34	Delaware	30
34	Hawaii	30
36	Michigan	29
36	Tennessee	29
38	Georgia	28
38	Kentucky	28
40	California	27
41	Florida	26
41	Nevada	26
41	South Carolina	26
44	Arkansas	25
45	Oklahoma	23
46	Mississippi	22
47	New Mexico	21
47	West Virginia	21
49	Louisiana	18
50	Alabama	17
	District of Columbia	19

Source: U.S. Department of Education, National Center for Education Statistics
"The Nation's Report Card: Mathematics 2015" (http://nces.ed.gov/nationsreportcard/)
*There are four achievement levels: Below Basic, Basic, Proficient, and Advanced. Proficient represents solid academic mastery for 8th graders. Students reaching this level have demonstrated competency over challenging subject matter, including subject matter knowledge, application of such knowledge to real-world situations, and analytical skills appropriate to the subject matter.

Percent of Population Graduated from High School in 2014

National Percent = 86.9%*

ALPHA ORDER

RANK	STATE	PERCENT
44	Alabama	84.7
1	Alaska	92.9
35	Arizona	86.1
41	Arkansas	85.3
50	California	82.1
14	Colorado	90.5
18	Connecticut	90.1
27	Delaware	89.0
33	Florida	87.2
40	Georgia	85.6
9	Hawaii	91.7
18	Idaho	90.1
31	Illinois	88.2
30	Indiana	88.4
7	Iowa	92.1
16	Kansas	90.3
45	Kentucky	84.5
47	Louisiana	83.6
9	Maine	91.7
23	Maryland	89.6
21	Massachusetts	89.7
20	Michigan	89.9
2	Minnesota	92.6
48	Mississippi	82.8
28	Missouri	88.9
2	Montana	92.6
16	Nebraska	90.3
43	Nevada	85.1
5	New Hampshire	92.2
26	New Jersey	89.1
46	New Mexico	84.2
39	New York	85.7
34	North Carolina	86.4
5	North Dakota	92.2
24	Ohio	89.4
32	Oklahoma	87.3
21	Oregon	89.7
24	Pennsylvania	89.4
37	Rhode Island	85.8
35	South Carolina	86.1
9	South Dakota	91.7
37	Tennessee	85.8
49	Texas	82.2
12	Utah	91.4
8	Vermont	92.0
29	Virginia	88.5
15	Washington	90.4
42	West Virginia	85.2
12	Wisconsin	91.4
2	Wyoming	92.6

RANK ORDER

RANK	STATE	PERCENT
1	Alaska	92.9
2	Minnesota	92.6
2	Montana	92.6
2	Wyoming	92.6
5	New Hampshire	92.2
5	North Dakota	92.2
7	Iowa	92.1
8	Vermont	92.0
9	Hawaii	91.7
9	Maine	91.7
9	South Dakota	91.7
12	Utah	91.4
12	Wisconsin	91.4
14	Colorado	90.5
15	Washington	90.4
16	Kansas	90.3
16	Nebraska	90.3
18	Connecticut	90.1
18	Idaho	90.1
20	Michigan	89.9
21	Massachusetts	89.7
21	Oregon	89.7
23	Maryland	89.6
24	Ohio	89.4
24	Pennsylvania	89.4
26	New Jersey	89.1
27	Delaware	89.0
28	Missouri	88.9
29	Virginia	88.5
30	Indiana	88.4
31	Illinois	88.2
32	Oklahoma	87.3
33	Florida	87.2
34	North Carolina	86.4
35	Arizona	86.1
35	South Carolina	86.1
37	Rhode Island	85.8
37	Tennessee	85.8
39	New York	85.7
40	Georgia	85.6
41	Arkansas	85.3
42	West Virginia	85.2
43	Nevada	85.1
44	Alabama	84.7
45	Kentucky	84.5
46	New Mexico	84.2
47	Louisiana	83.6
48	Mississippi	82.8
49	Texas	82.2
50	California	82.1
	District of Columbia	90.2

Source: U.S. Bureau of the Census
"2014 American Community Survey-Table R1501" (http://www.census.gov/programs-surveys/acs/)
*Persons age 25 and older. Includes equivalency status.

Public High School Graduates in 2013

National Total = 3,169,257 Graduates*

ALPHA ORDER

RANK	STATE	GRADUATES	% of USA
23	Alabama	44,233	1.4%
47	Alaska	7,860	0.2%
16	Arizona	62,208	2.0%
33	Arkansas	28,928	0.9%
1	California	422,125	13.3%
22	Colorado	50,968	1.6%
26	Connecticut	38,722	1.2%
46	Delaware	8,070	0.3%
4	Florida	158,029	5.0%
11	Georgia	92,416	2.9%
42	Hawaii	10,790	0.3%
39	Idaho	17,198	0.5%
5	Illinois	139,228	4.4%
13	Indiana	66,595	2.1%
31	Iowa	32,548	1.0%
32	Kansas	31,922	1.0%
24	Kentucky	42,888	1.4%
27	Louisiana	37,508	1.2%
41	Maine	13,170	0.4%
20	Maryland	58,896	1.9%
14	Massachusetts	66,360	2.1%
8	Michigan	104,210	3.3%
21	Minnesota	58,255	1.8%
34	Mississippi	26,502	0.8%
18	Missouri	61,407	1.9%
44	Montana	9,369	0.3%
36	Nebraska	20,442	0.6%
35	Nevada	23,038	0.7%
40	New Hampshire	14,262	0.5%
9	New Jersey	96,490	3.0%
37	New Mexico	19,232	0.6%
3	New York	180,351	5.7%
10	North Carolina	94,339	3.0%
48	North Dakota	6,900	0.2%
7	Ohio	122,491	3.9%
28	Oklahoma	37,033	1.2%
29	Oregon	33,899	1.1%
6	Pennsylvania	129,777	4.1%
43	Rhode Island	9,579	0.3%
25	South Carolina	42,246	1.3%
45	South Dakota	8,239	0.3%
19	Tennessee	61,323	1.9%
2	Texas	301,390	9.5%
30	Utah	33,186	1.0%
49	Vermont	6,491	0.2%
12	Virginia	83,279	2.6%
15	Washington	66,066	2.1%
38	West Virginia	17,924	0.6%
17	Wisconsin	61,425	1.9%
50	Wyoming	5,489	0.2%

RANK ORDER

RANK	STATE	GRADUATES	% of USA
1	California	422,125	13.3%
2	Texas	301,390	9.5%
3	New York	180,351	5.7%
4	Florida	158,029	5.0%
5	Illinois	139,228	4.4%
6	Pennsylvania	129,777	4.1%
7	Ohio	122,491	3.9%
8	Michigan	104,210	3.3%
9	New Jersey	96,490	3.0%
10	North Carolina	94,339	3.0%
11	Georgia	92,416	2.9%
12	Virginia	83,279	2.6%
13	Indiana	66,595	2.1%
14	Massachusetts	66,360	2.1%
15	Washington	66,066	2.1%
16	Arizona	62,208	2.0%
17	Wisconsin	61,425	1.9%
18	Missouri	61,407	1.9%
19	Tennessee	61,323	1.9%
20	Maryland	58,896	1.9%
21	Minnesota	58,255	1.8%
22	Colorado	50,968	1.6%
23	Alabama	44,233	1.4%
24	Kentucky	42,888	1.4%
25	South Carolina	42,246	1.3%
26	Connecticut	38,722	1.2%
27	Louisiana	37,508	1.2%
28	Oklahoma	37,033	1.2%
29	Oregon	33,899	1.1%
30	Utah	33,186	1.0%
31	Iowa	32,548	1.0%
32	Kansas	31,922	1.0%
33	Arkansas	28,928	0.9%
34	Mississippi	26,502	0.8%
35	Nevada	23,038	0.7%
36	Nebraska	20,442	0.6%
37	New Mexico	19,232	0.6%
38	West Virginia	17,924	0.6%
39	Idaho	17,198	0.5%
40	New Hampshire	14,262	0.5%
41	Maine	13,170	0.4%
42	Hawaii	10,790	0.3%
43	Rhode Island	9,579	0.3%
44	Montana	9,369	0.3%
45	South Dakota	8,239	0.3%
46	Delaware	8,070	0.3%
47	Alaska	7,860	0.2%
48	North Dakota	6,900	0.2%
49	Vermont	6,491	0.2%
50	Wyoming	5,489	0.2%
	District of Columbia	3,961	0.1%

Source: U.S. Department of Education, National Center for Education Statistics
"Digest of Education Statistics 2015" (http://nces.ed.gov/programs/digest/index.asp)
*Diploma recipients for school year 2012-2013. Excludes persons receiving high school equivalency certificates.

Adjusted Cohort Graduation Rate for Public High Schools in 2013

National Average = 81.4%*

ALPHA ORDER

RANK	STATE	RATE
32	Alabama	80.0
45	Alaska	71.8
43	Arizona	75.1
19	Arkansas	84.9
30	California	80.4
38	Colorado	76.9
15	Connecticut	85.5
30	Delaware	80.4
41	Florida	75.6
46	Georgia	71.7
27	Hawaii	82.4
NA	Idaho**	NA
23	Illinois	83.2
8	Indiana	87.0
1	Iowa	89.7
13	Kansas	85.7
12	Kentucky	86.1
44	Louisiana	73.5
10	Maine	86.4
17	Maryland	85.0
17	Massachusetts	85.0
36	Michigan	77.0
33	Minnesota	79.8
42	Mississippi	75.5
13	Missouri	85.7
22	Montana	84.4
2	Nebraska	88.5
47	Nevada	70.7
7	New Hampshire	87.3
5	New Jersey	87.5
48	New Mexico	70.3
39	New York	76.8
26	North Carolina	82.5
5	North Dakota	87.5
28	Ohio	82.2
20	Oklahoma	84.8
49	Oregon	68.7
15	Pennsylvania	85.5
34	Rhode Island	79.7
35	South Carolina	77.6
25	South Dakota	82.7
11	Tennessee	86.3
3	Texas	88.0
24	Utah	83.0
9	Vermont	86.6
21	Virginia	84.5
40	Washington	76.4
29	West Virginia	81.4
3	Wisconsin	88.0
36	Wyoming	77.0

RANK ORDER

RANK	STATE	RATE
1	Iowa	89.7
2	Nebraska	88.5
3	Texas	88.0
3	Wisconsin	88.0
5	New Jersey	87.5
5	North Dakota	87.5
7	New Hampshire	87.3
8	Indiana	87.0
9	Vermont	86.6
10	Maine	86.4
11	Tennessee	86.3
12	Kentucky	86.1
13	Kansas	85.7
13	Missouri	85.7
15	Connecticut	85.5
15	Pennsylvania	85.5
17	Maryland	85.0
17	Massachusetts	85.0
19	Arkansas	84.9
20	Oklahoma	84.8
21	Virginia	84.5
22	Montana	84.4
23	Illinois	83.2
24	Utah	83.0
25	South Dakota	82.7
26	North Carolina	82.5
27	Hawaii	82.4
28	Ohio	82.2
29	West Virginia	81.4
30	California	80.4
30	Delaware	80.4
32	Alabama	80.0
33	Minnesota	79.8
34	Rhode Island	79.7
35	South Carolina	77.6
36	Michigan	77.0
36	Wyoming	77.0
38	Colorado	76.9
39	New York	76.8
40	Washington	76.4
41	Florida	75.6
42	Mississippi	75.5
43	Arizona	75.1
44	Louisiana	73.5
45	Alaska	71.8
46	Georgia	71.7
47	Nevada	70.7
48	New Mexico	70.3
49	Oregon	68.7
NA	Idaho**	NA
	District of Columbia	62.3

Source: U.S. Department of Education, National Center for Education Statistics
"ED Data Express" (http://eddataexpress.ed.gov/index.cfm)
*The Adjusted Cohort Graduation Rate (ACGR) is the number of students who graduate in four years with a regular high school diploma divided by the number of students who form the adjusted cohort for the graduating class. From the beginning of 9th grade, students who are entering that grade for the first time form a cohort that is "adjusted" by adding any students who subsequently transfer into the cohort and subtracting any students who subsequently transfer out, emigrate to another country, or die. **Not available.

Public High School Dropout Rate in 2012

National Rate = 3.3%*

ALPHA ORDER

RANK	STATE	PERCENT
48	Alabama	1.4
1	Alaska	7.0
4	Arizona	5.9
21	Arkansas	3.2
12	California	4.0
6	Colorado	4.9
39	Connecticut	2.1
19	Delaware	3.5
39	Florida	2.1
13	Georgia	3.9
7	Hawaii	4.7
43	Idaho	1.9
37	Illinois	2.4
39	Indiana	2.1
21	Iowa	3.2
39	Kansas	2.1
31	Kentucky	2.5
5	Louisiana	5.7
21	Maine	3.2
15	Maryland	3.8
31	Massachusetts	2.5
2	Michigan	6.9
43	Minnesota	1.9
21	Mississippi	3.2
28	Missouri	2.9
11	Montana	4.1
38	Nebraska	2.2
13	Nevada	3.9
50	New Hampshire	1.3
48	New Jersey	1.4
3	New Mexico	6.4
15	New York	3.8
25	North Carolina	3.1
27	North Dakota	3.0
8	Ohio	4.6
31	Oklahoma	2.5
20	Oregon	3.4
29	Pennsylvania	2.8
10	Rhode Island	4.2
31	South Carolina	2.5
25	South Dakota	3.1
18	Tennessee	3.7
31	Texas	2.5
47	Utah	1.5
31	Vermont	2.5
43	Virginia	1.9
15	Washington	3.8
30	West Virginia	2.7
43	Wisconsin	1.9
9	Wyoming	4.3

RANK ORDER

RANK	STATE	PERCENT
1	Alaska	7.0
2	Michigan	6.9
3	New Mexico	6.4
4	Arizona	5.9
5	Louisiana	5.7
6	Colorado	4.9
7	Hawaii	4.7
8	Ohio	4.6
9	Wyoming	4.3
10	Rhode Island	4.2
11	Montana	4.1
12	California	4.0
13	Georgia	3.9
13	Nevada	3.9
15	Maryland	3.8
15	New York	3.8
15	Washington	3.8
18	Tennessee	3.7
19	Delaware	3.5
20	Oregon	3.4
21	Arkansas	3.2
21	Iowa	3.2
21	Maine	3.2
21	Mississippi	3.2
25	North Carolina	3.1
25	South Dakota	3.1
27	North Dakota	3.0
28	Missouri	2.9
29	Pennsylvania	2.8
30	West Virginia	2.7
31	Kentucky	2.5
31	Massachusetts	2.5
31	Oklahoma	2.5
31	South Carolina	2.5
31	Texas	2.5
31	Vermont	2.5
37	Illinois	2.4
38	Nebraska	2.2
39	Connecticut	2.1
39	Florida	2.1
39	Indiana	2.1
39	Kansas	2.1
43	Idaho	1.9
43	Minnesota	1.9
43	Virginia	1.9
43	Wisconsin	1.9
47	Utah	1.5
48	Alabama	1.4
48	New Jersey	1.4
50	New Hampshire	1.3
	District of Columbia	5.8

Source: U.S. Department of Education, National Center for Education Statistics
"Public High School Four-Year On-Time Graduation Rates and Event Dropout Rates: School Years 2010-11 and 2011-12"
(http://nces.ed.gov/pubsearch/pubsinfo.asp?pubid=2014391)
*"Event" dropout rates showing the number of 9th-12th grade dropouts divided by the number of students enrolled at the beginning of the school year in those grades.

ACT Average Composite Score in 2015

National Average = 21.0*

ALPHA ORDER

RANK	STATE	AVERAGE SCORE
47	Alabama	19.1
26	Alaska	21.1
43	Arizona	19.9
35	Arkansas	20.4
15	California	22.5
31	Colorado	20.7
1	Connecticut	24.4
6	Delaware	23.5
43	Florida	19.9
27	Georgia	21.0
50	Hawaii	18.5
12	Idaho	22.7
31	Illinois	20.7
19	Indiana	22.1
17	Iowa	22.2
21	Kansas	21.9
42	Kentucky	20.0
46	Louisiana	19.4
4	Maine	24.2
12	Maryland	22.7
1	Massachusetts	24.4
40	Michigan	20.1
12	Minnesota	22.7
48	Mississippi	19.0
23	Missouri	21.7
35	Montana	20.4
24	Nebraska	21.5
27	Nevada	21.0
3	New Hampshire	24.3
8	New Jersey	23.2
40	New Mexico	20.1
5	New York	23.7
48	North Carolina	19.0
34	North Dakota	20.6
20	Ohio	22.0
31	Oklahoma	20.7
24	Oregon	21.5
11	Pennsylvania	22.9
9	Rhode Island	23.1
35	South Carolina	20.4
21	South Dakota	21.9
45	Tennessee	19.8
29	Texas	20.9
38	Utah	20.2
6	Vermont	23.5
9	Virginia	23.1
16	Washington	22.4
30	West Virginia	20.8
17	Wisconsin	22.2
38	Wyoming	20.2

RANK ORDER

RANK	STATE	AVERAGE SCORE
1	Connecticut	24.4
1	Massachusetts	24.4
3	New Hampshire	24.3
4	Maine	24.2
5	New York	23.7
6	Delaware	23.5
6	Vermont	23.5
8	New Jersey	23.2
9	Rhode Island	23.1
9	Virginia	23.1
11	Pennsylvania	22.9
12	Idaho	22.7
12	Maryland	22.7
12	Minnesota	22.7
15	California	22.5
16	Washington	22.4
17	Iowa	22.2
17	Wisconsin	22.2
19	Indiana	22.1
20	Ohio	22.0
21	Kansas	21.9
21	South Dakota	21.9
23	Missouri	21.7
24	Nebraska	21.5
24	Oregon	21.5
26	Alaska	21.1
27	Georgia	21.0
27	Nevada	21.0
29	Texas	20.9
30	West Virginia	20.8
31	Colorado	20.7
31	Illinois	20.7
31	Oklahoma	20.7
34	North Dakota	20.6
35	Arkansas	20.4
35	Montana	20.4
35	South Carolina	20.4
38	Utah	20.2
38	Wyoming	20.2
40	Michigan	20.1
40	New Mexico	20.1
42	Kentucky	20.0
43	Arizona	19.9
43	Florida	19.9
45	Tennessee	19.8
46	Louisiana	19.4
47	Alabama	19.1
48	Mississippi	19.0
48	North Carolina	19.0
50	Hawaii	18.5
	District of Columbia	21.1

Source: The American College Testing Program (Copyright © 2015) "Average ACT Scores by State" (http://www.act.org/newsroom/)

*The ACT score range is 1 to 36. Approximately 1.9 million 2015 U.S. high school students took the test. Caution should be used in using ACT scores to compare states. The percentage of high school students taking the test varies greatly from one state to another. For example, all 11th grade students are required to take the test in thirteen states but, in Maine, only 10 percent of 11th grade students took the test.

Education Expenditures by State and Local Governments in 2013

National Total = $876,566,216,000*

ALPHA ORDER

RANK	STATE	EXPENDITURES	% of USA
23	Alabama	$13,372,920,000	1.5%
40	Alaska	3,624,902,000	0.4%
22	Arizona	13,455,713,000	1.5%
33	Arkansas	8,167,812,000	0.9%
1	California	106,083,661,000	12.1%
21	Colorado	13,507,081,000	1.5%
25	Connecticut	12,187,837,000	1.4%
41	Delaware	3,478,835,000	0.4%
5	Florida	37,468,374,000	4.3%
10	Georgia	25,183,893,000	2.9%
42	Hawaii	3,404,040,000	0.4%
45	Idaho	3,117,677,000	0.4%
6	Illinois	35,943,825,000	4.1%
17	Indiana	16,585,880,000	1.9%
29	Iowa	9,965,300,000	1.1%
32	Kansas	8,453,292,000	1.0%
27	Kentucky	11,645,301,000	1.3%
26	Louisiana	12,001,559,000	1.4%
43	Maine	3,224,107,000	0.4%
15	Maryland	18,446,253,000	2.1%
13	Massachusetts	20,964,585,000	2.4%
9	Michigan	27,992,574,000	3.2%
18	Minnesota	16,012,561,000	1.8%
34	Mississippi	7,319,139,000	0.8%
19	Missouri	14,347,248,000	1.6%
46	Montana	2,629,163,000	0.3%
36	Nebraska	6,106,021,000	0.7%
38	Nevada	5,440,717,000	0.6%
39	New Hampshire	3,714,697,000	0.4%
8	New Jersey	32,115,432,000	3.7%
35	New Mexico	6,183,067,000	0.7%
3	New York	71,143,627,000	8.1%
11	North Carolina	24,871,295,000	2.8%
48	North Dakota	2,522,474,000	0.3%
7	Ohio	32,380,740,000	3.7%
30	Oklahoma	9,594,931,000	1.1%
28	Oregon	10,446,679,000	1.2%
4	Pennsylvania	37,475,930,000	4.3%
44	Rhode Island	3,200,828,000	0.4%
24	South Carolina	12,606,392,000	1.4%
50	South Dakota	2,057,580,000	0.2%
20	Tennessee	13,745,616,000	1.6%
2	Texas	71,860,625,000	8.2%
31	Utah	8,468,406,000	1.0%
49	Vermont	2,459,146,000	0.3%
12	Virginia	24,528,812,000	2.8%
14	Washington	19,713,143,000	2.2%
37	West Virginia	5,482,118,000	0.6%
16	Wisconsin	16,775,852,000	1.9%
47	Wyoming	2,562,658,000	0.3%

RANK ORDER

RANK	STATE	EXPENDITURES	% of USA
1	California	$106,083,661,000	12.1%
2	Texas	71,860,625,000	8.2%
3	New York	71,143,627,000	8.1%
4	Pennsylvania	37,475,930,000	4.3%
5	Florida	37,468,374,000	4.3%
6	Illinois	35,943,825,000	4.1%
7	Ohio	32,380,740,000	3.7%
8	New Jersey	32,115,432,000	3.7%
9	Michigan	27,992,574,000	3.2%
10	Georgia	25,183,893,000	2.9%
11	North Carolina	24,871,295,000	2.8%
12	Virginia	24,528,812,000	2.8%
13	Massachusetts	20,964,585,000	2.4%
14	Washington	19,713,143,000	2.2%
15	Maryland	18,446,253,000	2.1%
16	Wisconsin	16,775,852,000	1.9%
17	Indiana	16,585,880,000	1.9%
18	Minnesota	16,012,561,000	1.8%
19	Missouri	14,347,248,000	1.6%
20	Tennessee	13,745,616,000	1.6%
21	Colorado	13,507,081,000	1.5%
22	Arizona	13,455,713,000	1.5%
23	Alabama	13,372,920,000	1.5%
24	South Carolina	12,606,392,000	1.4%
25	Connecticut	12,187,837,000	1.4%
26	Louisiana	12,001,559,000	1.4%
27	Kentucky	11,645,301,000	1.3%
28	Oregon	10,446,679,000	1.2%
29	Iowa	9,965,300,000	1.1%
30	Oklahoma	9,594,931,000	1.1%
31	Utah	8,468,406,000	1.0%
32	Kansas	8,453,292,000	1.0%
33	Arkansas	8,167,812,000	0.9%
34	Mississippi	7,319,139,000	0.8%
35	New Mexico	6,183,067,000	0.7%
36	Nebraska	6,106,021,000	0.7%
37	West Virginia	5,482,118,000	0.6%
38	Nevada	5,440,717,000	0.6%
39	New Hampshire	3,714,697,000	0.4%
40	Alaska	3,624,902,000	0.4%
41	Delaware	3,478,835,000	0.4%
42	Hawaii	3,404,040,000	0.4%
43	Maine	3,224,107,000	0.4%
44	Rhode Island	3,200,828,000	0.4%
45	Idaho	3,117,677,000	0.4%
46	Montana	2,629,163,000	0.3%
47	Wyoming	2,562,658,000	0.3%
48	North Dakota	2,522,474,000	0.3%
49	Vermont	2,459,146,000	0.3%
50	South Dakota	2,057,580,000	0.2%
	District of Columbia	2,525,898,000	0.3%

Source: U.S. Bureau of the Census, Governments Division
"2013 State and Local Government Finances" (http://www.census.gov/govs/local/)
*Direct general expenditures for higher, secondary, elementary, and, "other" education. Includes capital outlays.

Per Capita State and Local Government Expenditures for Education in 2013

National Per Capita = $2,770*

ALPHA ORDER

RANK	STATE	PER CAPITA
27	Alabama	$2,768
1	Alaska	4,916
47	Arizona	2,029
29	Arkansas	2,761
28	California	2,762
36	Colorado	2,562
8	Connecticut	3,388
4	Delaware	3,759
50	Florida	1,912
39	Georgia	2,521
44	Hawaii	2,416
49	Idaho	1,933
26	Illinois	2,789
38	Indiana	2,524
10	Iowa	3,223
20	Kansas	2,920
32	Kentucky	2,648
34	Louisiana	2,594
43	Maine	2,426
12	Maryland	3,108
11	Massachusetts	3,125
22	Michigan	2,827
17	Minnesota	2,954
41	Mississippi	2,447
45	Missouri	2,374
35	Montana	2,592
9	Nebraska	3,266
48	Nevada	1,950
24	New Hampshire	2,809
6	New Jersey	3,605
15	New Mexico	2,963
5	New York	3,613
37	North Carolina	2,526
7	North Dakota	3,486
25	Ohio	2,798
40	Oklahoma	2,490
31	Oregon	2,660
18	Pennsylvania	2,932
13	Rhode Island	3,040
33	South Carolina	2,644
42	South Dakota	2,434
46	Tennessee	2,116
30	Texas	2,712
21	Utah	2,916
3	Vermont	3,921
14	Virginia	2,967
22	Washington	2,827
16	West Virginia	2,959
19	Wisconsin	2,921
2	Wyoming	4,395

RANK ORDER

RANK	STATE	PER CAPITA
1	Alaska	$4,916
2	Wyoming	4,395
3	Vermont	3,921
4	Delaware	3,759
5	New York	3,613
6	New Jersey	3,605
7	North Dakota	3,486
8	Connecticut	3,388
9	Nebraska	3,266
10	Iowa	3,223
11	Massachusetts	3,125
12	Maryland	3,108
13	Rhode Island	3,040
14	Virginia	2,967
15	New Mexico	2,963
16	West Virginia	2,959
17	Minnesota	2,954
18	Pennsylvania	2,932
19	Wisconsin	2,921
20	Kansas	2,920
21	Utah	2,916
22	Michigan	2,827
22	Washington	2,827
24	New Hampshire	2,809
25	Ohio	2,798
26	Illinois	2,789
27	Alabama	2,768
28	California	2,762
29	Arkansas	2,761
30	Texas	2,712
31	Oregon	2,660
32	Kentucky	2,648
33	South Carolina	2,644
34	Louisiana	2,594
35	Montana	2,592
36	Colorado	2,562
37	North Carolina	2,526
38	Indiana	2,524
39	Georgia	2,521
40	Oklahoma	2,490
41	Mississippi	2,447
42	South Dakota	2,434
43	Maine	2,426
44	Hawaii	2,416
45	Missouri	2,374
46	Tennessee	2,116
47	Arizona	2,029
48	Nevada	1,950
49	Idaho	1,933
50	Florida	1,912

District of Columbia 3,889

Source: CQ Press using data from U.S. Bureau of the Census, Governments Division
"2013 State and Local Government Finances" (http://www.census.gov/govs/local/)
*Direct general expenditures for higher, secondary, elementary, and, "other" education. Includes capital outlays.

Expenditures for Education as a Percent of All State and Local Government Expenditures in 2013
National Percent = 33.2%*

ALPHA ORDER

RANK	STATE	PERCENT
13	Alabama	36.9
50	Alaska	26.7
35	Arizona	32.6
6	Arkansas	38.1
44	California	29.3
34	Colorado	32.7
22	Connecticut	34.9
12	Delaware	37.0
48	Florida	27.8
3	Georgia	38.6
49	Hawaii	27.7
42	Idaho	30.1
29	Illinois	33.4
19	Indiana	35.4
17	Iowa	35.7
15	Kansas	36.3
14	Kentucky	36.4
47	Louisiana	28.6
46	Maine	29.0
21	Maryland	35.0
40	Massachusetts	31.9
7	Michigan	37.5
36	Minnesota	32.5
41	Mississippi	30.5
33	Missouri	32.9
39	Montana	32.1
2	Nebraska	39.7
43	Nevada	30.0
11	New Hampshire	37.2
5	New Jersey	38.3
25	New Mexico	34.0
45	New York	29.1
25	North Carolina	34.0
28	North Dakota	33.8
23	Ohio	34.8
20	Oklahoma	35.1
37	Oregon	32.4
24	Pennsylvania	34.1
27	Rhode Island	33.9
16	South Carolina	36.0
30	South Dakota	33.1
38	Tennessee	32.2
4	Texas	38.4
1	Utah	39.8
7	Vermont	37.5
9	Virginia	37.4
30	Washington	33.1
10	West Virginia	37.3
18	Wisconsin	35.5
32	Wyoming	33.0

RANK ORDER

RANK	STATE	PERCENT
1	Utah	39.8
2	Nebraska	39.7
3	Georgia	38.6
4	Texas	38.4
5	New Jersey	38.3
6	Arkansas	38.1
7	Michigan	37.5
7	Vermont	37.5
9	Virginia	37.4
10	West Virginia	37.3
11	New Hampshire	37.2
12	Delaware	37.0
13	Alabama	36.9
14	Kentucky	36.4
15	Kansas	36.3
16	South Carolina	36.0
17	Iowa	35.7
18	Wisconsin	35.5
19	Indiana	35.4
20	Oklahoma	35.1
21	Maryland	35.0
22	Connecticut	34.9
23	Ohio	34.8
24	Pennsylvania	34.1
25	New Mexico	34.0
25	North Carolina	34.0
27	Rhode Island	33.9
28	North Dakota	33.8
29	Illinois	33.4
30	South Dakota	33.1
30	Washington	33.1
32	Wyoming	33.0
33	Missouri	32.9
34	Colorado	32.7
35	Arizona	32.6
36	Minnesota	32.5
37	Oregon	32.4
38	Tennessee	32.2
39	Montana	32.1
40	Massachusetts	31.9
41	Mississippi	30.5
42	Idaho	30.1
43	Nevada	30.0
44	California	29.3
45	New York	29.1
46	Maine	29.0
47	Louisiana	28.6
48	Florida	27.8
49	Hawaii	27.7
50	Alaska	26.7
	District of Columbia	21.9

Source: CQ Press using data from U.S. Bureau of the Census, Governments Division
"2013 State and Local Government Finances" (http://www.census.gov/govs/local/)
*Direct general expenditures for higher, secondary, elementary, and "other" education as a percent of all direct general expenditures. Includes capital outlays.

State and Local Government Expenditures for Elementary and Secondary Education in 2013
National Total = $569,808,329,000*

ALPHA ORDER

RANK	STATE	EXPENDITURES	% of USA
25	Alabama	$7,542,890,000	1.3%
40	Alaska	2,496,748,000	0.4%
26	Arizona	7,464,108,000	1.3%
32	Arkansas	4,910,061,000	0.9%
1	California	66,339,646,000	11.6%
22	Colorado	8,195,853,000	1.4%
21	Connecticut	8,848,480,000	1.6%
45	Delaware	1,847,436,000	0.3%
6	Florida	24,645,770,000	4.3%
9	Georgia	17,044,972,000	3.0%
44	Hawaii	1,886,487,000	0.3%
43	Idaho	1,914,356,000	0.3%
5	Illinois	25,012,192,000	4.4%
19	Indiana	9,609,909,000	1.7%
28	Iowa	5,961,490,000	1.0%
31	Kansas	5,146,082,000	0.9%
27	Kentucky	6,873,081,000	1.2%
23	Louisiana	7,957,996,000	1.4%
42	Maine	2,228,716,000	0.4%
14	Maryland	12,108,041,000	2.1%
12	Massachusetts	14,713,023,000	2.6%
10	Michigan	16,473,496,000	2.9%
16	Minnesota	10,346,467,000	1.8%
34	Mississippi	4,310,580,000	0.8%
18	Missouri	9,621,772,000	1.7%
47	Montana	1,640,721,000	0.3%
36	Nebraska	3,811,437,000	0.7%
35	Nevada	3,844,420,000	0.7%
39	New Hampshire	2,688,597,000	0.5%
7	New Jersey	24,520,537,000	4.3%
37	New Mexico	3,470,180,000	0.6%
2	New York	55,769,468,000	9.8%
13	North Carolina	14,178,231,000	2.5%
49	North Dakota	1,440,823,000	0.3%
8	Ohio	21,111,394,000	3.7%
30	Oklahoma	5,713,682,000	1.0%
29	Oregon	5,901,123,000	1.0%
4	Pennsylvania	25,908,977,000	4.5%
41	Rhode Island	2,270,819,000	0.4%
24	South Carolina	7,665,808,000	1.3%
50	South Dakota	1,292,102,000	0.2%
20	Tennessee	9,040,547,000	1.6%
3	Texas	45,039,672,000	7.9%
33	Utah	4,466,277,000	0.8%
48	Vermont	1,524,806,000	0.3%
11	Virginia	15,901,201,000	2.8%
15	Washington	11,677,102,000	2.0%
38	West Virginia	3,166,754,000	0.6%
17	Wisconsin	10,237,586,000	1.8%
46	Wyoming	1,659,222,000	0.3%

RANK ORDER

RANK	STATE	EXPENDITURES	% of USA
1	California	$66,339,646,000	11.6%
2	New York	55,769,468,000	9.8%
3	Texas	45,039,672,000	7.9%
4	Pennsylvania	25,908,977,000	4.5%
5	Illinois	25,012,192,000	4.4%
6	Florida	24,645,770,000	4.3%
7	New Jersey	24,520,537,000	4.3%
8	Ohio	21,111,394,000	3.7%
9	Georgia	17,044,972,000	3.0%
10	Michigan	16,473,496,000	2.9%
11	Virginia	15,901,201,000	2.8%
12	Massachusetts	14,713,023,000	2.6%
13	North Carolina	14,178,231,000	2.5%
14	Maryland	12,108,041,000	2.1%
15	Washington	11,677,102,000	2.0%
16	Minnesota	10,346,467,000	1.8%
17	Wisconsin	10,237,586,000	1.8%
18	Missouri	9,621,772,000	1.7%
19	Indiana	9,609,909,000	1.7%
20	Tennessee	9,040,547,000	1.6%
21	Connecticut	8,848,480,000	1.6%
22	Colorado	8,195,853,000	1.4%
23	Louisiana	7,957,996,000	1.4%
24	South Carolina	7,665,808,000	1.3%
25	Alabama	7,542,890,000	1.3%
26	Arizona	7,464,108,000	1.3%
27	Kentucky	6,873,081,000	1.2%
28	Iowa	5,961,490,000	1.0%
29	Oregon	5,901,123,000	1.0%
30	Oklahoma	5,713,682,000	1.0%
31	Kansas	5,146,082,000	0.9%
32	Arkansas	4,910,061,000	0.9%
33	Utah	4,466,277,000	0.8%
34	Mississippi	4,310,580,000	0.8%
35	Nevada	3,844,420,000	0.7%
36	Nebraska	3,811,437,000	0.7%
37	New Mexico	3,470,180,000	0.6%
38	West Virginia	3,166,754,000	0.6%
39	New Hampshire	2,688,597,000	0.5%
40	Alaska	2,496,748,000	0.4%
41	Rhode Island	2,270,819,000	0.4%
42	Maine	2,228,716,000	0.4%
43	Idaho	1,914,356,000	0.3%
44	Hawaii	1,886,487,000	0.3%
45	Delaware	1,847,436,000	0.3%
46	Wyoming	1,659,222,000	0.3%
47	Montana	1,640,721,000	0.3%
48	Vermont	1,524,806,000	0.3%
49	North Dakota	1,440,823,000	0.3%
50	South Dakota	1,292,102,000	0.2%
	District of Columbia	2,367,191,000	0.4%

Source: U.S. Bureau of the Census, Governments Division
 "2013 State and Local Government Finances" (http://www.census.gov/govs/local/)
*Direct general expenditures. Includes capital outlays.

Per Capita State and Local Government Expenditures for Elementary and Secondary Education in 2013
National Per Capita = $1,801*

ALPHA ORDER

RANK	STATE	PER CAPITA
36	Alabama	$1,562
1	Alaska	3,386
50	Arizona	1,126
31	Arkansas	1,660
22	California	1,727
37	Colorado	1,555
5	Connecticut	2,460
13	Delaware	1,996
48	Florida	1,258
25	Georgia	1,706
47	Hawaii	1,339
49	Idaho	1,187
15	Illinois	1,940
42	Indiana	1,463
16	Iowa	1,928
21	Kansas	1,778
35	Kentucky	1,563
23	Louisiana	1,720
27	Maine	1,677
9	Maryland	2,040
7	Massachusetts	2,193
29	Michigan	1,664
18	Minnesota	1,909
43	Mississippi	1,441
34	Missouri	1,592
32	Montana	1,617
10	Nebraska	2,039
46	Nevada	1,378
11	New Hampshire	2,033
4	New Jersey	2,753
30	New Mexico	1,663
3	New York	2,832
44	North Carolina	1,440
14	North Dakota	1,991
19	Ohio	1,824
41	Oklahoma	1,483
40	Oregon	1,502
12	Pennsylvania	2,027
8	Rhode Island	2,157
33	South Carolina	1,608
39	South Dakota	1,529
45	Tennessee	1,392
26	Texas	1,700
38	Utah	1,538
6	Vermont	2,431
17	Virginia	1,923
28	Washington	1,675
24	West Virginia	1,709
20	Wisconsin	1,782
2	Wyoming	2,845

RANK ORDER

RANK	STATE	PER CAPITA
1	Alaska	$3,386
2	Wyoming	2,845
3	New York	2,832
4	New Jersey	2,753
5	Connecticut	2,460
6	Vermont	2,431
7	Massachusetts	2,193
8	Rhode Island	2,157
9	Maryland	2,040
10	Nebraska	2,039
11	New Hampshire	2,033
12	Pennsylvania	2,027
13	Delaware	1,996
14	North Dakota	1,991
15	Illinois	1,940
16	Iowa	1,928
17	Virginia	1,923
18	Minnesota	1,909
19	Ohio	1,824
20	Wisconsin	1,782
21	Kansas	1,778
22	California	1,727
23	Louisiana	1,720
24	West Virginia	1,709
25	Georgia	1,706
26	Texas	1,700
27	Maine	1,677
28	Washington	1,675
29	Michigan	1,664
30	New Mexico	1,663
31	Arkansas	1,660
32	Montana	1,617
33	South Carolina	1,608
34	Missouri	1,592
35	Kentucky	1,563
36	Alabama	1,562
37	Colorado	1,555
38	Utah	1,538
39	South Dakota	1,529
40	Oregon	1,502
41	Oklahoma	1,483
42	Indiana	1,463
43	Mississippi	1,441
44	North Carolina	1,440
45	Tennessee	1,392
46	Nevada	1,378
47	Hawaii	1,339
48	Florida	1,258
49	Idaho	1,187
50	Arizona	1,126
	District of Columbia	3,644

Source: CQ Press using data from U.S. Bureau of the Census, Governments Division
"2013 State and Local Government Finances" (http://www.census.gov/govs/local/)
*Direct general expenditures. Includes capital outlays.

Expenditures for Elementary and Secondary Education as a Percent of All State and Local Government Expenditures in 2013
National Percent = 21.6%*

ALPHA ORDER

RANK	STATE	PERCENT
31	Alabama	20.8
44	Alaska	18.4
48	Arizona	18.1
13	Arkansas	22.9
45	California	18.3
36	Colorado	19.8
4	Connecticut	25.4
37	Delaware	19.6
45	Florida	18.3
3	Georgia	26.1
50	Hawaii	15.3
43	Idaho	18.5
10	Illinois	23.3
33	Indiana	20.5
25	Iowa	21.3
17	Kansas	22.1
23	Kentucky	21.5
42	Louisiana	18.9
34	Maine	20.0
12	Maryland	23.0
16	Massachusetts	22.4
17	Michigan	22.1
28	Minnesota	21.0
49	Mississippi	18.0
17	Missouri	22.1
34	Montana	20.0
5	Nebraska	24.8
26	Nevada	21.2
2	New Hampshire	26.9
1	New Jersey	29.2
41	New Mexico	19.1
14	New York	22.8
39	North Carolina	19.4
40	North Dakota	19.3
15	Ohio	22.7
30	Oklahoma	20.9
45	Oregon	18.3
9	Pennsylvania	23.6
7	Rhode Island	24.1
20	South Carolina	21.9
31	South Dakota	20.8
26	Tennessee	21.2
7	Texas	24.1
28	Utah	21.0
11	Vermont	23.2
6	Virginia	24.3
37	Washington	19.6
22	West Virginia	21.6
21	Wisconsin	21.7
24	Wyoming	21.4

RANK ORDER

RANK	STATE	PERCENT
1	New Jersey	29.2
2	New Hampshire	26.9
3	Georgia	26.1
4	Connecticut	25.4
5	Nebraska	24.8
6	Virginia	24.3
7	Rhode Island	24.1
7	Texas	24.1
9	Pennsylvania	23.6
10	Illinois	23.3
11	Vermont	23.2
12	Maryland	23.0
13	Arkansas	22.9
14	New York	22.8
15	Ohio	22.7
16	Massachusetts	22.4
17	Kansas	22.1
17	Michigan	22.1
17	Missouri	22.1
20	South Carolina	21.9
21	Wisconsin	21.7
22	West Virginia	21.6
23	Kentucky	21.5
24	Wyoming	21.4
25	Iowa	21.3
26	Nevada	21.2
26	Tennessee	21.2
28	Minnesota	21.0
28	Utah	21.0
30	Oklahoma	20.9
31	Alabama	20.8
31	South Dakota	20.8
33	Indiana	20.5
34	Maine	20.0
34	Montana	20.0
36	Colorado	19.8
37	Delaware	19.6
37	Washington	19.6
39	North Carolina	19.4
40	North Dakota	19.3
41	New Mexico	19.1
42	Louisiana	18.9
43	Idaho	18.5
44	Alaska	18.4
45	California	18.3
45	Florida	18.3
45	Oregon	18.3
48	Arizona	18.1
49	Mississippi	18.0
50	Hawaii	15.3

District of Columbia 20.5

Source: CQ Press using data from U.S. Bureau of the Census, Governments Division
"2013 State and Local Government Finances" (http://www.census.gov/govs/local/)
*Direct general expenditures as a percent of all direct general expenditures. Includes capital outlays.

Estimated Per Pupil Public Elementary and Secondary School Current Expenditures in 2015
National Per Pupil = $11,732*

ALPHA ORDER

RANK	STATE	PER PUPIL
43	Alabama	$8,797
4	Alaska	20,117
50	Arizona	7,461
34	Arkansas	9,573
20	California	11,145
23	Colorado	10,899
6	Connecticut	17,759
10	Delaware	15,858
36	Florida	9,223
35	Georgia	9,291
17	Hawaii	12,014
42	Idaho	8,928
14	Illinois	13,870
47	Indiana	8,034
27	Iowa	10,613
32	Kansas	9,822
33	Kentucky	9,635
28	Louisiana	10,511
40	Maine	8,957
13	Maryland	14,249
8	Massachusetts	16,678
12	Michigan	15,175
16	Minnesota	12,180
44	Mississippi	8,779
25	Missouri	10,755
24	Montana	10,859
30	Nebraska	10,012
41	Nevada	8,956
7	New Hampshire	17,115
3	New Jersey	20,925
26	New Mexico	10,633
2	New York	21,366
45	North Carolina	8,620
46	North Dakota	8,518
18	Ohio	11,530
48	Oklahoma	7,977
21	Oregon	11,127
11	Pennsylvania	15,691
5	Rhode Island	19,676
31	South Carolina	10,005
38	South Dakota	8,989
37	Tennessee	9,105
39	Texas	8,962
49	Utah	7,711
1	Vermont	23,149
22	Virginia	10,980
29	Washington	10,055
15	West Virginia	12,859
19	Wisconsin	11,424
9	Wyoming	16,127

RANK ORDER

RANK	STATE	PER PUPIL
1	Vermont	$23,149
2	New York	21,366
3	New Jersey	20,925
4	Alaska	20,117
5	Rhode Island	19,676
6	Connecticut	17,759
7	New Hampshire	17,115
8	Massachusetts	16,678
9	Wyoming	16,127
10	Delaware	15,858
11	Pennsylvania	15,691
12	Michigan	15,175
13	Maryland	14,249
14	Illinois	13,870
15	West Virginia	12,859
16	Minnesota	12,180
17	Hawaii	12,014
18	Ohio	11,530
19	Wisconsin	11,424
20	California	11,145
21	Oregon	11,127
22	Virginia	10,980
23	Colorado	10,899
24	Montana	10,859
25	Missouri	10,755
26	New Mexico	10,633
27	Iowa	10,613
28	Louisiana	10,511
29	Washington	10,055
30	Nebraska	10,012
31	South Carolina	10,005
32	Kansas	9,822
33	Kentucky	9,635
34	Arkansas	9,573
35	Georgia	9,291
36	Florida	9,223
37	Tennessee	9,105
38	South Dakota	8,989
39	Texas	8,962
40	Maine	8,957
41	Nevada	8,956
42	Idaho	8,928
43	Alabama	8,797
44	Mississippi	8,779
45	North Carolina	8,620
46	North Dakota	8,518
47	Indiana	8,034
48	Oklahoma	7,977
49	Utah	7,711
50	Arizona	7,461
	District of Columbia	14,779

Source: National Education Association, Washington, D.C.
"Rankings and Estimates" (Copyright © 2015, NEA, used with permission, http://www.nea.org/home/44479.htm)
*Estimates for school year 2014-2015. Based on student membership.

Higher Education Expenditures by State and Local Governments in 2013

National Total = $261,153,244,000*

ALPHA ORDER

RANK	STATE	EXPENDITURES	% of USA
19	Alabama	$4,977,347,000	1.9%
42	Alaska	985,698,000	0.4%
18	Arizona	5,075,263,000	1.9%
33	Arkansas	2,607,159,000	1.0%
1	California	34,610,395,000	13.3%
20	Colorado	4,662,517,000	1.8%
32	Connecticut	2,610,141,000	1.0%
39	Delaware	1,252,274,000	0.5%
7	Florida	9,531,771,000	3.6%
11	Georgia	6,297,952,000	2.4%
38	Hawaii	1,410,793,000	0.5%
41	Idaho	1,046,022,000	0.4%
9	Illinois	9,253,792,000	3.5%
14	Indiana	5,884,919,000	2.3%
28	Iowa	3,554,648,000	1.4%
31	Kansas	3,053,623,000	1.2%
24	Kentucky	3,781,413,000	1.4%
30	Louisiana	3,115,463,000	1.2%
46	Maine	791,682,000	0.3%
16	Maryland	5,632,108,000	2.2%
17	Massachusetts	5,215,076,000	2.0%
4	Michigan	10,482,543,000	4.0%
21	Minnesota	4,648,241,000	1.8%
34	Mississippi	2,572,748,000	1.0%
23	Missouri	3,989,691,000	1.5%
45	Montana	809,883,000	0.3%
36	Nebraska	2,014,872,000	0.8%
40	Nevada	1,230,699,000	0.5%
44	New Hampshire	846,535,000	0.3%
13	New Jersey	5,940,340,000	2.3%
35	New Mexico	2,333,632,000	0.9%
3	New York	13,641,632,000	5.2%
8	North Carolina	9,435,853,000	3.6%
43	North Dakota	980,924,000	0.4%
5	Ohio	9,754,306,000	3.7%
29	Oklahoma	3,348,446,000	1.3%
22	Oregon	4,119,532,000	1.6%
6	Pennsylvania	9,593,303,000	3.7%
49	Rhode Island	660,004,000	0.3%
25	South Carolina	3,696,772,000	1.4%
50	South Dakota	652,450,000	0.2%
26	Tennessee	3,669,656,000	1.4%
2	Texas	24,648,872,000	9.4%
27	Utah	3,619,850,000	1.4%
47	Vermont	757,850,000	0.3%
10	Virginia	7,714,628,000	3.0%
12	Washington	6,221,366,000	2.4%
37	West Virginia	1,683,869,000	0.6%
15	Wisconsin	5,842,762,000	2.2%
48	Wyoming	733,222,000	0.3%

RANK ORDER

RANK	STATE	EXPENDITURES	% of USA
1	California	$34,610,395,000	13.3%
2	Texas	24,648,872,000	9.4%
3	New York	13,641,632,000	5.2%
4	Michigan	10,482,543,000	4.0%
5	Ohio	9,754,306,000	3.7%
6	Pennsylvania	9,593,303,000	3.7%
7	Florida	9,531,771,000	3.6%
8	North Carolina	9,435,853,000	3.6%
9	Illinois	9,253,792,000	3.5%
10	Virginia	7,714,628,000	3.0%
11	Georgia	6,297,952,000	2.4%
12	Washington	6,221,366,000	2.4%
13	New Jersey	5,940,340,000	2.3%
14	Indiana	5,884,919,000	2.3%
15	Wisconsin	5,842,762,000	2.2%
16	Maryland	5,632,108,000	2.2%
17	Massachusetts	5,215,076,000	2.0%
18	Arizona	5,075,263,000	1.9%
19	Alabama	4,977,347,000	1.9%
20	Colorado	4,662,517,000	1.8%
21	Minnesota	4,648,241,000	1.8%
22	Oregon	4,119,532,000	1.6%
23	Missouri	3,989,691,000	1.5%
24	Kentucky	3,781,413,000	1.4%
25	South Carolina	3,696,772,000	1.4%
26	Tennessee	3,669,656,000	1.4%
27	Utah	3,619,850,000	1.4%
28	Iowa	3,554,648,000	1.4%
29	Oklahoma	3,348,446,000	1.3%
30	Louisiana	3,115,463,000	1.2%
31	Kansas	3,053,623,000	1.2%
32	Connecticut	2,610,141,000	1.0%
33	Arkansas	2,607,159,000	1.0%
34	Mississippi	2,572,748,000	1.0%
35	New Mexico	2,333,632,000	0.9%
36	Nebraska	2,014,872,000	0.8%
37	West Virginia	1,683,869,000	0.6%
38	Hawaii	1,410,793,000	0.5%
39	Delaware	1,252,274,000	0.5%
40	Nevada	1,230,699,000	0.5%
41	Idaho	1,046,022,000	0.4%
42	Alaska	985,698,000	0.4%
43	North Dakota	980,924,000	0.4%
44	New Hampshire	846,535,000	0.3%
45	Montana	809,883,000	0.3%
46	Maine	791,682,000	0.3%
47	Vermont	757,850,000	0.3%
48	Wyoming	733,222,000	0.3%
49	Rhode Island	660,004,000	0.3%
50	South Dakota	652,450,000	0.2%
	District of Columbia	158,707,000	0.1%

Source: U.S. Bureau of the Census, Governments Division
"2013 State and Local Government Finances" (http://www.census.gov/govs/local/)
*Direct general expenditures. Includes capital outlays.

Per Capita State and Local Government Expenditures for Higher Education in 2013
National Per Capita = $825*

ALPHA ORDER

RANK	STATE	PER CAPITA
13	Alabama	$1,030
3	Alaska	1,337
35	Arizona	765
25	Arkansas	881
21	California	901
24	Colorado	885
37	Connecticut	726
2	Delaware	1,353
49	Florida	486
45	Georgia	630
15	Hawaii	1,001
43	Idaho	649
38	Illinois	718
22	Indiana	896
7	Iowa	1,150
11	Kansas	1,055
27	Kentucky	860
40	Louisiana	673
47	Maine	596
17	Maryland	949
32	Massachusetts	777
10	Michigan	1,059
29	Minnesota	858
27	Mississippi	860
42	Missouri	660
31	Montana	798
9	Nebraska	1,078
50	Nevada	441
44	New Hampshire	640
41	New Jersey	667
8	New Mexico	1,118
39	New York	693
16	North Carolina	958
1	North Dakota	1,356
30	Ohio	843
26	Oklahoma	869
12	Oregon	1,049
36	Pennsylvania	750
46	Rhode Island	627
33	South Carolina	775
34	South Dakota	772
48	Tennessee	565
19	Texas	930
5	Utah	1,247
6	Vermont	1,208
18	Virginia	933
23	Washington	892
20	West Virginia	909
14	Wisconsin	1,017
4	Wyoming	1,257

RANK ORDER

RANK	STATE	PER CAPITA
1	North Dakota	$1,356
2	Delaware	1,353
3	Alaska	1,337
4	Wyoming	1,257
5	Utah	1,247
6	Vermont	1,208
7	Iowa	1,150
8	New Mexico	1,118
9	Nebraska	1,078
10	Michigan	1,059
11	Kansas	1,055
12	Oregon	1,049
13	Alabama	1,030
14	Wisconsin	1,017
15	Hawaii	1,001
16	North Carolina	958
17	Maryland	949
18	Virginia	933
19	Texas	930
20	West Virginia	909
21	California	901
22	Indiana	896
23	Washington	892
24	Colorado	885
25	Arkansas	881
26	Oklahoma	869
27	Kentucky	860
27	Mississippi	860
29	Minnesota	858
30	Ohio	843
31	Montana	798
32	Massachusetts	777
33	South Carolina	775
34	South Dakota	772
35	Arizona	765
36	Pennsylvania	750
37	Connecticut	726
38	Illinois	718
39	New York	693
40	Louisiana	673
41	New Jersey	667
42	Missouri	660
43	Idaho	649
44	New Hampshire	640
45	Georgia	630
46	Rhode Island	627
47	Maine	596
48	Tennessee	565
49	Florida	486
50	Nevada	441
	District of Columbia	244

Source: CQ Press using data from U.S. Bureau of the Census, Governments Division
"2013 State and Local Government Finances" (http://www.census.gov/govs/local/)
*Direct general expenditures. Includes capital outlays.

Expenditures for Higher Education as a Percent of All State and Local Government Expenditures in 2013
National Percent = 9.9%*

ALPHA ORDER

RANK	STATE	PERCENT
3	Alabama	13.7
44	Alaska	7.3
15	Arizona	12.3
17	Arkansas	12.2
32	California	9.6
23	Colorado	11.3
42	Connecticut	7.5
4	Delaware	13.3
45	Florida	7.1
32	Georgia	9.6
20	Hawaii	11.5
30	Idaho	10.1
38	Illinois	8.6
13	Indiana	12.6
12	Iowa	12.7
7	Kansas	13.1
18	Kentucky	11.8
43	Louisiana	7.4
45	Maine	7.1
24	Maryland	10.7
41	Massachusetts	7.9
2	Michigan	14.0
34	Minnesota	9.4
24	Mississippi	10.7
36	Missouri	9.1
31	Montana	9.9
7	Nebraska	13.1
49	Nevada	6.8
40	New Hampshire	8.5
45	New Jersey	7.1
10	New Mexico	12.8
50	New York	5.6
9	North Carolina	12.9
5	North Dakota	13.2
26	Ohio	10.5
15	Oklahoma	12.3
10	Oregon	12.8
37	Pennsylvania	8.7
48	Rhode Island	7.0
26	South Carolina	10.5
26	South Dakota	10.5
38	Tennessee	8.6
5	Texas	13.2
1	Utah	17.0
20	Vermont	11.5
18	Virginia	11.8
26	Washington	10.5
20	West Virginia	11.5
14	Wisconsin	12.4
34	Wyoming	9.4

RANK ORDER

RANK	STATE	PERCENT
1	Utah	17.0
2	Michigan	14.0
3	Alabama	13.7
4	Delaware	13.3
5	North Dakota	13.2
5	Texas	13.2
7	Kansas	13.1
7	Nebraska	13.1
9	North Carolina	12.9
10	New Mexico	12.8
10	Oregon	12.8
12	Iowa	12.7
13	Indiana	12.6
14	Wisconsin	12.4
15	Arizona	12.3
15	Oklahoma	12.3
17	Arkansas	12.2
18	Kentucky	11.8
18	Virginia	11.8
20	Hawaii	11.5
20	Vermont	11.5
20	West Virginia	11.5
23	Colorado	11.3
24	Maryland	10.7
24	Mississippi	10.7
26	Ohio	10.5
26	South Carolina	10.5
26	South Dakota	10.5
26	Washington	10.5
30	Idaho	10.1
31	Montana	9.9
32	California	9.6
32	Georgia	9.6
34	Minnesota	9.4
34	Wyoming	9.4
36	Missouri	9.1
37	Pennsylvania	8.7
38	Illinois	8.6
38	Tennessee	8.6
40	New Hampshire	8.5
41	Massachusetts	7.9
42	Connecticut	7.5
43	Louisiana	7.4
44	Alaska	7.3
45	Florida	7.1
45	Maine	7.1
45	New Jersey	7.1
48	Rhode Island	7.0
49	Nevada	6.8
50	New York	5.6

| | District of Columbia | 1.4 |

Source: CQ Press using data from U.S. Bureau of the Census, Governments Division
"2013 State and Local Government Finances" (http://www.census.gov/govs/local/)
*Direct general expenditures for higher education as a percent of all direct general expenditures. Includes capital outlays.

Average Faculty Salary at Institutions of Higher Education in 2014

National Average = $78,625*

ALPHA ORDER

RANK	STATE	AVERAGE SALARY
37	Alabama	$68,313
17	Alaska	75,825
13	Arizona	79,704
49	Arkansas	58,545
5	California	92,595
19	Colorado	75,433
3	Connecticut	96,841
4	Delaware	93,436
23	Florida	73,391
35	Georgia	69,731
12	Hawaii	80,704
48	Idaho	60,003
11	Illinois	83,057
18	Indiana	75,527
30	Iowa	71,252
40	Kansas	64,913
44	Kentucky	63,504
43	Louisiana	64,609
22	Maine	73,444
15	Maryland	78,110
1	Massachusetts	99,515
10	Michigan	83,540
20	Minnesota	74,191
50	Mississippi	58,187
32	Missouri	70,919
38	Montana	67,559
28	Nebraska	71,781
14	Nevada	78,430
8	New Hampshire	87,923
2	New Jersey	98,143
45	New Mexico	63,318
6	New York	91,351
29	North Carolina	71,647
39	North Dakota	64,948
24	Ohio	72,993
41	Oklahoma	64,838
27	Oregon	71,791
9	Pennsylvania	84,832
7	Rhode Island	91,302
42	South Carolina	64,711
47	South Dakota	60,294
34	Tennessee	69,840
21	Texas	74,014
36	Utah	68,825
16	Vermont	76,077
25	Virginia	72,630
31	Washington	71,189
46	West Virginia	62,353
26	Wisconsin	71,855
33	Wyoming	70,158

RANK ORDER

RANK	STATE	AVERAGE SALARY
1	Massachusetts	$99,515
2	New Jersey	98,143
3	Connecticut	96,841
4	Delaware	93,436
5	California	92,595
6	New York	91,351
7	Rhode Island	91,302
8	New Hampshire	87,923
9	Pennsylvania	84,832
10	Michigan	83,540
11	Illinois	83,057
12	Hawaii	80,704
13	Arizona	79,704
14	Nevada	78,430
15	Maryland	78,110
16	Vermont	76,077
17	Alaska	75,825
18	Indiana	75,527
19	Colorado	75,433
20	Minnesota	74,191
21	Texas	74,014
22	Maine	73,444
23	Florida	73,391
24	Ohio	72,993
25	Virginia	72,630
26	Wisconsin	71,855
27	Oregon	71,791
28	Nebraska	71,781
29	North Carolina	71,647
30	Iowa	71,252
31	Washington	71,189
32	Missouri	70,919
33	Wyoming	70,158
34	Tennessee	69,840
35	Georgia	69,731
36	Utah	68,825
37	Alabama	68,313
38	Montana	67,559
39	North Dakota	64,948
40	Kansas	64,913
41	Oklahoma	64,838
42	South Carolina	64,711
43	Louisiana	64,609
44	Kentucky	63,504
45	New Mexico	63,318
46	West Virginia	62,353
47	South Dakota	60,294
48	Idaho	60,003
49	Arkansas	58,545
50	Mississippi	58,187
	District of Columbia	101,098

Source: U.S. Department of Education, National Center for Education Statistics
  "Digest of Education Statistics" (http://nces.ed.gov/programs/digest/index.asp)
*For 2013-2014 school year. For full-time instructional faculty on 9-month contracts at four-year and two-year public and private degree-granting institutions.

Average Student Costs at Public Institutions of Higher Education in 2014

National Average = $18,110*

ALPHA ORDER

RANK	STATE	AVERAGE COSTS
26	Alabama	$17,247
34	Alaska	15,697
14	Arizona	19,784
39	Arkansas	14,653
10	California	21,283
20	Colorado	18,979
9	Connecticut	21,642
6	Delaware	22,685
43	Florida	14,372
31	Georgia	16,062
24	Hawaii	18,027
46	Idaho	13,819
4	Illinois	23,096
23	Indiana	18,253
28	Iowa	16,534
40	Kansas	14,634
25	Kentucky	17,281
36	Louisiana	15,240
19	Maine	19,123
21	Maryland	18,881
7	Massachusetts	21,817
11	Michigan	20,415
22	Minnesota	18,389
42	Mississippi	14,414
27	Missouri	16,787
45	Montana	14,082
35	Nebraska	15,637
32	Nevada	16,036
1	New Hampshire	25,248
2	New Jersey	24,246
44	New Mexico	14,106
15	New York	19,757
37	North Carolina	15,197
47	North Dakota	13,714
12	Ohio	20,000
48	Oklahoma	13,496
18	Oregon	19,153
5	Pennsylvania	22,771
8	Rhode Island	21,761
16	South Carolina	19,504
41	South Dakota	14,430
29	Tennessee	16,265
30	Texas	16,211
50	Utah	12,802
3	Vermont	24,073
13	Virginia	19,847
17	Washington	19,286
38	West Virginia	14,835
33	Wisconsin	15,722
49	Wyoming	12,949

RANK ORDER

RANK	STATE	AVERAGE COSTS
1	New Hampshire	$25,248
2	New Jersey	24,246
3	Vermont	24,073
4	Illinois	23,096
5	Pennsylvania	22,771
6	Delaware	22,685
7	Massachusetts	21,817
8	Rhode Island	21,761
9	Connecticut	21,642
10	California	21,283
11	Michigan	20,415
12	Ohio	20,000
13	Virginia	19,847
14	Arizona	19,784
15	New York	19,757
16	South Carolina	19,504
17	Washington	19,286
18	Oregon	19,153
19	Maine	19,123
20	Colorado	18,979
21	Maryland	18,881
22	Minnesota	18,389
23	Indiana	18,253
24	Hawaii	18,027
25	Kentucky	17,281
26	Alabama	17,247
27	Missouri	16,787
28	Iowa	16,534
29	Tennessee	16,265
30	Texas	16,211
31	Georgia	16,062
32	Nevada	16,036
33	Wisconsin	15,722
34	Alaska	15,697
35	Nebraska	15,637
36	Louisiana	15,240
37	North Carolina	15,197
38	West Virginia	14,835
39	Arkansas	14,653
40	Kansas	14,634
41	South Dakota	14,430
42	Mississippi	14,414
43	Florida	14,372
44	New Mexico	14,106
45	Montana	14,082
46	Idaho	13,819
47	North Dakota	13,714
48	Oklahoma	13,496
49	Wyoming	12,949
50	Utah	12,802
	District of Columbia**	NA

Source: U.S. Department of Education, National Center for Education Statistics
"Digest of Education Statistics" (http://nces.ed.gov/programs/digest/index.asp)
*Data for 2013-2014 school year. Based on average in-state tuition, room and board, and fees for full-time students in public four-year institutions for an entire academic year.
**Not available.

Average Student Costs at Private Institutions of Higher Education in 2014

National Average = $36,589*

ALPHA ORDER

RANK	STATE	AVERAGE COSTS
43	Alabama	$22,974
28	Alaska	30,261
45	Arizona	20,196
40	Arkansas	26,475
12	California	41,891
25	Colorado	31,473
2	Connecticut	48,718
42	Delaware	24,221
26	Florida	31,288
22	Georgia	34,659
39	Hawaii	27,266
49	Idaho	14,163
15	Illinois	38,629
16	Indiana	37,964
41	Iowa	24,517
34	Kansas	27,963
31	Kentucky	29,527
14	Louisiana	41,044
9	Maine	44,057
5	Maryland	47,023
1	Massachusetts	51,484
36	Michigan	27,836
20	Minnesota	36,247
44	Mississippi	21,699
33	Missouri	28,415
32	Montana	28,733
35	Nebraska	27,884
27	Nevada	30,745
10	New Hampshire	43,490
8	New Jersey	44,239
38	New Mexico	27,468
4	New York	47,055
17	North Carolina	37,542
47	North Dakota	18,123
18	Ohio	36,856
30	Oklahoma	29,990
11	Oregon	42,385
7	Pennsylvania	46,239
6	Rhode Island	46,706
29	South Carolina	30,169
37	South Dakota	27,523
24	Tennessee	31,709
19	Texas	36,292
48	Utah	15,365
3	Vermont	47,909
23	Virginia	31,828
13	Washington	41,865
46	West Virginia	19,697
21	Wisconsin	35,654
NA	Wyoming**	NA

RANK ORDER

RANK	STATE	AVERAGE COSTS
1	Massachusetts	$51,484
2	Connecticut	48,718
3	Vermont	47,909
4	New York	47,055
5	Maryland	47,023
6	Rhode Island	46,706
7	Pennsylvania	46,239
8	New Jersey	44,239
9	Maine	44,057
10	New Hampshire	43,490
11	Oregon	42,385
12	California	41,891
13	Washington	41,865
14	Louisiana	41,044
15	Illinois	38,629
16	Indiana	37,964
17	North Carolina	37,542
18	Ohio	36,856
19	Texas	36,292
20	Minnesota	36,247
21	Wisconsin	35,654
22	Georgia	34,659
23	Virginia	31,828
24	Tennessee	31,709
25	Colorado	31,473
26	Florida	31,288
27	Nevada	30,745
28	Alaska	30,261
29	South Carolina	30,169
30	Oklahoma	29,990
31	Kentucky	29,527
32	Montana	28,733
33	Missouri	28,415
34	Kansas	27,963
35	Nebraska	27,884
36	Michigan	27,836
37	South Dakota	27,523
38	New Mexico	27,468
39	Hawaii	27,266
40	Arkansas	26,475
41	Iowa	24,517
42	Delaware	24,221
43	Alabama	22,974
44	Mississippi	21,699
45	Arizona	20,196
46	West Virginia	19,697
47	North Dakota	18,123
48	Utah	15,365
49	Idaho	14,163
NA	Wyoming**	NA
	District of Columbia	49,894

Source: U.S. Department of Education, National Center for Education Statistics
"Digest of Education Statistics" (http://nces.ed.gov/programs/digest/index.asp)
*Data for 2013-2014 school year. Based on average in-state tuition, room and board, and fees for full-time students in private four-year institutions for an entire academic year.
**Not available.

Average College Graduate Debt: Class of 2014

National Average Debt = $28,950*

ALPHA ORDER

RANK	STATE	AVERAGE DEBT
10	Alabama	$29,425
23	Alaska	26,742
45	Arizona	22,609
36	Arkansas	25,344
46	California	21,382
38	Colorado	25,064
7	Connecticut	29,750
1	Delaware	33,808
39	Florida	24,947
24	Georgia	26,518
41	Hawaii	24,554
30	Idaho	26,091
16	Illinois	28,984
13	Indiana	29,222
8	Iowa	29,732
34	Kansas	25,521
32	Kentucky	25,939
44	Louisiana	23,025
6	Maine	30,908
20	Maryland	27,457
11	Massachusetts	29,391
9	Michigan	29,450
5	Minnesota	31,579
28	Mississippi	26,177
33	Missouri	25,844
21	Montana	26,946
26	Nebraska	26,278
47	Nevada	20,211
2	New Hampshire	33,410
18	New Jersey	28,318
48	New Mexico	18,969
19	New York	27,822
37	North Carolina	25,218
NA	North Dakota**	NA
12	Ohio	29,353
43	Oklahoma	23,430
29	Oregon	26,106
3	Pennsylvania	33,264
4	Rhode Island	31,841
14	South Carolina	29,163
31	South Dakota	26,023
35	Tennessee	25,510
27	Texas	26,250
49	Utah	18,921
15	Vermont	29,060
25	Virginia	26,432
40	Washington	24,804
22	West Virginia	26,854
17	Wisconsin	28,810
42	Wyoming	23,708

RANK ORDER

RANK	STATE	AVERAGE DEBT
1	Delaware	$33,808
2	New Hampshire	33,410
3	Pennsylvania	33,264
4	Rhode Island	31,841
5	Minnesota	31,579
6	Maine	30,908
7	Connecticut	29,750
8	Iowa	29,732
9	Michigan	29,450
10	Alabama	29,425
11	Massachusetts	29,391
12	Ohio	29,353
13	Indiana	29,222
14	South Carolina	29,163
15	Vermont	29,060
16	Illinois	28,984
17	Wisconsin	28,810
18	New Jersey	28,318
19	New York	27,822
20	Maryland	27,457
21	Montana	26,946
22	West Virginia	26,854
23	Alaska	26,742
24	Georgia	26,518
25	Virginia	26,432
26	Nebraska	26,278
27	Texas	26,250
28	Mississippi	26,177
29	Oregon	26,106
30	Idaho	26,091
31	South Dakota	26,023
32	Kentucky	25,939
33	Missouri	25,844
34	Kansas	25,521
35	Tennessee	25,510
36	Arkansas	25,344
37	North Carolina	25,218
38	Colorado	25,064
39	Florida	24,947
40	Washington	24,804
41	Hawaii	24,554
42	Wyoming	23,708
43	Oklahoma	23,430
44	Louisiana	23,025
45	Arizona	22,609
46	California	21,382
47	Nevada	20,211
48	New Mexico	18,969
49	Utah	18,921
NA	North Dakota**	NA
	District of Columbia**	NA

Source: The Project on Student Debt
"Student Debt and The Class of 2014" (October 2015, http://ticas.org/posd/map-state-data)
*For students receiving a bachelor's degree in 2014.
**Not available.

Percent of College Graduates with Debt: Class of 2014

National Percent = 69%*

ALPHA ORDER

RANK	STATE	PERCENT
41	Alabama	54
44	Alaska	50
36	Arizona	57
38	Arkansas	55
38	California	55
37	Colorado	56
20	Connecticut	62
20	Delaware	62
41	Florida	54
20	Georgia	62
46	Hawaii	47
2	Idaho	72
11	Illinois	67
25	Indiana	61
8	Iowa	68
14	Kansas	65
18	Kentucky	64
46	Louisiana	47
8	Maine	68
34	Maryland	58
14	Massachusetts	65
20	Michigan	62
3	Minnesota	70
28	Mississippi	60
31	Missouri	59
11	Montana	67
19	Nebraska	63
48	Nevada	46
1	New Hampshire	76
8	New Jersey	68
45	New Mexico	48
25	New York	61
25	North Carolina	61
NA	North Dakota**	NA
11	Ohio	67
38	Oklahoma	55
20	Oregon	62
3	Pennsylvania	70
14	Rhode Island	65
31	South Carolina	59
6	South Dakota	69
28	Tennessee	60
31	Texas	59
41	Utah	54
14	Vermont	65
28	Virginia	60
34	Washington	58
6	West Virginia	69
3	Wisconsin	70
48	Wyoming	46

RANK ORDER

RANK	STATE	PERCENT
1	New Hampshire	76
2	Idaho	72
3	Minnesota	70
3	Pennsylvania	70
3	Wisconsin	70
6	South Dakota	69
6	West Virginia	69
8	Iowa	68
8	Maine	68
8	New Jersey	68
11	Illinois	67
11	Montana	67
11	Ohio	67
14	Kansas	65
14	Massachusetts	65
14	Rhode Island	65
14	Vermont	65
18	Kentucky	64
19	Nebraska	63
20	Connecticut	62
20	Delaware	62
20	Georgia	62
20	Michigan	62
20	Oregon	62
25	Indiana	61
25	New York	61
25	North Carolina	61
28	Mississippi	60
28	Tennessee	60
28	Virginia	60
31	Missouri	59
31	South Carolina	59
31	Texas	59
34	Maryland	58
34	Washington	58
36	Arizona	57
37	Colorado	56
38	Arkansas	55
38	California	55
38	Oklahoma	55
41	Alabama	54
41	Florida	54
41	Utah	54
44	Alaska	50
45	New Mexico	48
46	Hawaii	47
46	Louisiana	47
48	Nevada	46
48	Wyoming	46
NA	North Dakota**	NA
	District of Columbia**	NA

Source: The Project on Student Debt
  "Student Debt and The Class of 2014" (October 2015, http://ticas.org/posd/map-state-data)
*For students receiving a bachelor's degree in 2014.
**Not available.

Institutions of Higher Education in 2014

National Total = 4,724 Institutions*

ALPHA ORDER

RANK	STATE	INSTITUTIONS	% of USA
23	Alabama	77	1.6%
49	Alaska	11	0.2%
17	Arizona	91	1.9%
31	Arkansas	52	1.1%
1	California	469	9.9%
16	Colorado	92	1.9%
32	Connecticut	46	1.0%
48	Delaware	12	0.3%
5	Florida	235	5.0%
9	Georgia	136	2.9%
43	Hawaii	22	0.5%
46	Idaho	19	0.4%
7	Illinois	185	3.9%
20	Indiana	84	1.8%
27	Iowa	66	1.4%
24	Kansas	74	1.6%
21	Kentucky	79	1.7%
25	Louisiana	70	1.5%
38	Maine	31	0.7%
30	Maryland	62	1.3%
12	Massachusetts	125	2.6%
14	Michigan	117	2.5%
13	Minnesota	118	2.5%
36	Mississippi	42	0.9%
9	Missouri	136	2.9%
43	Montana	22	0.5%
35	Nebraska	43	0.9%
40	Nevada	26	0.6%
39	New Hampshire	27	0.6%
25	New Jersey	70	1.5%
33	New Mexico	44	0.9%
2	New York	304	6.4%
8	North Carolina	151	3.2%
45	North Dakota	21	0.4%
6	Ohio	219	4.6%
27	Oklahoma	66	1.4%
29	Oregon	65	1.4%
4	Pennsylvania	263	5.6%
47	Rhode Island	13	0.3%
22	South Carolina	78	1.7%
41	South Dakota	25	0.5%
15	Tennessee	113	2.4%
3	Texas	275	5.8%
37	Utah	41	0.9%
42	Vermont	24	0.5%
11	Virginia	130	2.8%
19	Washington	86	1.8%
33	West Virginia	44	0.9%
18	Wisconsin	88	1.9%
50	Wyoming	10	0.2%

RANK ORDER

RANK	STATE	INSTITUTIONS	% of USA
1	California	469	9.9%
2	New York	304	6.4%
3	Texas	275	5.8%
4	Pennsylvania	263	5.6%
5	Florida	235	5.0%
6	Ohio	219	4.6%
7	Illinois	185	3.9%
8	North Carolina	151	3.2%
9	Georgia	136	2.9%
9	Missouri	136	2.9%
11	Virginia	130	2.8%
12	Massachusetts	125	2.6%
13	Minnesota	118	2.5%
14	Michigan	117	2.5%
15	Tennessee	113	2.4%
16	Colorado	92	1.9%
17	Arizona	91	1.9%
18	Wisconsin	88	1.9%
19	Washington	86	1.8%
20	Indiana	84	1.8%
21	Kentucky	79	1.7%
22	South Carolina	78	1.7%
23	Alabama	77	1.6%
24	Kansas	74	1.6%
25	Louisiana	70	1.5%
25	New Jersey	70	1.5%
27	Iowa	66	1.4%
27	Oklahoma	66	1.4%
29	Oregon	65	1.4%
30	Maryland	62	1.3%
31	Arkansas	52	1.1%
32	Connecticut	46	1.0%
33	New Mexico	44	0.9%
33	West Virginia	44	0.9%
35	Nebraska	43	0.9%
36	Mississippi	42	0.9%
37	Utah	41	0.9%
38	Maine	31	0.7%
39	New Hampshire	27	0.6%
40	Nevada	26	0.6%
41	South Dakota	25	0.5%
42	Vermont	24	0.5%
43	Hawaii	22	0.5%
43	Montana	22	0.5%
45	North Dakota	21	0.4%
46	Idaho	19	0.4%
47	Rhode Island	13	0.3%
48	Delaware	12	0.3%
49	Alaska	11	0.2%
50	Wyoming	10	0.2%
	District of Columbia	20	0.4%

Source: U.S. Department of Education, National Center for Education Statistics
"Digest of Education Statistics" (http://nces.ed.gov/programs/digest/index.asp)
*For 2013-2014 school year. Consists of 3,039 four-year and 1,685 two-year public and private (profit and not-for-profit) degree-granting institutions. Includes five U.S. Service Schools not shown by state.

Enrollment in Institutions of Higher Education in 2013

National Total = 20,375,789 Students*

ALPHA ORDER

RANK	STATE	STUDENTS	% of USA
24	Alabama	305,712	1.5%
50	Alaska	34,890	0.2%
8	Arizona	694,123	3.4%
34	Arkansas	172,224	0.8%
1	California	2,636,921	12.9%
21	Colorado	358,723	1.8%
32	Connecticut	200,966	1.0%
44	Delaware	59,615	0.3%
4	Florida	1,125,810	5.5%
12	Georgia	533,424	2.6%
42	Hawaii	76,434	0.4%
39	Idaho	109,318	0.5%
5	Illinois	842,888	4.1%
14	Indiana	444,364	2.2%
22	Iowa	339,738	1.7%
31	Kansas	215,855	1.1%
25	Kentucky	273,073	1.3%
28	Louisiana	251,887	1.2%
43	Maine	70,849	0.3%
19	Maryland	363,771	1.8%
13	Massachusetts	514,008	2.5%
9	Michigan	643,592	3.2%
15	Minnesota	441,491	2.2%
33	Mississippi	173,634	0.9%
16	Missouri	438,222	2.2%
47	Montana	52,777	0.3%
37	Nebraska	137,943	0.7%
38	Nevada	116,738	0.6%
40	New Hampshire	92,440	0.5%
17	New Jersey	436,939	2.1%
36	New Mexico	153,455	0.8%
3	New York	1,304,230	6.4%
11	North Carolina	575,198	2.8%
46	North Dakota	55,063	0.3%
7	Ohio	697,647	3.4%
30	Oklahoma	220,897	1.1%
29	Oregon	251,106	1.2%
6	Pennsylvania	765,582	3.8%
41	Rhode Island	83,460	0.4%
27	South Carolina	257,844	1.3%
45	South Dakota	55,129	0.3%
23	Tennessee	338,197	1.7%
2	Texas	1,541,378	7.6%
26	Utah	264,255	1.3%
48	Vermont	43,534	0.2%
10	Virginia	583,755	2.9%
20	Washington	363,377	1.8%
35	West Virginia	157,954	0.8%
18	Wisconsin	364,021	1.8%
49	Wyoming	37,084	0.2%

RANK ORDER

RANK	STATE	STUDENTS	% of USA
1	California	2,636,921	12.9%
2	Texas	1,541,378	7.6%
3	New York	1,304,230	6.4%
4	Florida	1,125,810	5.5%
5	Illinois	842,888	4.1%
6	Pennsylvania	765,582	3.8%
7	Ohio	697,647	3.4%
8	Arizona	694,123	3.4%
9	Michigan	643,592	3.2%
10	Virginia	583,755	2.9%
11	North Carolina	575,198	2.8%
12	Georgia	533,424	2.6%
13	Massachusetts	514,008	2.5%
14	Indiana	444,364	2.2%
15	Minnesota	441,491	2.2%
16	Missouri	438,222	2.2%
17	New Jersey	436,939	2.1%
18	Wisconsin	364,021	1.8%
19	Maryland	363,771	1.8%
20	Washington	363,377	1.8%
21	Colorado	358,723	1.8%
22	Iowa	339,738	1.7%
23	Tennessee	338,197	1.7%
24	Alabama	305,712	1.5%
25	Kentucky	273,073	1.3%
26	Utah	264,255	1.3%
27	South Carolina	257,844	1.3%
28	Louisiana	251,887	1.2%
29	Oregon	251,106	1.2%
30	Oklahoma	220,897	1.1%
31	Kansas	215,855	1.1%
32	Connecticut	200,966	1.0%
33	Mississippi	173,634	0.9%
34	Arkansas	172,224	0.8%
35	West Virginia	157,954	0.8%
36	New Mexico	153,455	0.8%
37	Nebraska	137,943	0.7%
38	Nevada	116,738	0.6%
39	Idaho	109,318	0.5%
40	New Hampshire	92,440	0.5%
41	Rhode Island	83,460	0.4%
42	Hawaii	76,434	0.4%
43	Maine	70,849	0.3%
44	Delaware	59,615	0.3%
45	South Dakota	55,129	0.3%
46	North Dakota	55,063	0.3%
47	Montana	52,777	0.3%
48	Vermont	43,534	0.2%
49	Wyoming	37,084	0.2%
50	Alaska	34,890	0.2%
	District of Columbia	89,257	0.4%

Source: U.S. Department of Education, National Center for Education Statistics
"Digest of Education Statistics" (http://nces.ed.gov/programs/digest/index.asp)
*Fall 2013 enrollment. Includes full-time and part-time students at Title IV eligible, degree-granting four-year and two-year institutions. National total includes 14,997 students at U.S. Service Schools not shown by state.

Enrollment Rate in Institutions of Higher Education in 2013

National Rate = 648 Students per 1,000 Population 18 to 24 Years Old*

ALPHA ORDER

RANK	STATE	RATE
30	Alabama	629
50	Alaska	424
2	Arizona	1,042
34	Arkansas	597
19	California	658
15	Colorado	696
36	Connecticut	584
24	Delaware	647
29	Florida	632
48	Georgia	524
40	Hawaii	558
14	Idaho	702
17	Illinois	669
18	Indiana	667
1	Iowa	1,071
11	Kansas	719
26	Kentucky	640
45	Louisiana	532
32	Maine	623
25	Maryland	645
6	Massachusetts	744
26	Michigan	640
4	Minnesota	871
41	Mississippi	553
7	Missouri	736
47	Montana	526
8	Nebraska	731
49	Nevada	458
10	New Hampshire	728
42	New Jersey	552
9	New Mexico	729
19	New York	658
36	North Carolina	584
35	North Dakota	594
30	Ohio	629
39	Oklahoma	562
16	Oregon	683
33	Pennsylvania	615
12	Rhode Island	708
46	South Carolina	528
23	South Dakota	649
44	Tennessee	537
38	Texas	568
5	Utah	795
22	Vermont	650
13	Virginia	704
43	Washington	545
3	West Virginia	919
21	Wisconsin	651
28	Wyoming	633

RANK ORDER

RANK	STATE	RATE
1	Iowa	1,071
2	Arizona	1,042
3	West Virginia	919
4	Minnesota	871
5	Utah	795
6	Massachusetts	744
7	Missouri	736
8	Nebraska	731
9	New Mexico	729
10	New Hampshire	728
11	Kansas	719
12	Rhode Island	708
13	Virginia	704
14	Idaho	702
15	Colorado	696
16	Oregon	683
17	Illinois	669
18	Indiana	667
19	California	658
19	New York	658
21	Wisconsin	651
22	Vermont	650
23	South Dakota	649
24	Delaware	647
25	Maryland	645
26	Kentucky	640
26	Michigan	640
28	Wyoming	633
29	Florida	632
30	Alabama	629
30	Ohio	629
32	Maine	623
33	Pennsylvania	615
34	Arkansas	597
35	North Dakota	594
36	Connecticut	584
36	North Carolina	584
38	Texas	568
39	Oklahoma	562
40	Hawaii	558
41	Mississippi	553
42	New Jersey	552
43	Washington	545
44	Tennessee	537
45	Louisiana	532
46	South Carolina	528
47	Montana	526
48	Georgia	524
49	Nevada	458
50	Alaska	424
	District of Columbia	1,102

Source: CQ Press using data from U.S. Department of Education, National Center for Education Statistics "Digest of Education Statistics" (http://nces.ed.gov/programs/digest/index.asp)

*Based on fall 2013 enrollment and population. National rate includes U.S. Service Schools. Includes students at four-year and two-year public and private degree-granting institutions. Enrollment based on location of institution. Population based on residence.

Enrollment in Public Institutions of Higher Education in 2013

National Total = 14,745,558 Students*

ALPHA ORDER

RANK	STATE	STUDENTS	% of USA
21	Alabama	248,284	1.7%
49	Alaska	31,600	0.2%
12	Arizona	354,462	2.4%
33	Arkansas	153,690	1.0%
1	California	2,148,147	14.6%
18	Colorado	271,223	1.8%
35	Connecticut	123,093	0.8%
47	Delaware	40,992	0.3%
3	Florida	795,860	5.4%
10	Georgia	413,706	2.8%
40	Hawaii	58,941	0.4%
39	Idaho	75,910	0.5%
5	Illinois	546,483	3.7%
14	Indiana	335,923	2.3%
30	Iowa	168,644	1.1%
29	Kansas	184,075	1.2%
24	Kentucky	218,472	1.5%
25	Louisiana	215,653	1.5%
41	Maine	49,602	0.3%
16	Maryland	301,565	2.0%
23	Massachusetts	228,255	1.5%
6	Michigan	527,740	3.6%
19	Minnesota	266,440	1.8%
32	Mississippi	154,916	1.1%
20	Missouri	254,650	1.7%
43	Montana	47,851	0.3%
37	Nebraska	101,893	0.7%
36	Nevada	102,538	0.7%
46	New Hampshire	42,711	0.3%
13	New Jersey	352,822	2.4%
34	New Mexico	144,381	1.0%
4	New York	720,934	4.9%
8	North Carolina	460,100	3.1%
42	North Dakota	48,751	0.3%
7	Ohio	520,039	3.5%
28	Oklahoma	187,078	1.3%
26	Oregon	208,317	1.4%
9	Pennsylvania	419,849	2.8%
45	Rhode Island	42,786	0.3%
27	South Carolina	207,717	1.4%
44	South Dakota	44,272	0.3%
22	Tennessee	229,302	1.6%
2	Texas	1,349,609	9.2%
31	Utah	168,311	1.1%
50	Vermont	25,852	0.2%
11	Virginia	405,915	2.8%
15	Washington	310,192	2.1%
38	West Virginia	90,782	0.6%
17	Wisconsin	289,339	2.0%
48	Wyoming	35,547	0.2%

RANK ORDER

RANK	STATE	STUDENTS	% of USA
1	California	2,148,147	14.6%
2	Texas	1,349,609	9.2%
3	Florida	795,860	5.4%
4	New York	720,934	4.9%
5	Illinois	546,483	3.7%
6	Michigan	527,740	3.6%
7	Ohio	520,039	3.5%
8	North Carolina	460,100	3.1%
9	Pennsylvania	419,849	2.8%
10	Georgia	413,706	2.8%
11	Virginia	405,915	2.8%
12	Arizona	354,462	2.4%
13	New Jersey	352,822	2.4%
14	Indiana	335,923	2.3%
15	Washington	310,192	2.1%
16	Maryland	301,565	2.0%
17	Wisconsin	289,339	2.0%
18	Colorado	271,223	1.8%
19	Minnesota	266,440	1.8%
20	Missouri	254,650	1.7%
21	Alabama	248,284	1.7%
22	Tennessee	229,302	1.6%
23	Massachusetts	228,255	1.5%
24	Kentucky	218,472	1.5%
25	Louisiana	215,653	1.5%
26	Oregon	208,317	1.4%
27	South Carolina	207,717	1.4%
28	Oklahoma	187,078	1.3%
29	Kansas	184,075	1.2%
30	Iowa	168,644	1.1%
31	Utah	168,311	1.1%
32	Mississippi	154,916	1.1%
33	Arkansas	153,690	1.0%
34	New Mexico	144,381	1.0%
35	Connecticut	123,093	0.8%
36	Nevada	102,538	0.7%
37	Nebraska	101,893	0.7%
38	West Virginia	90,782	0.6%
39	Idaho	75,910	0.5%
40	Hawaii	58,941	0.4%
41	Maine	49,602	0.3%
42	North Dakota	48,751	0.3%
43	Montana	47,851	0.3%
44	South Dakota	44,272	0.3%
45	Rhode Island	42,786	0.3%
46	New Hampshire	42,711	0.3%
47	Delaware	40,992	0.3%
48	Wyoming	35,547	0.2%
49	Alaska	31,600	0.2%
50	Vermont	25,852	0.2%
	District of Columbia	5,347	0.0%

Source: U.S. Department of Education, National Center for Education Statistics
"Digest of Education Statistics" (http://nces.ed.gov/programs/digest/index.asp)
*Fall 2013 enrollment. Includes full-time and part-time students at Title IV eligible, degree-granting four-year and two-year institutions. National total includes 14,997 students at U.S. Service Schools not shown by state.

Enrollment in Private Institutions of Higher Education in 2013

National Total = 5,630,231 Students*

ALPHA ORDER

RANK	STATE	STUDENTS	% of USA
26	Alabama	57,428	1.0%
49	Alaska	3,290	0.1%
4	Arizona	339,661	6.0%
41	Arkansas	18,534	0.3%
2	California	488,774	8.7%
20	Colorado	87,500	1.6%
22	Connecticut	77,873	1.4%
40	Delaware	18,623	0.3%
5	Florida	329,950	5.9%
14	Georgia	119,718	2.1%
43	Hawaii	17,493	0.3%
36	Idaho	33,408	0.6%
6	Illinois	296,405	5.3%
18	Indiana	108,441	1.9%
13	Iowa	171,094	3.0%
37	Kansas	31,780	0.6%
27	Kentucky	54,601	1.0%
33	Louisiana	36,234	0.6%
38	Maine	21,247	0.4%
25	Maryland	62,206	1.1%
7	Massachusetts	285,753	5.1%
15	Michigan	115,852	2.1%
12	Minnesota	175,051	3.1%
39	Mississippi	18,718	0.3%
9	Missouri	183,572	3.3%
48	Montana	4,926	0.1%
34	Nebraska	36,050	0.6%
44	Nevada	14,200	0.3%
30	New Hampshire	49,729	0.9%
21	New Jersey	84,117	1.5%
46	New Mexico	9,074	0.2%
1	New York	583,296	10.4%
16	North Carolina	115,098	2.0%
47	North Dakota	6,312	0.1%
11	Ohio	177,608	3.2%
35	Oklahoma	33,819	0.6%
31	Oregon	42,789	0.8%
3	Pennsylvania	345,733	6.1%
32	Rhode Island	40,674	0.7%
29	South Carolina	50,127	0.9%
45	South Dakota	10,857	0.2%
17	Tennessee	108,895	1.9%
8	Texas	191,769	3.4%
19	Utah	95,944	1.7%
42	Vermont	17,682	0.3%
10	Virginia	177,840	3.2%
28	Washington	53,185	0.9%
24	West Virginia	67,172	1.2%
23	Wisconsin	74,682	1.3%
50	Wyoming	1,537	0.0%

RANK ORDER

RANK	STATE	STUDENTS	% of USA
1	New York	583,296	10.4%
2	California	488,774	8.7%
3	Pennsylvania	345,733	6.1%
4	Arizona	339,661	6.0%
5	Florida	329,950	5.9%
6	Illinois	296,405	5.3%
7	Massachusetts	285,753	5.1%
8	Texas	191,769	3.4%
9	Missouri	183,572	3.3%
10	Virginia	177,840	3.2%
11	Ohio	177,608	3.2%
12	Minnesota	175,051	3.1%
13	Iowa	171,094	3.0%
14	Georgia	119,718	2.1%
15	Michigan	115,852	2.1%
16	North Carolina	115,098	2.0%
17	Tennessee	108,895	1.9%
18	Indiana	108,441	1.9%
19	Utah	95,944	1.7%
20	Colorado	87,500	1.6%
21	New Jersey	84,117	1.5%
22	Connecticut	77,873	1.4%
23	Wisconsin	74,682	1.3%
24	West Virginia	67,172	1.2%
25	Maryland	62,206	1.1%
26	Alabama	57,428	1.0%
27	Kentucky	54,601	1.0%
28	Washington	53,185	0.9%
29	South Carolina	50,127	0.9%
30	New Hampshire	49,729	0.9%
31	Oregon	42,789	0.8%
32	Rhode Island	40,674	0.7%
33	Louisiana	36,234	0.6%
34	Nebraska	36,050	0.6%
35	Oklahoma	33,819	0.6%
36	Idaho	33,408	0.6%
37	Kansas	31,780	0.6%
38	Maine	21,247	0.4%
39	Mississippi	18,718	0.3%
40	Delaware	18,623	0.3%
41	Arkansas	18,534	0.3%
42	Vermont	17,682	0.3%
43	Hawaii	17,493	0.3%
44	Nevada	14,200	0.3%
45	South Dakota	10,857	0.2%
46	New Mexico	9,074	0.2%
47	North Dakota	6,312	0.1%
48	Montana	4,926	0.1%
49	Alaska	3,290	0.1%
50	Wyoming	1,537	0.0%
	District of Columbia	83,910	1.5%

Source: U.S. Department of Education, National Center for Education Statistics
"Digest of Education Statistics" (http://nces.ed.gov/programs/digest/index.asp)
*Fall 2013 enrollment. Includes full-time and part-time students at Title IV eligible, degree-granting four-year and two-year institutions.

Percent of Population with a Bachelor's Degree or More in 2014

National Percent = 30.1%*

ALPHA ORDER

RANK	STATE	PERCENT
44	Alabama	23.5
27	Alaska	28.0
31	Arizona	27.6
48	Arkansas	21.4
13	California	31.7
2	Colorado	38.3
4	Connecticut	38.0
18	Delaware	30.6
35	Florida	27.3
23	Georgia	29.1
16	Hawaii	31.0
41	Idaho	25.0
12	Illinois	32.8
42	Indiana	24.7
30	Iowa	27.7
14	Kansas	31.5
47	Kentucky	22.2
46	Louisiana	22.9
21	Maine	29.4
3	Maryland	38.2
1	Massachusetts	41.2
33	Michigan	27.4
10	Minnesota	34.3
49	Mississippi	21.1
32	Missouri	27.5
22	Montana	29.3
20	Nebraska	29.5
45	Nevada	23.1
7	New Hampshire	35.0
5	New Jersey	37.4
38	New Mexico	26.4
9	New York	34.5
25	North Carolina	28.7
33	North Dakota	27.4
36	Ohio	26.6
43	Oklahoma	24.2
17	Oregon	30.8
24	Pennsylvania	29.0
19	Rhode Island	30.4
39	South Carolina	26.3
28	South Dakota	27.8
40	Tennessee	25.3
28	Texas	27.8
15	Utah	31.1
8	Vermont	34.9
6	Virginia	36.7
11	Washington	33.1
50	West Virginia	19.2
26	Wisconsin	28.4
36	Wyoming	26.6

RANK ORDER

RANK	STATE	PERCENT
1	Massachusetts	41.2
2	Colorado	38.3
3	Maryland	38.2
4	Connecticut	38.0
5	New Jersey	37.4
6	Virginia	36.7
7	New Hampshire	35.0
8	Vermont	34.9
9	New York	34.5
10	Minnesota	34.3
11	Washington	33.1
12	Illinois	32.8
13	California	31.7
14	Kansas	31.5
15	Utah	31.1
16	Hawaii	31.0
17	Oregon	30.8
18	Delaware	30.6
19	Rhode Island	30.4
20	Nebraska	29.5
21	Maine	29.4
22	Montana	29.3
23	Georgia	29.1
24	Pennsylvania	29.0
25	North Carolina	28.7
26	Wisconsin	28.4
27	Alaska	28.0
28	South Dakota	27.8
28	Texas	27.8
30	Iowa	27.7
31	Arizona	27.6
32	Missouri	27.5
33	Michigan	27.4
33	North Dakota	27.4
35	Florida	27.3
36	Ohio	26.6
36	Wyoming	26.6
38	New Mexico	26.4
39	South Carolina	26.3
40	Tennessee	25.3
41	Idaho	25.0
42	Indiana	24.7
43	Oklahoma	24.2
44	Alabama	23.5
45	Nevada	23.1
46	Louisiana	22.9
47	Kentucky	22.2
48	Arkansas	21.4
49	Mississippi	21.1
50	West Virginia	19.2
	District of Columbia	55.0

Source: U.S. Bureau of the Census
"2014 American Community Survey-Table R1502" (http://www.census.gov/programs-surveys/acs/)
*Persons age 25 and older.

Percent of Population Who Have Completed an Advanced Degree in 2014

National Percent = 11.4%*

ALPHA ORDER

RANK	STATE	PERCENT
40	Alabama	8.8
31	Alaska	9.6
24	Arizona	10.3
49	Arkansas	7.5
14	California	11.8
6	Colorado	14.3
3	Connecticut	16.7
11	Delaware	12.3
29	Florida	9.8
20	Georgia	10.8
22	Hawaii	10.5
42	Idaho	8.3
10	Illinois	12.7
39	Indiana	8.9
38	Iowa	9.0
19	Kansas	11.3
36	Kentucky	9.2
46	Louisiana	7.8
28	Maine	10.0
2	Maryland	17.5
1	Massachusetts	18.0
20	Michigan	10.8
15	Minnesota	11.6
44	Mississippi	8.0
23	Missouri	10.4
29	Montana	9.8
35	Nebraska	9.3
45	Nevada	7.9
9	New Hampshire	13.3
6	New Jersey	14.3
17	New Mexico	11.4
5	New York	14.9
26	North Carolina	10.1
48	North Dakota	7.6
26	Ohio	10.1
43	Oklahoma	8.1
15	Oregon	11.6
17	Pennsylvania	11.4
11	Rhode Island	12.3
31	South Carolina	9.6
46	South Dakota	7.8
37	Tennessee	9.1
31	Texas	9.6
24	Utah	10.3
8	Vermont	14.0
4	Virginia	15.9
13	Washington	12.1
50	West Virginia	7.4
34	Wisconsin	9.5
41	Wyoming	8.7

RANK ORDER

RANK	STATE	PERCENT
1	Massachusetts	18.0
2	Maryland	17.5
3	Connecticut	16.7
4	Virginia	15.9
5	New York	14.9
6	Colorado	14.3
6	New Jersey	14.3
8	Vermont	14.0
9	New Hampshire	13.3
10	Illinois	12.7
11	Delaware	12.3
11	Rhode Island	12.3
13	Washington	12.1
14	California	11.8
15	Minnesota	11.6
15	Oregon	11.6
17	New Mexico	11.4
17	Pennsylvania	11.4
19	Kansas	11.3
20	Georgia	10.8
20	Michigan	10.8
22	Hawaii	10.5
23	Missouri	10.4
24	Arizona	10.3
24	Utah	10.3
26	North Carolina	10.1
26	Ohio	10.1
28	Maine	10.0
29	Florida	9.8
29	Montana	9.8
31	Alaska	9.6
31	South Carolina	9.6
31	Texas	9.6
34	Wisconsin	9.5
35	Nebraska	9.3
36	Kentucky	9.2
37	Tennessee	9.1
38	Iowa	9.0
39	Indiana	8.9
40	Alabama	8.8
41	Wyoming	8.7
42	Idaho	8.3
43	Oklahoma	8.1
44	Mississippi	8.0
45	Nevada	7.9
46	Louisiana	7.8
46	South Dakota	7.8
48	North Dakota	7.6
49	Arkansas	7.5
50	West Virginia	7.4

| | District of Columbia | 30.6 |

Source: U.S. Bureau of the Census
"2014 American Community Survey-Table R1503" (http://www.census.gov/programs-surveys/acs/)
*Persons age 25 and older who have earned a master's degree or higher.

Public Libraries and Branches in 2012

National Total = 16,536 Libraries and Branches*

ALPHA ORDER

RANK	STATE	LIBRARIES	% of USA
22	Alabama	294	1.8%
44	Alaska	93	0.6%
30	Arizona	219	1.3%
32	Arkansas	218	1.3%
1	California	1,103	6.7%
25	Colorado	251	1.5%
28	Connecticut	229	1.4%
50	Delaware	32	0.2%
9	Florida	527	3.2%
14	Georgia	393	2.4%
49	Hawaii	50	0.3%
40	Idaho	142	0.9%
4	Illinois	779	4.7%
13	Indiana	434	2.6%
8	Iowa	557	3.4%
16	Kansas	369	2.2%
34	Kentucky	203	1.2%
21	Louisiana	338	2.0%
27	Maine	235	1.4%
36	Maryland	187	1.1%
11	Massachusetts	452	2.7%
6	Michigan	645	3.9%
18	Minnesota	356	2.2%
26	Mississippi	236	1.4%
17	Missouri	359	2.2%
42	Montana	114	0.7%
24	Nebraska	284	1.7%
45	Nevada	88	0.5%
29	New Hampshire	223	1.3%
12	New Jersey	442	2.7%
43	New Mexico	111	0.7%
2	New York	1,064	6.4%
15	North Carolina	384	2.3%
46	North Dakota	80	0.5%
5	Ohio	712	4.3%
33	Oklahoma	212	1.3%
30	Oregon	219	1.3%
7	Pennsylvania	629	3.8%
48	Rhode Island	69	0.4%
35	South Carolina	191	1.2%
39	South Dakota	146	0.9%
23	Tennessee	287	1.7%
3	Texas	857	5.2%
41	Utah	125	0.8%
38	Vermont	165	1.0%
18	Virginia	356	2.2%
20	Washington	340	2.1%
37	West Virginia	175	1.1%
10	Wisconsin	461	2.8%
47	Wyoming	76	0.5%

RANK ORDER

RANK	STATE	LIBRARIES	% of USA
1	California	1,103	6.7%
2	New York	1,064	6.4%
3	Texas	857	5.2%
4	Illinois	779	4.7%
5	Ohio	712	4.3%
6	Michigan	645	3.9%
7	Pennsylvania	629	3.8%
8	Iowa	557	3.4%
9	Florida	527	3.2%
10	Wisconsin	461	2.8%
11	Massachusetts	452	2.7%
12	New Jersey	442	2.7%
13	Indiana	434	2.6%
14	Georgia	393	2.4%
15	North Carolina	384	2.3%
16	Kansas	369	2.2%
17	Missouri	359	2.2%
18	Minnesota	356	2.2%
18	Virginia	356	2.2%
20	Washington	340	2.1%
21	Louisiana	338	2.0%
22	Alabama	294	1.8%
23	Tennessee	287	1.7%
24	Nebraska	284	1.7%
25	Colorado	251	1.5%
26	Mississippi	236	1.4%
27	Maine	235	1.4%
28	Connecticut	229	1.4%
29	New Hampshire	223	1.3%
30	Arizona	219	1.3%
30	Oregon	219	1.3%
32	Arkansas	218	1.3%
33	Oklahoma	212	1.3%
34	Kentucky	203	1.2%
35	South Carolina	191	1.2%
36	Maryland	187	1.1%
37	West Virginia	175	1.1%
38	Vermont	165	1.0%
39	South Dakota	146	0.9%
40	Idaho	142	0.9%
41	Utah	125	0.8%
42	Montana	114	0.7%
43	New Mexico	111	0.7%
44	Alaska	93	0.6%
45	Nevada	88	0.5%
46	North Dakota	80	0.5%
47	Wyoming	76	0.5%
48	Rhode Island	69	0.4%
49	Hawaii	50	0.3%
50	Delaware	32	0.2%
	District of Columbia	25	0.2%

Source: Institute of Museum and Library Services
"Public Library Survey Fiscal Year 2012" (December 2014, http://www.imls.gov/research/default.aspx)
*For fiscal year 2012. Total of central and branch outlets. Does not include bookmobiles. There are 9,082 public libraries.

Rate of Public Libraries and Branches in 2012

National Average = 18,995 Population per Library*

RANK	STATE (ALPHA ORDER)	RATE	RANK	STATE (RANK ORDER)	RATE
26	Alabama	16,381	1	Florida	36,721
42	Alaska	7,863	2	California	34,502
6	Arizona	29,924	3	Maryland	31,501
35	Arkansas	13,530	4	Nevada	31,305
2	California	34,502	5	Texas	30,443
16	Colorado	20,684	6	Arizona	29,924
28	Connecticut	15,692	7	Delaware	28,659
7	Delaware	28,659	8	Hawaii	27,853
1	Florida	36,721	9	North Carolina	25,383
10	Georgia	25,236	10	Georgia	25,236
8	Hawaii	27,853	11	South Carolina	24,719
38	Idaho	11,240	12	Virginia	23,015
25	Illinois	16,528	13	Utah	22,851
32	Indiana	15,065	14	Tennessee	22,493
49	Iowa	5,524	15	Kentucky	21,589
43	Kansas	7,822	16	Colorado	20,684
15	Kentucky	21,589	17	Pennsylvania	20,307
34	Louisiana	13,620	18	Washington	20,286
48	Maine	5,655	19	New Jersey	20,079
3	Maryland	31,501	20	New Mexico	18,782
33	Massachusetts	14,730	21	New York	18,428
29	Michigan	15,328	22	Oklahoma	18,008
31	Minnesota	15,114	23	Oregon	17,806
36	Mississippi	12,651	24	Missouri	16,784
24	Missouri	16,784	25	Illinois	16,528
40	Montana	8,817	26	Alabama	16,381
45	Nebraska	6,535	27	Ohio	16,224
4	Nevada	31,305	28	Connecticut	15,692
46	New Hampshire	5,926	29	Michigan	15,328
19	New Jersey	20,079	30	Rhode Island	15,252
20	New Mexico	18,782	31	Minnesota	15,114
21	New York	18,428	32	Indiana	15,065
9	North Carolina	25,383	33	Massachusetts	14,730
41	North Dakota	8,778	34	Louisiana	13,620
27	Ohio	16,224	35	Arkansas	13,530
22	Oklahoma	18,008	36	Mississippi	12,651
23	Oregon	17,806	37	Wisconsin	12,422
17	Pennsylvania	20,307	38	Idaho	11,240
30	Rhode Island	15,252	39	West Virginia	10,607
11	South Carolina	24,719	40	Montana	8,817
47	South Dakota	5,717	41	North Dakota	8,778
14	Tennessee	22,493	42	Alaska	7,863
5	Texas	30,443	43	Kansas	7,822
13	Utah	22,851	44	Wyoming	7,593
50	Vermont	3,796	45	Nebraska	6,535
12	Virginia	23,015	46	New Hampshire	5,926
18	Washington	20,286	47	South Dakota	5,717
39	West Virginia	10,607	48	Maine	5,655
37	Wisconsin	12,422	49	Iowa	5,524
44	Wyoming	7,593	50	Vermont	3,796
				District of Columbia	25,414

Source: CQ Press using data from Institute of Museum and Library Services
"Public Library Survey Fiscal Year 2012" (December 2014, http://www.imls.gov/research/default.aspx)
*For fiscal year 2012. Based on total of central and branch outlets. Does not include bookmobiles.

Rate of Books in Public Libraries in 2012

National Rate = 2,496 Books per 1,000 Population*

ALPHA ORDER

RANK	STATE	RATE
38	Alabama	2,008
19	Alaska	3,219
50	Arizona	1,282
32	Arkansas	2,204
43	California	1,811
33	Colorado	2,189
7	Connecticut	4,041
42	Delaware	1,850
46	Florida	1,678
46	Georgia	1,678
29	Hawaii	2,437
24	Idaho	2,725
14	Illinois	3,405
10	Indiana	3,720
8	Iowa	3,934
16	Kansas	3,282
37	Kentucky	2,009
26	Louisiana	2,592
3	Maine	4,488
31	Maryland	2,211
1	Massachusetts	4,907
13	Michigan	3,411
22	Minnesota	2,818
41	Mississippi	1,921
21	Missouri	2,858
25	Montana	2,686
20	Nebraska	3,205
48	Nevada	1,612
4	New Hampshire	4,445
17	New Jersey	3,276
36	New Mexico	2,049
12	New York	3,574
45	North Carolina	1,695
18	North Dakota	3,267
9	Ohio	3,819
40	Oklahoma	1,949
27	Oregon	2,545
35	Pennsylvania	2,090
6	Rhode Island	4,208
39	South Carolina	1,979
11	South Dakota	3,580
44	Tennessee	1,785
49	Texas	1,560
28	Utah	2,438
2	Vermont	4,599
30	Virginia	2,237
34	Washington	2,152
23	West Virginia	2,769
15	Wisconsin	3,364
5	Wyoming	4,311

RANK ORDER

RANK	STATE	RATE
1	Massachusetts	4,907
2	Vermont	4,599
3	Maine	4,488
4	New Hampshire	4,445
5	Wyoming	4,311
6	Rhode Island	4,208
7	Connecticut	4,041
8	Iowa	3,934
9	Ohio	3,819
10	Indiana	3,720
11	South Dakota	3,580
12	New York	3,574
13	Michigan	3,411
14	Illinois	3,405
15	Wisconsin	3,364
16	Kansas	3,282
17	New Jersey	3,276
18	North Dakota	3,267
19	Alaska	3,219
20	Nebraska	3,205
21	Missouri	2,858
22	Minnesota	2,818
23	West Virginia	2,769
24	Idaho	2,725
25	Montana	2,686
26	Louisiana	2,592
27	Oregon	2,545
28	Utah	2,438
29	Hawaii	2,437
30	Virginia	2,237
31	Maryland	2,211
32	Arkansas	2,204
33	Colorado	2,189
34	Washington	2,152
35	Pennsylvania	2,090
36	New Mexico	2,049
37	Kentucky	2,009
38	Alabama	2,008
39	South Carolina	1,979
40	Oklahoma	1,949
41	Mississippi	1,921
42	Delaware	1,850
43	California	1,811
44	Tennessee	1,785
45	North Carolina	1,695
46	Florida	1,678
46	Georgia	1,678
48	Nevada	1,612
49	Texas	1,560
50	Arizona	1,282
	District of Columbia	2,100

Source: CQ Press using data from Institute of Museum and Library Services
"Public Library Survey Fiscal Year 2012" (December 2014, http://www.imls.gov/research/default.aspx)
*For fiscal year 2012. Includes serial back files in print.

Rate of Electronic Books in Public Libraries in 2012

National Rate = 278 Electronic Books per 1,000 Population*

ALPHA ORDER

RANK	STATE	RATE
24	Alabama	182
11	Alaska	417
16	Arizona	324
36	Arkansas	53
41	California	36
28	Colorado	120
20	Connecticut	198
14	Delaware	350
32	Florida	72
42	Georgia	28
48	Hawaii	8
42	Idaho	28
23	Illinois	185
22	Indiana	191
7	Iowa	656
45	Kansas	17
5	Kentucky	739
33	Louisiana	71
8	Maine	580
31	Maryland	100
13	Massachusetts	373
27	Michigan	125
10	Minnesota	511
46	Mississippi	16
34	Missouri	69
4	Montana	797
9	Nebraska	519
37	Nevada	44
2	New Hampshire	1,537
21	New Jersey	195
44	New Mexico	26
18	New York	257
17	North Carolina	286
15	North Dakota	333
3	Ohio	1,533
35	Oklahoma	64
6	Oregon	658
19	Pennsylvania	218
12	Rhode Island	410
40	South Carolina	38
39	South Dakota	43
47	Tennessee	12
37	Texas	44
29	Utah	117
25	Vermont	144
26	Virginia	129
30	Washington	106
50	West Virginia	2
1	Wisconsin	3,533
49	Wyoming	7

RANK ORDER

RANK	STATE	RATE
1	Wisconsin	3,533
2	New Hampshire	1,537
3	Ohio	1,533
4	Montana	797
5	Kentucky	739
6	Oregon	658
7	Iowa	656
8	Maine	580
9	Nebraska	519
10	Minnesota	511
11	Alaska	417
12	Rhode Island	410
13	Massachusetts	373
14	Delaware	350
15	North Dakota	333
16	Arizona	324
17	North Carolina	286
18	New York	257
19	Pennsylvania	218
20	Connecticut	198
21	New Jersey	195
22	Indiana	191
23	Illinois	185
24	Alabama	182
25	Vermont	144
26	Virginia	129
27	Michigan	125
28	Colorado	120
29	Utah	117
30	Washington	106
31	Maryland	100
32	Florida	72
33	Louisiana	71
34	Missouri	69
35	Oklahoma	64
36	Arkansas	53
37	Nevada	44
37	Texas	44
39	South Dakota	43
40	South Carolina	38
41	California	36
42	Georgia	28
42	Idaho	28
44	New Mexico	26
45	Kansas	17
46	Mississippi	16
47	Tennessee	12
48	Hawaii	8
49	Wyoming	7
50	West Virginia	2
	District of Columbia	31

Source: CQ Press using data from Institute of Museum and Library Services
"Public Library Survey Fiscal Year 2012" (December 2014, http://www.imls.gov/research/default.aspx)
*For fiscal year 2012.

Internet Terminals in Public Libraries in 2012

National Total = 271,146 Terminals*

ALPHA ORDER				RANK ORDER			
RANK	STATE	TERMINALS	% of USA	RANK	STATE	TERMINALS	% of USA
20	Alabama	5,272	1.9%	1	California	20,340	7.5%
47	Alaska	754	0.3%	2	Texas	19,115	7.0%
19	Arizona	5,290	2.0%	3	New York	17,856	6.6%
34	Arkansas	2,235	0.8%	4	Florida	15,735	5.8%
1	California	20,340	7.5%	5	Illinois	13,854	5.1%
16	Colorado	5,874	2.2%	6	Michigan	12,072	4.5%
27	Connecticut	4,176	1.5%	7	Ohio	11,980	4.4%
49	Delaware	576	0.2%	8	Indiana	8,383	3.1%
4	Florida	15,735	5.8%	9	Pennsylvania	7,885	2.9%
11	Georgia	7,516	2.8%	10	New Jersey	7,867	2.9%
50	Hawaii	453	0.2%	11	Georgia	7,516	2.8%
39	Idaho	1,650	0.6%	12	North Carolina	7,246	2.7%
5	Illinois	13,854	5.1%	13	Washington	6,906	2.5%
8	Indiana	8,383	3.1%	14	Wisconsin	6,164	2.3%
26	Iowa	4,469	1.6%	15	Massachusetts	6,049	2.2%
29	Kansas	3,639	1.3%	16	Colorado	5,874	2.2%
25	Kentucky	4,497	1.7%	17	Virginia	5,699	2.1%
21	Louisiana	5,054	1.9%	18	Minnesota	5,675	2.1%
37	Maine	1,789	0.7%	19	Arizona	5,290	2.0%
24	Maryland	4,531	1.7%	20	Alabama	5,272	1.9%
15	Massachusetts	6,049	2.2%	21	Louisiana	5,054	1.9%
6	Michigan	12,072	4.5%	22	Missouri	4,913	1.8%
18	Minnesota	5,675	2.1%	23	Tennessee	4,896	1.8%
33	Mississippi	2,696	1.0%	24	Maryland	4,531	1.7%
22	Missouri	4,913	1.8%	25	Kentucky	4,497	1.7%
43	Montana	1,248	0.5%	26	Iowa	4,469	1.6%
32	Nebraska	2,793	1.0%	27	Connecticut	4,176	1.5%
38	Nevada	1,654	0.6%	28	South Carolina	3,823	1.4%
42	New Hampshire	1,403	0.5%	29	Kansas	3,639	1.3%
10	New Jersey	7,867	2.9%	30	Oregon	3,032	1.1%
36	New Mexico	1,891	0.7%	31	Oklahoma	2,994	1.1%
3	New York	17,856	6.6%	32	Nebraska	2,793	1.0%
12	North Carolina	7,246	2.7%	33	Mississippi	2,696	1.0%
48	North Dakota	650	0.2%	34	Arkansas	2,235	0.8%
7	Ohio	11,980	4.4%	35	Utah	1,974	0.7%
31	Oklahoma	2,994	1.1%	36	New Mexico	1,891	0.7%
30	Oregon	3,032	1.1%	37	Maine	1,789	0.7%
9	Pennsylvania	7,885	2.9%	38	Nevada	1,654	0.6%
40	Rhode Island	1,426	0.5%	39	Idaho	1,650	0.6%
28	South Carolina	3,823	1.4%	40	Rhode Island	1,426	0.5%
45	South Dakota	973	0.4%	41	West Virginia	1,405	0.5%
23	Tennessee	4,896	1.8%	42	New Hampshire	1,403	0.5%
2	Texas	19,115	7.0%	43	Montana	1,248	0.5%
35	Utah	1,974	0.7%	44	Vermont	1,059	0.4%
44	Vermont	1,059	0.4%	45	South Dakota	973	0.4%
17	Virginia	5,699	2.1%	46	Wyoming	815	0.3%
13	Washington	6,906	2.5%	47	Alaska	754	0.3%
41	West Virginia	1,405	0.5%	48	North Dakota	650	0.2%
14	Wisconsin	6,164	2.3%	49	Delaware	576	0.2%
46	Wyoming	815	0.3%	50	Hawaii	453	0.2%
					District of Columbia	900	0.3%

Source: Institute of Museum and Library Services
"Public Library Survey Fiscal Year 2012" (December 2014, http://www.imls.gov/research/default.aspx)
*For fiscal year 2012. Total of public-use Internet terminals in central and branch outlets.

Rate of Internet Terminals in Public Libraries in 2012

National Rate = 16.4 Terminals per Library*

ALPHA ORDER				RANK ORDER		
RANK	STATE	RATE		RANK	STATE	RATE
18	Alabama	17.9		1	Florida	29.9
43	Alaska	8.1		2	Arizona	24.2
2	Arizona	24.2		2	Maryland	24.2
39	Arkansas	10.3		4	Colorado	23.4
15	California	18.4		5	Texas	22.3
4	Colorado	23.4		6	Kentucky	22.2
16	Connecticut	18.2		7	Rhode Island	20.7
17	Delaware	18.0		8	Washington	20.3
1	Florida	29.9		9	South Carolina	20.0
11	Georgia	19.1		10	Indiana	19.3
42	Hawaii	9.1		11	Georgia	19.1
35	Idaho	11.6		12	North Carolina	18.9
19	Illinois	17.8		13	Nevada	18.8
10	Indiana	19.3		14	Michigan	18.7
45	Iowa	8.0		15	California	18.4
40	Kansas	9.9		16	Connecticut	18.2
6	Kentucky	22.2		17	Delaware	18.0
28	Louisiana	15.0		18	Alabama	17.9
47	Maine	7.6		19	Illinois	17.8
2	Maryland	24.2		19	New Jersey	17.8
32	Massachusetts	13.4		21	Tennessee	17.1
14	Michigan	18.7		22	New Mexico	17.0
26	Minnesota	15.9		23	New York	16.8
36	Mississippi	11.4		23	Ohio	16.8
31	Missouri	13.7		25	Virginia	16.0
37	Montana	10.9		26	Minnesota	15.9
41	Nebraska	9.8		27	Utah	15.8
13	Nevada	18.8		28	Louisiana	15.0
50	New Hampshire	6.3		29	Oklahoma	14.1
19	New Jersey	17.8		30	Oregon	13.8
22	New Mexico	17.0		31	Missouri	13.7
23	New York	16.8		32	Massachusetts	13.4
12	North Carolina	18.9		32	Wisconsin	13.4
43	North Dakota	8.1		34	Pennsylvania	12.5
23	Ohio	16.8		35	Idaho	11.6
29	Oklahoma	14.1		36	Mississippi	11.4
30	Oregon	13.8		37	Montana	10.9
34	Pennsylvania	12.5		38	Wyoming	10.7
7	Rhode Island	20.7		39	Arkansas	10.3
9	South Carolina	20.0		40	Kansas	9.9
48	South Dakota	6.7		41	Nebraska	9.8
21	Tennessee	17.1		42	Hawaii	9.1
5	Texas	22.3		43	Alaska	8.1
27	Utah	15.8		43	North Dakota	8.1
49	Vermont	6.4		45	Iowa	8.0
25	Virginia	16.0		45	West Virginia	8.0
8	Washington	20.3		47	Maine	7.6
45	West Virginia	8.0		48	South Dakota	6.7
32	Wisconsin	13.4		49	Vermont	6.4
38	Wyoming	10.7		50	New Hampshire	6.3
					District of Columbia	36.0

Source: CQ Press using data from Institute of Museum and Library Services
"Public Library Survey Fiscal Year 2012" (December 2014, http://www.imls.gov/research/default.aspx)
*For fiscal year 2012. Total of public-use Internet terminals in central and branch outlets divided by the number of outlets.

Per Capita State Art Agencies' Legislative Appropriations in 2016

National Per Capita = $1.12*

ALPHA ORDER

RANK	STATE	PER CAPITA
25	Alabama	0.82
17	Alaska	0.99
50	Arizona	0.00
31	Arkansas	0.56
44	California	0.28
42	Colorado	0.39
11	Connecticut	1.67
3	Delaware	3.66
9	Florida	1.98
48	Georgia	0.09
2	Hawaii	3.73
38	Idaho	0.46
29	Illinois	0.63
35	Indiana	0.51
41	Iowa	0.40
49	Kansas	0.07
29	Kentucky	0.63
36	Louisiana	0.48
27	Maine	0.73
5	Maryland	2.79
8	Massachusetts	2.10
19	Michigan	0.91
1	Minnesota	6.29
33	Mississippi	0.53
14	Missouri	1.13
32	Montana	0.54
24	Nebraska	0.83
38	Nevada	0.46
45	New Hampshire	0.22
10	New Jersey	1.83
26	New Mexico	0.75
6	New York	2.34
27	North Carolina	0.73
13	North Dakota	1.19
12	Ohio	1.23
19	Oklahoma	0.91
34	Oregon	0.52
21	Pennsylvania	0.90
4	Rhode Island	3.09
22	South Carolina	0.87
18	South Dakota	0.95
15	Tennessee	1.07
42	Texas	0.39
22	Utah	0.87
16	Vermont	1.03
40	Virginia	0.42
46	Washington	0.16
37	West Virginia	0.47
47	Wisconsin	0.14
7	Wyoming	2.12

RANK ORDER

RANK	STATE	PER CAPITA
1	Minnesota	6.29
2	Hawaii	3.73
3	Delaware	3.66
4	Rhode Island	3.09
5	Maryland	2.79
6	New York	2.34
7	Wyoming	2.12
8	Massachusetts	2.10
9	Florida	1.98
10	New Jersey	1.83
11	Connecticut	1.67
12	Ohio	1.23
13	North Dakota	1.19
14	Missouri	1.13
15	Tennessee	1.07
16	Vermont	1.03
17	Alaska	0.99
18	South Dakota	0.95
19	Michigan	0.91
19	Oklahoma	0.91
21	Pennsylvania	0.90
22	South Carolina	0.87
22	Utah	0.87
24	Nebraska	0.83
25	Alabama	0.82
26	New Mexico	0.75
27	Maine	0.73
27	North Carolina	0.73
29	Illinois	0.63
29	Kentucky	0.63
31	Arkansas	0.56
32	Montana	0.54
33	Mississippi	0.53
34	Oregon	0.52
35	Indiana	0.51
36	Louisiana	0.48
37	West Virginia	0.47
38	Idaho	0.46
38	Nevada	0.46
40	Virginia	0.42
41	Iowa	0.40
42	Colorado	0.39
42	Texas	0.39
44	California	0.28
45	New Hampshire	0.22
46	Washington	0.16
47	Wisconsin	0.14
48	Georgia	0.09
49	Kansas	0.07
50	Arizona	0.00
	District of Columbia	22.30

Source: National Assembly of State Arts Agencies
"State Arts Agency Legislative Appropriations Preview Fiscal Year 2016" (http://www.nasaa-arts.org/Research/Funding/)
*Projected figures for fiscal year 2016. Includes line item appropriations. Line items are legislative appropriations that are not controlled by the state art agencies but are passed through their budgets directly to another entity.

Federal Allocations for Head Start Program in 2014

National Total = $8,098,095,000*

ALPHA ORDER

RANK	STATE	EXPENDITURES	% of USA
18	Alabama	$124,377,203	1.6%
49	Alaska	14,677,625	0.2%
20	Arizona	121,586,377	1.6%
29	Arkansas	73,063,664	0.9%
1	California	979,754,551	12.6%
28	Colorado	83,043,878	1.1%
31	Connecticut	62,589,568	0.8%
48	Delaware	15,172,449	0.2%
5	Florida	318,389,657	4.1%
9	Georgia	203,399,319	2.6%
41	Hawaii	26,060,039	0.3%
40	Idaho	26,697,173	0.3%
4	Illinois	321,387,029	4.1%
22	Indiana	113,430,566	1.5%
34	Iowa	60,129,449	0.8%
33	Kansas	60,237,400	0.8%
16	Kentucky	128,035,469	1.6%
12	Louisiana	166,131,337	2.1%
38	Maine	32,208,621	0.4%
26	Maryland	91,807,269	1.2%
17	Massachusetts	124,459,511	1.6%
7	Michigan	271,485,932	3.5%
27	Minnesota	85,086,710	1.1%
10	Mississippi	182,885,459	2.3%
14	Missouri	141,473,617	1.8%
43	Montana	24,385,336	0.3%
37	Nebraska	42,962,702	0.6%
39	Nevada	28,416,227	0.4%
46	New Hampshire	15,739,084	0.2%
13	New Jersey	156,698,017	2.0%
32	New Mexico	61,861,561	0.8%
3	New York	505,464,030	6.5%
11	North Carolina	171,279,580	2.2%
45	North Dakota	20,359,378	0.3%
6	Ohio	291,584,452	3.7%
25	Oklahoma	99,351,062	1.3%
30	Oregon	71,691,114	0.9%
8	Pennsylvania	270,312,578	3.5%
42	Rhode Island	25,484,182	0.3%
24	South Carolina	101,263,106	1.3%
44	South Dakota	21,988,051	0.3%
15	Tennessee	136,892,761	1.8%
2	Texas	570,538,533	7.3%
36	Utah	48,418,043	0.6%
47	Vermont	15,535,073	0.2%
21	Virginia	117,220,586	1.5%
19	Washington	123,638,128	1.6%
35	West Virginia	59,476,634	0.8%
23	Wisconsin	105,704,455	1.4%
50	Wyoming	13,750,805	0.2%

RANK ORDER

RANK	STATE	EXPENDITURES	% of USA
1	California	$979,754,551	12.6%
2	Texas	570,538,533	7.3%
3	New York	505,464,030	6.5%
4	Illinois	321,387,029	4.1%
5	Florida	318,389,657	4.1%
6	Ohio	291,584,452	3.7%
7	Michigan	271,485,932	3.5%
8	Pennsylvania	270,312,578	3.5%
9	Georgia	203,399,319	2.6%
10	Mississippi	182,885,459	2.3%
11	North Carolina	171,279,580	2.2%
12	Louisiana	166,131,337	2.1%
13	New Jersey	156,698,017	2.0%
14	Missouri	141,473,617	1.8%
15	Tennessee	136,892,761	1.8%
16	Kentucky	128,035,469	1.6%
17	Massachusetts	124,459,511	1.6%
18	Alabama	124,377,203	1.6%
19	Washington	123,638,128	1.6%
20	Arizona	121,586,377	1.6%
21	Virginia	117,220,586	1.5%
22	Indiana	113,430,566	1.5%
23	Wisconsin	105,704,455	1.4%
24	South Carolina	101,263,106	1.3%
25	Oklahoma	99,351,062	1.3%
26	Maryland	91,807,269	1.2%
27	Minnesota	85,086,710	1.1%
28	Colorado	83,043,878	1.1%
29	Arkansas	73,063,664	0.9%
30	Oregon	71,691,114	0.9%
31	Connecticut	62,589,568	0.8%
32	New Mexico	61,861,561	0.8%
33	Kansas	60,237,400	0.8%
34	Iowa	60,129,449	0.8%
35	West Virginia	59,476,634	0.8%
36	Utah	48,418,043	0.6%
37	Nebraska	42,962,702	0.6%
38	Maine	32,208,621	0.4%
39	Nevada	28,416,227	0.4%
40	Idaho	26,697,173	0.3%
41	Hawaii	26,060,039	0.3%
42	Rhode Island	25,484,182	0.3%
43	Montana	24,385,336	0.3%
44	South Dakota	21,988,051	0.3%
45	North Dakota	20,359,378	0.3%
46	New Hampshire	15,739,084	0.2%
47	Vermont	15,535,073	0.2%
48	Delaware	15,172,449	0.2%
49	Alaska	14,677,625	0.2%
50	Wyoming	13,750,805	0.2%
	District of Columbia	27,977,602	0.4%

Source: U.S. Department of Health and Human Services, Administration for Children and Families "Head Start Fact Sheet Fiscal Year 2014" (http://eclkc.ohs.acf.hhs.gov/hslc/mr/factsheets)

*For fiscal year 2014. National total includes $555,124,621 to Migrant and Native American programs not included in state totals and $296,456,348 to U.S. territories. Does not include $315,675,000 in "support activities" expenditures or $500,000,000 to expand access to high-quality early learning and development opportunities for infants and toddlers through Early Head Start-Child Care Partnerships.

Head Start Program Enrollment in 2014

National Total = 927,275 Children*

ALPHA ORDER

RANK	STATE	ENROLLMENT	% of USA
15	Alabama	16,606	1.8%
49	Alaska	1,632	0.2%
21	Arizona	14,065	1.5%
30	Arkansas	10,034	1.1%
1	California	101,189	10.9%
28	Colorado	10,538	1.1%
35	Connecticut	6,701	0.7%
46	Delaware	2,209	0.2%
6	Florida	37,609	4.1%
10	Georgia	24,191	2.6%
39	Hawaii	3,152	0.3%
40	Idaho	3,111	0.3%
4	Illinois	40,898	4.4%
17	Indiana	15,179	1.6%
33	Iowa	7,680	0.8%
31	Kansas	8,556	0.9%
16	Kentucky	15,960	1.7%
11	Louisiana	21,772	2.3%
38	Maine	3,237	0.3%
29	Maryland	10,273	1.1%
25	Massachusetts	12,501	1.3%
8	Michigan	32,708	3.5%
27	Minnesota	11,288	1.2%
9	Mississippi	26,782	2.9%
13	Missouri	17,527	1.9%
41	Montana	3,055	0.3%
37	Nebraska	5,204	0.6%
43	Nevada	2,852	0.3%
48	New Hampshire	1,650	0.2%
18	New Jersey	15,074	1.6%
34	New Mexico	7,672	0.8%
3	New York	50,216	5.4%
12	North Carolina	20,278	2.2%
45	North Dakota	2,378	0.3%
5	Ohio	39,293	4.2%
22	Oklahoma	13,986	1.5%
24	Oregon	12,741	1.4%
7	Pennsylvania	36,626	3.9%
44	Rhode Island	2,811	0.3%
23	South Carolina	12,860	1.4%
42	South Dakota	2,890	0.3%
14	Tennessee	16,841	1.8%
2	Texas	71,465	7.7%
36	Utah	6,080	0.7%
50	Vermont	1,448	0.2%
19	Virginia	14,590	1.6%
26	Washington	12,423	1.3%
32	West Virginia	7,978	0.9%
20	Wisconsin	14,218	1.5%
47	Wyoming	1,658	0.2%

RANK ORDER

RANK	STATE	ENROLLMENT	% of USA
1	California	101,189	10.9%
2	Texas	71,465	7.7%
3	New York	50,216	5.4%
4	Illinois	40,898	4.4%
5	Ohio	39,293	4.2%
6	Florida	37,609	4.1%
7	Pennsylvania	36,626	3.9%
8	Michigan	32,708	3.5%
9	Mississippi	26,782	2.9%
10	Georgia	24,191	2.6%
11	Louisiana	21,772	2.3%
12	North Carolina	20,278	2.2%
13	Missouri	17,527	1.9%
14	Tennessee	16,841	1.8%
15	Alabama	16,606	1.8%
16	Kentucky	15,960	1.7%
17	Indiana	15,179	1.6%
18	New Jersey	15,074	1.6%
19	Virginia	14,590	1.6%
20	Wisconsin	14,218	1.5%
21	Arizona	14,065	1.5%
22	Oklahoma	13,986	1.5%
23	South Carolina	12,860	1.4%
24	Oregon	12,741	1.4%
25	Massachusetts	12,501	1.3%
26	Washington	12,423	1.3%
27	Minnesota	11,288	1.2%
28	Colorado	10,538	1.1%
29	Maryland	10,273	1.1%
30	Arkansas	10,034	1.1%
31	Kansas	8,556	0.9%
32	West Virginia	7,978	0.9%
33	Iowa	7,680	0.8%
34	New Mexico	7,672	0.8%
35	Connecticut	6,701	0.7%
36	Utah	6,080	0.7%
37	Nebraska	5,204	0.6%
38	Maine	3,237	0.3%
39	Hawaii	3,152	0.3%
40	Idaho	3,111	0.3%
41	Montana	3,055	0.3%
42	South Dakota	2,890	0.3%
43	Nevada	2,852	0.3%
44	Rhode Island	2,811	0.3%
45	North Dakota	2,378	0.3%
46	Delaware	2,209	0.2%
47	Wyoming	1,658	0.2%
48	New Hampshire	1,650	0.2%
49	Alaska	1,632	0.2%
50	Vermont	1,448	0.2%
	District of Columbia	3,106	0.3%

Source: U.S. Department of Health and Human Services, Administration for Children and Families "Head Start Fact Sheet Fiscal Year 2014" (http://eclkc.ohs.acf.hhs.gov/hslc/mr/factsheets)

*For fiscal year 2014. National total includes 52,264 enrollees not included in state totals enrolled in Migrant and Native American programs and 40,220 enrollees in U.S. territories.

VI. Employment and Labor

Average Annual Pay in 2014. 169
Percent Change in Average Annual Pay: 2013 to 2014 . . . 170
Median Earnings of Male Full-Time Workers in 2014. . . . 171
Median Earnings of Female Full-Time Workers in 2014 . . 172
State Minimum Wage Rates in 2016. 173
Average Hourly Earnings of Production Workers on
    Manufacturing Payrolls in 2015. 174
Average Weekly Earnings of Production Workers on
    Manufacturing Payrolls in 2015. 175
Average Work Week of Production Workers on
    Manufacturing Payrolls in 2015. 176
Average Weekly Unemployment Benefit in 2015. 177
Workers' Compensation Benefit Payments in 2013 178
Workers' Compensation Benefit Payment per Covered
    Worker in 2013. 179
Percent Change in Workers' Compensation Benefit
    Payments: 2012 to 2013. 180
Civilian Labor Force in 2015 181
Employed Civilian Labor Force in 2015 182
Employment to Population Ratio in 2015. 183
Unemployed Civilian Labor Force in 2015 184
Unemployment Rate in 2015 185
Women in Civilian Labor Force in 2014 186
Percent of Women in the Civilian Labor Force in 2014 . . . 187
Percent of Civilian Labor Force Comprised of Women
    in 2014 188
Job Growth: 2014 to 2015. 189
Employees on Nonfarm Payrolls in 2015. 190

Employees in Construction in 2015 191
Percent of Nonfarm Employees in Construction in 2015 . . 192
Employees in Education and Health Services in 2015 193
Percent of Nonfarm Employees in Education and Health
    Services in 2015. 194
Employees in Financial Activities in 2015 195
Percent of Nonfarm Employees in Financial Activities
    in 2015 196
Employees in Government in 2015. 197
Percent of Nonfarm Employees in Government in 2015 . . 198
Employees in Leisure and Hospitality in 2015. 199
Percent of Nonfarm Employees in Leisure and Hospitality
    in 2015 200
Employees in Manufacturing in 2015. 201
Percent of Nonfarm Employees in Manufacturing
    in 2015 202
Employees in Mining and Logging in 2015 203
Percent of Nonfarm Employees in Mining and Logging
    in 2015 204
Employees in Professional and Business Services
    in 2015 205
Percent of Nonfarm Employees in Professional and
    Business Services in 2015 206
Employees in Trade, Transportation, and Public Utilities
    in 2015 207
Percent of Nonfarm Employees in Trade, Transportation,
    and Public Utilities in 2015 208

Average Annual Pay in 2014

National Average = $51,364*

ALPHA ORDER

RANK	STATE	ANNUAL PAY
34	Alabama	$43,287
9	Alaska	53,418
21	Arizona	46,919
46	Arkansas	39,975
5	California	59,042
13	Colorado	52,724
3	Connecticut	63,919
11	Delaware	53,212
29	Florida	44,803
20	Georgia	48,138
26	Hawaii	45,210
49	Idaho	37,982
8	Illinois	54,106
38	Indiana	42,553
39	Iowa	42,538
37	Kansas	42,716
40	Kentucky	41,941
25	Louisiana	45,336
45	Maine	40,442
6	Maryland	55,389
2	Massachusetts	64,103
19	Michigan	48,487
14	Minnesota	51,602
50	Mississippi	37,111
31	Missouri	44,258
47	Montana	38,878
43	Nebraska	41,185
30	Nevada	44,727
15	New Hampshire	51,165
4	New Jersey	60,597
41	New Mexico	41,925
1	New York	65,880
28	North Carolina	44,973
16	North Dakota	50,855
24	Ohio	46,000
33	Oklahoma	43,773
22	Oregon	46,529
17	Pennsylvania	50,567
18	Rhode Island	49,297
44	South Carolina	40,797
48	South Dakota	38,690
27	Tennessee	45,202
10	Texas	53,218
36	Utah	42,942
35	Vermont	43,025
12	Virginia	52,929
7	Washington	55,016
42	West Virginia	41,201
32	Wisconsin	43,829
23	Wyoming	46,492

RANK ORDER

RANK	STATE	ANNUAL PAY
1	New York	$65,880
2	Massachusetts	64,103
3	Connecticut	63,919
4	New Jersey	60,597
5	California	59,042
6	Maryland	55,389
7	Washington	55,016
8	Illinois	54,106
9	Alaska	53,418
10	Texas	53,218
11	Delaware	53,212
12	Virginia	52,929
13	Colorado	52,724
14	Minnesota	51,602
15	New Hampshire	51,165
16	North Dakota	50,855
17	Pennsylvania	50,567
18	Rhode Island	49,297
19	Michigan	48,487
20	Georgia	48,138
21	Arizona	46,919
22	Oregon	46,529
23	Wyoming	46,492
24	Ohio	46,000
25	Louisiana	45,336
26	Hawaii	45,210
27	Tennessee	45,202
28	North Carolina	44,973
29	Florida	44,803
30	Nevada	44,727
31	Missouri	44,258
32	Wisconsin	43,829
33	Oklahoma	43,773
34	Alabama	43,287
35	Vermont	43,025
36	Utah	42,942
37	Kansas	42,716
38	Indiana	42,553
39	Iowa	42,538
40	Kentucky	41,941
41	New Mexico	41,925
42	West Virginia	41,201
43	Nebraska	41,185
44	South Carolina	40,797
45	Maine	40,442
46	Arkansas	39,975
47	Montana	38,878
48	South Dakota	38,690
49	Idaho	37,982
50	Mississippi	37,111
	District of Columbia	85,877

Source: U.S. Department of Labor, Bureau of Labor Statistics
"Quarterly Census of Employment and Wages" (http://www.bls.gov/cew/data.htm)
*Computed by dividing total annual wages of employees covered by unemployment insurance programs by the average monthly number of these employees. Includes bonuses, cash value of meals and lodging, tips and, in many states, employer contributions to certain deferred compensation plans such as 401(k) plans.

Percent Change in Average Annual Pay: 2013 to 2014

National Percent Change = 3.1% Increase*

ALPHA ORDER

RANK	STATE	PERCENT CHANGE
42	Alabama	2.4
8	Alaska	3.6
45	Arizona	2.2
32	Arkansas	2.7
12	California	3.4
8	Colorado	3.6
36	Connecticut	2.5
43	Delaware	2.3
35	Florida	2.6
25	Georgia	2.9
16	Hawaii	3.1
16	Idaho	3.1
25	Illinois	2.9
46	Indiana	2.1
10	Iowa	3.5
28	Kansas	2.8
28	Kentucky	2.8
20	Louisiana	3.0
20	Maine	3.0
36	Maryland	2.5
6	Massachusetts	3.7
25	Michigan	2.9
20	Minnesota	3.0
49	Mississippi	1.8
28	Missouri	2.8
10	Montana	3.5
16	Nebraska	3.1
50	Nevada	1.4
2	New Hampshire	4.5
47	New Jersey	1.9
32	New Mexico	2.7
3	New York	4.4
32	North Carolina	2.7
1	North Dakota	6.4
20	Ohio	3.0
16	Oklahoma	3.1
12	Oregon	3.4
20	Pennsylvania	3.0
15	Rhode Island	3.3
36	South Carolina	2.5
4	South Dakota	3.9
36	Tennessee	2.5
4	Texas	3.9
28	Utah	2.8
43	Vermont	2.3
47	Virginia	1.9
6	Washington	3.7
36	West Virginia	2.5
36	Wisconsin	2.5
12	Wyoming	3.4

RANK ORDER

RANK	STATE	PERCENT CHANGE
1	North Dakota	6.4
2	New Hampshire	4.5
3	New York	4.4
4	South Dakota	3.9
4	Texas	3.9
6	Massachusetts	3.7
6	Washington	3.7
8	Alaska	3.6
8	Colorado	3.6
10	Iowa	3.5
10	Montana	3.5
12	California	3.4
12	Oregon	3.4
12	Wyoming	3.4
15	Rhode Island	3.3
16	Hawaii	3.1
16	Idaho	3.1
16	Nebraska	3.1
16	Oklahoma	3.1
20	Louisiana	3.0
20	Maine	3.0
20	Minnesota	3.0
20	Ohio	3.0
20	Pennsylvania	3.0
25	Georgia	2.9
25	Illinois	2.9
25	Michigan	2.9
28	Kansas	2.8
28	Kentucky	2.8
28	Missouri	2.8
28	Utah	2.8
32	Arkansas	2.7
32	New Mexico	2.7
32	North Carolina	2.7
35	Florida	2.6
36	Connecticut	2.5
36	Maryland	2.5
36	South Carolina	2.5
36	Tennessee	2.5
36	West Virginia	2.5
36	Wisconsin	2.5
42	Alabama	2.4
43	Delaware	2.3
43	Vermont	2.3
45	Arizona	2.2
46	Indiana	2.1
47	New Jersey	1.9
47	Virginia	1.9
49	Mississippi	1.8
50	Nevada	1.4
	District of Columbia	3.4

Source: CQ Press using data from U.S. Department of Labor, Bureau of Labor Statistics
"Quarterly Census of Employment and Wages" (http://www.bls.gov/cew/data.htm)
*Includes bonuses, cash value of meals and lodging, tips and, in many states, employer contributions to certain deferred compensation plans such as 401(k) plans.

Median Earnings of Male Full-Time Workers in 2014

National Median = $48,745

ALPHA ORDER

RANK	STATE	EARNINGS
36	Alabama	$44,245
5	Alaska	57,318
37	Arizona	43,945
50	Arkansas	39,916
18	California	50,539
15	Colorado	50,898
2	Connecticut	61,385
13	Delaware	50,976
48	Florida	40,971
34	Georgia	44,623
28	Hawaii	46,786
40	Idaho	42,624
10	Illinois	51,652
29	Indiana	46,273
24	Iowa	47,202
26	Kansas	46,951
42	Kentucky	42,203
21	Louisiana	48,382
31	Maine	45,784
4	Maryland	59,085
1	Massachusetts	61,611
20	Michigan	50,157
11	Minnesota	51,625
49	Mississippi	40,850
32	Missouri	45,611
39	Montana	42,679
35	Nebraska	44,533
41	Nevada	42,294
6	New Hampshire	55,617
3	New Jersey	60,870
47	New Mexico	41,561
12	New York	51,580
45	North Carolina	41,857
17	North Dakota	50,624
22	Ohio	47,737
38	Oklahoma	43,803
25	Oregon	47,194
19	Pennsylvania	50,412
16	Rhode Island	50,765
44	South Carolina	41,991
43	South Dakota	42,034
46	Tennessee	41,661
30	Texas	46,235
14	Utah	50,937
27	Vermont	46,911
8	Virginia	52,864
7	Washington	54,358
33	West Virginia	45,272
23	Wisconsin	47,518
9	Wyoming	51,926

RANK ORDER

RANK	STATE	EARNINGS
1	Massachusetts	$61,611
2	Connecticut	61,385
3	New Jersey	60,870
4	Maryland	59,085
5	Alaska	57,318
6	New Hampshire	55,617
7	Washington	54,358
8	Virginia	52,864
9	Wyoming	51,926
10	Illinois	51,652
11	Minnesota	51,625
12	New York	51,580
13	Delaware	50,976
14	Utah	50,937
15	Colorado	50,898
16	Rhode Island	50,765
17	North Dakota	50,624
18	California	50,539
19	Pennsylvania	50,412
20	Michigan	50,157
21	Louisiana	48,382
22	Ohio	47,737
23	Wisconsin	47,518
24	Iowa	47,202
25	Oregon	47,194
26	Kansas	46,951
27	Vermont	46,911
28	Hawaii	46,786
29	Indiana	46,273
30	Texas	46,235
31	Maine	45,784
32	Missouri	45,611
33	West Virginia	45,272
34	Georgia	44,623
35	Nebraska	44,533
36	Alabama	44,245
37	Arizona	43,945
38	Oklahoma	43,803
39	Montana	42,679
40	Idaho	42,624
41	Nevada	42,294
42	Kentucky	42,203
43	South Dakota	42,034
44	South Carolina	41,991
45	North Carolina	41,857
46	Tennessee	41,661
47	New Mexico	41,561
48	Florida	40,971
49	Mississippi	40,850
50	Arkansas	39,916
	District of Columbia	68,932

Source: U.S. Bureau of the Census
"2014 American Community Survey-Table R2001" (http://www.census.gov/programs-surveys/acs/)

Median Earnings of Female Full-Time Workers in 2014

National Median = $38,941

ALPHA ORDER

RANK	STATE	EARNINGS
43	Alabama	$32,136
5	Alaska	46,288
23	Arizona	36,916
49	Arkansas	31,161
7	California	42,486
12	Colorado	41,690
1	Connecticut	50,706
14	Delaware	41,278
36	Florida	34,768
25	Georgia	36,468
16	Hawaii	40,162
50	Idaho	31,019
15	Illinois	40,898
35	Indiana	34,846
24	Iowa	36,522
27	Kansas	36,162
40	Kentucky	33,704
47	Louisiana	31,586
28	Maine	36,137
2	Maryland	50,481
3	Massachusetts	50,459
21	Michigan	37,419
9	Minnesota	42,066
48	Mississippi	31,465
33	Missouri	35,311
46	Montana	31,696
34	Nebraska	35,101
30	Nevada	35,993
10	New Hampshire	42,052
4	New Jersey	48,943
41	New Mexico	32,473
6	New York	44,781
32	North Carolina	35,481
29	North Dakota	36,087
22	Ohio	37,140
42	Oklahoma	32,186
19	Oregon	38,801
17	Pennsylvania	39,905
13	Rhode Island	41,469
39	South Carolina	33,719
44	South Dakota	32,048
38	Tennessee	34,009
26	Texas	36,428
37	Utah	34,351
18	Vermont	39,322
8	Virginia	42,445
11	Washington	41,926
45	West Virginia	31,712
20	Wisconsin	37,481
31	Wyoming	35,652

RANK ORDER

RANK	STATE	EARNINGS
1	Connecticut	$50,706
2	Maryland	50,481
3	Massachusetts	50,459
4	New Jersey	48,943
5	Alaska	46,288
6	New York	44,781
7	California	42,486
8	Virginia	42,445
9	Minnesota	42,066
10	New Hampshire	42,052
11	Washington	41,926
12	Colorado	41,690
13	Rhode Island	41,469
14	Delaware	41,278
15	Illinois	40,898
16	Hawaii	40,162
17	Pennsylvania	39,905
18	Vermont	39,322
19	Oregon	38,801
20	Wisconsin	37,481
21	Michigan	37,419
22	Ohio	37,140
23	Arizona	36,916
24	Iowa	36,522
25	Georgia	36,468
26	Texas	36,428
27	Kansas	36,162
28	Maine	36,137
29	North Dakota	36,087
30	Nevada	35,993
31	Wyoming	35,652
32	North Carolina	35,481
33	Missouri	35,311
34	Nebraska	35,101
35	Indiana	34,846
36	Florida	34,768
37	Utah	34,351
38	Tennessee	34,009
39	South Carolina	33,719
40	Kentucky	33,704
41	New Mexico	32,473
42	Oklahoma	32,186
43	Alabama	32,136
44	South Dakota	32,048
45	West Virginia	31,712
46	Montana	31,696
47	Louisiana	31,586
48	Mississippi	31,465
49	Arkansas	31,161
50	Idaho	31,019
	District of Columbia	61,718

Source: U.S. Bureau of the Census
"2014 American Community Survey-Table R2002" (http://www.census.gov/programs-surveys/acs/)

State Minimum Wage Rates in 2016

National Rate = $7.25 per Hour*

ALPHA ORDER

RANK	STATE	MINIMUM WAGE
NA	Alabama**	NA
3	Alaska	9.75
23	Arizona	8.05
26	Arkansas	8.00
1	California	10.00
17	Colorado	8.31
4	Connecticut	9.60
18	Delaware	8.25
23	Florida	8.05
44	Georgia	5.15
14	Hawaii	8.50
30	Idaho	7.25
18	Illinois	8.25
30	Indiana	7.25
30	Iowa	7.25
30	Kansas	7.25
30	Kentucky	7.25
NA	Louisiana**	NA
28	Maine	7.50
18	Maryland	8.25
1	Massachusetts	10.00
14	Michigan	8.50
9	Minnesota	9.00
NA	Mississippi**	NA
27	Missouri	7.65
23	Montana	8.05
9	Nebraska	9.00
18	Nevada	8.25
30	New Hampshire	7.25
16	New Jersey	8.38
28	New Mexico	7.50
9	New York	9.00
30	North Carolina	7.25
30	North Dakota	7.25
22	Ohio	8.10
30	Oklahoma	7.25
8	Oregon	9.25
30	Pennsylvania	7.25
4	Rhode Island	9.60
NA	South Carolina**	NA
13	South Dakota	8.55
NA	Tennessee**	NA
30	Texas	7.25
30	Utah	7.25
4	Vermont	9.60
30	Virginia	7.25
7	Washington	9.47
12	West Virginia	8.75
30	Wisconsin	7.25
44	Wyoming	5.15

RANK ORDER

RANK	STATE	MINIMUM WAGE
1	California	$10.00
1	Massachusetts	10.00
3	Alaska	9.75
4	Connecticut	9.60
4	Rhode Island	9.60
4	Vermont	9.60
7	Washington	9.47
8	Oregon	9.25
9	Minnesota	9.00
9	Nebraska	9.00
9	New York	9.00
12	West Virginia	8.75
13	South Dakota	8.55
14	Hawaii	8.50
14	Michigan	8.50
16	New Jersey	8.38
17	Colorado	8.31
18	Delaware	8.25
18	Illinois	8.25
18	Maryland	8.25
18	Nevada	8.25
22	Ohio	8.10
23	Arizona	8.05
23	Florida	8.05
23	Montana	8.05
26	Arkansas	8.00
27	Missouri	7.65
28	Maine	7.50
28	New Mexico	7.50
30	Idaho	7.25
30	Indiana	7.25
30	Iowa	7.25
30	Kansas	7.25
30	Kentucky	7.25
30	New Hampshire	7.25
30	North Carolina	7.25
30	North Dakota	7.25
30	Oklahoma	7.25
30	Pennsylvania	7.25
30	Texas	7.25
30	Utah	7.25
30	Virginia	7.25
30	Wisconsin	7.25
44	Georgia	5.15
44	Wyoming	5.15
NA	Alabama**	NA
NA	Louisiana**	NA
NA	Mississippi**	NA
NA	South Carolina**	NA
NA	Tennessee**	NA
	District of Columbia	10.50

Source: U.S. Department of Labor, Employment Standards Administration
"Minimum Wage Laws in the States" (http://www.dol.gov/whd/minwage/america.htm)
*As of January 1, 2016. State minimum wage rates are for those employers and jobs not covered by the federal program.
**No separate state program.

Average Hourly Earnings of Production Workers on Manufacturing Payrolls in 2015
National Average = $25.49*

ALPHA ORDER

RANK	STATE	HOURLY EARNINGS
34	Alabama	$18.80
1	Alaska	29.78
43	Arizona	17.64
50	Arkansas	16.39
9	California	21.61
3	Colorado	27.13
2	Connecticut	27.16
41	Delaware	17.74
14	Florida	20.31
40	Georgia	18.33
13	Hawaii	20.72
10	Idaho	21.36
16	Illinois	20.26
35	Indiana	18.71
36	Iowa	18.51
26	Kansas	19.35
12	Kentucky	20.73
7	Louisiana	22.04
8	Maine	21.66
27	Maryland	19.26
5	Massachusetts	22.37
11	Michigan	21.03
19	Minnesota	20.07
30	Mississippi	19.07
22	Missouri	19.93
42	Montana	17.67
44	Nebraska	17.59
38	Nevada	18.36
20	New Hampshire	19.96
18	New Jersey	20.10
49	New Mexico	16.73
27	New York	19.26
46	North Carolina	17.47
14	North Dakota	20.31
17	Ohio	20.15
37	Oklahoma	18.43
20	Oregon	19.96
31	Pennsylvania	18.99
46	Rhode Island	17.47
32	South Carolina	18.94
39	South Dakota	18.34
48	Tennessee	17.37
6	Texas	22.18
29	Utah	19.24
25	Vermont	19.46
24	Virginia	19.48
4	Washington	26.64
33	West Virginia	18.83
45	Wisconsin	17.53
23	Wyoming	19.52

RANK ORDER

RANK	STATE	HOURLY EARNINGS
1	Alaska	$29.78
2	Connecticut	27.16
3	Colorado	27.13
4	Washington	26.64
5	Massachusetts	22.37
6	Texas	22.18
7	Louisiana	22.04
8	Maine	21.66
9	California	21.61
10	Idaho	21.36
11	Michigan	21.03
12	Kentucky	20.73
13	Hawaii	20.72
14	Florida	20.31
14	North Dakota	20.31
16	Illinois	20.26
17	Ohio	20.15
18	New Jersey	20.10
19	Minnesota	20.07
20	New Hampshire	19.96
20	Oregon	19.96
22	Missouri	19.93
23	Wyoming	19.52
24	Virginia	19.48
25	Vermont	19.46
26	Kansas	19.35
27	Maryland	19.26
27	New York	19.26
29	Utah	19.24
30	Mississippi	19.07
31	Pennsylvania	18.99
32	South Carolina	18.94
33	West Virginia	18.83
34	Alabama	18.80
35	Indiana	18.71
36	Iowa	18.51
37	Oklahoma	18.43
38	Nevada	18.36
39	South Dakota	18.34
40	Georgia	18.33
41	Delaware	17.74
42	Montana	17.67
43	Arizona	17.64
44	Nebraska	17.59
45	Wisconsin	17.53
46	North Carolina	17.47
46	Rhode Island	17.47
48	Tennessee	17.37
49	New Mexico	16.73
50	Arkansas	16.39
	District of Columbia**	NA

Source: U.S. Department of Labor, Bureau of Labor Statistics
"State and Metro Area Employment, Hours and Earnings" (http://www.bls.gov/sae/home.htm)
*Preliminary data for December 2015. Not seasonally adjusted except for national figure.
**Not available.

Average Weekly Earnings of Production Workers on Manufacturing Payrolls in 2015
National Average = $1,034.89*

ALPHA ORDER

RANK	STATE	WEEKLY EARNINGS
27	Alabama	$808.40
48	Alaska	667.07
44	Arizona	721.48
48	Arkansas	667.07
10	California	916.26
3	Colorado	1,101.48
1	Connecticut	1,148.87
45	Delaware	718.47
16	Florida	855.05
29	Georgia	802.85
13	Hawaii	868.17
12	Idaho	875.76
11	Illinois	877.26
25	Indiana	810.14
30	Iowa	794.08
18	Kansas	839.79
4	Kentucky	970.16
5	Louisiana	963.15
8	Maine	927.05
34	Maryland	780.03
9	Massachusetts	926.12
7	Michigan	944.25
21	Minnesota	824.88
24	Mississippi	812.38
15	Missouri	856.99
50	Montana	659.09
43	Nebraska	731.74
31	Nevada	789.48
19	New Hampshire	838.32
22	New Jersey	824.10
47	New Mexico	669.20
35	New York	778.10
40	North Carolina	744.22
20	North Dakota	832.71
14	Ohio	860.41
36	Oklahoma	766.69
23	Oregon	814.37
32	Pennsylvania	788.09
46	Rhode Island	690.07
28	South Carolina	803.06
38	South Dakota	755.61
39	Tennessee	748.65
6	Texas	955.96
42	Utah	733.04
37	Vermont	762.83
17	Virginia	847.38
2	Washington	1,110.89
41	West Virginia	743.79
33	Wisconsin	780.09
26	Wyoming	810.08

RANK ORDER

RANK	STATE	WEEKLY EARNINGS
1	Connecticut	$1,148.87
2	Washington	1,110.89
3	Colorado	1,101.48
4	Kentucky	970.16
5	Louisiana	963.15
6	Texas	955.96
7	Michigan	944.25
8	Maine	927.05
9	Massachusetts	926.12
10	California	916.26
11	Illinois	877.26
12	Idaho	875.76
13	Hawaii	868.17
14	Ohio	860.41
15	Missouri	856.99
16	Florida	855.05
17	Virginia	847.38
18	Kansas	839.79
19	New Hampshire	838.32
20	North Dakota	832.71
21	Minnesota	824.88
22	New Jersey	824.10
23	Oregon	814.37
24	Mississippi	812.38
25	Indiana	810.14
26	Wyoming	810.08
27	Alabama	808.40
28	South Carolina	803.06
29	Georgia	802.85
30	Iowa	794.08
31	Nevada	789.48
32	Pennsylvania	788.09
33	Wisconsin	780.09
34	Maryland	780.03
35	New York	778.10
36	Oklahoma	766.69
37	Vermont	762.83
38	South Dakota	755.61
39	Tennessee	748.65
40	North Carolina	744.22
41	West Virginia	743.79
42	Utah	733.04
43	Nebraska	731.74
44	Arizona	721.48
45	Delaware	718.47
46	Rhode Island	690.07
47	New Mexico	669.20
48	Alaska	667.07
48	Arkansas	667.07
50	Montana	659.09
	District of Columbia**	NA

Source: U.S. Department of Labor, Bureau of Labor Statistics
"State and Metro Area Employment, Hours and Earnings" (http://www.bls.gov/sae/home.htm)
*Preliminary data for December 2015. Not seasonally adjusted except for national figure.
**Not available.

Average Work Week of Production Workers on Manufacturing Payrolls in 2015
National Average = 40.6 Hours per Week*

ALPHA ORDER

RANK	STATE	WEEKLY HOURS
12	Alabama	43.0
50	Alaska	22.4
37	Arizona	40.9
39	Arkansas	40.7
20	California	42.4
40	Colorado	40.6
22	Connecticut	42.3
41	Delaware	40.5
23	Florida	42.1
4	Georgia	43.8
25	Hawaii	41.9
34	Idaho	41.0
8	Illinois	43.3
8	Indiana	43.3
15	Iowa	42.9
7	Kansas	43.4
1	Kentucky	46.8
5	Louisiana	43.7
16	Maine	42.8
41	Maryland	40.5
31	Massachusetts	41.4
2	Michigan	44.9
33	Minnesota	41.1
18	Mississippi	42.6
12	Missouri	43.0
49	Montana	37.3
27	Nebraska	41.6
12	Nevada	43.0
24	New Hampshire	42.0
34	New Jersey	41.0
44	New Mexico	40.0
43	New York	40.4
18	North Carolina	42.6
34	North Dakota	41.0
17	Ohio	42.7
27	Oklahoma	41.6
38	Oregon	40.8
29	Pennsylvania	41.5
45	Rhode Island	39.5
20	South Carolina	42.4
32	South Dakota	41.2
10	Tennessee	43.1
10	Texas	43.1
48	Utah	38.1
47	Vermont	39.2
6	Virginia	43.5
26	Washington	41.7
45	West Virginia	39.5
3	Wisconsin	44.5
29	Wyoming	41.5

RANK ORDER

RANK	STATE	WEEKLY HOURS
1	Kentucky	46.8
2	Michigan	44.9
3	Wisconsin	44.5
4	Georgia	43.8
5	Louisiana	43.7
6	Virginia	43.5
7	Kansas	43.4
8	Illinois	43.3
8	Indiana	43.3
10	Tennessee	43.1
10	Texas	43.1
12	Alabama	43.0
12	Missouri	43.0
12	Nevada	43.0
15	Iowa	42.9
16	Maine	42.8
17	Ohio	42.7
18	Mississippi	42.6
18	North Carolina	42.6
20	California	42.4
20	South Carolina	42.4
22	Connecticut	42.3
23	Florida	42.1
24	New Hampshire	42.0
25	Hawaii	41.9
26	Washington	41.7
27	Nebraska	41.6
27	Oklahoma	41.6
29	Pennsylvania	41.5
29	Wyoming	41.5
31	Massachusetts	41.4
32	South Dakota	41.2
33	Minnesota	41.1
34	Idaho	41.0
34	New Jersey	41.0
34	North Dakota	41.0
37	Arizona	40.9
38	Oregon	40.8
39	Arkansas	40.7
40	Colorado	40.6
41	Delaware	40.5
41	Maryland	40.5
43	New York	40.4
44	New Mexico	40.0
45	Rhode Island	39.5
45	West Virginia	39.5
47	Vermont	39.2
48	Utah	38.1
49	Montana	37.3
50	Alaska	22.4
	District of Columbia**	NA

Source: U.S. Department of Labor, Bureau of Labor Statistics
"State and Metro Area Employment, Hours and Earnings" (http://www.bls.gov/sae/home.htm)
*Preliminary data for December 2015. Not seasonally adjusted except for national figure.
**Not available.

Average Weekly Unemployment Benefit in 2015

National Average = $328.73 a Week

ALPHA ORDER

RANK	STATE	BENEFIT
48	Alabama	$216.02
39	Alaska	266.62
47	Arizona	222.79
29	Arkansas	303.29
26	California	306.56
8	Colorado	385.99
15	Connecticut	355.57
41	Delaware	253.25
44	Florida	237.28
38	Georgia	275.97
3	Hawaii	441.42
35	Idaho	297.47
18	Illinois	338.14
40	Indiana	258.44
12	Iowa	369.52
14	Kansas	364.30
27	Kentucky	306.51
49	Louisiana	214.91
30	Maine	301.98
20	Maryland	328.90
2	Massachusetts	454.50
37	Michigan	284.70
5	Minnesota	410.88
50	Mississippi	203.19
43	Missouri	247.11
25	Montana	313.78
32	Nebraska	299.81
23	Nevada	320.66
28	New Hampshire	306.13
6	New Jersey	410.60
22	New Mexico	321.65
24	New York	317.01
45	North Carolina	236.57
1	North Dakota	504.11
17	Ohio	341.53
13	Oklahoma	366.90
16	Oregon	349.42
10	Pennsylvania	376.70
19	Rhode Island	333.10
42	South Carolina	252.69
34	South Dakota	299.10
46	Tennessee	226.04
9	Texas	384.09
11	Utah	370.80
21	Vermont	326.39
33	Virginia	299.75
4	Washington	418.67
31	West Virginia	301.23
36	Wisconsin	295.09
7	Wyoming	402.53

RANK ORDER

RANK	STATE	BENEFIT
1	North Dakota	$504.11
2	Massachusetts	454.50
3	Hawaii	441.42
4	Washington	418.67
5	Minnesota	410.88
6	New Jersey	410.60
7	Wyoming	402.53
8	Colorado	385.99
9	Texas	384.09
10	Pennsylvania	376.70
11	Utah	370.80
12	Iowa	369.52
13	Oklahoma	366.90
14	Kansas	364.30
15	Connecticut	355.57
16	Oregon	349.42
17	Ohio	341.53
18	Illinois	338.14
19	Rhode Island	333.10
20	Maryland	328.90
21	Vermont	326.39
22	New Mexico	321.65
23	Nevada	320.66
24	New York	317.01
25	Montana	313.78
26	California	306.56
27	Kentucky	306.51
28	New Hampshire	306.13
29	Arkansas	303.29
30	Maine	301.98
31	West Virginia	301.23
32	Nebraska	299.81
33	Virginia	299.75
34	South Dakota	299.10
35	Idaho	297.47
36	Wisconsin	295.09
37	Michigan	284.70
38	Georgia	275.97
39	Alaska	266.62
40	Indiana	258.44
41	Delaware	253.25
42	South Carolina	252.69
43	Missouri	247.11
44	Florida	237.28
45	North Carolina	236.57
46	Tennessee	226.04
47	Arizona	222.79
48	Alabama	216.02
49	Louisiana	214.91
50	Mississippi	203.19
	District of Columbia	297.82

Source: CQ Press using data from U.S. Department of Labor, Bureau of Labor Statistics
"Unemployment Insurance Data Summary" (http://workforcesecurity.doleta.gov/unemploy/finance.asp)

Workers' Compensation Benefit Payments in 2013

National Total = $63,574,440,000*

ALPHA ORDER

RANK	STATE	PAYMENTS	% of USA
30	Alabama	$639,311,000	1.0%
39	Alaska	253,081,000	0.4%
25	Arizona	752,123,000	1.2%
45	Arkansas	202,235,000	0.3%
1	California	12,100,181,000	19.0%
23	Colorado	858,947,000	1.4%
17	Connecticut	950,065,000	1.5%
43	Delaware	240,313,000	0.4%
3	Florida	3,131,293,000	4.9%
11	Georgia	1,566,186,000	2.5%
38	Hawaii	260,352,000	0.4%
40	Idaho	251,846,000	0.4%
5	Illinois	2,923,024,000	4.6%
27	Indiana	674,206,000	1.1%
29	Iowa	668,646,000	1.1%
32	Kansas	387,384,000	0.6%
26	Kentucky	697,974,000	1.1%
22	Louisiana	870,086,000	1.4%
41	Maine	247,766,000	0.4%
18	Maryland	944,612,000	1.5%
15	Massachusetts	1,061,981,000	1.7%
12	Michigan	1,134,005,000	1.8%
14	Minnesota	1,064,684,000	1.7%
34	Mississippi	332,790,000	0.5%
21	Missouri	873,946,000	1.4%
42	Montana	247,003,000	0.4%
35	Nebraska	305,001,000	0.5%
33	Nevada	358,740,000	0.6%
44	New Hampshire	214,560,000	0.3%
7	New Jersey	2,239,166,000	3.5%
37	New Mexico	267,330,000	0.4%
2	New York	5,543,750,000	8.7%
10	North Carolina	1,568,586,000	2.5%
46	North Dakota	193,975,000	0.3%
8	Ohio	2,070,022,000	3.3%
20	Oklahoma	878,022,000	1.4%
28	Oregon	668,686,000	1.1%
4	Pennsylvania	2,966,353,000	4.7%
48	Rhode Island	162,356,000	0.3%
19	South Carolina	878,428,000	1.4%
50	South Dakota	94,015,000	0.1%
24	Tennessee	808,055,000	1.3%
9	Texas	1,767,908,000	2.8%
36	Utah	282,462,000	0.4%
49	Vermont	141,511,000	0.2%
16	Virginia	953,165,000	1.5%
6	Washington	2,331,783,000	3.7%
31	West Virginia	436,017,000	0.7%
13	Wisconsin	1,126,058,000	1.8%
47	Wyoming	191,807,000	0.3%

RANK ORDER

RANK	STATE	PAYMENTS	% of USA
1	California	$12,100,181,000	19.0%
2	New York	5,543,750,000	8.7%
3	Florida	3,131,293,000	4.9%
4	Pennsylvania	2,966,353,000	4.7%
5	Illinois	2,923,024,000	4.6%
6	Washington	2,331,783,000	3.7%
7	New Jersey	2,239,166,000	3.5%
8	Ohio	2,070,022,000	3.3%
9	Texas	1,767,908,000	2.8%
10	North Carolina	1,568,586,000	2.5%
11	Georgia	1,566,186,000	2.5%
12	Michigan	1,134,005,000	1.8%
13	Wisconsin	1,126,058,000	1.8%
14	Minnesota	1,064,684,000	1.7%
15	Massachusetts	1,061,981,000	1.7%
16	Virginia	953,165,000	1.5%
17	Connecticut	950,065,000	1.5%
18	Maryland	944,612,000	1.5%
19	South Carolina	878,428,000	1.4%
20	Oklahoma	878,022,000	1.4%
21	Missouri	873,946,000	1.4%
22	Louisiana	870,086,000	1.4%
23	Colorado	858,947,000	1.4%
24	Tennessee	808,055,000	1.3%
25	Arizona	752,123,000	1.2%
26	Kentucky	697,974,000	1.1%
27	Indiana	674,206,000	1.1%
28	Oregon	668,686,000	1.1%
29	Iowa	668,646,000	1.1%
30	Alabama	639,311,000	1.0%
31	West Virginia	436,017,000	0.7%
32	Kansas	387,384,000	0.6%
33	Nevada	358,740,000	0.6%
34	Mississippi	332,790,000	0.5%
35	Nebraska	305,001,000	0.5%
36	Utah	282,462,000	0.4%
37	New Mexico	267,330,000	0.4%
38	Hawaii	260,352,000	0.4%
39	Alaska	253,081,000	0.4%
40	Idaho	251,846,000	0.4%
41	Maine	247,766,000	0.4%
42	Montana	247,003,000	0.4%
43	Delaware	240,313,000	0.4%
44	New Hampshire	214,560,000	0.3%
45	Arkansas	202,235,000	0.3%
46	North Dakota	193,975,000	0.3%
47	Wyoming	191,807,000	0.3%
48	Rhode Island	162,356,000	0.3%
49	Vermont	141,511,000	0.2%
50	South Dakota	94,015,000	0.1%
	District of Columbia	101,630,000	0.2%

Source: National Academy of Social Insurance (Washington, DC)
"Workers' Compensation: Benefits, Coverage, and Costs, 2013" (http://www.nasi.org)
*Estimated payments from private insurance, state and federal funds, and self insurance. National total includes payments for federal civilian employee program, Black Lung Program, and other federal programs.

Workers' Compensation Benefit Payment per Covered Worker in 2013

National Average = $491*

ALPHA ORDER

RANK	STATE	AVERAGE
32	Alabama	$373
2	Alaska	809
42	Arizona	309
50	Arkansas	189
3	California	799
31	Colorado	378
11	Connecticut	585
9	Delaware	590
19	Florida	452
23	Georgia	430
20	Hawaii	447
26	Idaho	408
13	Illinois	523
47	Indiana	241
18	Iowa	457
44	Kansas	297
29	Kentucky	402
17	Louisiana	468
22	Maine	435
30	Maryland	396
38	Massachusetts	327
43	Michigan	300
28	Minnesota	403
38	Mississippi	327
35	Missouri	354
10	Montana	587
37	Nebraska	337
41	Nevada	315
36	New Hampshire	351
8	New Jersey	594
33	New Mexico	372
6	New York	648
24	North Carolina	422
16	North Dakota	469
25	Ohio	411
7	Oklahoma	613
27	Oregon	405
12	Pennsylvania	541
34	Rhode Island	365
14	South Carolina	507
46	South Dakota	242
40	Tennessee	317
49	Texas	205
48	Utah	232
15	Vermont	485
45	Virginia	287
1	Washington	827
5	West Virginia	669
21	Wisconsin	438
4	Wyoming	705

RANK ORDER

RANK	STATE	AVERAGE
1	Washington	$827
2	Alaska	809
3	California	799
4	Wyoming	705
5	West Virginia	669
6	New York	648
7	Oklahoma	613
8	New Jersey	594
9	Delaware	590
10	Montana	587
11	Connecticut	585
12	Pennsylvania	541
13	Illinois	523
14	South Carolina	507
15	Vermont	485
16	North Dakota	469
17	Louisiana	468
18	Iowa	457
19	Florida	452
20	Hawaii	447
21	Wisconsin	438
22	Maine	435
23	Georgia	430
24	North Carolina	422
25	Ohio	411
26	Idaho	408
27	Oregon	405
28	Minnesota	403
29	Kentucky	402
30	Maryland	396
31	Colorado	378
32	Alabama	373
33	New Mexico	372
34	Rhode Island	365
35	Missouri	354
36	New Hampshire	351
37	Nebraska	337
38	Massachusetts	327
38	Mississippi	327
40	Tennessee	317
41	Nevada	315
42	Arizona	309
43	Michigan	300
44	Kansas	297
45	Virginia	287
46	South Dakota	242
47	Indiana	241
48	Utah	232
49	Texas	205
50	Arkansas	189
	District of Columbia	196

Source: CQ Press using data from National Academy of Social Insurance (Washington, DC)
"Workers' Compensation: Benefits, Coverage, and Costs, 2013" (http://www.nasi.org)
*Estimated payments from private insurance, state and federal funds, and self insurance. National rate includes payments for federal civilian employee program, Black Lung Program, and other federal programs. Total divided by number of workers covered by workers' compensation.

Percent Change in Workers' Compensation Benefit Payments: 2012 to 2013

National Percent Change = 0.9% Increase*

ALPHA ORDER

RANK	STATE	PERCENT CHANGE
34	Alabama	(1.6)
14	Alaska	2.0
29	Arizona	(0.4)
36	Arkansas	(2.4)
7	California	5.1
36	Colorado	(2.4)
9	Connecticut	3.3
3	Delaware	11.0
18	Florida	1.5
30	Georgia	(0.6)
8	Hawaii	4.8
6	Idaho	6.2
32	Illinois	(1.0)
10	Indiana	3.2
20	Iowa	1.4
49	Kansas	(9.5)
17	Kentucky	1.8
15	Louisiana	1.9
23	Maine	0.7
38	Maryland	(2.7)
4	Massachusetts	8.2
44	Michigan	(4.7)
13	Minnesota	2.1
32	Mississippi	(1.0)
24	Missouri	0.5
31	Montana	(0.7)
18	Nebraska	1.5
35	Nevada	(2.3)
45	New Hampshire	(4.8)
27	New Jersey	(0.3)
50	New Mexico	(12.7)
10	New York	3.2
26	North Carolina	0.0
1	North Dakota	28.4
43	Ohio	(4.6)
45	Oklahoma	(4.8)
22	Oregon	0.8
15	Pennsylvania	1.9
47	Rhode Island	(5.2)
40	South Carolina	(3.0)
5	South Dakota	8.0
41	Tennessee	(3.6)
42	Texas	(3.8)
27	Utah	(0.3)
12	Vermont	2.2
38	Virginia	(2.7)
21	Washington	0.9
48	West Virginia	(8.4)
25	Wisconsin	0.2
2	Wyoming	18.2

RANK ORDER

RANK	STATE	PERCENT CHANGE
1	North Dakota	28.4
2	Wyoming	18.2
3	Delaware	11.0
4	Massachusetts	8.2
5	South Dakota	8.0
6	Idaho	6.2
7	California	5.1
8	Hawaii	4.8
9	Connecticut	3.3
10	Indiana	3.2
10	New York	3.2
12	Vermont	2.2
13	Minnesota	2.1
14	Alaska	2.0
15	Louisiana	1.9
15	Pennsylvania	1.9
17	Kentucky	1.8
18	Florida	1.5
18	Nebraska	1.5
20	Iowa	1.4
21	Washington	0.9
22	Oregon	0.8
23	Maine	0.7
24	Missouri	0.5
25	Wisconsin	0.2
26	North Carolina	0.0
27	New Jersey	(0.3)
27	Utah	(0.3)
29	Arizona	(0.4)
30	Georgia	(0.6)
31	Montana	(0.7)
32	Illinois	(1.0)
32	Mississippi	(1.0)
34	Alabama	(1.6)
35	Nevada	(2.3)
36	Arkansas	(2.4)
36	Colorado	(2.4)
38	Maryland	(2.7)
38	Virginia	(2.7)
40	South Carolina	(3.0)
41	Tennessee	(3.6)
42	Texas	(3.8)
43	Ohio	(4.6)
44	Michigan	(4.7)
45	New Hampshire	(4.8)
45	Oklahoma	(4.8)
47	Rhode Island	(5.2)
48	West Virginia	(8.4)
49	Kansas	(9.5)
50	New Mexico	(12.7)
	District of Columbia	12.3

Source: CQ Press using data from National Academy of Social Insurance (Washington, DC)
"Workers' Compensation: Benefits, Coverage, and Costs, 2013" (http://www.nasi.org)
*Estimated payments from private insurance, state and federal funds, and self insurance. National rate includes payments for federal civilian employee program, Black Lung Program, and other federal programs.

Civilian Labor Force in 2015

National Total = 157,833,000 Workers*

ALPHA ORDER

RANK	STATE	LABOR FORCE	% of USA
24	Alabama	2,154,800	1.4%
48	Alaska	362,700	0.2%
17	Arizona	3,167,100	2.0%
34	Arkansas	1,337,600	0.8%
1	California	18,996,500	12.0%
22	Colorado	2,819,100	1.8%
28	Connecticut	1,893,600	1.2%
45	Delaware	470,700	0.3%
4	Florida	9,666,900	6.1%
10	Georgia	4,764,700	3.0%
41	Hawaii	682,800	0.4%
38	Idaho	806,000	0.5%
5	Illinois	6,556,400	4.2%
15	Indiana	3,291,300	2.1%
30	Iowa	1,708,700	1.1%
31	Kansas	1,510,300	1.0%
27	Kentucky	1,950,400	1.2%
25	Louisiana	2,133,600	1.4%
42	Maine	676,600	0.4%
16	Maryland	3,174,200	2.0%
13	Massachusetts	3,559,000	2.3%
9	Michigan	4,787,200	3.0%
21	Minnesota	3,030,500	1.9%
35	Mississippi	1,296,000	0.8%
18	Missouri	3,127,800	2.0%
44	Montana	523,800	0.3%
36	Nebraska	1,015,100	0.6%
33	Nevada	1,430,600	0.9%
40	New Hampshire	737,200	0.5%
11	New Jersey	4,568,000	2.9%
37	New Mexico	912,200	0.6%
3	New York	9,740,900	6.2%
8	North Carolina	4,792,100	3.0%
47	North Dakota	412,900	0.3%
7	Ohio	5,726,600	3.6%
29	Oklahoma	1,855,900	1.2%
26	Oregon	1,982,500	1.3%
6	Pennsylvania	6,446,000	4.1%
43	Rhode Island	554,900	0.4%
23	South Carolina	2,271,700	1.4%
46	South Dakota	456,200	0.3%
20	Tennessee	3,082,800	2.0%
2	Texas	13,097,100	8.3%
32	Utah	1,465,400	0.9%
49	Vermont	343,000	0.2%
12	Virginia	4,231,700	2.7%
14	Washington	3,541,300	2.2%
39	West Virginia	788,200	0.5%
19	Wisconsin	3,107,100	2.0%
50	Wyoming	304,500	0.2%

RANK ORDER

RANK	STATE	LABOR FORCE	% of USA
1	California	18,996,500	12.0%
2	Texas	13,097,100	8.3%
3	New York	9,740,900	6.2%
4	Florida	9,666,900	6.1%
5	Illinois	6,556,400	4.2%
6	Pennsylvania	6,446,000	4.1%
7	Ohio	5,726,600	3.6%
8	North Carolina	4,792,100	3.0%
9	Michigan	4,787,200	3.0%
10	Georgia	4,764,700	3.0%
11	New Jersey	4,568,000	2.9%
12	Virginia	4,231,700	2.7%
13	Massachusetts	3,559,000	2.3%
14	Washington	3,541,300	2.2%
15	Indiana	3,291,300	2.1%
16	Maryland	3,174,200	2.0%
17	Arizona	3,167,100	2.0%
18	Missouri	3,127,800	2.0%
19	Wisconsin	3,107,100	2.0%
20	Tennessee	3,082,800	2.0%
21	Minnesota	3,030,500	1.9%
22	Colorado	2,819,100	1.8%
23	South Carolina	2,271,700	1.4%
24	Alabama	2,154,800	1.4%
25	Louisiana	2,133,600	1.4%
26	Oregon	1,982,500	1.3%
27	Kentucky	1,950,400	1.2%
28	Connecticut	1,893,600	1.2%
29	Oklahoma	1,855,900	1.2%
30	Iowa	1,708,700	1.1%
31	Kansas	1,510,300	1.0%
32	Utah	1,465,400	0.9%
33	Nevada	1,430,600	0.9%
34	Arkansas	1,337,600	0.8%
35	Mississippi	1,296,000	0.8%
36	Nebraska	1,015,100	0.6%
37	New Mexico	912,200	0.6%
38	Idaho	806,000	0.5%
39	West Virginia	788,200	0.5%
40	New Hampshire	737,200	0.5%
41	Hawaii	682,800	0.4%
42	Maine	676,600	0.4%
43	Rhode Island	554,900	0.4%
44	Montana	523,800	0.3%
45	Delaware	470,700	0.3%
46	South Dakota	456,200	0.3%
47	North Dakota	412,900	0.3%
48	Alaska	362,700	0.2%
49	Vermont	343,000	0.2%
50	Wyoming	304,500	0.2%
	District of Columbia	389,400	0.2%

Source: U.S. Department of Labor, Bureau of Labor Statistics
"Regional and State Employment and Unemployment" (press release, January 26, 2016, www.bls.gov/bls/newsrels.htm)
*Seasonally adjusted preliminary data as of December 2015. National total calculated through a different formula.

Employed Civilian Labor Force in 2015

National Total = 149,929,000 Employed Workers*

ALPHA ORDER

RANK	STATE	EMPLOYED	% of USA
24	Alabama	2,021,900	1.3%
48	Alaska	339,000	0.2%
18	Arizona	2,983,000	2.0%
34	Arkansas	1,273,100	0.8%
1	California	17,900,400	11.9%
22	Colorado	2,719,800	1.8%
28	Connecticut	1,794,600	1.2%
45	Delaware	447,400	0.3%
4	Florida	9,180,200	6.1%
10	Georgia	4,502,600	3.0%
41	Hawaii	660,600	0.4%
38	Idaho	774,500	0.5%
5	Illinois	6,166,400	4.1%
15	Indiana	3,145,300	2.1%
30	Iowa	1,650,400	1.1%
31	Kansas	1,451,200	1.0%
27	Kentucky	1,846,100	1.2%
25	Louisiana	2,003,800	1.3%
42	Maine	649,800	0.4%
16	Maryland	3,012,100	2.0%
13	Massachusetts	3,390,500	2.3%
8	Michigan	4,541,200	3.0%
20	Minnesota	2,923,000	1.9%
35	Mississippi	1,213,300	0.8%
17	Missouri	2,989,000	2.0%
44	Montana	502,700	0.3%
36	Nebraska	985,400	0.7%
33	Nevada	1,338,800	0.9%
40	New Hampshire	714,100	0.5%
11	New Jersey	4,332,900	2.9%
37	New Mexico	851,100	0.6%
3	New York	9,270,300	6.2%
9	North Carolina	4,522,300	3.0%
47	North Dakota	401,600	0.3%
7	Ohio	5,457,600	3.6%
29	Oklahoma	1,779,100	1.2%
26	Oregon	1,874,700	1.3%
6	Pennsylvania	6,139,500	4.1%
43	Rhode Island	526,500	0.4%
23	South Carolina	2,147,700	1.4%
46	South Dakota	442,800	0.3%
21	Tennessee	2,909,700	1.9%
2	Texas	12,486,800	8.3%
32	Utah	1,414,700	0.9%
49	Vermont	330,800	0.2%
12	Virginia	4,055,300	2.7%
14	Washington	3,348,100	2.2%
39	West Virginia	738,900	0.5%
19	Wisconsin	2,972,100	2.0%
50	Wyoming	291,400	0.2%

RANK ORDER

RANK	STATE	EMPLOYED	% of USA
1	California	17,900,400	11.9%
2	Texas	12,486,800	8.3%
3	New York	9,270,300	6.2%
4	Florida	9,180,200	6.1%
5	Illinois	6,166,400	4.1%
6	Pennsylvania	6,139,500	4.1%
7	Ohio	5,457,600	3.6%
8	Michigan	4,541,200	3.0%
9	North Carolina	4,522,300	3.0%
10	Georgia	4,502,600	3.0%
11	New Jersey	4,332,900	2.9%
12	Virginia	4,055,300	2.7%
13	Massachusetts	3,390,500	2.3%
14	Washington	3,348,100	2.2%
15	Indiana	3,145,300	2.1%
16	Maryland	3,012,100	2.0%
17	Missouri	2,989,000	2.0%
18	Arizona	2,983,000	2.0%
19	Wisconsin	2,972,100	2.0%
20	Minnesota	2,923,000	1.9%
21	Tennessee	2,909,700	1.9%
22	Colorado	2,719,800	1.8%
23	South Carolina	2,147,700	1.4%
24	Alabama	2,021,900	1.3%
25	Louisiana	2,003,800	1.3%
26	Oregon	1,874,700	1.3%
27	Kentucky	1,846,100	1.2%
28	Connecticut	1,794,600	1.2%
29	Oklahoma	1,779,100	1.2%
30	Iowa	1,650,400	1.1%
31	Kansas	1,451,200	1.0%
32	Utah	1,414,700	0.9%
33	Nevada	1,338,800	0.9%
34	Arkansas	1,273,100	0.8%
35	Mississippi	1,213,300	0.8%
36	Nebraska	985,400	0.7%
37	New Mexico	851,100	0.6%
38	Idaho	774,500	0.5%
39	West Virginia	738,900	0.5%
40	New Hampshire	714,100	0.5%
41	Hawaii	660,600	0.4%
42	Maine	649,800	0.4%
43	Rhode Island	526,500	0.4%
44	Montana	502,700	0.3%
45	Delaware	447,400	0.3%
46	South Dakota	442,800	0.3%
47	North Dakota	401,600	0.3%
48	Alaska	339,000	0.2%
49	Vermont	330,800	0.2%
50	Wyoming	291,400	0.2%
	District of Columbia	363,800	0.2%

Source: CQ Press using data from U.S. Department of Labor, Bureau of Labor Statistics
"Regional and State Employment and Unemployment" (press release, January 26, 2016, www.bls.gov/bls/newsrels.htm)
*Seasonally adjusted preliminary data as of December 2015. National total calculated through a different formula.

Employment to Population Ratio in 2015

National Percent = 59.1% of Population 16 Years and Older Employed*

ALPHA ORDER

RANK	STATE	PERCENT
47	Alabama	52.3
26	Alaska	59.4
40	Arizona	56.4
45	Arkansas	54.4
34	California	58.3
10	Colorado	64.1
16	Connecticut	61.5
28	Delaware	59.3
41	Florida	56.3
38	Georgia	57.1
36	Hawaii	57.8
14	Idaho	61.9
24	Illinois	60.2
22	Indiana	60.5
4	Iowa	67.0
9	Kansas	64.2
46	Kentucky	52.5
44	Louisiana	54.8
30	Maine	58.9
13	Maryland	63.0
17	Massachusetts	61.4
38	Michigan	57.1
2	Minnesota	67.7
49	Mississippi	51.8
14	Missouri	61.9
18	Montana	61.0
3	Nebraska	67.3
25	Nevada	59.5
7	New Hampshire	65.3
22	New Jersey	60.5
48	New Mexico	51.9
35	New York	57.9
37	North Carolina	57.2
1	North Dakota	68.2
30	Ohio	58.9
32	Oklahoma	58.8
33	Oregon	58.4
29	Pennsylvania	59.0
20	Rhode Island	60.6
43	South Carolina	55.5
5	South Dakota	66.6
42	Tennessee	55.7
20	Texas	60.6
6	Utah	66.4
11	Vermont	63.6
19	Virginia	60.8
26	Washington	59.4
50	West Virginia	48.8
8	Wisconsin	64.5
12	Wyoming	63.2

RANK ORDER

RANK	STATE	PERCENT
1	North Dakota	68.2
2	Minnesota	67.7
3	Nebraska	67.3
4	Iowa	67.0
5	South Dakota	66.6
6	Utah	66.4
7	New Hampshire	65.3
8	Wisconsin	64.5
9	Kansas	64.2
10	Colorado	64.1
11	Vermont	63.6
12	Wyoming	63.2
13	Maryland	63.0
14	Idaho	61.9
14	Missouri	61.9
16	Connecticut	61.5
17	Massachusetts	61.4
18	Montana	61.0
19	Virginia	60.8
20	Rhode Island	60.6
20	Texas	60.6
22	Indiana	60.5
22	New Jersey	60.5
24	Illinois	60.2
25	Nevada	59.5
26	Alaska	59.4
26	Washington	59.4
28	Delaware	59.3
29	Pennsylvania	59.0
30	Maine	58.9
30	Ohio	58.9
32	Oklahoma	58.8
33	Oregon	58.4
34	California	58.3
35	New York	57.9
36	Hawaii	57.8
37	North Carolina	57.2
38	Georgia	57.1
38	Michigan	57.1
40	Arizona	56.4
41	Florida	56.3
42	Tennessee	55.7
43	South Carolina	55.5
44	Louisiana	54.8
45	Arkansas	54.4
46	Kentucky	52.5
47	Alabama	52.3
48	New Mexico	51.9
49	Mississippi	51.8
50	West Virginia	48.8

District of Columbia — 65.7

Source: CQ Press using data from U.S. Department of Labor, Bureau of Labor Statistics
"Regional and State Employment and Unemployment" (press release, January 26, 2016, www.bls.gov/bls/newsrels.htm)
*Seasonally adjusted preliminary data as of December 2015. Calculated with 2014 population data.

Unemployed Civilian Labor Force in 2015

National Total = 7,904,000 Unemployed Workers*

ALPHA ORDER

RANK	STATE	UNEMPLOYED	% of USA
21	Alabama	132,900	1.7%
42	Alaska	23,700	0.3%
13	Arizona	184,100	2.3%
32	Arkansas	64,500	0.8%
1	California	1,096,100	13.9%
27	Colorado	99,300	1.3%
28	Connecticut	99,000	1.3%
43	Delaware	23,300	0.3%
3	Florida	486,700	6.2%
9	Georgia	262,100	3.3%
45	Hawaii	22,200	0.3%
38	Idaho	31,500	0.4%
5	Illinois	390,000	4.9%
18	Indiana	146,000	1.8%
35	Iowa	58,300	0.7%
34	Kansas	59,100	0.7%
26	Kentucky	104,300	1.3%
22	Louisiana	129,800	1.6%
41	Maine	26,800	0.3%
17	Maryland	162,100	2.1%
16	Massachusetts	168,500	2.1%
10	Michigan	246,000	3.1%
25	Minnesota	107,500	1.4%
30	Mississippi	82,700	1.0%
19	Missouri	138,800	1.8%
46	Montana	21,100	0.3%
39	Nebraska	29,700	0.4%
29	Nevada	91,800	1.2%
44	New Hampshire	23,100	0.3%
11	New Jersey	235,100	3.0%
33	New Mexico	61,100	0.8%
4	New York	470,600	6.0%
7	North Carolina	269,800	3.4%
50	North Dakota	11,300	0.1%
8	Ohio	269,000	3.4%
31	Oklahoma	76,800	1.0%
24	Oregon	107,800	1.4%
6	Pennsylvania	306,500	3.9%
40	Rhode Island	28,400	0.4%
23	South Carolina	124,000	1.6%
47	South Dakota	13,400	0.2%
15	Tennessee	173,100	2.2%
2	Texas	610,300	7.7%
36	Utah	50,700	0.6%
49	Vermont	12,200	0.2%
14	Virginia	176,400	2.2%
12	Washington	193,200	2.4%
37	West Virginia	49,300	0.6%
20	Wisconsin	135,000	1.7%
48	Wyoming	13,100	0.2%

RANK ORDER

RANK	STATE	UNEMPLOYED	% of USA
1	California	1,096,100	13.9%
2	Texas	610,300	7.7%
3	Florida	486,700	6.2%
4	New York	470,600	6.0%
5	Illinois	390,000	4.9%
6	Pennsylvania	306,500	3.9%
7	North Carolina	269,800	3.4%
8	Ohio	269,000	3.4%
9	Georgia	262,100	3.3%
10	Michigan	246,000	3.1%
11	New Jersey	235,100	3.0%
12	Washington	193,200	2.4%
13	Arizona	184,100	2.3%
14	Virginia	176,400	2.2%
15	Tennessee	173,100	2.2%
16	Massachusetts	168,500	2.1%
17	Maryland	162,100	2.1%
18	Indiana	146,000	1.8%
19	Missouri	138,800	1.8%
20	Wisconsin	135,000	1.7%
21	Alabama	132,900	1.7%
22	Louisiana	129,800	1.6%
23	South Carolina	124,000	1.6%
24	Oregon	107,800	1.4%
25	Minnesota	107,500	1.4%
26	Kentucky	104,300	1.3%
27	Colorado	99,300	1.3%
28	Connecticut	99,000	1.3%
29	Nevada	91,800	1.2%
30	Mississippi	82,700	1.0%
31	Oklahoma	76,800	1.0%
32	Arkansas	64,500	0.8%
33	New Mexico	61,100	0.8%
34	Kansas	59,100	0.7%
35	Iowa	58,300	0.7%
36	Utah	50,700	0.6%
37	West Virginia	49,300	0.6%
38	Idaho	31,500	0.4%
39	Nebraska	29,700	0.4%
40	Rhode Island	28,400	0.4%
41	Maine	26,800	0.3%
42	Alaska	23,700	0.3%
43	Delaware	23,300	0.3%
44	New Hampshire	23,100	0.3%
45	Hawaii	22,200	0.3%
46	Montana	21,100	0.3%
47	South Dakota	13,400	0.2%
48	Wyoming	13,100	0.2%
49	Vermont	12,200	0.2%
50	North Dakota	11,300	0.1%
	District of Columbia	25,600	0.3%

Source: U.S. Department of Labor, Bureau of Labor Statistics
"Regional and State Employment and Unemployment" (press release, January 26, 2016, www.bls.gov/bls/newsrels.htm)
*Seasonally adjusted preliminary data as of December 2015. National total calculated through a different formula.

Unemployment Rate in 2015

National Rate = 5.0% of Labor Force Unemployed*

ALPHA ORDER

RANK	STATE	PERCENT
6	Alabama	6.2
2	Alaska	6.5
9	Arizona	5.8
25	Arkansas	4.8
9	California	5.8
42	Colorado	3.5
18	Connecticut	5.2
23	Delaware	5.0
23	Florida	5.0
13	Georgia	5.5
46	Hawaii	3.2
39	Idaho	3.9
8	Illinois	5.9
31	Indiana	4.4
45	Iowa	3.4
39	Kansas	3.9
17	Kentucky	5.3
7	Louisiana	6.1
37	Maine	4.0
19	Maryland	5.1
28	Massachusetts	4.7
19	Michigan	5.1
42	Minnesota	3.5
3	Mississippi	6.4
31	Missouri	4.4
37	Montana	4.0
48	Nebraska	2.9
3	Nevada	6.4
47	New Hampshire	3.1
19	New Jersey	5.1
1	New Mexico	6.7
25	New York	4.8
11	North Carolina	5.6
50	North Dakota	2.7
28	Ohio	4.7
36	Oklahoma	4.1
16	Oregon	5.4
25	Pennsylvania	4.8
19	Rhode Island	5.1
13	South Carolina	5.5
48	South Dakota	2.9
11	Tennessee	5.6
28	Texas	4.7
42	Utah	3.5
41	Vermont	3.6
35	Virginia	4.2
13	Washington	5.5
5	West Virginia	6.3
33	Wisconsin	4.3
33	Wyoming	4.3

RANK ORDER

RANK	STATE	PERCENT
1	New Mexico	6.7
2	Alaska	6.5
3	Mississippi	6.4
3	Nevada	6.4
5	West Virginia	6.3
6	Alabama	6.2
7	Louisiana	6.1
8	Illinois	5.9
9	Arizona	5.8
9	California	5.8
11	North Carolina	5.6
11	Tennessee	5.6
13	Georgia	5.5
13	South Carolina	5.5
13	Washington	5.5
16	Oregon	5.4
17	Kentucky	5.3
18	Connecticut	5.2
19	Maryland	5.1
19	Michigan	5.1
19	New Jersey	5.1
19	Rhode Island	5.1
23	Delaware	5.0
23	Florida	5.0
25	Arkansas	4.8
25	New York	4.8
25	Pennsylvania	4.8
28	Massachusetts	4.7
28	Ohio	4.7
28	Texas	4.7
31	Indiana	4.4
31	Missouri	4.4
33	Wisconsin	4.3
33	Wyoming	4.3
35	Virginia	4.2
36	Oklahoma	4.1
37	Maine	4.0
37	Montana	4.0
39	Idaho	3.9
39	Kansas	3.9
41	Vermont	3.6
42	Colorado	3.5
42	Minnesota	3.5
42	Utah	3.5
45	Iowa	3.4
46	Hawaii	3.2
47	New Hampshire	3.1
48	Nebraska	2.9
48	South Dakota	2.9
50	North Dakota	2.7

District of Columbia   6.6

Source: U.S. Department of Labor, Bureau of Labor Statistics
"Regional and State Employment and Unemployment" (press release, January 26, 2016, www.bls.gov/bls/newsrels.htm)
*Seasonally adjusted preliminary data as of December 2015. National figure calculated through a different formula.

Women in Civilian Labor Force in 2014

National Total = 73,039,000 Women*

ALPHA ORDER

RANK	STATE	WOMEN	% of USA
24	Alabama	1,031,000	1.4%
48	Alaska	169,000	0.2%
19	Arizona	1,432,000	2.0%
33	Arkansas	617,000	0.8%
1	California	8,565,000	11.7%
22	Colorado	1,300,000	1.8%
27	Connecticut	915,000	1.3%
45	Delaware	224,000	0.3%
3	Florida	4,582,000	6.3%
9	Georgia	2,225,000	3.0%
42	Hawaii	317,000	0.4%
40	Idaho	348,000	0.5%
5	Illinois	3,110,000	4.3%
15	Indiana	1,525,000	2.1%
29	Iowa	813,000	1.1%
31	Kansas	696,000	1.0%
26	Kentucky	959,000	1.3%
25	Louisiana	999,000	1.4%
41	Maine	336,000	0.5%
16	Maryland	1,502,000	2.1%
13	Massachusetts	1,723,000	2.4%
8	Michigan	2,281,000	3.1%
21	Minnesota	1,410,000	1.9%
35	Mississippi	590,000	0.8%
17	Missouri	1,467,000	2.0%
44	Montana	247,000	0.3%
36	Nebraska	481,000	0.7%
32	Nevada	628,000	0.9%
39	New Hampshire	355,000	0.5%
11	New Jersey	2,092,000	2.9%
37	New Mexico	426,000	0.6%
4	New York	4,524,000	6.2%
10	North Carolina	2,210,000	3.0%
47	North Dakota	188,000	0.3%
7	Ohio	2,751,000	3.8%
30	Oklahoma	806,000	1.1%
28	Oregon	914,000	1.3%
6	Pennsylvania	3,019,000	4.1%
43	Rhode Island	268,000	0.4%
23	South Carolina	1,066,000	1.5%
46	South Dakota	211,000	0.3%
20	Tennessee	1,412,000	1.9%
2	Texas	5,869,000	8.0%
34	Utah	602,000	0.8%
49	Vermont	168,000	0.2%
12	Virginia	2,028,000	2.8%
14	Washington	1,608,000	2.2%
38	West Virginia	372,000	0.5%
17	Wisconsin	1,467,000	2.0%
50	Wyoming	136,000	0.2%

RANK ORDER

RANK	STATE	WOMEN	% of USA
1	California	8,565,000	11.7%
2	Texas	5,869,000	8.0%
3	Florida	4,582,000	6.3%
4	New York	4,524,000	6.2%
5	Illinois	3,110,000	4.3%
6	Pennsylvania	3,019,000	4.1%
7	Ohio	2,751,000	3.8%
8	Michigan	2,281,000	3.1%
9	Georgia	2,225,000	3.0%
10	North Carolina	2,210,000	3.0%
11	New Jersey	2,092,000	2.9%
12	Virginia	2,028,000	2.8%
13	Massachusetts	1,723,000	2.4%
14	Washington	1,608,000	2.2%
15	Indiana	1,525,000	2.1%
16	Maryland	1,502,000	2.1%
17	Missouri	1,467,000	2.0%
17	Wisconsin	1,467,000	2.0%
19	Arizona	1,432,000	2.0%
20	Tennessee	1,412,000	1.9%
21	Minnesota	1,410,000	1.9%
22	Colorado	1,300,000	1.8%
23	South Carolina	1,066,000	1.5%
24	Alabama	1,031,000	1.4%
25	Louisiana	999,000	1.4%
26	Kentucky	959,000	1.3%
27	Connecticut	915,000	1.3%
28	Oregon	914,000	1.3%
29	Iowa	813,000	1.1%
30	Oklahoma	806,000	1.1%
31	Kansas	696,000	1.0%
32	Nevada	628,000	0.9%
33	Arkansas	617,000	0.8%
34	Utah	602,000	0.8%
35	Mississippi	590,000	0.8%
36	Nebraska	481,000	0.7%
37	New Mexico	426,000	0.6%
38	West Virginia	372,000	0.5%
39	New Hampshire	355,000	0.5%
40	Idaho	348,000	0.5%
41	Maine	336,000	0.5%
42	Hawaii	317,000	0.4%
43	Rhode Island	268,000	0.4%
44	Montana	247,000	0.3%
45	Delaware	224,000	0.3%
46	South Dakota	211,000	0.3%
47	North Dakota	188,000	0.3%
48	Alaska	169,000	0.2%
49	Vermont	168,000	0.2%
50	Wyoming	136,000	0.2%
	District of Columbia	191,000	0.3%

Source: U.S. Department of Labor, Bureau of Labor Statistics
"Geographic Profiles of Employment and Unemployment, 2014" (http://www.bls.gov/gps/)
*Annual averages.

Percent of Women in the Civilian Labor Force in 2014

National Percent = 57.0% of Women*

ALPHA ORDER

RANK	STATE	PERCENT
47	Alabama	51.8
7	Alaska	64.0
41	Arizona	53.9
46	Arkansas	52.0
35	California	55.5
11	Colorado	61.8
12	Connecticut	61.3
24	Delaware	57.5
37	Florida	55.1
36	Georgia	55.2
26	Hawaii	57.0
34	Idaho	55.9
19	Illinois	59.9
23	Indiana	58.1
2	Iowa	66.1
10	Kansas	61.9
40	Kentucky	54.0
43	Louisiana	53.6
21	Maine	59.8
13	Maryland	60.9
16	Massachusetts	60.6
32	Michigan	56.3
4	Minnesota	65.2
49	Mississippi	49.0
19	Missouri	59.9
14	Montana	60.8
3	Nebraska	65.9
31	Nevada	56.5
5	New Hampshire	64.5
26	New Jersey	57.0
48	New Mexico	51.7
38	New York	54.8
39	North Carolina	54.6
1	North Dakota	67.1
22	Ohio	58.3
44	Oklahoma	53.0
32	Oregon	56.3
26	Pennsylvania	57.0
18	Rhode Island	60.0
42	South Carolina	53.7
5	South Dakota	64.5
45	Tennessee	52.8
29	Texas	56.9
29	Utah	56.9
7	Vermont	64.0
17	Virginia	60.3
25	Washington	57.3
50	West Virginia	48.9
9	Wisconsin	63.5
14	Wyoming	60.8

RANK ORDER

RANK	STATE	PERCENT
1	North Dakota	67.1
2	Iowa	66.1
3	Nebraska	65.9
4	Minnesota	65.2
5	New Hampshire	64.5
5	South Dakota	64.5
7	Alaska	64.0
7	Vermont	64.0
9	Wisconsin	63.5
10	Kansas	61.9
11	Colorado	61.8
12	Connecticut	61.3
13	Maryland	60.9
14	Montana	60.8
14	Wyoming	60.8
16	Massachusetts	60.6
17	Virginia	60.3
18	Rhode Island	60.0
19	Illinois	59.9
19	Missouri	59.9
21	Maine	59.8
22	Ohio	58.3
23	Indiana	58.1
24	Delaware	57.5
25	Washington	57.3
26	Hawaii	57.0
26	New Jersey	57.0
26	Pennsylvania	57.0
29	Texas	56.9
29	Utah	56.9
31	Nevada	56.5
32	Michigan	56.3
32	Oregon	56.3
34	Idaho	55.9
35	California	55.5
36	Georgia	55.2
37	Florida	55.1
38	New York	54.8
39	North Carolina	54.6
40	Kentucky	54.0
41	Arizona	53.9
42	South Carolina	53.7
43	Louisiana	53.6
44	Oklahoma	53.0
45	Tennessee	52.8
46	Arkansas	52.0
47	Alabama	51.8
48	New Mexico	51.7
49	Mississippi	49.0
50	West Virginia	48.9
	District of Columbia	65.5

Source: U.S. Department of Labor, Bureau of Labor Statistics
"Geographic Profiles of Employment and Unemployment, 2014" (http://www.bls.gov/gps/)
*Annual averages.

Percent of Civilian Labor Force Comprised of Women in 2014

National Percent = 46.8% of Civilian Labor Force*

ALPHA ORDER

RANK	STATE	PERCENT
17	Alabama	47.6
42	Alaska	45.9
39	Arizona	46.1
16	Arkansas	47.7
43	California	45.6
39	Colorado	46.1
5	Connecticut	48.3
1	Delaware	49.4
25	Florida	47.3
30	Georgia	47.0
27	Hawaii	47.2
47	Idaho	44.9
14	Illinois	47.8
28	Indiana	47.1
17	Iowa	47.6
36	Kansas	46.3
14	Kentucky	47.8
36	Louisiana	46.3
5	Maine	48.3
2	Maryland	48.5
3	Massachusetts	48.4
11	Michigan	48.0
19	Minnesota	47.5
13	Mississippi	47.9
10	Missouri	48.1
28	Montana	47.1
25	Nebraska	47.3
46	Nevada	45.0
11	New Hampshire	48.0
36	New Jersey	46.3
35	New Mexico	46.5
22	New York	47.4
19	North Carolina	47.5
45	North Dakota	45.1
8	Ohio	48.2
43	Oklahoma	45.6
30	Oregon	47.0
22	Pennsylvania	47.4
3	Rhode Island	48.4
8	South Carolina	48.2
30	South Dakota	47.0
34	Tennessee	46.7
48	Texas	44.8
50	Utah	42.2
5	Vermont	48.3
22	Virginia	47.4
39	Washington	46.1
30	West Virginia	47.0
19	Wisconsin	47.5
49	Wyoming	44.2

RANK ORDER

RANK	STATE	PERCENT
1	Delaware	49.4
2	Maryland	48.5
3	Massachusetts	48.4
3	Rhode Island	48.4
5	Connecticut	48.3
5	Maine	48.3
5	Vermont	48.3
8	Ohio	48.2
8	South Carolina	48.2
10	Missouri	48.1
11	Michigan	48.0
11	New Hampshire	48.0
13	Mississippi	47.9
14	Illinois	47.8
14	Kentucky	47.8
16	Arkansas	47.7
17	Alabama	47.6
17	Iowa	47.6
19	Minnesota	47.5
19	North Carolina	47.5
19	Wisconsin	47.5
22	New York	47.4
22	Pennsylvania	47.4
22	Virginia	47.4
25	Florida	47.3
25	Nebraska	47.3
27	Hawaii	47.2
28	Indiana	47.1
28	Montana	47.1
30	Georgia	47.0
30	Oregon	47.0
30	South Dakota	47.0
30	West Virginia	47.0
34	Tennessee	46.7
35	New Mexico	46.5
36	Kansas	46.3
36	Louisiana	46.3
36	New Jersey	46.3
39	Arizona	46.1
39	Colorado	46.1
39	Washington	46.1
42	Alaska	45.9
43	California	45.6
43	Oklahoma	45.6
45	North Dakota	45.1
46	Nevada	45.0
47	Idaho	44.9
48	Texas	44.8
49	Wyoming	44.2
50	Utah	42.2

District of Columbia 50.5

Source: CQ Press using data from U.S. Department of Labor, Bureau of Labor Statistics
"Geographic Profiles of Employment and Unemployment, 2014" (http://www.bls.gov/gps/)
*Annual averages.

Job Growth: 2014 to 2015

National Percent Change = 1.9% Increase*

ALPHA ORDER

RANK	STATE	PERCENT CHANGE
34	Alabama	1.0
44	Alaska	(0.1)
8	Arizona	2.5
24	Arkansas	1.6
4	California	2.9
18	Colorado	1.9
33	Connecticut	1.3
22	Delaware	1.7
4	Florida	2.9
11	Georgia	2.2
8	Hawaii	2.5
1	Idaho	4.4
44	Illinois	(0.1)
18	Indiana	1.9
24	Iowa	1.6
40	Kansas	0.5
13	Kentucky	2.1
47	Louisiana	(0.9)
30	Maine	1.4
13	Maryland	2.1
13	Massachusetts	2.1
18	Michigan	1.9
27	Minnesota	1.5
35	Mississippi	0.9
35	Missouri	0.9
40	Montana	0.5
30	Nebraska	1.4
17	Nevada	2.0
40	New Hampshire	0.5
24	New Jersey	1.6
43	New Mexico	0.3
22	New York	1.7
13	North Carolina	2.1
50	North Dakota	(4.0)
27	Ohio	1.5
46	Oklahoma	(0.5)
7	Oregon	2.7
39	Pennsylvania	0.7
21	Rhode Island	1.8
2	South Carolina	3.3
11	South Dakota	2.2
10	Tennessee	2.3
30	Texas	1.4
3	Utah	3.2
38	Vermont	0.8
27	Virginia	1.5
6	Washington	2.8
48	West Virginia	(1.5)
35	Wisconsin	0.9
49	Wyoming	(2.2)

RANK ORDER

RANK	STATE	PERCENT CHANGE
1	Idaho	4.4
2	South Carolina	3.3
3	Utah	3.2
4	California	2.9
4	Florida	2.9
6	Washington	2.8
7	Oregon	2.7
8	Arizona	2.5
8	Hawaii	2.5
10	Tennessee	2.3
11	Georgia	2.2
11	South Dakota	2.2
13	Kentucky	2.1
13	Maryland	2.1
13	Massachusetts	2.1
13	North Carolina	2.1
17	Nevada	2.0
18	Colorado	1.9
18	Indiana	1.9
18	Michigan	1.9
21	Rhode Island	1.8
22	Delaware	1.7
22	New York	1.7
24	Arkansas	1.6
24	Iowa	1.6
24	New Jersey	1.6
27	Minnesota	1.5
27	Ohio	1.5
27	Virginia	1.5
30	Maine	1.4
30	Nebraska	1.4
30	Texas	1.4
33	Connecticut	1.3
34	Alabama	1.0
35	Mississippi	0.9
35	Missouri	0.9
35	Wisconsin	0.9
38	Vermont	0.8
39	Pennsylvania	0.7
40	Kansas	0.5
40	Montana	0.5
40	New Hampshire	0.5
43	New Mexico	0.3
44	Alaska	(0.1)
44	Illinois	(0.1)
46	Oklahoma	(0.5)
47	Louisiana	(0.9)
48	West Virginia	(1.5)
49	Wyoming	(2.2)
50	North Dakota	(4.0)

District of Columbia	1.4

Source: CQ Press using data from U.S. Department of Labor, Bureau of Labor Statistics
"Regional and State Employment and Unemployment" (press release, January 26, 2016, www.bls.gov/bls/newsrels.htm)
*Nonfarm jobs. December 2014 to December 2015, seasonally adjusted. National figure based on nonfarm employment from a different survey.

Employees on Nonfarm Payrolls in 2015

National Total = 143,242,000 Employees*

ALPHA ORDER

RANK	STATE	EMPLOYEES	% of USA
25	Alabama	1,963,100	1.4%
48	Alaska	340,300	0.2%
21	Arizona	2,671,800	1.9%
34	Arkansas	1,223,900	0.9%
1	California	16,320,100	11.4%
22	Colorado	2,539,400	1.8%
28	Connecticut	1,700,700	1.2%
46	Delaware	450,300	0.3%
4	Florida	8,198,800	5.7%
8	Georgia	4,317,600	3.0%
41	Hawaii	641,700	0.4%
39	Idaho	688,200	0.5%
5	Illinois	5,904,000	4.1%
15	Indiana	3,069,200	2.1%
30	Iowa	1,584,700	1.1%
31	Kansas	1,408,800	1.0%
26	Kentucky	1,920,200	1.3%
24	Louisiana	1,979,000	1.4%
42	Maine	613,300	0.4%
20	Maryland	2,696,200	1.9%
13	Massachusetts	3,519,700	2.5%
9	Michigan	4,297,400	3.0%
18	Minnesota	2,873,700	2.0%
35	Mississippi	1,135,000	0.8%
19	Missouri	2,770,600	1.9%
44	Montana	457,200	0.3%
36	Nebraska	1,011,000	0.7%
33	Nevada	1,255,700	0.9%
40	New Hampshire	656,400	0.5%
11	New Jersey	4,047,500	2.8%
37	New Mexico	830,000	0.6%
3	New York	9,316,200	6.5%
10	North Carolina	4,289,900	3.0%
45	North Dakota	451,000	0.3%
7	Ohio	5,451,500	3.8%
29	Oklahoma	1,659,400	1.2%
27	Oregon	1,798,600	1.3%
6	Pennsylvania	5,863,500	4.1%
43	Rhode Island	487,700	0.3%
23	South Carolina	2,040,200	1.4%
47	South Dakota	434,100	0.3%
16	Tennessee	2,915,800	2.0%
2	Texas	11,916,400	8.3%
32	Utah	1,396,800	1.0%
49	Vermont	314,300	0.2%
12	Virginia	3,856,100	2.7%
14	Washington	3,210,500	2.2%
38	West Virginia	751,300	0.5%
17	Wisconsin	2,897,700	2.0%
50	Wyoming	288,600	0.2%

RANK ORDER

RANK	STATE	EMPLOYEES	% of USA
1	California	16,320,100	11.4%
2	Texas	11,916,400	8.3%
3	New York	9,316,200	6.5%
4	Florida	8,198,800	5.7%
5	Illinois	5,904,000	4.1%
6	Pennsylvania	5,863,500	4.1%
7	Ohio	5,451,500	3.8%
8	Georgia	4,317,600	3.0%
9	Michigan	4,297,400	3.0%
10	North Carolina	4,289,900	3.0%
11	New Jersey	4,047,500	2.8%
12	Virginia	3,856,100	2.7%
13	Massachusetts	3,519,700	2.5%
14	Washington	3,210,500	2.2%
15	Indiana	3,069,200	2.1%
16	Tennessee	2,915,800	2.0%
17	Wisconsin	2,897,700	2.0%
18	Minnesota	2,873,700	2.0%
19	Missouri	2,770,600	1.9%
20	Maryland	2,696,200	1.9%
21	Arizona	2,671,800	1.9%
22	Colorado	2,539,400	1.8%
23	South Carolina	2,040,200	1.4%
24	Louisiana	1,979,000	1.4%
25	Alabama	1,963,100	1.4%
26	Kentucky	1,920,200	1.3%
27	Oregon	1,798,600	1.3%
28	Connecticut	1,700,700	1.2%
29	Oklahoma	1,659,400	1.2%
30	Iowa	1,584,700	1.1%
31	Kansas	1,408,800	1.0%
32	Utah	1,396,800	1.0%
33	Nevada	1,255,700	0.9%
34	Arkansas	1,223,900	0.9%
35	Mississippi	1,135,000	0.8%
36	Nebraska	1,011,000	0.7%
37	New Mexico	830,000	0.6%
38	West Virginia	751,300	0.5%
39	Idaho	688,200	0.5%
40	New Hampshire	656,400	0.5%
41	Hawaii	641,700	0.4%
42	Maine	613,300	0.4%
43	Rhode Island	487,700	0.3%
44	Montana	457,200	0.3%
45	North Dakota	451,000	0.3%
46	Delaware	450,300	0.3%
47	South Dakota	434,100	0.3%
48	Alaska	340,300	0.2%
49	Vermont	314,300	0.2%
50	Wyoming	288,600	0.2%
	District of Columbia	772,100	0.5%

Source: U.S. Department of Labor, Bureau of Labor Statistics
"Regional and State Employment and Unemployment" (press release, January 26, 2016, www.bls.gov/bls/newsrels.htm)
*Seasonally adjusted preliminary data as of December 2015. National total calculated through a different formula.

Employees in Construction in 2015

National Total = 6,538,000 Employees*

ALPHA ORDER

RANK	STATE	EMPLOYEES	% of USA
27	Alabama	84,900	1.3%
48	Alaska	18,500	0.3%
18	Arizona	132,900	2.0%
34	Arkansas	52,600	0.8%
1	California	745,800	11.4%
12	Colorado	159,900	2.4%
33	Connecticut	57,100	0.9%
47	Delaware**	22,100	0.3%
3	Florida	438,400	6.7%
11	Georgia	166,300	2.5%
39	Hawaii**	35,700	0.5%
38	Idaho	41,500	0.6%
6	Illinois	215,000	3.3%
19	Indiana	124,800	1.9%
25	Iowa	87,500	1.3%
32	Kansas	65,200	1.0%
30	Kentucky	78,900	1.2%
16	Louisiana	147,700	2.3%
42	Maine	26,700	0.4%
13	Maryland**	159,800	2.4%
17	Massachusetts	137,800	2.1%
14	Michigan	155,600	2.4%
23	Minnesota	108,200	1.7%
35	Mississippi	47,400	0.7%
21	Missouri	116,900	1.8%
43	Montana	25,800	0.4%
36	Nebraska**	46,900	0.7%
31	Nevada	69,700	1.1%
45	New Hampshire	24,400	0.4%
15	New Jersey	155,100	2.4%
37	New Mexico	41,600	0.6%
4	New York	373,400	5.7%
8	North Carolina	191,500	2.9%
40	North Dakota	34,200	0.5%
7	Ohio	194,500	3.0%
28	Oklahoma	82,800	1.3%
29	Oregon	82,200	1.3%
5	Pennsylvania	231,600	3.5%
49	Rhode Island	16,500	0.3%
24	South Carolina	89,700	1.4%
44	South Dakota**	24,700	0.4%
20	Tennessee**	117,000	1.8%
2	Texas	684,800	10.5%
26	Utah	85,600	1.3%
50	Vermont	15,300	0.2%
9	Virginia	186,200	2.8%
10	Washington	177,600	2.7%
41	West Virginia	30,000	0.5%
22	Wisconsin	110,200	1.7%
46	Wyoming	23,400	0.4%

RANK ORDER

RANK	STATE	EMPLOYEES	% of USA
1	California	745,800	11.4%
2	Texas	684,800	10.5%
3	Florida	438,400	6.7%
4	New York	373,400	5.7%
5	Pennsylvania	231,600	3.5%
6	Illinois	215,000	3.3%
7	Ohio	194,500	3.0%
8	North Carolina	191,500	2.9%
9	Virginia	186,200	2.8%
10	Washington	177,600	2.7%
11	Georgia	166,300	2.5%
12	Colorado	159,900	2.4%
13	Maryland**	159,800	2.4%
14	Michigan	155,600	2.4%
15	New Jersey	155,100	2.4%
16	Louisiana	147,700	2.3%
17	Massachusetts	137,800	2.1%
18	Arizona	132,900	2.0%
19	Indiana	124,800	1.9%
20	Tennessee**	117,000	1.8%
21	Missouri	116,900	1.8%
22	Wisconsin	110,200	1.7%
23	Minnesota	108,200	1.7%
24	South Carolina	89,700	1.4%
25	Iowa	87,500	1.3%
26	Utah	85,600	1.3%
27	Alabama	84,900	1.3%
28	Oklahoma	82,800	1.3%
29	Oregon	82,200	1.3%
30	Kentucky	78,900	1.2%
31	Nevada	69,700	1.1%
32	Kansas	65,200	1.0%
33	Connecticut	57,100	0.9%
34	Arkansas	52,600	0.8%
35	Mississippi	47,400	0.7%
36	Nebraska**	46,900	0.7%
37	New Mexico	41,600	0.6%
38	Idaho	41,500	0.6%
39	Hawaii**	35,700	0.5%
40	North Dakota	34,200	0.5%
41	West Virginia	30,000	0.5%
42	Maine	26,700	0.4%
43	Montana	25,800	0.4%
44	South Dakota**	24,700	0.4%
45	New Hampshire	24,400	0.4%
46	Wyoming	23,400	0.4%
47	Delaware**	22,100	0.3%
48	Alaska	18,500	0.3%
49	Rhode Island	16,500	0.3%
50	Vermont	15,300	0.2%
	District of Columbia**	14,900	0.2%

Source: U.S. Department of Labor, Bureau of Labor Statistics
"Regional and State Employment and Unemployment" (press release, January 26, 2016, www.bls.gov/bls/newsrels.htm)
*Seasonally adjusted preliminary data as of December 2015. National total calculated through a different formula.
**Figures for states include employees in mining and logging.

Percent of Nonfarm Employees in Construction in 2015

National Percent = 4.6% of Employees*

ALPHA ORDER

RANK	STATE	PERCENT
30	Alabama	4.3
15	Alaska	5.4
17	Arizona	5.0
30	Arkansas	4.3
23	California	4.6
4	Colorado	6.3
49	Connecticut	3.4
20	Delaware**	4.9
16	Florida	5.3
39	Georgia	3.9
10	Hawaii**	5.6
6	Idaho	6.0
46	Illinois	3.6
34	Indiana	4.1
13	Iowa	5.5
23	Kansas	4.6
34	Kentucky	4.1
3	Louisiana	7.5
28	Maine	4.4
7	Maryland**	5.9
39	Massachusetts	3.9
46	Michigan	3.6
42	Minnesota	3.8
32	Mississippi	4.2
32	Missouri	4.2
10	Montana	5.6
23	Nebraska**	4.6
10	Nevada	5.6
45	New Hampshire	3.7
42	New Jersey	3.8
17	New Mexico	5.0
36	New York	4.0
27	North Carolina	4.5
2	North Dakota	7.6
46	Ohio	3.6
17	Oklahoma	5.0
23	Oregon	4.6
39	Pennsylvania	3.9
49	Rhode Island	3.4
28	South Carolina	4.4
8	South Dakota**	5.7
36	Tennessee**	4.0
8	Texas	5.7
5	Utah	6.1
20	Vermont	4.9
22	Virginia	4.8
13	Washington	5.5
36	West Virginia	4.0
42	Wisconsin	3.8
1	Wyoming	8.1

RANK ORDER

RANK	STATE	PERCENT
1	Wyoming	8.1
2	North Dakota	7.6
3	Louisiana	7.5
4	Colorado	6.3
5	Utah	6.1
6	Idaho	6.0
7	Maryland**	5.9
8	South Dakota**	5.7
8	Texas	5.7
10	Hawaii**	5.6
10	Montana	5.6
10	Nevada	5.6
13	Iowa	5.5
13	Washington	5.5
15	Alaska	5.4
16	Florida	5.3
17	Arizona	5.0
17	New Mexico	5.0
17	Oklahoma	5.0
20	Delaware**	4.9
20	Vermont	4.9
22	Virginia	4.8
23	California	4.6
23	Kansas	4.6
23	Nebraska**	4.6
23	Oregon	4.6
27	North Carolina	4.5
28	Maine	4.4
28	South Carolina	4.4
30	Alabama	4.3
30	Arkansas	4.3
32	Mississippi	4.2
32	Missouri	4.2
34	Indiana	4.1
34	Kentucky	4.1
36	New York	4.0
36	Tennessee**	4.0
36	West Virginia	4.0
39	Georgia	3.9
39	Massachusetts	3.9
39	Pennsylvania	3.9
42	Minnesota	3.8
42	New Jersey	3.8
42	Wisconsin	3.8
45	New Hampshire	3.7
46	Illinois	3.6
46	Michigan	3.6
46	Ohio	3.6
49	Connecticut	3.4
49	Rhode Island	3.4
	District of Columbia**	1.9

Source: CQ Press using data from U.S. Department of Labor, Bureau of Labor Statistics
"Regional and State Employment and Unemployment" (press release, January 26, 2016, www.bls.gov/bls/newsrels.htm)
*Seasonally adjusted preliminary data as of December 2015. National figure calculated through a different formula.
**Figures for states include employees in mining and logging.

Employees in Education and Health Services in 2015

National Total = 22,373,000 Employees*

ALPHA ORDER

RANK	STATE	EMPLOYEES	% of USA
28	Alabama	232,100	1.0%
49	Alaska	48,300	0.2%
21	Arizona	401,300	1.8%
33	Arkansas	180,500	0.8%
1	California	2,516,000	11.2%
23	Colorado	315,400	1.4%
22	Connecticut	332,900	1.5%
44	Delaware	74,500	0.3%
4	Florida	1,226,000	5.5%
12	Georgia	545,900	2.4%
43	Hawaii	81,600	0.4%
42	Idaho	98,600	0.4%
7	Illinois	900,300	4.0%
16	Indiana	457,700	2.0%
30	Iowa	230,400	1.0%
31	Kansas	194,800	0.9%
25	Kentucky	273,900	1.2%
24	Louisiana	311,600	1.4%
39	Maine	124,000	0.6%
18	Maryland	447,500	2.0%
8	Massachusetts	766,600	3.4%
9	Michigan	667,900	3.0%
13	Minnesota	514,200	2.3%
35	Mississippi	138,100	0.6%
17	Missouri	447,700	2.0%
45	Montana	71,200	0.3%
34	Nebraska	157,200	0.7%
38	Nevada	124,100	0.6%
40	New Hampshire	118,600	0.5%
10	New Jersey	656,700	2.9%
36	New Mexico	134,200	0.6%
2	New York	1,944,100	8.7%
11	North Carolina	585,700	2.6%
48	North Dakota	59,200	0.3%
6	Ohio	914,100	4.1%
29	Oklahoma	230,600	1.0%
26	Oregon	263,600	1.2%
5	Pennsylvania	1,204,900	5.4%
41	Rhode Island	105,700	0.5%
27	South Carolina	239,300	1.1%
46	South Dakota	69,700	0.3%
20	Tennessee	414,800	1.9%
3	Texas	1,621,400	7.2%
32	Utah	188,200	0.8%
47	Vermont	64,800	0.3%
14	Virginia	508,000	2.3%
15	Washington	473,800	2.1%
37	West Virginia	128,900	0.6%
19	Wisconsin	445,000	2.0%
50	Wyoming	27,700	0.1%

RANK ORDER

RANK	STATE	EMPLOYEES	% of USA
1	California	2,516,000	11.2%
2	New York	1,944,100	8.7%
3	Texas	1,621,400	7.2%
4	Florida	1,226,000	5.5%
5	Pennsylvania	1,204,900	5.4%
6	Ohio	914,100	4.1%
7	Illinois	900,300	4.0%
8	Massachusetts	766,600	3.4%
9	Michigan	667,900	3.0%
10	New Jersey	656,700	2.9%
11	North Carolina	585,700	2.6%
12	Georgia	545,900	2.4%
13	Minnesota	514,200	2.3%
14	Virginia	508,000	2.3%
15	Washington	473,800	2.1%
16	Indiana	457,700	2.0%
17	Missouri	447,700	2.0%
18	Maryland	447,500	2.0%
19	Wisconsin	445,000	2.0%
20	Tennessee	414,800	1.9%
21	Arizona	401,300	1.8%
22	Connecticut	332,900	1.5%
23	Colorado	315,400	1.4%
24	Louisiana	311,600	1.4%
25	Kentucky	273,900	1.2%
26	Oregon	263,600	1.2%
27	South Carolina	239,300	1.1%
28	Alabama	232,100	1.0%
29	Oklahoma	230,600	1.0%
30	Iowa	230,400	1.0%
31	Kansas	194,800	0.9%
32	Utah	188,200	0.8%
33	Arkansas	180,500	0.8%
34	Nebraska	157,200	0.7%
35	Mississippi	138,100	0.6%
36	New Mexico	134,200	0.6%
37	West Virginia	128,900	0.6%
38	Nevada	124,100	0.6%
39	Maine	124,000	0.6%
40	New Hampshire	118,600	0.5%
41	Rhode Island	105,700	0.5%
42	Idaho	98,600	0.4%
43	Hawaii	81,600	0.4%
44	Delaware	74,500	0.3%
45	Montana	71,200	0.3%
46	South Dakota	69,700	0.3%
47	Vermont	64,800	0.3%
48	North Dakota	59,200	0.3%
49	Alaska	48,300	0.2%
50	Wyoming	27,700	0.1%
	District of Columbia	130,100	0.6%

Source: U.S. Department of Labor, Bureau of Labor Statistics
 "Regional and State Employment and Unemployment" (press release, January 26, 2016, www.bls.gov/bls/newsrels.htm)
*Seasonally adjusted preliminary data as of December 2015. National total calculated through a different formula.

Percent of Nonfarm Employees in Education and Health Services in 2015

National Percent = 15.6% of Employees*

ALPHA ORDER

RANK	STATE	PERCENT
47	Alabama	11.8
34	Alaska	14.2
25	Arizona	15.0
29	Arkansas	14.7
22	California	15.4
45	Colorado	12.4
7	Connecticut	19.6
13	Delaware	16.5
25	Florida	15.0
44	Georgia	12.6
43	Hawaii	12.7
32	Idaho	14.3
24	Illinois	15.2
27	Indiana	14.9
31	Iowa	14.5
37	Kansas	13.8
32	Kentucky	14.3
18	Louisiana	15.7
6	Maine	20.2
12	Maryland	16.6
1	Massachusetts	21.8
20	Michigan	15.5
9	Minnesota	17.9
46	Mississippi	12.2
14	Missouri	16.2
19	Montana	15.6
20	Nebraska	15.5
49	Nevada	9.9
8	New Hampshire	18.1
14	New Jersey	16.2
14	New Mexico	16.2
3	New York	20.9
38	North Carolina	13.7
42	North Dakota	13.1
11	Ohio	16.8
36	Oklahoma	13.9
29	Oregon	14.7
5	Pennsylvania	20.5
2	Rhode Island	21.7
48	South Carolina	11.7
17	South Dakota	16.1
34	Tennessee	14.2
39	Texas	13.6
40	Utah	13.5
4	Vermont	20.6
41	Virginia	13.2
28	Washington	14.8
10	West Virginia	17.2
22	Wisconsin	15.4
50	Wyoming	9.6

RANK ORDER

RANK	STATE	PERCENT
1	Massachusetts	21.8
2	Rhode Island	21.7
3	New York	20.9
4	Vermont	20.6
5	Pennsylvania	20.5
6	Maine	20.2
7	Connecticut	19.6
8	New Hampshire	18.1
9	Minnesota	17.9
10	West Virginia	17.2
11	Ohio	16.8
12	Maryland	16.6
13	Delaware	16.5
14	Missouri	16.2
14	New Jersey	16.2
14	New Mexico	16.2
17	South Dakota	16.1
18	Louisiana	15.7
19	Montana	15.6
20	Michigan	15.5
20	Nebraska	15.5
22	California	15.4
22	Wisconsin	15.4
24	Illinois	15.2
25	Arizona	15.0
25	Florida	15.0
27	Indiana	14.9
28	Washington	14.8
29	Arkansas	14.7
29	Oregon	14.7
31	Iowa	14.5
32	Idaho	14.3
32	Kentucky	14.3
34	Alaska	14.2
34	Tennessee	14.2
36	Oklahoma	13.9
37	Kansas	13.8
38	North Carolina	13.7
39	Texas	13.6
40	Utah	13.5
41	Virginia	13.2
42	North Dakota	13.1
43	Hawaii	12.7
44	Georgia	12.6
45	Colorado	12.4
46	Mississippi	12.2
47	Alabama	11.8
48	South Carolina	11.7
49	Nevada	9.9
50	Wyoming	9.6
	District of Columbia	16.9

Source: CQ Press using data from U.S. Department of Labor, Bureau of Labor Statistics
"Regional and State Employment and Unemployment" (press release, January 26, 2016, www.bls.gov/bls/newsrels.htm)
*Seasonally adjusted preliminary data as of December 2015. National figure calculated through a different formula.

Employees in Financial Activities in 2015

National Total = 8,196,000 Employees*

ALPHA ORDER

RANK	STATE	EMPLOYEES	% of USA
25	Alabama	97,100	1.2%
49	Alaska	12,000	0.1%
14	Arizona	198,400	2.4%
35	Arkansas	50,400	0.6%
1	California	797,400	9.7%
17	Colorado	159,800	1.9%
22	Connecticut	130,900	1.6%
36	Delaware	47,000	0.6%
4	Florida	546,800	6.7%
9	Georgia	236,800	2.9%
45	Hawaii	28,000	0.3%
39	Idaho	35,500	0.4%
5	Illinois	368,900	4.5%
23	Indiana	129,200	1.6%
24	Iowa	107,800	1.3%
31	Kansas	80,800	1.0%
27	Kentucky	95,200	1.2%
29	Louisiana	91,600	1.1%
42	Maine	31,300	0.4%
21	Maryland	146,500	1.8%
12	Massachusetts	212,500	2.6%
11	Michigan	212,900	2.6%
15	Minnesota	183,400	2.2%
37	Mississippi	44,200	0.5%
16	Missouri	166,200	2.0%
46	Montana	26,700	0.3%
33	Nebraska	75,700	0.9%
34	Nevada	55,700	0.7%
38	New Hampshire	36,700	0.4%
8	New Jersey	248,300	3.0%
40	New Mexico	34,100	0.4%
3	New York	699,200	8.5%
10	North Carolina	222,400	2.7%
47	North Dakota	23,900	0.3%
7	Ohio	296,800	3.6%
30	Oklahoma	81,200	1.0%
26	Oregon	95,300	1.2%
6	Pennsylvania	321,300	3.9%
41	Rhode Island	32,800	0.4%
28	South Carolina	95,000	1.2%
44	South Dakota	29,900	0.4%
20	Tennessee	147,400	1.8%
2	Texas	715,500	8.7%
32	Utah	80,500	1.0%
48	Vermont	12,200	0.1%
13	Virginia	200,000	2.4%
18	Washington	158,400	1.9%
43	West Virginia	30,300	0.4%
19	Wisconsin	155,800	1.9%
50	Wyoming	11,700	0.1%

RANK ORDER

RANK	STATE	EMPLOYEES	% of USA
1	California	797,400	9.7%
2	Texas	715,500	8.7%
3	New York	699,200	8.5%
4	Florida	546,800	6.7%
5	Illinois	368,900	4.5%
6	Pennsylvania	321,300	3.9%
7	Ohio	296,800	3.6%
8	New Jersey	248,300	3.0%
9	Georgia	236,800	2.9%
10	North Carolina	222,400	2.7%
11	Michigan	212,900	2.6%
12	Massachusetts	212,500	2.6%
13	Virginia	200,000	2.4%
14	Arizona	198,400	2.4%
15	Minnesota	183,400	2.2%
16	Missouri	166,200	2.0%
17	Colorado	159,800	1.9%
18	Washington	158,400	1.9%
19	Wisconsin	155,800	1.9%
20	Tennessee	147,400	1.8%
21	Maryland	146,500	1.8%
22	Connecticut	130,900	1.6%
23	Indiana	129,200	1.6%
24	Iowa	107,800	1.3%
25	Alabama	97,100	1.2%
26	Oregon	95,300	1.2%
27	Kentucky	95,200	1.2%
28	South Carolina	95,000	1.2%
29	Louisiana	91,600	1.1%
30	Oklahoma	81,200	1.0%
31	Kansas	80,800	1.0%
32	Utah	80,500	1.0%
33	Nebraska	75,700	0.9%
34	Nevada	55,700	0.7%
35	Arkansas	50,400	0.6%
36	Delaware	47,000	0.6%
37	Mississippi	44,200	0.5%
38	New Hampshire	36,700	0.4%
39	Idaho	35,500	0.4%
40	New Mexico	34,100	0.4%
41	Rhode Island	32,800	0.4%
42	Maine	31,300	0.4%
43	West Virginia	30,300	0.4%
44	South Dakota	29,900	0.4%
45	Hawaii	28,000	0.3%
46	Montana	26,700	0.3%
47	North Dakota	23,900	0.3%
48	Vermont	12,200	0.1%
49	Alaska	12,000	0.1%
50	Wyoming	11,700	0.1%
	District of Columbia	31,200	0.4%

Source: U.S. Department of Labor, Bureau of Labor Statistics
"Regional and State Employment and Unemployment" (press release, January 26, 2016, www.bls.gov/bls/newsrels.htm)
*Seasonally adjusted preliminary data as of December 2015. National total calculated through a different formula. Financial activities include insurance and real estate.

Percent of Nonfarm Employees in Financial Activities in 2015

National Percent = 5.7% of Employees*

ALPHA ORDER

RANK	STATE	PERCENT
35	Alabama	4.9
50	Alaska	3.5
5	Arizona	7.4
44	Arkansas	4.1
35	California	4.9
11	Colorado	6.3
2	Connecticut	7.7
1	Delaware	10.4
8	Florida	6.7
21	Georgia	5.5
41	Hawaii	4.4
28	Idaho	5.2
12	Illinois	6.2
43	Indiana	4.2
7	Iowa	6.8
19	Kansas	5.7
33	Kentucky	5.0
40	Louisiana	4.6
31	Maine	5.1
23	Maryland	5.4
14	Massachusetts	6.0
33	Michigan	5.0
10	Minnesota	6.4
48	Mississippi	3.9
14	Missouri	6.0
17	Montana	5.8
3	Nebraska	7.5
41	Nevada	4.4
20	New Hampshire	5.6
13	New Jersey	6.1
44	New Mexico	4.1
3	New York	7.5
28	North Carolina	5.2
26	North Dakota	5.3
23	Ohio	5.4
35	Oklahoma	4.9
26	Oregon	5.3
21	Pennsylvania	5.5
8	Rhode Island	6.7
39	South Carolina	4.7
6	South Dakota	6.9
31	Tennessee	5.1
14	Texas	6.0
17	Utah	5.8
48	Vermont	3.9
28	Virginia	5.2
35	Washington	4.9
47	West Virginia	4.0
23	Wisconsin	5.4
44	Wyoming	4.1

RANK ORDER

RANK	STATE	PERCENT
1	Delaware	10.4
2	Connecticut	7.7
3	Nebraska	7.5
3	New York	7.5
5	Arizona	7.4
6	South Dakota	6.9
7	Iowa	6.8
8	Florida	6.7
8	Rhode Island	6.7
10	Minnesota	6.4
11	Colorado	6.3
12	Illinois	6.2
13	New Jersey	6.1
14	Massachusetts	6.0
14	Missouri	6.0
14	Texas	6.0
17	Montana	5.8
17	Utah	5.8
19	Kansas	5.7
20	New Hampshire	5.6
21	Georgia	5.5
21	Pennsylvania	5.5
23	Maryland	5.4
23	Ohio	5.4
23	Wisconsin	5.4
26	North Dakota	5.3
26	Oregon	5.3
28	Idaho	5.2
28	North Carolina	5.2
28	Virginia	5.2
31	Maine	5.1
31	Tennessee	5.1
33	Kentucky	5.0
33	Michigan	5.0
35	Alabama	4.9
35	California	4.9
35	Oklahoma	4.9
35	Washington	4.9
39	South Carolina	4.7
40	Louisiana	4.6
41	Hawaii	4.4
41	Nevada	4.4
43	Indiana	4.2
44	Arkansas	4.1
44	New Mexico	4.1
44	Wyoming	4.1
47	West Virginia	4.0
48	Mississippi	3.9
48	Vermont	3.9
50	Alaska	3.5
	District of Columbia	4.0

Source: CQ Press using data from U.S. Department of Labor, Bureau of Labor Statistics
"Regional and State Employment and Unemployment" (press release, January 26, 2016, www.bls.gov/bls/newsrels.htm)
*Seasonally adjusted preliminary data as of December 2015. National figure calculated through a different formula. Financial activities include insurance and real estate.

Employees in Government in 2015

National Total = 22,001,000 Employees*

ALPHA ORDER

RANK	STATE	EMPLOYEES	% of USA
23	Alabama	379,500	1.7%
45	Alaska	80,300	0.4%
22	Arizona	411,000	1.9%
34	Arkansas	212,700	1.0%
1	California	2,467,200	11.2%
20	Colorado	414,400	1.9%
32	Connecticut	237,300	1.1%
48	Delaware	65,900	0.3%
4	Florida	1,073,500	4.9%
10	Georgia	693,300	3.2%
39	Hawaii	125,400	0.6%
40	Idaho	121,200	0.6%
5	Illinois	831,000	3.8%
16	Indiana	435,800	2.0%
29	Iowa	256,300	1.2%
30	Kansas	255,200	1.2%
26	Kentucky	325,900	1.5%
27	Louisiana	321,100	1.5%
41	Maine	99,700	0.5%
14	Maryland	513,600	2.3%
15	Massachusetts	463,400	2.1%
12	Michigan	587,900	2.7%
19	Minnesota	421,900	1.9%
31	Mississippi	245,700	1.1%
17	Missouri	433,400	2.0%
42	Montana	88,300	0.4%
36	Nebraska	173,500	0.8%
37	Nevada	156,000	0.7%
43	New Hampshire	87,800	0.4%
11	New Jersey	623,200	2.8%
35	New Mexico	192,300	0.9%
3	New York	1,436,200	6.5%
7	North Carolina	717,100	3.3%
44	North Dakota	80,500	0.4%
6	Ohio	759,800	3.5%
25	Oklahoma	348,700	1.6%
28	Oregon	304,500	1.4%
9	Pennsylvania	706,500	3.2%
49	Rhode Island	59,300	0.3%
24	South Carolina	364,000	1.7%
46	South Dakota	78,800	0.4%
18	Tennessee	429,100	2.0%
2	Texas	1,866,900	8.5%
33	Utah	234,200	1.1%
50	Vermont	56,900	0.3%
8	Virginia	707,200	3.2%
13	Washington	565,900	2.6%
38	West Virginia	152,100	0.7%
20	Wisconsin	414,400	1.9%
47	Wyoming	72,400	0.3%

RANK ORDER

RANK	STATE	EMPLOYEES	% of USA
1	California	2,467,200	11.2%
2	Texas	1,866,900	8.5%
3	New York	1,436,200	6.5%
4	Florida	1,073,500	4.9%
5	Illinois	831,000	3.8%
6	Ohio	759,800	3.5%
7	North Carolina	717,100	3.3%
8	Virginia	707,200	3.2%
9	Pennsylvania	706,500	3.2%
10	Georgia	693,300	3.2%
11	New Jersey	623,200	2.8%
12	Michigan	587,900	2.7%
13	Washington	565,900	2.6%
14	Maryland	513,600	2.3%
15	Massachusetts	463,400	2.1%
16	Indiana	435,800	2.0%
17	Missouri	433,400	2.0%
18	Tennessee	429,100	2.0%
19	Minnesota	421,900	1.9%
20	Colorado	414,400	1.9%
20	Wisconsin	414,400	1.9%
22	Arizona	411,000	1.9%
23	Alabama	379,500	1.7%
24	South Carolina	364,000	1.7%
25	Oklahoma	348,700	1.6%
26	Kentucky	325,900	1.5%
27	Louisiana	321,100	1.5%
28	Oregon	304,500	1.4%
29	Iowa	256,300	1.2%
30	Kansas	255,200	1.2%
31	Mississippi	245,700	1.1%
32	Connecticut	237,300	1.1%
33	Utah	234,200	1.1%
34	Arkansas	212,700	1.0%
35	New Mexico	192,300	0.9%
36	Nebraska	173,500	0.8%
37	Nevada	156,000	0.7%
38	West Virginia	152,100	0.7%
39	Hawaii	125,400	0.6%
40	Idaho	121,200	0.6%
41	Maine	99,700	0.5%
42	Montana	88,300	0.4%
43	New Hampshire	87,800	0.4%
44	North Dakota	80,500	0.4%
45	Alaska	80,300	0.4%
46	South Dakota	78,800	0.4%
47	Wyoming	72,400	0.3%
48	Delaware	65,900	0.3%
49	Rhode Island	59,300	0.3%
50	Vermont	56,900	0.3%
	District of Columbia	236,700	1.1%

Source: U.S. Department of Labor, Bureau of Labor Statistics
"Regional and State Employment and Unemployment" (press release, January 26, 2016, www.bls.gov/bls/newsrels.htm)
*Seasonally adjusted preliminary data as of December 2015. National total calculated through a different formula.

Percent of Nonfarm Employees in Government in 2015

National Percent = 15.4% of Employees*

ALPHA ORDER

RANK	STATE	PERCENT
8	Alabama	19.3
2	Alaska	23.6
32	Arizona	15.4
19	Arkansas	17.4
35	California	15.1
25	Colorado	16.3
42	Connecticut	14.0
38	Delaware	14.6
47	Florida	13.1
29	Georgia	16.1
7	Hawaii	19.5
17	Idaho	17.6
41	Illinois	14.1
40	Indiana	14.2
27	Iowa	16.2
13	Kansas	18.1
21	Kentucky	17.0
27	Louisiana	16.2
25	Maine	16.3
10	Maryland	19.0
46	Massachusetts	13.2
44	Michigan	13.7
36	Minnesota	14.7
4	Mississippi	21.6
31	Missouri	15.6
8	Montana	19.3
20	Nebraska	17.2
48	Nevada	12.4
45	New Hampshire	13.4
32	New Jersey	15.4
3	New Mexico	23.2
32	New York	15.4
24	North Carolina	16.7
15	North Dakota	17.8
43	Ohio	13.9
5	Oklahoma	21.0
22	Oregon	16.9
50	Pennsylvania	12.0
49	Rhode Island	12.2
15	South Carolina	17.8
12	South Dakota	18.2
36	Tennessee	14.7
30	Texas	15.7
23	Utah	16.8
13	Vermont	18.1
11	Virginia	18.3
17	Washington	17.6
6	West Virginia	20.2
39	Wisconsin	14.3
1	Wyoming	25.1

RANK ORDER

RANK	STATE	PERCENT
1	Wyoming	25.1
2	Alaska	23.6
3	New Mexico	23.2
4	Mississippi	21.6
5	Oklahoma	21.0
6	West Virginia	20.2
7	Hawaii	19.5
8	Alabama	19.3
8	Montana	19.3
10	Maryland	19.0
11	Virginia	18.3
12	South Dakota	18.2
13	Kansas	18.1
13	Vermont	18.1
15	North Dakota	17.8
15	South Carolina	17.8
17	Idaho	17.6
17	Washington	17.6
19	Arkansas	17.4
20	Nebraska	17.2
21	Kentucky	17.0
22	Oregon	16.9
23	Utah	16.8
24	North Carolina	16.7
25	Colorado	16.3
25	Maine	16.3
27	Iowa	16.2
27	Louisiana	16.2
29	Georgia	16.1
30	Texas	15.7
31	Missouri	15.6
32	Arizona	15.4
32	New Jersey	15.4
32	New York	15.4
35	California	15.1
36	Minnesota	14.7
36	Tennessee	14.7
38	Delaware	14.6
39	Wisconsin	14.3
40	Indiana	14.2
41	Illinois	14.1
42	Connecticut	14.0
43	Ohio	13.9
44	Michigan	13.7
45	New Hampshire	13.4
46	Massachusetts	13.2
47	Florida	13.1
48	Nevada	12.4
49	Rhode Island	12.2
50	Pennsylvania	12.0
	District of Columbia	30.7

Source: CQ Press using data from U.S. Department of Labor, Bureau of Labor Statistics
"Regional and State Employment and Unemployment" (press release, January 26, 2016, www.bls.gov/bls/newsrels.htm)
*Seasonally adjusted preliminary data as of December 2015. National figure calculated through a different formula.

Employees in Leisure and Hospitality in 2015

National Total = 15,367,000 Employees*

ALPHA ORDER

RANK	STATE	EMPLOYEES	% of USA
26	Alabama	192,900	1.3%
50	Alaska	34,300	0.2%
19	Arizona	301,900	2.0%
36	Arkansas	116,000	0.8%
1	California	1,861,100	12.1%
15	Colorado	322,100	2.1%
30	Connecticut	159,100	1.0%
45	Delaware	49,900	0.3%
3	Florida	1,153,100	7.5%
9	Georgia	457,600	3.0%
35	Hawaii	116,500	0.8%
40	Idaho	70,700	0.5%
5	Illinois	563,100	3.7%
18	Indiana	306,400	2.0%
31	Iowa	142,600	0.9%
34	Kansas	125,800	0.8%
28	Kentucky	189,500	1.2%
25	Louisiana	225,400	1.5%
42	Maine	64,300	0.4%
21	Maryland	271,800	1.8%
13	Massachusetts	354,800	2.3%
10	Michigan	415,300	2.7%
22	Minnesota	268,000	1.7%
33	Mississippi	130,400	0.8%
20	Missouri	287,200	1.9%
44	Montana	58,400	0.4%
38	Nebraska	87,500	0.6%
14	Nevada	351,800	2.3%
41	New Hampshire	67,900	0.4%
12	New Jersey	368,400	2.4%
37	New Mexico	95,000	0.6%
4	New York	891,600	5.8%
8	North Carolina	465,100	3.0%
47	North Dakota	40,300	0.3%
6	Ohio	557,300	3.6%
29	Oklahoma	161,300	1.0%
27	Oregon	190,700	1.2%
7	Pennsylvania	556,200	3.6%
43	Rhode Island	58,600	0.4%
24	South Carolina	243,600	1.6%
46	South Dakota	45,600	0.3%
17	Tennessee	311,300	2.0%
2	Texas	1,267,800	8.3%
32	Utah	140,700	0.9%
48	Vermont	36,100	0.2%
11	Virginia	385,700	2.5%
16	Washington	311,800	2.0%
39	West Virginia	70,900	0.5%
23	Wisconsin	263,900	1.7%
49	Wyoming	35,600	0.2%

RANK ORDER

RANK	STATE	EMPLOYEES	% of USA
1	California	1,861,100	12.1%
2	Texas	1,267,800	8.3%
3	Florida	1,153,100	7.5%
4	New York	891,600	5.8%
5	Illinois	563,100	3.7%
6	Ohio	557,300	3.6%
7	Pennsylvania	556,200	3.6%
8	North Carolina	465,100	3.0%
9	Georgia	457,600	3.0%
10	Michigan	415,300	2.7%
11	Virginia	385,700	2.5%
12	New Jersey	368,400	2.4%
13	Massachusetts	354,800	2.3%
14	Nevada	351,800	2.3%
15	Colorado	322,100	2.1%
16	Washington	311,800	2.0%
17	Tennessee	311,300	2.0%
18	Indiana	306,400	2.0%
19	Arizona	301,900	2.0%
20	Missouri	287,200	1.9%
21	Maryland	271,800	1.8%
22	Minnesota	268,000	1.7%
23	Wisconsin	263,900	1.7%
24	South Carolina	243,600	1.6%
25	Louisiana	225,400	1.5%
26	Alabama	192,900	1.3%
27	Oregon	190,700	1.2%
28	Kentucky	189,500	1.2%
29	Oklahoma	161,300	1.0%
30	Connecticut	159,100	1.0%
31	Iowa	142,600	0.9%
32	Utah	140,700	0.9%
33	Mississippi	130,400	0.8%
34	Kansas	125,800	0.8%
35	Hawaii	116,500	0.8%
36	Arkansas	116,000	0.8%
37	New Mexico	95,000	0.6%
38	Nebraska	87,500	0.6%
39	West Virginia	70,900	0.5%
40	Idaho	70,700	0.5%
41	New Hampshire	67,900	0.4%
42	Maine	64,300	0.4%
43	Rhode Island	58,600	0.4%
44	Montana	58,400	0.4%
45	Delaware	49,900	0.3%
46	South Dakota	45,600	0.3%
47	North Dakota	40,300	0.3%
48	Vermont	36,100	0.2%
49	Wyoming	35,600	0.2%
50	Alaska	34,300	0.2%
	District of Columbia	71,500	0.5%

Source: U.S. Department of Labor, Bureau of Labor Statistics
 "Regional and State Employment and Unemployment" (press release, January 26, 2016, www.bls.gov/bls/newsrels.htm)
*Seasonally adjusted preliminary data as of December 2015. National total calculated through a different formula.

Percent of Nonfarm Employees in Leisure and Hospitality in 2015

National Percent = 10.7% of Employees*

ALPHA ORDER

RANK	STATE	PERCENT
34	Alabama	9.8
27	Alaska	10.1
14	Arizona	11.3
39	Arkansas	9.5
11	California	11.4
5	Colorado	12.7
42	Connecticut	9.4
15	Delaware	11.1
3	Florida	14.1
18	Georgia	10.6
2	Hawaii	18.2
24	Idaho	10.3
39	Illinois	9.5
31	Indiana	10.0
47	Iowa	9.0
48	Kansas	8.9
33	Kentucky	9.9
11	Louisiana	11.4
21	Maine	10.5
27	Maryland	10.1
27	Massachusetts	10.1
35	Michigan	9.7
44	Minnesota	9.3
9	Mississippi	11.5
23	Missouri	10.4
4	Montana	12.8
50	Nebraska	8.7
1	Nevada	28.0
24	New Hampshire	10.3
45	New Jersey	9.1
11	New Mexico	11.4
38	New York	9.6
16	North Carolina	10.8
48	North Dakota	8.9
26	Ohio	10.2
35	Oklahoma	9.7
18	Oregon	10.6
39	Pennsylvania	9.5
7	Rhode Island	12.0
8	South Carolina	11.9
21	South Dakota	10.5
17	Tennessee	10.7
18	Texas	10.6
27	Utah	10.1
9	Vermont	11.5
31	Virginia	10.0
35	Washington	9.7
42	West Virginia	9.4
45	Wisconsin	9.1
6	Wyoming	12.3

RANK ORDER

RANK	STATE	PERCENT
1	Nevada	28.0
2	Hawaii	18.2
3	Florida	14.1
4	Montana	12.8
5	Colorado	12.7
6	Wyoming	12.3
7	Rhode Island	12.0
8	South Carolina	11.9
9	Mississippi	11.5
9	Vermont	11.5
11	California	11.4
11	Louisiana	11.4
11	New Mexico	11.4
14	Arizona	11.3
15	Delaware	11.1
16	North Carolina	10.8
17	Tennessee	10.7
18	Georgia	10.6
18	Oregon	10.6
18	Texas	10.6
21	Maine	10.5
21	South Dakota	10.5
23	Missouri	10.4
24	Idaho	10.3
24	New Hampshire	10.3
26	Ohio	10.2
27	Alaska	10.1
27	Maryland	10.1
27	Massachusetts	10.1
27	Utah	10.1
31	Indiana	10.0
31	Virginia	10.0
33	Kentucky	9.9
34	Alabama	9.8
35	Michigan	9.7
35	Oklahoma	9.7
35	Washington	9.7
38	New York	9.6
39	Arkansas	9.5
39	Illinois	9.5
39	Pennsylvania	9.5
42	Connecticut	9.4
42	West Virginia	9.4
44	Minnesota	9.3
45	New Jersey	9.1
45	Wisconsin	9.1
47	Iowa	9.0
48	Kansas	8.9
48	North Dakota	8.9
50	Nebraska	8.7

District of Columbia 9.3

Source: CQ Press using data from U.S. Department of Labor, Bureau of Labor Statistics
"Regional and State Employment and Unemployment" (press release, January 26, 2016, www.bls.gov/bls/newsrels.htm)
*Seasonally adjusted preliminary data as of December 2015. National figure calculated through a different formula.

Employees in Manufacturing in 2015

National Total = 12,331,000 Employees*

ALPHA ORDER

RANK	STATE	EMPLOYEES	% of USA
NA	Alabama**	NA	NA
46	Alaska	14,400	0.1%
26	Arizona	156,700	1.3%
27	Arkansas	152,900	1.2%
1	California	1,269,200	10.3%
29	Colorado	143,200	1.2%
25	Connecticut	161,300	1.3%
43	Delaware	25,800	0.2%
12	Florida	341,000	2.8%
11	Georgia	377,200	3.1%
47	Hawaii	13,400	0.1%
35	Idaho	64,400	0.5%
6	Illinois	567,000	4.6%
7	Indiana	519,700	4.2%
22	Iowa	215,000	1.7%
24	Kansas	162,900	1.3%
19	Kentucky	245,300	2.0%
28	Louisiana	144,300	1.2%
36	Maine	50,000	0.4%
32	Maryland	104,300	0.8%
17	Massachusetts	250,300	2.0%
4	Michigan	603,500	4.9%
14	Minnesota	315,600	2.6%
30	Mississippi	142,000	1.2%
16	Missouri	262,000	2.1%
45	Montana	19,000	0.2%
33	Nebraska	94,200	0.8%
39	Nevada	42,400	0.3%
34	New Hampshire	67,400	0.5%
18	New Jersey	245,600	2.0%
42	New Mexico	27,600	0.2%
10	New York	448,500	3.6%
9	North Carolina	459,900	3.7%
44	North Dakota	25,300	0.2%
3	Ohio	691,700	5.6%
NA	Oklahoma**	NA	NA
23	Oregon	186,900	1.5%
5	Pennsylvania	567,200	4.6%
40	Rhode Island	42,000	0.3%
21	South Carolina	232,000	1.9%
38	South Dakota	43,600	0.4%
13	Tennessee	335,300	2.7%
2	Texas	849,300	6.9%
31	Utah	126,200	1.0%
41	Vermont	30,200	0.2%
20	Virginia	234,000	1.9%
15	Washington	291,000	2.4%
37	West Virginia	47,600	0.4%
8	Wisconsin	473,500	3.8%
48	Wyoming	9,700	0.1%

RANK ORDER

RANK	STATE	EMPLOYEES	% of USA
1	California	1,269,200	10.3%
2	Texas	849,300	6.9%
3	Ohio	691,700	5.6%
4	Michigan	603,500	4.9%
5	Pennsylvania	567,200	4.6%
6	Illinois	567,000	4.6%
7	Indiana	519,700	4.2%
8	Wisconsin	473,500	3.8%
9	North Carolina	459,900	3.7%
10	New York	448,500	3.6%
11	Georgia	377,200	3.1%
12	Florida	341,000	2.8%
13	Tennessee	335,300	2.7%
14	Minnesota	315,600	2.6%
15	Washington	291,000	2.4%
16	Missouri	262,000	2.1%
17	Massachusetts	250,300	2.0%
18	New Jersey	245,600	2.0%
19	Kentucky	245,300	2.0%
20	Virginia	234,000	1.9%
21	South Carolina	232,000	1.9%
22	Iowa	215,000	1.7%
23	Oregon	186,900	1.5%
24	Kansas	162,900	1.3%
25	Connecticut	161,300	1.3%
26	Arizona	156,700	1.3%
27	Arkansas	152,900	1.2%
28	Louisiana	144,300	1.2%
29	Colorado	143,200	1.2%
30	Mississippi	142,000	1.2%
31	Utah	126,200	1.0%
32	Maryland	104,300	0.8%
33	Nebraska	94,200	0.8%
34	New Hampshire	67,400	0.5%
35	Idaho	64,400	0.5%
36	Maine	50,000	0.4%
37	West Virginia	47,600	0.4%
38	South Dakota	43,600	0.4%
39	Nevada	42,400	0.3%
40	Rhode Island	42,000	0.3%
41	Vermont	30,200	0.2%
42	New Mexico	27,600	0.2%
43	Delaware	25,800	0.2%
44	North Dakota	25,300	0.2%
45	Montana	19,000	0.2%
46	Alaska	14,400	0.1%
47	Hawaii	13,400	0.1%
48	Wyoming	9,700	0.1%
NA	Alabama**	NA	NA
NA	Oklahoma**	NA	NA
	District of Columbia**	NA	NA

Source: U.S. Department of Labor, Bureau of Labor Statistics
"Regional and State Employment and Unemployment" (press release, January 26, 2016, www.bls.gov/bls/newsrels.htm)
*Seasonally adjusted preliminary data as of December 2015. National total calculated through a different formula.
**The Bureau of Labor Statistics does not publish seasonally adjusted figures in this category for these states.

Percent of Nonfarm Employees in Manufacturing in 2015

National Percent = 8.6% of Employees*

ALPHA ORDER

RANK	STATE	PERCENT
NA	Alabama**	NA
41	Alaska	4.2
36	Arizona	5.9
7	Arkansas	12.5
29	California	7.8
38	Colorado	5.6
20	Connecticut	9.5
37	Delaware	5.7
41	Florida	4.2
26	Georgia	8.7
48	Hawaii	2.1
22	Idaho	9.4
18	Illinois	9.6
1	Indiana	16.9
4	Iowa	13.6
9	Kansas	11.6
5	Kentucky	12.8
30	Louisiana	7.3
28	Maine	8.2
44	Maryland	3.9
31	Massachusetts	7.1
3	Michigan	14.0
12	Minnesota	11.0
7	Mississippi	12.5
20	Missouri	9.5
41	Montana	4.2
23	Nebraska	9.3
45	Nevada	3.4
15	New Hampshire	10.3
34	New Jersey	6.1
47	New Mexico	3.3
40	New York	4.8
13	North Carolina	10.7
38	North Dakota	5.6
6	Ohio	12.7
NA	Oklahoma**	NA
14	Oregon	10.4
17	Pennsylvania	9.7
27	Rhode Island	8.6
11	South Carolina	11.4
16	South Dakota	10.0
10	Tennessee	11.5
31	Texas	7.1
25	Utah	9.0
18	Vermont	9.6
34	Virginia	6.1
24	Washington	9.1
33	West Virginia	6.3
2	Wisconsin	16.3
45	Wyoming	3.4

RANK ORDER

RANK	STATE	PERCENT
1	Indiana	16.9
2	Wisconsin	16.3
3	Michigan	14.0
4	Iowa	13.6
5	Kentucky	12.8
6	Ohio	12.7
7	Arkansas	12.5
7	Mississippi	12.5
9	Kansas	11.6
10	Tennessee	11.5
11	South Carolina	11.4
12	Minnesota	11.0
13	North Carolina	10.7
14	Oregon	10.4
15	New Hampshire	10.3
16	South Dakota	10.0
17	Pennsylvania	9.7
18	Illinois	9.6
18	Vermont	9.6
20	Connecticut	9.5
20	Missouri	9.5
22	Idaho	9.4
23	Nebraska	9.3
24	Washington	9.1
25	Utah	9.0
26	Georgia	8.7
27	Rhode Island	8.6
28	Maine	8.2
29	California	7.8
30	Louisiana	7.3
31	Massachusetts	7.1
31	Texas	7.1
33	West Virginia	6.3
34	New Jersey	6.1
34	Virginia	6.1
36	Arizona	5.9
37	Delaware	5.7
38	Colorado	5.6
38	North Dakota	5.6
40	New York	4.8
41	Alaska	4.2
41	Florida	4.2
41	Montana	4.2
44	Maryland	3.9
45	Nevada	3.4
45	Wyoming	3.4
47	New Mexico	3.3
48	Hawaii	2.1
NA	Alabama**	NA
NA	Oklahoma**	NA
	District of Columbia**	NA

Source: CQ Press using data from U.S. Department of Labor, Bureau of Labor Statistics
"Regional and State Employment and Unemployment" (press release, January 26, 2016, www.bls.gov/bls/newsrels.htm)
*Seasonally adjusted preliminary data as of December 2015. National figure calculated through a different formula.
**The Bureau of Labor Statistics does not publish seasonally adjusted figures in this category for these states.

Employees in Mining and Logging in 2015

National Total = 781,000 Employees*

ALPHA ORDER

RANK	STATE	EMPLOYEES	% of USA
17	Alabama	10,300	1.3%
11	Alaska	16,600	2.1%
15	Arizona	12,000	1.5%
22	Arkansas	8,100	1.0%
6	California	27,800	3.6%
4	Colorado	34,100	4.4%
43	Connecticut	500	0.1%
NA	Delaware**	NA	NA
30	Florida	5,500	0.7%
20	Georgia	8,500	1.1%
NA	Hawaii**	NA	NA
36	Idaho	3,400	0.4%
19	Illinois	9,100	1.2%
27	Indiana	6,500	0.8%
38	Iowa	2,100	0.3%
18	Kansas	9,600	1.2%
12	Kentucky	14,300	1.8%
3	Louisiana	42,500	5.4%
37	Maine	2,600	0.3%
NA	Maryland**	NA	NA
40	Massachusetts	900	0.1%
25	Michigan	7,900	1.0%
28	Minnesota	5,600	0.7%
22	Mississippi	8,100	1.0%
35	Missouri	3,700	0.5%
21	Montana	8,400	1.1%
NA	Nebraska**	NA	NA
14	Nevada	12,700	1.6%
40	New Hampshire	900	0.1%
39	New Jersey	1,300	0.2%
7	New Mexico	25,800	3.3%
32	New York	4,700	0.6%
30	North Carolina	5,500	0.7%
9	North Dakota	24,200	3.1%
13	Ohio	13,700	1.8%
2	Oklahoma	51,000	6.5%
26	Oregon	6,800	0.9%
5	Pennsylvania	33,900	4.3%
44	Rhode Island	200	0.0%
34	South Carolina	3,800	0.5%
NA	South Dakota**	NA	NA
NA	Tennessee**	NA	NA
1	Texas	283,600	36.3%
16	Utah	11,300	1.4%
42	Vermont	700	0.1%
22	Virginia	8,100	1.0%
28	Washington	5,600	0.7%
8	West Virginia	24,900	3.2%
33	Wisconsin	3,900	0.5%
10	Wyoming	22,100	2.8%

RANK ORDER

RANK	STATE	EMPLOYEES	% of USA
1	Texas	283,600	36.3%
2	Oklahoma	51,000	6.5%
3	Louisiana	42,500	5.4%
4	Colorado	34,100	4.4%
5	Pennsylvania	33,900	4.3%
6	California	27,800	3.6%
7	New Mexico	25,800	3.3%
8	West Virginia	24,900	3.2%
9	North Dakota	24,200	3.1%
10	Wyoming	22,100	2.8%
11	Alaska	16,600	2.1%
12	Kentucky	14,300	1.8%
13	Ohio	13,700	1.8%
14	Nevada	12,700	1.6%
15	Arizona	12,000	1.5%
16	Utah	11,300	1.4%
17	Alabama	10,300	1.3%
18	Kansas	9,600	1.2%
19	Illinois	9,100	1.2%
20	Georgia	8,500	1.1%
21	Montana	8,400	1.1%
22	Arkansas	8,100	1.0%
22	Mississippi	8,100	1.0%
22	Virginia	8,100	1.0%
25	Michigan	7,900	1.0%
26	Oregon	6,800	0.9%
27	Indiana	6,500	0.8%
28	Minnesota	5,600	0.7%
28	Washington	5,600	0.7%
30	Florida	5,500	0.7%
30	North Carolina	5,500	0.7%
32	New York	4,700	0.6%
33	Wisconsin	3,900	0.5%
34	South Carolina	3,800	0.5%
35	Missouri	3,700	0.5%
36	Idaho	3,400	0.4%
37	Maine	2,600	0.3%
38	Iowa	2,100	0.3%
39	New Jersey	1,300	0.2%
40	Massachusetts	900	0.1%
40	New Hampshire	900	0.1%
42	Vermont	700	0.1%
43	Connecticut	500	0.1%
44	Rhode Island	200	0.0%
NA	Delaware**	NA	NA
NA	Hawaii**	NA	NA
NA	Maryland**	NA	NA
NA	Nebraska**	NA	NA
NA	South Dakota**	NA	NA
NA	Tennessee**	NA	NA
	District of Columbia**	NA	NA

Source: U.S. Department of Labor, Bureau of Labor Statistics
"Regional and State Employment and Unemployment" (press release, January 26, 2016, www.bls.gov/bls/newsrels.htm)
*Not seasonally adjusted preliminary data as of December 2015. National total calculated through a different formula.
**The Bureau of Labor Statistics does not publish figures in this category for these states.

Percent of Nonfarm Employees in Mining and Logging in 2015

National Percent = 0.5% of Employees*

ALPHA ORDER

RANK	STATE	PERCENT
18	Alabama	0.5
3	Alaska	5.1
20	Arizona	0.4
13	Arkansas	0.7
24	California	0.2
10	Colorado	1.3
40	Connecticut	0.0
NA	Delaware**	NA
34	Florida	0.1
24	Georgia	0.2
NA	Hawaii**	NA
18	Idaho	0.5
24	Illinois	0.2
24	Indiana	0.2
34	Iowa	0.1
13	Kansas	0.7
13	Kentucky	0.7
8	Louisiana	2.1
20	Maine	0.4
NA	Maryland**	NA
40	Massachusetts	0.0
24	Michigan	0.2
24	Minnesota	0.2
13	Mississippi	0.7
34	Missouri	0.1
9	Montana	1.8
NA	Nebraska**	NA
11	Nevada	1.0
34	New Hampshire	0.1
40	New Jersey	0.0
5	New Mexico	3.1
40	New York	0.0
34	North Carolina	0.1
2	North Dakota	5.3
23	Ohio	0.3
5	Oklahoma	3.1
20	Oregon	0.4
17	Pennsylvania	0.6
40	Rhode Island	0.0
24	South Carolina	0.2
NA	South Dakota**	NA
NA	Tennessee**	NA
7	Texas	2.4
12	Utah	0.8
24	Vermont	0.2
24	Virginia	0.2
24	Washington	0.2
4	West Virginia	3.3
34	Wisconsin	0.1
1	Wyoming	7.7

RANK ORDER

RANK	STATE	PERCENT
1	Wyoming	7.7
2	North Dakota	5.3
3	Alaska	5.1
4	West Virginia	3.3
5	New Mexico	3.1
5	Oklahoma	3.1
7	Texas	2.4
8	Louisiana	2.1
9	Montana	1.8
10	Colorado	1.3
11	Nevada	1.0
12	Utah	0.8
13	Arkansas	0.7
13	Kansas	0.7
13	Kentucky	0.7
13	Mississippi	0.7
17	Pennsylvania	0.6
18	Alabama	0.5
18	Idaho	0.5
20	Arizona	0.4
20	Maine	0.4
20	Oregon	0.4
23	Ohio	0.3
24	California	0.2
24	Georgia	0.2
24	Illinois	0.2
24	Indiana	0.2
24	Michigan	0.2
24	Minnesota	0.2
24	South Carolina	0.2
24	Vermont	0.2
24	Virginia	0.2
24	Washington	0.2
34	Florida	0.1
34	Iowa	0.1
34	Missouri	0.1
34	New Hampshire	0.1
34	North Carolina	0.1
34	Wisconsin	0.1
40	Connecticut	0.0
40	Massachusetts	0.0
40	New Jersey	0.0
40	New York	0.0
40	Rhode Island	0.0
NA	Delaware**	NA
NA	Hawaii**	NA
NA	Maryland**	NA
NA	Nebraska**	NA
NA	South Dakota**	NA
NA	Tennessee**	NA

| | District of Columbia** | NA |

Source: CQ Press using data from U.S. Department of Labor, Bureau of Labor Statistics
    "Regional and State Employment and Unemployment" (press release, January 26, 2016, www.bls.gov/bls/newsrels.htm)
*Not seasonally adjusted preliminary data as of December 2015. National figure calculated through a different formula.
**The Bureau of Labor Statistics does not publish seasonally adjusted figures in this category for these states.

Employees in Professional and Business Services in 2015

National Total = 20,044,000 Employees*

ALPHA ORDER

RANK	STATE	EMPLOYEES	% of USA
25	Alabama	228,300	1.1%
48	Alaska	27,900	0.1%
15	Arizona	409,800	2.0%
33	Arkansas	141,300	0.7%
1	California	2,618,100	13.1%
18	Colorado	385,300	1.9%
27	Connecticut	217,200	1.1%
44	Delaware	62,600	0.3%
4	Florida	1,244,300	6.2%
9	Georgia	659,100	3.3%
38	Hawaii	84,200	0.4%
39	Idaho	82,900	0.4%
5	Illinois	929,600	4.6%
21	Indiana	324,100	1.6%
34	Iowa	139,500	0.7%
31	Kansas	170,600	0.9%
26	Kentucky	221,000	1.1%
28	Louisiana	216,500	1.1%
42	Maine	66,500	0.3%
14	Maryland	438,200	2.2%
13	Massachusetts	546,300	2.7%
10	Michigan	645,800	3.2%
19	Minnesota	368,500	1.8%
36	Mississippi	104,700	0.5%
20	Missouri	357,500	1.8%
45	Montana	39,700	0.2%
35	Nebraska	113,300	0.6%
32	Nevada	161,200	0.8%
40	New Hampshire	72,900	0.4%
11	New Jersey	643,400	3.2%
37	New Mexico	102,800	0.5%
3	New York	1,269,300	6.3%
12	North Carolina	607,000	3.0%
46	North Dakota	36,300	0.2%
7	Ohio	717,800	3.6%
30	Oklahoma	188,000	0.9%
24	Oregon	235,500	1.2%
6	Pennsylvania	772,200	3.9%
43	Rhode Island	64,800	0.3%
23	South Carolina	281,100	1.4%
47	South Dakota	32,400	0.2%
17	Tennessee	393,800	2.0%
2	Texas	1,620,900	8.1%
29	Utah	193,600	1.0%
49	Vermont	26,800	0.1%
8	Virginia	701,800	3.5%
16	Washington	394,700	2.0%
41	West Virginia	67,100	0.3%
22	Wisconsin	312,400	1.6%
50	Wyoming	19,100	0.1%

RANK ORDER

RANK	STATE	EMPLOYEES	% of USA
1	California	2,618,100	13.1%
2	Texas	1,620,900	8.1%
3	New York	1,269,300	6.3%
4	Florida	1,244,300	6.2%
5	Illinois	929,600	4.6%
6	Pennsylvania	772,200	3.9%
7	Ohio	717,800	3.6%
8	Virginia	701,800	3.5%
9	Georgia	659,100	3.3%
10	Michigan	645,800	3.2%
11	New Jersey	643,400	3.2%
12	North Carolina	607,000	3.0%
13	Massachusetts	546,300	2.7%
14	Maryland	438,200	2.2%
15	Arizona	409,800	2.0%
16	Washington	394,700	2.0%
17	Tennessee	393,800	2.0%
18	Colorado	385,300	1.9%
19	Minnesota	368,500	1.8%
20	Missouri	357,500	1.8%
21	Indiana	324,100	1.6%
22	Wisconsin	312,400	1.6%
23	South Carolina	281,100	1.4%
24	Oregon	235,500	1.2%
25	Alabama	228,300	1.1%
26	Kentucky	221,000	1.1%
27	Connecticut	217,200	1.1%
28	Louisiana	216,500	1.1%
29	Utah	193,600	1.0%
30	Oklahoma	188,000	0.9%
31	Kansas	170,600	0.9%
32	Nevada	161,200	0.8%
33	Arkansas	141,300	0.7%
34	Iowa	139,500	0.7%
35	Nebraska	113,300	0.6%
36	Mississippi	104,700	0.5%
37	New Mexico	102,800	0.5%
38	Hawaii	84,200	0.4%
39	Idaho	82,900	0.4%
40	New Hampshire	72,900	0.4%
41	West Virginia	67,100	0.3%
42	Maine	66,500	0.3%
43	Rhode Island	64,800	0.3%
44	Delaware	62,600	0.3%
45	Montana	39,700	0.2%
46	North Dakota	36,300	0.2%
47	South Dakota	32,400	0.2%
48	Alaska	27,900	0.1%
49	Vermont	26,800	0.1%
50	Wyoming	19,100	0.1%
	District of Columbia	164,900	0.8%

Source: U.S. Department of Labor, Bureau of Labor Statistics
 "Regional and State Employment and Unemployment" (press release, January 26, 2016, www.bls.gov/bls/newsrels.htm)
*Seasonally adjusted preliminary data as of December 2015. National total calculated through a different formula.

Percent of Nonfarm Employees in Professional and Business Services in 2015

National Percent = 14.0% of Employees*

ALPHA ORDER

RANK	STATE	PERCENT
32	Alabama	11.6
47	Alaska	8.2
7	Arizona	15.3
33	Arkansas	11.5
3	California	16.0
9	Colorado	15.2
25	Connecticut	12.8
13	Delaware	13.9
9	Florida	15.2
7	Georgia	15.3
22	Hawaii	13.1
31	Idaho	12.0
5	Illinois	15.7
41	Indiana	10.6
44	Iowa	8.8
30	Kansas	12.1
33	Kentucky	11.5
38	Louisiana	10.9
39	Maine	10.8
2	Maryland	16.3
6	Massachusetts	15.5
11	Michigan	15.0
25	Minnesota	12.8
42	Mississippi	9.2
24	Missouri	12.9
45	Montana	8.7
36	Nebraska	11.2
25	Nevada	12.8
37	New Hampshire	11.1
4	New Jersey	15.9
28	New Mexico	12.4
16	New York	13.6
12	North Carolina	14.1
48	North Dakota	8.0
20	Ohio	13.2
35	Oklahoma	11.3
22	Oregon	13.1
20	Pennsylvania	13.2
19	Rhode Island	13.3
15	South Carolina	13.8
49	South Dakota	7.5
18	Tennessee	13.5
16	Texas	13.6
13	Utah	13.9
46	Vermont	8.5
1	Virginia	18.2
29	Washington	12.3
43	West Virginia	8.9
39	Wisconsin	10.8
50	Wyoming	6.6

RANK ORDER

RANK	STATE	PERCENT
1	Virginia	18.2
2	Maryland	16.3
3	California	16.0
4	New Jersey	15.9
5	Illinois	15.7
6	Massachusetts	15.5
7	Arizona	15.3
7	Georgia	15.3
9	Colorado	15.2
9	Florida	15.2
11	Michigan	15.0
12	North Carolina	14.1
13	Delaware	13.9
13	Utah	13.9
15	South Carolina	13.8
16	New York	13.6
16	Texas	13.6
18	Tennessee	13.5
19	Rhode Island	13.3
20	Ohio	13.2
20	Pennsylvania	13.2
22	Hawaii	13.1
22	Oregon	13.1
24	Missouri	12.9
25	Connecticut	12.8
25	Minnesota	12.8
25	Nevada	12.8
28	New Mexico	12.4
29	Washington	12.3
30	Kansas	12.1
31	Idaho	12.0
32	Alabama	11.6
33	Arkansas	11.5
33	Kentucky	11.5
35	Oklahoma	11.3
36	Nebraska	11.2
37	New Hampshire	11.1
38	Louisiana	10.9
39	Maine	10.8
39	Wisconsin	10.8
41	Indiana	10.6
42	Mississippi	9.2
43	West Virginia	8.9
44	Iowa	8.8
45	Montana	8.7
46	Vermont	8.5
47	Alaska	8.2
48	North Dakota	8.0
49	South Dakota	7.5
50	Wyoming	6.6

District of Columbia 21.4

Source: CQ Press using data from U.S. Department of Labor, Bureau of Labor Statistics
"Regional and State Employment and Unemployment" (press release, January 26, 2016, www.bls.gov/bls/newsrels.htm)
*Seasonally adjusted preliminary data as of December 2015. National figure calculated through a different formula.

Employees in Trade, Transportation, and Public Utilities in 2015

National Total = 27,114,000 Employees*

ALPHA ORDER

RANK	STATE	EMPLOYEES	% of USA
25	Alabama	382,700	1.4%
48	Alaska	69,000	0.3%
20	Arizona	508,400	1.9%
33	Arkansas	249,500	0.9%
1	California	2,984,700	11.0%
22	Colorado	436,600	1.6%
29	Connecticut	308,800	1.1%
46	Delaware	80,100	0.3%
3	Florida	1,694,500	6.2%
8	Georgia	909,200	3.4%
41	Hawaii	120,000	0.4%
38	Idaho	137,100	0.5%
5	Illinois	1,170,000	4.3%
14	Indiana	605,000	2.2%
28	Iowa	315,000	1.2%
31	Kansas	266,300	1.0%
24	Kentucky	385,100	1.4%
26	Louisiana	381,500	1.4%
42	Maine	119,700	0.4%
21	Maryland	464,900	1.7%
16	Massachusetts	560,200	2.1%
11	Michigan	769,500	2.8%
19	Minnesota	521,500	1.9%
35	Mississippi	222,900	0.8%
18	Missouri	525,100	1.9%
44	Montana	94,800	0.3%
36	Nebraska	206,300	0.8%
34	Nevada	231,300	0.9%
37	New Hampshire	140,600	0.5%
9	New Jersey	855,700	3.2%
39	New Mexico	136,400	0.5%
4	New York	1,569,500	5.8%
10	North Carolina	801,900	3.0%
43	North Dakota	102,400	0.4%
7	Ohio	1,017,300	3.8%
30	Oklahoma	306,000	1.1%
27	Oregon	337,700	1.2%
6	Pennsylvania	1,127,400	4.2%
47	Rhode Island	75,300	0.3%
23	South Carolina	390,400	1.4%
45	South Dakota	88,000	0.3%
13	Tennessee	620,300	2.3%
2	Texas	2,378,400	8.8%
32	Utah	263,500	1.0%
49	Vermont	55,800	0.2%
12	Virginia	655,300	2.4%
15	Washington	597,900	2.2%
40	West Virginia	134,900	0.5%
17	Wisconsin	530,200	2.0%
50	Wyoming	53,800	0.2%

RANK ORDER

RANK	STATE	EMPLOYEES	% of USA
1	California	2,984,700	11.0%
2	Texas	2,378,400	8.8%
3	Florida	1,694,500	6.2%
4	New York	1,569,500	5.8%
5	Illinois	1,170,000	4.3%
6	Pennsylvania	1,127,400	4.2%
7	Ohio	1,017,300	3.8%
8	Georgia	909,200	3.4%
9	New Jersey	855,700	3.2%
10	North Carolina	801,900	3.0%
11	Michigan	769,500	2.8%
12	Virginia	655,300	2.4%
13	Tennessee	620,300	2.3%
14	Indiana	605,000	2.2%
15	Washington	597,900	2.2%
16	Massachusetts	560,200	2.1%
17	Wisconsin	530,200	2.0%
18	Missouri	525,100	1.9%
19	Minnesota	521,500	1.9%
20	Arizona	508,400	1.9%
21	Maryland	464,900	1.7%
22	Colorado	436,600	1.6%
23	South Carolina	390,400	1.4%
24	Kentucky	385,100	1.4%
25	Alabama	382,700	1.4%
26	Louisiana	381,500	1.4%
27	Oregon	337,700	1.2%
28	Iowa	315,000	1.2%
29	Connecticut	308,800	1.1%
30	Oklahoma	306,000	1.1%
31	Kansas	266,300	1.0%
32	Utah	263,500	1.0%
33	Arkansas	249,500	0.9%
34	Nevada	231,300	0.9%
35	Mississippi	222,900	0.8%
36	Nebraska	206,300	0.8%
37	New Hampshire	140,600	0.5%
38	Idaho	137,100	0.5%
39	New Mexico	136,400	0.5%
40	West Virginia	134,900	0.5%
41	Hawaii	120,000	0.4%
42	Maine	119,700	0.4%
43	North Dakota	102,400	0.4%
44	Montana	94,800	0.3%
45	South Dakota	88,000	0.3%
46	Delaware	80,100	0.3%
47	Rhode Island	75,300	0.3%
48	Alaska	69,000	0.3%
49	Vermont	55,800	0.2%
50	Wyoming	53,800	0.2%
	District of Columbia	32,400	0.1%

Source: U.S. Department of Labor, Bureau of Labor Statistics
 "Regional and State Employment and Unemployment" (press release, January 26, 2016, www.bls.gov/bls/newsrels.htm)
*Seasonally adjusted preliminary data as of December 2015. National total calculated through a different formula.

Percent of Nonfarm Employees in Trade, Transportation, and Public Utilities in 2015
National Percent = 18.9% of Employees*

ALPHA ORDER

RANK	STATE	PERCENT
19	Alabama	19.5
10	Alaska	20.3
24	Arizona	19.0
8	Arkansas	20.4
36	California	18.3
44	Colorado	17.2
38	Connecticut	18.2
42	Delaware	17.8
6	Florida	20.7
4	Georgia	21.1
29	Hawaii	18.7
14	Idaho	19.9
16	Illinois	19.8
17	Indiana	19.7
14	Iowa	19.9
26	Kansas	18.9
12	Kentucky	20.1
21	Louisiana	19.3
19	Maine	19.5
44	Maryland	17.2
49	Massachusetts	15.9
41	Michigan	17.9
39	Minnesota	18.1
18	Mississippi	19.6
24	Missouri	19.0
6	Montana	20.7
8	Nebraska	20.4
34	Nevada	18.4
2	New Hampshire	21.4
4	New Jersey	21.1
48	New Mexico	16.4
47	New York	16.8
29	North Carolina	18.7
1	North Dakota	22.7
29	Ohio	18.7
34	Oklahoma	18.4
28	Oregon	18.8
22	Pennsylvania	19.2
50	Rhode Island	15.4
23	South Carolina	19.1
10	South Dakota	20.3
3	Tennessee	21.3
13	Texas	20.0
26	Utah	18.9
42	Vermont	17.8
46	Virginia	17.0
32	Washington	18.6
40	West Virginia	18.0
36	Wisconsin	18.3
32	Wyoming	18.6

RANK ORDER

RANK	STATE	PERCENT
1	North Dakota	22.7
2	New Hampshire	21.4
3	Tennessee	21.3
4	Georgia	21.1
4	New Jersey	21.1
6	Florida	20.7
6	Montana	20.7
8	Arkansas	20.4
8	Nebraska	20.4
10	Alaska	20.3
10	South Dakota	20.3
12	Kentucky	20.1
13	Texas	20.0
14	Idaho	19.9
14	Iowa	19.9
16	Illinois	19.8
17	Indiana	19.7
18	Mississippi	19.6
19	Alabama	19.5
19	Maine	19.5
21	Louisiana	19.3
22	Pennsylvania	19.2
23	South Carolina	19.1
24	Arizona	19.0
24	Missouri	19.0
26	Kansas	18.9
26	Utah	18.9
28	Oregon	18.8
29	Hawaii	18.7
29	North Carolina	18.7
29	Ohio	18.7
32	Washington	18.6
32	Wyoming	18.6
34	Nevada	18.4
34	Oklahoma	18.4
36	California	18.3
36	Wisconsin	18.3
38	Connecticut	18.2
39	Minnesota	18.1
40	West Virginia	18.0
41	Michigan	17.9
42	Delaware	17.8
42	Vermont	17.8
44	Colorado	17.2
44	Maryland	17.2
46	Virginia	17.0
47	New York	16.8
48	New Mexico	16.4
49	Massachusetts	15.9
50	Rhode Island	15.4
	District of Columbia	4.2

Source: CQ Press using data from U.S. Department of Labor, Bureau of Labor Statistics
"Regional and State Employment and Unemployment" (press release, January 26, 2016, www.bls.gov/bls/newsrels.htm)
*Seasonally adjusted preliminary data as of December 2015. National figure calculated through a different formula.

VII. Energy and Environment

Energy Consumption in 2013 211
Per Capita Energy Consumption in 2013 212
Energy Prices in 2013 213
Energy Expenditures in 2013 214
Per Capita Energy Expenditures in 2013 215
Average Monthly Electric Bill for Industrial Customers
    in 2014 216
Average Monthly Electric Bill for Commercial Customers
    in 2014 217
Average Monthly Electric Bill for Residential Customers
    in 2014 218
Electricity Generated through Renewable Sources
    in 2014 219
Percent of Electricity Generated through Renewable
    Sources in 2014 220
Average Price of Natural Gas Delivered to Industrial
    Customers in 2014 221
Average Price of Natural Gas Delivered to Commercial
    Customers in 2014 222

Average Price of Natural Gas Delivered to Residential
    Customers in 2014 223
Natural Gas Consumption in 2014 224
Coal Mines in 2013 225
Coal Production in 2013 226
Gasoline Used in 2014 227
Per Capita Gasoline Used in 2014 228
Daily Production of Crude Oil in 2014 229
Fossil Fuel Emissions in 2013 230
Per Capita Fossil Fuel Emissions in 2013 231
Percent Change in Fossil Fuel Emissions: 2009 to 2013 .. 232
Toxic Releases: Total Pollution Released in 2014 233
Toxic Releases: Total Air Emissions in 2014 234
Toxic Releases: Total Surface Water Discharges in 2014 .. 235
Hazardous Waste Sites on the National Priority List
    in 2016 236
Hazardous Waste Sites on the National Priority List per
    10,000 Square Miles in 2016 237
Hazardous Waste Sites Deleted from the National
    Priorities List as of 2016 238

Energy Consumption in 2013

National Total = 97,144,700,000,000,000 BTUs*

ALPHA ORDER

RANK	STATE	BTUs	% of USA
17	Alabama	1,931,400,000,000,000	2.0%
39	Alaska	609,000,000,000,000	0.6%
27	Arizona	1,414,800,000,000,000	1.5%
31	Arkansas	1,093,000,000,000,000	1.1%
2	California	7,684,100,000,000,000	7.9%
25	Colorado	1,471,800,000,000,000	1.5%
35	Connecticut	748,100,000,000,000	0.8%
48	Delaware	274,500,000,000,000	0.3%
3	Florida	4,077,900,000,000,000	4.2%
11	Georgia	2,795,400,000,000,000	2.9%
47	Hawaii	277,100,000,000,000	0.3%
42	Idaho	529,500,000,000,000	0.5%
4	Illinois	4,011,500,000,000,000	4.1%
9	Indiana	2,900,000,000,000,000	3.0%
24	Iowa	1,516,500,000,000,000	1.6%
29	Kansas	1,163,100,000,000,000	1.2%
20	Kentucky	1,822,700,000,000,000	1.9%
5	Louisiana	3,835,000,000,000,000	3.9%
43	Maine	407,100,000,000,000	0.4%
28	Maryland	1,403,800,000,000,000	1.4%
26	Massachusetts	1,442,600,000,000,000	1.5%
10	Michigan	2,843,200,000,000,000	2.9%
18	Minnesota	1,859,800,000,000,000	1.9%
30	Mississippi	1,141,800,000,000,000	1.2%
19	Missouri	1,857,000,000,000,000	1.9%
44	Montana	401,200,000,000,000	0.4%
33	Nebraska	871,800,000,000,000	0.9%
38	Nevada	657,100,000,000,000	0.7%
46	New Hampshire	302,800,000,000,000	0.3%
14	New Jersey	2,314,500,000,000,000	2.4%
37	New Mexico	688,500,000,000,000	0.7%
8	New York	3,625,300,000,000,000	3.7%
12	North Carolina	2,524,100,000,000,000	2.6%
40	North Dakota	588,600,000,000,000	0.6%
7	Ohio	3,745,400,000,000,000	3.9%
22	Oklahoma	1,622,800,000,000,000	1.7%
32	Oregon	996,700,000,000,000	1.0%
6	Pennsylvania	3,795,000,000,000,000	3.9%
49	Rhode Island	193,600,000,000,000	0.2%
23	South Carolina	1,591,400,000,000,000	1.6%
45	South Dakota	390,400,000,000,000	0.4%
15	Tennessee	2,135,900,000,000,000	2.2%
1	Texas	12,944,100,000,000,000	13.3%
34	Utah	830,600,000,000,000	0.9%
50	Vermont	133,600,000,000,000	0.1%
13	Virginia	2,410,700,000,000,000	2.5%
16	Washington	2,039,300,000,000,000	2.1%
36	West Virginia	737,800,000,000,000	0.8%
21	Wisconsin	1,804,000,000,000,000	1.9%
41	Wyoming	535,500,000,000,000	0.6%

RANK ORDER

RANK	STATE	BTUs	% of USA
1	Texas	12,944,100,000,000,000	13.3%
2	California	7,684,100,000,000,000	7.9%
3	Florida	4,077,900,000,000,000	4.2%
4	Illinois	4,011,500,000,000,000	4.1%
5	Louisiana	3,835,000,000,000,000	3.9%
6	Pennsylvania	3,795,000,000,000,000	3.9%
7	Ohio	3,745,400,000,000,000	3.9%
8	New York	3,625,300,000,000,000	3.7%
9	Indiana	2,900,000,000,000,000	3.0%
10	Michigan	2,843,200,000,000,000	2.9%
11	Georgia	2,795,400,000,000,000	2.9%
12	North Carolina	2,524,100,000,000,000	2.6%
13	Virginia	2,410,700,000,000,000	2.5%
14	New Jersey	2,314,500,000,000,000	2.4%
15	Tennessee	2,135,900,000,000,000	2.2%
16	Washington	2,039,300,000,000,000	2.1%
17	Alabama	1,931,400,000,000,000	2.0%
18	Minnesota	1,859,800,000,000,000	1.9%
19	Missouri	1,857,000,000,000,000	1.9%
20	Kentucky	1,822,700,000,000,000	1.9%
21	Wisconsin	1,804,000,000,000,000	1.9%
22	Oklahoma	1,622,800,000,000,000	1.7%
23	South Carolina	1,591,400,000,000,000	1.6%
24	Iowa	1,516,500,000,000,000	1.6%
25	Colorado	1,471,800,000,000,000	1.5%
26	Massachusetts	1,442,600,000,000,000	1.5%
27	Arizona	1,414,800,000,000,000	1.5%
28	Maryland	1,403,800,000,000,000	1.4%
29	Kansas	1,163,100,000,000,000	1.2%
30	Mississippi	1,141,800,000,000,000	1.2%
31	Arkansas	1,093,000,000,000,000	1.1%
32	Oregon	996,700,000,000,000	1.0%
33	Nebraska	871,800,000,000,000	0.9%
34	Utah	830,600,000,000,000	0.9%
35	Connecticut	748,100,000,000,000	0.8%
36	West Virginia	737,800,000,000,000	0.8%
37	New Mexico	688,500,000,000,000	0.7%
38	Nevada	657,100,000,000,000	0.7%
39	Alaska	609,000,000,000,000	0.6%
40	North Dakota	588,600,000,000,000	0.6%
41	Wyoming	535,500,000,000,000	0.6%
42	Idaho	529,500,000,000,000	0.5%
43	Maine	407,100,000,000,000	0.4%
44	Montana	401,200,000,000,000	0.4%
45	South Dakota	390,400,000,000,000	0.4%
46	New Hampshire	302,800,000,000,000	0.3%
47	Hawaii	277,100,000,000,000	0.3%
48	Delaware	274,500,000,000,000	0.3%
49	Rhode Island	193,600,000,000,000	0.2%
50	Vermont	133,600,000,000,000	0.1%
	District of Columbia	170,900,000,000,000	0.2%

Source: U.S. Department of Energy, Energy Information Administration
"State Energy Data 2013: Consumption" (http://www.eia.gov/state/seds/)
*British Thermal Units: The amount of heat required to raise the temperature of one pound of water one degree. National total includes 17.4 trillion Btu of net imports of coal coke that are not allocated to the states.

Per Capita Energy Consumption in 2013

National Per Capita = 307,004,708 BTUs*

ALPHA ORDER

RANK	STATE	PER CAPITA
13	Alabama	399,831,654
3	Alaska	825,827,658
43	Arizona	213,367,952
17	Arkansas	369,511,795
47	California	200,033,175
35	Colorado	279,218,961
46	Connecticut	207,969,158
29	Delaware	296,643,551
45	Florida	208,114,872
34	Georgia	279,776,075
48	Hawaii	196,697,107
22	Idaho	328,314,065
25	Illinois	311,220,381
9	Indiana	441,365,506
5	Iowa	490,423,721
12	Kansas	401,813,012
11	Kentucky	414,391,270
2	Louisiana	828,742,833
27	Maine	306,371,719
39	Maryland	236,487,625
42	Massachusetts	215,030,684
32	Michigan	287,177,241
18	Minnesota	343,102,284
16	Mississippi	381,748,299
26	Missouri	307,261,701
15	Montana	395,503,952
7	Nebraska	466,377,788
40	Nevada	235,488,821
41	New Hampshire	228,932,606
36	New Jersey	259,840,600
20	New Mexico	329,916,766
49	New York	184,109,192
37	North Carolina	256,372,702
4	North Dakota	813,403,609
23	Ohio	323,654,071
10	Oklahoma	421,134,036
38	Oregon	253,740,425
28	Pennsylvania	296,866,219
50	Rhode Island	183,880,797
19	South Carolina	333,731,921
8	South Dakota	461,864,256
21	Tennessee	328,795,760
6	Texas	488,444,181
33	Utah	286,050,312
44	Vermont	213,034,320
31	Virginia	291,574,316
30	Washington	292,444,833
14	West Virginia	398,168,361
24	Wisconsin	314,085,827
1	Wyoming	918,318,525

RANK ORDER

RANK	STATE	PER CAPITA
1	Wyoming	918,318,525
2	Louisiana	828,742,833
3	Alaska	825,827,658
4	North Dakota	813,403,609
5	Iowa	490,423,721
6	Texas	488,444,181
7	Nebraska	466,377,788
8	South Dakota	461,864,256
9	Indiana	441,365,506
10	Oklahoma	421,134,036
11	Kentucky	414,391,270
12	Kansas	401,813,012
13	Alabama	399,831,654
14	West Virginia	398,168,361
15	Montana	395,503,952
16	Mississippi	381,748,299
17	Arkansas	369,511,795
18	Minnesota	343,102,284
19	South Carolina	333,731,921
20	New Mexico	329,916,766
21	Tennessee	328,795,760
22	Idaho	328,314,065
23	Ohio	323,654,071
24	Wisconsin	314,085,827
25	Illinois	311,220,381
26	Missouri	307,261,701
27	Maine	306,371,719
28	Pennsylvania	296,866,219
29	Delaware	296,643,551
30	Washington	292,444,833
31	Virginia	291,574,316
32	Michigan	287,177,241
33	Utah	286,050,312
34	Georgia	279,776,075
35	Colorado	279,218,961
36	New Jersey	259,840,600
37	North Carolina	256,372,702
38	Oregon	253,740,425
39	Maryland	236,487,625
40	Nevada	235,488,821
41	New Hampshire	228,932,606
42	Massachusetts	215,030,684
43	Arizona	213,367,952
44	Vermont	213,034,320
45	Florida	208,114,872
46	Connecticut	207,969,158
47	California	200,033,175
48	Hawaii	196,697,107
49	New York	184,109,192
50	Rhode Island	183,880,797
	District of Columbia	263,109,277

Source: CQ Press using data from U.S. Department of Energy, Energy Information Administration
"State Energy Data 2013: Consumption" (http://www.eia.gov/state/seds/)
*British Thermal Units: The amount of heat required to raise the temperature of one pound of water one degree. National figure includes 17.4 trillion Btu of net imports of coal coke that are not allocated to the states.

Energy Prices in 2013

National Rate = $21.41 per Million BTUs*

ALPHA ORDER

RANK	STATE	RATE
43	Alabama	$18.90
10	Alaska	24.92
7	Arizona	25.98
41	Arkansas	19.51
12	California	24.77
30	Colorado	21.15
4	Connecticut	27.89
13	Delaware	24.18
9	Florida	25.11
28	Georgia	21.27
1	Hawaii	38.90
38	Idaho	19.96
46	Illinois	18.46
48	Indiana	17.79
48	Iowa	17.79
27	Kansas	21.32
31	Kentucky	20.85
50	Louisiana	15.88
23	Maine	21.87
8	Maryland	25.44
6	Massachusetts	26.35
35	Michigan	20.39
40	Minnesota	19.70
29	Mississippi	21.20
18	Missouri	22.43
19	Montana	22.15
42	Nebraska	19.34
17	Nevada	22.86
3	New Hampshire	27.90
14	New Jersey	23.60
16	New Mexico	22.92
11	New York	24.82
15	North Carolina	23.36
45	North Dakota	18.53
36	Ohio	20.01
39	Oklahoma	19.82
21	Oregon	22.04
24	Pennsylvania	21.73
5	Rhode Island	26.51
22	South Carolina	21.95
36	South Dakota	20.01
25	Tennessee	21.61
43	Texas	18.90
33	Utah	20.45
2	Vermont	28.72
20	Virginia	22.05
26	Washington	21.39
32	West Virginia	20.53
34	Wisconsin	20.41
47	Wyoming	18.39

RANK ORDER

RANK	STATE	RATE
1	Hawaii	$38.90
2	Vermont	28.72
3	New Hampshire	27.90
4	Connecticut	27.89
5	Rhode Island	26.51
6	Massachusetts	26.35
7	Arizona	25.98
8	Maryland	25.44
9	Florida	25.11
10	Alaska	24.92
11	New York	24.82
12	California	24.77
13	Delaware	24.18
14	New Jersey	23.60
15	North Carolina	23.36
16	New Mexico	22.92
17	Nevada	22.86
18	Missouri	22.43
19	Montana	22.15
20	Virginia	22.05
21	Oregon	22.04
22	South Carolina	21.95
23	Maine	21.87
24	Pennsylvania	21.73
25	Tennessee	21.61
26	Washington	21.39
27	Kansas	21.32
28	Georgia	21.27
29	Mississippi	21.20
30	Colorado	21.15
31	Kentucky	20.85
32	West Virginia	20.53
33	Utah	20.45
34	Wisconsin	20.41
35	Michigan	20.39
36	Ohio	20.01
36	South Dakota	20.01
38	Idaho	19.96
39	Oklahoma	19.82
40	Minnesota	19.70
41	Arkansas	19.51
42	Nebraska	19.34
43	Alabama	18.90
43	Texas	18.90
45	North Dakota	18.53
46	Illinois	18.46
47	Wyoming	18.39
48	Indiana	17.79
48	Iowa	17.79
50	Louisiana	15.88
	District of Columbia	25.53

Source: U.S. Department of Energy, Energy Information Administration
"State Energy Data 2013: Prices and Expenditures" (http://www.eia.gov/state/seds/)
*British Thermal Units: The amount of heat required to raise the temperature of one pound of water one degree.

Energy Expenditures in 2013

National Total = $1,375,305,900,000*

ALPHA ORDER

RANK	STATE	EXPENDITURES	% of USA
21	Alabama	$24,155,600,000	1.8%
42	Alaska	7,074,500,000	0.5%
23	Arizona	22,785,400,000	1.7%
33	Arkansas	14,001,500,000	1.0%
2	California	136,935,800,000	10.0%
26	Colorado	19,701,200,000	1.4%
30	Connecticut	15,334,600,000	1.1%
49	Delaware	3,853,800,000	0.3%
3	Florida	66,153,000,000	4.8%
9	Georgia	40,021,300,000	2.9%
40	Hawaii	7,537,800,000	0.5%
43	Idaho	6,962,900,000	0.5%
7	Illinois	49,296,600,000	3.6%
14	Indiana	33,371,600,000	2.4%
28	Iowa	17,265,400,000	1.3%
31	Kansas	15,253,100,000	1.1%
24	Kentucky	22,422,900,000	1.6%
10	Louisiana	39,557,800,000	2.9%
41	Maine	7,449,100,000	0.5%
22	Maryland	22,971,600,000	1.7%
16	Massachusetts	27,837,200,000	2.0%
8	Michigan	40,646,900,000	3.0%
20	Minnesota	24,689,500,000	1.8%
29	Mississippi	15,761,600,000	1.1%
17	Missouri	26,721,700,000	1.9%
45	Montana	5,532,800,000	0.4%
35	Nebraska	10,293,800,000	0.7%
36	Nevada	10,178,200,000	0.7%
44	New Hampshire	6,083,400,000	0.4%
11	New Jersey	39,242,800,000	2.9%
37	New Mexico	9,155,100,000	0.7%
4	New York	65,971,700,000	4.8%
12	North Carolina	37,331,500,000	2.7%
39	North Dakota	7,629,200,000	0.6%
6	Ohio	50,156,400,000	3.6%
27	Oklahoma	19,545,900,000	1.4%
32	Oregon	14,878,700,000	1.1%
5	Pennsylvania	54,066,800,000	3.9%
48	Rhode Island	3,912,900,000	0.3%
25	South Carolina	21,726,300,000	1.6%
47	South Dakota	4,708,900,000	0.3%
15	Tennessee	28,924,700,000	2.1%
1	Texas	162,054,400,000	11.8%
34	Utah	11,005,200,000	0.8%
50	Vermont	3,256,900,000	0.2%
13	Virginia	34,283,200,000	2.5%
18	Washington	26,508,900,000	1.9%
38	West Virginia	8,886,000,000	0.6%
19	Wisconsin	24,715,900,000	1.8%
46	Wyoming	5,457,500,000	0.4%

RANK ORDER

RANK	STATE	EXPENDITURES	% of USA
1	Texas	$162,054,400,000	11.8%
2	California	136,935,800,000	10.0%
3	Florida	66,153,000,000	4.8%
4	New York	65,971,700,000	4.8%
5	Pennsylvania	54,066,800,000	3.9%
6	Ohio	50,156,400,000	3.6%
7	Illinois	49,296,600,000	3.6%
8	Michigan	40,646,900,000	3.0%
9	Georgia	40,021,300,000	2.9%
10	Louisiana	39,557,800,000	2.9%
11	New Jersey	39,242,800,000	2.9%
12	North Carolina	37,331,500,000	2.7%
13	Virginia	34,283,200,000	2.5%
14	Indiana	33,371,600,000	2.4%
15	Tennessee	28,924,700,000	2.1%
16	Massachusetts	27,837,200,000	2.0%
17	Missouri	26,721,700,000	1.9%
18	Washington	26,508,900,000	1.9%
19	Wisconsin	24,715,900,000	1.8%
20	Minnesota	24,689,500,000	1.8%
21	Alabama	24,155,600,000	1.8%
22	Maryland	22,971,600,000	1.7%
23	Arizona	22,785,400,000	1.7%
24	Kentucky	22,422,900,000	1.6%
25	South Carolina	21,726,300,000	1.6%
26	Colorado	19,701,200,000	1.4%
27	Oklahoma	19,545,900,000	1.4%
28	Iowa	17,265,400,000	1.3%
29	Mississippi	15,761,600,000	1.1%
30	Connecticut	15,334,600,000	1.1%
31	Kansas	15,253,100,000	1.1%
32	Oregon	14,878,700,000	1.1%
33	Arkansas	14,001,500,000	1.0%
34	Utah	11,005,200,000	0.8%
35	Nebraska	10,293,800,000	0.7%
36	Nevada	10,178,200,000	0.7%
37	New Mexico	9,155,100,000	0.7%
38	West Virginia	8,886,000,000	0.6%
39	North Dakota	7,629,200,000	0.6%
40	Hawaii	7,537,800,000	0.5%
41	Maine	7,449,100,000	0.5%
42	Alaska	7,074,500,000	0.5%
43	Idaho	6,962,900,000	0.5%
44	New Hampshire	6,083,400,000	0.4%
45	Montana	5,532,800,000	0.4%
46	Wyoming	5,457,500,000	0.4%
47	South Dakota	4,708,900,000	0.3%
48	Rhode Island	3,912,900,000	0.3%
49	Delaware	3,853,800,000	0.3%
50	Vermont	3,256,900,000	0.2%
	District of Columbia	2,192,600,000	0.2%

Source: U.S. Department of Energy, Energy Information Administration
"State Energy Data 2013: Prices and Expenditures" (http://www.eia.gov/state/seds/)
*The national total includes a negative $156 million for coal coke net imports, which is not allocated to the states.

Per Capita Energy Expenditures in 2013

National Per Capita = $4,346

ALPHA ORDER

RANK	STATE	PER CAPITA
18	Alabama	$5,001
2	Alaska	9,593
48	Arizona	3,436
20	Arkansas	4,734
47	California	3,565
44	Colorado	3,738
31	Connecticut	4,263
33	Delaware	4,165
49	Florida	3,376
37	Georgia	4,006
11	Hawaii	5,351
29	Idaho	4,317
39	Illinois	3,825
16	Indiana	5,079
7	Iowa	5,583
13	Kansas	5,269
15	Kentucky	5,098
4	Louisiana	8,548
6	Maine	5,606
38	Maryland	3,870
34	Massachusetts	4,149
36	Michigan	4,106
23	Minnesota	4,555
12	Mississippi	5,270
25	Missouri	4,421
10	Montana	5,454
9	Nebraska	5,507
46	Nevada	3,648
21	New Hampshire	4,599
26	New Jersey	4,406
27	New Mexico	4,387
50	New York	3,350
41	North Carolina	3,792
1	North Dakota	10,543
28	Ohio	4,334
17	Oklahoma	5,072
43	Oregon	3,788
32	Pennsylvania	4,229
45	Rhode Island	3,716
22	South Carolina	4,556
8	South Dakota	5,571
24	Tennessee	4,453
5	Texas	6,115
42	Utah	3,790
14	Vermont	5,193
35	Virginia	4,147
40	Washington	3,801
19	West Virginia	4,796
30	Wisconsin	4,303
3	Wyoming	9,359

RANK ORDER

RANK	STATE	PER CAPITA
1	North Dakota	$10,543
2	Alaska	9,593
3	Wyoming	9,359
4	Louisiana	8,548
5	Texas	6,115
6	Maine	5,606
7	Iowa	5,583
8	South Dakota	5,571
9	Nebraska	5,507
10	Montana	5,454
11	Hawaii	5,351
12	Mississippi	5,270
13	Kansas	5,269
14	Vermont	5,193
15	Kentucky	5,098
16	Indiana	5,079
17	Oklahoma	5,072
18	Alabama	5,001
19	West Virginia	4,796
20	Arkansas	4,734
21	New Hampshire	4,599
22	South Carolina	4,556
23	Minnesota	4,555
24	Tennessee	4,453
25	Missouri	4,421
26	New Jersey	4,406
27	New Mexico	4,387
28	Ohio	4,334
29	Idaho	4,317
30	Wisconsin	4,303
31	Connecticut	4,263
32	Pennsylvania	4,229
33	Delaware	4,165
34	Massachusetts	4,149
35	Virginia	4,147
36	Michigan	4,106
37	Georgia	4,006
38	Maryland	3,870
39	Illinois	3,825
40	Washington	3,801
41	North Carolina	3,792
42	Utah	3,790
43	Oregon	3,788
44	Colorado	3,738
45	Rhode Island	3,716
46	Nevada	3,648
47	California	3,565
48	Arizona	3,436
49	Florida	3,376
50	New York	3,350
	District of Columbia	3,376

Source: CQ Press using data from U.S. Department of Energy, Energy Information Administration "State Energy Data 2013: Prices and Expenditures" (http://www.eia.gov/state/seds/)

Average Monthly Electric Bill for Industrial Customers in 2014

National Average = $7,036 per Month

ALPHA ORDER

RANK	STATE	MONTHLY BILL
8	Alabama	$24,540
16	Alaska	13,791
21	Arizona	10,243
47	Arkansas	2,341
42	California	3,701
38	Colorado	4,893
27	Connecticut	8,139
10	Delaware	20,707
29	Florida	5,796
24	Georgia	8,685
1	Hawaii	129,766
49	Idaho	1,763
4	Illinois	41,506
12	Indiana	15,738
17	Iowa	13,143
45	Kansas	2,789
11	Kentucky	20,704
23	Louisiana	8,950
25	Maine	8,281
44	Maryland	3,300
31	Massachusetts	5,674
13	Michigan	15,621
18	Minnesota	13,064
26	Mississippi	8,218
22	Missouri	8,966
48	Montana	2,017
50	Nebraska	1,157
9	Nevada	22,065
28	New Hampshire	5,857
30	New Jersey	5,792
40	New Mexico	4,551
19	New York	12,553
15	North Carolina	14,097
33	North Dakota	5,518
14	Ohio	14,928
39	Oklahoma	4,747
46	Oregon	2,695
20	Pennsylvania	12,320
37	Rhode Island	5,047
5	South Carolina	33,581
41	South Dakota	4,525
2	Tennessee	101,542
34	Texas	5,516
35	Utah	5,229
3	Vermont	53,985
6	Virginia	27,823
43	Washington	3,331
36	West Virginia	5,167
7	Wisconsin	27,304
32	Wyoming	5,540

RANK ORDER

RANK	STATE	MONTHLY BILL
1	Hawaii	$129,766
2	Tennessee	101,542
3	Vermont	53,985
4	Illinois	41,506
5	South Carolina	33,581
6	Virginia	27,823
7	Wisconsin	27,304
8	Alabama	24,540
9	Nevada	22,065
10	Delaware	20,707
11	Kentucky	20,704
12	Indiana	15,738
13	Michigan	15,621
14	Ohio	14,928
15	North Carolina	14,097
16	Alaska	13,791
17	Iowa	13,143
18	Minnesota	13,064
19	New York	12,553
20	Pennsylvania	12,320
21	Arizona	10,243
22	Missouri	8,966
23	Louisiana	8,950
24	Georgia	8,685
25	Maine	8,281
26	Mississippi	8,218
27	Connecticut	8,139
28	New Hampshire	5,857
29	Florida	5,796
30	New Jersey	5,792
31	Massachusetts	5,674
32	Wyoming	5,540
33	North Dakota	5,518
34	Texas	5,516
35	Utah	5,229
36	West Virginia	5,167
37	Rhode Island	5,047
38	Colorado	4,893
39	Oklahoma	4,747
40	New Mexico	4,551
41	South Dakota	4,525
42	California	3,701
43	Washington	3,331
44	Maryland	3,300
45	Kansas	2,789
46	Oregon	2,695
47	Arkansas	2,341
48	Montana	2,017
49	Idaho	1,763
50	Nebraska	1,157
	District of Columbia	1,697,258

Source: U.S. Department of Energy, Energy Information Administration
"Electric Sales, Revenue and Average Price 2014" (http://www.eia.gov/electricity/sales_revenue_price/index.cfm)

Average Monthly Electric Bill for Commercial Customers in 2014

National Average = $678 per Month

ALPHA ORDER

RANK	STATE	MONTHLY BILL
28	Alabama	$571
9	Alaska	771
8	Arizona	792
46	Arkansas	433
5	California	928
43	Colorado	469
3	Connecticut	1,075
13	Delaware	703
19	Florida	647
12	Georgia	728
1	Hawaii	1,504
49	Idaho	380
17	Illinois	651
26	Indiana	574
47	Iowa	398
26	Kansas	574
37	Kentucky	507
20	Louisiana	624
44	Maine	461
2	Maryland	1,116
7	Massachusetts	800
18	Michigan	648
16	Minnesota	658
29	Mississippi	552
24	Missouri	612
48	Montana	382
45	Nebraska	458
41	Nevada	471
38	New Hampshire	504
6	New Jersey	817
30	New Mexico	549
4	New York	984
33	North Carolina	528
25	North Dakota	583
21	Ohio	621
39	Oklahoma	501
34	Oregon	509
34	Pennsylvania	509
11	Rhode Island	761
32	South Carolina	531
40	South Dakota	486
23	Tennessee	614
15	Texas	662
14	Utah	667
42	Vermont	470
10	Virginia	767
31	Washington	537
50	West Virginia	373
22	Wisconsin	616
34	Wyoming	509

RANK ORDER

RANK	STATE	MONTHLY BILL
1	Hawaii	$1,504
2	Maryland	1,116
3	Connecticut	1,075
4	New York	984
5	California	928
6	New Jersey	817
7	Massachusetts	800
8	Arizona	792
9	Alaska	771
10	Virginia	767
11	Rhode Island	761
12	Georgia	728
13	Delaware	703
14	Utah	667
15	Texas	662
16	Minnesota	658
17	Illinois	651
18	Michigan	648
19	Florida	647
20	Louisiana	624
21	Ohio	621
22	Wisconsin	616
23	Tennessee	614
24	Missouri	612
25	North Dakota	583
26	Indiana	574
26	Kansas	574
28	Alabama	571
29	Mississippi	552
30	New Mexico	549
31	Washington	537
32	South Carolina	531
33	North Carolina	528
34	Oregon	509
34	Pennsylvania	509
34	Wyoming	509
37	Kentucky	507
38	New Hampshire	504
39	Oklahoma	501
40	South Dakota	486
41	Nevada	471
42	Vermont	470
43	Colorado	469
44	Maine	461
45	Nebraska	458
46	Arkansas	433
47	Iowa	398
48	Montana	382
49	Idaho	380
50	West Virginia	373
	District of Columbia	3,283

Source: U.S. Department of Energy, Energy Information Administration
"Electric Sales, Revenue and Average Price 2014" (http://www.eia.gov/electricity/sales_revenue_price/index.cfm)

Average Monthly Electric Bill for Residential Customers in 2014

National Average = $114 per Month

ALPHA ORDER

RANK	STATE	MONTHLY BILL
3	Alabama	$145
18	Alaska	116
15	Arizona	121
27	Arkansas	109
42	California	91
47	Colorado	84
4	Connecticut	144
12	Delaware	126
10	Florida	130
8	Georgia	134
1	Hawaii	188
39	Idaho	96
44	Illinois	89
18	Indiana	116
35	Iowa	99
24	Kansas	113
16	Kentucky	120
14	Louisiana	124
47	Maine	84
6	Maryland	140
31	Massachusetts	107
40	Michigan	95
37	Minnesota	97
5	Mississippi	141
18	Missouri	116
45	Montana	87
32	Nebraska	106
18	Nevada	116
27	New Hampshire	109
32	New Jersey	106
50	New Mexico	78
17	New York	119
12	North Carolina	126
24	North Dakota	113
24	Ohio	113
22	Oklahoma	114
37	Oregon	97
22	Pennsylvania	114
34	Rhode Island	100
2	South Carolina	148
27	South Dakota	109
9	Tennessee	133
7	Texas	137
49	Utah	79
35	Vermont	99
10	Virginia	130
45	Washington	87
30	West Virginia	108
40	Wisconsin	95
42	Wyoming	91

RANK ORDER

RANK	STATE	MONTHLY BILL
1	Hawaii	$188
2	South Carolina	148
3	Alabama	145
4	Connecticut	144
5	Mississippi	141
6	Maryland	140
7	Texas	137
8	Georgia	134
9	Tennessee	133
10	Florida	130
10	Virginia	130
12	Delaware	126
12	North Carolina	126
14	Louisiana	124
15	Arizona	121
16	Kentucky	120
17	New York	119
18	Alaska	116
18	Indiana	116
18	Missouri	116
18	Nevada	116
22	Oklahoma	114
22	Pennsylvania	114
24	Kansas	113
24	North Dakota	113
24	Ohio	113
27	Arkansas	109
27	New Hampshire	109
27	South Dakota	109
30	West Virginia	108
31	Massachusetts	107
32	Nebraska	106
32	New Jersey	106
34	Rhode Island	100
35	Iowa	99
35	Vermont	99
37	Minnesota	97
37	Oregon	97
39	Idaho	96
40	Michigan	95
40	Wisconsin	95
42	California	91
42	Wyoming	91
44	Illinois	89
45	Montana	87
45	Washington	87
47	Colorado	84
47	Maine	84
49	Utah	79
50	New Mexico	78
	District of Columbia	92

Source: U.S. Department of Energy, Energy Information Administration "Electric Sales, Revenue and Average Price 2014" (http://www.eia.gov/electricity/sales_revenue_price/index.cfm)

Electricity Generated through Renewable Sources in 2014

National Total = 538,579,319,800 Kilowatthours*

ALPHA ORDER

RANK	STATE	KWH	% of USA
10	Alabama	12,245,893,030	2.3%
44	Alaska	1,753,206,680	0.3%
15	Arizona	9,958,627,070	1.8%
31	Arkansas	4,169,992,660	0.8%
2	California	58,448,097,440	10.9%
16	Colorado	9,517,186,730	1.8%
48	Connecticut	1,202,806,220	0.2%
50	Delaware	131,080,380	0.0%
26	Florida	5,284,496,340	1.0%
23	Georgia	7,346,955,800	1.4%
47	Hawaii	1,299,832,920	0.2%
9	Idaho	12,479,328,510	2.3%
13	Illinois	10,831,681,260	2.0%
30	Indiana	4,359,860,330	0.8%
6	Iowa	17,451,604,920	3.2%
12	Kansas	10,920,291,690	2.0%
34	Kentucky	3,591,556,370	0.7%
33	Louisiana	3,869,642,160	0.7%
20	Maine	8,114,963,270	1.5%
39	Maryland	2,604,397,430	0.5%
38	Massachusetts	2,632,028,050	0.5%
19	Michigan	8,274,373,880	1.5%
11	Minnesota	12,005,328,200	2.2%
46	Mississippi	1,507,948,560	0.3%
42	Missouri	1,952,782,580	0.4%
8	Montana	13,469,554,080	2.5%
32	Nebraska	3,958,905,250	0.7%
24	Nevada	6,456,172,000	1.2%
35	New Hampshire	3,333,750,700	0.6%
45	New Jersey	1,552,829,730	0.3%
36	New Mexico	2,911,100,640	0.5%
5	New York	32,533,527,180	6.0%
21	North Carolina	8,031,914,520	1.5%
17	North Dakota	8,736,424,000	1.6%
40	Ohio	2,503,800,710	0.5%
7	Oklahoma	13,703,661,160	2.5%
3	Oregon	44,175,468,480	8.2%
18	Pennsylvania	8,721,580,330	1.6%
49	Rhode Island	230,378,350	0.0%
28	South Carolina	5,011,621,270	0.9%
22	South Dakota	7,834,507,260	1.5%
14	Tennessee	10,041,648,550	1.9%
4	Texas	42,481,611,920	7.9%
43	Utah	1,889,121,170	0.4%
41	Vermont	1,962,874,390	0.4%
29	Virginia	4,806,991,170	0.9%
1	Washington	88,571,311,220	16.4%
37	West Virginia	2,697,972,040	0.5%
25	Wisconsin	5,734,164,130	1.1%
27	Wyoming	5,274,467,150	1.0%

RANK ORDER

RANK	STATE	KWH	% of USA
1	Washington	88,571,311,220	16.4%
2	California	58,448,097,440	10.9%
3	Oregon	44,175,468,480	8.2%
4	Texas	42,481,611,920	7.9%
5	New York	32,533,527,180	6.0%
6	Iowa	17,451,604,920	3.2%
7	Oklahoma	13,703,661,160	2.5%
8	Montana	13,469,554,080	2.5%
9	Idaho	12,479,328,510	2.3%
10	Alabama	12,245,893,030	2.3%
11	Minnesota	12,005,328,200	2.2%
12	Kansas	10,920,291,690	2.0%
13	Illinois	10,831,681,260	2.0%
14	Tennessee	10,041,648,550	1.9%
15	Arizona	9,958,627,070	1.8%
16	Colorado	9,517,186,730	1.8%
17	North Dakota	8,736,424,000	1.6%
18	Pennsylvania	8,721,580,330	1.6%
19	Michigan	8,274,373,880	1.5%
20	Maine	8,114,963,270	1.5%
21	North Carolina	8,031,914,520	1.5%
22	South Dakota	7,834,507,260	1.5%
23	Georgia	7,346,955,800	1.4%
24	Nevada	6,456,172,000	1.2%
25	Wisconsin	5,734,164,130	1.1%
26	Florida	5,284,496,340	1.0%
27	Wyoming	5,274,467,150	1.0%
28	South Carolina	5,011,621,270	0.9%
29	Virginia	4,806,991,170	0.9%
30	Indiana	4,359,860,330	0.8%
31	Arkansas	4,169,992,660	0.8%
32	Nebraska	3,958,905,250	0.7%
33	Louisiana	3,869,642,160	0.7%
34	Kentucky	3,591,556,370	0.7%
35	New Hampshire	3,333,750,700	0.6%
36	New Mexico	2,911,100,640	0.5%
37	West Virginia	2,697,972,040	0.5%
38	Massachusetts	2,632,028,050	0.5%
39	Maryland	2,604,397,430	0.5%
40	Ohio	2,503,800,710	0.5%
41	Vermont	1,962,874,390	0.4%
42	Missouri	1,952,782,580	0.4%
43	Utah	1,889,121,170	0.4%
44	Alaska	1,753,206,680	0.3%
45	New Jersey	1,552,829,730	0.3%
46	Mississippi	1,507,948,560	0.3%
47	Hawaii	1,299,832,920	0.2%
48	Connecticut	1,202,806,220	0.2%
49	Rhode Island	230,378,350	0.0%
50	Delaware	131,080,380	0.0%
	District of Columbia	0	0.0%

Source: U.S. Department of Energy, Energy Information Administration
"Electricity" (http://www.eia.gov/electricity/data/state/)
*Includes hydroelectric, geothermal, solar thermal and photovoltaic, wind, wood and wood-derived fuels, and other biomass.

Percent of Electricity Generated through Renewable Sources in 2014

National Percent = 13.2%*

ALPHA ORDER

RANK	STATE	PERCENT
28	Alabama	8.2
9	Alaska	29.0
26	Arizona	8.9
31	Arkansas	6.8
8	California	29.4
17	Colorado	17.7
43	Connecticut	3.6
50	Delaware	1.7
46	Florida	2.3
34	Georgia	5.8
19	Hawaii	12.7
1	Idaho	82.2
35	Illinois	5.4
40	Indiana	3.8
7	Iowa	30.7
13	Kansas	22.0
38	Kentucky	4.0
41	Louisiana	3.7
5	Maine	61.3
30	Maryland	6.9
27	Massachusetts	8.5
29	Michigan	7.7
14	Minnesota	21.1
45	Mississippi	2.7
48	Missouri	2.2
6	Montana	44.5
22	Nebraska	10.0
16	Nevada	17.9
18	New Hampshire	17.1
46	New Jersey	2.3
25	New Mexico	9.0
12	New York	23.7
32	North Carolina	6.3
11	North Dakota	24.0
49	Ohio	1.9
15	Oklahoma	19.5
3	Oregon	73.5
39	Pennsylvania	3.9
41	Rhode Island	3.7
36	South Carolina	5.2
4	South Dakota	71.3
20	Tennessee	12.6
23	Texas	9.7
37	Utah	4.3
10	Vermont	27.9
33	Virginia	6.2
2	Washington	76.1
44	West Virginia	3.3
24	Wisconsin	9.4
21	Wyoming	10.6

RANK ORDER

RANK	STATE	PERCENT
1	Idaho	82.2
2	Washington	76.1
3	Oregon	73.5
4	South Dakota	71.3
5	Maine	61.3
6	Montana	44.5
7	Iowa	30.7
8	California	29.4
9	Alaska	29.0
10	Vermont	27.9
11	North Dakota	24.0
12	New York	23.7
13	Kansas	22.0
14	Minnesota	21.1
15	Oklahoma	19.5
16	Nevada	17.9
17	Colorado	17.7
18	New Hampshire	17.1
19	Hawaii	12.7
20	Tennessee	12.6
21	Wyoming	10.6
22	Nebraska	10.0
23	Texas	9.7
24	Wisconsin	9.4
25	New Mexico	9.0
26	Arizona	8.9
27	Massachusetts	8.5
28	Alabama	8.2
29	Michigan	7.7
30	Maryland	6.9
31	Arkansas	6.8
32	North Carolina	6.3
33	Virginia	6.2
34	Georgia	5.8
35	Illinois	5.4
36	South Carolina	5.2
37	Utah	4.3
38	Kentucky	4.0
39	Pennsylvania	3.9
40	Indiana	3.8
41	Louisiana	3.7
41	Rhode Island	3.7
43	Connecticut	3.6
44	West Virginia	3.3
45	Mississippi	2.7
46	Florida	2.3
46	New Jersey	2.3
48	Missouri	2.2
49	Ohio	1.9
50	Delaware	1.7
	District of Columbia	0.0

Source: CQ Press using data from U.S. Department of Energy, Energy Information Administration "Electricity" (http://www.eia.gov/electricity/data/state/)

*Includes hydroelectric, geothermal, solar thermal and photovoltaic, wind, wood and wood-derived fuels, and other biomass.

Average Price of Natural Gas Delivered to Industrial Customers in 2014

National Average = $5.55 per Thousand Cubic Feet

ALPHA ORDER

RANK	STATE	RATE
47	Alabama	$5.49
17	Alaska	7.97
23	Arizona	7.52
27	Arkansas	6.99
21	California	7.65
30	Colorado	6.84
14	Connecticut	8.07
4	Delaware	10.95
28	Florida	6.89
39	Georgia	6.07
1	Hawaii	26.75
40	Idaho	5.96
20	Illinois	7.75
24	Indiana	7.45
25	Iowa	7.40
44	Kansas	5.70
43	Kentucky	5.80
50	Louisiana	4.68
2	Maine	11.93
8	Maryland	9.94
3	Massachusetts	11.53
18	Michigan	7.84
32	Minnesota	6.57
37	Mississippi	6.15
15	Missouri	8.00
16	Montana	7.99
45	Nebraska	5.69
19	Nevada	7.83
9	New Hampshire	9.46
5	New Jersey	10.45
33	New Mexico	6.45
12	New York	8.13
22	North Carolina	7.55
46	North Dakota	5.61
26	Ohio	7.06
11	Oklahoma	8.27
36	Oregon	6.20
7	Pennsylvania	9.95
6	Rhode Island	10.27
38	South Carolina	6.13
29	South Dakota	6.88
35	Tennessee	6.31
49	Texas	4.71
42	Utah	5.83
31	Vermont	6.63
34	Virginia	6.43
10	Washington	8.55
48	West Virginia	5.00
13	Wisconsin	8.08
41	Wyoming	5.89

RANK ORDER

RANK	STATE	RATE
1	Hawaii	$26.75
2	Maine	11.93
3	Massachusetts	11.53
4	Delaware	10.95
5	New Jersey	10.45
6	Rhode Island	10.27
7	Pennsylvania	9.95
8	Maryland	9.94
9	New Hampshire	9.46
10	Washington	8.55
11	Oklahoma	8.27
12	New York	8.13
13	Wisconsin	8.08
14	Connecticut	8.07
15	Missouri	8.00
16	Montana	7.99
17	Alaska	7.97
18	Michigan	7.84
19	Nevada	7.83
20	Illinois	7.75
21	California	7.65
22	North Carolina	7.55
23	Arizona	7.52
24	Indiana	7.45
25	Iowa	7.40
26	Ohio	7.06
27	Arkansas	6.99
28	Florida	6.89
29	South Dakota	6.88
30	Colorado	6.84
31	Vermont	6.63
32	Minnesota	6.57
33	New Mexico	6.45
34	Virginia	6.43
35	Tennessee	6.31
36	Oregon	6.20
37	Mississippi	6.15
38	South Carolina	6.13
39	Georgia	6.07
40	Idaho	5.96
41	Wyoming	5.89
42	Utah	5.83
43	Kentucky	5.80
44	Kansas	5.70
45	Nebraska	5.69
46	North Dakota	5.61
47	Alabama	5.49
48	West Virginia	5.00
49	Texas	4.71
50	Louisiana	4.68
	District of Columbia*	NA

Source: U.S. Department of Energy, Energy Information Administration
"Natural Gas" (http://www.eia.gov/naturalgas/annual/)
*Not available.

Average Price of Natural Gas Delivered to Commercial Customers in 2014

National Average = $8.90 per Thousand Cubic Feet

ALPHA ORDER

RANK	STATE	RATE
6	Alabama	$11.92
34	Alaska	8.30
10	Arizona	10.34
42	Arkansas	7.88
22	California	9.05
40	Colorado	8.15
11	Connecticut	10.24
7	Delaware	11.42
8	Florida	11.38
14	Georgia	9.86
1	Hawaii	40.42
47	Idaho	7.70
28	Illinois	8.86
39	Indiana	8.19
40	Iowa	8.15
16	Kansas	9.53
23	Kentucky	9.04
25	Louisiana	9.01
2	Maine	15.13
9	Maryland	10.52
5	Massachusetts	12.48
35	Michigan	8.28
31	Minnesota	8.66
32	Mississippi	8.36
26	Missouri	8.96
29	Montana	8.77
50	Nebraska	7.27
38	Nevada	8.21
3	New Hampshire	14.96
13	New Jersey	10.08
43	New Mexico	7.87
33	New York	8.31
21	North Carolina	9.12
45	North Dakota	7.74
44	Ohio	7.82
36	Oklahoma	8.26
17	Oregon	9.44
12	Pennsylvania	10.13
4	Rhode Island	12.89
15	South Carolina	9.55
49	South Dakota	7.65
18	Tennessee	9.30
36	Texas	8.26
46	Utah	7.71
20	Vermont	9.13
19	Virginia	9.17
24	Washington	9.03
27	West Virginia	8.92
30	Wisconsin	8.74
48	Wyoming	7.69

RANK ORDER

RANK	STATE	RATE
1	Hawaii	$40.42
2	Maine	15.13
3	New Hampshire	14.96
4	Rhode Island	12.89
5	Massachusetts	12.48
6	Alabama	11.92
7	Delaware	11.42
8	Florida	11.38
9	Maryland	10.52
10	Arizona	10.34
11	Connecticut	10.24
12	Pennsylvania	10.13
13	New Jersey	10.08
14	Georgia	9.86
15	South Carolina	9.55
16	Kansas	9.53
17	Oregon	9.44
18	Tennessee	9.30
19	Virginia	9.17
20	Vermont	9.13
21	North Carolina	9.12
22	California	9.05
23	Kentucky	9.04
24	Washington	9.03
25	Louisiana	9.01
26	Missouri	8.96
27	West Virginia	8.92
28	Illinois	8.86
29	Montana	8.77
30	Wisconsin	8.74
31	Minnesota	8.66
32	Mississippi	8.36
33	New York	8.31
34	Alaska	8.30
35	Michigan	8.28
36	Oklahoma	8.26
36	Texas	8.26
38	Nevada	8.21
39	Indiana	8.19
40	Colorado	8.15
40	Iowa	8.15
42	Arkansas	7.88
43	New Mexico	7.87
44	Ohio	7.82
45	North Dakota	7.74
46	Utah	7.71
47	Idaho	7.70
48	Wyoming	7.69
49	South Dakota	7.65
50	Nebraska	7.27
	District of Columbia	12.18

Source: U.S. Department of Energy, Energy Information Administration "Natural Gas" (http://www.eia.gov/naturalgas/annual/)

Average Price of Natural Gas Delivered to Residential Customers in 2014

National Average = $10.97 per Thousand Cubic Feet

ALPHA ORDER

RANK	STATE	RATE
8	Alabama	$14.59
44	Alaska	9.11
3	Arizona	17.20
29	Arkansas	10.39
20	California	11.51
47	Colorado	8.89
11	Connecticut	14.13
12	Delaware	13.21
2	Florida	19.02
10	Georgia	14.45
1	Hawaii	47.51
50	Idaho	8.54
38	Illinois	9.59
46	Indiana	9.02
35	Iowa	10.02
26	Kansas	10.59
25	Kentucky	10.62
23	Louisiana	10.89
4	Maine	16.90
15	Maryland	12.21
9	Massachusetts	14.50
42	Michigan	9.33
36	Minnesota	9.89
39	Mississippi	9.49
24	Missouri	10.83
44	Montana	9.11
49	Nebraska	8.77
21	Nevada	11.44
5	New Hampshire	16.27
37	New Jersey	9.69
32	New Mexico	10.13
14	New York	12.54
17	North Carolina	11.88
48	North Dakota	8.86
31	Ohio	10.16
34	Oklahoma	10.10
19	Oregon	11.72
18	Pennsylvania	11.77
6	Rhode Island	15.14
13	South Carolina	12.65
43	South Dakota	9.27
32	Tennessee	10.13
22	Texas	11.16
40	Utah	9.48
7	Vermont	14.68
16	Virginia	12.07
26	Washington	10.59
30	West Virginia	10.21
28	Wisconsin	10.52
41	Wyoming	9.34

RANK ORDER

RANK	STATE	RATE
1	Hawaii	$47.51
2	Florida	19.02
3	Arizona	17.20
4	Maine	16.90
5	New Hampshire	16.27
6	Rhode Island	15.14
7	Vermont	14.68
8	Alabama	14.59
9	Massachusetts	14.50
10	Georgia	14.45
11	Connecticut	14.13
12	Delaware	13.21
13	South Carolina	12.65
14	New York	12.54
15	Maryland	12.21
16	Virginia	12.07
17	North Carolina	11.88
18	Pennsylvania	11.77
19	Oregon	11.72
20	California	11.51
21	Nevada	11.44
22	Texas	11.16
23	Louisiana	10.89
24	Missouri	10.83
25	Kentucky	10.62
26	Kansas	10.59
26	Washington	10.59
28	Wisconsin	10.52
29	Arkansas	10.39
30	West Virginia	10.21
31	Ohio	10.16
32	New Mexico	10.13
32	Tennessee	10.13
34	Oklahoma	10.10
35	Iowa	10.02
36	Minnesota	9.89
37	New Jersey	9.69
38	Illinois	9.59
39	Mississippi	9.49
40	Utah	9.48
41	Wyoming	9.34
42	Michigan	9.33
43	South Dakota	9.27
44	Alaska	9.11
44	Montana	9.11
46	Indiana	9.02
47	Colorado	8.89
48	North Dakota	8.86
49	Nebraska	8.77
50	Idaho	8.54
	District of Columbia	13.05

Source: U.S. Department of Energy, Energy Information Administration "Natural Gas" (http://www.eia.gov/naturalgas/annual/)

Natural Gas Consumption in 2014

National Total = 26,698,069,000,000 Cubic Feet*

ALPHA ORDER

RANK	STATE	CUBIC FEET	% of USA
14	Alabama	634,678,000,000	2.4%
23	Alaska	327,428,000,000	1.2%
24	Arizona	307,946,000,000	1.2%
29	Arkansas	268,453,000,000	1.0%
2	California	2,344,977,000,000	8.8%
15	Colorado	480,747,000,000	1.8%
34	Connecticut	235,205,000,000	0.9%
41	Delaware	100,776,000,000	0.4%
5	Florida	1,231,957,000,000	4.6%
12	Georgia	652,230,000,000	2.4%
50	Hawaii	2,928,000,000	0.0%
42	Idaho	91,514,000,000	0.3%
7	Illinois	1,092,999,000,000	4.1%
11	Indiana	710,838,000,000	2.7%
22	Iowa	330,433,000,000	1.2%
28	Kansas	285,969,000,000	1.1%
30	Kentucky	254,244,000,000	1.0%
3	Louisiana	1,460,031,000,000	5.5%
47	Maine	60,661,000,000	0.2%
37	Maryland	207,527,000,000	0.8%
20	Massachusetts	418,526,000,000	1.6%
9	Michigan	850,974,000,000	3.2%
16	Minnesota	473,310,000,000	1.8%
21	Mississippi	412,979,000,000	1.5%
27	Missouri	296,605,000,000	1.1%
46	Montana	78,010,000,000	0.3%
38	Nebraska	172,749,000,000	0.6%
31	Nevada	252,097,000,000	0.9%
48	New Hampshire	57,017,000,000	0.2%
10	New Jersey	762,200,000,000	2.9%
32	New Mexico	246,178,000,000	0.9%
4	New York	1,345,315,000,000	5.0%
18	North Carolina	453,212,000,000	1.7%
44	North Dakota	83,330,000,000	0.3%
8	Ohio	1,000,231,000,000	3.7%
13	Oklahoma	640,607,000,000	2.4%
36	Oregon	220,076,000,000	0.8%
6	Pennsylvania	1,203,418,000,000	4.5%
43	Rhode Island	88,673,000,000	0.3%
35	South Carolina	231,863,000,000	0.9%
45	South Dakota	79,964,000,000	0.3%
26	Tennessee	303,996,000,000	1.1%
1	Texas	4,088,445,000,000	15.3%
33	Utah	242,457,000,000	0.9%
49	Vermont	10,678,000,000	0.0%
19	Virginia	419,615,000,000	1.6%
25	Washington	307,021,000,000	1.1%
39	West Virginia	150,766,000,000	0.6%
17	Wisconsin	462,627,000,000	1.7%
40	Wyoming	135,678,000,000	0.5%

RANK ORDER

RANK	STATE	CUBIC FEET	% of USA
1	Texas	4,088,445,000,000	15.3%
2	California	2,344,977,000,000	8.8%
3	Louisiana	1,460,031,000,000	5.5%
4	New York	1,345,315,000,000	5.0%
5	Florida	1,231,957,000,000	4.6%
6	Pennsylvania	1,203,418,000,000	4.5%
7	Illinois	1,092,999,000,000	4.1%
8	Ohio	1,000,231,000,000	3.7%
9	Michigan	850,974,000,000	3.2%
10	New Jersey	762,200,000,000	2.9%
11	Indiana	710,838,000,000	2.7%
12	Georgia	652,230,000,000	2.4%
13	Oklahoma	640,607,000,000	2.4%
14	Alabama	634,678,000,000	2.4%
15	Colorado	480,747,000,000	1.8%
16	Minnesota	473,310,000,000	1.8%
17	Wisconsin	462,627,000,000	1.7%
18	North Carolina	453,212,000,000	1.7%
19	Virginia	419,615,000,000	1.6%
20	Massachusetts	418,526,000,000	1.6%
21	Mississippi	412,979,000,000	1.5%
22	Iowa	330,433,000,000	1.2%
23	Alaska	327,428,000,000	1.2%
24	Arizona	307,946,000,000	1.2%
25	Washington	307,021,000,000	1.1%
26	Tennessee	303,996,000,000	1.1%
27	Missouri	296,605,000,000	1.1%
28	Kansas	285,969,000,000	1.1%
29	Arkansas	268,453,000,000	1.0%
30	Kentucky	254,244,000,000	1.0%
31	Nevada	252,097,000,000	0.9%
32	New Mexico	246,178,000,000	0.9%
33	Utah	242,457,000,000	0.9%
34	Connecticut	235,205,000,000	0.9%
35	South Carolina	231,863,000,000	0.9%
36	Oregon	220,076,000,000	0.8%
37	Maryland	207,527,000,000	0.8%
38	Nebraska	172,749,000,000	0.6%
39	West Virginia	150,766,000,000	0.6%
40	Wyoming	135,678,000,000	0.5%
41	Delaware	100,776,000,000	0.4%
42	Idaho	91,514,000,000	0.3%
43	Rhode Island	88,673,000,000	0.3%
44	North Dakota	83,330,000,000	0.3%
45	South Dakota	79,964,000,000	0.3%
46	Montana	78,010,000,000	0.3%
47	Maine	60,661,000,000	0.2%
48	New Hampshire	57,017,000,000	0.2%
49	Vermont	10,678,000,000	0.0%
50	Hawaii	2,928,000,000	0.0%
	District of Columbia	34,057,000,000	0.1%

Source: U.S. Department of Energy, Energy Information Administration
"Natural Gas" (http://www.eia.gov/naturalgas/annual/)
*National total includes 93,855,000,000 cubic feet of consumption in the Gulf of Mexico not shown by state.

Coal Mines in 2013

National Total = 1,061 Mines*

ALPHA ORDER

RANK	STATE	MINES	% of USA
5	Alabama	39	3.7%
22	Alaska	1	0.1%
22	Arizona	1	0.1%
19	Arkansas	2	0.2%
NA	California**	NA	NA
13	Colorado	10	0.9%
NA	Connecticut**	NA	NA
NA	Delaware**	NA	NA
NA	Florida**	NA	NA
NA	Georgia**	NA	NA
NA	Hawaii**	NA	NA
NA	Idaho**	NA	NA
8	Illinois	24	2.3%
7	Indiana	27	2.5%
NA	Iowa**	NA	NA
22	Kansas	1	0.1%
1	Kentucky	270	25.4%
19	Louisiana	2	0.2%
NA	Maine**	NA	NA
9	Maryland	21	2.0%
NA	Massachusetts**	NA	NA
NA	Michigan**	NA	NA
NA	Minnesota**	NA	NA
19	Mississippi	2	0.2%
22	Missouri	1	0.1%
16	Montana	6	0.6%
NA	Nebraska**	NA	NA
NA	Nevada**	NA	NA
NA	New Hampshire**	NA	NA
NA	New Jersey**	NA	NA
17	New Mexico	4	0.4%
NA	New York**	NA	NA
NA	North Carolina**	NA	NA
17	North Dakota	4	0.4%
6	Ohio	31	2.9%
14	Oklahoma	9	0.8%
NA	Oregon**	NA	NA
2	Pennsylvania	228	21.5%
NA	Rhode Island**	NA	NA
NA	South Carolina**	NA	NA
NA	South Dakota**	NA	NA
11	Tennessee	11	1.0%
11	Texas	11	1.0%
14	Utah	9	0.8%
NA	Vermont**	NA	NA
4	Virginia	82	7.7%
NA	Washington**	NA	NA
3	West Virginia	219	20.6%
NA	Wisconsin**	NA	NA
10	Wyoming	17	1.6%

RANK ORDER

RANK	STATE	MINES	% of USA
1	Kentucky	270	25.4%
2	Pennsylvania	228	21.5%
3	West Virginia	219	20.6%
4	Virginia	82	7.7%
5	Alabama	39	3.7%
6	Ohio	31	2.9%
7	Indiana	27	2.5%
8	Illinois	24	2.3%
9	Maryland	21	2.0%
10	Wyoming	17	1.6%
11	Tennessee	11	1.0%
11	Texas	11	1.0%
13	Colorado	10	0.9%
14	Oklahoma	9	0.8%
14	Utah	9	0.8%
16	Montana	6	0.6%
17	New Mexico	4	0.4%
17	North Dakota	4	0.4%
19	Arkansas	2	0.2%
19	Louisiana	2	0.2%
19	Mississippi	2	0.2%
22	Alaska	1	0.1%
22	Arizona	1	0.1%
22	Kansas	1	0.1%
22	Missouri	1	0.1%
NA	California**	NA	NA
NA	Connecticut**	NA	NA
NA	Delaware**	NA	NA
NA	Florida**	NA	NA
NA	Georgia**	NA	NA
NA	Hawaii**	NA	NA
NA	Idaho**	NA	NA
NA	Iowa**	NA	NA
NA	Maine**	NA	NA
NA	Massachusetts**	NA	NA
NA	Michigan**	NA	NA
NA	Minnesota**	NA	NA
NA	Nebraska**	NA	NA
NA	Nevada**	NA	NA
NA	New Hampshire**	NA	NA
NA	New Jersey**	NA	NA
NA	New York**	NA	NA
NA	North Carolina**	NA	NA
NA	Oregon**	NA	NA
NA	Rhode Island**	NA	NA
NA	South Carolina**	NA	NA
NA	South Dakota**	NA	NA
NA	Vermont**	NA	NA
NA	Washington**	NA	NA
NA	Wisconsin**	NA	NA
	District of Columbia**	NA	NA

Source: U.S. Department of Energy, Energy Information Administration
"Annual Coal Report" (released January 20, 2015, http://www.eia.gov/coal/annual/)
*National total includes 29 coal mines in refuse recovery not shown by state.
**Not available or no mines.

Coal Production in 2013

National Total = 984,842,000 Short Tons*

ALPHA ORDER

RANK	STATE	SHORT TONS	% of USA
13	Alabama	18,620,000	1.9%
20	Alaska	1,632,000	0.2%
16	Arizona	7,603,000	0.8%
24	Arkansas	59,000	0.0%
NA	California**	NA	NA
11	Colorado	24,236,000	2.5%
NA	Connecticut**	NA	NA
NA	Delaware**	NA	NA
NA	Florida**	NA	NA
NA	Georgia**	NA	NA
NA	Hawaii**	NA	NA
NA	Idaho**	NA	NA
4	Illinois	52,147,000	5.3%
8	Indiana	39,102,000	4.0%
NA	Iowa**	NA	NA
25	Kansas	22,000	0.0%
3	Kentucky	80,380,000	8.2%
18	Louisiana	2,810,000	0.3%
NA	Maine**	NA	NA
19	Maryland	1,925,000	0.2%
NA	Massachusetts**	NA	NA
NA	Michigan**	NA	NA
NA	Minnesota**	NA	NA
17	Mississippi	3,575,000	0.4%
23	Missouri	414,000	0.0%
7	Montana	42,231,000	4.3%
NA	Nebraska**	NA	NA
NA	Nevada**	NA	NA
NA	New Hampshire**	NA	NA
NA	New Jersey**	NA	NA
12	New Mexico	21,969,000	2.2%
NA	New York**	NA	NA
NA	North Carolina**	NA	NA
9	North Dakota	27,639,000	2.8%
10	Ohio	25,113,000	2.5%
21	Oklahoma	1,136,000	0.1%
NA	Oregon**	NA	NA
5	Pennsylvania	50,870,000	5.2%
NA	Rhode Island**	NA	NA
NA	South Carolina**	NA	NA
NA	South Dakota**	NA	NA
22	Tennessee	1,098,000	0.1%
6	Texas	42,851,000	4.4%
14	Utah	16,977,000	1.7%
NA	Vermont**	NA	NA
15	Virginia	16,619,000	1.7%
NA	Washington**	NA	NA
2	West Virginia	115,925,000	11.8%
NA	Wisconsin**	NA	NA
1	Wyoming	387,924,000	39.4%

RANK ORDER

RANK	STATE	SHORT TONS	% of USA
1	Wyoming	387,924,000	39.4%
2	West Virginia	115,925,000	11.8%
3	Kentucky	80,380,000	8.2%
4	Illinois	52,147,000	5.3%
5	Pennsylvania	50,870,000	5.2%
6	Texas	42,851,000	4.4%
7	Montana	42,231,000	4.3%
8	Indiana	39,102,000	4.0%
9	North Dakota	27,639,000	2.8%
10	Ohio	25,113,000	2.5%
11	Colorado	24,236,000	2.5%
12	New Mexico	21,969,000	2.2%
13	Alabama	18,620,000	1.9%
14	Utah	16,977,000	1.7%
15	Virginia	16,619,000	1.7%
16	Arizona	7,603,000	0.8%
17	Mississippi	3,575,000	0.4%
18	Louisiana	2,810,000	0.3%
19	Maryland	1,925,000	0.2%
20	Alaska	1,632,000	0.2%
21	Oklahoma	1,136,000	0.1%
22	Tennessee	1,098,000	0.1%
23	Missouri	414,000	0.0%
24	Arkansas	59,000	0.0%
25	Kansas	22,000	0.0%
NA	California**	NA	NA
NA	Connecticut**	NA	NA
NA	Delaware**	NA	NA
NA	Florida**	NA	NA
NA	Georgia**	NA	NA
NA	Hawaii**	NA	NA
NA	Idaho**	NA	NA
NA	Iowa**	NA	NA
NA	Maine**	NA	NA
NA	Massachusetts**	NA	NA
NA	Michigan**	NA	NA
NA	Minnesota**	NA	NA
NA	Nebraska**	NA	NA
NA	Nevada**	NA	NA
NA	New Hampshire**	NA	NA
NA	New Jersey**	NA	NA
NA	New York**	NA	NA
NA	North Carolina**	NA	NA
NA	Oregon**	NA	NA
NA	Rhode Island**	NA	NA
NA	South Carolina**	NA	NA
NA	South Dakota**	NA	NA
NA	Vermont**	NA	NA
NA	Washington**	NA	NA
NA	Wisconsin**	NA	NA
	District of Columbia**	NA	NA

Source: U.S. Department of Energy, Energy Information Administration
"Annual Coal Report" (released January 20, 2015, http://www.eia.gov/coal/annual/)
*National total includes 1,966,000 short tons from refuse recovery not shown by state.
**Not available or no production.

Gasoline Used in 2014

National Total = 137,526,812,000 Gallons*

ALPHA ORDER

RANK	STATE	GALLONS	% of USA
22	Alabama	2,591,750,000	1.9%
50	Alaska	283,915,000	0.2%
19	Arizona	2,689,150,000	2.0%
32	Arkansas	1,425,619,000	1.0%
1	California	14,717,868,000	10.7%
25	Colorado	2,198,040,000	1.6%
31	Connecticut	1,429,346,000	1.0%
46	Delaware	434,698,000	0.3%
3	Florida	8,434,775,000	6.1%
7	Georgia	4,687,434,000	3.4%
45	Hawaii	451,097,000	0.3%
40	Idaho	718,173,000	0.5%
8	Illinois	4,652,347,000	3.4%
15	Indiana	3,053,601,000	2.2%
29	Iowa	1,677,591,000	1.2%
33	Kansas	1,307,128,000	1.0%
26	Kentucky	2,116,465,000	1.5%
24	Louisiana	2,259,110,000	1.6%
39	Maine	781,011,000	0.6%
17	Maryland	2,743,520,000	2.0%
18	Massachusetts	2,723,193,000	2.0%
9	Michigan	4,619,493,000	3.4%
23	Minnesota	2,534,766,000	1.8%
28	Mississippi	1,682,292,000	1.2%
14	Missouri	3,094,063,000	2.2%
42	Montana	518,748,000	0.4%
37	Nebraska	890,105,000	0.6%
34	Nevada	1,109,995,000	0.8%
41	New Hampshire	709,009,000	0.5%
11	New Jersey	4,102,520,000	3.0%
36	New Mexico	961,826,000	0.7%
4	New York	5,560,191,000	4.0%
10	North Carolina	4,340,720,000	3.2%
43	North Dakota	472,512,000	0.3%
5	Ohio	4,961,728,000	3.6%
27	Oklahoma	1,995,855,000	1.5%
30	Oregon	1,499,270,000	1.1%
6	Pennsylvania	4,945,316,000	3.6%
47	Rhode Island	367,314,000	0.3%
20	South Carolina	2,683,640,000	2.0%
44	South Dakota	452,825,000	0.3%
13	Tennessee	3,197,840,000	2.3%
2	Texas	13,364,215,000	9.7%
35	Utah	1,106,392,000	0.8%
49	Vermont	314,898,000	0.2%
12	Virginia	4,020,470,000	2.9%
16	Washington	2,751,602,000	2.0%
38	West Virginia	818,810,000	0.6%
21	Wisconsin	2,617,177,000	1.9%
48	Wyoming	353,601,000	0.3%

RANK ORDER

RANK	STATE	GALLONS	% of USA
1	California	14,717,868,000	10.7%
2	Texas	13,364,215,000	9.7%
3	Florida	8,434,775,000	6.1%
4	New York	5,560,191,000	4.0%
5	Ohio	4,961,728,000	3.6%
6	Pennsylvania	4,945,316,000	3.6%
7	Georgia	4,687,434,000	3.4%
8	Illinois	4,652,347,000	3.4%
9	Michigan	4,619,493,000	3.4%
10	North Carolina	4,340,720,000	3.2%
11	New Jersey	4,102,520,000	3.0%
12	Virginia	4,020,470,000	2.9%
13	Tennessee	3,197,840,000	2.3%
14	Missouri	3,094,063,000	2.2%
15	Indiana	3,053,601,000	2.2%
16	Washington	2,751,602,000	2.0%
17	Maryland	2,743,520,000	2.0%
18	Massachusetts	2,723,193,000	2.0%
19	Arizona	2,689,150,000	2.0%
20	South Carolina	2,683,640,000	2.0%
21	Wisconsin	2,617,177,000	1.9%
22	Alabama	2,591,750,000	1.9%
23	Minnesota	2,534,766,000	1.8%
24	Louisiana	2,259,110,000	1.6%
25	Colorado	2,198,040,000	1.6%
26	Kentucky	2,116,465,000	1.5%
27	Oklahoma	1,995,855,000	1.5%
28	Mississippi	1,682,292,000	1.2%
29	Iowa	1,677,591,000	1.2%
30	Oregon	1,499,270,000	1.1%
31	Connecticut	1,429,346,000	1.0%
32	Arkansas	1,425,619,000	1.0%
33	Kansas	1,307,128,000	1.0%
34	Nevada	1,109,995,000	0.8%
35	Utah	1,106,392,000	0.8%
36	New Mexico	961,826,000	0.7%
37	Nebraska	890,105,000	0.6%
38	West Virginia	818,810,000	0.6%
39	Maine	781,011,000	0.6%
40	Idaho	718,173,000	0.5%
41	New Hampshire	709,009,000	0.5%
42	Montana	518,748,000	0.4%
43	North Dakota	472,512,000	0.3%
44	South Dakota	452,825,000	0.3%
45	Hawaii	451,097,000	0.3%
46	Delaware	434,698,000	0.3%
47	Rhode Island	367,314,000	0.3%
48	Wyoming	353,601,000	0.3%
49	Vermont	314,898,000	0.2%
50	Alaska	283,915,000	0.2%
	District of Columbia	103,788,000	0.1%

Source: U.S. Department of Transportation, Federal Highway Administration
"Highway Statistics 2014" (Table MF-21, http://www.fhwa.dot.gov/policyinformation/statistics/2014/)
*Includes gasoline for highway and nonhighway uses as well as for losses allowed for evaporation and handling. "Gasoline" includes gasohol but excludes "special fuels" such as diesel.

Per Capita Gasoline Used in 2014

National Per Capita = 431 Gallons*

ALPHA ORDER

RANK	STATE	PER CAPITA
7	Alabama	535
43	Alaska	385
38	Arizona	400
18	Arkansas	481
44	California	379
36	Colorado	410
39	Connecticut	398
22	Delaware	464
35	Florida	424
22	Georgia	464
49	Hawaii	318
32	Idaho	439
47	Illinois	361
25	Indiana	463
6	Iowa	540
30	Kansas	450
19	Kentucky	480
16	Louisiana	486
3	Maine	587
27	Maryland	459
37	Massachusetts	403
21	Michigan	466
22	Minnesota	464
4	Mississippi	562
11	Missouri	510
12	Montana	507
20	Nebraska	473
40	Nevada	391
8	New Hampshire	534
27	New Jersey	459
26	New Mexico	461
50	New York	282
33	North Carolina	437
1	North Dakota	638
34	Ohio	428
10	Oklahoma	514
45	Oregon	378
42	Pennsylvania	387
48	Rhode Island	348
5	South Carolina	556
9	South Dakota	531
15	Tennessee	488
14	Texas	495
46	Utah	376
13	Vermont	502
17	Virginia	483
41	Washington	390
31	West Virginia	443
29	Wisconsin	454
2	Wyoming	605

RANK ORDER

RANK	STATE	PER CAPITA
1	North Dakota	638
2	Wyoming	605
3	Maine	587
4	Mississippi	562
5	South Carolina	556
6	Iowa	540
7	Alabama	535
8	New Hampshire	534
9	South Dakota	531
10	Oklahoma	514
11	Missouri	510
12	Montana	507
13	Vermont	502
14	Texas	495
15	Tennessee	488
16	Louisiana	486
17	Virginia	483
18	Arkansas	481
19	Kentucky	480
20	Nebraska	473
21	Michigan	466
22	Delaware	464
22	Georgia	464
22	Minnesota	464
25	Indiana	463
26	New Mexico	461
27	Maryland	459
27	New Jersey	459
29	Wisconsin	454
30	Kansas	450
31	West Virginia	443
32	Idaho	439
33	North Carolina	437
34	Ohio	428
35	Florida	424
36	Colorado	410
37	Massachusetts	403
38	Arizona	400
39	Connecticut	398
40	Nevada	391
41	Washington	390
42	Pennsylvania	387
43	Alaska	385
44	California	379
45	Oregon	378
46	Utah	376
47	Illinois	361
48	Rhode Island	348
49	Hawaii	318
50	New York	282
	District of Columbia	157

Source: CQ Press using data from U.S. Department of Transportation, Federal Highway Administration "Highway Statistics 2014" (Table MF-21, http://www.fhwa.dot.gov/policyinformation/statistics/2014/)

*Includes gasoline for highway and nonhighway uses as well as for losses allowed for evaporation and handling. "Gasoline" includes gasohol but excludes "special fuels" such as diesel.

Daily Production of Crude Oil in 2014

National Total = 8,708,370 Barrels a Day*

ALPHA ORDER

RANK	STATE	BARRELS	% of USA
15	Alabama	26,926	0.3%
4	Alaska	497,055	5.7%
30	Arizona	153	0.0%
19	Arkansas	18,753	0.2%
3	California	559,641	6.4%
7	Colorado	260,800	3.0%
NA	Connecticut**	NA	NA
NA	Delaware**	NA	NA
24	Florida	6,101	0.1%
NA	Georgia**	NA	NA
NA	Hawaii**	NA	NA
NA	Idaho**	NA	NA
16	Illinois	26,156	0.3%
23	Indiana	6,868	0.1%
NA	Iowa**	NA	NA
10	Kansas	135,644	1.6%
21	Kentucky	9,249	0.1%
9	Louisiana	187,277	2.2%
NA	Maine**	NA	NA
NA	Maryland**	NA	NA
NA	Massachusetts**	NA	NA
18	Michigan	19,970	0.2%
NA	Minnesota**	NA	NA
13	Mississippi	66,701	0.8%
29	Missouri	537	0.0%
12	Montana	81,863	0.9%
22	Nebraska	8,356	0.1%
28	Nevada	866	0.0%
NA	New Hampshire**	NA	NA
NA	New Jersey**	NA	NA
6	New Mexico	338,866	3.9%
26	New York	934	0.0%
NA	North Carolina**	NA	NA
2	North Dakota	1,087,304	12.5%
14	Ohio	40,871	0.5%
5	Oklahoma	348,074	4.0%
NA	Oregon**	NA	NA
20	Pennsylvania	18,334	0.2%
NA	Rhode Island**	NA	NA
NA	South Carolina**	NA	NA
25	South Dakota	4,926	0.1%
27	Tennessee	904	0.0%
1	Texas	3,166,258	36.4%
11	Utah	112,068	1.3%
NA	Vermont**	NA	NA
31	Virginia	38	0.0%
NA	Washington**	NA	NA
17	West Virginia	20,614	0.2%
NA	Wisconsin**	NA	NA
8	Wyoming	208,433	2.4%

RANK ORDER

RANK	STATE	BARRELS	% of USA
1	Texas	3,166,258	36.4%
2	North Dakota	1,087,304	12.5%
3	California	559,641	6.4%
4	Alaska	497,055	5.7%
5	Oklahoma	348,074	4.0%
6	New Mexico	338,866	3.9%
7	Colorado	260,800	3.0%
8	Wyoming	208,433	2.4%
9	Louisiana	187,277	2.2%
10	Kansas	135,644	1.6%
11	Utah	112,068	1.3%
12	Montana	81,863	0.9%
13	Mississippi	66,701	0.8%
14	Ohio	40,871	0.5%
15	Alabama	26,926	0.3%
16	Illinois	26,156	0.3%
17	West Virginia	20,614	0.2%
18	Michigan	19,970	0.2%
19	Arkansas	18,753	0.2%
20	Pennsylvania	18,334	0.2%
21	Kentucky	9,249	0.1%
22	Nebraska	8,356	0.1%
23	Indiana	6,868	0.1%
24	Florida	6,101	0.1%
25	South Dakota	4,926	0.1%
26	New York	934	0.0%
27	Tennessee	904	0.0%
28	Nevada	866	0.0%
29	Missouri	537	0.0%
30	Arizona	153	0.0%
31	Virginia	38	0.0%
NA	Connecticut**	NA	NA
NA	Delaware**	NA	NA
NA	Georgia**	NA	NA
NA	Hawaii**	NA	NA
NA	Idaho**	NA	NA
NA	Iowa**	NA	NA
NA	Maine**	NA	NA
NA	Maryland**	NA	NA
NA	Massachusetts**	NA	NA
NA	Minnesota**	NA	NA
NA	New Hampshire**	NA	NA
NA	New Jersey**	NA	NA
NA	North Carolina**	NA	NA
NA	Oregon**	NA	NA
NA	Rhode Island**	NA	NA
NA	South Carolina**	NA	NA
NA	Vermont**	NA	NA
NA	Washington**	NA	NA
NA	Wisconsin**	NA	NA
	District of Columbia**	NA	NA

Source: CQ Press using data from U.S. Department of Energy, Energy Information Administration
"Petroleum Supply Annual 2014, Volume 1" (http://tonto.eia.doe.gov/dnav/pet/pet_crd_crpdn_adc_mbbl_m.htm)
*National total includes 1,447,830 barrels a day in federal offshore production. Figures for Alaska, California, Louisiana, and Texas include state offshore production.
**No reported production.

Fossil Fuel Emissions in 2013

National Total = 5,157,700,000 Metric Tons of Carbon Dioxide (CO_2)*

ALPHA ORDER

RANK	STATE	TONS OF CO_2	% of USA
15	Alabama	121,040,000	2.3%
40	Alaska	36,030,000	0.7%
21	Arizona	96,340,000	1.9%
29	Arkansas	69,070,000	1.3%
2	California	371,070,000	7.2%
23	Colorado	92,170,000	1.8%
41	Connecticut	35,970,000	0.7%
48	Delaware	13,910,000	0.3%
6	Florida	225,800,000	4.4%
12	Georgia	136,970,000	2.7%
43	Hawaii	18,640,000	0.4%
44	Idaho	17,490,000	0.3%
4	Illinois	234,620,000	4.5%
8	Indiana	199,640,000	3.9%
25	Iowa	83,270,000	1.6%
27	Kansas	71,860,000	1.4%
11	Kentucky	137,880,000	2.7%
7	Louisiana	201,670,000	3.9%
45	Maine	17,030,000	0.3%
33	Maryland	61,700,000	1.2%
30	Massachusetts	68,560,000	1.3%
10	Michigan	164,450,000	3.2%
24	Minnesota	91,240,000	1.8%
34	Mississippi	61,630,000	1.2%
13	Missouri	133,480,000	2.6%
42	Montana	32,220,000	0.6%
37	Nebraska	53,550,000	1.0%
39	Nevada	36,870,000	0.7%
47	New Hampshire	14,720,000	0.3%
16	New Jersey	110,310,000	2.1%
36	New Mexico	54,360,000	1.1%
9	New York	166,720,000	3.2%
14	North Carolina	126,110,000	2.4%
35	North Dakota	58,910,000	1.1%
5	Ohio	231,870,000	4.5%
18	Oklahoma	104,470,000	2.0%
38	Oregon	39,860,000	0.8%
3	Pennsylvania	246,220,000	4.8%
49	Rhode Island	10,420,000	0.2%
28	South Carolina	71,730,000	1.4%
46	South Dakota	15,580,000	0.3%
20	Tennessee	99,680,000	1.9%
1	Texas	712,860,000	13.8%
32	Utah	66,610,000	1.3%
50	Vermont	5,970,000	0.1%
17	Virginia	106,900,000	2.1%
26	Washington	75,980,000	1.5%
22	West Virginia	92,930,000	1.8%
19	Wisconsin	101,770,000	2.0%
31	Wyoming	68,330,000	1.3%

RANK ORDER

RANK	STATE	TONS OF CO_2	% of USA
1	Texas	712,860,000	13.8%
2	California	371,070,000	7.2%
3	Pennsylvania	246,220,000	4.8%
4	Illinois	234,620,000	4.5%
5	Ohio	231,870,000	4.5%
6	Florida	225,800,000	4.4%
7	Louisiana	201,670,000	3.9%
8	Indiana	199,640,000	3.9%
9	New York	166,720,000	3.2%
10	Michigan	164,450,000	3.2%
11	Kentucky	137,880,000	2.7%
12	Georgia	136,970,000	2.7%
13	Missouri	133,480,000	2.6%
14	North Carolina	126,110,000	2.4%
15	Alabama	121,040,000	2.3%
16	New Jersey	110,310,000	2.1%
17	Virginia	106,900,000	2.1%
18	Oklahoma	104,470,000	2.0%
19	Wisconsin	101,770,000	2.0%
20	Tennessee	99,680,000	1.9%
21	Arizona	96,340,000	1.9%
22	West Virginia	92,930,000	1.8%
23	Colorado	92,170,000	1.8%
24	Minnesota	91,240,000	1.8%
25	Iowa	83,270,000	1.6%
26	Washington	75,980,000	1.5%
27	Kansas	71,860,000	1.4%
28	South Carolina	71,730,000	1.4%
29	Arkansas	69,070,000	1.3%
30	Massachusetts	68,560,000	1.3%
31	Wyoming	68,330,000	1.3%
32	Utah	66,610,000	1.3%
33	Maryland	61,700,000	1.2%
34	Mississippi	61,630,000	1.2%
35	North Dakota	58,910,000	1.1%
36	New Mexico	54,360,000	1.1%
37	Nebraska	53,550,000	1.0%
38	Oregon	39,860,000	0.8%
39	Nevada	36,870,000	0.7%
40	Alaska	36,030,000	0.7%
41	Connecticut	35,970,000	0.7%
42	Montana	32,220,000	0.6%
43	Hawaii	18,640,000	0.4%
44	Idaho	17,490,000	0.3%
45	Maine	17,030,000	0.3%
46	South Dakota	15,580,000	0.3%
47	New Hampshire	14,720,000	0.3%
48	Delaware	13,910,000	0.3%
49	Rhode Island	10,420,000	0.2%
50	Vermont	5,970,000	0.1%
	District of Columbia	2,910,000	0.1%

Source: U.S. Environmental Protection Agency
"Energy CO2 Emissions by State" (http://www.epa.gov/statelocalclimate/resources/state_energyco2inv.html)
*Carbon dioxide (CO_2) emissions from fossil fuel combustion. This represents the largest source (94%) of total CO_2 emissions from all emission sources. Emissions are based on the location where fossil fuels are used. Fuels can be used in one state to generate electricity consumed in another. National figure no longer includes non-energy use of fuels.

Per Capita Fossil Fuel Emissions in 2013

National Per Capita = 16.3 Metric Tons of Carbon Dioxide (CO_2)*

ALPHA ORDER

RANK	STATE	PER CAPITA
14	Alabama	25.1
4	Alaska	48.9
31	Arizona	14.5
16	Arkansas	23.4
48	California	9.7
25	Colorado	17.5
46	Connecticut	10.0
29	Delaware	15.0
39	Florida	11.5
32	Georgia	13.7
33	Hawaii	13.2
42	Idaho	10.8
23	Illinois	18.2
8	Indiana	30.4
11	Iowa	26.9
15	Kansas	24.8
7	Kentucky	31.3
5	Louisiana	43.6
36	Maine	12.8
43	Maryland	10.4
44	Massachusetts	10.2
27	Michigan	16.6
26	Minnesota	16.8
19	Mississippi	20.6
18	Missouri	22.1
6	Montana	31.8
9	Nebraska	28.6
33	Nevada	13.2
40	New Hampshire	11.1
38	New Jersey	12.4
13	New Mexico	26.0
50	New York	8.5
36	North Carolina	12.8
2	North Dakota	81.4
20	Ohio	20.0
10	Oklahoma	27.1
45	Oregon	10.1
21	Pennsylvania	19.3
47	Rhode Island	9.9
29	South Carolina	15.0
22	South Dakota	18.4
28	Tennessee	15.3
11	Texas	26.9
17	Utah	22.9
49	Vermont	9.5
35	Virginia	12.9
41	Washington	10.9
3	West Virginia	50.2
24	Wisconsin	17.7
1	Wyoming	117.2

RANK ORDER

RANK	STATE	PER CAPITA
1	Wyoming	117.2
2	North Dakota	81.4
3	West Virginia	50.2
4	Alaska	48.9
5	Louisiana	43.6
6	Montana	31.8
7	Kentucky	31.3
8	Indiana	30.4
9	Nebraska	28.6
10	Oklahoma	27.1
11	Iowa	26.9
11	Texas	26.9
13	New Mexico	26.0
14	Alabama	25.1
15	Kansas	24.8
16	Arkansas	23.4
17	Utah	22.9
18	Missouri	22.1
19	Mississippi	20.6
20	Ohio	20.0
21	Pennsylvania	19.3
22	South Dakota	18.4
23	Illinois	18.2
24	Wisconsin	17.7
25	Colorado	17.5
26	Minnesota	16.8
27	Michigan	16.6
28	Tennessee	15.3
29	Delaware	15.0
29	South Carolina	15.0
31	Arizona	14.5
32	Georgia	13.7
33	Hawaii	13.2
33	Nevada	13.2
35	Virginia	12.9
36	Maine	12.8
36	North Carolina	12.8
38	New Jersey	12.4
39	Florida	11.5
40	New Hampshire	11.1
41	Washington	10.9
42	Idaho	10.8
43	Maryland	10.4
44	Massachusetts	10.2
45	Oregon	10.1
46	Connecticut	10.0
47	Rhode Island	9.9
48	California	9.7
49	Vermont	9.5
50	New York	8.5
	District of Columbia	4.5

Source: CQ Press using data from U.S. Environmental Protection Agency
"Energy CO2 Emissions by State" (http://www.epa.gov/statelocalclimate/resources/state_energyco2inv.html)
*Carbon dioxide (CO_2) emissions from fossil fuel combustion. This represents the largest source (94%) of total CO_2 emissions from all emission sources. Emissions are based on the location where fossil fuels are used. Fuels can be used in one state to generate electricity consumed in another. National figure no longer includes non-energy use of fuels.

Energy and Environment

Percent Change in Fossil Fuel Emissions: 2009 to 2013

National Percent Change = 0.8% Decrease*

ALPHA ORDER

RANK	STATE	PERCENT CHANGE
17	Alabama	1.9
39	Alaska	(3.8)
14	Arizona	3.4
6	Arkansas	12.7
23	California	(0.4)
24	Colorado	(0.5)
22	Connecticut	(0.2)
2	Delaware	17.0
20	Florida	1.3
50	Georgia	(15.0)
25	Hawaii	(0.7)
3	Idaho	15.0
13	Illinois	4.1
34	Indiana	(2.4)
29	Iowa	(1.7)
37	Kansas	(2.6)
40	Kentucky	(4.0)
10	Louisiana	5.2
45	Maine	(7.2)
48	Maryland	(13.0)
36	Massachusetts	(2.5)
21	Michigan	0.7
25	Minnesota	(0.7)
16	Mississippi	2.0
15	Missouri	2.2
33	Montana	(2.1)
4	Nebraska	14.1
44	Nevada	(6.2)
49	New Hampshire	(13.3)
30	New Jersey	(1.8)
43	New Mexico	(5.8)
42	New York	(4.2)
40	North Carolina	(4.0)
1	North Dakota	23.4
31	Ohio	(1.9)
27	Oklahoma	(1.4)
34	Oregon	(2.4)
18	Pennsylvania	1.8
46	Rhode Island	(7.5)
47	South Carolina	(11.8)
8	South Dakota	6.3
32	Tennessee	(2.0)
4	Texas	14.1
12	Utah	4.3
38	Vermont	(3.6)
19	Virginia	1.7
28	Washington	(1.6)
11	West Virginia	5.1
9	Wisconsin	6.2
7	Wyoming	7.8

RANK ORDER

RANK	STATE	PERCENT CHANGE
1	North Dakota	23.4
2	Delaware	17.0
3	Idaho	15.0
4	Nebraska	14.1
4	Texas	14.1
6	Arkansas	12.7
7	Wyoming	7.8
8	South Dakota	6.3
9	Wisconsin	6.2
10	Louisiana	5.2
11	West Virginia	5.1
12	Utah	4.3
13	Illinois	4.1
14	Arizona	3.4
15	Missouri	2.2
16	Mississippi	2.0
17	Alabama	1.9
18	Pennsylvania	1.8
19	Virginia	1.7
20	Florida	1.3
21	Michigan	0.7
22	Connecticut	(0.2)
23	California	(0.4)
24	Colorado	(0.5)
25	Hawaii	(0.7)
25	Minnesota	(0.7)
27	Oklahoma	(1.4)
28	Washington	(1.6)
29	Iowa	(1.7)
30	New Jersey	(1.8)
31	Ohio	(1.9)
32	Tennessee	(2.0)
33	Montana	(2.1)
34	Indiana	(2.4)
34	Oregon	(2.4)
36	Massachusetts	(2.5)
37	Kansas	(2.6)
38	Vermont	(3.6)
39	Alaska	(3.8)
40	Kentucky	(4.0)
40	North Carolina	(4.0)
42	New York	(4.2)
43	New Mexico	(5.8)
44	Nevada	(6.2)
45	Maine	(7.2)
46	Rhode Island	(7.5)
47	South Carolina	(11.8)
48	Maryland	(13.0)
49	New Hampshire	(13.3)
50	Georgia	(15.0)
	District of Columbia	(8.8)

Source: CQ Press using data from U.S. Environmental Protection Agency
"Energy CO2 Emissions by State" (http://www.epa.gov/statelocalclimate/resources/state_energyco2inv.html)
*Based on metric tons of carbon dioxide (CO_2).

Toxic Releases: Total Pollution Released in 2014

National Total = 3,891,985,158 Pounds of Toxins*

ALPHA ORDER

RANK	STATE	POUNDS	% of USA
9	Alabama	90,487,048	2.3%
1	Alaska	1,163,914,639	29.9%
12	Arizona	78,532,846	2.0%
25	Arkansas	37,702,693	1.0%
31	California	27,772,599	0.7%
29	Colorado	29,492,190	0.8%
47	Connecticut	2,057,482	0.1%
44	Delaware	6,077,932	0.2%
17	Florida	64,074,864	1.6%
16	Georgia	68,185,289	1.8%
46	Hawaii	2,672,526	0.1%
20	Idaho	50,331,326	1.3%
7	Illinois	119,243,321	3.1%
5	Indiana	157,943,798	4.1%
23	Iowa	39,090,377	1.0%
34	Kansas	21,867,453	0.6%
13	Kentucky	71,048,302	1.8%
6	Louisiana	136,800,102	3.5%
41	Maine	10,165,309	0.3%
42	Maryland	8,242,964	0.2%
45	Massachusetts	3,392,136	0.1%
19	Michigan	61,199,227	1.6%
30	Minnesota	28,709,025	0.7%
15	Mississippi	69,718,632	1.8%
14	Missouri	69,722,750	1.8%
24	Montana	37,726,270	1.0%
32	Nebraska	26,269,911	0.7%
2	Nevada	285,297,668	7.3%
48	New Hampshire	702,056	0.0%
40	New Jersey	10,882,909	0.3%
36	New Mexico	20,332,074	0.5%
38	New York	16,835,684	0.4%
18	North Carolina	61,903,968	1.6%
28	North Dakota	32,784,568	0.8%
8	Ohio	113,253,572	2.9%
33	Oklahoma	26,149,369	0.7%
39	Oregon	16,404,351	0.4%
11	Pennsylvania	84,911,213	2.2%
49	Rhode Island	383,794	0.0%
21	South Carolina	46,356,720	1.2%
43	South Dakota	6,160,781	0.2%
10	Tennessee	85,776,149	2.2%
3	Texas	237,757,999	6.1%
4	Utah	208,795,963	5.4%
50	Vermont	309,125	0.0%
22	Virginia	42,393,279	1.1%
35	Washington	20,967,837	0.5%
26	West Virginia	36,208,292	0.9%
27	Wisconsin	36,014,861	0.9%
37	Wyoming	18,373,457	0.5%

RANK ORDER

RANK	STATE	POUNDS	% of USA
1	Alaska	1,163,914,639	29.9%
2	Nevada	285,297,668	7.3%
3	Texas	237,757,999	6.1%
4	Utah	208,795,963	5.4%
5	Indiana	157,943,798	4.1%
6	Louisiana	136,800,102	3.5%
7	Illinois	119,243,321	3.1%
8	Ohio	113,253,572	2.9%
9	Alabama	90,487,048	2.3%
10	Tennessee	85,776,149	2.2%
11	Pennsylvania	84,911,213	2.2%
12	Arizona	78,532,846	2.0%
13	Kentucky	71,048,302	1.8%
14	Missouri	69,722,750	1.8%
15	Mississippi	69,718,632	1.8%
16	Georgia	68,185,289	1.8%
17	Florida	64,074,864	1.6%
18	North Carolina	61,903,968	1.6%
19	Michigan	61,199,227	1.6%
20	Idaho	50,331,326	1.3%
21	South Carolina	46,356,720	1.2%
22	Virginia	42,393,279	1.1%
23	Iowa	39,090,377	1.0%
24	Montana	37,726,270	1.0%
25	Arkansas	37,702,693	1.0%
26	West Virginia	36,208,292	0.9%
27	Wisconsin	36,014,861	0.9%
28	North Dakota	32,784,568	0.8%
29	Colorado	29,492,190	0.8%
30	Minnesota	28,709,025	0.7%
31	California	27,772,599	0.7%
32	Nebraska	26,269,911	0.7%
33	Oklahoma	26,149,369	0.7%
34	Kansas	21,867,453	0.6%
35	Washington	20,967,837	0.5%
36	New Mexico	20,332,074	0.5%
37	Wyoming	18,373,457	0.5%
38	New York	16,835,684	0.4%
39	Oregon	16,404,351	0.4%
40	New Jersey	10,882,909	0.3%
41	Maine	10,165,309	0.3%
42	Maryland	8,242,964	0.2%
43	South Dakota	6,160,781	0.2%
44	Delaware	6,077,932	0.2%
45	Massachusetts	3,392,136	0.1%
46	Hawaii	2,672,526	0.1%
47	Connecticut	2,057,482	0.1%
48	New Hampshire	702,056	0.0%
49	Rhode Island	383,794	0.0%
50	Vermont	309,125	0.0%
	District of Columbia	588,458	0.0%

Source: U.S. Environmental Protection Agency, Office of Pollution Prevention and Toxics Information Management "2014 Toxics Release Inventory" (http://www.epa.gov/triexplorer/)

*National total does not include 2,900,892 pounds of toxins in U.S. territories. Includes discharges to air, surface water, underground injection, and surface land. Includes both original (or manufacturing) industries and those added by EPA since it began tracking releases.

Toxic Releases: Total Air Emissions in 2014

National Total = 735,987,481 Pounds*

ALPHA ORDER

RANK	STATE	POUNDS	% of USA
7	Alabama	34,638,814	4.7%
48	Alaska	355,045	0.0%
35	Arizona	2,278,256	0.3%
19	Arkansas	16,329,494	2.2%
27	California	8,432,275	1.1%
36	Colorado	2,223,343	0.3%
44	Connecticut	1,018,050	0.1%
45	Delaware	805,127	0.1%
13	Florida	24,865,537	3.4%
5	Georgia	40,242,974	5.5%
40	Hawaii	1,567,674	0.2%
33	Idaho	4,826,010	0.7%
9	Illinois	28,109,479	3.8%
4	Indiana	43,737,527	5.9%
16	Iowa	22,733,876	3.1%
22	Kansas	10,314,691	1.4%
6	Kentucky	39,094,763	5.3%
2	Louisiana	49,184,501	6.7%
34	Maine	3,517,975	0.5%
32	Maryland	5,015,926	0.7%
43	Massachusetts	1,199,286	0.2%
18	Michigan	18,066,535	2.5%
23	Minnesota	9,972,174	1.4%
12	Mississippi	25,344,368	3.4%
24	Missouri	9,838,175	1.3%
39	Montana	2,037,612	0.3%
31	Nebraska	5,629,703	0.8%
41	Nevada	1,510,612	0.2%
47	New Hampshire	518,243	0.1%
37	New Jersey	2,101,415	0.3%
46	New Mexico	759,066	0.1%
29	New York	6,553,409	0.9%
14	North Carolina	23,079,735	3.1%
26	North Dakota	9,046,680	1.2%
3	Ohio	44,944,789	6.1%
20	Oklahoma	12,798,354	1.7%
28	Oregon	6,569,173	0.9%
10	Pennsylvania	28,061,208	3.8%
49	Rhode Island	156,033	0.0%
11	South Carolina	26,538,763	3.6%
42	South Dakota	1,219,198	0.2%
8	Tennessee	28,781,971	3.9%
1	Texas	60,462,539	8.2%
30	Utah	6,484,932	0.9%
50	Vermont	31,500	0.0%
15	Virginia	23,005,746	3.1%
25	Washington	9,506,745	1.3%
17	West Virginia	18,224,835	2.5%
21	Wisconsin	12,215,196	1.7%
38	Wyoming	2,037,715	0.3%

RANK ORDER

RANK	STATE	POUNDS	% of USA
1	Texas	60,462,539	8.2%
2	Louisiana	49,184,501	6.7%
3	Ohio	44,944,789	6.1%
4	Indiana	43,737,527	5.9%
5	Georgia	40,242,974	5.5%
6	Kentucky	39,094,763	5.3%
7	Alabama	34,638,814	4.7%
8	Tennessee	28,781,971	3.9%
9	Illinois	28,109,479	3.8%
10	Pennsylvania	28,061,208	3.8%
11	South Carolina	26,538,763	3.6%
12	Mississippi	25,344,368	3.4%
13	Florida	24,865,537	3.4%
14	North Carolina	23,079,735	3.1%
15	Virginia	23,005,746	3.1%
16	Iowa	22,733,876	3.1%
17	West Virginia	18,224,835	2.5%
18	Michigan	18,066,535	2.5%
19	Arkansas	16,329,494	2.2%
20	Oklahoma	12,798,354	1.7%
21	Wisconsin	12,215,196	1.7%
22	Kansas	10,314,691	1.4%
23	Minnesota	9,972,174	1.4%
24	Missouri	9,838,175	1.3%
25	Washington	9,506,745	1.3%
26	North Dakota	9,046,680	1.2%
27	California	8,432,275	1.1%
28	Oregon	6,569,173	0.9%
29	New York	6,553,409	0.9%
30	Utah	6,484,932	0.9%
31	Nebraska	5,629,703	0.8%
32	Maryland	5,015,926	0.7%
33	Idaho	4,826,010	0.7%
34	Maine	3,517,975	0.5%
35	Arizona	2,278,256	0.3%
36	Colorado	2,223,343	0.3%
37	New Jersey	2,101,415	0.3%
38	Wyoming	2,037,715	0.3%
39	Montana	2,037,612	0.3%
40	Hawaii	1,567,674	0.2%
41	Nevada	1,510,612	0.2%
42	South Dakota	1,219,198	0.2%
43	Massachusetts	1,199,286	0.2%
44	Connecticut	1,018,050	0.1%
45	Delaware	805,127	0.1%
46	New Mexico	759,066	0.1%
47	New Hampshire	518,243	0.1%
48	Alaska	355,045	0.0%
49	Rhode Island	156,033	0.0%
50	Vermont	31,500	0.0%
	District of Columbia	434	0.0%

Source: U.S. Environmental Protection Agency, Office of Pollution Prevention and Toxics Information Management "2014 Toxics Release Inventory" (http://www.epa.gov/triexplorer/)
*Includes fugitive and point source air emissions. National total does not include 2,237,804 pounds of emissions in U.S. territories. Includes both original (or manufacturing) industries and those added by EPA since it began tracking releases.

Toxic Releases: Total Surface Water Discharges in 2014

National Total = 215,359,033 Pounds*

ALPHA ORDER

RANK	STATE	POUNDS	% of USA
4	Alabama	14,042,176	6.5%
37	Alaska	586,237	0.3%
48	Arizona	1,156	0.0%
16	Arkansas	4,598,199	2.1%
23	California	2,908,488	1.4%
33	Colorado	1,494,986	0.7%
43	Connecticut	84,869	0.0%
22	Delaware	2,931,067	1.4%
30	Florida	1,664,083	0.8%
3	Georgia	16,037,731	7.4%
38	Hawaii	534,190	0.2%
24	Idaho	2,852,758	1.3%
14	Illinois	5,422,281	2.5%
1	Indiana	22,455,054	10.4%
19	Iowa	3,589,600	1.7%
34	Kansas	1,253,830	0.6%
13	Kentucky	5,794,185	2.7%
5	Louisiana	13,311,011	6.2%
26	Maine	2,814,144	1.3%
36	Maryland	921,854	0.4%
45	Massachusetts	35,205	0.0%
27	Michigan	2,264,288	1.1%
32	Minnesota	1,608,869	0.7%
10	Mississippi	7,580,520	3.5%
28	Missouri	2,253,728	1.0%
39	Montana	225,755	0.1%
6	Nebraska	11,626,513	5.4%
47	Nevada	3,703	0.0%
50	New Hampshire	658	0.0%
15	New Jersey	5,394,428	2.5%
44	New Mexico	35,625	0.0%
12	New York	6,432,966	3.0%
8	North Carolina	8,643,534	4.0%
40	North Dakota	202,150	0.1%
11	Ohio	6,909,608	3.2%
20	Oklahoma	3,582,303	1.7%
35	Oregon	1,193,378	0.6%
9	Pennsylvania	8,188,891	3.8%
49	Rhode Island	758	0.0%
21	South Carolina	3,318,281	1.5%
25	South Dakota	2,829,537	1.3%
17	Tennessee	4,258,163	2.0%
2	Texas	16,303,947	7.6%
41	Utah	126,185	0.1%
42	Vermont	124,825	0.1%
7	Virginia	11,219,129	5.2%
29	Washington	2,213,777	1.0%
31	West Virginia	1,614,469	0.7%
18	Wisconsin	3,855,892	1.8%
46	Wyoming	12,160	0.0%

RANK ORDER

RANK	STATE	POUNDS	% of USA
1	Indiana	22,455,054	10.4%
2	Texas	16,303,947	7.6%
3	Georgia	16,037,731	7.4%
4	Alabama	14,042,176	6.5%
5	Louisiana	13,311,011	6.2%
6	Nebraska	11,626,513	5.4%
7	Virginia	11,219,129	5.2%
8	North Carolina	8,643,534	4.0%
9	Pennsylvania	8,188,891	3.8%
10	Mississippi	7,580,520	3.5%
11	Ohio	6,909,608	3.2%
12	New York	6,432,966	3.0%
13	Kentucky	5,794,185	2.7%
14	Illinois	5,422,281	2.5%
15	New Jersey	5,394,428	2.5%
16	Arkansas	4,598,199	2.1%
17	Tennessee	4,258,163	2.0%
18	Wisconsin	3,855,892	1.8%
19	Iowa	3,589,600	1.7%
20	Oklahoma	3,582,303	1.7%
21	South Carolina	3,318,281	1.5%
22	Delaware	2,931,067	1.4%
23	California	2,908,488	1.4%
24	Idaho	2,852,758	1.3%
25	South Dakota	2,829,537	1.3%
26	Maine	2,814,144	1.3%
27	Michigan	2,264,288	1.1%
28	Missouri	2,253,728	1.0%
29	Washington	2,213,777	1.0%
30	Florida	1,664,083	0.8%
31	West Virginia	1,614,469	0.7%
32	Minnesota	1,608,869	0.7%
33	Colorado	1,494,986	0.7%
34	Kansas	1,253,830	0.6%
35	Oregon	1,193,378	0.6%
36	Maryland	921,854	0.4%
37	Alaska	586,237	0.3%
38	Hawaii	534,190	0.2%
39	Montana	225,755	0.1%
40	North Dakota	202,150	0.1%
41	Utah	126,185	0.1%
42	Vermont	124,825	0.1%
43	Connecticut	84,869	0.0%
44	New Mexico	35,625	0.0%
45	Massachusetts	35,205	0.0%
46	Wyoming	12,160	0.0%
47	Nevada	3,703	0.0%
48	Arizona	1,156	0.0%
49	Rhode Island	758	0.0%
50	New Hampshire	658	0.0%
	District of Columbia	1,889	0.0%

Source: U.S. Environmental Protection Agency, Office of Pollution Prevention and Toxics Information Management "2014 Toxics Release Inventory" (http://www.epa.gov/triexplorer/)

*National total does not include 191,222 pounds of discharges in U.S. territories. Includes both original (or manufacturing) industries and those added by EPA since it began tracking releases.

Hazardous Waste Sites on the National Priority List in 2016

National Total = 1,376 Sites*

ALPHA ORDER

RANK	STATE	SITES	% of USA
28	Alabama	15	1.1%
45	Alaska	6	0.4%
39	Arizona	9	0.7%
39	Arkansas	9	0.7%
2	California	98	7.1%
21	Colorado	20	1.5%
28	Connecticut	15	1.1%
31	Delaware	14	1.0%
6	Florida	54	3.9%
24	Georgia	17	1.2%
46	Hawaii	3	0.2%
39	Idaho	9	0.7%
9	Illinois	49	3.6%
11	Indiana	39	2.8%
33	Iowa	13	0.9%
33	Kansas	13	0.9%
33	Kentucky	13	0.9%
28	Louisiana	15	1.1%
33	Maine	13	0.9%
19	Maryland	21	1.5%
14	Massachusetts	33	2.4%
5	Michigan	67	4.9%
17	Minnesota	25	1.8%
39	Mississippi	9	0.7%
14	Missouri	33	2.4%
22	Montana	19	1.4%
26	Nebraska	16	1.2%
49	Nevada	1	0.1%
19	New Hampshire	21	1.5%
1	New Jersey	115	8.4%
26	New Mexico	16	1.2%
4	New York	86	6.3%
11	North Carolina	39	2.8%
50	North Dakota	0	0.0%
10	Ohio	43	3.1%
44	Oklahoma	8	0.6%
31	Oregon	14	1.0%
3	Pennsylvania	97	7.0%
37	Rhode Island	12	0.9%
17	South Carolina	25	1.8%
47	South Dakota	2	0.1%
24	Tennessee	17	1.2%
7	Texas	52	3.8%
23	Utah	18	1.3%
37	Vermont	12	0.9%
16	Virginia	31	2.3%
8	Washington	51	3.7%
39	West Virginia	9	0.7%
13	Wisconsin	38	2.8%
47	Wyoming	2	0.1%

RANK ORDER

RANK	STATE	SITES	% of USA
1	New Jersey	115	8.4%
2	California	98	7.1%
3	Pennsylvania	97	7.0%
4	New York	86	6.3%
5	Michigan	67	4.9%
6	Florida	54	3.9%
7	Texas	52	3.8%
8	Washington	51	3.7%
9	Illinois	49	3.6%
10	Ohio	43	3.1%
11	Indiana	39	2.8%
11	North Carolina	39	2.8%
13	Wisconsin	38	2.8%
14	Massachusetts	33	2.4%
14	Missouri	33	2.4%
16	Virginia	31	2.3%
17	Minnesota	25	1.8%
17	South Carolina	25	1.8%
19	Maryland	21	1.5%
19	New Hampshire	21	1.5%
21	Colorado	20	1.5%
22	Montana	19	1.4%
23	Utah	18	1.3%
24	Georgia	17	1.2%
24	Tennessee	17	1.2%
26	Nebraska	16	1.2%
26	New Mexico	16	1.2%
28	Alabama	15	1.1%
28	Connecticut	15	1.1%
28	Louisiana	15	1.1%
31	Delaware	14	1.0%
31	Oregon	14	1.0%
33	Iowa	13	0.9%
33	Kansas	13	0.9%
33	Kentucky	13	0.9%
33	Maine	13	0.9%
37	Rhode Island	12	0.9%
37	Vermont	12	0.9%
39	Arizona	9	0.7%
39	Arkansas	9	0.7%
39	Idaho	9	0.7%
39	Mississippi	9	0.7%
39	West Virginia	9	0.7%
44	Oklahoma	8	0.6%
45	Alaska	6	0.4%
46	Hawaii	3	0.2%
47	South Dakota	2	0.1%
47	Wyoming	2	0.1%
49	Nevada	1	0.1%
50	North Dakota	0	0.0%
	District of Columbia	1	0.1%

Source: U.S. Environmental Protection Agency
"National Priorities List (NPL) Sites in the United States" (http://www.epa.gov/superfund/sites/npl/)
*As of January 22, 2016. Includes final and proposed General Superfund and Federal Facilities Sites. National total includes 16 sites in Puerto Rico, two in Guam, and one in the U.S. Virgin Islands.

Hazardous Waste Sites on the National Priority List per 10,000 Square Miles in 2016
National Rate = 3.6 Sites per 10,000 Square Miles*

ALPHA ORDER

RANK	STATE	RATE
27	Alabama	2.9
48	Alaska	0.1
45	Arizona	0.8
38	Arkansas	1.7
20	California	6.0
35	Colorado	1.9
5	Connecticut	27.1
3	Delaware	56.2
14	Florida	8.2
27	Georgia	2.9
31	Hawaii	2.7
43	Idaho	1.1
13	Illinois	8.5
11	Indiana	10.7
32	Iowa	2.3
39	Kansas	1.6
26	Kentucky	3.2
27	Louisiana	2.9
24	Maine	3.7
8	Maryland	16.9
4	Massachusetts	31.3
19	Michigan	6.9
27	Minnesota	2.9
35	Mississippi	1.9
22	Missouri	4.7
41	Montana	1.3
33	Nebraska	2.1
48	Nevada	0.1
6	New Hampshire	22.5
1	New Jersey	131.8
41	New Mexico	1.3
9	New York	15.8
16	North Carolina	7.2
50	North Dakota	0.0
12	Ohio	9.6
43	Oklahoma	1.1
40	Oregon	1.4
7	Pennsylvania	21.1
2	Rhode Island	77.7
15	South Carolina	7.8
46	South Dakota	0.3
23	Tennessee	4.0
35	Texas	1.9
33	Utah	2.1
10	Vermont	12.5
16	Virginia	7.2
16	Washington	7.2
24	West Virginia	3.7
21	Wisconsin	5.8
47	Wyoming	0.2

RANK ORDER

RANK	STATE	RATE
1	New Jersey	131.8
2	Rhode Island	77.7
3	Delaware	56.2
4	Massachusetts	31.3
5	Connecticut	27.1
6	New Hampshire	22.5
7	Pennsylvania	21.1
8	Maryland	16.9
9	New York	15.8
10	Vermont	12.5
11	Indiana	10.7
12	Ohio	9.6
13	Illinois	8.5
14	Florida	8.2
15	South Carolina	7.8
16	North Carolina	7.2
16	Virginia	7.2
16	Washington	7.2
19	Michigan	6.9
20	California	6.0
21	Wisconsin	5.8
22	Missouri	4.7
23	Tennessee	4.0
24	Maine	3.7
24	West Virginia	3.7
26	Kentucky	3.2
27	Alabama	2.9
27	Georgia	2.9
27	Louisiana	2.9
27	Minnesota	2.9
31	Hawaii	2.7
32	Iowa	2.3
33	Nebraska	2.1
33	Utah	2.1
35	Colorado	1.9
35	Mississippi	1.9
35	Texas	1.9
38	Arkansas	1.7
39	Kansas	1.6
40	Oregon	1.4
41	Montana	1.3
41	New Mexico	1.3
43	Idaho	1.1
43	Oklahoma	1.1
45	Arizona	0.8
46	South Dakota	0.3
47	Wyoming	0.2
48	Alaska	0.1
48	Nevada	0.1
50	North Dakota	0.0
	District of Columbia**	NA

Source: CQ Press using data from U.S. Environmental Protection Agency
"National Priorities List (NPL) Sites in the United States" (http://www.epa.gov/superfund/sites/npl/)
*As of January 22, 2016. Includes final and proposed General Superfund and Federal Facilities Sites. National rate excludes sites and square miles in Puerto Rico, Guam and the Virgin Islands. Based on land and water area of states.
**The District of Columbia has one site in its 68 square miles.

Hazardous Waste Sites Deleted from the National Priorities List as of 2016

National Total = 391 Sites*

ALPHA ORDER

RANK	STATE	SITES	% of USA
39	Alabama	2	0.5%
31	Alaska	3	0.8%
31	Arizona	3	0.8%
13	Arkansas	8	2.0%
8	California	13	3.3%
31	Colorado	3	0.8%
31	Connecticut	3	0.8%
14	Delaware	7	1.8%
4	Florida	26	6.6%
24	Georgia	5	1.3%
44	Hawaii	1	0.3%
31	Idaho	3	0.8%
19	Illinois	6	1.5%
11	Indiana	10	2.6%
11	Iowa	10	2.6%
24	Kansas	5	1.3%
14	Kentucky	7	1.8%
9	Louisiana	12	3.1%
31	Maine	3	0.8%
28	Maryland	4	1.0%
19	Massachusetts	6	1.5%
6	Michigan	20	5.1%
5	Minnesota	21	5.4%
31	Mississippi	3	0.8%
24	Missouri	5	1.3%
49	Montana	0	0.0%
44	Nebraska	1	0.3%
49	Nevada	0	0.0%
44	New Hampshire	1	0.3%
1	New Jersey	35	9.0%
28	New Mexico	4	1.0%
2	New York	31	7.9%
31	North Carolina	3	0.8%
39	North Dakota	2	0.5%
14	Ohio	7	1.8%
14	Oklahoma	7	1.8%
24	Oregon	5	1.3%
3	Pennsylvania	30	7.7%
44	Rhode Island	1	0.3%
19	South Carolina	6	1.5%
39	South Dakota	2	0.5%
19	Tennessee	6	1.5%
9	Texas	12	3.1%
19	Utah	6	1.5%
39	Vermont	2	0.5%
28	Virginia	4	1.0%
7	Washington	17	4.3%
39	West Virginia	2	0.5%
14	Wisconsin	7	1.8%
44	Wyoming	1	0.3%

RANK ORDER

RANK	STATE	SITES	% of USA
1	New Jersey	35	9.0%
2	New York	31	7.9%
3	Pennsylvania	30	7.7%
4	Florida	26	6.6%
5	Minnesota	21	5.4%
6	Michigan	20	5.1%
7	Washington	17	4.3%
8	California	13	3.3%
9	Louisiana	12	3.1%
9	Texas	12	3.1%
11	Indiana	10	2.6%
11	Iowa	10	2.6%
13	Arkansas	8	2.0%
14	Delaware	7	1.8%
14	Kentucky	7	1.8%
14	Ohio	7	1.8%
14	Oklahoma	7	1.8%
14	Wisconsin	7	1.8%
19	Illinois	6	1.5%
19	Massachusetts	6	1.5%
19	South Carolina	6	1.5%
19	Tennessee	6	1.5%
19	Utah	6	1.5%
24	Georgia	5	1.3%
24	Kansas	5	1.3%
24	Missouri	5	1.3%
24	Oregon	5	1.3%
28	Maryland	4	1.0%
28	New Mexico	4	1.0%
28	Virginia	4	1.0%
31	Alaska	3	0.8%
31	Arizona	3	0.8%
31	Colorado	3	0.8%
31	Connecticut	3	0.8%
31	Idaho	3	0.8%
31	Maine	3	0.8%
31	Mississippi	3	0.8%
31	North Carolina	3	0.8%
39	Alabama	2	0.5%
39	North Dakota	2	0.5%
39	South Dakota	2	0.5%
39	Vermont	2	0.5%
39	West Virginia	2	0.5%
44	Hawaii	1	0.3%
44	Nebraska	1	0.3%
44	New Hampshire	1	0.3%
44	Rhode Island	1	0.3%
44	Wyoming	1	0.3%
49	Montana	0	0.0%
49	Nevada	0	0.0%
	District of Columbia	0	0.0%

Source: U.S. Environmental Protection Agency
"National Priorities List (NPL) Sites in the United States" (http://www.epa.gov/superfund/sites/npl/)
*Cumulative total as of January 22, 2016. National total includes six sites in Puerto Rico and four in other U.S. territories.

VIII. Geography

Total Area of States in Square Miles in 2010 241
Land Area of States in Square Miles in 2010 242
Water Area of States in Square Miles in 2010 243
Highest Point of Elevation in Feet 244
Lowest Point of Elevation in Feet. 245
Approximate Mean Elevation in Feet. 246
Normal Daily Mean Temperature* 247
Percent of Days That Are Sunny* 248
Average Wind Speed (MPH)* 249

Hazardous Weather Fatalities in 2014 250
Tornadoes in 2015. 251
Fatalities Caused by Tornadoes: 2008 to 2015 252
Cost of Damage from Hazardous Weather in 2014 253
National Park Service Land in 2014. 254
Recreation Visits to National Park Service Areas in 2014. . 255
Percent Change in National Park Service Recreation
    Visits: 2013 to 2014 256

Total Area of States in Square Miles in 2010

National Total = 3,796,742 Square Miles*

ALPHA ORDER

RANK	STATE	MILES	% of USA
30	Alabama	52,420	1.4%
1	Alaska	665,384	17.5%
6	Arizona	113,990	3.0%
29	Arkansas	53,179	1.4%
3	California	163,695	4.3%
8	Colorado	104,094	2.7%
48	Connecticut	5,543	0.1%
49	Delaware	2,489	0.1%
22	Florida	65,758	1.7%
24	Georgia	59,425	1.6%
43	Hawaii	10,932	0.3%
14	Idaho	83,569	2.2%
25	Illinois	57,914	1.5%
38	Indiana	36,420	1.0%
26	Iowa	56,273	1.5%
15	Kansas	82,278	2.2%
37	Kentucky	40,408	1.1%
31	Louisiana	52,378	1.4%
39	Maine	35,380	0.9%
42	Maryland	12,406	0.3%
44	Massachusetts	10,554	0.3%
11	Michigan	96,714	2.5%
12	Minnesota	86,936	2.3%
32	Mississippi	48,432	1.3%
21	Missouri	69,707	1.8%
4	Montana	147,040	3.9%
16	Nebraska	77,348	2.0%
7	Nevada	110,572	2.9%
46	New Hampshire	9,349	0.2%
47	New Jersey	8,723	0.2%
5	New Mexico	121,590	3.2%
27	New York	54,555	1.4%
28	North Carolina	53,819	1.4%
19	North Dakota	70,698	1.9%
34	Ohio	44,826	1.2%
20	Oklahoma	69,899	1.8%
9	Oregon	98,379	2.6%
33	Pennsylvania	46,054	1.2%
50	Rhode Island	1,545	0.0%
40	South Carolina	32,020	0.8%
17	South Dakota	77,116	2.0%
36	Tennessee	42,144	1.1%
2	Texas	268,596	7.1%
13	Utah	84,897	2.2%
45	Vermont	9,616	0.3%
35	Virginia	42,775	1.1%
18	Washington	71,298	1.9%
41	West Virginia	24,230	0.6%
23	Wisconsin	65,496	1.7%
10	Wyoming	97,813	2.6%

RANK ORDER

RANK	STATE	MILES	% of USA
1	Alaska	665,384	17.5%
2	Texas	268,596	7.1%
3	California	163,695	4.3%
4	Montana	147,040	3.9%
5	New Mexico	121,590	3.2%
6	Arizona	113,990	3.0%
7	Nevada	110,572	2.9%
8	Colorado	104,094	2.7%
9	Oregon	98,379	2.6%
10	Wyoming	97,813	2.6%
11	Michigan	96,714	2.5%
12	Minnesota	86,936	2.3%
13	Utah	84,897	2.2%
14	Idaho	83,569	2.2%
15	Kansas	82,278	2.2%
16	Nebraska	77,348	2.0%
17	South Dakota	77,116	2.0%
18	Washington	71,298	1.9%
19	North Dakota	70,698	1.9%
20	Oklahoma	69,899	1.8%
21	Missouri	69,707	1.8%
22	Florida	65,758	1.7%
23	Wisconsin	65,496	1.7%
24	Georgia	59,425	1.6%
25	Illinois	57,914	1.5%
26	Iowa	56,273	1.5%
27	New York	54,555	1.4%
28	North Carolina	53,819	1.4%
29	Arkansas	53,179	1.4%
30	Alabama	52,420	1.4%
31	Louisiana	52,378	1.4%
32	Mississippi	48,432	1.3%
33	Pennsylvania	46,054	1.2%
34	Ohio	44,826	1.2%
35	Virginia	42,775	1.1%
36	Tennessee	42,144	1.1%
37	Kentucky	40,408	1.1%
38	Indiana	36,420	1.0%
39	Maine	35,380	0.9%
40	South Carolina	32,020	0.8%
41	West Virginia	24,230	0.6%
42	Maryland	12,406	0.3%
43	Hawaii	10,932	0.3%
44	Massachusetts	10,554	0.3%
45	Vermont	9,616	0.3%
46	New Hampshire	9,349	0.2%
47	New Jersey	8,723	0.2%
48	Connecticut	5,543	0.1%
49	Delaware	2,489	0.1%
50	Rhode Island	1,545	0.0%
	District of Columbia	68	0.0%

Source: U.S. Bureau of the Census
"State Area Measurements" (http://www.census.gov/geo/reference/state-area.html)
*Total of land and water area. Revised figures as of January 1, 2010

Land Area of States in Square Miles in 2010

National Total = 3,531,905 Square Miles of Land Area*

<u>ALPHA ORDER</u>

RANK	STATE	MILES	% of USA
28	Alabama	50,645	1.4%
1	Alaska	570,641	16.2%
6	Arizona	113,594	3.2%
27	Arkansas	52,035	1.5%
3	California	155,779	4.4%
8	Colorado	103,642	2.9%
48	Connecticut	4,842	0.1%
49	Delaware	1,949	0.1%
26	Florida	53,625	1.5%
21	Georgia	57,513	1.6%
47	Hawaii	6,423	0.2%
11	Idaho	82,643	2.3%
24	Illinois	55,519	1.6%
38	Indiana	35,826	1.0%
23	Iowa	55,857	1.6%
13	Kansas	81,759	2.3%
37	Kentucky	39,486	1.1%
33	Louisiana	43,204	1.2%
39	Maine	30,843	0.9%
42	Maryland	9,707	0.3%
45	Massachusetts	7,800	0.2%
22	Michigan	56,539	1.6%
14	Minnesota	79,627	2.3%
31	Mississippi	46,923	1.3%
18	Missouri	68,742	1.9%
4	Montana	145,546	4.1%
15	Nebraska	76,824	2.2%
7	Nevada	109,781	3.1%
44	New Hampshire	8,953	0.3%
46	New Jersey	7,354	0.2%
5	New Mexico	121,298	3.4%
30	New York	47,126	1.3%
29	North Carolina	48,618	1.4%
17	North Dakota	69,001	2.0%
35	Ohio	40,861	1.2%
19	Oklahoma	68,595	1.9%
10	Oregon	95,988	2.7%
32	Pennsylvania	44,743	1.3%
50	Rhode Island	1,034	0.0%
40	South Carolina	30,061	0.9%
16	South Dakota	75,811	2.1%
34	Tennessee	41,235	1.2%
2	Texas	261,232	7.4%
12	Utah	82,170	2.3%
43	Vermont	9,217	0.3%
36	Virginia	39,490	1.1%
20	Washington	66,456	1.9%
41	West Virginia	24,038	0.7%
25	Wisconsin	54,158	1.5%
9	Wyoming	97,093	2.7%

<u>RANK ORDER</u>

RANK	STATE	MILES	% of USA
1	Alaska	570,641	16.2%
2	Texas	261,232	7.4%
3	California	155,779	4.4%
4	Montana	145,546	4.1%
5	New Mexico	121,298	3.4%
6	Arizona	113,594	3.2%
7	Nevada	109,781	3.1%
8	Colorado	103,642	2.9%
9	Wyoming	97,093	2.7%
10	Oregon	95,988	2.7%
11	Idaho	82,643	2.3%
12	Utah	82,170	2.3%
13	Kansas	81,759	2.3%
14	Minnesota	79,627	2.3%
15	Nebraska	76,824	2.2%
16	South Dakota	75,811	2.1%
17	North Dakota	69,001	2.0%
18	Missouri	68,742	1.9%
19	Oklahoma	68,595	1.9%
20	Washington	66,456	1.9%
21	Georgia	57,513	1.6%
22	Michigan	56,539	1.6%
23	Iowa	55,857	1.6%
24	Illinois	55,519	1.6%
25	Wisconsin	54,158	1.5%
26	Florida	53,625	1.5%
27	Arkansas	52,035	1.5%
28	Alabama	50,645	1.4%
29	North Carolina	48,618	1.4%
30	New York	47,126	1.3%
31	Mississippi	46,923	1.3%
32	Pennsylvania	44,743	1.3%
33	Louisiana	43,204	1.2%
34	Tennessee	41,235	1.2%
35	Ohio	40,861	1.2%
36	Virginia	39,490	1.1%
37	Kentucky	39,486	1.1%
38	Indiana	35,826	1.0%
39	Maine	30,843	0.9%
40	South Carolina	30,061	0.9%
41	West Virginia	24,038	0.7%
42	Maryland	9,707	0.3%
43	Vermont	9,217	0.3%
44	New Hampshire	8,953	0.3%
45	Massachusetts	7,800	0.2%
46	New Jersey	7,354	0.2%
47	Hawaii	6,423	0.2%
48	Connecticut	4,842	0.1%
49	Delaware	1,949	0.1%
50	Rhode Island	1,034	0.0%
	District of Columbia	61	0.0%

Source: U.S. Bureau of the Census
   "State Area Measurements" (http://www.census.gov/geo/reference/state-area.html)
*Includes dry land temporarily or partially covered by water, such as marshland, swamps, etc.; streams and canals under one-eighth mile wide; and lakes, reservoirs, and ponds under 40 acres. Revised figures as of August 2010.

Water Area of States in Square Miles in 2010

National Total = 264,837 Square Miles of Water*

ALPHA ORDER

RANK	STATE	MILES	% of USA
23	Alabama	1,775	0.7%
1	Alaska	94,743	35.8%
48	Arizona	396	0.1%
31	Arkansas	1,143	0.4%
6	California	7,916	3.0%
44	Colorado	452	0.2%
38	Connecticut	701	0.3%
40	Delaware	540	0.2%
3	Florida	12,133	4.6%
22	Georgia	1,912	0.7%
13	Hawaii	4,509	1.7%
33	Idaho	926	0.3%
19	Illinois	2,395	0.9%
39	Indiana	593	0.2%
45	Iowa	416	0.2%
42	Kansas	520	0.2%
34	Kentucky	921	0.3%
5	Louisiana	9,174	3.5%
12	Maine	4,537	1.7%
18	Maryland	2,699	1.0%
16	Massachusetts	2,754	1.0%
2	Michigan	40,175	15.2%
9	Minnesota	7,309	2.8%
25	Mississippi	1,509	0.6%
32	Missouri	965	0.4%
26	Montana	1,494	0.6%
41	Nebraska	524	0.2%
36	Nevada	791	0.3%
47	New Hampshire	397	0.1%
27	New Jersey	1,368	0.5%
49	New Mexico	292	0.1%
7	New York	7,429	2.8%
10	North Carolina	5,201	2.0%
24	North Dakota	1,698	0.6%
14	Ohio	3,965	1.5%
30	Oklahoma	1,304	0.5%
20	Oregon	2,391	0.9%
28	Pennsylvania	1,312	0.5%
43	Rhode Island	511	0.2%
21	South Carolina	1,960	0.7%
29	South Dakota	1,305	0.5%
35	Tennessee	909	0.3%
8	Texas	7,365	2.8%
17	Utah	2,727	1.0%
46	Vermont	400	0.2%
15	Virginia	3,285	1.2%
11	Washington	4,842	1.8%
50	West Virginia	192	0.1%
4	Wisconsin	11,339	4.3%
37	Wyoming	720	0.3%

RANK ORDER

RANK	STATE	MILES	% of USA
1	Alaska	94,743	35.8%
2	Michigan	40,175	15.2%
3	Florida	12,133	4.6%
4	Wisconsin	11,339	4.3%
5	Louisiana	9,174	3.5%
6	California	7,916	3.0%
7	New York	7,429	2.8%
8	Texas	7,365	2.8%
9	Minnesota	7,309	2.8%
10	North Carolina	5,201	2.0%
11	Washington	4,842	1.8%
12	Maine	4,537	1.7%
13	Hawaii	4,509	1.7%
14	Ohio	3,965	1.5%
15	Virginia	3,285	1.2%
16	Massachusetts	2,754	1.0%
17	Utah	2,727	1.0%
18	Maryland	2,699	1.0%
19	Illinois	2,395	0.9%
20	Oregon	2,391	0.9%
21	South Carolina	1,960	0.7%
22	Georgia	1,912	0.7%
23	Alabama	1,775	0.7%
24	North Dakota	1,698	0.6%
25	Mississippi	1,509	0.6%
26	Montana	1,494	0.6%
27	New Jersey	1,368	0.5%
28	Pennsylvania	1,312	0.5%
29	South Dakota	1,305	0.5%
30	Oklahoma	1,304	0.5%
31	Arkansas	1,143	0.4%
32	Missouri	965	0.4%
33	Idaho	926	0.3%
34	Kentucky	921	0.3%
35	Tennessee	909	0.3%
36	Nevada	791	0.3%
37	Wyoming	720	0.3%
38	Connecticut	701	0.3%
39	Indiana	593	0.2%
40	Delaware	540	0.2%
41	Nebraska	524	0.2%
42	Kansas	520	0.2%
43	Rhode Island	511	0.2%
44	Colorado	452	0.2%
45	Iowa	416	0.2%
46	Vermont	400	0.2%
47	New Hampshire	397	0.1%
48	Arizona	396	0.1%
49	New Mexico	292	0.1%
50	West Virginia	192	0.1%
	District of Columbia	7	0.0%

Source: U.S. Bureau of the Census
   "State Area Measurements" (http://www.census.gov/geo/reference/state-area.html)
*Includes permanent inland water surface, such as lakes, reservoirs, and ponds having an area of 40 acres or more, canals one-eighth mile or more in width; coastal waters behind or sheltered by headlands or islands separated by less than 1 nautical mile of water, and islands under 40 acres in area. Excludes areas of oceans, bays, etc., lying within U.S. jurisdiction but not defined as inland water. Revised figures as of August 2010.

Highest Point of Elevation in Feet

National High Point = 20,320 Feet Above Sea Level (Mt. McKinley, Alaska)

ALPHA ORDER

RANK	STATE	HIGHEST POINT
35	Alabama	2,407
1	Alaska	20,320
12	Arizona	12,633
34	Arkansas	2,753
2	California	14,494
3	Colorado	14,433
36	Connecticut	2,380
49	Delaware	448
50	Florida	345
25	Georgia	4,784
6	Hawaii	13,796
11	Idaho	12,662
45	Illinois	1,235
44	Indiana	1,257
42	Iowa	1,670
28	Kansas	4,039
27	Kentucky	4,145
48	Louisiana	535
22	Maine	5,268
32	Maryland	3,360
31	Massachusetts	3,491
38	Michigan	1,979
37	Minnesota	2,301
47	Mississippi	806
41	Missouri	1,772
10	Montana	12,799
20	Nebraska	5,424
9	Nevada	13,140
18	New Hampshire	6,288
40	New Jersey	1,803
8	New Mexico	13,161
21	New York	5,344
16	North Carolina	6,684
30	North Dakota	3,506
43	Ohio	1,550
23	Oklahoma	4,973
13	Oregon	11,239
33	Pennsylvania	3,213
46	Rhode Island	812
29	South Carolina	3,560
15	South Dakota	7,242
17	Tennessee	6,643
14	Texas	8,749
7	Utah	13,528
26	Vermont	4,393
19	Virginia	5,729
4	Washington	14,411
24	West Virginia	4,863
39	Wisconsin	1,951
5	Wyoming	13,804

RANK ORDER

RANK	STATE	HIGHEST POINT
1	Alaska	20,320
2	California	14,494
3	Colorado	14,433
4	Washington	14,411
5	Wyoming	13,804
6	Hawaii	13,796
7	Utah	13,528
8	New Mexico	13,161
9	Nevada	13,140
10	Montana	12,799
11	Idaho	12,662
12	Arizona	12,633
13	Oregon	11,239
14	Texas	8,749
15	South Dakota	7,242
16	North Carolina	6,684
17	Tennessee	6,643
18	New Hampshire	6,288
19	Virginia	5,729
20	Nebraska	5,424
21	New York	5,344
22	Maine	5,268
23	Oklahoma	4,973
24	West Virginia	4,863
25	Georgia	4,784
26	Vermont	4,393
27	Kentucky	4,145
28	Kansas	4,039
29	South Carolina	3,560
30	North Dakota	3,506
31	Massachusetts	3,491
32	Maryland	3,360
33	Pennsylvania	3,213
34	Arkansas	2,753
35	Alabama	2,407
36	Connecticut	2,380
37	Minnesota	2,301
38	Michigan	1,979
39	Wisconsin	1,951
40	New Jersey	1,803
41	Missouri	1,772
42	Iowa	1,670
43	Ohio	1,550
44	Indiana	1,257
45	Illinois	1,235
46	Rhode Island	812
47	Mississippi	806
48	Louisiana	535
49	Delaware	448
50	Florida	345
	District of Columbia	410

Source: U.S. Department of Interior, U.S. Geological Survey
"Elevations and Distances in the United States" (http://erg.usgs.gov/isb/pubs/booklets/elvadist/elvadist.html)

Lowest Point of Elevation in Feet

National Low Point = 282 Feet Below Sea Level (Death Valley, California)*

ALPHA ORDER

RANK	STATE	LOWEST POINT
3	Alabama	0
3	Alaska	0
26	Arizona	70
25	Arkansas	55
1	California	(282)
50	Colorado	3,315
3	Connecticut	0
3	Delaware	0
3	Florida	0
3	Georgia	0
3	Hawaii	0
42	Idaho	710
32	Illinois	279
34	Indiana	320
37	Iowa	480
41	Kansas	679
31	Kentucky	257
2	Louisiana	(8)
3	Maine	0
3	Maryland	0
3	Massachusetts	0
38	Michigan	571
40	Minnesota	601
3	Mississippi	0
29	Missouri	230
46	Montana	1,800
44	Nebraska	840
36	Nevada	479
3	New Hampshire	0
3	New Jersey	0
48	New Mexico	2,842
3	New York	0
3	North Carolina	0
43	North Dakota	750
35	Ohio	455
33	Oklahoma	289
3	Oregon	0
3	Pennsylvania	0
3	Rhode Island	0
3	South Carolina	0
45	South Dakota	966
28	Tennessee	178
3	Texas	0
47	Utah	2,000
27	Vermont	95
3	Virginia	0
3	Washington	0
30	West Virginia	240
39	Wisconsin	579
49	Wyoming	3,099

RANK ORDER

RANK	STATE	LOWEST POINT
1	California	(282)
2	Louisiana	(8)
3	Alabama*	0
3	Alaska	0
3	Connecticut	0
3	Delaware	0
3	Florida	0
3	Georgia	0
3	Hawaii	0
3	Maine	0
3	Maryland	0
3	Massachusetts	0
3	Mississippi	0
3	New Hampshire	0
3	New Jersey	0
3	New York	0
3	North Carolina	0
3	Oregon	0
3	Pennsylvania	0
3	Rhode Island	0
3	South Carolina	0
3	Texas	0
3	Virginia	0
3	Washington	0
25	Arkansas	55
26	Arizona	70
27	Vermont	95
28	Tennessee	178
29	Missouri	230
30	West Virginia	240
31	Kentucky	257
32	Illinois	279
33	Oklahoma	289
34	Indiana	320
35	Ohio	455
36	Nevada	479
37	Iowa	480
38	Michigan	571
39	Wisconsin	579
40	Minnesota	601
41	Kansas	679
42	Idaho	710
43	North Dakota	750
44	Nebraska	840
45	South Dakota	966
46	Montana	1,800
47	Utah	2,000
48	New Mexico	2,842
49	Wyoming	3,099
50	Colorado	3,315

| | District of Columbia | 1 |

Source: U.S. Department of Interior, U.S. Geological Survey
  "Elevations and Distances in the United States" (http://erg.usgs.gov/isb/pubs/booklets/elvadist/elvadist.html)
*States with "0" have sea level as lowest point.

Approximate Mean Elevation in Feet

Approximate National Mean Elevation = 2,500 Feet Above Sea Level

ALPHA ORDER

RANK	STATE	MEAN ELEVATION
40	Alabama	500
15	Alaska	1,900
7	Arizona	4,100
36	Arkansas	650
11	California	2,900
1	Colorado	6,800
40	Connecticut	500
50	Delaware	60
48	Florida	100
37	Georgia	600
10	Hawaii	3,030
6	Idaho	5,000
37	Illinois	600
34	Indiana	700
22	Iowa	1,100
14	Kansas	2,000
33	Kentucky	750
48	Louisiana	100
37	Maine	600
43	Maryland	350
40	Massachusetts	500
29	Michigan	900
21	Minnesota	1,200
45	Mississippi	300
32	Missouri	800
8	Montana	3,400
12	Nebraska	2,600
5	Nevada	5,500
25	New Hampshire	1,000
46	New Jersey	250
4	New Mexico	5,700
25	New York	1,000
34	North Carolina	700
15	North Dakota	1,900
31	Ohio	850
20	Oklahoma	1,300
9	Oregon	3,300
22	Pennsylvania	1,100
47	Rhode Island	200
43	South Carolina	350
13	South Dakota	2,200
29	Tennessee	900
17	Texas	1,700
3	Utah	6,100
25	Vermont	1,000
28	Virginia	950
17	Washington	1,700
19	West Virginia	1,500
24	Wisconsin	1,050
2	Wyoming	6,700

RANK ORDER

RANK	STATE	MEAN ELEVATION
1	Colorado	6,800
2	Wyoming	6,700
3	Utah	6,100
4	New Mexico	5,700
5	Nevada	5,500
6	Idaho	5,000
7	Arizona	4,100
8	Montana	3,400
9	Oregon	3,300
10	Hawaii	3,030
11	California	2,900
12	Nebraska	2,600
13	South Dakota	2,200
14	Kansas	2,000
15	Alaska	1,900
15	North Dakota	1,900
17	Texas	1,700
17	Washington	1,700
19	West Virginia	1,500
20	Oklahoma	1,300
21	Minnesota	1,200
22	Iowa	1,100
22	Pennsylvania	1,100
24	Wisconsin	1,050
25	New Hampshire	1,000
25	New York	1,000
25	Vermont	1,000
28	Virginia	950
29	Michigan	900
29	Tennessee	900
31	Ohio	850
32	Missouri	800
33	Kentucky	750
34	Indiana	700
34	North Carolina	700
36	Arkansas	650
37	Georgia	600
37	Illinois	600
37	Maine	600
40	Alabama	500
40	Connecticut	500
40	Massachusetts	500
43	Maryland	350
43	South Carolina	350
45	Mississippi	300
46	New Jersey	250
47	Rhode Island	200
48	Florida	100
48	Louisiana	100
50	Delaware	60
	District of Columbia	150

Source: U.S. Department of Interior, U.S. Geological Survey
"Elevations and Distances in the United States" (http://erg.usgs.gov/isb/pubs/booklets/elvadist/elvadist.html)

Normal Daily Mean Temperature*

ALPHA ORDER

RANK	STATE	MEAN TEMPERATURE
7	Alabama	63.7
50	Alaska	31.9
6	Arizona	63.9
10	Arkansas	62.0
12	California	60.3
38	Colorado	48.4
27	Connecticut	51.2
20	Delaware**	54.4
2	Florida	72.0
8	Georgia	63.6
1	Hawaii	75.7
31	Idaho	50.3
33	Illinois	50.1
24	Indiana	52.0
39	Iowa	48.1
22	Kansas	54.0
17	Kentucky	55.8
3	Louisiana	67.4
47	Maine	42.5
19	Maryland**	54.6
37	Massachusetts	49.3
45	Michigan	44.7
48	Minnesota	41.4
9	Mississippi	63.4
18	Missouri	55.2
46	Montana	44.0
36	Nebraska	49.4
24	Nevada	52.0
41	New Hampshire**	45.9
20	New Jersey	54.4
16	New Mexico	57.0
32	New York	50.2
13	North Carolina	60.1
49	North Dakota	41.3
34	Ohio	50.0
11	Oklahoma	60.5
28	Oregon	51.1
26	Pennsylvania	51.6
28	Rhode Island**	51.1
5	South Carolina	64.0
42	South Dakota	45.2
14	Tennessee	58.7
4	Texas	66.8
28	Utah	51.1
42	Vermont**	45.2
15	Virginia	57.2
34	Washington	50.0
23	West Virginia	52.7
40	Wisconsin	46.3
44	Wyoming	44.8

RANK ORDER

RANK	STATE	MEAN TEMPERATURE
1	Hawaii	75.7
2	Florida	72.0
3	Louisiana	67.4
4	Texas	66.8
5	South Carolina	64.0
6	Arizona	63.9
7	Alabama	63.7
8	Georgia	63.6
9	Mississippi	63.4
10	Arkansas	62.0
11	Oklahoma	60.5
12	California	60.3
13	North Carolina	60.1
14	Tennessee	58.7
15	Virginia	57.2
16	New Mexico	57.0
17	Kentucky	55.8
18	Missouri	55.2
19	Maryland**	54.6
20	Delaware**	54.4
20	New Jersey	54.4
22	Kansas	54.0
23	West Virginia	52.7
24	Indiana	52.0
24	Nevada	52.0
26	Pennsylvania	51.6
27	Connecticut	51.2
28	Oregon	51.1
28	Rhode Island**	51.1
28	Utah	51.1
31	Idaho	50.3
32	New York	50.2
33	Illinois	50.1
34	Ohio	50.0
34	Washington	50.0
36	Nebraska	49.4
37	Massachusetts	49.3
38	Colorado	48.4
39	Iowa	48.1
40	Wisconsin	46.3
41	New Hampshire**	45.9
42	South Dakota	45.2
42	Vermont**	45.2
44	Wyoming	44.8
45	Michigan	44.7
46	Montana	44.0
47	Maine	42.5
48	Minnesota	41.4
49	North Dakota	41.3
50	Alaska	31.9
	District of Columbia	55.9

Source: CQ Press using data from U.S. Department of Commerce, National Oceanic and Atmospheric Administration "Comparative Climatic Data Through 2012" (ftp://ftp.ncdc.noaa.gov/pub/data/ccd-data/CCD-2012.pdf)

*Based on 30-year averages, 1971-2000.

**Percentages from these states are from a single location. All other states are from two or more reporting cities within each state, which were averaged to determine each state's average.

Percent of Days That Are Sunny*

ALPHA ORDER

RANK	STATE	PERCENT OF DAYS SUNNY
26	Alabama	58
50	Alaska	38
1	Arizona	85
8	Arkansas	66
4	California	72
4	Colorado	72
34	Connecticut**	56
36	Delaware**	55
7	Florida	67
16	Georgia	63
8	Hawaii	66
14	Idaho	64
31	Illinois	57
26	Indiana	58
22	Iowa	60
8	Kansas	66
36	Kentucky	55
14	Louisiana	64
31	Maine**	57
31	Maryland**	57
36	Massachusetts	55
44	Michigan	49
36	Minnesota	55
16	Mississippi	63
26	Missouri	58
24	Montana	59
16	Nebraska	63
2	Nevada	76
48	New Hampshire	44
34	New Jersey**	56
3	New Mexico	75
42	New York	51
22	North Carolina	60
24	North Dakota	59
42	Ohio	51
12	Oklahoma	65
46	Oregon**	48
41	Pennsylvania	53
26	Rhode Island**	58
20	South Carolina	62
16	South Dakota	63
26	Tennessee	58
12	Texas	65
6	Utah	68
44	Vermont**	49
21	Virginia	61
47	Washington	45
49	West Virginia**	40
40	Wisconsin	54
8	Wyoming	66

RANK ORDER

RANK	STATE	PERCENT OF DAYS SUNNY
1	Arizona	85
2	Nevada	76
3	New Mexico	75
4	California	72
4	Colorado	72
6	Utah	68
7	Florida	67
8	Arkansas	66
8	Hawaii	66
8	Kansas	66
8	Wyoming	66
12	Oklahoma	65
12	Texas	65
14	Idaho	64
14	Louisiana	64
16	Georgia	63
16	Mississippi	63
16	Nebraska	63
16	South Dakota	63
20	South Carolina	62
21	Virginia	61
22	Iowa	60
22	North Carolina	60
24	Montana	59
24	North Dakota	59
26	Alabama	58
26	Indiana	58
26	Missouri	58
26	Rhode Island**	58
26	Tennessee	58
31	Illinois	57
31	Maine**	57
31	Maryland**	57
34	Connecticut**	56
34	New Jersey**	56
36	Delaware**	55
36	Kentucky	55
36	Massachusetts	55
36	Minnesota	55
40	Wisconsin	54
41	Pennsylvania	53
42	New York	51
42	Ohio	51
44	Michigan	49
44	Vermont**	49
46	Oregon**	48
47	Washington	45
48	New Hampshire	44
49	West Virginia**	40
50	Alaska	38
	District of Columbia**	56

Source: CQ Press using data from U.S. Department of Commerce, National Oceanic and Atmospheric Administration "Comparative Climatic Data Through 2012" (ftp://ftp.ncdc.noaa.gov/pub/data/ccd-data/CCD-2012.pdf)

*As a percent of possible sunshine updated through 2012.

**Percentages from these states are from a single location. All other states are from two or more reporting cities within each state, which were averaged to determine each state's average.

Average Wind Speed (MPH)*

ALPHA ORDER

RANK	STATE	MILES PER HOUR
41	Alabama	7.6
24	Alaska	9.3
42	Arizona	7.5
40	Arkansas	7.7
46	California	6.9
32	Colorado	8.5
19	Connecticut	9.6
26	Delaware**	9.0
33	Florida	8.3
45	Georgia	7.4
5	Hawaii	10.9
22	Idaho	9.4
18	Illinois	9.8
22	Indiana	9.4
6	Iowa	10.7
2	Kansas	12.0
39	Kentucky	7.8
36	Louisiana	8.1
27	Maine	8.9
30	Maryland**	8.6
1	Massachusetts	12.5
21	Michigan	9.5
11	Minnesota	10.2
48	Mississippi	6.5
13	Missouri	10.1
25	Montana	9.2
9	Nebraska	10.3
37	Nevada	8.0
47	New Hampshire**	6.7
15	New Jersey	10.0
16	New Mexico	9.9
11	New York	10.2
34	North Carolina	8.2
7	North Dakota	10.6
19	Ohio	9.6
3	Oklahoma	11.2
38	Oregon	7.9
30	Pennsylvania	8.6
8	Rhode Island	10.5
42	South Carolina	7.5
4	South Dakota	11.1
48	Tennessee	6.5
9	Texas	10.3
29	Utah**	8.8
27	Vermont**	8.9
34	Virginia	8.2
42	Washington	7.5
48	West Virginia	6.5
16	Wisconsin	9.9
13	Wyoming	10.1

RANK ORDER

RANK	STATE	MILES PER HOUR
1	Massachusetts	12.5
2	Kansas	12.0
3	Oklahoma	11.2
4	South Dakota	11.1
5	Hawaii	10.9
6	Iowa	10.7
7	North Dakota	10.6
8	Rhode Island	10.5
9	Nebraska	10.3
9	Texas	10.3
11	Minnesota	10.2
11	New York	10.2
13	Missouri	10.1
13	Wyoming	10.1
15	New Jersey	10.0
16	New Mexico	9.9
16	Wisconsin	9.9
18	Illinois	9.8
19	Connecticut	9.6
19	Ohio	9.6
21	Michigan	9.5
22	Idaho	9.4
22	Indiana	9.4
24	Alaska	9.3
25	Montana	9.2
26	Delaware**	9.0
27	Maine	8.9
27	Vermont**	8.9
29	Utah**	8.8
30	Maryland**	8.6
30	Pennsylvania	8.6
32	Colorado	8.5
33	Florida	8.3
34	North Carolina	8.2
34	Virginia	8.2
36	Louisiana	8.1
37	Nevada	8.0
38	Oregon	7.9
39	Kentucky	7.8
40	Arkansas	7.7
41	Alabama	7.6
42	Arizona	7.5
42	South Carolina	7.5
42	Washington	7.5
45	Georgia	7.4
46	California	6.9
47	New Hampshire**	6.7
48	Mississippi	6.5
48	Tennessee	6.5
48	West Virginia	6.5

District of Columbia 8.4

Source: CQ Press using data from U.S. Department of Commerce, National Oceanic and Atmospheric Administration "Comparative Climatic Data Through 2012" (ftp://ftp.ncdc.noaa.gov/pub/data/ccd-data/CCD-2012.pdf)
*Updated through 2012.
**Averages from these states are from a single location. All other states are from two or more reporting cities within each state, which were averaged to determine each state's average.

Hazardous Weather Fatalities in 2014

National Total = 356 Fatalities*

ALPHA ORDER

RANK	STATE	FATALITIES	% of USA
9	Alabama	10	2.8%
37	Alaska	1	0.3%
20	Arizona	6	1.7%
2	Arkansas	23	6.5%
4	California	20	5.6%
9	Colorado	10	2.8%
46	Connecticut	0	0.0%
37	Delaware	1	0.3%
4	Florida	20	5.6%
31	Georgia	2	0.6%
46	Hawaii	0	0.0%
16	Idaho	7	2.0%
2	Illinois	23	6.5%
26	Indiana	5	1.4%
20	Iowa	6	1.7%
37	Kansas	1	0.3%
14	Kentucky	8	2.2%
20	Louisiana	6	1.7%
31	Maine	2	0.6%
20	Maryland	6	1.7%
31	Massachusetts	2	0.6%
37	Michigan	1	0.3%
16	Minnesota	7	2.0%
4	Mississippi	20	5.6%
31	Missouri	2	0.6%
20	Montana	6	1.7%
29	Nebraska	3	0.8%
8	Nevada	14	3.9%
46	New Hampshire	0	0.0%
26	New Jersey	5	1.4%
29	New Mexico	3	0.8%
14	New York	8	2.2%
13	North Carolina	9	2.5%
46	North Dakota	0	0.0%
37	Ohio	1	0.3%
31	Oklahoma	2	0.6%
9	Oregon	10	2.8%
31	Pennsylvania	2	0.6%
37	Rhode Island	1	0.3%
16	South Carolina	7	2.0%
37	South Dakota	1	0.3%
20	Tennessee	6	1.7%
9	Texas	10	2.8%
26	Utah	5	1.4%
46	Vermont	0	0.0%
16	Virginia	7	2.0%
1	Washington	50	14.0%
37	West Virginia	1	0.3%
7	Wisconsin	15	4.2%
37	Wyoming	1	0.3%

RANK ORDER

RANK	STATE	FATALITIES	% of USA
1	Washington	50	14.0%
2	Arkansas	23	6.5%
2	Illinois	23	6.5%
4	California	20	5.6%
4	Florida	20	5.6%
4	Mississippi	20	5.6%
7	Wisconsin	15	4.2%
8	Nevada	14	3.9%
9	Alabama	10	2.8%
9	Colorado	10	2.8%
9	Oregon	10	2.8%
9	Texas	10	2.8%
13	North Carolina	9	2.5%
14	Kentucky	8	2.2%
14	New York	8	2.2%
16	Idaho	7	2.0%
16	Minnesota	7	2.0%
16	South Carolina	7	2.0%
16	Virginia	7	2.0%
20	Arizona	6	1.7%
20	Iowa	6	1.7%
20	Louisiana	6	1.7%
20	Maryland	6	1.7%
20	Montana	6	1.7%
20	Tennessee	6	1.7%
26	Indiana	5	1.4%
26	New Jersey	5	1.4%
26	Utah	5	1.4%
29	Nebraska	3	0.8%
29	New Mexico	3	0.8%
31	Georgia	2	0.6%
31	Maine	2	0.6%
31	Massachusetts	2	0.6%
31	Missouri	2	0.6%
31	Oklahoma	2	0.6%
31	Pennsylvania	2	0.6%
37	Alaska	1	0.3%
37	Delaware	1	0.3%
37	Kansas	1	0.3%
37	Michigan	1	0.3%
37	Ohio	1	0.3%
37	Rhode Island	1	0.3%
37	South Dakota	1	0.3%
37	West Virginia	1	0.3%
37	Wyoming	1	0.3%
46	Connecticut	0	0.0%
46	Hawaii	0	0.0%
46	New Hampshire	0	0.0%
46	North Dakota	0	0.0%
46	Vermont	0	0.0%
	District of Columbia	0	0.0%

Source: National Weather Service, Water and Weather Services
"2014 Summary of Hazardous Weather Fatalities" (http://www.nws.noaa.gov/om/hazstats.shtml)
*Includes lightning, tornado, thunderstorm, extreme temperature, flood, coastal storm, rip current, hurricane, winter storm, fog, avalanche, and other weather events. National total does not include 28 fatalities in U.S. waters or territories.

Tornadoes in 2015

National Total = 1,259 Tornadoes*

ALPHA ORDER

RANK	STATE	TORNADOES	% of USA
12	Alabama	32	2.5%
44	Alaska	0	0.0%
32	Arizona	3	0.2%
14	Arkansas	25	2.0%
23	California	13	1.0%
6	Colorado	52	4.1%
44	Connecticut	0	0.0%
39	Delaware	1	0.1%
15	Florida	24	1.9%
15	Georgia	24	1.9%
44	Hawaii	0	0.0%
39	Idaho	1	0.1%
4	Illinois	82	6.5%
20	Indiana	17	1.4%
8	Iowa	46	3.7%
2	Kansas	178	14.1%
20	Kentucky	17	1.4%
11	Louisiana	34	2.7%
44	Maine	0	0.0%
32	Maryland	3	0.2%
37	Massachusetts	2	0.2%
27	Michigan	9	0.7%
15	Minnesota	24	1.9%
5	Mississippi	63	5.0%
7	Missouri	48	3.8%
39	Montana	1	0.1%
9	Nebraska	38	3.0%
37	Nevada	2	0.2%
39	New Hampshire	1	0.1%
44	New Jersey	0	0.0%
30	New Mexico	4	0.3%
32	New York	3	0.2%
26	North Carolina	10	0.8%
10	North Dakota	35	2.8%
29	Ohio	6	0.5%
3	Oklahoma	111	8.8%
39	Oregon	1	0.1%
25	Pennsylvania	12	1.0%
44	Rhode Island	0	0.0%
23	South Carolina	13	1.0%
13	South Dakota	26	2.1%
19	Tennessee	18	1.4%
1	Texas	228	18.1%
32	Utah	3	0.2%
44	Vermont	0	0.0%
28	Virginia	7	0.6%
30	Washington	4	0.3%
32	West Virginia	3	0.2%
18	Wisconsin	20	1.6%
22	Wyoming	15	1.2%

RANK ORDER

RANK	STATE	TORNADOES	% of USA
1	Texas	228	18.1%
2	Kansas	178	14.1%
3	Oklahoma	111	8.8%
4	Illinois	82	6.5%
5	Mississippi	63	5.0%
6	Colorado	52	4.1%
7	Missouri	48	3.8%
8	Iowa	46	3.7%
9	Nebraska	38	3.0%
10	North Dakota	35	2.8%
11	Louisiana	34	2.7%
12	Alabama	32	2.5%
13	South Dakota	26	2.1%
14	Arkansas	25	2.0%
15	Florida	24	1.9%
15	Georgia	24	1.9%
15	Minnesota	24	1.9%
18	Wisconsin	20	1.6%
19	Tennessee	18	1.4%
20	Indiana	17	1.4%
20	Kentucky	17	1.4%
22	Wyoming	15	1.2%
23	California	13	1.0%
23	South Carolina	13	1.0%
25	Pennsylvania	12	1.0%
26	North Carolina	10	0.8%
27	Michigan	9	0.7%
28	Virginia	7	0.6%
29	Ohio	6	0.5%
30	New Mexico	4	0.3%
30	Washington	4	0.3%
32	Arizona	3	0.2%
32	Maryland	3	0.2%
32	New York	3	0.2%
32	Utah	3	0.2%
32	West Virginia	3	0.2%
37	Massachusetts	2	0.2%
37	Nevada	2	0.2%
39	Delaware	1	0.1%
39	Idaho	1	0.1%
39	Montana	1	0.1%
39	New Hampshire	1	0.1%
39	Oregon	1	0.1%
44	Alaska	0	0.0%
44	Connecticut	0	0.0%
44	Hawaii	0	0.0%
44	Maine	0	0.0%
44	New Jersey	0	0.0%
44	Rhode Island	0	0.0%
44	Vermont	0	0.0%
	District of Columbia	0	0.0%

Source: National Weather Service, Storm Prediction Center
"Annual Severe Weather Report Summary - 2015" (http://www.spc.noaa.gov/climo/online/monthly/2015_annual_summary.html)
*Preliminary figures. Tornadoes striking more than one state are counted in each state.

Fatalities Caused by Tornadoes: 2008 to 2015

National Total = 951 Fatalities

ALPHA ORDER

RANK	STATE	FATALITIES	% of USA
1	Alabama	257	27.0%
31	Alaska	0	0.0%
31	Arizona	0	0.0%
6	Arkansas	63	6.6%
31	California	0	0.0%
25	Colorado	1	0.1%
31	Connecticut	0	0.0%
31	Delaware	0	0.0%
22	Florida	2	0.2%
10	Georgia	23	2.4%
31	Hawaii	0	0.0%
31	Idaho	0	0.0%
11	Illinois	20	2.1%
12	Indiana	17	1.8%
13	Iowa	16	1.7%
15	Kansas	8	0.8%
7	Kentucky	31	3.3%
19	Louisiana	4	0.4%
31	Maine	0	0.0%
31	Maryland	0	0.0%
20	Massachusetts	3	0.3%
25	Michigan	1	0.1%
17	Minnesota	5	0.5%
3	Mississippi	75	7.9%
2	Missouri	191	20.1%
22	Montana	2	0.2%
22	Nebraska	2	0.2%
31	Nevada	0	0.0%
25	New Hampshire	1	0.1%
31	New Jersey	0	0.0%
31	New Mexico	0	0.0%
17	New York	5	0.5%
8	North Carolina	30	3.2%
25	North Dakota	1	0.1%
14	Ohio	11	1.2%
4	Oklahoma	74	7.8%
31	Oregon	0	0.0%
31	Pennsylvania	0	0.0%
31	Rhode Island	0	0.0%
20	South Carolina	3	0.3%
31	South Dakota	0	0.0%
5	Tennessee	73	7.7%
9	Texas	24	2.5%
31	Utah	0	0.0%
31	Vermont	0	0.0%
16	Virginia	6	0.6%
31	Washington	0	0.0%
25	West Virginia	1	0.1%
25	Wisconsin	1	0.1%
31	Wyoming	0	0.0%

RANK ORDER

RANK	STATE	FATALITIES	% of USA
1	Alabama	257	27.0%
2	Missouri	191	20.1%
3	Mississippi	75	7.9%
4	Oklahoma	74	7.8%
5	Tennessee	73	7.7%
6	Arkansas	63	6.6%
7	Kentucky	31	3.3%
8	North Carolina	30	3.2%
9	Texas	24	2.5%
10	Georgia	23	2.4%
11	Illinois	20	2.1%
12	Indiana	17	1.8%
13	Iowa	16	1.7%
14	Ohio	11	1.2%
15	Kansas	8	0.8%
16	Virginia	6	0.6%
17	Minnesota	5	0.5%
17	New York	5	0.5%
19	Louisiana	4	0.4%
20	Massachusetts	3	0.3%
20	South Carolina	3	0.3%
22	Florida	2	0.2%
22	Montana	2	0.2%
22	Nebraska	2	0.2%
25	Colorado	1	0.1%
25	Michigan	1	0.1%
25	New Hampshire	1	0.1%
25	North Dakota	1	0.1%
25	West Virginia	1	0.1%
25	Wisconsin	1	0.1%
31	Alaska	0	0.0%
31	Arizona	0	0.0%
31	California	0	0.0%
31	Connecticut	0	0.0%
31	Delaware	0	0.0%
31	Hawaii	0	0.0%
31	Idaho	0	0.0%
31	Maine	0	0.0%
31	Maryland	0	0.0%
31	Nevada	0	0.0%
31	New Jersey	0	0.0%
31	New Mexico	0	0.0%
31	Oregon	0	0.0%
31	Pennsylvania	0	0.0%
31	Rhode Island	0	0.0%
31	South Dakota	0	0.0%
31	Utah	0	0.0%
31	Vermont	0	0.0%
31	Washington	0	0.0%
31	Wyoming	0	0.0%
	District of Columbia	0	0.0%

Source: National Weather Service, Storm Prediction Center
"Annual U.S. Killer Tornado Statistics" (http://www.spc.noaa.gov/climo/torn/fatalmap.php)

Cost of Damage from Hazardous Weather in 2014

National Total = $7,677,060,000*

ALPHA ORDER

RANK	STATE	DAMAGE	% of USA
21	Alabama	$38,220,000	0.5%
46	Alaska	1,470,000	0.0%
22	Arizona	28,050,000	0.4%
6	Arkansas	280,770,000	3.7%
2	California	1,628,080,000	21.2%
9	Colorado	215,770,000	2.8%
47	Connecticut	510,000	0.0%
48	Delaware	420,000	0.0%
10	Florida	210,240,000	2.7%
34	Georgia	9,040,000	0.1%
50	Hawaii	110,000	0.0%
13	Idaho	87,570,000	1.1%
7	Illinois	256,600,000	3.3%
15	Indiana	75,470,000	1.0%
14	Iowa	87,440,000	1.1%
16	Kansas	60,470,000	0.8%
28	Kentucky	12,540,000	0.2%
32	Louisiana	10,250,000	0.1%
42	Maine	3,690,000	0.0%
40	Maryland	5,960,000	0.1%
30	Massachusetts	11,820,000	0.2%
1	Michigan	1,880,370,000	24.5%
20	Minnesota	48,090,000	0.6%
8	Mississippi	222,260,000	2.9%
36	Missouri	7,300,000	0.1%
44	Montana	2,800,000	0.0%
4	Nebraska	493,410,000	6.4%
27	Nevada	13,360,000	0.2%
41	New Hampshire	3,770,000	0.0%
26	New Jersey	13,790,000	0.2%
39	New Mexico	6,100,000	0.1%
12	New York	93,450,000	1.2%
18	North Carolina	54,620,000	0.7%
23	North Dakota	26,420,000	0.3%
11	Ohio	97,020,000	1.3%
33	Oklahoma	9,790,000	0.1%
43	Oregon	3,360,000	0.0%
25	Pennsylvania	18,890,000	0.2%
49	Rhode Island	160,000	0.0%
29	South Carolina	12,080,000	0.2%
24	South Dakota	19,440,000	0.3%
17	Tennessee	57,260,000	0.7%
3	Texas	1,150,440,000	15.0%
38	Utah	7,090,000	0.1%
37	Vermont	7,250,000	0.1%
35	Virginia	7,580,000	0.1%
5	Washington	329,280,000	4.3%
31	West Virginia	10,390,000	0.1%
19	Wisconsin	54,590,000	0.7%
45	Wyoming	2,200,000	0.0%

RANK ORDER

RANK	STATE	DAMAGE	% of USA
1	Michigan	$1,880,370,000	24.5%
2	California	1,628,080,000	21.2%
3	Texas	1,150,440,000	15.0%
4	Nebraska	493,410,000	6.4%
5	Washington	329,280,000	4.3%
6	Arkansas	280,770,000	3.7%
7	Illinois	256,600,000	3.3%
8	Mississippi	222,260,000	2.9%
9	Colorado	215,770,000	2.8%
10	Florida	210,240,000	2.7%
11	Ohio	97,020,000	1.3%
12	New York	93,450,000	1.2%
13	Idaho	87,570,000	1.1%
14	Iowa	87,440,000	1.1%
15	Indiana	75,470,000	1.0%
16	Kansas	60,470,000	0.8%
17	Tennessee	57,260,000	0.7%
18	North Carolina	54,620,000	0.7%
19	Wisconsin	54,590,000	0.7%
20	Minnesota	48,090,000	0.6%
21	Alabama	38,220,000	0.5%
22	Arizona	28,050,000	0.4%
23	North Dakota	26,420,000	0.3%
24	South Dakota	19,440,000	0.3%
25	Pennsylvania	18,890,000	0.2%
26	New Jersey	13,790,000	0.2%
27	Nevada	13,360,000	0.2%
28	Kentucky	12,540,000	0.2%
29	South Carolina	12,080,000	0.2%
30	Massachusetts	11,820,000	0.2%
31	West Virginia	10,390,000	0.1%
32	Louisiana	10,250,000	0.1%
33	Oklahoma	9,790,000	0.1%
34	Georgia	9,040,000	0.1%
35	Virginia	7,580,000	0.1%
36	Missouri	7,300,000	0.1%
37	Vermont	7,250,000	0.1%
38	Utah	7,090,000	0.1%
39	New Mexico	6,100,000	0.1%
40	Maryland	5,960,000	0.1%
41	New Hampshire	3,770,000	0.0%
42	Maine	3,690,000	0.0%
43	Oregon	3,360,000	0.0%
44	Montana	2,800,000	0.0%
45	Wyoming	2,200,000	0.0%
46	Alaska	1,470,000	0.0%
47	Connecticut	510,000	0.0%
48	Delaware	420,000	0.0%
49	Rhode Island	160,000	0.0%
50	Hawaii	110,000	0.0%
	District of Columbia	10,000	0.0%

Source: National Weather Service, Water and Weather Services
"2014 Summary of Hazardous Weather Fatalities" (http://www.nws.noaa.gov/om/hazstats.shtml)
*Includes property and crop damage from lightning, tornado, thunderstorm, extreme temperature, flood, coastal storm, rip current, hurricane, winter storm, fog, avalanche, and other weather events. National total does not include damage costs in U.S. territories.

National Park Service Land in 2014

National Total = 84,479,064 Acres*

ALPHA ORDER

RANK	STATE	ACRES	% of USA
41	Alabama	22,737	0.0%
1	Alaska	54,654,154	64.7%
3	Arizona	2,947,312	3.5%
25	Arkansas	104,977	0.1%
2	California	8,144,518	9.6%
11	Colorado	737,812	0.9%
46	Connecticut	7,782	0.0%
48	Delaware	900	0.0%
4	Florida	2,638,658	3.1%
34	Georgia	63,338	0.1%
17	Hawaii	369,166	0.4%
13	Idaho	518,224	0.6%
49	Illinois	115	0.0%
43	Indiana	15,540	0.0%
47	Iowa	2,713	0.0%
44	Kansas	11,636	0.0%
27	Kentucky	95,942	0.1%
39	Louisiana	23,545	0.0%
29	Maine	91,826	0.1%
31	Maryland	73,893	0.1%
35	Massachusetts	57,962	0.1%
12	Michigan	718,148	0.9%
20	Minnesota	301,330	0.4%
24	Mississippi	118,587	0.1%
30	Missouri	83,476	0.1%
8	Montana	1,274,364	1.5%
36	Nebraska	45,735	0.1%
10	Nevada	778,512	0.9%
42	New Hampshire	21,015	0.0%
26	New Jersey	99,313	0.1%
15	New Mexico	391,078	0.5%
32	New York	72,992	0.1%
14	North Carolina	407,225	0.5%
33	North Dakota	72,568	0.1%
37	Ohio	34,544	0.0%
45	Oklahoma	10,241	0.0%
21	Oregon	199,319	0.2%
22	Pennsylvania	138,683	0.2%
50	Rhode Island	5	0.0%
38	South Carolina	32,348	0.0%
19	South Dakota	302,998	0.4%
16	Tennessee	384,978	0.5%
9	Texas	1,247,918	1.5%
6	Utah	2,117,683	2.5%
40	Vermont	23,265	0.0%
18	Virginia	364,371	0.4%
7	Washington	1,967,532	2.3%
28	West Virginia	92,721	0.1%
23	Wisconsin	133,755	0.2%
5	Wyoming	2,396,424	2.8%

RANK ORDER

RANK	STATE	ACRES	% of USA
1	Alaska	54,654,154	64.7%
2	California	8,144,518	9.6%
3	Arizona	2,947,312	3.5%
4	Florida	2,638,658	3.1%
5	Wyoming	2,396,424	2.8%
6	Utah	2,117,683	2.5%
7	Washington	1,967,532	2.3%
8	Montana	1,274,364	1.5%
9	Texas	1,247,918	1.5%
10	Nevada	778,512	0.9%
11	Colorado	737,812	0.9%
12	Michigan	718,148	0.9%
13	Idaho	518,224	0.6%
14	North Carolina	407,225	0.5%
15	New Mexico	391,078	0.5%
16	Tennessee	384,978	0.5%
17	Hawaii	369,166	0.4%
18	Virginia	364,371	0.4%
19	South Dakota	302,998	0.4%
20	Minnesota	301,330	0.4%
21	Oregon	199,319	0.2%
22	Pennsylvania	138,683	0.2%
23	Wisconsin	133,755	0.2%
24	Mississippi	118,587	0.1%
25	Arkansas	104,977	0.1%
26	New Jersey	99,313	0.1%
27	Kentucky	95,942	0.1%
28	West Virginia	92,721	0.1%
29	Maine	91,826	0.1%
30	Missouri	83,476	0.1%
31	Maryland	73,893	0.1%
32	New York	72,992	0.1%
33	North Dakota	72,568	0.1%
34	Georgia	63,338	0.1%
35	Massachusetts	57,962	0.1%
36	Nebraska	45,735	0.1%
37	Ohio	34,544	0.0%
38	South Carolina	32,348	0.0%
39	Louisiana	23,545	0.0%
40	Vermont	23,265	0.0%
41	Alabama	22,737	0.0%
42	New Hampshire	21,015	0.0%
43	Indiana	15,540	0.0%
44	Kansas	11,636	0.0%
45	Oklahoma	10,241	0.0%
46	Connecticut	7,782	0.0%
47	Iowa	2,713	0.0%
48	Delaware	900	0.0%
49	Illinois	115	0.0%
50	Rhode Island	5	0.0%
	District of Columbia	7,131	0.0%

Source: National Park Service
"Listing of Acreage by State" (unpublished data)

*As of December 31, 2014. Includes federal and nonfederal land in national parks, monuments, historic sites, recreation areas, preserves, battlefields, grasslands, seashores, parkways, trails, and rivers. Does not include land in national forest or wildlife areas. Includes 58,057 acres in U.S. territories.

Recreation Visits to National Park Service Areas in 2014

National Total = 292,800,082 Visits*

ALPHA ORDER

RANK	STATE	VISITS	% of USA
37	Alabama	753,178	0.3%
25	Alaska	2,684,693	0.9%
5	Arizona	10,747,219	3.7%
24	Arkansas	3,132,898	1.1%
1	California	37,363,392	12.8%
16	Colorado	6,031,874	2.1%
49	Connecticut	34,082	0.0%
50	Delaware	0	0.0%
6	Florida	10,667,459	3.6%
12	Georgia	7,491,109	2.6%
18	Hawaii	5,213,817	1.8%
40	Idaho	553,739	0.2%
43	Illinois	218,132	0.1%
30	Indiana	1,778,385	0.6%
44	Iowa	216,898	0.1%
45	Kansas	98,591	0.0%
29	Kentucky	1,828,192	0.6%
41	Louisiana	510,522	0.2%
26	Maine	2,574,717	0.9%
13	Maryland	6,815,195	2.3%
8	Massachusetts	9,850,586	3.4%
28	Michigan	1,993,139	0.7%
36	Minnesota	811,616	0.3%
14	Mississippi	6,557,120	2.2%
23	Missouri	3,385,772	1.2%
20	Montana	4,590,398	1.6%
42	Nebraska	254,198	0.1%
17	Nevada	5,314,681	1.8%
48	New Hampshire	37,785	0.0%
21	New Jersey	4,389,637	1.5%
31	New Mexico	1,602,114	0.5%
4	New York	16,141,397	5.5%
3	North Carolina	16,710,759	5.7%
39	North Dakota	581,851	0.2%
27	Ohio	2,470,177	0.8%
34	Oklahoma	1,165,269	0.4%
35	Oregon	1,033,254	0.4%
9	Pennsylvania	9,005,244	3.1%
46	Rhode Island	51,523	0.0%
33	South Carolina	1,519,746	0.5%
22	South Dakota	3,861,090	1.3%
10	Tennessee	8,470,460	2.9%
19	Texas	4,680,387	1.6%
7	Utah	10,551,040	3.6%
47	Vermont	39,086	0.0%
2	Virginia	22,870,531	7.8%
11	Washington	7,652,073	2.6%
32	West Virginia	1,541,805	0.5%
38	Wisconsin	625,850	0.2%
15	Wyoming	6,387,455	2.2%

RANK ORDER

RANK	STATE	VISITS	% of USA
1	California	37,363,392	12.8%
2	Virginia	22,870,531	7.8%
3	North Carolina	16,710,759	5.7%
4	New York	16,141,397	5.5%
5	Arizona	10,747,219	3.7%
6	Florida	10,667,459	3.6%
7	Utah	10,551,040	3.6%
8	Massachusetts	9,850,586	3.4%
9	Pennsylvania	9,005,244	3.1%
10	Tennessee	8,470,460	2.9%
11	Washington	7,652,073	2.6%
12	Georgia	7,491,109	2.6%
13	Maryland	6,815,195	2.3%
14	Mississippi	6,557,120	2.2%
15	Wyoming	6,387,455	2.2%
16	Colorado	6,031,874	2.1%
17	Nevada	5,314,681	1.8%
18	Hawaii	5,213,817	1.8%
19	Texas	4,680,387	1.6%
20	Montana	4,590,398	1.6%
21	New Jersey	4,389,637	1.5%
22	South Dakota	3,861,090	1.3%
23	Missouri	3,385,772	1.2%
24	Arkansas	3,132,898	1.1%
25	Alaska	2,684,693	0.9%
26	Maine	2,574,717	0.9%
27	Ohio	2,470,177	0.8%
28	Michigan	1,993,139	0.7%
29	Kentucky	1,828,192	0.6%
30	Indiana	1,778,385	0.6%
31	New Mexico	1,602,114	0.5%
32	West Virginia	1,541,805	0.5%
33	South Carolina	1,519,746	0.5%
34	Oklahoma	1,165,269	0.4%
35	Oregon	1,033,254	0.4%
36	Minnesota	811,616	0.3%
37	Alabama	753,178	0.3%
38	Wisconsin	625,850	0.2%
39	North Dakota	581,851	0.2%
40	Idaho	553,739	0.2%
41	Louisiana	510,522	0.2%
42	Nebraska	254,198	0.1%
43	Illinois	218,132	0.1%
44	Iowa	216,898	0.1%
45	Kansas	98,591	0.0%
46	Rhode Island	51,523	0.0%
47	Vermont	39,086	0.0%
48	New Hampshire	37,785	0.0%
49	Connecticut	34,082	0.0%
50	Delaware	0	0.0%
	District of Columbia	37,701,216	12.9%

Source: National Park Service, Public Use Statistics Office
"National Park Service Statistical Abstract 2014" (https://irma.nps.gov/Stats/Reports/AbstractsandForecasts)
*National total includes 2,238,731 visits in U.S. territories.

Percent Change in National Park Service Recreation Visits: 2013 to 2014

National Percent Change = 7.0% Increase*

ALPHA ORDER

RANK	STATE	PERCENT CHANGE
37	Alabama	0.4
28	Alaska	3.8
17	Arizona	6.4
10	Arkansas	12.9
24	California	5.0
11	Colorado	11.8
2	Connecticut	49.1
NA	Delaware**	NA
30	Florida	3.7
19	Georgia	6.3
17	Hawaii	6.4
46	Idaho	(9.9)
26	Illinois	4.2
45	Indiana	(8.1)
13	Iowa	8.5
14	Kansas	7.3
8	Kentucky	13.9
49	Louisiana	(18.2)
9	Maine	13.6
32	Maryland	3.0
35	Massachusetts	1.8
38	Michigan	0.2
5	Minnesota	23.3
44	Mississippi	(3.4)
48	Missouri	(12.9)
15	Montana	7.2
41	Nebraska	(1.4)
12	Nevada	9.6
40	New Hampshire	(0.1)
47	New Jersey	(12.7)
20	New Mexico	5.9
3	New York	46.9
31	North Carolina	3.6
36	North Dakota	1.6
34	Ohio	2.7
22	Oklahoma	5.2
16	Oregon	6.6
43	Pennsylvania	(1.5)
20	Rhode Island	5.9
38	South Carolina	0.2
41	South Dakota	(1.4)
25	Tennessee	4.7
4	Texas	34.4
6	Utah	17.5
7	Vermont	14.6
28	Virginia	3.8
26	Washington	4.2
33	West Virginia	2.9
1	Wisconsin	95.6
23	Wyoming	5.1

RANK ORDER

RANK	STATE	PERCENT CHANGE
1	Wisconsin	95.6
2	Connecticut	49.1
3	New York	46.9
4	Texas	34.4
5	Minnesota	23.3
6	Utah	17.5
7	Vermont	14.6
8	Kentucky	13.9
9	Maine	13.6
10	Arkansas	12.9
11	Colorado	11.8
12	Nevada	9.6
13	Iowa	8.5
14	Kansas	7.3
15	Montana	7.2
16	Oregon	6.6
17	Arizona	6.4
17	Hawaii	6.4
19	Georgia	6.3
20	New Mexico	5.9
20	Rhode Island	5.9
22	Oklahoma	5.2
23	Wyoming	5.1
24	California	5.0
25	Tennessee	4.7
26	Illinois	4.2
26	Washington	4.2
28	Alaska	3.8
28	Virginia	3.8
30	Florida	3.7
31	North Carolina	3.6
32	Maryland	3.0
33	West Virginia	2.9
34	Ohio	2.7
35	Massachusetts	1.8
36	North Dakota	1.6
37	Alabama	0.4
38	Michigan	0.2
38	South Carolina	0.2
40	New Hampshire	(0.1)
41	Nebraska	(1.4)
41	South Dakota	(1.4)
43	Pennsylvania	(1.5)
44	Mississippi	(3.4)
45	Indiana	(8.1)
46	Idaho	(9.9)
47	New Jersey	(12.7)
48	Missouri	(12.9)
49	Louisiana	(18.2)
NA	Delaware**	NA
	District of Columbia	10.2

Source: National Park Service, Public Use Statistics Office
"National Park Service Statistical Abstract 2014" (https://irma.nps.gov/Stats/Reports/AbstractsandForecasts)
*National percent change includes visits in U.S. territories.
**Not applicable.

IX. Government Finances: Federal

Internal Revenue Service Gross Collections in 2014 259
Per Capita Internal Revenue Service Gross Collections
    in 2014 260
Federal Individual Income Tax Collections in 2014 261
Average Revenue Collection per Federal Individual
    Income Tax Return in 2014 262
Adjusted Gross Income in 2013 263
Per Capita Adjusted Gross Income in 2013 264
Federal Business Income Tax Collections in 2014 265
Average Revenue Collection per Federal Business
    Income Tax Return in 2014 266
Federal Tax Returns Filed in 2014 267
Percent of Federal Returns Filed Electronically in 2014 . . 268
Federal Individual Income Tax Returns Filed in 2014 269
Percent of Federal Individual Income Tax Returns Filed
    Electronically in 2014 270
Federal Business Income Tax Returns Filed in 2014 271
Federal Tax Refunds in 2014 272
Value of Federal Tax Refunds in 2014 273
Average Value of Federal Tax Refunds in 2014 274
Value of Federal Individual Income Tax Refunds
    in 2014 275
Average Value of Federal Individual Income Tax
    Refunds in 2014 276
Value of Federal Business Income Tax Refunds in 2014 . . 277
Average Value of Federal Business Income Tax Refunds
    in 2014 278
Federal Government Expenditures in 2014 279
Per Capita Federal Government Expenditures in 2014 280
Federal Government Contract Awards in 2014 281
Per Capita Expenditures for Federal Government Contract
    Awards in 2014 282
Federal Government Assistance in 2014 283
Per Capita Federal Government Assistance in 2014 284
Federal Government Grants in 2014 285
Per Capita Expenditures for Federal Government Grants
    in 2014 286
Federal Government Loans in 2014 287
Per Capita Federal Government Loans in 2014 288
Federal Government "Other Financial Assistance"
    in 2014 289
Per Capita Federal Government "Other Financial
    Assistance" in 2014 290
Federal Civilian Employees in 2014 291
Rate of Federal Civilian Employees in 2014 292

Internal Revenue Service Gross Collections in 2014

National Total = $3,064,301,358,000*

ALPHA ORDER

RANK	STATE	COLLECTIONS	% of USA
31	Alabama	$23,789,249,000	0.8%
47	Alaska	5,449,061,000	0.2%
24	Arizona	40,530,219,000	1.3%
26	Arkansas	30,728,862,000	1.0%
1	California	369,193,162,000	12.0%
21	Colorado	52,002,903,000	1.7%
18	Connecticut	57,697,380,000	1.9%
34	Delaware	19,039,980,000	0.6%
4	Florida	154,353,070,000	5.0%
11	Georgia	79,565,715,000	2.6%
42	Hawaii	7,722,840,000	0.3%
40	Idaho	9,223,749,000	0.3%
5	Illinois	148,332,148,000	4.8%
20	Indiana	54,606,571,000	1.8%
32	Iowa	22,309,198,000	0.7%
29	Kansas	25,896,981,000	0.8%
27	Kentucky	30,128,276,000	1.0%
23	Louisiana	43,023,097,000	1.4%
44	Maine	6,901,517,000	0.2%
17	Maryland	59,613,635,000	1.9%
9	Massachusetts	100,160,858,000	3.3%
14	Michigan	71,183,803,000	2.3%
10	Minnesota	96,227,262,000	3.1%
39	Mississippi	11,011,288,000	0.4%
16	Missouri	61,511,933,000	2.0%
48	Montana	5,338,004,000	0.2%
30	Nebraska	23,884,904,000	0.8%
36	Nevada	16,578,585,000	0.5%
38	New Hampshire	11,043,784,000	0.4%
6	New Jersey	134,869,876,000	4.4%
41	New Mexico	8,758,418,000	0.3%
3	New York	250,618,177,000	8.2%
13	North Carolina	72,471,513,000	2.4%
43	North Dakota	7,585,145,000	0.2%
7	Ohio	129,901,095,000	4.2%
25	Oklahoma	32,610,983,000	1.1%
28	Oregon	28,409,241,000	0.9%
8	Pennsylvania	126,374,146,000	4.1%
37	Rhode Island	13,887,904,000	0.5%
33	South Carolina	22,242,016,000	0.7%
46	South Dakota	6,733,600,000	0.2%
19	Tennessee	56,936,715,000	1.9%
2	Texas	265,336,183,000	8.7%
35	Utah	18,389,171,000	0.6%
50	Vermont	4,324,613,000	0.1%
12	Virginia	75,048,791,000	2.4%
15	Washington	67,812,753,000	2.2%
45	West Virginia	6,885,260,000	0.2%
22	Wisconsin	49,592,070,000	1.6%
49	Wyoming	4,891,559,000	0.2%

RANK ORDER

RANK	STATE	COLLECTIONS	% of USA
1	California	$369,193,162,000	12.0%
2	Texas	265,336,183,000	8.7%
3	New York	250,618,177,000	8.2%
4	Florida	154,353,070,000	5.0%
5	Illinois	148,332,148,000	4.8%
6	New Jersey	134,869,876,000	4.4%
7	Ohio	129,901,095,000	4.2%
8	Pennsylvania	126,374,146,000	4.1%
9	Massachusetts	100,160,858,000	3.3%
10	Minnesota	96,227,262,000	3.1%
11	Georgia	79,565,715,000	2.6%
12	Virginia	75,048,791,000	2.4%
13	North Carolina	72,471,513,000	2.4%
14	Michigan	71,183,803,000	2.3%
15	Washington	67,812,753,000	2.2%
16	Missouri	61,511,933,000	2.0%
17	Maryland	59,613,635,000	1.9%
18	Connecticut	57,697,380,000	1.9%
19	Tennessee	56,936,715,000	1.9%
20	Indiana	54,606,571,000	1.8%
21	Colorado	52,002,903,000	1.7%
22	Wisconsin	49,592,070,000	1.6%
23	Louisiana	43,023,097,000	1.4%
24	Arizona	40,530,219,000	1.3%
25	Oklahoma	32,610,983,000	1.1%
26	Arkansas	30,728,862,000	1.0%
27	Kentucky	30,128,276,000	1.0%
28	Oregon	28,409,241,000	0.9%
29	Kansas	25,896,981,000	0.8%
30	Nebraska	23,884,904,000	0.8%
31	Alabama	23,789,249,000	0.8%
32	Iowa	22,309,198,000	0.7%
33	South Carolina	22,242,016,000	0.7%
34	Delaware	19,039,980,000	0.6%
35	Utah	18,389,171,000	0.6%
36	Nevada	16,578,585,000	0.5%
37	Rhode Island	13,887,904,000	0.5%
38	New Hampshire	11,043,784,000	0.4%
39	Mississippi	11,011,288,000	0.4%
40	Idaho	9,223,749,000	0.3%
41	New Mexico	8,758,418,000	0.3%
42	Hawaii	7,722,840,000	0.3%
43	North Dakota	7,585,145,000	0.2%
44	Maine	6,901,517,000	0.2%
45	West Virginia	6,885,260,000	0.2%
46	South Dakota	6,733,600,000	0.2%
47	Alaska	5,449,061,000	0.2%
48	Montana	5,338,004,000	0.2%
49	Wyoming	4,891,559,000	0.2%
50	Vermont	4,324,613,000	0.1%
	District of Columbia	26,432,733,000	0.9%

Source: U.S. Department of the Treasury, Internal Revenue Service
"Fiscal Year 2014 IRS Data Book" (http://www.irs.gov/uac/SOI-Tax-Stats-IRS-Data-Book)
*Total includes $17,141,364,000 from U.S. citizens abroad and other miscellaneous returns not shown separately.

Per Capita Internal Revenue Service Gross Collections in 2014

National Per Capita = $9,555*

ALPHA ORDER

RANK	STATE	PER CAPITA
46	Alabama	$4,909
32	Alaska	7,393
40	Arizona	6,023
11	Arkansas	10,357
19	California	9,517
17	Colorado	9,710
3	Connecticut	16,050
1	Delaware	20,343
31	Florida	7,754
30	Georgia	7,880
43	Hawaii	5,438
42	Idaho	5,642
9	Illinois	11,515
28	Indiana	8,276
35	Iowa	7,175
22	Kansas	8,922
38	Kentucky	6,828
20	Louisiana	9,254
45	Maine	5,188
14	Maryland	9,977
5	Massachusetts	14,827
34	Michigan	7,178
2	Minnesota	17,633
50	Mississippi	3,678
13	Missouri	10,144
44	Montana	5,217
8	Nebraska	12,685
41	Nevada	5,841
27	New Hampshire	8,316
4	New Jersey	15,088
48	New Mexico	4,200
7	New York	12,690
33	North Carolina	7,291
12	North Dakota	10,250
10	Ohio	11,201
25	Oklahoma	8,406
36	Oregon	7,154
15	Pennsylvania	9,878
6	Rhode Island	13,165
47	South Carolina	4,606
29	South Dakota	7,891
23	Tennessee	8,696
16	Texas	9,835
39	Utah	6,245
37	Vermont	6,900
21	Virginia	9,012
18	Washington	9,601
49	West Virginia	3,724
24	Wisconsin	8,611
26	Wyoming	8,372

RANK ORDER

RANK	STATE	PER CAPITA
1	Delaware	$20,343
2	Minnesota	17,633
3	Connecticut	16,050
4	New Jersey	15,088
5	Massachusetts	14,827
6	Rhode Island	13,165
7	New York	12,690
8	Nebraska	12,685
9	Illinois	11,515
10	Ohio	11,201
11	Arkansas	10,357
12	North Dakota	10,250
13	Missouri	10,144
14	Maryland	9,977
15	Pennsylvania	9,878
16	Texas	9,835
17	Colorado	9,710
18	Washington	9,601
19	California	9,517
20	Louisiana	9,254
21	Virginia	9,012
22	Kansas	8,922
23	Tennessee	8,696
24	Wisconsin	8,611
25	Oklahoma	8,406
26	Wyoming	8,372
27	New Hampshire	8,316
28	Indiana	8,276
29	South Dakota	7,891
30	Georgia	7,880
31	Florida	7,754
32	Alaska	7,393
33	North Carolina	7,291
34	Michigan	7,178
35	Iowa	7,175
36	Oregon	7,154
37	Vermont	6,900
38	Kentucky	6,828
39	Utah	6,245
40	Arizona	6,023
41	Nevada	5,841
42	Idaho	5,642
43	Hawaii	5,438
44	Montana	5,217
45	Maine	5,188
46	Alabama	4,909
47	South Carolina	4,606
48	New Mexico	4,200
49	West Virginia	3,724
50	Mississippi	3,678
	District of Columbia	40,060

Source: CQ Press using data from U.S. Department of the Treasury, Internal Revenue Service
"Fiscal Year 2014 IRS Data Book" (http://www.irs.gov/uac/SOI-Tax-Stats-IRS-Data-Book)
*National per capita does not include collections from U.S. citizens abroad and other miscellaneous returns not shown separately.

Federal Individual Income Tax Collections in 2014

National Total = $2,619,847,215,000*

ALPHA ORDER

RANK	STATE	COLLECTIONS	% of USA
29	Alabama	$21,820,797,000	0.8%
47	Alaska	5,213,654,000	0.2%
24	Arizona	34,357,778,000	1.3%
28	Arkansas	22,353,431,000	0.9%
1	California	314,319,084,000	12.0%
21	Colorado	43,660,813,000	1.7%
20	Connecticut	47,265,116,000	1.8%
36	Delaware	14,146,624,000	0.5%
4	Florida	141,912,552,000	5.4%
12	Georgia	64,674,241,000	2.5%
42	Hawaii	7,090,806,000	0.3%
40	Idaho	8,788,307,000	0.3%
5	Illinois	123,885,426,000	4.7%
19	Indiana	48,027,054,000	1.8%
31	Iowa	20,398,887,000	0.8%
30	Kansas	21,819,357,000	0.8%
25	Kentucky	26,911,767,000	1.0%
23	Louisiana	40,613,155,000	1.6%
44	Maine	6,452,674,000	0.2%
16	Maryland	55,800,282,000	2.1%
9	Massachusetts	89,106,987,000	3.4%
11	Michigan	65,478,941,000	2.5%
10	Minnesota	74,153,885,000	2.8%
38	Mississippi	10,122,056,000	0.4%
17	Missouri	50,072,510,000	1.9%
48	Montana	5,053,198,000	0.2%
33	Nebraska	16,416,668,000	0.6%
35	Nevada	15,264,612,000	0.6%
37	New Hampshire	10,437,649,000	0.4%
7	New Jersey	109,983,681,000	4.2%
41	New Mexico	8,233,829,000	0.3%
2	New York	217,823,234,000	8.3%
13	North Carolina	63,172,182,000	2.4%
43	North Dakota	6,939,582,000	0.3%
6	Ohio	113,211,893,000	4.3%
27	Oklahoma	24,339,580,000	0.9%
26	Oregon	25,598,367,000	1.0%
8	Pennsylvania	109,883,768,000	4.2%
39	Rhode Island	10,058,643,000	0.4%
32	South Carolina	20,290,724,000	0.8%
46	South Dakota	6,256,818,000	0.2%
18	Tennessee	49,504,974,000	1.9%
3	Texas	211,993,178,000	8.1%
34	Utah	16,186,263,000	0.6%
50	Vermont	3,912,161,000	0.1%
14	Virginia	63,044,178,000	2.4%
15	Washington	60,801,922,000	2.3%
45	West Virginia	6,438,716,000	0.2%
22	Wisconsin	42,831,333,000	1.6%
49	Wyoming	4,570,938,000	0.2%

RANK ORDER

RANK	STATE	COLLECTIONS	% of USA
1	California	$314,319,084,000	12.0%
2	New York	217,823,234,000	8.3%
3	Texas	211,993,178,000	8.1%
4	Florida	141,912,552,000	5.4%
5	Illinois	123,885,426,000	4.7%
6	Ohio	113,211,893,000	4.3%
7	New Jersey	109,983,681,000	4.2%
8	Pennsylvania	109,883,768,000	4.2%
9	Massachusetts	89,106,987,000	3.4%
10	Minnesota	74,153,885,000	2.8%
11	Michigan	65,478,941,000	2.5%
12	Georgia	64,674,241,000	2.5%
13	North Carolina	63,172,182,000	2.4%
14	Virginia	63,044,178,000	2.4%
15	Washington	60,801,922,000	2.3%
16	Maryland	55,800,282,000	2.1%
17	Missouri	50,072,510,000	1.9%
18	Tennessee	49,504,974,000	1.9%
19	Indiana	48,027,054,000	1.8%
20	Connecticut	47,265,116,000	1.8%
21	Colorado	43,660,813,000	1.7%
22	Wisconsin	42,831,333,000	1.6%
23	Louisiana	40,613,155,000	1.6%
24	Arizona	34,357,778,000	1.3%
25	Kentucky	26,911,767,000	1.0%
26	Oregon	25,598,367,000	1.0%
27	Oklahoma	24,339,580,000	0.9%
28	Arkansas	22,353,431,000	0.9%
29	Alabama	21,820,797,000	0.8%
30	Kansas	21,819,357,000	0.8%
31	Iowa	20,398,887,000	0.8%
32	South Carolina	20,290,724,000	0.8%
33	Nebraska	16,416,668,000	0.6%
34	Utah	16,186,263,000	0.6%
35	Nevada	15,264,612,000	0.6%
36	Delaware	14,146,624,000	0.5%
37	New Hampshire	10,437,649,000	0.4%
38	Mississippi	10,122,056,000	0.4%
39	Rhode Island	10,058,643,000	0.4%
40	Idaho	8,788,307,000	0.3%
41	New Mexico	8,233,829,000	0.3%
42	Hawaii	7,090,806,000	0.3%
43	North Dakota	6,939,582,000	0.3%
44	Maine	6,452,674,000	0.2%
45	West Virginia	6,438,716,000	0.2%
46	South Dakota	6,256,818,000	0.2%
47	Alaska	5,213,654,000	0.2%
48	Montana	5,053,198,000	0.2%
49	Wyoming	4,570,938,000	0.2%
50	Vermont	3,912,161,000	0.1%
	District of Columbia	25,049,824,000	1.0%

Source: U.S. Department of the Treasury, Internal Revenue Service
"Fiscal Year 2014 IRS Data Book" (http://www.irs.gov/uac/SOI-Tax-Stats-IRS-Data-Book)
*Total includes $14,103,115,000 from U.S. citizens abroad and other miscellaneous returns not shown separately.

Average Revenue Collection per Federal Individual Income Tax Return in 2014

National Average = $17,768 per Return*

ALPHA ORDER

RANK	STATE	PER RETURN
43	Alabama	$10,652
33	Alaska	14,574
40	Arizona	12,245
15	Arkansas	18,325
16	California	18,322
20	Colorado	17,493
4	Connecticut	26,964
1	Delaware	32,281
28	Florida	15,177
31	Georgia	14,850
44	Hawaii	10,492
39	Idaho	12,760
9	Illinois	20,238
25	Indiana	15,754
36	Iowa	14,214
23	Kansas	16,421
35	Kentucky	14,258
8	Louisiana	20,258
46	Maine	10,183
12	Maryland	18,979
3	Massachusetts	27,008
37	Michigan	14,041
2	Minnesota	27,959
50	Mississippi	8,117
17	Missouri	18,255
45	Montana	10,385
13	Nebraska	18,604
42	Nevada	11,676
26	New Hampshire	15,333
5	New Jersey	25,384
48	New Mexico	9,085
6	New York	23,010
32	North Carolina	14,629
11	North Dakota	19,173
7	Ohio	20,431
30	Oklahoma	14,953
34	Oregon	14,307
19	Pennsylvania	17,853
10	Rhode Island	19,415
47	South Carolina	9,712
29	South Dakota	15,031
21	Tennessee	17,044
18	Texas	18,129
38	Utah	13,552
41	Vermont	12,188
22	Virginia	16,446
14	Washington	18,531
49	West Virginia	8,204
27	Wisconsin	15,276
24	Wyoming	15,818

RANK ORDER

RANK	STATE	PER RETURN
1	Delaware	$32,281
2	Minnesota	27,959
3	Massachusetts	27,008
4	Connecticut	26,964
5	New Jersey	25,384
6	New York	23,010
7	Ohio	20,431
8	Louisiana	20,258
9	Illinois	20,238
10	Rhode Island	19,415
11	North Dakota	19,173
12	Maryland	18,979
13	Nebraska	18,604
14	Washington	18,531
15	Arkansas	18,325
16	California	18,322
17	Missouri	18,255
18	Texas	18,129
19	Pennsylvania	17,853
20	Colorado	17,493
21	Tennessee	17,044
22	Virginia	16,446
23	Kansas	16,421
24	Wyoming	15,818
25	Indiana	15,754
26	New Hampshire	15,333
27	Wisconsin	15,276
28	Florida	15,177
29	South Dakota	15,031
30	Oklahoma	14,953
31	Georgia	14,850
32	North Carolina	14,629
33	Alaska	14,574
34	Oregon	14,307
35	Kentucky	14,258
36	Iowa	14,214
37	Michigan	14,041
38	Utah	13,552
39	Idaho	12,760
40	Arizona	12,245
41	Vermont	12,188
42	Nevada	11,676
43	Alabama	10,652
44	Hawaii	10,492
45	Montana	10,385
46	Maine	10,183
47	South Carolina	9,712
48	New Mexico	9,085
49	West Virginia	8,204
50	Mississippi	8,117
	District of Columbia	75,361

Source: CQ Press using data from U.S. Department of the Treasury, Internal Revenue Service
"Fiscal Year 2014 IRS Data Book" (http://www.irs.gov/uac/SOI-Tax-Stats-IRS-Data-Book)
*National Rate includes collections and returns from U.S. citizens abroad and other miscellaneous returns not shown separately.

Adjusted Gross Income in 2013

National Total = $9,057,169,217,000*

ALPHA ORDER

RANK	STATE	A.G.I.	% of USA
26	Alabama	$103,844,557,000	1.1%
48	Alaska	22,931,040,000	0.3%
21	Arizona	152,738,303,000	1.7%
34	Arkansas	61,472,759,000	0.7%
1	California	1,181,367,138,000	13.0%
17	Colorado	164,067,142,000	1.8%
20	Connecticut	155,370,730,000	1.7%
44	Delaware	26,108,080,000	0.3%
4	Florida	520,165,734,000	5.7%
12	Georgia	235,981,563,000	2.6%
40	Hawaii	37,478,298,000	0.4%
41	Idaho	34,403,673,000	0.4%
5	Illinois	399,201,505,000	4.4%
19	Indiana	158,756,695,000	1.8%
30	Iowa	81,928,471,000	0.9%
31	Kansas	78,516,041,000	0.9%
28	Kentucky	93,260,866,000	1.0%
24	Louisiana	109,192,972,000	1.2%
42	Maine	32,699,679,000	0.4%
15	Maryland	203,829,474,000	2.3%
10	Massachusetts	262,985,516,000	2.9%
11	Michigan	252,105,817,000	2.8%
16	Minnesota	172,891,877,000	1.9%
35	Mississippi	56,011,854,000	0.6%
23	Missouri	148,434,377,000	1.6%
46	Montana	24,976,187,000	0.3%
36	Nebraska	50,727,108,000	0.6%
32	Nevada	75,468,050,000	0.8%
37	New Hampshire	44,790,417,000	0.5%
7	New Jersey	335,599,912,000	3.7%
38	New Mexico	43,941,015,000	0.5%
3	New York	698,576,291,000	7.7%
13	North Carolina	232,421,512,000	2.6%
45	North Dakota	25,006,410,000	0.3%
8	Ohio	296,428,083,000	3.3%
29	Oklahoma	91,922,944,000	1.0%
27	Oregon	101,826,339,000	1.1%
6	Pennsylvania	368,059,936,000	4.1%
43	Rhode Island	30,572,463,000	0.3%
25	South Carolina	105,954,068,000	1.2%
47	South Dakota	23,166,962,000	0.3%
22	Tennessee	151,117,321,000	1.7%
2	Texas	737,452,938,000	8.1%
33	Utah	68,993,676,000	0.8%
50	Vermont	17,451,163,000	0.2%
9	Virginia	264,027,441,000	2.9%
14	Washington	222,348,557,000	2.5%
39	West Virginia	37,820,826,000	0.4%
18	Wisconsin	159,418,292,000	1.8%
49	Wyoming	20,544,887,000	0.2%

RANK ORDER

RANK	STATE	A.G.I.	% of USA
1	California	$1,181,367,138,000	13.0%
2	Texas	737,452,938,000	8.1%
3	New York	698,576,291,000	7.7%
4	Florida	520,165,734,000	5.7%
5	Illinois	399,201,505,000	4.4%
6	Pennsylvania	368,059,936,000	4.1%
7	New Jersey	335,599,912,000	3.7%
8	Ohio	296,428,083,000	3.3%
9	Virginia	264,027,441,000	2.9%
10	Massachusetts	262,985,516,000	2.9%
11	Michigan	252,105,817,000	2.8%
12	Georgia	235,981,563,000	2.6%
13	North Carolina	232,421,512,000	2.6%
14	Washington	222,348,557,000	2.5%
15	Maryland	203,829,474,000	2.3%
16	Minnesota	172,891,877,000	1.9%
17	Colorado	164,067,142,000	1.8%
18	Wisconsin	159,418,292,000	1.8%
19	Indiana	158,756,695,000	1.8%
20	Connecticut	155,370,730,000	1.7%
21	Arizona	152,738,303,000	1.7%
22	Tennessee	151,117,321,000	1.7%
23	Missouri	148,434,377,000	1.6%
24	Louisiana	109,192,972,000	1.2%
25	South Carolina	105,954,068,000	1.2%
26	Alabama	103,844,557,000	1.1%
27	Oregon	101,826,339,000	1.1%
28	Kentucky	93,260,866,000	1.0%
29	Oklahoma	91,922,944,000	1.0%
30	Iowa	81,928,471,000	0.9%
31	Kansas	78,516,041,000	0.9%
32	Nevada	75,468,050,000	0.8%
33	Utah	68,993,676,000	0.8%
34	Arkansas	61,472,759,000	0.7%
35	Mississippi	56,011,854,000	0.6%
36	Nebraska	50,727,108,000	0.6%
37	New Hampshire	44,790,417,000	0.5%
38	New Mexico	43,941,015,000	0.5%
39	West Virginia	37,820,826,000	0.4%
40	Hawaii	37,478,298,000	0.4%
41	Idaho	34,403,673,000	0.4%
42	Maine	32,699,679,000	0.4%
43	Rhode Island	30,572,463,000	0.3%
44	Delaware	26,108,080,000	0.3%
45	North Dakota	25,006,410,000	0.3%
46	Montana	24,976,187,000	0.3%
47	South Dakota	23,166,962,000	0.3%
48	Alaska	22,931,040,000	0.3%
49	Wyoming	20,544,887,000	0.2%
50	Vermont	17,451,163,000	0.2%
	District of Columbia	27,259,627,000	0.3%

Source: U.S. Department of the Treasury, Internal Revenue Service
"Individual Tax Statistics, State Income" (http://www.irs.gov/taxstats/index.html)
*Total includes $55,552,629,000 from U.S. citizens abroad and other miscellaneous returns not shown separately.

Per Capita Adjusted Gross Income in 2013

National Per Capita = $28,448*

ALPHA ORDER

RANK	STATE	PER CAPITA
44	Alabama	$21,498
13	Alaska	31,095
42	Arizona	23,035
48	Arkansas	20,782
15	California	30,753
12	Colorado	31,126
1	Connecticut	43,193
18	Delaware	28,214
27	Florida	26,547
38	Georgia	23,618
26	Hawaii	26,604
45	Idaho	21,332
14	Illinois	30,971
35	Indiana	24,162
28	Iowa	26,495
24	Kansas	27,125
46	Kentucky	21,203
40	Louisiana	23,597
33	Maine	24,609
7	Maryland	34,338
2	Massachusetts	39,200
31	Michigan	25,464
10	Minnesota	31,896
50	Mississippi	18,727
34	Missouri	24,560
32	Montana	24,622
23	Nebraska	27,137
25	Nevada	27,046
8	New Hampshire	33,864
3	New Jersey	37,677
47	New Mexico	21,056
4	New York	35,477
39	North Carolina	23,607
6	North Dakota	34,557
30	Ohio	25,615
36	Oklahoma	23,855
29	Oregon	25,923
17	Pennsylvania	28,792
16	Rhode Island	29,038
43	South Carolina	22,220
22	South Dakota	27,408
41	Tennessee	23,263
19	Texas	27,828
37	Utah	23,761
20	Vermont	27,827
9	Virginia	31,934
11	Washington	31,886
49	West Virginia	20,411
21	Wisconsin	27,756
5	Wyoming	35,232

RANK ORDER

RANK	STATE	PER CAPITA
1	Connecticut	$43,193
2	Massachusetts	39,200
3	New Jersey	37,677
4	New York	35,477
5	Wyoming	35,232
6	North Dakota	34,557
7	Maryland	34,338
8	New Hampshire	33,864
9	Virginia	31,934
10	Minnesota	31,896
11	Washington	31,886
12	Colorado	31,126
13	Alaska	31,095
14	Illinois	30,971
15	California	30,753
16	Rhode Island	29,038
17	Pennsylvania	28,792
18	Delaware	28,214
19	Texas	27,828
20	Vermont	27,827
21	Wisconsin	27,756
22	South Dakota	27,408
23	Nebraska	27,137
24	Kansas	27,125
25	Nevada	27,046
26	Hawaii	26,604
27	Florida	26,547
28	Iowa	26,495
29	Oregon	25,923
30	Ohio	25,615
31	Michigan	25,464
32	Montana	24,622
33	Maine	24,609
34	Missouri	24,560
35	Indiana	24,162
36	Oklahoma	23,855
37	Utah	23,761
38	Georgia	23,618
39	North Carolina	23,607
40	Louisiana	23,597
41	Tennessee	23,263
42	Arizona	23,035
43	South Carolina	22,220
44	Alabama	21,498
45	Idaho	21,332
46	Kentucky	21,203
47	New Mexico	21,056
48	Arkansas	20,782
49	West Virginia	20,411
50	Mississippi	18,727
	District of Columbia	41,968

Source: CQ Press using data from U.S. Department of the Treasury, Internal Revenue Service
"Individual Tax Statistics, State Income" (http://www.irs.gov/taxstats/index.html)
*National per capita does not include income from U.S. citizens abroad and other miscellaneous returns not shown separately.

Federal Business Income Tax Collections in 2014

National Total = $353,141,112,000*

ALPHA ORDER

RANK	STATE	COLLECTIONS	% of USA
36	Alabama	$1,484,582,000	0.4%
50	Alaska	179,898,000	0.1%
24	Arizona	4,380,014,000	1.2%
16	Arkansas	7,611,308,000	2.2%
1	California	46,236,808,000	13.1%
17	Colorado	7,339,139,000	2.1%
15	Connecticut	8,633,070,000	2.4%
25	Delaware	4,335,398,000	1.2%
13	Florida	9,015,856,000	2.6%
10	Georgia	10,736,886,000	3.0%
41	Hawaii	376,857,000	0.1%
44	Idaho	333,880,000	0.1%
5	Illinois	20,034,959,000	5.7%
23	Indiana	4,561,915,000	1.3%
35	Iowa	1,544,385,000	0.4%
30	Kansas	2,166,100,000	0.6%
29	Kentucky	2,324,359,000	0.7%
32	Louisiana	1,604,433,000	0.5%
45	Maine	292,164,000	0.1%
28	Maryland	3,176,203,000	0.9%
12	Massachusetts	9,277,736,000	2.6%
22	Michigan	5,022,559,000	1.4%
6	Minnesota	19,417,565,000	5.5%
38	Mississippi	693,586,000	0.2%
11	Missouri	9,946,571,000	2.8%
48	Montana	194,463,000	0.1%
18	Nebraska	7,269,170,000	2.1%
37	Nevada	777,910,000	0.2%
46	New Hampshire	236,410,000	0.1%
4	New Jersey	21,813,832,000	6.2%
47	New Mexico	231,314,000	0.1%
3	New York	28,664,811,000	8.1%
14	North Carolina	8,698,479,000	2.5%
39	North Dakota	560,449,000	0.2%
8	Ohio	12,286,168,000	3.5%
26	Oklahoma	4,049,061,000	1.1%
31	Oregon	1,920,303,000	0.5%
7	Pennsylvania	12,619,448,000	3.6%
27	Rhode Island	3,683,902,000	1.0%
33	South Carolina	1,567,705,000	0.4%
40	South Dakota	404,686,000	0.1%
20	Tennessee	5,905,079,000	1.7%
2	Texas	32,585,544,000	9.2%
34	Utah	1,557,838,000	0.4%
43	Vermont	351,999,000	0.1%
9	Virginia	11,378,112,000	3.2%
21	Washington	5,612,788,000	1.6%
42	West Virginia	374,563,000	0.1%
19	Wisconsin	6,021,437,000	1.7%
49	Wyoming	185,588,000	0.1%

RANK ORDER

RANK	STATE	COLLECTIONS	% of USA
1	California	$46,236,808,000	13.1%
2	Texas	32,585,544,000	9.2%
3	New York	28,664,811,000	8.1%
4	New Jersey	21,813,832,000	6.2%
5	Illinois	20,034,959,000	5.7%
6	Minnesota	19,417,565,000	5.5%
7	Pennsylvania	12,619,448,000	3.6%
8	Ohio	12,286,168,000	3.5%
9	Virginia	11,378,112,000	3.2%
10	Georgia	10,736,886,000	3.0%
11	Missouri	9,946,571,000	2.8%
12	Massachusetts	9,277,736,000	2.6%
13	Florida	9,015,856,000	2.6%
14	North Carolina	8,698,479,000	2.5%
15	Connecticut	8,633,070,000	2.4%
16	Arkansas	7,611,308,000	2.2%
17	Colorado	7,339,139,000	2.1%
18	Nebraska	7,269,170,000	2.1%
19	Wisconsin	6,021,437,000	1.7%
20	Tennessee	5,905,079,000	1.7%
21	Washington	5,612,788,000	1.6%
22	Michigan	5,022,559,000	1.4%
23	Indiana	4,561,915,000	1.3%
24	Arizona	4,380,014,000	1.2%
25	Delaware	4,335,398,000	1.2%
26	Oklahoma	4,049,061,000	1.1%
27	Rhode Island	3,683,902,000	1.0%
28	Maryland	3,176,203,000	0.9%
29	Kentucky	2,324,359,000	0.7%
30	Kansas	2,166,100,000	0.6%
31	Oregon	1,920,303,000	0.5%
32	Louisiana	1,604,433,000	0.5%
33	South Carolina	1,567,705,000	0.4%
34	Utah	1,557,838,000	0.4%
35	Iowa	1,544,385,000	0.4%
36	Alabama	1,484,582,000	0.4%
37	Nevada	777,910,000	0.2%
38	Mississippi	693,586,000	0.2%
39	North Dakota	560,449,000	0.2%
40	South Dakota	404,686,000	0.1%
41	Hawaii	376,857,000	0.1%
42	West Virginia	374,563,000	0.1%
43	Vermont	351,999,000	0.1%
44	Idaho	333,880,000	0.1%
45	Maine	292,164,000	0.1%
46	New Hampshire	236,410,000	0.1%
47	New Mexico	231,314,000	0.1%
48	Montana	194,463,000	0.1%
49	Wyoming	185,588,000	0.1%
50	Alaska	179,898,000	0.1%
	District of Columbia	1,322,308,000	0.4%

Source: U.S. Department of the Treasury, Internal Revenue Service
  "Fiscal Year 2014 IRS Data Book" (http://www.irs.gov/uac/SOI-Tax-Stats-IRS-Data-Book)
*Total includes collections and returns from international sources and others not distributed by state. Includes taxes on corporation income (Form 1120 series) and unrelated business income from tax-exempt organizations.

Average Revenue Collection per Federal Business Income Tax Return in 2014

National Average = $51,488 per Return*

ALPHA ORDER

RANK	STATE	PER RETURN
34	Alabama	$21,816
41	Alaska	14,367
26	Arizona	37,185
6	Arkansas	141,751
15	California	58,440
20	Colorado	47,916
3	Connecticut	162,716
1	Delaware	175,757
43	Florida	11,174
19	Georgia	48,862
42	Hawaii	13,805
48	Idaho	9,604
17	Illinois	57,740
25	Indiana	40,726
31	Iowa	24,997
23	Kansas	42,109
28	Kentucky	34,794
37	Louisiana	18,697
47	Maine	9,678
32	Maryland	24,497
14	Massachusetts	64,277
29	Michigan	26,274
5	Minnesota	153,342
40	Mississippi	17,010
8	Missouri	100,588
50	Montana	5,614
2	Nebraska	166,164
44	Nevada	11,111
45	New Hampshire	10,723
7	New Jersey	114,094
49	New Mexico	7,798
22	New York	44,344
21	North Carolina	45,179
27	North Dakota	35,273
11	Ohio	70,041
18	Oklahoma	55,451
30	Oregon	25,702
16	Pennsylvania	58,071
4	Rhode Island	154,988
39	South Carolina	18,552
35	South Dakota	21,774
9	Tennessee	88,629
10	Texas	72,519
36	Utah	21,561
33	Vermont	22,025
12	Virginia	67,957
24	Washington	41,469
38	West Virginia	18,685
13	Wisconsin	65,780
46	Wyoming	10,212

RANK ORDER

RANK	STATE	PER RETURN
1	Delaware	$175,757
2	Nebraska	166,164
3	Connecticut	162,716
4	Rhode Island	154,988
5	Minnesota	153,342
6	Arkansas	141,751
7	New Jersey	114,094
8	Missouri	100,588
9	Tennessee	88,629
10	Texas	72,519
11	Ohio	70,041
12	Virginia	67,957
13	Wisconsin	65,780
14	Massachusetts	64,277
15	California	58,440
16	Pennsylvania	58,071
17	Illinois	57,740
18	Oklahoma	55,451
19	Georgia	48,862
20	Colorado	47,916
21	North Carolina	45,179
22	New York	44,344
23	Kansas	42,109
24	Washington	41,469
25	Indiana	40,726
26	Arizona	37,185
27	North Dakota	35,273
28	Kentucky	34,794
29	Michigan	26,274
30	Oregon	25,702
31	Iowa	24,997
32	Maryland	24,497
33	Vermont	22,025
34	Alabama	21,816
35	South Dakota	21,774
36	Utah	21,561
37	Louisiana	18,697
38	West Virginia	18,685
39	South Carolina	18,552
40	Mississippi	17,010
41	Alaska	14,367
42	Hawaii	13,805
43	Florida	11,174
44	Nevada	11,111
45	New Hampshire	10,723
46	Wyoming	10,212
47	Maine	9,678
48	Idaho	9,604
49	New Mexico	7,798
50	Montana	5,614
	District of Columbia	74,698

Source: CQ Press using data from U.S. Department of the Treasury, Internal Revenue Service
"Fiscal Year 2014 IRS Data Book" (http://www.irs.gov/uac/SOI-Tax-Stats-IRS-Data-Book)
*National average does not include income from U.S. citizens abroad and other miscellaneous returns not shown separately. Includes taxes on corporation income (Form 1120 series) and unrelated business income from tax-exempt organizations.

Federal Tax Returns Filed in 2014

National Total = 239,874,741 Returns*

ALPHA ORDER

RANK	STATE	RETURNS	% of USA
26	Alabama	3,074,293	1.3%
48	Alaska	584,480	0.2%
18	Arizona	4,485,975	1.9%
34	Arkansas	1,933,942	0.8%
1	California	28,720,123	12.0%
19	Colorado	4,407,894	1.8%
27	Connecticut	2,948,257	1.2%
45	Delaware	757,208	0.3%
3	Florida	16,408,264	6.8%
10	Georgia	6,826,489	2.8%
40	Hawaii	1,108,736	0.5%
38	Idaho	1,176,813	0.5%
5	Illinois	9,998,165	4.2%
16	Indiana	4,593,690	1.9%
30	Iowa	2,398,672	1.0%
31	Kansas	2,204,297	0.9%
28	Kentucky	2,859,381	1.2%
24	Louisiana	3,191,882	1.3%
42	Maine	1,083,248	0.5%
15	Maryland	4,693,024	2.0%
13	Massachusetts	5,537,843	2.3%
9	Michigan	7,210,281	3.0%
20	Minnesota	4,406,209	1.8%
35	Mississippi	1,847,620	0.8%
17	Missouri	4,488,629	1.9%
43	Montana	929,618	0.4%
36	Nebraska	1,487,400	0.6%
32	Nevada	2,069,872	0.9%
41	New Hampshire	1,107,000	0.5%
8	New Jersey	7,347,485	3.1%
37	New Mexico	1,410,550	0.6%
4	New York	15,866,679	6.6%
11	North Carolina	6,747,162	2.8%
47	North Dakota	667,690	0.3%
7	Ohio	8,416,238	3.5%
29	Oklahoma	2,708,287	1.1%
25	Oregon	3,099,035	1.3%
6	Pennsylvania	9,699,299	4.0%
44	Rhode Island	850,759	0.4%
23	South Carolina	3,196,445	1.3%
46	South Dakota	745,690	0.3%
22	Tennessee	4,278,396	1.8%
2	Texas	18,551,291	7.7%
33	Utah	2,040,447	0.9%
49	Vermont	572,375	0.2%
12	Virginia	6,118,884	2.6%
14	Washington	5,472,716	2.3%
39	West Virginia	1,157,042	0.5%
21	Wisconsin	4,395,017	1.8%
50	Wyoming	535,781	0.2%

RANK ORDER

RANK	STATE	RETURNS	% of USA
1	California	28,720,123	12.0%
2	Texas	18,551,291	7.7%
3	Florida	16,408,264	6.8%
4	New York	15,866,679	6.6%
5	Illinois	9,998,165	4.2%
6	Pennsylvania	9,699,299	4.0%
7	Ohio	8,416,238	3.5%
8	New Jersey	7,347,485	3.1%
9	Michigan	7,210,281	3.0%
10	Georgia	6,826,489	2.8%
11	North Carolina	6,747,162	2.8%
12	Virginia	6,118,884	2.6%
13	Massachusetts	5,537,843	2.3%
14	Washington	5,472,716	2.3%
15	Maryland	4,693,024	2.0%
16	Indiana	4,593,690	1.9%
17	Missouri	4,488,629	1.9%
18	Arizona	4,485,975	1.9%
19	Colorado	4,407,894	1.8%
20	Minnesota	4,406,209	1.8%
21	Wisconsin	4,395,017	1.8%
22	Tennessee	4,278,396	1.8%
23	South Carolina	3,196,445	1.3%
24	Louisiana	3,191,882	1.3%
25	Oregon	3,099,035	1.3%
26	Alabama	3,074,293	1.3%
27	Connecticut	2,948,257	1.2%
28	Kentucky	2,859,381	1.2%
29	Oklahoma	2,708,287	1.1%
30	Iowa	2,398,672	1.0%
31	Kansas	2,204,297	0.9%
32	Nevada	2,069,872	0.9%
33	Utah	2,040,447	0.9%
34	Arkansas	1,933,942	0.8%
35	Mississippi	1,847,620	0.8%
36	Nebraska	1,487,400	0.6%
37	New Mexico	1,410,550	0.6%
38	Idaho	1,176,813	0.5%
39	West Virginia	1,157,042	0.5%
40	Hawaii	1,108,736	0.5%
41	New Hampshire	1,107,000	0.5%
42	Maine	1,083,248	0.5%
43	Montana	929,618	0.4%
44	Rhode Island	850,759	0.4%
45	Delaware	757,208	0.3%
46	South Dakota	745,690	0.3%
47	North Dakota	667,690	0.3%
48	Alaska	584,480	0.2%
49	Vermont	572,375	0.2%
50	Wyoming	535,781	0.2%
	District of Columbia	585,665	0.2%

Source: U.S. Department of the Treasury, Internal Revenue Service "Fiscal Year 2014 IRS Data Book" (http://www.irs.gov/uac/SOI-Tax-Stats-IRS-Data-Book)

*Total includes returns from international sources and other miscellaneous returns not shown separately.

Percent of Federal Returns Filed Electronically in 2014

National Percent = 65.5%*

ALPHA ORDER

RANK	STATE	PERCENT
4	Alabama	69.0
38	Alaska	63.5
24	Arizona	65.5
16	Arkansas	66.6
29	California	64.9
43	Colorado	62.3
32	Connecticut	64.5
34	Delaware	64.2
33	Florida	64.4
3	Georgia	69.7
50	Hawaii	57.1
39	Idaho	63.4
29	Illinois	64.9
12	Indiana	67.8
36	Iowa	64.1
20	Kansas	66.0
13	Kentucky	67.7
19	Louisiana	66.4
44	Maine	62.0
42	Maryland	62.4
8	Massachusetts	68.3
14	Michigan	67.5
22	Minnesota	65.7
6	Mississippi	68.8
21	Missouri	65.9
48	Montana	59.7
27	Nebraska	65.1
10	Nevada	68.0
34	New Hampshire	64.2
17	New Jersey	66.5
36	New Mexico	64.1
1	New York	70.2
22	North Carolina	65.7
49	North Dakota	58.2
11	Ohio	67.9
25	Oklahoma	65.4
41	Oregon	62.6
26	Pennsylvania	65.2
2	Rhode Island	69.8
9	South Carolina	68.1
45	South Dakota	61.5
4	Tennessee	69.0
17	Texas	66.5
7	Utah	68.4
47	Vermont	59.8
27	Virginia	65.1
40	Washington	63.3
31	West Virginia	64.7
15	Wisconsin	66.9
46	Wyoming	61.4

RANK ORDER

RANK	STATE	PERCENT
1	New York	70.2
2	Rhode Island	69.8
3	Georgia	69.7
4	Alabama	69.0
4	Tennessee	69.0
6	Mississippi	68.8
7	Utah	68.4
8	Massachusetts	68.3
9	South Carolina	68.1
10	Nevada	68.0
11	Ohio	67.9
12	Indiana	67.8
13	Kentucky	67.7
14	Michigan	67.5
15	Wisconsin	66.9
16	Arkansas	66.6
17	New Jersey	66.5
17	Texas	66.5
19	Louisiana	66.4
20	Kansas	66.0
21	Missouri	65.9
22	Minnesota	65.7
22	North Carolina	65.7
24	Arizona	65.5
25	Oklahoma	65.4
26	Pennsylvania	65.2
27	Nebraska	65.1
27	Virginia	65.1
29	California	64.9
29	Illinois	64.9
31	West Virginia	64.7
32	Connecticut	64.5
33	Florida	64.4
34	Delaware	64.2
34	New Hampshire	64.2
36	Iowa	64.1
36	New Mexico	64.1
38	Alaska	63.5
39	Idaho	63.4
40	Washington	63.3
41	Oregon	62.6
42	Maryland	62.4
43	Colorado	62.3
44	Maine	62.0
45	South Dakota	61.5
46	Wyoming	61.4
47	Vermont	59.8
48	Montana	59.7
49	North Dakota	58.2
50	Hawaii	57.1
	District of Columbia	62.9

Source: CQ Press using data from U.S. Department of the Treasury, Internal Revenue Service
"Fiscal Year 2014 IRS Data Book" (http://www.irs.gov/uac/SOI-Tax-Stats-IRS-Data-Book)
*Total includes returns from international sources and other miscellaneous returns. Includes corporate, individual, partnership, estate, employment and other returns. Excludes returns that cannot be filed electronically including informational returns.

Federal Individual Income Tax Returns Filed in 2014

National Total = 147,444,789 Returns*

ALPHA ORDER

RANK	STATE	RETURNS	% of USA
24	Alabama	2,048,463	1.4%
48	Alaska	357,733	0.2%
18	Arizona	2,805,861	1.9%
34	Arkansas	1,219,841	0.8%
1	California	17,155,206	11.6%
22	Colorado	2,495,936	1.7%
28	Connecticut	1,752,898	1.2%
45	Delaware	438,240	0.3%
4	Florida	9,350,393	6.3%
9	Georgia	4,355,079	3.0%
41	Hawaii	675,858	0.5%
39	Idaho	688,751	0.5%
6	Illinois	6,121,352	4.2%
15	Indiana	3,048,651	2.1%
30	Iowa	1,435,089	1.0%
31	Kansas	1,328,787	0.9%
26	Kentucky	1,887,430	1.3%
25	Louisiana	2,004,832	1.4%
42	Maine	633,662	0.4%
16	Maryland	2,940,059	2.0%
13	Massachusetts	3,299,297	2.2%
8	Michigan	4,663,269	3.2%
21	Minnesota	2,652,227	1.8%
33	Mississippi	1,246,984	0.8%
20	Missouri	2,742,888	1.9%
44	Montana	486,592	0.3%
37	Nebraska	882,429	0.6%
32	Nevada	1,307,349	0.9%
40	New Hampshire	680,729	0.5%
10	New Jersey	4,332,769	2.9%
36	New Mexico	906,337	0.6%
3	New York	9,466,459	6.4%
11	North Carolina	4,318,220	2.9%
47	North Dakota	361,952	0.2%
7	Ohio	5,541,252	3.8%
29	Oklahoma	1,627,694	1.1%
27	Oregon	1,789,210	1.2%
5	Pennsylvania	6,154,779	4.2%
43	Rhode Island	518,077	0.4%
23	South Carolina	2,089,348	1.4%
46	South Dakota	416,267	0.3%
17	Tennessee	2,904,567	2.0%
2	Texas	11,693,399	7.9%
35	Utah	1,194,382	0.8%
49	Vermont	320,980	0.2%
12	Virginia	3,833,510	2.6%
14	Washington	3,281,026	2.2%
38	West Virginia	784,830	0.5%
19	Wisconsin	2,803,790	1.9%
50	Wyoming	288,969	0.2%

RANK ORDER

RANK	STATE	RETURNS	% of USA
1	California	17,155,206	11.6%
2	Texas	11,693,399	7.9%
3	New York	9,466,459	6.4%
4	Florida	9,350,393	6.3%
5	Pennsylvania	6,154,779	4.2%
6	Illinois	6,121,352	4.2%
7	Ohio	5,541,252	3.8%
8	Michigan	4,663,269	3.2%
9	Georgia	4,355,079	3.0%
10	New Jersey	4,332,769	2.9%
11	North Carolina	4,318,220	2.9%
12	Virginia	3,833,510	2.6%
13	Massachusetts	3,299,297	2.2%
14	Washington	3,281,026	2.2%
15	Indiana	3,048,651	2.1%
16	Maryland	2,940,059	2.0%
17	Tennessee	2,904,567	2.0%
18	Arizona	2,805,861	1.9%
19	Wisconsin	2,803,790	1.9%
20	Missouri	2,742,888	1.9%
21	Minnesota	2,652,227	1.8%
22	Colorado	2,495,936	1.7%
23	South Carolina	2,089,348	1.4%
24	Alabama	2,048,463	1.4%
25	Louisiana	2,004,832	1.4%
26	Kentucky	1,887,430	1.3%
27	Oregon	1,789,210	1.2%
28	Connecticut	1,752,898	1.2%
29	Oklahoma	1,627,694	1.1%
30	Iowa	1,435,089	1.0%
31	Kansas	1,328,787	0.9%
32	Nevada	1,307,349	0.9%
33	Mississippi	1,246,984	0.8%
34	Arkansas	1,219,841	0.8%
35	Utah	1,194,382	0.8%
36	New Mexico	906,337	0.6%
37	Nebraska	882,429	0.6%
38	West Virginia	784,830	0.5%
39	Idaho	688,751	0.5%
40	New Hampshire	680,729	0.5%
41	Hawaii	675,858	0.5%
42	Maine	633,662	0.4%
43	Rhode Island	518,077	0.4%
44	Montana	486,592	0.3%
45	Delaware	438,240	0.3%
46	South Dakota	416,267	0.3%
47	North Dakota	361,952	0.2%
48	Alaska	357,733	0.2%
49	Vermont	320,980	0.2%
50	Wyoming	288,969	0.2%
	District of Columbia	332,396	0.2%

Source: U.S. Department of the Treasury, Internal Revenue Service
"Fiscal Year 2014 IRS Data Book" (http://www.irs.gov/uac/SOI-Tax-Stats-IRS-Data-Book)
*Total includes returns from international sources and other miscellaneous returns not shown separately.

Percent of Federal Individual Income Tax Returns Filed Electronically in 2014

National Percent = 84.5%*

ALPHA ORDER

RANK	STATE	PERCENT
14	Alabama	87.2
35	Alaska	84.4
46	Arizona	83.4
10	Arkansas	87.6
47	California	83.1
45	Colorado	83.7
30	Connecticut	84.8
38	Delaware	84.3
42	Florida	83.8
24	Georgia	86.3
50	Hawaii	78.4
14	Idaho	87.2
32	Illinois	84.6
7	Indiana	88.1
1	Iowa	91.2
4	Kansas	89.2
5	Kentucky	88.4
29	Louisiana	85.1
47	Maine	83.1
49	Maryland	79.4
30	Massachusetts	84.8
24	Michigan	86.3
14	Minnesota	87.2
10	Mississippi	87.6
21	Missouri	86.4
10	Montana	87.6
2	Nebraska	90.6
40	Nevada	84.0
32	New Hampshire	84.6
39	New Jersey	84.1
35	New Mexico	84.4
8	New York	87.7
21	North Carolina	86.4
5	North Dakota	88.4
26	Ohio	86.0
13	Oklahoma	87.3
42	Oregon	83.8
40	Pennsylvania	84.0
21	Rhode Island	86.4
19	South Carolina	87.1
3	South Dakota	89.3
20	Tennessee	87.0
42	Texas	83.8
14	Utah	87.2
28	Vermont	85.2
32	Virginia	84.6
35	Washington	84.4
27	West Virginia	85.5
14	Wisconsin	87.2
8	Wyoming	87.7

RANK ORDER

RANK	STATE	PERCENT
1	Iowa	91.2
2	Nebraska	90.6
3	South Dakota	89.3
4	Kansas	89.2
5	Kentucky	88.4
5	North Dakota	88.4
7	Indiana	88.1
8	New York	87.7
8	Wyoming	87.7
10	Arkansas	87.6
10	Mississippi	87.6
10	Montana	87.6
13	Oklahoma	87.3
14	Alabama	87.2
14	Idaho	87.2
14	Minnesota	87.2
14	Utah	87.2
14	Wisconsin	87.2
19	South Carolina	87.1
20	Tennessee	87.0
21	Missouri	86.4
21	North Carolina	86.4
21	Rhode Island	86.4
24	Georgia	86.3
24	Michigan	86.3
26	Ohio	86.0
27	West Virginia	85.5
28	Vermont	85.2
29	Louisiana	85.1
30	Connecticut	84.8
30	Massachusetts	84.8
32	Illinois	84.6
32	New Hampshire	84.6
32	Virginia	84.6
35	Alaska	84.4
35	New Mexico	84.4
35	Washington	84.4
38	Delaware	84.3
39	New Jersey	84.1
40	Nevada	84.0
40	Pennsylvania	84.0
42	Florida	83.8
42	Oregon	83.8
42	Texas	83.8
45	Colorado	83.7
46	Arizona	83.4
47	California	83.1
47	Maine	83.1
49	Maryland	79.4
50	Hawaii	78.4
	District of Columbia	80.5

Source: CQ Press using data from U.S. Department of the Treasury, Internal Revenue Service
"Fiscal Year 2014 IRS Data Book" (http://www.irs.gov/uac/SOI-Tax-Stats-IRS-Data-Book)
*Total includes returns from international sources and other miscellaneous returns. Includes returns filed electronically by practitioners.

Federal Business Income Tax Returns Filed in 2014

National Total = 6,863,738 Returns*

ALPHA ORDER

RANK	STATE	RETURNS	% of USA
28	Alabama	68,051	1.0%
50	Alaska	12,522	0.2%
18	Arizona	117,789	1.7%
32	Arkansas	53,695	0.8%
2	California	791,187	11.5%
13	Colorado	153,166	2.2%
33	Connecticut	53,056	0.8%
42	Delaware	24,667	0.4%
1	Florida	806,869	11.8%
6	Georgia	219,740	3.2%
41	Hawaii	27,299	0.4%
37	Idaho	34,763	0.5%
5	Illinois	346,988	5.1%
19	Indiana	112,015	1.6%
31	Iowa	61,783	0.9%
34	Kansas	51,440	0.7%
29	Kentucky	66,804	1.0%
22	Louisiana	85,814	1.3%
39	Maine	30,188	0.4%
16	Maryland	129,656	1.9%
14	Massachusetts	144,340	2.1%
10	Michigan	191,159	2.8%
17	Minnesota	126,629	1.8%
36	Mississippi	40,775	0.6%
20	Missouri	98,884	1.4%
38	Montana	34,636	0.5%
35	Nebraska	43,747	0.6%
27	Nevada	70,013	1.0%
44	New Hampshire	22,048	0.3%
9	New Jersey	191,192	2.8%
40	New Mexico	29,664	0.4%
3	New York	646,415	9.4%
8	North Carolina	192,534	2.8%
49	North Dakota	15,889	0.2%
11	Ohio	175,414	2.6%
25	Oklahoma	73,021	1.1%
24	Oregon	74,714	1.1%
7	Pennsylvania	217,311	3.2%
43	Rhode Island	23,769	0.3%
23	South Carolina	84,504	1.2%
46	South Dakota	18,586	0.3%
30	Tennessee	66,627	1.0%
4	Texas	449,338	6.5%
26	Utah	72,253	1.1%
48	Vermont	15,982	0.2%
12	Virginia	167,431	2.4%
15	Washington	135,348	2.0%
45	West Virginia	20,046	0.3%
21	Wisconsin	91,539	1.3%
47	Wyoming	18,174	0.3%

RANK ORDER

RANK	STATE	RETURNS	% of USA
1	Florida	806,869	11.8%
2	California	791,187	11.5%
3	New York	646,415	9.4%
4	Texas	449,338	6.5%
5	Illinois	346,988	5.1%
6	Georgia	219,740	3.2%
7	Pennsylvania	217,311	3.2%
8	North Carolina	192,534	2.8%
9	New Jersey	191,192	2.8%
10	Michigan	191,159	2.8%
11	Ohio	175,414	2.6%
12	Virginia	167,431	2.4%
13	Colorado	153,166	2.2%
14	Massachusetts	144,340	2.1%
15	Washington	135,348	2.0%
16	Maryland	129,656	1.9%
17	Minnesota	126,629	1.8%
18	Arizona	117,789	1.7%
19	Indiana	112,015	1.6%
20	Missouri	98,884	1.4%
21	Wisconsin	91,539	1.3%
22	Louisiana	85,814	1.3%
23	South Carolina	84,504	1.2%
24	Oregon	74,714	1.1%
25	Oklahoma	73,021	1.1%
26	Utah	72,253	1.1%
27	Nevada	70,013	1.0%
28	Alabama	68,051	1.0%
29	Kentucky	66,804	1.0%
30	Tennessee	66,627	1.0%
31	Iowa	61,783	0.9%
32	Arkansas	53,695	0.8%
33	Connecticut	53,056	0.8%
34	Kansas	51,440	0.7%
35	Nebraska	43,747	0.6%
36	Mississippi	40,775	0.6%
37	Idaho	34,763	0.5%
38	Montana	34,636	0.5%
39	Maine	30,188	0.4%
40	New Mexico	29,664	0.4%
41	Hawaii	27,299	0.4%
42	Delaware	24,667	0.4%
43	Rhode Island	23,769	0.3%
44	New Hampshire	22,048	0.3%
45	West Virginia	20,046	0.3%
46	South Dakota	18,586	0.3%
47	Wyoming	18,174	0.3%
48	Vermont	15,982	0.2%
49	North Dakota	15,889	0.2%
50	Alaska	12,522	0.2%
	District of Columbia	17,702	0.3%

Source: U.S. Department of the Treasury, Internal Revenue Service
"Fiscal Year 2014 IRS Data Book" (http://www.irs.gov/uac/SOI-Tax-Stats-IRS-Data-Book)
*Total includes returns from international sources and other miscellaneous returns not shown separately.

Federal Tax Refunds in 2014

National Total = 118,694,299 Refunds*

ALPHA ORDER

RANK	STATE	REFUNDS	% of USA
23	Alabama	1,702,744	1.4%
47	Alaska	287,182	0.2%
20	Arizona	2,175,590	1.8%
34	Arkansas	1,003,190	0.8%
1	California	13,283,040	11.2%
22	Colorado	1,932,768	1.6%
27	Connecticut	1,405,931	1.2%
45	Delaware	360,809	0.3%
4	Florida	7,606,995	6.4%
9	Georgia	3,618,237	3.0%
41	Hawaii	536,883	0.5%
40	Idaho	546,456	0.5%
5	Illinois	5,096,556	4.3%
15	Indiana	2,565,469	2.2%
30	Iowa	1,149,923	1.0%
33	Kansas	1,052,716	0.9%
26	Kentucky	1,594,872	1.3%
25	Louisiana	1,672,605	1.4%
42	Maine	514,012	0.4%
17	Maryland	2,313,936	1.9%
14	Massachusetts	2,636,735	2.2%
8	Michigan	3,789,560	3.2%
21	Minnesota	2,067,438	1.7%
32	Mississippi	1,055,448	0.9%
19	Missouri	2,227,989	1.9%
44	Montana	372,925	0.3%
37	Nebraska	708,888	0.6%
31	Nevada	1,068,420	0.9%
39	New Hampshire	554,811	0.5%
10	New Jersey	3,482,558	2.9%
36	New Mexico	738,963	0.6%
3	New York	7,686,707	6.5%
11	North Carolina	3,476,410	2.9%
48	North Dakota	278,156	0.2%
7	Ohio	4,605,489	3.9%
29	Oklahoma	1,320,261	1.1%
28	Oregon	1,374,235	1.2%
6	Pennsylvania	5,085,356	4.3%
43	Rhode Island	433,443	0.4%
24	South Carolina	1,677,347	1.4%
46	South Dakota	326,389	0.3%
16	Tennessee	2,444,675	2.1%
2	Texas	9,802,282	8.3%
35	Utah	987,266	0.8%
49	Vermont	257,560	0.2%
12	Virginia	3,112,499	2.6%
13	Washington	2,640,001	2.2%
38	West Virginia	674,868	0.6%
18	Wisconsin	2,253,326	1.9%
50	Wyoming	232,612	0.2%

RANK ORDER

RANK	STATE	REFUNDS	% of USA
1	California	13,283,040	11.2%
2	Texas	9,802,282	8.3%
3	New York	7,686,707	6.5%
4	Florida	7,606,995	6.4%
5	Illinois	5,096,556	4.3%
6	Pennsylvania	5,085,356	4.3%
7	Ohio	4,605,489	3.9%
8	Michigan	3,789,560	3.2%
9	Georgia	3,618,237	3.0%
10	New Jersey	3,482,558	2.9%
11	North Carolina	3,476,410	2.9%
12	Virginia	3,112,499	2.6%
13	Washington	2,640,001	2.2%
14	Massachusetts	2,636,735	2.2%
15	Indiana	2,565,469	2.2%
16	Tennessee	2,444,675	2.1%
17	Maryland	2,313,936	1.9%
18	Wisconsin	2,253,326	1.9%
19	Missouri	2,227,989	1.9%
20	Arizona	2,175,590	1.8%
21	Minnesota	2,067,438	1.7%
22	Colorado	1,932,768	1.6%
23	Alabama	1,702,744	1.4%
24	South Carolina	1,677,347	1.4%
25	Louisiana	1,672,605	1.4%
26	Kentucky	1,594,872	1.3%
27	Connecticut	1,405,931	1.2%
28	Oregon	1,374,235	1.2%
29	Oklahoma	1,320,261	1.1%
30	Iowa	1,149,923	1.0%
31	Nevada	1,068,420	0.9%
32	Mississippi	1,055,448	0.9%
33	Kansas	1,052,716	0.9%
34	Arkansas	1,003,190	0.8%
35	Utah	987,266	0.8%
36	New Mexico	738,963	0.6%
37	Nebraska	708,888	0.6%
38	West Virginia	674,868	0.6%
39	New Hampshire	554,811	0.5%
40	Idaho	546,456	0.5%
41	Hawaii	536,883	0.5%
42	Maine	514,012	0.4%
43	Rhode Island	433,443	0.4%
44	Montana	372,925	0.3%
45	Delaware	360,809	0.3%
46	South Dakota	326,389	0.3%
47	Alaska	287,182	0.2%
48	North Dakota	278,156	0.2%
49	Vermont	257,560	0.2%
50	Wyoming	232,612	0.2%
	District of Columbia	265,764	0.2%

Source: U.S. Department of the Treasury, Internal Revenue Service
"Fiscal Year 2014 IRS Data Book" (http://www.irs.gov/uac/SOI-Tax-Stats-IRS-Data-Book)
*Total includes refunds to international sources and other miscellaneous refunds not shown separately.

Value of Federal Tax Refunds in 2014

National Total = $373,545,926,000*

ALPHA ORDER

RANK	STATE	REFUNDS	% of USA
25	Alabama	$4,951,091,000	1.3%
47	Alaska	820,566,000	0.2%
19	Arizona	6,117,312,000	1.6%
36	Arkansas	2,922,525,000	0.8%
1	California	42,112,601,000	11.3%
21	Colorado	5,750,477,000	1.5%
23	Connecticut	5,354,519,000	1.4%
30	Delaware	3,251,375,000	0.9%
4	Florida	22,313,006,000	6.0%
9	Georgia	10,684,039,000	2.9%
40	Hawaii	1,452,114,000	0.4%
42	Idaho	1,369,447,000	0.4%
5	Illinois	17,151,666,000	4.6%
17	Indiana	6,876,981,000	1.8%
32	Iowa	3,066,502,000	0.8%
34	Kansas	2,976,769,000	0.8%
27	Kentucky	4,307,783,000	1.2%
24	Louisiana	5,067,969,000	1.4%
43	Maine	1,323,953,000	0.4%
18	Maryland	6,858,448,000	1.8%
13	Massachusetts	8,018,069,000	2.1%
10	Michigan	9,936,380,000	2.7%
16	Minnesota	7,009,210,000	1.9%
31	Mississippi	3,137,665,000	0.8%
20	Missouri	6,111,154,000	1.6%
45	Montana	866,466,000	0.2%
38	Nebraska	1,871,763,000	0.5%
33	Nevada	3,045,267,000	0.8%
41	New Hampshire	1,444,791,000	0.4%
7	New Jersey	12,430,351,000	3.3%
37	New Mexico	1,940,170,000	0.5%
3	New York	26,226,700,000	7.0%
11	North Carolina	9,424,292,000	2.5%
48	North Dakota	738,591,000	0.2%
8	Ohio	12,064,238,000	3.2%
28	Oklahoma	4,249,198,000	1.1%
29	Oregon	3,317,872,000	0.9%
6	Pennsylvania	15,116,043,000	4.0%
44	Rhode Island	1,128,851,000	0.3%
26	South Carolina	4,391,486,000	1.2%
46	South Dakota	838,698,000	0.2%
15	Tennessee	7,076,525,000	1.9%
2	Texas	33,727,956,000	9.0%
35	Utah	2,957,729,000	0.8%
50	Vermont	610,494,000	0.2%
12	Virginia	8,972,589,000	2.4%
14	Washington	7,302,638,000	2.0%
39	West Virginia	1,744,747,000	0.5%
22	Wisconsin	5,629,268,000	1.5%
49	Wyoming	626,003,000	0.2%

RANK ORDER

RANK	STATE	REFUNDS	% of USA
1	California	$42,112,601,000	11.3%
2	Texas	33,727,956,000	9.0%
3	New York	26,226,700,000	7.0%
4	Florida	22,313,006,000	6.0%
5	Illinois	17,151,666,000	4.6%
6	Pennsylvania	15,116,043,000	4.0%
7	New Jersey	12,430,351,000	3.3%
8	Ohio	12,064,238,000	3.2%
9	Georgia	10,684,039,000	2.9%
10	Michigan	9,936,380,000	2.7%
11	North Carolina	9,424,292,000	2.5%
12	Virginia	8,972,589,000	2.4%
13	Massachusetts	8,018,069,000	2.1%
14	Washington	7,302,638,000	2.0%
15	Tennessee	7,076,525,000	1.9%
16	Minnesota	7,009,210,000	1.9%
17	Indiana	6,876,981,000	1.8%
18	Maryland	6,858,448,000	1.8%
19	Arizona	6,117,312,000	1.6%
20	Missouri	6,111,154,000	1.6%
21	Colorado	5,750,477,000	1.5%
22	Wisconsin	5,629,268,000	1.5%
23	Connecticut	5,354,519,000	1.4%
24	Louisiana	5,067,969,000	1.4%
25	Alabama	4,951,091,000	1.3%
26	South Carolina	4,391,486,000	1.2%
27	Kentucky	4,307,783,000	1.2%
28	Oklahoma	4,249,198,000	1.1%
29	Oregon	3,317,872,000	0.9%
30	Delaware	3,251,375,000	0.9%
31	Mississippi	3,137,665,000	0.8%
32	Iowa	3,066,502,000	0.8%
33	Nevada	3,045,267,000	0.8%
34	Kansas	2,976,769,000	0.8%
35	Utah	2,957,729,000	0.8%
36	Arkansas	2,922,525,000	0.8%
37	New Mexico	1,940,170,000	0.5%
38	Nebraska	1,871,763,000	0.5%
39	West Virginia	1,744,747,000	0.5%
40	Hawaii	1,452,114,000	0.4%
41	New Hampshire	1,444,791,000	0.4%
42	Idaho	1,369,447,000	0.4%
43	Maine	1,323,953,000	0.4%
44	Rhode Island	1,128,851,000	0.3%
45	Montana	866,466,000	0.2%
46	South Dakota	838,698,000	0.2%
47	Alaska	820,566,000	0.2%
48	North Dakota	738,591,000	0.2%
49	Wyoming	626,003,000	0.2%
50	Vermont	610,494,000	0.2%
	District of Columbia	849,615,000	0.2%

Source: U.S. Department of the Treasury, Internal Revenue Service
"Fiscal Year 2014 IRS Data Book" (http://www.irs.gov/uac/SOI-Tax-Stats-IRS-Data-Book)
*Total includes refunds to international sources and other miscellaneous refunds not shown separately.

Average Value of Federal Tax Refunds in 2014

National Average = $3,147*

ALPHA ORDER

RANK	STATE	AVERAGE REFUND
20	Alabama	$2,908
23	Alaska	2,857
26	Arizona	2,812
19	Arkansas	2,913
9	California	3,170
13	Colorado	2,975
2	Connecticut	3,809
1	Delaware	9,011
18	Florida	2,933
17	Georgia	2,953
30	Hawaii	2,705
46	Idaho	2,506
7	Illinois	3,365
33	Indiana	2,681
34	Iowa	2,667
25	Kansas	2,828
31	Kentucky	2,701
11	Louisiana	3,030
44	Maine	2,576
16	Maryland	2,964
10	Massachusetts	3,041
38	Michigan	2,622
6	Minnesota	3,390
14	Mississippi	2,973
28	Missouri	2,743
50	Montana	2,323
36	Nebraska	2,640
24	Nevada	2,850
41	New Hampshire	2,604
3	New Jersey	3,569
37	New Mexico	2,626
5	New York	3,412
29	North Carolina	2,711
35	North Dakota	2,655
39	Ohio	2,620
8	Oklahoma	3,218
48	Oregon	2,414
15	Pennsylvania	2,972
41	Rhode Island	2,604
40	South Carolina	2,618
45	South Dakota	2,570
21	Tennessee	2,895
4	Texas	3,441
12	Utah	2,996
49	Vermont	2,370
22	Virginia	2,883
27	Washington	2,766
43	West Virginia	2,585
47	Wisconsin	2,498
32	Wyoming	2,691

RANK ORDER

RANK	STATE	AVERAGE REFUND
1	Delaware	$9,011
2	Connecticut	3,809
3	New Jersey	3,569
4	Texas	3,441
5	New York	3,412
6	Minnesota	3,390
7	Illinois	3,365
8	Oklahoma	3,218
9	California	3,170
10	Massachusetts	3,041
11	Louisiana	3,030
12	Utah	2,996
13	Colorado	2,975
14	Mississippi	2,973
15	Pennsylvania	2,972
16	Maryland	2,964
17	Georgia	2,953
18	Florida	2,933
19	Arkansas	2,913
20	Alabama	2,908
21	Tennessee	2,895
22	Virginia	2,883
23	Alaska	2,857
24	Nevada	2,850
25	Kansas	2,828
26	Arizona	2,812
27	Washington	2,766
28	Missouri	2,743
29	North Carolina	2,711
30	Hawaii	2,705
31	Kentucky	2,701
32	Wyoming	2,691
33	Indiana	2,681
34	Iowa	2,667
35	North Dakota	2,655
36	Nebraska	2,640
37	New Mexico	2,626
38	Michigan	2,622
39	Ohio	2,620
40	South Carolina	2,618
41	New Hampshire	2,604
41	Rhode Island	2,604
43	West Virginia	2,585
44	Maine	2,576
45	South Dakota	2,570
46	Idaho	2,506
47	Wisconsin	2,498
48	Oregon	2,414
49	Vermont	2,370
50	Montana	2,323
	District of Columbia	3,197

Source: CQ Press using data from U.S. Department of the Treasury, Internal Revenue Service
"Fiscal Year 2014 IRS Data Book" (http://www.irs.gov/uac/SOI-Tax-Stats-IRS-Data-Book)
*National average includes refunds to international sources and other miscellaneous refunds not shown separately.

Value of Federal Individual Income Tax Refunds in 2014

National Total = $330,561,145,000*

ALPHA ORDER

RANK	STATE	REFUNDS	% of USA
24	Alabama	$4,724,766,000	1.4%
47	Alaska	762,026,000	0.2%
18	Arizona	5,652,704,000	1.7%
34	Arkansas	2,648,474,000	0.8%
1	California	36,675,433,000	11.1%
22	Colorado	4,812,689,000	1.5%
25	Connecticut	4,314,033,000	1.3%
44	Delaware	903,684,000	0.3%
4	Florida	21,204,143,000	6.4%
9	Georgia	9,868,301,000	3.0%
40	Hawaii	1,349,655,000	0.4%
41	Idaho	1,287,214,000	0.4%
5	Illinois	14,184,482,000	4.3%
15	Indiana	6,509,854,000	2.0%
32	Iowa	2,796,185,000	0.8%
35	Kansas	2,628,567,000	0.8%
27	Kentucky	4,091,732,000	1.2%
21	Louisiana	4,818,487,000	1.5%
42	Maine	1,149,887,000	0.3%
17	Maryland	6,260,116,000	1.9%
13	Massachusetts	6,953,479,000	2.1%
10	Michigan	9,242,438,000	2.8%
23	Minnesota	4,810,182,000	1.5%
30	Mississippi	3,050,351,000	0.9%
19	Missouri	5,572,044,000	1.7%
45	Montana	830,495,000	0.3%
37	Nebraska	1,733,840,000	0.5%
31	Nevada	2,878,499,000	0.9%
39	New Hampshire	1,358,494,000	0.4%
8	New Jersey	10,116,765,000	3.1%
36	New Mexico	1,889,991,000	0.6%
3	New York	22,357,499,000	6.8%
11	North Carolina	8,781,827,000	2.7%
48	North Dakota	679,340,000	0.2%
7	Ohio	11,198,465,000	3.4%
28	Oklahoma	3,553,877,000	1.1%
29	Oregon	3,139,457,000	0.9%
6	Pennsylvania	12,824,424,000	3.9%
43	Rhode Island	1,082,405,000	0.3%
26	South Carolina	4,181,137,000	1.3%
46	South Dakota	781,149,000	0.2%
16	Tennessee	6,461,409,000	2.0%
2	Texas	29,138,140,000	8.8%
33	Utah	2,692,102,000	0.8%
50	Vermont	566,260,000	0.2%
12	Virginia	8,238,539,000	2.5%
14	Washington	6,692,115,000	2.0%
38	West Virginia	1,691,829,000	0.5%
20	Wisconsin	5,163,132,000	1.6%
49	Wyoming	604,827,000	0.2%

RANK ORDER

RANK	STATE	REFUNDS	% of USA
1	California	$36,675,433,000	11.1%
2	Texas	29,138,140,000	8.8%
3	New York	22,357,499,000	6.8%
4	Florida	21,204,143,000	6.4%
5	Illinois	14,184,482,000	4.3%
6	Pennsylvania	12,824,424,000	3.9%
7	Ohio	11,198,465,000	3.4%
8	New Jersey	10,116,765,000	3.1%
9	Georgia	9,868,301,000	3.0%
10	Michigan	9,242,438,000	2.8%
11	North Carolina	8,781,827,000	2.7%
12	Virginia	8,238,539,000	2.5%
13	Massachusetts	6,953,479,000	2.1%
14	Washington	6,692,115,000	2.0%
15	Indiana	6,509,854,000	2.0%
16	Tennessee	6,461,409,000	2.0%
17	Maryland	6,260,116,000	1.9%
18	Arizona	5,652,704,000	1.7%
19	Missouri	5,572,044,000	1.7%
20	Wisconsin	5,163,132,000	1.6%
21	Louisiana	4,818,487,000	1.5%
22	Colorado	4,812,689,000	1.5%
23	Minnesota	4,810,182,000	1.5%
24	Alabama	4,724,766,000	1.4%
25	Connecticut	4,314,033,000	1.3%
26	South Carolina	4,181,137,000	1.3%
27	Kentucky	4,091,732,000	1.2%
28	Oklahoma	3,553,877,000	1.1%
29	Oregon	3,139,457,000	0.9%
30	Mississippi	3,050,351,000	0.9%
31	Nevada	2,878,499,000	0.9%
32	Iowa	2,796,185,000	0.8%
33	Utah	2,692,102,000	0.8%
34	Arkansas	2,648,474,000	0.8%
35	Kansas	2,628,567,000	0.8%
36	New Mexico	1,889,991,000	0.6%
37	Nebraska	1,733,840,000	0.5%
38	West Virginia	1,691,829,000	0.5%
39	New Hampshire	1,358,494,000	0.4%
40	Hawaii	1,349,655,000	0.4%
41	Idaho	1,287,214,000	0.4%
42	Maine	1,149,887,000	0.3%
43	Rhode Island	1,082,405,000	0.3%
44	Delaware	903,684,000	0.3%
45	Montana	830,495,000	0.3%
46	South Dakota	781,149,000	0.2%
47	Alaska	762,026,000	0.2%
48	North Dakota	679,340,000	0.2%
49	Wyoming	604,827,000	0.2%
50	Vermont	566,260,000	0.2%
	District of Columbia	756,962,000	0.2%

Source: U.S. Department of the Treasury, Internal Revenue Service
"Fiscal Year 2014 IRS Data Book" (http://www.irs.gov/uac/SOI-Tax-Stats-IRS-Data-Book)
*Total includes refunds to international sources and other miscellaneous refunds not shown separately.

Average Value of Federal Individual Income Tax Refunds in 2014

National Average = $2,836*

ALPHA ORDER

RANK	STATE	AVERAGE REFUND
9	Alabama	$2,821
16	Alaska	2,721
22	Arizona	2,640
18	Arkansas	2,691
10	California	2,810
35	Colorado	2,540
1	Connecticut	3,125
28	Delaware	2,563
7	Florida	2,844
12	Georgia	2,767
30	Hawaii	2,559
44	Idaho	2,414
8	Illinois	2,835
26	Indiana	2,572
40	Iowa	2,483
31	Kansas	2,551
24	Kentucky	2,602
6	Louisiana	2,940
49	Maine	2,278
13	Maryland	2,748
21	Massachusetts	2,683
41	Michigan	2,482
45	Minnesota	2,372
5	Mississippi	2,943
33	Missouri	2,547
48	Montana	2,298
38	Nebraska	2,502
15	Nevada	2,738
39	New Hampshire	2,495
4	New Jersey	2,960
23	New Mexico	2,604
3	New York	2,964
27	North Carolina	2,566
37	North Dakota	2,513
42	Ohio	2,466
13	Oklahoma	2,748
46	Oregon	2,332
29	Pennsylvania	2,562
34	Rhode Island	2,542
36	South Carolina	2,532
43	South Dakota	2,464
19	Tennessee	2,688
2	Texas	3,033
11	Utah	2,779
50	Vermont	2,254
17	Virginia	2,693
25	Washington	2,589
32	West Virginia	2,548
47	Wisconsin	2,330
20	Wyoming	2,685

RANK ORDER

RANK	STATE	AVERAGE REFUND
1	Connecticut	$3,125
2	Texas	3,033
3	New York	2,964
4	New Jersey	2,960
5	Mississippi	2,943
6	Louisiana	2,940
7	Florida	2,844
8	Illinois	2,835
9	Alabama	2,821
10	California	2,810
11	Utah	2,779
12	Georgia	2,767
13	Maryland	2,748
13	Oklahoma	2,748
15	Nevada	2,738
16	Alaska	2,721
17	Virginia	2,693
18	Arkansas	2,691
19	Tennessee	2,688
20	Wyoming	2,685
21	Massachusetts	2,683
22	Arizona	2,640
23	New Mexico	2,604
24	Kentucky	2,602
25	Washington	2,589
26	Indiana	2,572
27	North Carolina	2,566
28	Delaware	2,563
29	Pennsylvania	2,562
30	Hawaii	2,559
31	Kansas	2,551
32	West Virginia	2,548
33	Missouri	2,547
34	Rhode Island	2,542
35	Colorado	2,540
36	South Carolina	2,532
37	North Dakota	2,513
38	Nebraska	2,502
39	New Hampshire	2,495
40	Iowa	2,483
41	Michigan	2,482
42	Ohio	2,466
43	South Dakota	2,464
44	Idaho	2,414
45	Minnesota	2,372
46	Oregon	2,332
47	Wisconsin	2,330
48	Montana	2,298
49	Maine	2,278
50	Vermont	2,254
	District of Columbia	2,910

Source: CQ Press using data from U.S. Department of the Treasury, Internal Revenue Service
"Fiscal Year 2014 IRS Data Book" (http://www.irs.gov/uac/SOI-Tax-Stats-IRS-Data-Book)
*National average includes refunds to international sources and other miscellaneous refunds not shown separately.

Value of Federal Business Income Tax Refunds in 2014

National Total = $35,313,521,000*

ALPHA ORDER

RANK	STATE	REFUNDS	% of USA
30	Alabama	$186,726,000	0.5%
43	Alaska	45,817,000	0.1%
24	Arizona	378,771,000	1.1%
27	Arkansas	242,638,000	0.7%
1	California	4,520,744,000	12.8%
11	Colorado	845,191,000	2.4%
9	Connecticut	919,537,000	2.6%
5	Delaware	2,265,613,000	6.4%
12	Florida	750,891,000	2.1%
13	Georgia	649,439,000	1.8%
38	Hawaii	87,680,000	0.2%
40	Idaho	60,746,000	0.2%
4	Illinois	2,647,968,000	7.5%
26	Indiana	277,248,000	0.8%
28	Iowa	237,162,000	0.7%
25	Kansas	289,642,000	0.8%
33	Kentucky	170,035,000	0.5%
31	Louisiana	184,568,000	0.5%
34	Maine	160,713,000	0.5%
20	Maryland	491,109,000	1.4%
10	Massachusetts	907,568,000	2.6%
17	Michigan	528,950,000	1.5%
8	Minnesota	2,037,770,000	5.8%
39	Mississippi	64,580,000	0.2%
22	Missouri	443,565,000	1.3%
48	Montana	23,855,000	0.1%
37	Nebraska	108,318,000	0.3%
36	Nevada	115,366,000	0.3%
41	New Hampshire	50,862,000	0.1%
6	New Jersey	2,100,883,000	5.9%
46	New Mexico	26,624,000	0.1%
3	New York	3,216,598,000	9.1%
18	North Carolina	522,845,000	1.5%
42	North Dakota	47,301,000	0.1%
15	Ohio	582,159,000	1.6%
21	Oklahoma	460,117,000	1.3%
35	Oregon	123,725,000	0.4%
7	Pennsylvania	2,085,626,000	5.9%
49	Rhode Island	18,224,000	0.1%
32	South Carolina	173,677,000	0.5%
47	South Dakota	24,317,000	0.1%
16	Tennessee	531,706,000	1.5%
2	Texas	3,816,828,000	10.8%
29	Utah	216,322,000	0.6%
45	Vermont	30,232,000	0.1%
14	Virginia	610,428,000	1.7%
19	Washington	499,621,000	1.4%
44	West Virginia	40,088,000	0.1%
23	Wisconsin	383,199,000	1.1%
50	Wyoming	11,520,000	0.0%

RANK ORDER

RANK	STATE	REFUNDS	% of USA
1	California	$4,520,744,000	12.8%
2	Texas	3,816,828,000	10.8%
3	New York	3,216,598,000	9.1%
4	Illinois	2,647,968,000	7.5%
5	Delaware	2,265,613,000	6.4%
6	New Jersey	2,100,883,000	5.9%
7	Pennsylvania	2,085,626,000	5.9%
8	Minnesota	2,037,770,000	5.8%
9	Connecticut	919,537,000	2.6%
10	Massachusetts	907,568,000	2.6%
11	Colorado	845,191,000	2.4%
12	Florida	750,891,000	2.1%
13	Georgia	649,439,000	1.8%
14	Virginia	610,428,000	1.7%
15	Ohio	582,159,000	1.6%
16	Tennessee	531,706,000	1.5%
17	Michigan	528,950,000	1.5%
18	North Carolina	522,845,000	1.5%
19	Washington	499,621,000	1.4%
20	Maryland	491,109,000	1.4%
21	Oklahoma	460,117,000	1.3%
22	Missouri	443,565,000	1.3%
23	Wisconsin	383,199,000	1.1%
24	Arizona	378,771,000	1.1%
25	Kansas	289,642,000	0.8%
26	Indiana	277,248,000	0.8%
27	Arkansas	242,638,000	0.7%
28	Iowa	237,162,000	0.7%
29	Utah	216,322,000	0.6%
30	Alabama	186,726,000	0.5%
31	Louisiana	184,568,000	0.5%
32	South Carolina	173,677,000	0.5%
33	Kentucky	170,035,000	0.5%
34	Maine	160,713,000	0.5%
35	Oregon	123,725,000	0.4%
36	Nevada	115,366,000	0.3%
37	Nebraska	108,318,000	0.3%
38	Hawaii	87,680,000	0.2%
39	Mississippi	64,580,000	0.2%
40	Idaho	60,746,000	0.2%
41	New Hampshire	50,862,000	0.1%
42	North Dakota	47,301,000	0.1%
43	Alaska	45,817,000	0.1%
44	West Virginia	40,088,000	0.1%
45	Vermont	30,232,000	0.1%
46	New Mexico	26,624,000	0.1%
47	South Dakota	24,317,000	0.1%
48	Montana	23,855,000	0.1%
49	Rhode Island	18,224,000	0.1%
50	Wyoming	11,520,000	0.0%
	District of Columbia	73,096,000	0.2%

Source: U.S. Department of the Treasury, Internal Revenue Service
"Fiscal Year 2014 IRS Data Book" (http://www.irs.gov/uac/SOI-Tax-Stats-IRS-Data-Book)
*Total includes refunds to international sources and other miscellaneous refunds not shown separately. Includes taxes on corporation income (Form 1120 series) and unrelated business income from tax-exempt organizations.

Average Value of Federal Business Income Tax Refunds in 2014

National Average = $97,154*

ALPHA ORDER

RANK	STATE	AVERAGE REFUND
27	Alabama	$49,688
25	Alaska	55,806
18	Arizona	76,535
14	Arkansas	83,755
12	California	103,815
7	Colorado	138,692
3	Connecticut	230,634
1	Delaware	1,561,415
37	Florida	34,998
19	Georgia	74,614
33	Hawaii	41,812
39	Idaho	31,705
5	Illinois	171,501
29	Indiana	46,170
34	Iowa	37,161
22	Kansas	60,017
26	Kentucky	50,606
35	Louisiana	36,995
15	Maine	80,357
16	Maryland	79,084
10	Massachusetts	123,917
32	Michigan	42,743
2	Minnesota	230,752
45	Mississippi	22,261
23	Missouri	59,205
50	Montana	7,941
38	Nebraska	31,933
36	Nevada	36,041
41	New Hampshire	27,962
4	New Jersey	214,507
47	New Mexico	14,260
8	New York	135,424
24	North Carolina	56,256
40	North Dakota	29,343
30	Ohio	46,035
11	Oklahoma	108,903
44	Oregon	22,769
6	Pennsylvania	154,858
46	Rhode Island	17,423
28	South Carolina	47,067
48	South Dakota	12,599
13	Tennessee	101,879
9	Texas	132,944
17	Utah	78,292
42	Vermont	24,699
20	Virginia	68,045
21	Washington	62,359
43	West Virginia	23,416
31	Wisconsin	44,203
49	Wyoming	8,446

RANK ORDER

RANK	STATE	AVERAGE REFUND
1	Delaware	$1,561,415
2	Minnesota	230,752
3	Connecticut	230,634
4	New Jersey	214,507
5	Illinois	171,501
6	Pennsylvania	154,858
7	Colorado	138,692
8	New York	135,424
9	Texas	132,944
10	Massachusetts	123,917
11	Oklahoma	108,903
12	California	103,815
13	Tennessee	101,879
14	Arkansas	83,755
15	Maine	80,357
16	Maryland	79,084
17	Utah	78,292
18	Arizona	76,535
19	Georgia	74,614
20	Virginia	68,045
21	Washington	62,359
22	Kansas	60,017
23	Missouri	59,205
24	North Carolina	56,256
25	Alaska	55,806
26	Kentucky	50,606
27	Alabama	49,688
28	South Carolina	47,067
29	Indiana	46,170
30	Ohio	46,035
31	Wisconsin	44,203
32	Michigan	42,743
33	Hawaii	41,812
34	Iowa	37,161
35	Louisiana	36,995
36	Nevada	36,041
37	Florida	34,998
38	Nebraska	31,933
39	Idaho	31,705
40	North Dakota	29,343
41	New Hampshire	27,962
42	Vermont	24,699
43	West Virginia	23,416
44	Oregon	22,769
45	Mississippi	22,261
46	Rhode Island	17,423
47	New Mexico	14,260
48	South Dakota	12,599
49	Wyoming	8,446
50	Montana	7,941
	District of Columbia	70,015

Source: CQ Press using data from U.S. Department of the Treasury, Internal Revenue Service
"Fiscal Year 2014 IRS Data Book" (http://www.irs.gov/uac/SOI-Tax-Stats-IRS-Data-Book)
*National average includes refunds to international sources and other miscellaneous refunds not shown separately.

Federal Government Expenditures in 2014

National Total = $2,763,203,837,000*

ALPHA ORDER

RANK	STATE	EXPENDITURES	% of USA
18	Alabama	$61,812,106,952	2.2%
45	Alaska	7,501,789,534	0.3%
21	Arizona	58,751,881,246	2.1%
33	Arkansas	20,461,175,426	0.7%
1	California	248,142,440,096	9.0%
27	Colorado	35,613,880,360	1.3%
16	Connecticut	65,030,407,440	2.4%
47	Delaware	6,099,294,775	0.2%
3	Florida	150,212,196,570	5.4%
24	Georgia	55,465,329,763	2.0%
41	Hawaii	10,713,258,761	0.4%
40	Idaho	10,923,059,849	0.4%
13	Illinois	70,130,445,567	2.5%
6	Indiana	106,552,071,750	3.9%
34	Iowa	19,416,818,069	0.7%
35	Kansas	14,725,742,925	0.5%
12	Kentucky	71,541,488,779	2.6%
28	Louisiana	29,388,024,698	1.1%
42	Maine	10,557,494,153	0.4%
17	Maryland	62,512,613,302	2.3%
15	Massachusetts	67,944,981,966	2.5%
14	Michigan	69,036,500,374	2.5%
20	Minnesota	59,189,261,326	2.1%
31	Mississippi	21,874,021,741	0.8%
26	Missouri	44,594,740,280	1.6%
46	Montana	7,271,660,284	0.3%
39	Nebraska	11,325,933,972	0.4%
36	Nevada	14,683,678,982	0.5%
43	New Hampshire	8,522,868,920	0.3%
23	New Jersey	56,013,480,592	2.0%
32	New Mexico	21,202,348,062	0.8%
5	New York	145,955,854,156	5.3%
19	North Carolina	59,909,461,664	2.2%
22	North Dakota	56,985,406,585	2.1%
9	Ohio	73,328,691,417	2.7%
30	Oklahoma	25,352,485,176	0.9%
29	Oregon	28,451,073,295	1.0%
2	Pennsylvania	181,852,368,457	6.6%
44	Rhode Island	8,376,956,374	0.3%
10	South Carolina	73,100,663,883	2.6%
48	South Dakota	6,050,180,763	0.2%
11	Tennessee	72,694,385,607	2.6%
4	Texas	147,422,868,581	5.3%
38	Utah	13,445,127,058	0.5%
49	Vermont	4,695,670,970	0.2%
7	Virginia	91,884,112,022	3.3%
25	Washington	51,094,950,829	1.8%
37	West Virginia	14,616,617,913	0.5%
8	Wisconsin	78,687,162,046	2.8%
50	Wyoming	3,561,215,299	0.1%

RANK ORDER

RANK	STATE	EXPENDITURES	% of USA
1	California	$248,142,440,096	9.0%
2	Pennsylvania	181,852,368,457	6.6%
3	Florida	150,212,196,570	5.4%
4	Texas	147,422,868,581	5.3%
5	New York	145,955,854,156	5.3%
6	Indiana	106,552,071,750	3.9%
7	Virginia	91,884,112,022	3.3%
8	Wisconsin	78,687,162,046	2.8%
9	Ohio	73,328,691,417	2.7%
10	South Carolina	73,100,663,883	2.6%
11	Tennessee	72,694,385,607	2.6%
12	Kentucky	71,541,488,779	2.6%
13	Illinois	70,130,445,567	2.5%
14	Michigan	69,036,500,374	2.5%
15	Massachusetts	67,944,981,966	2.5%
16	Connecticut	65,030,407,440	2.4%
17	Maryland	62,512,613,302	2.3%
18	Alabama	61,812,106,952	2.2%
19	North Carolina	59,909,461,664	2.2%
20	Minnesota	59,189,261,326	2.1%
21	Arizona	58,751,881,246	2.1%
22	North Dakota	56,985,406,585	2.1%
23	New Jersey	56,013,480,592	2.0%
24	Georgia	55,465,329,763	2.0%
25	Washington	51,094,950,829	1.8%
26	Missouri	44,594,740,280	1.6%
27	Colorado	35,613,880,360	1.3%
28	Louisiana	29,388,024,698	1.1%
29	Oregon	28,451,073,295	1.0%
30	Oklahoma	25,352,485,176	0.9%
31	Mississippi	21,874,021,741	0.8%
32	New Mexico	21,202,348,062	0.8%
33	Arkansas	20,461,175,426	0.7%
34	Iowa	19,416,818,069	0.7%
35	Kansas	14,725,742,925	0.5%
36	Nevada	14,683,678,982	0.5%
37	West Virginia	14,616,617,913	0.5%
38	Utah	13,445,127,058	0.5%
39	Nebraska	11,325,933,972	0.4%
40	Idaho	10,923,059,849	0.4%
41	Hawaii	10,713,258,761	0.4%
42	Maine	10,557,494,153	0.4%
43	New Hampshire	8,522,868,920	0.3%
44	Rhode Island	8,376,956,374	0.3%
45	Alaska	7,501,789,534	0.3%
46	Montana	7,271,660,284	0.3%
47	Delaware	6,099,294,775	0.2%
48	South Dakota	6,050,180,763	0.2%
49	Vermont	4,695,670,970	0.2%
50	Wyoming	3,561,215,299	0.1%
	District of Columbia	26,420,553,125	1.0%

Source: U.S. Office of Management and Budget, USAspending.gov
"Prime Award Spending Data Summary" (https://www.usaspending.gov/, as of January 29, 2016)
*Total includes $76,829,666,000 in U.S. territories and internationally as well as $25,277,369,000 in expenditures not distributed by state. Expenditures allocated based on place of performance of a contract. Includes Contracts, Grants, Loans, and "Other Financial Assistance."

Per Capita Federal Government Expenditures in 2014

National Per Capita = $8,344*

ALPHA ORDER

RANK	STATE	PER CAPITA
8	Alabama	$12,754
13	Alaska	10,178
16	Arizona	8,731
31	Arkansas	6,897
37	California	6,397
33	Colorado	6,650
2	Connecticut	18,090
35	Delaware	6,517
20	Florida	7,546
45	Georgia	5,493
21	Hawaii	7,543
32	Idaho	6,682
47	Illinois	5,444
4	Indiana	16,149
41	Iowa	6,244
49	Kansas	5,073
3	Kentucky	16,213
39	Louisiana	6,321
18	Maine	7,936
12	Maryland	10,462
15	Massachusetts	10,058
30	Michigan	6,962
11	Minnesota	10,846
25	Mississippi	7,307
24	Missouri	7,354
28	Montana	7,106
44	Nebraska	6,015
48	Nevada	5,173
36	New Hampshire	6,418
40	New Jersey	6,266
14	New Mexico	10,166
23	New York	7,391
43	North Carolina	6,027
1	North Dakota	77,003
38	Ohio	6,323
34	Oklahoma	6,535
27	Oregon	7,164
6	Pennsylvania	14,214
17	Rhode Island	7,941
5	South Carolina	15,137
29	South Dakota	7,090
9	Tennessee	11,102
46	Texas	5,464
50	Utah	4,566
22	Vermont	7,492
10	Virginia	11,033
26	Washington	7,234
19	West Virginia	7,906
7	Wisconsin	13,662
42	Wyoming	6,095

RANK ORDER

RANK	STATE	PER CAPITA
1	North Dakota	$77,003
2	Connecticut	18,090
3	Kentucky	16,213
4	Indiana	16,149
5	South Carolina	15,137
6	Pennsylvania	14,214
7	Wisconsin	13,662
8	Alabama	12,754
9	Tennessee	11,102
10	Virginia	11,033
11	Minnesota	10,846
12	Maryland	10,462
13	Alaska	10,178
14	New Mexico	10,166
15	Massachusetts	10,058
16	Arizona	8,731
17	Rhode Island	7,941
18	Maine	7,936
19	West Virginia	7,906
20	Florida	7,546
21	Hawaii	7,543
22	Vermont	7,492
23	New York	7,391
24	Missouri	7,354
25	Mississippi	7,307
26	Washington	7,234
27	Oregon	7,164
28	Montana	7,106
29	South Dakota	7,090
30	Michigan	6,962
31	Arkansas	6,897
32	Idaho	6,682
33	Colorado	6,650
34	Oklahoma	6,535
35	Delaware	6,517
36	New Hampshire	6,418
37	California	6,397
38	Ohio	6,323
39	Louisiana	6,321
40	New Jersey	6,266
41	Iowa	6,244
42	Wyoming	6,095
43	North Carolina	6,027
44	Nebraska	6,015
45	Georgia	5,493
46	Texas	5,464
47	Illinois	5,444
48	Nevada	5,173
49	Kansas	5,073
50	Utah	4,566
	District of Columbia	40,041

Source: CQ Press using data from U.S. Office of Management and Budget, USAspending.gov
"Prime Award Spending Data Summary" (https://www.usaspending.gov/, as of January 29, 2016)
*National per capita excludes expenditures and population for territories and undistributed amounts. Expenditures allocated based on place of performance of a contract. Includes Contracts, Grants, Loans, and "Other Financial Assistance."

Federal Government Contract Awards in 2014

National Total = $445,673,098,000*

ALPHA ORDER

RANK	STATE	EXPENDITURES	% of USA
10	Alabama	$10,568,848,447	2.4%
36	Alaska	1,922,562,398	0.4%
11	Arizona	9,950,586,777	2.2%
42	Arkansas	1,153,329,245	0.3%
2	California	46,084,397,043	10.3%
13	Colorado	9,834,816,223	2.2%
6	Connecticut	13,692,995,092	3.1%
48	Delaware	514,936,305	0.1%
7	Florida	13,572,388,741	3.0%
15	Georgia	8,735,383,250	2.0%
30	Hawaii	2,429,357,543	0.5%
31	Idaho	2,347,758,199	0.5%
16	Illinois	7,536,676,181	1.7%
27	Indiana	3,497,197,023	0.8%
37	Iowa	1,739,607,028	0.4%
35	Kansas	1,949,721,034	0.4%
18	Kentucky	6,888,250,576	1.5%
28	Louisiana	3,411,359,508	0.8%
38	Maine	1,560,156,497	0.4%
4	Maryland	27,933,095,149	6.3%
8	Massachusetts	12,605,914,706	2.8%
25	Michigan	4,738,129,107	1.1%
23	Minnesota	5,132,656,895	1.2%
26	Mississippi	3,709,812,206	0.8%
14	Missouri	9,057,327,946	2.0%
46	Montana	550,346,654	0.1%
43	Nebraska	1,130,546,357	0.3%
32	Nevada	2,290,907,000	0.5%
39	New Hampshire	1,507,967,695	0.3%
19	New Jersey	6,870,810,352	1.5%
17	New Mexico	7,501,008,985	1.7%
12	New York	9,853,493,705	2.2%
24	North Carolina	4,890,997,684	1.1%
47	North Dakota	535,491,098	0.1%
21	Ohio	6,294,091,563	1.4%
29	Oklahoma	2,552,582,538	0.6%
41	Oregon	1,241,045,032	0.3%
5	Pennsylvania	16,671,453,284	3.7%
44	Rhode Island	930,699,561	0.2%
22	South Carolina	5,604,309,699	1.3%
45	South Dakota	609,131,135	0.1%
20	Tennessee	6,643,181,467	1.5%
3	Texas	29,635,985,604	6.6%
33	Utah	2,284,384,328	0.5%
49	Vermont	300,475,174	0.1%
1	Virginia	51,996,368,048	11.7%
9	Washington	11,811,762,604	2.7%
40	West Virginia	1,366,802,704	0.3%
34	Wisconsin	2,206,634,839	0.5%
50	Wyoming	280,474,891	0.1%

RANK ORDER

RANK	STATE	EXPENDITURES	% of USA
1	Virginia	$51,996,368,048	11.7%
2	California	46,084,397,043	10.3%
3	Texas	29,635,985,604	6.6%
4	Maryland	27,933,095,149	6.3%
5	Pennsylvania	16,671,453,284	3.7%
6	Connecticut	13,692,995,092	3.1%
7	Florida	13,572,388,741	3.0%
8	Massachusetts	12,605,914,706	2.8%
9	Washington	11,811,762,604	2.7%
10	Alabama	10,568,848,447	2.4%
11	Arizona	9,950,586,777	2.2%
12	New York	9,853,493,705	2.2%
13	Colorado	9,834,816,223	2.2%
14	Missouri	9,057,327,946	2.0%
15	Georgia	8,735,383,250	2.0%
16	Illinois	7,536,676,181	1.7%
17	New Mexico	7,501,008,985	1.7%
18	Kentucky	6,888,250,576	1.5%
19	New Jersey	6,870,810,352	1.5%
20	Tennessee	6,643,181,467	1.5%
21	Ohio	6,294,091,563	1.4%
22	South Carolina	5,604,309,699	1.3%
23	Minnesota	5,132,656,895	1.2%
24	North Carolina	4,890,997,684	1.1%
25	Michigan	4,738,129,107	1.1%
26	Mississippi	3,709,812,206	0.8%
27	Indiana	3,497,197,023	0.8%
28	Louisiana	3,411,359,508	0.8%
29	Oklahoma	2,552,582,538	0.6%
30	Hawaii	2,429,357,543	0.5%
31	Idaho	2,347,758,199	0.5%
32	Nevada	2,290,907,000	0.5%
33	Utah	2,284,384,328	0.5%
34	Wisconsin	2,206,634,839	0.5%
35	Kansas	1,949,721,034	0.4%
36	Alaska	1,922,562,398	0.4%
37	Iowa	1,739,607,028	0.4%
38	Maine	1,560,156,497	0.4%
39	New Hampshire	1,507,967,695	0.3%
40	West Virginia	1,366,802,704	0.3%
41	Oregon	1,241,045,032	0.3%
42	Arkansas	1,153,329,245	0.3%
43	Nebraska	1,130,546,357	0.3%
44	Rhode Island	930,699,561	0.2%
45	South Dakota	609,131,135	0.1%
46	Montana	550,346,654	0.1%
47	North Dakota	535,491,098	0.1%
48	Delaware	514,936,305	0.1%
49	Vermont	300,475,174	0.1%
50	Wyoming	280,474,891	0.1%
	District of Columbia	18,950,224,212	4.3%

Source: U.S. Office of Management and Budget, USAspending.gov
"Prime Award Spending Data Summary" (https://www.usaspending.gov/, as of January 29, 2016)
*Total includes $34,761,848,000 in U.S. territories and internationally as well as $5,832,811,000 in expenditures not distributed by state. Expenditures allocated based on place of performance of a contract. Does not include grants, co-operative agreements, or contracts under grants.

Per Capita Expenditures for Federal Government Contract Awards in 2014
National Per Capita = $1,270*

ALPHA ORDER

RANK	STATE	PER CAPITA
6	Alabama	$2,181
5	Alaska	2,608
13	Arizona	1,479
48	Arkansas	389
17	California	1,188
8	Colorado	1,836
3	Connecticut	3,809
39	Delaware	550
33	Florida	682
25	Georgia	865
9	Hawaii	1,711
14	Idaho	1,436
37	Illinois	585
42	Indiana	530
38	Iowa	559
34	Kansas	672
11	Kentucky	1,561
30	Louisiana	734
18	Maine	1,173
2	Maryland	4,675
7	Massachusetts	1,866
47	Michigan	478
23	Minnesota	941
16	Mississippi	1,239
12	Missouri	1,494
41	Montana	538
36	Nebraska	600
26	Nevada	807
20	New Hampshire	1,136
28	New Jersey	769
4	New Mexico	3,597
43	New York	499
44	North Carolina	492
31	North Dakota	724
40	Ohio	543
35	Oklahoma	658
50	Oregon	313
15	Pennsylvania	1,303
24	Rhode Island	882
19	South Carolina	1,161
32	South Dakota	714
22	Tennessee	1,015
21	Texas	1,098
27	Utah	776
46	Vermont	479
1	Virginia	6,243
10	Washington	1,672
29	West Virginia	739
49	Wisconsin	383
45	Wyoming	480

RANK ORDER

RANK	STATE	PER CAPITA
1	Virginia	$6,243
2	Maryland	4,675
3	Connecticut	3,809
4	New Mexico	3,597
5	Alaska	2,608
6	Alabama	2,181
7	Massachusetts	1,866
8	Colorado	1,836
9	Hawaii	1,711
10	Washington	1,672
11	Kentucky	1,561
12	Missouri	1,494
13	Arizona	1,479
14	Idaho	1,436
15	Pennsylvania	1,303
16	Mississippi	1,239
17	California	1,188
18	Maine	1,173
19	South Carolina	1,161
20	New Hampshire	1,136
21	Texas	1,098
22	Tennessee	1,015
23	Minnesota	941
24	Rhode Island	882
25	Georgia	865
26	Nevada	807
27	Utah	776
28	New Jersey	769
29	West Virginia	739
30	Louisiana	734
31	North Dakota	724
32	South Dakota	714
33	Florida	682
34	Kansas	672
35	Oklahoma	658
36	Nebraska	600
37	Illinois	585
38	Iowa	559
39	Delaware	550
40	Ohio	543
41	Montana	538
42	Indiana	530
43	New York	499
44	North Carolina	492
45	Wyoming	480
46	Vermont	479
47	Michigan	478
48	Arkansas	389
49	Wisconsin	383
50	Oregon	313
	District of Columbia	28,720

Source: CQ Press using data from U.S. Office of Management and Budget, USAspending.gov
"Prime Award Spending Data Summary" (https://www.usaspending.gov/, as of January 29, 2016)
*National per capita excludes expenditures and population for territories and undistributed amounts. Expenditures allocated based on place of performance of a contract. Does not include grants, co-operative agreements, or contracts under grants.

Federal Government Assistance in 2014

National Total = $2,317,530,739,000*

ALPHA ORDER

RANK	STATE	EXPENDITURES	% of USA
19	Alabama	$51,243,258,505	2.2%
47	Alaska	5,579,227,136	0.2%
21	Arizona	48,801,294,469	2.1%
31	Arkansas	19,307,846,181	0.8%
1	California	202,058,043,053	8.7%
29	Colorado	25,779,064,137	1.1%
18	Connecticut	51,337,412,348	2.2%
46	Delaware	5,584,358,470	0.2%
3	Florida	136,639,807,829	5.9%
22	Georgia	46,729,946,513	2.0%
42	Hawaii	8,283,901,218	0.4%
41	Idaho	8,575,301,650	0.4%
13	Illinois	62,593,769,386	2.7%
6	Indiana	103,054,874,727	4.4%
33	Iowa	17,677,211,041	0.8%
36	Kansas	12,776,021,891	0.6%
11	Kentucky	64,653,238,203	2.8%
28	Louisiana	25,976,665,190	1.1%
40	Maine	8,997,337,656	0.4%
26	Maryland	34,579,518,153	1.5%
15	Massachusetts	55,339,067,260	2.4%
12	Michigan	64,298,371,267	2.8%
17	Minnesota	54,056,604,431	2.3%
32	Mississippi	18,164,209,535	0.8%
25	Missouri	35,537,412,334	1.5%
45	Montana	6,721,313,630	0.3%
39	Nebraska	10,195,387,615	0.4%
37	Nevada	12,392,771,982	0.5%
44	New Hampshire	7,014,901,225	0.3%
20	New Jersey	49,142,670,240	2.1%
34	New Mexico	13,701,339,077	0.6%
4	New York	136,102,360,451	5.9%
16	North Carolina	55,018,463,980	2.4%
14	North Dakota	56,449,915,487	2.4%
9	Ohio	67,034,599,854	2.9%
30	Oklahoma	22,799,902,638	1.0%
27	Oregon	27,210,028,263	1.2%
2	Pennsylvania	165,180,915,173	7.1%
43	Rhode Island	7,446,256,813	0.3%
8	South Carolina	67,496,354,184	2.9%
48	South Dakota	5,441,049,628	0.2%
10	Tennessee	66,051,204,140	2.9%
5	Texas	117,786,882,977	5.1%
38	Utah	11,160,742,730	0.5%
49	Vermont	4,395,195,796	0.2%
23	Virginia	39,887,743,974	1.7%
24	Washington	39,283,188,225	1.7%
35	West Virginia	13,249,815,209	0.6%
7	Wisconsin	76,480,527,207	3.3%
50	Wyoming	3,280,740,408	0.1%

RANK ORDER

RANK	STATE	EXPENDITURES	% of USA
1	California	$202,058,043,053	8.7%
2	Pennsylvania	165,180,915,173	7.1%
3	Florida	136,639,807,829	5.9%
4	New York	136,102,360,451	5.9%
5	Texas	117,786,882,977	5.1%
6	Indiana	103,054,874,727	4.4%
7	Wisconsin	76,480,527,207	3.3%
8	South Carolina	67,496,354,184	2.9%
9	Ohio	67,034,599,854	2.9%
10	Tennessee	66,051,204,140	2.9%
11	Kentucky	64,653,238,203	2.8%
12	Michigan	64,298,371,267	2.8%
13	Illinois	62,593,769,386	2.7%
14	North Dakota	56,449,915,487	2.4%
15	Massachusetts	55,339,067,260	2.4%
16	North Carolina	55,018,463,980	2.4%
17	Minnesota	54,056,604,431	2.3%
18	Connecticut	51,337,412,348	2.2%
19	Alabama	51,243,258,505	2.2%
20	New Jersey	49,142,670,240	2.1%
21	Arizona	48,801,294,469	2.1%
22	Georgia	46,729,946,513	2.0%
23	Virginia	39,887,743,974	1.7%
24	Washington	39,283,188,225	1.7%
25	Missouri	35,537,412,334	1.5%
26	Maryland	34,579,518,153	1.5%
27	Oregon	27,210,028,263	1.2%
28	Louisiana	25,976,665,190	1.1%
29	Colorado	25,779,064,137	1.1%
30	Oklahoma	22,799,902,638	1.0%
31	Arkansas	19,307,846,181	0.8%
32	Mississippi	18,164,209,535	0.8%
33	Iowa	17,677,211,041	0.8%
34	New Mexico	13,701,339,077	0.6%
35	West Virginia	13,249,815,209	0.6%
36	Kansas	12,776,021,891	0.6%
37	Nevada	12,392,771,982	0.5%
38	Utah	11,160,742,730	0.5%
39	Nebraska	10,195,387,615	0.4%
40	Maine	8,997,337,656	0.4%
41	Idaho	8,575,301,650	0.4%
42	Hawaii	8,283,901,218	0.4%
43	Rhode Island	7,446,256,813	0.3%
44	New Hampshire	7,014,901,225	0.3%
45	Montana	6,721,313,630	0.3%
46	Delaware	5,584,358,470	0.2%
47	Alaska	5,579,227,136	0.2%
48	South Dakota	5,441,049,628	0.2%
49	Vermont	4,395,195,796	0.2%
50	Wyoming	3,280,740,408	0.1%
	District of Columbia	7,470,328,913	0.3%

Source: CQ Press using data from U.S. Office of Management and Budget, USAspending.gov
"Prime Award Spending Data Summary" (https://www.usaspending.gov/, as of January 29, 2016)
*Total includes $42,067,819,000 in U.S. territories and internationally as well as $19,444,558,000 in expenditures not distributed by state. Expenditures allocated based on place of performance of a contract. Includes grants, loans, and other financial assistance.

Per Capita Federal Government Assistance in 2014

National Per Capita = $7,074*

ALPHA ORDER

RANK	STATE	PER CAPITA
8	Alabama	$10,573
12	Alaska	7,570
13	Arizona	7,253
23	Arkansas	6,508
42	California	5,209
44	Colorado	4,813
4	Connecticut	14,281
27	Delaware	5,966
18	Florida	6,864
46	Georgia	4,628
30	Hawaii	5,833
41	Idaho	5,245
43	Illinois	4,859
2	Indiana	15,619
33	Iowa	5,685
47	Kansas	4,402
3	Kentucky	14,652
35	Louisiana	5,588
20	Maine	6,764
31	Maryland	5,787
11	Massachusetts	8,192
24	Michigan	6,484
10	Minnesota	9,906
26	Mississippi	6,068
29	Missouri	5,861
22	Montana	6,569
39	Nebraska	5,414
48	Nevada	4,366
40	New Hampshire	5,282
38	New Jersey	5,498
21	New Mexico	6,570
17	New York	6,892
37	North Carolina	5,535
1	North Dakota	76,280
32	Ohio	5,780
28	Oklahoma	5,877
19	Oregon	6,852
7	Pennsylvania	12,911
15	Rhode Island	7,059
5	South Carolina	13,977
25	South Dakota	6,376
9	Tennessee	10,088
48	Texas	4,366
50	Utah	3,790
16	Vermont	7,012
45	Virginia	4,790
36	Washington	5,562
14	West Virginia	7,167
6	Wisconsin	13,279
34	Wyoming	5,615

RANK ORDER

RANK	STATE	PER CAPITA
1	North Dakota	$76,280
2	Indiana	15,619
3	Kentucky	14,652
4	Connecticut	14,281
5	South Carolina	13,977
6	Wisconsin	13,279
7	Pennsylvania	12,911
8	Alabama	10,573
9	Tennessee	10,088
10	Minnesota	9,906
11	Massachusetts	8,192
12	Alaska	7,570
13	Arizona	7,253
14	West Virginia	7,167
15	Rhode Island	7,059
16	Vermont	7,012
17	New York	6,892
18	Florida	6,864
19	Oregon	6,852
20	Maine	6,764
21	New Mexico	6,570
22	Montana	6,569
23	Arkansas	6,508
24	Michigan	6,484
25	South Dakota	6,376
26	Mississippi	6,068
27	Delaware	5,966
28	Oklahoma	5,877
29	Missouri	5,861
30	Hawaii	5,833
31	Maryland	5,787
32	Ohio	5,780
33	Iowa	5,685
34	Wyoming	5,615
35	Louisiana	5,588
36	Washington	5,562
37	North Carolina	5,535
38	New Jersey	5,498
39	Nebraska	5,414
40	New Hampshire	5,282
41	Idaho	5,245
42	California	5,209
43	Illinois	4,859
44	Colorado	4,813
45	Virginia	4,790
46	Georgia	4,628
47	Kansas	4,402
48	Nevada	4,366
48	Texas	4,366
50	Utah	3,790
	District of Columbia	11,321

Source: CQ Press using data from U.S. Office of Management and Budget, USAspending.gov
"Prime Award Spending Data Summary" (https://www.usaspending.gov/, as of January 29, 2016)
*National per capita excludes expenditures and population for territories and undistributed amounts. Expenditures allocated based on place of performance of a contract. Includes grants, loans and other financial assistance.

Federal Government Grants in 2014

National Total = $602,601,800,000*

ALPHA ORDER

RANK	STATE	EXPENDITURES	% of USA
26	Alabama	$7,667,366,914	1.3%
37	Alaska	3,031,293,372	0.5%
15	Arizona	12,112,099,455	2.0%
31	Arkansas	6,256,516,899	1.0%
1	California	73,893,563,133	12.3%
25	Colorado	8,419,714,804	1.4%
27	Connecticut	7,575,089,113	1.3%
45	Delaware	1,947,550,070	0.3%
4	Florida	23,079,843,278	3.8%
12	Georgia	13,725,709,396	2.3%
40	Hawaii	2,801,530,765	0.5%
42	Idaho	2,531,610,255	0.4%
7	Illinois	19,631,701,004	3.3%
17	Indiana	10,450,906,694	1.7%
33	Iowa	5,080,990,856	0.8%
44	Kansas	1,947,764,250	0.3%
19	Kentucky	9,803,349,653	1.6%
22	Louisiana	9,241,225,894	1.5%
38	Maine	2,872,062,824	0.5%
16	Maryland	11,278,179,583	1.9%
9	Massachusetts	16,375,258,352	2.7%
8	Michigan	19,344,405,723	3.2%
18	Minnesota	10,105,845,910	1.7%
30	Mississippi	6,401,985,061	1.1%
21	Missouri	9,250,657,594	1.5%
43	Montana	2,224,761,898	0.4%
41	Nebraska	2,673,923,825	0.4%
36	Nevada	3,045,846,980	0.5%
47	New Hampshire	1,751,775,339	0.3%
11	New Jersey	15,179,790,453	2.5%
32	New Mexico	5,246,684,711	0.9%
2	New York	57,133,624,407	9.5%
10	North Carolina	16,111,263,190	2.7%
49	North Dakota	1,661,560,474	0.3%
6	Ohio	21,332,965,645	3.5%
29	Oklahoma	6,662,955,819	1.1%
23	Oregon	8,714,247,812	1.4%
5	Pennsylvania	22,700,162,306	3.8%
39	Rhode Island	2,824,976,225	0.5%
28	South Carolina	7,246,787,204	1.2%
48	South Dakota	1,667,824,342	0.3%
14	Tennessee	12,126,446,015	2.0%
3	Texas	37,034,490,998	6.1%
35	Utah	3,690,842,317	0.6%
46	Vermont	1,858,382,450	0.3%
20	Virginia	9,444,600,058	1.6%
13	Washington	13,135,172,120	2.2%
34	West Virginia	4,266,251,333	0.7%
24	Wisconsin	8,567,794,978	1.4%
50	Wyoming	1,147,095,403	0.2%

RANK ORDER

RANK	STATE	EXPENDITURES	% of USA
1	California	$73,893,563,133	12.3%
2	New York	57,133,624,407	9.5%
3	Texas	37,034,490,998	6.1%
4	Florida	23,079,843,278	3.8%
5	Pennsylvania	22,700,162,306	3.8%
6	Ohio	21,332,965,645	3.5%
7	Illinois	19,631,701,004	3.3%
8	Michigan	19,344,405,723	3.2%
9	Massachusetts	16,375,258,352	2.7%
10	North Carolina	16,111,263,190	2.7%
11	New Jersey	15,179,790,453	2.5%
12	Georgia	13,725,709,396	2.3%
13	Washington	13,135,172,120	2.2%
14	Tennessee	12,126,446,015	2.0%
15	Arizona	12,112,099,455	2.0%
16	Maryland	11,278,179,583	1.9%
17	Indiana	10,450,906,694	1.7%
18	Minnesota	10,105,845,910	1.7%
19	Kentucky	9,803,349,653	1.6%
20	Virginia	9,444,600,058	1.6%
21	Missouri	9,250,657,594	1.5%
22	Louisiana	9,241,225,894	1.5%
23	Oregon	8,714,247,812	1.4%
24	Wisconsin	8,567,794,978	1.4%
25	Colorado	8,419,714,804	1.4%
26	Alabama	7,667,366,914	1.3%
27	Connecticut	7,575,089,113	1.3%
28	South Carolina	7,246,787,204	1.2%
29	Oklahoma	6,662,955,819	1.1%
30	Mississippi	6,401,985,061	1.1%
31	Arkansas	6,256,516,899	1.0%
32	New Mexico	5,246,684,711	0.9%
33	Iowa	5,080,990,856	0.8%
34	West Virginia	4,266,251,333	0.7%
35	Utah	3,690,842,317	0.6%
36	Nevada	3,045,846,980	0.5%
37	Alaska	3,031,293,372	0.5%
38	Maine	2,872,062,824	0.5%
39	Rhode Island	2,824,976,225	0.5%
40	Hawaii	2,801,530,765	0.5%
41	Nebraska	2,673,923,825	0.4%
42	Idaho	2,531,610,255	0.4%
43	Montana	2,224,761,898	0.4%
44	Kansas	1,947,764,250	0.3%
45	Delaware	1,947,550,070	0.3%
46	Vermont	1,858,382,450	0.3%
47	New Hampshire	1,751,775,339	0.3%
48	South Dakota	1,667,824,342	0.3%
49	North Dakota	1,661,560,474	0.3%
50	Wyoming	1,147,095,403	0.2%
	District of Columbia	5,392,361,193	0.9%

Source: U.S. Office of Management and Budget, USAspending.gov
"Prime Award Spending Data Summary" (https://www.usaspending.gov/, as of January 29, 2016)
*Total includes $15,496,662,000 in U.S. territories and internationally as well as $19,436,330,000 in expenditures not distributed by state. Expenditures allocated based on place of performance of a contract. Includes funds awarded to a non-federal entity for a defined public or private purpose in which services are not rendered to the federal government.

Per Capita Expenditures for Federal Government Grants in 2014

National Per Capita = $1,780*

ALPHA ORDER

RANK	STATE	PER CAPITA
35	Alabama	$1,582
1	Alaska	4,113
28	Arizona	1,800
14	Arkansas	2,109
22	California	1,905
36	Colorado	1,572
15	Connecticut	2,107
16	Delaware	2,081
47	Florida	1,159
44	Georgia	1,359
18	Hawaii	1,973
37	Idaho	1,549
39	Illinois	1,524
34	Indiana	1,584
32	Iowa	1,634
50	Kansas	671
9	Kentucky	2,222
17	Louisiana	1,988
12	Maine	2,159
23	Maryland	1,887
6	Massachusetts	2,424
21	Michigan	1,951
25	Minnesota	1,852
13	Mississippi	2,139
38	Missouri	1,526
11	Montana	2,174
42	Nebraska	1,420
49	Nevada	1,073
45	New Hampshire	1,319
31	New Jersey	1,698
5	New Mexico	2,516
3	New York	2,893
33	North Carolina	1,621
8	North Dakota	2,245
27	Ohio	1,840
30	Oklahoma	1,717
10	Oregon	2,194
29	Pennsylvania	1,774
4	Rhode Island	2,678
40	South Carolina	1,501
20	South Dakota	1,955
25	Tennessee	1,852
43	Texas	1,373
46	Utah	1,253
2	Vermont	2,965
48	Virginia	1,134
24	Washington	1,860
7	West Virginia	2,308
41	Wisconsin	1,488
19	Wyoming	1,963

RANK ORDER

RANK	STATE	PER CAPITA
1	Alaska	$4,113
2	Vermont	2,965
3	New York	2,893
4	Rhode Island	2,678
5	New Mexico	2,516
6	Massachusetts	2,424
7	West Virginia	2,308
8	North Dakota	2,245
9	Kentucky	2,222
10	Oregon	2,194
11	Montana	2,174
12	Maine	2,159
13	Mississippi	2,139
14	Arkansas	2,109
15	Connecticut	2,107
16	Delaware	2,081
17	Louisiana	1,988
18	Hawaii	1,973
19	Wyoming	1,963
20	South Dakota	1,955
21	Michigan	1,951
22	California	1,905
23	Maryland	1,887
24	Washington	1,860
25	Minnesota	1,852
25	Tennessee	1,852
27	Ohio	1,840
28	Arizona	1,800
29	Pennsylvania	1,774
30	Oklahoma	1,717
31	New Jersey	1,698
32	Iowa	1,634
33	North Carolina	1,621
34	Indiana	1,584
35	Alabama	1,582
36	Colorado	1,572
37	Idaho	1,549
38	Missouri	1,526
39	Illinois	1,524
40	South Carolina	1,501
41	Wisconsin	1,488
42	Nebraska	1,420
43	Texas	1,373
44	Georgia	1,359
45	New Hampshire	1,319
46	Utah	1,253
47	Florida	1,159
48	Virginia	1,134
49	Nevada	1,073
50	Kansas	671
	District of Columbia	8,172

Source: CQ Press using data from U.S. Office of Management and Budget, USAspending.gov
"Prime Award Spending Data Summary" (https://www.usaspending.gov/, as of January 29, 2016)
*National per capita excludes expenditures and population for territories and undistributed amounts. Expenditures allocated based on place of performance of a contract. Includes funds awarded to a non-federal entity for a defined public or private purpose in which services are not rendered to the federal government.

Federal Government Loans in 2014

National Total = $6,586,595,000*

ALPHA ORDER

RANK	STATE	EXPENDITURES	% of USA
30	Alabama	$4,205,392	0.1%
45	Alaska	184,419	0.0%
41	Arizona	899,356	0.0%
28	Arkansas	5,428,500	0.1%
3	California	1,291,249,179	19.6%
8	Colorado	76,253,495	1.2%
19	Connecticut	12,638,621	0.2%
37	Delaware	2,493,374	0.0%
44	Florida	285,598	0.0%
9	Georgia	45,919,220	0.7%
46	Hawaii	178,549	0.0%
32	Idaho	3,801,331	0.1%
49	Illinois	(15,418,631)	
38	Indiana	2,399,326	0.0%
13	Iowa	25,072,637	0.4%
23	Kansas	8,780,965	0.1%
6	Kentucky	480,194,832	7.3%
7	Louisiana	170,944,996	2.6%
10	Maine	30,662,921	0.5%
39	Maryland	2,096,242	0.0%
12	Massachusetts	29,085,718	0.4%
18	Michigan	12,843,632	0.2%
15	Minnesota	14,542,685	0.2%
27	Mississippi	5,498,341	0.1%
26	Missouri	5,795,887	0.1%
16	Montana	14,052,481	0.2%
22	Nebraska	10,874,356	0.2%
43	Nevada	558,158	0.0%
42	New Hampshire	873,060	0.0%
5	New Jersey	486,669,590	7.4%
33	New Mexico	3,521,277	0.1%
1	New York	1,680,513,750	25.5%
11	North Carolina	29,484,408	0.4%
17	North Dakota	13,545,978	0.2%
24	Ohio	7,840,668	0.1%
21	Oklahoma	11,139,959	0.2%
31	Oregon	4,138,143	0.1%
48	Pennsylvania	(4,208,872)	
47	Rhode Island	64,249	0.0%
50	South Carolina	(101,891,757)	
20	South Dakota	11,423,650	0.2%
25	Tennessee	7,380,733	0.1%
4	Texas	845,952,352	12.8%
34	Utah	3,393,918	0.1%
40	Vermont	1,577,420	0.0%
2	Virginia	1,291,889,906	19.6%
36	Washington	2,583,167	0.0%
29	West Virginia	4,264,476	0.1%
14	Wisconsin	24,908,948	0.4%
35	Wyoming	3,263,416	0.0%

RANK ORDER

RANK	STATE	EXPENDITURES	% of USA
1	New York	$1,680,513,750	25.5%
2	Virginia	1,291,889,906	19.6%
3	California	1,291,249,179	19.6%
4	Texas	845,952,352	12.8%
5	New Jersey	486,669,590	7.4%
6	Kentucky	480,194,832	7.3%
7	Louisiana	170,944,996	2.6%
8	Colorado	76,253,495	1.2%
9	Georgia	45,919,220	0.7%
10	Maine	30,662,921	0.5%
11	North Carolina	29,484,408	0.4%
12	Massachusetts	29,085,718	0.4%
13	Iowa	25,072,637	0.4%
14	Wisconsin	24,908,948	0.4%
15	Minnesota	14,542,685	0.2%
16	Montana	14,052,481	0.2%
17	North Dakota	13,545,978	0.2%
18	Michigan	12,843,632	0.2%
19	Connecticut	12,638,621	0.2%
20	South Dakota	11,423,650	0.2%
21	Oklahoma	11,139,959	0.2%
22	Nebraska	10,874,356	0.2%
23	Kansas	8,780,965	0.1%
24	Ohio	7,840,668	0.1%
25	Tennessee	7,380,733	0.1%
26	Missouri	5,795,887	0.1%
27	Mississippi	5,498,341	0.1%
28	Arkansas	5,428,500	0.1%
29	West Virginia	4,264,476	0.1%
30	Alabama	4,205,392	0.1%
31	Oregon	4,138,143	0.1%
32	Idaho	3,801,331	0.1%
33	New Mexico	3,521,277	0.1%
34	Utah	3,393,918	0.1%
35	Wyoming	3,263,416	0.0%
36	Washington	2,583,167	0.0%
37	Delaware	2,493,374	0.0%
38	Indiana	2,399,326	0.0%
39	Maryland	2,096,242	0.0%
40	Vermont	1,577,420	0.0%
41	Arizona	899,356	0.0%
42	New Hampshire	873,060	0.0%
43	Nevada	558,158	0.0%
44	Florida	285,598	0.0%
45	Alaska	184,419	0.0%
46	Hawaii	178,549	0.0%
47	Rhode Island	64,249	0.0%
48	Pennsylvania	(4,208,872)	
49	Illinois	(15,418,631)	
50	South Carolina	(101,891,757)	
	District of Columbia	(167,570)	0.0%

Source: CQ Press using data from U.S. Office of Management and Budget, USAspending.gov
"Prime Award Spending Data Summary" (https://www.usaspending.gov/, as of January 29, 2016)
*Total includes $17,987,000 in U.S. territories and internationally as well as negative $1,074,000 in expenditures not distributed by state. Expenditures allocated based on place of performance of a contract. Includes federal awards that the borrowers will eventually pay back to the government. Guaranteed loans require the federal government to pay the bank and take over the loan if the borrower defaults.

Per Capita Federal Government Loans in 2014

National Per Capita = $20.60*

ALPHA ORDER

RANK	STATE	PER CAPITA
36	Alabama	$0.87
42	Alaska	0.25
44	Arizona	0.13
29	Arkansas	1.83
6	California	33.29
10	Colorado	14.24
19	Connecticut	3.52
23	Delaware	2.66
47	Florida	0.01
16	Georgia	4.55
44	Hawaii	0.13
26	Idaho	2.33
49	Illinois	(1.20)
40	Indiana	0.36
13	Iowa	8.06
20	Kansas	3.03
2	Kentucky	108.82
5	Louisiana	36.77
8	Maine	23.05
41	Maryland	0.35
18	Massachusetts	4.31
31	Michigan	1.30
23	Minnesota	2.66
28	Mississippi	1.84
35	Missouri	0.96
11	Montana	13.73
14	Nebraska	5.78
43	Nevada	0.20
38	New Hampshire	0.66
4	New Jersey	54.44
30	New Mexico	1.69
3	New York	85.09
21	North Carolina	2.97
9	North Dakota	18.30
37	Ohio	0.68
22	Oklahoma	2.87
34	Oregon	1.04
48	Pennsylvania	(0.33)
46	Rhode Island	0.06
50	South Carolina	(21.10)
12	South Dakota	13.39
33	Tennessee	1.13
7	Texas	31.36
32	Utah	1.15
25	Vermont	2.52
1	Virginia	155.12
39	Washington	0.37
27	West Virginia	2.31
17	Wisconsin	4.32
15	Wyoming	5.59

RANK ORDER

RANK	STATE	PER CAPITA
1	Virginia	$155.12
2	Kentucky	108.82
3	New York	85.09
4	New Jersey	54.44
5	Louisiana	36.77
6	California	33.29
7	Texas	31.36
8	Maine	23.05
9	North Dakota	18.30
10	Colorado	14.24
11	Montana	13.73
12	South Dakota	13.39
13	Iowa	8.06
14	Nebraska	5.78
15	Wyoming	5.59
16	Georgia	4.55
17	Wisconsin	4.32
18	Massachusetts	4.31
19	Connecticut	3.52
20	Kansas	3.03
21	North Carolina	2.97
22	Oklahoma	2.87
23	Delaware	2.66
23	Minnesota	2.66
25	Vermont	2.52
26	Idaho	2.33
27	West Virginia	2.31
28	Mississippi	1.84
29	Arkansas	1.83
30	New Mexico	1.69
31	Michigan	1.30
32	Utah	1.15
33	Tennessee	1.13
34	Oregon	1.04
35	Missouri	0.96
36	Alabama	0.87
37	Ohio	0.68
38	New Hampshire	0.66
39	Washington	0.37
40	Indiana	0.36
41	Maryland	0.35
42	Alaska	0.25
43	Nevada	0.20
44	Arizona	0.13
44	Hawaii	0.13
46	Rhode Island	0.06
47	Florida	0.01
48	Pennsylvania	(0.33)
49	Illinois	(1.20)
50	South Carolina	(21.10)
	District of Columbia	(0.25)

Source: CQ Press using data from U.S. Office of Management and Budget, USAspending.gov
"Prime Award Spending Data Summary" (https://www.usaspending.gov/, as of January 29, 2016)
*National per capita excludes expenditures and population for territories and undistributed amounts. Expenditures allocated based on place of performance of a contract. Includes Federal awards that the borrowers will eventually pay back to the government. Guaranteed loans require the federal government to pay the bank and take over the loan if the borrower defaults.

Federal Government "Other Financial Assistance" in 2014

National Total = $1,708,342,343,000*

ALPHA ORDER

RANK	STATE	EXPENDITURES	% of USA
16	Alabama	$43,571,686,199	2.6%
48	Alaska	2,547,749,345	0.1%
20	Arizona	36,688,295,658	2.1%
31	Arkansas	13,045,900,782	0.8%
2	California	126,873,230,741	7.4%
28	Colorado	17,283,095,838	1.0%
15	Connecticut	43,749,684,614	2.6%
47	Delaware	3,634,315,026	0.2%
3	Florida	113,559,678,953	6.6%
22	Georgia	32,958,317,897	1.9%
42	Hawaii	5,482,191,904	0.3%
41	Idaho	6,039,890,064	0.4%
17	Illinois	42,977,487,013	2.5%
4	Indiana	92,601,568,707	5.4%
32	Iowa	12,571,147,548	0.7%
34	Kansas	10,819,476,676	0.6%
10	Kentucky	54,369,693,718	3.2%
29	Louisiana	16,564,494,300	1.0%
40	Maine	6,094,611,911	0.4%
26	Maryland	23,299,242,328	1.4%
18	Massachusetts	38,934,723,190	2.3%
13	Michigan	44,941,121,912	2.6%
14	Minnesota	43,936,215,836	2.6%
33	Mississippi	11,756,726,133	0.7%
24	Missouri	26,280,958,853	1.5%
45	Montana	4,482,499,251	0.3%
38	Nebraska	7,510,589,434	0.4%
35	Nevada	9,346,366,844	0.5%
43	New Hampshire	5,262,252,826	0.3%
21	New Jersey	33,476,210,197	2.0%
37	New Mexico	8,451,133,089	0.5%
6	New York	77,288,222,294	4.5%
19	North Carolina	38,877,716,382	2.3%
9	North Dakota	54,774,809,035	3.2%
12	Ohio	45,693,793,541	2.7%
30	Oklahoma	16,125,806,860	0.9%
27	Oregon	18,491,642,308	1.1%
1	Pennsylvania	142,484,961,739	8.3%
44	Rhode Island	4,621,216,339	0.3%
8	South Carolina	60,351,458,737	3.5%
46	South Dakota	3,761,801,636	0.2%
11	Tennessee	53,917,377,392	3.2%
5	Texas	79,906,439,627	4.7%
39	Utah	7,466,506,495	0.4%
49	Vermont	2,535,235,926	0.1%
23	Virginia	29,151,254,010	1.7%
25	Washington	26,145,432,938	1.5%
36	West Virginia	8,979,299,400	0.5%
7	Wisconsin	67,887,823,281	4.0%
50	Wyoming	2,130,381,589	0.1%

RANK ORDER

RANK	STATE	EXPENDITURES	% of USA
1	Pennsylvania	$142,484,961,739	8.3%
2	California	126,873,230,741	7.4%
3	Florida	113,559,678,953	6.6%
4	Indiana	92,601,568,707	5.4%
5	Texas	79,906,439,627	4.7%
6	New York	77,288,222,294	4.5%
7	Wisconsin	67,887,823,281	4.0%
8	South Carolina	60,351,458,737	3.5%
9	North Dakota	54,774,809,035	3.2%
10	Kentucky	54,369,693,718	3.2%
11	Tennessee	53,917,377,392	3.2%
12	Ohio	45,693,793,541	2.7%
13	Michigan	44,941,121,912	2.6%
14	Minnesota	43,936,215,836	2.6%
15	Connecticut	43,749,684,614	2.6%
16	Alabama	43,571,686,199	2.6%
17	Illinois	42,977,487,013	2.5%
18	Massachusetts	38,934,723,190	2.3%
19	North Carolina	38,877,716,382	2.3%
20	Arizona	36,688,295,658	2.1%
21	New Jersey	33,476,210,197	2.0%
22	Georgia	32,958,317,897	1.9%
23	Virginia	29,151,254,010	1.7%
24	Missouri	26,280,958,853	1.5%
25	Washington	26,145,432,938	1.5%
26	Maryland	23,299,242,328	1.4%
27	Oregon	18,491,642,308	1.1%
28	Colorado	17,283,095,838	1.0%
29	Louisiana	16,564,494,300	1.0%
30	Oklahoma	16,125,806,860	0.9%
31	Arkansas	13,045,900,782	0.8%
32	Iowa	12,571,147,548	0.7%
33	Mississippi	11,756,726,133	0.7%
34	Kansas	10,819,476,676	0.6%
35	Nevada	9,346,366,844	0.5%
36	West Virginia	8,979,299,400	0.5%
37	New Mexico	8,451,133,089	0.5%
38	Nebraska	7,510,589,434	0.4%
39	Utah	7,466,506,495	0.4%
40	Maine	6,094,611,911	0.4%
41	Idaho	6,039,890,064	0.4%
42	Hawaii	5,482,191,904	0.3%
43	New Hampshire	5,262,252,826	0.3%
44	Rhode Island	4,621,216,339	0.3%
45	Montana	4,482,499,251	0.3%
46	South Dakota	3,761,801,636	0.2%
47	Delaware	3,634,315,026	0.2%
48	Alaska	2,547,749,345	0.1%
49	Vermont	2,535,235,926	0.1%
50	Wyoming	2,130,381,589	0.1%
	District of Columbia	2,078,135,290	0.1%

Source: CQ Press using data from U.S. Office of Management and Budget, USAspending.gov
"Prime Award Spending Data Summary" (https://www.usaspending.gov/, as of January 29, 2016)
*Total includes $26,553,169,000 in U.S. territories and internationally as well as $9,302,000 in expenditures not distributed by state. Expenditures allocated based on place of performance of a contract. Includes direct payments to individuals (such as Medicare and food stamps), insurance payments (such as, unemployment benefits, flood insurance), and other types of assistance payments (such as, reimbursements for prescriptions for veterans).

Per Capita Federal Government "Other Financial Assistance" in 2014

National Per Capita = $5,274*

ALPHA ORDER

RANK	STATE	PER CAPITA
8	Alabama	$8,991
43	Alaska	3,457
13	Arizona	5,452
19	Arkansas	4,397
46	California	3,271
48	Colorado	3,227
5	Connecticut	12,170
34	Delaware	3,883
12	Florida	5,705
47	Georgia	3,264
35	Hawaii	3,860
39	Idaho	3,695
44	Illinois	3,336
2	Indiana	14,035
26	Iowa	4,043
37	Kansas	3,728
4	Kentucky	12,321
41	Louisiana	3,563
16	Maine	4,582
33	Maryland	3,899
11	Massachusetts	5,764
17	Michigan	4,532
10	Minnesota	8,051
30	Mississippi	3,927
22	Missouri	4,334
20	Montana	4,381
27	Nebraska	3,989
45	Nevada	3,293
28	New Hampshire	3,963
36	New Jersey	3,745
24	New Mexico	4,052
31	New York	3,914
32	North Carolina	3,911
1	North Dakota	74,016
29	Ohio	3,940
23	Oklahoma	4,157
15	Oregon	4,656
7	Pennsylvania	11,137
20	Rhode Island	4,381
3	South Carolina	12,497
18	South Dakota	4,409
9	Tennessee	8,234
49	Texas	2,962
50	Utah	2,536
25	Vermont	4,045
42	Virginia	3,500
38	Washington	3,702
14	West Virginia	4,857
6	Wisconsin	11,787
40	Wyoming	3,646

RANK ORDER

RANK	STATE	PER CAPITA
1	North Dakota	$74,016
2	Indiana	14,035
3	South Carolina	12,497
4	Kentucky	12,321
5	Connecticut	12,170
6	Wisconsin	11,787
7	Pennsylvania	11,137
8	Alabama	8,991
9	Tennessee	8,234
10	Minnesota	8,051
11	Massachusetts	5,764
12	Florida	5,705
13	Arizona	5,452
14	West Virginia	4,857
15	Oregon	4,656
16	Maine	4,582
17	Michigan	4,532
18	South Dakota	4,409
19	Arkansas	4,397
20	Montana	4,381
20	Rhode Island	4,381
22	Missouri	4,334
23	Oklahoma	4,157
24	New Mexico	4,052
25	Vermont	4,045
26	Iowa	4,043
27	Nebraska	3,989
28	New Hampshire	3,963
29	Ohio	3,940
30	Mississippi	3,927
31	New York	3,914
32	North Carolina	3,911
33	Maryland	3,899
34	Delaware	3,883
35	Hawaii	3,860
36	New Jersey	3,745
37	Kansas	3,728
38	Washington	3,702
39	Idaho	3,695
40	Wyoming	3,646
41	Louisiana	3,563
42	Virginia	3,500
43	Alaska	3,457
44	Illinois	3,336
45	Nevada	3,293
46	California	3,271
47	Georgia	3,264
48	Colorado	3,227
49	Texas	2,962
50	Utah	2,536
	District of Columbia	3,149

Source: CQ Press using data from U.S. Office of Management and Budget, USAspending.gov
"Prime Award Spending Data Summary" (https://www.usaspending.gov/, as of January 29, 2016)
*National per capita excludes expenditures and population for territories and undistributed amounts. Expenditures allocated based on place of performance of a contract. Includes direct payments to individuals (such as Medicare and food stamps), insurance payments (such as, unemployment benefits, flood insurance), and other types of assistance payments (such as, reimbursements for prescriptions for veterans).

Federal Civilian Employees in 2014

National Total = 1,825,762 Employees*

ALPHA ORDER

RANK	STATE	EMPLOYEES	% of USA
13	Alabama	37,500	2.1%
37	Alaska	10,382	0.6%
14	Arizona	36,766	2.0%
35	Arkansas	12,791	0.7%
1	California	148,781	8.1%
16	Colorado	35,791	2.0%
41	Connecticut	7,950	0.4%
50	Delaware	3,025	0.2%
5	Florida	84,572	4.6%
6	Georgia	70,158	3.8%
23	Hawaii	22,669	1.2%
43	Idaho	7,323	0.4%
11	Illinois	44,867	2.5%
26	Indiana	21,507	1.2%
42	Iowa	7,834	0.4%
33	Kansas	15,286	0.8%
24	Kentucky	22,197	1.2%
28	Louisiana	18,961	1.0%
38	Maine	10,093	0.6%
4	Maryland	118,906	6.5%
21	Massachusetts	24,627	1.3%
18	Michigan	27,238	1.5%
32	Minnesota	15,853	0.9%
30	Mississippi	17,189	0.9%
17	Missouri	32,740	1.8%
40	Montana	8,416	0.5%
39	Nebraska	10,087	0.6%
36	Nevada	11,537	0.6%
49	New Hampshire	4,229	0.2%
22	New Jersey	24,538	1.3%
25	New Mexico	21,823	1.2%
8	New York	60,866	3.3%
12	North Carolina	40,618	2.2%
46	North Dakota	5,292	0.3%
10	Ohio	47,814	2.6%
15	Oklahoma	35,913	2.0%
31	Oregon	16,721	0.9%
7	Pennsylvania	61,320	3.4%
45	Rhode Island	6,270	0.3%
27	South Carolina	20,414	1.1%
44	South Dakota	7,157	0.4%
20	Tennessee	24,930	1.4%
3	Texas	130,066	7.1%
19	Utah	25,012	1.4%
48	Vermont	4,528	0.2%
2	Virginia	141,913	7.8%
9	Washington	49,890	2.7%
29	West Virginia	18,161	1.0%
34	Wisconsin	13,673	0.7%
47	Wyoming	4,719	0.3%

RANK ORDER

RANK	STATE	EMPLOYEES	% of USA
1	California	148,781	8.1%
2	Virginia	141,913	7.8%
3	Texas	130,066	7.1%
4	Maryland	118,906	6.5%
5	Florida	84,572	4.6%
6	Georgia	70,158	3.8%
7	Pennsylvania	61,320	3.4%
8	New York	60,866	3.3%
9	Washington	49,890	2.7%
10	Ohio	47,814	2.6%
11	Illinois	44,867	2.5%
12	North Carolina	40,618	2.2%
13	Alabama	37,500	2.1%
14	Arizona	36,766	2.0%
15	Oklahoma	35,913	2.0%
16	Colorado	35,791	2.0%
17	Missouri	32,740	1.8%
18	Michigan	27,238	1.5%
19	Utah	25,012	1.4%
20	Tennessee	24,930	1.4%
21	Massachusetts	24,627	1.3%
22	New Jersey	24,538	1.3%
23	Hawaii	22,669	1.2%
24	Kentucky	22,197	1.2%
25	New Mexico	21,823	1.2%
26	Indiana	21,507	1.2%
27	South Carolina	20,414	1.1%
28	Louisiana	18,961	1.0%
29	West Virginia	18,161	1.0%
30	Mississippi	17,189	0.9%
31	Oregon	16,721	0.9%
32	Minnesota	15,853	0.9%
33	Kansas	15,286	0.8%
34	Wisconsin	13,673	0.7%
35	Arkansas	12,791	0.7%
36	Nevada	11,537	0.6%
37	Alaska	10,382	0.6%
38	Maine	10,093	0.6%
39	Nebraska	10,087	0.6%
40	Montana	8,416	0.5%
41	Connecticut	7,950	0.4%
42	Iowa	7,834	0.4%
43	Idaho	7,323	0.4%
44	South Dakota	7,157	0.4%
45	Rhode Island	6,270	0.3%
46	North Dakota	5,292	0.3%
47	Wyoming	4,719	0.3%
48	Vermont	4,528	0.2%
49	New Hampshire	4,229	0.2%
50	Delaware	3,025	0.2%
	District of Columbia	140,308	7.7%

Source: U.S. Office of Personnel Management
"Common Characteristics of the Government" (http://www.opm.gov/feddata/)
*Head count based on place of employment. There were an average of 2,739,234 federal civilian employees in 2013. Total includes 34,541 employees either outside the U.S. or unspecified. Excludes Central Intelligence Agency, Defense Intelligence Agency, and National Security Agency.

Rate of Federal Civilian Employees in 2014

National Rate = 57 Employees per 10,000 Population*

ALPHA ORDER

RANK	STATE	RATE
12	Alabama	77
4	Alaska	141
21	Arizona	55
29	Arkansas	43
37	California	38
18	Colorado	67
50	Connecticut	22
42	Delaware	32
30	Florida	42
17	Georgia	69
3	Hawaii	160
28	Idaho	45
40	Illinois	35
41	Indiana	33
48	Iowa	25
24	Kansas	53
25	Kentucky	50
33	Louisiana	41
13	Maine	76
1	Maryland	199
39	Massachusetts	36
46	Michigan	27
45	Minnesota	29
20	Mississippi	57
22	Missouri	54
10	Montana	82
22	Nebraska	54
33	Nevada	41
42	New Hampshire	32
46	New Jersey	27
5	New Mexico	105
44	New York	31
33	North Carolina	41
14	North Dakota	72
33	Ohio	41
7	Oklahoma	93
30	Oregon	42
26	Pennsylvania	48
19	Rhode Island	59
30	South Carolina	42
9	South Dakota	84
37	Tennessee	38
26	Texas	48
8	Utah	85
14	Vermont	72
2	Virginia	170
16	Washington	71
6	West Virginia	98
49	Wisconsin	24
11	Wyoming	81

RANK ORDER

RANK	STATE	RATE
1	Maryland	199
2	Virginia	170
3	Hawaii	160
4	Alaska	141
5	New Mexico	105
6	West Virginia	98
7	Oklahoma	93
8	Utah	85
9	South Dakota	84
10	Montana	82
11	Wyoming	81
12	Alabama	77
13	Maine	76
14	North Dakota	72
14	Vermont	72
16	Washington	71
17	Georgia	69
18	Colorado	67
19	Rhode Island	59
20	Mississippi	57
21	Arizona	55
22	Missouri	54
22	Nebraska	54
24	Kansas	53
25	Kentucky	50
26	Pennsylvania	48
26	Texas	48
28	Idaho	45
29	Arkansas	43
30	Florida	42
30	Oregon	42
30	South Carolina	42
33	Louisiana	41
33	Nevada	41
33	North Carolina	41
33	Ohio	41
37	California	38
37	Tennessee	38
39	Massachusetts	36
40	Illinois	35
41	Indiana	33
42	Delaware	32
42	New Hampshire	32
44	New York	31
45	Minnesota	29
46	Michigan	27
46	New Jersey	27
48	Iowa	25
49	Wisconsin	24
50	Connecticut	22
	District of Columbia	2,126

Source: CQ Press using data from U.S. Office of Personnel Management
"Common Characteristics of the Government" (http://www.opm.gov/feddata/)

*Head count based on place of employment. There were an average of 2,739,234 federal civilian employees in 2013. National rate excludes employees either outside the U.S. or unspecified. Excludes Central Intelligence Agency, Defense Intelligence Agency, and National Security Agency.

X. Government Finances: State and Local

State and Local Government Total Revenue in 2013 295
Per Capita State and Local Government Revenue in 2013 296
State and Local Government Revenue from the Federal Government in 2013 297
Per Capita State and Local Government Revenue from the Federal Government in 2013 298
Percent of State and Local Government Revenue from the Federal Government in 2013 299
State and Local Government Own Source Revenue in 2013 300
Per Capita State and Local Government Own Source Revenue in 2013 301
State and Local Government Tax Revenue in 2013 302
Per Capita State and Local Government Tax Revenue in 2013 303
Percent of State and Local Government Revenue from Taxes in 2013 304
State and Local Government Tax Revenue as a Percent of Personal Income in 2013 305
State and Local Government General Sales Tax Revenue in 2013 306
Per Capita State and Local Government General Sales Tax Revenue in 2013 307
State and Local Government Property Tax Revenue in 2013 308
Per Capita State and Local Government Property Tax Revenue in 2013 309
State and Local Government Property Tax as a Percent of State and Local Government Total Revenue in 2013 ... 310
State and Local Government Property Tax Revenue as a Percent of State and Local Government Own Source Revenue in 2013 311
State and Local Tax Burden as a Percent of Income in 2012 312
State and Local Government Total Expenditures in 2013 313
Per Capita State and Local Government Total Expenditures in 2013 314
State and Local Government Direct General Expenditures in 2013 315
Per Capita State and Local Government Direct General Expenditures in 2013 316
State and Local Government Debt Outstanding in 2013 .. 317
Per Capita State and Local Government Debt Outstanding in 2013 318
State and Local Government Full-Time Equivalent Employees in 2014 319
Rate of State and Local Government Full-Time Equivalent Employees in 2014 320
Average Annual Earnings of Full-Time State and Local Government Employees in 2014 321
State Government Total Revenue in 2013 322
Per Capita State Government Total Revenue in 2013 323
State Government Intergovernmental Revenue in 2013 ... 324
Per Capita State Government Intergovernmental Revenue in 2013 325
State Government Own Source Revenue in 2013 326
Per Capita State Government Own Source Revenue in 2013 327
Per Capita Profits of State Lotteries in 2014 328
Projected vs. Actual State Tax Collections in 2015 329
State Government Tax Revenue in 2014 330
Per Capita State Government Tax Revenue in 2014 331
State Government Tax Revenue as a Percent of Personal Income in 2014 332
State Government Individual Income Tax Revenue in 2014 333
Per Capita State Government Individual Income Tax Revenue in 2014 334
State Government Corporation Net Income Tax Revenue in 2014 335
Per Capita State Government Corporation Net Income Tax Revenue in 2014 336
State Government General Sales Tax Revenue in 2014 ... 337
Per Capita State Government General Sales Tax Revenue in 2014 338

(Continued)

(Continued)

State Government Motor Fuels Sales Tax Revenue
in 2014 339
Per Capita State Government Motor Fuel Sales Tax
Revenue in 2014 340
State Tax Rates on Gasoline in 2016 341
State Government Motor Vehicle and Operators' License
Tax Revenue in 2014 342
Per Capita State Government Motor Vehicle and
Operators' License Tax Revenue in 2014 343
State Government Tobacco Product Sales Tax Revenue
in 2014 344
Per Capita State Government Tobacco Sales Tax Revenue
in 2014 345
State Tax on a Pack of Cigarettes in 2016 346
State Government Alcoholic Beverage Sales Tax Revenue
in 2014 347
Per Capita State Government Alcoholic Beverage Sales
Tax Revenue in 2014 348
State Government Total Expenditures in 2013 349
Per Capita State Government Total Expenditures in 2013 .. 350
State Government Direct General Expenditures in 2013 .. 351
Per Capita State Government Direct General Expenditures
in 2013 352
State Government Debt Outstanding in 2013 353
Per Capita State Government Debt Outstanding in 2013 .. 354
State Government Full-Time Equivalent Employees
in 2014 355
Rate of State Government Full-Time Equivalent
Employees in 2014 356

Average Annual Earnings of Full-Time State Government
Employees in 2014 357
Local Government Total Revenue in 2013 358
Per Capita Local Government Total Revenue in 2013 359
Local Government Revenue from the Federal
Government in 2013 360
Per Capita Local Government Revenue from the Federal
Government in 2013 361
Local Government Own Source Revenue in 2013 362
Per Capita Local Government Own Source Revenue
in 2013 363
Local Government Tax Revenue in 2013 364
Per Capita Local Government Tax Revenue in 2013 365
Local Government Total Expenditures in 2013 366
Per Capita Local Government Total Expenditures
in 2013 367
Local Government Direct General Expenditures
in 2013 368
Per Capita Local Government Direct General
Expenditures in 2013 369
Local Government Debt Outstanding in 2013 370
Per Capita Local Government Debt Outstanding
in 2013 371
Local Government Full-Time Equivalent Employees
in 2014 372
Rate of Local Government Full-Time Equivalent
Employees in 2014 373
Average Annual Earnings of Full-Time Local
Government Employees in 2014 374

State and Local Government Total Revenue in 2013

National Total = $3,419,868,195,000*

ALPHA ORDER

RANK	STATE	REVENUE	% of USA
26	Alabama	$44,644,352,000	1.3%
39	Alaska	17,371,758,000	0.5%
20	Arizona	57,247,325,000	1.7%
34	Arkansas	26,683,523,000	0.8%
1	California	503,939,325,000	14.7%
22	Colorado	54,853,161,000	1.6%
25	Connecticut	45,506,342,000	1.3%
46	Delaware	10,912,225,000	0.3%
4	Florida	171,135,006,000	5.0%
11	Georgia	86,216,256,000	2.5%
40	Hawaii	16,384,826,000	0.5%
42	Idaho	12,646,888,000	0.4%
5	Illinois	139,251,764,000	4.1%
21	Indiana	56,115,760,000	1.6%
30	Iowa	34,018,505,000	1.0%
32	Kansas	28,650,412,000	0.8%
28	Kentucky	38,093,383,000	1.1%
23	Louisiana	47,106,791,000	1.4%
41	Maine	13,061,463,000	0.4%
17	Maryland	63,917,692,000	1.9%
12	Massachusetts	80,495,430,000	2.4%
9	Michigan	95,183,919,000	2.8%
15	Minnesota	65,110,610,000	1.9%
31	Mississippi	29,791,795,000	0.9%
19	Missouri	57,500,264,000	1.7%
47	Montana	10,436,893,000	0.3%
36	Nebraska	22,609,379,000	0.7%
35	Nevada	25,330,520,000	0.7%
44	New Hampshire	12,078,693,000	0.4%
8	New Jersey	103,183,092,000	3.0%
37	New Mexico	22,493,944,000	0.7%
2	New York	330,872,844,000	9.7%
10	North Carolina	91,365,819,000	2.7%
45	North Dakota	11,147,294,000	0.3%
7	Ohio	128,180,245,000	3.7%
29	Oklahoma	35,911,747,000	1.1%
24	Oregon	45,524,579,000	1.3%
6	Pennsylvania	132,023,885,000	3.9%
43	Rhode Island	12,129,769,000	0.4%
27	South Carolina	44,391,906,000	1.3%
49	South Dakota	8,381,653,000	0.2%
18	Tennessee	57,552,372,000	1.7%
3	Texas	232,876,013,000	6.8%
33	Utah	27,032,915,000	0.8%
50	Vermont	7,423,978,000	0.2%
13	Virginia	78,047,201,000	2.3%
14	Washington	77,878,070,000	2.3%
38	West Virginia	18,057,824,000	0.5%
16	Wisconsin	64,640,604,000	1.9%
48	Wyoming	10,364,859,000	0.3%

RANK ORDER

RANK	STATE	REVENUE	% of USA
1	California	$503,939,325,000	14.7%
2	New York	330,872,844,000	9.7%
3	Texas	232,876,013,000	6.8%
4	Florida	171,135,006,000	5.0%
5	Illinois	139,251,764,000	4.1%
6	Pennsylvania	132,023,885,000	3.9%
7	Ohio	128,180,245,000	3.7%
8	New Jersey	103,183,092,000	3.0%
9	Michigan	95,183,919,000	2.8%
10	North Carolina	91,365,819,000	2.7%
11	Georgia	86,216,256,000	2.5%
12	Massachusetts	80,495,430,000	2.4%
13	Virginia	78,047,201,000	2.3%
14	Washington	77,878,070,000	2.3%
15	Minnesota	65,110,610,000	1.9%
16	Wisconsin	64,640,604,000	1.9%
17	Maryland	63,917,692,000	1.9%
18	Tennessee	57,552,372,000	1.7%
19	Missouri	57,500,264,000	1.7%
20	Arizona	57,247,325,000	1.7%
21	Indiana	56,115,760,000	1.6%
22	Colorado	54,853,161,000	1.6%
23	Louisiana	47,106,791,000	1.4%
24	Oregon	45,524,579,000	1.3%
25	Connecticut	45,506,342,000	1.3%
26	Alabama	44,644,352,000	1.3%
27	South Carolina	44,391,906,000	1.3%
28	Kentucky	38,093,383,000	1.1%
29	Oklahoma	35,911,747,000	1.1%
30	Iowa	34,018,505,000	1.0%
31	Mississippi	29,791,795,000	0.9%
32	Kansas	28,650,412,000	0.8%
33	Utah	27,032,915,000	0.8%
34	Arkansas	26,683,523,000	0.8%
35	Nevada	25,330,520,000	0.7%
36	Nebraska	22,609,379,000	0.7%
37	New Mexico	22,493,944,000	0.7%
38	West Virginia	18,057,824,000	0.5%
39	Alaska	17,371,758,000	0.5%
40	Hawaii	16,384,826,000	0.5%
41	Maine	13,061,463,000	0.4%
42	Idaho	12,646,888,000	0.4%
43	Rhode Island	12,129,769,000	0.4%
44	New Hampshire	12,078,693,000	0.4%
45	North Dakota	11,147,294,000	0.3%
46	Delaware	10,912,225,000	0.3%
47	Montana	10,436,893,000	0.3%
48	Wyoming	10,364,859,000	0.3%
49	South Dakota	8,381,653,000	0.2%
50	Vermont	7,423,978,000	0.2%
	District of Columbia	14,093,322,000	0.4%

Source: U.S. Bureau of the Census, Governments Division
"2013 State and Local Government Finances" (http://www.census.gov/govs/local/)
*Total revenue includes all money received from external sources. This includes taxes, intergovernmental transfers and insurance trust revenue, and revenue from government owned utilities and other commercial or auxiliary enterprise.

Per Capita State and Local Government Revenue in 2013

National Per Capita = $10,808*

ALPHA ORDER

RANK	STATE	PER CAPITA
39	Alabama	$9,242
1	Alaska	23,557
47	Arizona	8,634
42	Arkansas	9,021
5	California	13,119
23	Colorado	10,406
6	Connecticut	12,651
11	Delaware	11,792
45	Florida	8,734
48	Georgia	8,629
12	Hawaii	11,631
50	Idaho	7,842
20	Illinois	10,803
49	Indiana	8,541
19	Iowa	11,001
29	Kansas	9,898
46	Kentucky	8,661
26	Louisiana	10,180
30	Maine	9,830
22	Maryland	10,768
9	Massachusetts	11,998
32	Michigan	9,614
8	Minnesota	12,012
27	Mississippi	9,961
33	Missouri	9,514
25	Montana	10,289
7	Nebraska	12,095
41	Nevada	9,078
40	New Hampshire	9,132
14	New Jersey	11,584
21	New Mexico	10,779
3	New York	16,803
38	North Carolina	9,280
4	North Dakota	15,405
18	Ohio	11,077
35	Oklahoma	9,319
13	Oregon	11,590
24	Pennsylvania	10,328
15	Rhode Island	11,521
37	South Carolina	9,309
28	South Dakota	9,916
43	Tennessee	8,859
44	Texas	8,788
36	Utah	9,310
10	Vermont	11,838
34	Virginia	9,440
17	Washington	11,168
31	West Virginia	9,745
16	Wisconsin	11,254
2	Wyoming	17,774

RANK ORDER

RANK	STATE	PER CAPITA
1	Alaska	$23,557
2	Wyoming	17,774
3	New York	16,803
4	North Dakota	15,405
5	California	13,119
6	Connecticut	12,651
7	Nebraska	12,095
8	Minnesota	12,012
9	Massachusetts	11,998
10	Vermont	11,838
11	Delaware	11,792
12	Hawaii	11,631
13	Oregon	11,590
14	New Jersey	11,584
15	Rhode Island	11,521
16	Wisconsin	11,254
17	Washington	11,168
18	Ohio	11,077
19	Iowa	11,001
20	Illinois	10,803
21	New Mexico	10,779
22	Maryland	10,768
23	Colorado	10,406
24	Pennsylvania	10,328
25	Montana	10,289
26	Louisiana	10,180
27	Mississippi	9,961
28	South Dakota	9,916
29	Kansas	9,898
30	Maine	9,830
31	West Virginia	9,745
32	Michigan	9,614
33	Missouri	9,514
34	Virginia	9,440
35	Oklahoma	9,319
36	Utah	9,310
37	South Carolina	9,309
38	North Carolina	9,280
39	Alabama	9,242
40	New Hampshire	9,132
41	Nevada	9,078
42	Arkansas	9,021
43	Tennessee	8,859
44	Texas	8,788
45	Florida	8,734
46	Kentucky	8,661
47	Arizona	8,634
48	Georgia	8,629
49	Indiana	8,541
50	Idaho	7,842

District of Columbia   21,697

Source: CQ Press using data from U.S. Bureau of the Census, Governments Division
"2013 State and Local Government Finances" (http://www.census.gov/govs/local/)
*Total revenue includes all money received from external sources. This includes taxes, intergovernmental transfers and insurance trust revenue, and revenue from government owned utilities and other commercial or auxiliary enterprise.

State and Local Government Revenue from the Federal Government in 2013

National Total = $584,651,830,000

ALPHA ORDER

RANK	STATE	REVENUE	% of USA
23	Alabama	$9,186,815,000	1.6%
39	Alaska	3,004,845,000	0.5%
19	Arizona	11,173,613,000	1.9%
32	Arkansas	6,015,670,000	1.0%
1	California	66,803,001,000	11.4%
27	Colorado	7,795,888,000	1.3%
30	Connecticut	6,584,182,000	1.1%
46	Delaware	2,004,163,000	0.3%
4	Florida	28,094,171,000	4.8%
10	Georgia	15,775,358,000	2.7%
41	Hawaii	2,714,227,000	0.5%
42	Idaho	2,655,625,000	0.5%
7	Illinois	20,196,640,000	3.5%
13	Indiana	11,818,797,000	2.0%
31	Iowa	6,520,575,000	1.1%
36	Kansas	4,036,095,000	0.7%
25	Kentucky	8,509,786,000	1.5%
14	Louisiana	11,604,895,000	2.0%
40	Maine	2,962,691,000	0.5%
17	Maryland	11,275,358,000	1.9%
12	Massachusetts	14,654,174,000	2.5%
8	Michigan	19,757,302,000	3.4%
21	Minnesota	10,036,723,000	1.7%
26	Mississippi	7,946,976,000	1.4%
20	Missouri	11,053,312,000	1.9%
44	Montana	2,407,873,000	0.4%
37	Nebraska	3,509,525,000	0.6%
38	Nevada	3,349,652,000	0.6%
48	New Hampshire	1,822,584,000	0.3%
11	New Jersey	14,754,857,000	2.5%
33	New Mexico	5,610,376,000	1.0%
2	New York	53,782,083,000	9.2%
9	North Carolina	17,692,359,000	3.0%
50	North Dakota	1,735,565,000	0.3%
6	Ohio	23,058,726,000	3.9%
28	Oklahoma	7,445,216,000	1.3%
24	Oregon	9,069,578,000	1.6%
5	Pennsylvania	24,022,824,000	4.1%
43	Rhode Island	2,512,543,000	0.4%
29	South Carolina	7,108,172,000	1.2%
49	South Dakota	1,760,610,000	0.3%
15	Tennessee	11,597,532,000	2.0%
3	Texas	41,527,742,000	7.1%
34	Utah	4,875,132,000	0.8%
47	Vermont	1,943,820,000	0.3%
18	Virginia	11,205,968,000	1.9%
16	Washington	11,498,164,000	2.0%
35	West Virginia	4,474,847,000	0.8%
22	Wisconsin	9,520,627,000	1.6%
45	Wyoming	2,202,148,000	0.4%

RANK ORDER

RANK	STATE	REVENUE	% of USA
1	California	$66,803,001,000	11.4%
2	New York	53,782,083,000	9.2%
3	Texas	41,527,742,000	7.1%
4	Florida	28,094,171,000	4.8%
5	Pennsylvania	24,022,824,000	4.1%
6	Ohio	23,058,726,000	3.9%
7	Illinois	20,196,640,000	3.5%
8	Michigan	19,757,302,000	3.4%
9	North Carolina	17,692,359,000	3.0%
10	Georgia	15,775,358,000	2.7%
11	New Jersey	14,754,857,000	2.5%
12	Massachusetts	14,654,174,000	2.5%
13	Indiana	11,818,797,000	2.0%
14	Louisiana	11,604,895,000	2.0%
15	Tennessee	11,597,532,000	2.0%
16	Washington	11,498,164,000	2.0%
17	Maryland	11,275,358,000	1.9%
18	Virginia	11,205,968,000	1.9%
19	Arizona	11,173,613,000	1.9%
20	Missouri	11,053,312,000	1.9%
21	Minnesota	10,036,723,000	1.7%
22	Wisconsin	9,520,627,000	1.6%
23	Alabama	9,186,815,000	1.6%
24	Oregon	9,069,578,000	1.6%
25	Kentucky	8,509,786,000	1.5%
26	Mississippi	7,946,976,000	1.4%
27	Colorado	7,795,888,000	1.3%
28	Oklahoma	7,445,216,000	1.3%
29	South Carolina	7,108,172,000	1.2%
30	Connecticut	6,584,182,000	1.1%
31	Iowa	6,520,575,000	1.1%
32	Arkansas	6,015,670,000	1.0%
33	New Mexico	5,610,376,000	1.0%
34	Utah	4,875,132,000	0.8%
35	West Virginia	4,474,847,000	0.8%
36	Kansas	4,036,095,000	0.7%
37	Nebraska	3,509,525,000	0.6%
38	Nevada	3,349,652,000	0.6%
39	Alaska	3,004,845,000	0.5%
40	Maine	2,962,691,000	0.5%
41	Hawaii	2,714,227,000	0.5%
42	Idaho	2,655,625,000	0.5%
43	Rhode Island	2,512,543,000	0.4%
44	Montana	2,407,873,000	0.4%
45	Wyoming	2,202,148,000	0.4%
46	Delaware	2,004,163,000	0.3%
47	Vermont	1,943,820,000	0.3%
48	New Hampshire	1,822,584,000	0.3%
49	South Dakota	1,760,610,000	0.3%
50	North Dakota	1,735,565,000	0.3%
	District of Columbia	3,982,425,000	0.7%

Source: U.S. Bureau of the Census, Governments Division
"2013 State and Local Government Finances" (http://www.census.gov/govs/local/)

Per Capita State and Local Government Revenue from the Federal Government in 2013
National Per Capita = $1,848

ALPHA ORDER

RANK	STATE	PER CAPITA
24	Alabama	$1,902
1	Alaska	4,075
35	Arizona	1,685
18	Arkansas	2,034
34	California	1,739
45	Colorado	1,479
29	Connecticut	1,830
15	Delaware	2,166
46	Florida	1,434
41	Georgia	1,579
23	Hawaii	1,927
40	Idaho	1,647
42	Illinois	1,567
31	Indiana	1,799
16	Iowa	2,109
47	Kansas	1,394
21	Kentucky	1,935
7	Louisiana	2,508
13	Maine	2,230
25	Maryland	1,899
14	Massachusetts	2,184
19	Michigan	1,996
28	Minnesota	1,852
6	Mississippi	2,657
30	Missouri	1,829
11	Montana	2,374
27	Nebraska	1,877
50	Nevada	1,200
48	New Hampshire	1,378
38	New Jersey	1,656
5	New Mexico	2,688
4	New York	2,731
32	North Carolina	1,797
9	North Dakota	2,398
20	Ohio	1,993
22	Oklahoma	1,932
12	Oregon	2,309
26	Pennsylvania	1,879
10	Rhode Island	2,386
44	South Carolina	1,491
17	South Dakota	2,083
33	Tennessee	1,785
42	Texas	1,567
36	Utah	1,679
3	Vermont	3,100
49	Virginia	1,355
39	Washington	1,649
8	West Virginia	2,415
37	Wisconsin	1,658
2	Wyoming	3,776

RANK ORDER

RANK	STATE	PER CAPITA
1	Alaska	$4,075
2	Wyoming	3,776
3	Vermont	3,100
4	New York	2,731
5	New Mexico	2,688
6	Mississippi	2,657
7	Louisiana	2,508
8	West Virginia	2,415
9	North Dakota	2,398
10	Rhode Island	2,386
11	Montana	2,374
12	Oregon	2,309
13	Maine	2,230
14	Massachusetts	2,184
15	Delaware	2,166
16	Iowa	2,109
17	South Dakota	2,083
18	Arkansas	2,034
19	Michigan	1,996
20	Ohio	1,993
21	Kentucky	1,935
22	Oklahoma	1,932
23	Hawaii	1,927
24	Alabama	1,902
25	Maryland	1,899
26	Pennsylvania	1,879
27	Nebraska	1,877
28	Minnesota	1,852
29	Connecticut	1,830
30	Missouri	1,829
31	Indiana	1,799
32	North Carolina	1,797
33	Tennessee	1,785
34	California	1,739
35	Arizona	1,685
36	Utah	1,679
37	Wisconsin	1,658
38	New Jersey	1,656
39	Washington	1,649
40	Idaho	1,647
41	Georgia	1,579
42	Illinois	1,567
42	Texas	1,567
44	South Carolina	1,491
45	Colorado	1,479
46	Florida	1,434
47	Kansas	1,394
48	New Hampshire	1,378
49	Virginia	1,355
50	Nevada	1,200
	District of Columbia	6,131

Source: CQ Press using data from U.S. Bureau of the Census, Governments Division
"2013 State and Local Government Finances" (http://www.census.gov/govs/local/)

Percent of State and Local Government Revenue from the Federal Government in 2013
National Percent = 17.1%*

ALPHA ORDER

RANK	STATE	PERCENT
17	Alabama	20.6
32	Alaska	17.3
20	Arizona	19.5
8	Arkansas	22.5
49	California	13.3
47	Colorado	14.2
43	Connecticut	14.5
24	Delaware	18.4
34	Florida	16.4
25	Georgia	18.3
33	Hawaii	16.6
12	Idaho	21.0
43	Illinois	14.5
11	Indiana	21.1
22	Iowa	19.2
48	Kansas	14.1
9	Kentucky	22.3
5	Louisiana	24.6
7	Maine	22.7
31	Maryland	17.6
26	Massachusetts	18.2
14	Michigan	20.8
39	Minnesota	15.4
1	Mississippi	26.7
22	Missouri	19.2
6	Montana	23.1
38	Nebraska	15.5
50	Nevada	13.2
40	New Hampshire	15.1
46	New Jersey	14.3
3	New Mexico	24.9
35	New York	16.3
21	North Carolina	19.4
37	North Dakota	15.6
28	Ohio	18.0
15	Oklahoma	20.7
19	Oregon	19.9
26	Pennsylvania	18.2
15	Rhode Island	20.7
36	South Carolina	16.0
12	South Dakota	21.0
18	Tennessee	20.2
30	Texas	17.8
28	Utah	18.0
2	Vermont	26.2
45	Virginia	14.4
41	Washington	14.8
4	West Virginia	24.8
42	Wisconsin	14.7
10	Wyoming	21.2

RANK ORDER

RANK	STATE	PERCENT
1	Mississippi	26.7
2	Vermont	26.2
3	New Mexico	24.9
4	West Virginia	24.8
5	Louisiana	24.6
6	Montana	23.1
7	Maine	22.7
8	Arkansas	22.5
9	Kentucky	22.3
10	Wyoming	21.2
11	Indiana	21.1
12	Idaho	21.0
12	South Dakota	21.0
14	Michigan	20.8
15	Oklahoma	20.7
15	Rhode Island	20.7
17	Alabama	20.6
18	Tennessee	20.2
19	Oregon	19.9
20	Arizona	19.5
21	North Carolina	19.4
22	Iowa	19.2
22	Missouri	19.2
24	Delaware	18.4
25	Georgia	18.3
26	Massachusetts	18.2
26	Pennsylvania	18.2
28	Ohio	18.0
28	Utah	18.0
30	Texas	17.8
31	Maryland	17.6
32	Alaska	17.3
33	Hawaii	16.6
34	Florida	16.4
35	New York	16.3
36	South Carolina	16.0
37	North Dakota	15.6
38	Nebraska	15.5
39	Minnesota	15.4
40	New Hampshire	15.1
41	Washington	14.8
42	Wisconsin	14.7
43	Connecticut	14.5
43	Illinois	14.5
45	Virginia	14.4
46	New Jersey	14.3
47	Colorado	14.2
48	Kansas	14.1
49	California	13.3
50	Nevada	13.2
	District of Columbia	28.3

Source: CQ Press using data from U.S. Bureau of the Census, Governments Division
"2013 State and Local Government Finances" (http://www.census.gov/govs/local/)
*As a percent of total revenue.

State and Local Government Own Source Revenue in 2013

National Total = $2,105,774,905,000*

ALPHA ORDER

RANK	STATE	REVENUE	% of USA
26	Alabama	$25,799,712,000	1.2%
38	Alaska	12,224,253,000	0.6%
20	Arizona	33,162,914,000	1.6%
35	Arkansas	15,391,842,000	0.7%
1	California	291,210,951,000	13.8%
19	Colorado	35,714,337,000	1.7%
23	Connecticut	30,915,557,000	1.5%
46	Delaware	7,254,014,000	0.3%
4	Florida	108,648,986,000	5.2%
13	Georgia	49,576,083,000	2.4%
39	Hawaii	11,180,350,000	0.5%
44	Idaho	7,717,848,000	0.4%
5	Illinois	89,601,596,000	4.3%
18	Indiana	37,407,230,000	1.8%
29	Iowa	21,852,512,000	1.0%
31	Kansas	20,229,643,000	1.0%
28	Kentucky	22,212,974,000	1.1%
25	Louisiana	27,887,662,000	1.3%
42	Maine	8,365,555,000	0.4%
15	Maryland	42,897,552,000	2.0%
12	Massachusetts	50,917,659,000	2.4%
9	Michigan	57,885,366,000	2.7%
16	Minnesota	41,431,292,000	2.0%
32	Mississippi	16,581,993,000	0.8%
21	Missouri	32,056,721,000	1.5%
48	Montana	5,656,881,000	0.3%
36	Nebraska	12,779,621,000	0.6%
34	Nevada	15,421,764,000	0.7%
43	New Hampshire	8,043,559,000	0.4%
7	New Jersey	73,035,390,000	3.5%
37	New Mexico	12,698,570,000	0.6%
2	New York	205,653,807,000	9.8%
10	North Carolina	56,065,490,000	2.7%
41	North Dakota	8,397,024,000	0.4%
8	Ohio	72,427,993,000	3.4%
30	Oklahoma	21,315,513,000	1.0%
27	Oregon	24,935,738,000	1.2%
6	Pennsylvania	84,267,573,000	4.0%
45	Rhode Island	7,557,320,000	0.4%
24	South Carolina	28,081,177,000	1.3%
50	South Dakota	4,471,893,000	0.2%
22	Tennessee	31,008,388,000	1.5%
3	Texas	150,601,489,000	7.2%
33	Utah	16,493,589,000	0.8%
49	Vermont	4,588,612,000	0.2%
11	Virginia	53,118,492,000	2.5%
14	Washington	47,175,808,000	2.2%
40	West Virginia	11,104,102,000	0.5%
17	Wisconsin	38,539,288,000	1.8%
47	Wyoming	6,244,277,000	0.3%

RANK ORDER

RANK	STATE	REVENUE	% of USA
1	California	$291,210,951,000	13.8%
2	New York	205,653,807,000	9.8%
3	Texas	150,601,489,000	7.2%
4	Florida	108,648,986,000	5.2%
5	Illinois	89,601,596,000	4.3%
6	Pennsylvania	84,267,573,000	4.0%
7	New Jersey	73,035,390,000	3.5%
8	Ohio	72,427,993,000	3.4%
9	Michigan	57,885,366,000	2.7%
10	North Carolina	56,065,490,000	2.7%
11	Virginia	53,118,492,000	2.5%
12	Massachusetts	50,917,659,000	2.4%
13	Georgia	49,576,083,000	2.4%
14	Washington	47,175,808,000	2.2%
15	Maryland	42,897,552,000	2.0%
16	Minnesota	41,431,292,000	2.0%
17	Wisconsin	38,539,288,000	1.8%
18	Indiana	37,407,230,000	1.8%
19	Colorado	35,714,337,000	1.7%
20	Arizona	33,162,914,000	1.6%
21	Missouri	32,056,721,000	1.5%
22	Tennessee	31,008,388,000	1.5%
23	Connecticut	30,915,557,000	1.5%
24	South Carolina	28,081,177,000	1.3%
25	Louisiana	27,887,662,000	1.3%
26	Alabama	25,799,712,000	1.2%
27	Oregon	24,935,738,000	1.2%
28	Kentucky	22,212,974,000	1.1%
29	Iowa	21,852,512,000	1.0%
30	Oklahoma	21,315,513,000	1.0%
31	Kansas	20,229,643,000	1.0%
32	Mississippi	16,581,993,000	0.8%
33	Utah	16,493,589,000	0.8%
34	Nevada	15,421,764,000	0.7%
35	Arkansas	15,391,842,000	0.7%
36	Nebraska	12,779,621,000	0.6%
37	New Mexico	12,698,570,000	0.6%
38	Alaska	12,224,253,000	0.6%
39	Hawaii	11,180,350,000	0.5%
40	West Virginia	11,104,102,000	0.5%
41	North Dakota	8,397,024,000	0.4%
42	Maine	8,365,555,000	0.4%
43	New Hampshire	8,043,559,000	0.4%
44	Idaho	7,717,848,000	0.4%
45	Rhode Island	7,557,320,000	0.4%
46	Delaware	7,254,014,000	0.3%
47	Wyoming	6,244,277,000	0.3%
48	Montana	5,656,881,000	0.3%
49	Vermont	4,588,612,000	0.2%
50	South Dakota	4,471,893,000	0.2%
	District of Columbia	7,966,945,000	0.4%

Source: U.S. Bureau of the Census, Governments Division
"2013 State and Local Government Finances" (http://www.census.gov/govs/local/)
*Own source revenue includes taxes, current charges, and miscellaneous general revenue. Excluded are intergovernmental transfers, insurance trust revenue, and revenue from government owned utilities and other commercial or auxiliary enterprise.

Per Capita State and Local Government Own Source Revenue in 2013

National Per Capita = $6,655*

ALPHA ORDER

RANK	STATE	PER CAPITA
42	Alabama	$5,341
1	Alaska	16,577
47	Arizona	5,001
45	Arkansas	5,204
11	California	7,581
19	Colorado	6,775
5	Connecticut	8,594
8	Delaware	7,839
38	Florida	5,545
48	Georgia	4,962
7	Hawaii	7,936
49	Idaho	4,785
17	Illinois	6,951
34	Indiana	5,693
15	Iowa	7,067
16	Kansas	6,989
46	Kentucky	5,050
29	Louisiana	6,027
25	Maine	6,296
13	Maryland	7,227
10	Massachusetts	7,590
32	Michigan	5,847
9	Minnesota	7,643
39	Mississippi	5,544
43	Missouri	5,304
37	Montana	5,577
18	Nebraska	6,837
41	Nevada	5,527
28	New Hampshire	6,081
6	New Jersey	8,199
27	New Mexico	6,085
4	New York	10,444
33	North Carolina	5,695
2	North Dakota	11,604
26	Ohio	6,259
40	Oklahoma	5,532
24	Oregon	6,348
22	Pennsylvania	6,592
14	Rhode Island	7,178
31	South Carolina	5,889
44	South Dakota	5,290
50	Tennessee	4,773
35	Texas	5,683
36	Utah	5,680
12	Vermont	7,317
23	Virginia	6,425
20	Washington	6,765
30	West Virginia	5,993
21	Wisconsin	6,710
3	Wyoming	10,708

RANK ORDER

RANK	STATE	PER CAPITA
1	Alaska	$16,577
2	North Dakota	11,604
3	Wyoming	10,708
4	New York	10,444
5	Connecticut	8,594
6	New Jersey	8,199
7	Hawaii	7,936
8	Delaware	7,839
9	Minnesota	7,643
10	Massachusetts	7,590
11	California	7,581
12	Vermont	7,317
13	Maryland	7,227
14	Rhode Island	7,178
15	Iowa	7,067
16	Kansas	6,989
17	Illinois	6,951
18	Nebraska	6,837
19	Colorado	6,775
20	Washington	6,765
21	Wisconsin	6,710
22	Pennsylvania	6,592
23	Virginia	6,425
24	Oregon	6,348
25	Maine	6,296
26	Ohio	6,259
27	New Mexico	6,085
28	New Hampshire	6,081
29	Louisiana	6,027
30	West Virginia	5,993
31	South Carolina	5,889
32	Michigan	5,847
33	North Carolina	5,695
34	Indiana	5,693
35	Texas	5,683
36	Utah	5,680
37	Montana	5,577
38	Florida	5,545
39	Mississippi	5,544
40	Oklahoma	5,532
41	Nevada	5,527
42	Alabama	5,341
43	Missouri	5,304
44	South Dakota	5,290
45	Arkansas	5,204
46	Kentucky	5,050
47	Arizona	5,001
48	Georgia	4,962
49	Idaho	4,785
50	Tennessee	4,773
	District of Columbia	12,266

Source: CQ Press using data from U.S. Bureau of the Census, Governments Division "2013 State and Local Government Finances" (http://www.census.gov/govs/local/)

*Own source revenue includes taxes, current charges, and miscellaneous general revenue. Excluded are intergovernmental transfers, insurance trust revenue, and revenue from government owned utilities and other commercial or auxiliary enterprise.

State and Local Government Tax Revenue in 2013

National Total = $1,455,498,630,000

ALPHA ORDER

RANK	STATE	REVENUE	% of USA
28	Alabama	$14,724,783,000	1.0%
40	Alaska	6,792,745,000	0.5%
21	Arizona	22,656,410,000	1.6%
33	Arkansas	10,764,696,000	0.7%
1	California	204,653,383,000	14.1%
20	Colorado	22,870,573,000	1.6%
18	Connecticut	26,125,481,000	1.8%
46	Delaware	4,266,923,000	0.3%
5	Florida	66,199,688,000	4.5%
13	Georgia	33,215,010,000	2.3%
37	Hawaii	8,041,176,000	0.6%
45	Idaho	5,104,976,000	0.4%
4	Illinois	69,268,459,000	4.8%
19	Indiana	24,919,642,000	1.7%
29	Iowa	13,787,267,000	0.9%
31	Kansas	12,902,577,000	0.9%
25	Kentucky	15,431,580,000	1.1%
24	Louisiana	17,566,975,000	1.2%
41	Maine	6,402,709,000	0.4%
14	Maryland	32,470,068,000	2.2%
9	Massachusetts	38,394,358,000	2.6%
10	Michigan	37,122,183,000	2.6%
16	Minnesota	30,075,762,000	2.1%
34	Mississippi	10,262,494,000	0.7%
22	Missouri	20,909,857,000	1.4%
47	Montana	3,852,584,000	0.3%
36	Nebraska	8,697,819,000	0.6%
32	Nevada	10,817,783,000	0.7%
43	New Hampshire	5,551,156,000	0.4%
7	New Jersey	56,199,438,000	3.9%
38	New Mexico	7,666,140,000	0.5%
2	New York	158,492,164,000	10.9%
11	North Carolina	35,538,649,000	2.4%
42	North Dakota	6,384,310,000	0.4%
8	Ohio	49,464,684,000	3.4%
30	Oklahoma	13,455,922,000	0.9%
26	Oregon	15,353,218,000	1.1%
6	Pennsylvania	59,135,426,000	4.1%
44	Rhode Island	5,402,158,000	0.4%
27	South Carolina	15,241,839,000	1.0%
50	South Dakota	2,965,725,000	0.2%
23	Tennessee	20,177,658,000	1.4%
3	Texas	102,372,906,000	7.0%
35	Utah	10,188,214,000	0.7%
48	Vermont	3,399,212,000	0.2%
12	Virginia	35,046,760,000	2.4%
15	Washington	30,792,952,000	2.1%
39	West Virginia	7,224,929,000	0.5%
17	Wisconsin	27,588,284,000	1.9%
49	Wyoming	3,379,158,000	0.2%

RANK ORDER

RANK	STATE	REVENUE	% of USA
1	California	$204,653,383,000	14.1%
2	New York	158,492,164,000	10.9%
3	Texas	102,372,906,000	7.0%
4	Illinois	69,268,459,000	4.8%
5	Florida	66,199,688,000	4.5%
6	Pennsylvania	59,135,426,000	4.1%
7	New Jersey	56,199,438,000	3.9%
8	Ohio	49,464,684,000	3.4%
9	Massachusetts	38,394,358,000	2.6%
10	Michigan	37,122,183,000	2.6%
11	North Carolina	35,538,649,000	2.4%
12	Virginia	35,046,760,000	2.4%
13	Georgia	33,215,010,000	2.3%
14	Maryland	32,470,068,000	2.2%
15	Washington	30,792,952,000	2.1%
16	Minnesota	30,075,762,000	2.1%
17	Wisconsin	27,588,284,000	1.9%
18	Connecticut	26,125,481,000	1.8%
19	Indiana	24,919,642,000	1.7%
20	Colorado	22,870,573,000	1.6%
21	Arizona	22,656,410,000	1.6%
22	Missouri	20,909,857,000	1.4%
23	Tennessee	20,177,658,000	1.4%
24	Louisiana	17,566,975,000	1.2%
25	Kentucky	15,431,580,000	1.1%
26	Oregon	15,353,218,000	1.1%
27	South Carolina	15,241,839,000	1.0%
28	Alabama	14,724,783,000	1.0%
29	Iowa	13,787,267,000	0.9%
30	Oklahoma	13,455,922,000	0.9%
31	Kansas	12,902,577,000	0.9%
32	Nevada	10,817,783,000	0.7%
33	Arkansas	10,764,696,000	0.7%
34	Mississippi	10,262,494,000	0.7%
35	Utah	10,188,214,000	0.7%
36	Nebraska	8,697,819,000	0.6%
37	Hawaii	8,041,176,000	0.6%
38	New Mexico	7,666,140,000	0.5%
39	West Virginia	7,224,929,000	0.5%
40	Alaska	6,792,745,000	0.5%
41	Maine	6,402,709,000	0.4%
42	North Dakota	6,384,310,000	0.4%
43	New Hampshire	5,551,156,000	0.4%
44	Rhode Island	5,402,158,000	0.4%
45	Idaho	5,104,976,000	0.4%
46	Delaware	4,266,923,000	0.3%
47	Montana	3,852,584,000	0.3%
48	Vermont	3,399,212,000	0.2%
49	Wyoming	3,379,158,000	0.2%
50	South Dakota	2,965,725,000	0.2%
	District of Columbia	6,179,767,000	0.4%

Source: U.S. Bureau of the Census, Governments Division
"2013 State and Local Government Finances" (http://www.census.gov/govs/local/)

Per Capita State and Local Government Tax Revenue in 2013

National Per Capita = $4,600

ALPHA ORDER

RANK	STATE	PER CAPITA
50	Alabama	$3,048
1	Alaska	9,211
44	Arizona	3,417
36	Arkansas	3,639
13	California	5,328
23	Colorado	4,339
4	Connecticut	7,263
19	Delaware	4,611
45	Florida	3,378
46	Georgia	3,324
8	Hawaii	5,708
48	Idaho	3,165
12	Illinois	5,374
33	Indiana	3,793
20	Iowa	4,459
21	Kansas	4,457
40	Kentucky	3,508
32	Louisiana	3,796
15	Maine	4,818
10	Maryland	5,470
7	Massachusetts	5,723
34	Michigan	3,750
9	Minnesota	5,548
43	Mississippi	3,431
42	Missouri	3,460
31	Montana	3,798
17	Nebraska	4,653
29	Nevada	3,877
26	New Hampshire	4,197
5	New Jersey	6,309
35	New Mexico	3,673
3	New York	8,049
37	North Carolina	3,610
2	North Dakota	8,823
24	Ohio	4,274
41	Oklahoma	3,492
27	Oregon	3,909
18	Pennsylvania	4,626
14	Rhode Island	5,131
47	South Carolina	3,196
38	South Dakota	3,509
49	Tennessee	3,106
30	Texas	3,863
38	Utah	3,509
11	Vermont	5,420
25	Virginia	4,239
22	Washington	4,416
28	West Virginia	3,899
16	Wisconsin	4,803
6	Wyoming	5,795

RANK ORDER

RANK	STATE	PER CAPITA
1	Alaska	$9,211
2	North Dakota	8,823
3	New York	8,049
4	Connecticut	7,263
5	New Jersey	6,309
6	Wyoming	5,795
7	Massachusetts	5,723
8	Hawaii	5,708
9	Minnesota	5,548
10	Maryland	5,470
11	Vermont	5,420
12	Illinois	5,374
13	California	5,328
14	Rhode Island	5,131
15	Maine	4,818
16	Wisconsin	4,803
17	Nebraska	4,653
18	Pennsylvania	4,626
19	Delaware	4,611
20	Iowa	4,459
21	Kansas	4,457
22	Washington	4,416
23	Colorado	4,339
24	Ohio	4,274
25	Virginia	4,239
26	New Hampshire	4,197
27	Oregon	3,909
28	West Virginia	3,899
29	Nevada	3,877
30	Texas	3,863
31	Montana	3,798
32	Louisiana	3,796
33	Indiana	3,793
34	Michigan	3,750
35	New Mexico	3,673
36	Arkansas	3,639
37	North Carolina	3,610
38	South Dakota	3,509
38	Utah	3,509
40	Kentucky	3,508
41	Oklahoma	3,492
42	Missouri	3,460
43	Mississippi	3,431
44	Arizona	3,417
45	Florida	3,378
46	Georgia	3,324
47	South Carolina	3,196
48	Idaho	3,165
49	Tennessee	3,106
50	Alabama	3,048
	District of Columbia	9,514

Source: CQ Press using data from U.S. Bureau of the Census, Governments Division
"2013 State and Local Government Finances" (http://www.census.gov/govs/local/)

Percent of State and Local Government Revenue from Taxes in 2013

National Percent = 42.6%

ALPHA ORDER

RANK	STATE	PERCENT
49	Alabama	33.0
30	Alaska	39.1
28	Arizona	39.6
26	Arkansas	40.3
22	California	40.6
21	Colorado	41.7
1	Connecticut	57.4
30	Delaware	39.1
34	Florida	38.7
36	Georgia	38.5
6	Hawaii	49.1
25	Idaho	40.4
5	Illinois	49.7
17	Indiana	44.4
23	Iowa	40.5
13	Kansas	45.0
23	Kentucky	40.5
40	Louisiana	37.3
7	Maine	49.0
4	Maryland	50.8
9	Massachusetts	47.7
32	Michigan	39.0
10	Minnesota	46.2
45	Mississippi	34.4
42	Missouri	36.4
41	Montana	36.9
36	Nebraska	38.5
19	Nevada	42.7
11	New Hampshire	46.0
3	New Jersey	54.5
47	New Mexico	34.1
8	New York	47.9
33	North Carolina	38.9
2	North Dakota	57.3
35	Ohio	38.6
39	Oklahoma	37.5
48	Oregon	33.7
15	Pennsylvania	44.8
16	Rhode Island	44.5
46	South Carolina	34.3
43	South Dakota	35.4
44	Tennessee	35.1
18	Texas	44.0
38	Utah	37.7
12	Vermont	45.8
14	Virginia	44.9
29	Washington	39.5
27	West Virginia	40.0
19	Wisconsin	42.7
50	Wyoming	32.6

RANK ORDER

RANK	STATE	PERCENT
1	Connecticut	57.4
2	North Dakota	57.3
3	New Jersey	54.5
4	Maryland	50.8
5	Illinois	49.7
6	Hawaii	49.1
7	Maine	49.0
8	New York	47.9
9	Massachusetts	47.7
10	Minnesota	46.2
11	New Hampshire	46.0
12	Vermont	45.8
13	Kansas	45.0
14	Virginia	44.9
15	Pennsylvania	44.8
16	Rhode Island	44.5
17	Indiana	44.4
18	Texas	44.0
19	Nevada	42.7
19	Wisconsin	42.7
21	Colorado	41.7
22	California	40.6
23	Iowa	40.5
23	Kentucky	40.5
25	Idaho	40.4
26	Arkansas	40.3
27	West Virginia	40.0
28	Arizona	39.6
29	Washington	39.5
30	Alaska	39.1
30	Delaware	39.1
32	Michigan	39.0
33	North Carolina	38.9
34	Florida	38.7
35	Ohio	38.6
36	Georgia	38.5
36	Nebraska	38.5
38	Utah	37.7
39	Oklahoma	37.5
40	Louisiana	37.3
41	Montana	36.9
42	Missouri	36.4
43	South Dakota	35.4
44	Tennessee	35.1
45	Mississippi	34.4
46	South Carolina	34.3
47	New Mexico	34.1
48	Oregon	33.7
49	Alabama	33.0
50	Wyoming	32.6
	District of Columbia	43.8

Source: CQ Press using data from U.S. Bureau of the Census, Governments Division
"2013 State and Local Government Finances" (http://www.census.gov/govs/local/)

State and Local Government Tax Revenue as a Percent of Personal Income in 2013
National Percent = 10.3% of Personal Income*

ALPHA ORDER

RANK	STATE	PERCENT
45	Alabama	8.4
1	Alaska	18.0
35	Arizona	9.3
26	Arkansas	10.0
13	California	11.1
35	Colorado	9.3
7	Connecticut	11.7
19	Delaware	10.3
48	Florida	8.2
41	Georgia	8.8
4	Hawaii	12.9
40	Idaho	8.9
9	Illinois	11.6
27	Indiana	9.9
20	Iowa	10.2
22	Kansas	10.1
30	Kentucky	9.8
35	Louisiana	9.3
5	Maine	12.2
17	Maryland	10.4
22	Massachusetts	10.1
32	Michigan	9.6
7	Minnesota	11.7
20	Mississippi	10.2
44	Missouri	8.6
30	Montana	9.8
22	Nebraska	10.1
27	Nevada	9.9
46	New Hampshire	8.3
10	New Jersey	11.4
17	New Mexico	10.4
3	New York	15.0
32	North Carolina	9.6
2	North Dakota	16.2
16	Ohio	10.5
46	Oklahoma	8.3
27	Oregon	9.9
22	Pennsylvania	10.1
13	Rhode Island	11.1
39	South Carolina	9.0
50	South Dakota	7.8
49	Tennessee	7.9
41	Texas	8.8
32	Utah	9.6
6	Vermont	12.1
43	Virginia	8.7
35	Washington	9.3
13	West Virginia	11.1
11	Wisconsin	11.2
11	Wyoming	11.2

RANK ORDER

RANK	STATE	PERCENT
1	Alaska	18.0
2	North Dakota	16.2
3	New York	15.0
4	Hawaii	12.9
5	Maine	12.2
6	Vermont	12.1
7	Connecticut	11.7
7	Minnesota	11.7
9	Illinois	11.6
10	New Jersey	11.4
11	Wisconsin	11.2
11	Wyoming	11.2
13	California	11.1
13	Rhode Island	11.1
13	West Virginia	11.1
16	Ohio	10.5
17	Maryland	10.4
17	New Mexico	10.4
19	Delaware	10.3
20	Iowa	10.2
20	Mississippi	10.2
22	Kansas	10.1
22	Massachusetts	10.1
22	Nebraska	10.1
22	Pennsylvania	10.1
26	Arkansas	10.0
27	Indiana	9.9
27	Nevada	9.9
27	Oregon	9.9
30	Kentucky	9.8
30	Montana	9.8
32	Michigan	9.6
32	North Carolina	9.6
32	Utah	9.6
35	Arizona	9.3
35	Colorado	9.3
35	Louisiana	9.3
35	Washington	9.3
39	South Carolina	9.0
40	Idaho	8.9
41	Georgia	8.8
41	Texas	8.8
43	Virginia	8.7
44	Missouri	8.6
45	Alabama	8.4
46	New Hampshire	8.3
46	Oklahoma	8.3
48	Florida	8.2
49	Tennessee	7.9
50	South Dakota	7.8
	District of Columbia	13.9

Source: CQ Press using data from Bureau of Economic Analysis and U.S. Census Bureau
"Annual State Personal Income" (http://www.bea.gov/iTable/index_regional.cfm) and
"2013 State and Local Government Finances" (http://www.census.gov/govs/local/)
*The personal income total used for this table is the sum of state estimates. This total differs from the national income and product accounts (NIPA) estimate of personal income because it omits the earnings of federal civilian and military personnel stationed abroad and of U.S. residents employed abroad temporarily by private U.S. firms.

State and Local Government General Sales Tax Revenue in 2013

National Total = $327,065,751,000*

ALPHA ORDER

RANK	STATE	REVENUE	% of USA
24	Alabama	$4,358,304,000	1.3%
46	Alaska	216,932,000	0.1%
10	Arizona	9,023,805,000	2.8%
28	Arkansas	3,854,132,000	1.2%
1	California	44,509,896,000	13.6%
17	Colorado	6,126,955,000	1.9%
27	Connecticut	3,855,861,000	1.2%
47	Delaware	0	0.0%
4	Florida	22,622,591,000	6.9%
9	Georgia	9,156,191,000	2.8%
32	Hawaii	3,118,310,000	1.0%
39	Idaho	1,324,182,000	0.4%
8	Illinois	9,782,752,000	3.0%
15	Indiana	6,793,923,000	2.1%
35	Iowa	2,823,606,000	0.9%
29	Kansas	3,782,309,000	1.2%
33	Kentucky	3,021,794,000	0.9%
16	Louisiana	6,780,420,000	2.1%
42	Maine	1,071,886,000	0.3%
25	Maryland	4,114,296,000	1.3%
19	Massachusetts	5,184,312,000	1.6%
11	Michigan	8,465,895,000	2.6%
20	Minnesota	5,129,434,000	1.6%
31	Mississippi	3,191,683,000	1.0%
18	Missouri	5,317,028,000	1.6%
47	Montana	0	0.0%
37	Nebraska	2,009,918,000	0.6%
26	Nevada	3,975,983,000	1.2%
47	New Hampshire	0	0.0%
12	New Jersey	8,454,788,000	2.6%
34	New Mexico	2,927,961,000	0.9%
3	New York	25,793,108,000	7.9%
14	North Carolina	7,829,797,000	2.4%
38	North Dakota	1,464,946,000	0.4%
6	Ohio	10,586,135,000	3.2%
23	Oklahoma	4,512,843,000	1.4%
47	Oregon	0	0.0%
7	Pennsylvania	9,948,187,000	3.0%
43	Rhode Island	881,458,000	0.3%
30	South Carolina	3,571,238,000	1.1%
41	South Dakota	1,181,985,000	0.4%
13	Tennessee	8,098,789,000	2.5%
2	Texas	32,627,176,000	10.0%
36	Utah	2,534,680,000	0.8%
45	Vermont	357,818,000	0.1%
21	Virginia	4,906,526,000	1.5%
5	Washington	13,795,696,000	4.2%
40	West Virginia	1,255,377,000	0.4%
22	Wisconsin	4,770,922,000	1.5%
44	Wyoming	868,376,000	0.3%

RANK ORDER

RANK	STATE	REVENUE	% of USA
1	California	$44,509,896,000	13.6%
2	Texas	32,627,176,000	10.0%
3	New York	25,793,108,000	7.9%
4	Florida	22,622,591,000	6.9%
5	Washington	13,795,696,000	4.2%
6	Ohio	10,586,135,000	3.2%
7	Pennsylvania	9,948,187,000	3.0%
8	Illinois	9,782,752,000	3.0%
9	Georgia	9,156,191,000	2.8%
10	Arizona	9,023,805,000	2.8%
11	Michigan	8,465,895,000	2.6%
12	New Jersey	8,454,788,000	2.6%
13	Tennessee	8,098,789,000	2.5%
14	North Carolina	7,829,797,000	2.4%
15	Indiana	6,793,923,000	2.1%
16	Louisiana	6,780,420,000	2.1%
17	Colorado	6,126,955,000	1.9%
18	Missouri	5,317,028,000	1.6%
19	Massachusetts	5,184,312,000	1.6%
20	Minnesota	5,129,434,000	1.6%
21	Virginia	4,906,526,000	1.5%
22	Wisconsin	4,770,922,000	1.5%
23	Oklahoma	4,512,843,000	1.4%
24	Alabama	4,358,304,000	1.3%
25	Maryland	4,114,296,000	1.3%
26	Nevada	3,975,983,000	1.2%
27	Connecticut	3,855,861,000	1.2%
28	Arkansas	3,854,132,000	1.2%
29	Kansas	3,782,309,000	1.2%
30	South Carolina	3,571,238,000	1.1%
31	Mississippi	3,191,683,000	1.0%
32	Hawaii	3,118,310,000	1.0%
33	Kentucky	3,021,794,000	0.9%
34	New Mexico	2,927,961,000	0.9%
35	Iowa	2,823,606,000	0.9%
36	Utah	2,534,680,000	0.8%
37	Nebraska	2,009,918,000	0.6%
38	North Dakota	1,464,946,000	0.4%
39	Idaho	1,324,182,000	0.4%
40	West Virginia	1,255,377,000	0.4%
41	South Dakota	1,181,985,000	0.4%
42	Maine	1,071,886,000	0.3%
43	Rhode Island	881,458,000	0.3%
44	Wyoming	868,376,000	0.3%
45	Vermont	357,818,000	0.1%
46	Alaska	216,932,000	0.1%
47	Delaware	0	0.0%
47	Montana	0	0.0%
47	New Hampshire	0	0.0%
47	Oregon	0	0.0%
	District of Columbia	1,085,547,000	0.3%

Source: U.S. Bureau of the Census, Governments Division
"2013 State and Local Government Finances" (http://www.census.gov/govs/local/)
*Does not include special sales taxes such as those on sale of alcohol, gasoline, or tobacco.

Per Capita State and Local Government General Sales Tax Revenue in 2013

National Per Capita = $1,034*

ALPHA ORDER

RANK	STATE	PER CAPITA
28	Alabama	$902
46	Alaska	294
9	Arizona	1,361
12	Arkansas	1,303
17	California	1,159
16	Colorado	1,162
20	Connecticut	1,072
47	Delaware	0
18	Florida	1,155
25	Georgia	916
1	Hawaii	2,214
34	Idaho	821
39	Illinois	759
22	Indiana	1,034
27	Iowa	913
11	Kansas	1,307
42	Kentucky	687
5	Louisiana	1,465
35	Maine	807
41	Maryland	693
38	Massachusetts	773
31	Michigan	855
24	Minnesota	946
21	Mississippi	1,067
29	Missouri	880
47	Montana	0
19	Nebraska	1,075
6	Nevada	1,425
47	New Hampshire	0
23	New Jersey	949
7	New Mexico	1,403
10	New York	1,310
36	North Carolina	795
2	North Dakota	2,024
26	Ohio	915
15	Oklahoma	1,171
47	Oregon	0
37	Pennsylvania	778
32	Rhode Island	837
40	South Carolina	749
8	South Dakota	1,398
13	Tennessee	1,247
14	Texas	1,231
30	Utah	873
45	Vermont	571
44	Virginia	593
3	Washington	1,978
43	West Virginia	677
33	Wisconsin	831
4	Wyoming	1,489

RANK ORDER

RANK	STATE	PER CAPITA
1	Hawaii	$2,214
2	North Dakota	2,024
3	Washington	1,978
4	Wyoming	1,489
5	Louisiana	1,465
6	Nevada	1,425
7	New Mexico	1,403
8	South Dakota	1,398
9	Arizona	1,361
10	New York	1,310
11	Kansas	1,307
12	Arkansas	1,303
13	Tennessee	1,247
14	Texas	1,231
15	Oklahoma	1,171
16	Colorado	1,162
17	California	1,159
18	Florida	1,155
19	Nebraska	1,075
20	Connecticut	1,072
21	Mississippi	1,067
22	Indiana	1,034
23	New Jersey	949
24	Minnesota	946
25	Georgia	916
26	Ohio	915
27	Iowa	913
28	Alabama	902
29	Missouri	880
30	Utah	873
31	Michigan	855
32	Rhode Island	837
33	Wisconsin	831
34	Idaho	821
35	Maine	807
36	North Carolina	795
37	Pennsylvania	778
38	Massachusetts	773
39	Illinois	759
40	South Carolina	749
41	Maryland	693
42	Kentucky	687
43	West Virginia	677
44	Virginia	593
45	Vermont	571
46	Alaska	294
47	Delaware	0
47	Montana	0
47	New Hampshire	0
47	Oregon	0
	District of Columbia	1,671

Source: CQ Press using data from U.S. Bureau of the Census, Governments Division
"2013 State and Local Government Finances" (http://www.census.gov/govs/local/)
*Does not include special sales taxes such as those on sale of alcohol, gasoline, or tobacco.

State and Local Government Property Tax Revenue in 2013

National Total = $455,441,810,000

ALPHA ORDER

RANK	STATE	REVENUE	% of USA
35	Alabama	$2,645,349,000	0.6%
45	Alaska	1,411,018,000	0.3%
20	Arizona	6,688,638,000	1.5%
39	Arkansas	1,949,568,000	0.4%
1	California	52,442,692,000	11.5%
19	Colorado	7,027,778,000	1.5%
14	Connecticut	9,806,529,000	2.2%
50	Delaware	763,406,000	0.2%
6	Florida	23,817,726,000	5.2%
13	Georgia	10,100,046,000	2.2%
46	Hawaii	1,328,624,000	0.3%
42	Idaho	1,431,374,000	0.3%
5	Illinois	25,541,107,000	5.6%
21	Indiana	6,358,368,000	1.4%
26	Iowa	4,683,787,000	1.0%
27	Kansas	4,125,384,000	0.9%
30	Kentucky	3,217,861,000	0.7%
28	Louisiana	3,931,013,000	0.9%
36	Maine	2,533,872,000	0.6%
16	Maryland	8,927,867,000	2.0%
9	Massachusetts	13,883,777,000	3.0%
10	Michigan	13,069,522,000	2.9%
18	Minnesota	8,386,600,000	1.8%
34	Mississippi	2,689,489,000	0.6%
22	Missouri	5,901,969,000	1.3%
44	Montana	1,426,817,000	0.3%
31	Nebraska	3,081,714,000	0.7%
33	Nevada	2,713,097,000	0.6%
29	New Hampshire	3,558,546,000	0.8%
4	New Jersey	26,624,057,000	5.8%
43	New Mexico	1,428,570,000	0.3%
2	New York	49,100,972,000	10.8%
17	North Carolina	8,891,965,000	2.0%
49	North Dakota	825,158,000	0.2%
8	Ohio	14,060,448,000	3.1%
38	Oklahoma	2,293,338,000	0.5%
25	Oregon	5,047,590,000	1.1%
7	Pennsylvania	17,591,680,000	3.9%
37	Rhode Island	2,402,791,000	0.5%
24	South Carolina	5,137,971,000	1.1%
48	South Dakota	1,040,165,000	0.2%
23	Tennessee	5,444,910,000	1.2%
3	Texas	41,341,895,000	9.1%
32	Utah	2,763,278,000	0.6%
41	Vermont	1,462,078,000	0.3%
11	Virginia	11,826,422,000	2.6%
15	Washington	9,415,715,000	2.1%
40	West Virginia	1,479,014,000	0.3%
12	Wisconsin	10,583,547,000	2.3%
47	Wyoming	1,266,990,000	0.3%

RANK ORDER

RANK	STATE	REVENUE	% of USA
1	California	$52,442,692,000	11.5%
2	New York	49,100,972,000	10.8%
3	Texas	41,341,895,000	9.1%
4	New Jersey	26,624,057,000	5.8%
5	Illinois	25,541,107,000	5.6%
6	Florida	23,817,726,000	5.2%
7	Pennsylvania	17,591,680,000	3.9%
8	Ohio	14,060,448,000	3.1%
9	Massachusetts	13,883,777,000	3.0%
10	Michigan	13,069,522,000	2.9%
11	Virginia	11,826,422,000	2.6%
12	Wisconsin	10,583,547,000	2.3%
13	Georgia	10,100,046,000	2.2%
14	Connecticut	9,806,529,000	2.2%
15	Washington	9,415,715,000	2.1%
16	Maryland	8,927,867,000	2.0%
17	North Carolina	8,891,965,000	2.0%
18	Minnesota	8,386,600,000	1.8%
19	Colorado	7,027,778,000	1.5%
20	Arizona	6,688,638,000	1.5%
21	Indiana	6,358,368,000	1.4%
22	Missouri	5,901,969,000	1.3%
23	Tennessee	5,444,910,000	1.2%
24	South Carolina	5,137,971,000	1.1%
25	Oregon	5,047,590,000	1.1%
26	Iowa	4,683,787,000	1.0%
27	Kansas	4,125,384,000	0.9%
28	Louisiana	3,931,013,000	0.9%
29	New Hampshire	3,558,546,000	0.8%
30	Kentucky	3,217,861,000	0.7%
31	Nebraska	3,081,714,000	0.7%
32	Utah	2,763,278,000	0.6%
33	Nevada	2,713,097,000	0.6%
34	Mississippi	2,689,489,000	0.6%
35	Alabama	2,645,349,000	0.6%
36	Maine	2,533,872,000	0.6%
37	Rhode Island	2,402,791,000	0.5%
38	Oklahoma	2,293,338,000	0.5%
39	Arkansas	1,949,568,000	0.4%
40	West Virginia	1,479,014,000	0.3%
41	Vermont	1,462,078,000	0.3%
42	Idaho	1,431,374,000	0.3%
43	New Mexico	1,428,570,000	0.3%
44	Montana	1,426,817,000	0.3%
45	Alaska	1,411,018,000	0.3%
46	Hawaii	1,328,624,000	0.3%
47	Wyoming	1,266,990,000	0.3%
48	South Dakota	1,040,165,000	0.2%
49	North Dakota	825,158,000	0.2%
50	Delaware	763,406,000	0.2%
	District of Columbia	1,969,718,000	0.4%

Source: U.S. Bureau of the Census, Governments Division
"2013 State and Local Government Finances" (http://www.census.gov/govs/local/)

Per Capita State and Local Government Property Tax Revenue in 2013

National Per Capita = $1,439

ALPHA ORDER

RANK	STATE	PER CAPITA
50	Alabama	$548
10	Alaska	1,913
33	Arizona	1,009
48	Arkansas	659
22	California	1,365
24	Colorado	1,333
2	Connecticut	2,726
44	Delaware	825
28	Florida	1,216
32	Georgia	1,011
38	Hawaii	943
41	Idaho	888
9	Illinois	1,982
36	Indiana	968
16	Iowa	1,515
19	Kansas	1,425
46	Kentucky	732
42	Louisiana	849
11	Maine	1,907
17	Maryland	1,504
8	Massachusetts	2,069
25	Michigan	1,320
15	Minnesota	1,547
40	Mississippi	899
34	Missouri	977
20	Montana	1,407
13	Nebraska	1,649
35	Nevada	972
3	New Hampshire	2,690
1	New Jersey	2,989
47	New Mexico	685
4	New York	2,494
39	North Carolina	903
30	North Dakota	1,140
29	Ohio	1,215
49	Oklahoma	595
26	Oregon	1,285
21	Pennsylvania	1,376
6	Rhode Island	2,282
31	South Carolina	1,077
27	South Dakota	1,231
43	Tennessee	838
14	Texas	1,560
37	Utah	952
5	Vermont	2,331
18	Virginia	1,430
23	Washington	1,350
45	West Virginia	798
12	Wisconsin	1,843
7	Wyoming	2,173

RANK ORDER

RANK	STATE	PER CAPITA
1	New Jersey	$2,989
2	Connecticut	2,726
3	New Hampshire	2,690
4	New York	2,494
5	Vermont	2,331
6	Rhode Island	2,282
7	Wyoming	2,173
8	Massachusetts	2,069
9	Illinois	1,982
10	Alaska	1,913
11	Maine	1,907
12	Wisconsin	1,843
13	Nebraska	1,649
14	Texas	1,560
15	Minnesota	1,547
16	Iowa	1,515
17	Maryland	1,504
18	Virginia	1,430
19	Kansas	1,425
20	Montana	1,407
21	Pennsylvania	1,376
22	California	1,365
23	Washington	1,350
24	Colorado	1,333
25	Michigan	1,320
26	Oregon	1,285
27	South Dakota	1,231
28	Florida	1,216
29	Ohio	1,215
30	North Dakota	1,140
31	South Carolina	1,077
32	Georgia	1,011
33	Arizona	1,009
34	Missouri	977
35	Nevada	972
36	Indiana	968
37	Utah	952
38	Hawaii	943
39	North Carolina	903
40	Mississippi	899
41	Idaho	888
42	Louisiana	849
43	Tennessee	838
44	Delaware	825
45	West Virginia	798
46	Kentucky	732
47	New Mexico	685
48	Arkansas	659
49	Oklahoma	595
50	Alabama	548
	District of Columbia	3,032

Source: CQ Press using data from U.S. Bureau of the Census, Governments Division
"2013 State and Local Government Finances" (http://www.census.gov/govs/local/)

State and Local Government Property Tax as a Percent of State and Local Government Total Revenue in 2013
National Percent = 13.3%

ALPHA ORDER

RANK	STATE	PERCENT
50	Alabama	5.9
43	Alaska	8.1
26	Arizona	11.7
46	Arkansas	7.3
34	California	10.4
22	Colorado	12.8
3	Connecticut	21.5
47	Delaware	7.0
15	Florida	13.9
26	Georgia	11.7
43	Hawaii	8.1
29	Idaho	11.3
7	Illinois	18.3
29	Indiana	11.3
16	Iowa	13.8
13	Kansas	14.4
40	Kentucky	8.4
41	Louisiana	8.3
6	Maine	19.4
14	Maryland	14.0
9	Massachusetts	17.2
17	Michigan	13.7
21	Minnesota	12.9
39	Mississippi	9.0
35	Missouri	10.3
17	Montana	13.7
19	Nebraska	13.6
33	Nevada	10.7
1	New Hampshire	29.5
2	New Jersey	25.8
48	New Mexico	6.4
12	New York	14.8
37	North Carolina	9.7
45	North Dakota	7.4
32	Ohio	11.0
48	Oklahoma	6.4
31	Oregon	11.1
20	Pennsylvania	13.3
4	Rhode Island	19.8
28	South Carolina	11.6
23	South Dakota	12.4
38	Tennessee	9.5
8	Texas	17.8
36	Utah	10.2
5	Vermont	19.7
11	Virginia	15.2
25	Washington	12.1
42	West Virginia	8.2
10	Wisconsin	16.4
24	Wyoming	12.2

RANK ORDER

RANK	STATE	PERCENT
1	New Hampshire	29.5
2	New Jersey	25.8
3	Connecticut	21.5
4	Rhode Island	19.8
5	Vermont	19.7
6	Maine	19.4
7	Illinois	18.3
8	Texas	17.8
9	Massachusetts	17.2
10	Wisconsin	16.4
11	Virginia	15.2
12	New York	14.8
13	Kansas	14.4
14	Maryland	14.0
15	Florida	13.9
16	Iowa	13.8
17	Michigan	13.7
17	Montana	13.7
19	Nebraska	13.6
20	Pennsylvania	13.3
21	Minnesota	12.9
22	Colorado	12.8
23	South Dakota	12.4
24	Wyoming	12.2
25	Washington	12.1
26	Arizona	11.7
26	Georgia	11.7
28	South Carolina	11.6
29	Idaho	11.3
29	Indiana	11.3
31	Oregon	11.1
32	Ohio	11.0
33	Nevada	10.7
34	California	10.4
35	Missouri	10.3
36	Utah	10.2
37	North Carolina	9.7
38	Tennessee	9.5
39	Mississippi	9.0
40	Kentucky	8.4
41	Louisiana	8.3
42	West Virginia	8.2
43	Alaska	8.1
43	Hawaii	8.1
45	North Dakota	7.4
46	Arkansas	7.3
47	Delaware	7.0
48	New Mexico	6.4
48	Oklahoma	6.4
50	Alabama	5.9

District of Columbia   14.0

Source: CQ Press using data from U.S. Bureau of the Census, Governments Division
"2013 State and Local Government Finances" (http://www.census.gov/govs/local/)

State and Local Government Property Tax Revenue as a Percent of State and Local Government Own Source Revenue in 2013
National Percent = 21.6%*

ALPHA ORDER

RANK	STATE	PERCENT
49	Alabama	10.3
45	Alaska	11.5
24	Arizona	20.2
43	Arkansas	12.7
33	California	18.0
28	Colorado	19.7
5	Connecticut	31.7
48	Delaware	10.5
17	Florida	21.9
21	Georgia	20.4
44	Hawaii	11.9
30	Idaho	18.5
7	Illinois	28.5
36	Indiana	17.0
18	Iowa	21.4
21	Kansas	20.4
40	Kentucky	14.5
41	Louisiana	14.1
6	Maine	30.3
20	Maryland	20.8
10	Massachusetts	27.3
15	Michigan	22.6
24	Minnesota	20.2
38	Mississippi	16.2
31	Missouri	18.4
11	Montana	25.2
12	Nebraska	24.1
34	Nevada	17.6
1	New Hampshire	44.2
2	New Jersey	36.5
46	New Mexico	11.2
13	New York	23.9
39	North Carolina	15.9
50	North Dakota	9.8
29	Ohio	19.4
47	Oklahoma	10.8
24	Oregon	20.2
19	Pennsylvania	20.9
4	Rhode Island	31.8
32	South Carolina	18.3
14	South Dakota	23.3
34	Tennessee	17.6
8	Texas	27.5
37	Utah	16.8
3	Vermont	31.9
16	Virginia	22.3
27	Washington	20.0
42	West Virginia	13.3
8	Wisconsin	27.5
23	Wyoming	20.3

RANK ORDER

RANK	STATE	PERCENT
1	New Hampshire	44.2
2	New Jersey	36.5
3	Vermont	31.9
4	Rhode Island	31.8
5	Connecticut	31.7
6	Maine	30.3
7	Illinois	28.5
8	Texas	27.5
8	Wisconsin	27.5
10	Massachusetts	27.3
11	Montana	25.2
12	Nebraska	24.1
13	New York	23.9
14	South Dakota	23.3
15	Michigan	22.6
16	Virginia	22.3
17	Florida	21.9
18	Iowa	21.4
19	Pennsylvania	20.9
20	Maryland	20.8
21	Georgia	20.4
21	Kansas	20.4
23	Wyoming	20.3
24	Arizona	20.2
24	Minnesota	20.2
24	Oregon	20.2
27	Washington	20.0
28	Colorado	19.7
29	Ohio	19.4
30	Idaho	18.5
31	Missouri	18.4
32	South Carolina	18.3
33	California	18.0
34	Nevada	17.6
34	Tennessee	17.6
36	Indiana	17.0
37	Utah	16.8
38	Mississippi	16.2
39	North Carolina	15.9
40	Kentucky	14.5
41	Louisiana	14.1
42	West Virginia	13.3
43	Arkansas	12.7
44	Hawaii	11.9
45	Alaska	11.5
46	New Mexico	11.2
47	Oklahoma	10.8
48	Delaware	10.5
49	Alabama	10.3
50	North Dakota	9.8
	District of Columbia	24.7

Source: CQ Press using data from U.S. Bureau of the Census, Governments Division
"2013 State and Local Government Finances" (http://www.census.gov/govs/local/)
*Own source revenue includes taxes, current charges, and miscellaneous general revenue. Excluded are intergovernmental transfers, insurance trust revenue, and revenue from government owned utilities and other commercial or auxiliary enterprise.

State and Local Tax Burden as a Percent of Income in 2012

National Percent = 9.8% of Income*

ALPHA ORDER

RANK	STATE	PERCENT
37	Alabama	8.7
50	Alaska	6.5
36	Arizona	8.8
17	Arkansas	10.1
4	California	11.0
34	Colorado	8.9
2	Connecticut	12.6
13	Delaware	10.2
34	Florida	8.9
32	Georgia	9.1
13	Hawaii	10.2
26	Idaho	9.3
4	Illinois	11.0
22	Indiana	9.5
30	Iowa	9.2
22	Kansas	9.5
22	Kentucky	9.5
45	Louisiana	7.6
13	Maine	10.2
7	Maryland	10.9
10	Massachusetts	10.3
25	Michigan	9.4
8	Minnesota	10.8
40	Mississippi	8.6
26	Missouri	9.3
37	Montana	8.7
30	Nebraska	9.2
43	Nevada	8.1
44	New Hampshire	7.9
3	New Jersey	12.2
37	New Mexico	8.7
1	New York	12.7
18	North Carolina	9.8
33	North Dakota	9.0
18	Ohio	9.8
40	Oklahoma	8.6
10	Oregon	10.3
13	Pennsylvania	10.2
8	Rhode Island	10.8
42	South Carolina	8.4
48	South Dakota	7.1
47	Tennessee	7.3
45	Texas	7.6
21	Utah	9.6
10	Vermont	10.3
26	Virginia	9.3
26	Washington	9.3
18	West Virginia	9.8
4	Wisconsin	11.0
48	Wyoming	7.1

RANK ORDER

RANK	STATE	PERCENT
1	New York	12.7
2	Connecticut	12.6
3	New Jersey	12.2
4	California	11.0
4	Illinois	11.0
4	Wisconsin	11.0
7	Maryland	10.9
8	Minnesota	10.8
8	Rhode Island	10.8
10	Massachusetts	10.3
10	Oregon	10.3
10	Vermont	10.3
13	Delaware	10.2
13	Hawaii	10.2
13	Maine	10.2
13	Pennsylvania	10.2
17	Arkansas	10.1
18	North Carolina	9.8
18	Ohio	9.8
18	West Virginia	9.8
21	Utah	9.6
22	Indiana	9.5
22	Kansas	9.5
22	Kentucky	9.5
25	Michigan	9.4
26	Idaho	9.3
26	Missouri	9.3
26	Virginia	9.3
26	Washington	9.3
30	Iowa	9.2
30	Nebraska	9.2
32	Georgia	9.1
33	North Dakota	9.0
34	Colorado	8.9
34	Florida	8.9
36	Arizona	8.8
37	Alabama	8.7
37	Montana	8.7
37	New Mexico	8.7
40	Mississippi	8.6
40	Oklahoma	8.6
42	South Carolina	8.4
43	Nevada	8.1
44	New Hampshire	7.9
45	Louisiana	7.6
45	Texas	7.6
47	Tennessee	7.3
48	South Dakota	7.1
48	Wyoming	7.1
50	Alaska	6.5

| District of Columbia | 10.6 |

Source: The Tax Foundation
"State and Local Tax Burdens: All States, One Year, 1977-2012"
(http://taxfoundation.org/article/state-and-local-tax-burdens-1977-2012)
*All state and local taxes.

State and Local Government Total Expenditures in 2013

National Total = $3,204,487,884,000*

ALPHA ORDER

RANK	STATE	EXPENDITURES	% of USA
24	Alabama	$43,041,699,000	1.3%
39	Alaska	15,626,824,000	0.5%
21	Arizona	51,462,487,000	1.6%
34	Arkansas	24,394,331,000	0.8%
1	California	463,132,983,000	14.5%
22	Colorado	51,340,931,000	1.6%
26	Connecticut	41,888,206,000	1.3%
45	Delaware	10,725,350,000	0.3%
4	Florida	157,029,147,000	4.9%
12	Georgia	78,828,922,000	2.5%
40	Hawaii	14,585,252,000	0.5%
42	Idaho	11,746,790,000	0.4%
5	Illinois	134,071,551,000	4.2%
19	Indiana	53,147,205,000	1.7%
30	Iowa	31,708,866,000	1.0%
32	Kansas	26,591,136,000	0.8%
28	Kentucky	38,579,749,000	1.2%
23	Louisiana	47,925,501,000	1.5%
41	Maine	12,375,971,000	0.4%
15	Maryland	60,749,114,000	1.9%
11	Massachusetts	80,941,048,000	2.5%
9	Michigan	89,255,645,000	2.8%
16	Minnesota	57,052,565,000	1.8%
31	Mississippi	27,657,530,000	0.9%
20	Missouri	51,633,679,000	1.6%
46	Montana	9,374,477,000	0.3%
37	Nebraska	20,624,289,000	0.6%
35	Nevada	22,095,908,000	0.7%
44	New Hampshire	11,402,651,000	0.4%
8	New Jersey	102,439,151,000	3.2%
36	New Mexico	21,135,363,000	0.7%
2	New York	310,406,218,000	9.7%
10	North Carolina	85,915,026,000	2.7%
48	North Dakota	8,334,366,000	0.3%
7	Ohio	113,759,659,000	3.6%
29	Oklahoma	32,320,196,000	1.0%
27	Oregon	40,042,315,000	1.2%
6	Pennsylvania	131,934,153,000	4.1%
43	Rhode Island	11,473,066,000	0.4%
25	South Carolina	42,805,953,000	1.3%
50	South Dakota	7,100,532,000	0.2%
18	Tennessee	55,309,480,000	1.7%
3	Texas	223,761,832,000	7.0%
33	Utah	25,408,155,000	0.8%
49	Vermont	7,264,928,000	0.2%
14	Virginia	73,865,631,000	2.3%
13	Washington	76,011,346,000	2.4%
38	West Virginia	16,673,260,000	0.5%
17	Wisconsin	55,719,362,000	1.7%
47	Wyoming	8,869,282,000	0.3%

RANK ORDER

RANK	STATE	EXPENDITURES	% of USA
1	California	$463,132,983,000	14.5%
2	New York	310,406,218,000	9.7%
3	Texas	223,761,832,000	7.0%
4	Florida	157,029,147,000	4.9%
5	Illinois	134,071,551,000	4.2%
6	Pennsylvania	131,934,153,000	4.1%
7	Ohio	113,759,659,000	3.6%
8	New Jersey	102,439,151,000	3.2%
9	Michigan	89,255,645,000	2.8%
10	North Carolina	85,915,026,000	2.7%
11	Massachusetts	80,941,048,000	2.5%
12	Georgia	78,828,922,000	2.5%
13	Washington	76,011,346,000	2.4%
14	Virginia	73,865,631,000	2.3%
15	Maryland	60,749,114,000	1.9%
16	Minnesota	57,052,565,000	1.8%
17	Wisconsin	55,719,362,000	1.7%
18	Tennessee	55,309,480,000	1.7%
19	Indiana	53,147,205,000	1.7%
20	Missouri	51,633,679,000	1.6%
21	Arizona	51,462,487,000	1.6%
22	Colorado	51,340,931,000	1.6%
23	Louisiana	47,925,501,000	1.5%
24	Alabama	43,041,699,000	1.3%
25	South Carolina	42,805,953,000	1.3%
26	Connecticut	41,888,206,000	1.3%
27	Oregon	40,042,315,000	1.2%
28	Kentucky	38,579,749,000	1.2%
29	Oklahoma	32,320,196,000	1.0%
30	Iowa	31,708,866,000	1.0%
31	Mississippi	27,657,530,000	0.9%
32	Kansas	26,591,136,000	0.8%
33	Utah	25,408,155,000	0.8%
34	Arkansas	24,394,331,000	0.8%
35	Nevada	22,095,908,000	0.7%
36	New Mexico	21,135,363,000	0.7%
37	Nebraska	20,624,289,000	0.6%
38	West Virginia	16,673,260,000	0.5%
39	Alaska	15,626,824,000	0.5%
40	Hawaii	14,585,252,000	0.5%
41	Maine	12,375,971,000	0.4%
42	Idaho	11,746,790,000	0.4%
43	Rhode Island	11,473,066,000	0.4%
44	New Hampshire	11,402,651,000	0.4%
45	Delaware	10,725,350,000	0.3%
46	Montana	9,374,477,000	0.3%
47	Wyoming	8,869,282,000	0.3%
48	North Dakota	8,334,366,000	0.3%
49	Vermont	7,264,928,000	0.2%
50	South Dakota	7,100,532,000	0.2%
	District of Columbia	14,948,803,000	0.5%

Source: U.S. Bureau of the Census, Governments Division
 "2013 State and Local Government Finances" (http://www.census.gov/govs/local/)
*Total expenditures includes all money paid other than for retirement of debt and extension of loans. Includes payments from all sources of funds including current revenues and proceeds from borrowing and prior year fund balances. Includes intergovernmental transfers and expenditures for government owned utilities and other commercial or auxiliary enterprise, and insurance trust expenditures.

Per Capita State and Local Government Total Expenditures in 2013

National Per Capita = $10,127*

ALPHA ORDER

RANK	STATE	PER CAPITA
34	Alabama	$8,910
1	Alaska	21,191
49	Arizona	7,761
44	Arkansas	8,247
5	California	12,056
24	Colorado	9,740
6	Connecticut	11,645
7	Delaware	11,591
46	Florida	8,014
48	Georgia	7,890
17	Hawaii	10,353
50	Idaho	7,284
15	Illinois	10,402
45	Indiana	8,089
19	Iowa	10,254
29	Kansas	9,186
35	Kentucky	8,771
16	Louisiana	10,357
26	Maine	9,314
20	Maryland	10,234
4	Massachusetts	12,065
30	Michigan	9,015
14	Minnesota	10,525
27	Mississippi	9,247
39	Missouri	8,543
28	Montana	9,241
11	Nebraska	11,033
47	Nevada	7,919
38	New Hampshire	8,621
10	New Jersey	11,500
22	New Mexico	10,128
2	New York	15,764
37	North Carolina	8,726
9	North Dakota	11,518
23	Ohio	9,830
43	Oklahoma	8,387
21	Oregon	10,194
18	Pennsylvania	10,321
13	Rhode Island	10,897
32	South Carolina	8,977
42	South Dakota	8,400
40	Tennessee	8,514
41	Texas	8,444
36	Utah	8,750
8	Vermont	11,584
33	Virginia	8,934
12	Washington	10,900
31	West Virginia	8,998
25	Wisconsin	9,701
3	Wyoming	15,210

RANK ORDER

RANK	STATE	PER CAPITA
1	Alaska	$21,191
2	New York	15,764
3	Wyoming	15,210
4	Massachusetts	12,065
5	California	12,056
6	Connecticut	11,645
7	Delaware	11,591
8	Vermont	11,584
9	North Dakota	11,518
10	New Jersey	11,500
11	Nebraska	11,033
12	Washington	10,900
13	Rhode Island	10,897
14	Minnesota	10,525
15	Illinois	10,402
16	Louisiana	10,357
17	Hawaii	10,353
18	Pennsylvania	10,321
19	Iowa	10,254
20	Maryland	10,234
21	Oregon	10,194
22	New Mexico	10,128
23	Ohio	9,830
24	Colorado	9,740
25	Wisconsin	9,701
26	Maine	9,314
27	Mississippi	9,247
28	Montana	9,241
29	Kansas	9,186
30	Michigan	9,015
31	West Virginia	8,998
32	South Carolina	8,977
33	Virginia	8,934
34	Alabama	8,910
35	Kentucky	8,771
36	Utah	8,750
37	North Carolina	8,726
38	New Hampshire	8,621
39	Missouri	8,543
40	Tennessee	8,514
41	Texas	8,444
42	South Dakota	8,400
43	Oklahoma	8,387
44	Arkansas	8,247
45	Indiana	8,089
46	Florida	8,014
47	Nevada	7,919
48	Georgia	7,890
49	Arizona	7,761
50	Idaho	7,284

| | District of Columbia | 23,014 |

Source: CQ Press using data from U.S. Bureau of the Census, Governments Division
"2013 State and Local Government Finances" (http://www.census.gov/govs/local/)
*Total expenditures includes all money paid other than for retirement of debt and extension of loans. Includes payments from all sources of funds including current revenues and proceeds from borrowing and prior year fund balances. Includes intergovernmental transfers and expenditures for government owned utilities and other commercial or auxiliary enterprise, and insurance trust expenditures.

State and Local Government Direct General Expenditures in 2013

National Total = $2,639,728,963,000*

ALPHA ORDER

RANK	STATE	EXPENDITURES	% of USA
24	Alabama	$36,239,383,000	1.4%
39	Alaska	13,566,156,000	0.5%
23	Arizona	41,310,180,000	1.6%
33	Arkansas	21,426,843,000	0.8%
1	California	361,925,163,000	13.7%
22	Colorado	41,358,346,000	1.6%
26	Connecticut	34,903,862,000	1.3%
45	Delaware	9,405,869,000	0.4%
4	Florida	134,866,755,000	5.1%
13	Georgia	65,267,254,000	2.5%
40	Hawaii	12,308,513,000	0.5%
42	Idaho	10,360,853,000	0.4%
6	Illinois	107,508,949,000	4.1%
18	Indiana	46,801,710,000	1.8%
29	Iowa	27,945,223,000	1.1%
32	Kansas	23,263,029,000	0.9%
28	Kentucky	32,001,953,000	1.2%
21	Louisiana	42,029,526,000	1.6%
41	Maine	11,116,839,000	0.4%
15	Maryland	52,690,523,000	2.0%
11	Massachusetts	65,732,817,000	2.5%
9	Michigan	74,701,665,000	2.8%
16	Minnesota	49,238,065,000	1.9%
31	Mississippi	23,963,270,000	0.9%
19	Missouri	43,624,126,000	1.7%
46	Montana	8,197,323,000	0.3%
37	Nebraska	15,367,289,000	0.6%
36	Nevada	18,126,737,000	0.7%
43	New Hampshire	9,984,176,000	0.4%
8	New Jersey	83,871,785,000	3.2%
35	New Mexico	18,190,316,000	0.7%
2	New York	244,723,886,000	9.3%
10	North Carolina	73,098,434,000	2.8%
48	North Dakota	7,457,949,000	0.3%
7	Ohio	93,034,688,000	3.5%
30	Oklahoma	27,301,462,000	1.0%
27	Oregon	32,203,065,000	1.2%
5	Pennsylvania	109,848,970,000	4.2%
44	Rhode Island	9,430,522,000	0.4%
25	South Carolina	35,049,710,000	1.3%
50	South Dakota	6,215,850,000	0.2%
20	Tennessee	42,732,652,000	1.6%
3	Texas	187,242,949,000	7.1%
34	Utah	21,257,316,000	0.8%
49	Vermont	6,566,374,000	0.2%
12	Virginia	65,558,194,000	2.5%
14	Washington	59,513,021,000	2.3%
38	West Virginia	14,684,925,000	0.6%
17	Wisconsin	47,194,955,000	1.8%
47	Wyoming	7,762,819,000	0.3%

RANK ORDER

RANK	STATE	EXPENDITURES	% of USA
1	California	$361,925,163,000	13.7%
2	New York	244,723,886,000	9.3%
3	Texas	187,242,949,000	7.1%
4	Florida	134,866,755,000	5.1%
5	Pennsylvania	109,848,970,000	4.2%
6	Illinois	107,508,949,000	4.1%
7	Ohio	93,034,688,000	3.5%
8	New Jersey	83,871,785,000	3.2%
9	Michigan	74,701,665,000	2.8%
10	North Carolina	73,098,434,000	2.8%
11	Massachusetts	65,732,817,000	2.5%
12	Virginia	65,558,194,000	2.5%
13	Georgia	65,267,254,000	2.5%
14	Washington	59,513,021,000	2.3%
15	Maryland	52,690,523,000	2.0%
16	Minnesota	49,238,065,000	1.9%
17	Wisconsin	47,194,955,000	1.8%
18	Indiana	46,801,710,000	1.8%
19	Missouri	43,624,126,000	1.7%
20	Tennessee	42,732,652,000	1.6%
21	Louisiana	42,029,526,000	1.6%
22	Colorado	41,358,346,000	1.6%
23	Arizona	41,310,180,000	1.6%
24	Alabama	36,239,383,000	1.4%
25	South Carolina	35,049,710,000	1.3%
26	Connecticut	34,903,862,000	1.3%
27	Oregon	32,203,065,000	1.2%
28	Kentucky	32,001,953,000	1.2%
29	Iowa	27,945,223,000	1.1%
30	Oklahoma	27,301,462,000	1.0%
31	Mississippi	23,963,270,000	0.9%
32	Kansas	23,263,029,000	0.9%
33	Arkansas	21,426,843,000	0.8%
34	Utah	21,257,316,000	0.8%
35	New Mexico	18,190,316,000	0.7%
36	Nevada	18,126,737,000	0.7%
37	Nebraska	15,367,289,000	0.6%
38	West Virginia	14,684,925,000	0.6%
39	Alaska	13,566,156,000	0.5%
40	Hawaii	12,308,513,000	0.5%
41	Maine	11,116,839,000	0.4%
42	Idaho	10,360,853,000	0.4%
43	New Hampshire	9,984,176,000	0.4%
44	Rhode Island	9,430,522,000	0.4%
45	Delaware	9,405,869,000	0.4%
46	Montana	8,197,323,000	0.3%
47	Wyoming	7,762,819,000	0.3%
48	North Dakota	7,457,949,000	0.3%
49	Vermont	6,566,374,000	0.2%
50	South Dakota	6,215,850,000	0.2%
	District of Columbia	11,556,724,000	0.4%

Source: U.S. Bureau of the Census, Governments Division
    "2013 State and Local Government Finances" (http://www.census.gov/govs/local/)
*Direct general expenditures include expenditures for current operations, assistance and subsidies, interest on debt, and capital outlay. Excludes intergovernmental transfers, expenditures for government owned utilities and other commercial or auxiliary enterprise, and insurance trust expenditures.

Per Capita State and Local Government Direct General Expenditures in 2013

National Per Capita = $8,342*

ALPHA ORDER

RANK	STATE	PER CAPITA
34	Alabama	$7,502
1	Alaska	18,396
50	Arizona	6,230
40	Arkansas	7,244
9	California	9,422
31	Colorado	7,846
8	Connecticut	9,703
6	Delaware	10,165
45	Florida	6,883
47	Georgia	6,532
16	Hawaii	8,737
49	Idaho	6,424
21	Illinois	8,341
42	Indiana	7,123
13	Iowa	9,037
27	Kansas	8,037
39	Kentucky	7,276
12	Louisiana	9,083
20	Maine	8,366
15	Maryland	8,876
7	Massachusetts	9,798
33	Michigan	7,545
11	Minnesota	9,084
28	Mississippi	8,012
41	Missouri	7,218
25	Montana	8,081
22	Nebraska	8,221
48	Nevada	6,496
32	New Hampshire	7,549
10	New Jersey	9,416
17	New Mexico	8,716
3	New York	12,428
35	North Carolina	7,425
5	North Dakota	10,306
26	Ohio	8,039
43	Oklahoma	7,085
24	Oregon	8,198
18	Pennsylvania	8,593
14	Rhode Island	8,957
37	South Carolina	7,350
36	South Dakota	7,354
46	Tennessee	6,578
44	Texas	7,066
38	Utah	7,321
4	Vermont	10,471
29	Virginia	7,929
19	Washington	8,534
30	West Virginia	7,925
23	Wisconsin	8,217
2	Wyoming	13,312

RANK ORDER

RANK	STATE	PER CAPITA
1	Alaska	$18,396
2	Wyoming	13,312
3	New York	12,428
4	Vermont	10,471
5	North Dakota	10,306
6	Delaware	10,165
7	Massachusetts	9,798
8	Connecticut	9,703
9	California	9,422
10	New Jersey	9,416
11	Minnesota	9,084
12	Louisiana	9,083
13	Iowa	9,037
14	Rhode Island	8,957
15	Maryland	8,876
16	Hawaii	8,737
17	New Mexico	8,716
18	Pennsylvania	8,593
19	Washington	8,534
20	Maine	8,366
21	Illinois	8,341
22	Nebraska	8,221
23	Wisconsin	8,217
24	Oregon	8,198
25	Montana	8,081
26	Ohio	8,039
27	Kansas	8,037
28	Mississippi	8,012
29	Virginia	7,929
30	West Virginia	7,925
31	Colorado	7,846
32	New Hampshire	7,549
33	Michigan	7,545
34	Alabama	7,502
35	North Carolina	7,425
36	South Dakota	7,354
37	South Carolina	7,350
38	Utah	7,321
39	Kentucky	7,276
40	Arkansas	7,244
41	Missouri	7,218
42	Indiana	7,123
43	Oklahoma	7,085
44	Texas	7,066
45	Florida	6,883
46	Tennessee	6,578
47	Georgia	6,532
48	Nevada	6,496
49	Idaho	6,424
50	Arizona	6,230
	District of Columbia	17,792

Source: CQ Press using data from U.S. Bureau of the Census, Governments Division "2013 State and Local Government Finances" (http://www.census.gov/govs/local/)

*Direct general expenditures include expenditures for current operations, assistance and subsidies, interest on debt, and capital outlay. Excludes intergovernmental transfers, expenditures for government owned utilities and other commercial or auxiliary enterprise, and insurance trust expenditures.

State and Local Government Debt Outstanding in 2013

National Total = $2,954,722,052,000*

ALPHA ORDER

RANK	STATE	DEBT	% of USA
28	Alabama	$31,620,925,000	1.1%
42	Alaska	9,615,550,000	0.3%
18	Arizona	48,660,963,000	1.6%
37	Arkansas	14,150,578,000	0.5%
1	California	420,283,803,000	14.2%
14	Colorado	53,198,127,000	1.8%
22	Connecticut	43,374,345,000	1.5%
44	Delaware	8,332,959,000	0.3%
5	Florida	146,427,382,000	5.0%
13	Georgia	55,679,279,000	1.9%
36	Hawaii	14,299,877,000	0.5%
45	Idaho	5,878,981,000	0.2%
4	Illinois	148,688,795,000	5.0%
16	Indiana	49,410,078,000	1.7%
33	Iowa	18,497,531,000	0.6%
30	Kansas	25,835,557,000	0.9%
24	Kentucky	41,694,574,000	1.4%
25	Louisiana	39,032,085,000	1.3%
43	Maine	8,405,987,000	0.3%
17	Maryland	48,900,843,000	1.7%
8	Massachusetts	95,353,347,000	3.2%
11	Michigan	76,315,075,000	2.6%
19	Minnesota	48,041,557,000	1.6%
38	Mississippi	14,130,863,000	0.5%
20	Missouri	45,574,074,000	1.5%
47	Montana	5,306,828,000	0.2%
35	Nebraska	14,969,244,000	0.5%
29	Nevada	26,803,967,000	0.9%
40	New Hampshire	11,431,139,000	0.4%
7	New Jersey	100,956,778,000	3.4%
34	New Mexico	16,325,689,000	0.6%
2	New York	346,238,031,000	11.7%
15	North Carolina	51,523,898,000	1.7%
48	North Dakota	4,658,980,000	0.2%
9	Ohio	82,483,154,000	2.8%
32	Oklahoma	18,876,298,000	0.6%
27	Oregon	34,795,871,000	1.2%
6	Pennsylvania	130,237,853,000	4.4%
39	Rhode Island	12,310,381,000	0.4%
23	South Carolina	42,313,778,000	1.4%
46	South Dakota	5,878,042,000	0.2%
26	Tennessee	36,811,078,000	1.2%
3	Texas	264,722,521,000	9.0%
31	Utah	19,624,986,000	0.7%
49	Vermont	4,544,926,000	0.2%
12	Virginia	65,472,437,000	2.2%
10	Washington	77,294,131,000	2.6%
41	West Virginia	10,899,714,000	0.4%
21	Wisconsin	44,435,936,000	1.5%
50	Wyoming	1,994,509,000	0.1%

RANK ORDER

RANK	STATE	DEBT	% of USA
1	California	$420,283,803,000	14.2%
2	New York	346,238,031,000	11.7%
3	Texas	264,722,521,000	9.0%
4	Illinois	148,688,795,000	5.0%
5	Florida	146,427,382,000	5.0%
6	Pennsylvania	130,237,853,000	4.4%
7	New Jersey	100,956,778,000	3.4%
8	Massachusetts	95,353,347,000	3.2%
9	Ohio	82,483,154,000	2.8%
10	Washington	77,294,131,000	2.6%
11	Michigan	76,315,075,000	2.6%
12	Virginia	65,472,437,000	2.2%
13	Georgia	55,679,279,000	1.9%
14	Colorado	53,198,127,000	1.8%
15	North Carolina	51,523,898,000	1.7%
16	Indiana	49,410,078,000	1.7%
17	Maryland	48,900,843,000	1.7%
18	Arizona	48,660,963,000	1.6%
19	Minnesota	48,041,557,000	1.6%
20	Missouri	45,574,074,000	1.5%
21	Wisconsin	44,435,936,000	1.5%
22	Connecticut	43,374,345,000	1.5%
23	South Carolina	42,313,778,000	1.4%
24	Kentucky	41,694,574,000	1.4%
25	Louisiana	39,032,085,000	1.3%
26	Tennessee	36,811,078,000	1.2%
27	Oregon	34,795,871,000	1.2%
28	Alabama	31,620,925,000	1.1%
29	Nevada	26,803,967,000	0.9%
30	Kansas	25,835,557,000	0.9%
31	Utah	19,624,986,000	0.7%
32	Oklahoma	18,876,298,000	0.6%
33	Iowa	18,497,531,000	0.6%
34	New Mexico	16,325,689,000	0.6%
35	Nebraska	14,969,244,000	0.5%
36	Hawaii	14,299,877,000	0.5%
37	Arkansas	14,150,578,000	0.5%
38	Mississippi	14,130,863,000	0.5%
39	Rhode Island	12,310,381,000	0.4%
40	New Hampshire	11,431,139,000	0.4%
41	West Virginia	10,899,714,000	0.4%
42	Alaska	9,615,550,000	0.3%
43	Maine	8,405,987,000	0.3%
44	Delaware	8,332,959,000	0.3%
45	Idaho	5,878,981,000	0.2%
46	South Dakota	5,878,042,000	0.2%
47	Montana	5,306,828,000	0.2%
48	North Dakota	4,658,980,000	0.2%
49	Vermont	4,544,926,000	0.2%
50	Wyoming	1,994,509,000	0.1%
	District of Columbia	12,408,748,000	0.4%

Source: U.S. Bureau of the Census, Governments Division
"2013 State and Local Government Finances" (http://www.census.gov/govs/local/)
*Includes short-term, long-term, full faith and credit, nonguaranteed, and public debt for private purposes.

Per Capita State and Local Government Debt Outstanding in 2013

National Per Capita = $9,338*

ALPHA ORDER

RANK	STATE	PER CAPITA
37	Alabama	$6,546
3	Alaska	13,039
32	Arizona	7,339
47	Arkansas	4,784
9	California	10,941
12	Colorado	10,092
4	Connecticut	12,058
16	Delaware	9,005
31	Florida	7,473
43	Georgia	5,573
11	Hawaii	10,151
49	Idaho	3,645
6	Illinois	11,536
30	Indiana	7,520
40	Iowa	5,982
17	Kansas	8,925
15	Kentucky	9,479
22	Louisiana	8,435
39	Maine	6,326
23	Maryland	8,238
2	Massachusetts	14,213
28	Michigan	7,708
19	Minnesota	8,863
48	Mississippi	4,724
29	Missouri	7,541
45	Montana	5,231
24	Nebraska	8,008
14	Nevada	9,606
21	New Hampshire	8,643
7	New Jersey	11,334
26	New Mexico	7,823
1	New York	17,584
44	North Carolina	5,233
38	North Dakota	6,438
34	Ohio	7,128
46	Oklahoma	4,899
20	Oregon	8,858
10	Pennsylvania	10,188
5	Rhode Island	11,692
18	South Carolina	8,874
35	South Dakota	6,954
42	Tennessee	5,667
13	Texas	9,989
36	Utah	6,759
33	Vermont	7,247
25	Virginia	7,919
8	Washington	11,084
41	West Virginia	5,882
27	Wisconsin	7,737
50	Wyoming	3,420

RANK ORDER

RANK	STATE	PER CAPITA
1	New York	$17,584
2	Massachusetts	14,213
3	Alaska	13,039
4	Connecticut	12,058
5	Rhode Island	11,692
6	Illinois	11,536
7	New Jersey	11,334
8	Washington	11,084
9	California	10,941
10	Pennsylvania	10,188
11	Hawaii	10,151
12	Colorado	10,092
13	Texas	9,989
14	Nevada	9,606
15	Kentucky	9,479
16	Delaware	9,005
17	Kansas	8,925
18	South Carolina	8,874
19	Minnesota	8,863
20	Oregon	8,858
21	New Hampshire	8,643
22	Louisiana	8,435
23	Maryland	8,238
24	Nebraska	8,008
25	Virginia	7,919
26	New Mexico	7,823
27	Wisconsin	7,737
28	Michigan	7,708
29	Missouri	7,541
30	Indiana	7,520
31	Florida	7,473
32	Arizona	7,339
33	Vermont	7,247
34	Ohio	7,128
35	South Dakota	6,954
36	Utah	6,759
37	Alabama	6,546
38	North Dakota	6,438
39	Maine	6,326
40	Iowa	5,982
41	West Virginia	5,882
42	Tennessee	5,667
43	Georgia	5,573
44	North Carolina	5,233
45	Montana	5,231
46	Oklahoma	4,899
47	Arkansas	4,784
48	Mississippi	4,724
49	Idaho	3,645
50	Wyoming	3,420
	District of Columbia	19,104

Source: CQ Press using data from U.S. Bureau of the Census, Governments Division
"2013 State and Local Government Finances" (http://www.census.gov/govs/local/)
*Includes short-term, long-term, full faith and credit, nonguaranteed, and public debt for private purposes.

State and Local Government Full-Time Equivalent Employees in 2014

National Total = 16,188,581 FTE Employees*

ALPHA ORDER

RANK	STATE	EMPLOYEES	% of USA
20	Alabama	283,141	1.7%
44	Alaska	54,435	0.3%
19	Arizona	287,144	1.8%
33	Arkansas	167,493	1.0%
1	California	1,752,729	10.8%
22	Colorado	280,486	1.7%
30	Connecticut	190,660	1.2%
46	Delaware	49,042	0.3%
4	Florida	863,896	5.3%
9	Georgia	508,642	3.1%
40	Hawaii	74,920	0.5%
39	Idaho	80,704	0.5%
5	Illinois	628,231	3.9%
16	Indiana	318,963	2.0%
32	Iowa	181,805	1.1%
28	Kansas	195,140	1.2%
26	Kentucky	242,987	1.5%
24	Louisiana	262,918	1.6%
42	Maine	70,717	0.4%
18	Maryland	301,853	1.9%
14	Massachusetts	329,701	2.0%
12	Michigan	437,560	2.7%
21	Minnesota	282,992	1.7%
29	Mississippi	192,077	1.2%
17	Missouri	316,651	2.0%
43	Montana	57,077	0.4%
36	Nebraska	118,556	0.7%
37	Nevada	109,862	0.7%
41	New Hampshire	71,316	0.4%
10	New Jersey	475,254	2.9%
35	New Mexico	125,761	0.8%
3	New York	1,166,793	7.2%
8	North Carolina	549,747	3.4%
48	North Dakota	45,825	0.3%
6	Ohio	578,629	3.6%
27	Oklahoma	215,278	1.3%
31	Oregon	190,330	1.2%
7	Pennsylvania	569,375	3.5%
47	Rhode Island	47,922	0.3%
25	South Carolina	256,341	1.6%
49	South Dakota	45,382	0.3%
15	Tennessee	323,676	2.0%
2	Texas	1,436,297	8.9%
34	Utah	140,418	0.9%
50	Vermont	39,900	0.2%
11	Virginia	447,594	2.8%
13	Washington	341,924	2.1%
38	West Virginia	103,675	0.6%
23	Wisconsin	279,515	1.7%
45	Wyoming	51,003	0.3%

RANK ORDER

RANK	STATE	EMPLOYEES	% of USA
1	California	1,752,729	10.8%
2	Texas	1,436,297	8.9%
3	New York	1,166,793	7.2%
4	Florida	863,896	5.3%
5	Illinois	628,231	3.9%
6	Ohio	578,629	3.6%
7	Pennsylvania	569,375	3.5%
8	North Carolina	549,747	3.4%
9	Georgia	508,642	3.1%
10	New Jersey	475,254	2.9%
11	Virginia	447,594	2.8%
12	Michigan	437,560	2.7%
13	Washington	341,924	2.1%
14	Massachusetts	329,701	2.0%
15	Tennessee	323,676	2.0%
16	Indiana	318,963	2.0%
17	Missouri	316,651	2.0%
18	Maryland	301,853	1.9%
19	Arizona	287,144	1.8%
20	Alabama	283,141	1.7%
21	Minnesota	282,992	1.7%
22	Colorado	280,486	1.7%
23	Wisconsin	279,515	1.7%
24	Louisiana	262,918	1.6%
25	South Carolina	256,341	1.6%
26	Kentucky	242,987	1.5%
27	Oklahoma	215,278	1.3%
28	Kansas	195,140	1.2%
29	Mississippi	192,077	1.2%
30	Connecticut	190,660	1.2%
31	Oregon	190,330	1.2%
32	Iowa	181,805	1.1%
33	Arkansas	167,493	1.0%
34	Utah	140,418	0.9%
35	New Mexico	125,761	0.8%
36	Nebraska	118,556	0.7%
37	Nevada	109,862	0.7%
38	West Virginia	103,675	0.6%
39	Idaho	80,704	0.5%
40	Hawaii	74,920	0.5%
41	New Hampshire	71,316	0.4%
42	Maine	70,717	0.4%
43	Montana	57,077	0.4%
44	Alaska	54,435	0.3%
45	Wyoming	51,003	0.3%
46	Delaware	49,042	0.3%
47	Rhode Island	47,922	0.3%
48	North Dakota	45,825	0.3%
49	South Dakota	45,382	0.3%
50	Vermont	39,900	0.2%
	District of Columbia	46,244	0.3%

Source: U.S. Bureau of the Census, Governments Division
"Government Employment and Payroll" (http://www.census.gov/govs/apes/index.html)
*Full-time equivalent as of March 2014.

Rate of State and Local Government Full-Time Equivalent Employees in 2014

National Rate = 508 FTE Employees per 10,000 Population*

ALPHA ORDER

RANK	STATE	RATE
11	Alabama	584
2	Alaska	739
49	Arizona	427
13	Arkansas	565
45	California	452
28	Colorado	524
26	Connecticut	530
28	Delaware	524
48	Florida	434
33	Georgia	504
27	Hawaii	528
35	Idaho	494
37	Illinois	488
41	Indiana	483
10	Iowa	585
3	Kansas	672
18	Kentucky	551
12	Louisiana	566
21	Maine	532
32	Maryland	505
37	Massachusetts	488
47	Michigan	441
31	Minnesota	519
4	Mississippi	642
30	Missouri	522
15	Montana	558
6	Nebraska	630
50	Nevada	387
19	New Hampshire	537
21	New Jersey	532
8	New Mexico	603
9	New York	591
17	North Carolina	553
7	North Dakota	619
34	Ohio	499
16	Oklahoma	555
42	Oregon	479
46	Pennsylvania	445
44	Rhode Island	454
25	South Carolina	531
21	South Dakota	532
35	Tennessee	494
21	Texas	532
43	Utah	477
5	Vermont	637
19	Virginia	537
40	Washington	484
14	West Virginia	561
39	Wisconsin	485
1	Wyoming	873

RANK ORDER

RANK	STATE	RATE
1	Wyoming	873
2	Alaska	739
3	Kansas	672
4	Mississippi	642
5	Vermont	637
6	Nebraska	630
7	North Dakota	619
8	New Mexico	603
9	New York	591
10	Iowa	585
11	Alabama	584
12	Louisiana	566
13	Arkansas	565
14	West Virginia	561
15	Montana	558
16	Oklahoma	555
17	North Carolina	553
18	Kentucky	551
19	New Hampshire	537
19	Virginia	537
21	Maine	532
21	New Jersey	532
21	South Dakota	532
21	Texas	532
25	South Carolina	531
26	Connecticut	530
27	Hawaii	528
28	Colorado	524
28	Delaware	524
30	Missouri	522
31	Minnesota	519
32	Maryland	505
33	Georgia	504
34	Ohio	499
35	Idaho	494
35	Tennessee	494
37	Illinois	488
37	Massachusetts	488
39	Wisconsin	485
40	Washington	484
41	Indiana	483
42	Oregon	479
43	Utah	477
44	Rhode Island	454
45	California	452
46	Pennsylvania	445
47	Michigan	441
48	Florida	434
49	Arizona	427
50	Nevada	387
	District of Columbia	701

Source: CQ Press using data from U.S. Bureau of the Census, Governments Division
  "Government Employment and Payroll" (http://www.census.gov/govs/apes/index.html)
*Full-time equivalent as of March 2014.

Average Annual Earnings of Full-Time State and Local Government Employees in 2014
National Average = $56,293*

ALPHA ORDER

RANK	STATE	SALARY
42	Alabama	$44,375
6	Alaska	65,541
23	Arizona	52,565
48	Arkansas	41,959
1	California	76,431
16	Colorado	56,848
4	Connecticut	69,231
18	Delaware	56,077
30	Florida	49,180
46	Georgia	43,409
20	Hawaii	55,074
38	Idaho	45,208
11	Illinois	62,335
36	Indiana	46,702
17	Iowa	56,417
37	Kansas	45,801
43	Kentucky	44,110
40	Louisiana	44,635
35	Maine	46,765
10	Maryland	62,552
8	Massachusetts	63,322
14	Michigan	58,742
12	Minnesota	59,886
50	Mississippi	39,602
45	Missouri	43,527
32	Montana	47,986
29	Nebraska	50,509
9	Nevada	62,832
24	New Hampshire	52,463
2	New Jersey	71,692
34	New Mexico	46,867
3	New York	69,626
33	North Carolina	47,849
28	North Dakota	50,914
21	Ohio	53,022
47	Oklahoma	42,144
13	Oregon	58,910
15	Pennsylvania	57,181
7	Rhode Island	64,918
39	South Carolina	45,183
44	South Dakota	43,631
41	Tennessee	44,590
31	Texas	48,657
27	Utah	51,613
25	Vermont	52,355
26	Virginia	52,100
5	Washington	67,856
49	West Virginia	41,827
19	Wisconsin	55,995
22	Wyoming	52,775

RANK ORDER

RANK	STATE	SALARY
1	California	$76,431
2	New Jersey	71,692
3	New York	69,626
4	Connecticut	69,231
5	Washington	67,856
6	Alaska	65,541
7	Rhode Island	64,918
8	Massachusetts	63,322
9	Nevada	62,832
10	Maryland	62,552
11	Illinois	62,335
12	Minnesota	59,886
13	Oregon	58,910
14	Michigan	58,742
15	Pennsylvania	57,181
16	Colorado	56,848
17	Iowa	56,417
18	Delaware	56,077
19	Wisconsin	55,995
20	Hawaii	55,074
21	Ohio	53,022
22	Wyoming	52,775
23	Arizona	52,565
24	New Hampshire	52,463
25	Vermont	52,355
26	Virginia	52,100
27	Utah	51,613
28	North Dakota	50,914
29	Nebraska	50,509
30	Florida	49,180
31	Texas	48,657
32	Montana	47,986
33	North Carolina	47,849
34	New Mexico	46,867
35	Maine	46,765
36	Indiana	46,702
37	Kansas	45,801
38	Idaho	45,208
39	South Carolina	45,183
40	Louisiana	44,635
41	Tennessee	44,590
42	Alabama	44,375
43	Kentucky	44,110
44	South Dakota	43,631
45	Missouri	43,527
46	Georgia	43,409
47	Oklahoma	42,144
48	Arkansas	41,959
49	West Virginia	41,827
50	Mississippi	39,602
	District of Columbia	78,512

Source: CQ Press using data from U.S. Bureau of the Census, Governments Division "Government Employment and Payroll" (http://www.census.gov/govs/apes/index.html)
*March 2014 full-time payroll (multiplied by 12) divided by full-time employees.

State Government Total Revenue in 2013

National Total = $2,193,443,291,000*

ALPHA ORDER

RANK	STATE	REVENUE	% of USA
27	Alabama	$29,092,950,000	1.3%
38	Alaska	14,020,580,000	0.6%
20	Arizona	36,947,686,000	1.7%
32	Arkansas	21,541,707,000	1.0%
1	California	316,235,067,000	14.4%
25	Colorado	31,004,478,000	1.4%
22	Connecticut	31,852,785,000	1.5%
43	Delaware	8,937,707,000	0.4%
4	Florida	95,222,070,000	4.3%
12	Georgia	53,510,459,000	2.4%
39	Hawaii	12,944,952,000	0.6%
42	Idaho	9,391,142,000	0.4%
7	Illinois	84,493,376,000	3.9%
18	Indiana	38,141,709,000	1.7%
30	Iowa	23,123,901,000	1.1%
34	Kansas	18,013,265,000	0.8%
28	Kentucky	28,607,106,000	1.3%
24	Louisiana	31,472,244,000	1.4%
41	Maine	9,571,311,000	0.4%
17	Maryland	41,802,233,000	1.9%
11	Massachusetts	55,451,223,000	2.5%
9	Michigan	66,401,159,000	3.0%
15	Minnesota	46,561,172,000	2.1%
31	Mississippi	21,865,219,000	1.0%
19	Missouri	37,535,142,000	1.7%
47	Montana	8,007,799,000	0.4%
40	Nebraska	11,484,492,000	0.5%
36	Nevada	17,040,569,000	0.8%
46	New Hampshire	8,163,715,000	0.4%
8	New Jersey	67,982,088,000	3.1%
35	New Mexico	17,808,300,000	0.8%
2	New York	188,460,985,000	8.6%
10	North Carolina	60,004,493,000	2.7%
44	North Dakota	8,848,268,000	0.4%
5	Ohio	90,385,483,000	4.1%
29	Oklahoma	26,344,587,000	1.2%
21	Oregon	32,914,634,000	1.5%
6	Pennsylvania	87,910,876,000	4.0%
45	Rhode Island	8,681,540,000	0.4%
26	South Carolina	29,638,637,000	1.4%
50	South Dakota	5,759,268,000	0.3%
23	Tennessee	31,718,284,000	1.4%
3	Texas	136,985,717,000	6.2%
33	Utah	18,442,304,000	0.8%
49	Vermont	6,295,755,000	0.3%
13	Virginia	50,851,769,000	2.3%
14	Washington	47,862,480,000	2.2%
37	West Virginia	14,593,283,000	0.7%
16	Wisconsin	45,891,806,000	2.1%
48	Wyoming	7,625,516,000	0.3%

RANK ORDER

RANK	STATE	REVENUE	% of USA
1	California	$316,235,067,000	14.4%
2	New York	188,460,985,000	8.6%
3	Texas	136,985,717,000	6.2%
4	Florida	95,222,070,000	4.3%
5	Ohio	90,385,483,000	4.1%
6	Pennsylvania	87,910,876,000	4.0%
7	Illinois	84,493,376,000	3.9%
8	New Jersey	67,982,088,000	3.1%
9	Michigan	66,401,159,000	3.0%
10	North Carolina	60,004,493,000	2.7%
11	Massachusetts	55,451,223,000	2.5%
12	Georgia	53,510,459,000	2.4%
13	Virginia	50,851,769,000	2.3%
14	Washington	47,862,480,000	2.2%
15	Minnesota	46,561,172,000	2.1%
16	Wisconsin	45,891,806,000	2.1%
17	Maryland	41,802,233,000	1.9%
18	Indiana	38,141,709,000	1.7%
19	Missouri	37,535,142,000	1.7%
20	Arizona	36,947,686,000	1.7%
21	Oregon	32,914,634,000	1.5%
22	Connecticut	31,852,785,000	1.5%
23	Tennessee	31,718,284,000	1.4%
24	Louisiana	31,472,244,000	1.4%
25	Colorado	31,004,478,000	1.4%
26	South Carolina	29,638,637,000	1.4%
27	Alabama	29,092,950,000	1.3%
28	Kentucky	28,607,106,000	1.3%
29	Oklahoma	26,344,587,000	1.2%
30	Iowa	23,123,901,000	1.1%
31	Mississippi	21,865,219,000	1.0%
32	Arkansas	21,541,707,000	1.0%
33	Utah	18,442,304,000	0.8%
34	Kansas	18,013,265,000	0.8%
35	New Mexico	17,808,300,000	0.8%
36	Nevada	17,040,569,000	0.8%
37	West Virginia	14,593,283,000	0.7%
38	Alaska	14,020,580,000	0.6%
39	Hawaii	12,944,952,000	0.6%
40	Nebraska	11,484,492,000	0.5%
41	Maine	9,571,311,000	0.4%
42	Idaho	9,391,142,000	0.4%
43	Delaware	8,937,707,000	0.4%
44	North Dakota	8,848,268,000	0.4%
45	Rhode Island	8,681,540,000	0.4%
46	New Hampshire	8,163,715,000	0.4%
47	Montana	8,007,799,000	0.4%
48	Wyoming	7,625,516,000	0.3%
49	Vermont	6,295,755,000	0.3%
50	South Dakota	5,759,268,000	0.3%
	District of Columbia**	NA	NA

Source: U.S. Bureau of the Census, Governments Division
"2012 Census of Governments" (http://www.census.gov/govs/local/)
*Total revenue includes all money received from external sources. This includes taxes, intergovernmental transfers and insurance trust revenue, and revenue from government owned utilities and other commercial or auxiliary enterprise.
**Not applicable.

Per Capita State Government Total Revenue in 2013

National Per Capita = $6,946*

ALPHA ORDER				RANK ORDER		
RANK	STATE	PER CAPITA		RANK	STATE	PER CAPITA
42	Alabama	$6,023		1	Alaska	$19,012
1	Alaska	19,012		2	Wyoming	13,077
46	Arizona	5,572		3	North Dakota	12,228
22	Arkansas	7,283		4	Vermont	10,039
14	California	8,232		5	Delaware	9,659
43	Colorado	5,882		6	New York	9,571
8	Connecticut	8,855		7	Hawaii	9,189
5	Delaware	9,659		8	Connecticut	8,855
50	Florida	4,860		9	Minnesota	8,590
47	Georgia	5,356		10	New Mexico	8,533
7	Hawaii	9,189		11	Oregon	8,379
44	Idaho	5,823		12	Massachusetts	8,265
31	Illinois	6,555		13	Rhode Island	8,246
45	Indiana	5,805		14	California	8,232
20	Iowa	7,478		15	Wisconsin	7,990
34	Kansas	6,223		16	Montana	7,894
32	Kentucky	6,504		17	West Virginia	7,876
29	Louisiana	6,801		18	Ohio	7,811
23	Maine	7,203		19	New Jersey	7,632
24	Maryland	7,042		20	Iowa	7,478
12	Massachusetts	8,265		21	Mississippi	7,310
30	Michigan	6,707		22	Arkansas	7,283
9	Minnesota	8,590		23	Maine	7,203
21	Mississippi	7,310		24	Maryland	7,042
36	Missouri	6,211		25	Pennsylvania	6,877
16	Montana	7,894		26	Washington	6,864
39	Nebraska	6,144		27	Oklahoma	6,837
40	Nevada	6,107		28	South Dakota	6,814
37	New Hampshire	6,172		29	Louisiana	6,801
19	New Jersey	7,632		30	Michigan	6,707
10	New Mexico	8,533		31	Illinois	6,555
6	New York	9,571		32	Kentucky	6,504
41	North Carolina	6,095		33	Utah	6,351
3	North Dakota	12,228		34	Kansas	6,223
18	Ohio	7,811		35	South Carolina	6,216
27	Oklahoma	6,837		36	Missouri	6,211
11	Oregon	8,379		37	New Hampshire	6,172
25	Pennsylvania	6,877		38	Virginia	6,151
13	Rhode Island	8,246		39	Nebraska	6,144
35	South Carolina	6,216		40	Nevada	6,107
28	South Dakota	6,814		41	North Carolina	6,095
49	Tennessee	4,883		42	Alabama	6,023
48	Texas	5,169		43	Colorado	5,882
33	Utah	6,351		44	Idaho	5,823
4	Vermont	10,039		45	Indiana	5,805
38	Virginia	6,151		46	Arizona	5,572
26	Washington	6,864		47	Georgia	5,356
17	West Virginia	7,876		48	Texas	5,169
15	Wisconsin	7,990		49	Tennessee	4,883
2	Wyoming	13,077		50	Florida	4,860
					District of Columbia**	NA

Source: CQ Press using data from U.S. Bureau of the Census, Governments Division
"2012 Census of Governments" (http://www.census.gov/govs/local/)
*Total revenue includes all money received from external sources. This includes taxes, intergovernmental transfers and insurance trust revenue, and revenue from government owned utilities and other commercial or auxiliary enterprise.
**Not applicable.

State Government Intergovernmental Revenue in 2013

National Total = $527,066,355,000*

ALPHA ORDER

RANK	STATE	REVENUE	% of USA
23	Alabama	$8,338,033,000	1.6%
40	Alaska	2,754,412,000	0.5%
16	Arizona	10,580,523,000	2.0%
32	Arkansas	5,724,598,000	1.1%
1	California	58,096,373,000	11.0%
29	Colorado	6,508,932,000	1.2%
31	Connecticut	5,962,699,000	1.1%
46	Delaware	1,996,011,000	0.4%
4	Florida	23,880,229,000	4.5%
10	Georgia	14,619,221,000	2.8%
43	Hawaii	2,331,449,000	0.4%
41	Idaho	2,541,438,000	0.5%
8	Illinois	17,312,790,000	3.3%
13	Indiana	11,267,810,000	2.1%
30	Iowa	5,991,401,000	1.1%
36	Kansas	3,845,073,000	0.7%
24	Kentucky	8,083,482,000	1.5%
15	Louisiana	10,660,261,000	2.0%
39	Maine	2,830,353,000	0.5%
18	Maryland	10,325,181,000	2.0%
12	Massachusetts	13,706,498,000	2.6%
7	Michigan	18,007,780,000	3.4%
21	Minnesota	9,315,259,000	1.8%
26	Mississippi	7,649,292,000	1.5%
17	Missouri	10,497,449,000	2.0%
45	Montana	2,161,997,000	0.4%
37	Nebraska	3,212,304,000	0.6%
38	Nevada	3,080,240,000	0.6%
47	New Hampshire	1,883,424,000	0.4%
11	New Jersey	14,471,986,000	2.7%
33	New Mexico	5,416,068,000	1.0%
2	New York	47,284,329,000	9.0%
9	North Carolina	15,769,950,000	3.0%
50	North Dakota	1,572,480,000	0.3%
6	Ohio	21,113,847,000	4.0%
28	Oklahoma	7,159,511,000	1.4%
25	Oregon	8,003,252,000	1.5%
5	Pennsylvania	21,412,638,000	4.1%
42	Rhode Island	2,369,822,000	0.4%
27	South Carolina	7,202,824,000	1.4%
49	South Dakota	1,605,537,000	0.3%
14	Tennessee	10,900,626,000	2.1%
3	Texas	37,580,061,000	7.1%
35	Utah	4,304,061,000	0.8%
48	Vermont	1,872,013,000	0.4%
20	Virginia	9,959,041,000	1.9%
19	Washington	10,030,961,000	1.9%
34	West Virginia	4,325,052,000	0.8%
22	Wisconsin	9,228,907,000	1.8%
44	Wyoming	2,318,877,000	0.4%

RANK ORDER

RANK	STATE	REVENUE	% of USA
1	California	$58,096,373,000	11.0%
2	New York	47,284,329,000	9.0%
3	Texas	37,580,061,000	7.1%
4	Florida	23,880,229,000	4.5%
5	Pennsylvania	21,412,638,000	4.1%
6	Ohio	21,113,847,000	4.0%
7	Michigan	18,007,780,000	3.4%
8	Illinois	17,312,790,000	3.3%
9	North Carolina	15,769,950,000	3.0%
10	Georgia	14,619,221,000	2.8%
11	New Jersey	14,471,986,000	2.7%
12	Massachusetts	13,706,498,000	2.6%
13	Indiana	11,267,810,000	2.1%
14	Tennessee	10,900,626,000	2.1%
15	Louisiana	10,660,261,000	2.0%
16	Arizona	10,580,523,000	2.0%
17	Missouri	10,497,449,000	2.0%
18	Maryland	10,325,181,000	2.0%
19	Washington	10,030,961,000	1.9%
20	Virginia	9,959,041,000	1.9%
21	Minnesota	9,315,259,000	1.8%
22	Wisconsin	9,228,907,000	1.8%
23	Alabama	8,338,033,000	1.6%
24	Kentucky	8,083,482,000	1.5%
25	Oregon	8,003,252,000	1.5%
26	Mississippi	7,649,292,000	1.5%
27	South Carolina	7,202,824,000	1.4%
28	Oklahoma	7,159,511,000	1.4%
29	Colorado	6,508,932,000	1.2%
30	Iowa	5,991,401,000	1.1%
31	Connecticut	5,962,699,000	1.1%
32	Arkansas	5,724,598,000	1.1%
33	New Mexico	5,416,068,000	1.0%
34	West Virginia	4,325,052,000	0.8%
35	Utah	4,304,061,000	0.8%
36	Kansas	3,845,073,000	0.7%
37	Nebraska	3,212,304,000	0.6%
38	Nevada	3,080,240,000	0.6%
39	Maine	2,830,353,000	0.5%
40	Alaska	2,754,412,000	0.5%
41	Idaho	2,541,438,000	0.5%
42	Rhode Island	2,369,822,000	0.4%
43	Hawaii	2,331,449,000	0.4%
44	Wyoming	2,318,877,000	0.4%
45	Montana	2,161,997,000	0.4%
46	Delaware	1,996,011,000	0.4%
47	New Hampshire	1,883,424,000	0.4%
48	Vermont	1,872,013,000	0.4%
49	South Dakota	1,605,537,000	0.3%
50	North Dakota	1,572,480,000	0.3%
	District of Columbia**	NA	NA

Source: U.S. Bureau of the Census, Governments Division
 "2013 State and Local Government Finances" (http://www.census.gov/govs/local/)
*Includes revenue from federal and local government sources.
**Not applicable.

Per Capita State Government Intergovernmental Revenue in 2013

National Per Capita = $1,669*

ALPHA ORDER

RANK	STATE	PER CAPITA
25	Alabama	$1,726
2	Alaska	3,735
36	Arizona	1,596
17	Arkansas	1,935
38	California	1,512
47	Colorado	1,235
31	Connecticut	1,658
11	Delaware	2,157
48	Florida	1,219
41	Georgia	1,463
32	Hawaii	1,655
37	Idaho	1,576
45	Illinois	1,343
28	Indiana	1,715
16	Iowa	1,938
46	Kansas	1,328
20	Kentucky	1,838
8	Louisiana	2,304
13	Maine	2,130
23	Maryland	1,739
14	Massachusetts	2,043
22	Michigan	1,819
26	Minnesota	1,719
5	Mississippi	2,557
24	Missouri	1,737
12	Montana	2,131
27	Nebraska	1,718
50	Nevada	1,104
43	New Hampshire	1,424
33	New Jersey	1,625
4	New Mexico	2,595
6	New York	2,401
35	North Carolina	1,602
10	North Dakota	2,173
21	Ohio	1,825
19	Oklahoma	1,858
15	Oregon	2,037
30	Pennsylvania	1,675
9	Rhode Island	2,251
39	South Carolina	1,511
18	South Dakota	1,899
29	Tennessee	1,678
44	Texas	1,418
40	Utah	1,482
3	Vermont	2,985
49	Virginia	1,205
42	Washington	1,438
7	West Virginia	2,334
34	Wisconsin	1,607
1	Wyoming	3,977

RANK ORDER

RANK	STATE	PER CAPITA
1	Wyoming	$3,977
2	Alaska	3,735
3	Vermont	2,985
4	New Mexico	2,595
5	Mississippi	2,557
6	New York	2,401
7	West Virginia	2,334
8	Louisiana	2,304
9	Rhode Island	2,251
10	North Dakota	2,173
11	Delaware	2,157
12	Montana	2,131
13	Maine	2,130
14	Massachusetts	2,043
15	Oregon	2,037
16	Iowa	1,938
17	Arkansas	1,935
18	South Dakota	1,899
19	Oklahoma	1,858
20	Kentucky	1,838
21	Ohio	1,825
22	Michigan	1,819
23	Maryland	1,739
24	Missouri	1,737
25	Alabama	1,726
26	Minnesota	1,719
27	Nebraska	1,718
28	Indiana	1,715
29	Tennessee	1,678
30	Pennsylvania	1,675
31	Connecticut	1,658
32	Hawaii	1,655
33	New Jersey	1,625
34	Wisconsin	1,607
35	North Carolina	1,602
36	Arizona	1,596
37	Idaho	1,576
38	California	1,512
39	South Carolina	1,511
40	Utah	1,482
41	Georgia	1,463
42	Washington	1,438
43	New Hampshire	1,424
44	Texas	1,418
45	Illinois	1,343
46	Kansas	1,328
47	Colorado	1,235
48	Florida	1,219
49	Virginia	1,205
50	Nevada	1,104

District of Columbia**   NA

Source: CQ Press using data from U.S. Bureau of the Census, Governments Division
"2013 State and Local Government Finances" (http://www.census.gov/govs/local/)
*Includes revenue from federal and local government sources.
**Not applicable.

State Government Own Source Revenue in 2013

National Total = $1,158,679,491,000*

ALPHA ORDER

RANK	STATE	REVENUE	% of USA
28	Alabama	$14,421,612,000	1.2%
35	Alaska	9,525,903,000	0.8%
20	Arizona	18,595,751,000	1.6%
31	Arkansas	11,585,470,000	1.0%
1	California	161,596,347,000	13.9%
21	Colorado	16,620,348,000	1.4%
19	Connecticut	19,483,715,000	1.7%
42	Delaware	5,797,909,000	0.5%
4	Florida	50,845,694,000	4.4%
16	Georgia	23,796,038,000	2.1%
37	Hawaii	8,493,665,000	0.7%
44	Idaho	4,798,825,000	0.4%
6	Illinois	48,248,729,000	4.2%
18	Indiana	22,231,342,000	1.9%
30	Iowa	12,542,278,000	1.1%
32	Kansas	11,400,905,000	1.0%
25	Kentucky	14,843,124,000	1.3%
27	Louisiana	14,595,098,000	1.3%
43	Maine	5,160,626,000	0.4%
15	Maryland	24,454,140,000	2.1%
10	Massachusetts	32,473,820,000	2.8%
9	Michigan	36,335,514,000	3.1%
13	Minnesota	26,296,254,000	2.3%
34	Mississippi	9,861,240,000	0.9%
22	Missouri	16,164,587,000	1.4%
49	Montana	3,605,557,000	0.3%
40	Nebraska	6,607,023,000	0.6%
38	Nevada	8,322,156,000	0.7%
46	New Hampshire	4,249,015,000	0.4%
8	New Jersey	39,391,848,000	3.4%
36	New Mexico	8,879,293,000	0.8%
2	New York	93,518,424,000	8.1%
11	North Carolina	31,804,580,000	2.7%
41	North Dakota	6,487,449,000	0.6%
7	Ohio	39,831,671,000	3.4%
29	Oklahoma	13,640,191,000	1.2%
26	Oregon	14,829,764,000	1.3%
5	Pennsylvania	48,343,093,000	4.2%
45	Rhode Island	4,563,674,000	0.4%
24	South Carolina	14,958,035,000	1.3%
50	South Dakota	2,430,143,000	0.2%
23	Tennessee	15,863,120,000	1.4%
3	Texas	75,355,849,000	6.5%
33	Utah	10,506,594,000	0.9%
47	Vermont	3,763,196,000	0.3%
12	Virginia	31,181,368,000	2.7%
14	Washington	25,638,865,000	2.2%
39	West Virginia	8,077,544,000	0.7%
17	Wisconsin	23,051,930,000	2.0%
48	Wyoming	3,610,175,000	0.3%

RANK ORDER

RANK	STATE	REVENUE	% of USA
1	California	$161,596,347,000	13.9%
2	New York	93,518,424,000	8.1%
3	Texas	75,355,849,000	6.5%
4	Florida	50,845,694,000	4.4%
5	Pennsylvania	48,343,093,000	4.2%
6	Illinois	48,248,729,000	4.2%
7	Ohio	39,831,671,000	3.4%
8	New Jersey	39,391,848,000	3.4%
9	Michigan	36,335,514,000	3.1%
10	Massachusetts	32,473,820,000	2.8%
11	North Carolina	31,804,580,000	2.7%
12	Virginia	31,181,368,000	2.7%
13	Minnesota	26,296,254,000	2.3%
14	Washington	25,638,865,000	2.2%
15	Maryland	24,454,140,000	2.1%
16	Georgia	23,796,038,000	2.1%
17	Wisconsin	23,051,930,000	2.0%
18	Indiana	22,231,342,000	1.9%
19	Connecticut	19,483,715,000	1.7%
20	Arizona	18,595,751,000	1.6%
21	Colorado	16,620,348,000	1.4%
22	Missouri	16,164,587,000	1.4%
23	Tennessee	15,863,120,000	1.4%
24	South Carolina	14,958,035,000	1.3%
25	Kentucky	14,843,124,000	1.3%
26	Oregon	14,829,764,000	1.3%
27	Louisiana	14,595,098,000	1.3%
28	Alabama	14,421,612,000	1.2%
29	Oklahoma	13,640,191,000	1.2%
30	Iowa	12,542,278,000	1.1%
31	Arkansas	11,585,470,000	1.0%
32	Kansas	11,400,905,000	1.0%
33	Utah	10,506,594,000	0.9%
34	Mississippi	9,861,240,000	0.9%
35	Alaska	9,525,903,000	0.8%
36	New Mexico	8,879,293,000	0.8%
37	Hawaii	8,493,665,000	0.7%
38	Nevada	8,322,156,000	0.7%
39	West Virginia	8,077,544,000	0.7%
40	Nebraska	6,607,023,000	0.6%
41	North Dakota	6,487,449,000	0.6%
42	Delaware	5,797,909,000	0.5%
43	Maine	5,160,626,000	0.4%
44	Idaho	4,798,825,000	0.4%
45	Rhode Island	4,563,674,000	0.4%
46	New Hampshire	4,249,015,000	0.4%
47	Vermont	3,763,196,000	0.3%
48	Wyoming	3,610,175,000	0.3%
49	Montana	3,605,557,000	0.3%
50	South Dakota	2,430,143,000	0.2%
	District of Columbia**	NA	NA

Source: U.S. Bureau of the Census, Governments Division
"2013 State and Local Government Finances" (http://www.census.gov/govs/local/)
*Own source revenue includes taxes, current charges, and miscellaneous general revenue. Excluded are intergovernmental transfers, insurance trust revenue, and revenue from government owned utilities and other commercial or auxiliary enterprise.
**Not applicable.

Per Capita State Government Own Source Revenue in 2013

National Per Capita = $3,669*

ALPHA ORDER

RANK	STATE	PER CAPITA
41	Alabama	$2,986
1	Alaska	12,917
46	Arizona	2,804
20	Arkansas	3,917
15	California	4,207
39	Colorado	3,153
7	Connecticut	5,416
3	Delaware	6,266
48	Florida	2,595
50	Georgia	2,382
5	Hawaii	6,029
43	Idaho	2,975
25	Illinois	3,743
33	Indiana	3,383
17	Iowa	4,056
19	Kansas	3,939
34	Kentucky	3,375
38	Louisiana	3,154
21	Maine	3,884
16	Maryland	4,120
9	Massachusetts	4,840
27	Michigan	3,670
8	Minnesota	4,851
35	Mississippi	3,297
47	Missouri	2,675
29	Montana	3,554
31	Nebraska	3,534
42	Nevada	2,982
37	New Hampshire	3,212
11	New Jersey	4,422
14	New Mexico	4,255
10	New York	4,749
36	North Carolina	3,230
2	North Dakota	8,965
32	Ohio	3,442
30	Oklahoma	3,540
23	Oregon	3,775
22	Pennsylvania	3,782
13	Rhode Island	4,335
40	South Carolina	3,137
44	South Dakota	2,875
49	Tennessee	2,442
45	Texas	2,844
28	Utah	3,618
6	Vermont	6,001
24	Virginia	3,771
26	Washington	3,677
12	West Virginia	4,359
18	Wisconsin	4,013
4	Wyoming	6,191

RANK ORDER

RANK	STATE	PER CAPITA
1	Alaska	$12,917
2	North Dakota	8,965
3	Delaware	6,266
4	Wyoming	6,191
5	Hawaii	6,029
6	Vermont	6,001
7	Connecticut	5,416
8	Minnesota	4,851
9	Massachusetts	4,840
10	New York	4,749
11	New Jersey	4,422
12	West Virginia	4,359
13	Rhode Island	4,335
14	New Mexico	4,255
15	California	4,207
16	Maryland	4,120
17	Iowa	4,056
18	Wisconsin	4,013
19	Kansas	3,939
20	Arkansas	3,917
21	Maine	3,884
22	Pennsylvania	3,782
23	Oregon	3,775
24	Virginia	3,771
25	Illinois	3,743
26	Washington	3,677
27	Michigan	3,670
28	Utah	3,618
29	Montana	3,554
30	Oklahoma	3,540
31	Nebraska	3,534
32	Ohio	3,442
33	Indiana	3,383
34	Kentucky	3,375
35	Mississippi	3,297
36	North Carolina	3,230
37	New Hampshire	3,212
38	Louisiana	3,154
39	Colorado	3,153
40	South Carolina	3,137
41	Alabama	2,986
42	Nevada	2,982
43	Idaho	2,975
44	South Dakota	2,875
45	Texas	2,844
46	Arizona	2,804
47	Missouri	2,675
48	Florida	2,595
49	Tennessee	2,442
50	Georgia	2,382

District of Columbia**   NA

Source: CQ Press using data from U.S. Bureau of the Census, Governments Division
"2013 State and Local Government Finances" (http://www.census.gov/govs/local/)
*Own source revenue includes taxes, current charges, and miscellaneous general revenue. Excluded are intergovernmental transfers, insurance trust revenue, and revenue from government owned utilities and other commercial or auxiliary enterprise.
**Not applicable.

Per Capita Profits of State Lotteries in 2014

National Per Capita = $65.89*

ALPHA ORDER

RANK	STATE	PER CAPITA
NA	Alabama**	NA
NA	Alaska**	NA
32	Arizona	26.06
31	Arkansas	27.47
28	California	34.97
34	Colorado	24.29
10	Connecticut	88.83
2	Delaware	229.26
13	Florida	75.17
9	Georgia	93.60
NA	Hawaii**	NA
29	Idaho	29.98
17	Illinois	63.30
24	Indiana	38.01
35	Iowa	23.80
33	Kansas	25.58
20	Kentucky	51.09
26	Louisiana	36.70
23	Maine	38.98
4	Maryland	157.58
5	Massachusetts	143.95
14	Michigan	74.99
36	Minnesota	23.44
NA	Mississippi**	NA
22	Missouri	44.08
41	Montana	11.82
38	Nebraska	20.20
NA	Nevada**	NA
18	New Hampshire	54.63
8	New Jersey	107.96
39	New Mexico	19.61
3	New York	160.69
21	North Carolina	50.59
42	North Dakota	10.57
12	Ohio	78.00
40	Oklahoma	17.25
6	Oregon	130.14
11	Pennsylvania	84.58
1	Rhode Island	356.62
15	South Carolina	66.92
7	South Dakota	122.76
19	Tennessee	51.50
25	Texas	36.93
NA	Utah**	NA
27	Vermont	36.07
16	Virginia	64.68
37	Washington	21.00
43	West Virginia	0.00
30	Wisconsin	29.23
NA	Wyoming**	NA

RANK ORDER

RANK	STATE	PER CAPITA
1	Rhode Island	$356.62
2	Delaware	229.26
3	New York	160.69
4	Maryland	157.58
5	Massachusetts	143.95
6	Oregon	130.14
7	South Dakota	122.76
8	New Jersey	107.96
9	Georgia	93.60
10	Connecticut	88.83
11	Pennsylvania	84.58
12	Ohio	78.00
13	Florida	75.17
14	Michigan	74.99
15	South Carolina	66.92
16	Virginia	64.68
17	Illinois	63.30
18	New Hampshire	54.63
19	Tennessee	51.50
20	Kentucky	51.09
21	North Carolina	50.59
22	Missouri	44.08
23	Maine	38.98
24	Indiana	38.01
25	Texas	36.93
26	Louisiana	36.70
27	Vermont	36.07
28	California	34.97
29	Idaho	29.98
30	Wisconsin	29.23
31	Arkansas	27.47
32	Arizona	26.06
33	Kansas	25.58
34	Colorado	24.29
35	Iowa	23.80
36	Minnesota	23.44
37	Washington	21.00
38	Nebraska	20.20
39	New Mexico	19.61
40	Oklahoma	17.25
41	Montana	11.82
42	North Dakota	10.57
43	West Virginia	0.00
NA	Alabama**	NA
NA	Alaska**	NA
NA	Hawaii**	NA
NA	Mississippi**	NA
NA	Nevada**	NA
NA	Utah**	NA
NA	Wyoming**	NA
	District of Columbia	83.47

Source: CQ Press using data from North American Association of State and Provincial Lotteries, Willoughby Hills, OH
"Lottery Sales and Profits" (http://www.naspl.org/index.cfm?fuseaction=content&menuid=17&pageid=1025)
*For fiscal year 2014. National rate is based on population of states with a lottery.
**No lottery as of fiscal year 2014.

Projected vs. Actual State Tax Collections in 2015

National Percent = 102.2% of Projected Taxes*

ALPHA ORDER

RANK	STATE	PERCENT
26	Alabama	101.1
48	Alaska	54.1
30	Arizona	100.4
28	Arkansas	100.8
3	California	105.7
9	Colorado	103.9
32	Connecticut	100.3
2	Delaware	105.8
30	Florida	100.4
15	Georgia	102.6
5	Hawaii	105.6
14	Idaho	103.1
NA	Illinois**	NA
45	Indiana	98.5
47	Iowa	98.3
40	Kansas	99.4
12	Kentucky	103.6
34	Louisiana	100.0
6	Maine	104.9
23	Maryland	101.5
18	Massachusetts	102.5
37	Michigan	99.6
9	Minnesota	103.9
39	Mississippi	99.5
42	Missouri	98.9
11	Montana	103.7
35	Nebraska	99.8
26	Nevada	101.1
42	New Hampshire	98.9
21	New Jersey	102.2
24	New Mexico	101.3
24	New York	101.3
19	North Carolina	102.4
13	North Dakota	103.4
41	Ohio	99.3
44	Oklahoma	98.8
7	Oregon	104.7
NA	Pennsylvania**	NA
29	Rhode Island	100.7
8	South Carolina	104.0
46	South Dakota	98.4
3	Tennessee	105.7
15	Texas	102.6
19	Utah	102.4
22	Vermont	101.9
32	Virginia	100.3
15	Washington	102.6
37	West Virginia	99.6
35	Wisconsin	99.8
1	Wyoming	107.7

RANK ORDER

RANK	STATE	PERCENT
1	Wyoming	107.7
2	Delaware	105.8
3	California	105.7
3	Tennessee	105.7
5	Hawaii	105.6
6	Maine	104.9
7	Oregon	104.7
8	South Carolina	104.0
9	Colorado	103.9
9	Minnesota	103.9
11	Montana	103.7
12	Kentucky	103.6
13	North Dakota	103.4
14	Idaho	103.1
15	Georgia	102.6
15	Texas	102.6
15	Washington	102.6
18	Massachusetts	102.5
19	North Carolina	102.4
19	Utah	102.4
21	New Jersey	102.2
22	Vermont	101.9
23	Maryland	101.5
24	New Mexico	101.3
24	New York	101.3
26	Alabama	101.1
26	Nevada	101.1
28	Arkansas	100.8
29	Rhode Island	100.7
30	Arizona	100.4
30	Florida	100.4
32	Connecticut	100.3
32	Virginia	100.3
34	Louisiana	100.0
35	Nebraska	99.8
35	Wisconsin	99.8
37	Michigan	99.6
37	West Virginia	99.6
39	Mississippi	99.5
40	Kansas	99.4
41	Ohio	99.3
42	Missouri	98.9
42	New Hampshire	98.9
44	Oklahoma	98.8
45	Indiana	98.5
46	South Dakota	98.4
47	Iowa	98.3
48	Alaska	54.1
NA	Illinois**	NA
NA	Pennsylvania**	NA
	District of Columbia**	NA

Source: CQ Press using data from National Association of State Budget Officers
"The Fiscal Survey of States" (Fall 2015, http://www.nasbo.org)
*For fiscal year 2015. This table compares sales, personal, and corporate income tax collections projected in adopting budgets with the amount collected.
**Not available.

Government Finances: State and Local

State Government Tax Revenue in 2014

National Total = $865,752,089,000

ALPHA ORDER

RANK	STATE	REVENUE	% of USA
27	Alabama	$9,293,754,000	1.1%
43	Alaska	3,392,869,000	0.4%
20	Arizona	13,084,043,000	1.5%
29	Arkansas	8,936,781,000	1.0%
1	California	138,069,870,000	15.9%
22	Colorado	11,755,394,000	1.4%
19	Connecticut	15,937,742,000	1.8%
44	Delaware	3,176,169,000	0.4%
5	Florida	35,384,350,000	4.1%
16	Georgia	18,628,502,000	2.2%
37	Hawaii	6,033,331,000	0.7%
42	Idaho	3,671,715,000	0.4%
4	Illinois	39,182,894,000	4.5%
17	Indiana	16,846,961,000	1.9%
31	Iowa	8,271,839,000	1.0%
33	Kansas	7,334,481,000	0.8%
24	Kentucky	11,103,545,000	1.3%
25	Louisiana	9,695,281,000	1.1%
41	Maine	3,847,181,000	0.4%
15	Maryland	18,929,069,000	2.2%
9	Massachusetts	25,235,726,000	2.9%
10	Michigan	24,803,973,000	2.9%
12	Minnesota	23,128,901,000	2.7%
32	Mississippi	7,574,515,000	0.9%
23	Missouri	11,240,657,000	1.3%
47	Montana	2,655,553,000	0.3%
40	Nebraska	4,877,401,000	0.6%
34	Nevada	7,143,169,000	0.8%
48	New Hampshire	2,282,507,000	0.3%
7	New Jersey	29,679,226,000	3.4%
38	New Mexico	5,757,432,000	0.7%
2	New York	76,978,982,000	8.9%
11	North Carolina	23,396,751,000	2.7%
36	North Dakota	6,120,435,000	0.7%
8	Ohio	27,020,625,000	3.1%
28	Oklahoma	9,103,302,000	1.1%
26	Oregon	9,683,640,000	1.1%
6	Pennsylvania	34,192,869,000	3.9%
45	Rhode Island	2,965,975,000	0.3%
30	South Carolina	8,932,564,000	1.0%
50	South Dakota	1,608,496,000	0.2%
21	Tennessee	11,806,329,000	1.4%
3	Texas	55,260,850,000	6.4%
35	Utah	6,312,489,000	0.7%
46	Vermont	2,962,531,000	0.3%
14	Virginia	18,949,272,000	2.2%
13	Washington	19,447,899,000	2.2%
39	West Virginia	5,379,937,000	0.6%
18	Wisconsin	16,410,925,000	1.9%
49	Wyoming	2,263,387,000	0.3%

RANK ORDER

RANK	STATE	REVENUE	% of USA
1	California	$138,069,870,000	15.9%
2	New York	76,978,982,000	8.9%
3	Texas	55,260,850,000	6.4%
4	Illinois	39,182,894,000	4.5%
5	Florida	35,384,350,000	4.1%
6	Pennsylvania	34,192,869,000	3.9%
7	New Jersey	29,679,226,000	3.4%
8	Ohio	27,020,625,000	3.1%
9	Massachusetts	25,235,726,000	2.9%
10	Michigan	24,803,973,000	2.9%
11	North Carolina	23,396,751,000	2.7%
12	Minnesota	23,128,901,000	2.7%
13	Washington	19,447,899,000	2.2%
14	Virginia	18,949,272,000	2.2%
15	Maryland	18,929,069,000	2.2%
16	Georgia	18,628,502,000	2.2%
17	Indiana	16,846,961,000	1.9%
18	Wisconsin	16,410,925,000	1.9%
19	Connecticut	15,937,742,000	1.8%
20	Arizona	13,084,043,000	1.5%
21	Tennessee	11,806,329,000	1.4%
22	Colorado	11,755,394,000	1.4%
23	Missouri	11,240,657,000	1.3%
24	Kentucky	11,103,545,000	1.3%
25	Louisiana	9,695,281,000	1.1%
26	Oregon	9,683,640,000	1.1%
27	Alabama	9,293,754,000	1.1%
28	Oklahoma	9,103,302,000	1.1%
29	Arkansas	8,936,781,000	1.0%
30	South Carolina	8,932,564,000	1.0%
31	Iowa	8,271,839,000	1.0%
32	Mississippi	7,574,515,000	0.9%
33	Kansas	7,334,481,000	0.8%
34	Nevada	7,143,169,000	0.8%
35	Utah	6,312,489,000	0.7%
36	North Dakota	6,120,435,000	0.7%
37	Hawaii	6,033,331,000	0.7%
38	New Mexico	5,757,432,000	0.7%
39	West Virginia	5,379,937,000	0.6%
40	Nebraska	4,877,401,000	0.6%
41	Maine	3,847,181,000	0.4%
42	Idaho	3,671,715,000	0.4%
43	Alaska	3,392,869,000	0.4%
44	Delaware	3,176,169,000	0.4%
45	Rhode Island	2,965,975,000	0.3%
46	Vermont	2,962,531,000	0.3%
47	Montana	2,655,553,000	0.3%
48	New Hampshire	2,282,507,000	0.3%
49	Wyoming	2,263,387,000	0.3%
50	South Dakota	1,608,496,000	0.2%
	District of Columbia*	NA	NA

Source: U.S. Bureau of the Census, Governments Division
"2014 State Government Tax Collections" (http://www.census.gov/govs/statetax/)
*Not applicable.

Per Capita State Government Tax Revenue in 2014

National Per Capita = $2,721

ALPHA ORDER

RANK	STATE	PER CAPITA
43	Alabama	$1,916
3	Alaska	4,605
42	Arizona	1,944
15	Arkansas	3,013
10	California	3,558
38	Colorado	2,195
4	Connecticut	4,431
11	Delaware	3,395
49	Florida	1,779
47	Georgia	1,845
5	Hawaii	4,250
37	Idaho	2,246
14	Illinois	3,042
26	Indiana	2,554
23	Iowa	2,662
28	Kansas	2,526
29	Kentucky	2,516
40	Louisiana	2,085
17	Maine	2,892
13	Maryland	3,167
9	Massachusetts	3,741
31	Michigan	2,503
6	Minnesota	4,238
27	Mississippi	2,530
45	Missouri	1,854
24	Montana	2,594
25	Nebraska	2,592
29	Nevada	2,516
50	New Hampshire	1,720
12	New Jersey	3,321
20	New Mexico	2,761
7	New York	3,898
33	North Carolina	2,353
1	North Dakota	8,277
35	Ohio	2,331
34	Oklahoma	2,347
32	Oregon	2,439
22	Pennsylvania	2,674
19	Rhode Island	2,811
46	South Carolina	1,848
44	South Dakota	1,885
48	Tennessee	1,803
41	Texas	2,050
39	Utah	2,145
2	Vermont	4,728
36	Virginia	2,276
21	Washington	2,754
16	West Virginia	2,908
18	Wisconsin	2,850
8	Wyoming	3,875

RANK ORDER

RANK	STATE	PER CAPITA
1	North Dakota	$8,277
2	Vermont	4,728
3	Alaska	4,605
4	Connecticut	4,431
5	Hawaii	4,250
6	Minnesota	4,238
7	New York	3,898
8	Wyoming	3,875
9	Massachusetts	3,741
10	California	3,558
11	Delaware	3,395
12	New Jersey	3,321
13	Maryland	3,167
14	Illinois	3,042
15	Arkansas	3,013
16	West Virginia	2,908
17	Maine	2,892
18	Wisconsin	2,850
19	Rhode Island	2,811
20	New Mexico	2,761
21	Washington	2,754
22	Pennsylvania	2,674
23	Iowa	2,662
24	Montana	2,594
25	Nebraska	2,592
26	Indiana	2,554
27	Mississippi	2,530
28	Kansas	2,526
29	Kentucky	2,516
29	Nevada	2,516
31	Michigan	2,503
32	Oregon	2,439
33	North Carolina	2,353
34	Oklahoma	2,347
35	Ohio	2,331
36	Virginia	2,276
37	Idaho	2,246
38	Colorado	2,195
39	Utah	2,145
40	Louisiana	2,085
41	Texas	2,050
42	Arizona	1,944
43	Alabama	1,916
44	South Dakota	1,885
45	Missouri	1,854
46	South Carolina	1,848
47	Georgia	1,845
48	Tennessee	1,803
49	Florida	1,779
50	New Hampshire	1,720
	District of Columbia*	NA

Source: CQ Press using data from U.S. Bureau of the Census, Governments Division
"2014 State Government Tax Collections" (http://www.census.gov/govs/statetax/)
*Not applicable.

State Government Tax Revenue as a Percent of Personal Income in 2014

National Percent = 5.9% of Personal Income*

ALPHA ORDER

RANK	STATE	PERCENT
38	Alabama	5.1
4	Alaska	8.7
38	Arizona	5.1
6	Arkansas	8.0
11	California	7.1
44	Colorado	4.5
11	Connecticut	7.1
8	Delaware	7.4
48	Florida	4.2
42	Georgia	4.7
3	Hawaii	9.2
24	Idaho	6.0
20	Illinois	6.3
17	Indiana	6.5
25	Iowa	5.9
34	Kansas	5.5
16	Kentucky	6.7
41	Louisiana	4.9
14	Maine	6.9
30	Maryland	5.7
20	Massachusetts	6.3
23	Michigan	6.2
4	Minnesota	8.7
8	Mississippi	7.4
44	Missouri	4.5
18	Montana	6.4
34	Nebraska	5.5
20	Nevada	6.3
50	New Hampshire	3.2
28	New Jersey	5.8
10	New Mexico	7.3
14	New York	6.9
25	North Carolina	5.9
1	North Dakota	15.1
34	Ohio	5.5
37	Oklahoma	5.4
25	Oregon	5.9
32	Pennsylvania	5.6
28	Rhode Island	5.8
40	South Carolina	5.0
49	South Dakota	4.1
47	Tennessee	4.4
44	Texas	4.5
30	Utah	5.7
2	Vermont	10.0
43	Virginia	4.6
32	Washington	5.6
7	West Virginia	7.9
18	Wisconsin	6.4
11	Wyoming	7.1

RANK ORDER

RANK	STATE	PERCENT
1	North Dakota	15.1
2	Vermont	10.0
3	Hawaii	9.2
4	Alaska	8.7
4	Minnesota	8.7
6	Arkansas	8.0
7	West Virginia	7.9
8	Delaware	7.4
8	Mississippi	7.4
10	New Mexico	7.3
11	California	7.1
11	Connecticut	7.1
11	Wyoming	7.1
14	Maine	6.9
14	New York	6.9
16	Kentucky	6.7
17	Indiana	6.5
18	Montana	6.4
18	Wisconsin	6.4
20	Illinois	6.3
20	Massachusetts	6.3
20	Nevada	6.3
23	Michigan	6.2
24	Idaho	6.0
25	Iowa	5.9
25	North Carolina	5.9
25	Oregon	5.9
28	New Jersey	5.8
28	Rhode Island	5.8
30	Maryland	5.7
30	Utah	5.7
32	Pennsylvania	5.6
32	Washington	5.6
34	Kansas	5.5
34	Nebraska	5.5
34	Ohio	5.5
37	Oklahoma	5.4
38	Alabama	5.1
38	Arizona	5.1
40	South Carolina	5.0
41	Louisiana	4.9
42	Georgia	4.7
43	Virginia	4.6
44	Colorado	4.5
44	Missouri	4.5
44	Texas	4.5
47	Tennessee	4.4
48	Florida	4.2
49	South Dakota	4.1
50	New Hampshire	3.2
	District of Columbia**	NA

Source: CQ Press using data from U.S. Bureau of the Census, Governments Division
"2014 State Government Tax Collections" (http://www.census.gov/govs/statetax/) and
U.S. Department of Commerce, Bureau of Economic Analysis
"Annual State Personal Income" (http://www.bea.gov/iTable/index.cfm)
*National figure does not include personal income or taxes from the District of Columbia.
**Not applicable.

State Government Individual Income Tax Revenue in 2014

National Total = $310,828,815,000

ALPHA ORDER

RANK	STATE	REVENUE	% of USA
23	Alabama	$3,206,583,000	1.0%
44	Alaska	0	0.0%
21	Arizona	3,462,413,000	1.1%
28	Arkansas	2,602,160,000	0.8%
1	California	67,995,659,000	21.9%
17	Colorado	5,658,457,000	1.8%
14	Connecticut	7,772,602,000	2.5%
39	Delaware	1,040,341,000	0.3%
44	Florida	0	0.0%
10	Georgia	8,965,572,000	2.9%
32	Hawaii	1,745,461,000	0.6%
35	Idaho	1,338,075,000	0.4%
3	Illinois	16,058,396,000	5.2%
19	Indiana	4,896,317,000	1.6%
24	Iowa	3,197,578,000	1.0%
29	Kansas	2,511,660,000	0.8%
20	Kentucky	3,749,258,000	1.2%
27	Louisiana	2,753,680,000	0.9%
34	Maine	1,414,110,000	0.5%
13	Maryland	7,773,773,000	2.5%
4	Massachusetts	13,246,221,000	4.3%
12	Michigan	7,874,712,000	2.5%
9	Minnesota	9,528,454,000	3.1%
33	Mississippi	1,667,344,000	0.5%
18	Missouri	5,361,976,000	1.7%
38	Montana	1,063,261,000	0.3%
30	Nebraska	2,124,164,000	0.7%
44	Nevada	0	0.0%
43	New Hampshire	92,743,000	0.0%
5	New Jersey	11,973,673,000	3.9%
36	New Mexico	1,297,493,000	0.4%
2	New York	42,964,774,000	13.8%
8	North Carolina	10,390,520,000	3.3%
41	North Dakota	498,528,000	0.2%
11	Ohio	8,424,843,000	2.7%
25	Oklahoma	2,962,128,000	1.0%
16	Oregon	6,649,418,000	2.1%
7	Pennsylvania	10,809,736,000	3.5%
37	Rhode Island	1,088,405,000	0.4%
22	South Carolina	3,422,532,000	1.1%
44	South Dakota	0	0.0%
42	Tennessee	239,219,000	0.1%
44	Texas	0	0.0%
26	Utah	2,889,912,000	0.9%
40	Vermont	675,240,000	0.2%
6	Virginia	10,877,689,000	3.5%
44	Washington	0	0.0%
31	West Virginia	1,770,466,000	0.6%
15	Wisconsin	6,793,269,000	2.2%
44	Wyoming	0	0.0%

RANK ORDER

RANK	STATE	REVENUE	% of USA
1	California	$67,995,659,000	21.9%
2	New York	42,964,774,000	13.8%
3	Illinois	16,058,396,000	5.2%
4	Massachusetts	13,246,221,000	4.3%
5	New Jersey	11,973,673,000	3.9%
6	Virginia	10,877,689,000	3.5%
7	Pennsylvania	10,809,736,000	3.5%
8	North Carolina	10,390,520,000	3.3%
9	Minnesota	9,528,454,000	3.1%
10	Georgia	8,965,572,000	2.9%
11	Ohio	8,424,843,000	2.7%
12	Michigan	7,874,712,000	2.5%
13	Maryland	7,773,773,000	2.5%
14	Connecticut	7,772,602,000	2.5%
15	Wisconsin	6,793,269,000	2.2%
16	Oregon	6,649,418,000	2.1%
17	Colorado	5,658,457,000	1.8%
18	Missouri	5,361,976,000	1.7%
19	Indiana	4,896,317,000	1.6%
20	Kentucky	3,749,258,000	1.2%
21	Arizona	3,462,413,000	1.1%
22	South Carolina	3,422,532,000	1.1%
23	Alabama	3,206,583,000	1.0%
24	Iowa	3,197,578,000	1.0%
25	Oklahoma	2,962,128,000	1.0%
26	Utah	2,889,912,000	0.9%
27	Louisiana	2,753,680,000	0.9%
28	Arkansas	2,602,160,000	0.8%
29	Kansas	2,511,660,000	0.8%
30	Nebraska	2,124,164,000	0.7%
31	West Virginia	1,770,466,000	0.6%
32	Hawaii	1,745,461,000	0.6%
33	Mississippi	1,667,344,000	0.5%
34	Maine	1,414,110,000	0.5%
35	Idaho	1,338,075,000	0.4%
36	New Mexico	1,297,493,000	0.4%
37	Rhode Island	1,088,405,000	0.4%
38	Montana	1,063,261,000	0.3%
39	Delaware	1,040,341,000	0.3%
40	Vermont	675,240,000	0.2%
41	North Dakota	498,528,000	0.2%
42	Tennessee	239,219,000	0.1%
43	New Hampshire	92,743,000	0.0%
44	Alaska	0	0.0%
44	Florida	0	0.0%
44	Nevada	0	0.0%
44	South Dakota	0	0.0%
44	Texas	0	0.0%
44	Washington	0	0.0%
44	Wyoming	0	0.0%
District of Columbia*		NA	NA

Source: U.S. Bureau of the Census, Governments Division
"2014 State Government Tax Collections" (http://www.census.gov/govs/statetax/)
*Not applicable.

Per Capita State Government Individual Income Tax Revenue in 2014

National Per Capita = $977

ALPHA ORDER

RANK	STATE	PER CAPITA
37	Alabama	$661
44	Alaska	0
41	Arizona	514
26	Arkansas	877
4	California	1,752
17	Colorado	1,056
2	Connecticut	2,161
14	Delaware	1,112
44	Florida	0
24	Georgia	888
11	Hawaii	1,230
30	Idaho	819
10	Illinois	1,247
33	Indiana	742
21	Iowa	1,029
27	Kansas	865
28	Kentucky	850
39	Louisiana	592
16	Maine	1,063
9	Maryland	1,301
3	Massachusetts	1,964
31	Michigan	795
5	Minnesota	1,746
40	Mississippi	557
25	Missouri	884
19	Montana	1,039
13	Nebraska	1,129
44	Nevada	0
42	New Hampshire	70
7	New Jersey	1,340
38	New Mexico	622
1	New York	2,176
18	North Carolina	1,045
36	North Dakota	674
34	Ohio	727
32	Oklahoma	764
6	Oregon	1,675
29	Pennsylvania	845
20	Rhode Island	1,031
35	South Carolina	708
44	South Dakota	0
43	Tennessee	37
44	Texas	0
22	Utah	982
15	Vermont	1,078
8	Virginia	1,306
44	Washington	0
23	West Virginia	957
12	Wisconsin	1,180
44	Wyoming	0

RANK ORDER

RANK	STATE	PER CAPITA
1	New York	$2,176
2	Connecticut	2,161
3	Massachusetts	1,964
4	California	1,752
5	Minnesota	1,746
6	Oregon	1,675
7	New Jersey	1,340
8	Virginia	1,306
9	Maryland	1,301
10	Illinois	1,247
11	Hawaii	1,230
12	Wisconsin	1,180
13	Nebraska	1,129
14	Delaware	1,112
15	Vermont	1,078
16	Maine	1,063
17	Colorado	1,056
18	North Carolina	1,045
19	Montana	1,039
20	Rhode Island	1,031
21	Iowa	1,029
22	Utah	982
23	West Virginia	957
24	Georgia	888
25	Missouri	884
26	Arkansas	877
27	Kansas	865
28	Kentucky	850
29	Pennsylvania	845
30	Idaho	819
31	Michigan	795
32	Oklahoma	764
33	Indiana	742
34	Ohio	727
35	South Carolina	708
36	North Dakota	674
37	Alabama	661
38	New Mexico	622
39	Louisiana	592
40	Mississippi	557
41	Arizona	514
42	New Hampshire	70
43	Tennessee	37
44	Alaska	0
44	Florida	0
44	Nevada	0
44	South Dakota	0
44	Texas	0
44	Washington	0
44	Wyoming	0
	District of Columbia*	NA

Source: CQ Press using data from U.S. Bureau of the Census, Governments Division
"2014 State Government Tax Collections" (http://www.census.gov/govs/statetax/)
*Not applicable.

State Government Corporation Net Income Tax Revenue in 2014

National Total = $46,275,970,000

ALPHA ORDER

RANK	STATE	REVENUE	% of USA
26	Alabama	$406,408,000	0.9%
25	Alaska	408,938,000	0.9%
20	Arizona	575,180,000	1.2%
27	Arkansas	398,493,000	0.9%
1	California	8,858,498,000	19.1%
17	Colorado	717,506,000	1.6%
19	Connecticut	627,358,000	1.4%
35	Delaware	278,872,000	0.6%
7	Florida	2,043,750,000	4.4%
13	Georgia	943,806,000	2.0%
42	Hawaii	126,045,000	0.3%
39	Idaho	190,002,000	0.4%
3	Illinois	4,284,646,000	9.3%
15	Indiana	866,747,000	1.9%
29	Iowa	388,699,000	0.8%
31	Kansas	330,181,000	0.7%
18	Kentucky	674,464,000	1.5%
24	Louisiana	481,212,000	1.0%
40	Maine	182,928,000	0.4%
12	Maryland	982,784,000	2.1%
6	Massachusetts	2,194,620,000	4.7%
14	Michigan	881,011,000	1.9%
9	Minnesota	1,315,762,000	2.8%
22	Mississippi	526,302,000	1.1%
30	Missouri	357,724,000	0.8%
41	Montana	150,139,000	0.3%
34	Nebraska	306,591,000	0.7%
46	Nevada	0	0.0%
21	New Hampshire	542,847,000	1.2%
4	New Jersey	2,368,068,000	5.1%
37	New Mexico	205,702,000	0.4%
2	New York	4,861,687,000	10.5%
8	North Carolina	1,360,628,000	2.9%
36	North Dakota	250,438,000	0.5%
46	Ohio	0	0.0%
28	Oklahoma	397,290,000	0.9%
23	Oregon	495,134,000	1.1%
5	Pennsylvania	2,301,589,000	5.0%
43	Rhode Island	120,112,000	0.3%
32	South Carolina	327,809,000	0.7%
45	South Dakota	24,819,000	0.1%
10	Tennessee	1,176,971,000	2.5%
46	Texas	0	0.0%
33	Utah	307,910,000	0.7%
44	Vermont	105,817,000	0.2%
16	Virginia	740,511,000	1.6%
46	Washington	0	0.0%
38	West Virginia	203,508,000	0.4%
11	Wisconsin	986,464,000	2.1%
46	Wyoming	0	0.0%

RANK ORDER

RANK	STATE	REVENUE	% of USA
1	California	$8,858,498,000	19.1%
2	New York	4,861,687,000	10.5%
3	Illinois	4,284,646,000	9.3%
4	New Jersey	2,368,068,000	5.1%
5	Pennsylvania	2,301,589,000	5.0%
6	Massachusetts	2,194,620,000	4.7%
7	Florida	2,043,750,000	4.4%
8	North Carolina	1,360,628,000	2.9%
9	Minnesota	1,315,762,000	2.8%
10	Tennessee	1,176,971,000	2.5%
11	Wisconsin	986,464,000	2.1%
12	Maryland	982,784,000	2.1%
13	Georgia	943,806,000	2.0%
14	Michigan	881,011,000	1.9%
15	Indiana	866,747,000	1.9%
16	Virginia	740,511,000	1.6%
17	Colorado	717,506,000	1.6%
18	Kentucky	674,464,000	1.5%
19	Connecticut	627,358,000	1.4%
20	Arizona	575,180,000	1.2%
21	New Hampshire	542,847,000	1.2%
22	Mississippi	526,302,000	1.1%
23	Oregon	495,134,000	1.1%
24	Louisiana	481,212,000	1.0%
25	Alaska	408,938,000	0.9%
26	Alabama	406,408,000	0.9%
27	Arkansas	398,493,000	0.9%
28	Oklahoma	397,290,000	0.9%
29	Iowa	388,699,000	0.8%
30	Missouri	357,724,000	0.8%
31	Kansas	330,181,000	0.7%
32	South Carolina	327,809,000	0.7%
33	Utah	307,910,000	0.7%
34	Nebraska	306,591,000	0.7%
35	Delaware	278,872,000	0.6%
36	North Dakota	250,438,000	0.5%
37	New Mexico	205,702,000	0.4%
38	West Virginia	203,508,000	0.4%
39	Idaho	190,002,000	0.4%
40	Maine	182,928,000	0.4%
41	Montana	150,139,000	0.3%
42	Hawaii	126,045,000	0.3%
43	Rhode Island	120,112,000	0.3%
44	Vermont	105,817,000	0.2%
45	South Dakota	24,819,000	0.1%
46	Nevada	0	0.0%
46	Ohio	0	0.0%
46	Texas	0	0.0%
46	Washington	0	0.0%
46	Wyoming	0	0.0%
	District of Columbia*	NA	NA

Source: U.S. Bureau of the Census, Governments Division
"2014 State Government Tax Collections" (http://www.census.gov/govs/statetax/)
*Not applicable.

Per Capita State Government Corporation Net Income Tax Revenue in 2014

National Per Capita = $145

ALPHA ORDER

RANK	STATE	PER CAPITA
42	Alabama	$84
1	Alaska	555
41	Arizona	85
23	Arkansas	134
10	California	228
23	Colorado	134
14	Connecticut	174
6	Delaware	298
33	Florida	103
37	Georgia	93
38	Hawaii	89
28	Idaho	116
4	Illinois	333
25	Indiana	131
26	Iowa	125
29	Kansas	114
19	Kentucky	153
33	Louisiana	103
21	Maine	138
17	Maryland	164
5	Massachusetts	325
38	Michigan	89
9	Minnesota	241
13	Mississippi	176
44	Missouri	59
20	Montana	147
18	Nebraska	163
46	Nevada	0
2	New Hampshire	409
7	New Jersey	265
36	New Mexico	99
8	New York	246
22	North Carolina	137
3	North Dakota	339
46	Ohio	0
35	Oklahoma	102
26	Oregon	125
11	Pennsylvania	180
29	Rhode Island	114
43	South Carolina	68
45	South Dakota	29
11	Tennessee	180
46	Texas	0
32	Utah	105
16	Vermont	169
38	Virginia	89
46	Washington	0
31	West Virginia	110
15	Wisconsin	171
46	Wyoming	0

RANK ORDER

RANK	STATE	PER CAPITA
1	Alaska	$555
2	New Hampshire	409
3	North Dakota	339
4	Illinois	333
5	Massachusetts	325
6	Delaware	298
7	New Jersey	265
8	New York	246
9	Minnesota	241
10	California	228
11	Pennsylvania	180
11	Tennessee	180
13	Mississippi	176
14	Connecticut	174
15	Wisconsin	171
16	Vermont	169
17	Maryland	164
18	Nebraska	163
19	Kentucky	153
20	Montana	147
21	Maine	138
22	North Carolina	137
23	Arkansas	134
23	Colorado	134
25	Indiana	131
26	Iowa	125
26	Oregon	125
28	Idaho	116
29	Kansas	114
29	Rhode Island	114
31	West Virginia	110
32	Utah	105
33	Florida	103
33	Louisiana	103
35	Oklahoma	102
36	New Mexico	99
37	Georgia	93
38	Hawaii	89
38	Michigan	89
38	Virginia	89
41	Arizona	85
42	Alabama	84
43	South Carolina	68
44	Missouri	59
45	South Dakota	29
46	Nevada	0
46	Ohio	0
46	Texas	0
46	Washington	0
46	Wyoming	0
	District of Columbia*	NA

Source: CQ Press using data from U.S. Bureau of the Census, Governments Division
"2014 State Government Tax Collections" (http://www.census.gov/govs/statetax/)
*Not applicable.

State Government General Sales Tax Revenue in 2014

National Total = $271,286,848,000*

ALPHA ORDER

RANK	STATE	REVENUE	% of USA
34	Alabama	$2,393,192,000	0.9%
46	Alaska	0	0.0%
13	Arizona	5,994,048,000	2.2%
27	Arkansas	3,130,274,000	1.2%
1	California	37,224,077,000	13.7%
32	Colorado	2,615,601,000	1.0%
20	Connecticut	3,981,362,000	1.5%
46	Delaware	0	0.0%
3	Florida	21,480,910,000	7.9%
17	Georgia	5,125,502,000	1.9%
30	Hawaii	2,825,041,000	1.0%
38	Idaho	1,373,666,000	0.5%
9	Illinois	8,515,410,000	3.1%
11	Indiana	7,003,426,000	2.6%
31	Iowa	2,659,231,000	1.0%
28	Kansas	2,983,664,000	1.1%
26	Kentucky	3,131,157,000	1.2%
29	Louisiana	2,923,336,000	1.1%
41	Maine	1,191,685,000	0.4%
19	Maryland	4,195,996,000	1.5%
15	Massachusetts	5,518,580,000	2.0%
10	Michigan	8,419,195,000	3.1%
16	Minnesota	5,441,934,000	2.0%
24	Mississippi	3,304,632,000	1.2%
25	Missouri	3,285,563,000	1.2%
46	Montana	0	0.0%
37	Nebraska	1,763,695,000	0.7%
21	Nevada	3,828,869,000	1.4%
46	New Hampshire	0	0.0%
8	New Jersey	8,885,847,000	3.3%
35	New Mexico	2,098,676,000	0.8%
4	New York	12,668,587,000	4.7%
14	North Carolina	5,842,182,000	2.2%
39	North Dakota	1,320,196,000	0.5%
6	Ohio	10,217,826,000	3.8%
33	Oklahoma	2,599,203,000	1.0%
46	Oregon	0	0.0%
7	Pennsylvania	9,497,906,000	3.5%
42	Rhode Island	915,468,000	0.3%
23	South Carolina	3,370,643,000	1.2%
43	South Dakota	914,979,000	0.3%
12	Tennessee	6,192,281,000	2.3%
2	Texas	32,336,032,000	11.9%
36	Utah	1,823,355,000	0.7%
45	Vermont	354,541,000	0.1%
22	Virginia	3,555,745,000	1.3%
5	Washington	11,767,488,000	4.3%
40	West Virginia	1,221,966,000	0.5%
18	Wisconsin	4,628,338,000	1.7%
44	Wyoming	765,543,000	0.3%

RANK ORDER

RANK	STATE	REVENUE	% of USA
1	California	$37,224,077,000	13.7%
2	Texas	32,336,032,000	11.9%
3	Florida	21,480,910,000	7.9%
4	New York	12,668,587,000	4.7%
5	Washington	11,767,488,000	4.3%
6	Ohio	10,217,826,000	3.8%
7	Pennsylvania	9,497,906,000	3.5%
8	New Jersey	8,885,847,000	3.3%
9	Illinois	8,515,410,000	3.1%
10	Michigan	8,419,195,000	3.1%
11	Indiana	7,003,426,000	2.6%
12	Tennessee	6,192,281,000	2.3%
13	Arizona	5,994,048,000	2.2%
14	North Carolina	5,842,182,000	2.2%
15	Massachusetts	5,518,580,000	2.0%
16	Minnesota	5,441,934,000	2.0%
17	Georgia	5,125,502,000	1.9%
18	Wisconsin	4,628,338,000	1.7%
19	Maryland	4,195,996,000	1.5%
20	Connecticut	3,981,362,000	1.5%
21	Nevada	3,828,869,000	1.4%
22	Virginia	3,555,745,000	1.3%
23	South Carolina	3,370,643,000	1.2%
24	Mississippi	3,304,632,000	1.2%
25	Missouri	3,285,563,000	1.2%
26	Kentucky	3,131,157,000	1.2%
27	Arkansas	3,130,274,000	1.2%
28	Kansas	2,983,664,000	1.1%
29	Louisiana	2,923,336,000	1.1%
30	Hawaii	2,825,041,000	1.0%
31	Iowa	2,659,231,000	1.0%
32	Colorado	2,615,601,000	1.0%
33	Oklahoma	2,599,203,000	1.0%
34	Alabama	2,393,192,000	0.9%
35	New Mexico	2,098,676,000	0.8%
36	Utah	1,823,355,000	0.7%
37	Nebraska	1,763,695,000	0.7%
38	Idaho	1,373,666,000	0.5%
39	North Dakota	1,320,196,000	0.5%
40	West Virginia	1,221,966,000	0.5%
41	Maine	1,191,685,000	0.4%
42	Rhode Island	915,468,000	0.3%
43	South Dakota	914,979,000	0.3%
44	Wyoming	765,543,000	0.3%
45	Vermont	354,541,000	0.1%
46	Alaska	0	0.0%
46	Delaware	0	0.0%
46	Montana	0	0.0%
46	New Hampshire	0	0.0%
46	Oregon	0	0.0%
District of Columbia**		NA	NA

Source: U.S. Bureau of the Census, Governments Division
"2014 State Government Tax Collections" (http://www.census.gov/govs/statetax/)
*Does not include special sales taxes such as those on sale of alcohol, gasoline, or tobacco.
**Not applicable.

Per Capita State Government General Sales Tax Revenue in 2014

National Per Capita = $853*

ALPHA ORDER

RANK	STATE	PER CAPITA
43	Alabama	$494
46	Alaska	0
21	Arizona	890
12	Arkansas	1,055
17	California	959
44	Colorado	488
7	Connecticut	1,107
46	Delaware	0
9	Florida	1,080
42	Georgia	508
1	Hawaii	1,990
26	Idaho	840
34	Illinois	661
11	Indiana	1,062
24	Iowa	856
13	Kansas	1,027
30	Kentucky	709
37	Louisiana	629
20	Maine	896
31	Maryland	702
27	Massachusetts	818
25	Michigan	850
15	Minnesota	997
8	Mississippi	1,104
41	Missouri	542
46	Montana	0
19	Nebraska	937
4	Nevada	1,349
46	New Hampshire	0
16	New Jersey	994
14	New Mexico	1,006
36	New York	642
39	North Carolina	588
2	North Dakota	1,785
22	Ohio	881
33	Oklahoma	670
46	Oregon	0
29	Pennsylvania	743
23	Rhode Island	868
32	South Carolina	697
10	South Dakota	1,072
18	Tennessee	945
6	Texas	1,200
38	Utah	620
40	Vermont	566
45	Virginia	427
3	Washington	1,666
35	West Virginia	660
28	Wisconsin	804
5	Wyoming	1,311

RANK ORDER

RANK	STATE	PER CAPITA
1	Hawaii	$1,990
2	North Dakota	1,785
3	Washington	1,666
4	Nevada	1,349
5	Wyoming	1,311
6	Texas	1,200
7	Connecticut	1,107
8	Mississippi	1,104
9	Florida	1,080
10	South Dakota	1,072
11	Indiana	1,062
12	Arkansas	1,055
13	Kansas	1,027
14	New Mexico	1,006
15	Minnesota	997
16	New Jersey	994
17	California	959
18	Tennessee	945
19	Nebraska	937
20	Maine	896
21	Arizona	890
22	Ohio	881
23	Rhode Island	868
24	Iowa	856
25	Michigan	850
26	Idaho	840
27	Massachusetts	818
28	Wisconsin	804
29	Pennsylvania	743
30	Kentucky	709
31	Maryland	702
32	South Carolina	697
33	Oklahoma	670
34	Illinois	661
35	West Virginia	660
36	New York	642
37	Louisiana	629
38	Utah	620
39	North Carolina	588
40	Vermont	566
41	Missouri	542
42	Georgia	508
43	Alabama	494
44	Colorado	488
45	Virginia	427
46	Alaska	0
46	Delaware	0
46	Montana	0
46	New Hampshire	0
46	Oregon	0
	District of Columbia**	NA

Source: CQ Press using data from U.S. Bureau of the Census, Governments Division
"2014 State Government Tax Collections" (http://www.census.gov/govs/statetax/)
*Does not include special sales taxes such as those on sale of alcohol, gasoline, or tobacco.
**Not applicable.

State Government Motor Fuels Sales Tax Revenue in 2014

National Total = $41,499,698,000

ALPHA ORDER

RANK	STATE	REVENUE	% of USA
25	Alabama	$534,396,000	1.3%
50	Alaska	42,467,000	0.1%
18	Arizona	779,970,000	1.9%
29	Arkansas	454,909,000	1.1%
1	California	6,063,356,000	14.6%
22	Colorado	647,104,000	1.6%
28	Connecticut	503,252,000	1.2%
45	Delaware	113,326,000	0.3%
3	Florida	2,422,718,000	5.8%
10	Georgia	1,006,494,000	2.4%
49	Hawaii	93,598,000	0.2%
38	Idaho	248,454,000	0.6%
8	Illinois	1,293,967,000	3.1%
16	Indiana	814,549,000	2.0%
30	Iowa	452,596,000	1.1%
32	Kansas	441,843,000	1.1%
14	Kentucky	886,161,000	2.1%
23	Louisiana	588,860,000	1.4%
39	Maine	240,901,000	0.6%
17	Maryland	812,739,000	2.0%
19	Massachusetts	732,207,000	1.8%
12	Michigan	964,119,000	2.3%
13	Minnesota	893,351,000	2.2%
34	Mississippi	409,836,000	1.0%
20	Missouri	696,458,000	1.7%
42	Montana	196,965,000	0.5%
36	Nebraska	335,153,000	0.8%
37	Nevada	296,649,000	0.7%
43	New Hampshire	146,101,000	0.4%
24	New Jersey	539,155,000	1.3%
40	New Mexico	234,881,000	0.6%
7	New York	1,630,358,000	3.9%
5	North Carolina	1,915,670,000	4.6%
41	North Dakota	228,022,000	0.5%
6	Ohio	1,839,594,000	4.4%
31	Oklahoma	450,807,000	1.1%
27	Oregon	512,342,000	1.2%
4	Pennsylvania	2,231,348,000	5.4%
48	Rhode Island	95,828,000	0.2%
26	South Carolina	529,655,000	1.3%
44	South Dakota	138,087,000	0.3%
15	Tennessee	845,395,000	2.0%
2	Texas	3,325,916,000	8.0%
35	Utah	372,935,000	0.9%
46	Vermont	103,551,000	0.2%
21	Virginia	694,833,000	1.7%
9	Washington	1,156,242,000	2.8%
33	West Virginia	441,096,000	1.1%
11	Wisconsin	1,000,595,000	2.4%
47	Wyoming	100,889,000	0.2%

RANK ORDER

RANK	STATE	REVENUE	% of USA
1	California	$6,063,356,000	14.6%
2	Texas	3,325,916,000	8.0%
3	Florida	2,422,718,000	5.8%
4	Pennsylvania	2,231,348,000	5.4%
5	North Carolina	1,915,670,000	4.6%
6	Ohio	1,839,594,000	4.4%
7	New York	1,630,358,000	3.9%
8	Illinois	1,293,967,000	3.1%
9	Washington	1,156,242,000	2.8%
10	Georgia	1,006,494,000	2.4%
11	Wisconsin	1,000,595,000	2.4%
12	Michigan	964,119,000	2.3%
13	Minnesota	893,351,000	2.2%
14	Kentucky	886,161,000	2.1%
15	Tennessee	845,395,000	2.0%
16	Indiana	814,549,000	2.0%
17	Maryland	812,739,000	2.0%
18	Arizona	779,970,000	1.9%
19	Massachusetts	732,207,000	1.8%
20	Missouri	696,458,000	1.7%
21	Virginia	694,833,000	1.7%
22	Colorado	647,104,000	1.6%
23	Louisiana	588,860,000	1.4%
24	New Jersey	539,155,000	1.3%
25	Alabama	534,396,000	1.3%
26	South Carolina	529,655,000	1.3%
27	Oregon	512,342,000	1.2%
28	Connecticut	503,252,000	1.2%
29	Arkansas	454,909,000	1.1%
30	Iowa	452,596,000	1.1%
31	Oklahoma	450,807,000	1.1%
32	Kansas	441,843,000	1.1%
33	West Virginia	441,096,000	1.1%
34	Mississippi	409,836,000	1.0%
35	Utah	372,935,000	0.9%
36	Nebraska	335,153,000	0.8%
37	Nevada	296,649,000	0.7%
38	Idaho	248,454,000	0.6%
39	Maine	240,901,000	0.6%
40	New Mexico	234,881,000	0.6%
41	North Dakota	228,022,000	0.5%
42	Montana	196,965,000	0.5%
43	New Hampshire	146,101,000	0.4%
44	South Dakota	138,087,000	0.3%
45	Delaware	113,326,000	0.3%
46	Vermont	103,551,000	0.2%
47	Wyoming	100,889,000	0.2%
48	Rhode Island	95,828,000	0.2%
49	Hawaii	93,598,000	0.2%
50	Alaska	42,467,000	0.1%
	District of Columbia*	NA	NA

Source: U.S. Bureau of the Census, Governments Division
"2014 State Government Tax Collections" (http://www.census.gov/govs/statetax/)
*Not applicable.

Per Capita State Government Motor Fuel Sales Tax Revenue in 2014

National Per Capita = $130

ALPHA ORDER

RANK	STATE	PER CAPITA
37	Alabama	$110
50	Alaska	58
33	Arizona	116
17	Arkansas	153
16	California	156
31	Colorado	121
21	Connecticut	140
31	Delaware	121
30	Florida	122
42	Georgia	100
48	Hawaii	66
18	Idaho	152
42	Illinois	100
28	Indiana	123
20	Iowa	146
18	Kansas	152
3	Kentucky	201
26	Louisiana	127
6	Maine	181
23	Maryland	136
40	Massachusetts	109
44	Michigan	97
12	Minnesota	164
22	Mississippi	137
35	Missouri	115
5	Montana	192
7	Nebraska	178
41	Nevada	104
37	New Hampshire	110
49	New Jersey	60
36	New Mexico	113
46	New York	83
4	North Carolina	193
1	North Dakota	308
15	Ohio	159
33	Oklahoma	116
24	Oregon	129
8	Pennsylvania	174
45	Rhode Island	91
37	South Carolina	110
14	South Dakota	162
24	Tennessee	129
28	Texas	123
26	Utah	127
11	Vermont	165
46	Virginia	83
12	Washington	164
2	West Virginia	238
8	Wisconsin	174
10	Wyoming	173

RANK ORDER

RANK	STATE	PER CAPITA
1	North Dakota	$308
2	West Virginia	238
3	Kentucky	201
4	North Carolina	193
5	Montana	192
6	Maine	181
7	Nebraska	178
8	Pennsylvania	174
8	Wisconsin	174
10	Wyoming	173
11	Vermont	165
12	Minnesota	164
12	Washington	164
14	South Dakota	162
15	Ohio	159
16	California	156
17	Arkansas	153
18	Idaho	152
18	Kansas	152
20	Iowa	146
21	Connecticut	140
22	Mississippi	137
23	Maryland	136
24	Oregon	129
24	Tennessee	129
26	Louisiana	127
26	Utah	127
28	Indiana	123
28	Texas	123
30	Florida	122
31	Colorado	121
31	Delaware	121
33	Arizona	116
33	Oklahoma	116
35	Missouri	115
36	New Mexico	113
37	Alabama	110
37	New Hampshire	110
37	South Carolina	110
40	Massachusetts	109
41	Nevada	104
42	Georgia	100
42	Illinois	100
44	Michigan	97
45	Rhode Island	91
46	New York	83
46	Virginia	83
48	Hawaii	66
49	New Jersey	60
50	Alaska	58
	District of Columbia*	NA

Source: CQ Press using data from U.S. Bureau of the Census, Governments Division
"2014 State Government Tax Collections" (http://www.census.gov/govs/statetax/)
*Not applicable.

State Tax Rates on Gasoline in 2016

National Median = 24.00 Cents per Gallon*

ALPHA ORDER				RANK ORDER		
RANK	STATE	CENTS PER GALLON		RANK	STATE	CENTS PER GALLON
42	Alabama	18.00		1	Pennsylvania	50.30
50	Alaska	8.95		2	Washington	44.50
38	Arizona	19.00		3	North Carolina	35.25
33	Arkansas	21.80		4	California	35.00
4	California	35.00		5	Rhode Island	34.00
32	Colorado	22.00		6	West Virginia	33.20
24	Connecticut	25.00		7	Idaho	33.00
30	Delaware	23.00		8	Wisconsin	32.90
17	Florida	28.40		9	Maryland	32.60
21	Georgia	26.00		10	Iowa	31.80
45	Hawaii	17.00		11	Vermont	30.46
7	Idaho	33.00		12	Maine	30.00
36	Illinois	20.10		12	Oregon	30.00
42	Indiana	18.00		12	South Dakota	30.00
10	Iowa	31.80		15	Utah	29.40
23	Kansas	25.03		16	Minnesota	28.60
21	Kentucky	26.00		17	Florida	28.40
35	Louisiana	20.13		18	Ohio	28.00
12	Maine	30.00		19	Nebraska	27.70
9	Maryland	32.60		20	Montana	27.00
26	Massachusetts	24.00		21	Georgia	26.00
38	Michigan	19.00		21	Kentucky	26.00
16	Minnesota	28.60		23	Kansas	25.03
41	Mississippi	18.40		24	Connecticut	25.00
44	Missouri	17.30		24	New York	25.00
20	Montana	27.00		26	Massachusetts	24.00
19	Nebraska	27.70		26	Wyoming	24.00
29	Nevada	23.81		28	New Hampshire	23.83
28	New Hampshire	23.83		29	Nevada	23.81
49	New Jersey	14.50		30	Delaware	23.00
40	New Mexico	18.88		30	North Dakota	23.00
24	New York	25.00		32	Colorado	22.00
3	North Carolina	35.25		33	Arkansas	21.80
30	North Dakota	23.00		34	Tennessee	21.40
18	Ohio	28.00		35	Louisiana	20.13
45	Oklahoma	17.00		36	Illinois	20.10
12	Oregon	30.00		37	Texas	20.00
1	Pennsylvania	50.30		38	Arizona	19.00
5	Rhode Island	34.00		38	Michigan	19.00
47	South Carolina	16.75		40	New Mexico	18.88
12	South Dakota	30.00		41	Mississippi	18.40
34	Tennessee	21.40		42	Alabama	18.00
37	Texas	20.00		42	Indiana	18.00
15	Utah	29.40		44	Missouri	17.30
11	Vermont	30.46		45	Hawaii	17.00
48	Virginia	16.20		45	Oklahoma	17.00
2	Washington	44.50		47	South Carolina	16.75
6	West Virginia	33.20		48	Virginia	16.20
8	Wisconsin	32.90		49	New Jersey	14.50
26	Wyoming	24.00		50	Alaska	8.95
					District of Columbia	23.50

Source: Federation of Tax Administrators
   "Motor Fuel Excise Tax Rates" (http://www.taxadmin.org/current-tax-rates)
*As of January 1, 2016. Federal gasoline tax rate is an additional 18.4 cents per gallon. Many states also allow additional local option taxes on gasoline.

State Government Motor Vehicle and Operators' License Tax Revenue in 2014

National Total = $26,317,525,000

ALPHA ORDER

RANK	STATE	REVENUE	% of USA
29	Alabama	$210,265,000	0.8%
49	Alaska	59,497,000	0.2%
27	Arizona	228,442,000	0.9%
35	Arkansas	171,102,000	0.7%
1	California	4,025,415,000	15.3%
18	Colorado	503,194,000	1.9%
25	Connecticut	254,808,000	1.0%
50	Delaware	57,502,000	0.2%
4	Florida	1,568,092,000	6.0%
21	Georgia	428,573,000	1.6%
36	Hawaii	169,340,000	0.6%
37	Idaho	145,112,000	0.6%
3	Illinois	1,739,777,000	6.6%
22	Indiana	415,669,000	1.6%
14	Iowa	570,537,000	2.2%
26	Kansas	231,686,000	0.9%
30	Kentucky	206,970,000	0.8%
44	Louisiana	87,209,000	0.3%
40	Maine	112,370,000	0.4%
16	Maryland	511,334,000	1.9%
19	Massachusetts	496,201,000	1.9%
6	Michigan	1,033,756,000	3.9%
10	Minnesota	739,340,000	2.8%
31	Mississippi	194,763,000	0.7%
24	Missouri	288,371,000	1.1%
38	Montana	144,829,000	0.6%
43	Nebraska	98,662,000	0.4%
32	Nevada	192,584,000	0.7%
42	New Hampshire	106,520,000	0.4%
12	New Jersey	670,444,000	2.5%
33	New Mexico	191,827,000	0.7%
5	New York	1,503,053,000	5.7%
11	North Carolina	702,589,000	2.7%
39	North Dakota	124,601,000	0.5%
8	Ohio	807,651,000	3.1%
9	Oklahoma	774,544,000	2.9%
15	Oregon	555,487,000	2.1%
7	Pennsylvania	892,670,000	3.4%
47	Rhode Island	74,337,000	0.3%
28	South Carolina	223,005,000	0.8%
45	South Dakota	79,916,000	0.3%
23	Tennessee	316,511,000	1.2%
2	Texas	2,316,908,000	8.8%
34	Utah	191,412,000	0.7%
46	Vermont	78,193,000	0.3%
20	Virginia	491,585,000	1.9%
13	Washington	638,560,000	2.4%
41	West Virginia	110,948,000	0.4%
17	Wisconsin	507,193,000	1.9%
48	Wyoming	74,171,000	0.3%

RANK ORDER

RANK	STATE	REVENUE	% of USA
1	California	$4,025,415,000	15.3%
2	Texas	2,316,908,000	8.8%
3	Illinois	1,739,777,000	6.6%
4	Florida	1,568,092,000	6.0%
5	New York	1,503,053,000	5.7%
6	Michigan	1,033,756,000	3.9%
7	Pennsylvania	892,670,000	3.4%
8	Ohio	807,651,000	3.1%
9	Oklahoma	774,544,000	2.9%
10	Minnesota	739,340,000	2.8%
11	North Carolina	702,589,000	2.7%
12	New Jersey	670,444,000	2.5%
13	Washington	638,560,000	2.4%
14	Iowa	570,537,000	2.2%
15	Oregon	555,487,000	2.1%
16	Maryland	511,334,000	1.9%
17	Wisconsin	507,193,000	1.9%
18	Colorado	503,194,000	1.9%
19	Massachusetts	496,201,000	1.9%
20	Virginia	491,585,000	1.9%
21	Georgia	428,573,000	1.6%
22	Indiana	415,669,000	1.6%
23	Tennessee	316,511,000	1.2%
24	Missouri	288,371,000	1.1%
25	Connecticut	254,808,000	1.0%
26	Kansas	231,686,000	0.9%
27	Arizona	228,442,000	0.9%
28	South Carolina	223,005,000	0.8%
29	Alabama	210,265,000	0.8%
30	Kentucky	206,970,000	0.8%
31	Mississippi	194,763,000	0.7%
32	Nevada	192,584,000	0.7%
33	New Mexico	191,827,000	0.7%
34	Utah	191,412,000	0.7%
35	Arkansas	171,102,000	0.7%
36	Hawaii	169,340,000	0.6%
37	Idaho	145,112,000	0.6%
38	Montana	144,829,000	0.6%
39	North Dakota	124,601,000	0.5%
40	Maine	112,370,000	0.4%
41	West Virginia	110,948,000	0.4%
42	New Hampshire	106,520,000	0.4%
43	Nebraska	98,662,000	0.4%
44	Louisiana	87,209,000	0.3%
45	South Dakota	79,916,000	0.3%
46	Vermont	78,193,000	0.3%
47	Rhode Island	74,337,000	0.3%
48	Wyoming	74,171,000	0.3%
49	Alaska	59,497,000	0.2%
50	Delaware	57,502,000	0.2%
	District of Columbia*	NA	NA

Source: U.S. Bureau of the Census, Governments Division
"2013 State Government Tax Collections" (http://www.census.gov/govs/statetax/)
*Not applicable.

Per Capita State Government Motor Vehicle and Operators' License Tax Revenue in 2014
National Per Capita = $82.71

ALPHA ORDER

RANK	STATE	PER CAPITA
47	Alabama	$43.36
22	Alaska	80.76
49	Arizona	33.94
41	Arkansas	57.68
12	California	103.74
13	Colorado	93.95
29	Connecticut	70.85
38	Delaware	61.46
25	Florida	78.83
48	Georgia	42.44
10	Hawaii	119.29
17	Idaho	88.78
7	Illinois	135.07
37	Indiana	63.01
2	Iowa	183.62
24	Kansas	79.78
45	Kentucky	46.90
50	Louisiana	18.76
21	Maine	84.48
20	Maryland	85.56
28	Massachusetts	73.56
11	Michigan	104.32
6	Minnesota	135.48
35	Mississippi	65.05
44	Missouri	47.56
4	Montana	141.49
42	Nebraska	52.44
34	Nevada	67.83
23	New Hampshire	80.28
27	New Jersey	75.01
15	New Mexico	91.98
26	New York	76.12
30	North Carolina	70.65
3	North Dakota	168.50
33	Ohio	69.66
1	Oklahoma	199.73
5	Oregon	139.91
32	Pennsylvania	69.81
31	Rhode Island	70.45
46	South Carolina	46.15
14	South Dakota	93.67
43	Tennessee	48.33
19	Texas	85.95
36	Utah	65.04
9	Vermont	124.80
40	Virginia	59.04
16	Washington	90.43
39	West Virginia	59.96
18	Wisconsin	88.09
8	Wyoming	126.97

RANK ORDER

RANK	STATE	PER CAPITA
1	Oklahoma	$199.73
2	Iowa	183.62
3	North Dakota	168.50
4	Montana	141.49
5	Oregon	139.91
6	Minnesota	135.48
7	Illinois	135.07
8	Wyoming	126.97
9	Vermont	124.80
10	Hawaii	119.29
11	Michigan	104.32
12	California	103.74
13	Colorado	93.95
14	South Dakota	93.67
15	New Mexico	91.98
16	Washington	90.43
17	Idaho	88.78
18	Wisconsin	88.09
19	Texas	85.95
20	Maryland	85.56
21	Maine	84.48
22	Alaska	80.76
23	New Hampshire	80.28
24	Kansas	79.78
25	Florida	78.83
26	New York	76.12
27	New Jersey	75.01
28	Massachusetts	73.56
29	Connecticut	70.85
30	North Carolina	70.65
31	Rhode Island	70.45
32	Pennsylvania	69.81
33	Ohio	69.66
34	Nevada	67.83
35	Mississippi	65.05
36	Utah	65.04
37	Indiana	63.01
38	Delaware	61.46
39	West Virginia	59.96
40	Virginia	59.04
41	Arkansas	57.68
42	Nebraska	52.44
43	Tennessee	48.33
44	Missouri	47.56
45	Kentucky	46.90
46	South Carolina	46.15
47	Alabama	43.36
48	Georgia	42.44
49	Arizona	33.94
50	Louisiana	18.76

District of Columbia*   NA

Source: CQ Press using data from U.S. Bureau of the Census, Governments Division
"2014 State Government Tax Collections" (http://www.census.gov/govs/statetax/)
*Not applicable.

State Government Tobacco Product Sales Tax Revenue in 2014

National Total = $16,912,535,000

ALPHA ORDER

RANK	STATE	REVENUE	% of USA
33	Alabama	$117,112,000	0.7%
43	Alaska	72,004,000	0.4%
17	Arizona	311,811,000	1.8%
23	Arkansas	225,809,000	1.3%
6	California	833,126,000	4.9%
27	Colorado	194,192,000	1.1%
15	Connecticut	376,489,000	2.2%
34	Delaware	114,659,000	0.7%
16	Florida	370,993,000	2.2%
25	Georgia	216,640,000	1.3%
36	Hawaii	107,685,000	0.6%
47	Idaho	47,816,000	0.3%
5	Illinois	859,865,000	5.1%
12	Indiana	447,561,000	2.6%
24	Iowa	225,375,000	1.3%
40	Kansas	97,813,000	0.6%
22	Kentucky	248,979,000	1.5%
32	Louisiana	130,045,000	0.8%
30	Maine	136,160,000	0.8%
14	Maryland	402,403,000	2.4%
9	Massachusetts	660,029,000	3.9%
4	Michigan	942,148,000	5.6%
11	Minnesota	581,872,000	3.4%
29	Mississippi	146,050,000	0.9%
39	Missouri	99,527,000	0.6%
41	Montana	85,404,000	0.5%
45	Nebraska	63,425,000	0.4%
37	Nevada	102,116,000	0.6%
26	New Hampshire	215,012,000	1.3%
8	New Jersey	740,605,000	4.4%
42	New Mexico	81,272,000	0.5%
1	New York	1,446,184,000	8.6%
19	North Carolina	281,773,000	1.7%
48	North Dakota	31,262,000	0.2%
7	Ohio	815,532,000	4.8%
18	Oklahoma	292,752,000	1.7%
21	Oregon	257,583,000	1.5%
3	Pennsylvania	1,028,006,000	6.1%
31	Rhode Island	134,805,000	0.8%
49	South Carolina	25,632,000	0.2%
46	South Dakota	61,811,000	0.4%
20	Tennessee	261,101,000	1.5%
2	Texas	1,446,144,000	8.6%
35	Utah	113,184,000	0.7%
44	Vermont	71,854,000	0.4%
28	Virginia	180,733,000	1.1%
13	Washington	443,185,000	2.6%
38	West Virginia	101,779,000	0.6%
10	Wisconsin	640,728,000	3.8%
50	Wyoming	24,490,000	0.1%

RANK ORDER

RANK	STATE	REVENUE	% of USA
1	New York	$1,446,184,000	8.6%
2	Texas	1,446,144,000	8.6%
3	Pennsylvania	1,028,006,000	6.1%
4	Michigan	942,148,000	5.6%
5	Illinois	859,865,000	5.1%
6	California	833,126,000	4.9%
7	Ohio	815,532,000	4.8%
8	New Jersey	740,605,000	4.4%
9	Massachusetts	660,029,000	3.9%
10	Wisconsin	640,728,000	3.8%
11	Minnesota	581,872,000	3.4%
12	Indiana	447,561,000	2.6%
13	Washington	443,185,000	2.6%
14	Maryland	402,403,000	2.4%
15	Connecticut	376,489,000	2.2%
16	Florida	370,993,000	2.2%
17	Arizona	311,811,000	1.8%
18	Oklahoma	292,752,000	1.7%
19	North Carolina	281,773,000	1.7%
20	Tennessee	261,101,000	1.5%
21	Oregon	257,583,000	1.5%
22	Kentucky	248,979,000	1.5%
23	Arkansas	225,809,000	1.3%
24	Iowa	225,375,000	1.3%
25	Georgia	216,640,000	1.3%
26	New Hampshire	215,012,000	1.3%
27	Colorado	194,192,000	1.1%
28	Virginia	180,733,000	1.1%
29	Mississippi	146,050,000	0.9%
30	Maine	136,160,000	0.8%
31	Rhode Island	134,805,000	0.8%
32	Louisiana	130,045,000	0.8%
33	Alabama	117,112,000	0.7%
34	Delaware	114,659,000	0.7%
35	Utah	113,184,000	0.7%
36	Hawaii	107,685,000	0.6%
37	Nevada	102,116,000	0.6%
38	West Virginia	101,779,000	0.6%
39	Missouri	99,527,000	0.6%
40	Kansas	97,813,000	0.6%
41	Montana	85,404,000	0.5%
42	New Mexico	81,272,000	0.5%
43	Alaska	72,004,000	0.4%
44	Vermont	71,854,000	0.4%
45	Nebraska	63,425,000	0.4%
46	South Dakota	61,811,000	0.4%
47	Idaho	47,816,000	0.3%
48	North Dakota	31,262,000	0.2%
49	South Carolina	25,632,000	0.2%
50	Wyoming	24,490,000	0.1%
	District of Columbia*	NA	NA

Source: U.S. Bureau of the Census, Governments Division
"2014 State Government Tax Collections" (http://www.census.gov/govs/statetax/)
*Not applicable.

Per Capita State Government Tobacco Sales Tax Revenue in 2014

National Per Capita = $53.15

ALPHA ORDER

RANK	STATE	PER CAPITA
44	Alabama	$24.15
10	Alaska	97.73
31	Arizona	46.32
15	Arkansas	76.12
46	California	21.47
37	Colorado	36.26
7	Connecticut	104.68
3	Delaware	122.55
48	Florida	18.65
47	Georgia	21.46
16	Hawaii	75.86
41	Idaho	29.25
24	Illinois	66.76
22	Indiana	67.84
19	Iowa	72.53
40	Kansas	33.68
27	Kentucky	56.41
43	Louisiana	27.97
8	Maine	102.37
23	Maryland	67.33
9	Massachusetts	97.85
11	Michigan	95.07
6	Minnesota	106.63
30	Mississippi	48.78
49	Missouri	16.41
12	Montana	83.44
39	Nebraska	33.71
38	Nevada	35.97
1	New Hampshire	162.05
13	New Jersey	82.86
35	New Mexico	38.97
18	New York	73.24
42	North Carolina	28.34
32	North Dakota	42.28
21	Ohio	70.34
17	Oklahoma	75.49
25	Oregon	64.88
14	Pennsylvania	80.39
2	Rhode Island	127.76
50	South Carolina	5.30
20	South Dakota	72.45
34	Tennessee	39.87
29	Texas	53.65
36	Utah	38.46
4	Vermont	114.68
45	Virginia	21.71
26	Washington	62.76
28	West Virginia	55.01
5	Wisconsin	111.28
33	Wyoming	41.92

RANK ORDER

RANK	STATE	PER CAPITA
1	New Hampshire	$162.05
2	Rhode Island	127.76
3	Delaware	122.55
4	Vermont	114.68
5	Wisconsin	111.28
6	Minnesota	106.63
7	Connecticut	104.68
8	Maine	102.37
9	Massachusetts	97.85
10	Alaska	97.73
11	Michigan	95.07
12	Montana	83.44
13	New Jersey	82.86
14	Pennsylvania	80.39
15	Arkansas	76.12
16	Hawaii	75.86
17	Oklahoma	75.49
18	New York	73.24
19	Iowa	72.53
20	South Dakota	72.45
21	Ohio	70.34
22	Indiana	67.84
23	Maryland	67.33
24	Illinois	66.76
25	Oregon	64.88
26	Washington	62.76
27	Kentucky	56.41
28	West Virginia	55.01
29	Texas	53.65
30	Mississippi	48.78
31	Arizona	46.32
32	North Dakota	42.28
33	Wyoming	41.92
34	Tennessee	39.87
35	New Mexico	38.97
36	Utah	38.46
37	Colorado	36.26
38	Nevada	35.97
39	Nebraska	33.71
40	Kansas	33.68
41	Idaho	29.25
42	North Carolina	28.34
43	Louisiana	27.97
44	Alabama	24.15
45	Virginia	21.71
46	California	21.47
47	Georgia	21.46
48	Florida	18.65
49	Missouri	16.41
50	South Carolina	5.30

District of Columbia* NA

Source: CQ Press using data from U.S. Bureau of the Census, Governments Division
"2014 State Government Tax Collections" (http://www.census.gov/govs/statetax/)
*Not applicable.

State Tax on a Pack of Cigarettes in 2016

National Median = $1.53 per Pack*

ALPHA ORDER

RANK	STATE	TAX PER PACK
37	Alabama	$0.68
11	Alaska	2.00
11	Arizona	2.00
31	Arkansas	1.15
34	California	0.87
36	Colorado	0.84
3	Connecticut	3.65
22	Delaware	1.60
28	Florida	1.34
48	Georgia	0.37
5	Hawaii	3.20
43	Idaho	0.57
16	Illinois	1.98
33	Indiana	1.00
27	Iowa	1.36
30	Kansas	1.29
41	Kentucky	0.60
35	Louisiana	0.86
11	Maine	2.00
11	Maryland	2.00
4	Massachusetts	3.51
11	Michigan	2.00
8	Minnesota	3.00
37	Mississippi	0.68
50	Missouri	0.17
19	Montana	1.70
39	Nebraska	0.64
17	Nevada	1.80
18	New Hampshire	1.78
9	New Jersey	2.70
21	New Mexico	1.66
1	New York	4.35
46	North Carolina	0.45
47	North Dakota	0.44
22	Ohio	1.60
32	Oklahoma	1.03
29	Oregon	1.32
22	Pennsylvania	1.60
2	Rhode Island	3.75
43	South Carolina	0.57
25	South Dakota	1.53
40	Tennessee	0.62
26	Texas	1.41
19	Utah	1.70
6	Vermont	3.08
49	Virginia	0.30
7	Washington	3.03
45	West Virginia	0.55
10	Wisconsin	2.52
41	Wyoming	0.60

RANK ORDER

RANK	STATE	TAX PER PACK
1	New York	$4.35
2	Rhode Island	3.75
3	Connecticut	3.65
4	Massachusetts	3.51
5	Hawaii	3.20
6	Vermont	3.08
7	Washington	3.03
8	Minnesota	3.00
9	New Jersey	2.70
10	Wisconsin	2.52
11	Alaska	2.00
11	Arizona	2.00
11	Maine	2.00
11	Maryland	2.00
11	Michigan	2.00
16	Illinois	1.98
17	Nevada	1.80
18	New Hampshire	1.78
19	Montana	1.70
19	Utah	1.70
21	New Mexico	1.66
22	Delaware	1.60
22	Ohio	1.60
22	Pennsylvania	1.60
25	South Dakota	1.53
26	Texas	1.41
27	Iowa	1.36
28	Florida	1.34
29	Oregon	1.32
30	Kansas	1.29
31	Arkansas	1.15
32	Oklahoma	1.03
33	Indiana	1.00
34	California	0.87
35	Louisiana	0.86
36	Colorado	0.84
37	Alabama	0.68
37	Mississippi	0.68
39	Nebraska	0.64
40	Tennessee	0.62
41	Kentucky	0.60
41	Wyoming	0.60
43	Idaho	0.57
43	South Carolina	0.57
45	West Virginia	0.55
46	North Carolina	0.45
47	North Dakota	0.44
48	Georgia	0.37
49	Virginia	0.30
50	Missouri	0.17
	District of Columbia	2.50

Source: Federation of Tax Administrators
"State Excise Tax Rates on Cigarettes" (http://www.taxadmin.org/current-tax-rates)
*As of January 1, 2016. Many states also allow additional local option taxes on cigarettes.

State Government Alcoholic Beverage Sales Tax Revenue in 2014

National Total = $6,154,774,000

ALPHA ORDER

RANK	STATE	REVENUE	% of USA
11	Alabama	$181,427,000	2.9%
34	Alaska	39,078,000	0.6%
22	Arizona	71,136,000	1.2%
26	Arkansas	51,618,000	0.8%
3	California	354,297,000	5.8%
33	Colorado	40,886,000	0.7%
23	Connecticut	60,686,000	1.0%
40	Delaware	19,616,000	0.3%
2	Florida	452,370,000	7.3%
10	Georgia	181,875,000	3.0%
28	Hawaii	48,305,000	0.8%
49	Idaho	8,780,000	0.1%
7	Illinois	279,587,000	4.5%
29	Indiana	45,955,000	0.7%
46	Iowa	14,187,000	0.2%
17	Kansas	126,861,000	2.1%
16	Kentucky	128,534,000	2.1%
25	Louisiana	56,967,000	0.9%
41	Maine	17,923,000	0.3%
36	Maryland	30,808,000	0.5%
21	Massachusetts	78,817,000	1.3%
14	Michigan	143,641,000	2.3%
20	Minnesota	81,328,000	1.3%
32	Mississippi	42,402,000	0.7%
35	Missouri	35,760,000	0.6%
38	Montana	30,053,000	0.5%
37	Nebraska	30,258,000	0.5%
31	Nevada	42,917,000	0.7%
47	New Hampshire	9,545,000	0.2%
15	New Jersey	139,438,000	2.3%
30	New Mexico	44,968,000	0.7%
8	New York	250,926,000	4.1%
5	North Carolina	343,344,000	5.6%
48	North Dakota	9,220,000	0.1%
19	Ohio	98,397,000	1.6%
18	Oklahoma	110,941,000	1.8%
42	Oregon	17,627,000	0.3%
4	Pennsylvania	346,008,000	5.6%
44	Rhode Island	16,803,000	0.3%
12	South Carolina	162,313,000	2.6%
45	South Dakota	16,205,000	0.3%
13	Tennessee	147,812,000	2.4%
1	Texas	1,066,512,000	17.3%
27	Utah	48,413,000	0.8%
39	Vermont	24,065,000	0.4%
9	Virginia	207,672,000	3.4%
6	Washington	321,412,000	5.2%
43	West Virginia	17,295,000	0.3%
24	Wisconsin	57,958,000	0.9%
50	Wyoming	1,828,000	0.0%

RANK ORDER

RANK	STATE	REVENUE	% of USA
1	Texas	$1,066,512,000	17.3%
2	Florida	452,370,000	7.3%
3	California	354,297,000	5.8%
4	Pennsylvania	346,008,000	5.6%
5	North Carolina	343,344,000	5.6%
6	Washington	321,412,000	5.2%
7	Illinois	279,587,000	4.5%
8	New York	250,926,000	4.1%
9	Virginia	207,672,000	3.4%
10	Georgia	181,875,000	3.0%
11	Alabama	181,427,000	2.9%
12	South Carolina	162,313,000	2.6%
13	Tennessee	147,812,000	2.4%
14	Michigan	143,641,000	2.3%
15	New Jersey	139,438,000	2.3%
16	Kentucky	128,534,000	2.1%
17	Kansas	126,861,000	2.1%
18	Oklahoma	110,941,000	1.8%
19	Ohio	98,397,000	1.6%
20	Minnesota	81,328,000	1.3%
21	Massachusetts	78,817,000	1.3%
22	Arizona	71,136,000	1.2%
23	Connecticut	60,686,000	1.0%
24	Wisconsin	57,958,000	0.9%
25	Louisiana	56,967,000	0.9%
26	Arkansas	51,618,000	0.8%
27	Utah	48,413,000	0.8%
28	Hawaii	48,305,000	0.8%
29	Indiana	45,955,000	0.7%
30	New Mexico	44,968,000	0.7%
31	Nevada	42,917,000	0.7%
32	Mississippi	42,402,000	0.7%
33	Colorado	40,886,000	0.7%
34	Alaska	39,078,000	0.6%
35	Missouri	35,760,000	0.6%
36	Maryland	30,808,000	0.5%
37	Nebraska	30,258,000	0.5%
38	Montana	30,053,000	0.5%
39	Vermont	24,065,000	0.4%
40	Delaware	19,616,000	0.3%
41	Maine	17,923,000	0.3%
42	Oregon	17,627,000	0.3%
43	West Virginia	17,295,000	0.3%
44	Rhode Island	16,803,000	0.3%
45	South Dakota	16,205,000	0.3%
46	Iowa	14,187,000	0.2%
47	New Hampshire	9,545,000	0.2%
48	North Dakota	9,220,000	0.1%
49	Idaho	8,780,000	0.1%
50	Wyoming	1,828,000	0.0%
	District of Columbia*	NA	NA

Source: U.S. Bureau of the Census, Governments Division
 "2014 State Government Tax Collections" (http://www.census.gov/govs/statetax/)
*Not applicable.

Per Capita State Government Alcoholic Beverage Sales Tax Revenue in 2014

National Per Capita = $19.34

ALPHA ORDER

RANK	STATE	PER CAPITA
6	Alabama	$37.41
1	Alaska	53.04
37	Arizona	10.57
22	Arkansas	17.40
40	California	9.13
42	Colorado	7.63
23	Connecticut	16.87
19	Delaware	20.97
15	Florida	22.74
21	Georgia	18.01
8	Hawaii	34.03
46	Idaho	5.37
17	Illinois	21.71
44	Indiana	6.97
48	Iowa	4.57
3	Kansas	43.68
11	Kentucky	29.12
35	Louisiana	12.25
32	Maine	13.48
47	Maryland	5.15
36	Massachusetts	11.68
30	Michigan	14.49
29	Minnesota	14.90
31	Mississippi	14.16
45	Missouri	5.90
10	Montana	29.36
25	Nebraska	16.08
28	Nevada	15.12
43	New Hampshire	7.19
27	New Jersey	15.60
18	New Mexico	21.56
33	New York	12.71
7	North Carolina	34.53
34	North Dakota	12.47
41	Ohio	8.49
12	Oklahoma	28.61
49	Oregon	4.44
13	Pennsylvania	27.06
26	Rhode Island	15.92
9	South Carolina	33.59
20	South Dakota	18.99
16	Tennessee	22.57
4	Texas	39.56
24	Utah	16.45
5	Vermont	38.41
14	Virginia	24.94
2	Washington	45.52
39	West Virginia	9.35
38	Wisconsin	10.07
50	Wyoming	3.13

RANK ORDER

RANK	STATE	PER CAPITA
1	Alaska	$53.04
2	Washington	45.52
3	Kansas	43.68
4	Texas	39.56
5	Vermont	38.41
6	Alabama	37.41
7	North Carolina	34.53
8	Hawaii	34.03
9	South Carolina	33.59
10	Montana	29.36
11	Kentucky	29.12
12	Oklahoma	28.61
13	Pennsylvania	27.06
14	Virginia	24.94
15	Florida	22.74
16	Tennessee	22.57
17	Illinois	21.71
18	New Mexico	21.56
19	Delaware	20.97
20	South Dakota	18.99
21	Georgia	18.01
22	Arkansas	17.40
23	Connecticut	16.87
24	Utah	16.45
25	Nebraska	16.08
26	Rhode Island	15.92
27	New Jersey	15.60
28	Nevada	15.12
29	Minnesota	14.90
30	Michigan	14.49
31	Mississippi	14.16
32	Maine	13.48
33	New York	12.71
34	North Dakota	12.47
35	Louisiana	12.25
36	Massachusetts	11.68
37	Arizona	10.57
38	Wisconsin	10.07
39	West Virginia	9.35
40	California	9.13
41	Ohio	8.49
42	Colorado	7.63
43	New Hampshire	7.19
44	Indiana	6.97
45	Missouri	5.90
46	Idaho	5.37
47	Maryland	5.15
48	Iowa	4.57
49	Oregon	4.44
50	Wyoming	3.13
	District of Columbia*	NA

Source: CQ Press using data from U.S. Bureau of the Census, Governments Division
"2014 State Government Tax Collections" (http://www.census.gov/govs/statetax/)
*Not applicable.

State Government Total Expenditures in 2013

National Total = $2,006,144,436,000*

ALPHA ORDER

RANK	STATE	EXPENDITURES	% of USA
27	Alabama	$28,203,759,000	1.4%
38	Alaska	12,214,629,000	0.6%
20	Arizona	31,968,081,000	1.6%
32	Arkansas	19,522,252,000	1.0%
1	California	283,572,491,000	14.1%
25	Colorado	28,743,913,000	1.4%
23	Connecticut	29,302,715,000	1.5%
42	Delaware	8,648,250,000	0.4%
5	Florida	80,436,036,000	4.0%
14	Georgia	45,483,779,000	2.3%
39	Hawaii	11,477,711,000	0.6%
43	Idaho	8,530,858,000	0.4%
7	Illinois	75,324,720,000	3.8%
18	Indiana	36,793,639,000	1.8%
30	Iowa	20,517,934,000	1.0%
35	Kansas	16,436,706,000	0.8%
24	Kentucky	28,887,783,000	1.4%
19	Louisiana	32,037,578,000	1.6%
41	Maine	8,950,407,000	0.4%
16	Maryland	39,556,993,000	2.0%
10	Massachusetts	56,773,938,000	2.8%
9	Michigan	63,142,907,000	3.1%
15	Minnesota	39,943,492,000	2.0%
31	Mississippi	20,101,926,000	1.0%
22	Missouri	30,451,378,000	1.5%
46	Montana	7,075,444,000	0.4%
40	Nebraska	9,880,837,000	0.5%
36	Nevada	13,273,807,000	0.7%
45	New Hampshire	7,420,420,000	0.4%
8	New Jersey	67,362,610,000	3.4%
33	New Mexico	17,200,474,000	0.9%
2	New York	184,040,200,000	9.2%
11	North Carolina	53,625,862,000	2.7%
47	North Dakota	6,410,161,000	0.3%
6	Ohio	76,291,671,000	3.8%
29	Oklahoma	22,920,374,000	1.1%
28	Oregon	26,850,084,000	1.3%
4	Pennsylvania	87,532,654,000	4.4%
44	Rhode Island	8,189,015,000	0.4%
26	South Carolina	28,245,704,000	1.4%
50	South Dakota	4,476,725,000	0.2%
21	Tennessee	30,586,320,000	1.5%
3	Texas	124,963,671,000	6.2%
34	Utah	16,822,502,000	0.8%
48	Vermont	6,018,247,000	0.3%
12	Virginia	47,614,065,000	2.4%
13	Washington	45,725,863,000	2.3%
37	West Virginia	13,234,155,000	0.7%
17	Wisconsin	37,524,804,000	1.9%
49	Wyoming	5,834,892,000	0.3%

RANK ORDER

RANK	STATE	EXPENDITURES	% of USA
1	California	$283,572,491,000	14.1%
2	New York	184,040,200,000	9.2%
3	Texas	124,963,671,000	6.2%
4	Pennsylvania	87,532,654,000	4.4%
5	Florida	80,436,036,000	4.0%
6	Ohio	76,291,671,000	3.8%
7	Illinois	75,324,720,000	3.8%
8	New Jersey	67,362,610,000	3.4%
9	Michigan	63,142,907,000	3.1%
10	Massachusetts	56,773,938,000	2.8%
11	North Carolina	53,625,862,000	2.7%
12	Virginia	47,614,065,000	2.4%
13	Washington	45,725,863,000	2.3%
14	Georgia	45,483,779,000	2.3%
15	Minnesota	39,943,492,000	2.0%
16	Maryland	39,556,993,000	2.0%
17	Wisconsin	37,524,804,000	1.9%
18	Indiana	36,793,639,000	1.8%
19	Louisiana	32,037,578,000	1.6%
20	Arizona	31,968,081,000	1.6%
21	Tennessee	30,586,320,000	1.5%
22	Missouri	30,451,378,000	1.5%
23	Connecticut	29,302,715,000	1.5%
24	Kentucky	28,887,783,000	1.4%
25	Colorado	28,743,913,000	1.4%
26	South Carolina	28,245,704,000	1.4%
27	Alabama	28,203,759,000	1.4%
28	Oregon	26,850,084,000	1.3%
29	Oklahoma	22,920,374,000	1.1%
30	Iowa	20,517,934,000	1.0%
31	Mississippi	20,101,926,000	1.0%
32	Arkansas	19,522,252,000	1.0%
33	New Mexico	17,200,474,000	0.9%
34	Utah	16,822,502,000	0.8%
35	Kansas	16,436,706,000	0.8%
36	Nevada	13,273,807,000	0.7%
37	West Virginia	13,234,155,000	0.7%
38	Alaska	12,214,629,000	0.6%
39	Hawaii	11,477,711,000	0.6%
40	Nebraska	9,880,837,000	0.5%
41	Maine	8,950,407,000	0.4%
42	Delaware	8,648,250,000	0.4%
43	Idaho	8,530,858,000	0.4%
44	Rhode Island	8,189,015,000	0.4%
45	New Hampshire	7,420,420,000	0.4%
46	Montana	7,075,444,000	0.4%
47	North Dakota	6,410,161,000	0.3%
48	Vermont	6,018,247,000	0.3%
49	Wyoming	5,834,892,000	0.3%
50	South Dakota	4,476,725,000	0.2%
	District of Columbia**	NA	NA

Source: U.S. Bureau of the Census, Governments Division
 "2013 State and Local Government Finances" (http://www.census.gov/govs/local/)
*Total expenditures includes all money paid other than for retirement of debt and extension of loans. Includes payments from all sources of funds including current revenues and proceeds from borrowing and prior year fund balances. Includes intergovernmental transfers and expenditures for government owned utilities and other commercial or auxiliary enterprise, and insurance trust expenditures. **Not applicable.

Per Capita State Government Total Expenditures in 2013

National Per Capita = $6,353*

ALPHA ORDER

RANK	STATE	PER CAPITA
33	Alabama	$5,839
1	Alaska	16,564
45	Arizona	4,821
24	Arkansas	6,600
13	California	7,382
39	Colorado	5,453
10	Connecticut	8,146
4	Delaware	9,346
50	Florida	4,105
49	Georgia	4,552
9	Hawaii	8,147
42	Idaho	5,290
32	Illinois	5,844
38	Indiana	5,600
23	Iowa	6,635
36	Kansas	5,678
26	Kentucky	6,568
17	Louisiana	6,923
20	Maine	6,736
22	Maryland	6,664
7	Massachusetts	8,463
29	Michigan	6,378
14	Minnesota	7,369
21	Mississippi	6,721
44	Missouri	5,039
16	Montana	6,975
43	Nebraska	5,286
46	Nevada	4,757
37	New Hampshire	5,610
12	New Jersey	7,563
8	New Mexico	8,242
4	New York	9,346
40	North Carolina	5,447
6	North Dakota	8,858
25	Ohio	6,593
30	Oklahoma	5,948
19	Oregon	6,836
18	Pennsylvania	6,847
11	Rhode Island	7,778
31	South Carolina	5,923
41	South Dakota	5,296
48	Tennessee	4,708
47	Texas	4,715
34	Utah	5,794
3	Vermont	9,597
35	Virginia	5,759
27	Washington	6,557
15	West Virginia	7,142
28	Wisconsin	6,533
2	Wyoming	10,006

RANK ORDER

RANK	STATE	PER CAPITA
1	Alaska	$16,564
2	Wyoming	10,006
3	Vermont	9,597
4	Delaware	9,346
4	New York	9,346
6	North Dakota	8,858
7	Massachusetts	8,463
8	New Mexico	8,242
9	Hawaii	8,147
10	Connecticut	8,146
11	Rhode Island	7,778
12	New Jersey	7,563
13	California	7,382
14	Minnesota	7,369
15	West Virginia	7,142
16	Montana	6,975
17	Louisiana	6,923
18	Pennsylvania	6,847
19	Oregon	6,836
20	Maine	6,736
21	Mississippi	6,721
22	Maryland	6,664
23	Iowa	6,635
24	Arkansas	6,600
25	Ohio	6,593
26	Kentucky	6,568
27	Washington	6,557
28	Wisconsin	6,533
29	Michigan	6,378
30	Oklahoma	5,948
31	South Carolina	5,923
32	Illinois	5,844
33	Alabama	5,839
34	Utah	5,794
35	Virginia	5,759
36	Kansas	5,678
37	New Hampshire	5,610
38	Indiana	5,600
39	Colorado	5,453
40	North Carolina	5,447
41	South Dakota	5,296
42	Idaho	5,290
43	Nebraska	5,286
44	Missouri	5,039
45	Arizona	4,821
46	Nevada	4,757
47	Texas	4,715
48	Tennessee	4,708
49	Georgia	4,552
50	Florida	4,105
	District of Columbia**	NA

Source: CQ Press using data from U.S. Bureau of the Census, Governments Division
"2013 State and Local Government Finances" (http://www.census.gov/govs/local/)
*Total expenditures includes all money paid other than for retirement of debt and extension of loans. Includes payments from all sources of funds including current revenues and proceeds from borrowing and prior year fund balances. Includes intergovernmental transfers and expenditures for government owned utilities and other commercial or auxiliary enterprise, and insurance trust expenditures. **Not applicable.

State Government Direct General Expenditures in 2013

National Total = $1,194,387,197,000*

ALPHA ORDER

RANK	STATE	EXPENDITURES	% of USA
25	Alabama	$18,125,628,000	1.5%
38	Alaska	8,675,133,000	0.7%
23	Arizona	19,540,815,000	1.6%
31	Arkansas	12,622,186,000	1.1%
1	California	138,384,757,000	11.6%
26	Colorado	16,897,688,000	1.4%
24	Connecticut	18,810,763,000	1.6%
41	Delaware	6,511,612,000	0.5%
5	Florida	53,288,137,000	4.5%
13	Georgia	28,341,131,000	2.4%
36	Hawaii	9,877,260,000	0.8%
43	Idaho	5,396,576,000	0.5%
6	Illinois	45,672,784,000	3.8%
16	Indiana	24,157,778,000	2.0%
30	Iowa	13,147,905,000	1.1%
35	Kansas	10,458,360,000	0.9%
22	Kentucky	19,655,285,000	1.6%
19	Louisiana	21,558,589,000	1.8%
40	Maine	6,638,363,000	0.6%
15	Maryland	25,529,588,000	2.1%
9	Massachusetts	36,958,903,000	3.1%
10	Michigan	34,299,888,000	2.9%
18	Minnesota	22,083,061,000	1.8%
32	Mississippi	12,333,637,000	1.0%
21	Missouri	20,267,204,000	1.7%
46	Montana	4,687,532,000	0.4%
39	Nebraska	7,013,823,000	0.6%
42	Nevada	6,424,819,000	0.5%
45	New Hampshire	4,906,661,000	0.4%
8	New Jersey	38,950,015,000	3.3%
34	New Mexico	10,514,610,000	0.9%
2	New York	90,919,576,000	7.6%
11	North Carolina	32,930,088,000	2.8%
47	North Dakota	4,154,086,000	0.3%
7	Ohio	42,984,443,000	3.6%
29	Oklahoma	15,365,888,000	1.3%
28	Oregon	15,970,092,000	1.3%
4	Pennsylvania	53,409,816,000	4.5%
44	Rhode Island	5,392,328,000	0.5%
27	South Carolina	16,877,434,000	1.4%
50	South Dakota	3,270,982,000	0.3%
20	Tennessee	20,756,525,000	1.7%
3	Texas	80,434,631,000	6.7%
33	Utah	11,887,142,000	1.0%
48	Vermont	4,106,222,000	0.3%
12	Virginia	31,274,147,000	2.6%
14	Washington	28,087,169,000	2.4%
37	West Virginia	9,239,315,000	0.8%
17	Wisconsin	22,241,212,000	1.9%
49	Wyoming	3,355,610,000	0.3%

RANK ORDER

RANK	STATE	EXPENDITURES	% of USA
1	California	$138,384,757,000	11.6%
2	New York	90,919,576,000	7.6%
3	Texas	80,434,631,000	6.7%
4	Pennsylvania	53,409,816,000	4.5%
5	Florida	53,288,137,000	4.5%
6	Illinois	45,672,784,000	3.8%
7	Ohio	42,984,443,000	3.6%
8	New Jersey	38,950,015,000	3.3%
9	Massachusetts	36,958,903,000	3.1%
10	Michigan	34,299,888,000	2.9%
11	North Carolina	32,930,088,000	2.8%
12	Virginia	31,274,147,000	2.6%
13	Georgia	28,341,131,000	2.4%
14	Washington	28,087,169,000	2.4%
15	Maryland	25,529,588,000	2.1%
16	Indiana	24,157,778,000	2.0%
17	Wisconsin	22,241,212,000	1.9%
18	Minnesota	22,083,061,000	1.8%
19	Louisiana	21,558,589,000	1.8%
20	Tennessee	20,756,525,000	1.7%
21	Missouri	20,267,204,000	1.7%
22	Kentucky	19,655,285,000	1.6%
23	Arizona	19,540,815,000	1.6%
24	Connecticut	18,810,763,000	1.6%
25	Alabama	18,125,628,000	1.5%
26	Colorado	16,897,688,000	1.4%
27	South Carolina	16,877,434,000	1.4%
28	Oregon	15,970,092,000	1.3%
29	Oklahoma	15,365,888,000	1.3%
30	Iowa	13,147,905,000	1.1%
31	Arkansas	12,622,186,000	1.1%
32	Mississippi	12,333,637,000	1.0%
33	Utah	11,887,142,000	1.0%
34	New Mexico	10,514,610,000	0.9%
35	Kansas	10,458,360,000	0.9%
36	Hawaii	9,877,260,000	0.8%
37	West Virginia	9,239,315,000	0.8%
38	Alaska	8,675,133,000	0.7%
39	Nebraska	7,013,823,000	0.6%
40	Maine	6,638,363,000	0.6%
41	Delaware	6,511,612,000	0.5%
42	Nevada	6,424,819,000	0.5%
43	Idaho	5,396,576,000	0.5%
44	Rhode Island	5,392,328,000	0.5%
45	New Hampshire	4,906,661,000	0.4%
46	Montana	4,687,532,000	0.4%
47	North Dakota	4,154,086,000	0.3%
48	Vermont	4,106,222,000	0.3%
49	Wyoming	3,355,610,000	0.3%
50	South Dakota	3,270,982,000	0.3%
	District of Columbia**	NA	NA

Source: U.S. Bureau of the Census, Governments Division
 "2013 State and Local Government Finances" (http://www.census.gov/govs/local/)
*Direct general expenditures include expenditures for current operations, assistance and subsidies, interest on debt, and capital outlay. Excludes intergovernmental transfers, expenditures for government owned utilities and other commercial or auxiliary enterprise, and insurance trust expenditures.
**Not applicable.

Per Capita State Government Direct General Expenditures in 2013

National Per Capita = $3,782*

ALPHA ORDER

RANK	STATE	PER CAPITA
31	Alabama	$3,752
1	Alaska	11,764
47	Arizona	2,947
19	Arkansas	4,267
37	California	3,602
44	Colorado	3,206
8	Connecticut	5,229
2	Delaware	7,037
49	Florida	2,720
48	Georgia	2,837
3	Hawaii	7,011
42	Idaho	3,346
38	Illinois	3,543
35	Indiana	3,677
20	Iowa	4,252
36	Kansas	3,613
16	Kentucky	4,469
13	Louisiana	4,659
11	Maine	4,996
18	Maryland	4,301
7	Massachusetts	5,509
40	Michigan	3,464
24	Minnesota	4,074
22	Mississippi	4,124
41	Missouri	3,353
14	Montana	4,621
31	Nebraska	3,752
50	Nevada	2,303
34	New Hampshire	3,710
17	New Jersey	4,373
10	New Mexico	5,038
15	New York	4,617
43	North Carolina	3,345
6	North Dakota	5,741
33	Ohio	3,714
27	Oklahoma	3,988
25	Oregon	4,066
21	Pennsylvania	4,178
9	Rhode Island	5,122
39	South Carolina	3,539
29	South Dakota	3,870
45	Tennessee	3,195
46	Texas	3,035
23	Utah	4,094
4	Vermont	6,548
30	Virginia	3,783
26	Washington	4,028
12	West Virginia	4,986
28	Wisconsin	3,872
5	Wyoming	5,754

RANK ORDER

RANK	STATE	PER CAPITA
1	Alaska	$11,764
2	Delaware	7,037
3	Hawaii	7,011
4	Vermont	6,548
5	Wyoming	5,754
6	North Dakota	5,741
7	Massachusetts	5,509
8	Connecticut	5,229
9	Rhode Island	5,122
10	New Mexico	5,038
11	Maine	4,996
12	West Virginia	4,986
13	Louisiana	4,659
14	Montana	4,621
15	New York	4,617
16	Kentucky	4,469
17	New Jersey	4,373
18	Maryland	4,301
19	Arkansas	4,267
20	Iowa	4,252
21	Pennsylvania	4,178
22	Mississippi	4,124
23	Utah	4,094
24	Minnesota	4,074
25	Oregon	4,066
26	Washington	4,028
27	Oklahoma	3,988
28	Wisconsin	3,872
29	South Dakota	3,870
30	Virginia	3,783
31	Alabama	3,752
31	Nebraska	3,752
33	Ohio	3,714
34	New Hampshire	3,710
35	Indiana	3,677
36	Kansas	3,613
37	California	3,602
38	Illinois	3,543
39	South Carolina	3,539
40	Michigan	3,464
41	Missouri	3,353
42	Idaho	3,346
43	North Carolina	3,345
44	Colorado	3,206
45	Tennessee	3,195
46	Texas	3,035
47	Arizona	2,947
48	Georgia	2,837
49	Florida	2,720
50	Nevada	2,303
	District of Columbia**	NA

Source: CQ Press using data from U.S. Bureau of the Census, Governments Division
"2013 State and Local Government Finances" (http://www.census.gov/govs/local/)
*Direct general expenditures include expenditures for current operations, assistance and subsidies, interest on debt, and capital outlay. Excludes intergovernmental transfers, expenditures for government owned utilities and other commercial or auxiliary enterprise, and insurance trust expenditures.
**Not applicable.

State Government Debt Outstanding in 2013

National Total = $1,137,388,671,000*

ALPHA ORDER

RANK	STATE	DEBT	% of USA
29	Alabama	$9,055,227,000	0.8%
38	Alaska	6,218,363,000	0.5%
23	Arizona	13,723,166,000	1.2%
42	Arkansas	3,947,169,000	0.3%
1	California	152,186,012,000	13.4%
20	Colorado	16,309,217,000	1.4%
10	Connecticut	32,356,807,000	2.8%
40	Delaware	5,754,587,000	0.5%
8	Florida	37,892,165,000	3.3%
26	Georgia	13,292,965,000	1.2%
31	Hawaii	8,318,403,000	0.7%
43	Idaho	3,647,841,000	0.3%
5	Illinois	63,660,340,000	5.6%
16	Indiana	22,564,017,000	2.0%
37	Iowa	6,672,785,000	0.6%
36	Kansas	6,825,293,000	0.6%
21	Kentucky	14,983,712,000	1.3%
19	Louisiana	18,589,438,000	1.6%
41	Maine	5,374,528,000	0.5%
14	Maryland	26,066,617,000	2.3%
3	Massachusetts	76,160,503,000	6.7%
12	Michigan	30,377,220,000	2.7%
25	Minnesota	13,572,769,000	1.2%
34	Mississippi	7,112,560,000	0.6%
17	Missouri	19,307,770,000	1.7%
45	Montana	3,558,343,000	0.3%
48	Nebraska	1,846,583,000	0.2%
44	Nevada	3,609,752,000	0.3%
30	New Hampshire	8,763,339,000	0.8%
4	New Jersey	64,264,050,000	5.7%
33	New Mexico	7,232,938,000	0.6%
2	New York	136,014,460,000	12.0%
18	North Carolina	19,054,585,000	1.7%
49	North Dakota	1,834,319,000	0.2%
9	Ohio	33,132,906,000	2.9%
28	Oklahoma	9,514,281,000	0.8%
24	Oregon	13,598,468,000	1.2%
6	Pennsylvania	47,020,552,000	4.1%
27	Rhode Island	9,568,297,000	0.8%
22	South Carolina	14,723,546,000	1.3%
46	South Dakota	3,425,424,000	0.3%
39	Tennessee	6,191,955,000	0.5%
7	Texas	39,624,672,000	3.5%
35	Utah	7,049,552,000	0.6%
47	Vermont	3,330,238,000	0.3%
13	Virginia	28,022,656,000	2.5%
11	Washington	30,474,333,000	2.7%
32	West Virginia	7,355,630,000	0.6%
15	Wisconsin	23,187,772,000	2.0%
50	Wyoming	1,020,546,000	0.1%

RANK ORDER

RANK	STATE	DEBT	% of USA
1	California	$152,186,012,000	13.4%
2	New York	136,014,460,000	12.0%
3	Massachusetts	76,160,503,000	6.7%
4	New Jersey	64,264,050,000	5.7%
5	Illinois	63,660,340,000	5.6%
6	Pennsylvania	47,020,552,000	4.1%
7	Texas	39,624,672,000	3.5%
8	Florida	37,892,165,000	3.3%
9	Ohio	33,132,906,000	2.9%
10	Connecticut	32,356,807,000	2.8%
11	Washington	30,474,333,000	2.7%
12	Michigan	30,377,220,000	2.7%
13	Virginia	28,022,656,000	2.5%
14	Maryland	26,066,617,000	2.3%
15	Wisconsin	23,187,772,000	2.0%
16	Indiana	22,564,017,000	2.0%
17	Missouri	19,307,770,000	1.7%
18	North Carolina	19,054,585,000	1.7%
19	Louisiana	18,589,438,000	1.6%
20	Colorado	16,309,217,000	1.4%
21	Kentucky	14,983,712,000	1.3%
22	South Carolina	14,723,546,000	1.3%
23	Arizona	13,723,166,000	1.2%
24	Oregon	13,598,468,000	1.2%
25	Minnesota	13,572,769,000	1.2%
26	Georgia	13,292,965,000	1.2%
27	Rhode Island	9,568,297,000	0.8%
28	Oklahoma	9,514,281,000	0.8%
29	Alabama	9,055,227,000	0.8%
30	New Hampshire	8,763,339,000	0.8%
31	Hawaii	8,318,403,000	0.7%
32	West Virginia	7,355,630,000	0.6%
33	New Mexico	7,232,938,000	0.6%
34	Mississippi	7,112,560,000	0.6%
35	Utah	7,049,552,000	0.6%
36	Kansas	6,825,293,000	0.6%
37	Iowa	6,672,785,000	0.6%
38	Alaska	6,218,363,000	0.5%
39	Tennessee	6,191,955,000	0.5%
40	Delaware	5,754,587,000	0.5%
41	Maine	5,374,528,000	0.5%
42	Arkansas	3,947,169,000	0.3%
43	Idaho	3,647,841,000	0.3%
44	Nevada	3,609,752,000	0.3%
45	Montana	3,558,343,000	0.3%
46	South Dakota	3,425,424,000	0.3%
47	Vermont	3,330,238,000	0.3%
48	Nebraska	1,846,583,000	0.2%
49	North Dakota	1,834,319,000	0.2%
50	Wyoming	1,020,546,000	0.1%
	District of Columbia**	NA	NA

Source: U.S. Bureau of the Census, Governments Division
 "2013 State and Local Government Finances" (http://www.census.gov/govs/local/)
*Includes short-term, long-term, full faith and credit, nonguaranteed, and public debt for private purposes.
**Not applicable.

Per Capita State Government Debt Outstanding in 2013

National Per Capita = $3,602*

ALPHA ORDER				RANK ORDER		
RANK	STATE	PER CAPITA		RANK	STATE	PER CAPITA
43	Alabama	$1,875		1	Massachusetts	$11,352
4	Alaska	8,432		2	Rhode Island	9,088
40	Arizona	2,070		3	Connecticut	8,995
46	Arkansas	1,334		4	Alaska	8,432
19	California	3,962		5	New Jersey	7,215
28	Colorado	3,094		6	New York	6,907
3	Connecticut	8,995		7	New Hampshire	6,626
8	Delaware	6,219		8	Delaware	6,219
42	Florida	1,934		9	Hawaii	5,905
47	Georgia	1,330		10	Vermont	5,310
9	Hawaii	5,905		11	Illinois	4,939
38	Idaho	2,262		12	Maryland	4,391
11	Illinois	4,939		13	Washington	4,370
24	Indiana	3,434		14	South Dakota	4,052
39	Iowa	2,158		15	Maine	4,045
37	Kansas	2,358		16	Wisconsin	4,037
25	Kentucky	3,407		17	Louisiana	4,017
17	Louisiana	4,017		18	West Virginia	3,970
15	Maine	4,045		19	California	3,962
12	Maryland	4,391		20	Pennsylvania	3,678
1	Massachusetts	11,352		21	Montana	3,508
30	Michigan	3,068		22	New Mexico	3,466
33	Minnesota	2,504		23	Oregon	3,462
36	Mississippi	2,378		24	Indiana	3,434
27	Missouri	3,195		25	Kentucky	3,407
21	Montana	3,508		26	Virginia	3,389
49	Nebraska	988		27	Missouri	3,195
48	Nevada	1,294		28	Colorado	3,094
7	New Hampshire	6,626		29	South Carolina	3,088
5	New Jersey	7,215		30	Michigan	3,068
22	New Mexico	3,466		31	Ohio	2,863
6	New York	6,907		32	North Dakota	2,535
41	North Carolina	1,935		33	Minnesota	2,504
32	North Dakota	2,535		34	Oklahoma	2,469
31	Ohio	2,863		35	Utah	2,428
34	Oklahoma	2,469		36	Mississippi	2,378
23	Oregon	3,462		37	Kansas	2,358
20	Pennsylvania	3,678		38	Idaho	2,262
2	Rhode Island	9,088		39	Iowa	2,158
29	South Carolina	3,088		40	Arizona	2,070
14	South Dakota	4,052		41	North Carolina	1,935
50	Tennessee	953		42	Florida	1,934
45	Texas	1,495		43	Alabama	1,875
35	Utah	2,428		44	Wyoming	1,750
10	Vermont	5,310		45	Texas	1,495
26	Virginia	3,389		46	Arkansas	1,334
13	Washington	4,370		47	Georgia	1,330
18	West Virginia	3,970		48	Nevada	1,294
16	Wisconsin	4,037		49	Nebraska	988
44	Wyoming	1,750		50	Tennessee	953
					District of Columbia**	NA

Source: CQ Press using data from U.S. Bureau of the Census, Governments Division
"2013 State and Local Government Finances" (http://www.census.gov/govs/local/)
*Includes short-term, long-term, full faith and credit, nonguaranteed, and public debt for private purposes.
**Not applicable.

State Government Full-Time Equivalent Employees in 2014

National Total = 4,341,163 FTE Employees*

ALPHA ORDER

RANK	STATE	EMPLOYEES	% of USA
15	Alabama	88,687	2.0%
40	Alaska	27,049	0.6%
24	Arizona	78,689	1.8%
30	Arkansas	62,079	1.4%
1	California	406,842	9.4%
21	Colorado	79,518	1.8%
29	Connecticut	63,013	1.5%
41	Delaware	26,135	0.6%
4	Florida	176,990	4.1%
10	Georgia	131,916	3.0%
31	Hawaii	58,409	1.3%
42	Idaho	23,814	0.5%
12	Illinois	123,001	2.8%
17	Indiana	87,692	2.0%
34	Iowa	49,888	1.1%
35	Kansas	49,469	1.1%
19	Kentucky	83,409	1.9%
25	Louisiana	76,207	1.8%
43	Maine	20,990	0.5%
18	Maryland	86,771	2.0%
14	Massachusetts	98,985	2.3%
8	Michigan	142,057	3.3%
20	Minnesota	82,223	1.9%
32	Mississippi	56,884	1.3%
16	Missouri	88,133	2.0%
44	Montana	20,721	0.5%
38	Nebraska	32,101	0.7%
39	Nevada	27,236	0.6%
46	New Hampshire	18,698	0.4%
7	New Jersey	143,707	3.3%
36	New Mexico	46,114	1.1%
3	New York	240,744	5.5%
6	North Carolina	145,187	3.3%
45	North Dakota	18,752	0.4%
9	Ohio	136,486	3.1%
28	Oklahoma	66,939	1.5%
27	Oregon	66,966	1.5%
5	Pennsylvania	161,369	3.7%
47	Rhode Island	18,691	0.4%
23	South Carolina	78,690	1.8%
48	South Dakota	14,625	0.3%
22	Tennessee	79,258	1.8%
2	Texas	313,284	7.2%
33	Utah	54,038	1.2%
49	Vermont	14,483	0.3%
11	Virginia	127,408	2.9%
13	Washington	120,091	2.8%
37	West Virginia	40,281	0.9%
26	Wisconsin	72,960	1.7%
50	Wyoming	13,484	0.3%

RANK ORDER

RANK	STATE	EMPLOYEES	% of USA
1	California	406,842	9.4%
2	Texas	313,284	7.2%
3	New York	240,744	5.5%
4	Florida	176,990	4.1%
5	Pennsylvania	161,369	3.7%
6	North Carolina	145,187	3.3%
7	New Jersey	143,707	3.3%
8	Michigan	142,057	3.3%
9	Ohio	136,486	3.1%
10	Georgia	131,916	3.0%
11	Virginia	127,408	2.9%
12	Illinois	123,001	2.8%
13	Washington	120,091	2.8%
14	Massachusetts	98,985	2.3%
15	Alabama	88,687	2.0%
16	Missouri	88,133	2.0%
17	Indiana	87,692	2.0%
18	Maryland	86,771	2.0%
19	Kentucky	83,409	1.9%
20	Minnesota	82,223	1.9%
21	Colorado	79,518	1.8%
22	Tennessee	79,258	1.8%
23	South Carolina	78,690	1.8%
24	Arizona	78,689	1.8%
25	Louisiana	76,207	1.8%
26	Wisconsin	72,960	1.7%
27	Oregon	66,966	1.5%
28	Oklahoma	66,939	1.5%
29	Connecticut	63,013	1.5%
30	Arkansas	62,079	1.4%
31	Hawaii	58,409	1.3%
32	Mississippi	56,884	1.3%
33	Utah	54,038	1.2%
34	Iowa	49,888	1.1%
35	Kansas	49,469	1.1%
36	New Mexico	46,114	1.1%
37	West Virginia	40,281	0.9%
38	Nebraska	32,101	0.7%
39	Nevada	27,236	0.6%
40	Alaska	27,049	0.6%
41	Delaware	26,135	0.6%
42	Idaho	23,814	0.5%
43	Maine	20,990	0.5%
44	Montana	20,721	0.5%
45	North Dakota	18,752	0.4%
46	New Hampshire	18,698	0.4%
47	Rhode Island	18,691	0.4%
48	South Dakota	14,625	0.3%
49	Vermont	14,483	0.3%
50	Wyoming	13,484	0.3%
	District of Columbia**	NA	NA

Source: U.S. Bureau of the Census, Governments Division
"Government Employment and Payroll" (http://www.census.gov/govs/apes/index.html)
*Full-time equivalent as of March 2014.
**Not applicable.

Rate of State Government Full-Time Equivalent Employees in 2014

National Rate = 136 FTE Employees per 10,000 Population*

ALPHA ORDER

RANK	STATE	RATE
14	Alabama	183
2	Alaska	367
45	Arizona	117
9	Arkansas	209
47	California	105
30	Colorado	148
16	Connecticut	175
3	Delaware	279
50	Florida	89
39	Georgia	131
1	Hawaii	411
32	Idaho	146
49	Illinois	95
38	Indiana	133
26	Iowa	160
19	Kansas	170
12	Kentucky	189
23	Louisiana	164
27	Maine	158
34	Maryland	145
31	Massachusetts	147
36	Michigan	143
29	Minnesota	151
11	Mississippi	190
34	Missouri	145
10	Montana	203
19	Nebraska	170
48	Nevada	96
37	New Hampshire	141
25	New Jersey	161
7	New Mexico	221
42	New York	122
32	North Carolina	146
4	North Dakota	253
44	Ohio	118
17	Oklahoma	173
22	Oregon	169
41	Pennsylvania	126
15	Rhode Island	177
24	South Carolina	163
18	South Dakota	171
43	Tennessee	121
46	Texas	116
13	Utah	184
5	Vermont	231
28	Virginia	153
19	Washington	170
8	West Virginia	218
40	Wisconsin	127
5	Wyoming	231

RANK ORDER

RANK	STATE	RATE
1	Hawaii	411
2	Alaska	367
3	Delaware	279
4	North Dakota	253
5	Vermont	231
5	Wyoming	231
7	New Mexico	221
8	West Virginia	218
9	Arkansas	209
10	Montana	203
11	Mississippi	190
12	Kentucky	189
13	Utah	184
14	Alabama	183
15	Rhode Island	177
16	Connecticut	175
17	Oklahoma	173
18	South Dakota	171
19	Kansas	170
19	Nebraska	170
19	Washington	170
22	Oregon	169
23	Louisiana	164
24	South Carolina	163
25	New Jersey	161
26	Iowa	160
27	Maine	158
28	Virginia	153
29	Minnesota	151
30	Colorado	148
31	Massachusetts	147
32	Idaho	146
32	North Carolina	146
34	Maryland	145
34	Missouri	145
36	Michigan	143
37	New Hampshire	141
38	Indiana	133
39	Georgia	131
40	Wisconsin	127
41	Pennsylvania	126
42	New York	122
43	Tennessee	121
44	Ohio	118
45	Arizona	117
46	Texas	116
47	California	105
48	Nevada	96
49	Illinois	95
50	Florida	89
	District of Columbia**	NA

Source: CQ Press using data from U.S. Bureau of the Census, Governments Division
"Government Employment and Payroll" (http://www.census.gov/govs/apes/index.html)
*Full-time equivalent as of March 2014.
**Not applicable.

Average Annual Earnings of Full-Time State Government Employees in 2014

National Average = $60,546*

ALPHA ORDER

RANK	STATE	SALARY
34	Alabama	$52,801
7	Alaska	67,771
24	Arizona	56,372
45	Arkansas	48,315
1	California	80,263
12	Colorado	64,579
2	Connecticut	78,146
29	Delaware	54,178
39	Florida	51,020
47	Georgia	47,155
31	Hawaii	54,006
28	Idaho	54,693
6	Illinois	68,984
38	Indiana	51,405
3	Iowa	74,192
30	Kansas	54,124
40	Kentucky	50,324
32	Louisiana	53,246
37	Maine	51,409
16	Maryland	60,097
10	Massachusetts	67,145
8	Michigan	67,515
9	Minnesota	67,156
48	Mississippi	45,837
49	Missouri	45,149
35	Montana	51,891
41	Nebraska	50,314
21	Nevada	58,511
17	New Hampshire	59,937
4	New Jersey	73,572
33	New Mexico	52,901
5	New York	72,159
26	North Carolina	55,609
27	North Dakota	55,111
13	Ohio	62,602
43	Oklahoma	49,286
18	Oregon	59,467
20	Pennsylvania	58,756
11	Rhode Island	67,141
46	South Carolina	47,816
44	South Dakota	49,080
42	Tennessee	49,742
23	Texas	57,535
25	Utah	56,234
19	Vermont	59,331
22	Virginia	58,051
14	Washington	62,016
50	West Virginia	44,246
15	Wisconsin	61,503
36	Wyoming	51,807

RANK ORDER

RANK	STATE	SALARY
1	California	$80,263
2	Connecticut	78,146
3	Iowa	74,192
4	New Jersey	73,572
5	New York	72,159
6	Illinois	68,984
7	Alaska	67,771
8	Michigan	67,515
9	Minnesota	67,156
10	Massachusetts	67,145
11	Rhode Island	67,141
12	Colorado	64,579
13	Ohio	62,602
14	Washington	62,016
15	Wisconsin	61,503
16	Maryland	60,097
17	New Hampshire	59,937
18	Oregon	59,467
19	Vermont	59,331
20	Pennsylvania	58,756
21	Nevada	58,511
22	Virginia	58,051
23	Texas	57,535
24	Arizona	56,372
25	Utah	56,234
26	North Carolina	55,609
27	North Dakota	55,111
28	Idaho	54,693
29	Delaware	54,178
30	Kansas	54,124
31	Hawaii	54,006
32	Louisiana	53,246
33	New Mexico	52,901
34	Alabama	52,801
35	Montana	51,891
36	Wyoming	51,807
37	Maine	51,409
38	Indiana	51,405
39	Florida	51,020
40	Kentucky	50,324
41	Nebraska	50,314
42	Tennessee	49,742
43	Oklahoma	49,286
44	South Dakota	49,080
45	Arkansas	48,315
46	South Carolina	47,816
47	Georgia	47,155
48	Mississippi	45,837
49	Missouri	45,149
50	West Virginia	44,246
	District of Columbia**	NA

Source: CQ Press using data from U.S. Bureau of the Census, Governments Division "Government Employment and Payroll" (http://www.census.gov/govs/apes/index.html)
*March 2014 full-time payroll (multiplied by 12) divided by full-time employees.
**Not applicable.

Local Government Total Revenue in 2013

National Total = $1,709,268,981,000*

ALPHA ORDER

RANK	STATE	REVENUE	% of USA
24	Alabama	$21,180,567,000	1.2%
40	Alaska	5,267,139,000	0.3%
19	Arizona	28,079,502,000	1.6%
36	Arkansas	9,820,237,000	0.6%
1	California	277,446,692,000	16.2%
17	Colorado	29,824,625,000	1.7%
26	Connecticut	18,095,438,000	1.1%
49	Delaware	3,393,443,000	0.2%
4	Florida	94,549,133,000	5.5%
11	Georgia	43,338,694,000	2.5%
46	Hawaii	3,681,970,000	0.2%
41	Idaho	5,232,415,000	0.3%
5	Illinois	72,992,366,000	4.3%
20	Indiana	28,032,541,000	1.6%
28	Iowa	15,778,635,000	0.9%
29	Kansas	14,551,604,000	0.9%
30	Kentucky	13,961,273,000	0.8%
23	Louisiana	22,275,292,000	1.3%
42	Maine	4,763,314,000	0.3%
18	Maryland	29,805,151,000	1.7%
14	Massachusetts	34,211,120,000	2.0%
9	Michigan	46,914,313,000	2.7%
16	Minnesota	30,017,974,000	1.8%
34	Mississippi	12,528,607,000	0.7%
22	Missouri	26,308,603,000	1.5%
47	Montana	3,681,574,000	0.2%
32	Nebraska	13,281,075,000	0.8%
33	Nevada	13,270,773,000	0.8%
38	New Hampshire	5,686,212,000	0.3%
8	New Jersey	47,603,949,000	2.8%
37	New Mexico	8,499,903,000	0.5%
2	New York	193,254,540,000	11.3%
10	North Carolina	45,802,233,000	2.7%
45	North Dakota	3,810,131,000	0.2%
7	Ohio	55,199,296,000	3.2%
31	Oklahoma	13,578,879,000	0.8%
27	Oregon	18,022,561,000	1.1%
6	Pennsylvania	64,386,442,000	3.8%
43	Rhode Island	4,583,894,000	0.3%
25	South Carolina	20,263,171,000	1.2%
48	South Dakota	3,399,885,000	0.2%
15	Tennessee	32,706,444,000	1.9%
3	Texas	124,646,403,000	7.3%
35	Utah	11,570,532,000	0.7%
50	Vermont	2,787,762,000	0.2%
13	Virginia	38,644,207,000	2.3%
12	Washington	40,659,965,000	2.4%
39	West Virginia	5,479,402,000	0.3%
21	Wisconsin	27,755,022,000	1.6%
44	Wyoming	4,550,756,000	0.3%

RANK ORDER

RANK	STATE	REVENUE	% of USA
1	California	$277,446,692,000	16.2%
2	New York	193,254,540,000	11.3%
3	Texas	124,646,403,000	7.3%
4	Florida	94,549,133,000	5.5%
5	Illinois	72,992,366,000	4.3%
6	Pennsylvania	64,386,442,000	3.8%
7	Ohio	55,199,296,000	3.2%
8	New Jersey	47,603,949,000	2.8%
9	Michigan	46,914,313,000	2.7%
10	North Carolina	45,802,233,000	2.7%
11	Georgia	43,338,694,000	2.5%
12	Washington	40,659,965,000	2.4%
13	Virginia	38,644,207,000	2.3%
14	Massachusetts	34,211,120,000	2.0%
15	Tennessee	32,706,444,000	1.9%
16	Minnesota	30,017,974,000	1.8%
17	Colorado	29,824,625,000	1.7%
18	Maryland	29,805,151,000	1.7%
19	Arizona	28,079,502,000	1.6%
20	Indiana	28,032,541,000	1.6%
21	Wisconsin	27,755,022,000	1.6%
22	Missouri	26,308,603,000	1.5%
23	Louisiana	22,275,292,000	1.3%
24	Alabama	21,180,567,000	1.2%
25	South Carolina	20,263,171,000	1.2%
26	Connecticut	18,095,438,000	1.1%
27	Oregon	18,022,561,000	1.1%
28	Iowa	15,778,635,000	0.9%
29	Kansas	14,551,604,000	0.9%
30	Kentucky	13,961,273,000	0.8%
31	Oklahoma	13,578,879,000	0.8%
32	Nebraska	13,281,075,000	0.8%
33	Nevada	13,270,773,000	0.8%
34	Mississippi	12,528,607,000	0.7%
35	Utah	11,570,532,000	0.7%
36	Arkansas	9,820,237,000	0.6%
37	New Mexico	8,499,903,000	0.5%
38	New Hampshire	5,686,212,000	0.3%
39	West Virginia	5,479,402,000	0.3%
40	Alaska	5,267,139,000	0.3%
41	Idaho	5,232,415,000	0.3%
42	Maine	4,763,314,000	0.3%
43	Rhode Island	4,583,894,000	0.3%
44	Wyoming	4,550,756,000	0.3%
45	North Dakota	3,810,131,000	0.2%
46	Hawaii	3,681,970,000	0.2%
47	Montana	3,681,574,000	0.2%
48	South Dakota	3,399,885,000	0.2%
49	Delaware	3,393,443,000	0.2%
50	Vermont	2,787,762,000	0.2%
	District of Columbia	14,093,322,000	0.8%

Source: U.S. Bureau of the Census, Governments Division
"2013 State and Local Government Finances" (http://www.census.gov/govs/local/)
*Total revenue includes all money received from external sources. This includes taxes, intergovernmental transfers and insurance trust revenue, and revenue from government owned utilities and other commercial or auxiliary enterprise.

Per Capita Local Government Total Revenue in 2013

National Per Capita = $5,402*

ALPHA ORDER

RANK	STATE	PER CAPITA
30	Alabama	$4,385
4	Alaska	7,142
37	Arizona	4,235
46	Arkansas	3,320
3	California	7,223
8	Colorado	5,658
16	Connecticut	5,030
42	Delaware	3,667
20	Florida	4,825
33	Georgia	4,338
50	Hawaii	2,614
47	Idaho	3,244
7	Illinois	5,663
35	Indiana	4,266
12	Iowa	5,103
17	Kansas	5,027
48	Kentucky	3,174
21	Louisiana	4,814
44	Maine	3,585
18	Maryland	5,021
13	Massachusetts	5,099
24	Michigan	4,739
9	Minnesota	5,538
38	Mississippi	4,189
32	Missouri	4,353
43	Montana	3,629
5	Nebraska	7,105
23	Nevada	4,756
34	New Hampshire	4,299
10	New Jersey	5,344
39	New Mexico	4,073
1	New York	9,814
27	North Carolina	4,652
11	North Dakota	5,265
22	Ohio	4,770
45	Oklahoma	3,524
28	Oregon	4,588
14	Pennsylvania	5,037
31	Rhode Island	4,354
36	South Carolina	4,249
40	South Dakota	4,022
15	Tennessee	5,035
25	Texas	4,704
41	Utah	3,985
29	Vermont	4,445
26	Virginia	4,674
6	Washington	5,831
49	West Virginia	2,957
19	Wisconsin	4,832
2	Wyoming	7,804

RANK ORDER

RANK	STATE	PER CAPITA
1	New York	$9,814
2	Wyoming	7,804
3	California	7,223
4	Alaska	7,142
5	Nebraska	7,105
6	Washington	5,831
7	Illinois	5,663
8	Colorado	5,658
9	Minnesota	5,538
10	New Jersey	5,344
11	North Dakota	5,265
12	Iowa	5,103
13	Massachusetts	5,099
14	Pennsylvania	5,037
15	Tennessee	5,035
16	Connecticut	5,030
17	Kansas	5,027
18	Maryland	5,021
19	Wisconsin	4,832
20	Florida	4,825
21	Louisiana	4,814
22	Ohio	4,770
23	Nevada	4,756
24	Michigan	4,739
25	Texas	4,704
26	Virginia	4,674
27	North Carolina	4,652
28	Oregon	4,588
29	Vermont	4,445
30	Alabama	4,385
31	Rhode Island	4,354
32	Missouri	4,353
33	Georgia	4,338
34	New Hampshire	4,299
35	Indiana	4,266
36	South Carolina	4,249
37	Arizona	4,235
38	Mississippi	4,189
39	New Mexico	4,073
40	South Dakota	4,022
41	Utah	3,985
42	Delaware	3,667
43	Montana	3,629
44	Maine	3,585
45	Oklahoma	3,524
46	Arkansas	3,320
47	Idaho	3,244
48	Kentucky	3,174
49	West Virginia	2,957
50	Hawaii	2,614
	District of Columbia	21,697

Source: CQ Press using data from U.S. Bureau of the Census, Governments Division
"2013 State and Local Government Finances" (http://www.census.gov/govs/local/)
*Total revenue includes all money received from external sources. This includes taxes, intergovernmental transfers and insurance trust revenue, and revenue from government owned utilities and other commercial or auxiliary enterprise.

Local Government Revenue from the Federal Government in 2013

National Total = $71,172,879,000

ALPHA ORDER

RANK	STATE	REVENUE	% of USA
20	Alabama	$959,848,000	1.3%
38	Alaska	257,537,000	0.4%
18	Arizona	1,007,135,000	1.4%
37	Arkansas	326,280,000	0.5%
1	California	11,975,476,000	16.8%
14	Colorado	1,368,036,000	1.9%
24	Connecticut	635,023,000	0.9%
49	Delaware	74,978,000	0.1%
4	Florida	4,587,917,000	6.4%
12	Georgia	1,452,195,000	2.0%
34	Hawaii	387,625,000	0.5%
47	Idaho	132,859,000	0.2%
5	Illinois	3,223,063,000	4.5%
25	Indiana	626,345,000	0.9%
26	Iowa	605,354,000	0.9%
40	Kansas	247,133,000	0.3%
30	Kentucky	462,693,000	0.7%
17	Louisiana	1,012,238,000	1.4%
46	Maine	141,546,000	0.2%
15	Maryland	1,322,398,000	1.9%
13	Massachusetts	1,420,930,000	2.0%
9	Michigan	1,927,420,000	2.7%
21	Minnesota	894,728,000	1.3%
31	Mississippi	437,387,000	0.6%
22	Missouri	865,040,000	1.2%
39	Montana	249,646,000	0.4%
36	Nebraska	354,855,000	0.5%
29	Nevada	504,679,000	0.7%
45	New Hampshire	162,731,000	0.2%
19	New Jersey	999,309,000	1.4%
35	New Mexico	382,235,000	0.5%
2	New York	7,509,232,000	10.6%
8	North Carolina	2,221,551,000	3.1%
42	North Dakota	206,430,000	0.3%
7	Ohio	2,576,151,000	3.6%
32	Oklahoma	416,483,000	0.6%
16	Oregon	1,082,439,000	1.5%
6	Pennsylvania	2,803,708,000	3.9%
44	Rhode Island	181,070,000	0.3%
33	South Carolina	409,220,000	0.6%
43	South Dakota	185,398,000	0.3%
23	Tennessee	777,555,000	1.1%
3	Texas	4,683,006,000	6.6%
27	Utah	576,215,000	0.8%
50	Vermont	73,989,000	0.1%
10	Virginia	1,793,625,000	2.5%
11	Washington	1,760,735,000	2.5%
41	West Virginia	244,184,000	0.3%
28	Wisconsin	568,607,000	0.8%
48	Wyoming	116,217,000	0.2%

RANK ORDER

RANK	STATE	REVENUE	% of USA
1	California	$11,975,476,000	16.8%
2	New York	7,509,232,000	10.6%
3	Texas	4,683,006,000	6.6%
4	Florida	4,587,917,000	6.4%
5	Illinois	3,223,063,000	4.5%
6	Pennsylvania	2,803,708,000	3.9%
7	Ohio	2,576,151,000	3.6%
8	North Carolina	2,221,551,000	3.1%
9	Michigan	1,927,420,000	2.7%
10	Virginia	1,793,625,000	2.5%
11	Washington	1,760,735,000	2.5%
12	Georgia	1,452,195,000	2.0%
13	Massachusetts	1,420,930,000	2.0%
14	Colorado	1,368,036,000	1.9%
15	Maryland	1,322,398,000	1.9%
16	Oregon	1,082,439,000	1.5%
17	Louisiana	1,012,238,000	1.4%
18	Arizona	1,007,135,000	1.4%
19	New Jersey	999,309,000	1.4%
20	Alabama	959,848,000	1.3%
21	Minnesota	894,728,000	1.3%
22	Missouri	865,040,000	1.2%
23	Tennessee	777,555,000	1.1%
24	Connecticut	635,023,000	0.9%
25	Indiana	626,345,000	0.9%
26	Iowa	605,354,000	0.9%
27	Utah	576,215,000	0.8%
28	Wisconsin	568,607,000	0.8%
29	Nevada	504,679,000	0.7%
30	Kentucky	462,693,000	0.7%
31	Mississippi	437,387,000	0.6%
32	Oklahoma	416,483,000	0.6%
33	South Carolina	409,220,000	0.6%
34	Hawaii	387,625,000	0.5%
35	New Mexico	382,235,000	0.5%
36	Nebraska	354,855,000	0.5%
37	Arkansas	326,280,000	0.5%
38	Alaska	257,537,000	0.4%
39	Montana	249,646,000	0.4%
40	Kansas	247,133,000	0.3%
41	West Virginia	244,184,000	0.3%
42	North Dakota	206,430,000	0.3%
43	South Dakota	185,398,000	0.3%
44	Rhode Island	181,070,000	0.3%
45	New Hampshire	162,731,000	0.2%
46	Maine	141,546,000	0.2%
47	Idaho	132,859,000	0.2%
48	Wyoming	116,217,000	0.2%
49	Delaware	74,978,000	0.1%
50	Vermont	73,989,000	0.1%
	District of Columbia	3,982,425,000	5.6%

Source: U.S. Bureau of the Census, Governments Division
"2013 State and Local Government Finances" (http://www.census.gov/govs/local/)

Per Capita Local Government Revenue from the Federal Government in 2013

National Per Capita = $225

ALPHA ORDER

RANK	STATE	PER CAPITA
20	Alabama	$199
2	Alaska	349
32	Arizona	152
41	Arkansas	110
3	California	312
7	Colorado	260
28	Connecticut	177
50	Delaware	81
11	Florida	234
34	Georgia	145
6	Hawaii	275
49	Idaho	82
9	Illinois	250
46	Indiana	95
23	Iowa	196
48	Kansas	85
44	Kentucky	105
15	Louisiana	219
43	Maine	107
13	Maryland	223
19	Massachusetts	212
24	Michigan	195
31	Minnesota	165
33	Mississippi	146
35	Missouri	143
10	Montana	246
25	Nebraska	190
27	Nevada	181
37	New Hampshire	123
40	New Jersey	112
26	New Mexico	183
1	New York	381
12	North Carolina	226
4	North Dakota	285
13	Ohio	223
42	Oklahoma	108
5	Oregon	276
15	Pennsylvania	219
30	Rhode Island	172
47	South Carolina	86
15	South Dakota	219
38	Tennessee	120
28	Texas	177
22	Utah	198
39	Vermont	118
18	Virginia	217
8	Washington	252
36	West Virginia	132
45	Wisconsin	99
20	Wyoming	199

RANK ORDER

RANK	STATE	PER CAPITA
1	New York	$381
2	Alaska	349
3	California	312
4	North Dakota	285
5	Oregon	276
6	Hawaii	275
7	Colorado	260
8	Washington	252
9	Illinois	250
10	Montana	246
11	Florida	234
12	North Carolina	226
13	Maryland	223
13	Ohio	223
15	Louisiana	219
15	Pennsylvania	219
15	South Dakota	219
18	Virginia	217
19	Massachusetts	212
20	Alabama	199
20	Wyoming	199
22	Utah	198
23	Iowa	196
24	Michigan	195
25	Nebraska	190
26	New Mexico	183
27	Nevada	181
28	Connecticut	177
28	Texas	177
30	Rhode Island	172
31	Minnesota	165
32	Arizona	152
33	Mississippi	146
34	Georgia	145
35	Missouri	143
36	West Virginia	132
37	New Hampshire	123
38	Tennessee	120
39	Vermont	118
40	New Jersey	112
41	Arkansas	110
42	Oklahoma	108
43	Maine	107
44	Kentucky	105
45	Wisconsin	99
46	Indiana	95
47	South Carolina	86
48	Kansas	85
49	Idaho	82
50	Delaware	81
	District of Columbia	6,131

Source: CQ Press using data from U.S. Bureau of the Census, Governments Division
"2013 State and Local Government Finances" (http://www.census.gov/govs/local/)

Local Government Own Source Revenue in 2013

National Total = $947,095,414,000*

ALPHA ORDER

RANK	STATE	REVENUE	% of USA
26	Alabama	$11,378,100,000	1.2%
43	Alaska	2,698,350,000	0.3%
22	Arizona	14,567,163,000	1.5%
37	Arkansas	3,806,372,000	0.4%
1	California	129,614,604,000	13.7%
14	Colorado	19,093,989,000	2.0%
25	Connecticut	11,431,842,000	1.2%
49	Delaware	1,456,105,000	0.2%
4	Florida	57,803,292,000	6.1%
9	Georgia	25,780,045,000	2.7%
44	Hawaii	2,686,685,000	0.3%
42	Idaho	2,919,023,000	0.3%
5	Illinois	41,352,867,000	4.4%
19	Indiana	15,175,888,000	1.6%
28	Iowa	9,310,234,000	1.0%
29	Kansas	8,828,738,000	0.9%
31	Kentucky	7,369,850,000	0.8%
23	Louisiana	13,292,564,000	1.4%
39	Maine	3,204,929,000	0.3%
16	Maryland	18,443,412,000	1.9%
15	Massachusetts	18,443,839,000	1.9%
12	Michigan	21,549,852,000	2.3%
21	Minnesota	15,135,038,000	1.6%
33	Mississippi	6,720,753,000	0.7%
17	Missouri	15,892,134,000	1.7%
46	Montana	2,051,324,000	0.2%
34	Nebraska	6,172,598,000	0.7%
32	Nevada	7,099,608,000	0.7%
38	New Hampshire	3,794,544,000	0.4%
7	New Jersey	33,643,542,000	3.6%
36	New Mexico	3,819,277,000	0.4%
2	New York	112,135,383,000	11.8%
10	North Carolina	24,260,910,000	2.6%
48	North Dakota	1,909,575,000	0.2%
8	Ohio	32,596,322,000	3.4%
30	Oklahoma	7,675,322,000	0.8%
27	Oregon	10,105,974,000	1.1%
6	Pennsylvania	35,924,480,000	3.8%
41	Rhode Island	2,993,646,000	0.3%
24	South Carolina	13,123,142,000	1.4%
47	South Dakota	2,041,750,000	0.2%
20	Tennessee	15,145,268,000	1.6%
3	Texas	75,245,640,000	7.9%
35	Utah	5,986,995,000	0.6%
50	Vermont	825,416,000	0.1%
11	Virginia	21,937,124,000	2.3%
13	Washington	21,536,943,000	2.3%
40	West Virginia	3,026,558,000	0.3%
18	Wisconsin	15,487,358,000	1.6%
45	Wyoming	2,634,102,000	0.3%

RANK ORDER

RANK	STATE	REVENUE	% of USA
1	California	$129,614,604,000	13.7%
2	New York	112,135,383,000	11.8%
3	Texas	75,245,640,000	7.9%
4	Florida	57,803,292,000	6.1%
5	Illinois	41,352,867,000	4.4%
6	Pennsylvania	35,924,480,000	3.8%
7	New Jersey	33,643,542,000	3.6%
8	Ohio	32,596,322,000	3.4%
9	Georgia	25,780,045,000	2.7%
10	North Carolina	24,260,910,000	2.6%
11	Virginia	21,937,124,000	2.3%
12	Michigan	21,549,852,000	2.3%
13	Washington	21,536,943,000	2.3%
14	Colorado	19,093,989,000	2.0%
15	Massachusetts	18,443,839,000	1.9%
16	Maryland	18,443,412,000	1.9%
17	Missouri	15,892,134,000	1.7%
18	Wisconsin	15,487,358,000	1.6%
19	Indiana	15,175,888,000	1.6%
20	Tennessee	15,145,268,000	1.6%
21	Minnesota	15,135,038,000	1.6%
22	Arizona	14,567,163,000	1.5%
23	Louisiana	13,292,564,000	1.4%
24	South Carolina	13,123,142,000	1.4%
25	Connecticut	11,431,842,000	1.2%
26	Alabama	11,378,100,000	1.2%
27	Oregon	10,105,974,000	1.1%
28	Iowa	9,310,234,000	1.0%
29	Kansas	8,828,738,000	0.9%
30	Oklahoma	7,675,322,000	0.8%
31	Kentucky	7,369,850,000	0.8%
32	Nevada	7,099,608,000	0.7%
33	Mississippi	6,720,753,000	0.7%
34	Nebraska	6,172,598,000	0.7%
35	Utah	5,986,995,000	0.6%
36	New Mexico	3,819,277,000	0.4%
37	Arkansas	3,806,372,000	0.4%
38	New Hampshire	3,794,544,000	0.4%
39	Maine	3,204,929,000	0.3%
40	West Virginia	3,026,558,000	0.3%
41	Rhode Island	2,993,646,000	0.3%
42	Idaho	2,919,023,000	0.3%
43	Alaska	2,698,350,000	0.3%
44	Hawaii	2,686,685,000	0.3%
45	Wyoming	2,634,102,000	0.3%
46	Montana	2,051,324,000	0.2%
47	South Dakota	2,041,750,000	0.2%
48	North Dakota	1,909,575,000	0.2%
49	Delaware	1,456,105,000	0.2%
50	Vermont	825,416,000	0.1%
	District of Columbia	7,966,945,000	0.8%

Source: U.S. Bureau of the Census, Governments Division
"2013 State and Local Government Finances" (http://www.census.gov/govs/local/)
*Own source revenue includes taxes, current charges, and miscellaneous general revenue. Excluded are intergovernmental transfers, insurance trust revenue, and revenue from government owned utilities and other commercial or auxiliary enterprise.

Per Capita Local Government Own Source Revenue in 2013

National Per Capita = $2,993*

ALPHA ORDER

RANK	STATE	PER CAPITA
34	Alabama	$2,355
4	Alaska	3,659
38	Arizona	2,197
50	Arkansas	1,287
6	California	3,374
5	Colorado	3,622
9	Connecticut	3,178
48	Delaware	1,574
14	Florida	2,950
28	Georgia	2,580
43	Hawaii	1,907
45	Idaho	1,810
8	Illinois	3,208
36	Indiana	2,310
13	Iowa	3,011
12	Kansas	3,050
46	Kentucky	1,676
15	Louisiana	2,873
33	Maine	2,412
10	Maryland	3,107
23	Massachusetts	2,749
39	Michigan	2,177
21	Minnesota	2,792
37	Mississippi	2,247
27	Missouri	2,630
41	Montana	2,022
7	Nebraska	3,302
30	Nevada	2,544
16	New Hampshire	2,869
3	New Jersey	3,777
44	New Mexico	1,830
1	New York	5,695
31	North Carolina	2,464
26	North Dakota	2,639
19	Ohio	2,817
42	Oklahoma	1,992
29	Oregon	2,573
20	Pennsylvania	2,810
17	Rhode Island	2,843
22	South Carolina	2,752
32	South Dakota	2,416
35	Tennessee	2,331
18	Texas	2,839
40	Utah	2,062
49	Vermont	1,316
25	Virginia	2,653
11	Washington	3,088
47	West Virginia	1,633
24	Wisconsin	2,696
2	Wyoming	4,517

RANK ORDER

RANK	STATE	PER CAPITA
1	New York	$5,695
2	Wyoming	4,517
3	New Jersey	3,777
4	Alaska	3,659
5	Colorado	3,622
6	California	3,374
7	Nebraska	3,302
8	Illinois	3,208
9	Connecticut	3,178
10	Maryland	3,107
11	Washington	3,088
12	Kansas	3,050
13	Iowa	3,011
14	Florida	2,950
15	Louisiana	2,873
16	New Hampshire	2,869
17	Rhode Island	2,843
18	Texas	2,839
19	Ohio	2,817
20	Pennsylvania	2,810
21	Minnesota	2,792
22	South Carolina	2,752
23	Massachusetts	2,749
24	Wisconsin	2,696
25	Virginia	2,653
26	North Dakota	2,639
27	Missouri	2,630
28	Georgia	2,580
29	Oregon	2,573
30	Nevada	2,544
31	North Carolina	2,464
32	South Dakota	2,416
33	Maine	2,412
34	Alabama	2,355
35	Tennessee	2,331
36	Indiana	2,310
37	Mississippi	2,247
38	Arizona	2,197
39	Michigan	2,177
40	Utah	2,062
41	Montana	2,022
42	Oklahoma	1,992
43	Hawaii	1,907
44	New Mexico	1,830
45	Idaho	1,810
46	Kentucky	1,676
47	West Virginia	1,633
48	Delaware	1,574
49	Vermont	1,316
50	Arkansas	1,287
	District of Columbia	12,266

Source: CQ Press using data from U.S. Bureau of the Census, Governments Division
"2013 State and Local Government Finances" (http://www.census.gov/govs/local/)
*Own source revenue includes taxes, current charges, and miscellaneous general revenue. Excluded are intergovernmental transfers, insurance trust revenue, and revenue from government owned utilities and other commercial or auxiliary enterprise.

Local Government Tax Revenue in 2013

National Total = $608,064,019,000

ALPHA ORDER

RANK	STATE	REVENUE	% of USA
27	Alabama	$5,457,216,000	0.9%
43	Alaska	1,659,934,000	0.3%
20	Arizona	9,184,720,000	1.5%
40	Arkansas	2,178,289,000	0.4%
2	California	71,469,137,000	11.8%
16	Colorado	11,624,911,000	1.9%
18	Connecticut	9,935,956,000	1.6%
49	Delaware	920,607,000	0.2%
4	Florida	30,822,122,000	5.1%
10	Georgia	15,397,393,000	2.5%
41	Hawaii	1,948,283,000	0.3%
44	Idaho	1,525,883,000	0.3%
5	Illinois	30,539,137,000	5.0%
24	Indiana	7,988,911,000	1.3%
28	Iowa	5,412,891,000	0.9%
29	Kansas	5,282,295,000	0.9%
30	Kentucky	4,615,626,000	0.8%
22	Louisiana	8,343,146,000	1.4%
37	Maine	2,518,259,000	0.4%
12	Maryland	14,351,877,000	2.4%
11	Massachusetts	14,493,311,000	2.4%
13	Michigan	12,186,096,000	2.0%
23	Minnesota	8,083,918,000	1.3%
36	Mississippi	2,859,769,000	0.5%
19	Missouri	9,770,463,000	1.6%
46	Montana	1,207,974,000	0.2%
32	Nebraska	3,978,875,000	0.7%
34	Nevada	3,791,157,000	0.6%
35	New Hampshire	3,201,463,000	0.5%
6	New Jersey	27,122,557,000	4.5%
38	New Mexico	2,464,564,000	0.4%
1	New York	84,824,993,000	14.0%
15	North Carolina	11,770,071,000	1.9%
48	North Dakota	1,085,540,000	0.2%
8	Ohio	21,947,737,000	3.6%
31	Oklahoma	4,563,419,000	0.8%
26	Oregon	6,192,331,000	1.0%
7	Pennsylvania	25,169,800,000	4.1%
39	Rhode Island	2,461,725,000	0.4%
25	South Carolina	6,520,534,000	1.1%
45	South Dakota	1,432,062,000	0.2%
21	Tennessee	8,448,831,000	1.4%
3	Texas	50,658,611,000	8.3%
33	Utah	3,863,088,000	0.6%
50	Vermont	520,282,000	0.1%
9	Virginia	15,859,907,000	2.6%
14	Washington	12,125,908,000	2.0%
42	West Virginia	1,834,977,000	0.3%
17	Wisconsin	11,074,592,000	1.8%
47	Wyoming	1,193,104,000	0.2%

RANK ORDER

RANK	STATE	REVENUE	% of USA
1	New York	$84,824,993,000	14.0%
2	California	71,469,137,000	11.8%
3	Texas	50,658,611,000	8.3%
4	Florida	30,822,122,000	5.1%
5	Illinois	30,539,137,000	5.0%
6	New Jersey	27,122,557,000	4.5%
7	Pennsylvania	25,169,800,000	4.1%
8	Ohio	21,947,737,000	3.6%
9	Virginia	15,859,907,000	2.6%
10	Georgia	15,397,393,000	2.5%
11	Massachusetts	14,493,311,000	2.4%
12	Maryland	14,351,877,000	2.4%
13	Michigan	12,186,096,000	2.0%
14	Washington	12,125,908,000	2.0%
15	North Carolina	11,770,071,000	1.9%
16	Colorado	11,624,911,000	1.9%
17	Wisconsin	11,074,592,000	1.8%
18	Connecticut	9,935,956,000	1.6%
19	Missouri	9,770,463,000	1.6%
20	Arizona	9,184,720,000	1.5%
21	Tennessee	8,448,831,000	1.4%
22	Louisiana	8,343,146,000	1.4%
23	Minnesota	8,083,918,000	1.3%
24	Indiana	7,988,911,000	1.3%
25	South Carolina	6,520,534,000	1.1%
26	Oregon	6,192,331,000	1.0%
27	Alabama	5,457,216,000	0.9%
28	Iowa	5,412,891,000	0.9%
29	Kansas	5,282,295,000	0.9%
30	Kentucky	4,615,626,000	0.8%
31	Oklahoma	4,563,419,000	0.8%
32	Nebraska	3,978,875,000	0.7%
33	Utah	3,863,088,000	0.6%
34	Nevada	3,791,157,000	0.6%
35	New Hampshire	3,201,463,000	0.5%
36	Mississippi	2,859,769,000	0.5%
37	Maine	2,518,259,000	0.4%
38	New Mexico	2,464,564,000	0.4%
39	Rhode Island	2,461,725,000	0.4%
40	Arkansas	2,178,289,000	0.4%
41	Hawaii	1,948,283,000	0.3%
42	West Virginia	1,834,977,000	0.3%
43	Alaska	1,659,934,000	0.3%
44	Idaho	1,525,883,000	0.3%
45	South Dakota	1,432,062,000	0.2%
46	Montana	1,207,974,000	0.2%
47	Wyoming	1,193,104,000	0.2%
48	North Dakota	1,085,540,000	0.2%
49	Delaware	920,607,000	0.2%
50	Vermont	520,282,000	0.1%
	District of Columbia	6,179,767,000	1.0%

Source: U.S. Bureau of the Census, Governments Division
"2013 State and Local Government Finances" (http://www.census.gov/govs/local/)

Per Capita Local Government Tax Revenue in 2013

National Per Capita = $1,922

ALPHA ORDER

RANK	STATE	PER CAPITA
43	Alabama	$1,130
8	Alaska	2,251
31	Arizona	1,385
50	Arkansas	736
19	California	1,860
9	Colorado	2,205
3	Connecticut	2,762
45	Delaware	995
27	Florida	1,573
28	Georgia	1,541
32	Hawaii	1,383
48	Idaho	946
6	Illinois	2,369
38	Indiana	1,216
22	Iowa	1,750
20	Kansas	1,825
44	Kentucky	1,049
21	Louisiana	1,803
18	Maine	1,895
5	Maryland	2,418
10	Massachusetts	2,160
37	Michigan	1,231
30	Minnesota	1,491
47	Mississippi	956
25	Missouri	1,617
40	Montana	1,191
11	Nebraska	2,129
34	Nevada	1,359
4	New Hampshire	2,420
2	New Jersey	3,045
42	New Mexico	1,181
1	New York	4,308
39	North Carolina	1,195
29	North Dakota	1,500
17	Ohio	1,897
41	Oklahoma	1,184
26	Oregon	1,576
13	Pennsylvania	1,969
7	Rhode Island	2,338
33	South Carolina	1,367
24	South Dakota	1,694
36	Tennessee	1,301
16	Texas	1,912
35	Utah	1,330
49	Vermont	830
15	Virginia	1,918
23	Washington	1,739
46	West Virginia	990
14	Wisconsin	1,928
12	Wyoming	2,046

RANK ORDER

RANK	STATE	PER CAPITA
1	New York	$4,308
2	New Jersey	3,045
3	Connecticut	2,762
4	New Hampshire	2,420
5	Maryland	2,418
6	Illinois	2,369
7	Rhode Island	2,338
8	Alaska	2,251
9	Colorado	2,205
10	Massachusetts	2,160
11	Nebraska	2,129
12	Wyoming	2,046
13	Pennsylvania	1,969
14	Wisconsin	1,928
15	Virginia	1,918
16	Texas	1,912
17	Ohio	1,897
18	Maine	1,895
19	California	1,860
20	Kansas	1,825
21	Louisiana	1,803
22	Iowa	1,750
23	Washington	1,739
24	South Dakota	1,694
25	Missouri	1,617
26	Oregon	1,576
27	Florida	1,573
28	Georgia	1,541
29	North Dakota	1,500
30	Minnesota	1,491
31	Arizona	1,385
32	Hawaii	1,383
33	South Carolina	1,367
34	Nevada	1,359
35	Utah	1,330
36	Tennessee	1,301
37	Michigan	1,231
38	Indiana	1,216
39	North Carolina	1,195
40	Montana	1,191
41	Oklahoma	1,184
42	New Mexico	1,181
43	Alabama	1,130
44	Kentucky	1,049
45	Delaware	995
46	West Virginia	990
47	Mississippi	956
48	Idaho	946
49	Vermont	830
50	Arkansas	736
	District of Columbia	9,514

Source: CQ Press using data from U.S. Bureau of the Census, Governments Division
"2013 State and Local Government Finances" (http://www.census.gov/govs/local/)

Local Government Total Expenditures in 2013

National Total = $1,698,603,400,000*

ALPHA ORDER

RANK	STATE	EXPENDITURES	% of USA
24	Alabama	$21,346,826,000	1.3%
39	Alaska	5,465,933,000	0.3%
19	Arizona	27,885,581,000	1.6%
36	Arkansas	9,818,232,000	0.6%
1	California	272,244,866,000	16.0%
18	Colorado	28,927,890,000	1.7%
27	Connecticut	17,497,154,000	1.0%
48	Delaware	3,348,947,000	0.2%
4	Florida	94,775,788,000	5.6%
11	Georgia	43,751,404,000	2.6%
49	Hawaii	3,328,003,000	0.2%
41	Idaho	5,199,360,000	0.3%
5	Illinois	74,287,088,000	4.4%
22	Indiana	25,629,871,000	1.5%
28	Iowa	15,992,216,000	0.9%
30	Kansas	14,215,083,000	0.8%
29	Kentucky	14,515,399,000	0.9%
23	Louisiana	22,150,197,000	1.3%
43	Maine	4,660,377,000	0.3%
17	Maryland	29,935,351,000	1.8%
14	Massachusetts	34,194,911,000	2.0%
9	Michigan	45,608,174,000	2.7%
16	Minnesota	30,170,873,000	1.8%
34	Mississippi	12,609,692,000	0.7%
21	Missouri	26,889,407,000	1.6%
45	Montana	3,672,526,000	0.2%
33	Nebraska	12,874,645,000	0.8%
32	Nevada	13,055,349,000	0.8%
40	New Hampshire	5,359,498,000	0.3%
8	New Jersey	46,577,717,000	2.7%
37	New Mexico	8,459,044,000	0.5%
2	New York	193,532,070,000	11.4%
10	North Carolina	45,588,251,000	2.7%
46	North Dakota	3,565,415,000	0.2%
7	Ohio	54,454,051,000	3.2%
31	Oklahoma	13,559,503,000	0.8%
26	Oregon	18,690,943,000	1.1%
6	Pennsylvania	63,122,172,000	3.7%
44	Rhode Island	4,436,287,000	0.3%
25	South Carolina	20,035,208,000	1.2%
47	South Dakota	3,364,710,000	0.2%
15	Tennessee	31,799,023,000	1.9%
3	Texas	126,422,750,000	7.4%
35	Utah	11,721,039,000	0.7%
50	Vermont	2,752,353,000	0.2%
13	Virginia	37,540,640,000	2.2%
12	Washington	40,130,476,000	2.4%
38	West Virginia	5,913,511,000	0.3%
20	Wisconsin	27,865,037,000	1.6%
42	Wyoming	4,713,756,000	0.3%

RANK ORDER

RANK	STATE	EXPENDITURES	% of USA
1	California	$272,244,866,000	16.0%
2	New York	193,532,070,000	11.4%
3	Texas	126,422,750,000	7.4%
4	Florida	94,775,788,000	5.6%
5	Illinois	74,287,088,000	4.4%
6	Pennsylvania	63,122,172,000	3.7%
7	Ohio	54,454,051,000	3.2%
8	New Jersey	46,577,717,000	2.7%
9	Michigan	45,608,174,000	2.7%
10	North Carolina	45,588,251,000	2.7%
11	Georgia	43,751,404,000	2.6%
12	Washington	40,130,476,000	2.4%
13	Virginia	37,540,640,000	2.2%
14	Massachusetts	34,194,911,000	2.0%
15	Tennessee	31,799,023,000	1.9%
16	Minnesota	30,170,873,000	1.8%
17	Maryland	29,935,351,000	1.8%
18	Colorado	28,927,890,000	1.7%
19	Arizona	27,885,581,000	1.6%
20	Wisconsin	27,865,037,000	1.6%
21	Missouri	26,889,407,000	1.6%
22	Indiana	25,629,871,000	1.5%
23	Louisiana	22,150,197,000	1.3%
24	Alabama	21,346,826,000	1.3%
25	South Carolina	20,035,208,000	1.2%
26	Oregon	18,690,943,000	1.1%
27	Connecticut	17,497,154,000	1.0%
28	Iowa	15,992,216,000	0.9%
29	Kentucky	14,515,399,000	0.9%
30	Kansas	14,215,083,000	0.8%
31	Oklahoma	13,559,503,000	0.8%
32	Nevada	13,055,349,000	0.8%
33	Nebraska	12,874,645,000	0.8%
34	Mississippi	12,609,692,000	0.7%
35	Utah	11,721,039,000	0.7%
36	Arkansas	9,818,232,000	0.6%
37	New Mexico	8,459,044,000	0.5%
38	West Virginia	5,913,511,000	0.3%
39	Alaska	5,465,933,000	0.3%
40	New Hampshire	5,359,498,000	0.3%
41	Idaho	5,199,360,000	0.3%
42	Wyoming	4,713,756,000	0.3%
43	Maine	4,660,377,000	0.3%
44	Rhode Island	4,436,287,000	0.3%
45	Montana	3,672,526,000	0.2%
46	North Dakota	3,565,415,000	0.2%
47	South Dakota	3,364,710,000	0.2%
48	Delaware	3,348,947,000	0.2%
49	Hawaii	3,328,003,000	0.2%
50	Vermont	2,752,353,000	0.2%
	District of Columbia	14,948,803,000	0.9%

Source: U.S. Bureau of the Census, Governments Division
"2013 State and Local Government Finances" (http://www.census.gov/govs/local/)
*Total expenditures includes all money paid other than for retirement of debt and extension of loans. Includes payments from all sources of funds including current revenues and proceeds from borrowing and prior year fund balances. Includes intergovernmental transfers and expenditures for government owned utilities and other commercial or auxiliary enterprise and insurance trust expenditures.

Per Capita Local Government Total Expenditures in 2013

National Per Capita = $5,368*

ALPHA ORDER

RANK	STATE	PER CAPITA
30	Alabama	$4,419
3	Alaska	7,412
35	Arizona	4,205
46	Arkansas	3,319
4	California	7,087
9	Colorado	5,488
18	Connecticut	4,864
43	Delaware	3,619
20	Florida	4,837
32	Georgia	4,379
50	Hawaii	2,362
48	Idaho	3,224
6	Illinois	5,763
41	Indiana	3,901
11	Iowa	5,172
16	Kansas	4,911
47	Kentucky	3,300
21	Louisiana	4,787
45	Maine	3,507
13	Maryland	5,043
12	Massachusetts	5,097
27	Michigan	4,607
8	Minnesota	5,566
33	Mississippi	4,216
29	Missouri	4,449
42	Montana	3,620
5	Nebraska	6,887
25	Nevada	4,679
38	New Hampshire	4,052
10	New Jersey	5,229
37	New Mexico	4,053
1	New York	9,828
26	North Carolina	4,630
15	North Dakota	4,927
24	Ohio	4,706
44	Oklahoma	3,519
23	Oregon	4,758
14	Pennsylvania	4,938
34	Rhode Island	4,214
36	South Carolina	4,202
40	South Dakota	3,981
17	Tennessee	4,895
22	Texas	4,771
39	Utah	4,037
31	Vermont	4,389
28	Virginia	4,541
7	Washington	5,755
49	West Virginia	3,191
19	Wisconsin	4,851
2	Wyoming	8,084

RANK ORDER

RANK	STATE	PER CAPITA
1	New York	$9,828
2	Wyoming	8,084
3	Alaska	7,412
4	California	7,087
5	Nebraska	6,887
6	Illinois	5,763
7	Washington	5,755
8	Minnesota	5,566
9	Colorado	5,488
10	New Jersey	5,229
11	Iowa	5,172
12	Massachusetts	5,097
13	Maryland	5,043
14	Pennsylvania	4,938
15	North Dakota	4,927
16	Kansas	4,911
17	Tennessee	4,895
18	Connecticut	4,864
19	Wisconsin	4,851
20	Florida	4,837
21	Louisiana	4,787
22	Texas	4,771
23	Oregon	4,758
24	Ohio	4,706
25	Nevada	4,679
26	North Carolina	4,630
27	Michigan	4,607
28	Virginia	4,541
29	Missouri	4,449
30	Alabama	4,419
31	Vermont	4,389
32	Georgia	4,379
33	Mississippi	4,216
34	Rhode Island	4,214
35	Arizona	4,205
36	South Carolina	4,202
37	New Mexico	4,053
38	New Hampshire	4,052
39	Utah	4,037
40	South Dakota	3,981
41	Indiana	3,901
42	Montana	3,620
43	Delaware	3,619
44	Oklahoma	3,519
45	Maine	3,507
46	Arkansas	3,319
47	Kentucky	3,300
48	Idaho	3,224
49	West Virginia	3,191
50	Hawaii	2,362
	District of Columbia	23,014

Source: CQ Press using data from U.S. Bureau of the Census, Governments Division
"2013 State and Local Government Finances" (http://www.census.gov/govs/local/)
*Total expenditures includes all money paid other than for retirement of debt and extension of loans. Includes payments from all sources of funds including current revenues and proceeds from borrowing and prior year fund balances. Includes intergovernmental transfers and expenditures for government owned utilities and other commercial or auxiliary enterprise and insurance trust expenditures.

Local Government Direct General Expenditures in 2013

National Total = $1,445,341,766,000*

ALPHA ORDER

RANK	STATE	EXPENDITURES	% of USA
25	Alabama	$18,113,755,000	1.3%
41	Alaska	4,891,023,000	0.3%
22	Arizona	21,769,365,000	1.5%
35	Arkansas	8,804,657,000	0.6%
1	California	223,540,406,000	15.5%
18	Colorado	24,460,658,000	1.7%
27	Connecticut	16,093,099,000	1.1%
48	Delaware	2,894,257,000	0.2%
4	Florida	81,578,618,000	5.6%
11	Georgia	36,926,123,000	2.6%
50	Hawaii	2,431,253,000	0.2%
40	Idaho	4,964,277,000	0.3%
5	Illinois	61,836,165,000	4.3%
20	Indiana	22,643,932,000	1.6%
28	Iowa	14,797,318,000	1.0%
29	Kansas	12,804,669,000	0.9%
30	Kentucky	12,346,668,000	0.9%
23	Louisiana	20,470,937,000	1.4%
42	Maine	4,478,476,000	0.3%
15	Maryland	27,160,935,000	1.9%
14	Massachusetts	28,773,914,000	2.0%
9	Michigan	40,401,777,000	2.8%
16	Minnesota	27,155,004,000	1.9%
33	Mississippi	11,629,633,000	0.8%
19	Missouri	23,356,922,000	1.6%
45	Montana	3,509,791,000	0.2%
36	Nebraska	8,353,466,000	0.6%
32	Nevada	11,701,918,000	0.8%
39	New Hampshire	5,077,515,000	0.4%
8	New Jersey	44,921,770,000	3.1%
37	New Mexico	7,675,706,000	0.5%
2	New York	153,804,310,000	10.6%
10	North Carolina	40,168,346,000	2.8%
46	North Dakota	3,303,863,000	0.2%
7	Ohio	50,050,245,000	3.5%
31	Oklahoma	11,935,574,000	0.8%
26	Oregon	16,232,973,000	1.1%
6	Pennsylvania	56,439,154,000	3.9%
44	Rhode Island	4,038,194,000	0.3%
24	South Carolina	18,172,276,000	1.3%
47	South Dakota	2,944,868,000	0.2%
21	Tennessee	21,976,127,000	1.5%
3	Texas	106,808,318,000	7.4%
34	Utah	9,370,174,000	0.6%
49	Vermont	2,460,152,000	0.2%
12	Virginia	34,284,047,000	2.4%
13	Washington	31,425,852,000	2.2%
38	West Virginia	5,445,610,000	0.4%
17	Wisconsin	24,953,743,000	1.7%
43	Wyoming	4,407,209,000	0.3%

RANK ORDER

RANK	STATE	EXPENDITURES	% of USA
1	California	$223,540,406,000	15.5%
2	New York	153,804,310,000	10.6%
3	Texas	106,808,318,000	7.4%
4	Florida	81,578,618,000	5.6%
5	Illinois	61,836,165,000	4.3%
6	Pennsylvania	56,439,154,000	3.9%
7	Ohio	50,050,245,000	3.5%
8	New Jersey	44,921,770,000	3.1%
9	Michigan	40,401,777,000	2.8%
10	North Carolina	40,168,346,000	2.8%
11	Georgia	36,926,123,000	2.6%
12	Virginia	34,284,047,000	2.4%
13	Washington	31,425,852,000	2.2%
14	Massachusetts	28,773,914,000	2.0%
15	Maryland	27,160,935,000	1.9%
16	Minnesota	27,155,004,000	1.9%
17	Wisconsin	24,953,743,000	1.7%
18	Colorado	24,460,658,000	1.7%
19	Missouri	23,356,922,000	1.6%
20	Indiana	22,643,932,000	1.6%
21	Tennessee	21,976,127,000	1.5%
22	Arizona	21,769,365,000	1.5%
23	Louisiana	20,470,937,000	1.4%
24	South Carolina	18,172,276,000	1.3%
25	Alabama	18,113,755,000	1.3%
26	Oregon	16,232,973,000	1.1%
27	Connecticut	16,093,099,000	1.1%
28	Iowa	14,797,318,000	1.0%
29	Kansas	12,804,669,000	0.9%
30	Kentucky	12,346,668,000	0.9%
31	Oklahoma	11,935,574,000	0.8%
32	Nevada	11,701,918,000	0.8%
33	Mississippi	11,629,633,000	0.8%
34	Utah	9,370,174,000	0.6%
35	Arkansas	8,804,657,000	0.6%
36	Nebraska	8,353,466,000	0.6%
37	New Mexico	7,675,706,000	0.5%
38	West Virginia	5,445,610,000	0.4%
39	New Hampshire	5,077,515,000	0.4%
40	Idaho	4,964,277,000	0.3%
41	Alaska	4,891,023,000	0.3%
42	Maine	4,478,476,000	0.3%
43	Wyoming	4,407,209,000	0.3%
44	Rhode Island	4,038,194,000	0.3%
45	Montana	3,509,791,000	0.2%
46	North Dakota	3,303,863,000	0.2%
47	South Dakota	2,944,868,000	0.2%
48	Delaware	2,894,257,000	0.2%
49	Vermont	2,460,152,000	0.2%
50	Hawaii	2,431,253,000	0.2%
	District of Columbia	11,556,724,000	0.8%

Source: U.S. Bureau of the Census, Governments Division
 "2013 State and Local Government Finances" (http://www.census.gov/govs/local/)
*Direct general expenditures include expenditures for current operations, assistance and subsidies, interest on debt, and capital outlay. Excludes intergovernmental transfers, expenditures for government owned utilities and other commercial or auxiliary enterprise, and insurance trust expenditures.

Per Capita Local Government Direct General Expenditures in 2013

National Per Capita = $4,568*

ALPHA ORDER

RANK	STATE	PER CAPITA
34	Alabama	$3,750
3	Alaska	6,632
42	Arizona	3,283
47	Arkansas	2,977
4	California	5,819
9	Colorado	4,640
13	Connecticut	4,474
44	Delaware	3,128
22	Florida	4,163
35	Georgia	3,696
50	Hawaii	1,726
46	Idaho	3,078
7	Illinois	4,797
39	Indiana	3,446
8	Iowa	4,785
15	Kansas	4,424
49	Kentucky	2,807
15	Louisiana	4,424
41	Maine	3,370
10	Maryland	4,576
20	Massachusetts	4,289
25	Michigan	4,081
6	Minnesota	5,010
29	Mississippi	3,888
30	Missouri	3,865
38	Montana	3,460
14	Nebraska	4,469
21	Nevada	4,194
31	New Hampshire	3,839
5	New Jersey	5,043
36	New Mexico	3,678
1	New York	7,811
26	North Carolina	4,080
11	North Dakota	4,566
19	Ohio	4,325
45	Oklahoma	3,097
24	Oregon	4,133
17	Pennsylvania	4,415
32	Rhode Island	3,835
33	South Carolina	3,811
37	South Dakota	3,484
40	Tennessee	3,383
27	Texas	4,030
43	Utah	3,227
28	Vermont	3,923
23	Virginia	4,147
12	Washington	4,507
48	West Virginia	2,939
18	Wisconsin	4,345
2	Wyoming	7,558

RANK ORDER

RANK	STATE	PER CAPITA
1	New York	$7,811
2	Wyoming	7,558
3	Alaska	6,632
4	California	5,819
5	New Jersey	5,043
6	Minnesota	5,010
7	Illinois	4,797
8	Iowa	4,785
9	Colorado	4,640
10	Maryland	4,576
11	North Dakota	4,566
12	Washington	4,507
13	Connecticut	4,474
14	Nebraska	4,469
15	Kansas	4,424
15	Louisiana	4,424
17	Pennsylvania	4,415
18	Wisconsin	4,345
19	Ohio	4,325
20	Massachusetts	4,289
21	Nevada	4,194
22	Florida	4,163
23	Virginia	4,147
24	Oregon	4,133
25	Michigan	4,081
26	North Carolina	4,080
27	Texas	4,030
28	Vermont	3,923
29	Mississippi	3,888
30	Missouri	3,865
31	New Hampshire	3,839
32	Rhode Island	3,835
33	South Carolina	3,811
34	Alabama	3,750
35	Georgia	3,696
36	New Mexico	3,678
37	South Dakota	3,484
38	Montana	3,460
39	Indiana	3,446
40	Tennessee	3,383
41	Maine	3,370
42	Arizona	3,283
43	Utah	3,227
44	Delaware	3,128
45	Oklahoma	3,097
46	Idaho	3,078
47	Arkansas	2,977
48	West Virginia	2,939
49	Kentucky	2,807
50	Hawaii	1,726
	District of Columbia	17,792

Source: CQ Press using data from U.S. Bureau of the Census, Governments Division
"2013 State and Local Government Finances" (http://www.census.gov/govs/local/)
*Direct general expenditures include expenditures for current operations, assistance and subsidies, interest on debt, and capital outlay. Excludes intergovernmental transfers, expenditures for government owned utilities and other commercial or auxiliary enterprise, and insurance trust expenditures.

Local Government Debt Outstanding in 2013

National Total = $1,817,333,381,000*

ALPHA ORDER

RANK	STATE	DEBT	% of USA
24	Alabama	$22,565,698,000	1.2%
40	Alaska	3,397,187,000	0.2%
14	Arizona	34,937,797,000	1.9%
34	Arkansas	10,203,409,000	0.6%
1	California	268,097,791,000	14.8%
12	Colorado	36,888,910,000	2.0%
33	Connecticut	11,017,538,000	0.6%
45	Delaware	2,578,372,000	0.1%
4	Florida	108,535,217,000	6.0%
10	Georgia	42,386,314,000	2.3%
38	Hawaii	5,981,474,000	0.3%
47	Idaho	2,231,140,000	0.1%
5	Illinois	85,028,455,000	4.7%
19	Indiana	26,846,061,000	1.5%
32	Iowa	11,824,746,000	0.7%
29	Kansas	19,010,264,000	1.0%
20	Kentucky	26,710,862,000	1.5%
27	Louisiana	20,442,647,000	1.1%
41	Maine	3,031,459,000	0.2%
23	Maryland	22,834,226,000	1.3%
28	Massachusetts	19,192,844,000	1.1%
9	Michigan	45,937,855,000	2.5%
15	Minnesota	34,468,788,000	1.9%
37	Mississippi	7,018,303,000	0.4%
21	Missouri	26,266,304,000	1.4%
48	Montana	1,748,485,000	0.1%
30	Nebraska	13,122,661,000	0.7%
22	Nevada	23,194,215,000	1.3%
44	New Hampshire	2,667,800,000	0.1%
13	New Jersey	36,692,728,000	2.0%
36	New Mexico	9,092,751,000	0.5%
3	New York	210,223,571,000	11.6%
16	North Carolina	32,469,313,000	1.8%
42	North Dakota	2,824,661,000	0.2%
7	Ohio	49,350,248,000	2.7%
35	Oklahoma	9,362,017,000	0.5%
26	Oregon	21,197,403,000	1.2%
6	Pennsylvania	83,217,301,000	4.6%
43	Rhode Island	2,742,084,000	0.2%
18	South Carolina	27,590,232,000	1.5%
46	South Dakota	2,452,618,000	0.1%
17	Tennessee	30,619,123,000	1.7%
2	Texas	225,097,849,000	12.4%
31	Utah	12,575,434,000	0.7%
49	Vermont	1,214,688,000	0.1%
11	Virginia	37,449,781,000	2.1%
8	Washington	46,819,798,000	2.6%
39	West Virginia	3,544,084,000	0.2%
25	Wisconsin	21,248,164,000	1.2%
50	Wyoming	973,963,000	0.1%

RANK ORDER

RANK	STATE	DEBT	% of USA
1	California	$268,097,791,000	14.8%
2	Texas	225,097,849,000	12.4%
3	New York	210,223,571,000	11.6%
4	Florida	108,535,217,000	6.0%
5	Illinois	85,028,455,000	4.7%
6	Pennsylvania	83,217,301,000	4.6%
7	Ohio	49,350,248,000	2.7%
8	Washington	46,819,798,000	2.6%
9	Michigan	45,937,855,000	2.5%
10	Georgia	42,386,314,000	2.3%
11	Virginia	37,449,781,000	2.1%
12	Colorado	36,888,910,000	2.0%
13	New Jersey	36,692,728,000	2.0%
14	Arizona	34,937,797,000	1.9%
15	Minnesota	34,468,788,000	1.9%
16	North Carolina	32,469,313,000	1.8%
17	Tennessee	30,619,123,000	1.7%
18	South Carolina	27,590,232,000	1.5%
19	Indiana	26,846,061,000	1.5%
20	Kentucky	26,710,862,000	1.5%
21	Missouri	26,266,304,000	1.4%
22	Nevada	23,194,215,000	1.3%
23	Maryland	22,834,226,000	1.3%
24	Alabama	22,565,698,000	1.2%
25	Wisconsin	21,248,164,000	1.2%
26	Oregon	21,197,403,000	1.2%
27	Louisiana	20,442,647,000	1.1%
28	Massachusetts	19,192,844,000	1.1%
29	Kansas	19,010,264,000	1.0%
30	Nebraska	13,122,661,000	0.7%
31	Utah	12,575,434,000	0.7%
32	Iowa	11,824,746,000	0.7%
33	Connecticut	11,017,538,000	0.6%
34	Arkansas	10,203,409,000	0.6%
35	Oklahoma	9,362,017,000	0.5%
36	New Mexico	9,092,751,000	0.5%
37	Mississippi	7,018,303,000	0.4%
38	Hawaii	5,981,474,000	0.3%
39	West Virginia	3,544,084,000	0.2%
40	Alaska	3,397,187,000	0.2%
41	Maine	3,031,459,000	0.2%
42	North Dakota	2,824,661,000	0.2%
43	Rhode Island	2,742,084,000	0.2%
44	New Hampshire	2,667,800,000	0.1%
45	Delaware	2,578,372,000	0.1%
46	South Dakota	2,452,618,000	0.1%
47	Idaho	2,231,140,000	0.1%
48	Montana	1,748,485,000	0.1%
49	Vermont	1,214,688,000	0.1%
50	Wyoming	973,963,000	0.1%
	District of Columbia	12,408,748,000	0.7%

Source: U.S. Bureau of the Census, Governments Division
"2013 State and Local Government Finances" (http://www.census.gov/govs/local/)
*Includes short-term, long-term, full faith and credit, nonguaranteed, and public debt for private purposes.

Per Capita Local Government Debt Outstanding in 2013

National Per Capita = $5,743*

ALPHA ORDER

RANK	STATE	PER CAPITA
18	Alabama	$4,671
20	Alaska	4,607
16	Arizona	5,269
35	Arkansas	3,449
6	California	6,979
5	Colorado	6,998
37	Connecticut	3,063
40	Delaware	2,786
14	Florida	5,539
28	Georgia	4,242
27	Hawaii	4,246
50	Idaho	1,383
8	Illinois	6,597
30	Indiana	4,086
33	Iowa	3,824
9	Kansas	6,567
12	Kentucky	6,073
22	Louisiana	4,418
44	Maine	2,281
32	Maryland	3,847
39	Massachusetts	2,861
19	Michigan	4,640
11	Minnesota	6,359
43	Mississippi	2,346
24	Missouri	4,346
48	Montana	1,724
4	Nebraska	7,020
3	Nevada	8,312
45	New Hampshire	2,017
29	New Jersey	4,119
23	New Mexico	4,357
1	New York	10,676
36	North Carolina	3,298
31	North Dakota	3,903
26	Ohio	4,265
42	Oklahoma	2,430
15	Oregon	5,396
10	Pennsylvania	6,510
41	Rhode Island	2,604
13	South Carolina	5,786
38	South Dakota	2,902
17	Tennessee	4,713
2	Texas	8,494
25	Utah	4,331
46	Vermont	1,937
21	Virginia	4,530
7	Washington	6,714
47	West Virginia	1,913
34	Wisconsin	3,699
49	Wyoming	1,670

RANK ORDER

RANK	STATE	PER CAPITA
1	New York	$10,676
2	Texas	8,494
3	Nevada	8,312
4	Nebraska	7,020
5	Colorado	6,998
6	California	6,979
7	Washington	6,714
8	Illinois	6,597
9	Kansas	6,567
10	Pennsylvania	6,510
11	Minnesota	6,359
12	Kentucky	6,073
13	South Carolina	5,786
14	Florida	5,539
15	Oregon	5,396
16	Arizona	5,269
17	Tennessee	4,713
18	Alabama	4,671
19	Michigan	4,640
20	Alaska	4,607
21	Virginia	4,530
22	Louisiana	4,418
23	New Mexico	4,357
24	Missouri	4,346
25	Utah	4,331
26	Ohio	4,265
27	Hawaii	4,246
28	Georgia	4,242
29	New Jersey	4,119
30	Indiana	4,086
31	North Dakota	3,903
32	Maryland	3,847
33	Iowa	3,824
34	Wisconsin	3,699
35	Arkansas	3,449
36	North Carolina	3,298
37	Connecticut	3,063
38	South Dakota	2,902
39	Massachusetts	2,861
40	Delaware	2,786
41	Rhode Island	2,604
42	Oklahoma	2,430
43	Mississippi	2,346
44	Maine	2,281
45	New Hampshire	2,017
46	Vermont	1,937
47	West Virginia	1,913
48	Montana	1,724
49	Wyoming	1,670
50	Idaho	1,383
	District of Columbia	19,104

Source: CQ Press using data from U.S. Bureau of the Census, Governments Division
"2013 State and Local Government Finances" (http://www.census.gov/govs/local/)
*Includes short-term, long-term, full faith and credit, nonguaranteed, and public debt for private purposes.

Local Government Full-Time Equivalent Employees in 2014

National Total = 11,847,418 FTE Employees*

ALPHA ORDER

RANK	STATE	EMPLOYEES	% of USA
23	Alabama	194,454	1.6%
46	Alaska	27,386	0.2%
19	Arizona	208,455	1.8%
33	Arkansas	105,414	0.9%
1	California	1,345,887	11.4%
21	Colorado	200,968	1.7%
31	Connecticut	127,647	1.1%
49	Delaware	22,907	0.2%
4	Florida	686,906	5.8%
9	Georgia	376,726	3.2%
50	Hawaii	16,511	0.1%
39	Idaho	56,890	0.5%
5	Illinois	505,230	4.3%
14	Indiana	231,271	2.0%
30	Iowa	131,917	1.1%
28	Kansas	145,671	1.2%
26	Kentucky	159,578	1.3%
24	Louisiana	186,711	1.6%
41	Maine	49,727	0.4%
18	Maryland	215,082	1.8%
15	Massachusetts	230,716	1.9%
12	Michigan	295,503	2.5%
22	Minnesota	200,769	1.7%
29	Mississippi	135,193	1.1%
16	Missouri	228,518	1.9%
43	Montana	36,356	0.3%
34	Nebraska	86,455	0.7%
36	Nevada	82,626	0.7%
40	New Hampshire	52,618	0.4%
10	New Jersey	331,547	2.8%
37	New Mexico	79,647	0.7%
3	New York	926,049	7.8%
8	North Carolina	404,560	3.4%
47	North Dakota	27,073	0.2%
6	Ohio	442,143	3.7%
27	Oklahoma	148,339	1.3%
32	Oregon	123,364	1.0%
7	Pennsylvania	408,006	3.4%
45	Rhode Island	29,231	0.2%
25	South Carolina	177,651	1.5%
44	South Dakota	30,757	0.3%
13	Tennessee	244,418	2.1%
2	Texas	1,123,013	9.5%
35	Utah	86,380	0.7%
48	Vermont	25,417	0.2%
11	Virginia	320,186	2.7%
17	Washington	221,833	1.9%
38	West Virginia	63,394	0.5%
20	Wisconsin	206,555	1.7%
42	Wyoming	37,519	0.3%

RANK ORDER

RANK	STATE	EMPLOYEES	% of USA
1	California	1,345,887	11.4%
2	Texas	1,123,013	9.5%
3	New York	926,049	7.8%
4	Florida	686,906	5.8%
5	Illinois	505,230	4.3%
6	Ohio	442,143	3.7%
7	Pennsylvania	408,006	3.4%
8	North Carolina	404,560	3.4%
9	Georgia	376,726	3.2%
10	New Jersey	331,547	2.8%
11	Virginia	320,186	2.7%
12	Michigan	295,503	2.5%
13	Tennessee	244,418	2.1%
14	Indiana	231,271	2.0%
15	Massachusetts	230,716	1.9%
16	Missouri	228,518	1.9%
17	Washington	221,833	1.9%
18	Maryland	215,082	1.8%
19	Arizona	208,455	1.8%
20	Wisconsin	206,555	1.7%
21	Colorado	200,968	1.7%
22	Minnesota	200,769	1.7%
23	Alabama	194,454	1.6%
24	Louisiana	186,711	1.6%
25	South Carolina	177,651	1.5%
26	Kentucky	159,578	1.3%
27	Oklahoma	148,339	1.3%
28	Kansas	145,671	1.2%
29	Mississippi	135,193	1.1%
30	Iowa	131,917	1.1%
31	Connecticut	127,647	1.1%
32	Oregon	123,364	1.0%
33	Arkansas	105,414	0.9%
34	Nebraska	86,455	0.7%
35	Utah	86,380	0.7%
36	Nevada	82,626	0.7%
37	New Mexico	79,647	0.7%
38	West Virginia	63,394	0.5%
39	Idaho	56,890	0.5%
40	New Hampshire	52,618	0.4%
41	Maine	49,727	0.4%
42	Wyoming	37,519	0.3%
43	Montana	36,356	0.3%
44	South Dakota	30,757	0.3%
45	Rhode Island	29,231	0.2%
46	Alaska	27,386	0.2%
47	North Dakota	27,073	0.2%
48	Vermont	25,417	0.2%
49	Delaware	22,907	0.2%
50	Hawaii	16,511	0.1%
	District of Columbia	46,244	0.4%

Source: U.S. Bureau of the Census, Governments Division
"Government Employment and Payroll" (http://www.census.gov/govs/apes/index.html)
*As of March 2014.

Rate of Local Government Full-Time Equivalent Employees in 2014

National Rate = 372 FTE Employees per 10,000 Population*

ALPHA ORDER

RANK	STATE	RATE
11	Alabama	401
23	Alaska	372
44	Arizona	310
32	Arkansas	355
37	California	347
19	Colorado	375
32	Connecticut	355
49	Delaware	245
38	Florida	345
21	Georgia	373
50	Hawaii	116
36	Idaho	348
13	Illinois	392
35	Indiana	351
6	Iowa	424
2	Kansas	502
28	Kentucky	362
10	Louisiana	402
20	Maine	374
29	Maryland	360
40	Massachusetts	342
45	Michigan	298
25	Minnesota	368
5	Mississippi	452
18	Missouri	377
32	Montana	355
4	Nebraska	459
47	Nevada	291
12	New Hampshire	396
24	New Jersey	371
15	New Mexico	382
3	New York	469
8	North Carolina	407
27	North Dakota	366
17	Ohio	381
15	Oklahoma	382
43	Oregon	311
41	Pennsylvania	319
48	Rhode Island	277
25	South Carolina	368
29	South Dakota	360
21	Tennessee	373
7	Texas	416
46	Utah	293
9	Vermont	406
14	Virginia	384
42	Washington	314
39	West Virginia	343
31	Wisconsin	359
1	Wyoming	642

RANK ORDER

RANK	STATE	RATE
1	Wyoming	642
2	Kansas	502
3	New York	469
4	Nebraska	459
5	Mississippi	452
6	Iowa	424
7	Texas	416
8	North Carolina	407
9	Vermont	406
10	Louisiana	402
11	Alabama	401
12	New Hampshire	396
13	Illinois	392
14	Virginia	384
15	New Mexico	382
15	Oklahoma	382
17	Ohio	381
18	Missouri	377
19	Colorado	375
20	Maine	374
21	Georgia	373
21	Tennessee	373
23	Alaska	372
24	New Jersey	371
25	Minnesota	368
25	South Carolina	368
27	North Dakota	366
28	Kentucky	362
29	Maryland	360
29	South Dakota	360
31	Wisconsin	359
32	Arkansas	355
32	Connecticut	355
32	Montana	355
35	Indiana	351
36	Idaho	348
37	California	347
38	Florida	345
39	West Virginia	343
40	Massachusetts	342
41	Pennsylvania	319
42	Washington	314
43	Oregon	311
44	Arizona	310
45	Michigan	298
46	Utah	293
47	Nevada	291
48	Rhode Island	277
49	Delaware	245
50	Hawaii	116
	District of Columbia	701

Source: CQ Press using data from U.S. Bureau of the Census, Governments Division "Government Employment and Payroll" (http://www.census.gov/govs/apes/index.html)
*Full-time equivalent as of March 2014.

Average Annual Earnings of Full-Time Local Government Employees in 2014

National Average = $54,783*

ALPHA ORDER

RANK	STATE	SALARY
46	Alabama	$40,762
9	Alaska	63,286
21	Arizona	51,192
49	Arkansas	38,300
1	California	75,308
18	Colorado	54,296
5	Connecticut	64,976
14	Delaware	58,260
27	Florida	48,719
41	Georgia	42,172
13	Hawaii	58,553
42	Idaho	41,391
11	Illinois	60,802
34	Indiana	44,957
25	Iowa	49,919
38	Kansas	42,998
45	Kentucky	40,989
43	Louisiana	41,219
35	Maine	44,758
7	Maryland	63,568
10	Massachusetts	61,685
17	Michigan	54,707
15	Minnesota	56,907
50	Mississippi	37,049
40	Missouri	42,916
32	Montana	45,859
22	Nebraska	50,578
6	Nevada	64,369
24	New Hampshire	49,944
3	New Jersey	70,870
37	New Mexico	43,510
4	New York	68,960
33	North Carolina	45,194
30	North Dakota	47,989
23	Ohio	50,343
48	Oklahoma	39,119
12	Oregon	58,593
16	Pennsylvania	56,562
8	Rhode Island	63,489
36	South Carolina	44,063
44	South Dakota	41,102
39	Tennessee	42,986
31	Texas	46,325
28	Utah	48,571
29	Vermont	48,008
26	Virginia	49,904
2	Washington	71,127
47	West Virginia	40,304
19	Wisconsin	54,150
20	Wyoming	53,149

RANK ORDER

RANK	STATE	SALARY
1	California	$75,308
2	Washington	71,127
3	New Jersey	70,870
4	New York	68,960
5	Connecticut	64,976
6	Nevada	64,369
7	Maryland	63,568
8	Rhode Island	63,489
9	Alaska	63,286
10	Massachusetts	61,685
11	Illinois	60,802
12	Oregon	58,593
13	Hawaii	58,553
14	Delaware	58,260
15	Minnesota	56,907
16	Pennsylvania	56,562
17	Michigan	54,707
18	Colorado	54,296
19	Wisconsin	54,150
20	Wyoming	53,149
21	Arizona	51,192
22	Nebraska	50,578
23	Ohio	50,343
24	New Hampshire	49,944
25	Iowa	49,919
26	Virginia	49,904
27	Florida	48,719
28	Utah	48,571
29	Vermont	48,008
30	North Dakota	47,989
31	Texas	46,325
32	Montana	45,859
33	North Carolina	45,194
34	Indiana	44,957
35	Maine	44,758
36	South Carolina	44,063
37	New Mexico	43,510
38	Kansas	42,998
39	Tennessee	42,986
40	Missouri	42,916
41	Georgia	42,172
42	Idaho	41,391
43	Louisiana	41,219
44	South Dakota	41,102
45	Kentucky	40,989
46	Alabama	40,762
47	West Virginia	40,304
48	Oklahoma	39,119
49	Arkansas	38,300
50	Mississippi	37,049
	District of Columbia	78,512

Source: CQ Press using data from U.S. Bureau of the Census, Governments Division
"Government Employment and Payroll" (http://www.census.gov/govs/apes/index.html)
*March 2014 full-time payroll (multiplied by 12) divided by full-time employees.

XI. Health

Average Annual Single Coverage Health Insurance
    Premium per Enrolled Employee in 2014 377
Average Annual Family Coverage Health Insurance
    Premium per Enrolled Employee in 2014 378
Percent of Private-Sector Establishments That Offer
    Health Insurance: 2014 379
Persons Not Covered by Health Insurance in 2014 380
Percent of Population Not Covered by Health Insurance
    in 2014 381
Percent of Population Lacking Access to Primary Care
    in 2013 382
Physicians in 2013 383
Rate of Physicians in 2013 384
Rate of Registered Nurses in 2014 385
Rate of Dentists in 2016 386
Community Hospitals in 2014 387
Rate of Community Hospitals in 2014 388
Births in 2014 389
Birth Rate in 2014................................. 390
Births of Low Birthweight as a Percent of All Births
    in 2014 391
Births to Teenage Mothers as a Percent of All Births
    in 2013 392
Births to Unmarried Women as a Percent of All Births
    in 2014 393
Percent of Women Receiving Late or No Prenatal Care
    in 2013 394
Reported Legal Abortions in 2012 395
Reported Legal Abortions per 1,000 Live Births in 2012.. 396
Infant Deaths in 2013 397
Infant Mortality Rate in 2013 398
Deaths in 2013 399
Age-Adjusted Death Rate in 2013 400
Estimated Deaths by Cancer in 2015 401
Estimated Death Rate by Cancer in 2015.............. 402
Estimated New Cancer Cases in 2015 403
Estimated Rate of New Cancer Cases in 2015 404
Deaths by Accidents in 2013........................ 405
Age-Adjusted Death Rate by Accidents in 2013 406
Deaths by Cerebrovascular Diseases in 2013.......... 407
Age-Adjusted Death Rate by Cerebrovascular Diseases
    in 2013 408
Deaths by Diseases of the Heart in 2013 409
Age-Adjusted Death Rate by Diseases of the Heart
    in 2013 410
Deaths by Suicide in 2013 411
Age-Adjusted Death Rate by Suicide in 2013 412
Deaths by AIDS in 2013............................ 413
Age-Adjusted Death Rate by AIDS in 2013........... 414
Adult Per Capita Alcohol Consumption in 2013 415
Percent of Adults Who Smoke: 2013 416
Percent of Adults Overweight or Obese: 2013 417
Percent of Children Aged 19 to 35 Months Fully
    Immunized in 2014 418

Average Annual Single Coverage Health Insurance Premium per Enrolled Employee in 2014
National Average = $5,832*

ALPHA ORDER

RANK	STATE	PREMIUM
39	Alabama	$5,526
1	Alaska	7,099
46	Arizona	5,356
50	Arkansas	4,846
24	California	5,841
23	Colorado	5,848
6	Connecticut	6,223
10	Delaware	6,145
27	Florida	5,767
35	Georgia	5,570
47	Hawaii	5,316
49	Idaho	4,978
11	Illinois	6,126
13	Indiana	6,041
36	Iowa	5,557
45	Kansas	5,365
15	Kentucky	5,914
31	Louisiana	5,700
17	Maine	5,903
12	Maryland	6,059
3	Massachusetts	6,348
33	Michigan	5,610
26	Minnesota	5,832
42	Mississippi	5,443
41	Missouri	5,517
19	Montana	5,876
36	Nebraska	5,557
43	Nevada	5,426
4	New Hampshire	6,336
2	New Jersey	6,447
29	New Mexico	5,725
5	New York	6,307
34	North Carolina	5,593
40	North Dakota	5,521
14	Ohio	5,930
32	Oklahoma	5,649
30	Oregon	5,707
18	Pennsylvania	5,888
8	Rhode Island	6,156
22	South Carolina	5,850
21	South Dakota	5,859
48	Tennessee	5,310
28	Texas	5,740
38	Utah	5,538
7	Vermont	6,180
44	Virginia	5,422
16	Washington	5,910
9	West Virginia	6,149
20	Wisconsin	5,868
25	Wyoming	5,840

RANK ORDER

RANK	STATE	PREMIUM
1	Alaska	$7,099
2	New Jersey	6,447
3	Massachusetts	6,348
4	New Hampshire	6,336
5	New York	6,307
6	Connecticut	6,223
7	Vermont	6,180
8	Rhode Island	6,156
9	West Virginia	6,149
10	Delaware	6,145
11	Illinois	6,126
12	Maryland	6,059
13	Indiana	6,041
14	Ohio	5,930
15	Kentucky	5,914
16	Washington	5,910
17	Maine	5,903
18	Pennsylvania	5,888
19	Montana	5,876
20	Wisconsin	5,868
21	South Dakota	5,859
22	South Carolina	5,850
23	Colorado	5,848
24	California	5,841
25	Wyoming	5,840
26	Minnesota	5,832
27	Florida	5,767
28	Texas	5,740
29	New Mexico	5,725
30	Oregon	5,707
31	Louisiana	5,700
32	Oklahoma	5,649
33	Michigan	5,610
34	North Carolina	5,593
35	Georgia	5,570
36	Iowa	5,557
36	Nebraska	5,557
38	Utah	5,538
39	Alabama	5,526
40	North Dakota	5,521
41	Missouri	5,517
42	Mississippi	5,443
43	Nevada	5,426
44	Virginia	5,422
45	Kansas	5,365
46	Arizona	5,356
47	Hawaii	5,316
48	Tennessee	5,310
49	Idaho	4,978
50	Arkansas	4,846
	District of Columbia	6,097

Source: U.S. Department of Health and Human Services, Agency for Healthcare Research and Quality "Private-Sector Data by Firm Size and State" (Table II Series, Medical Expenditures Panel Survey) (http://www.meps.ahrq.gov/mepsweb/survey_comp/Insurance.jsp)

*Enrolled employees at private-sector establishments that offer health insurance coverage.

Average Annual Family Coverage Health Insurance Premium per Enrolled Employee in 2014
National Average = $16,655*

ALPHA ORDER

RANK	STATE	PREMIUM
49	Alabama	$14,352
1	Alaska	19,713
42	Arizona	15,535
50	Arkansas	14,143
8	California	17,444
35	Colorado	15,932
4	Connecticut	18,123
6	Delaware	17,514
37	Florida	15,915
28	Georgia	16,209
47	Hawaii	14,848
48	Idaho	14,729
14	Illinois	17,193
12	Indiana	17,223
38	Iowa	15,899
40	Kansas	15,652
16	Kentucky	16,711
36	Louisiana	15,928
19	Maine	16,514
11	Maryland	17,232
5	Massachusetts	17,702
41	Michigan	15,608
21	Minnesota	16,361
45	Mississippi	15,092
43	Missouri	15,493
46	Montana	15,005
30	Nebraska	16,139
29	Nevada	16,152
3	New Hampshire	18,126
2	New Jersey	19,143
39	New Mexico	15,766
10	New York	17,396
27	North Carolina	16,210
44	North Dakota	15,446
33	Ohio	15,974
26	Oklahoma	16,280
23	Oregon	16,330
24	Pennsylvania	16,328
20	Rhode Island	16,419
31	South Carolina	16,044
22	South Dakota	16,352
32	Tennessee	16,001
15	Texas	16,967
34	Utah	15,963
17	Vermont	16,659
18	Virginia	16,601
7	Washington	17,445
9	West Virginia	17,433
13	Wisconsin	17,209
25	Wyoming	16,299

RANK ORDER

RANK	STATE	PREMIUM
1	Alaska	$19,713
2	New Jersey	19,143
3	New Hampshire	18,126
4	Connecticut	18,123
5	Massachusetts	17,702
6	Delaware	17,514
7	Washington	17,445
8	California	17,444
9	West Virginia	17,433
10	New York	17,396
11	Maryland	17,232
12	Indiana	17,223
13	Wisconsin	17,209
14	Illinois	17,193
15	Texas	16,967
16	Kentucky	16,711
17	Vermont	16,659
18	Virginia	16,601
19	Maine	16,514
20	Rhode Island	16,419
21	Minnesota	16,361
22	South Dakota	16,352
23	Oregon	16,330
24	Pennsylvania	16,328
25	Wyoming	16,299
26	Oklahoma	16,280
27	North Carolina	16,210
28	Georgia	16,209
29	Nevada	16,152
30	Nebraska	16,139
31	South Carolina	16,044
32	Tennessee	16,001
33	Ohio	15,974
34	Utah	15,963
35	Colorado	15,932
36	Louisiana	15,928
37	Florida	15,915
38	Iowa	15,899
39	New Mexico	15,766
40	Kansas	15,652
41	Michigan	15,608
42	Arizona	15,535
43	Missouri	15,493
44	North Dakota	15,446
45	Mississippi	15,092
46	Montana	15,005
47	Hawaii	14,848
48	Idaho	14,729
49	Alabama	14,352
50	Arkansas	14,143
	District of Columbia	17,039

Source: U.S. Department of Health and Human Services, Agency for Healthcare Research and Quality "Private-Sector Data by Firm Size and State" (Table II Series, Medical Expenditures Panel Survey) (http://www.meps.ahrq.gov/mepsweb/survey_comp/Insurance.jsp)

*Enrolled employees at private-sector establishments that offer health insurance coverage.

Percent of Private-Sector Establishments That Offer Health Insurance: 2014

National Percent = 47.5%

ALPHA ORDER

RANK	STATE	PERCENT
5	Alabama	54.9
46	Alaska	39.7
24	Arizona	47.3
44	Arkansas	39.8
27	California	46.5
22	Colorado	47.7
11	Connecticut	52.3
17	Delaware	49.1
48	Florida	37.6
42	Georgia	40.9
1	Hawaii	86.4
49	Idaho	37.5
24	Illinois	47.3
16	Indiana	49.5
26	Iowa	47.1
19	Kansas	48.4
14	Kentucky	50.4
28	Louisiana	46.0
34	Maine	44.4
4	Maryland	55.0
2	Massachusetts	59.0
30	Michigan	45.9
39	Minnesota	42.2
36	Mississippi	43.0
21	Missouri	47.9
49	Montana	37.5
47	Nebraska	39.5
8	Nevada	53.0
10	New Hampshire	52.7
3	New Jersey	57.3
41	New Mexico	41.7
19	New York	48.4
35	North Carolina	43.5
28	North Dakota	46.0
9	Ohio	52.8
13	Oklahoma	50.6
38	Oregon	42.7
6	Pennsylvania	54.6
12	Rhode Island	52.1
33	South Carolina	45.3
37	South Dakota	42.9
18	Tennessee	48.5
30	Texas	45.9
44	Utah	39.8
40	Vermont	42.0
7	Virginia	53.4
32	Washington	45.7
15	West Virginia	50.2
23	Wisconsin	47.5
43	Wyoming	40.2

RANK ORDER

RANK	STATE	PERCENT
1	Hawaii	86.4
2	Massachusetts	59.0
3	New Jersey	57.3
4	Maryland	55.0
5	Alabama	54.9
6	Pennsylvania	54.6
7	Virginia	53.4
8	Nevada	53.0
9	Ohio	52.8
10	New Hampshire	52.7
11	Connecticut	52.3
12	Rhode Island	52.1
13	Oklahoma	50.6
14	Kentucky	50.4
15	West Virginia	50.2
16	Indiana	49.5
17	Delaware	49.1
18	Tennessee	48.5
19	Kansas	48.4
19	New York	48.4
21	Missouri	47.9
22	Colorado	47.7
23	Wisconsin	47.5
24	Arizona	47.3
24	Illinois	47.3
26	Iowa	47.1
27	California	46.5
28	Louisiana	46.0
28	North Dakota	46.0
30	Michigan	45.9
30	Texas	45.9
32	Washington	45.7
33	South Carolina	45.3
34	Maine	44.4
35	North Carolina	43.5
36	Mississippi	43.0
37	South Dakota	42.9
38	Oregon	42.7
39	Minnesota	42.2
40	Vermont	42.0
41	New Mexico	41.7
42	Georgia	40.9
43	Wyoming	40.2
44	Arkansas	39.8
44	Utah	39.8
46	Alaska	39.7
47	Nebraska	39.5
48	Florida	37.6
49	Idaho	37.5
49	Montana	37.5
	District of Columbia	64.9

Source: U.S. Department of Health and Human Services, Agency for Healthcare Research and Quality "Private-Sector Data by Firm Size and State" (Table II Series, Medical Expenditures Panel Survey) (http://www.meps.ahrq.gov/mepsweb/survey_comp/Insurance.jsp)

Persons Not Covered by Health Insurance in 2014

National Total = 36,670,223 Uninsured

ALPHA ORDER

RANK	STATE	UNINSURED	% of USA
21	Alabama	579,169	1.6%
42	Alaska	122,436	0.3%
11	Arizona	903,328	2.5%
30	Arkansas	343,171	0.9%
2	California	4,766,711	13.0%
22	Colorado	542,611	1.5%
34	Connecticut	245,399	0.7%
47	Delaware	71,597	0.2%
3	Florida	3,245,161	8.8%
5	Georgia	1,568,381	4.3%
46	Hawaii	72,111	0.2%
36	Idaho	218,707	0.6%
7	Illinois	1,237,926	3.4%
15	Indiana	775,884	2.1%
37	Iowa	188,885	0.5%
33	Kansas	291,474	0.8%
28	Kentucky	366,062	1.0%
17	Louisiana	671,753	1.8%
41	Maine	133,531	0.4%
23	Maryland	463,268	1.3%
35	Massachusetts	218,722	0.6%
13	Michigan	836,728	2.3%
31	Minnesota	317,257	0.9%
25	Mississippi	424,130	1.2%
16	Missouri	693,878	1.9%
40	Montana	143,321	0.4%
38	Nebraska	179,206	0.5%
24	Nevada	426,653	1.2%
43	New Hampshire	120,456	0.3%
9	New Jersey	965,411	2.6%
32	New Mexico	297,749	0.8%
4	New York	1,696,559	4.6%
6	North Carolina	1,276,054	3.5%
49	North Dakota	56,898	0.2%
10	Ohio	955,205	2.6%
20	Oklahoma	583,512	1.6%
27	Oregon	382,661	1.0%
8	Pennsylvania	1,064,577	2.9%
45	Rhode Island	77,119	0.2%
19	South Carolina	641,557	1.7%
44	South Dakota	81,931	0.2%
14	Tennessee	776,319	2.1%
1	Texas	5,047,477	13.8%
29	Utah	365,523	1.0%
50	Vermont	30,716	0.1%
12	Virginia	883,636	2.4%
18	Washington	642,654	1.8%
39	West Virginia	156,090	0.4%
26	Wisconsin	417,723	1.1%
48	Wyoming	68,748	0.2%

RANK ORDER

RANK	STATE	UNINSURED	% of USA
1	Texas	5,047,477	13.8%
2	California	4,766,711	13.0%
3	Florida	3,245,161	8.8%
4	New York	1,696,559	4.6%
5	Georgia	1,568,381	4.3%
6	North Carolina	1,276,054	3.5%
7	Illinois	1,237,926	3.4%
8	Pennsylvania	1,064,577	2.9%
9	New Jersey	965,411	2.6%
10	Ohio	955,205	2.6%
11	Arizona	903,328	2.5%
12	Virginia	883,636	2.4%
13	Michigan	836,728	2.3%
14	Tennessee	776,319	2.1%
15	Indiana	775,884	2.1%
16	Missouri	693,878	1.9%
17	Louisiana	671,753	1.8%
18	Washington	642,654	1.8%
19	South Carolina	641,557	1.7%
20	Oklahoma	583,512	1.6%
21	Alabama	579,169	1.6%
22	Colorado	542,611	1.5%
23	Maryland	463,268	1.3%
24	Nevada	426,653	1.2%
25	Mississippi	424,130	1.2%
26	Wisconsin	417,723	1.1%
27	Oregon	382,661	1.0%
28	Kentucky	366,062	1.0%
29	Utah	365,523	1.0%
30	Arkansas	343,171	0.9%
31	Minnesota	317,257	0.9%
32	New Mexico	297,749	0.8%
33	Kansas	291,474	0.8%
34	Connecticut	245,399	0.7%
35	Massachusetts	218,722	0.6%
36	Idaho	218,707	0.6%
37	Iowa	188,885	0.5%
38	Nebraska	179,206	0.5%
39	West Virginia	156,090	0.4%
40	Montana	143,321	0.4%
41	Maine	133,531	0.4%
42	Alaska	122,436	0.3%
43	New Hampshire	120,456	0.3%
44	South Dakota	81,931	0.2%
45	Rhode Island	77,119	0.2%
46	Hawaii	72,111	0.2%
47	Delaware	71,597	0.2%
48	Wyoming	68,748	0.2%
49	North Dakota	56,898	0.2%
50	Vermont	30,716	0.1%
	District of Columbia	34,188	0.1%

Source: U.S. Bureau of the Census
"2014 American Community Survey-Table S2701" (http://www.census.gov/programs-surveys/acs/)

Percent of Population Not Covered by Health Insurance in 2014

National Percent = 11.7% of Population*

ALPHA ORDER

RANK	STATE	PERCENT
17	Alabama	12.1
2	Alaska	17.2
11	Arizona	13.6
21	Arkansas	11.8
16	California	12.4
25	Colorado	10.3
45	Connecticut	6.9
42	Delaware	7.8
3	Florida	16.6
4	Georgia	15.8
48	Hawaii	5.3
11	Idaho	13.6
29	Illinois	9.7
20	Indiana	11.9
46	Iowa	6.2
26	Kansas	10.2
36	Kentucky	8.5
7	Louisiana	14.8
27	Maine	10.1
40	Maryland	7.9
50	Massachusetts	3.3
36	Michigan	8.5
47	Minnesota	5.9
8	Mississippi	14.5
22	Missouri	11.7
10	Montana	14.2
29	Nebraska	9.7
6	Nevada	15.2
32	New Hampshire	9.2
23	New Jersey	10.9
8	New Mexico	14.5
34	New York	8.7
14	North Carolina	13.1
40	North Dakota	7.9
39	Ohio	8.4
5	Oklahoma	15.4
29	Oregon	9.7
36	Pennsylvania	8.5
43	Rhode Island	7.4
11	South Carolina	13.6
28	South Dakota	9.8
18	Tennessee	12.0
1	Texas	19.1
15	Utah	12.5
49	Vermont	5.0
23	Virginia	10.9
32	Washington	9.2
35	West Virginia	8.6
44	Wisconsin	7.3
18	Wyoming	12.0

RANK ORDER

RANK	STATE	PERCENT
1	Texas	19.1
2	Alaska	17.2
3	Florida	16.6
4	Georgia	15.8
5	Oklahoma	15.4
6	Nevada	15.2
7	Louisiana	14.8
8	Mississippi	14.5
8	New Mexico	14.5
10	Montana	14.2
11	Arizona	13.6
11	Idaho	13.6
11	South Carolina	13.6
14	North Carolina	13.1
15	Utah	12.5
16	California	12.4
17	Alabama	12.1
18	Tennessee	12.0
18	Wyoming	12.0
20	Indiana	11.9
21	Arkansas	11.8
22	Missouri	11.7
23	New Jersey	10.9
23	Virginia	10.9
25	Colorado	10.3
26	Kansas	10.2
27	Maine	10.1
28	South Dakota	9.8
29	Illinois	9.7
29	Nebraska	9.7
29	Oregon	9.7
32	New Hampshire	9.2
32	Washington	9.2
34	New York	8.7
35	West Virginia	8.6
36	Kentucky	8.5
36	Michigan	8.5
36	Pennsylvania	8.5
39	Ohio	8.4
40	Maryland	7.9
40	North Dakota	7.9
42	Delaware	7.8
43	Rhode Island	7.4
44	Wisconsin	7.3
45	Connecticut	6.9
46	Iowa	6.2
47	Minnesota	5.9
48	Hawaii	5.3
49	Vermont	5.0
50	Massachusetts	3.3
	District of Columbia	5.3

Source: U.S. Bureau of the Census
"2014 American Community Survey-Table S2701" (http://www.census.gov/programs-surveys/acs/)
*This is a one-year figure. Census has discontinued three-year averages that had been used previously.

Percent of Population Lacking Access to Primary Care in 2013

National Percent = 10.9% of Population*

ALPHA ORDER

RANK	STATE	PERCENT
9	Alabama	19.5
11	Alaska	17.7
10	Arizona	18.6
31	Arkansas	8.7
34	California	8.3
25	Colorado	10.8
29	Connecticut	9.5
27	Delaware	9.7
13	Florida	16.4
23	Georgia	11.8
45	Hawaii	2.5
12	Idaho	17.4
14	Illinois	16.2
32	Indiana	8.6
19	Iowa	12.3
17	Kansas	13.0
30	Kentucky	9.0
3	Louisiana	24.4
43	Maine	3.2
28	Maryland	9.6
42	Massachusetts	3.4
26	Michigan	9.9
41	Minnesota	4.6
1	Mississippi	34.3
4	Missouri	23.4
15	Montana	15.9
47	Nebraska	1.2
21	Nevada	11.9
46	New Hampshire	2.3
49	New Jersey	0.1
2	New Mexico	30.8
24	New York	11.4
39	North Carolina	6.7
6	North Dakota	20.3
40	Ohio	4.9
5	Oklahoma	23.2
21	Oregon	11.9
43	Pennsylvania	3.2
50	Rhode Island	0.0
16	South Carolina	13.7
7	South Dakota	20.2
38	Tennessee	7.0
20	Texas	12.0
36	Utah	7.6
48	Vermont	1.0
37	Virginia	7.4
18	Washington	12.7
35	West Virginia	8.1
32	Wisconsin	8.6
7	Wyoming	20.2

RANK ORDER

RANK	STATE	PERCENT
1	Mississippi	34.3
2	New Mexico	30.8
3	Louisiana	24.4
4	Missouri	23.4
5	Oklahoma	23.2
6	North Dakota	20.3
7	South Dakota	20.2
7	Wyoming	20.2
9	Alabama	19.5
10	Arizona	18.6
11	Alaska	17.7
12	Idaho	17.4
13	Florida	16.4
14	Illinois	16.2
15	Montana	15.9
16	South Carolina	13.7
17	Kansas	13.0
18	Washington	12.7
19	Iowa	12.3
20	Texas	12.0
21	Nevada	11.9
21	Oregon	11.9
23	Georgia	11.8
24	New York	11.4
25	Colorado	10.8
26	Michigan	9.9
27	Delaware	9.7
28	Maryland	9.6
29	Connecticut	9.5
30	Kentucky	9.0
31	Arkansas	8.7
32	Indiana	8.6
32	Wisconsin	8.6
34	California	8.3
35	West Virginia	8.1
36	Utah	7.6
37	Virginia	7.4
38	Tennessee	7.0
39	North Carolina	6.7
40	Ohio	4.9
41	Minnesota	4.6
42	Massachusetts	3.4
43	Maine	3.2
43	Pennsylvania	3.2
45	Hawaii	2.5
46	New Hampshire	2.3
47	Nebraska	1.2
48	Vermont	1.0
49	New Jersey	0.1
50	Rhode Island	0.0
	District of Columbia	24.9

Source: CQ Press using data from U.S. Department of Health and Human Services, Division of Shortage Designation
"State Population and HPSA Designation Population Statistics" (as of January 9, 2013)
(http://datawarehouse.hrsa.gov/hpsadetail.aspx)

*Percent of population considered under-served by primary medical practitioners (Family and General Practice doctors, Internists, Ob/Gyns, and Pediatricians). An under-served population does not have primary medical care within reasonable economic and geographic bounds.

Physicians in 2013

National Total = 1,032,056 Physicians*

ALPHA ORDER

RANK	STATE	PHYSICIANS	% of USA
27	Alabama	12,209	1.2%
49	Alaska	1,924	0.2%
18	Arizona	18,313	1.8%
32	Arkansas	7,188	0.7%
1	California	126,034	12.2%
21	Colorado	17,065	1.7%
23	Connecticut	16,138	1.6%
46	Delaware	2,722	0.3%
4	Florida	62,290	6.0%
14	Georgia	26,434	2.6%
38	Hawaii	5,184	0.5%
43	Idaho	3,350	0.3%
6	Illinois	44,055	4.3%
22	Indiana	16,793	1.6%
33	Iowa	7,047	0.7%
30	Kansas	7,941	0.8%
28	Kentucky	11,865	1.1%
24	Louisiana	14,528	1.4%
42	Maine	4,638	0.4%
12	Maryland	28,869	2.8%
8	Massachusetts	37,205	3.6%
10	Michigan	30,913	3.0%
17	Minnesota	19,398	1.9%
34	Mississippi	6,491	0.6%
20	Missouri	17,693	1.7%
45	Montana	2,824	0.3%
37	Nebraska	5,421	0.5%
35	Nevada	6,299	0.6%
40	New Hampshire	4,815	0.5%
9	New Jersey	32,455	3.1%
36	New Mexico	6,159	0.6%
2	New York	91,188	8.8%
11	North Carolina	29,840	2.9%
48	North Dakota	2,060	0.2%
7	Ohio	38,265	3.7%
29	Oklahoma	8,060	0.8%
25	Oregon	14,030	1.4%
5	Pennsylvania	46,647	4.5%
41	Rhode Island	4,806	0.5%
26	South Carolina	13,093	1.3%
47	South Dakota	2,310	0.2%
16	Tennessee	20,234	2.0%
3	Texas	66,659	6.5%
31	Utah	7,236	0.7%
44	Vermont	2,886	0.3%
13	Virginia	27,130	2.6%
15	Washington	23,143	2.2%
39	West Virginia	5,083	0.5%
19	Wisconsin	17,986	1.7%
50	Wyoming	1,287	0.1%

RANK ORDER

RANK	STATE	PHYSICIANS	% of USA
1	California	126,034	12.2%
2	New York	91,188	8.8%
3	Texas	66,659	6.5%
4	Florida	62,290	6.0%
5	Pennsylvania	46,647	4.5%
6	Illinois	44,055	4.3%
7	Ohio	38,265	3.7%
8	Massachusetts	37,205	3.6%
9	New Jersey	32,455	3.1%
10	Michigan	30,913	3.0%
11	North Carolina	29,840	2.9%
12	Maryland	28,869	2.8%
13	Virginia	27,130	2.6%
14	Georgia	26,434	2.6%
15	Washington	23,143	2.2%
16	Tennessee	20,234	2.0%
17	Minnesota	19,398	1.9%
18	Arizona	18,313	1.8%
19	Wisconsin	17,986	1.7%
20	Missouri	17,693	1.7%
21	Colorado	17,065	1.7%
22	Indiana	16,793	1.6%
23	Connecticut	16,138	1.6%
24	Louisiana	14,528	1.4%
25	Oregon	14,030	1.4%
26	South Carolina	13,093	1.3%
27	Alabama	12,209	1.2%
28	Kentucky	11,865	1.1%
29	Oklahoma	8,060	0.8%
30	Kansas	7,941	0.8%
31	Utah	7,236	0.7%
32	Arkansas	7,188	0.7%
33	Iowa	7,047	0.7%
34	Mississippi	6,491	0.6%
35	Nevada	6,299	0.6%
36	New Mexico	6,159	0.6%
37	Nebraska	5,421	0.5%
38	Hawaii	5,184	0.5%
39	West Virginia	5,083	0.5%
40	New Hampshire	4,815	0.5%
41	Rhode Island	4,806	0.5%
42	Maine	4,638	0.4%
43	Idaho	3,350	0.3%
44	Vermont	2,886	0.3%
45	Montana	2,824	0.3%
46	Delaware	2,722	0.3%
47	South Dakota	2,310	0.2%
48	North Dakota	2,060	0.2%
49	Alaska	1,924	0.2%
50	Wyoming	1,287	0.1%
	District of Columbia	5,853	0.6%

Source: American Medical Association (Chicago, Illinois)
 "Physician Characteristics and Distribution in the U.S." (2015 Edition)
*As of December 31, 2013. Total does not include 13,854 physicians in the U.S. territories and possessions, at APOs and FPOs, or whose addresses are unknown.

Rate of Physicians in 2013

National Rate = 326 Physicians per 100,000 Population*

ALPHA ORDER

RANK	STATE	RATE
41	Alabama	253
39	Alaska	262
32	Arizona	276
44	Arkansas	243
17	California	329
19	Colorado	324
6	Connecticut	449
27	Delaware	294
20	Florida	319
38	Georgia	265
7	Hawaii	369
50	Idaho	208
14	Illinois	342
40	Indiana	256
45	Iowa	228
33	Kansas	274
37	Kentucky	270
21	Louisiana	314
13	Maine	349
2	Maryland	487
1	Massachusetts	556
23	Michigan	312
11	Minnesota	358
48	Mississippi	217
28	Missouri	293
31	Montana	278
29	Nebraska	290
46	Nevada	226
10	New Hampshire	364
8	New Jersey	365
26	New Mexico	295
3	New York	464
25	North Carolina	303
30	North Dakota	285
16	Ohio	331
49	Oklahoma	209
12	Oregon	357
8	Pennsylvania	365
5	Rhode Island	457
33	South Carolina	274
36	South Dakota	273
24	Tennessee	311
42	Texas	252
43	Utah	249
4	Vermont	461
18	Virginia	328
15	Washington	332
33	West Virginia	274
22	Wisconsin	313
47	Wyoming	221

RANK ORDER

RANK	STATE	RATE
1	Massachusetts	556
2	Maryland	487
3	New York	464
4	Vermont	461
5	Rhode Island	457
6	Connecticut	449
7	Hawaii	369
8	New Jersey	365
8	Pennsylvania	365
10	New Hampshire	364
11	Minnesota	358
12	Oregon	357
13	Maine	349
14	Illinois	342
15	Washington	332
16	Ohio	331
17	California	329
18	Virginia	328
19	Colorado	324
20	Florida	319
21	Louisiana	314
22	Wisconsin	313
23	Michigan	312
24	Tennessee	311
25	North Carolina	303
26	New Mexico	295
27	Delaware	294
28	Missouri	293
29	Nebraska	290
30	North Dakota	285
31	Montana	278
32	Arizona	276
33	Kansas	274
33	South Carolina	274
33	West Virginia	274
36	South Dakota	273
37	Kentucky	270
38	Georgia	265
39	Alaska	262
40	Indiana	256
41	Alabama	253
42	Texas	252
43	Utah	249
44	Arkansas	243
45	Iowa	228
46	Nevada	226
47	Wyoming	221
48	Mississippi	217
49	Oklahoma	209
50	Idaho	208
	District of Columbia	905

Source: CQ Press using data from American Medical Association (Chicago, Illinois)
"Physician Characteristics and Distribution in the U.S." (2015 Edition)

*As of December 31, 2013. National rate does not include physicians in the U.S. territories and possessions, at APOs and FPOs, or whose addresses are unknown.

Rate of Registered Nurses in 2014

National Rate = 843 Nurses per 100,000 Population*

ALPHA ORDER

RANK	STATE	RATE
24	Alabama	901
36	Alaska	784
45	Arizona	699
38	Arkansas	768
49	California	653
33	Colorado	828
17	Connecticut	940
7	Delaware	1,078
34	Florida	824
47	Georgia	674
40	Hawaii	750
42	Idaho	727
27	Illinois	866
23	Indiana	903
13	Iowa	1,025
22	Kansas	909
16	Kentucky	991
26	Louisiana	870
6	Maine	1,087
35	Maryland	800
2	Massachusetts	1,183
21	Michigan	911
12	Minnesota	1,026
18	Mississippi	938
4	Missouri	1,109
20	Montana	928
8	Nebraska	1,064
50	Nevada	649
19	New Hampshire	933
28	New Jersey	859
43	New Mexico	716
28	New York	859
25	North Carolina	896
10	North Dakota	1,038
5	Ohio	1,094
46	Oklahoma	680
37	Oregon	782
14	Pennsylvania	1,006
3	Rhode Island	1,119
30	South Carolina	855
1	South Dakota	1,362
31	Tennessee	849
44	Texas	705
48	Utah	664
9	Vermont	1,043
39	Virginia	753
41	Washington	731
11	West Virginia	1,034
15	Wisconsin	994
32	Wyoming	830

RANK ORDER

RANK	STATE	RATE
1	South Dakota	1,362
2	Massachusetts	1,183
3	Rhode Island	1,119
4	Missouri	1,109
5	Ohio	1,094
6	Maine	1,087
7	Delaware	1,078
8	Nebraska	1,064
9	Vermont	1,043
10	North Dakota	1,038
11	West Virginia	1,034
12	Minnesota	1,026
13	Iowa	1,025
14	Pennsylvania	1,006
15	Wisconsin	994
16	Kentucky	991
17	Connecticut	940
18	Mississippi	938
19	New Hampshire	933
20	Montana	928
21	Michigan	911
22	Kansas	909
23	Indiana	903
24	Alabama	901
25	North Carolina	896
26	Louisiana	870
27	Illinois	866
28	New Jersey	859
28	New York	859
30	South Carolina	855
31	Tennessee	849
32	Wyoming	830
33	Colorado	828
34	Florida	824
35	Maryland	800
36	Alaska	784
37	Oregon	782
38	Arkansas	768
39	Virginia	753
40	Hawaii	750
41	Washington	731
42	Idaho	727
43	New Mexico	716
44	Texas	705
45	Arizona	699
46	Oklahoma	680
47	Georgia	674
48	Utah	664
49	California	653
50	Nevada	649
	District of Columbia	1,672

Source: CQ Press using data from U.S. Department of Labor, Bureau of Labor Statistics
"Occupational Employment and Wages, 2014" (http://www.bls.gov/oes/)
*Does not include self-employed.

Rate of Dentists in 2016

National Rate = 65 Dentists per 100,000 Population*

ALPHA ORDER

RANK	STATE	RATE
46	Alabama	47
5	Alaska	82
21	Arizona	59
50	Arkansas	43
3	California	85
10	Colorado	75
6	Connecticut	81
46	Delaware	47
23	Florida	57
42	Georgia	50
7	Hawaii	79
42	Idaho	50
11	Illinois	71
42	Indiana	50
25	Iowa	56
31	Kansas	54
20	Kentucky	62
40	Louisiana	51
34	Maine	53
7	Maryland	79
1	Massachusetts	93
17	Michigan	64
18	Minnesota	63
49	Mississippi	45
38	Missouri	52
18	Montana	63
12	Nebraska	69
25	Nevada	56
15	New Hampshire	67
2	New Jersey	87
31	New Mexico	54
4	New York	83
34	North Carolina	53
23	North Dakota	57
25	Ohio	56
38	Oklahoma	52
46	Oregon	47
13	Pennsylvania	68
28	Rhode Island	55
40	South Carolina	51
34	South Dakota	53
31	Tennessee	54
28	Texas	55
16	Utah	65
45	Vermont	48
13	Virginia	68
9	Washington	77
34	West Virginia	53
21	Wisconsin	59
28	Wyoming	55

RANK ORDER

RANK	STATE	RATE
1	Massachusetts	93
2	New Jersey	87
3	California	85
4	New York	83
5	Alaska	82
6	Connecticut	81
7	Hawaii	79
7	Maryland	79
9	Washington	77
10	Colorado	75
11	Illinois	71
12	Nebraska	69
13	Pennsylvania	68
13	Virginia	68
15	New Hampshire	67
16	Utah	65
17	Michigan	64
18	Minnesota	63
18	Montana	63
20	Kentucky	62
21	Arizona	59
21	Wisconsin	59
23	Florida	57
23	North Dakota	57
25	Iowa	56
25	Nevada	56
25	Ohio	56
28	Rhode Island	55
28	Texas	55
28	Wyoming	55
31	Kansas	54
31	New Mexico	54
31	Tennessee	54
34	Maine	53
34	North Carolina	53
34	South Dakota	53
34	West Virginia	53
38	Missouri	52
38	Oklahoma	52
40	Louisiana	51
40	South Carolina	51
42	Georgia	50
42	Idaho	50
42	Indiana	50
45	Vermont	48
46	Alabama	47
46	Delaware	47
46	Oregon	47
49	Mississippi	45
50	Arkansas	43

District of Columbia 110

Source: CQ Press using data from American Dental Association as reported by The Henry J. Kaiser Family Foundation "Professionally Active Dentists" (http://kff.org/other/state-indicator/total-dentists/)
*Professionally active dentists. Rates calculated using 2015 Census population estimates.

Community Hospitals in 2014

National Total = 4,926 Hospitals*

ALPHA ORDER

RANK	STATE	HOSPITALS	% of USA
22	Alabama	96	1.9%
47	Alaska	22	0.4%
30	Arizona	72	1.5%
27	Arkansas	81	1.6%
2	California	344	7.0%
26	Colorado	82	1.7%
43	Connecticut	32	0.6%
50	Delaware	7	0.1%
3	Florida	211	4.3%
9	Georgia	142	2.9%
45	Hawaii	25	0.5%
38	Idaho	40	0.8%
4	Illinois	189	3.8%
16	Indiana	121	2.5%
17	Iowa	118	2.4%
10	Kansas	133	2.7%
20	Kentucky	104	2.1%
14	Louisiana	122	2.5%
42	Maine	35	0.7%
35	Maryland	50	1.0%
28	Massachusetts	79	1.6%
8	Michigan	148	3.0%
11	Minnesota	131	2.7%
21	Mississippi	97	2.0%
14	Missouri	122	2.5%
35	Montana	50	1.0%
25	Nebraska	89	1.8%
40	Nevada	37	0.8%
44	New Hampshire	28	0.6%
29	New Jersey	75	1.5%
40	New Mexico	37	0.8%
7	New York	174	3.5%
18	North Carolina	116	2.4%
38	North Dakota	40	0.8%
6	Ohio	182	3.7%
19	Oklahoma	114	2.3%
32	Oregon	59	1.2%
5	Pennsylvania	185	3.8%
49	Rhode Island	11	0.2%
31	South Carolina	70	1.4%
34	South Dakota	53	1.1%
13	Tennessee	125	2.5%
1	Texas	417	8.5%
37	Utah	47	1.0%
48	Vermont	14	0.3%
23	Virginia	93	1.9%
24	Washington	90	1.8%
33	West Virginia	54	1.1%
12	Wisconsin	129	2.6%
46	Wyoming	23	0.5%

RANK ORDER

RANK	STATE	HOSPITALS	% of USA
1	Texas	417	8.5%
2	California	344	7.0%
3	Florida	211	4.3%
4	Illinois	189	3.8%
5	Pennsylvania	185	3.8%
6	Ohio	182	3.7%
7	New York	174	3.5%
8	Michigan	148	3.0%
9	Georgia	142	2.9%
10	Kansas	133	2.7%
11	Minnesota	131	2.7%
12	Wisconsin	129	2.6%
13	Tennessee	125	2.5%
14	Louisiana	122	2.5%
14	Missouri	122	2.5%
16	Indiana	121	2.5%
17	Iowa	118	2.4%
18	North Carolina	116	2.4%
19	Oklahoma	114	2.3%
20	Kentucky	104	2.1%
21	Mississippi	97	2.0%
22	Alabama	96	1.9%
23	Virginia	93	1.9%
24	Washington	90	1.8%
25	Nebraska	89	1.8%
26	Colorado	82	1.7%
27	Arkansas	81	1.6%
28	Massachusetts	79	1.6%
29	New Jersey	75	1.5%
30	Arizona	72	1.5%
31	South Carolina	70	1.4%
32	Oregon	59	1.2%
33	West Virginia	54	1.1%
34	South Dakota	53	1.1%
35	Maryland	50	1.0%
35	Montana	50	1.0%
37	Utah	47	1.0%
38	Idaho	40	0.8%
38	North Dakota	40	0.8%
40	Nevada	37	0.8%
40	New Mexico	37	0.8%
42	Maine	35	0.7%
43	Connecticut	32	0.6%
44	New Hampshire	28	0.6%
45	Hawaii	25	0.5%
46	Wyoming	23	0.5%
47	Alaska	22	0.4%
48	Vermont	14	0.3%
49	Rhode Island	11	0.2%
50	Delaware	7	0.1%
	District of Columbia	11	0.2%

Source: American Hospital Association (Chicago, IL)
"Hospital Statistics" (2016 edition)

*Community hospitals are all nonfederal, short-term general, and special hospitals whose facilities and services are available to the public.

Rate of Community Hospitals in 2014

National Rate = 1.5 Community Hospitals per 100,000 Population*

ALPHA ORDER

RANK	STATE	RATE
21	Alabama	2.0
9	Alaska	3.0
41	Arizona	1.1
12	Arkansas	2.7
45	California	0.9
29	Colorado	1.5
45	Connecticut	0.9
50	Delaware	0.7
41	Florida	1.1
34	Georgia	1.4
24	Hawaii	1.8
15	Idaho	2.4
29	Illinois	1.5
24	Indiana	1.8
7	Iowa	3.8
5	Kansas	4.6
15	Kentucky	2.4
13	Louisiana	2.6
13	Maine	2.6
48	Maryland	0.8
39	Massachusetts	1.2
29	Michigan	1.5
15	Minnesota	2.4
8	Mississippi	3.2
21	Missouri	2.0
3	Montana	4.9
4	Nebraska	4.7
37	Nevada	1.3
20	New Hampshire	2.1
48	New Jersey	0.8
24	New Mexico	1.8
45	New York	0.9
39	North Carolina	1.2
2	North Dakota	5.4
27	Ohio	1.6
10	Oklahoma	2.9
29	Oregon	1.5
34	Pennsylvania	1.4
44	Rhode Island	1.0
34	South Carolina	1.4
1	South Dakota	6.2
23	Tennessee	1.9
29	Texas	1.5
27	Utah	1.6
18	Vermont	2.2
41	Virginia	1.1
37	Washington	1.3
10	West Virginia	2.9
18	Wisconsin	2.2
6	Wyoming	3.9

RANK ORDER

RANK	STATE	RATE
1	South Dakota	6.2
2	North Dakota	5.4
3	Montana	4.9
4	Nebraska	4.7
5	Kansas	4.6
6	Wyoming	3.9
7	Iowa	3.8
8	Mississippi	3.2
9	Alaska	3.0
10	Oklahoma	2.9
10	West Virginia	2.9
12	Arkansas	2.7
13	Louisiana	2.6
13	Maine	2.6
15	Idaho	2.4
15	Kentucky	2.4
15	Minnesota	2.4
18	Vermont	2.2
18	Wisconsin	2.2
20	New Hampshire	2.1
21	Alabama	2.0
21	Missouri	2.0
23	Tennessee	1.9
24	Hawaii	1.8
24	Indiana	1.8
24	New Mexico	1.8
27	Ohio	1.6
27	Utah	1.6
29	Colorado	1.5
29	Illinois	1.5
29	Michigan	1.5
29	Oregon	1.5
29	Texas	1.5
34	Georgia	1.4
34	Pennsylvania	1.4
34	South Carolina	1.4
37	Nevada	1.3
37	Washington	1.3
39	Massachusetts	1.2
39	North Carolina	1.2
41	Arizona	1.1
41	Florida	1.1
41	Virginia	1.1
44	Rhode Island	1.0
45	California	0.9
45	Connecticut	0.9
45	New York	0.9
48	Maryland	0.8
48	New Jersey	0.8
50	Delaware	0.7
	District of Columbia	1.7

Source: CQ Press using data from American Hospital Association (Chicago, IL)
"Hospital Statistics" (2016 edition)

*Community hospitals are all nonfederal, short-term general, and special hospitals whose facilities and services are available to the public.

Births in 2014

National Total = 3,988,076 Live Births*

ALPHA ORDER					RANK ORDER			
RANK	STATE	BIRTHS	% of USA		RANK	STATE	BIRTHS	% of USA
24	Alabama	59,422	1.5%		1	California	502,879	12.6%
45	Alaska	11,392	0.3%		2	Texas	399,766	10.0%
14	Arizona	86,887	2.2%		3	New York	238,773	6.0%
33	Arkansas	38,511	1.0%		4	Florida	219,991	5.5%
1	California	502,879	12.6%		5	Illinois	158,556	4.0%
22	Colorado	65,830	1.7%		6	Pennsylvania	142,268	3.6%
34	Connecticut	36,285	0.9%		7	Ohio	139,467	3.5%
47	Delaware	10,972	0.3%		8	Georgia	130,946	3.3%
4	Florida	219,991	5.5%		9	North Carolina	120,975	3.0%
8	Georgia	130,946	3.3%		10	Michigan	114,375	2.9%
40	Hawaii	18,550	0.5%		11	New Jersey	103,305	2.6%
38	Idaho	22,876	0.6%		12	Virginia	103,300	2.6%
5	Illinois	158,556	4.0%		13	Washington	88,585	2.2%
15	Indiana	84,080	2.1%		14	Arizona	86,887	2.2%
30	Iowa	39,687	1.0%		15	Indiana	84,080	2.1%
31	Kansas	39,223	1.0%		16	Tennessee	81,602	2.0%
26	Kentucky	56,170	1.4%		17	Missouri	75,360	1.9%
23	Louisiana	64,497	1.6%		18	Maryland	73,921	1.9%
41	Maine	12,698	0.3%		19	Massachusetts	71,908	1.8%
18	Maryland	73,921	1.9%		20	Minnesota	69,904	1.8%
19	Massachusetts	71,908	1.8%		21	Wisconsin	67,161	1.7%
10	Michigan	114,375	2.9%		22	Colorado	65,830	1.7%
20	Minnesota	69,904	1.8%		23	Louisiana	64,497	1.6%
32	Mississippi	38,736	1.0%		24	Alabama	59,422	1.5%
17	Missouri	75,360	1.9%		25	South Carolina	57,627	1.4%
42	Montana	12,432	0.3%		26	Kentucky	56,170	1.4%
36	Nebraska	26,794	0.7%		27	Oklahoma	53,339	1.3%
35	Nevada	35,861	0.9%		28	Utah	51,154	1.3%
43	New Hampshire	12,302	0.3%		29	Oregon	45,556	1.1%
11	New Jersey	103,305	2.6%		30	Iowa	39,687	1.0%
37	New Mexico	26,052	0.7%		31	Kansas	39,223	1.0%
3	New York	238,773	6.0%		32	Mississippi	38,736	1.0%
9	North Carolina	120,975	3.0%		33	Arkansas	38,511	1.0%
46	North Dakota	11,359	0.3%		34	Connecticut	36,285	0.9%
7	Ohio	139,467	3.5%		35	Nevada	35,861	0.9%
27	Oklahoma	53,339	1.3%		36	Nebraska	26,794	0.7%
29	Oregon	45,556	1.1%		37	New Mexico	26,052	0.7%
6	Pennsylvania	142,268	3.6%		38	Idaho	22,876	0.6%
48	Rhode Island	10,823	0.3%		39	West Virginia	20,301	0.5%
25	South Carolina	57,627	1.4%		40	Hawaii	18,550	0.5%
44	South Dakota	12,283	0.3%		41	Maine	12,698	0.3%
16	Tennessee	81,602	2.0%		42	Montana	12,432	0.3%
2	Texas	399,766	10.0%		43	New Hampshire	12,302	0.3%
28	Utah	51,154	1.3%		44	South Dakota	12,283	0.3%
50	Vermont	6,130	0.2%		45	Alaska	11,392	0.3%
12	Virginia	103,300	2.6%		46	North Dakota	11,359	0.3%
13	Washington	88,585	2.2%		47	Delaware	10,972	0.3%
39	West Virginia	20,301	0.5%		48	Rhode Island	10,823	0.3%
21	Wisconsin	67,161	1.7%		49	Wyoming	7,696	0.2%
49	Wyoming	7,696	0.2%		50	Vermont	6,130	0.2%
						District of Columbia	9,509	0.2%

Source: U.S. Department of Health and Human Services, National Center for Health Statistics
  "National Vital Statistics Reports" (Vol. 64, No. 12, December 23, 2015, http://www.cdc.gov/nchs/births.htm)
*Final data by state of residence.

Birth Rate in 2014

National Rate = 12.5 Live Births per 1,000 Population*

ALPHA ORDER

RANK	STATE	RATE
29	Alabama	12.3
2	Alaska	15.5
16	Arizona	12.9
13	Arkansas	13.0
13	California	13.0
29	Colorado	12.3
47	Connecticut	10.1
37	Delaware	11.7
42	Florida	11.1
13	Georgia	13.0
12	Hawaii	13.1
7	Idaho	14.0
29	Illinois	12.3
20	Indiana	12.7
18	Iowa	12.8
10	Kansas	13.5
20	Kentucky	12.7
8	Louisiana	13.9
49	Maine	9.5
26	Maryland	12.4
45	Massachusetts	10.7
40	Michigan	11.5
18	Minnesota	12.8
16	Mississippi	12.9
26	Missouri	12.4
33	Montana	12.1
6	Nebraska	14.2
22	Nevada	12.6
50	New Hampshire	9.3
39	New Jersey	11.6
23	New Mexico	12.5
33	New York	12.1
32	North Carolina	12.2
3	North Dakota	15.4
35	Ohio	12.0
9	Oklahoma	13.8
40	Oregon	11.5
42	Pennsylvania	11.1
46	Rhode Island	10.3
36	South Carolina	11.9
5	South Dakota	14.4
23	Tennessee	12.5
4	Texas	14.8
1	Utah	17.4
48	Vermont	9.8
26	Virginia	12.4
23	Washington	12.5
44	West Virginia	11.0
37	Wisconsin	11.7
11	Wyoming	13.2

RANK ORDER

RANK	STATE	RATE
1	Utah	17.4
2	Alaska	15.5
3	North Dakota	15.4
4	Texas	14.8
5	South Dakota	14.4
6	Nebraska	14.2
7	Idaho	14.0
8	Louisiana	13.9
9	Oklahoma	13.8
10	Kansas	13.5
11	Wyoming	13.2
12	Hawaii	13.1
13	Arkansas	13.0
13	California	13.0
13	Georgia	13.0
16	Arizona	12.9
16	Mississippi	12.9
18	Iowa	12.8
18	Minnesota	12.8
20	Indiana	12.7
20	Kentucky	12.7
22	Nevada	12.6
23	New Mexico	12.5
23	Tennessee	12.5
23	Washington	12.5
26	Maryland	12.4
26	Missouri	12.4
26	Virginia	12.4
29	Alabama	12.3
29	Colorado	12.3
29	Illinois	12.3
32	North Carolina	12.2
33	Montana	12.1
33	New York	12.1
35	Ohio	12.0
36	South Carolina	11.9
37	Delaware	11.7
37	Wisconsin	11.7
39	New Jersey	11.6
40	Michigan	11.5
40	Oregon	11.5
42	Florida	11.1
42	Pennsylvania	11.1
44	West Virginia	11.0
45	Massachusetts	10.7
46	Rhode Island	10.3
47	Connecticut	10.1
48	Vermont	9.8
49	Maine	9.5
50	New Hampshire	9.3
	District of Columbia	14.4

Source: U.S. Department of Health and Human Services, National Center for Health Statistics
"National Vital Statistics Reports" (Vol. 64, No. 12, December 23, 2015, http://www.cdc.gov/nchs/births.htm)
*Final data by state of residence.

Births of Low Birthweight as a Percent of All Births in 2014

National Percent = 8.0% of Live Births*

ALPHA ORDER

RANK	STATE	PERCENT
3	Alabama	10.1
50	Alaska	5.9
37	Arizona	7.0
9	Arkansas	8.9
41	California	6.7
11	Colorado	8.8
30	Connecticut	7.6
18	Delaware	8.3
14	Florida	8.7
4	Georgia	9.5
27	Hawaii	7.9
46	Idaho	6.4
21	Illinois	8.2
25	Indiana	8.0
41	Iowa	6.7
37	Kansas	7.0
11	Kentucky	8.8
2	Louisiana	10.5
30	Maine	7.6
15	Maryland	8.6
32	Massachusetts	7.5
17	Michigan	8.4
43	Minnesota	6.6
1	Mississippi	11.3
21	Missouri	8.2
33	Montana	7.4
43	Nebraska	6.6
18	Nevada	8.3
40	New Hampshire	6.9
24	New Jersey	8.1
11	New Mexico	8.8
27	New York	7.9
9	North Carolina	8.9
48	North Dakota	6.2
16	Ohio	8.5
25	Oklahoma	8.0
48	Oregon	6.2
18	Pennsylvania	8.3
35	Rhode Island	7.1
5	South Carolina	9.4
45	South Dakota	6.5
8	Tennessee	9.0
21	Texas	8.2
37	Utah	7.0
35	Vermont	7.1
27	Virginia	7.9
46	Washington	6.4
7	West Virginia	9.1
34	Wisconsin	7.3
6	Wyoming	9.2

RANK ORDER

RANK	STATE	PERCENT
1	Mississippi	11.3
2	Louisiana	10.5
3	Alabama	10.1
4	Georgia	9.5
5	South Carolina	9.4
6	Wyoming	9.2
7	West Virginia	9.1
8	Tennessee	9.0
9	Arkansas	8.9
9	North Carolina	8.9
11	Colorado	8.8
11	Kentucky	8.8
11	New Mexico	8.8
14	Florida	8.7
15	Maryland	8.6
16	Ohio	8.5
17	Michigan	8.4
18	Delaware	8.3
18	Nevada	8.3
18	Pennsylvania	8.3
21	Illinois	8.2
21	Missouri	8.2
21	Texas	8.2
24	New Jersey	8.1
25	Indiana	8.0
25	Oklahoma	8.0
27	Hawaii	7.9
27	New York	7.9
27	Virginia	7.9
30	Connecticut	7.6
30	Maine	7.6
32	Massachusetts	7.5
33	Montana	7.4
34	Wisconsin	7.3
35	Rhode Island	7.1
35	Vermont	7.1
37	Arizona	7.0
37	Kansas	7.0
37	Utah	7.0
40	New Hampshire	6.9
41	California	6.7
41	Iowa	6.7
43	Minnesota	6.6
43	Nebraska	6.6
45	South Dakota	6.5
46	Idaho	6.4
46	Washington	6.4
48	North Dakota	6.2
48	Oregon	6.2
50	Alaska	5.9
	District of Columbia	9.8

Source: U.S. Department of Health and Human Services, National Center for Health Statistics
"National Vital Statistics Reports" (Vol. 64, No. 12, December 23, 2015, http://www.cdc.gov/nchs/births.htm)
*Final data by state of residence. Births of less than 2,500 grams (5 pounds 8 ounces).

Births to Teenage Mothers as a Percent of All Births in 2013

National Percent = 6.9% of Live Births*

ALPHA ORDER

RANK	STATE	PERCENT
8	Alabama	9.3
28	Alaska	6.2
11	Arizona	8.4
3	Arkansas	11.0
28	California	6.2
32	Colorado	5.9
45	Connecticut	4.5
23	Delaware	6.7
26	Florida	6.5
14	Georgia	8.0
41	Hawaii	5.1
27	Idaho	6.4
23	Illinois	6.7
13	Indiana	8.1
32	Iowa	5.9
18	Kansas	7.4
6	Kentucky	9.7
9	Louisiana	9.2
36	Maine	5.5
41	Maryland	5.1
50	Massachusetts	3.8
21	Michigan	6.9
48	Minnesota	4.3
1	Mississippi	11.3
15	Missouri	7.7
21	Montana	6.9
32	Nebraska	5.9
18	Nevada	7.4
45	New Hampshire	4.5
49	New Jersey	4.1
2	New Mexico	11.2
44	New York	4.7
16	North Carolina	7.6
38	North Dakota	5.3
17	Ohio	7.5
5	Oklahoma	9.9
35	Oregon	5.7
30	Pennsylvania	6.1
30	Rhode Island	6.1
11	South Carolina	8.4
25	South Dakota	6.6
10	Tennessee	8.9
6	Texas	9.7
47	Utah	4.4
38	Vermont	5.3
40	Virginia	5.2
41	Washington	5.1
4	West Virginia	10.5
36	Wisconsin	5.5
20	Wyoming	7.1

RANK ORDER

RANK	STATE	PERCENT
1	Mississippi	11.3
2	New Mexico	11.2
3	Arkansas	11.0
4	West Virginia	10.5
5	Oklahoma	9.9
6	Kentucky	9.7
6	Texas	9.7
8	Alabama	9.3
9	Louisiana	9.2
10	Tennessee	8.9
11	Arizona	8.4
11	South Carolina	8.4
13	Indiana	8.1
14	Georgia	8.0
15	Missouri	7.7
16	North Carolina	7.6
17	Ohio	7.5
18	Kansas	7.4
18	Nevada	7.4
20	Wyoming	7.1
21	Michigan	6.9
21	Montana	6.9
23	Delaware	6.7
23	Illinois	6.7
25	South Dakota	6.6
26	Florida	6.5
27	Idaho	6.4
28	Alaska	6.2
28	California	6.2
30	Pennsylvania	6.1
30	Rhode Island	6.1
32	Colorado	5.9
32	Iowa	5.9
32	Nebraska	5.9
35	Oregon	5.7
36	Maine	5.5
36	Wisconsin	5.5
38	North Dakota	5.3
38	Vermont	5.3
40	Virginia	5.2
41	Hawaii	5.1
41	Maryland	5.1
41	Washington	5.1
44	New York	4.7
45	Connecticut	4.5
45	New Hampshire	4.5
47	Utah	4.4
48	Minnesota	4.3
49	New Jersey	4.1
50	Massachusetts	3.8

District of Columbia 6.9

Source: CQ Press using data from U.S. Department of Health and Human Services, Centers for Disease Control and Prevention
 "CDC Wonder" (http://wonder.cdc.gov)
*Final data. Live births to women 15 to 19 years old by state of residence.

Births to Unmarried Women as a Percent of All Births in 2014

National Percent = 40.2% of Live Births*

ALPHA ORDER				RANK ORDER		
RANK	STATE	PERCENT		RANK	STATE	PERCENT
15	Alabama	43.3		1	Mississippi	54.0
37	Alaska	35.6		2	Louisiana	52.7
10	Arizona	45.1		3	New Mexico	51.3
13	Arkansas	43.9		4	Florida	47.9
29	California	38.8		5	South Carolina	47.3
49	Colorado	22.4		6	Delaware	46.6
32	Connecticut	37.1		7	Nevada	45.8
6	Delaware	46.6		8	Georgia	45.4
4	Florida	47.9		8	Rhode Island	45.4
8	Georgia	45.4		10	Arizona	45.1
32	Hawaii	37.1		11	West Virginia	44.9
48	Idaho	27.8		12	Tennessee	44.0
25	Illinois	40.1		13	Arkansas	43.9
15	Indiana	43.3		14	Ohio	43.5
39	Iowa	35.1		15	Alabama	43.3
35	Kansas	36.5		15	Indiana	43.3
18	Kentucky	41.9		17	Oklahoma	42.2
2	Louisiana	52.7		18	Kentucky	41.9
21	Maine	41.2		19	Michigan	41.8
26	Maryland	39.7		20	Texas	41.7
42	Massachusetts	33.2		21	Maine	41.2
19	Michigan	41.8		22	North Carolina	41.0
46	Minnesota	32.3		22	Pennsylvania	41.0
1	Mississippi	54.0		24	Missouri	40.2
24	Missouri	40.2		25	Illinois	40.1
34	Montana	36.9		26	Maryland	39.7
44	Nebraska	33.0		27	New York	39.6
7	Nevada	45.8		28	Vermont	39.5
41	New Hampshire	33.7		29	California	38.8
38	New Jersey	35.5		30	Wisconsin	37.8
3	New Mexico	51.3		31	South Dakota	37.7
27	New York	39.6		32	Connecticut	37.1
22	North Carolina	41.0		32	Hawaii	37.1
45	North Dakota	32.4		34	Montana	36.9
14	Ohio	43.5		35	Kansas	36.5
17	Oklahoma	42.2		36	Oregon	36.1
36	Oregon	36.1		37	Alaska	35.6
22	Pennsylvania	41.0		38	New Jersey	35.5
8	Rhode Island	45.4		39	Iowa	35.1
5	South Carolina	47.3		40	Virginia	33.9
31	South Dakota	37.7		41	New Hampshire	33.7
12	Tennessee	44.0		42	Massachusetts	33.2
20	Texas	41.7		42	Wyoming	33.2
50	Utah	18.6		44	Nebraska	33.0
28	Vermont	39.5		45	North Dakota	32.4
40	Virginia	33.9		46	Minnesota	32.3
47	Washington	32.1		47	Washington	32.1
11	West Virginia	44.9		48	Idaho	27.8
30	Wisconsin	37.8		49	Colorado	22.4
42	Wyoming	33.2		50	Utah	18.6
					District of Columbia	50.2

Source: U.S. Department of Health and Human Services, National Center for Health Statistics
"National Vital Statistics Reports" (Vol. 64, No. 12, December 23, 2015, http://www.cdc.gov/nchs/births.htm)
*Final data by state of residence.

Percent of Women Receiving Late or No Prenatal Care in 2013

National Percent = 6.1% of Women*

ALPHA ORDER

RANK	STATE	PERCENT
NA	Alabama**	NA
9	Alaska	7.0
NA	Arizona**	NA
NA	Arkansas**	NA
38	California	3.7
11	Colorado	6.9
NA	Connecticut**	NA
16	Delaware	6.5
20	Florida	6.1
6	Georgia	7.4
NA	Hawaii**	NA
24	Idaho	5.5
31	Illinois	4.7
14	Indiana	6.6
34	Iowa	4.0
37	Kansas	3.8
27	Kentucky	5.1
11	Louisiana	6.9
NA	Maine**	NA
3	Maryland	9.2
39	Massachusetts	3.6
26	Michigan	5.3
35	Minnesota	3.9
29	Mississippi	4.8
24	Missouri	5.5
7	Montana	7.1
28	Nebraska	4.9
1	Nevada	10.5
35	New Hampshire	3.9
NA	New Jersey**	NA
4	New Mexico	8.9
22	New York	5.8
16	North Carolina	6.5
14	North Dakota	6.6
16	Ohio	6.5
5	Oklahoma	8.0
32	Oregon	4.4
13	Pennsylvania	6.8
NA	Rhode Island**	NA
7	South Carolina	7.1
23	South Dakota	5.6
19	Tennessee	6.4
1	Texas	10.5
39	Utah	3.6
41	Vermont	2.6
29	Virginia	4.8
21	Washington	5.9
NA	West Virginia**	NA
33	Wisconsin	4.2
9	Wyoming	7.0

RANK ORDER

RANK	STATE	PERCENT
1	Nevada	10.5
1	Texas	10.5
3	Maryland	9.2
4	New Mexico	8.9
5	Oklahoma	8.0
6	Georgia	7.4
7	Montana	7.1
7	South Carolina	7.1
9	Alaska	7.0
9	Wyoming	7.0
11	Colorado	6.9
11	Louisiana	6.9
13	Pennsylvania	6.8
14	Indiana	6.6
14	North Dakota	6.6
16	Delaware	6.5
16	North Carolina	6.5
16	Ohio	6.5
19	Tennessee	6.4
20	Florida	6.1
21	Washington	5.9
22	New York	5.8
23	South Dakota	5.6
24	Idaho	5.5
24	Missouri	5.5
26	Michigan	5.3
27	Kentucky	5.1
28	Nebraska	4.9
29	Mississippi	4.8
29	Virginia	4.8
31	Illinois	4.7
32	Oregon	4.4
33	Wisconsin	4.2
34	Iowa	4.0
35	Minnesota	3.9
35	New Hampshire	3.9
37	Kansas	3.8
38	California	3.7
39	Massachusetts	3.6
39	Utah	3.6
41	Vermont	2.6
NA	Alabama**	NA
NA	Arizona**	NA
NA	Arkansas**	NA
NA	Connecticut**	NA
NA	Hawaii**	NA
NA	Maine**	NA
NA	New Jersey**	NA
NA	Rhode Island**	NA
NA	West Virginia**	NA

District of Columbia 10.5

Source: CQ Press using data from U.S. Department of Health and Human Services, Centers for Disease Control and Prevention "CDC Wonder" (http://wonder.cdc.gov)
*Final data by state of residence. "Late" means care begun in third trimester. National figure is for reporting states only.
**Not available.

Reported Legal Abortions in 2012

Reporting States' Total = 699,202 Abortions*

ALPHA ORDER

RANK	STATE	ABORTIONS	% of USA
20	Alabama	9,076	1.3%
41	Alaska	1,632	0.2%
15	Arizona	13,340	1.9%
32	Arkansas	3,782	0.5%
NA	California**	NA	NA
18	Colorado	9,972	1.4%
16	Connecticut	11,955	1.7%
30	Delaware	3,823	0.5%
2	Florida	76,151	10.9%
6	Georgia	31,370	4.5%
36	Hawaii	2,824	0.4%
42	Idaho	1,458	0.2%
4	Illinois	43,203	6.2%
22	Indiana	8,808	1.3%
29	Iowa	4,648	0.7%
23	Kansas	7,451	1.1%
31	Kentucky	3,810	0.5%
19	Louisiana	9,225	1.3%
45	Maine	1,004	0.1%
NA	Maryland**	NA	NA
12	Massachusetts	20,062	2.9%
9	Michigan	23,230	3.3%
17	Minnesota	10,701	1.5%
38	Mississippi	2,176	0.3%
27	Missouri	5,624	0.8%
39	Montana	2,031	0.3%
37	Nebraska	2,299	0.3%
24	Nevada	7,218	1.0%
NA	New Hampshire**	NA	NA
10	New Jersey	22,953	3.3%
34	New Mexico	3,517	0.5%
1	New York	104,370	14.9%
8	North Carolina	24,439	3.5%
43	North Dakota	1,330	0.2%
7	Ohio	25,473	3.6%
28	Oklahoma	5,150	0.7%
21	Oregon	9,016	1.3%
5	Pennsylvania	34,536	4.9%
33	Rhode Island	3,549	0.5%
26	South Carolina	6,084	0.9%
46	South Dakota	634	0.1%
14	Tennessee	15,859	2.3%
3	Texas	68,201	9.8%
35	Utah	3,273	0.5%
44	Vermont	1,270	0.2%
11	Virginia	22,916	3.3%
13	Washington	18,386	2.6%
40	West Virginia	1,828	0.3%
25	Wisconsin	6,927	1.0%
NA	Wyoming**	NA	NA

RANK ORDER

RANK	STATE	ABORTIONS	% of USA
1	New York	104,370	14.9%
2	Florida	76,151	10.9%
3	Texas	68,201	9.8%
4	Illinois	43,203	6.2%
5	Pennsylvania	34,536	4.9%
6	Georgia	31,370	4.5%
7	Ohio	25,473	3.6%
8	North Carolina	24,439	3.5%
9	Michigan	23,230	3.3%
10	New Jersey	22,953	3.3%
11	Virginia	22,916	3.3%
12	Massachusetts	20,062	2.9%
13	Washington	18,386	2.6%
14	Tennessee	15,859	2.3%
15	Arizona	13,340	1.9%
16	Connecticut	11,955	1.7%
17	Minnesota	10,701	1.5%
18	Colorado	9,972	1.4%
19	Louisiana	9,225	1.3%
20	Alabama	9,076	1.3%
21	Oregon	9,016	1.3%
22	Indiana	8,808	1.3%
23	Kansas	7,451	1.1%
24	Nevada	7,218	1.0%
25	Wisconsin	6,927	1.0%
26	South Carolina	6,084	0.9%
27	Missouri	5,624	0.8%
28	Oklahoma	5,150	0.7%
29	Iowa	4,648	0.7%
30	Delaware	3,823	0.5%
31	Kentucky	3,810	0.5%
32	Arkansas	3,782	0.5%
33	Rhode Island	3,549	0.5%
34	New Mexico	3,517	0.5%
35	Utah	3,273	0.5%
36	Hawaii	2,824	0.4%
37	Nebraska	2,299	0.3%
38	Mississippi	2,176	0.3%
39	Montana	2,031	0.3%
40	West Virginia	1,828	0.3%
41	Alaska	1,632	0.2%
42	Idaho	1,458	0.2%
43	North Dakota	1,330	0.2%
44	Vermont	1,270	0.2%
45	Maine	1,004	0.1%
46	South Dakota	634	0.1%
NA	California**	NA	NA
NA	Maryland**	NA	NA
NA	New Hampshire**	NA	NA
NA	Wyoming**	NA	NA
	District of Columbia	2,615	0.4%

Source: U.S. Department of Health and Human Services, Centers for Disease Control and Prevention
"Abortion Surveillance-United States, 2012" (MMWR, Vol. 64, No. SS-10, 11/27/15, www.cdc.gov/mmwr/mmwr_ss/ss_pvol.html)
*By state of occurrence. Total is for reporting states only.
**Not reported.

Reported Legal Abortions per 1,000 Live Births in 2012

Reporting States' Ratio = 210 Abortions per 1,000 Live Births*

ALPHA ORDER

RANK	STATE	RATIO
24	Alabama	155
29	Alaska	146
25	Arizona	154
36	Arkansas	99
NA	California**	NA
26	Colorado	153
4	Connecticut	327
3	Delaware	347
2	Florida	357
9	Georgia	241
27	Hawaii	149
44	Idaho	63
7	Illinois	271
33	Indiana	106
32	Iowa	120
19	Kansas	185
42	Kentucky	68
28	Louisiana	147
40	Maine	78
NA	Maryland**	NA
6	Massachusetts	277
15	Michigan	205
23	Minnesota	156
45	Mississippi	56
41	Missouri	75
22	Montana	168
38	Nebraska	89
14	Nevada	207
NA	New Hampshire**	NA
11	New Jersey	220
31	New Mexico	130
1	New York	433
16	North Carolina	204
30	North Dakota	132
20	Ohio	184
37	Oklahoma	98
17	Oregon	200
8	Pennsylvania	242
5	Rhode Island	325
33	South Carolina	106
46	South Dakota	52
18	Tennessee	197
21	Texas	178
43	Utah	64
12	Vermont	211
10	Virginia	222
13	Washington	210
39	West Virginia	88
35	Wisconsin	103
NA	Wyoming**	NA

RANK ORDER

RANK	STATE	RATIO
1	New York	433
2	Florida	357
3	Delaware	347
4	Connecticut	327
5	Rhode Island	325
6	Massachusetts	277
7	Illinois	271
8	Pennsylvania	242
9	Georgia	241
10	Virginia	222
11	New Jersey	220
12	Vermont	211
13	Washington	210
14	Nevada	207
15	Michigan	205
16	North Carolina	204
17	Oregon	200
18	Tennessee	197
19	Kansas	185
20	Ohio	184
21	Texas	178
22	Montana	168
23	Minnesota	156
24	Alabama	155
25	Arizona	154
26	Colorado	153
27	Hawaii	149
28	Louisiana	147
29	Alaska	146
30	North Dakota	132
31	New Mexico	130
32	Iowa	120
33	Indiana	106
33	South Carolina	106
35	Wisconsin	103
36	Arkansas	99
37	Oklahoma	98
38	Nebraska	89
39	West Virginia	88
40	Maine	78
41	Missouri	75
42	Kentucky	68
43	Utah	64
44	Idaho	63
45	Mississippi	56
46	South Dakota	52
NA	California**	NA
NA	Maryland**	NA
NA	New Hampshire**	NA
NA	Wyoming**	NA

District of Columbia 278

Source: U.S. Department of Health and Human Services, Centers for Disease Control and Prevention
    "Abortion Surveillance-United States, 2012" (MMWR, Vol. 64, No. SS-10, 11/27/15, www.cdc.gov/mmwr/mmwr_ss/ss_pvol.html)
*By state of occurrence. National figure is for reporting states only.
**Not reported.

Infant Deaths in 2013

National Total = 23,440 Infant Deaths*

ALPHA ORDER

RANK	STATE	DEATHS	% of USA
15	Alabama	501	2.1%
48	Alaska	64	0.3%
19	Arizona	451	1.9%
29	Arkansas	288	1.2%
1	California	2,353	10.0%
27	Colorado	331	1.4%
34	Connecticut	169	0.7%
46	Delaware	68	0.3%
3	Florida	1,326	5.7%
8	Georgia	894	3.8%
40	Hawaii	124	0.5%
39	Idaho	126	0.5%
6	Illinois	942	4.0%
12	Indiana	600	2.6%
35	Iowa	162	0.7%
31	Kansas	250	1.1%
25	Kentucky	355	1.5%
13	Louisiana	547	2.3%
41	Maine	90	0.4%
17	Maryland	477	2.0%
28	Massachusetts	298	1.3%
10	Michigan	799	3.4%
26	Minnesota	349	1.5%
23	Mississippi	373	1.6%
16	Missouri	491	2.1%
43	Montana	70	0.3%
38	Nebraska	139	0.6%
33	Nevada	191	0.8%
43	New Hampshire	70	0.3%
18	New Jersey	460	2.0%
37	New Mexico	144	0.6%
4	New York	1,167	5.0%
9	North Carolina	832	3.5%
47	North Dakota	65	0.3%
5	Ohio	1,018	4.3%
24	Oklahoma	364	1.6%
32	Oregon	224	1.0%
7	Pennsylvania	938	4.0%
43	Rhode Island	70	0.3%
21	South Carolina	389	1.7%
42	South Dakota	80	0.3%
14	Tennessee	544	2.3%
2	Texas	2,264	9.7%
30	Utah	263	1.1%
50	Vermont	26	0.1%
11	Virginia	634	2.7%
22	Washington	388	1.7%
36	West Virginia	158	0.7%
20	Wisconsin	416	1.8%
49	Wyoming	35	0.1%

RANK ORDER

RANK	STATE	DEATHS	% of USA
1	California	2,353	10.0%
2	Texas	2,264	9.7%
3	Florida	1,326	5.7%
4	New York	1,167	5.0%
5	Ohio	1,018	4.3%
6	Illinois	942	4.0%
7	Pennsylvania	938	4.0%
8	Georgia	894	3.8%
9	North Carolina	832	3.5%
10	Michigan	799	3.4%
11	Virginia	634	2.7%
12	Indiana	600	2.6%
13	Louisiana	547	2.3%
14	Tennessee	544	2.3%
15	Alabama	501	2.1%
16	Missouri	491	2.1%
17	Maryland	477	2.0%
18	New Jersey	460	2.0%
19	Arizona	451	1.9%
20	Wisconsin	416	1.8%
21	South Carolina	389	1.7%
22	Washington	388	1.7%
23	Mississippi	373	1.6%
24	Oklahoma	364	1.6%
25	Kentucky	355	1.5%
26	Minnesota	349	1.5%
27	Colorado	331	1.4%
28	Massachusetts	298	1.3%
29	Arkansas	288	1.2%
30	Utah	263	1.1%
31	Kansas	250	1.1%
32	Oregon	224	1.0%
33	Nevada	191	0.8%
34	Connecticut	169	0.7%
35	Iowa	162	0.7%
36	West Virginia	158	0.7%
37	New Mexico	144	0.6%
38	Nebraska	139	0.6%
39	Idaho	126	0.5%
40	Hawaii	124	0.5%
41	Maine	90	0.4%
42	South Dakota	80	0.3%
43	Montana	70	0.3%
43	New Hampshire	70	0.3%
43	Rhode Island	70	0.3%
46	Delaware	68	0.3%
47	North Dakota	65	0.3%
48	Alaska	64	0.3%
49	Wyoming	35	0.1%
50	Vermont	26	0.1%
	District of Columbia	63	0.3%

Source: U.S. Department of Health and Human Services, National Center for Health Statistics
"National Vital Statistics Reports" (Vol. 64, No. 2, 2015, http://www.cdc.gov/nchs/deaths.htm)
*Final data. Deaths of infants under 1 year old by state of residence.

Infant Mortality Rate in 2013

National Rate = 6.0 Infant Deaths per 1,000 Live Births*

ALPHA ORDER

RANK	STATE	RATE
3	Alabama	8.6
32	Alaska	5.6
36	Arizona	5.3
4	Arkansas	7.6
43	California	4.8
39	Colorado	5.1
44	Connecticut	4.7
23	Delaware	6.3
24	Florida	6.2
11	Georgia	6.9
17	Hawaii	6.5
32	Idaho	5.6
28	Illinois	6.0
7	Indiana	7.2
50	Iowa	4.1
21	Kansas	6.4
21	Kentucky	6.4
2	Louisiana	8.7
8	Maine	7.0
16	Maryland	6.6
49	Massachusetts	4.2
8	Michigan	7.0
39	Minnesota	5.1
1	Mississippi	9.7
17	Missouri	6.5
30	Montana	5.7
36	Nebraska	5.3
34	Nevada	5.5
30	New Hampshire	5.7
46	New Jersey	4.5
34	New Mexico	5.5
42	New York	4.9
8	North Carolina	7.0
27	North Dakota	6.1
6	Ohio	7.3
13	Oklahoma	6.8
41	Oregon	5.0
15	Pennsylvania	6.7
17	Rhode Island	6.5
11	South Carolina	6.9
17	South Dakota	6.5
13	Tennessee	6.8
29	Texas	5.8
38	Utah	5.2
48	Vermont	4.4
24	Virginia	6.2
46	Washington	4.5
4	West Virginia	7.6
24	Wisconsin	6.2
45	Wyoming	4.6

RANK ORDER

RANK	STATE	RATE
1	Mississippi	9.7
2	Louisiana	8.7
3	Alabama	8.6
4	Arkansas	7.6
4	West Virginia	7.6
6	Ohio	7.3
7	Indiana	7.2
8	Maine	7.0
8	Michigan	7.0
8	North Carolina	7.0
11	Georgia	6.9
11	South Carolina	6.9
13	Oklahoma	6.8
13	Tennessee	6.8
15	Pennsylvania	6.7
16	Maryland	6.6
17	Hawaii	6.5
17	Missouri	6.5
17	Rhode Island	6.5
17	South Dakota	6.5
21	Kansas	6.4
21	Kentucky	6.4
23	Delaware	6.3
24	Florida	6.2
24	Virginia	6.2
24	Wisconsin	6.2
27	North Dakota	6.1
28	Illinois	6.0
29	Texas	5.8
30	Montana	5.7
30	New Hampshire	5.7
32	Alaska	5.6
32	Idaho	5.6
34	Nevada	5.5
34	New Mexico	5.5
36	Arizona	5.3
36	Nebraska	5.3
38	Utah	5.2
39	Colorado	5.1
39	Minnesota	5.1
41	Oregon	5.0
42	New York	4.9
43	California	4.8
44	Connecticut	4.7
45	Wyoming	4.6
46	New Jersey	4.5
46	Washington	4.5
48	Vermont	4.4
49	Massachusetts	4.2
50	Iowa	4.1
	District of Columbia	6.8

Source: U.S. Department of Health and Human Services, National Center for Health Statistics
"National Vital Statistics Reports" (Vol. 64, No. 2, 2015, http://www.cdc.gov/nchs/deaths.htm)
*Final data. Deaths of infants under 1 year old by state of residence.

Deaths in 2013

National Total = 2,596,993 Deaths*

ALPHA ORDER

RANK	STATE	DEATHS	% of USA
19	Alabama	50,189	1.9%
50	Alaska	3,997	0.2%
18	Arizona	50,534	1.9%
30	Arkansas	30,437	1.2%
1	California	248,359	9.6%
28	Colorado	33,712	1.3%
31	Connecticut	29,632	1.1%
45	Delaware	7,967	0.3%
2	Florida	181,112	7.0%
10	Georgia	75,088	2.9%
42	Hawaii	10,505	0.4%
40	Idaho	12,434	0.5%
7	Illinois	103,401	4.0%
14	Indiana	60,716	2.3%
32	Iowa	28,948	1.1%
33	Kansas	25,414	1.0%
23	Kentucky	43,759	1.7%
24	Louisiana	43,270	1.7%
39	Maine	13,547	0.5%
21	Maryland	45,689	1.8%
16	Massachusetts	54,567	2.1%
8	Michigan	92,408	3.6%
25	Minnesota	40,987	1.6%
29	Mississippi	30,703	1.2%
15	Missouri	57,444	2.2%
44	Montana	9,511	0.4%
38	Nebraska	15,754	0.6%
35	Nevada	21,468	0.8%
41	New Hampshire	10,897	0.4%
11	New Jersey	71,403	2.7%
36	New Mexico	16,805	0.6%
4	New York	150,919	5.8%
9	North Carolina	83,329	3.2%
47	North Dakota	6,233	0.2%
6	Ohio	113,258	4.4%
26	Oklahoma	38,384	1.5%
27	Oregon	33,939	1.3%
5	Pennsylvania	129,123	5.0%
43	Rhode Island	9,792	0.4%
22	South Carolina	44,582	1.7%
46	South Dakota	7,099	0.3%
12	Tennessee	63,406	2.4%
3	Texas	179,183	6.9%
37	Utah	16,366	0.6%
48	Vermont	5,639	0.2%
13	Virginia	62,716	2.4%
17	Washington	51,264	2.0%
34	West Virginia	21,843	0.8%
20	Wisconsin	50,026	1.9%
49	Wyoming	4,516	0.2%

RANK ORDER

RANK	STATE	DEATHS	% of USA
1	California	248,359	9.6%
2	Florida	181,112	7.0%
3	Texas	179,183	6.9%
4	New York	150,919	5.8%
5	Pennsylvania	129,123	5.0%
6	Ohio	113,258	4.4%
7	Illinois	103,401	4.0%
8	Michigan	92,408	3.6%
9	North Carolina	83,329	3.2%
10	Georgia	75,088	2.9%
11	New Jersey	71,403	2.7%
12	Tennessee	63,406	2.4%
13	Virginia	62,716	2.4%
14	Indiana	60,716	2.3%
15	Missouri	57,444	2.2%
16	Massachusetts	54,567	2.1%
17	Washington	51,264	2.0%
18	Arizona	50,534	1.9%
19	Alabama	50,189	1.9%
20	Wisconsin	50,026	1.9%
21	Maryland	45,689	1.8%
22	South Carolina	44,582	1.7%
23	Kentucky	43,759	1.7%
24	Louisiana	43,270	1.7%
25	Minnesota	40,987	1.6%
26	Oklahoma	38,384	1.5%
27	Oregon	33,939	1.3%
28	Colorado	33,712	1.3%
29	Mississippi	30,703	1.2%
30	Arkansas	30,437	1.2%
31	Connecticut	29,632	1.1%
32	Iowa	28,948	1.1%
33	Kansas	25,414	1.0%
34	West Virginia	21,843	0.8%
35	Nevada	21,468	0.8%
36	New Mexico	16,805	0.6%
37	Utah	16,366	0.6%
38	Nebraska	15,754	0.6%
39	Maine	13,547	0.5%
40	Idaho	12,434	0.5%
41	New Hampshire	10,897	0.4%
42	Hawaii	10,505	0.4%
43	Rhode Island	9,792	0.4%
44	Montana	9,511	0.4%
45	Delaware	7,967	0.3%
46	South Dakota	7,099	0.3%
47	North Dakota	6,233	0.2%
48	Vermont	5,639	0.2%
49	Wyoming	4,516	0.2%
50	Alaska	3,997	0.2%
	District of Columbia	4,719	0.2%

Source: U.S. Department of Health and Human Services, National Center for Health Statistics "National Vital Statistics Reports" (Vol. 64, No. 2, 2015, http://www.cdc.gov/nchs/deaths.htm)
*Final data by state of residence.

Age-Adjusted Death Rate in 2013

National Rate = 731.9 Deaths per 100,000 Population*

ALPHA ORDER

RANK	STATE	RATE
2	Alabama	925.2
27	Alaska	724.4
42	Arizona	674.2
7	Arkansas	893.8
49	California	630.1
45	Colorado	655.4
48	Connecticut	646.3
25	Delaware	726.8
44	Florida	663.4
13	Georgia	806.2
50	Hawaii	590.8
24	Idaho	730.6
28	Illinois	724.0
10	Indiana	832.2
29	Iowa	723.7
19	Kansas	757.7
5	Kentucky	899.9
6	Louisiana	897.7
20	Maine	754.2
34	Maryland	710.4
43	Massachusetts	663.5
14	Michigan	782.3
46	Minnesota	651.0
1	Mississippi	959.6
12	Missouri	807.7
17	Montana	761.3
32	Nebraska	714.7
16	Nevada	769.8
40	New Hampshire	679.1
41	New Jersey	676.4
22	New Mexico	731.8
47	New York	649.3
15	North Carolina	777.6
36	North Dakota	709.7
11	Ohio	811.2
4	Oklahoma	910.7
31	Oregon	717.5
17	Pennsylvania	761.3
37	Rhode Island	709.6
9	South Carolina	837.8
38	South Dakota	679.3
8	Tennessee	881.1
21	Texas	751.6
34	Utah	710.4
33	Vermont	710.6
26	Virginia	724.8
38	Washington	679.3
3	West Virginia	923.8
30	Wisconsin	720.1
23	Wyoming	731.7

RANK ORDER

RANK	STATE	RATE
1	Mississippi	959.6
2	Alabama	925.2
3	West Virginia	923.8
4	Oklahoma	910.7
5	Kentucky	899.9
6	Louisiana	897.7
7	Arkansas	893.8
8	Tennessee	881.1
9	South Carolina	837.8
10	Indiana	832.2
11	Ohio	811.2
12	Missouri	807.7
13	Georgia	806.2
14	Michigan	782.3
15	North Carolina	777.6
16	Nevada	769.8
17	Montana	761.3
17	Pennsylvania	761.3
19	Kansas	757.7
20	Maine	754.2
21	Texas	751.6
22	New Mexico	731.8
23	Wyoming	731.7
24	Idaho	730.6
25	Delaware	726.8
26	Virginia	724.8
27	Alaska	724.4
28	Illinois	724.0
29	Iowa	723.7
30	Wisconsin	720.1
31	Oregon	717.5
32	Nebraska	714.7
33	Vermont	710.6
34	Maryland	710.4
34	Utah	710.4
36	North Dakota	709.7
37	Rhode Island	709.6
38	South Dakota	679.3
38	Washington	679.3
40	New Hampshire	679.1
41	New Jersey	676.4
42	Arizona	674.2
43	Massachusetts	663.5
44	Florida	663.4
45	Colorado	655.4
46	Minnesota	651.0
47	New York	649.3
48	Connecticut	646.3
49	California	630.1
50	Hawaii	590.8
	District of Columbia	752.0

Source: U.S. Department of Health and Human Services, National Center for Health Statistics
"National Vital Statistics Reports" (Vol. 64, No. 2, 2015, http://www.cdc.gov/nchs/deaths.htm)
*Final data by state of residence. Age-adjusted rates eliminate the distorting effects of the aging of the population. Rates based on the year 2000 standard population.

Estimated Deaths by Cancer in 2015

National Estimated Total = 589,430 Deaths

ALPHA ORDER

RANK	STATE	DEATHS	% of USA
20	Alabama	10,560	1.8%
49	Alaska	1,040	0.2%
19	Arizona	11,540	2.0%
30	Arkansas	6,760	1.1%
1	California	58,180	9.9%
28	Colorado	7,590	1.3%
29	Connecticut	6,840	1.2%
45	Delaware	2,010	0.3%
2	Florida	43,050	7.3%
10	Georgia	16,460	2.8%
42	Hawaii	2,470	0.4%
40	Idaho	2,790	0.5%
7	Illinois	23,940	4.1%
14	Indiana	13,420	2.3%
31	Iowa	6,440	1.1%
33	Kansas	5,510	0.9%
22	Kentucky	10,200	1.7%
25	Louisiana	9,040	1.5%
38	Maine	3,300	0.6%
21	Maryland	10,470	1.8%
16	Massachusetts	12,710	2.2%
8	Michigan	20,920	3.5%
24	Minnesota	9,820	1.7%
32	Mississippi	6,360	1.1%
15	Missouri	12,830	2.2%
44	Montana	2,020	0.3%
37	Nebraska	3,480	0.6%
34	Nevada	4,880	0.8%
41	New Hampshire	2,730	0.5%
11	New Jersey	16,250	2.8%
36	New Mexico	3,620	0.6%
4	New York	34,600	5.9%
9	North Carolina	19,310	3.3%
48	North Dakota	1,280	0.2%
6	Ohio	25,400	4.3%
26	Oklahoma	8,100	1.4%
27	Oregon	8,040	1.4%
5	Pennsylvania	28,640	4.9%
43	Rhode Island	2,120	0.4%
23	South Carolina	10,130	1.7%
46	South Dakota	1,630	0.3%
13	Tennessee	14,370	2.4%
3	Texas	38,520	6.5%
39	Utah	2,900	0.5%
47	Vermont	1,360	0.2%
12	Virginia	14,830	2.5%
17	Washington	12,700	2.2%
35	West Virginia	4,710	0.8%
18	Wisconsin	11,550	2.0%
50	Wyoming	1,000	0.2%

RANK ORDER

RANK	STATE	DEATHS	% of USA
1	California	58,180	9.9%
2	Florida	43,050	7.3%
3	Texas	38,520	6.5%
4	New York	34,600	5.9%
5	Pennsylvania	28,640	4.9%
6	Ohio	25,400	4.3%
7	Illinois	23,940	4.1%
8	Michigan	20,920	3.5%
9	North Carolina	19,310	3.3%
10	Georgia	16,460	2.8%
11	New Jersey	16,250	2.8%
12	Virginia	14,830	2.5%
13	Tennessee	14,370	2.4%
14	Indiana	13,420	2.3%
15	Missouri	12,830	2.2%
16	Massachusetts	12,710	2.2%
17	Washington	12,700	2.2%
18	Wisconsin	11,550	2.0%
19	Arizona	11,540	2.0%
20	Alabama	10,560	1.8%
21	Maryland	10,470	1.8%
22	Kentucky	10,200	1.7%
23	South Carolina	10,130	1.7%
24	Minnesota	9,820	1.7%
25	Louisiana	9,040	1.5%
26	Oklahoma	8,100	1.4%
27	Oregon	8,040	1.4%
28	Colorado	7,590	1.3%
29	Connecticut	6,840	1.2%
30	Arkansas	6,760	1.1%
31	Iowa	6,440	1.1%
32	Mississippi	6,360	1.1%
33	Kansas	5,510	0.9%
34	Nevada	4,880	0.8%
35	West Virginia	4,710	0.8%
36	New Mexico	3,620	0.6%
37	Nebraska	3,480	0.6%
38	Maine	3,300	0.6%
39	Utah	2,900	0.5%
40	Idaho	2,790	0.5%
41	New Hampshire	2,730	0.5%
42	Hawaii	2,470	0.4%
43	Rhode Island	2,120	0.4%
44	Montana	2,020	0.3%
45	Delaware	2,010	0.3%
46	South Dakota	1,630	0.3%
47	Vermont	1,360	0.2%
48	North Dakota	1,280	0.2%
49	Alaska	1,040	0.2%
50	Wyoming	1,000	0.2%
	District of Columbia	990	0.2%

Source: American Cancer Society
"Cancer Facts & Figures 2015" (Copyright 2015, American Cancer Society, www.cancer.org/research/cancerfactsstatistics/index)

Estimated Death Rate by Cancer in 2015

National Estimated Rate = 183.4 Deaths per 100,000 Population*

ALPHA ORDER

RANK	STATE	RATE
8	Alabama	217.3
47	Alaska	140.8
42	Arizona	169.0
4	Arkansas	227.0
46	California	148.6
49	Colorado	139.1
26	Connecticut	190.5
10	Delaware	212.5
12	Florida	212.4
45	Georgia	161.1
39	Hawaii	172.5
44	Idaho	168.6
30	Illinois	186.2
19	Indiana	202.7
17	Iowa	206.2
28	Kansas	189.2
3	Kentucky	230.5
24	Louisiana	193.5
2	Maine	248.2
37	Maryland	174.3
29	Massachusetts	187.1
14	Michigan	210.8
33	Minnesota	178.9
10	Mississippi	212.5
13	Missouri	210.9
23	Montana	195.6
31	Nebraska	183.5
43	Nevada	168.8
18	New Hampshire	205.2
32	New Jersey	181.4
38	New Mexico	173.6
36	New York	174.8
25	North Carolina	192.3
41	North Dakota	169.1
6	Ohio	218.7
15	Oklahoma	207.1
22	Oregon	199.6
5	Pennsylvania	223.7
20	Rhode Island	200.7
16	South Carolina	206.9
27	South Dakota	189.9
7	Tennessee	217.7
48	Texas	140.2
50	Utah	96.8
9	Vermont	217.2
35	Virginia	176.9
34	Washington	177.1
1	West Virginia	255.4
21	Wisconsin	200.1
40	Wyoming	170.6

RANK ORDER

RANK	STATE	RATE
1	West Virginia	255.4
2	Maine	248.2
3	Kentucky	230.5
4	Arkansas	227.0
5	Pennsylvania	223.7
6	Ohio	218.7
7	Tennessee	217.7
8	Alabama	217.3
9	Vermont	217.2
10	Delaware	212.5
10	Mississippi	212.5
12	Florida	212.4
13	Missouri	210.9
14	Michigan	210.8
15	Oklahoma	207.1
16	South Carolina	206.9
17	Iowa	206.2
18	New Hampshire	205.2
19	Indiana	202.7
20	Rhode Island	200.7
21	Wisconsin	200.1
22	Oregon	199.6
23	Montana	195.6
24	Louisiana	193.5
25	North Carolina	192.3
26	Connecticut	190.5
27	South Dakota	189.9
28	Kansas	189.2
29	Massachusetts	187.1
30	Illinois	186.2
31	Nebraska	183.5
32	New Jersey	181.4
33	Minnesota	178.9
34	Washington	177.1
35	Virginia	176.9
36	New York	174.8
37	Maryland	174.3
38	New Mexico	173.6
39	Hawaii	172.5
40	Wyoming	170.6
41	North Dakota	169.1
42	Arizona	169.0
43	Nevada	168.8
44	Idaho	168.6
45	Georgia	161.1
46	California	148.6
47	Alaska	140.8
48	Texas	140.2
49	Colorado	139.1
50	Utah	96.8
	District of Columbia	147.3

Source: CQ Press using data from American Cancer Society
"Cancer Facts & Figures 2015" (Copyright 2015, American Cancer Society, www.cancer.org/research/cancerfactsstatistics/index)
*Rates calculated using 2015 Census resident population estimates. Not age-adjusted.

Estimated New Cancer Cases in 2015

National Estimated Total = 1,658,370 New Cases*

ALPHA ORDER

RANK	STATE	CASES	% of USA
23	Alabama	26,150	1.6%
49	Alaska	3,700	0.2%
19	Arizona	32,440	2.0%
32	Arkansas	15,830	1.0%
1	California	172,090	10.4%
25	Colorado	24,540	1.5%
28	Connecticut	21,970	1.3%
45	Delaware	5,280	0.3%
2	Florida	114,040	6.9%
11	Georgia	48,070	2.9%
42	Hawaii	6,730	0.4%
41	Idaho	8,080	0.5%
6	Illinois	65,460	3.9%
16	Indiana	35,620	2.1%
30	Iowa	17,140	1.0%
33	Kansas	14,440	0.9%
22	Kentucky	26,490	1.6%
26	Louisiana	24,100	1.5%
39	Maine	8,810	0.5%
20	Maryland	30,050	1.8%
15	Massachusetts	37,790	2.3%
8	Michigan	57,420	3.5%
21	Minnesota	29,730	1.8%
31	Mississippi	16,260	1.0%
17	Missouri	34,680	2.1%
44	Montana	5,950	0.4%
38	Nebraska	9,540	0.6%
34	Nevada	13,640	0.8%
40	New Hampshire	8,090	0.5%
9	New Jersey	51,410	3.1%
37	New Mexico	9,970	0.6%
4	New York	107,840	6.5%
10	North Carolina	50,420	3.0%
48	North Dakota	3,840	0.2%
7	Ohio	65,010	3.9%
29	Oklahoma	19,280	1.2%
27	Oregon	22,410	1.4%
5	Pennsylvania	81,540	4.9%
43	Rhode Island	6,040	0.4%
24	South Carolina	25,550	1.5%
46	South Dakota	4,520	0.3%
13	Tennessee	38,300	2.3%
3	Texas	113,630	6.9%
36	Utah	11,050	0.7%
47	Vermont	4,020	0.2%
12	Virginia	41,170	2.5%
14	Washington	38,180	2.3%
35	West Virginia	11,730	0.7%
18	Wisconsin	32,700	2.0%
50	Wyoming	2,860	0.2%

RANK ORDER

RANK	STATE	CASES	% of USA
1	California	172,090	10.4%
2	Florida	114,040	6.9%
3	Texas	113,630	6.9%
4	New York	107,840	6.5%
5	Pennsylvania	81,540	4.9%
6	Illinois	65,460	3.9%
7	Ohio	65,010	3.9%
8	Michigan	57,420	3.5%
9	New Jersey	51,410	3.1%
10	North Carolina	50,420	3.0%
11	Georgia	48,070	2.9%
12	Virginia	41,170	2.5%
13	Tennessee	38,300	2.3%
14	Washington	38,180	2.3%
15	Massachusetts	37,790	2.3%
16	Indiana	35,620	2.1%
17	Missouri	34,680	2.1%
18	Wisconsin	32,700	2.0%
19	Arizona	32,440	2.0%
20	Maryland	30,050	1.8%
21	Minnesota	29,730	1.8%
22	Kentucky	26,490	1.6%
23	Alabama	26,150	1.6%
24	South Carolina	25,550	1.5%
25	Colorado	24,540	1.5%
26	Louisiana	24,100	1.5%
27	Oregon	22,410	1.4%
28	Connecticut	21,970	1.3%
29	Oklahoma	19,280	1.2%
30	Iowa	17,140	1.0%
31	Mississippi	16,260	1.0%
32	Arkansas	15,830	1.0%
33	Kansas	14,440	0.9%
34	Nevada	13,640	0.8%
35	West Virginia	11,730	0.7%
36	Utah	11,050	0.7%
37	New Mexico	9,970	0.6%
38	Nebraska	9,540	0.6%
39	Maine	8,810	0.5%
40	New Hampshire	8,090	0.5%
41	Idaho	8,080	0.5%
42	Hawaii	6,730	0.4%
43	Rhode Island	6,040	0.4%
44	Montana	5,950	0.4%
45	Delaware	5,280	0.3%
46	South Dakota	4,520	0.3%
47	Vermont	4,020	0.2%
48	North Dakota	3,840	0.2%
49	Alaska	3,700	0.2%
50	Wyoming	2,860	0.2%
	District of Columbia	2,800	0.2%

Source: American Cancer Society
"Cancer Facts & Figures 2015" (Copyright 2015, American Cancer Society, www.cancer.org/research/cancerfactsstatistics/index)
*These estimates are offered as a rough guide and should not be regarded as definitive. They are calculated by the American Cancer Society using a model based on 1995-2011 incidence data. Totals do not include basal and squamous cell skin cancers or in situ carcinomas except urinary bladder.

Estimated Rate of New Cancer Cases in 2015

National Estimated Rate = 516.0 New Cases per 100,000 Population*

ALPHA ORDER

RANK	STATE	RATE
24	Alabama	538.2
35	Alaska	501.1
43	Arizona	475.1
27	Arkansas	531.5
48	California	439.6
47	Colorado	449.7
5	Connecticut	611.8
17	Delaware	558.2
15	Florida	562.6
45	Georgia	470.6
46	Hawaii	470.1
40	Idaho	488.2
31	Illinois	509.0
25	Indiana	538.1
20	Iowa	548.7
37	Kansas	495.9
7	Kentucky	598.6
30	Louisiana	516.0
1	Maine	662.7
36	Maryland	500.3
18	Massachusetts	556.2
9	Michigan	578.7
23	Minnesota	541.6
22	Mississippi	543.4
13	Missouri	570.1
10	Montana	576.0
33	Nebraska	503.1
44	Nevada	471.8
6	New Hampshire	608.0
11	New Jersey	573.9
42	New Mexico	478.2
21	New York	544.8
34	North Carolina	502.1
32	North Dakota	507.3
16	Ohio	559.8
38	Oklahoma	492.9
18	Oregon	556.2
3	Pennsylvania	636.9
12	Rhode Island	571.8
29	South Carolina	521.8
28	South Dakota	526.5
8	Tennessee	580.3
49	Texas	413.7
50	Utah	368.8
2	Vermont	642.1
39	Virginia	491.1
26	Washington	532.5
4	West Virginia	636.1
14	Wisconsin	566.6
41	Wyoming	488.0

RANK ORDER

RANK	STATE	RATE
1	Maine	662.7
2	Vermont	642.1
3	Pennsylvania	636.9
4	West Virginia	636.1
5	Connecticut	611.8
6	New Hampshire	608.0
7	Kentucky	598.6
8	Tennessee	580.3
9	Michigan	578.7
10	Montana	576.0
11	New Jersey	573.9
12	Rhode Island	571.8
13	Missouri	570.1
14	Wisconsin	566.6
15	Florida	562.6
16	Ohio	559.8
17	Delaware	558.2
18	Massachusetts	556.2
18	Oregon	556.2
20	Iowa	548.7
21	New York	544.8
22	Mississippi	543.4
23	Minnesota	541.6
24	Alabama	538.2
25	Indiana	538.1
26	Washington	532.5
27	Arkansas	531.5
28	South Dakota	526.5
29	South Carolina	521.8
30	Louisiana	516.0
31	Illinois	509.0
32	North Dakota	507.3
33	Nebraska	503.1
34	North Carolina	502.1
35	Alaska	501.1
36	Maryland	500.3
37	Kansas	495.9
38	Oklahoma	492.9
39	Virginia	491.1
40	Idaho	488.2
41	Wyoming	488.0
42	New Mexico	478.2
43	Arizona	475.1
44	Nevada	471.8
45	Georgia	470.6
46	Hawaii	470.1
47	Colorado	449.7
48	California	439.6
49	Texas	413.7
50	Utah	368.8
	District of Columbia	416.5

Source: CQ Press using data from American Cancer Society
"Cancer Facts & Figures 2015" (Copyright 2015, American Cancer Society, www.cancer.org/research/cancerfactsstatistics/index)
*These estimates are offered as a rough guide and should not be regarded as definitive. They are calculated by the American Cancer Society using a model based on 1995-2011 incidence data. Totals do not include basal and squamous cell skin cancers or in situ carcinomas except urinary bladder. Rates calculated using 2015 Census resident population estimates.

Deaths by Accidents in 2013

National Total = 130,557 Deaths*

ALPHA ORDER

RANK	STATE	DEATHS	% of USA
25	Alabama	2,329	1.8%
47	Alaska	353	0.3%
12	Arizona	3,349	2.6%
33	Arkansas	1,373	1.1%
1	California	11,538	8.8%
21	Colorado	2,422	1.9%
30	Connecticut	1,582	1.2%
46	Delaware	412	0.3%
3	Florida	8,736	6.7%
10	Georgia	3,727	2.9%
44	Hawaii	467	0.4%
38	Idaho	776	0.6%
7	Illinois	4,511	3.5%
17	Indiana	2,898	2.2%
31	Iowa	1,422	1.1%
34	Kansas	1,359	1.0%
19	Kentucky	2,513	1.9%
24	Louisiana	2,333	1.8%
40	Maine	644	0.5%
28	Maryland	1,732	1.3%
23	Massachusetts	2,393	1.8%
9	Michigan	4,225	3.2%
22	Minnesota	2,405	1.8%
29	Mississippi	1,692	1.3%
14	Missouri	2,981	2.3%
41	Montana	623	0.5%
39	Nebraska	703	0.5%
36	Nevada	1,184	0.9%
42	New Hampshire	619	0.5%
13	New Jersey	3,028	2.3%
35	New Mexico	1,245	1.0%
5	New York	5,927	4.5%
8	North Carolina	4,324	3.3%
49	North Dakota	326	0.2%
6	Ohio	5,497	4.2%
20	Oklahoma	2,474	1.9%
27	Oregon	1,755	1.3%
4	Pennsylvania	6,359	4.9%
43	Rhode Island	537	0.4%
26	South Carolina	2,287	1.8%
45	South Dakota	425	0.3%
11	Tennessee	3,540	2.7%
2	Texas	9,395	7.2%
37	Utah	1,103	0.8%
48	Vermont	352	0.3%
16	Virginia	2,951	2.3%
18	Washington	2,826	2.2%
32	West Virginia	1,395	1.1%
15	Wisconsin	2,969	2.3%
50	Wyoming	325	0.2%

RANK ORDER

RANK	STATE	DEATHS	% of USA
1	California	11,538	8.8%
2	Texas	9,395	7.2%
3	Florida	8,736	6.7%
4	Pennsylvania	6,359	4.9%
5	New York	5,927	4.5%
6	Ohio	5,497	4.2%
7	Illinois	4,511	3.5%
8	North Carolina	4,324	3.3%
9	Michigan	4,225	3.2%
10	Georgia	3,727	2.9%
11	Tennessee	3,540	2.7%
12	Arizona	3,349	2.6%
13	New Jersey	3,028	2.3%
14	Missouri	2,981	2.3%
15	Wisconsin	2,969	2.3%
16	Virginia	2,951	2.3%
17	Indiana	2,898	2.2%
18	Washington	2,826	2.2%
19	Kentucky	2,513	1.9%
20	Oklahoma	2,474	1.9%
21	Colorado	2,422	1.9%
22	Minnesota	2,405	1.8%
23	Massachusetts	2,393	1.8%
24	Louisiana	2,333	1.8%
25	Alabama	2,329	1.8%
26	South Carolina	2,287	1.8%
27	Oregon	1,755	1.3%
28	Maryland	1,732	1.3%
29	Mississippi	1,692	1.3%
30	Connecticut	1,582	1.2%
31	Iowa	1,422	1.1%
32	West Virginia	1,395	1.1%
33	Arkansas	1,373	1.1%
34	Kansas	1,359	1.0%
35	New Mexico	1,245	1.0%
36	Nevada	1,184	0.9%
37	Utah	1,103	0.8%
38	Idaho	776	0.6%
39	Nebraska	703	0.5%
40	Maine	644	0.5%
41	Montana	623	0.5%
42	New Hampshire	619	0.5%
43	Rhode Island	537	0.4%
44	Hawaii	467	0.4%
45	South Dakota	425	0.3%
46	Delaware	412	0.3%
47	Alaska	353	0.3%
48	Vermont	352	0.3%
49	North Dakota	326	0.2%
50	Wyoming	325	0.2%
	District of Columbia	216	0.2%

Source: U.S. Department of Health and Human Services, National Center for Health Statistics
"National Vital Statistics Reports" (Vol. 64, No. 2, 2015, http://www.cdc.gov/nchs/deaths.htm)
*Final data by state of residence. Includes motor vehicle deaths, poisoning, falls, drowning, and other accidents.

Age-Adjusted Death Rate by Accidents in 2013

National Rate = 39.4 Deaths per 100,000 Population*

ALPHA ORDER

RANK	STATE	RATE
14	Alabama	47.2
9	Alaska	52.5
12	Arizona	48.6
23	Arkansas	44.8
48	California	29.2
19	Colorado	46.4
37	Connecticut	39.3
27	Delaware	42.9
38	Florida	39.1
40	Georgia	38.3
47	Hawaii	30.1
13	Idaho	47.7
44	Illinois	33.6
26	Indiana	43.1
36	Iowa	40.0
24	Kansas	44.4
5	Kentucky	55.7
10	Louisiana	50.5
29	Maine	42.6
49	Maryland	27.9
45	Massachusetts	32.5
33	Michigan	40.1
33	Minnesota	40.1
6	Mississippi	55.6
15	Missouri	47.0
4	Montana	57.7
42	Nebraska	34.9
31	Nevada	41.9
30	New Hampshire	42.5
46	New Jersey	31.8
3	New Mexico	59.0
50	New York	27.7
28	North Carolina	42.7
32	North Dakota	41.7
21	Ohio	45.0
2	Oklahoma	62.7
33	Oregon	40.1
22	Pennsylvania	44.9
20	Rhode Island	45.3
18	South Carolina	46.6
17	South Dakota	46.7
8	Tennessee	52.7
41	Texas	37.0
25	Utah	43.4
11	Vermont	49.6
42	Virginia	34.9
39	Washington	38.7
1	West Virginia	71.7
16	Wisconsin	46.8
7	Wyoming	55.2

RANK ORDER

RANK	STATE	RATE
1	West Virginia	71.7
2	Oklahoma	62.7
3	New Mexico	59.0
4	Montana	57.7
5	Kentucky	55.7
6	Mississippi	55.6
7	Wyoming	55.2
8	Tennessee	52.7
9	Alaska	52.5
10	Louisiana	50.5
11	Vermont	49.6
12	Arizona	48.6
13	Idaho	47.7
14	Alabama	47.2
15	Missouri	47.0
16	Wisconsin	46.8
17	South Dakota	46.7
18	South Carolina	46.6
19	Colorado	46.4
20	Rhode Island	45.3
21	Ohio	45.0
22	Pennsylvania	44.9
23	Arkansas	44.8
24	Kansas	44.4
25	Utah	43.4
26	Indiana	43.1
27	Delaware	42.9
28	North Carolina	42.7
29	Maine	42.6
30	New Hampshire	42.5
31	Nevada	41.9
32	North Dakota	41.7
33	Michigan	40.1
33	Minnesota	40.1
33	Oregon	40.1
36	Iowa	40.0
37	Connecticut	39.3
38	Florida	39.1
39	Washington	38.7
40	Georgia	38.3
41	Texas	37.0
42	Nebraska	34.9
42	Virginia	34.9
44	Illinois	33.6
45	Massachusetts	32.5
46	New Jersey	31.8
47	Hawaii	30.1
48	California	29.2
49	Maryland	27.9
50	New York	27.7
	District of Columbia	33.6

Source: U.S. Department of Health and Human Services, National Center for Health Statistics
"National Vital Statistics Reports" (Vol. 64, No. 2, 2015, http://www.cdc.gov/nchs/deaths.htm)
*Final data by state of residence. Includes motor vehicle deaths, poisoning, falls, drowning, and other accidents. Age-adjusted rates based on the year 2000 standard population.

Deaths by Cerebrovascular Diseases in 2013

National Total = 128,978 Deaths*

ALPHA ORDER

RANK	STATE	DEATHS	% of USA
17	Alabama	2,604	2.0%
50	Alaska	189	0.1%
22	Arizona	2,162	1.7%
28	Arkansas	1,637	1.3%
1	California	13,698	10.6%
29	Colorado	1,588	1.2%
32	Connecticut	1,348	1.0%
45	Delaware	409	0.3%
3	Florida	8,698	6.7%
10	Georgia	3,694	2.9%
39	Hawaii	634	0.5%
41	Idaho	598	0.5%
7	Illinois	5,294	4.1%
14	Indiana	2,996	2.3%
31	Iowa	1,409	1.1%
33	Kansas	1,320	1.0%
25	Kentucky	1,990	1.5%
23	Louisiana	2,098	1.6%
40	Maine	620	0.5%
21	Maryland	2,315	1.8%
20	Massachusetts	2,354	1.8%
9	Michigan	4,373	3.4%
24	Minnesota	2,073	1.6%
30	Mississippi	1,500	1.2%
15	Missouri	2,935	2.3%
42	Montana	480	0.4%
37	Nebraska	820	0.6%
35	Nevada	905	0.7%
43	New Hampshire	441	0.3%
11	New Jersey	3,456	2.7%
38	New Mexico	689	0.5%
5	New York	6,176	4.8%
8	North Carolina	4,503	3.5%
47	North Dakota	306	0.2%
6	Ohio	5,690	4.4%
26	Oklahoma	1,880	1.5%
27	Oregon	1,775	1.4%
4	Pennsylvania	6,604	5.1%
46	Rhode Island	397	0.3%
19	South Carolina	2,508	1.9%
44	South Dakota	418	0.3%
13	Tennessee	3,157	2.4%
2	Texas	9,283	7.2%
36	Utah	836	0.6%
48	Vermont	260	0.2%
12	Virginia	3,287	2.5%
16	Washington	2,652	2.1%
34	West Virginia	983	0.8%
18	Wisconsin	2,536	2.0%
49	Wyoming	213	0.2%

RANK ORDER

RANK	STATE	DEATHS	% of USA
1	California	13,698	10.6%
2	Texas	9,283	7.2%
3	Florida	8,698	6.7%
4	Pennsylvania	6,604	5.1%
5	New York	6,176	4.8%
6	Ohio	5,690	4.4%
7	Illinois	5,294	4.1%
8	North Carolina	4,503	3.5%
9	Michigan	4,373	3.4%
10	Georgia	3,694	2.9%
11	New Jersey	3,456	2.7%
12	Virginia	3,287	2.5%
13	Tennessee	3,157	2.4%
14	Indiana	2,996	2.3%
15	Missouri	2,935	2.3%
16	Washington	2,652	2.1%
17	Alabama	2,604	2.0%
18	Wisconsin	2,536	2.0%
19	South Carolina	2,508	1.9%
20	Massachusetts	2,354	1.8%
21	Maryland	2,315	1.8%
22	Arizona	2,162	1.7%
23	Louisiana	2,098	1.6%
24	Minnesota	2,073	1.6%
25	Kentucky	1,990	1.5%
26	Oklahoma	1,880	1.5%
27	Oregon	1,775	1.4%
28	Arkansas	1,637	1.3%
29	Colorado	1,588	1.2%
30	Mississippi	1,500	1.2%
31	Iowa	1,409	1.1%
32	Connecticut	1,348	1.0%
33	Kansas	1,320	1.0%
34	West Virginia	983	0.8%
35	Nevada	905	0.7%
36	Utah	836	0.6%
37	Nebraska	820	0.6%
38	New Mexico	689	0.5%
39	Hawaii	634	0.5%
40	Maine	620	0.5%
41	Idaho	598	0.5%
42	Montana	480	0.4%
43	New Hampshire	441	0.3%
44	South Dakota	418	0.3%
45	Delaware	409	0.3%
46	Rhode Island	397	0.3%
47	North Dakota	306	0.2%
48	Vermont	260	0.2%
49	Wyoming	213	0.2%
50	Alaska	189	0.1%
	District of Columbia	187	0.1%

Source: U.S. Department of Health and Human Services, National Center for Health Statistics
  "National Vital Statistics Reports" (Vol. 64, No. 2, 2015, http://www.cdc.gov/nchs/deaths.htm)
*Final data by state of residence. Cerebrovascular diseases include stroke and other disorders of the blood vessels of the brain.

Age-Adjusted Death Rate by Cerebrovascular Diseases in 2013

National Rate = 36.2 Deaths per 100,000 Population*

ALPHA ORDER

RANK	STATE	RATE
1	Alabama	48.1
11	Alaska	40.7
45	Arizona	28.6
2	Arkansas	47.6
33	California	34.9
40	Colorado	32.0
46	Connecticut	28.3
24	Delaware	37.0
43	Florida	30.6
10	Georgia	41.4
34	Hawaii	34.8
31	Idaho	35.4
25	Illinois	36.7
11	Indiana	40.7
35	Iowa	33.9
19	Kansas	38.1
9	Kentucky	41.7
7	Louisiana	44.0
36	Maine	33.4
28	Maryland	36.1
47	Massachusetts	27.7
27	Michigan	36.3
40	Minnesota	32.0
4	Mississippi	47.2
14	Missouri	40.6
21	Montana	37.6
26	Nebraska	36.4
37	Nevada	33.3
49	New Hampshire	27.6
38	New Jersey	32.4
44	New Mexico	30.0
50	New York	26.3
8	North Carolina	42.4
38	North Dakota	32.4
16	Ohio	39.9
5	Oklahoma	44.5
22	Oregon	37.3
23	Pennsylvania	37.2
47	Rhode Island	27.7
2	South Carolina	47.6
20	South Dakota	38.0
6	Tennessee	44.4
15	Texas	40.2
18	Utah	38.2
42	Vermont	31.7
17	Virginia	38.6
30	Washington	35.5
11	West Virginia	40.7
29	Wisconsin	36.0
32	Wyoming	35.1

RANK ORDER

RANK	STATE	RATE
1	Alabama	48.1
2	Arkansas	47.6
2	South Carolina	47.6
4	Mississippi	47.2
5	Oklahoma	44.5
6	Tennessee	44.4
7	Louisiana	44.0
8	North Carolina	42.4
9	Kentucky	41.7
10	Georgia	41.4
11	Alaska	40.7
11	Indiana	40.7
11	West Virginia	40.7
14	Missouri	40.6
15	Texas	40.2
16	Ohio	39.9
17	Virginia	38.6
18	Utah	38.2
19	Kansas	38.1
20	South Dakota	38.0
21	Montana	37.6
22	Oregon	37.3
23	Pennsylvania	37.2
24	Delaware	37.0
25	Illinois	36.7
26	Nebraska	36.4
27	Michigan	36.3
28	Maryland	36.1
29	Wisconsin	36.0
30	Washington	35.5
31	Idaho	35.4
32	Wyoming	35.1
33	California	34.9
34	Hawaii	34.8
35	Iowa	33.9
36	Maine	33.4
37	Nevada	33.3
38	New Jersey	32.4
38	North Dakota	32.4
40	Colorado	32.0
40	Minnesota	32.0
42	Vermont	31.7
43	Florida	30.6
44	New Mexico	30.0
45	Arizona	28.6
46	Connecticut	28.3
47	Massachusetts	27.7
47	Rhode Island	27.7
49	New Hampshire	27.6
50	New York	26.3
	District of Columbia	30.1

Source: U.S. Department of Health and Human Services, National Center for Health Statistics
"National Vital Statistics Reports" (Vol. 64, No. 2, 2015, http://www.cdc.gov/nchs/deaths.htm)
*Final data by state of residence. Cerebrovascular diseases include stroke and other disorders of the blood vessels of the brain. Age-adjusted rates based on the year 2000 standard population.

Deaths by Diseases of the Heart in 2013

National Total = 611,105 Deaths*

ALPHA ORDER

RANK	STATE	DEATHS	% of USA
16	Alabama	12,472	2.0%
50	Alaska	706	0.1%
20	Arizona	10,755	1.8%
28	Arkansas	7,377	1.2%
1	California	60,299	9.9%
32	Colorado	6,456	1.1%
29	Connecticut	7,090	1.2%
45	Delaware	1,861	0.3%
3	Florida	42,656	7.0%
11	Georgia	16,550	2.7%
40	Hawaii	2,521	0.4%
41	Idaho	2,495	0.4%
7	Illinois	24,839	4.1%
14	Indiana	13,773	2.3%
30	Iowa	6,995	1.1%
34	Kansas	5,364	0.9%
23	Kentucky	9,971	1.6%
22	Louisiana	10,346	1.7%
39	Maine	2,807	0.5%
19	Maryland	11,244	1.8%
17	Massachusetts	12,023	2.0%
8	Michigan	24,156	4.0%
27	Minnesota	7,714	1.3%
26	Mississippi	7,715	1.3%
13	Missouri	14,095	2.3%
44	Montana	2,004	0.3%
37	Nebraska	3,381	0.6%
33	Nevada	5,434	0.9%
42	New Hampshire	2,434	0.4%
9	New Jersey	18,460	3.0%
36	New Mexico	3,425	0.6%
2	New York	44,039	7.2%
10	North Carolina	17,830	2.9%
47	North Dakota	1,382	0.2%
6	Ohio	26,878	4.4%
24	Oklahoma	9,721	1.6%
31	Oregon	6,523	1.1%
5	Pennsylvania	31,629	5.2%
43	Rhode Island	2,364	0.4%
25	South Carolina	9,648	1.6%
46	South Dakota	1,630	0.3%
12	Tennessee	14,803	2.4%
4	Texas	40,203	6.6%
38	Utah	3,323	0.5%
48	Vermont	1,220	0.2%
15	Virginia	13,663	2.2%
21	Washington	10,524	1.7%
35	West Virginia	4,666	0.8%
18	Wisconsin	11,362	1.9%
49	Wyoming	939	0.2%

RANK ORDER

RANK	STATE	DEATHS	% of USA
1	California	60,299	9.9%
2	New York	44,039	7.2%
3	Florida	42,656	7.0%
4	Texas	40,203	6.6%
5	Pennsylvania	31,629	5.2%
6	Ohio	26,878	4.4%
7	Illinois	24,839	4.1%
8	Michigan	24,156	4.0%
9	New Jersey	18,460	3.0%
10	North Carolina	17,830	2.9%
11	Georgia	16,550	2.7%
12	Tennessee	14,803	2.4%
13	Missouri	14,095	2.3%
14	Indiana	13,773	2.3%
15	Virginia	13,663	2.2%
16	Alabama	12,472	2.0%
17	Massachusetts	12,023	2.0%
18	Wisconsin	11,362	1.9%
19	Maryland	11,244	1.8%
20	Arizona	10,755	1.8%
21	Washington	10,524	1.7%
22	Louisiana	10,346	1.7%
23	Kentucky	9,971	1.6%
24	Oklahoma	9,721	1.6%
25	South Carolina	9,648	1.6%
26	Mississippi	7,715	1.3%
27	Minnesota	7,714	1.3%
28	Arkansas	7,377	1.2%
29	Connecticut	7,090	1.2%
30	Iowa	6,995	1.1%
31	Oregon	6,523	1.1%
32	Colorado	6,456	1.1%
33	Nevada	5,434	0.9%
34	Kansas	5,364	0.9%
35	West Virginia	4,666	0.8%
36	New Mexico	3,425	0.6%
37	Nebraska	3,381	0.6%
38	Utah	3,323	0.5%
39	Maine	2,807	0.5%
40	Hawaii	2,521	0.4%
41	Idaho	2,495	0.4%
42	New Hampshire	2,434	0.4%
43	Rhode Island	2,364	0.4%
44	Montana	2,004	0.3%
45	Delaware	1,861	0.3%
46	South Dakota	1,630	0.3%
47	North Dakota	1,382	0.2%
48	Vermont	1,220	0.2%
49	Wyoming	939	0.2%
50	Alaska	706	0.1%
	District of Columbia	1,340	0.2%

Source: U.S. Department of Health and Human Services, National Center for Health Statistics
"National Vital Statistics Reports" (Vol. 64, No. 2, 2015, http://www.cdc.gov/nchs/deaths.htm)
*Final data by state of residence.

Age-Adjusted Death Rate by Diseases of the Heart in 2013

National Rate = 169.8 Deaths per 100,000 Population*

ALPHA ORDER

RANK	STATE	RATE
3	Alabama	228.4
48	Alaska	135.0
44	Arizona	141.1
4	Arkansas	214.1
32	California	151.8
49	Colorado	125.7
38	Connecticut	148.9
23	Delaware	168.0
35	Florida	149.8
17	Georgia	178.7
45	Hawaii	139.0
42	Idaho	145.4
19	Illinois	170.9
13	Indiana	186.2
22	Iowa	168.8
28	Kansas	156.1
7	Kentucky	203.4
4	Louisiana	214.1
31	Maine	152.3
18	Maryland	172.7
43	Massachusetts	141.5
8	Michigan	199.8
50	Minnesota	119.6
1	Mississippi	240.0
10	Missouri	194.7
29	Montana	154.3
40	Nebraska	147.9
9	Nevada	195.1
38	New Hampshire	148.9
21	New Jersey	170.1
41	New Mexico	147.1
14	New York	184.8
24	North Carolina	165.3
33	North Dakota	150.7
12	Ohio	187.9
2	Oklahoma	228.5
47	Oregon	135.1
16	Pennsylvania	179.0
25	Rhode Island	163.4
15	South Carolina	180.0
34	South Dakota	150.1
6	Tennessee	204.1
20	Texas	170.7
37	Utah	149.0
36	Vermont	149.6
27	Virginia	157.2
46	Washington	138.2
11	West Virginia	193.7
26	Wisconsin	159.3
30	Wyoming	152.4

RANK ORDER

RANK	STATE	RATE
1	Mississippi	240.0
2	Oklahoma	228.5
3	Alabama	228.4
4	Arkansas	214.1
4	Louisiana	214.1
6	Tennessee	204.1
7	Kentucky	203.4
8	Michigan	199.8
9	Nevada	195.1
10	Missouri	194.7
11	West Virginia	193.7
12	Ohio	187.9
13	Indiana	186.2
14	New York	184.8
15	South Carolina	180.0
16	Pennsylvania	179.0
17	Georgia	178.7
18	Maryland	172.7
19	Illinois	170.9
20	Texas	170.7
21	New Jersey	170.1
22	Iowa	168.8
23	Delaware	168.0
24	North Carolina	165.3
25	Rhode Island	163.4
26	Wisconsin	159.3
27	Virginia	157.2
28	Kansas	156.1
29	Montana	154.3
30	Wyoming	152.4
31	Maine	152.3
32	California	151.8
33	North Dakota	150.7
34	South Dakota	150.1
35	Florida	149.8
36	Vermont	149.6
37	Utah	149.0
38	Connecticut	148.9
38	New Hampshire	148.9
40	Nebraska	147.9
41	New Mexico	147.1
42	Idaho	145.4
43	Massachusetts	141.5
44	Arizona	141.1
45	Hawaii	139.0
46	Washington	138.2
47	Oregon	135.1
48	Alaska	135.0
49	Colorado	125.7
50	Minnesota	119.6
	District of Columbia	213.5

Source: U.S. Department of Health and Human Services, National Center for Health Statistics
"National Vital Statistics Reports" (Vol. 64, No. 2, 2015, http://www.cdc.gov/nchs/deaths.htm)
*Final data by state of residence. Age-adjusted rates based on the year 2000 standard population.

Deaths by Suicide in 2013

National Total = 41,149 Suicides*

ALPHA ORDER

RANK	STATE	DEATHS	% of USA
20	Alabama	721	1.8%
43	Alaska	171	0.4%
11	Arizona	1,163	2.8%
31	Arkansas	516	1.3%
1	California	4,025	9.8%
15	Colorado	1,007	2.4%
36	Connecticut	330	0.8%
49	Delaware	122	0.3%
3	Florida	2,928	7.1%
10	Georgia	1,212	2.9%
43	Hawaii	171	0.4%
38	Idaho	308	0.7%
7	Illinois	1,321	3.2%
17	Indiana	944	2.3%
32	Iowa	447	1.1%
34	Kansas	425	1.0%
21	Kentucky	701	1.7%
26	Louisiana	583	1.4%
39	Maine	245	0.6%
29	Maryland	569	1.4%
28	Massachusetts	572	1.4%
8	Michigan	1,295	3.1%
24	Minnesota	678	1.6%
35	Mississippi	388	0.9%
16	Missouri	960	2.3%
40	Montana	243	0.6%
41	Nebraska	220	0.5%
30	Nevada	541	1.3%
42	New Hampshire	185	0.4%
19	New Jersey	757	1.8%
33	New Mexico	431	1.0%
5	New York	1,687	4.1%
9	North Carolina	1,284	3.1%
48	North Dakota	128	0.3%
6	Ohio	1,526	3.7%
25	Oklahoma	665	1.6%
22	Oregon	698	1.7%
4	Pennsylvania	1,788	4.3%
46	Rhode Island	132	0.3%
23	South Carolina	696	1.7%
45	South Dakota	147	0.4%
13	Tennessee	1,030	2.5%
2	Texas	3,059	7.4%
27	Utah	579	1.4%
50	Vermont	112	0.3%
12	Virginia	1,072	2.6%
14	Washington	1,027	2.5%
37	West Virginia	323	0.8%
18	Wisconsin	850	2.1%
47	Wyoming	129	0.3%

RANK ORDER

RANK	STATE	DEATHS	% of USA
1	California	4,025	9.8%
2	Texas	3,059	7.4%
3	Florida	2,928	7.1%
4	Pennsylvania	1,788	4.3%
5	New York	1,687	4.1%
6	Ohio	1,526	3.7%
7	Illinois	1,321	3.2%
8	Michigan	1,295	3.1%
9	North Carolina	1,284	3.1%
10	Georgia	1,212	2.9%
11	Arizona	1,163	2.8%
12	Virginia	1,072	2.6%
13	Tennessee	1,030	2.5%
14	Washington	1,027	2.5%
15	Colorado	1,007	2.4%
16	Missouri	960	2.3%
17	Indiana	944	2.3%
18	Wisconsin	850	2.1%
19	New Jersey	757	1.8%
20	Alabama	721	1.8%
21	Kentucky	701	1.7%
22	Oregon	698	1.7%
23	South Carolina	696	1.7%
24	Minnesota	678	1.6%
25	Oklahoma	665	1.6%
26	Louisiana	583	1.4%
27	Utah	579	1.4%
28	Massachusetts	572	1.4%
29	Maryland	569	1.4%
30	Nevada	541	1.3%
31	Arkansas	516	1.3%
32	Iowa	447	1.1%
33	New Mexico	431	1.0%
34	Kansas	425	1.0%
35	Mississippi	388	0.9%
36	Connecticut	330	0.8%
37	West Virginia	323	0.8%
38	Idaho	308	0.7%
39	Maine	245	0.6%
40	Montana	243	0.6%
41	Nebraska	220	0.5%
42	New Hampshire	185	0.4%
43	Alaska	171	0.4%
43	Hawaii	171	0.4%
45	South Dakota	147	0.4%
46	Rhode Island	132	0.3%
47	Wyoming	129	0.3%
48	North Dakota	128	0.3%
49	Delaware	122	0.3%
50	Vermont	112	0.3%
	District of Columbia	38	0.1%

Source: U.S. Department of Health and Human Services, National Center for Health Statistics
"National Vital Statistics Reports" (Vol. 64, No. 2, 2015, http://www.cdc.gov/nchs/deaths.htm)
*Final data by state of residence. Also referred to as "Intentional self-harm."

Age-Adjusted Death Rate by Suicide in 2013

National Rate = 12.6 Deaths per 100,000 Population*

ALPHA ORDER				RANK ORDER		
RANK	STATE	RATE		RANK	STATE	RATE
22	Alabama	14.4		1	Montana	23.7
2	Alaska	23.2		2	Alaska	23.2
10	Arizona	17.5		3	Wyoming	21.5
12	Arkansas	17.3		4	Utah	21.4
44	California	10.2		5	New Mexico	20.3
7	Colorado	18.6		6	Idaho	19.2
47	Connecticut	8.7		7	Colorado	18.6
35	Delaware	12.5		7	Nevada	18.6
28	Florida	13.8		9	South Dakota	18.0
40	Georgia	12.0		10	Arizona	17.5
41	Hawaii	11.8		11	Maine	17.4
6	Idaho	19.2		12	Arkansas	17.3
45	Illinois	9.9		12	North Dakota	17.3
25	Indiana	14.2		14	Oklahoma	17.2
22	Iowa	14.4		15	Oregon	16.8
21	Kansas	14.7		15	Vermont	16.8
19	Kentucky	15.5		17	West Virginia	16.4
37	Louisiana	12.4		18	Missouri	15.6
11	Maine	17.4		19	Kentucky	15.5
46	Maryland	9.2		20	Tennessee	15.4
48	Massachusetts	8.2		21	Kansas	14.7
31	Michigan	12.9		22	Alabama	14.4
39	Minnesota	12.1		22	Iowa	14.4
30	Mississippi	13.0		22	Wisconsin	14.4
18	Missouri	15.6		25	Indiana	14.2
1	Montana	23.7		26	South Carolina	14.0
43	Nebraska	11.6		26	Washington	14.0
7	Nevada	18.6		28	Florida	13.8
33	New Hampshire	12.8		29	Pennsylvania	13.4
50	New Jersey	8.0		30	Mississippi	13.0
5	New Mexico	20.3		31	Michigan	12.9
49	New York	8.1		31	Ohio	12.9
34	North Carolina	12.6		33	New Hampshire	12.8
12	North Dakota	17.3		34	North Carolina	12.6
31	Ohio	12.9		35	Delaware	12.5
14	Oklahoma	17.2		35	Virginia	12.5
15	Oregon	16.8		37	Louisiana	12.4
29	Pennsylvania	13.4		38	Rhode Island	12.2
38	Rhode Island	12.2		39	Minnesota	12.1
26	South Carolina	14.0		40	Georgia	12.0
9	South Dakota	18.0		41	Hawaii	11.8
20	Tennessee	15.4		42	Texas	11.7
42	Texas	11.7		43	Nebraska	11.6
4	Utah	21.4		44	California	10.2
15	Vermont	16.8		45	Illinois	9.9
35	Virginia	12.5		46	Maryland	9.2
26	Washington	14.0		47	Connecticut	8.7
17	West Virginia	16.4		48	Massachusetts	8.2
22	Wisconsin	14.4		49	New York	8.1
3	Wyoming	21.5		50	New Jersey	8.0
					District of Columbia	5.7

Source: U.S. Department of Health and Human Services, National Center for Health Statistics
"National Vital Statistics Reports" (Vol. 64, No. 2, 2015, http://www.cdc.gov/nchs/deaths.htm)
*Final data by state of residence. Also referred to as "Intentional self-harm." Age-adjusted rates based on the year 2000 standard population.

Deaths by AIDS in 2013

National Total = 6,955 Deaths*

ALPHA ORDER

RANK	STATE	DEATHS	% of USA
16	Alabama	122	1.8%
43	Alaska	7	0.1%
19	Arizona	97	1.4%
24	Arkansas	68	1.0%
3	California	696	10.0%
27	Colorado	58	0.8%
25	Connecticut	67	1.0%
32	Delaware	36	0.5%
1	Florida	940	13.5%
5	Georgia	385	5.5%
42	Hawaii	8	0.1%
43	Idaho	7	0.1%
11	Illinois	188	2.7%
22	Indiana	77	1.1%
38	Iowa	18	0.3%
34	Kansas	29	0.4%
29	Kentucky	51	0.7%
10	Louisiana	214	3.1%
39	Maine	17	0.2%
9	Maryland	229	3.3%
20	Massachusetts	86	1.2%
15	Michigan	125	1.8%
31	Minnesota	38	0.5%
18	Mississippi	119	1.7%
21	Missouri	80	1.2%
47	Montana	5	0.1%
39	Nebraska	17	0.2%
23	Nevada	71	1.0%
43	New Hampshire	7	0.1%
6	New Jersey	295	4.2%
36	New Mexico	23	0.3%
2	New York	719	10.3%
7	North Carolina	266	3.8%
49	North Dakota	2	0.0%
14	Ohio	139	2.0%
28	Oklahoma	57	0.8%
30	Oregon	50	0.7%
8	Pennsylvania	247	3.6%
39	Rhode Island	17	0.2%
13	South Carolina	146	2.1%
48	South Dakota	4	0.1%
12	Tennessee	153	2.2%
4	Texas	624	9.0%
35	Utah	24	0.3%
43	Vermont	7	0.1%
16	Virginia	122	1.8%
26	Washington	63	0.9%
37	West Virginia	19	0.3%
33	Wisconsin	35	0.5%
49	Wyoming	2	0.0%

RANK ORDER

RANK	STATE	DEATHS	% of USA
1	Florida	940	13.5%
2	New York	719	10.3%
3	California	696	10.0%
4	Texas	624	9.0%
5	Georgia	385	5.5%
6	New Jersey	295	4.2%
7	North Carolina	266	3.8%
8	Pennsylvania	247	3.6%
9	Maryland	229	3.3%
10	Louisiana	214	3.1%
11	Illinois	188	2.7%
12	Tennessee	153	2.2%
13	South Carolina	146	2.1%
14	Ohio	139	2.0%
15	Michigan	125	1.8%
16	Alabama	122	1.8%
16	Virginia	122	1.8%
18	Mississippi	119	1.7%
19	Arizona	97	1.4%
20	Massachusetts	86	1.2%
21	Missouri	80	1.2%
22	Indiana	77	1.1%
23	Nevada	71	1.0%
24	Arkansas	68	1.0%
25	Connecticut	67	1.0%
26	Washington	63	0.9%
27	Colorado	58	0.8%
28	Oklahoma	57	0.8%
29	Kentucky	51	0.7%
30	Oregon	50	0.7%
31	Minnesota	38	0.5%
32	Delaware	36	0.5%
33	Wisconsin	35	0.5%
34	Kansas	29	0.4%
35	Utah	24	0.3%
36	New Mexico	23	0.3%
37	West Virginia	19	0.3%
38	Iowa	18	0.3%
39	Maine	17	0.2%
39	Nebraska	17	0.2%
39	Rhode Island	17	0.2%
42	Hawaii	8	0.1%
43	Alaska	7	0.1%
43	Idaho	7	0.1%
43	New Hampshire	7	0.1%
43	Vermont	7	0.1%
47	Montana	5	0.1%
48	South Dakota	4	0.1%
49	North Dakota	2	0.0%
49	Wyoming	2	0.0%
	District of Columbia	79	1.1%

Source: U.S. Department of Health and Human Services, National Center for Health Statistics
"National Vital Statistics Reports" (Vol. 64, No. 2, 2015, http://www.cdc.gov/nchs/deaths.htm)
*Final data by state of residence. AIDS is Acquired Immunodeficiency Syndrome. It is a specific group of diseases or conditions which are indicative of severe immunosuppression related to infection with the Human Immunodeficiency Virus (HIV).

Age-Adjusted Death Rate by AIDS in 2013

National Rate = 2.1 Deaths per 100,000 Population*

ALPHA ORDER

RANK	STATE	RATE
11	Alabama	2.5
NA	Alaska**	NA
19	Arizona	1.5
10	Arkansas	2.6
16	California	1.8
30	Colorado	1.0
18	Connecticut	1.6
6	Delaware	3.4
2	Florida	4.5
4	Georgia	3.7
NA	Hawaii**	NA
NA	Idaho**	NA
21	Illinois	1.4
27	Indiana	1.1
NA	Iowa**	NA
30	Kansas	1.0
27	Kentucky	1.1
1	Louisiana	4.7
NA	Maine**	NA
5	Maryland	3.5
30	Massachusetts	1.0
24	Michigan	1.2
35	Minnesota	0.7
3	Mississippi	4.0
23	Missouri	1.3
NA	Montana**	NA
NA	Nebraska**	NA
13	Nevada	2.4
NA	New Hampshire**	NA
9	New Jersey	2.8
27	New Mexico	1.1
7	New York	3.3
11	North Carolina	2.5
NA	North Dakota**	NA
24	Ohio	1.2
19	Oklahoma	1.5
24	Oregon	1.2
16	Pennsylvania	1.8
NA	Rhode Island**	NA
8	South Carolina	3.0
NA	South Dakota**	NA
15	Tennessee	2.3
13	Texas	2.4
30	Utah	1.0
NA	Vermont**	NA
21	Virginia	1.4
34	Washington	0.8
NA	West Virginia**	NA
36	Wisconsin	0.6
NA	Wyoming**	NA

RANK ORDER

RANK	STATE	RATE
1	Louisiana	4.7
2	Florida	4.5
3	Mississippi	4.0
4	Georgia	3.7
5	Maryland	3.5
6	Delaware	3.4
7	New York	3.3
8	South Carolina	3.0
9	New Jersey	2.8
10	Arkansas	2.6
11	Alabama	2.5
11	North Carolina	2.5
13	Nevada	2.4
13	Texas	2.4
15	Tennessee	2.3
16	California	1.8
16	Pennsylvania	1.8
18	Connecticut	1.6
19	Arizona	1.5
19	Oklahoma	1.5
21	Illinois	1.4
21	Virginia	1.4
23	Missouri	1.3
24	Michigan	1.2
24	Ohio	1.2
24	Oregon	1.2
27	Indiana	1.1
27	Kentucky	1.1
27	New Mexico	1.1
30	Colorado	1.0
30	Kansas	1.0
30	Massachusetts	1.0
30	Utah	1.0
34	Washington	0.8
35	Minnesota	0.7
36	Wisconsin	0.6
NA	Alaska**	NA
NA	Hawaii**	NA
NA	Idaho**	NA
NA	Iowa**	NA
NA	Maine**	NA
NA	Montana**	NA
NA	Nebraska**	NA
NA	New Hampshire**	NA
NA	North Dakota**	NA
NA	Rhode Island**	NA
NA	South Dakota**	NA
NA	Vermont**	NA
NA	West Virginia**	NA
NA	Wyoming**	NA

District of Columbia 12.0

Source: U.S. Department of Health and Human Services, National Center for Health Statistics
"National Vital Statistics Reports" (Vol. 64, No. 2, 2015, http://www.cdc.gov/nchs/deaths.htm)
*Final data by state of residence. AIDS is Acquired Immunodeficiency Syndrome. It is a specific group of diseases or conditions which are indicative of severe immunosuppression related to infection with the Human Immunodeficiency Virus (HIV). Age-adjusted rates based on the year 2000 standard population.
**Insufficient data to determine a reliable rate.

Adult Per Capita Alcohol Consumption in 2013

National Per Capita = 2.6 Gallons Consumed per Adult 21 Years and Older*

ALPHA ORDER

RANK	STATE	GALLONS
40	Alabama	2.3
11	Alaska	3.1
23	Arizona	2.7
48	Arkansas	2.0
23	California	2.7
8	Colorado	3.2
23	Connecticut	2.7
2	Delaware	4.0
13	Florida	3.0
40	Georgia	2.3
17	Hawaii	2.9
8	Idaho	3.2
28	Illinois	2.6
37	Indiana	2.4
23	Iowa	2.7
46	Kansas	2.1
46	Kentucky	2.1
17	Louisiana	2.9
13	Maine	3.0
37	Maryland	2.4
17	Massachusetts	2.9
34	Michigan	2.5
11	Minnesota	3.1
28	Mississippi	2.6
22	Missouri	2.8
5	Montana	3.5
28	Nebraska	2.6
4	Nevada	3.7
1	New Hampshire	5.3
17	New Jersey	2.9
23	New Mexico	2.7
34	New York	2.5
40	North Carolina	2.3
3	North Dakota	3.8
40	Ohio	2.3
44	Oklahoma	2.2
13	Oregon	3.0
28	Pennsylvania	2.6
17	Rhode Island	2.9
28	South Carolina	2.6
8	South Dakota	3.2
44	Tennessee	2.2
28	Texas	2.6
50	Utah	1.6
6	Vermont	3.4
37	Virginia	2.4
34	Washington	2.5
48	West Virginia	2.0
6	Wisconsin	3.4
13	Wyoming	3.0

RANK ORDER

RANK	STATE	GALLONS
1	New Hampshire	5.3
2	Delaware	4.0
3	North Dakota	3.8
4	Nevada	3.7
5	Montana	3.5
6	Vermont	3.4
6	Wisconsin	3.4
8	Colorado	3.2
8	Idaho	3.2
8	South Dakota	3.2
11	Alaska	3.1
11	Minnesota	3.1
13	Florida	3.0
13	Maine	3.0
13	Oregon	3.0
13	Wyoming	3.0
17	Hawaii	2.9
17	Louisiana	2.9
17	Massachusetts	2.9
17	New Jersey	2.9
17	Rhode Island	2.9
22	Missouri	2.8
23	Arizona	2.7
23	California	2.7
23	Connecticut	2.7
23	Iowa	2.7
23	New Mexico	2.7
28	Illinois	2.6
28	Mississippi	2.6
28	Nebraska	2.6
28	Pennsylvania	2.6
28	South Carolina	2.6
28	Texas	2.6
34	Michigan	2.5
34	New York	2.5
34	Washington	2.5
37	Indiana	2.4
37	Maryland	2.4
37	Virginia	2.4
40	Alabama	2.3
40	Georgia	2.3
40	North Carolina	2.3
40	Ohio	2.3
44	Oklahoma	2.2
44	Tennessee	2.2
46	Kansas	2.1
46	Kentucky	2.1
48	Arkansas	2.0
48	West Virginia	2.0
50	Utah	1.6
	District of Columbia	4.3

Source: CQ Press using data from U.S. Dept of Health and Human Services, National Institute on Alcohol Abuse and Alcoholism "Apparent Per Capita Alcohol Consumption, 1977-2013" (http://pubs.niaaa.nih.gov/publications/surveillance102/CONS13.htm)

*This is apparent consumption of actual alcohol, not entire volume of an alcoholic beverage (for example, wine is roughly 11% absolute alcohol content). Apparent consumption is based on several sources which together approximate sales but do not actually measure consumption. Accordingly, figures for some states may be skewed by purchases by nonresidents.

Percent of Adults Who Smoke: 2013

National Median = 19.0% of Adults*

ALPHA ORDER

RANK	STATE	PERCENT
13	Alabama	21.5
9	Alaska	22.6
42	Arizona	16.3
3	Arkansas	25.9
49	California	12.5
33	Colorado	17.7
47	Connecticut	15.5
21	Delaware	19.6
37	Florida	16.8
28	Georgia	18.8
48	Hawaii	13.3
36	Idaho	17.2
31	Illinois	18.0
12	Indiana	21.9
23	Iowa	19.5
20	Kansas	20.0
2	Kentucky	26.5
7	Louisiana	23.5
19	Maine	20.2
41	Maryland	16.4
38	Massachusetts	16.6
14	Michigan	21.4
31	Minnesota	18.0
4	Mississippi	24.8
10	Missouri	22.1
26	Montana	19.0
30	Nebraska	18.5
24	Nevada	19.4
43	New Hampshire	16.2
46	New Jersey	15.7
25	New Mexico	19.1
38	New York	16.6
18	North Carolina	20.3
15	North Dakota	21.2
8	Ohio	23.4
6	Oklahoma	23.7
35	Oregon	17.3
16	Pennsylvania	21.0
34	Rhode Island	17.4
11	South Carolina	22.0
21	South Dakota	19.6
5	Tennessee	24.3
45	Texas	15.9
50	Utah	10.3
38	Vermont	16.6
26	Virginia	19.0
44	Washington	16.1
1	West Virginia	27.3
29	Wisconsin	18.7
17	Wyoming	20.6

RANK ORDER

RANK	STATE	PERCENT
1	West Virginia	27.3
2	Kentucky	26.5
3	Arkansas	25.9
4	Mississippi	24.8
5	Tennessee	24.3
6	Oklahoma	23.7
7	Louisiana	23.5
8	Ohio	23.4
9	Alaska	22.6
10	Missouri	22.1
11	South Carolina	22.0
12	Indiana	21.9
13	Alabama	21.5
14	Michigan	21.4
15	North Dakota	21.2
16	Pennsylvania	21.0
17	Wyoming	20.6
18	North Carolina	20.3
19	Maine	20.2
20	Kansas	20.0
21	Delaware	19.6
21	South Dakota	19.6
23	Iowa	19.5
24	Nevada	19.4
25	New Mexico	19.1
26	Montana	19.0
26	Virginia	19.0
28	Georgia	18.8
29	Wisconsin	18.7
30	Nebraska	18.5
31	Illinois	18.0
31	Minnesota	18.0
33	Colorado	17.7
34	Rhode Island	17.4
35	Oregon	17.3
36	Idaho	17.2
37	Florida	16.8
38	Massachusetts	16.6
38	New York	16.6
38	Vermont	16.6
41	Maryland	16.4
42	Arizona	16.3
43	New Hampshire	16.2
44	Washington	16.1
45	Texas	15.9
46	New Jersey	15.7
47	Connecticut	15.5
48	Hawaii	13.3
49	California	12.5
50	Utah	10.3
	District of Columbia	18.8

Source: U.S. Department of Health and Human Services, Centers for Disease Control and Prevention "2013 Behavioral Risk Factor Surveillance Summary Prevalence Data" (http://apps.nccd.cdc.gov/brfss/)

*Persons 18 and older who have smoked more than 100 cigarettes during their lifetime and who currently smoke every day or some days.

Percent of Adults Overweight or Obese: 2013

National Median = 64.8% of Adults*

ALPHA ORDER

RANK	STATE	PERCENT
5	Alabama	68.1
17	Alaska	66.1
38	Arizona	61.9
1	Arkansas	69.9
45	California	60.1
49	Colorado	56.4
37	Connecticut	62.6
28	Delaware	64.6
34	Florida	62.8
19	Georgia	65.7
50	Hawaii	55.4
24	Idaho	65.0
27	Illinois	64.7
10	Indiana	67.2
11	Iowa	67.0
22	Kansas	65.3
9	Kentucky	67.3
8	Louisiana	67.4
25	Maine	64.9
32	Maryland	64.2
48	Massachusetts	58.0
15	Michigan	66.2
44	Minnesota	61.1
2	Mississippi	69.3
20	Missouri	65.5
42	Montana	61.4
20	Nebraska	65.5
26	Nevada	64.8
40	New Hampshire	61.7
34	New Jersey	62.8
36	New Mexico	62.7
43	New York	61.3
17	North Carolina	66.1
7	North Dakota	67.6
23	Ohio	65.1
6	Oklahoma	67.9
46	Oregon	59.9
30	Pennsylvania	64.5
28	Rhode Island	64.6
14	South Carolina	66.4
11	South Dakota	67.0
4	Tennessee	68.4
15	Texas	66.2
47	Utah	59.1
38	Vermont	61.9
33	Virginia	64.0
41	Washington	61.5
3	West Virginia	68.8
13	Wisconsin	66.5
31	Wyoming	64.4

RANK ORDER

RANK	STATE	PERCENT
1	Arkansas	69.9
2	Mississippi	69.3
3	West Virginia	68.8
4	Tennessee	68.4
5	Alabama	68.1
6	Oklahoma	67.9
7	North Dakota	67.6
8	Louisiana	67.4
9	Kentucky	67.3
10	Indiana	67.2
11	Iowa	67.0
11	South Dakota	67.0
13	Wisconsin	66.5
14	South Carolina	66.4
15	Michigan	66.2
15	Texas	66.2
17	Alaska	66.1
17	North Carolina	66.1
19	Georgia	65.7
20	Missouri	65.5
20	Nebraska	65.5
22	Kansas	65.3
23	Ohio	65.1
24	Idaho	65.0
25	Maine	64.9
26	Nevada	64.8
27	Illinois	64.7
28	Delaware	64.6
28	Rhode Island	64.6
30	Pennsylvania	64.5
31	Wyoming	64.4
32	Maryland	64.2
33	Virginia	64.0
34	Florida	62.8
34	New Jersey	62.8
36	New Mexico	62.7
37	Connecticut	62.6
38	Arizona	61.9
38	Vermont	61.9
40	New Hampshire	61.7
41	Washington	61.5
42	Montana	61.4
43	New York	61.3
44	Minnesota	61.1
45	California	60.1
46	Oregon	59.9
47	Utah	59.1
48	Massachusetts	58.0
49	Colorado	56.4
50	Hawaii	55.4
	District of Columbia	53.8

Source: CQ Press using data from U.S. Department of Health and Human Services, Centers for Disease Control and Prevention "2013 Behavioral Risk Factor Surveillance Summary Prevalence Data" (http://apps.nccd.cdc.gov/brfss/)

*Persons 18 and older. Overweight is defined as a Body Mass Index (BMI) of 25.0 to 29.9 regardless of sex. Obese is a BMI of 30.0 or greater. BMI is a ratio of height to weight. As an example, a person 5' 8" and weighing 165 pounds has a BMI of 25. The same height at 197 pounds has a BMI of 30. See http://www.cdc.gov/healthyweight/assessing/bmi/index.html.

Percent of Children Aged 19 to 35 Months Fully Immunized in 2014

National Percent = 71.6%*

ALPHA ORDER

RANK	STATE	PERCENT
7	Alabama	76.9
39	Alaska	67.3
43	Arizona	66.1
44	Arkansas	66.0
6	California	77.9
21	Colorado	72.8
20	Connecticut	73.0
13	Delaware	74.5
22	Florida	72.7
15	Georgia	74.0
16	Hawaii	73.7
45	Idaho	65.9
35	Illinois	68.3
42	Indiana	66.3
27	Iowa	71.3
8	Kansas	76.5
24	Kentucky	72.3
19	Louisiana	73.2
1	Maine	84.7
14	Maryland	74.4
12	Massachusetts	75.4
47	Michigan	65.0
33	Minnesota	70.5
31	Mississippi	70.7
34	Missouri	70.0
41	Montana	67.1
4	Nebraska	80.2
37	Nevada	67.7
3	New Hampshire	80.4
40	New Jersey	67.2
10	New Mexico	75.9
31	New York	70.7
2	North Carolina	80.8
27	North Dakota	71.3
36	Ohio	68.1
18	Oklahoma	73.3
46	Oregon	65.3
5	Pennsylvania	78.6
11	Rhode Island	75.6
23	South Carolina	72.6
9	South Dakota	76.3
25	Tennessee	71.9
48	Texas	64.0
30	Utah	70.8
26	Vermont	71.8
16	Virginia	73.7
38	Washington	67.4
50	West Virginia	63.4
29	Wisconsin	70.9
48	Wyoming	64.0

RANK ORDER

RANK	STATE	PERCENT
1	Maine	84.7
2	North Carolina	80.8
3	New Hampshire	80.4
4	Nebraska	80.2
5	Pennsylvania	78.6
6	California	77.9
7	Alabama	76.9
8	Kansas	76.5
9	South Dakota	76.3
10	New Mexico	75.9
11	Rhode Island	75.6
12	Massachusetts	75.4
13	Delaware	74.5
14	Maryland	74.4
15	Georgia	74.0
16	Hawaii	73.7
16	Virginia	73.7
18	Oklahoma	73.3
19	Louisiana	73.2
20	Connecticut	73.0
21	Colorado	72.8
22	Florida	72.7
23	South Carolina	72.6
24	Kentucky	72.3
25	Tennessee	71.9
26	Vermont	71.8
27	Iowa	71.3
27	North Dakota	71.3
29	Wisconsin	70.9
30	Utah	70.8
31	Mississippi	70.7
31	New York	70.7
33	Minnesota	70.5
34	Missouri	70.0
35	Illinois	68.3
36	Ohio	68.1
37	Nevada	67.7
38	Washington	67.4
39	Alaska	67.3
40	New Jersey	67.2
41	Montana	67.1
42	Indiana	66.3
43	Arizona	66.1
44	Arkansas	66.0
45	Idaho	65.9
46	Oregon	65.3
47	Michigan	65.0
48	Texas	64.0
48	Wyoming	64.0
50	West Virginia	63.4
	District of Columbia	71.1

Source: U.S. Department of Health and Human Services, Centers for Disease Control and Prevention "State Vaccination Coverage Levels" (MMWR, Vol. 64, No. 33, August 28, 2015, http://www.cdc.gov/mmwr/)

*Fully immunized (4:3:1:3:3:1:4 series) children received four doses of DTaP (Diphtheria, Tetanus Toxoids, Pertussis [Whooping Cough]), three doses of Poliovirus Vaccine, one dose of MCV (Measles-Containing Vaccine), full series (3 or 4 doses depending on product type) of Hib (Haemophilus influenzae type b), three doses of Hepatitis B vaccine, one dose of Varicella (chickenpox) vaccine, and four doses of PCV (pneumococcal conjugate vaccine). This differs from previous "fully" immunized tables.

XII. Households and Housing

Households in 2014. 421
Persons per Household in 2014. 422
Percent of Households with One Person in 2014 423
Percent of Households Headed by Married Couples
    in 2014 424
Percent of Households Headed by Single Mothers
    in 2014 425
Percent of Households Headed by Single Fathers
    in 2014 426
Same-Sex Couple Households in 2014. 427
Percent of Same-Sex Household Couples Who Are
    Married: 2014. 428
Housing Units in 2014 429
Housing Units per Square Mile in 2014 430
Percent of Housing Units That Are Owner-Occupied
    in 2014 431
New Housing Units Authorized in 2015. 432
Value of New Housing Units Authorized in 2015 433
Average Value of New Housing Units in 2015. 434
Median Value of Owner-Occupied Housing in 2014 435
Percent Change in House Prices: 2014 to 2015 436
Percent Change in House Prices: 2011 to 2015 437
Percent of Owner-Occupied Housing Units with a
    Mortgage in 2014. 438
Median Monthly Mortgage Payment in 2014. 439
Percent of Home Owners Spending 30% or More of
    Household Income on Housing Costs in 2014. 440
Median Annual Real Estate Taxes in 2014 441
Homeownership Rate in 2014. 442
Percent of Housing Units That Are Renter-Occupied
    in 2014 443
Median Monthly Rental Payment in 2014 444
Percent of Renters Spending 30% or More of Household
    Income on Rent and Utilities in 2014 445
State and Local Government Expenditures for Housing
    and Community Development in 2013 446
Per Capita State and Local Government Expenditures for
    Housing and Community Development in 2013 447
State & Local Government Spending for Housing and
    Community Development as a Percent of All State and
    Local Government Expenditures in 2013 448

Households in 2014

National Total = 117,259,427 Households*

ALPHA ORDER

RANK	STATE	HOUSEHOLDS	% of USA
23	Alabama	1,841,217	1.6%
49	Alaska	249,659	0.2%
17	Arizona	2,428,743	2.1%
31	Arkansas	1,131,288	1.0%
1	California	12,758,648	10.9%
22	Colorado	2,039,592	1.7%
29	Connecticut	1,355,817	1.2%
45	Delaware	349,743	0.3%
3	Florida	7,328,046	6.2%
10	Georgia	3,587,521	3.1%
42	Hawaii	450,769	0.4%
39	Idaho	591,587	0.5%
6	Illinois	4,772,421	4.1%
16	Indiana	2,502,739	2.1%
30	Iowa	1,241,471	1.1%
32	Kansas	1,109,280	0.9%
26	Kentucky	1,712,094	1.5%
25	Louisiana	1,718,194	1.5%
40	Maine	549,841	0.5%
20	Maryland	2,165,438	1.8%
14	Massachusetts	2,549,336	2.2%
8	Michigan	3,834,574	3.3%
21	Minnesota	2,129,195	1.8%
33	Mississippi	1,095,823	0.9%
18	Missouri	2,354,809	2.0%
43	Montana	410,962	0.4%
37	Nebraska	740,765	0.6%
34	Nevada	1,021,519	0.9%
41	New Hampshire	519,756	0.4%
11	New Jersey	3,194,844	2.7%
36	New Mexico	760,916	0.6%
4	New York	7,282,398	6.2%
9	North Carolina	3,790,620	3.2%
47	North Dakota	305,431	0.3%
7	Ohio	4,593,172	3.9%
28	Oklahoma	1,459,759	1.2%
27	Oregon	1,535,511	1.3%
5	Pennsylvania	4,945,972	4.2%
44	Rhode Island	409,654	0.3%
24	South Carolina	1,826,914	1.6%
46	South Dakota	334,475	0.3%
15	Tennessee	2,509,665	2.1%
2	Texas	9,277,197	7.9%
35	Utah	918,370	0.8%
48	Vermont	257,229	0.2%
12	Virginia	3,083,820	2.6%
13	Washington	2,679,601	2.3%
38	West Virginia	735,375	0.6%
19	Wisconsin	2,307,685	2.0%
50	Wyoming	232,594	0.2%

RANK ORDER

RANK	STATE	HOUSEHOLDS	% of USA
1	California	12,758,648	10.9%
2	Texas	9,277,197	7.9%
3	Florida	7,328,046	6.2%
4	New York	7,282,398	6.2%
5	Pennsylvania	4,945,972	4.2%
6	Illinois	4,772,421	4.1%
7	Ohio	4,593,172	3.9%
8	Michigan	3,834,574	3.3%
9	North Carolina	3,790,620	3.2%
10	Georgia	3,587,521	3.1%
11	New Jersey	3,194,844	2.7%
12	Virginia	3,083,820	2.6%
13	Washington	2,679,601	2.3%
14	Massachusetts	2,549,336	2.2%
15	Tennessee	2,509,665	2.1%
16	Indiana	2,502,739	2.1%
17	Arizona	2,428,743	2.1%
18	Missouri	2,354,809	2.0%
19	Wisconsin	2,307,685	2.0%
20	Maryland	2,165,438	1.8%
21	Minnesota	2,129,195	1.8%
22	Colorado	2,039,592	1.7%
23	Alabama	1,841,217	1.6%
24	South Carolina	1,826,914	1.6%
25	Louisiana	1,718,194	1.5%
26	Kentucky	1,712,094	1.5%
27	Oregon	1,535,511	1.3%
28	Oklahoma	1,459,759	1.2%
29	Connecticut	1,355,817	1.2%
30	Iowa	1,241,471	1.1%
31	Arkansas	1,131,288	1.0%
32	Kansas	1,109,280	0.9%
33	Mississippi	1,095,823	0.9%
34	Nevada	1,021,519	0.9%
35	Utah	918,370	0.8%
36	New Mexico	760,916	0.6%
37	Nebraska	740,765	0.6%
38	West Virginia	735,375	0.6%
39	Idaho	591,587	0.5%
40	Maine	549,841	0.5%
41	New Hampshire	519,756	0.4%
42	Hawaii	450,769	0.4%
43	Montana	410,962	0.4%
44	Rhode Island	409,654	0.3%
45	Delaware	349,743	0.3%
46	South Dakota	334,475	0.3%
47	North Dakota	305,431	0.3%
48	Vermont	257,229	0.2%
49	Alaska	249,659	0.2%
50	Wyoming	232,594	0.2%
	District of Columbia	277,378	0.2%

Source: U.S. Bureau of the Census
"2014 American Community Survey-Table S2501" (http://www.census.gov/programs-surveys/acs/)
*A household includes all persons who occupy a housing unit. A household consists of a single family, one person living alone, two or more families living together, or any other group of related or unrelated persons who share living arrangements.

Persons per Household in 2014

National Rate = 2.65 Persons per Household*

ALPHA ORDER

RANK	STATE	PERSONS
22	Alabama	2.57
4	Alaska	2.84
9	Arizona	2.71
28	Arkansas	2.55
3	California	2.98
22	Colorado	2.57
22	Connecticut	2.57
19	Delaware	2.60
13	Florida	2.66
6	Georgia	2.74
2	Hawaii	3.05
9	Idaho	2.71
14	Illinois	2.64
26	Indiana	2.56
46	Iowa	2.42
28	Kansas	2.55
34	Kentucky	2.50
16	Louisiana	2.63
48	Maine	2.35
11	Maryland	2.70
28	Massachusetts	2.55
32	Michigan	2.53
34	Minnesota	2.50
14	Mississippi	2.64
34	Missouri	2.50
46	Montana	2.42
38	Nebraska	2.47
6	Nevada	2.74
38	New Hampshire	2.47
6	New Jersey	2.74
12	New Mexico	2.68
16	New York	2.63
26	North Carolina	2.56
50	North Dakota	2.33
41	Ohio	2.46
20	Oklahoma	2.58
32	Oregon	2.53
34	Pennsylvania	2.50
38	Rhode Island	2.47
22	South Carolina	2.57
42	South Dakota	2.45
28	Tennessee	2.55
4	Texas	2.84
1	Utah	3.16
49	Vermont	2.34
18	Virginia	2.62
20	Washington	2.58
42	West Virginia	2.45
45	Wisconsin	2.43
42	Wyoming	2.45

RANK ORDER

RANK	STATE	PERSONS
1	Utah	3.16
2	Hawaii	3.05
3	California	2.98
4	Alaska	2.84
4	Texas	2.84
6	Georgia	2.74
6	Nevada	2.74
6	New Jersey	2.74
9	Arizona	2.71
9	Idaho	2.71
11	Maryland	2.70
12	New Mexico	2.68
13	Florida	2.66
14	Illinois	2.64
14	Mississippi	2.64
16	Louisiana	2.63
16	New York	2.63
18	Virginia	2.62
19	Delaware	2.60
20	Oklahoma	2.58
20	Washington	2.58
22	Alabama	2.57
22	Colorado	2.57
22	Connecticut	2.57
22	South Carolina	2.57
26	Indiana	2.56
26	North Carolina	2.56
28	Arkansas	2.55
28	Kansas	2.55
28	Massachusetts	2.55
28	Tennessee	2.55
32	Michigan	2.53
32	Oregon	2.53
34	Kentucky	2.50
34	Minnesota	2.50
34	Missouri	2.50
34	Pennsylvania	2.50
38	Nebraska	2.47
38	New Hampshire	2.47
38	Rhode Island	2.47
41	Ohio	2.46
42	South Dakota	2.45
42	West Virginia	2.45
42	Wyoming	2.45
45	Wisconsin	2.43
46	Iowa	2.42
46	Montana	2.42
48	Maine	2.35
49	Vermont	2.34
50	North Dakota	2.33
	District of Columbia	2.23

Source: U.S. Bureau of the Census
"2014 American Community Survey-Table R1105" (http://www.census.gov/programs-surveys/acs/)
*A household includes all persons who occupy a housing unit. A household consists of a single family, one person living alone, two or more families living together, or any other group of related or unrelated persons who share living arrangements.

Percent of Households with One Person in 2014

National Percent = 27.8% of Households*

ALPHA ORDER

RANK	STATE	PERCENT
20	Alabama	28.8
44	Alaska	25.6
37	Arizona	27.6
25	Arkansas	28.6
48	California	24.0
38	Colorado	27.5
17	Connecticut	28.9
38	Delaware	27.5
14	Florida	29.1
41	Georgia	26.9
49	Hawaii	23.6
44	Idaho	25.6
17	Illinois	28.9
35	Indiana	27.7
23	Iowa	28.7
17	Kansas	28.9
29	Kentucky	28.5
7	Louisiana	29.7
12	Maine	29.4
41	Maryland	26.9
16	Massachusetts	29.0
14	Michigan	29.1
23	Minnesota	28.7
25	Mississippi	28.6
6	Missouri	29.8
1	Montana	31.2
25	Nebraska	28.6
13	Nevada	29.2
46	New Hampshire	25.4
43	New Jersey	25.9
5	New Mexico	29.9
7	New York	29.7
31	North Carolina	28.4
2	North Dakota	30.8
4	Ohio	30.4
33	Oklahoma	28.2
34	Oregon	28.1
10	Pennsylvania	29.6
7	Rhode Island	29.7
20	South Carolina	28.8
3	South Dakota	30.7
32	Tennessee	28.3
47	Texas	25.3
50	Utah	19.3
25	Vermont	28.6
40	Virginia	27.0
35	Washington	27.7
10	West Virginia	29.6
29	Wisconsin	28.5
20	Wyoming	28.8

RANK ORDER

RANK	STATE	PERCENT
1	Montana	31.2
2	North Dakota	30.8
3	South Dakota	30.7
4	Ohio	30.4
5	New Mexico	29.9
6	Missouri	29.8
7	Louisiana	29.7
7	New York	29.7
7	Rhode Island	29.7
10	Pennsylvania	29.6
10	West Virginia	29.6
12	Maine	29.4
13	Nevada	29.2
14	Florida	29.1
14	Michigan	29.1
16	Massachusetts	29.0
17	Connecticut	28.9
17	Illinois	28.9
17	Kansas	28.9
20	Alabama	28.8
20	South Carolina	28.8
20	Wyoming	28.8
23	Iowa	28.7
23	Minnesota	28.7
25	Arkansas	28.6
25	Mississippi	28.6
25	Nebraska	28.6
25	Vermont	28.6
29	Kentucky	28.5
29	Wisconsin	28.5
31	North Carolina	28.4
32	Tennessee	28.3
33	Oklahoma	28.2
34	Oregon	28.1
35	Indiana	27.7
35	Washington	27.7
37	Arizona	27.6
38	Colorado	27.5
38	Delaware	27.5
40	Virginia	27.0
41	Georgia	26.9
41	Maryland	26.9
43	New Jersey	25.9
44	Alaska	25.6
44	Idaho	25.6
46	New Hampshire	25.4
47	Texas	25.3
48	California	24.0
49	Hawaii	23.6
50	Utah	19.3
	District of Columbia	44.6

Source: U.S. Bureau of the Census
"2014 American Community Survey-Table S2501" (http://www.census.gov/programs-surveys/acs/)
*A household includes all persons who occupy a housing unit. A household consists of a single family, one person living alone, two or more families living together, or any other group of related or unrelated persons who share living arrangements.

Percent of Households Headed by Married Couples in 2014

National Percent = 47.9% of Households*

ALPHA ORDER

RANK	STATE	PERCENT
35	Alabama	47.3
12	Alaska	49.7
40	Arizona	47.0
26	Arkansas	48.3
18	California	48.9
16	Colorado	49.3
27	Connecticut	48.0
35	Delaware	47.3
43	Florida	46.1
38	Georgia	47.2
4	Hawaii	51.5
2	Idaho	54.9
32	Illinois	47.6
21	Indiana	48.7
5	Iowa	51.3
6	Kansas	50.9
24	Kentucky	48.4
50	Louisiana	43.2
27	Maine	48.0
38	Maryland	47.2
41	Massachusetts	46.4
35	Michigan	47.3
7	Minnesota	50.5
46	Mississippi	44.0
30	Missouri	47.8
23	Montana	48.5
10	Nebraska	50.2
47	Nevada	43.8
3	New Hampshire	52.1
8	New Jersey	50.3
45	New Mexico	44.8
49	New York	43.6
32	North Carolina	47.6
20	North Dakota	48.8
44	Ohio	45.8
21	Oklahoma	48.7
32	Oregon	47.6
30	Pennsylvania	47.8
48	Rhode Island	43.7
41	South Carolina	46.4
15	South Dakota	49.5
29	Tennessee	47.9
13	Texas	49.6
1	Utah	61.7
18	Vermont	48.9
11	Virginia	50.1
13	Washington	49.6
24	West Virginia	48.4
17	Wisconsin	49.1
8	Wyoming	50.3

RANK ORDER

RANK	STATE	PERCENT
1	Utah	61.7
2	Idaho	54.9
3	New Hampshire	52.1
4	Hawaii	51.5
5	Iowa	51.3
6	Kansas	50.9
7	Minnesota	50.5
8	New Jersey	50.3
8	Wyoming	50.3
10	Nebraska	50.2
11	Virginia	50.1
12	Alaska	49.7
13	Texas	49.6
13	Washington	49.6
15	South Dakota	49.5
16	Colorado	49.3
17	Wisconsin	49.1
18	California	48.9
18	Vermont	48.9
20	North Dakota	48.8
21	Indiana	48.7
21	Oklahoma	48.7
23	Montana	48.5
24	Kentucky	48.4
24	West Virginia	48.4
26	Arkansas	48.3
27	Connecticut	48.0
27	Maine	48.0
29	Tennessee	47.9
30	Missouri	47.8
30	Pennsylvania	47.8
32	Illinois	47.6
32	North Carolina	47.6
32	Oregon	47.6
35	Alabama	47.3
35	Delaware	47.3
35	Michigan	47.3
38	Georgia	47.2
38	Maryland	47.2
40	Arizona	47.0
41	Massachusetts	46.4
41	South Carolina	46.4
43	Florida	46.1
44	Ohio	45.8
45	New Mexico	44.8
46	Mississippi	44.0
47	Nevada	43.8
48	Rhode Island	43.7
49	New York	43.6
50	Louisiana	43.2
	District of Columbia	23.9

Source: U.S. Bureau of the Census
"2014 American Community Survey-Table R1101" (http://www.census.gov/programs-surveys/acs/)
*A household includes all persons who occupy a housing unit. A household consists of a single family, one person living alone, two or more families living together, or any other group of related or unrelated persons who share living arrangements. Includes married same-sex couple households.

Percent of Households Headed by Single Mothers in 2014

National Percent = 7.0% of Households*

ALPHA ORDER

RANK	STATE	PERCENT
5	Alabama	8.1
29	Alaska	6.6
24	Arizona	6.8
9	Arkansas	7.5
18	California	6.9
38	Colorado	6.0
18	Connecticut	6.9
12	Delaware	7.4
27	Florida	6.7
3	Georgia	8.8
48	Hawaii	5.2
44	Idaho	5.6
24	Illinois	6.8
12	Indiana	7.4
44	Iowa	5.6
36	Kansas	6.2
18	Kentucky	6.9
2	Louisiana	9.1
39	Maine	5.9
12	Maryland	7.4
18	Massachusetts	6.9
18	Michigan	6.9
39	Minnesota	5.9
1	Mississippi	9.5
29	Missouri	6.6
50	Montana	4.6
27	Nebraska	6.7
24	Nevada	6.8
41	New Hampshire	5.8
18	New Jersey	6.9
7	New Mexico	7.8
17	New York	7.2
9	North Carolina	7.5
41	North Dakota	5.8
9	Ohio	7.5
16	Oklahoma	7.3
37	Oregon	6.1
33	Pennsylvania	6.3
6	Rhode Island	8.0
7	South Carolina	7.8
33	South Dakota	6.3
12	Tennessee	7.4
4	Texas	8.2
44	Utah	5.6
33	Vermont	6.3
29	Virginia	6.6
43	Washington	5.7
44	West Virginia	5.6
32	Wisconsin	6.5
49	Wyoming	4.9

RANK ORDER

RANK	STATE	PERCENT
1	Mississippi	9.5
2	Louisiana	9.1
3	Georgia	8.8
4	Texas	8.2
5	Alabama	8.1
6	Rhode Island	8.0
7	New Mexico	7.8
7	South Carolina	7.8
9	Arkansas	7.5
9	North Carolina	7.5
9	Ohio	7.5
12	Delaware	7.4
12	Indiana	7.4
12	Maryland	7.4
12	Tennessee	7.4
16	Oklahoma	7.3
17	New York	7.2
18	California	6.9
18	Connecticut	6.9
18	Kentucky	6.9
18	Massachusetts	6.9
18	Michigan	6.9
18	New Jersey	6.9
24	Arizona	6.8
24	Illinois	6.8
24	Nevada	6.8
27	Florida	6.7
27	Nebraska	6.7
29	Alaska	6.6
29	Missouri	6.6
29	Virginia	6.6
32	Wisconsin	6.5
33	Pennsylvania	6.3
33	South Dakota	6.3
33	Vermont	6.3
36	Kansas	6.2
37	Oregon	6.1
38	Colorado	6.0
39	Maine	5.9
39	Minnesota	5.9
41	New Hampshire	5.8
41	North Dakota	5.8
43	Washington	5.7
44	Idaho	5.6
44	Iowa	5.6
44	Utah	5.6
44	West Virginia	5.6
48	Hawaii	5.2
49	Wyoming	4.9
50	Montana	4.6
	District of Columbia	7.5

Source: U.S. Bureau of the Census
 "2014 American Community Survey-Table CP02" (http://www.census.gov/programs-surveys/acs/)
*No spouse present in household with children under 18 years old. A household includes all persons who occupy a housing unit. A household consists of a single family, one person living alone, two or more families living together, or any other group of related or unrelated persons who share living arrangements.

Percent of Households Headed by Single Fathers in 2014

National Percent = 2.3% of Households*

ALPHA ORDER

RANK	STATE	PERCENT
49	Alabama	1.7
1	Alaska	3.5
6	Arizona	2.7
20	Arkansas	2.4
6	California	2.7
6	Colorado	2.7
37	Connecticut	2.1
37	Delaware	2.1
37	Florida	2.1
20	Georgia	2.4
37	Hawaii	2.1
14	Idaho	2.6
37	Illinois	2.1
18	Indiana	2.5
6	Iowa	2.7
6	Kansas	2.7
29	Kentucky	2.3
20	Louisiana	2.4
6	Maine	2.7
29	Maryland	2.3
49	Massachusetts	1.7
20	Michigan	2.4
29	Minnesota	2.3
18	Mississippi	2.5
20	Missouri	2.4
6	Montana	2.7
29	Nebraska	2.3
2	Nevada	3.2
14	New Hampshire	2.6
45	New Jersey	2.0
3	New Mexico	2.9
45	New York	2.0
29	North Carolina	2.3
6	North Dakota	2.7
29	Ohio	2.3
14	Oklahoma	2.6
20	Oregon	2.4
37	Pennsylvania	2.1
29	Rhode Island	2.3
45	South Carolina	2.0
29	South Dakota	2.3
37	Tennessee	2.1
20	Texas	2.4
37	Utah	2.1
14	Vermont	2.6
45	Virginia	2.0
20	Washington	2.4
20	West Virginia	2.4
3	Wisconsin	2.9
5	Wyoming	2.8

RANK ORDER

RANK	STATE	PERCENT
1	Alaska	3.5
2	Nevada	3.2
3	New Mexico	2.9
3	Wisconsin	2.9
5	Wyoming	2.8
6	Arizona	2.7
6	California	2.7
6	Colorado	2.7
6	Iowa	2.7
6	Kansas	2.7
6	Maine	2.7
6	Montana	2.7
6	North Dakota	2.7
14	Idaho	2.6
14	New Hampshire	2.6
14	Oklahoma	2.6
14	Vermont	2.6
18	Indiana	2.5
18	Mississippi	2.5
20	Arkansas	2.4
20	Georgia	2.4
20	Louisiana	2.4
20	Michigan	2.4
20	Missouri	2.4
20	Oregon	2.4
20	Texas	2.4
20	Washington	2.4
20	West Virginia	2.4
29	Kentucky	2.3
29	Maryland	2.3
29	Minnesota	2.3
29	Nebraska	2.3
29	North Carolina	2.3
29	Ohio	2.3
29	Rhode Island	2.3
29	South Dakota	2.3
37	Connecticut	2.1
37	Delaware	2.1
37	Florida	2.1
37	Hawaii	2.1
37	Illinois	2.1
37	Pennsylvania	2.1
37	Tennessee	2.1
37	Utah	2.1
45	New Jersey	2.0
45	New York	2.0
45	South Carolina	2.0
45	Virginia	2.0
49	Alabama	1.7
49	Massachusetts	1.7
	District of Columbia	1.3

Source: U.S. Bureau of the Census
   "2014 American Community Survey-Table CP02" (http://www.census.gov/programs-surveys/acs/)
*No spouse present in household with children under 18 years old. A household includes all persons who occupy a housing unit. A household consists of a single family, one person living alone, two or more families living together, or any other group of related or unrelated persons who share living arrangements.

Same-Sex Couple Households in 2014

National Total = 783,100 Households*

ALPHA ORDER

RANK	STATE	HOUSEHOLDS	% of USA
32	Alabama	6,797	0.9%
46	Alaska	1,816	0.2%
15	Arizona	17,515	2.2%
35	Arkansas	5,399	0.7%
1	California	109,296	14.0%
17	Colorado	15,402	2.0%
25	Connecticut	9,701	1.2%
38	Delaware	3,850	0.5%
4	Florida	55,372	7.1%
8	Georgia	24,707	3.2%
39	Hawaii	3,831	0.5%
43	Idaho	2,599	0.3%
5	Illinois	29,115	3.7%
16	Indiana	15,431	2.0%
30	Iowa	7,080	0.9%
33	Kansas	5,674	0.7%
27	Kentucky	8,310	1.1%
26	Louisiana	8,906	1.1%
34	Maine	5,442	0.7%
18	Maryland	14,977	1.9%
9	Massachusetts	24,461	3.1%
14	Michigan	18,742	2.4%
19	Minnesota	14,539	1.9%
40	Mississippi	3,628	0.5%
23	Missouri	12,371	1.6%
47	Montana	1,235	0.2%
41	Nebraska	3,349	0.4%
28	Nevada	7,365	0.9%
37	New Hampshire	4,166	0.5%
12	New Jersey	20,061	2.6%
31	New Mexico	6,838	0.9%
2	New York	59,405	7.6%
10	North Carolina	23,127	3.0%
50	North Dakota	774	0.1%
7	Ohio	26,021	3.3%
29	Oklahoma	7,283	0.9%
20	Oregon	13,380	1.7%
6	Pennsylvania	28,654	3.7%
42	Rhode Island	2,917	0.4%
24	South Carolina	9,908	1.3%
48	South Dakota	1,094	0.1%
21	Tennessee	13,140	1.7%
3	Texas	58,654	7.5%
36	Utah	5,099	0.7%
44	Vermont	2,433	0.3%
13	Virginia	19,027	2.4%
11	Washington	22,981	2.9%
45	West Virginia	2,353	0.3%
22	Wisconsin	12,706	1.6%
49	Wyoming	945	0.1%

RANK ORDER

RANK	STATE	HOUSEHOLDS	% of USA
1	California	109,296	14.0%
2	New York	59,405	7.6%
3	Texas	58,654	7.5%
4	Florida	55,372	7.1%
5	Illinois	29,115	3.7%
6	Pennsylvania	28,654	3.7%
7	Ohio	26,021	3.3%
8	Georgia	24,707	3.2%
9	Massachusetts	24,461	3.1%
10	North Carolina	23,127	3.0%
11	Washington	22,981	2.9%
12	New Jersey	20,061	2.6%
13	Virginia	19,027	2.4%
14	Michigan	18,742	2.4%
15	Arizona	17,515	2.2%
16	Indiana	15,431	2.0%
17	Colorado	15,402	2.0%
18	Maryland	14,977	1.9%
19	Minnesota	14,539	1.9%
20	Oregon	13,380	1.7%
21	Tennessee	13,140	1.7%
22	Wisconsin	12,706	1.6%
23	Missouri	12,371	1.6%
24	South Carolina	9,908	1.3%
25	Connecticut	9,701	1.2%
26	Louisiana	8,906	1.1%
27	Kentucky	8,310	1.1%
28	Nevada	7,365	0.9%
29	Oklahoma	7,283	0.9%
30	Iowa	7,080	0.9%
31	New Mexico	6,838	0.9%
32	Alabama	6,797	0.9%
33	Kansas	5,674	0.7%
34	Maine	5,442	0.7%
35	Arkansas	5,399	0.7%
36	Utah	5,099	0.7%
37	New Hampshire	4,166	0.5%
38	Delaware	3,850	0.5%
39	Hawaii	3,831	0.5%
40	Mississippi	3,628	0.5%
41	Nebraska	3,349	0.4%
42	Rhode Island	2,917	0.4%
43	Idaho	2,599	0.3%
44	Vermont	2,433	0.3%
45	West Virginia	2,353	0.3%
46	Alaska	1,816	0.2%
47	Montana	1,235	0.2%
48	South Dakota	1,094	0.1%
49	Wyoming	945	0.1%
50	North Dakota	774	0.1%
	District of Columbia	5,224	0.7%

Source: U.S. Bureau of the Census
"Same Sex Couples Main" (http://www.census.gov/hhes/samesex/)
*The total is comprised of 334,829 married couples and 448,271 unmarried couples. Male couples are 377,903 of the households. Female couples are 405,197 of the households.

Percent of Same-Sex Household Couples Who Are Married: 2014

National Percent = 42.8% of Same-Sex Households*

ALPHA ORDER

RANK	STATE	PERCENT
24	Alabama	43.2
50	Alaska	27.4
43	Arizona	33.9
17	Arkansas	45.6
12	California	48.8
35	Colorado	36.2
4	Connecticut	60.9
9	Delaware	52.3
44	Florida	33.2
47	Georgia	29.2
15	Hawaii	46.2
49	Idaho	28.2
21	Illinois	44.1
33	Indiana	36.9
3	Iowa	65.7
20	Kansas	44.8
42	Kentucky	34.2
37	Louisiana	35.8
18	Maine	45.5
6	Maryland	56.9
7	Massachusetts	56.5
39	Michigan	34.8
10	Minnesota	52.0
21	Mississippi	44.1
29	Missouri	39.9
23	Montana	43.7
48	Nebraska	28.7
45	Nevada	30.8
4	New Hampshire	60.9
14	New Jersey	47.9
38	New Mexico	35.3
11	New York	49.2
36	North Carolina	36.0
19	North Dakota	45.1
41	Ohio	34.5
13	Oklahoma	48.2
16	Oregon	46.0
28	Pennsylvania	40.7
31	Rhode Island	37.3
26	South Carolina	42.0
46	South Dakota	30.3
32	Tennessee	37.0
40	Texas	34.6
2	Utah	65.8
1	Vermont	66.8
27	Virginia	40.9
8	Washington	54.5
25	West Virginia	42.7
34	Wisconsin	36.5
30	Wyoming	39.4

RANK ORDER

RANK	STATE	PERCENT
1	Vermont	66.8
2	Utah	65.8
3	Iowa	65.7
4	Connecticut	60.9
4	New Hampshire	60.9
6	Maryland	56.9
7	Massachusetts	56.5
8	Washington	54.5
9	Delaware	52.3
10	Minnesota	52.0
11	New York	49.2
12	California	48.8
13	Oklahoma	48.2
14	New Jersey	47.9
15	Hawaii	46.2
16	Oregon	46.0
17	Arkansas	45.6
18	Maine	45.5
19	North Dakota	45.1
20	Kansas	44.8
21	Illinois	44.1
21	Mississippi	44.1
23	Montana	43.7
24	Alabama	43.2
25	West Virginia	42.7
26	South Carolina	42.0
27	Virginia	40.9
28	Pennsylvania	40.7
29	Missouri	39.9
30	Wyoming	39.4
31	Rhode Island	37.3
32	Tennessee	37.0
33	Indiana	36.9
34	Wisconsin	36.5
35	Colorado	36.2
36	North Carolina	36.0
37	Louisiana	35.8
38	New Mexico	35.3
39	Michigan	34.8
40	Texas	34.6
41	Ohio	34.5
42	Kentucky	34.2
43	Arizona	33.9
44	Florida	33.2
45	Nevada	30.8
46	South Dakota	30.3
47	Georgia	29.2
48	Nebraska	28.7
49	Idaho	28.2
50	Alaska	27.4
	District of Columbia	45.7

Source: U.S. Bureau of the Census
 "Same Sex Couples Main" (http://www.census.gov/hhes/samesex/)
*Male-couple households are 43.2 percent married. Female couple households are 42.3 percent married.

Housing Units in 2014

National Total = 133,962,970 Housing Units*

ALPHA ORDER

RANK	STATE	HOUSING UNITS	% of USA
23	Alabama	2,208,030	1.6%
49	Alaska	308,571	0.2%
14	Arizona	2,909,336	2.2%
31	Arkansas	1,341,081	1.0%
1	California	13,901,594	10.4%
22	Colorado	2,276,280	1.7%
29	Connecticut	1,493,632	1.1%
45	Delaware	417,413	0.3%
3	Florida	9,144,650	6.8%
10	Georgia	4,151,387	3.1%
42	Hawaii	530,118	0.4%
40	Idaho	685,098	0.5%
6	Illinois	5,307,508	4.0%
16	Indiana	2,829,630	2.1%
30	Iowa	1,362,034	1.0%
33	Kansas	1,248,861	0.9%
26	Kentucky	1,950,504	1.5%
25	Louisiana	2,011,037	1.5%
39	Maine	727,693	0.5%
20	Maryland	2,422,317	1.8%
17	Massachusetts	2,828,592	2.1%
8	Michigan	4,540,088	3.4%
21	Minnesota	2,385,261	1.8%
32	Mississippi	1,294,738	1.0%
18	Missouri	2,735,803	2.0%
43	Montana	491,515	0.4%
38	Nebraska	814,957	0.6%
34	Nevada	1,198,969	0.9%
41	New Hampshire	619,865	0.5%
11	New Jersey	3,591,847	2.7%
36	New Mexico	912,910	0.7%
4	New York	8,191,528	6.1%
9	North Carolina	4,452,464	3.3%
47	North Dakota	350,534	0.3%
7	Ohio	5,147,282	3.8%
28	Oklahoma	1,699,556	1.3%
27	Oregon	1,700,611	1.3%
5	Pennsylvania	5,590,712	4.2%
44	Rhode Island	462,630	0.3%
24	South Carolina	2,188,258	1.6%
46	South Dakota	376,347	0.3%
15	Tennessee	2,869,419	2.1%
2	Texas	10,426,760	7.8%
35	Utah	1,022,593	0.8%
48	Vermont	325,774	0.2%
12	Virginia	3,446,585	2.6%
13	Washington	2,963,293	2.2%
37	West Virginia	884,574	0.7%
19	Wisconsin	2,648,342	2.0%
50	Wyoming	268,205	0.2%

RANK ORDER

RANK	STATE	HOUSING UNITS	% of USA
1	California	13,901,594	10.4%
2	Texas	10,426,760	7.8%
3	Florida	9,144,650	6.8%
4	New York	8,191,528	6.1%
5	Pennsylvania	5,590,712	4.2%
6	Illinois	5,307,508	4.0%
7	Ohio	5,147,282	3.8%
8	Michigan	4,540,088	3.4%
9	North Carolina	4,452,464	3.3%
10	Georgia	4,151,387	3.1%
11	New Jersey	3,591,847	2.7%
12	Virginia	3,446,585	2.6%
13	Washington	2,963,293	2.2%
14	Arizona	2,909,336	2.2%
15	Tennessee	2,869,419	2.1%
16	Indiana	2,829,630	2.1%
17	Massachusetts	2,828,592	2.1%
18	Missouri	2,735,803	2.0%
19	Wisconsin	2,648,342	2.0%
20	Maryland	2,422,317	1.8%
21	Minnesota	2,385,261	1.8%
22	Colorado	2,276,280	1.7%
23	Alabama	2,208,030	1.6%
24	South Carolina	2,188,258	1.6%
25	Louisiana	2,011,037	1.5%
26	Kentucky	1,950,504	1.5%
27	Oregon	1,700,611	1.3%
28	Oklahoma	1,699,556	1.3%
29	Connecticut	1,493,632	1.1%
30	Iowa	1,362,034	1.0%
31	Arkansas	1,341,081	1.0%
32	Mississippi	1,294,738	1.0%
33	Kansas	1,248,861	0.9%
34	Nevada	1,198,969	0.9%
35	Utah	1,022,593	0.8%
36	New Mexico	912,910	0.7%
37	West Virginia	884,574	0.7%
38	Nebraska	814,957	0.6%
39	Maine	727,693	0.5%
40	Idaho	685,098	0.5%
41	New Hampshire	619,865	0.5%
42	Hawaii	530,118	0.4%
43	Montana	491,515	0.4%
44	Rhode Island	462,630	0.3%
45	Delaware	417,413	0.3%
46	South Dakota	376,347	0.3%
47	North Dakota	350,534	0.3%
48	Vermont	325,774	0.2%
49	Alaska	308,571	0.2%
50	Wyoming	268,205	0.2%
	District of Columbia	306,184	0.2%

Source: U.S. Bureau of the Census
"2014 American Community Survey-Table B25001" (http://www.census.gov/programs-surveys/acs/)

*A housing unit is a house, an apartment, a mobile home, a group of rooms, or a single room that is occupied (or if vacant, is intended for occupancy) as separate living quarters. Separate living quarters are those in which the occupants live and eat separately from any other persons in the building and which have direct access from the outside of the building or through a common hall.

Housing Units per Square Mile in 2014

National Average = 37.9 Housing Units*

ALPHA ORDER

RANK	STATE	RATE
26	Alabama	43.5
50	Alaska	0.5
34	Arizona	25.6
33	Arkansas	25.8
13	California	89.1
38	Colorado	21.9
4	Connecticut	308.3
6	Delaware	213.6
8	Florida	169.6
19	Georgia	71.7
15	Hawaii	82.5
44	Idaho	8.3
11	Illinois	95.5
17	Indiana	78.9
36	Iowa	24.4
40	Kansas	15.3
22	Kentucky	49.1
24	Louisiana	46.2
37	Maine	23.6
5	Maryland	247.8
3	Massachusetts	360.8
16	Michigan	79.9
31	Minnesota	30.0
32	Mississippi	27.6
28	Missouri	39.7
48	Montana	3.4
43	Nebraska	10.6
42	Nevada	10.9
21	New Hampshire	69.1
1	New Jersey	484.3
45	New Mexico	7.5
7	New York	173.5
12	North Carolina	91.4
46	North Dakota	5.1
9	Ohio	125.7
35	Oklahoma	24.8
39	Oregon	17.7
10	Pennsylvania	124.7
2	Rhode Island	442.7
18	South Carolina	72.7
47	South Dakota	5.0
20	Tennessee	69.6
27	Texas	39.8
41	Utah	12.4
30	Vermont	35.2
14	Virginia	87.0
25	Washington	44.5
29	West Virginia	36.7
23	Wisconsin	48.8
49	Wyoming	2.8

RANK ORDER

RANK	STATE	RATE
1	New Jersey	484.3
2	Rhode Island	442.7
3	Massachusetts	360.8
4	Connecticut	308.3
5	Maryland	247.8
6	Delaware	213.6
7	New York	173.5
8	Florida	169.6
9	Ohio	125.7
10	Pennsylvania	124.7
11	Illinois	95.5
12	North Carolina	91.4
13	California	89.1
14	Virginia	87.0
15	Hawaii	82.5
16	Michigan	79.9
17	Indiana	78.9
18	South Carolina	72.7
19	Georgia	71.7
20	Tennessee	69.6
21	New Hampshire	69.1
22	Kentucky	49.1
23	Wisconsin	48.8
24	Louisiana	46.2
25	Washington	44.5
26	Alabama	43.5
27	Texas	39.8
28	Missouri	39.7
29	West Virginia	36.7
30	Vermont	35.2
31	Minnesota	30.0
32	Mississippi	27.6
33	Arkansas	25.8
34	Arizona	25.6
35	Oklahoma	24.8
36	Iowa	24.4
37	Maine	23.6
38	Colorado	21.9
39	Oregon	17.7
40	Kansas	15.3
41	Utah	12.4
42	Nevada	10.9
43	Nebraska	10.6
44	Idaho	8.3
45	New Mexico	7.5
46	North Dakota	5.1
47	South Dakota	5.0
48	Montana	3.4
49	Wyoming	2.8
50	Alaska	0.5

District of Columbia   5,019.4

Source: CQ Press using data from U.S. Bureau of the Census
"2014 American Community Survey-Table B25001" (http://www.census.gov/programs-surveys/acs/)
*Based on land area. A housing unit is a house, an apartment, a mobile home, a group of rooms, or a single room that is occupied (or if vacant, is intended for occupancy) as separate living quarters. Separate living quarters are those in which the occupants live and eat separately from any other persons in the building and which have direct access from the outside of the building or through a common hall.

Percent of Housing Units That Are Owner-Occupied in 2014

National Percent = 63.1% of Housing Units*

ALPHA ORDER

RANK	STATE	PERCENT
15	Alabama	67.7
39	Alaska	62.5
44	Arizona	61.1
28	Arkansas	65.8
48	California	53.7
36	Colorado	63.9
22	Connecticut	66.4
5	Delaware	70.3
35	Florida	64.1
40	Georgia	62.2
47	Hawaii	56.7
13	Idaho	68.0
29	Illinois	65.5
11	Indiana	68.6
4	Iowa	70.9
20	Kansas	66.6
24	Kentucky	66.1
33	Louisiana	64.4
3	Maine	71.3
26	Maryland	65.9
42	Massachusetts	61.6
6	Michigan	70.2
2	Minnesota	71.7
15	Mississippi	67.7
17	Missouri	66.9
22	Montana	66.4
26	Nebraska	65.9
49	Nevada	53.6
6	New Hampshire	70.2
38	New Jersey	63.3
17	New Mexico	66.9
50	New York	53.0
34	North Carolina	64.2
37	North Dakota	63.8
30	Ohio	65.3
32	Oklahoma	65.1
45	Oregon	60.7
10	Pennsylvania	68.8
46	Rhode Island	58.8
13	South Carolina	68.0
12	South Dakota	68.2
24	Tennessee	66.1
43	Texas	61.2
9	Utah	69.2
8	Vermont	70.0
30	Virginia	65.3
41	Washington	61.7
1	West Virginia	72.2
20	Wisconsin	66.6
17	Wyoming	66.9

RANK ORDER

RANK	STATE	PERCENT
1	West Virginia	72.2
2	Minnesota	71.7
3	Maine	71.3
4	Iowa	70.9
5	Delaware	70.3
6	Michigan	70.2
6	New Hampshire	70.2
8	Vermont	70.0
9	Utah	69.2
10	Pennsylvania	68.8
11	Indiana	68.6
12	South Dakota	68.2
13	Idaho	68.0
13	South Carolina	68.0
15	Alabama	67.7
15	Mississippi	67.7
17	Missouri	66.9
17	New Mexico	66.9
17	Wyoming	66.9
20	Kansas	66.6
20	Wisconsin	66.6
22	Connecticut	66.4
22	Montana	66.4
24	Kentucky	66.1
24	Tennessee	66.1
26	Maryland	65.9
26	Nebraska	65.9
28	Arkansas	65.8
29	Illinois	65.5
30	Ohio	65.3
30	Virginia	65.3
32	Oklahoma	65.1
33	Louisiana	64.4
34	North Carolina	64.2
35	Florida	64.1
36	Colorado	63.9
37	North Dakota	63.8
38	New Jersey	63.3
39	Alaska	62.5
40	Georgia	62.2
41	Washington	61.7
42	Massachusetts	61.6
43	Texas	61.2
44	Arizona	61.1
45	Oregon	60.7
46	Rhode Island	58.8
47	Hawaii	56.7
48	California	53.7
49	Nevada	53.6
50	New York	53.0
	District of Columbia	40.6

Source: U.S. Bureau of the Census
"2014 American Community Survey-Table R2512" (http://www.census.gov/programs-surveys/acs/)
*For occupied housing units.

New Housing Units Authorized in 2015

National Total = 1,178,138 Units*

ALPHA ORDER

RANK	STATE	UNITS	% of USA
28	Alabama	13,597	1.2%
49	Alaska	1,291	0.1%
11	Arizona	30,836	2.6%
33	Arkansas	8,534	0.7%
3	California	95,955	8.1%
9	Colorado	31,071	2.6%
37	Connecticut	5,883	0.5%
40	Delaware	5,299	0.4%
2	Florida	107,984	9.2%
6	Georgia	43,935	3.7%
39	Hawaii	5,422	0.5%
32	Idaho	9,370	0.8%
18	Illinois	19,472	1.7%
20	Indiana	17,891	1.5%
30	Iowa	11,252	1.0%
34	Kansas	7,936	0.7%
31	Kentucky	10,228	0.9%
26	Louisiana	14,548	1.2%
44	Maine	3,688	0.3%
25	Maryland	16,149	1.4%
22	Massachusetts	17,059	1.4%
15	Michigan	22,093	1.9%
16	Minnesota	21,873	1.9%
36	Mississippi	6,792	0.6%
21	Missouri	17,120	1.5%
43	Montana	3,853	0.3%
35	Nebraska	7,838	0.7%
27	Nevada	14,076	1.2%
45	New Hampshire	3,606	0.3%
10	New Jersey	31,050	2.6%
41	New Mexico	4,575	0.4%
4	New York	76,587	6.5%
5	North Carolina	53,512	4.5%
38	North Dakota	5,727	0.5%
17	Ohio	19,600	1.7%
29	Oklahoma	11,620	1.0%
23	Oregon	16,959	1.4%
14	Pennsylvania	22,497	1.9%
50	Rhode Island	990	0.1%
12	South Carolina	30,059	2.6%
42	South Dakota	4,314	0.4%
8	Tennessee	34,781	3.0%
1	Texas	173,990	14.8%
19	Utah	19,034	1.6%
47	Vermont	1,883	0.2%
13	Virginia	30,033	2.5%
7	Washington	39,963	3.4%
46	West Virginia	2,934	0.2%
24	Wisconsin	16,563	1.4%
48	Wyoming	1,860	0.2%

RANK ORDER

RANK	STATE	UNITS	% of USA
1	Texas	173,990	14.8%
2	Florida	107,984	9.2%
3	California	95,955	8.1%
4	New York	76,587	6.5%
5	North Carolina	53,512	4.5%
6	Georgia	43,935	3.7%
7	Washington	39,963	3.4%
8	Tennessee	34,781	3.0%
9	Colorado	31,071	2.6%
10	New Jersey	31,050	2.6%
11	Arizona	30,836	2.6%
12	South Carolina	30,059	2.6%
13	Virginia	30,033	2.5%
14	Pennsylvania	22,497	1.9%
15	Michigan	22,093	1.9%
16	Minnesota	21,873	1.9%
17	Ohio	19,600	1.7%
18	Illinois	19,472	1.7%
19	Utah	19,034	1.6%
20	Indiana	17,891	1.5%
21	Missouri	17,120	1.5%
22	Massachusetts	17,059	1.4%
23	Oregon	16,959	1.4%
24	Wisconsin	16,563	1.4%
25	Maryland	16,149	1.4%
26	Louisiana	14,548	1.2%
27	Nevada	14,076	1.2%
28	Alabama	13,597	1.2%
29	Oklahoma	11,620	1.0%
30	Iowa	11,252	1.0%
31	Kentucky	10,228	0.9%
32	Idaho	9,370	0.8%
33	Arkansas	8,534	0.7%
34	Kansas	7,936	0.7%
35	Nebraska	7,838	0.7%
36	Mississippi	6,792	0.6%
37	Connecticut	5,883	0.5%
38	North Dakota	5,727	0.5%
39	Hawaii	5,422	0.5%
40	Delaware	5,299	0.4%
41	New Mexico	4,575	0.4%
42	South Dakota	4,314	0.4%
43	Montana	3,853	0.3%
44	Maine	3,688	0.3%
45	New Hampshire	3,606	0.3%
46	West Virginia	2,934	0.2%
47	Vermont	1,883	0.2%
48	Wyoming	1,860	0.2%
49	Alaska	1,291	0.1%
50	Rhode Island	990	0.1%
	District of Columbia	4,956	0.4%

Source: U.S. Bureau of the Census
"Building Permits Survey" (https://www.census.gov/construction/bps/stateannual.html)
*Preliminary and unadjusted year-to-date monthly data as of December 2015. Includes single and multifamily privately owned units. All places issuing building permits for privately owned residential structures. More than 98 percent of all privately owned residential buildings constructed are in permit-issuing places.

Value of New Housing Units Authorized in 2015

National Total = $220,797,789,000*

ALPHA ORDER

RANK	STATE	VALUE	% of USA
27	Alabama	$2,391,505,000	1.1%
49	Alaska	322,779,000	0.1%
9	Arizona	7,065,048,000	3.2%
35	Arkansas	1,418,959,000	0.6%
3	California	21,977,064,000	10.0%
8	Colorado	7,230,770,000	3.3%
37	Connecticut	1,189,416,000	0.5%
45	Delaware	650,645,000	0.3%
2	Florida	23,128,992,000	10.5%
7	Georgia	7,760,704,000	3.5%
32	Hawaii	1,582,395,000	0.7%
31	Idaho	1,774,492,000	0.8%
15	Illinois	4,185,461,000	1.9%
21	Indiana	3,593,661,000	1.6%
30	Iowa	2,062,433,000	0.9%
33	Kansas	1,520,578,000	0.7%
34	Kentucky	1,487,944,000	0.7%
26	Louisiana	2,778,112,000	1.3%
44	Maine	656,531,000	0.3%
24	Maryland	2,946,334,000	1.3%
20	Massachusetts	3,777,376,000	1.7%
14	Michigan	4,252,759,000	1.9%
13	Minnesota	4,476,196,000	2.0%
38	Mississippi	1,105,235,000	0.5%
25	Missouri	2,929,938,000	1.3%
41	Montana	685,820,000	0.3%
36	Nebraska	1,285,071,000	0.6%
28	Nevada	2,335,865,000	1.1%
42	New Hampshire	684,086,000	0.3%
19	New Jersey	3,898,813,000	1.8%
40	New Mexico	881,103,000	0.4%
4	New York	11,207,582,000	5.1%
5	North Carolina	9,499,032,000	4.3%
39	North Dakota	927,659,000	0.4%
18	Ohio	3,939,423,000	1.8%
29	Oklahoma	2,212,689,000	1.0%
22	Oregon	3,460,811,000	1.6%
17	Pennsylvania	4,067,728,000	1.8%
50	Rhode Island	212,995,000	0.1%
10	South Carolina	5,933,255,000	2.7%
43	South Dakota	666,595,000	0.3%
11	Tennessee	5,664,195,000	2.6%
1	Texas	28,570,110,000	12.9%
16	Utah	4,127,273,000	1.9%
48	Vermont	397,673,000	0.2%
12	Virginia	4,839,801,000	2.2%
6	Washington	8,405,339,000	3.8%
47	West Virginia	422,597,000	0.2%
23	Wisconsin	3,106,257,000	1.4%
46	Wyoming	605,670,000	0.3%

RANK ORDER

RANK	STATE	VALUE	% of USA
1	Texas	$28,570,110,000	12.9%
2	Florida	23,128,992,000	10.5%
3	California	21,977,064,000	10.0%
4	New York	11,207,582,000	5.1%
5	North Carolina	9,499,032,000	4.3%
6	Washington	8,405,339,000	3.8%
7	Georgia	7,760,704,000	3.5%
8	Colorado	7,230,770,000	3.3%
9	Arizona	7,065,048,000	3.2%
10	South Carolina	5,933,255,000	2.7%
11	Tennessee	5,664,195,000	2.6%
12	Virginia	4,839,801,000	2.2%
13	Minnesota	4,476,196,000	2.0%
14	Michigan	4,252,759,000	1.9%
15	Illinois	4,185,461,000	1.9%
16	Utah	4,127,273,000	1.9%
17	Pennsylvania	4,067,728,000	1.8%
18	Ohio	3,939,423,000	1.8%
19	New Jersey	3,898,813,000	1.8%
20	Massachusetts	3,777,376,000	1.7%
21	Indiana	3,593,661,000	1.6%
22	Oregon	3,460,811,000	1.6%
23	Wisconsin	3,106,257,000	1.4%
24	Maryland	2,946,334,000	1.3%
25	Missouri	2,929,938,000	1.3%
26	Louisiana	2,778,112,000	1.3%
27	Alabama	2,391,505,000	1.1%
28	Nevada	2,335,865,000	1.1%
29	Oklahoma	2,212,689,000	1.0%
30	Iowa	2,062,433,000	0.9%
31	Idaho	1,774,492,000	0.8%
32	Hawaii	1,582,395,000	0.7%
33	Kansas	1,520,578,000	0.7%
34	Kentucky	1,487,944,000	0.7%
35	Arkansas	1,418,959,000	0.6%
36	Nebraska	1,285,071,000	0.6%
37	Connecticut	1,189,416,000	0.5%
38	Mississippi	1,105,235,000	0.5%
39	North Dakota	927,659,000	0.4%
40	New Mexico	881,103,000	0.4%
41	Montana	685,820,000	0.3%
42	New Hampshire	684,086,000	0.3%
43	South Dakota	666,595,000	0.3%
44	Maine	656,531,000	0.3%
45	Delaware	650,645,000	0.3%
46	Wyoming	605,670,000	0.3%
47	West Virginia	422,597,000	0.2%
48	Vermont	397,673,000	0.2%
49	Alaska	322,779,000	0.1%
50	Rhode Island	212,995,000	0.1%
	District of Columbia	495,021,000	0.2%

Source: U.S. Bureau of the Census
"Building Permits Survey" (https://www.census.gov/construction/bps/stateannual.html)
*Preliminary and unadjusted year-to-date monthly data as of December 2015. Includes single and multifamily privately owned units. All places issuing building permits for privately owned residential structures. More than 98 percent of all privately owned residential buildings constructed are in permit-issuing places.

Average Value of New Housing Units in 2015

National Average = $187,413 per Unit*

ALPHA ORDER

RANK	STATE	VALUE
35	Alabama	$175,885
3	Alaska	250,022
5	Arizona	229,117
37	Arkansas	166,271
6	California	229,035
4	Colorado	232,718
16	Connecticut	202,178
50	Delaware	122,786
11	Florida	214,189
34	Georgia	176,641
2	Hawaii	291,847
26	Idaho	189,380
10	Illinois	214,948
18	Indiana	200,864
28	Iowa	183,295
22	Kansas	191,605
47	Kentucky	145,478
23	Louisiana	190,962
31	Maine	178,018
29	Maryland	182,447
7	Massachusetts	221,430
21	Michigan	192,494
14	Minnesota	204,645
42	Mississippi	162,726
36	Missouri	171,141
32	Montana	177,996
40	Nebraska	163,954
38	Nevada	165,947
25	New Hampshire	189,708
49	New Jersey	125,566
20	New Mexico	192,591
46	New York	146,338
33	North Carolina	177,512
43	North Dakota	161,980
17	Ohio	200,991
24	Oklahoma	190,421
15	Oregon	204,069
30	Pennsylvania	180,812
9	Rhode Island	215,146
19	South Carolina	197,387
45	South Dakota	154,519
41	Tennessee	162,853
39	Texas	164,205
8	Utah	216,837
12	Vermont	211,191
44	Virginia	161,149
13	Washington	210,328
48	West Virginia	144,034
27	Wisconsin	187,542
1	Wyoming	325,629

RANK ORDER

RANK	STATE	VALUE
1	Wyoming	$325,629
2	Hawaii	291,847
3	Alaska	250,022
4	Colorado	232,718
5	Arizona	229,117
6	California	229,035
7	Massachusetts	221,430
8	Utah	216,837
9	Rhode Island	215,146
10	Illinois	214,948
11	Florida	214,189
12	Vermont	211,191
13	Washington	210,328
14	Minnesota	204,645
15	Oregon	204,069
16	Connecticut	202,178
17	Ohio	200,991
18	Indiana	200,864
19	South Carolina	197,387
20	New Mexico	192,591
21	Michigan	192,494
22	Kansas	191,605
23	Louisiana	190,962
24	Oklahoma	190,421
25	New Hampshire	189,708
26	Idaho	189,380
27	Wisconsin	187,542
28	Iowa	183,295
29	Maryland	182,447
30	Pennsylvania	180,812
31	Maine	178,018
32	Montana	177,996
33	North Carolina	177,512
34	Georgia	176,641
35	Alabama	175,885
36	Missouri	171,141
37	Arkansas	166,271
38	Nevada	165,947
39	Texas	164,205
40	Nebraska	163,954
41	Tennessee	162,853
42	Mississippi	162,726
43	North Dakota	161,980
44	Virginia	161,149
45	South Dakota	154,519
46	New York	146,338
47	Kentucky	145,478
48	West Virginia	144,034
49	New Jersey	125,566
50	Delaware	122,786
	District of Columbia	99,883

Source: CQ Press using data from U.S. Bureau of the Census
"Building Permits Survey" (https://www.census.gov/construction/bps/stateannual.html)
*Preliminary and unadjusted year-to-date monthly data as of December 2015. Includes single and multifamily privately owned units. All places issuing building permits for privately owned residential structures. More than 98 percent of all privately owned residential buildings constructed are in permit-issuing places.

Median Value of Owner-Occupied Housing in 2014

National Median = $181,200*

ALPHA ORDER

RANK	STATE	MEDIAN
44	Alabama	$125,600
10	Alaska	254,500
22	Arizona	176,700
48	Arkansas	112,500
2	California	412,700
9	Colorado	255,200
7	Connecticut	267,200
15	Delaware	230,500
28	Florida	162,700
32	Georgia	147,900
1	Hawaii	528,000
26	Idaho	165,300
24	Illinois	171,900
45	Indiana	124,300
40	Iowa	133,100
41	Kansas	132,100
46	Kentucky	123,800
33	Louisiana	143,600
23	Maine	174,800
5	Maryland	288,500
3	Massachusetts	338,900
43	Michigan	125,700
21	Minnesota	188,300
49	Mississippi	104,000
38	Missouri	138,500
19	Montana	196,800
39	Nebraska	133,800
20	Nevada	192,100
13	New Hampshire	236,400
4	New Jersey	313,200
30	New Mexico	158,400
6	New York	279,100
31	North Carolina	155,000
29	North Dakota	161,800
42	Ohio	129,100
47	Oklahoma	119,800
12	Oregon	239,800
25	Pennsylvania	165,400
14	Rhode Island	236,000
36	South Carolina	140,000
35	South Dakota	142,300
34	Tennessee	142,900
37	Texas	139,600
16	Utah	223,200
17	Vermont	214,600
11	Virginia	247,800
8	Washington	266,200
50	West Virginia	103,900
27	Wisconsin	164,700
18	Wyoming	201,000

RANK ORDER

RANK	STATE	MEDIAN
1	Hawaii	$528,000
2	California	412,700
3	Massachusetts	338,900
4	New Jersey	313,200
5	Maryland	288,500
6	New York	279,100
7	Connecticut	267,200
8	Washington	266,200
9	Colorado	255,200
10	Alaska	254,500
11	Virginia	247,800
12	Oregon	239,800
13	New Hampshire	236,400
14	Rhode Island	236,000
15	Delaware	230,500
16	Utah	223,200
17	Vermont	214,600
18	Wyoming	201,000
19	Montana	196,800
20	Nevada	192,100
21	Minnesota	188,300
22	Arizona	176,700
23	Maine	174,800
24	Illinois	171,900
25	Pennsylvania	165,400
26	Idaho	165,300
27	Wisconsin	164,700
28	Florida	162,700
29	North Dakota	161,800
30	New Mexico	158,400
31	North Carolina	155,000
32	Georgia	147,900
33	Louisiana	143,600
34	Tennessee	142,900
35	South Dakota	142,300
36	South Carolina	140,000
37	Texas	139,600
38	Missouri	138,500
39	Nebraska	133,800
40	Iowa	133,100
41	Kansas	132,100
42	Ohio	129,100
43	Michigan	125,700
44	Alabama	125,600
45	Indiana	124,300
46	Kentucky	123,800
47	Oklahoma	119,800
48	Arkansas	112,500
49	Mississippi	104,000
50	West Virginia	103,900
	District of Columbia	486,900

Source: U.S. Bureau of the Census
"2014 American Community Survey-Table R2510" (http://www.census.gov/programs-surveys/acs/)
*Housing units with a mortgage.

Percent Change in House Prices: 2014 to 2015

National Percent Change = 5.7% Increase*

ALPHA ORDER

RANK	STATE	PERCENT CHANGE
28	Alabama	4.1
45	Alaska	2.5
6	Arizona	8.3
35	Arkansas	3.6
10	California	7.4
1	Colorado	12.7
49	Connecticut	1.1
36	Delaware	3.5
4	Florida	10.0
8	Georgia	8.0
46	Hawaii	2.4
7	Idaho	8.2
36	Illinois	3.5
33	Indiana	3.8
39	Iowa	3.3
25	Kansas	4.4
31	Kentucky	3.9
25	Louisiana	4.4
48	Maine	1.8
41	Maryland	3.1
40	Massachusetts	3.2
13	Michigan	5.9
19	Minnesota	5.0
41	Mississippi	3.1
21	Missouri	4.9
27	Montana	4.2
15	Nebraska	5.4
2	Nevada	12.4
14	New Hampshire	5.5
47	New Jersey	2.2
16	New Mexico	5.3
36	New York	3.5
12	North Carolina	6.8
23	North Dakota	4.7
31	Ohio	3.9
22	Oklahoma	4.8
3	Oregon	10.1
44	Pennsylvania	2.6
28	Rhode Island	4.1
19	South Carolina	5.0
18	South Dakota	5.1
16	Tennessee	5.3
9	Texas	7.5
11	Utah	7.3
33	Vermont	3.8
41	Virginia	3.1
5	Washington	9.4
50	West Virginia	(0.1)
30	Wisconsin	4.0
23	Wyoming	4.7

RANK ORDER

RANK	STATE	PERCENT CHANGE
1	Colorado	12.7
2	Nevada	12.4
3	Oregon	10.1
4	Florida	10.0
5	Washington	9.4
6	Arizona	8.3
7	Idaho	8.2
8	Georgia	8.0
9	Texas	7.5
10	California	7.4
11	Utah	7.3
12	North Carolina	6.8
13	Michigan	5.9
14	New Hampshire	5.5
15	Nebraska	5.4
16	New Mexico	5.3
16	Tennessee	5.3
18	South Dakota	5.1
19	Minnesota	5.0
19	South Carolina	5.0
21	Missouri	4.9
22	Oklahoma	4.8
23	North Dakota	4.7
23	Wyoming	4.7
25	Kansas	4.4
25	Louisiana	4.4
27	Montana	4.2
28	Alabama	4.1
28	Rhode Island	4.1
30	Wisconsin	4.0
31	Kentucky	3.9
31	Ohio	3.9
33	Indiana	3.8
33	Vermont	3.8
35	Arkansas	3.6
36	Delaware	3.5
36	Illinois	3.5
36	New York	3.5
39	Iowa	3.3
40	Massachusetts	3.2
41	Maryland	3.1
41	Mississippi	3.1
41	Virginia	3.1
44	Pennsylvania	2.6
45	Alaska	2.5
46	Hawaii	2.4
47	New Jersey	2.2
48	Maine	1.8
49	Connecticut	1.1
50	West Virginia	(0.1)
	District of Columbia	15.4

Source: Federal Housing Finance Agency
"State HPI Summary" (http://www.fhfa.gov/DataTools/Tools/Pages/House-Price-Index-%28HPI%29.aspx)
*Single-family house prices. As of September 31, 2015.

Percent Change in House Prices: 2011 to 2015

National Percent Change = 19.9% Increase*

ALPHA ORDER

RANK	STATE	PERCENT CHANGE
37	Alabama	9.0
35	Alaska	9.8
2	Arizona	43.2
29	Arkansas	12.1
3	California	41.6
4	Colorado	41.2
50	Connecticut	(1.4)
48	Delaware	3.4
6	Florida	36.8
12	Georgia	26.2
10	Hawaii	26.9
13	Idaho	24.0
44	Illinois	5.9
28	Indiana	12.9
24	Iowa	13.9
30	Kansas	11.3
33	Kentucky	10.5
27	Louisiana	13.2
46	Maine	5.3
33	Maryland	10.5
25	Massachusetts	13.8
8	Michigan	30.0
20	Minnesota	17.0
42	Mississippi	7.2
31	Missouri	10.9
16	Montana	18.2
16	Nebraska	18.2
1	Nevada	51.3
38	New Hampshire	8.8
49	New Jersey	1.2
46	New Mexico	5.3
43	New York	6.0
23	North Carolina	14.0
5	North Dakota	39.7
26	Ohio	13.5
22	Oklahoma	14.8
7	Oregon	30.4
40	Pennsylvania	8.3
45	Rhode Island	5.4
21	South Carolina	15.1
18	South Dakota	18.0
15	Tennessee	18.9
9	Texas	28.6
11	Utah	26.7
36	Vermont	9.1
32	Virginia	10.8
14	Washington	20.9
39	West Virginia	8.6
41	Wisconsin	8.0
19	Wyoming	17.4

RANK ORDER

RANK	STATE	PERCENT CHANGE
1	Nevada	51.3
2	Arizona	43.2
3	California	41.6
4	Colorado	41.2
5	North Dakota	39.7
6	Florida	36.8
7	Oregon	30.4
8	Michigan	30.0
9	Texas	28.6
10	Hawaii	26.9
11	Utah	26.7
12	Georgia	26.2
13	Idaho	24.0
14	Washington	20.9
15	Tennessee	18.9
16	Montana	18.2
16	Nebraska	18.2
18	South Dakota	18.0
19	Wyoming	17.4
20	Minnesota	17.0
21	South Carolina	15.1
22	Oklahoma	14.8
23	North Carolina	14.0
24	Iowa	13.9
25	Massachusetts	13.8
26	Ohio	13.5
27	Louisiana	13.2
28	Indiana	12.9
29	Arkansas	12.1
30	Kansas	11.3
31	Missouri	10.9
32	Virginia	10.8
33	Kentucky	10.5
33	Maryland	10.5
35	Alaska	9.8
36	Vermont	9.1
37	Alabama	9.0
38	New Hampshire	8.8
39	West Virginia	8.6
40	Pennsylvania	8.3
41	Wisconsin	8.0
42	Mississippi	7.2
43	New York	6.0
44	Illinois	5.9
45	Rhode Island	5.4
46	Maine	5.3
46	New Mexico	5.3
48	Delaware	3.4
49	New Jersey	1.2
50	Connecticut	(1.4)
	District of Columbia	51.6

Source: Federal Housing Finance Agency
"State HPI Summary" (http://www.fhfa.gov/DataTools/Tools/Pages/House-Price-Index-%28HPI%29.aspx)
*Single-family house prices. As of September 31, 2015.

Percent of Owner-Occupied Housing Units with a Mortgage in 2014

National Percent = 63.8% with Mortgages

ALPHA ORDER

RANK	STATE	PERCENT
41	Alabama	57.4
18	Alaska	66.1
23	Arizona	64.4
44	Arkansas	55.6
3	California	71.9
2	Colorado	72.8
5	Connecticut	69.9
9	Delaware	69.4
39	Florida	58.1
14	Georgia	66.9
17	Hawaii	66.3
20	Idaho	65.8
22	Illinois	65.0
16	Indiana	66.7
32	Iowa	60.7
34	Kansas	60.3
36	Kentucky	59.4
47	Louisiana	53.2
29	Maine	62.3
1	Maryland	73.5
8	Massachusetts	69.5
30	Michigan	61.6
15	Minnesota	66.8
49	Mississippi	51.2
27	Missouri	62.7
45	Montana	55.1
31	Nebraska	61.1
11	Nevada	68.4
13	New Hampshire	67.0
11	New Jersey	68.4
42	New Mexico	56.3
28	New York	62.4
23	North Carolina	64.4
48	North Dakota	51.9
25	Ohio	64.0
43	Oklahoma	56.0
18	Oregon	66.1
33	Pennsylvania	60.6
5	Rhode Island	69.9
37	South Carolina	58.6
46	South Dakota	54.7
35	Tennessee	59.9
38	Texas	58.3
4	Utah	71.0
26	Vermont	62.9
5	Virginia	69.9
10	Washington	69.0
50	West Virginia	46.3
21	Wisconsin	65.1
39	Wyoming	58.1

RANK ORDER

RANK	STATE	PERCENT
1	Maryland	73.5
2	Colorado	72.8
3	California	71.9
4	Utah	71.0
5	Connecticut	69.9
5	Rhode Island	69.9
5	Virginia	69.9
8	Massachusetts	69.5
9	Delaware	69.4
10	Washington	69.0
11	Nevada	68.4
11	New Jersey	68.4
13	New Hampshire	67.0
14	Georgia	66.9
15	Minnesota	66.8
16	Indiana	66.7
17	Hawaii	66.3
18	Alaska	66.1
18	Oregon	66.1
20	Idaho	65.8
21	Wisconsin	65.1
22	Illinois	65.0
23	Arizona	64.4
23	North Carolina	64.4
25	Ohio	64.0
26	Vermont	62.9
27	Missouri	62.7
28	New York	62.4
29	Maine	62.3
30	Michigan	61.6
31	Nebraska	61.1
32	Iowa	60.7
33	Pennsylvania	60.6
34	Kansas	60.3
35	Tennessee	59.9
36	Kentucky	59.4
37	South Carolina	58.6
38	Texas	58.3
39	Florida	58.1
39	Wyoming	58.1
41	Alabama	57.4
42	New Mexico	56.3
43	Oklahoma	56.0
44	Arkansas	55.6
45	Montana	55.1
46	South Dakota	54.7
47	Louisiana	53.2
48	North Dakota	51.9
49	Mississippi	51.2
50	West Virginia	46.3
	District of Columbia	76.0

Source: CQ Press using data from U.S. Bureau of the Census
"2014 American Community Survey-Table B25027" (http://www.census.gov/programs-surveys/acs/)

Median Monthly Mortgage Payment in 2014

National Median = $1,454*

ALPHA ORDER

RANK	STATE	MEDIAN
45	Alabama	$1,119
9	Alaska	1,797
28	Arizona	1,273
49	Arkansas	995
3	California	2,068
14	Colorado	1,536
5	Connecticut	1,994
17	Delaware	1,460
23	Florida	1,364
27	Georgia	1,285
2	Hawaii	2,173
44	Idaho	1,138
13	Illinois	1,584
47	Indiana	1,082
40	Iowa	1,173
31	Kansas	1,256
46	Kentucky	1,100
39	Louisiana	1,178
25	Maine	1,322
7	Maryland	1,903
4	Massachusetts	2,014
34	Michigan	1,217
18	Minnesota	1,454
48	Mississippi	1,079
38	Missouri	1,187
32	Montana	1,251
30	Nebraska	1,261
24	Nevada	1,331
8	New Hampshire	1,828
1	New Jersey	2,313
37	New Mexico	1,195
6	New York	1,982
33	North Carolina	1,224
29	North Dakota	1,267
35	Ohio	1,211
43	Oklahoma	1,143
16	Oregon	1,500
20	Pennsylvania	1,400
10	Rhode Island	1,745
42	South Carolina	1,164
36	South Dakota	1,201
41	Tennessee	1,167
19	Texas	1,419
21	Utah	1,393
15	Vermont	1,504
12	Virginia	1,664
11	Washington	1,673
50	West Virginia	945
22	Wisconsin	1,373
26	Wyoming	1,311

RANK ORDER

RANK	STATE	MEDIAN
1	New Jersey	$2,313
2	Hawaii	2,173
3	California	2,068
4	Massachusetts	2,014
5	Connecticut	1,994
6	New York	1,982
7	Maryland	1,903
8	New Hampshire	1,828
9	Alaska	1,797
10	Rhode Island	1,745
11	Washington	1,673
12	Virginia	1,664
13	Illinois	1,584
14	Colorado	1,536
15	Vermont	1,504
16	Oregon	1,500
17	Delaware	1,460
18	Minnesota	1,454
19	Texas	1,419
20	Pennsylvania	1,400
21	Utah	1,393
22	Wisconsin	1,373
23	Florida	1,364
24	Nevada	1,331
25	Maine	1,322
26	Wyoming	1,311
27	Georgia	1,285
28	Arizona	1,273
29	North Dakota	1,267
30	Nebraska	1,261
31	Kansas	1,256
32	Montana	1,251
33	North Carolina	1,224
34	Michigan	1,217
35	Ohio	1,211
36	South Dakota	1,201
37	New Mexico	1,195
38	Missouri	1,187
39	Louisiana	1,178
40	Iowa	1,173
41	Tennessee	1,167
42	South Carolina	1,164
43	Oklahoma	1,143
44	Idaho	1,138
45	Alabama	1,119
46	Kentucky	1,100
47	Indiana	1,082
48	Mississippi	1,079
49	Arkansas	995
50	West Virginia	945
	District of Columbia	2,194

Source: U.S. Bureau of the Census
"2014 American Community Survey-Table R2511" (http://www.census.gov/programs-surveys/acs/)
*Monthly housing costs for owner-occupied housing.

Percent of Home Owners Spending 30% or More of Household Income on Housing Costs in 2014
National Percent = 30.7% of Home Owners*

ALPHA ORDER

RANK	STATE	PERCENT
30	Alabama	28.0
35	Alaska	26.9
23	Arizona	29.1
42	Arkansas	24.4
1	California	40.3
25	Colorado	28.9
8	Connecticut	34.0
17	Delaware	31.1
5	Florida	36.9
21	Georgia	29.4
1	Hawaii	40.3
33	Idaho	27.1
15	Illinois	31.4
47	Indiana	22.6
49	Iowa	20.8
44	Kansas	23.5
37	Kentucky	25.7
29	Louisiana	28.1
15	Maine	31.4
18	Maryland	30.9
10	Massachusetts	32.5
36	Michigan	26.4
39	Minnesota	24.8
20	Mississippi	30.4
38	Missouri	25.2
19	Montana	30.5
45	Nebraska	22.9
13	Nevada	32.0
10	New Hampshire	32.5
3	New Jersey	39.3
12	New Mexico	32.1
4	New York	37.1
28	North Carolina	28.3
50	North Dakota	16.3
40	Ohio	24.7
41	Oklahoma	24.6
9	Oregon	32.7
26	Pennsylvania	28.5
6	Rhode Island	36.8
22	South Carolina	29.3
48	South Dakota	22.5
24	Tennessee	29.0
34	Texas	27.0
32	Utah	27.3
7	Vermont	35.4
26	Virginia	28.5
14	Washington	31.5
46	West Virginia	22.7
31	Wisconsin	27.9
43	Wyoming	23.6

RANK ORDER

RANK	STATE	PERCENT
1	California	40.3
1	Hawaii	40.3
3	New Jersey	39.3
4	New York	37.1
5	Florida	36.9
6	Rhode Island	36.8
7	Vermont	35.4
8	Connecticut	34.0
9	Oregon	32.7
10	Massachusetts	32.5
10	New Hampshire	32.5
12	New Mexico	32.1
13	Nevada	32.0
14	Washington	31.5
15	Illinois	31.4
15	Maine	31.4
17	Delaware	31.1
18	Maryland	30.9
19	Montana	30.5
20	Mississippi	30.4
21	Georgia	29.4
22	South Carolina	29.3
23	Arizona	29.1
24	Tennessee	29.0
25	Colorado	28.9
26	Pennsylvania	28.5
26	Virginia	28.5
28	North Carolina	28.3
29	Louisiana	28.1
30	Alabama	28.0
31	Wisconsin	27.9
32	Utah	27.3
33	Idaho	27.1
34	Texas	27.0
35	Alaska	26.9
36	Michigan	26.4
37	Kentucky	25.7
38	Missouri	25.2
39	Minnesota	24.8
40	Ohio	24.7
41	Oklahoma	24.6
42	Arkansas	24.4
43	Wyoming	23.6
44	Kansas	23.5
45	Nebraska	22.9
46	West Virginia	22.7
47	Indiana	22.6
48	South Dakota	22.5
49	Iowa	20.8
50	North Dakota	16.3
	District of Columbia	26.4

Source: U.S. Bureau of the Census
"2014 American Community Survey-Table R2513" (http://www.census.gov/programs-surveys/acs/)
*For owner-occupied housing units with a mortgage.

Median Annual Real Estate Taxes in 2014

National Median = $2,139*

ALPHA ORDER

RANK	STATE	MEDIAN
50	Alabama	$539
12	Alaska	2,987
35	Arizona	1,330
47	Arkansas	716
10	California	3,160
30	Colorado	1,472
2	Connecticut	5,369
38	Delaware	1,224
28	Florida	1,631
34	Georgia	1,346
32	Hawaii	1,401
37	Idaho	1,243
6	Illinois	3,952
41	Indiana	1,081
22	Iowa	1,965
25	Kansas	1,840
44	Kentucky	1,054
48	Louisiana	710
18	Maine	2,335
11	Maryland	3,154
5	Massachusetts	4,080
20	Michigan	2,147
19	Minnesota	2,148
45	Mississippi	854
33	Missouri	1,368
26	Montana	1,653
17	Nebraska	2,474
31	Nevada	1,426
3	New Hampshire	5,131
1	New Jersey	7,452
40	New Mexico	1,197
4	New York	4,703
36	North Carolina	1,324
27	North Dakota	1,652
21	Ohio	2,027
43	Oklahoma	1,062
15	Oregon	2,570
16	Pennsylvania	2,559
7	Rhode Island	3,855
46	South Carolina	808
24	South Dakota	1,876
42	Tennessee	1,066
14	Texas	2,595
29	Utah	1,480
8	Vermont	3,797
23	Virginia	1,956
13	Washington	2,798
49	West Virginia	616
9	Wisconsin	3,212
39	Wyoming	1,206

RANK ORDER

RANK	STATE	MEDIAN
1	New Jersey	$7,452
2	Connecticut	5,369
3	New Hampshire	5,131
4	New York	4,703
5	Massachusetts	4,080
6	Illinois	3,952
7	Rhode Island	3,855
8	Vermont	3,797
9	Wisconsin	3,212
10	California	3,160
11	Maryland	3,154
12	Alaska	2,987
13	Washington	2,798
14	Texas	2,595
15	Oregon	2,570
16	Pennsylvania	2,559
17	Nebraska	2,474
18	Maine	2,335
19	Minnesota	2,148
20	Michigan	2,147
21	Ohio	2,027
22	Iowa	1,965
23	Virginia	1,956
24	South Dakota	1,876
25	Kansas	1,840
26	Montana	1,653
27	North Dakota	1,652
28	Florida	1,631
29	Utah	1,480
30	Colorado	1,472
31	Nevada	1,426
32	Hawaii	1,401
33	Missouri	1,368
34	Georgia	1,346
35	Arizona	1,330
36	North Carolina	1,324
37	Idaho	1,243
38	Delaware	1,224
39	Wyoming	1,206
40	New Mexico	1,197
41	Indiana	1,081
42	Tennessee	1,066
43	Oklahoma	1,062
44	Kentucky	1,054
45	Mississippi	854
46	South Carolina	808
47	Arkansas	716
48	Louisiana	710
49	West Virginia	616
50	Alabama	539
	District of Columbia	2,614

Source: U.S. Bureau of the Census
"2014 American Community Survey-Table B25103" (http://www.census.gov/programs-surveys/acs/)
*For owner-occupied housing units with or without mortgages.

Homeownership Rate in 2014

National Rate = 64.5%*

ALPHA ORDER

RANK	STATE	PERCENT
8	Alabama	72.1
36	Alaska	64.9
41	Arizona	63.5
32	Arkansas	65.4
49	California	54.2
35	Colorado	65.0
23	Connecticut	67.4
2	Delaware	74.3
36	Florida	64.9
43	Georgia	62.9
47	Hawaii	58.4
16	Idaho	69.6
28	Illinois	66.4
14	Indiana	70.1
17	Iowa	69.4
38	Kansas	64.7
22	Kentucky	67.6
33	Louisiana	65.3
10	Maine	71.0
31	Maryland	66.2
42	Massachusetts	63.0
3	Michigan	73.8
9	Minnesota	71.4
5	Mississippi	73.2
13	Missouri	70.5
25	Montana	66.9
26	Nebraska	66.7
48	Nevada	56.0
7	New Hampshire	72.2
34	New Jersey	65.2
30	New Mexico	66.3
50	New York	52.9
28	North Carolina	66.4
39	North Dakota	64.5
24	Ohio	67.3
18	Oklahoma	69.3
44	Oregon	62.8
15	Pennsylvania	69.7
46	Rhode Island	61.8
6	South Carolina	72.9
19	South Dakota	69.2
26	Tennessee	66.7
45	Texas	62.2
11	Utah	70.9
4	Vermont	73.5
20	Virginia	68.7
40	Washington	63.6
1	West Virginia	75.6
21	Wisconsin	67.8
12	Wyoming	70.8

RANK ORDER

RANK	STATE	PERCENT
1	West Virginia	75.6
2	Delaware	74.3
3	Michigan	73.8
4	Vermont	73.5
5	Mississippi	73.2
6	South Carolina	72.9
7	New Hampshire	72.2
8	Alabama	72.1
9	Minnesota	71.4
10	Maine	71.0
11	Utah	70.9
12	Wyoming	70.8
13	Missouri	70.5
14	Indiana	70.1
15	Pennsylvania	69.7
16	Idaho	69.6
17	Iowa	69.4
18	Oklahoma	69.3
19	South Dakota	69.2
20	Virginia	68.7
21	Wisconsin	67.8
22	Kentucky	67.6
23	Connecticut	67.4
24	Ohio	67.3
25	Montana	66.9
26	Nebraska	66.7
26	Tennessee	66.7
28	Illinois	66.4
28	North Carolina	66.4
30	New Mexico	66.3
31	Maryland	66.2
32	Arkansas	65.4
33	Louisiana	65.3
34	New Jersey	65.2
35	Colorado	65.0
36	Alaska	64.9
36	Florida	64.9
38	Kansas	64.7
39	North Dakota	64.5
40	Washington	63.6
41	Arizona	63.5
42	Massachusetts	63.0
43	Georgia	62.9
44	Oregon	62.8
45	Texas	62.2
46	Rhode Island	61.8
47	Hawaii	58.4
48	Nevada	56.0
49	California	54.2
50	New York	52.9 |//
	District of Columbia	41.5

Source: U.S. Bureau of the Census
"Housing Vacancies and Homeownership, Annual Statistics: 2013" (http://www.census.gov/housing/hvs/data/ann14ind.html)
*Percent of households occupied by the owner.

Percent of Housing Units That Are Renter-Occupied in 2014

National Percent = 36.9% of Housing Units*

ALPHA ORDER

RANK	STATE	PERCENT
35	Alabama	32.3
12	Alaska	37.5
7	Arizona	38.9
23	Arkansas	34.2
3	California	46.3
15	Colorado	36.1
28	Connecticut	33.6
46	Delaware	29.7
16	Florida	35.9
11	Georgia	37.8
4	Hawaii	43.3
37	Idaho	32.0
22	Illinois	34.5
40	Indiana	31.4
47	Iowa	29.1
30	Kansas	33.4
26	Kentucky	33.9
18	Louisiana	35.6
48	Maine	28.7
24	Maryland	34.1
9	Massachusetts	38.4
44	Michigan	29.8
49	Minnesota	28.3
35	Mississippi	32.3
32	Missouri	33.1
28	Montana	33.6
24	Nebraska	34.1
2	Nevada	46.4
44	New Hampshire	29.8
13	New Jersey	36.7
32	New Mexico	33.1
1	New York	47.0
17	North Carolina	35.8
14	North Dakota	36.2
20	Ohio	34.7
19	Oklahoma	34.9
6	Oregon	39.3
41	Pennsylvania	31.2
5	Rhode Island	41.2
37	South Carolina	32.0
39	South Dakota	31.8
26	Tennessee	33.9
8	Texas	38.8
42	Utah	30.8
43	Vermont	30.0
20	Virginia	34.7
10	Washington	38.3
50	West Virginia	27.8
30	Wisconsin	33.4
32	Wyoming	33.1

RANK ORDER

RANK	STATE	PERCENT
1	New York	47.0
2	Nevada	46.4
3	California	46.3
4	Hawaii	43.3
5	Rhode Island	41.2
6	Oregon	39.3
7	Arizona	38.9
8	Texas	38.8
9	Massachusetts	38.4
10	Washington	38.3
11	Georgia	37.8
12	Alaska	37.5
13	New Jersey	36.7
14	North Dakota	36.2
15	Colorado	36.1
16	Florida	35.9
17	North Carolina	35.8
18	Louisiana	35.6
19	Oklahoma	34.9
20	Ohio	34.7
20	Virginia	34.7
22	Illinois	34.5
23	Arkansas	34.2
24	Maryland	34.1
24	Nebraska	34.1
26	Kentucky	33.9
26	Tennessee	33.9
28	Connecticut	33.6
28	Montana	33.6
30	Kansas	33.4
30	Wisconsin	33.4
32	Missouri	33.1
32	New Mexico	33.1
32	Wyoming	33.1
35	Alabama	32.3
35	Mississippi	32.3
37	Idaho	32.0
37	South Carolina	32.0
39	South Dakota	31.8
40	Indiana	31.4
41	Pennsylvania	31.2
42	Utah	30.8
43	Vermont	30.0
44	Michigan	29.8
44	New Hampshire	29.8
46	Delaware	29.7
47	Iowa	29.1
48	Maine	28.7
49	Minnesota	28.3
50	West Virginia	27.8
	District of Columbia	59.4

Source: U.S. Bureau of the Census
 "2014 American Community Survey-Table R2512" (http://www.census.gov/programs-surveys/acs/)
*For occupied housing units.

Median Monthly Rental Payment in 2014

National Median = $934*

ALPHA ORDER

RANK	STATE	MEDIAN
43	Alabama	$717
5	Alaska	1,183
19	Arizona	916
47	Arkansas	683
2	California	1,268
12	Colorado	1,020
9	Connecticut	1,076
11	Delaware	1,024
13	Florida	1,003
23	Georgia	882
1	Hawaii	1,448
36	Idaho	755
20	Illinois	905
38	Indiana	753
44	Iowa	711
34	Kansas	773
48	Kentucky	678
27	Louisiana	801
33	Maine	776
3	Maryland	1,242
8	Massachusetts	1,107
30	Michigan	788
24	Minnesota	859
44	Mississippi	711
37	Missouri	754
44	Montana	711
39	Nebraska	742
15	Nevada	955
14	New Hampshire	994
4	New Jersey	1,202
32	New Mexico	777
6	New York	1,148
26	North Carolina	803
42	North Dakota	728
41	Ohio	735
40	Oklahoma	737
17	Oregon	924
25	Pennsylvania	848
16	Rhode Island	934
29	South Carolina	791
50	South Dakota	647
35	Tennessee	770
21	Texas	896
22	Utah	886
18	Vermont	917
7	Virginia	1,116
10	Washington	1,032
49	West Virginia	656
31	Wisconsin	782
28	Wyoming	792

RANK ORDER

RANK	STATE	MEDIAN
1	Hawaii	$1,448
2	California	1,268
3	Maryland	1,242
4	New Jersey	1,202
5	Alaska	1,183
6	New York	1,148
7	Virginia	1,116
8	Massachusetts	1,107
9	Connecticut	1,076
10	Washington	1,032
11	Delaware	1,024
12	Colorado	1,020
13	Florida	1,003
14	New Hampshire	994
15	Nevada	955
16	Rhode Island	934
17	Oregon	924
18	Vermont	917
19	Arizona	916
20	Illinois	905
21	Texas	896
22	Utah	886
23	Georgia	882
24	Minnesota	859
25	Pennsylvania	848
26	North Carolina	803
27	Louisiana	801
28	Wyoming	792
29	South Carolina	791
30	Michigan	788
31	Wisconsin	782
32	New Mexico	777
33	Maine	776
34	Kansas	773
35	Tennessee	770
36	Idaho	755
37	Missouri	754
38	Indiana	753
39	Nebraska	742
40	Oklahoma	737
41	Ohio	735
42	North Dakota	728
43	Alabama	717
44	Iowa	711
44	Mississippi	711
44	Montana	711
47	Arkansas	683
48	Kentucky	678
49	West Virginia	656
50	South Dakota	647
	District of Columbia	1,360

Source: U.S. Bureau of the Census
"2014 American Community Survey-Table R2514" (http://www.census.gov/programs-surveys/acs/)
*Monthly housing costs for renter-occupied housing.

Percent of Renters Spending 30% or More of Household Income on Rent and Utilities in 2014
National Percent = 47.6% of Renters

ALPHA ORDER

RANK	STATE	PERCENT
35	Alabama	43.6
45	Alaska	39.8
21	Arizona	45.8
40	Arkansas	42.2
1	California	54.1
10	Colorado	49.0
8	Connecticut	49.3
17	Delaware	46.7
2	Florida	53.4
14	Georgia	47.8
4	Hawaii	50.8
38	Idaho	43.1
21	Illinois	45.8
26	Indiana	45.2
46	Iowa	39.6
41	Kansas	41.3
44	Kentucky	40.1
24	Louisiana	45.5
14	Maine	47.8
11	Maryland	48.4
16	Massachusetts	47.5
12	Michigan	48.2
29	Minnesota	44.8
37	Mississippi	43.5
30	Missouri	44.7
39	Montana	42.5
41	Nebraska	41.3
17	Nevada	46.7
25	New Hampshire	45.3
3	New Jersey	51.1
20	New Mexico	46.0
4	New York	50.8
28	North Carolina	45.1
47	North Dakota	38.6
31	Ohio	44.6
43	Oklahoma	40.4
7	Oregon	50.2
19	Pennsylvania	46.1
8	Rhode Island	49.3
26	South Carolina	45.2
50	South Dakota	36.4
31	Tennessee	44.6
34	Texas	44.2
35	Utah	43.6
6	Vermont	50.3
23	Virginia	45.6
13	Washington	48.0
48	West Virginia	38.4
33	Wisconsin	44.3
49	Wyoming	37.4

RANK ORDER

RANK	STATE	PERCENT
1	California	54.1
2	Florida	53.4
3	New Jersey	51.1
4	Hawaii	50.8
4	New York	50.8
6	Vermont	50.3
7	Oregon	50.2
8	Connecticut	49.3
8	Rhode Island	49.3
10	Colorado	49.0
11	Maryland	48.4
12	Michigan	48.2
13	Washington	48.0
14	Georgia	47.8
14	Maine	47.8
16	Massachusetts	47.5
17	Delaware	46.7
17	Nevada	46.7
19	Pennsylvania	46.1
20	New Mexico	46.0
21	Arizona	45.8
21	Illinois	45.8
23	Virginia	45.6
24	Louisiana	45.5
25	New Hampshire	45.3
26	Indiana	45.2
26	South Carolina	45.2
28	North Carolina	45.1
29	Minnesota	44.8
30	Missouri	44.7
31	Ohio	44.6
31	Tennessee	44.6
33	Wisconsin	44.3
34	Texas	44.2
35	Alabama	43.6
35	Utah	43.6
37	Mississippi	43.5
38	Idaho	43.1
39	Montana	42.5
40	Arkansas	42.2
41	Kansas	41.3
41	Nebraska	41.3
43	Oklahoma	40.4
44	Kentucky	40.1
45	Alaska	39.8
46	Iowa	39.6
47	North Dakota	38.6
48	West Virginia	38.4
49	Wyoming	37.4
50	South Dakota	36.4
	District of Columbia	46.7

Source: U.S. Bureau of the Census
"2014 American Community Survey-Table R2515" (http://www.census.gov/programs-surveys/acs/)

State and Local Government Expenditures for Housing and Community Development in 2013
National Total = $51,539,193,000*

ALPHA ORDER

RANK	STATE	EXPENDITURES	% of USA
26	Alabama	$461,483,000	0.9%
30	Alaska	336,571,000	0.7%
24	Arizona	570,244,000	1.1%
40	Arkansas	189,904,000	0.4%
1	California	8,411,311,000	16.3%
21	Colorado	789,656,000	1.5%
17	Connecticut	926,375,000	1.8%
44	Delaware	150,533,000	0.3%
3	Florida	2,920,648,000	5.7%
12	Georgia	1,303,676,000	2.5%
36	Hawaii	251,012,000	0.5%
46	Idaho	133,174,000	0.3%
7	Illinois	2,040,532,000	4.0%
18	Indiana	925,869,000	1.8%
39	Iowa	213,817,000	0.4%
38	Kansas	216,834,000	0.4%
28	Kentucky	412,659,000	0.8%
15	Louisiana	1,061,813,000	2.1%
32	Maine	308,033,000	0.6%
13	Maryland	1,300,069,000	2.5%
4	Massachusetts	2,823,735,000	5.5%
14	Michigan	1,247,097,000	2.4%
19	Minnesota	895,337,000	1.7%
35	Mississippi	265,701,000	0.5%
22	Missouri	663,472,000	1.3%
47	Montana	114,263,000	0.2%
41	Nebraska	179,542,000	0.3%
33	Nevada	297,834,000	0.6%
37	New Hampshire	218,653,000	0.4%
10	New Jersey	1,362,320,000	2.6%
42	New Mexico	172,416,000	0.3%
2	New York	5,780,948,000	11.2%
9	North Carolina	1,520,647,000	3.0%
49	North Dakota	81,118,000	0.2%
5	Ohio	2,319,455,000	4.5%
25	Oklahoma	481,122,000	0.9%
23	Oregon	633,608,000	1.2%
8	Pennsylvania	1,968,835,000	3.8%
34	Rhode Island	266,728,000	0.5%
27	South Carolina	446,355,000	0.9%
48	South Dakota	106,891,000	0.2%
20	Tennessee	863,056,000	1.7%
6	Texas	2,143,844,000	4.2%
29	Utah	338,934,000	0.7%
43	Vermont	160,811,000	0.3%
16	Virginia	961,788,000	1.9%
11	Washington	1,318,454,000	2.6%
45	West Virginia	135,118,000	0.3%
31	Wisconsin	326,913,000	0.6%
50	Wyoming	22,331,000	0.0%

RANK ORDER

RANK	STATE	EXPENDITURES	% of USA
1	California	$8,411,311,000	16.3%
2	New York	5,780,948,000	11.2%
3	Florida	2,920,648,000	5.7%
4	Massachusetts	2,823,735,000	5.5%
5	Ohio	2,319,455,000	4.5%
6	Texas	2,143,844,000	4.2%
7	Illinois	2,040,532,000	4.0%
8	Pennsylvania	1,968,835,000	3.8%
9	North Carolina	1,520,647,000	3.0%
10	New Jersey	1,362,320,000	2.6%
11	Washington	1,318,454,000	2.6%
12	Georgia	1,303,676,000	2.5%
13	Maryland	1,300,069,000	2.5%
14	Michigan	1,247,097,000	2.4%
15	Louisiana	1,061,813,000	2.1%
16	Virginia	961,788,000	1.9%
17	Connecticut	926,375,000	1.8%
18	Indiana	925,869,000	1.8%
19	Minnesota	895,337,000	1.7%
20	Tennessee	863,056,000	1.7%
21	Colorado	789,656,000	1.5%
22	Missouri	663,472,000	1.3%
23	Oregon	633,608,000	1.2%
24	Arizona	570,244,000	1.1%
25	Oklahoma	481,122,000	0.9%
26	Alabama	461,483,000	0.9%
27	South Carolina	446,355,000	0.9%
28	Kentucky	412,659,000	0.8%
29	Utah	338,934,000	0.7%
30	Alaska	336,571,000	0.7%
31	Wisconsin	326,913,000	0.6%
32	Maine	308,033,000	0.6%
33	Nevada	297,834,000	0.6%
34	Rhode Island	266,728,000	0.5%
35	Mississippi	265,701,000	0.5%
36	Hawaii	251,012,000	0.5%
37	New Hampshire	218,653,000	0.4%
38	Kansas	216,834,000	0.4%
39	Iowa	213,817,000	0.4%
40	Arkansas	189,904,000	0.4%
41	Nebraska	179,542,000	0.3%
42	New Mexico	172,416,000	0.3%
43	Vermont	160,811,000	0.3%
44	Delaware	150,533,000	0.3%
45	West Virginia	135,118,000	0.3%
46	Idaho	133,174,000	0.3%
47	Montana	114,263,000	0.2%
48	South Dakota	106,891,000	0.2%
49	North Dakota	81,118,000	0.2%
50	Wyoming	22,331,000	0.0%
	District of Columbia	497,654,000	1.0%

Source: U.S. Bureau of the Census, Governments Division
"2013 State and Local Government Finances" (http://www.census.gov/govs/local/)
*Direct general expenditures.

Per Capita State and Local Government Expenditures for Housing and Community Development in 2013
National Per Capita = $163*

ALPHA ORDER

RANK	STATE	PER CAPITA
36	Alabama	$96
1	Alaska	456
41	Arizona	86
48	Arkansas	64
9	California	219
22	Colorado	150
4	Connecticut	258
16	Delaware	163
23	Florida	149
26	Georgia	130
13	Hawaii	178
42	Idaho	83
18	Illinois	158
24	Indiana	141
47	Iowa	69
45	Kansas	75
38	Kentucky	94
8	Louisiana	229
7	Maine	232
9	Maryland	219
2	Massachusetts	421
27	Michigan	126
14	Minnesota	165
40	Mississippi	89
34	Missouri	110
32	Montana	113
36	Nebraska	96
35	Nevada	107
14	New Hampshire	165
21	New Jersey	153
42	New Mexico	83
3	New York	294
19	North Carolina	154
33	North Dakota	112
11	Ohio	200
29	Oklahoma	125
17	Oregon	161
19	Pennsylvania	154
6	Rhode Island	253
38	South Carolina	94
27	South Dakota	126
25	Tennessee	133
44	Texas	81
30	Utah	117
5	Vermont	256
31	Virginia	116
12	Washington	189
46	West Virginia	73
49	Wisconsin	57
50	Wyoming	38

RANK ORDER

RANK	STATE	PER CAPITA
1	Alaska	$456
2	Massachusetts	421
3	New York	294
4	Connecticut	258
5	Vermont	256
6	Rhode Island	253
7	Maine	232
8	Louisiana	229
9	California	219
9	Maryland	219
11	Ohio	200
12	Washington	189
13	Hawaii	178
14	Minnesota	165
14	New Hampshire	165
16	Delaware	163
17	Oregon	161
18	Illinois	158
19	North Carolina	154
19	Pennsylvania	154
21	New Jersey	153
22	Colorado	150
23	Florida	149
24	Indiana	141
25	Tennessee	133
26	Georgia	130
27	Michigan	126
27	South Dakota	126
29	Oklahoma	125
30	Utah	117
31	Virginia	116
32	Montana	113
33	North Dakota	112
34	Missouri	110
35	Nevada	107
36	Alabama	96
36	Nebraska	96
38	Kentucky	94
38	South Carolina	94
40	Mississippi	89
41	Arizona	86
42	Idaho	83
42	New Mexico	83
44	Texas	81
45	Kansas	75
46	West Virginia	73
47	Iowa	69
48	Arkansas	64
49	Wisconsin	57
50	Wyoming	38
	District of Columbia	766

Source: CQ Press using data from U.S. Bureau of the Census, Governments Division
"2013 State and Local Government Finances" (http://www.census.gov/govs/local/)
*Direct general expenditures.

State & Local Government Spending for Housing and Community Development as a Percent of All State and Local Government Expenditures in 2013
National Percent = 2.0%*

ALPHA ORDER

RANK	STATE	PERCENT
36	Alabama	1.3
5	Alaska	2.5
34	Arizona	1.4
44	Arkansas	0.9
11	California	2.3
21	Colorado	1.9
4	Connecticut	2.7
28	Delaware	1.6
12	Florida	2.2
16	Georgia	2.0
16	Hawaii	2.0
36	Idaho	1.3
21	Illinois	1.9
16	Indiana	2.0
48	Iowa	0.8
44	Kansas	0.9
36	Kentucky	1.3
5	Louisiana	2.5
2	Maine	2.8
5	Maryland	2.5
1	Massachusetts	4.3
26	Michigan	1.7
23	Minnesota	1.8
41	Mississippi	1.1
32	Missouri	1.5
34	Montana	1.4
40	Nebraska	1.2
28	Nevada	1.6
12	New Hampshire	2.2
28	New Jersey	1.6
44	New Mexico	0.9
9	New York	2.4
15	North Carolina	2.1
41	North Dakota	1.1
5	Ohio	2.5
23	Oklahoma	1.8
16	Oregon	2.0
23	Pennsylvania	1.8
2	Rhode Island	2.8
36	South Carolina	1.3
26	South Dakota	1.7
16	Tennessee	2.0
41	Texas	1.1
28	Utah	1.6
9	Vermont	2.4
32	Virginia	1.5
12	Washington	2.2
44	West Virginia	0.9
49	Wisconsin	0.7
50	Wyoming	0.3

RANK ORDER

RANK	STATE	PERCENT
1	Massachusetts	4.3
2	Maine	2.8
2	Rhode Island	2.8
4	Connecticut	2.7
5	Alaska	2.5
5	Louisiana	2.5
5	Maryland	2.5
5	Ohio	2.5
9	New York	2.4
9	Vermont	2.4
11	California	2.3
12	Florida	2.2
12	New Hampshire	2.2
12	Washington	2.2
15	North Carolina	2.1
16	Georgia	2.0
16	Hawaii	2.0
16	Indiana	2.0
16	Oregon	2.0
16	Tennessee	2.0
21	Colorado	1.9
21	Illinois	1.9
23	Minnesota	1.8
23	Oklahoma	1.8
23	Pennsylvania	1.8
26	Michigan	1.7
26	South Dakota	1.7
28	Delaware	1.6
28	Nevada	1.6
28	New Jersey	1.6
28	Utah	1.6
32	Missouri	1.5
32	Virginia	1.5
34	Arizona	1.4
34	Montana	1.4
36	Alabama	1.3
36	Idaho	1.3
36	Kentucky	1.3
36	South Carolina	1.3
40	Nebraska	1.2
41	Mississippi	1.1
41	North Dakota	1.1
41	Texas	1.1
44	Arkansas	0.9
44	Kansas	0.9
44	New Mexico	0.9
44	West Virginia	0.9
48	Iowa	0.8
49	Wisconsin	0.7
50	Wyoming	0.3
	District of Columbia	4.3

Source: CQ Press using data from U.S. Bureau of the Census, Governments Division
"2013 State and Local Government Finances" (http://www.census.gov/govs/local/)
*As a percent of direct general expenditures.

XIII. Population

Population in 2015	451
Population in 2014	452
Numerical Population Change: 2014 to 2015	453
Percent Change in Population: 2014 to 2015	454
Population in 2010 Census	455
Projected State Population in 2030	456
Population per Square Mile in 2015	457
Male Population in 2014	458
Female Population in 2014	459
Male to Female Ratio in 2014	460
White Population in 2014	461
Percent of Population White in 2014	462
Black Population in 2014	463
Percent of Population Black in 2014	464
Hispanic Population in 2014	465
Percent of Population Hispanic in 2014	466
Asian Population in 2014	467
Percent of Population Asian in 2014	468
American Indian Population in 2014	469
Percent of Population American Indian in 2014	470
Native Hawaiian or Other Pacific Islander Population in 2014	471
Percent of Population Native Hawaiian or Other Pacific Islander in 2014	472
Non-Hispanic White Population in 2014	473
Percent of Population Non-Hispanic White in 2014	474
Multiple Race Population in 2014	475
Percent of Population Multiple Races in 2014	476
Median Age in 2014	477
Population under 5 Years Old in 2014	478
Percent of Population under 5 Years Old in 2014	479
Population 5 to 17 Years Old in 2014	480
Percent of Population 5 to 17 Years Old in 2014	481
Population 18 Years Old and Older in 2014	482
Percent of Population 18 Years Old and Older in 2014	483
Population 18 to 24 Years Old in 2014	484
Percent of Population 18 to 24 Years Old in 2014	485
Population 25 to 44 Years Old in 2014	486
Percent of Population 25 to 44 Years Old in 2014	487
Population 45 to 64 Years Old in 2014	488
Percent of Population 45 to 64 Years Old in 2014	489
Population 65 Years Old and Older in 2014	490
Percent of Population 65 Years Old and Older in 2014	491
Population 85 Years Old and Older in 2014	492
Percent of Population 85 Years Old and Older in 2014	493
Percent of Native Population Born in Their State of Residence in 2014	494
Domestic Migration of Population: 2014 to 2015	495
Net International Migration: 2014 to 2015	496
Percent of Population Foreign Born in 2014	497
Percent of Population Speaking a Language Other Than English at Home in 2014	498
Percent of Population Speaking Spanish at Home in 2014	499
Marriage Rate for Men in 2014	500
Estimated Median Age of Men at First Marriage in 2014	501
Marriage Rate for Women in 2014	502
Estimated Median Age of Women at First Marriage in 2014	503
Ratio of Unmarried Men to Unmarried Women in 2014	504
Divorce Rate for Men in 2014	505
Divorce Rate for Women in 2014	506
Average Family Size in 2014	507
Seats in the U.S. House of Representatives in 2016	508
Estimated Population per U.S. House Seat in 2016	509
State Legislators in 2015	510
Population per State Legislator in 2015	511
Registered Voters in 2014	512
Percent of Eligible Voters Reported Registered in 2014	513
Persons Voting in 2014	514
Percent of Eligible Population Reported Voting in 2014	515
Percent of Registered Population Reported Voting in 2014	516

Population in 2015

National Total = 321,418,820*

ALPHA ORDER

RANK	STATE	POPULATION	% of USA
24	Alabama	4,858,979	1.5%
48	Alaska	738,432	0.2%
14	Arizona	6,828,065	2.1%
33	Arkansas	2,978,204	0.9%
1	California	39,144,818	12.2%
22	Colorado	5,456,574	1.7%
29	Connecticut	3,590,886	1.1%
45	Delaware	945,934	0.3%
3	Florida	20,271,272	6.3%
8	Georgia	10,214,860	3.2%
40	Hawaii	1,431,603	0.4%
39	Idaho	1,654,930	0.5%
5	Illinois	12,859,995	4.0%
16	Indiana	6,619,680	2.1%
30	Iowa	3,123,899	1.0%
34	Kansas	2,911,641	0.9%
26	Kentucky	4,425,092	1.4%
25	Louisiana	4,670,724	1.5%
42	Maine	1,329,328	0.4%
19	Maryland	6,006,401	1.9%
15	Massachusetts	6,794,422	2.1%
10	Michigan	9,922,576	3.1%
21	Minnesota	5,489,594	1.7%
32	Mississippi	2,992,333	0.9%
18	Missouri	6,083,672	1.9%
44	Montana	1,032,949	0.3%
37	Nebraska	1,896,190	0.6%
35	Nevada	2,890,845	0.9%
41	New Hampshire	1,330,608	0.4%
11	New Jersey	8,958,013	2.8%
36	New Mexico	2,085,109	0.6%
4	New York	19,795,791	6.2%
9	North Carolina	10,042,802	3.1%
47	North Dakota	756,927	0.2%
7	Ohio	11,613,423	3.6%
28	Oklahoma	3,911,338	1.2%
27	Oregon	4,028,977	1.3%
6	Pennsylvania	12,802,503	4.0%
43	Rhode Island	1,056,298	0.3%
23	South Carolina	4,896,146	1.5%
46	South Dakota	858,469	0.3%
17	Tennessee	6,600,299	2.1%
2	Texas	27,469,114	8.5%
31	Utah	2,995,919	0.9%
49	Vermont	626,042	0.2%
12	Virginia	8,382,993	2.6%
13	Washington	7,170,351	2.2%
38	West Virginia	1,844,128	0.6%
20	Wisconsin	5,771,337	1.8%
50	Wyoming	586,107	0.2%

RANK ORDER

RANK	STATE	POPULATION	% of USA
1	California	39,144,818	12.2%
2	Texas	27,469,114	8.5%
3	Florida	20,271,272	6.3%
4	New York	19,795,791	6.2%
5	Illinois	12,859,995	4.0%
6	Pennsylvania	12,802,503	4.0%
7	Ohio	11,613,423	3.6%
8	Georgia	10,214,860	3.2%
9	North Carolina	10,042,802	3.1%
10	Michigan	9,922,576	3.1%
11	New Jersey	8,958,013	2.8%
12	Virginia	8,382,993	2.6%
13	Washington	7,170,351	2.2%
14	Arizona	6,828,065	2.1%
15	Massachusetts	6,794,422	2.1%
16	Indiana	6,619,680	2.1%
17	Tennessee	6,600,299	2.1%
18	Missouri	6,083,672	1.9%
19	Maryland	6,006,401	1.9%
20	Wisconsin	5,771,337	1.8%
21	Minnesota	5,489,594	1.7%
22	Colorado	5,456,574	1.7%
23	South Carolina	4,896,146	1.5%
24	Alabama	4,858,979	1.5%
25	Louisiana	4,670,724	1.5%
26	Kentucky	4,425,092	1.4%
27	Oregon	4,028,977	1.3%
28	Oklahoma	3,911,338	1.2%
29	Connecticut	3,590,886	1.1%
30	Iowa	3,123,899	1.0%
31	Utah	2,995,919	0.9%
32	Mississippi	2,992,333	0.9%
33	Arkansas	2,978,204	0.9%
34	Kansas	2,911,641	0.9%
35	Nevada	2,890,845	0.9%
36	New Mexico	2,085,109	0.6%
37	Nebraska	1,896,190	0.6%
38	West Virginia	1,844,128	0.6%
39	Idaho	1,654,930	0.5%
40	Hawaii	1,431,603	0.4%
41	New Hampshire	1,330,608	0.4%
42	Maine	1,329,328	0.4%
43	Rhode Island	1,056,298	0.3%
44	Montana	1,032,949	0.3%
45	Delaware	945,934	0.3%
46	South Dakota	858,469	0.3%
47	North Dakota	756,927	0.2%
48	Alaska	738,432	0.2%
49	Vermont	626,042	0.2%
50	Wyoming	586,107	0.2%
	District of Columbia	672,228	0.2%

Source: U.S. Bureau of the Census
"Population Estimates" (December 2015, http://www.census.gov/popest/data/index.html)
*Resident population estimate as of July 1, 2015.

Population in 2014

National Total = 318,907,401*

ALPHA ORDER

RANK	STATE	POPULATION	% of USA
23	Alabama	4,846,411	1.5%
48	Alaska	737,046	0.2%
15	Arizona	6,728,783	2.1%
32	Arkansas	2,966,835	0.9%
1	California	38,792,291	12.2%
22	Colorado	5,355,588	1.7%
29	Connecticut	3,594,762	1.1%
45	Delaware	935,968	0.3%
3	Florida	19,905,569	6.2%
8	Georgia	10,097,132	3.2%
40	Hawaii	1,420,257	0.4%
39	Idaho	1,634,806	0.5%
5	Illinois	12,882,189	4.0%
16	Indiana	6,597,880	2.1%
30	Iowa	3,109,481	1.0%
34	Kansas	2,902,507	0.9%
26	Kentucky	4,412,617	1.4%
25	Louisiana	4,648,990	1.5%
41	Maine	1,330,256	0.4%
19	Maryland	5,975,346	1.9%
14	Massachusetts	6,755,124	2.1%
10	Michigan	9,916,306	3.1%
21	Minnesota	5,457,125	1.7%
31	Mississippi	2,993,443	0.9%
18	Missouri	6,063,827	1.9%
44	Montana	1,023,252	0.3%
37	Nebraska	1,882,980	0.6%
35	Nevada	2,838,281	0.9%
42	New Hampshire	1,327,996	0.4%
11	New Jersey	8,938,844	2.8%
36	New Mexico	2,085,567	0.7%
4	New York	19,748,858	6.2%
9	North Carolina	9,940,387	3.1%
47	North Dakota	740,040	0.2%
7	Ohio	11,596,998	3.6%
28	Oklahoma	3,879,610	1.2%
27	Oregon	3,971,202	1.2%
6	Pennsylvania	12,793,767	4.0%
43	Rhode Island	1,054,907	0.3%
24	South Carolina	4,829,160	1.5%
46	South Dakota	853,304	0.3%
17	Tennessee	6,547,779	2.1%
2	Texas	26,979,078	8.5%
33	Utah	2,944,498	0.9%
49	Vermont	626,767	0.2%
12	Virginia	8,328,098	2.6%
13	Washington	7,063,166	2.2%
38	West Virginia	1,848,751	0.6%
20	Wisconsin	5,759,432	1.8%
50	Wyoming	584,304	0.2%

RANK ORDER

RANK	STATE	POPULATION	% of USA
1	California	38,792,291	12.2%
2	Texas	26,979,078	8.5%
3	Florida	19,905,569	6.2%
4	New York	19,748,858	6.2%
5	Illinois	12,882,189	4.0%
6	Pennsylvania	12,793,767	4.0%
7	Ohio	11,596,998	3.6%
8	Georgia	10,097,132	3.2%
9	North Carolina	9,940,387	3.1%
10	Michigan	9,916,306	3.1%
11	New Jersey	8,938,844	2.8%
12	Virginia	8,328,098	2.6%
13	Washington	7,063,166	2.2%
14	Massachusetts	6,755,124	2.1%
15	Arizona	6,728,783	2.1%
16	Indiana	6,597,880	2.1%
17	Tennessee	6,547,779	2.1%
18	Missouri	6,063,827	1.9%
19	Maryland	5,975,346	1.9%
20	Wisconsin	5,759,432	1.8%
21	Minnesota	5,457,125	1.7%
22	Colorado	5,355,588	1.7%
23	Alabama	4,846,411	1.5%
24	South Carolina	4,829,160	1.5%
25	Louisiana	4,648,990	1.5%
26	Kentucky	4,412,617	1.4%
27	Oregon	3,971,202	1.2%
28	Oklahoma	3,879,610	1.2%
29	Connecticut	3,594,762	1.1%
30	Iowa	3,109,481	1.0%
31	Mississippi	2,993,443	0.9%
32	Arkansas	2,966,835	0.9%
33	Utah	2,944,498	0.9%
34	Kansas	2,902,507	0.9%
35	Nevada	2,838,281	0.9%
36	New Mexico	2,085,567	0.7%
37	Nebraska	1,882,980	0.6%
38	West Virginia	1,848,751	0.6%
39	Idaho	1,634,806	0.5%
40	Hawaii	1,420,257	0.4%
41	Maine	1,330,256	0.4%
42	New Hampshire	1,327,996	0.4%
43	Rhode Island	1,054,907	0.3%
44	Montana	1,023,252	0.3%
45	Delaware	935,968	0.3%
46	South Dakota	853,304	0.3%
47	North Dakota	740,040	0.2%
48	Alaska	737,046	0.2%
49	Vermont	626,767	0.2%
50	Wyoming	584,304	0.2%
	District of Columbia	659,836	0.2%

Source: U.S. Bureau of the Census
"Population Estimates" (December 2015, http://www.census.gov/popest/data/index.html)
*Resident population. Revised estimates of July 1, 2015.

Numerical Population Change: 2014 to 2015

National Total = 2,511,419 Increase*

ALPHA ORDER

RANK	STATE	GAIN/LOSS
29	Alabama	12,568
43	Alaska	1,386
8	Arizona	99,282
32	Arkansas	11,369
3	California	352,527
7	Colorado	100,986
48	Connecticut	(3,876)
34	Delaware	9,966
2	Florida	365,703
4	Georgia	117,728
33	Hawaii	11,346
22	Idaho	20,124
50	Illinois	(22,194)
20	Indiana	21,800
27	Iowa	14,418
36	Kansas	9,134
30	Kentucky	12,475
21	Louisiana	21,734
46	Maine	(928)
19	Maryland	31,055
16	Massachusetts	39,298
38	Michigan	6,270
17	Minnesota	32,469
47	Mississippi	(1,110)
23	Missouri	19,845
35	Montana	9,697
28	Nebraska	13,210
12	Nevada	52,564
40	New Hampshire	2,612
24	New Jersey	19,169
44	New Mexico	(458)
15	New York	46,933
6	North Carolina	102,415
25	North Dakota	16,887
26	Ohio	16,425
18	Oklahoma	31,728
10	Oregon	57,775
37	Pennsylvania	8,736
42	Rhode Island	1,391
9	South Carolina	66,986
39	South Dakota	5,165
13	Tennessee	52,520
1	Texas	490,036
14	Utah	51,421
45	Vermont	(725)
11	Virginia	54,895
5	Washington	107,185
49	West Virginia	(4,623)
31	Wisconsin	11,905
41	Wyoming	1,803

RANK ORDER

RANK	STATE	GAIN/LOSS
1	Texas	490,036
2	Florida	365,703
3	California	352,527
4	Georgia	117,728
5	Washington	107,185
6	North Carolina	102,415
7	Colorado	100,986
8	Arizona	99,282
9	South Carolina	66,986
10	Oregon	57,775
11	Virginia	54,895
12	Nevada	52,564
13	Tennessee	52,520
14	Utah	51,421
15	New York	46,933
16	Massachusetts	39,298
17	Minnesota	32,469
18	Oklahoma	31,728
19	Maryland	31,055
20	Indiana	21,800
21	Louisiana	21,734
22	Idaho	20,124
23	Missouri	19,845
24	New Jersey	19,169
25	North Dakota	16,887
26	Ohio	16,425
27	Iowa	14,418
28	Nebraska	13,210
29	Alabama	12,568
30	Kentucky	12,475
31	Wisconsin	11,905
32	Arkansas	11,369
33	Hawaii	11,346
34	Delaware	9,966
35	Montana	9,697
36	Kansas	9,134
37	Pennsylvania	8,736
38	Michigan	6,270
39	South Dakota	5,165
40	New Hampshire	2,612
41	Wyoming	1,803
42	Rhode Island	1,391
43	Alaska	1,386
44	New Mexico	(458)
45	Vermont	(725)
46	Maine	(928)
47	Mississippi	(1,110)
48	Connecticut	(3,876)
49	West Virginia	(4,623)
50	Illinois	(22,194)
	District of Columbia	12,392

Source: CQ Press using data from U.S. Bureau of the Census
"Population Estimates" (December 2015, http://www.census.gov/popest/data/index.html)
*Resident population from July 1, 2014 to July 1, 2015.

Percent Change in Population: 2014 to 2015

National Percent Change = 0.8% Increase*

ALPHA ORDER

RANK	STATE	PERCENT CHANGE
29	Alabama	0.3
35	Alaska	0.2
7	Arizona	1.5
28	Arkansas	0.4
15	California	0.9
2	Colorado	1.9
46	Connecticut	(0.1)
13	Delaware	1.1
4	Florida	1.8
11	Georgia	1.2
17	Hawaii	0.8
11	Idaho	1.2
49	Illinois	(0.2)
29	Indiana	0.3
25	Iowa	0.5
29	Kansas	0.3
29	Kentucky	0.3
25	Louisiana	0.5
46	Maine	(0.1)
25	Maryland	0.5
22	Massachusetts	0.6
40	Michigan	0.1
22	Minnesota	0.6
44	Mississippi	0.0
29	Missouri	0.3
15	Montana	0.9
20	Nebraska	0.7
2	Nevada	1.9
35	New Hampshire	0.2
35	New Jersey	0.2
44	New Mexico	0.0
35	New York	0.2
14	North Carolina	1.0
1	North Dakota	2.3
40	Ohio	0.1
17	Oklahoma	0.8
7	Oregon	1.5
40	Pennsylvania	0.1
40	Rhode Island	0.1
10	South Carolina	1.4
22	South Dakota	0.6
17	Tennessee	0.8
4	Texas	1.8
6	Utah	1.7
46	Vermont	(0.1)
20	Virginia	0.7
7	Washington	1.5
50	West Virginia	(0.3)
35	Wisconsin	0.2
29	Wyoming	0.3

RANK ORDER

RANK	STATE	PERCENT CHANGE
1	North Dakota	2.3
2	Colorado	1.9
2	Nevada	1.9
4	Florida	1.8
4	Texas	1.8
6	Utah	1.7
7	Arizona	1.5
7	Oregon	1.5
7	Washington	1.5
10	South Carolina	1.4
11	Georgia	1.2
11	Idaho	1.2
13	Delaware	1.1
14	North Carolina	1.0
15	California	0.9
15	Montana	0.9
17	Hawaii	0.8
17	Oklahoma	0.8
17	Tennessee	0.8
20	Nebraska	0.7
20	Virginia	0.7
22	Massachusetts	0.6
22	Minnesota	0.6
22	South Dakota	0.6
25	Iowa	0.5
25	Louisiana	0.5
25	Maryland	0.5
28	Arkansas	0.4
29	Alabama	0.3
29	Indiana	0.3
29	Kansas	0.3
29	Kentucky	0.3
29	Missouri	0.3
29	Wyoming	0.3
35	Alaska	0.2
35	New Hampshire	0.2
35	New Jersey	0.2
35	New York	0.2
35	Wisconsin	0.2
40	Michigan	0.1
40	Ohio	0.1
40	Pennsylvania	0.1
40	Rhode Island	0.1
44	Mississippi	0.0
44	New Mexico	0.0
46	Connecticut	(0.1)
46	Maine	(0.1)
46	Vermont	(0.1)
49	Illinois	(0.2)
50	West Virginia	(0.3)
	District of Columbia	1.9

Source: CQ Press using data from U.S. Bureau of the Census
"Population Estimates" (December 2015, http://www.census.gov/popest/data/index.html)
*Resident population from July 1, 2014 to July 1, 2015.

Population in 2010 Census

National Total = 308,745,538*

ALPHA ORDER

RANK	STATE	POPULATION	% of USA
23	Alabama	4,779,736	1.5%
47	Alaska	710,231	0.2%
16	Arizona	6,392,017	2.1%
32	Arkansas	2,915,918	0.9%
1	California	37,253,956	12.1%
22	Colorado	5,029,196	1.6%
29	Connecticut	3,574,097	1.2%
45	Delaware	897,934	0.3%
4	Florida	18,801,310	6.1%
9	Georgia	9,687,653	3.1%
40	Hawaii	1,360,301	0.4%
39	Idaho	1,567,582	0.5%
5	Illinois	12,830,632	4.2%
15	Indiana	6,483,802	2.1%
30	Iowa	3,046,355	1.0%
33	Kansas	2,853,118	0.9%
26	Kentucky	4,339,367	1.4%
25	Louisiana	4,533,372	1.5%
41	Maine	1,328,361	0.4%
19	Maryland	5,773,552	1.9%
14	Massachusetts	6,547,629	2.1%
8	Michigan	9,883,640	3.2%
21	Minnesota	5,303,925	1.7%
31	Mississippi	2,967,297	1.0%
18	Missouri	5,988,927	1.9%
44	Montana	989,415	0.3%
38	Nebraska	1,826,341	0.6%
35	Nevada	2,700,551	0.9%
42	New Hampshire	1,316,470	0.4%
11	New Jersey	8,791,894	2.8%
36	New Mexico	2,059,179	0.7%
3	New York	19,378,102	6.3%
10	North Carolina	9,535,483	3.1%
48	North Dakota	672,591	0.2%
7	Ohio	11,536,504	3.7%
28	Oklahoma	3,751,351	1.2%
27	Oregon	3,831,074	1.2%
6	Pennsylvania	12,702,379	4.1%
43	Rhode Island	1,052,567	0.3%
24	South Carolina	4,625,364	1.5%
46	South Dakota	814,180	0.3%
17	Tennessee	6,346,105	2.1%
2	Texas	25,145,561	8.1%
34	Utah	2,763,885	0.9%
49	Vermont	625,741	0.2%
12	Virginia	8,001,024	2.6%
13	Washington	6,724,540	2.2%
37	West Virginia	1,852,994	0.6%
20	Wisconsin	5,686,986	1.8%
50	Wyoming	563,626	0.2%

RANK ORDER

RANK	STATE	POPULATION	% of USA
1	California	37,253,956	12.1%
2	Texas	25,145,561	8.1%
3	New York	19,378,102	6.3%
4	Florida	18,801,310	6.1%
5	Illinois	12,830,632	4.2%
6	Pennsylvania	12,702,379	4.1%
7	Ohio	11,536,504	3.7%
8	Michigan	9,883,640	3.2%
9	Georgia	9,687,653	3.1%
10	North Carolina	9,535,483	3.1%
11	New Jersey	8,791,894	2.8%
12	Virginia	8,001,024	2.6%
13	Washington	6,724,540	2.2%
14	Massachusetts	6,547,629	2.1%
15	Indiana	6,483,802	2.1%
16	Arizona	6,392,017	2.1%
17	Tennessee	6,346,105	2.1%
18	Missouri	5,988,927	1.9%
19	Maryland	5,773,552	1.9%
20	Wisconsin	5,686,986	1.8%
21	Minnesota	5,303,925	1.7%
22	Colorado	5,029,196	1.6%
23	Alabama	4,779,736	1.5%
24	South Carolina	4,625,364	1.5%
25	Louisiana	4,533,372	1.5%
26	Kentucky	4,339,367	1.4%
27	Oregon	3,831,074	1.2%
28	Oklahoma	3,751,351	1.2%
29	Connecticut	3,574,097	1.2%
30	Iowa	3,046,355	1.0%
31	Mississippi	2,967,297	1.0%
32	Arkansas	2,915,918	0.9%
33	Kansas	2,853,118	0.9%
34	Utah	2,763,885	0.9%
35	Nevada	2,700,551	0.9%
36	New Mexico	2,059,179	0.7%
37	West Virginia	1,852,994	0.6%
38	Nebraska	1,826,341	0.6%
39	Idaho	1,567,582	0.5%
40	Hawaii	1,360,301	0.4%
41	Maine	1,328,361	0.4%
42	New Hampshire	1,316,470	0.4%
43	Rhode Island	1,052,567	0.3%
44	Montana	989,415	0.3%
45	Delaware	897,934	0.3%
46	South Dakota	814,180	0.3%
47	Alaska	710,231	0.2%
48	North Dakota	672,591	0.2%
49	Vermont	625,741	0.2%
50	Wyoming	563,626	0.2%
	District of Columbia	601,723	0.2%

Source: U.S. Bureau of the Census
"First 2010 Census Results" (http://www.census.gov/2010census/news/press-kits/apportionment/apport.html)
*Resident population as of April 2010 Census.

Projected State Population in 2030

National Total = 363,584,435*

ALPHA ORDER

RANK	STATE	POPULATION	% of USA
24	Alabama	4,874,243	1.3%
46	Alaska	867,674	0.2%
10	Arizona	10,712,397	2.9%
32	Arkansas	3,240,208	0.9%
1	California	46,444,861	12.8%
22	Colorado	5,792,357	1.6%
30	Connecticut	3,688,630	1.0%
45	Delaware	1,012,658	0.3%
3	Florida	28,685,769	7.9%
8	Georgia	12,017,838	3.3%
41	Hawaii	1,466,046	0.4%
37	Idaho	1,969,624	0.5%
5	Illinois	13,432,892	3.7%
18	Indiana	6,810,108	1.9%
34	Iowa	2,955,172	0.8%
35	Kansas	2,940,084	0.8%
27	Kentucky	4,554,998	1.3%
26	Louisiana	4,802,633	1.3%
42	Maine	1,411,097	0.4%
16	Maryland	7,022,251	1.9%
17	Massachusetts	7,012,009	1.9%
11	Michigan	10,694,172	2.9%
20	Minnesota	6,306,130	1.7%
33	Mississippi	3,092,410	0.9%
19	Missouri	6,430,173	1.8%
44	Montana	1,044,898	0.3%
38	Nebraska	1,820,247	0.5%
28	Nevada	4,282,102	1.2%
40	New Hampshire	1,646,471	0.5%
13	New Jersey	9,802,440	2.7%
36	New Mexico	2,099,708	0.6%
4	New York	19,477,429	5.4%
7	North Carolina	12,227,739	3.4%
49	North Dakota	606,566	0.2%
9	Ohio	11,550,528	3.2%
29	Oklahoma	3,913,251	1.1%
25	Oregon	4,833,918	1.3%
6	Pennsylvania	12,768,184	3.5%
43	Rhode Island	1,152,941	0.3%
23	South Carolina	5,148,569	1.4%
47	South Dakota	800,462	0.2%
15	Tennessee	7,380,634	2.0%
2	Texas	33,317,744	9.2%
31	Utah	3,485,367	1.0%
48	Vermont	711,867	0.2%
12	Virginia	9,825,019	2.7%
14	Washington	8,624,801	2.4%
39	West Virginia	1,719,959	0.5%
21	Wisconsin	6,150,764	1.7%
50	Wyoming	522,979	0.1%

RANK ORDER

RANK	STATE	POPULATION	% of USA
1	California	46,444,861	12.8%
2	Texas	33,317,744	9.2%
3	Florida	28,685,769	7.9%
4	New York	19,477,429	5.4%
5	Illinois	13,432,892	3.7%
6	Pennsylvania	12,768,184	3.5%
7	North Carolina	12,227,739	3.4%
8	Georgia	12,017,838	3.3%
9	Ohio	11,550,528	3.2%
10	Arizona	10,712,397	2.9%
11	Michigan	10,694,172	2.9%
12	Virginia	9,825,019	2.7%
13	New Jersey	9,802,440	2.7%
14	Washington	8,624,801	2.4%
15	Tennessee	7,380,634	2.0%
16	Maryland	7,022,251	1.9%
17	Massachusetts	7,012,009	1.9%
18	Indiana	6,810,108	1.9%
19	Missouri	6,430,173	1.8%
20	Minnesota	6,306,130	1.7%
21	Wisconsin	6,150,764	1.7%
22	Colorado	5,792,357	1.6%
23	South Carolina	5,148,569	1.4%
24	Alabama	4,874,243	1.3%
25	Oregon	4,833,918	1.3%
26	Louisiana	4,802,633	1.3%
27	Kentucky	4,554,998	1.3%
28	Nevada	4,282,102	1.2%
29	Oklahoma	3,913,251	1.1%
30	Connecticut	3,688,630	1.0%
31	Utah	3,485,367	1.0%
32	Arkansas	3,240,208	0.9%
33	Mississippi	3,092,410	0.9%
34	Iowa	2,955,172	0.8%
35	Kansas	2,940,084	0.8%
36	New Mexico	2,099,708	0.6%
37	Idaho	1,969,624	0.5%
38	Nebraska	1,820,247	0.5%
39	West Virginia	1,719,959	0.5%
40	New Hampshire	1,646,471	0.5%
41	Hawaii	1,466,046	0.4%
42	Maine	1,411,097	0.4%
43	Rhode Island	1,152,941	0.3%
44	Montana	1,044,898	0.3%
45	Delaware	1,012,658	0.3%
46	Alaska	867,674	0.2%
47	South Dakota	800,462	0.2%
48	Vermont	711,867	0.2%
49	North Dakota	606,566	0.2%
50	Wyoming	522,979	0.1%
	District of Columbia	433,414	0.1%

Source: U.S. Bureau of the Census
"State Interim Population Projections: 2004-2030"
(http://www.census.gov/population/www/projections/projectionsagesex.html)
*Based on 2000 Census.

Population per Square Mile in 2015

National Rate = 91.0 Persons per Square Mile*

ALPHA ORDER

RANK	STATE	RATE
27	Alabama	95.9
50	Alaska	1.3
33	Arizona	60.1
34	Arkansas	57.2
11	California	251.3
37	Colorado	52.6
4	Connecticut	741.6
6	Delaware	485.3
8	Florida	378.0
17	Georgia	177.6
13	Hawaii	222.9
44	Idaho	20.0
12	Illinois	231.6
16	Indiana	184.8
36	Iowa	55.9
41	Kansas	35.6
22	Kentucky	112.1
23	Louisiana	108.1
38	Maine	43.1
5	Maryland	618.8
3	Massachusetts	871.1
18	Michigan	175.5
30	Minnesota	68.9
32	Mississippi	63.8
28	Missouri	88.5
48	Montana	7.1
43	Nebraska	24.7
42	Nevada	26.3
21	New Hampshire	148.6
1	New Jersey	1,218.1
45	New Mexico	17.2
7	New York	420.1
15	North Carolina	206.6
47	North Dakota	11.0
10	Ohio	284.2
35	Oklahoma	57.0
39	Oregon	42.0
9	Pennsylvania	286.1
2	Rhode Island	1,021.6
19	South Carolina	162.9
46	South Dakota	11.3
20	Tennessee	160.1
26	Texas	105.2
40	Utah	36.5
31	Vermont	67.9
14	Virginia	212.3
24	Washington	107.9
29	West Virginia	76.7
25	Wisconsin	106.6
49	Wyoming	6.0

RANK ORDER

RANK	STATE	RATE
1	New Jersey	1,218.1
2	Rhode Island	1,021.6
3	Massachusetts	871.1
4	Connecticut	741.6
5	Maryland	618.8
6	Delaware	485.3
7	New York	420.1
8	Florida	378.0
9	Pennsylvania	286.1
10	Ohio	284.2
11	California	251.3
12	Illinois	231.6
13	Hawaii	222.9
14	Virginia	212.3
15	North Carolina	206.6
16	Indiana	184.8
17	Georgia	177.6
18	Michigan	175.5
19	South Carolina	162.9
20	Tennessee	160.1
21	New Hampshire	148.6
22	Kentucky	112.1
23	Louisiana	108.1
24	Washington	107.9
25	Wisconsin	106.6
26	Texas	105.2
27	Alabama	95.9
28	Missouri	88.5
29	West Virginia	76.7
30	Minnesota	68.9
31	Vermont	67.9
32	Mississippi	63.8
33	Arizona	60.1
34	Arkansas	57.2
35	Oklahoma	57.0
36	Iowa	55.9
37	Colorado	52.6
38	Maine	43.1
39	Oregon	42.0
40	Utah	36.5
41	Kansas	35.6
42	Nevada	26.3
43	Nebraska	24.7
44	Idaho	20.0
45	New Mexico	17.2
46	South Dakota	11.3
47	North Dakota	11.0
48	Montana	7.1
49	Wyoming	6.0
50	Alaska	1.3
	District of Columbia	11,020.1

Source: CQ Press using data from U.S. Bureau of the Census
"Population Estimates" (December 2015, http://www.census.gov/popest/data/index.html)
*Resident population. Based on land area of states.

Male Population in 2014

National Total = 156,936,487 Males

ALPHA ORDER

RANK	STATE	MALES	% of USA
23	Alabama	2,349,967	1.5%
47	Alaska	387,296	0.2%
14	Arizona	3,343,847	2.1%
32	Arkansas	1,457,316	0.9%
1	California	19,268,904	12.3%
22	Colorado	2,691,159	1.7%
29	Connecticut	1,754,549	1.1%
45	Delaware	452,689	0.3%
3	Florida	9,723,286	6.2%
8	Georgia	4,926,987	3.1%
40	Hawaii	718,099	0.5%
39	Idaho	818,496	0.5%
5	Illinois	6,320,886	4.0%
16	Indiana	3,249,444	2.1%
30	Iowa	1,543,045	1.0%
34	Kansas	1,447,355	0.9%
26	Kentucky	2,173,158	1.4%
25	Louisiana	2,273,939	1.4%
42	Maine	651,271	0.4%
19	Maryland	2,896,418	1.8%
15	Massachusetts	3,270,824	2.1%
9	Michigan	4,868,463	3.1%
21	Minnesota	2,712,041	1.7%
33	Mississippi	1,454,556	0.9%
18	Missouri	2,974,222	1.9%
43	Montana	514,123	0.3%
37	Nebraska	936,863	0.6%
35	Nevada	1,426,793	0.9%
41	New Hampshire	655,469	0.4%
11	New Jersey	4,361,952	2.8%
36	New Mexico	1,032,882	0.7%
4	New York	9,581,261	6.1%
10	North Carolina	4,844,593	3.1%
48	North Dakota	379,019	0.2%
7	Ohio	5,674,772	3.6%
28	Oklahoma	1,920,148	1.2%
27	Oregon	1,964,100	1.3%
6	Pennsylvania	6,253,817	4.0%
44	Rhode Island	511,363	0.3%
24	South Carolina	2,349,394	1.5%
46	South Dakota	429,313	0.3%
17	Tennessee	3,192,180	2.0%
2	Texas	13,382,386	8.5%
31	Utah	1,479,750	0.9%
49	Vermont	308,849	0.2%
12	Virginia	4,095,244	2.6%
13	Washington	3,529,935	2.2%
38	West Virginia	913,915	0.6%
20	Wisconsin	2,859,507	1.8%
50	Wyoming	298,042	0.2%

RANK ORDER

RANK	STATE	MALES	% of USA
1	California	19,268,904	12.3%
2	Texas	13,382,386	8.5%
3	Florida	9,723,286	6.2%
4	New York	9,581,261	6.1%
5	Illinois	6,320,886	4.0%
6	Pennsylvania	6,253,817	4.0%
7	Ohio	5,674,772	3.6%
8	Georgia	4,926,987	3.1%
9	Michigan	4,868,463	3.1%
10	North Carolina	4,844,593	3.1%
11	New Jersey	4,361,952	2.8%
12	Virginia	4,095,244	2.6%
13	Washington	3,529,935	2.2%
14	Arizona	3,343,847	2.1%
15	Massachusetts	3,270,824	2.1%
16	Indiana	3,249,444	2.1%
17	Tennessee	3,192,180	2.0%
18	Missouri	2,974,222	1.9%
19	Maryland	2,896,418	1.8%
20	Wisconsin	2,859,507	1.8%
21	Minnesota	2,712,041	1.7%
22	Colorado	2,691,159	1.7%
23	Alabama	2,349,967	1.5%
24	South Carolina	2,349,394	1.5%
25	Louisiana	2,273,939	1.4%
26	Kentucky	2,173,158	1.4%
27	Oregon	1,964,100	1.3%
28	Oklahoma	1,920,148	1.2%
29	Connecticut	1,754,549	1.1%
30	Iowa	1,543,045	1.0%
31	Utah	1,479,750	0.9%
32	Arkansas	1,457,316	0.9%
33	Mississippi	1,454,556	0.9%
34	Kansas	1,447,355	0.9%
35	Nevada	1,426,793	0.9%
36	New Mexico	1,032,882	0.7%
37	Nebraska	936,863	0.6%
38	West Virginia	913,915	0.6%
39	Idaho	818,496	0.5%
40	Hawaii	718,099	0.5%
41	New Hampshire	655,469	0.4%
42	Maine	651,271	0.4%
43	Montana	514,123	0.3%
44	Rhode Island	511,363	0.3%
45	Delaware	452,689	0.3%
46	South Dakota	429,313	0.3%
47	Alaska	387,296	0.2%
48	North Dakota	379,019	0.2%
49	Vermont	308,849	0.2%
50	Wyoming	298,042	0.2%
	District of Columbia	312,600	0.2%

Source: U.S. Bureau of the Census
"State Characteristics: Vintage 2014" (http://www.census.gov/popest/data/state/asrh/2014/index.html)

Female Population in 2014

National Total = 161,920,569 Females

ALPHA ORDER

RANK	STATE	FEMALES	% of USA
23	Alabama	2,499,410	1.5%
48	Alaska	349,436	0.2%
15	Arizona	3,387,637	2.1%
32	Arkansas	1,509,053	0.9%
1	California	19,533,596	12.1%
22	Colorado	2,664,707	1.6%
29	Connecticut	1,842,128	1.1%
45	Delaware	482,925	0.3%
3	Florida	10,170,011	6.3%
8	Georgia	5,170,356	3.2%
40	Hawaii	701,462	0.4%
39	Idaho	815,968	0.5%
5	Illinois	6,559,694	4.1%
17	Indiana	3,347,411	2.1%
30	Iowa	1,564,081	1.0%
34	Kansas	1,456,666	0.9%
26	Kentucky	2,240,299	1.4%
25	Louisiana	2,375,737	1.5%
41	Maine	678,818	0.4%
19	Maryland	3,079,989	1.9%
14	Massachusetts	3,474,584	2.1%
10	Michigan	5,041,414	3.1%
21	Minnesota	2,745,132	1.7%
31	Mississippi	1,539,523	1.0%
18	Missouri	3,089,367	1.9%
44	Montana	509,456	0.3%
37	Nebraska	944,640	0.6%
35	Nevada	1,412,306	0.9%
42	New Hampshire	671,344	0.4%
11	New Jersey	4,576,223	2.8%
36	New Mexico	1,052,690	0.7%
4	New York	10,164,966	6.3%
9	North Carolina	5,099,371	3.1%
47	North Dakota	360,463	0.2%
7	Ohio	5,919,391	3.7%
28	Oklahoma	1,957,903	1.2%
27	Oregon	2,006,139	1.2%
6	Pennsylvania	6,533,392	4.0%
43	Rhode Island	543,810	0.3%
24	South Carolina	2,483,088	1.5%
46	South Dakota	423,862	0.3%
16	Tennessee	3,357,172	2.1%
2	Texas	13,574,572	8.4%
33	Utah	1,463,152	0.9%
49	Vermont	317,713	0.2%
12	Virginia	4,231,045	2.6%
13	Washington	3,531,595	2.2%
38	West Virginia	936,411	0.6%
20	Wisconsin	2,898,057	1.8%
50	Wyoming	286,111	0.2%

RANK ORDER

RANK	STATE	FEMALES	% of USA
1	California	19,533,596	12.1%
2	Texas	13,574,572	8.4%
3	Florida	10,170,011	6.3%
4	New York	10,164,966	6.3%
5	Illinois	6,559,694	4.1%
6	Pennsylvania	6,533,392	4.0%
7	Ohio	5,919,391	3.7%
8	Georgia	5,170,356	3.2%
9	North Carolina	5,099,371	3.1%
10	Michigan	5,041,414	3.1%
11	New Jersey	4,576,223	2.8%
12	Virginia	4,231,045	2.6%
13	Washington	3,531,595	2.2%
14	Massachusetts	3,474,584	2.1%
15	Arizona	3,387,637	2.1%
16	Tennessee	3,357,172	2.1%
17	Indiana	3,347,411	2.1%
18	Missouri	3,089,367	1.9%
19	Maryland	3,079,989	1.9%
20	Wisconsin	2,898,057	1.8%
21	Minnesota	2,745,132	1.7%
22	Colorado	2,664,707	1.6%
23	Alabama	2,499,410	1.5%
24	South Carolina	2,483,088	1.5%
25	Louisiana	2,375,737	1.5%
26	Kentucky	2,240,299	1.4%
27	Oregon	2,006,139	1.2%
28	Oklahoma	1,957,903	1.2%
29	Connecticut	1,842,128	1.1%
30	Iowa	1,564,081	1.0%
31	Mississippi	1,539,523	1.0%
32	Arkansas	1,509,053	0.9%
33	Utah	1,463,152	0.9%
34	Kansas	1,456,666	0.9%
35	Nevada	1,412,306	0.9%
36	New Mexico	1,052,690	0.7%
37	Nebraska	944,640	0.6%
38	West Virginia	936,411	0.6%
39	Idaho	815,968	0.5%
40	Hawaii	701,462	0.4%
41	Maine	678,818	0.4%
42	New Hampshire	671,344	0.4%
43	Rhode Island	543,810	0.3%
44	Montana	509,456	0.3%
45	Delaware	482,925	0.3%
46	South Dakota	423,862	0.3%
47	North Dakota	360,463	0.2%
48	Alaska	349,436	0.2%
49	Vermont	317,713	0.2%
50	Wyoming	286,111	0.2%
	District of Columbia	346,293	0.2%

Source: U.S. Bureau of the Census
"State Characteristics: Vintage 2014" (http://www.census.gov/popest/data/state/asrh/2014/index.html)

Male to Female Ratio in 2014

National Ratio = 96.9 Males per 100 Females

ALPHA ORDER

RANK	STATE	RATIO
47	Alabama	94.0
1	Alaska	110.8
15	Arizona	98.7
29	Arkansas	96.6
18	California	98.6
7	Colorado	101.0
40	Connecticut	95.2
50	Delaware	93.7
37	Florida	95.6
38	Georgia	95.3
4	Hawaii	102.4
10	Idaho	100.3
31	Illinois	96.4
26	Indiana	97.1
15	Iowa	98.7
12	Kansas	99.4
27	Kentucky	97.0
35	Louisiana	95.7
33	Maine	95.9
47	Maryland	94.0
46	Massachusetts	94.1
29	Michigan	96.6
14	Minnesota	98.8
44	Mississippi	94.5
32	Missouri	96.3
9	Montana	100.9
13	Nebraska	99.2
7	Nevada	101.0
23	New Hampshire	97.6
38	New Jersey	95.3
20	New Mexico	98.1
45	New York	94.3
42	North Carolina	95.0
2	North Dakota	105.1
33	Ohio	95.9
20	Oklahoma	98.1
22	Oregon	97.9
35	Pennsylvania	95.7
47	Rhode Island	94.0
43	South Carolina	94.6
5	South Dakota	101.3
41	Tennessee	95.1
18	Texas	98.6
6	Utah	101.1
25	Vermont	97.2
28	Virginia	96.8
11	Washington	100.0
23	West Virginia	97.6
15	Wisconsin	98.7
3	Wyoming	104.2

RANK ORDER

RANK	STATE	RATIO
1	Alaska	110.8
2	North Dakota	105.1
3	Wyoming	104.2
4	Hawaii	102.4
5	South Dakota	101.3
6	Utah	101.1
7	Colorado	101.0
7	Nevada	101.0
9	Montana	100.9
10	Idaho	100.3
11	Washington	100.0
12	Kansas	99.4
13	Nebraska	99.2
14	Minnesota	98.8
15	Arizona	98.7
15	Iowa	98.7
15	Wisconsin	98.7
18	California	98.6
18	Texas	98.6
20	New Mexico	98.1
20	Oklahoma	98.1
22	Oregon	97.9
23	New Hampshire	97.6
23	West Virginia	97.6
25	Vermont	97.2
26	Indiana	97.1
27	Kentucky	97.0
28	Virginia	96.8
29	Arkansas	96.6
29	Michigan	96.6
31	Illinois	96.4
32	Missouri	96.3
33	Maine	95.9
33	Ohio	95.9
35	Louisiana	95.7
35	Pennsylvania	95.7
37	Florida	95.6
38	Georgia	95.3
38	New Jersey	95.3
40	Connecticut	95.2
41	Tennessee	95.1
42	North Carolina	95.0
43	South Carolina	94.6
44	Mississippi	94.5
45	New York	94.3
46	Massachusetts	94.1
47	Alabama	94.0
47	Maryland	94.0
47	Rhode Island	94.0
50	Delaware	93.7
	District of Columbia	90.3

Source: CQ Press using data from U.S. Bureau of the Census
"State Characteristics: Vintage 2014" (http://www.census.gov/popest/data/state/asrh/2014/index.html)

White Population in 2014

National Total = 246,660,710*

ALPHA ORDER

RANK	STATE	POPULATION	% of USA
25	Alabama	3,377,605	1.4%
49	Alaska	492,522	0.2%
15	Arizona	5,636,322	2.3%
33	Arkansas	2,364,132	1.0%
1	California	28,395,830	11.5%
20	Colorado	4,699,302	1.9%
28	Connecticut	2,919,746	1.2%
45	Delaware	662,176	0.3%
3	Florida	15,485,874	6.3%
11	Georgia	6,266,166	2.5%
50	Hawaii	378,323	0.2%
39	Idaho	1,528,744	0.6%
6	Illinois	9,984,775	4.0%
14	Indiana	5,678,447	2.3%
30	Iowa	2,860,661	1.2%
32	Kansas	2,521,932	1.0%
22	Kentucky	3,895,463	1.6%
27	Louisiana	2,945,869	1.2%
40	Maine	1,263,864	0.5%
23	Maryland	3,589,555	1.5%
16	Massachusetts	5,574,178	2.3%
8	Michigan	7,915,690	3.2%
21	Minnesota	4,677,716	1.9%
35	Mississippi	1,786,028	0.7%
18	Missouri	5,063,452	2.1%
42	Montana	914,674	0.4%
38	Nebraska	1,682,074	0.7%
34	Nevada	2,163,454	0.9%
41	New Hampshire	1,247,714	0.5%
10	New Jersey	6,526,416	2.6%
37	New Mexico	1,726,182	0.7%
4	New York	13,906,584	5.6%
9	North Carolina	7,108,057	2.9%
46	North Dakota	659,128	0.3%
7	Ohio	9,618,404	3.9%
29	Oklahoma	2,910,952	1.2%
24	Oregon	3,488,798	1.4%
5	Pennsylvania	10,598,587	4.3%
43	Rhode Island	898,297	0.4%
26	South Carolina	3,302,736	1.3%
44	South Dakota	731,359	0.3%
17	Tennessee	5,169,234	2.1%
2	Texas	21,565,643	8.7%
31	Utah	2,689,846	1.1%
47	Vermont	595,181	0.2%
12	Virginia	5,872,210	2.4%
13	Washington	5,699,754	2.3%
36	West Virginia	1,734,220	0.7%
19	Wisconsin	5,057,797	2.1%
48	Wyoming	541,596	0.2%

RANK ORDER

RANK	STATE	POPULATION	% of USA
1	California	28,395,830	11.5%
2	Texas	21,565,643	8.7%
3	Florida	15,485,874	6.3%
4	New York	13,906,584	5.6%
5	Pennsylvania	10,598,587	4.3%
6	Illinois	9,984,775	4.0%
7	Ohio	9,618,404	3.9%
8	Michigan	7,915,690	3.2%
9	North Carolina	7,108,057	2.9%
10	New Jersey	6,526,416	2.6%
11	Georgia	6,266,166	2.5%
12	Virginia	5,872,210	2.4%
13	Washington	5,699,754	2.3%
14	Indiana	5,678,447	2.3%
15	Arizona	5,636,322	2.3%
16	Massachusetts	5,574,178	2.3%
17	Tennessee	5,169,234	2.1%
18	Missouri	5,063,452	2.1%
19	Wisconsin	5,057,797	2.1%
20	Colorado	4,699,302	1.9%
21	Minnesota	4,677,716	1.9%
22	Kentucky	3,895,463	1.6%
23	Maryland	3,589,555	1.5%
24	Oregon	3,488,798	1.4%
25	Alabama	3,377,605	1.4%
26	South Carolina	3,302,736	1.3%
27	Louisiana	2,945,869	1.2%
28	Connecticut	2,919,746	1.2%
29	Oklahoma	2,910,952	1.2%
30	Iowa	2,860,661	1.2%
31	Utah	2,689,846	1.1%
32	Kansas	2,521,932	1.0%
33	Arkansas	2,364,132	1.0%
34	Nevada	2,163,454	0.9%
35	Mississippi	1,786,028	0.7%
36	West Virginia	1,734,220	0.7%
37	New Mexico	1,726,182	0.7%
38	Nebraska	1,682,074	0.7%
39	Idaho	1,528,744	0.6%
40	Maine	1,263,864	0.5%
41	New Hampshire	1,247,714	0.5%
42	Montana	914,674	0.4%
43	Rhode Island	898,297	0.4%
44	South Dakota	731,359	0.3%
45	Delaware	662,176	0.3%
46	North Dakota	659,128	0.3%
47	Vermont	595,181	0.2%
48	Wyoming	541,596	0.2%
49	Alaska	492,522	0.2%
50	Hawaii	378,323	0.2%
	District of Columbia	287,441	0.1%

Source: U.S. Bureau of the Census
"State Characteristics: Vintage 2014" (http://www.census.gov/popest/data/state/asrh/2014/index.html)
*Those who identified themselves as one race. "White" is defined by Census as a person having origins in any of the original peoples of Europe, North Africa, or the Middle East. There are 197,836,231 non-Hispanic whites. Census states "Race is a self-identification data item in which respondents choose the race or races with which they most closely identify."

Percent of Population White in 2014

National Percent = 77.4%*

ALPHA ORDER

RANK	STATE	PERCENT
43	Alabama	69.7
45	Alaska	66.9
21	Arizona	83.7
31	Arkansas	79.7
37	California	73.2
15	Colorado	87.7
27	Connecticut	81.2
40	Delaware	70.8
33	Florida	77.8
47	Georgia	62.1
50	Hawaii	26.7
5	Idaho	93.5
34	Illinois	77.5
17	Indiana	86.1
7	Iowa	92.1
16	Kansas	86.8
12	Kentucky	88.3
46	Louisiana	63.4
1	Maine	95.0
48	Maryland	60.1
26	Massachusetts	82.6
30	Michigan	79.9
18	Minnesota	85.7
49	Mississippi	59.7
22	Missouri	83.5
9	Montana	89.4
9	Nebraska	89.4
35	Nevada	76.2
3	New Hampshire	94.0
38	New Jersey	73.0
25	New Mexico	82.8
42	New York	70.4
39	North Carolina	71.5
11	North Dakota	89.1
23	Ohio	83.0
36	Oklahoma	75.1
13	Oregon	87.9
24	Pennsylvania	82.9
20	Rhode Island	85.1
44	South Carolina	68.3
18	South Dakota	85.7
32	Tennessee	78.9
29	Texas	80.0
8	Utah	91.4
1	Vermont	95.0
41	Virginia	70.5
28	Washington	80.7
4	West Virginia	93.7
14	Wisconsin	87.8
6	Wyoming	92.7

RANK ORDER

RANK	STATE	PERCENT
1	Maine	95.0
1	Vermont	95.0
3	New Hampshire	94.0
4	West Virginia	93.7
5	Idaho	93.5
6	Wyoming	92.7
7	Iowa	92.1
8	Utah	91.4
9	Montana	89.4
9	Nebraska	89.4
11	North Dakota	89.1
12	Kentucky	88.3
13	Oregon	87.9
14	Wisconsin	87.8
15	Colorado	87.7
16	Kansas	86.8
17	Indiana	86.1
18	Minnesota	85.7
18	South Dakota	85.7
20	Rhode Island	85.1
21	Arizona	83.7
22	Missouri	83.5
23	Ohio	83.0
24	Pennsylvania	82.9
25	New Mexico	82.8
26	Massachusetts	82.6
27	Connecticut	81.2
28	Washington	80.7
29	Texas	80.0
30	Michigan	79.9
31	Arkansas	79.7
32	Tennessee	78.9
33	Florida	77.8
34	Illinois	77.5
35	Nevada	76.2
36	Oklahoma	75.1
37	California	73.2
38	New Jersey	73.0
39	North Carolina	71.5
40	Delaware	70.8
41	Virginia	70.5
42	New York	70.4
43	Alabama	69.7
44	South Carolina	68.3
45	Alaska	66.9
46	Louisiana	63.4
47	Georgia	62.1
48	Maryland	60.1
49	Mississippi	59.7
50	Hawaii	26.7
	District of Columbia	43.6

Source: CQ Press using data from U.S. Bureau of the Census
"State Characteristics: Vintage 2014" (http://www.census.gov/popest/data/state/asrh/2014/index.html)
*Those who identified themselves as one race. "White" is defined by Census as a person having origins in any of the original peoples of Europe, North Africa, or the Middle East. Non-Hispanic whites comprise 62.6% of the total population. Census states "Race is a self-identification data item in which respondents choose the race or races with which they most closely identify."

Black Population in 2014

National Total = 42,158,238*

ALPHA ORDER

RANK	STATE	POPULATION	% of USA
16	Alabama	1,293,200	3.1%
42	Alaska	28,820	0.1%
27	Arizona	318,202	0.8%
22	Arkansas	463,360	1.1%
5	California	2,541,367	6.0%
31	Colorado	238,720	0.6%
23	Connecticut	413,814	1.0%
32	Delaware	208,081	0.5%
3	Florida	3,337,159	7.9%
4	Georgia	3,183,784	7.6%
41	Hawaii	34,864	0.1%
47	Idaho	13,507	0.0%
7	Illinois	1,892,255	4.5%
20	Indiana	630,754	1.5%
34	Iowa	106,073	0.3%
33	Kansas	181,546	0.4%
25	Kentucky	363,239	0.9%
10	Louisiana	1,510,676	3.6%
44	Maine	19,149	0.0%
8	Maryland	1,809,294	4.3%
21	Massachusetts	558,072	1.3%
13	Michigan	1,410,458	3.3%
26	Minnesota	320,423	0.8%
17	Mississippi	1,122,938	2.7%
19	Missouri	714,595	1.7%
50	Montana	6,108	0.0%
35	Nebraska	92,289	0.2%
30	Nevada	258,492	0.6%
43	New Hampshire	19,686	0.0%
15	New Jersey	1,321,105	3.1%
39	New Mexico	52,666	0.1%
1	New York	3,479,242	8.3%
6	North Carolina	2,196,390	5.2%
46	North Dakota	15,555	0.0%
12	Ohio	1,463,594	3.5%
28	Oklahoma	299,574	0.7%
37	Oregon	80,962	0.2%
11	Pennsylvania	1,484,746	3.5%
36	Rhode Island	81,149	0.2%
14	South Carolina	1,342,308	3.2%
45	South Dakota	15,971	0.0%
18	Tennessee	1,119,119	2.7%
2	Texas	3,364,416	8.0%
40	Utah	39,655	0.1%
49	Vermont	7,709	0.0%
9	Virginia	1,638,835	3.9%
29	Washington	286,779	0.7%
38	West Virginia	67,073	0.2%
24	Wisconsin	378,526	0.9%
48	Wyoming	9,112	0.0%

RANK ORDER

RANK	STATE	POPULATION	% of USA
1	New York	3,479,242	8.3%
2	Texas	3,364,416	8.0%
3	Florida	3,337,159	7.9%
4	Georgia	3,183,784	7.6%
5	California	2,541,367	6.0%
6	North Carolina	2,196,390	5.2%
7	Illinois	1,892,255	4.5%
8	Maryland	1,809,294	4.3%
9	Virginia	1,638,835	3.9%
10	Louisiana	1,510,676	3.6%
11	Pennsylvania	1,484,746	3.5%
12	Ohio	1,463,594	3.5%
13	Michigan	1,410,458	3.3%
14	South Carolina	1,342,308	3.2%
15	New Jersey	1,321,105	3.1%
16	Alabama	1,293,200	3.1%
17	Mississippi	1,122,938	2.7%
18	Tennessee	1,119,119	2.7%
19	Missouri	714,595	1.7%
20	Indiana	630,754	1.5%
21	Massachusetts	558,072	1.3%
22	Arkansas	463,360	1.1%
23	Connecticut	413,814	1.0%
24	Wisconsin	378,526	0.9%
25	Kentucky	363,239	0.9%
26	Minnesota	320,423	0.8%
27	Arizona	318,202	0.8%
28	Oklahoma	299,574	0.7%
29	Washington	286,779	0.7%
30	Nevada	258,492	0.6%
31	Colorado	238,720	0.6%
32	Delaware	208,081	0.5%
33	Kansas	181,546	0.4%
34	Iowa	106,073	0.3%
35	Nebraska	92,289	0.2%
36	Rhode Island	81,149	0.2%
37	Oregon	80,962	0.2%
38	West Virginia	67,073	0.2%
39	New Mexico	52,666	0.1%
40	Utah	39,655	0.1%
41	Hawaii	34,864	0.1%
42	Alaska	28,820	0.1%
43	New Hampshire	19,686	0.0%
44	Maine	19,149	0.0%
45	South Dakota	15,971	0.0%
46	North Dakota	15,555	0.0%
47	Idaho	13,507	0.0%
48	Wyoming	9,112	0.0%
49	Vermont	7,709	0.0%
50	Montana	6,108	0.0%
	District of Columbia	322,827	0.8%

Source: U.S. Bureau of the Census
"State Characteristics: Vintage 2014" (http://www.census.gov/popest/data/state/asrh/2014/index.html)
*Those who identified themselves as one race. "Black" is defined by Census as a person having origins in any of the Black racial groups of Africa. Census states "Race is a self-identification data item in which respondents choose the race or races with which they most closely identify."

Percent of Population Black in 2014

National Percent = 13.2%*

ALPHA ORDER

RANK	STATE	PERCENT
6	Alabama	26.7
36	Alaska	3.9
33	Arizona	4.7
13	Arkansas	15.6
29	California	6.5
34	Colorado	4.5
21	Connecticut	11.5
7	Delaware	22.2
12	Florida	16.8
3	Georgia	31.5
39	Hawaii	2.5
49	Idaho	0.8
15	Illinois	14.7
22	Indiana	9.6
38	Iowa	3.4
30	Kansas	6.3
25	Kentucky	8.2
2	Louisiana	32.5
46	Maine	1.4
4	Maryland	30.3
24	Massachusetts	8.3
16	Michigan	14.2
31	Minnesota	5.9
1	Mississippi	37.5
19	Missouri	11.8
50	Montana	0.6
32	Nebraska	4.9
23	Nevada	9.1
45	New Hampshire	1.5
14	New Jersey	14.8
39	New Mexico	2.5
10	New York	17.6
8	North Carolina	22.1
41	North Dakota	2.1
17	Ohio	12.6
26	Oklahoma	7.7
42	Oregon	2.0
20	Pennsylvania	11.6
26	Rhode Island	7.7
5	South Carolina	27.8
43	South Dakota	1.9
11	Tennessee	17.1
18	Texas	12.5
47	Utah	1.3
48	Vermont	1.2
9	Virginia	19.7
35	Washington	4.1
37	West Virginia	3.6
28	Wisconsin	6.6
44	Wyoming	1.6

RANK ORDER

RANK	STATE	PERCENT
1	Mississippi	37.5
2	Louisiana	32.5
3	Georgia	31.5
4	Maryland	30.3
5	South Carolina	27.8
6	Alabama	26.7
7	Delaware	22.2
8	North Carolina	22.1
9	Virginia	19.7
10	New York	17.6
11	Tennessee	17.1
12	Florida	16.8
13	Arkansas	15.6
14	New Jersey	14.8
15	Illinois	14.7
16	Michigan	14.2
17	Ohio	12.6
18	Texas	12.5
19	Missouri	11.8
20	Pennsylvania	11.6
21	Connecticut	11.5
22	Indiana	9.6
23	Nevada	9.1
24	Massachusetts	8.3
25	Kentucky	8.2
26	Oklahoma	7.7
26	Rhode Island	7.7
28	Wisconsin	6.6
29	California	6.5
30	Kansas	6.3
31	Minnesota	5.9
32	Nebraska	4.9
33	Arizona	4.7
34	Colorado	4.5
35	Washington	4.1
36	Alaska	3.9
37	West Virginia	3.6
38	Iowa	3.4
39	Hawaii	2.5
39	New Mexico	2.5
41	North Dakota	2.1
42	Oregon	2.0
43	South Dakota	1.9
44	Wyoming	1.6
45	New Hampshire	1.5
46	Maine	1.4
47	Utah	1.3
48	Vermont	1.2
49	Idaho	0.8
50	Montana	0.6
	District of Columbia	49.0

Source: CQ Press using data from U.S. Bureau of the Census
"State Characteristics: Vintage 2014" (http://www.census.gov/popest/data/state/asrh/2014/index.html)
*Those who identified themselves as one race. "Black" is defined by Census as a person having origins in any of the Black racial groups of Africa. Census states "Race is a self-identification data item in which respondents choose the race or races with which they most closely identify."

Hispanic Population in 2014

National Total = 55,387,539*

ALPHA ORDER

RANK	STATE	POPULATION	% of USA
33	Alabama	200,664	0.4%
43	Alaska	50,178	0.1%
6	Arizona	2,056,455	3.7%
32	Arkansas	208,821	0.4%
1	California	14,988,768	27.1%
8	Colorado	1,135,109	2.0%
18	Connecticut	541,152	1.0%
41	Delaware	83,325	0.2%
3	Florida	4,788,869	8.6%
10	Georgia	935,279	1.7%
39	Hawaii	143,239	0.3%
34	Idaho	196,502	0.4%
5	Illinois	2,152,974	3.9%
21	Indiana	432,305	0.8%
36	Iowa	173,594	0.3%
26	Kansas	329,627	0.6%
37	Kentucky	149,006	0.3%
31	Louisiana	224,867	0.4%
49	Maine	20,165	0.0%
17	Maryland	557,371	1.0%
16	Massachusetts	731,206	1.3%
20	Michigan	476,285	0.9%
28	Minnesota	277,009	0.5%
40	Mississippi	88,937	0.2%
30	Missouri	240,222	0.4%
45	Montana	35,362	0.1%
35	Nebraska	191,325	0.3%
14	Nevada	790,034	1.4%
44	New Hampshire	43,544	0.1%
7	New Jersey	1,729,172	3.1%
9	New Mexico	994,151	1.8%
4	New York	3,672,791	6.6%
11	North Carolina	894,276	1.6%
48	North Dakota	23,439	0.0%
22	Ohio	403,190	0.7%
24	Oklahoma	381,531	0.7%
19	Oregon	496,789	0.9%
13	Pennsylvania	838,823	1.5%
38	Rhode Island	148,095	0.3%
29	South Carolina	261,752	0.5%
46	South Dakota	30,537	0.1%
27	Tennessee	328,979	0.6%
2	Texas	10,411,340	18.8%
23	Utah	398,760	0.7%
50	Vermont	11,110	0.0%
15	Virginia	737,316	1.3%
12	Washington	858,779	1.6%
47	West Virginia	26,847	0.0%
25	Wisconsin	372,248	0.7%
42	Wyoming	57,065	0.1%

RANK ORDER

RANK	STATE	POPULATION	% of USA
1	California	14,988,768	27.1%
2	Texas	10,411,340	18.8%
3	Florida	4,788,869	8.6%
4	New York	3,672,791	6.6%
5	Illinois	2,152,974	3.9%
6	Arizona	2,056,455	3.7%
7	New Jersey	1,729,172	3.1%
8	Colorado	1,135,109	2.0%
9	New Mexico	994,151	1.8%
10	Georgia	935,279	1.7%
11	North Carolina	894,276	1.6%
12	Washington	858,779	1.6%
13	Pennsylvania	838,823	1.5%
14	Nevada	790,034	1.4%
15	Virginia	737,316	1.3%
16	Massachusetts	731,206	1.3%
17	Maryland	557,371	1.0%
18	Connecticut	541,152	1.0%
19	Oregon	496,789	0.9%
20	Michigan	476,285	0.9%
21	Indiana	432,305	0.8%
22	Ohio	403,190	0.7%
23	Utah	398,760	0.7%
24	Oklahoma	381,531	0.7%
25	Wisconsin	372,248	0.7%
26	Kansas	329,627	0.6%
27	Tennessee	328,979	0.6%
28	Minnesota	277,009	0.5%
29	South Carolina	261,752	0.5%
30	Missouri	240,222	0.4%
31	Louisiana	224,867	0.4%
32	Arkansas	208,821	0.4%
33	Alabama	200,664	0.4%
34	Idaho	196,502	0.4%
35	Nebraska	191,325	0.3%
36	Iowa	173,594	0.3%
37	Kentucky	149,006	0.3%
38	Rhode Island	148,095	0.3%
39	Hawaii	143,239	0.3%
40	Mississippi	88,937	0.2%
41	Delaware	83,325	0.2%
42	Wyoming	57,065	0.1%
43	Alaska	50,178	0.1%
44	New Hampshire	43,544	0.1%
45	Montana	35,362	0.1%
46	South Dakota	30,537	0.1%
47	West Virginia	26,847	0.0%
48	North Dakota	23,439	0.0%
49	Maine	20,165	0.0%
50	Vermont	11,110	0.0%
	District of Columbia	68,355	0.1%

Source: U.S. Bureau of the Census
"State Characteristics: Vintage 2014" (http://www.census.gov/popest/data/state/asrh/2014/index.html)
*Persons of Hispanic origin may be of any race. Census states "Race is a self-identification data item in which respondents choose the race or races with which they most closely identify."

Percent of Population Hispanic in 2014

National Percent = 17.4%*

ALPHA ORDER

RANK	STATE	PERCENT
39	Alabama	4.1
29	Alaska	6.8
4	Arizona	30.5
28	Arkansas	7.0
2	California	38.6
7	Colorado	21.2
11	Connecticut	15.0
26	Delaware	8.9
6	Florida	24.1
23	Georgia	9.3
20	Hawaii	10.1
16	Idaho	12.0
10	Illinois	16.7
30	Indiana	6.6
33	Iowa	5.6
17	Kansas	11.4
44	Kentucky	3.4
37	Louisiana	4.8
49	Maine	1.5
23	Maryland	9.3
18	Massachusetts	10.8
37	Michigan	4.8
35	Minnesota	5.1
47	Mississippi	3.0
40	Missouri	4.0
42	Montana	3.5
19	Nebraska	10.2
5	Nevada	27.8
45	New Hampshire	3.3
8	New Jersey	19.3
1	New Mexico	47.7
9	New York	18.6
25	North Carolina	9.0
46	North Dakota	3.2
42	Ohio	3.5
21	Oklahoma	9.8
14	Oregon	12.5
30	Pennsylvania	6.6
12	Rhode Island	14.0
34	South Carolina	5.4
41	South Dakota	3.6
36	Tennessee	5.0
2	Texas	38.6
13	Utah	13.5
48	Vermont	1.8
26	Virginia	8.9
15	Washington	12.2
49	West Virginia	1.5
32	Wisconsin	6.5
21	Wyoming	9.8

RANK ORDER

RANK	STATE	PERCENT
1	New Mexico	47.7
2	California	38.6
2	Texas	38.6
4	Arizona	30.5
5	Nevada	27.8
6	Florida	24.1
7	Colorado	21.2
8	New Jersey	19.3
9	New York	18.6
10	Illinois	16.7
11	Connecticut	15.0
12	Rhode Island	14.0
13	Utah	13.5
14	Oregon	12.5
15	Washington	12.2
16	Idaho	12.0
17	Kansas	11.4
18	Massachusetts	10.8
19	Nebraska	10.2
20	Hawaii	10.1
21	Oklahoma	9.8
21	Wyoming	9.8
23	Georgia	9.3
23	Maryland	9.3
25	North Carolina	9.0
26	Delaware	8.9
26	Virginia	8.9
28	Arkansas	7.0
29	Alaska	6.8
30	Indiana	6.6
30	Pennsylvania	6.6
32	Wisconsin	6.5
33	Iowa	5.6
34	South Carolina	5.4
35	Minnesota	5.1
36	Tennessee	5.0
37	Louisiana	4.8
37	Michigan	4.8
39	Alabama	4.1
40	Missouri	4.0
41	South Dakota	3.6
42	Montana	3.5
42	Ohio	3.5
44	Kentucky	3.4
45	New Hampshire	3.3
46	North Dakota	3.2
47	Mississippi	3.0
48	Vermont	1.8
49	Maine	1.5
49	West Virginia	1.5

District of Columbia 10.4

Source: CQ Press using data from U.S. Bureau of the Census
"State Characteristics: Vintage 2014" (http://www.census.gov/popest/data/state/asrh/2014/index.html)
*Persons of Hispanic origin may be of any race. Census states "Race is a self-identification data item in which respondents choose the race or races with which they most closely identify."

Asian Population in 2014

National Total = 17,339,053*

ALPHA ORDER

RANK	STATE	POPULATION	% of USA
33	Alabama	64,633	0.4%
35	Alaska	44,681	0.3%
19	Arizona	221,347	1.3%
36	Arkansas	44,193	0.3%
1	California	5,586,184	32.2%
21	Colorado	168,460	1.0%
22	Connecticut	161,770	0.9%
39	Delaware	35,093	0.2%
7	Florida	553,820	3.2%
12	Georgia	387,181	2.2%
8	Hawaii	532,371	3.1%
43	Idaho	23,180	0.1%
5	Illinois	684,715	3.9%
24	Indiana	132,406	0.8%
32	Iowa	69,062	0.4%
29	Kansas	81,152	0.5%
34	Kentucky	60,889	0.4%
27	Louisiana	83,181	0.5%
44	Maine	15,758	0.1%
13	Maryland	380,168	2.2%
10	Massachusetts	425,305	2.5%
14	Michigan	283,968	1.6%
16	Minnesota	256,896	1.5%
42	Mississippi	30,557	0.2%
25	Missouri	116,213	0.7%
49	Montana	8,256	0.0%
37	Nebraska	41,216	0.2%
17	Nevada	236,304	1.4%
41	New Hampshire	33,742	0.2%
4	New Jersey	844,324	4.9%
40	New Mexico	34,848	0.2%
2	New York	1,677,323	9.7%
15	North Carolina	267,385	1.5%
48	North Dakota	9,412	0.1%
18	Ohio	233,379	1.3%
28	Oklahoma	81,394	0.5%
20	Oregon	169,517	1.0%
11	Pennsylvania	417,607	2.4%
38	Rhode Island	36,785	0.2%
30	South Carolina	74,319	0.4%
46	South Dakota	10,739	0.1%
26	Tennessee	112,524	0.6%
3	Texas	1,223,865	7.1%
31	Utah	70,407	0.4%
47	Vermont	9,752	0.1%
9	Virginia	526,867	3.0%
6	Washington	576,147	3.3%
45	West Virginia	14,945	0.1%
23	Wisconsin	152,512	0.9%
50	Wyoming	5,821	0.0%

RANK ORDER

RANK	STATE	POPULATION	% of USA
1	California	5,586,184	32.2%
2	New York	1,677,323	9.7%
3	Texas	1,223,865	7.1%
4	New Jersey	844,324	4.9%
5	Illinois	684,715	3.9%
6	Washington	576,147	3.3%
7	Florida	553,820	3.2%
8	Hawaii	532,371	3.1%
9	Virginia	526,867	3.0%
10	Massachusetts	425,305	2.5%
11	Pennsylvania	417,607	2.4%
12	Georgia	387,181	2.2%
13	Maryland	380,168	2.2%
14	Michigan	283,968	1.6%
15	North Carolina	267,385	1.5%
16	Minnesota	256,896	1.5%
17	Nevada	236,304	1.4%
18	Ohio	233,379	1.3%
19	Arizona	221,347	1.3%
20	Oregon	169,517	1.0%
21	Colorado	168,460	1.0%
22	Connecticut	161,770	0.9%
23	Wisconsin	152,512	0.9%
24	Indiana	132,406	0.8%
25	Missouri	116,213	0.7%
26	Tennessee	112,524	0.6%
27	Louisiana	83,181	0.5%
28	Oklahoma	81,394	0.5%
29	Kansas	81,152	0.5%
30	South Carolina	74,319	0.4%
31	Utah	70,407	0.4%
32	Iowa	69,062	0.4%
33	Alabama	64,633	0.4%
34	Kentucky	60,889	0.4%
35	Alaska	44,681	0.3%
36	Arkansas	44,193	0.3%
37	Nebraska	41,216	0.2%
38	Rhode Island	36,785	0.2%
39	Delaware	35,093	0.2%
40	New Mexico	34,848	0.2%
41	New Hampshire	33,742	0.2%
42	Mississippi	30,557	0.2%
43	Idaho	23,180	0.1%
44	Maine	15,758	0.1%
45	West Virginia	14,945	0.1%
46	South Dakota	10,739	0.1%
47	Vermont	9,752	0.1%
48	North Dakota	9,412	0.1%
49	Montana	8,256	0.0%
50	Wyoming	5,821	0.0%
	District of Columbia	26,480	0.2%

Source: U.S. Bureau of the Census
"State Characteristics: Vintage 2014" (http://www.census.gov/popest/data/state/asrh/2014/index.html)
*Those who identified themselves as one race. Census states "Race is a self-identification data item in which respondents choose the race or races with which they most closely identify."

Percent of Population Asian in 2014

National Percent = 5.4%*

ALPHA ORDER

RANK	STATE	PERCENT
43	Alabama	1.3
10	Alaska	6.1
19	Arizona	3.3
39	Arkansas	1.5
2	California	14.4
21	Colorado	3.1
13	Connecticut	4.5
16	Delaware	3.8
23	Florida	2.8
16	Georgia	3.8
1	Hawaii	37.5
41	Idaho	1.4
11	Illinois	5.3
32	Indiana	2.0
29	Iowa	2.2
23	Kansas	2.8
41	Kentucky	1.4
35	Louisiana	1.8
46	Maine	1.2
7	Maryland	6.4
8	Massachusetts	6.3
22	Michigan	2.9
12	Minnesota	4.7
47	Mississippi	1.0
34	Missouri	1.9
49	Montana	0.8
29	Nebraska	2.2
5	Nevada	8.3
27	New Hampshire	2.5
3	New Jersey	9.4
36	New Mexico	1.7
4	New York	8.5
25	North Carolina	2.7
43	North Dakota	1.3
32	Ohio	2.0
31	Oklahoma	2.1
15	Oregon	4.3
19	Pennsylvania	3.3
18	Rhode Island	3.5
39	South Carolina	1.5
43	South Dakota	1.3
36	Tennessee	1.7
13	Texas	4.5
28	Utah	2.4
38	Vermont	1.6
8	Virginia	6.3
6	Washington	8.2
49	West Virginia	0.8
26	Wisconsin	2.6
47	Wyoming	1.0

RANK ORDER

RANK	STATE	PERCENT
1	Hawaii	37.5
2	California	14.4
3	New Jersey	9.4
4	New York	8.5
5	Nevada	8.3
6	Washington	8.2
7	Maryland	6.4
8	Massachusetts	6.3
8	Virginia	6.3
10	Alaska	6.1
11	Illinois	5.3
12	Minnesota	4.7
13	Connecticut	4.5
13	Texas	4.5
15	Oregon	4.3
16	Delaware	3.8
16	Georgia	3.8
18	Rhode Island	3.5
19	Arizona	3.3
19	Pennsylvania	3.3
21	Colorado	3.1
22	Michigan	2.9
23	Florida	2.8
23	Kansas	2.8
25	North Carolina	2.7
26	Wisconsin	2.6
27	New Hampshire	2.5
28	Utah	2.4
29	Iowa	2.2
29	Nebraska	2.2
31	Oklahoma	2.1
32	Indiana	2.0
32	Ohio	2.0
34	Missouri	1.9
35	Louisiana	1.8
36	New Mexico	1.7
36	Tennessee	1.7
38	Vermont	1.6
39	Arkansas	1.5
39	South Carolina	1.5
41	Idaho	1.4
41	Kentucky	1.4
43	Alabama	1.3
43	North Dakota	1.3
43	South Dakota	1.3
46	Maine	1.2
47	Mississippi	1.0
47	Wyoming	1.0
49	Montana	0.8
49	West Virginia	0.8
	District of Columbia	4.0

Source: CQ Press using data from U.S. Bureau of the Census
"State Characteristics: Vintage 2014" (http://www.census.gov/popest/data/state/asrh/2014/index.html)
*Those who identified themselves as one race. Census states "Race is a self-identification data item in which respondents choose the race or races with which they most closely identify."

American Indian Population in 2014

National Total = 3,960,971*

ALPHA ORDER

RANK	STATE	POPULATION	% of USA
28	Alabama	33,772	0.9%
9	Alaska	108,956	2.8%
2	Arizona	357,672	9.0%
34	Arkansas	28,689	0.7%
1	California	645,309	16.3%
11	Colorado	84,946	2.1%
39	Connecticut	18,443	0.5%
47	Delaware	6,188	0.2%
10	Florida	99,203	2.5%
20	Georgia	50,988	1.3%
46	Hawaii	6,356	0.2%
35	Idaho	28,152	0.7%
13	Illinois	75,293	1.9%
36	Indiana	26,354	0.7%
42	Iowa	15,183	0.4%
27	Kansas	34,741	0.9%
43	Kentucky	12,774	0.3%
26	Louisiana	35,276	0.9%
45	Maine	9,132	0.2%
29	Maryland	33,413	0.8%
31	Massachusetts	32,392	0.8%
15	Michigan	71,030	1.8%
14	Minnesota	71,960	1.8%
40	Mississippi	17,520	0.4%
30	Missouri	32,828	0.8%
17	Montana	67,065	1.7%
38	Nebraska	25,690	0.6%
21	Nevada	46,535	1.2%
49	New Hampshire	3,849	0.1%
19	New Jersey	53,223	1.3%
5	New Mexico	217,262	5.5%
6	New York	189,764	4.8%
7	North Carolina	154,735	3.9%
25	North Dakota	40,277	1.0%
32	Ohio	31,585	0.8%
3	Oklahoma	350,892	8.9%
16	Oregon	70,842	1.8%
24	Pennsylvania	44,142	1.1%
44	Rhode Island	9,965	0.3%
37	South Carolina	25,961	0.7%
12	South Dakota	75,879	1.9%
33	Tennessee	28,845	0.7%
4	Texas	274,452	6.9%
23	Utah	44,551	1.1%
50	Vermont	2,356	0.1%
22	Virginia	45,725	1.2%
8	Washington	132,935	3.4%
48	West Virginia	4,441	0.1%
18	Wisconsin	64,192	1.6%
41	Wyoming	15,541	0.4%

RANK ORDER

RANK	STATE	POPULATION	% of USA
1	California	645,309	16.3%
2	Arizona	357,672	9.0%
3	Oklahoma	350,892	8.9%
4	Texas	274,452	6.9%
5	New Mexico	217,262	5.5%
6	New York	189,764	4.8%
7	North Carolina	154,735	3.9%
8	Washington	132,935	3.4%
9	Alaska	108,956	2.8%
10	Florida	99,203	2.5%
11	Colorado	84,946	2.1%
12	South Dakota	75,879	1.9%
13	Illinois	75,293	1.9%
14	Minnesota	71,960	1.8%
15	Michigan	71,030	1.8%
16	Oregon	70,842	1.8%
17	Montana	67,065	1.7%
18	Wisconsin	64,192	1.6%
19	New Jersey	53,223	1.3%
20	Georgia	50,988	1.3%
21	Nevada	46,535	1.2%
22	Virginia	45,725	1.2%
23	Utah	44,551	1.1%
24	Pennsylvania	44,142	1.1%
25	North Dakota	40,277	1.0%
26	Louisiana	35,276	0.9%
27	Kansas	34,741	0.9%
28	Alabama	33,772	0.9%
29	Maryland	33,413	0.8%
30	Missouri	32,828	0.8%
31	Massachusetts	32,392	0.8%
32	Ohio	31,585	0.8%
33	Tennessee	28,845	0.7%
34	Arkansas	28,689	0.7%
35	Idaho	28,152	0.7%
36	Indiana	26,354	0.7%
37	South Carolina	25,961	0.7%
38	Nebraska	25,690	0.6%
39	Connecticut	18,443	0.5%
40	Mississippi	17,520	0.4%
41	Wyoming	15,541	0.4%
42	Iowa	15,183	0.4%
43	Kentucky	12,774	0.3%
44	Rhode Island	9,965	0.3%
45	Maine	9,132	0.2%
46	Hawaii	6,356	0.2%
47	Delaware	6,188	0.2%
48	West Virginia	4,441	0.1%
49	New Hampshire	3,849	0.1%
50	Vermont	2,356	0.1%
	District of Columbia	3,697	0.1%

Source: U.S. Bureau of the Census
"State Characteristics: Vintage 2014" (http://www.census.gov/popest/data/state/asrh/2014/index.html)
*Those who identified themselves as one race. Includes Alaska Native populations. Census states "Race is a self-identification data item in which respondents choose the race or races with which they most closely identify."

Percent of Population American Indian in 2014

National Percent = 1.2%*

ALPHA ORDER

RANK	STATE	PERCENT
26	Alabama	0.7
1	Alaska	14.8
7	Arizona	5.3
21	Arkansas	1.0
11	California	1.7
13	Colorado	1.6
34	Connecticut	0.5
26	Delaware	0.7
34	Florida	0.5
34	Georgia	0.5
42	Hawaii	0.4
11	Idaho	1.7
30	Illinois	0.6
42	Indiana	0.4
34	Iowa	0.5
19	Kansas	1.2
46	Kentucky	0.3
25	Louisiana	0.8
26	Maine	0.7
30	Maryland	0.6
34	Massachusetts	0.5
26	Michigan	0.7
18	Minnesota	1.3
30	Mississippi	0.6
34	Missouri	0.5
5	Montana	6.6
17	Nebraska	1.4
13	Nevada	1.6
46	New Hampshire	0.3
30	New Jersey	0.6
2	New Mexico	10.4
21	New York	1.0
13	North Carolina	1.6
6	North Dakota	5.4
46	Ohio	0.3
3	Oklahoma	9.0
10	Oregon	1.8
46	Pennsylvania	0.3
24	Rhode Island	0.9
34	South Carolina	0.5
4	South Dakota	8.9
42	Tennessee	0.4
21	Texas	1.0
16	Utah	1.5
42	Vermont	0.4
34	Virginia	0.5
9	Washington	1.9
50	West Virginia	0.2
20	Wisconsin	1.1
8	Wyoming	2.7

RANK ORDER

RANK	STATE	PERCENT
1	Alaska	14.8
2	New Mexico	10.4
3	Oklahoma	9.0
4	South Dakota	8.9
5	Montana	6.6
6	North Dakota	5.4
7	Arizona	5.3
8	Wyoming	2.7
9	Washington	1.9
10	Oregon	1.8
11	California	1.7
11	Idaho	1.7
13	Colorado	1.6
13	Nevada	1.6
13	North Carolina	1.6
16	Utah	1.5
17	Nebraska	1.4
18	Minnesota	1.3
19	Kansas	1.2
20	Wisconsin	1.1
21	Arkansas	1.0
21	New York	1.0
21	Texas	1.0
24	Rhode Island	0.9
25	Louisiana	0.8
26	Alabama	0.7
26	Delaware	0.7
26	Maine	0.7
26	Michigan	0.7
30	Illinois	0.6
30	Maryland	0.6
30	Mississippi	0.6
30	New Jersey	0.6
34	Connecticut	0.5
34	Florida	0.5
34	Georgia	0.5
34	Iowa	0.5
34	Massachusetts	0.5
34	Missouri	0.5
34	South Carolina	0.5
34	Virginia	0.5
42	Hawaii	0.4
42	Indiana	0.4
42	Tennessee	0.4
42	Vermont	0.4
46	Kentucky	0.3
46	New Hampshire	0.3
46	Ohio	0.3
46	Pennsylvania	0.3
50	West Virginia	0.2
	District of Columbia	0.6

Source: CQ Press using data from U.S. Bureau of the Census
"State Characteristics: Vintage 2014" (http://www.census.gov/popest/data/state/asrh/2014/index.html)
*Those who identified themselves as one race. Includes Alaska Native populations. Census states "Race is a self-identification data item in which respondents choose the race or races with which they most closely identify."

Native Hawaiian or Other Pacific Islander Population in 2014

National Total = 741,601*

ALPHA ORDER

RANK	STATE	POPULATION	% of USA
26	Alabama	5,089	0.7%
15	Alaska	9,296	1.3%
9	Arizona	17,740	2.4%
17	Arkansas	8,633	1.2%
1	California	194,088	26.2%
13	Colorado	10,071	1.4%
30	Connecticut	3,862	0.5%
43	Delaware	863	0.1%
7	Florida	21,978	3.0%
12	Georgia	11,895	1.6%
2	Hawaii	141,286	19.1%
34	Idaho	3,302	0.4%
20	Illinois	8,193	1.1%
28	Indiana	4,093	0.6%
37	Iowa	2,953	0.4%
35	Kansas	3,228	0.4%
31	Kentucky	3,693	0.5%
36	Louisiana	2,996	0.4%
49	Maine	469	0.1%
23	Maryland	6,319	0.9%
21	Massachusetts	6,679	0.9%
29	Michigan	3,917	0.5%
33	Minnesota	3,391	0.5%
40	Mississippi	1,811	0.2%
18	Missouri	8,527	1.1%
42	Montana	897	0.1%
39	Nebraska	2,235	0.3%
8	Nevada	21,140	2.9%
44	New Hampshire	636	0.1%
16	New Jersey	8,917	1.2%
32	New Mexico	3,472	0.5%
6	New York	26,223	3.5%
11	North Carolina	11,930	1.6%
48	North Dakota	545	0.1%
25	Ohio	5,846	0.8%
22	Oklahoma	6,393	0.9%
10	Oregon	16,861	2.3%
19	Pennsylvania	8,516	1.1%
41	Rhode Island	1,800	0.2%
27	South Carolina	4,520	0.6%
46	South Dakota	625	0.1%
24	Tennessee	6,192	0.8%
4	Texas	36,632	4.9%
5	Utah	29,046	3.9%
50	Vermont	227	0.0%
14	Virginia	9,558	1.3%
3	Washington	49,986	6.7%
47	West Virginia	553	0.1%
38	Wisconsin	2,858	0.4%
45	Wyoming	632	0.1%

RANK ORDER

RANK	STATE	POPULATION	% of USA
1	California	194,088	26.2%
2	Hawaii	141,286	19.1%
3	Washington	49,986	6.7%
4	Texas	36,632	4.9%
5	Utah	29,046	3.9%
6	New York	26,223	3.5%
7	Florida	21,978	3.0%
8	Nevada	21,140	2.9%
9	Arizona	17,740	2.4%
10	Oregon	16,861	2.3%
11	North Carolina	11,930	1.6%
12	Georgia	11,895	1.6%
13	Colorado	10,071	1.4%
14	Virginia	9,558	1.3%
15	Alaska	9,296	1.3%
16	New Jersey	8,917	1.2%
17	Arkansas	8,633	1.2%
18	Missouri	8,527	1.1%
19	Pennsylvania	8,516	1.1%
20	Illinois	8,193	1.1%
21	Massachusetts	6,679	0.9%
22	Oklahoma	6,393	0.9%
23	Maryland	6,319	0.9%
24	Tennessee	6,192	0.8%
25	Ohio	5,846	0.8%
26	Alabama	5,089	0.7%
27	South Carolina	4,520	0.6%
28	Indiana	4,093	0.6%
29	Michigan	3,917	0.5%
30	Connecticut	3,862	0.5%
31	Kentucky	3,693	0.5%
32	New Mexico	3,472	0.5%
33	Minnesota	3,391	0.5%
34	Idaho	3,302	0.4%
35	Kansas	3,228	0.4%
36	Louisiana	2,996	0.4%
37	Iowa	2,953	0.4%
38	Wisconsin	2,858	0.4%
39	Nebraska	2,235	0.3%
40	Mississippi	1,811	0.2%
41	Rhode Island	1,800	0.2%
42	Montana	897	0.1%
43	Delaware	863	0.1%
44	New Hampshire	636	0.1%
45	Wyoming	632	0.1%
46	South Dakota	625	0.1%
47	West Virginia	553	0.1%
48	North Dakota	545	0.1%
49	Maine	469	0.1%
50	Vermont	227	0.0%
	District of Columbia	989	0.1%

Source: U.S. Bureau of the Census
"State Characteristics: Vintage 2014" (http://www.census.gov/popest/data/state/asrh/2014/index.html)
*Those who identified themselves as one race. Census states "Race is a self-identification data item in which respondents choose the race or races with which they most closely identify."

Percent of Population Native Hawaiian or Other Pacific Islander in 2014

National Percent = 0.2%*

ALPHA ORDER

RANK	STATE	PERCENT
15	Alabama	0.1
2	Alaska	1.3
8	Arizona	0.3
8	Arkansas	0.3
6	California	0.5
10	Colorado	0.2
15	Connecticut	0.1
15	Delaware	0.1
15	Florida	0.1
15	Georgia	0.1
1	Hawaii	10.0
10	Idaho	0.2
15	Illinois	0.1
15	Indiana	0.1
15	Iowa	0.1
15	Kansas	0.1
15	Kentucky	0.1
15	Louisiana	0.1
45	Maine	0.0
15	Maryland	0.1
15	Massachusetts	0.1
45	Michigan	0.0
15	Minnesota	0.1
15	Mississippi	0.1
15	Missouri	0.1
15	Montana	0.1
15	Nebraska	0.1
4	Nevada	0.7
45	New Hampshire	0.0
15	New Jersey	0.1
10	New Mexico	0.2
15	New York	0.1
15	North Carolina	0.1
15	North Dakota	0.1
15	Ohio	0.1
10	Oklahoma	0.2
7	Oregon	0.4
15	Pennsylvania	0.1
10	Rhode Island	0.2
15	South Carolina	0.1
15	South Dakota	0.1
15	Tennessee	0.1
15	Texas	0.1
3	Utah	1.0
45	Vermont	0.0
15	Virginia	0.1
4	Washington	0.7
45	West Virginia	0.0
45	Wisconsin	0.0
15	Wyoming	0.1

RANK ORDER

RANK	STATE	PERCENT
1	Hawaii	10.0
2	Alaska	1.3
3	Utah	1.0
4	Nevada	0.7
4	Washington	0.7
6	California	0.5
7	Oregon	0.4
8	Arizona	0.3
8	Arkansas	0.3
10	Colorado	0.2
10	Idaho	0.2
10	New Mexico	0.2
10	Oklahoma	0.2
10	Rhode Island	0.2
15	Alabama	0.1
15	Connecticut	0.1
15	Delaware	0.1
15	Florida	0.1
15	Georgia	0.1
15	Illinois	0.1
15	Indiana	0.1
15	Iowa	0.1
15	Kansas	0.1
15	Kentucky	0.1
15	Louisiana	0.1
15	Maryland	0.1
15	Massachusetts	0.1
15	Minnesota	0.1
15	Mississippi	0.1
15	Missouri	0.1
15	Montana	0.1
15	Nebraska	0.1
15	New Jersey	0.1
15	New York	0.1
15	North Carolina	0.1
15	North Dakota	0.1
15	Ohio	0.1
15	Pennsylvania	0.1
15	South Carolina	0.1
15	South Dakota	0.1
15	Tennessee	0.1
15	Texas	0.1
15	Virginia	0.1
15	Wyoming	0.1
45	Maine	0.0
45	Michigan	0.0
45	New Hampshire	0.0
45	Vermont	0.0
45	West Virginia	0.0
45	Wisconsin	0.0
	District of Columbia	0.2

Source: CQ Press using data from U.S. Bureau of the Census
"State Characteristics: Vintage 2014" (http://www.census.gov/popest/data/state/asrh/2014/index.html)
*Those who identified themselves as one race. Census states "Race is a self-identification data item in which respondents choose the race or races with which they most closely identify."

Non-Hispanic White Population in 2014

National Total = 197,870,516*

ALPHA ORDER

RANK	STATE	POPULATION	% of USA
23	Alabama	3,209,637	1.6%
49	Alaska	456,312	0.2%
20	Arizona	3,784,049	1.9%
33	Arkansas	2,176,899	1.1%
1	California	14,920,185	7.5%
22	Colorado	3,694,912	1.9%
30	Connecticut	2,475,371	1.3%
46	Delaware	595,873	0.3%
4	Florida	11,103,313	5.6%
10	Georgia	5,487,103	2.8%
50	Hawaii	326,086	0.2%
38	Idaho	1,353,442	0.7%
7	Illinois	8,022,946	4.1%
11	Indiana	5,297,365	2.7%
28	Iowa	2,706,164	1.4%
32	Kansas	2,229,102	1.1%
21	Kentucky	3,767,608	1.9%
27	Louisiana	2,758,588	1.4%
39	Maine	1,247,075	0.6%
24	Maryland	3,144,704	1.6%
14	Massachusetts	5,010,742	2.5%
8	Michigan	7,512,721	3.8%
19	Minnesota	4,444,157	2.2%
34	Mississippi	1,714,269	0.9%
17	Missouri	4,858,040	2.5%
41	Montana	887,707	0.4%
36	Nebraska	1,514,386	0.8%
37	Nevada	1,462,027	0.7%
40	New Hampshire	1,211,057	0.6%
13	New Jersey	5,081,261	2.6%
42	New Mexico	811,400	0.4%
3	New York	11,162,574	5.6%
9	North Carolina	6,373,505	3.2%
45	North Dakota	640,384	0.3%
6	Ohio	9,288,260	4.7%
29	Oklahoma	2,599,234	1.3%
26	Oregon	3,058,538	1.5%
5	Pennsylvania	9,958,389	5.0%
43	Rhode Island	786,563	0.4%
25	South Carolina	3,085,711	1.6%
44	South Dakota	708,452	0.4%
16	Tennessee	4,888,331	2.5%
2	Texas	11,735,074	5.9%
31	Utah	2,335,011	1.2%
47	Vermont	586,013	0.3%
12	Virginia	5,257,382	2.7%
15	Washington	4,970,274	2.5%
35	West Virginia	1,711,447	0.9%
18	Wisconsin	4,733,409	2.4%
48	Wyoming	491,288	0.2%

RANK ORDER

RANK	STATE	POPULATION	% of USA
1	California	14,920,185	7.5%
2	Texas	11,735,074	5.9%
3	New York	11,162,574	5.6%
4	Florida	11,103,313	5.6%
5	Pennsylvania	9,958,389	5.0%
6	Ohio	9,288,260	4.7%
7	Illinois	8,022,946	4.1%
8	Michigan	7,512,721	3.8%
9	North Carolina	6,373,505	3.2%
10	Georgia	5,487,103	2.8%
11	Indiana	5,297,365	2.7%
12	Virginia	5,257,382	2.7%
13	New Jersey	5,081,261	2.6%
14	Massachusetts	5,010,742	2.5%
15	Washington	4,970,274	2.5%
16	Tennessee	4,888,331	2.5%
17	Missouri	4,858,040	2.5%
18	Wisconsin	4,733,409	2.4%
19	Minnesota	4,444,157	2.2%
20	Arizona	3,784,049	1.9%
21	Kentucky	3,767,608	1.9%
22	Colorado	3,694,912	1.9%
23	Alabama	3,209,637	1.6%
24	Maryland	3,144,704	1.6%
25	South Carolina	3,085,711	1.6%
26	Oregon	3,058,538	1.5%
27	Louisiana	2,758,588	1.4%
28	Iowa	2,706,164	1.4%
29	Oklahoma	2,599,234	1.3%
30	Connecticut	2,475,371	1.3%
31	Utah	2,335,011	1.2%
32	Kansas	2,229,102	1.1%
33	Arkansas	2,176,899	1.1%
34	Mississippi	1,714,269	0.9%
35	West Virginia	1,711,447	0.9%
36	Nebraska	1,514,386	0.8%
37	Nevada	1,462,027	0.7%
38	Idaho	1,353,442	0.7%
39	Maine	1,247,075	0.6%
40	New Hampshire	1,211,057	0.6%
41	Montana	887,707	0.4%
42	New Mexico	811,400	0.4%
43	Rhode Island	786,563	0.4%
44	South Dakota	708,452	0.4%
45	North Dakota	640,384	0.3%
46	Delaware	595,873	0.3%
47	Vermont	586,013	0.3%
48	Wyoming	491,288	0.2%
49	Alaska	456,312	0.2%
50	Hawaii	326,086	0.2%
	District of Columbia	236,176	0.1%

Source: U.S. Bureau of the Census
"State Characteristics: Vintage 2014" (http://www.census.gov/popest/data/state/asrh/2014/index.html)
*Those who identified themselves as one race. "White" is defined by Census as a person having origins in any of the original peoples of Europe, North Africa, or the Middle East. This is a subset of the 246,660,710 white population. Persons of Hispanic origin may be of any race. Census states "Race is a self-identification data item in which respondents choose the race or races with which they most closely identify."

Percent of Population Non-Hispanic White in 2014

National Percent = 62.1%*

ALPHA ORDER

RANK	STATE	PERCENT
31	Alabama	66.2
37	Alaska	61.9
42	Arizona	56.2
26	Arkansas	73.4
49	California	38.5
28	Colorado	69.0
29	Connecticut	68.8
34	Delaware	63.7
43	Florida	55.8
44	Georgia	54.3
50	Hawaii	23.0
11	Idaho	82.8
36	Illinois	62.3
15	Indiana	80.3
5	Iowa	87.1
21	Kansas	76.8
8	Kentucky	85.4
38	Louisiana	59.3
1	Maine	93.8
45	Maryland	52.6
25	Massachusetts	74.3
22	Michigan	75.8
13	Minnesota	81.4
39	Mississippi	57.3
16	Missouri	80.1
6	Montana	86.7
14	Nebraska	80.5
46	Nevada	51.5
4	New Hampshire	91.3
40	New Jersey	56.8
48	New Mexico	38.9
41	New York	56.5
32	North Carolina	64.1
7	North Dakota	86.6
16	Ohio	80.1
30	Oklahoma	67.0
20	Oregon	77.0
19	Pennsylvania	77.9
24	Rhode Island	74.5
33	South Carolina	63.9
10	South Dakota	83.0
23	Tennessee	74.6
47	Texas	43.5
18	Utah	79.3
2	Vermont	93.5
35	Virginia	63.1
27	Washington	70.4
3	West Virginia	92.5
12	Wisconsin	82.2
9	Wyoming	84.1

RANK ORDER

RANK	STATE	PERCENT
1	Maine	93.8
2	Vermont	93.5
3	West Virginia	92.5
4	New Hampshire	91.3
5	Iowa	87.1
6	Montana	86.7
7	North Dakota	86.6
8	Kentucky	85.4
9	Wyoming	84.1
10	South Dakota	83.0
11	Idaho	82.8
12	Wisconsin	82.2
13	Minnesota	81.4
14	Nebraska	80.5
15	Indiana	80.3
16	Missouri	80.1
16	Ohio	80.1
18	Utah	79.3
19	Pennsylvania	77.9
20	Oregon	77.0
21	Kansas	76.8
22	Michigan	75.8
23	Tennessee	74.6
24	Rhode Island	74.5
25	Massachusetts	74.3
26	Arkansas	73.4
27	Washington	70.4
28	Colorado	69.0
29	Connecticut	68.8
30	Oklahoma	67.0
31	Alabama	66.2
32	North Carolina	64.1
33	South Carolina	63.9
34	Delaware	63.7
35	Virginia	63.1
36	Illinois	62.3
37	Alaska	61.9
38	Louisiana	59.3
39	Mississippi	57.3
40	New Jersey	56.8
41	New York	56.5
42	Arizona	56.2
43	Florida	55.8
44	Georgia	54.3
45	Maryland	52.6
46	Nevada	51.5
47	Texas	43.5
48	New Mexico	38.9
49	California	38.5
50	Hawaii	23.0

District of Columbia 35.8

Source: CQ Press using data from U.S. Bureau of the Census
"State Characteristics: Vintage 2014" (http://www.census.gov/popest/data/state/asrh/2014/index.html)
*Those who identified themselves as one race. "White" is defined by Census as a person having origins in any of the original peoples of Europe, North Africa, or the Middle East. This non-Hispanic white subset is 80.2% of the total white population. Persons of Hispanic origin may be of any race. Census states "Race is a self-identification data item in which respondents choose the race or races with which they most closely identify."

Multiple Race Population in 2014

National Total = 7,996,483*

ALPHA ORDER

RANK	STATE	POPULATION	% of USA
31	Alabama	75,078	0.9%
36	Alaska	52,457	0.7%
16	Arizona	180,201	2.3%
34	Arkansas	57,362	0.7%
1	California	1,439,722	18.0%
18	Colorado	154,367	1.9%
29	Connecticut	79,042	1.0%
44	Delaware	23,213	0.3%
4	Florida	395,263	4.9%
14	Georgia	197,329	2.5%
5	Hawaii	326,361	4.1%
39	Idaho	37,579	0.5%
8	Illinois	235,349	2.9%
23	Indiana	124,801	1.6%
35	Iowa	53,194	0.7%
28	Kansas	81,422	1.0%
30	Kentucky	77,399	1.0%
32	Louisiana	71,678	0.9%
45	Maine	21,717	0.3%
17	Maryland	157,658	2.0%
19	Massachusetts	148,782	1.9%
12	Michigan	224,814	2.8%
22	Minnesota	126,787	1.6%
40	Mississippi	35,225	0.4%
21	Missouri	127,974	1.6%
43	Montana	26,579	0.3%
38	Nebraska	37,999	0.5%
25	Nevada	113,174	1.4%
46	New Hampshire	21,186	0.3%
15	New Jersey	184,190	2.3%
37	New Mexico	51,142	0.6%
3	New York	467,091	5.8%
13	North Carolina	205,467	2.6%
48	North Dakota	14,565	0.2%
7	Ohio	241,355	3.0%
11	Oklahoma	228,846	2.9%
20	Oregon	143,259	1.8%
9	Pennsylvania	233,611	2.9%
42	Rhode Island	27,177	0.3%
27	South Carolina	82,638	1.0%
47	South Dakota	18,602	0.2%
24	Tennessee	113,438	1.4%
2	Texas	491,950	6.2%
33	Utah	69,397	0.9%
50	Vermont	11,337	0.1%
10	Virginia	233,094	2.9%
6	Washington	315,929	4.0%
41	West Virginia	29,094	0.4%
26	Wisconsin	101,679	1.3%
49	Wyoming	11,451	0.1%

RANK ORDER

RANK	STATE	POPULATION	% of USA
1	California	1,439,722	18.0%
2	Texas	491,950	6.2%
3	New York	467,091	5.8%
4	Florida	395,263	4.9%
5	Hawaii	326,361	4.1%
6	Washington	315,929	4.0%
7	Ohio	241,355	3.0%
8	Illinois	235,349	2.9%
9	Pennsylvania	233,611	2.9%
10	Virginia	233,094	2.9%
11	Oklahoma	228,846	2.9%
12	Michigan	224,814	2.8%
13	North Carolina	205,467	2.6%
14	Georgia	197,329	2.5%
15	New Jersey	184,190	2.3%
16	Arizona	180,201	2.3%
17	Maryland	157,658	2.0%
18	Colorado	154,367	1.9%
19	Massachusetts	148,782	1.9%
20	Oregon	143,259	1.8%
21	Missouri	127,974	1.6%
22	Minnesota	126,787	1.6%
23	Indiana	124,801	1.6%
24	Tennessee	113,438	1.4%
25	Nevada	113,174	1.4%
26	Wisconsin	101,679	1.3%
27	South Carolina	82,638	1.0%
28	Kansas	81,422	1.0%
29	Connecticut	79,042	1.0%
30	Kentucky	77,399	1.0%
31	Alabama	75,078	0.9%
32	Louisiana	71,678	0.9%
33	Utah	69,397	0.9%
34	Arkansas	57,362	0.7%
35	Iowa	53,194	0.7%
36	Alaska	52,457	0.7%
37	New Mexico	51,142	0.6%
38	Nebraska	37,999	0.5%
39	Idaho	37,579	0.5%
40	Mississippi	35,225	0.4%
41	West Virginia	29,094	0.4%
42	Rhode Island	27,177	0.3%
43	Montana	26,579	0.3%
44	Delaware	23,213	0.3%
45	Maine	21,717	0.3%
46	New Hampshire	21,186	0.3%
47	South Dakota	18,602	0.2%
48	North Dakota	14,565	0.2%
49	Wyoming	11,451	0.1%
50	Vermont	11,337	0.1%
	District of Columbia	17,459	0.2%

Source: U.S. Bureau of the Census
"State Characteristics: Vintage 2014" (http://www.census.gov/popest/data/state/asrh/2014/index.html)
*This includes those who identified themselves as two or more races. This is the population who did not identify themselves as one race (White, Black, American Indian/Native Alaska Native, Asian, or Native Hawaiian or Other Pacific Islander) but as a member of multiple racial groups. Census states "Race is a self-identification data item in which respondents choose the race or races with which they most closely identify."

Percent of Population Multiple Races in 2014

National Percent = 2.5%*

ALPHA ORDER

RANK	STATE	PERCENT
48	Alabama	1.5
2	Alaska	7.1
11	Arizona	2.7
34	Arkansas	1.9
6	California	3.7
8	Colorado	2.9
22	Connecticut	2.2
15	Delaware	2.5
29	Florida	2.0
29	Georgia	2.0
1	Hawaii	23.0
19	Idaho	2.3
36	Illinois	1.8
34	Indiana	1.9
42	Iowa	1.7
9	Kansas	2.8
36	Kentucky	1.8
48	Louisiana	1.5
45	Maine	1.6
12	Maryland	2.6
22	Massachusetts	2.2
19	Michigan	2.3
19	Minnesota	2.3
50	Mississippi	1.2
25	Missouri	2.1
12	Montana	2.6
29	Nebraska	2.0
5	Nevada	4.0
45	New Hampshire	1.6
25	New Jersey	2.1
15	New Mexico	2.5
17	New York	2.4
25	North Carolina	2.1
29	North Dakota	2.0
25	Ohio	2.1
3	Oklahoma	5.9
7	Oregon	3.6
36	Pennsylvania	1.8
12	Rhode Island	2.6
42	South Carolina	1.7
22	South Dakota	2.2
42	Tennessee	1.7
36	Texas	1.8
17	Utah	2.4
36	Vermont	1.8
9	Virginia	2.8
4	Washington	4.5
45	West Virginia	1.6
36	Wisconsin	1.8
29	Wyoming	2.0

RANK ORDER

RANK	STATE	PERCENT
1	Hawaii	23.0
2	Alaska	7.1
3	Oklahoma	5.9
4	Washington	4.5
5	Nevada	4.0
6	California	3.7
7	Oregon	3.6
8	Colorado	2.9
9	Kansas	2.8
9	Virginia	2.8
11	Arizona	2.7
12	Maryland	2.6
12	Montana	2.6
12	Rhode Island	2.6
15	Delaware	2.5
15	New Mexico	2.5
17	New York	2.4
17	Utah	2.4
19	Idaho	2.3
19	Michigan	2.3
19	Minnesota	2.3
22	Connecticut	2.2
22	Massachusetts	2.2
22	South Dakota	2.2
25	Missouri	2.1
25	New Jersey	2.1
25	North Carolina	2.1
25	Ohio	2.1
29	Florida	2.0
29	Georgia	2.0
29	Nebraska	2.0
29	North Dakota	2.0
29	Wyoming	2.0
34	Arkansas	1.9
34	Indiana	1.9
36	Illinois	1.8
36	Kentucky	1.8
36	Pennsylvania	1.8
36	Texas	1.8
36	Vermont	1.8
36	Wisconsin	1.8
42	Iowa	1.7
42	South Carolina	1.7
42	Tennessee	1.7
45	Maine	1.6
45	New Hampshire	1.6
45	West Virginia	1.6
48	Alabama	1.5
48	Louisiana	1.5
50	Mississippi	1.2

District of Columbia 2.6

Source: CQ Press using data from U.S. Bureau of the Census
"State Characteristics: Vintage 2014" (http://www.census.gov/popest/data/state/asrh/2014/index.html)
*This includes those who identified themselves as two or more races. This is the population who did not identify themselves as one race (White, Black, American Indian/Native Alaska Native, Asian, or Native Hawaiian or Other Pacific Islander) but as a member of multiple racial groups. Census states "Race is a self-identification data item in which respondents choose the race or races with which they most closely identify."

Median Age in 2014

National Median = 37.7 Years Old

ALPHA ORDER

RANK	STATE	MEDIAN AGE
18	Alabama	38.6
49	Alaska	33.3
34	Arizona	37.1
27	Arkansas	37.8
45	California	36.0
39	Colorado	36.5
7	Connecticut	40.6
10	Delaware	39.7
5	Florida	41.8
43	Georgia	36.1
26	Hawaii	37.9
46	Idaho	35.7
30	Illinois	37.5
30	Indiana	37.5
25	Iowa	38.1
43	Kansas	36.1
18	Kentucky	38.6
40	Louisiana	36.3
1	Maine	44.2
23	Maryland	38.2
13	Massachusetts	39.4
11	Michigan	39.6
27	Minnesota	37.8
38	Mississippi	36.7
21	Missouri	38.3
9	Montana	39.8
41	Nebraska	36.2
30	Nevada	37.5
2	New Hampshire	42.6
12	New Jersey	39.5
34	New Mexico	37.1
21	New York	38.3
23	North Carolina	38.2
47	North Dakota	34.9
14	Ohio	39.3
41	Oklahoma	36.2
15	Oregon	39.2
6	Pennsylvania	40.7
8	Rhode Island	39.9
17	South Carolina	38.8
36	South Dakota	36.8
18	Tennessee	38.6
48	Texas	34.2
50	Utah	30.5
2	Vermont	42.6
29	Virginia	37.7
30	Washington	37.5
4	West Virginia	42.0
15	Wisconsin	39.2
36	Wyoming	36.8

RANK ORDER

RANK	STATE	MEDIAN AGE
1	Maine	44.2
2	New Hampshire	42.6
2	Vermont	42.6
4	West Virginia	42.0
5	Florida	41.8
6	Pennsylvania	40.7
7	Connecticut	40.6
8	Rhode Island	39.9
9	Montana	39.8
10	Delaware	39.7
11	Michigan	39.6
12	New Jersey	39.5
13	Massachusetts	39.4
14	Ohio	39.3
15	Oregon	39.2
15	Wisconsin	39.2
17	South Carolina	38.8
18	Alabama	38.6
18	Kentucky	38.6
18	Tennessee	38.6
21	Missouri	38.3
21	New York	38.3
23	Maryland	38.2
23	North Carolina	38.2
25	Iowa	38.1
26	Hawaii	37.9
27	Arkansas	37.8
27	Minnesota	37.8
29	Virginia	37.7
30	Illinois	37.5
30	Indiana	37.5
30	Nevada	37.5
30	Washington	37.5
34	Arizona	37.1
34	New Mexico	37.1
36	South Dakota	36.8
36	Wyoming	36.8
38	Mississippi	36.7
39	Colorado	36.5
40	Louisiana	36.3
41	Nebraska	36.2
41	Oklahoma	36.2
43	Georgia	36.1
43	Kansas	36.1
45	California	36.0
46	Idaho	35.7
47	North Dakota	34.9
48	Texas	34.2
49	Alaska	33.3
50	Utah	30.5
	District of Columbia	33.8

Source: U.S. Bureau of the Census
"State Characteristics: Vintage 2014" (http://www.census.gov/popest/data/state/asrh/2014/index.html)

Population under 5 Years Old in 2014

National Total = 19,876,883

ALPHA ORDER

RANK	STATE	POPULATION	% of USA
24	Alabama	294,705	1.5%
47	Alaska	54,708	0.3%
14	Arizona	430,888	2.2%
33	Arkansas	191,621	1.0%
1	California	2,515,727	12.7%
22	Colorado	334,931	1.7%
34	Connecticut	189,437	1.0%
45	Delaware	56,351	0.3%
4	Florida	1,084,349	5.5%
8	Georgia	662,675	3.3%
40	Hawaii	91,480	0.5%
38	Idaho	113,832	0.6%
5	Illinois	790,685	4.0%
15	Indiana	419,487	2.1%
31	Iowa	195,340	1.0%
30	Kansas	200,607	1.0%
26	Kentucky	276,233	1.4%
23	Louisiana	308,634	1.6%
41	Maine	64,779	0.3%
18	Maryland	369,754	1.9%
19	Massachusetts	366,055	1.8%
10	Michigan	570,292	2.9%
20	Minnesota	348,643	1.8%
32	Mississippi	194,108	1.0%
17	Missouri	374,318	1.9%
43	Montana	61,194	0.3%
37	Nebraska	130,178	0.7%
35	Nevada	176,397	0.9%
42	New Hampshire	64,545	0.3%
11	New Jersey	532,519	2.7%
36	New Mexico	137,133	0.7%
3	New York	1,184,591	6.0%
9	North Carolina	607,476	3.1%
48	North Dakota	51,016	0.3%
7	Ohio	690,576	3.5%
27	Oklahoma	265,474	1.3%
29	Oregon	229,463	1.2%
6	Pennsylvania	715,084	3.6%
46	Rhode Island	54,896	0.3%
25	South Carolina	290,519	1.5%
44	South Dakota	60,610	0.3%
16	Tennessee	400,431	2.0%
2	Texas	1,956,213	9.8%
28	Utah	252,131	1.3%
50	Vermont	30,417	0.2%
12	Virginia	514,893	2.6%
13	Washington	446,570	2.2%
39	West Virginia	102,485	0.5%
21	Wisconsin	341,368	1.7%
49	Wyoming	38,171	0.2%

RANK ORDER

RANK	STATE	POPULATION	% of USA
1	California	2,515,727	12.7%
2	Texas	1,956,213	9.8%
3	New York	1,184,591	6.0%
4	Florida	1,084,349	5.5%
5	Illinois	790,685	4.0%
6	Pennsylvania	715,084	3.6%
7	Ohio	690,576	3.5%
8	Georgia	662,675	3.3%
9	North Carolina	607,476	3.1%
10	Michigan	570,292	2.9%
11	New Jersey	532,519	2.7%
12	Virginia	514,893	2.6%
13	Washington	446,570	2.2%
14	Arizona	430,888	2.2%
15	Indiana	419,487	2.1%
16	Tennessee	400,431	2.0%
17	Missouri	374,318	1.9%
18	Maryland	369,754	1.9%
19	Massachusetts	366,055	1.8%
20	Minnesota	348,643	1.8%
21	Wisconsin	341,368	1.7%
22	Colorado	334,931	1.7%
23	Louisiana	308,634	1.6%
24	Alabama	294,705	1.5%
25	South Carolina	290,519	1.5%
26	Kentucky	276,233	1.4%
27	Oklahoma	265,474	1.3%
28	Utah	252,131	1.3%
29	Oregon	229,463	1.2%
30	Kansas	200,607	1.0%
31	Iowa	195,340	1.0%
32	Mississippi	194,108	1.0%
33	Arkansas	191,621	1.0%
34	Connecticut	189,437	1.0%
35	Nevada	176,397	0.9%
36	New Mexico	137,133	0.7%
37	Nebraska	130,178	0.7%
38	Idaho	113,832	0.6%
39	West Virginia	102,485	0.5%
40	Hawaii	91,480	0.5%
41	Maine	64,779	0.3%
42	New Hampshire	64,545	0.3%
43	Montana	61,194	0.3%
44	South Dakota	60,610	0.3%
45	Delaware	56,351	0.3%
46	Rhode Island	54,896	0.3%
47	Alaska	54,708	0.3%
48	North Dakota	51,016	0.3%
49	Wyoming	38,171	0.2%
50	Vermont	30,417	0.2%
	District of Columbia	42,894	0.2%

Source: U.S. Bureau of the Census
"State Characteristics: Vintage 2014" (http://www.census.gov/popest/data/state/asrh/2014/index.html)

Percent of Population under 5 Years Old in 2014

National Percent = 6.2% of Population

ALPHA ORDER

RANK	STATE	PERCENT
29	Alabama	6.1
2	Alaska	7.4
17	Arizona	6.4
13	Arkansas	6.5
13	California	6.5
21	Colorado	6.3
46	Connecticut	5.3
33	Delaware	6.0
43	Florida	5.5
10	Georgia	6.6
17	Hawaii	6.4
5	Idaho	7.0
29	Illinois	6.1
17	Indiana	6.4
21	Iowa	6.3
6	Kansas	6.9
21	Kentucky	6.3
10	Louisiana	6.6
48	Maine	4.9
25	Maryland	6.2
45	Massachusetts	5.4
40	Michigan	5.8
17	Minnesota	6.4
13	Mississippi	6.5
25	Missouri	6.2
33	Montana	6.0
6	Nebraska	6.9
25	Nevada	6.2
48	New Hampshire	4.9
33	New Jersey	6.0
10	New Mexico	6.6
33	New York	6.0
29	North Carolina	6.1
6	North Dakota	6.9
33	Ohio	6.0
9	Oklahoma	6.8
40	Oregon	5.8
42	Pennsylvania	5.6
47	Rhode Island	5.2
33	South Carolina	6.0
4	South Dakota	7.1
29	Tennessee	6.1
3	Texas	7.3
1	Utah	8.6
48	Vermont	4.9
25	Virginia	6.2
21	Washington	6.3
43	West Virginia	5.5
39	Wisconsin	5.9
13	Wyoming	6.5

RANK ORDER

RANK	STATE	PERCENT
1	Utah	8.6
2	Alaska	7.4
3	Texas	7.3
4	South Dakota	7.1
5	Idaho	7.0
6	Kansas	6.9
6	Nebraska	6.9
6	North Dakota	6.9
9	Oklahoma	6.8
10	Georgia	6.6
10	Louisiana	6.6
10	New Mexico	6.6
13	Arkansas	6.5
13	California	6.5
13	Mississippi	6.5
13	Wyoming	6.5
17	Arizona	6.4
17	Hawaii	6.4
17	Indiana	6.4
17	Minnesota	6.4
21	Colorado	6.3
21	Iowa	6.3
21	Kentucky	6.3
21	Washington	6.3
25	Maryland	6.2
25	Missouri	6.2
25	Nevada	6.2
25	Virginia	6.2
29	Alabama	6.1
29	Illinois	6.1
29	North Carolina	6.1
29	Tennessee	6.1
33	Delaware	6.0
33	Montana	6.0
33	New Jersey	6.0
33	New York	6.0
33	Ohio	6.0
33	South Carolina	6.0
39	Wisconsin	5.9
40	Michigan	5.8
40	Oregon	5.8
42	Pennsylvania	5.6
43	Florida	5.5
43	West Virginia	5.5
45	Massachusetts	5.4
46	Connecticut	5.3
47	Rhode Island	5.2
48	Maine	4.9
48	New Hampshire	4.9
48	Vermont	4.9

District of Columbia 6.5

Source: CQ Press using data from U.S. Bureau of the Census
"State Characteristics: Vintage 2014" (http://www.census.gov/popest/data/state/asrh/2014/index.html)

Population 5 to 17 Years Old in 2014

National Total = 53,706,735

ALPHA ORDER

RANK	STATE	POPULATION	% of USA
23	Alabama	812,866	1.5%
47	Alaska	131,835	0.2%
13	Arizona	1,190,804	2.2%
34	Arkansas	515,398	1.0%
1	California	6,637,425	12.4%
22	Colorado	911,441	1.7%
30	Connecticut	585,993	1.1%
46	Delaware	147,896	0.3%
4	Florida	2,969,235	5.5%
8	Georgia	1,830,607	3.4%
40	Hawaii	216,964	0.4%
38	Idaho	317,248	0.6%
5	Illinois	2,197,789	4.1%
14	Indiana	1,162,440	2.2%
32	Iowa	530,614	1.0%
33	Kansas	522,059	1.0%
26	Kentucky	736,381	1.4%
24	Louisiana	804,859	1.5%
42	Maine	194,198	0.4%
19	Maryland	980,790	1.8%
17	Massachusetts	1,024,413	1.9%
10	Michigan	1,653,498	3.1%
21	Minnesota	933,183	1.7%
31	Mississippi	537,161	1.0%
18	Missouri	1,018,305	1.9%
43	Montana	163,830	0.3%
37	Nebraska	336,431	0.6%
35	Nevada	486,828	0.9%
41	New Hampshire	202,596	0.4%
11	New Jersey	1,479,562	2.8%
36	New Mexico	364,816	0.7%
3	New York	3,044,315	5.7%
9	North Carolina	1,680,073	3.1%
48	North Dakota	117,511	0.2%
7	Ohio	1,947,728	3.6%
27	Oklahoma	687,225	1.3%
29	Oregon	628,559	1.2%
6	Pennsylvania	1,985,809	3.7%
44	Rhode Island	157,956	0.3%
25	South Carolina	794,229	1.5%
45	South Dakota	149,797	0.3%
16	Tennessee	1,094,095	2.0%
2	Texas	5,159,401	9.6%
28	Utah	651,984	1.2%
50	Vermont	91,169	0.2%
12	Virginia	1,354,222	2.5%
15	Washington	1,156,151	2.2%
39	West Virginia	277,662	0.5%
20	Wisconsin	958,821	1.8%
49	Wyoming	100,152	0.2%

RANK ORDER

RANK	STATE	POPULATION	% of USA
1	California	6,637,425	12.4%
2	Texas	5,159,401	9.6%
3	New York	3,044,315	5.7%
4	Florida	2,969,235	5.5%
5	Illinois	2,197,789	4.1%
6	Pennsylvania	1,985,809	3.7%
7	Ohio	1,947,728	3.6%
8	Georgia	1,830,607	3.4%
9	North Carolina	1,680,073	3.1%
10	Michigan	1,653,498	3.1%
11	New Jersey	1,479,562	2.8%
12	Virginia	1,354,222	2.5%
13	Arizona	1,190,804	2.2%
14	Indiana	1,162,440	2.2%
15	Washington	1,156,151	2.2%
16	Tennessee	1,094,095	2.0%
17	Massachusetts	1,024,413	1.9%
18	Missouri	1,018,305	1.9%
19	Maryland	980,790	1.8%
20	Wisconsin	958,821	1.8%
21	Minnesota	933,183	1.7%
22	Colorado	911,441	1.7%
23	Alabama	812,866	1.5%
24	Louisiana	804,859	1.5%
25	South Carolina	794,229	1.5%
26	Kentucky	736,381	1.4%
27	Oklahoma	687,225	1.3%
28	Utah	651,984	1.2%
29	Oregon	628,559	1.2%
30	Connecticut	585,993	1.1%
31	Mississippi	537,161	1.0%
32	Iowa	530,614	1.0%
33	Kansas	522,059	1.0%
34	Arkansas	515,398	1.0%
35	Nevada	486,828	0.9%
36	New Mexico	364,816	0.7%
37	Nebraska	336,431	0.6%
38	Idaho	317,248	0.6%
39	West Virginia	277,662	0.5%
40	Hawaii	216,964	0.4%
41	New Hampshire	202,596	0.4%
42	Maine	194,198	0.4%
43	Montana	163,830	0.3%
44	Rhode Island	157,956	0.3%
45	South Dakota	149,797	0.3%
46	Delaware	147,896	0.3%
47	Alaska	131,835	0.2%
48	North Dakota	117,511	0.2%
49	Wyoming	100,152	0.2%
50	Vermont	91,169	0.2%
	District of Columbia	72,411	0.1%

Source: CQ Press using data from U.S. Bureau of the Census
"State Characteristics: Vintage 2014" (http://www.census.gov/popest/data/state/asrh/2014/index.html)

Percent of Population 5 to 17 Years Old in 2014

National Percent = 16.8% of Population

ALPHA ORDER

RANK	STATE	PERCENT
24	Alabama	16.8
6	Alaska	17.9
9	Arizona	17.7
14	Arkansas	17.4
16	California	17.1
22	Colorado	17.0
35	Connecticut	16.3
39	Delaware	15.8
48	Florida	14.9
4	Georgia	18.1
43	Hawaii	15.3
2	Idaho	19.4
16	Illinois	17.1
11	Indiana	17.6
16	Iowa	17.1
5	Kansas	18.0
27	Kentucky	16.7
15	Louisiana	17.3
49	Maine	14.6
32	Maryland	16.4
45	Massachusetts	15.2
27	Michigan	16.7
16	Minnesota	17.1
6	Mississippi	17.9
24	Missouri	16.8
37	Montana	16.0
6	Nebraska	17.9
16	Nevada	17.1
43	New Hampshire	15.3
31	New Jersey	16.6
13	New Mexico	17.5
42	New York	15.4
23	North Carolina	16.9
38	North Dakota	15.9
24	Ohio	16.8
9	Oklahoma	17.7
39	Oregon	15.8
41	Pennsylvania	15.5
46	Rhode Island	15.0
32	South Carolina	16.4
11	South Dakota	17.6
27	Tennessee	16.7
3	Texas	19.1
1	Utah	22.2
49	Vermont	14.6
35	Virginia	16.3
32	Washington	16.4
46	West Virginia	15.0
27	Wisconsin	16.7
16	Wyoming	17.1

RANK ORDER

RANK	STATE	PERCENT
1	Utah	22.2
2	Idaho	19.4
3	Texas	19.1
4	Georgia	18.1
5	Kansas	18.0
6	Alaska	17.9
6	Mississippi	17.9
6	Nebraska	17.9
9	Arizona	17.7
9	Oklahoma	17.7
11	Indiana	17.6
11	South Dakota	17.6
13	New Mexico	17.5
14	Arkansas	17.4
15	Louisiana	17.3
16	California	17.1
16	Illinois	17.1
16	Iowa	17.1
16	Minnesota	17.1
16	Nevada	17.1
16	Wyoming	17.1
22	Colorado	17.0
23	North Carolina	16.9
24	Alabama	16.8
24	Missouri	16.8
24	Ohio	16.8
27	Kentucky	16.7
27	Michigan	16.7
27	Tennessee	16.7
27	Wisconsin	16.7
31	New Jersey	16.6
32	Maryland	16.4
32	South Carolina	16.4
32	Washington	16.4
35	Connecticut	16.3
35	Virginia	16.3
37	Montana	16.0
38	North Dakota	15.9
39	Delaware	15.8
39	Oregon	15.8
41	Pennsylvania	15.5
42	New York	15.4
43	Hawaii	15.3
43	New Hampshire	15.3
45	Massachusetts	15.2
46	Rhode Island	15.0
46	West Virginia	15.0
48	Florida	14.9
49	Maine	14.6
49	Vermont	14.6
	District of Columbia	11.0

Source: CQ Press using data from U.S. Bureau of the Census
"State Characteristics: Vintage 2014" (http://www.census.gov/popest/data/state/asrh/2014/index.html)

Population 18 Years Old and Older in 2014

National Total = 245,273,438

ALPHA ORDER

RANK	STATE	POPULATION	% of USA
24	Alabama	3,741,806	1.5%
48	Alaska	550,189	0.2%
15	Arizona	5,109,792	2.1%
32	Arkansas	2,259,350	0.9%
1	California	29,649,348	12.1%
22	Colorado	4,109,494	1.7%
29	Connecticut	2,821,247	1.2%
45	Delaware	731,367	0.3%
3	Florida	15,839,713	6.5%
10	Georgia	7,604,061	3.1%
40	Hawaii	1,111,117	0.5%
39	Idaho	1,203,384	0.5%
6	Illinois	9,892,106	4.0%
17	Indiana	5,014,928	2.0%
30	Iowa	2,381,172	1.0%
33	Kansas	2,181,355	0.9%
26	Kentucky	3,400,843	1.4%
25	Louisiana	3,536,183	1.4%
41	Maine	1,071,112	0.4%
19	Maryland	4,625,863	1.9%
14	Massachusetts	5,354,940	2.2%
8	Michigan	7,686,087	3.1%
21	Minnesota	4,175,347	1.7%
31	Mississippi	2,262,810	0.9%
18	Missouri	4,670,966	1.9%
44	Montana	798,555	0.3%
38	Nebraska	1,414,894	0.6%
34	Nevada	2,175,874	0.9%
42	New Hampshire	1,059,672	0.4%
11	New Jersey	6,926,094	2.8%
36	New Mexico	1,583,623	0.6%
4	New York	15,517,321	6.3%
9	North Carolina	7,656,415	3.1%
47	North Dakota	570,955	0.2%
7	Ohio	8,955,859	3.7%
28	Oklahoma	2,925,352	1.2%
27	Oregon	3,112,217	1.3%
5	Pennsylvania	10,086,316	4.1%
43	Rhode Island	842,321	0.3%
23	South Carolina	3,747,734	1.5%
46	South Dakota	642,768	0.3%
16	Tennessee	5,054,826	2.1%
2	Texas	19,841,344	8.1%
35	Utah	2,038,787	0.8%
49	Vermont	504,976	0.2%
12	Virginia	6,457,174	2.6%
13	Washington	5,458,809	2.2%
37	West Virginia	1,470,179	0.6%
20	Wisconsin	4,457,375	1.8%
50	Wyoming	445,830	0.2%

RANK ORDER

RANK	STATE	POPULATION	% of USA
1	California	29,649,348	12.1%
2	Texas	19,841,344	8.1%
3	Florida	15,839,713	6.5%
4	New York	15,517,321	6.3%
5	Pennsylvania	10,086,316	4.1%
6	Illinois	9,892,106	4.0%
7	Ohio	8,955,859	3.7%
8	Michigan	7,686,087	3.1%
9	North Carolina	7,656,415	3.1%
10	Georgia	7,604,061	3.1%
11	New Jersey	6,926,094	2.8%
12	Virginia	6,457,174	2.6%
13	Washington	5,458,809	2.2%
14	Massachusetts	5,354,940	2.2%
15	Arizona	5,109,792	2.1%
16	Tennessee	5,054,826	2.1%
17	Indiana	5,014,928	2.0%
18	Missouri	4,670,966	1.9%
19	Maryland	4,625,863	1.9%
20	Wisconsin	4,457,375	1.8%
21	Minnesota	4,175,347	1.7%
22	Colorado	4,109,494	1.7%
23	South Carolina	3,747,734	1.5%
24	Alabama	3,741,806	1.5%
25	Louisiana	3,536,183	1.4%
26	Kentucky	3,400,843	1.4%
27	Oregon	3,112,217	1.3%
28	Oklahoma	2,925,352	1.2%
29	Connecticut	2,821,247	1.2%
30	Iowa	2,381,172	1.0%
31	Mississippi	2,262,810	0.9%
32	Arkansas	2,259,350	0.9%
33	Kansas	2,181,355	0.9%
34	Nevada	2,175,874	0.9%
35	Utah	2,038,787	0.8%
36	New Mexico	1,583,623	0.6%
37	West Virginia	1,470,179	0.6%
38	Nebraska	1,414,894	0.6%
39	Idaho	1,203,384	0.5%
40	Hawaii	1,111,117	0.5%
41	Maine	1,071,112	0.4%
42	New Hampshire	1,059,672	0.4%
43	Rhode Island	842,321	0.3%
44	Montana	798,555	0.3%
45	Delaware	731,367	0.3%
46	South Dakota	642,768	0.3%
47	North Dakota	570,955	0.2%
48	Alaska	550,189	0.2%
49	Vermont	504,976	0.2%
50	Wyoming	445,830	0.2%
	District of Columbia	543,588	0.2%

Source: U.S. Bureau of the Census
"State Characteristics: Vintage 2014" (http://www.census.gov/popest/data/state/asrh/2014/index.html)

Percent of Population 18 Years Old and Older in 2014

National Percent = 76.9% of Population

ALPHA ORDER

RANK	STATE	PERCENT
22	Alabama	77.2
47	Alaska	74.7
39	Arizona	75.9
36	Arkansas	76.2
34	California	76.4
30	Colorado	76.7
10	Connecticut	78.4
13	Delaware	78.2
5	Florida	79.6
43	Georgia	75.3
12	Hawaii	78.3
48	Idaho	73.6
29	Illinois	76.8
38	Indiana	76.0
31	Iowa	76.6
46	Kansas	75.1
26	Kentucky	77.1
37	Louisiana	76.1
2	Maine	80.5
19	Maryland	77.4
7	Massachusetts	79.4
15	Michigan	77.6
33	Minnesota	76.5
41	Mississippi	75.6
27	Missouri	77.0
14	Montana	78.0
45	Nebraska	75.2
31	Nevada	76.6
3	New Hampshire	79.9
18	New Jersey	77.5
39	New Mexico	75.9
9	New York	78.6
27	North Carolina	77.0
22	North Dakota	77.2
22	Ohio	77.2
42	Oklahoma	75.4
10	Oregon	78.4
8	Pennsylvania	78.9
4	Rhode Island	79.8
15	South Carolina	77.6
43	South Dakota	75.3
22	Tennessee	77.2
48	Texas	73.6
50	Utah	69.3
1	Vermont	80.6
15	Virginia	77.6
21	Washington	77.3
6	West Virginia	79.5
19	Wisconsin	77.4
35	Wyoming	76.3

RANK ORDER

RANK	STATE	PERCENT
1	Vermont	80.6
2	Maine	80.5
3	New Hampshire	79.9
4	Rhode Island	79.8
5	Florida	79.6
6	West Virginia	79.5
7	Massachusetts	79.4
8	Pennsylvania	78.9
9	New York	78.6
10	Connecticut	78.4
10	Oregon	78.4
12	Hawaii	78.3
13	Delaware	78.2
14	Montana	78.0
15	Michigan	77.6
15	South Carolina	77.6
15	Virginia	77.6
18	New Jersey	77.5
19	Maryland	77.4
19	Wisconsin	77.4
21	Washington	77.3
22	Alabama	77.2
22	North Dakota	77.2
22	Ohio	77.2
22	Tennessee	77.2
26	Kentucky	77.1
27	Missouri	77.0
27	North Carolina	77.0
29	Illinois	76.8
30	Colorado	76.7
31	Iowa	76.6
31	Nevada	76.6
33	Minnesota	76.5
34	California	76.4
35	Wyoming	76.3
36	Arkansas	76.2
37	Louisiana	76.1
38	Indiana	76.0
39	Arizona	75.9
39	New Mexico	75.9
41	Mississippi	75.6
42	Oklahoma	75.4
43	Georgia	75.3
43	South Dakota	75.3
45	Nebraska	75.2
46	Kansas	75.1
47	Alaska	74.7
48	Idaho	73.6
48	Texas	73.6
50	Utah	69.3
	District of Columbia	82.5

Source: CQ Press using data from U.S. Bureau of the Census
"State Characteristics: Vintage 2014" (http://www.census.gov/popest/data/state/asrh/2014/index.html)

Population 18 to 24 Years Old in 2014

National Total = 31,464,158

ALPHA ORDER

RANK	STATE	POPULATION	% of USA
24	Alabama	479,836	1.5%
48	Alaska	81,767	0.3%
14	Arizona	671,820	2.1%
34	Arkansas	286,564	0.9%
1	California	3,994,433	12.7%
21	Colorado	523,398	1.7%
29	Connecticut	350,052	1.1%
46	Delaware	89,714	0.3%
4	Florida	1,783,370	5.7%
8	Georgia	1,021,569	3.2%
40	Hawaii	138,127	0.4%
39	Idaho	156,039	0.5%
5	Illinois	1,252,160	4.0%
15	Indiana	669,383	2.1%
31	Iowa	320,437	1.0%
33	Kansas	302,135	1.0%
26	Kentucky	430,215	1.4%
25	Louisiana	466,593	1.5%
43	Maine	112,622	0.4%
20	Maryland	562,215	1.8%
13	Massachusetts	698,660	2.2%
9	Michigan	1,003,659	3.2%
22	Minnesota	507,489	1.6%
32	Mississippi	311,100	1.0%
18	Missouri	593,858	1.9%
44	Montana	100,985	0.3%
37	Nebraska	191,618	0.6%
35	Nevada	254,965	0.8%
41	New Hampshire	128,406	0.4%
12	New Jersey	797,166	2.5%
36	New Mexico	208,435	0.7%
3	New York	1,975,382	6.3%
10	North Carolina	987,888	3.1%
45	North Dakota	93,952	0.3%
7	Ohio	1,099,710	3.5%
27	Oklahoma	392,303	1.2%
28	Oregon	364,879	1.2%
6	Pennsylvania	1,226,409	3.9%
42	Rhode Island	117,130	0.4%
23	South Carolina	481,976	1.5%
47	South Dakota	85,678	0.3%
17	Tennessee	631,656	2.0%
2	Texas	2,747,682	8.7%
30	Utah	333,388	1.1%
49	Vermont	67,545	0.2%
11	Virginia	829,381	2.6%
16	Washington	668,570	2.1%
38	West Virginia	170,509	0.5%
19	Wisconsin	563,324	1.8%
50	Wyoming	57,443	0.2%

RANK ORDER

RANK	STATE	POPULATION	% of USA
1	California	3,994,433	12.7%
2	Texas	2,747,682	8.7%
3	New York	1,975,382	6.3%
4	Florida	1,783,370	5.7%
5	Illinois	1,252,160	4.0%
6	Pennsylvania	1,226,409	3.9%
7	Ohio	1,099,710	3.5%
8	Georgia	1,021,569	3.2%
9	Michigan	1,003,659	3.2%
10	North Carolina	987,888	3.1%
11	Virginia	829,381	2.6%
12	New Jersey	797,166	2.5%
13	Massachusetts	698,660	2.2%
14	Arizona	671,820	2.1%
15	Indiana	669,383	2.1%
16	Washington	668,570	2.1%
17	Tennessee	631,656	2.0%
18	Missouri	593,858	1.9%
19	Wisconsin	563,324	1.8%
20	Maryland	562,215	1.8%
21	Colorado	523,398	1.7%
22	Minnesota	507,489	1.6%
23	South Carolina	481,976	1.5%
24	Alabama	479,836	1.5%
25	Louisiana	466,593	1.5%
26	Kentucky	430,215	1.4%
27	Oklahoma	392,303	1.2%
28	Oregon	364,879	1.2%
29	Connecticut	350,052	1.1%
30	Utah	333,388	1.1%
31	Iowa	320,437	1.0%
32	Mississippi	311,100	1.0%
33	Kansas	302,135	1.0%
34	Arkansas	286,564	0.9%
35	Nevada	254,965	0.8%
36	New Mexico	208,435	0.7%
37	Nebraska	191,618	0.6%
38	West Virginia	170,509	0.5%
39	Idaho	156,039	0.5%
40	Hawaii	138,127	0.4%
41	New Hampshire	128,406	0.4%
42	Rhode Island	117,130	0.4%
43	Maine	112,622	0.4%
44	Montana	100,985	0.3%
45	North Dakota	93,952	0.3%
46	Delaware	89,714	0.3%
47	South Dakota	85,678	0.3%
48	Alaska	81,767	0.3%
49	Vermont	67,545	0.2%
50	Wyoming	57,443	0.2%
	District of Columbia	80,563	0.3%

Source: U.S. Bureau of the Census
"State Characteristics: Vintage 2014" (http://www.census.gov/popest/data/state/asrh/2014/index.html)

Percent of Population 18 to 24 Years Old in 2014

National Percent = 9.9% of Population

ALPHA ORDER

RANK	STATE	PERCENT
24	Alabama	9.9
3	Alaska	11.1
17	Arizona	10.0
31	Arkansas	9.7
9	California	10.3
27	Colorado	9.8
31	Connecticut	9.7
37	Delaware	9.6
47	Florida	9.0
13	Georgia	10.1
31	Hawaii	9.7
40	Idaho	9.5
31	Illinois	9.7
13	Indiana	10.1
9	Iowa	10.3
6	Kansas	10.4
31	Kentucky	9.7
17	Louisiana	10.0
50	Maine	8.5
43	Maryland	9.4
6	Massachusetts	10.4
13	Michigan	10.1
44	Minnesota	9.3
6	Mississippi	10.4
27	Missouri	9.8
24	Montana	9.9
11	Nebraska	10.2
47	Nevada	9.0
31	New Hampshire	9.7
49	New Jersey	8.9
17	New Mexico	10.0
17	New York	10.0
24	North Carolina	9.9
1	North Dakota	12.7
40	Ohio	9.5
13	Oklahoma	10.1
45	Oregon	9.2
37	Pennsylvania	9.6
3	Rhode Island	11.1
17	South Carolina	10.0
17	South Dakota	10.0
37	Tennessee	9.6
11	Texas	10.2
2	Utah	11.3
5	Vermont	10.8
17	Virginia	10.0
40	Washington	9.5
45	West Virginia	9.2
27	Wisconsin	9.8
27	Wyoming	9.8

RANK ORDER

RANK	STATE	PERCENT
1	North Dakota	12.7
2	Utah	11.3
3	Alaska	11.1
3	Rhode Island	11.1
5	Vermont	10.8
6	Kansas	10.4
6	Massachusetts	10.4
6	Mississippi	10.4
9	California	10.3
9	Iowa	10.3
11	Nebraska	10.2
11	Texas	10.2
13	Georgia	10.1
13	Indiana	10.1
13	Michigan	10.1
13	Oklahoma	10.1
17	Arizona	10.0
17	Louisiana	10.0
17	New Mexico	10.0
17	New York	10.0
17	South Carolina	10.0
17	South Dakota	10.0
17	Virginia	10.0
24	Alabama	9.9
24	Montana	9.9
24	North Carolina	9.9
27	Colorado	9.8
27	Missouri	9.8
27	Wisconsin	9.8
27	Wyoming	9.8
31	Arkansas	9.7
31	Connecticut	9.7
31	Hawaii	9.7
31	Illinois	9.7
31	Kentucky	9.7
31	New Hampshire	9.7
37	Delaware	9.6
37	Pennsylvania	9.6
37	Tennessee	9.6
40	Idaho	9.5
40	Ohio	9.5
40	Washington	9.5
43	Maryland	9.4
44	Minnesota	9.3
45	Oregon	9.2
45	West Virginia	9.2
47	Florida	9.0
47	Nevada	9.0
49	New Jersey	8.9
50	Maine	8.5
	District of Columbia	12.2

Source: CQ Press using data from U.S. Bureau of the Census
"State Characteristics: Vintage 2014" (http://www.census.gov/popest/data/state/asrh/2014/index.html)

Population 25 to 44 Years Old in 2014

National Total = 84,029,637

ALPHA ORDER

RANK	STATE	POPULATION	% of USA
24	Alabama	1,231,977	1.5%
46	Alaska	208,376	0.2%
15	Arizona	1,734,338	2.1%
34	Arkansas	751,172	0.9%
1	California	10,898,724	13.0%
20	Colorado	1,521,480	1.8%
29	Connecticut	880,758	1.0%
45	Delaware	234,122	0.3%
4	Florida	4,953,966	5.9%
8	Georgia	2,753,221	3.3%
40	Hawaii	386,848	0.5%
39	Idaho	415,163	0.5%
5	Illinois	3,460,751	4.1%
17	Indiana	1,670,608	2.0%
33	Iowa	755,513	0.9%
35	Kansas	732,560	0.9%
26	Kentucky	1,127,059	1.3%
23	Louisiana	1,235,576	1.5%
42	Maine	308,098	0.4%
18	Maryland	1,598,270	1.9%
14	Massachusetts	1,768,134	2.1%
10	Michigan	2,390,244	2.8%
22	Minnesota	1,417,387	1.7%
32	Mississippi	760,594	0.9%
19	Missouri	1,534,078	1.8%
44	Montana	244,942	0.3%
37	Nebraska	478,399	0.6%
31	Nevada	789,656	0.9%
41	New Hampshire	312,573	0.4%
11	New Jersey	2,322,025	2.8%
36	New Mexico	522,878	0.6%
3	New York	5,355,346	6.4%
9	North Carolina	2,595,008	3.1%
48	North Dakota	190,044	0.2%
7	Ohio	2,877,749	3.4%
28	Oklahoma	1,004,754	1.2%
27	Oregon	1,060,571	1.3%
6	Pennsylvania	3,152,939	3.8%
43	Rhode Island	264,030	0.3%
25	South Carolina	1,223,680	1.5%
47	South Dakota	207,650	0.2%
16	Tennessee	1,698,473	2.0%
2	Texas	7,560,542	9.0%
30	Utah	826,972	1.0%
50	Vermont	143,370	0.2%
12	Virginia	2,264,027	2.7%
13	Washington	1,939,868	2.3%
38	West Virginia	448,654	0.5%
21	Wisconsin	1,421,268	1.7%
49	Wyoming	152,555	0.2%

RANK ORDER

RANK	STATE	POPULATION	% of USA
1	California	10,898,724	13.0%
2	Texas	7,560,542	9.0%
3	New York	5,355,346	6.4%
4	Florida	4,953,966	5.9%
5	Illinois	3,460,751	4.1%
6	Pennsylvania	3,152,939	3.8%
7	Ohio	2,877,749	3.4%
8	Georgia	2,753,221	3.3%
9	North Carolina	2,595,008	3.1%
10	Michigan	2,390,244	2.8%
11	New Jersey	2,322,025	2.8%
12	Virginia	2,264,027	2.7%
13	Washington	1,939,868	2.3%
14	Massachusetts	1,768,134	2.1%
15	Arizona	1,734,338	2.1%
16	Tennessee	1,698,473	2.0%
17	Indiana	1,670,608	2.0%
18	Maryland	1,598,270	1.9%
19	Missouri	1,534,078	1.8%
20	Colorado	1,521,480	1.8%
21	Wisconsin	1,421,268	1.7%
22	Minnesota	1,417,387	1.7%
23	Louisiana	1,235,576	1.5%
24	Alabama	1,231,977	1.5%
25	South Carolina	1,223,680	1.5%
26	Kentucky	1,127,059	1.3%
27	Oregon	1,060,571	1.3%
28	Oklahoma	1,004,754	1.2%
29	Connecticut	880,758	1.0%
30	Utah	826,972	1.0%
31	Nevada	789,656	0.9%
32	Mississippi	760,594	0.9%
33	Iowa	755,513	0.9%
34	Arkansas	751,172	0.9%
35	Kansas	732,560	0.9%
36	New Mexico	522,878	0.6%
37	Nebraska	478,399	0.6%
38	West Virginia	448,654	0.5%
39	Idaho	415,163	0.5%
40	Hawaii	386,848	0.5%
41	New Hampshire	312,573	0.4%
42	Maine	308,098	0.4%
43	Rhode Island	264,030	0.3%
44	Montana	244,942	0.3%
45	Delaware	234,122	0.3%
46	Alaska	208,376	0.2%
47	South Dakota	207,650	0.2%
48	North Dakota	190,044	0.2%
49	Wyoming	152,555	0.2%
50	Vermont	143,370	0.2%
	District of Columbia	242,647	0.3%

Source: U.S. Bureau of the Census
"State Characteristics: Vintage 2014" (http://www.census.gov/popest/data/state/asrh/2014/index.html)

Percent of Population 25 to 44 Years Old in 2014

National Percent = 26.4% of Population

ALPHA ORDER

RANK	STATE	PERCENT
26	Alabama	25.4
2	Alaska	28.3
23	Arizona	25.8
30	Arkansas	25.3
3	California	28.1
1	Colorado	28.4
42	Connecticut	24.5
36	Delaware	25.0
38	Florida	24.9
8	Georgia	27.3
8	Hawaii	27.3
26	Idaho	25.4
12	Illinois	26.9
30	Indiana	25.3
43	Iowa	24.3
34	Kansas	25.2
25	Kentucky	25.5
15	Louisiana	26.6
49	Maine	23.2
13	Maryland	26.7
16	Massachusetts	26.2
46	Michigan	24.1
19	Minnesota	26.0
26	Mississippi	25.4
30	Missouri	25.3
47	Montana	23.9
26	Nebraska	25.4
6	Nevada	27.8
48	New Hampshire	23.6
19	New Jersey	26.0
35	New Mexico	25.1
11	New York	27.1
17	North Carolina	26.1
24	North Dakota	25.7
39	Ohio	24.8
21	Oklahoma	25.9
13	Oregon	26.7
40	Pennsylvania	24.7
36	Rhode Island	25.0
30	South Carolina	25.3
43	South Dakota	24.3
21	Tennessee	25.9
5	Texas	28.0
3	Utah	28.1
50	Vermont	22.9
10	Virginia	27.2
7	Washington	27.5
45	West Virginia	24.2
40	Wisconsin	24.7
17	Wyoming	26.1

RANK ORDER

RANK	STATE	PERCENT
1	Colorado	28.4
2	Alaska	28.3
3	California	28.1
3	Utah	28.1
5	Texas	28.0
6	Nevada	27.8
7	Washington	27.5
8	Georgia	27.3
8	Hawaii	27.3
10	Virginia	27.2
11	New York	27.1
12	Illinois	26.9
13	Maryland	26.7
13	Oregon	26.7
15	Louisiana	26.6
16	Massachusetts	26.2
17	North Carolina	26.1
17	Wyoming	26.1
19	Minnesota	26.0
19	New Jersey	26.0
21	Oklahoma	25.9
21	Tennessee	25.9
23	Arizona	25.8
24	North Dakota	25.7
25	Kentucky	25.5
26	Alabama	25.4
26	Idaho	25.4
26	Mississippi	25.4
26	Nebraska	25.4
30	Arkansas	25.3
30	Indiana	25.3
30	Missouri	25.3
30	South Carolina	25.3
34	Kansas	25.2
35	New Mexico	25.1
36	Delaware	25.0
36	Rhode Island	25.0
38	Florida	24.9
39	Ohio	24.8
40	Pennsylvania	24.7
40	Wisconsin	24.7
42	Connecticut	24.5
43	Iowa	24.3
43	South Dakota	24.3
45	West Virginia	24.2
46	Michigan	24.1
47	Montana	23.9
48	New Hampshire	23.6
49	Maine	23.2
50	Vermont	22.9
	District of Columbia	36.8

Source: CQ Press using data from U.S. Bureau of the Census
"State Characteristics: Vintage 2014" (http://www.census.gov/popest/data/state/asrh/2014/index.html)

Population 45 to 64 Years Old in 2014

National Total = 83,536,432

ALPHA ORDER

RANK	STATE	POPULATION	% of USA
23	Alabama	1,286,061	1.5%
47	Alaska	190,633	0.2%
18	Arizona	1,633,417	2.0%
32	Arkansas	755,423	0.9%
1	California	9,763,144	11.7%
22	Colorado	1,384,601	1.7%
28	Connecticut	1,034,514	1.2%
45	Delaware	253,624	0.3%
3	Florida	5,310,833	6.4%
10	Georgia	2,577,733	3.1%
42	Hawaii	357,988	0.4%
41	Idaho	398,806	0.5%
6	Illinois	3,390,662	4.1%
16	Indiana	1,733,493	2.1%
30	Iowa	813,873	1.0%
33	Kansas	731,201	0.9%
26	Kentucky	1,189,055	1.4%
25	Louisiana	1,201,120	1.4%
40	Maine	406,885	0.5%
17	Maryland	1,643,118	2.0%
13	Massachusetts	1,871,909	2.2%
8	Michigan	2,762,132	3.3%
21	Minnesota	1,470,329	1.8%
31	Mississippi	762,733	0.9%
19	Missouri	1,610,815	1.9%
44	Montana	281,473	0.3%
38	Nebraska	473,888	0.6%
34	Nevada	729,406	0.9%
39	New Hampshire	407,630	0.5%
11	New Jersey	2,493,400	3.0%
36	New Mexico	533,455	0.6%
4	New York	5,288,499	6.3%
9	North Carolina	2,610,157	3.1%
49	North Dakota	181,961	0.2%
7	Ohio	3,179,231	3.8%
29	Oklahoma	965,764	1.2%
27	Oregon	1,052,880	1.3%
5	Pennsylvania	3,572,447	4.3%
43	Rhode Island	295,014	0.4%
24	South Carolina	1,280,213	1.5%
46	South Dakota	219,217	0.3%
15	Tennessee	1,738,997	2.1%
2	Texas	6,434,039	7.7%
35	Utah	583,167	0.7%
48	Vermont	187,862	0.2%
12	Virginia	2,216,880	2.7%
14	Washington	1,857,616	2.2%
37	West Virginia	522,404	0.6%
20	Wisconsin	1,596,915	1.9%
50	Wyoming	154,191	0.2%

RANK ORDER

RANK	STATE	POPULATION	% of USA
1	California	9,763,144	11.7%
2	Texas	6,434,039	7.7%
3	Florida	5,310,833	6.4%
4	New York	5,288,499	6.3%
5	Pennsylvania	3,572,447	4.3%
6	Illinois	3,390,662	4.1%
7	Ohio	3,179,231	3.8%
8	Michigan	2,762,132	3.3%
9	North Carolina	2,610,157	3.1%
10	Georgia	2,577,733	3.1%
11	New Jersey	2,493,400	3.0%
12	Virginia	2,216,880	2.7%
13	Massachusetts	1,871,909	2.2%
14	Washington	1,857,616	2.2%
15	Tennessee	1,738,997	2.1%
16	Indiana	1,733,493	2.1%
17	Maryland	1,643,118	2.0%
18	Arizona	1,633,417	2.0%
19	Missouri	1,610,815	1.9%
20	Wisconsin	1,596,915	1.9%
21	Minnesota	1,470,329	1.8%
22	Colorado	1,384,601	1.7%
23	Alabama	1,286,061	1.5%
24	South Carolina	1,280,213	1.5%
25	Louisiana	1,201,120	1.4%
26	Kentucky	1,189,055	1.4%
27	Oregon	1,052,880	1.3%
28	Connecticut	1,034,514	1.2%
29	Oklahoma	965,764	1.2%
30	Iowa	813,873	1.0%
31	Mississippi	762,733	0.9%
32	Arkansas	755,423	0.9%
33	Kansas	731,201	0.9%
34	Nevada	729,406	0.9%
35	Utah	583,167	0.7%
36	New Mexico	533,455	0.6%
37	West Virginia	522,404	0.6%
38	Nebraska	473,888	0.6%
39	New Hampshire	407,630	0.5%
40	Maine	406,885	0.5%
41	Idaho	398,806	0.5%
42	Hawaii	357,988	0.4%
43	Rhode Island	295,014	0.4%
44	Montana	281,473	0.3%
45	Delaware	253,624	0.3%
46	South Dakota	219,217	0.3%
47	Alaska	190,633	0.2%
48	Vermont	187,862	0.2%
49	North Dakota	181,961	0.2%
50	Wyoming	154,191	0.2%
	District of Columbia	145,624	0.2%

Source: U.S. Bureau of the Census
"State Characteristics: Vintage 2014" (http://www.census.gov/popest/data/state/asrh/2014/index.html)

Percent of Population 45 to 64 Years Old in 2014

National Percent = 26.2% of Population

ALPHA ORDER

RANK	STATE	PERCENT
23	Alabama	26.5
32	Alaska	25.9
48	Arizona	24.3
38	Arkansas	25.5
41	California	25.2
32	Colorado	25.9
4	Connecticut	28.8
15	Delaware	27.1
19	Florida	26.7
38	Georgia	25.5
41	Hawaii	25.2
47	Idaho	24.4
27	Illinois	26.3
27	Indiana	26.3
30	Iowa	26.2
41	Kansas	25.2
16	Kentucky	26.9
34	Louisiana	25.8
2	Maine	30.6
12	Maryland	27.5
10	Massachusetts	27.8
7	Michigan	27.9
16	Minnesota	26.9
38	Mississippi	25.5
20	Missouri	26.6
12	Montana	27.5
41	Nebraska	25.2
35	Nevada	25.7
1	New Hampshire	30.7
7	New Jersey	27.9
37	New Mexico	25.6
18	New York	26.8
30	North Carolina	26.2
46	North Dakota	24.6
14	Ohio	27.4
45	Oklahoma	24.9
23	Oregon	26.5
7	Pennsylvania	27.9
6	Rhode Island	28.0
23	South Carolina	26.5
35	South Dakota	25.7
20	Tennessee	26.6
49	Texas	23.9
50	Utah	19.8
3	Vermont	30.0
20	Virginia	26.6
27	Washington	26.3
5	West Virginia	28.2
11	Wisconsin	27.7
26	Wyoming	26.4

RANK ORDER

RANK	STATE	PERCENT
1	New Hampshire	30.7
2	Maine	30.6
3	Vermont	30.0
4	Connecticut	28.8
5	West Virginia	28.2
6	Rhode Island	28.0
7	Michigan	27.9
7	New Jersey	27.9
7	Pennsylvania	27.9
10	Massachusetts	27.8
11	Wisconsin	27.7
12	Maryland	27.5
12	Montana	27.5
14	Ohio	27.4
15	Delaware	27.1
16	Kentucky	26.9
16	Minnesota	26.9
18	New York	26.8
19	Florida	26.7
20	Missouri	26.6
20	Tennessee	26.6
20	Virginia	26.6
23	Alabama	26.5
23	Oregon	26.5
23	South Carolina	26.5
26	Wyoming	26.4
27	Illinois	26.3
27	Indiana	26.3
27	Washington	26.3
30	Iowa	26.2
30	North Carolina	26.2
32	Alaska	25.9
32	Colorado	25.9
34	Louisiana	25.8
35	Nevada	25.7
35	South Dakota	25.7
37	New Mexico	25.6
38	Arkansas	25.5
38	Georgia	25.5
38	Mississippi	25.5
41	California	25.2
41	Hawaii	25.2
41	Kansas	25.2
41	Nebraska	25.2
45	Oklahoma	24.9
46	North Dakota	24.6
47	Idaho	24.4
48	Arizona	24.3
49	Texas	23.9
50	Utah	19.8
	District of Columbia	22.1

Source: CQ Press using data from U.S. Bureau of the Census
"State Characteristics: Vintage 2014" (http://www.census.gov/popest/data/state/asrh/2014/index.html)

Population 65 Years Old and Older in 2014

National Total = 46,243,211

ALPHA ORDER

RANK	STATE	POPULATION	% of USA
23	Alabama	743,932	1.6%
50	Alaska	69,413	0.2%
13	Arizona	1,070,217	2.3%
31	Arkansas	466,191	1.0%
1	California	4,993,047	10.8%
24	Colorado	680,015	1.5%
29	Connecticut	555,923	1.2%
45	Delaware	153,907	0.3%
2	Florida	3,791,544	8.2%
11	Georgia	1,251,538	2.7%
41	Hawaii	228,154	0.5%
40	Idaho	233,376	0.5%
7	Illinois	1,788,533	3.9%
17	Indiana	941,444	2.0%
30	Iowa	491,349	1.1%
33	Kansas	415,459	0.9%
25	Kentucky	654,514	1.4%
27	Louisiana	632,894	1.4%
39	Maine	243,507	0.5%
20	Maryland	822,260	1.8%
14	Massachusetts	1,016,237	2.2%
8	Michigan	1,530,052	3.3%
21	Minnesota	780,142	1.7%
32	Mississippi	428,383	0.9%
18	Missouri	932,215	2.0%
43	Montana	171,155	0.4%
38	Nebraska	270,989	0.6%
34	Nevada	401,847	0.9%
42	New Hampshire	211,063	0.5%
10	New Jersey	1,313,503	2.8%
36	New Mexico	318,855	0.7%
4	New York	2,898,094	6.3%
9	North Carolina	1,463,362	3.2%
48	North Dakota	104,998	0.2%
6	Ohio	1,799,169	3.9%
28	Oklahoma	562,531	1.2%
26	Oregon	633,887	1.4%
5	Pennsylvania	2,134,521	4.6%
44	Rhode Island	166,147	0.4%
22	South Carolina	761,865	1.6%
46	South Dakota	130,223	0.3%
16	Tennessee	985,700	2.1%
3	Texas	3,099,081	6.7%
37	Utah	295,260	0.6%
47	Vermont	106,199	0.2%
12	Virginia	1,146,886	2.5%
15	Washington	992,755	2.1%
35	West Virginia	328,612	0.7%
19	Wisconsin	875,868	1.9%
49	Wyoming	81,641	0.2%

RANK ORDER

RANK	STATE	POPULATION	% of USA
1	California	4,993,047	10.8%
2	Florida	3,791,544	8.2%
3	Texas	3,099,081	6.7%
4	New York	2,898,094	6.3%
5	Pennsylvania	2,134,521	4.6%
6	Ohio	1,799,169	3.9%
7	Illinois	1,788,533	3.9%
8	Michigan	1,530,052	3.3%
9	North Carolina	1,463,362	3.2%
10	New Jersey	1,313,503	2.8%
11	Georgia	1,251,538	2.7%
12	Virginia	1,146,886	2.5%
13	Arizona	1,070,217	2.3%
14	Massachusetts	1,016,237	2.2%
15	Washington	992,755	2.1%
16	Tennessee	985,700	2.1%
17	Indiana	941,444	2.0%
18	Missouri	932,215	2.0%
19	Wisconsin	875,868	1.9%
20	Maryland	822,260	1.8%
21	Minnesota	780,142	1.7%
22	South Carolina	761,865	1.6%
23	Alabama	743,932	1.6%
24	Colorado	680,015	1.5%
25	Kentucky	654,514	1.4%
26	Oregon	633,887	1.4%
27	Louisiana	632,894	1.4%
28	Oklahoma	562,531	1.2%
29	Connecticut	555,923	1.2%
30	Iowa	491,349	1.1%
31	Arkansas	466,191	1.0%
32	Mississippi	428,383	0.9%
33	Kansas	415,459	0.9%
34	Nevada	401,847	0.9%
35	West Virginia	328,612	0.7%
36	New Mexico	318,855	0.7%
37	Utah	295,260	0.6%
38	Nebraska	270,989	0.6%
39	Maine	243,507	0.5%
40	Idaho	233,376	0.5%
41	Hawaii	228,154	0.5%
42	New Hampshire	211,063	0.5%
43	Montana	171,155	0.4%
44	Rhode Island	166,147	0.4%
45	Delaware	153,907	0.3%
46	South Dakota	130,223	0.3%
47	Vermont	106,199	0.2%
48	North Dakota	104,998	0.2%
49	Wyoming	81,641	0.2%
50	Alaska	69,413	0.2%
	District of Columbia	74,754	0.2%

Source: U.S. Bureau of the Census
"State Characteristics: Vintage 2014" (http://www.census.gov/popest/data/state/asrh/2014/index.html)

Percent of Population 65 Years Old and Older in 2014

National Percent = 14.5% of Population

ALPHA ORDER

RANK	STATE	PERCENT
20	Alabama	15.3
50	Alaska	9.4
10	Arizona	15.9
14	Arkansas	15.7
45	California	12.9
46	Colorado	12.7
16	Connecticut	15.5
7	Delaware	16.4
1	Florida	19.1
47	Georgia	12.4
8	Hawaii	16.1
32	Idaho	14.3
41	Illinois	13.9
32	Indiana	14.3
12	Iowa	15.8
32	Kansas	14.3
26	Kentucky	14.8
44	Louisiana	13.6
2	Maine	18.3
42	Maryland	13.8
24	Massachusetts	15.1
18	Michigan	15.4
32	Minnesota	14.3
32	Mississippi	14.3
18	Missouri	15.4
5	Montana	16.7
31	Nebraska	14.4
37	Nevada	14.2
10	New Hampshire	15.9
27	New Jersey	14.7
20	New Mexico	15.3
27	New York	14.7
27	North Carolina	14.7
37	North Dakota	14.2
16	Ohio	15.5
30	Oklahoma	14.5
9	Oregon	16.0
5	Pennsylvania	16.7
14	Rhode Island	15.7
12	South Carolina	15.8
20	South Dakota	15.3
24	Tennessee	15.1
48	Texas	11.5
49	Utah	10.0
4	Vermont	16.9
42	Virginia	13.8
39	Washington	14.1
3	West Virginia	17.8
23	Wisconsin	15.2
40	Wyoming	14.0

RANK ORDER

RANK	STATE	PERCENT
1	Florida	19.1
2	Maine	18.3
3	West Virginia	17.8
4	Vermont	16.9
5	Montana	16.7
5	Pennsylvania	16.7
7	Delaware	16.4
8	Hawaii	16.1
9	Oregon	16.0
10	Arizona	15.9
10	New Hampshire	15.9
12	Iowa	15.8
12	South Carolina	15.8
14	Arkansas	15.7
14	Rhode Island	15.7
16	Connecticut	15.5
16	Ohio	15.5
18	Michigan	15.4
18	Missouri	15.4
20	Alabama	15.3
20	New Mexico	15.3
20	South Dakota	15.3
23	Wisconsin	15.2
24	Massachusetts	15.1
24	Tennessee	15.1
26	Kentucky	14.8
27	New Jersey	14.7
27	New York	14.7
27	North Carolina	14.7
30	Oklahoma	14.5
31	Nebraska	14.4
32	Idaho	14.3
32	Indiana	14.3
32	Kansas	14.3
32	Minnesota	14.3
32	Mississippi	14.3
37	Nevada	14.2
37	North Dakota	14.2
39	Washington	14.1
40	Wyoming	14.0
41	Illinois	13.9
42	Maryland	13.8
42	Virginia	13.8
44	Louisiana	13.6
45	California	12.9
46	Colorado	12.7
47	Georgia	12.4
48	Texas	11.5
49	Utah	10.0
50	Alaska	9.4
	District of Columbia	11.3

Source: CQ Press using data from U.S. Bureau of the Census
"State Characteristics: Vintage 2014" (http://www.census.gov/popest/data/state/asrh/2014/index.html)

Population 85 Years Old and Older in 2014

National Total = 6,162,231

ALPHA ORDER

RANK	STATE	POPULATION	% of USA
23	Alabama	83,567	1.4%
50	Alaska	5,931	0.1%
18	Arizona	124,772	2.0%
32	Arkansas	55,050	0.9%
1	California	688,650	11.2%
25	Colorado	81,627	1.3%
22	Connecticut	89,785	1.5%
47	Delaware	17,951	0.3%
2	Florida	522,291	8.5%
13	Georgia	131,194	2.1%
38	Hawaii	36,891	0.6%
43	Idaho	27,349	0.4%
6	Illinois	256,052	4.2%
16	Indiana	126,423	2.1%
27	Iowa	78,702	1.3%
31	Kansas	63,827	1.0%
28	Kentucky	75,895	1.2%
29	Louisiana	74,426	1.2%
40	Maine	31,721	0.5%
21	Maryland	111,008	1.8%
11	Massachusetts	157,194	2.6%
8	Michigan	210,821	3.4%
19	Minnesota	116,662	1.9%
33	Mississippi	49,635	0.8%
17	Missouri	125,005	2.0%
44	Montana	21,985	0.4%
34	Nebraska	41,852	0.7%
36	Nevada	37,764	0.6%
42	New Hampshire	27,875	0.5%
9	New Jersey	194,960	3.2%
37	New Mexico	37,373	0.6%
3	New York	429,182	7.0%
10	North Carolina	170,382	2.8%
46	North Dakota	17,959	0.3%
7	Ohio	250,929	4.1%
30	Oklahoma	68,092	1.1%
24	Oregon	83,540	1.4%
5	Pennsylvania	331,229	5.4%
41	Rhode Island	28,309	0.5%
26	South Carolina	80,384	1.3%
45	South Dakota	20,871	0.3%
20	Tennessee	111,140	1.8%
4	Texas	361,502	5.9%
39	Utah	34,758	0.6%
48	Vermont	14,107	0.2%
12	Virginia	138,840	2.3%
14	Washington	128,688	2.1%
35	West Virginia	38,735	0.6%
15	Wisconsin	128,096	2.1%
49	Wyoming	10,047	0.2%

RANK ORDER

RANK	STATE	POPULATION	% of USA
1	California	688,650	11.2%
2	Florida	522,291	8.5%
3	New York	429,182	7.0%
4	Texas	361,502	5.9%
5	Pennsylvania	331,229	5.4%
6	Illinois	256,052	4.2%
7	Ohio	250,929	4.1%
8	Michigan	210,821	3.4%
9	New Jersey	194,960	3.2%
10	North Carolina	170,382	2.8%
11	Massachusetts	157,194	2.6%
12	Virginia	138,840	2.3%
13	Georgia	131,194	2.1%
14	Washington	128,688	2.1%
15	Wisconsin	128,096	2.1%
16	Indiana	126,423	2.1%
17	Missouri	125,005	2.0%
18	Arizona	124,772	2.0%
19	Minnesota	116,662	1.9%
20	Tennessee	111,140	1.8%
21	Maryland	111,008	1.8%
22	Connecticut	89,785	1.5%
23	Alabama	83,567	1.4%
24	Oregon	83,540	1.4%
25	Colorado	81,627	1.3%
26	South Carolina	80,384	1.3%
27	Iowa	78,702	1.3%
28	Kentucky	75,895	1.2%
29	Louisiana	74,426	1.2%
30	Oklahoma	68,092	1.1%
31	Kansas	63,827	1.0%
32	Arkansas	55,050	0.9%
33	Mississippi	49,635	0.8%
34	Nebraska	41,852	0.7%
35	West Virginia	38,735	0.6%
36	Nevada	37,764	0.6%
37	New Mexico	37,373	0.6%
38	Hawaii	36,891	0.6%
39	Utah	34,758	0.6%
40	Maine	31,721	0.5%
41	Rhode Island	28,309	0.5%
42	New Hampshire	27,875	0.5%
43	Idaho	27,349	0.4%
44	Montana	21,985	0.4%
45	South Dakota	20,871	0.3%
46	North Dakota	17,959	0.3%
47	Delaware	17,951	0.3%
48	Vermont	14,107	0.2%
49	Wyoming	10,047	0.2%
50	Alaska	5,931	0.1%
	District of Columbia	11,203	0.2%

Source: U.S. Bureau of the Census
"State Characteristics: Vintage 2014" (http://www.census.gov/popest/data/state/asrh/2014/index.html)

Percent of Population 85 Years Old and Older in 2014

National Percent = 1.9% of Population

ALPHA ORDER

RANK	STATE	PERCENT
35	Alabama	1.7
50	Alaska	0.8
26	Arizona	1.9
26	Arkansas	1.9
31	California	1.8
45	Colorado	1.5
5	Connecticut	2.5
26	Delaware	1.9
2	Florida	2.6
46	Georgia	1.3
2	Hawaii	2.6
35	Idaho	1.7
25	Illinois	2.0
26	Indiana	1.9
5	Iowa	2.5
12	Kansas	2.2
35	Kentucky	1.7
44	Louisiana	1.6
7	Maine	2.4
26	Maryland	1.9
10	Massachusetts	2.3
18	Michigan	2.1
18	Minnesota	2.1
35	Mississippi	1.7
18	Missouri	2.1
18	Montana	2.1
12	Nebraska	2.2
46	Nevada	1.3
18	New Hampshire	2.1
12	New Jersey	2.2
31	New Mexico	1.8
12	New York	2.2
35	North Carolina	1.7
7	North Dakota	2.4
12	Ohio	2.2
31	Oklahoma	1.8
18	Oregon	2.1
2	Pennsylvania	2.6
1	Rhode Island	2.7
35	South Carolina	1.7
7	South Dakota	2.4
35	Tennessee	1.7
46	Texas	1.3
49	Utah	1.2
10	Vermont	2.3
35	Virginia	1.7
31	Washington	1.8
18	West Virginia	2.1
12	Wisconsin	2.2
35	Wyoming	1.7

RANK ORDER

RANK	STATE	PERCENT
1	Rhode Island	2.7
2	Florida	2.6
2	Hawaii	2.6
2	Pennsylvania	2.6
5	Connecticut	2.5
5	Iowa	2.5
7	Maine	2.4
7	North Dakota	2.4
7	South Dakota	2.4
10	Massachusetts	2.3
10	Vermont	2.3
12	Kansas	2.2
12	Nebraska	2.2
12	New Jersey	2.2
12	New York	2.2
12	Ohio	2.2
12	Wisconsin	2.2
18	Michigan	2.1
18	Minnesota	2.1
18	Missouri	2.1
18	Montana	2.1
18	New Hampshire	2.1
18	Oregon	2.1
18	West Virginia	2.1
25	Illinois	2.0
26	Arizona	1.9
26	Arkansas	1.9
26	Delaware	1.9
26	Indiana	1.9
26	Maryland	1.9
31	California	1.8
31	New Mexico	1.8
31	Oklahoma	1.8
31	Washington	1.8
35	Alabama	1.7
35	Idaho	1.7
35	Kentucky	1.7
35	Mississippi	1.7
35	North Carolina	1.7
35	South Carolina	1.7
35	Tennessee	1.7
35	Virginia	1.7
35	Wyoming	1.7
44	Louisiana	1.6
45	Colorado	1.5
46	Georgia	1.3
46	Nevada	1.3
46	Texas	1.3
49	Utah	1.2
50	Alaska	0.8

District of Columbia 1.7

Source: CQ Press using data from U.S. Bureau of the Census
"State Characteristics: Vintage 2014" (http://www.census.gov/popest/data/state/asrh/2014/index.html)

Percent of Native Population Born in Their State of Residence in 2014

National Percent = 67.7%

ALPHA ORDER

RANK	STATE	PERCENT
13	Alabama	72.7
48	Alaska	44.6
46	Arizona	45.1
29	Arkansas	64.1
7	California	75.4
44	Colorado	47.7
28	Connecticut	64.2
43	Delaware	49.9
46	Florida	45.1
33	Georgia	61.7
27	Hawaii	64.4
41	Idaho	51.5
6	Illinois	78.2
16	Indiana	71.8
8	Iowa	74.9
31	Kansas	63.1
14	Kentucky	72.3
3	Louisiana	81.1
25	Maine	65.8
37	Maryland	55.8
11	Massachusetts	73.3
1	Michigan	81.9
10	Minnesota	74.0
12	Mississippi	73.1
19	Missouri	68.6
38	Montana	55.6
18	Nebraska	69.9
50	Nevada	32.0
45	New Hampshire	45.4
21	New Jersey	67.5
35	New Mexico	58.7
2	New York	81.8
32	North Carolina	62.3
23	North Dakota	67.2
5	Ohio	78.4
26	Oklahoma	64.6
42	Oregon	51.0
4	Pennsylvania	78.5
22	Rhode Island	67.3
34	South Carolina	60.6
24	South Dakota	67.0
30	Tennessee	64.0
15	Texas	72.2
20	Utah	67.9
40	Vermont	54.5
36	Virginia	56.0
39	Washington	55.1
17	West Virginia	71.2
9	Wisconsin	74.8
49	Wyoming	42.7

RANK ORDER

RANK	STATE	PERCENT
1	Michigan	81.9
2	New York	81.8
3	Louisiana	81.1
4	Pennsylvania	78.5
5	Ohio	78.4
6	Illinois	78.2
7	California	75.4
8	Iowa	74.9
9	Wisconsin	74.8
10	Minnesota	74.0
11	Massachusetts	73.3
12	Mississippi	73.1
13	Alabama	72.7
14	Kentucky	72.3
15	Texas	72.2
16	Indiana	71.8
17	West Virginia	71.2
18	Nebraska	69.9
19	Missouri	68.6
20	Utah	67.9
21	New Jersey	67.5
22	Rhode Island	67.3
23	North Dakota	67.2
24	South Dakota	67.0
25	Maine	65.8
26	Oklahoma	64.6
27	Hawaii	64.4
28	Connecticut	64.2
29	Arkansas	64.1
30	Tennessee	64.0
31	Kansas	63.1
32	North Carolina	62.3
33	Georgia	61.7
34	South Carolina	60.6
35	New Mexico	58.7
36	Virginia	56.0
37	Maryland	55.8
38	Montana	55.6
39	Washington	55.1
40	Vermont	54.5
41	Idaho	51.5
42	Oregon	51.0
43	Delaware	49.9
44	Colorado	47.7
45	New Hampshire	45.4
46	Arizona	45.1
46	Florida	45.1
48	Alaska	44.6
49	Wyoming	42.7
50	Nevada	32.0
	District of Columbia	42.1

Source: U.S. Bureau of the Census
"2014 American Community Survey-Table R0601" (http://www.census.gov/programs-surveys/acs/)

Domestic Migration of Population: 2014 to 2015

National Net Migration = 0 People*

ALPHA ORDER

RANK	STATE	NET MIGRATION
24	Alabama	(2,268)
32	Alaska	(7,678)
4	Arizona	45,934
19	Arkansas	(1,212)
48	California	(77,219)
3	Colorado	54,459
43	Connecticut	(27,619)
17	Delaware	4,225
1	Florida	202,510
9	Georgia	34,013
29	Hawaii	(7,026)
15	Idaho	6,880
49	Illinois	(105,217)
38	Indiana	(14,881)
26	Iowa	(3,949)
36	Kansas	(13,030)
31	Kentucky	(7,441)
30	Louisiana	(7,358)
20	Maine	(1,718)
42	Maryland	(24,738)
40	Massachusetts	(21,805)
45	Michigan	(38,911)
35	Minnesota	(12,242)
34	Mississippi	(12,230)
33	Missouri	(8,744)
16	Montana	5,268
25	Nebraska	(2,775)
10	Nevada	27,959
18	New Hampshire	(1,167)
47	New Jersey	(65,254)
37	New Mexico	(13,352)
50	New York	(157,992)
7	North Carolina	38,197
12	North Dakota	9,966
44	Ohio	(31,297)
14	Oklahoma	8,199
8	Oregon	34,824
46	Pennsylvania	(41,607)
28	Rhode Island	(4,693)
5	South Carolina	45,582
21	South Dakota	(1,780)
11	Tennessee	21,425
2	Texas	170,103
13	Utah	9,303
23	Vermont	(2,223)
41	Virginia	(23,813)
6	Washington	40,799
27	West Virginia	(4,685)
39	Wisconsin	(15,568)
22	Wyoming	(1,885)

RANK ORDER

RANK	STATE	NET MIGRATION
1	Florida	202,510
2	Texas	170,103
3	Colorado	54,459
4	Arizona	45,934
5	South Carolina	45,582
6	Washington	40,799
7	North Carolina	38,197
8	Oregon	34,824
9	Georgia	34,013
10	Nevada	27,959
11	Tennessee	21,425
12	North Dakota	9,966
13	Utah	9,303
14	Oklahoma	8,199
15	Idaho	6,880
16	Montana	5,268
17	Delaware	4,225
18	New Hampshire	(1,167)
19	Arkansas	(1,212)
20	Maine	(1,718)
21	South Dakota	(1,780)
22	Wyoming	(1,885)
23	Vermont	(2,223)
24	Alabama	(2,268)
25	Nebraska	(2,775)
26	Iowa	(3,949)
27	West Virginia	(4,685)
28	Rhode Island	(4,693)
29	Hawaii	(7,026)
30	Louisiana	(7,358)
31	Kentucky	(7,441)
32	Alaska	(7,678)
33	Missouri	(8,744)
34	Mississippi	(12,230)
35	Minnesota	(12,242)
36	Kansas	(13,030)
37	New Mexico	(13,352)
38	Indiana	(14,881)
39	Wisconsin	(15,568)
40	Massachusetts	(21,805)
41	Virginia	(23,813)
42	Maryland	(24,738)
43	Connecticut	(27,619)
44	Ohio	(31,297)
45	Michigan	(38,911)
46	Pennsylvania	(41,607)
47	New Jersey	(65,254)
48	California	(77,219)
49	Illinois	(105,217)
50	New York	(157,992)
	District of Columbia	3,731

Source: U.S. Bureau of the Census
  "Components of Population Change" (http://www.census.gov/popest/data/datasets.html)
*From July 1, 2014 to June 30, 2015. Includes armed forces residing in each state. Net Domestic Migration is the difference between domestic inmigration to an area and domestic outmigration from it during the period. Domestic inmigration and outmigration consist of moves where both the origins and destinations are within the United States (excluding Puerto Rico).

Net International Migration: 2014 to 2015

National Net = 1,150,528 Immigrants*

ALPHA ORDER

RANK	STATE	IMMIGRANTS	% of USA
34	Alabama	5,726	0.5%
41	Alaska	2,601	0.2%
17	Arizona	17,344	1.5%
37	Arkansas	3,893	0.3%
1	California	180,722	15.7%
19	Colorado	13,322	1.2%
16	Connecticut	18,769	1.6%
39	Delaware	2,953	0.3%
3	Florida	129,525	11.3%
11	Georgia	29,141	2.5%
23	Hawaii	10,128	0.9%
43	Idaho	2,217	0.2%
8	Illinois	37,682	3.3%
20	Indiana	12,574	1.1%
33	Iowa	6,409	0.6%
29	Kansas	7,317	0.6%
28	Kentucky	7,400	0.6%
26	Louisiana	8,273	0.7%
46	Maine	1,528	0.1%
10	Maryland	31,330	2.7%
6	Massachusetts	43,508	3.8%
14	Michigan	24,202	2.1%
18	Minnesota	15,473	1.3%
40	Mississippi	2,770	0.2%
22	Missouri	10,210	0.9%
49	Montana	751	0.1%
35	Nebraska	4,825	0.4%
24	Nevada	9,156	0.8%
42	New Hampshire	2,244	0.2%
5	New Jersey	57,083	5.0%
38	New Mexico	3,631	0.3%
2	New York	134,160	11.7%
13	North Carolina	25,066	2.2%
44	North Dakota	1,767	0.2%
15	Ohio	20,693	1.8%
30	Oklahoma	7,267	0.6%
27	Oregon	8,111	0.7%
9	Pennsylvania	35,942	3.1%
36	Rhode Island	4,727	0.4%
31	South Carolina	6,803	0.6%
45	South Dakota	1,696	0.1%
21	Tennessee	10,843	0.9%
4	Texas	101,558	8.8%
32	Utah	6,441	0.6%
48	Vermont	914	0.1%
7	Virginia	38,801	3.4%
12	Washington	27,906	2.4%
47	West Virginia	1,345	0.1%
25	Wisconsin	8,569	0.7%
50	Wyoming	661	0.1%

RANK ORDER

RANK	STATE	IMMIGRANTS	% of USA
1	California	180,722	15.7%
2	New York	134,160	11.7%
3	Florida	129,525	11.3%
4	Texas	101,558	8.8%
5	New Jersey	57,083	5.0%
6	Massachusetts	43,508	3.8%
7	Virginia	38,801	3.4%
8	Illinois	37,682	3.3%
9	Pennsylvania	35,942	3.1%
10	Maryland	31,330	2.7%
11	Georgia	29,141	2.5%
12	Washington	27,906	2.4%
13	North Carolina	25,066	2.2%
14	Michigan	24,202	2.1%
15	Ohio	20,693	1.8%
16	Connecticut	18,769	1.6%
17	Arizona	17,344	1.5%
18	Minnesota	15,473	1.3%
19	Colorado	13,322	1.2%
20	Indiana	12,574	1.1%
21	Tennessee	10,843	0.9%
22	Missouri	10,210	0.9%
23	Hawaii	10,128	0.9%
24	Nevada	9,156	0.8%
25	Wisconsin	8,569	0.7%
26	Louisiana	8,273	0.7%
27	Oregon	8,111	0.7%
28	Kentucky	7,400	0.6%
29	Kansas	7,317	0.6%
30	Oklahoma	7,267	0.6%
31	South Carolina	6,803	0.6%
32	Utah	6,441	0.6%
33	Iowa	6,409	0.6%
34	Alabama	5,726	0.5%
35	Nebraska	4,825	0.4%
36	Rhode Island	4,727	0.4%
37	Arkansas	3,893	0.3%
38	New Mexico	3,631	0.3%
39	Delaware	2,953	0.3%
40	Mississippi	2,770	0.2%
41	Alaska	2,601	0.2%
42	New Hampshire	2,244	0.2%
43	Idaho	2,217	0.2%
44	North Dakota	1,767	0.2%
45	South Dakota	1,696	0.1%
46	Maine	1,528	0.1%
47	West Virginia	1,345	0.1%
48	Vermont	914	0.1%
49	Montana	751	0.1%
50	Wyoming	661	0.1%
	District of Columbia	4,551	0.4%

Source: U.S. Bureau of the Census
"Components of Population Change" (http://www.census.gov/popest/data/datasets.html)
*From July 1, 2014 to June 30, 2015. Net International Migration is the difference between migration to an area from outside the United States (immigration) and migration from the area to outside the United States (emigration) during the period. Includes legal immigration and estimates of undocumented immigration.

Percent of Population Foreign Born in 2014

National Percent = 13.3% of Population*

ALPHA ORDER

RANK	STATE	PERCENT
46	Alabama	3.2
24	Alaska	7.4
11	Arizona	13.7
36	Arkansas	4.7
1	California	27.1
16	Colorado	10.0
11	Connecticut	13.7
20	Delaware	8.6
4	Florida	20.0
17	Georgia	9.9
6	Hawaii	17.6
29	Idaho	6.0
10	Illinois	13.9
35	Indiana	4.8
32	Iowa	4.9
25	Kansas	7.0
42	Kentucky	3.7
38	Louisiana	4.2
42	Maine	3.7
9	Maryland	14.9
8	Massachusetts	15.7
27	Michigan	6.4
22	Minnesota	7.8
49	Mississippi	2.2
42	Missouri	3.7
48	Montana	2.3
26	Nebraska	6.7
5	Nevada	19.4
29	New Hampshire	6.0
3	New Jersey	21.9
17	New Mexico	9.9
2	New York	22.6
23	North Carolina	7.7
45	North Dakota	3.3
38	Ohio	4.2
31	Oklahoma	5.8
17	Oregon	9.9
27	Pennsylvania	6.4
13	Rhode Island	13.4
36	South Carolina	4.7
47	South Dakota	2.9
32	Tennessee	4.9
7	Texas	16.8
21	Utah	8.5
40	Vermont	4.1
15	Virginia	12.1
13	Washington	13.4
50	West Virginia	1.4
32	Wisconsin	4.9
41	Wyoming	3.8

RANK ORDER

RANK	STATE	PERCENT
1	California	27.1
2	New York	22.6
3	New Jersey	21.9
4	Florida	20.0
5	Nevada	19.4
6	Hawaii	17.6
7	Texas	16.8
8	Massachusetts	15.7
9	Maryland	14.9
10	Illinois	13.9
11	Arizona	13.7
11	Connecticut	13.7
13	Rhode Island	13.4
13	Washington	13.4
15	Virginia	12.1
16	Colorado	10.0
17	Georgia	9.9
17	New Mexico	9.9
17	Oregon	9.9
20	Delaware	8.6
21	Utah	8.5
22	Minnesota	7.8
23	North Carolina	7.7
24	Alaska	7.4
25	Kansas	7.0
26	Nebraska	6.7
27	Michigan	6.4
27	Pennsylvania	6.4
29	Idaho	6.0
29	New Hampshire	6.0
31	Oklahoma	5.8
32	Iowa	4.9
32	Tennessee	4.9
32	Wisconsin	4.9
35	Indiana	4.8
36	Arkansas	4.7
36	South Carolina	4.7
38	Louisiana	4.2
38	Ohio	4.2
40	Vermont	4.1
41	Wyoming	3.8
42	Kentucky	3.7
42	Maine	3.7
42	Missouri	3.7
45	North Dakota	3.3
46	Alabama	3.2
47	South Dakota	2.9
48	Montana	2.3
49	Mississippi	2.2
50	West Virginia	1.4
	District of Columbia	14.0

Source: U.S. Bureau of the Census
"2014 American Community Survey-Table R0501" (http://www.census.gov/programs-surveys/acs/)
*"Foreign born" are persons not born in the United States, Puerto Rico, a U.S. Island Area, or abroad of American parent or parents.

Percent of Population Speaking a Language Other Than English at Home in 2014
National Percent = 21.1%*

ALPHA ORDER

RANK	STATE	PERCENT
47	Alabama	4.9
17	Alaska	16.6
8	Arizona	27.0
38	Arkansas	6.9
1	California	43.9
15	Colorado	17.2
12	Connecticut	21.8
22	Delaware	13.0
7	Florida	28.3
21	Georgia	13.6
9	Hawaii	25.2
28	Idaho	10.3
10	Illinois	22.6
33	Indiana	7.9
35	Iowa	7.2
23	Kansas	11.3
45	Kentucky	5.2
32	Louisiana	8.4
39	Maine	6.8
16	Maryland	17.1
10	Massachusetts	22.6
30	Michigan	9.2
25	Minnesota	11.1
49	Mississippi	3.7
43	Missouri	5.6
48	Montana	3.9
27	Nebraska	10.6
4	Nevada	30.7
34	New Hampshire	7.5
5	New Jersey	30.6
2	New Mexico	36.8
6	New York	30.4
24	North Carolina	11.2
44	North Dakota	5.5
41	Ohio	6.6
29	Oklahoma	10.0
19	Oregon	15.5
26	Pennsylvania	10.8
13	Rhode Island	21.0
39	South Carolina	6.8
42	South Dakota	5.7
36	Tennessee	7.0
3	Texas	35.5
20	Utah	14.7
46	Vermont	5.0
18	Virginia	15.6
14	Washington	18.8
50	West Virginia	2.0
31	Wisconsin	8.7
36	Wyoming	7.0

RANK ORDER

RANK	STATE	PERCENT
1	California	43.9
2	New Mexico	36.8
3	Texas	35.5
4	Nevada	30.7
5	New Jersey	30.6
6	New York	30.4
7	Florida	28.3
8	Arizona	27.0
9	Hawaii	25.2
10	Illinois	22.6
10	Massachusetts	22.6
12	Connecticut	21.8
13	Rhode Island	21.0
14	Washington	18.8
15	Colorado	17.2
16	Maryland	17.1
17	Alaska	16.6
18	Virginia	15.6
19	Oregon	15.5
20	Utah	14.7
21	Georgia	13.6
22	Delaware	13.0
23	Kansas	11.3
24	North Carolina	11.2
25	Minnesota	11.1
26	Pennsylvania	10.8
27	Nebraska	10.6
28	Idaho	10.3
29	Oklahoma	10.0
30	Michigan	9.2
31	Wisconsin	8.7
32	Louisiana	8.4
33	Indiana	7.9
34	New Hampshire	7.5
35	Iowa	7.2
36	Tennessee	7.0
36	Wyoming	7.0
38	Arkansas	6.9
39	Maine	6.8
39	South Carolina	6.8
41	Ohio	6.6
42	South Dakota	5.7
43	Missouri	5.6
44	North Dakota	5.5
45	Kentucky	5.2
46	Vermont	5.0
47	Alabama	4.9
48	Montana	3.9
49	Mississippi	3.7
50	West Virginia	2.0
	District of Columbia	17.8

Source: U.S. Bureau of the Census
 "2014 American Community Survey-Table R1601" (http://www.census.gov/programs-surveys/acs/)
*Population five years old and older.

Percent of Population Speaking Spanish at Home in 2014

National Percent = 13.1%*

ALPHA ORDER

RANK	STATE	PERCENT
37	Alabama	3.1
36	Alaska	3.3
6	Arizona	20.6
26	Arkansas	5.1
3	California	28.8
10	Colorado	12.0
11	Connecticut	11.4
23	Delaware	6.9
5	Florida	20.9
17	Georgia	8.0
43	Hawaii	1.9
18	Idaho	7.8
9	Illinois	13.3
30	Indiana	4.4
33	Iowa	3.8
19	Kansas	7.5
39	Kentucky	2.5
34	Louisiana	3.7
49	Maine	0.9
22	Maryland	7.1
15	Massachusetts	8.6
38	Michigan	2.9
35	Minnesota	3.6
40	Mississippi	2.4
41	Missouri	2.3
46	Montana	1.5
21	Nebraska	7.3
4	Nevada	21.4
43	New Hampshire	1.9
7	New Jersey	15.9
2	New Mexico	29.1
8	New York	15.1
20	North Carolina	7.4
47	North Dakota	1.4
42	Ohio	2.1
24	Oklahoma	6.7
14	Oregon	9.3
27	Pennsylvania	4.7
12	Rhode Island	11.2
30	South Carolina	4.4
45	South Dakota	1.7
32	Tennessee	4.0
1	Texas	29.8
13	Utah	10.0
48	Vermont	1.0
24	Virginia	6.7
16	Washington	8.4
50	West Virginia	0.8
29	Wisconsin	4.5
27	Wyoming	4.7

RANK ORDER

RANK	STATE	PERCENT
1	Texas	29.8
2	New Mexico	29.1
3	California	28.8
4	Nevada	21.4
5	Florida	20.9
6	Arizona	20.6
7	New Jersey	15.9
8	New York	15.1
9	Illinois	13.3
10	Colorado	12.0
11	Connecticut	11.4
12	Rhode Island	11.2
13	Utah	10.0
14	Oregon	9.3
15	Massachusetts	8.6
16	Washington	8.4
17	Georgia	8.0
18	Idaho	7.8
19	Kansas	7.5
20	North Carolina	7.4
21	Nebraska	7.3
22	Maryland	7.1
23	Delaware	6.9
24	Oklahoma	6.7
24	Virginia	6.7
26	Arkansas	5.1
27	Pennsylvania	4.7
27	Wyoming	4.7
29	Wisconsin	4.5
30	Indiana	4.4
30	South Carolina	4.4
32	Tennessee	4.0
33	Iowa	3.8
34	Louisiana	3.7
35	Minnesota	3.6
36	Alaska	3.3
37	Alabama	3.1
38	Michigan	2.9
39	Kentucky	2.5
40	Mississippi	2.4
41	Missouri	2.3
42	Ohio	2.1
43	Hawaii	1.9
43	New Hampshire	1.9
45	South Dakota	1.7
46	Montana	1.5
47	North Dakota	1.4
48	Vermont	1.0
49	Maine	0.9
50	West Virginia	0.8
	District of Columbia	8.6

Source: U.S. Bureau of the Census
"2014 American Community Survey-Table R1602" (http://www.census.gov/programs-surveys/acs/)
*Population five years old and older.

Marriage Rate for Men in 2014

National Rate = 18.1 Marriages per 1,000 Men*

ALPHA ORDER

RANK	STATE	RATE
20	Alabama	19.4
1	Alaska	29.4
33	Arizona	17.7
15	Arkansas	19.7
27	California	18.3
7	Colorado	22.1
50	Connecticut	14.1
33	Delaware	17.7
45	Florida	15.4
18	Georgia	19.5
10	Hawaii	20.9
5	Idaho	22.7
38	Illinois	16.5
13	Indiana	19.9
21	Iowa	18.9
11	Kansas	20.7
28	Kentucky	18.2
25	Louisiana	18.4
47	Maine	15.0
43	Maryland	16.0
49	Massachusetts	14.6
48	Michigan	14.9
31	Minnesota	17.9
11	Mississippi	20.7
35	Missouri	17.2
38	Montana	16.5
30	Nebraska	18.0
8	Nevada	21.3
24	New Hampshire	18.5
44	New Jersey	15.9
32	New Mexico	17.8
36	New York	16.7
22	North Carolina	18.8
22	North Dakota	18.8
41	Ohio	16.1
4	Oklahoma	23.5
25	Oregon	18.4
40	Pennsylvania	16.2
37	Rhode Island	16.6
18	South Carolina	19.5
5	South Dakota	22.7
14	Tennessee	19.8
9	Texas	21.1
3	Utah	24.3
46	Vermont	15.2
16	Virginia	19.6
16	Washington	19.6
29	West Virginia	18.1
41	Wisconsin	16.1
2	Wyoming	24.6

RANK ORDER

RANK	STATE	RATE
1	Alaska	29.4
2	Wyoming	24.6
3	Utah	24.3
4	Oklahoma	23.5
5	Idaho	22.7
5	South Dakota	22.7
7	Colorado	22.1
8	Nevada	21.3
9	Texas	21.1
10	Hawaii	20.9
11	Kansas	20.7
11	Mississippi	20.7
13	Indiana	19.9
14	Tennessee	19.8
15	Arkansas	19.7
16	Virginia	19.6
16	Washington	19.6
18	Georgia	19.5
18	South Carolina	19.5
20	Alabama	19.4
21	Iowa	18.9
22	North Carolina	18.8
22	North Dakota	18.8
24	New Hampshire	18.5
25	Louisiana	18.4
25	Oregon	18.4
27	California	18.3
28	Kentucky	18.2
29	West Virginia	18.1
30	Nebraska	18.0
31	Minnesota	17.9
32	New Mexico	17.8
33	Arizona	17.7
33	Delaware	17.7
35	Missouri	17.2
36	New York	16.7
37	Rhode Island	16.6
38	Illinois	16.5
38	Montana	16.5
40	Pennsylvania	16.2
41	Ohio	16.1
41	Wisconsin	16.1
43	Maryland	16.0
44	New Jersey	15.9
45	Florida	15.4
46	Vermont	15.2
47	Maine	15.0
48	Michigan	14.9
49	Massachusetts	14.6
50	Connecticut	14.1
	District of Columbia	30.4

Source: U.S. Bureau of the Census
"2014 American Community Survey-Table GCT1252" (http://www.census.gov/programs-surveys/acs/)
*Men age 15 and older. Marriages in the last year.

Estimated Median Age of Men at First Marriage in 2014

National Median = 29.5 Years*

ALPHA ORDER

RANK	STATE	PERCENT
35	Alabama	28.3
22	Alaska	29.2
18	Arizona	29.5
46	Arkansas	27.5
8	California	30.4
28	Colorado	28.9
1	Connecticut	31.0
4	Delaware	30.7
8	Florida	30.4
29	Georgia	28.8
40	Hawaii	28.1
49	Idaho	26.7
12	Illinois	30.0
33	Indiana	28.6
46	Iowa	27.5
36	Kansas	28.2
43	Kentucky	27.9
13	Louisiana	29.7
13	Maine	29.7
6	Maryland	30.5
3	Massachusetts	30.8
13	Michigan	29.7
18	Minnesota	29.5
36	Mississippi	28.2
34	Missouri	28.4
29	Montana	28.8
44	Nebraska	27.8
10	Nevada	30.1
13	New Hampshire	29.7
4	New Jersey	30.7
26	New Mexico	29.0
2	New York	30.9
26	North Carolina	29.0
40	North Dakota	28.1
20	Ohio	29.4
48	Oklahoma	27.0
23	Oregon	29.1
10	Pennsylvania	30.1
6	Rhode Island	30.5
29	South Carolina	28.8
42	South Dakota	28.0
36	Tennessee	28.2
36	Texas	28.2
50	Utah	26.5
13	Vermont	29.7
23	Virginia	29.1
23	Washington	29.1
32	West Virginia	28.7
21	Wisconsin	29.3
44	Wyoming	27.8

RANK ORDER

RANK	STATE	PERCENT
1	Connecticut	31.0
2	New York	30.9
3	Massachusetts	30.8
4	Delaware	30.7
4	New Jersey	30.7
6	Maryland	30.5
6	Rhode Island	30.5
8	California	30.4
8	Florida	30.4
10	Nevada	30.1
10	Pennsylvania	30.1
12	Illinois	30.0
13	Louisiana	29.7
13	Maine	29.7
13	Michigan	29.7
13	New Hampshire	29.7
13	Vermont	29.7
18	Arizona	29.5
18	Minnesota	29.5
20	Ohio	29.4
21	Wisconsin	29.3
22	Alaska	29.2
23	Oregon	29.1
23	Virginia	29.1
23	Washington	29.1
26	New Mexico	29.0
26	North Carolina	29.0
28	Colorado	28.9
29	Georgia	28.8
29	Montana	28.8
29	South Carolina	28.8
32	West Virginia	28.7
33	Indiana	28.6
34	Missouri	28.4
35	Alabama	28.3
36	Kansas	28.2
36	Mississippi	28.2
36	Tennessee	28.2
36	Texas	28.2
40	Hawaii	28.1
40	North Dakota	28.1
42	South Dakota	28.0
43	Kentucky	27.9
44	Nebraska	27.8
44	Wyoming	27.8
46	Arkansas	27.5
46	Iowa	27.5
48	Oklahoma	27.0
49	Idaho	26.7
50	Utah	26.5
	District of Columbia	29.9

Source: U.S. Bureau of the Census
"2014 American Community Survey-Table R1204" (http://www.census.gov/programs-surveys/acs/)
*The median age at first marriage is calculated indirectly by estimating the proportion of young people who will marry during their lifetime, calculating one-half of this proportion, and determining the age (at the time of the survey) of people at this half-way mark. It does not represent the actual median age of the population who married during the calendar year.

Marriage Rate for Women in 2014

National Rate = 17.0 Marriages per 1,000 Women*

ALPHA ORDER

RANK	STATE	RATE
29	Alabama	17.0
1	Alaska	28.7
25	Arizona	17.3
9	Arkansas	20.5
27	California	17.1
8	Colorado	21.0
50	Connecticut	13.5
12	Delaware	19.4
48	Florida	13.7
19	Georgia	18.5
21	Hawaii	18.4
5	Idaho	22.3
40	Illinois	15.1
14	Indiana	19.3
24	Iowa	17.6
12	Kansas	19.4
25	Kentucky	17.3
23	Louisiana	18.0
37	Maine	16.4
43	Maryland	14.7
45	Massachusetts	14.3
46	Michigan	14.1
31	Minnesota	16.9
15	Mississippi	19.2
34	Missouri	16.7
36	Montana	16.6
34	Nebraska	16.7
6	Nevada	21.2
17	New Hampshire	18.6
48	New Jersey	13.7
31	New Mexico	16.9
44	New York	14.4
27	North Carolina	17.1
19	North Dakota	18.5
39	Ohio	15.2
4	Oklahoma	22.6
22	Oregon	18.3
41	Pennsylvania	15.0
47	Rhode Island	13.9
33	South Carolina	16.8
7	South Dakota	21.1
17	Tennessee	18.6
11	Texas	19.5
2	Utah	26.4
42	Vermont	14.9
16	Virginia	18.9
10	Washington	19.8
29	West Virginia	17.0
37	Wisconsin	16.4
2	Wyoming	26.4

RANK ORDER

RANK	STATE	RATE
1	Alaska	28.7
2	Utah	26.4
2	Wyoming	26.4
4	Oklahoma	22.6
5	Idaho	22.3
6	Nevada	21.2
7	South Dakota	21.1
8	Colorado	21.0
9	Arkansas	20.5
10	Washington	19.8
11	Texas	19.5
12	Delaware	19.4
12	Kansas	19.4
14	Indiana	19.3
15	Mississippi	19.2
16	Virginia	18.9
17	New Hampshire	18.6
17	Tennessee	18.6
19	Georgia	18.5
19	North Dakota	18.5
21	Hawaii	18.4
22	Oregon	18.3
23	Louisiana	18.0
24	Iowa	17.6
25	Arizona	17.3
25	Kentucky	17.3
27	California	17.1
27	North Carolina	17.1
29	Alabama	17.0
29	West Virginia	17.0
31	Minnesota	16.9
31	New Mexico	16.9
33	South Carolina	16.8
34	Missouri	16.7
34	Nebraska	16.7
36	Montana	16.6
37	Maine	16.4
37	Wisconsin	16.4
39	Ohio	15.2
40	Illinois	15.1
41	Pennsylvania	15.0
42	Vermont	14.9
43	Maryland	14.7
44	New York	14.4
45	Massachusetts	14.3
46	Michigan	14.1
47	Rhode Island	13.9
48	Florida	13.7
48	New Jersey	13.7
50	Connecticut	13.5
	District of Columbia	23.6

Source: U.S. Bureau of the Census
"2014 American Community Survey-Table GCT1251" (http://www.census.gov/programs-surveys/acs/)
*Women age 15 and older. Marriages in the last year.

Estimated Median Age of Women at First Marriage in 2014

National Median = 27.6 Years*

ALPHA ORDER

RANK	STATE	PERCENT
38	Alabama	26.4
34	Alaska	26.6
20	Arizona	27.4
47	Arkansas	25.5
8	California	28.5
30	Colorado	26.9
5	Connecticut	29.2
6	Delaware	28.6
12	Florida	28.2
25	Georgia	27.1
27	Hawaii	27.0
48	Idaho	25.3
6	Illinois	28.6
30	Indiana	26.9
42	Iowa	26.1
45	Kansas	25.9
43	Kentucky	26.0
13	Louisiana	28.1
11	Maine	28.3
8	Maryland	28.5
1	Massachusetts	29.7
16	Michigan	27.7
19	Minnesota	27.5
33	Mississippi	26.7
27	Missouri	27.0
39	Montana	26.3
40	Nebraska	26.2
18	Nevada	27.6
16	New Hampshire	27.7
4	New Jersey	29.3
14	New Mexico	28.0
2	New York	29.4
27	North Carolina	27.0
37	North Dakota	26.5
21	Ohio	27.3
48	Oklahoma	25.3
15	Oregon	27.9
10	Pennsylvania	28.4
2	Rhode Island	29.4
23	South Carolina	27.2
40	South Dakota	26.2
34	Tennessee	26.6
34	Texas	26.6
50	Utah	24.1
30	Vermont	26.9
21	Virginia	27.3
25	Washington	27.1
43	West Virginia	26.0
23	Wisconsin	27.2
46	Wyoming	25.6

RANK ORDER

RANK	STATE	PERCENT
1	Massachusetts	29.7
2	New York	29.4
2	Rhode Island	29.4
4	New Jersey	29.3
5	Connecticut	29.2
6	Delaware	28.6
6	Illinois	28.6
8	California	28.5
8	Maryland	28.5
10	Pennsylvania	28.4
11	Maine	28.3
12	Florida	28.2
13	Louisiana	28.1
14	New Mexico	28.0
15	Oregon	27.9
16	Michigan	27.7
16	New Hampshire	27.7
18	Nevada	27.6
19	Minnesota	27.5
20	Arizona	27.4
21	Ohio	27.3
21	Virginia	27.3
23	South Carolina	27.2
23	Wisconsin	27.2
25	Georgia	27.1
25	Washington	27.1
27	Hawaii	27.0
27	Missouri	27.0
27	North Carolina	27.0
30	Colorado	26.9
30	Indiana	26.9
30	Vermont	26.9
33	Mississippi	26.7
34	Alaska	26.6
34	Tennessee	26.6
34	Texas	26.6
37	North Dakota	26.5
38	Alabama	26.4
39	Montana	26.3
40	Nebraska	26.2
40	South Dakota	26.2
42	Iowa	26.1
43	Kentucky	26.0
43	West Virginia	26.0
45	Kansas	25.9
46	Wyoming	25.6
47	Arkansas	25.5
48	Idaho	25.3
48	Oklahoma	25.3
50	Utah	24.1
	District of Columbia	30.3

Source: U.S. Bureau of the Census
"2014 American Community Survey-Table R1205" (http://www.census.gov/programs-surveys/acs/)
*The median age at first marriage is calculated indirectly by estimating the proportion of young people who will marry during their lifetime, calculating one-half of this proportion, and determining the age (at the time of the survey) of people at this half-way mark. It does not represent the actual median age of the population who married during the calendar year.

Ratio of Unmarried Men to Unmarried Women in 2014

National Ratio = 110.6 Unmarried Men for Every 100 Unmarried Women*

ALPHA ORDER

RANK	STATE	RATIO
49	Alabama	104.4
2	Alaska	131.4
12	Arizona	116.1
23	Arkansas	112.5
18	California	114.0
5	Colorado	118.9
37	Connecticut	107.6
40	Delaware	107.2
26	Florida	110.5
46	Georgia	105.6
4	Hawaii	123.2
14	Idaho	115.2
35	Illinois	108.8
31	Indiana	109.4
16	Iowa	114.4
6	Kansas	118.2
15	Kentucky	114.6
43	Louisiana	105.9
38	Maine	107.4
42	Maryland	106.4
47	Massachusetts	105.0
32	Michigan	109.3
18	Minnesota	114.0
43	Mississippi	105.9
35	Missouri	108.8
9	Montana	117.7
21	Nebraska	113.1
9	Nevada	117.7
30	New Hampshire	109.6
29	New Jersey	109.8
20	New Mexico	113.4
47	New York	105.0
39	North Carolina	107.3
1	North Dakota	133.5
34	Ohio	108.9
12	Oklahoma	116.1
23	Oregon	112.5
28	Pennsylvania	110.1
50	Rhode Island	103.0
43	South Carolina	105.9
11	South Dakota	117.4
41	Tennessee	106.7
25	Texas	112.1
6	Utah	118.2
26	Vermont	110.5
33	Virginia	109.0
8	Washington	117.8
16	West Virginia	114.4
22	Wisconsin	112.6
3	Wyoming	125.6

RANK ORDER

RANK	STATE	RATIO
1	North Dakota	133.5
2	Alaska	131.4
3	Wyoming	125.6
4	Hawaii	123.2
5	Colorado	118.9
6	Kansas	118.2
6	Utah	118.2
8	Washington	117.8
9	Montana	117.7
9	Nevada	117.7
11	South Dakota	117.4
12	Arizona	116.1
12	Oklahoma	116.1
14	Idaho	115.2
15	Kentucky	114.6
16	Iowa	114.4
16	West Virginia	114.4
18	California	114.0
18	Minnesota	114.0
20	New Mexico	113.4
21	Nebraska	113.1
22	Wisconsin	112.6
23	Arkansas	112.5
23	Oregon	112.5
25	Texas	112.1
26	Florida	110.5
26	Vermont	110.5
28	Pennsylvania	110.1
29	New Jersey	109.8
30	New Hampshire	109.6
31	Indiana	109.4
32	Michigan	109.3
33	Virginia	109.0
34	Ohio	108.9
35	Illinois	108.8
35	Missouri	108.8
37	Connecticut	107.6
38	Maine	107.4
39	North Carolina	107.3
40	Delaware	107.2
41	Tennessee	106.7
42	Maryland	106.4
43	Louisiana	105.9
43	Mississippi	105.9
43	South Carolina	105.9
46	Georgia	105.6
47	Massachusetts	105.0
47	New York	105.0
49	Alabama	104.4
50	Rhode Island	103.0
	District of Columbia	89.8

Source: U.S. Bureau of the Census
  "2014 American Community Survey-Table R1203" (http://www.census.gov/programs-surveys/acs/)
*Population 15 to 44 years old.

Divorce Rate for Men in 2014

National Rate = 8.1 Divorces per 1,000 Men*

ALPHA ORDER

RANK	STATE	RATE
17	Alabama	9.4
18	Alaska	9.1
33	Arizona	7.5
2	Arkansas	12.0
44	California	6.7
11	Colorado	9.8
37	Connecticut	7.3
8	Delaware	10.3
31	Florida	7.6
22	Georgia	8.7
40	Hawaii	6.9
36	Idaho	7.4
40	Illinois	6.9
9	Indiana	10.1
33	Iowa	7.5
10	Kansas	9.9
7	Kentucky	10.6
27	Louisiana	8.3
6	Maine	10.7
42	Maryland	6.8
47	Massachusetts	6.5
25	Michigan	8.5
31	Minnesota	7.6
4	Mississippi	11.3
14	Missouri	9.7
1	Montana	12.2
24	Nebraska	8.6
11	Nevada	9.8
18	New Hampshire	9.1
46	New Jersey	6.6
25	New Mexico	8.5
49	New York	5.9
29	North Carolina	7.8
50	North Dakota	5.0
29	Ohio	7.8
3	Oklahoma	11.6
22	Oregon	8.7
38	Pennsylvania	7.2
47	Rhode Island	6.5
20	South Carolina	8.9
39	South Dakota	7.1
5	Tennessee	11.0
11	Texas	9.8
15	Utah	9.5
44	Vermont	6.7
28	Virginia	8.1
21	Washington	8.8
15	West Virginia	9.5
33	Wisconsin	7.5
42	Wyoming	6.8

RANK ORDER

RANK	STATE	RATE
1	Montana	12.2
2	Arkansas	12.0
3	Oklahoma	11.6
4	Mississippi	11.3
5	Tennessee	11.0
6	Maine	10.7
7	Kentucky	10.6
8	Delaware	10.3
9	Indiana	10.1
10	Kansas	9.9
11	Colorado	9.8
11	Nevada	9.8
11	Texas	9.8
14	Missouri	9.7
15	Utah	9.5
15	West Virginia	9.5
17	Alabama	9.4
18	Alaska	9.1
18	New Hampshire	9.1
20	South Carolina	8.9
21	Washington	8.8
22	Georgia	8.7
22	Oregon	8.7
24	Nebraska	8.6
25	Michigan	8.5
25	New Mexico	8.5
27	Louisiana	8.3
28	Virginia	8.1
29	North Carolina	7.8
29	Ohio	7.8
31	Florida	7.6
31	Minnesota	7.6
33	Arizona	7.5
33	Iowa	7.5
33	Wisconsin	7.5
36	Idaho	7.4
37	Connecticut	7.3
38	Pennsylvania	7.2
39	South Dakota	7.1
40	Hawaii	6.9
40	Illinois	6.9
42	Maryland	6.8
42	Wyoming	6.8
44	California	6.7
44	Vermont	6.7
46	New Jersey	6.6
47	Massachusetts	6.5
47	Rhode Island	6.5
49	New York	5.9
50	North Dakota	5.0
	District of Columbia	5.8

Source: U.S. Bureau of the Census
"2014 American Community Survey-Table GCT1254" (http://www.census.gov/programs-surveys/acs/)
*Men age 15 and older. Divorces in the last year.

Divorce Rate for Women in 2014

National Rate = 8.7 Divorces per 1,000 Women*

ALPHA ORDER

RANK	STATE	RATE
12	Alabama	10.4
15	Alaska	10.3
25	Arizona	8.8
5	Arkansas	11.6
41	California	7.2
11	Colorado	10.5
35	Connecticut	8.0
25	Delaware	8.8
19	Florida	9.5
7	Georgia	11.2
49	Hawaii	5.9
1	Idaho	14.4
40	Illinois	7.3
6	Indiana	11.3
47	Iowa	6.6
10	Kansas	10.8
8	Kentucky	11.0
45	Louisiana	6.8
8	Maine	11.0
33	Maryland	8.2
43	Massachusetts	7.0
21	Michigan	9.2
37	Minnesota	7.8
17	Mississippi	10.0
32	Missouri	8.4
44	Montana	6.9
23	Nebraska	8.9
12	Nevada	10.4
25	New Hampshire	8.8
50	New Jersey	5.5
18	New Mexico	9.7
48	New York	6.3
22	North Carolina	9.0
38	North Dakota	7.6
28	Ohio	8.7
2	Oklahoma	12.5
12	Oregon	10.4
41	Pennsylvania	7.2
31	Rhode Island	8.6
23	South Carolina	8.9
38	South Dakota	7.6
19	Tennessee	9.5
16	Texas	10.2
4	Utah	11.9
46	Vermont	6.7
28	Virginia	8.7
28	Washington	8.7
3	West Virginia	12.4
36	Wisconsin	7.9
34	Wyoming	8.1

RANK ORDER

RANK	STATE	RATE
1	Idaho	14.4
2	Oklahoma	12.5
3	West Virginia	12.4
4	Utah	11.9
5	Arkansas	11.6
6	Indiana	11.3
7	Georgia	11.2
8	Kentucky	11.0
8	Maine	11.0
10	Kansas	10.8
11	Colorado	10.5
12	Alabama	10.4
12	Nevada	10.4
12	Oregon	10.4
15	Alaska	10.3
16	Texas	10.2
17	Mississippi	10.0
18	New Mexico	9.7
19	Florida	9.5
19	Tennessee	9.5
21	Michigan	9.2
22	North Carolina	9.0
23	Nebraska	8.9
23	South Carolina	8.9
25	Arizona	8.8
25	Delaware	8.8
25	New Hampshire	8.8
28	Ohio	8.7
28	Virginia	8.7
28	Washington	8.7
31	Rhode Island	8.6
32	Missouri	8.4
33	Maryland	8.2
34	Wyoming	8.1
35	Connecticut	8.0
36	Wisconsin	7.9
37	Minnesota	7.8
38	North Dakota	7.6
38	South Dakota	7.6
40	Illinois	7.3
41	California	7.2
41	Pennsylvania	7.2
43	Massachusetts	7.0
44	Montana	6.9
45	Louisiana	6.8
46	Vermont	6.7
47	Iowa	6.6
48	New York	6.3
49	Hawaii	5.9
50	New Jersey	5.5
	District of Columbia	8.6

Source: U.S. Bureau of the Census
 "2014 American Community Survey-Table GCT1253" (http://www.census.gov/programs-surveys/acs/)
*Women age 15 and older. Divorces in the last year.

Average Family Size in 2014

National Average = 3.26 Persons per Family

ALPHA ORDER

RANK	STATE	PERSONS
19	Alabama	3.18
6	Alaska	3.41
9	Arizona	3.34
28	Arkansas	3.14
3	California	3.56
26	Colorado	3.15
19	Connecticut	3.18
24	Delaware	3.16
11	Florida	3.31
8	Georgia	3.35
2	Hawaii	3.61
16	Idaho	3.27
14	Illinois	3.29
30	Indiana	3.13
45	Iowa	2.98
28	Kansas	3.14
39	Kentucky	3.07
13	Louisiana	3.30
49	Maine	2.88
14	Maryland	3.29
21	Massachusetts	3.17
32	Michigan	3.12
37	Minnesota	3.08
17	Mississippi	3.26
33	Missouri	3.11
42	Montana	3.04
41	Nebraska	3.05
5	Nevada	3.43
47	New Hampshire	2.97
10	New Jersey	3.32
7	New Mexico	3.38
11	New York	3.31
26	North Carolina	3.15
48	North Dakota	2.92
39	Ohio	3.07
21	Oklahoma	3.17
37	Oregon	3.08
33	Pennsylvania	3.11
35	Rhode Island	3.10
21	South Carolina	3.17
36	South Dakota	3.09
30	Tennessee	3.13
4	Texas	3.45
1	Utah	3.65
50	Vermont	2.84
18	Virginia	3.19
24	Washington	3.16
43	West Virginia	3.03
45	Wisconsin	2.98
44	Wyoming	3.02

RANK ORDER

RANK	STATE	PERSONS
1	Utah	3.65
2	Hawaii	3.61
3	California	3.56
4	Texas	3.45
5	Nevada	3.43
6	Alaska	3.41
7	New Mexico	3.38
8	Georgia	3.35
9	Arizona	3.34
10	New Jersey	3.32
11	Florida	3.31
11	New York	3.31
13	Louisiana	3.30
14	Illinois	3.29
14	Maryland	3.29
16	Idaho	3.27
17	Mississippi	3.26
18	Virginia	3.19
19	Alabama	3.18
19	Connecticut	3.18
21	Massachusetts	3.17
21	Oklahoma	3.17
21	South Carolina	3.17
24	Delaware	3.16
24	Washington	3.16
26	Colorado	3.15
26	North Carolina	3.15
28	Arkansas	3.14
28	Kansas	3.14
30	Indiana	3.13
30	Tennessee	3.13
32	Michigan	3.12
33	Missouri	3.11
33	Pennsylvania	3.11
35	Rhode Island	3.10
36	South Dakota	3.09
37	Minnesota	3.08
37	Oregon	3.08
39	Kentucky	3.07
39	Ohio	3.07
41	Nebraska	3.05
42	Montana	3.04
43	West Virginia	3.03
44	Wyoming	3.02
45	Iowa	2.98
45	Wisconsin	2.98
47	New Hampshire	2.97
48	North Dakota	2.92
49	Maine	2.88
50	Vermont	2.84
	District of Columbia	3.24

Source: U.S. Bureau of the Census
"2014 American Community Survey-Table DP02" (http://www.census.gov/programs-surveys/acs/)

Seats in the U.S. House of Representatives in 2016

National Total = 435 Seats*

ALPHA ORDER

RANK	STATE	SEATS	% of USA
22	Alabama	7	1.6%
44	Alaska	1	0.2%
14	Arizona	9	2.1%
30	Arkansas	4	0.9%
1	California	53	12.2%
22	Colorado	7	1.6%
27	Connecticut	5	1.1%
44	Delaware	1	0.2%
3	Florida	27	6.2%
8	Georgia	14	3.2%
39	Hawaii	2	0.5%
39	Idaho	2	0.5%
5	Illinois	18	4.1%
14	Indiana	9	2.1%
30	Iowa	4	0.9%
30	Kansas	4	0.9%
25	Kentucky	6	1.4%
25	Louisiana	6	1.4%
39	Maine	2	0.5%
18	Maryland	8	1.8%
14	Massachusetts	9	2.1%
8	Michigan	14	3.2%
18	Minnesota	8	1.8%
30	Mississippi	4	0.9%
18	Missouri	8	1.8%
44	Montana	1	0.2%
36	Nebraska	3	0.7%
30	Nevada	4	0.9%
39	New Hampshire	2	0.5%
11	New Jersey	12	2.8%
36	New Mexico	3	0.7%
3	New York	27	6.2%
10	North Carolina	13	3.0%
44	North Dakota	1	0.2%
7	Ohio	16	3.7%
27	Oklahoma	5	1.1%
27	Oregon	5	1.1%
5	Pennsylvania	18	4.1%
39	Rhode Island	2	0.5%
22	South Carolina	7	1.6%
44	South Dakota	1	0.2%
14	Tennessee	9	2.1%
2	Texas	36	8.3%
30	Utah	4	0.9%
44	Vermont	1	0.2%
12	Virginia	11	2.5%
13	Washington	10	2.3%
36	West Virginia	3	0.7%
18	Wisconsin	8	1.8%
44	Wyoming	1	0.2%

RANK ORDER

RANK	STATE	SEATS	% of USA
1	California	53	12.2%
2	Texas	36	8.3%
3	Florida	27	6.2%
3	New York	27	6.2%
5	Illinois	18	4.1%
5	Pennsylvania	18	4.1%
7	Ohio	16	3.7%
8	Georgia	14	3.2%
8	Michigan	14	3.2%
10	North Carolina	13	3.0%
11	New Jersey	12	2.8%
12	Virginia	11	2.5%
13	Washington	10	2.3%
14	Arizona	9	2.1%
14	Indiana	9	2.1%
14	Massachusetts	9	2.1%
14	Tennessee	9	2.1%
18	Maryland	8	1.8%
18	Minnesota	8	1.8%
18	Missouri	8	1.8%
18	Wisconsin	8	1.8%
22	Alabama	7	1.6%
22	Colorado	7	1.6%
22	South Carolina	7	1.6%
25	Kentucky	6	1.4%
25	Louisiana	6	1.4%
27	Connecticut	5	1.1%
27	Oklahoma	5	1.1%
27	Oregon	5	1.1%
30	Arkansas	4	0.9%
30	Iowa	4	0.9%
30	Kansas	4	0.9%
30	Mississippi	4	0.9%
30	Nevada	4	0.9%
30	Utah	4	0.9%
36	Nebraska	3	0.7%
36	New Mexico	3	0.7%
36	West Virginia	3	0.7%
39	Hawaii	2	0.5%
39	Idaho	2	0.5%
39	Maine	2	0.5%
39	New Hampshire	2	0.5%
39	Rhode Island	2	0.5%
44	Alaska	1	0.2%
44	Delaware	1	0.2%
44	Montana	1	0.2%
44	North Dakota	1	0.2%
44	South Dakota	1	0.2%
44	Vermont	1	0.2%
44	Wyoming	1	0.2%
	District of Columbia**	0	0.0%

Source: U.S. Bureau of the Census
"Congressional Apportionment" (http://www.census.gov/topics/public-sector/congressional-apportionment.html)
*This table shows the number of seats after reapportionment of the 2010 Census. This apportionment became effective with the Congress elected in November 2012 and that took office in January 2013.
**The District of Columbia has one non-voting delegate. Each state has two members in the U.S. Senate.

Estimated Population per U.S. House Seat in 2016

National Rate = 737,348 Persons per House Member*

ALPHA ORDER

RANK	STATE	RATE
42	Alabama	694,140
24	Alaska	738,432
14	Arizona	758,674
22	Arkansas	744,551
23	California	738,581
8	Colorado	779,511
34	Connecticut	718,177
2	Delaware	945,934
18	Florida	750,788
29	Georgia	729,633
36	Hawaii	715,802
4	Idaho	827,465
37	Illinois	714,444
26	Indiana	735,520
7	Iowa	780,975
30	Kansas	727,910
25	Kentucky	737,515
9	Louisiana	778,454
45	Maine	664,664
17	Maryland	750,800
16	Massachusetts	754,936
39	Michigan	708,755
43	Minnesota	686,199
20	Mississippi	748,083
13	Missouri	760,459
1	Montana	1,032,949
46	Nebraska	632,063
32	Nevada	722,711
44	New Hampshire	665,304
21	New Jersey	746,501
41	New Mexico	695,036
28	New York	733,177
10	North Carolina	772,523
15	North Dakota	756,927
31	Ohio	725,839
6	Oklahoma	782,268
5	Oregon	805,795
38	Pennsylvania	711,250
50	Rhode Island	528,149
40	South Carolina	699,449
3	South Dakota	858,469
27	Tennessee	733,367
11	Texas	763,031
19	Utah	748,980
47	Vermont	626,042
12	Virginia	762,090
35	Washington	717,035
48	West Virginia	614,709
33	Wisconsin	721,417
49	Wyoming	586,107

RANK ORDER

RANK	STATE	RATE
1	Montana	1,032,949
2	Delaware	945,934
3	South Dakota	858,469
4	Idaho	827,465
5	Oregon	805,795
6	Oklahoma	782,268
7	Iowa	780,975
8	Colorado	779,511
9	Louisiana	778,454
10	North Carolina	772,523
11	Texas	763,031
12	Virginia	762,090
13	Missouri	760,459
14	Arizona	758,674
15	North Dakota	756,927
16	Massachusetts	754,936
17	Maryland	750,800
18	Florida	750,788
19	Utah	748,980
20	Mississippi	748,083
21	New Jersey	746,501
22	Arkansas	744,551
23	California	738,581
24	Alaska	738,432
25	Kentucky	737,515
26	Indiana	735,520
27	Tennessee	733,367
28	New York	733,177
29	Georgia	729,633
30	Kansas	727,910
31	Ohio	725,839
32	Nevada	722,711
33	Wisconsin	721,417
34	Connecticut	718,177
35	Washington	717,035
36	Hawaii	715,802
37	Illinois	714,444
38	Pennsylvania	711,250
39	Michigan	708,755
40	South Carolina	699,449
41	New Mexico	695,036
42	Alabama	694,140
43	Minnesota	686,199
44	New Hampshire	665,304
45	Maine	664,664
46	Nebraska	632,063
47	Vermont	626,042
48	West Virginia	614,709
49	Wyoming	586,107
50	Rhode Island	528,149
	District of Columbia**	NA

Source: CQ Press using data from U.S. Bureau of the Census
"Congressional Apportionment" (http://www.census.gov/population/apportionment/)
*Rates calculated using 2015 population estimates and do not include population of the District of Columbia. The District has one non-voting delegate. Each state has two members in the U.S. Senate. This table is based only on U.S. Representatives and not U.S. Senate members. This table reflects reapportionment resulting from the 2010 census and taking effect after the 2012 election. **Not applicable.

State Legislators in 2015

National Total = 7,383 Legislators*

ALPHA ORDER

RANK	STATE	LEGISLATORS	% of USA
27	Alabama	140	1.9%
49	Alaska	60	0.8%
43	Arizona	90	1.2%
30	Arkansas	135	1.8%
35	California	120	1.6%
42	Colorado	100	1.4%
9	Connecticut	187	2.5%
48	Delaware	62	0.8%
18	Florida	160	2.2%
3	Georgia	236	3.2%
46	Hawaii	76	1.0%
39	Idaho	105	1.4%
13	Illinois	177	2.4%
19	Indiana	150	2.0%
19	Iowa	150	2.0%
17	Kansas	165	2.2%
29	Kentucky	138	1.9%
25	Louisiana	144	2.0%
10	Maine	186	2.5%
8	Maryland	188	2.5%
6	Massachusetts	200	2.7%
23	Michigan	148	2.0%
5	Minnesota	201	2.7%
14	Mississippi	174	2.4%
7	Missouri	197	2.7%
19	Montana	150	2.0%
50	Nebraska	49	0.7%
47	Nevada	63	0.9%
1	New Hampshire	424	5.7%
35	New Jersey	120	1.6%
38	New Mexico	112	1.5%
4	New York	213	2.9%
15	North Carolina	170	2.3%
26	North Dakota	141	1.9%
32	Ohio	132	1.8%
22	Oklahoma	149	2.0%
43	Oregon	90	1.2%
2	Pennsylvania	253	3.4%
37	Rhode Island	113	1.5%
15	South Carolina	170	2.3%
39	South Dakota	105	1.4%
32	Tennessee	132	1.8%
11	Texas	181	2.5%
41	Utah	104	1.4%
12	Vermont	180	2.4%
27	Virginia	140	1.9%
24	Washington	147	2.0%
31	West Virginia	134	1.8%
32	Wisconsin	132	1.8%
43	Wyoming	90	1.2%

RANK ORDER

RANK	STATE	LEGISLATORS	% of USA
1	New Hampshire	424	5.7%
2	Pennsylvania	253	3.4%
3	Georgia	236	3.2%
4	New York	213	2.9%
5	Minnesota	201	2.7%
6	Massachusetts	200	2.7%
7	Missouri	197	2.7%
8	Maryland	188	2.5%
9	Connecticut	187	2.5%
10	Maine	186	2.5%
11	Texas	181	2.5%
12	Vermont	180	2.4%
13	Illinois	177	2.4%
14	Mississippi	174	2.4%
15	North Carolina	170	2.3%
15	South Carolina	170	2.3%
17	Kansas	165	2.2%
18	Florida	160	2.2%
19	Indiana	150	2.0%
19	Iowa	150	2.0%
19	Montana	150	2.0%
22	Oklahoma	149	2.0%
23	Michigan	148	2.0%
24	Washington	147	2.0%
25	Louisiana	144	2.0%
26	North Dakota	141	1.9%
27	Alabama	140	1.9%
27	Virginia	140	1.9%
29	Kentucky	138	1.9%
30	Arkansas	135	1.8%
31	West Virginia	134	1.8%
32	Ohio	132	1.8%
32	Tennessee	132	1.8%
32	Wisconsin	132	1.8%
35	California	120	1.6%
35	New Jersey	120	1.6%
37	Rhode Island	113	1.5%
38	New Mexico	112	1.5%
39	Idaho	105	1.4%
39	South Dakota	105	1.4%
41	Utah	104	1.4%
42	Colorado	100	1.4%
43	Arizona	90	1.2%
43	Oregon	90	1.2%
43	Wyoming	90	1.2%
46	Hawaii	76	1.0%
47	Nevada	63	0.9%
48	Delaware	62	0.8%
49	Alaska	60	0.8%
50	Nebraska	49	0.7%
	District of Columbia**	NA	NA

Source: National Conference of State Legislatures (Denver, CO)
  "2015 Partisan Composition" (http://www.ncsl.org/research/about-state-legislatures/partisan-composition.aspx)
*There are 1,972 state senators (including Nebraska's 49 unicameral seats) and 5,411 state house members.
**Not applicable.

Population per State Legislator in 2015

National Rate = 43,444 Population per Legislator*

ALPHA ORDER

RANK	STATE	RATE
22	Alabama	34,707
42	Alaska	12,307
6	Arizona	75,867
32	Arkansas	22,061
1	California	326,207
12	Colorado	54,566
34	Connecticut	19,203
40	Delaware	15,257
3	Florida	126,695
20	Georgia	43,283
35	Hawaii	18,837
39	Idaho	15,761
8	Illinois	72,655
18	Indiana	44,131
33	Iowa	20,826
37	Kansas	17,646
25	Kentucky	32,066
24	Louisiana	32,436
45	Maine	7,147
26	Maryland	31,949
23	Massachusetts	33,972
9	Michigan	67,044
30	Minnesota	27,311
38	Mississippi	17,197
27	Missouri	30,882
46	Montana	6,886
21	Nebraska	38,698
16	Nevada	45,886
50	New Hampshire	3,138
7	New Jersey	74,650
36	New Mexico	18,617
4	New York	92,938
11	North Carolina	59,075
48	North Dakota	5,368
5	Ohio	87,980
31	Oklahoma	26,251
17	Oregon	44,766
13	Pennsylvania	50,603
43	Rhode Island	9,348
29	South Carolina	28,801
44	South Dakota	8,176
14	Tennessee	50,002
2	Texas	151,763
28	Utah	28,807
49	Vermont	3,478
10	Virginia	59,879
15	Washington	48,778
41	West Virginia	13,762
19	Wisconsin	43,722
47	Wyoming	6,512

RANK ORDER

RANK	STATE	RATE
1	California	326,207
2	Texas	151,763
3	Florida	126,695
4	New York	92,938
5	Ohio	87,980
6	Arizona	75,867
7	New Jersey	74,650
8	Illinois	72,655
9	Michigan	67,044
10	Virginia	59,879
11	North Carolina	59,075
12	Colorado	54,566
13	Pennsylvania	50,603
14	Tennessee	50,002
15	Washington	48,778
16	Nevada	45,886
17	Oregon	44,766
18	Indiana	44,131
19	Wisconsin	43,722
20	Georgia	43,283
21	Nebraska	38,698
22	Alabama	34,707
23	Massachusetts	33,972
24	Louisiana	32,436
25	Kentucky	32,066
26	Maryland	31,949
27	Missouri	30,882
28	Utah	28,807
29	South Carolina	28,801
30	Minnesota	27,311
31	Oklahoma	26,251
32	Arkansas	22,061
33	Iowa	20,826
34	Connecticut	19,203
35	Hawaii	18,837
36	New Mexico	18,617
37	Kansas	17,646
38	Mississippi	17,197
39	Idaho	15,761
40	Delaware	15,257
41	West Virginia	13,762
42	Alaska	12,307
43	Rhode Island	9,348
44	South Dakota	8,176
45	Maine	7,147
46	Montana	6,886
47	Wyoming	6,512
48	North Dakota	5,368
49	Vermont	3,478
50	New Hampshire	3,138
	District of Columbia**	NA

Source: CQ Press using data from National Conference of State Legislatures (Denver, CO)
"2015 Partisan Composition" (http://www.ncsl.org/research/about-state-legislatures/partisan-composition.aspx)
*There are 1,972 state senators (including Nebraska's 49 unicameral seats) and 5,411 state house members. National rate does not include population for the District of Columbia. Calculated using 2015 population estimates.
**Not applicable.

Registered Voters in 2014

National Total = 142,166,000

ALPHA ORDER

RANK	STATE	REGISTERED	% of USA
25	Alabama	2,366,000	1.7%
48	Alaska	336,000	0.2%
21	Arizona	2,738,000	1.9%
33	Arkansas	1,292,000	0.9%
1	California	14,113,000	9.9%
22	Colorado	2,654,000	1.9%
28	Connecticut	1,668,000	1.2%
45	Delaware	442,000	0.3%
3	Florida	8,691,000	6.1%
10	Georgia	4,306,000	3.0%
43	Hawaii	490,000	0.3%
41	Idaho	671,000	0.5%
6	Illinois	5,716,000	4.0%
17	Indiana	3,048,000	2.1%
31	Iowa	1,584,000	1.1%
32	Kansas	1,353,000	1.0%
26	Kentucky	2,298,000	1.6%
24	Louisiana	2,398,000	1.7%
39	Maine	799,000	0.6%
19	Maryland	2,995,000	2.1%
14	Massachusetts	3,250,000	2.3%
8	Michigan	5,159,000	3.6%
20	Minnesota	2,822,000	2.0%
30	Mississippi	1,628,000	1.1%
15	Missouri	3,194,000	2.2%
42	Montana	506,000	0.4%
38	Nebraska	873,000	0.6%
35	Nevada	1,088,000	0.8%
40	New Hampshire	694,000	0.5%
12	New Jersey	3,919,000	2.8%
36	New Mexico	919,000	0.6%
4	New York	8,078,000	5.7%
9	North Carolina	4,779,000	3.4%
47	North Dakota	363,000	0.3%
7	Ohio	5,657,000	4.0%
29	Oklahoma	1,644,000	1.2%
27	Oregon	2,008,000	1.4%
5	Pennsylvania	6,121,000	4.3%
44	Rhode Island	486,000	0.3%
23	South Carolina	2,458,000	1.7%
46	South Dakota	401,000	0.3%
16	Tennessee	3,088,000	2.2%
2	Texas	9,946,000	7.0%
34	Utah	1,101,000	0.8%
49	Vermont	324,000	0.2%
11	Virginia	3,924,000	2.8%
13	Washington	3,281,000	2.3%
37	West Virginia	896,000	0.6%
18	Wisconsin	3,005,000	2.1%
50	Wyoming	241,000	0.2%

RANK ORDER

RANK	STATE	REGISTERED	% of USA
1	California	14,113,000	9.9%
2	Texas	9,946,000	7.0%
3	Florida	8,691,000	6.1%
4	New York	8,078,000	5.7%
5	Pennsylvania	6,121,000	4.3%
6	Illinois	5,716,000	4.0%
7	Ohio	5,657,000	4.0%
8	Michigan	5,159,000	3.6%
9	North Carolina	4,779,000	3.4%
10	Georgia	4,306,000	3.0%
11	Virginia	3,924,000	2.8%
12	New Jersey	3,919,000	2.8%
13	Washington	3,281,000	2.3%
14	Massachusetts	3,250,000	2.3%
15	Missouri	3,194,000	2.2%
16	Tennessee	3,088,000	2.2%
17	Indiana	3,048,000	2.1%
18	Wisconsin	3,005,000	2.1%
19	Maryland	2,995,000	2.1%
20	Minnesota	2,822,000	2.0%
21	Arizona	2,738,000	1.9%
22	Colorado	2,654,000	1.9%
23	South Carolina	2,458,000	1.7%
24	Louisiana	2,398,000	1.7%
25	Alabama	2,366,000	1.7%
26	Kentucky	2,298,000	1.6%
27	Oregon	2,008,000	1.4%
28	Connecticut	1,668,000	1.2%
29	Oklahoma	1,644,000	1.2%
30	Mississippi	1,628,000	1.1%
31	Iowa	1,584,000	1.1%
32	Kansas	1,353,000	1.0%
33	Arkansas	1,292,000	0.9%
34	Utah	1,101,000	0.8%
35	Nevada	1,088,000	0.8%
36	New Mexico	919,000	0.6%
37	West Virginia	896,000	0.6%
38	Nebraska	873,000	0.6%
39	Maine	799,000	0.6%
40	New Hampshire	694,000	0.5%
41	Idaho	671,000	0.5%
42	Montana	506,000	0.4%
43	Hawaii	490,000	0.3%
44	Rhode Island	486,000	0.3%
45	Delaware	442,000	0.3%
46	South Dakota	401,000	0.3%
47	North Dakota	363,000	0.3%
48	Alaska	336,000	0.2%
49	Vermont	324,000	0.2%
50	Wyoming	241,000	0.2%
	District of Columbia	353,000	0.2%

Source: U.S. Bureau of the Census
"Voting and Registration" (Table 4a, http://www.census.gov/hhes/www/socdemo/voting/index.html)

Percent of Eligible Voters Reported Registered in 2014

National Percent = 64.6%*

ALPHA ORDER

RANK	STATE	PERCENT
19	Alabama	67.2
22	Alaska	66.8
40	Arizona	62.3
38	Arkansas	62.8
47	California	57.7
9	Colorado	71.1
28	Connecticut	65.1
22	Delaware	66.8
39	Florida	62.6
36	Georgia	63.7
50	Hawaii	51.3
43	Idaho	60.7
35	Illinois	63.9
29	Indiana	64.9
13	Iowa	69.6
17	Kansas	67.9
7	Kentucky	71.6
6	Louisiana	71.7
1	Maine	76.5
3	Maryland	72.2
18	Massachusetts	67.5
8	Michigan	71.2
5	Minnesota	71.8
2	Mississippi	76.0
4	Missouri	72.1
32	Montana	64.8
21	Nebraska	66.9
46	Nevada	58.5
16	New Hampshire	68.3
27	New Jersey	66.3
29	New Mexico	64.9
44	New York	59.4
12	North Carolina	69.7
26	North Dakota	66.4
25	Ohio	66.5
42	Oklahoma	61.1
11	Oregon	70.0
33	Pennsylvania	64.4
37	Rhode Island	63.6
14	South Carolina	68.9
29	South Dakota	64.9
34	Tennessee	64.1
45	Texas	59.1
48	Utah	57.2
19	Vermont	67.2
24	Virginia	66.6
15	Washington	68.7
41	West Virginia	62.2
10	Wisconsin	71.0
49	Wyoming	56.5

RANK ORDER

RANK	STATE	PERCENT
1	Maine	76.5
2	Mississippi	76.0
3	Maryland	72.2
4	Missouri	72.1
5	Minnesota	71.8
6	Louisiana	71.7
7	Kentucky	71.6
8	Michigan	71.2
9	Colorado	71.1
10	Wisconsin	71.0
11	Oregon	70.0
12	North Carolina	69.7
13	Iowa	69.6
14	South Carolina	68.9
15	Washington	68.7
16	New Hampshire	68.3
17	Kansas	67.9
18	Massachusetts	67.5
19	Alabama	67.2
19	Vermont	67.2
21	Nebraska	66.9
22	Alaska	66.8
22	Delaware	66.8
24	Virginia	66.6
25	Ohio	66.5
26	North Dakota	66.4
27	New Jersey	66.3
28	Connecticut	65.1
29	Indiana	64.9
29	New Mexico	64.9
29	South Dakota	64.9
32	Montana	64.8
33	Pennsylvania	64.4
34	Tennessee	64.1
35	Illinois	63.9
36	Georgia	63.7
37	Rhode Island	63.6
38	Arkansas	62.8
39	Florida	62.6
40	Arizona	62.3
41	West Virginia	62.2
42	Oklahoma	61.1
43	Idaho	60.7
44	New York	59.4
45	Texas	59.1
46	Nevada	58.5
47	California	57.7
48	Utah	57.2
49	Wyoming	56.5
50	Hawaii	51.3
	District of Columbia	73.5

Source: U.S. Bureau of the Census
"Voting and Registration" (Table 4a, http://www.census.gov/hhes/www/socdemo/voting/index.html)
*As a percent of citizen population 18 and older.

Persons Voting in 2014

National Total = 92,251,000

ALPHA ORDER

RANK	STATE	VOTERS	% of USA
27	Alabama	1,497,000	1.6%
48	Alaska	255,000	0.3%
19	Arizona	1,785,000	1.9%
33	Arkansas	798,000	0.9%
1	California	8,949,000	9.7%
15	Colorado	2,211,000	2.4%
29	Connecticut	1,195,000	1.3%
45	Delaware	299,000	0.3%
2	Florida	6,220,000	6.7%
10	Georgia	2,919,000	3.2%
42	Hawaii	399,000	0.4%
41	Idaho	462,000	0.5%
6	Illinois	3,734,000	4.0%
23	Indiana	1,646,000	1.8%
28	Iowa	1,203,000	1.3%
30	Kansas	962,000	1.0%
25	Kentucky	1,525,000	1.7%
22	Louisiana	1,677,000	1.8%
37	Maine	642,000	0.7%
18	Maryland	2,028,000	2.2%
14	Massachusetts	2,259,000	2.4%
7	Michigan	3,416,000	3.7%
17	Minnesota	2,047,000	2.2%
32	Mississippi	907,000	1.0%
21	Missouri	1,713,000	1.9%
43	Montana	391,000	0.4%
38	Nebraska	579,000	0.6%
35	Nevada	693,000	0.8%
39	New Hampshire	509,000	0.6%
16	New Jersey	2,151,000	2.3%
36	New Mexico	646,000	0.7%
4	New York	4,680,000	5.1%
9	North Carolina	3,170,000	3.4%
46	North Dakota	279,000	0.3%
8	Ohio	3,378,000	3.7%
31	Oklahoma	920,000	1.0%
24	Oregon	1,594,000	1.7%
5	Pennsylvania	3,803,000	4.1%
44	Rhode Island	331,000	0.4%
26	South Carolina	1,514,000	1.6%
47	South Dakota	273,000	0.3%
20	Tennessee	1,763,000	1.9%
3	Texas	5,836,000	6.3%
34	Utah	703,000	0.8%
49	Vermont	205,000	0.2%
11	Virginia	2,453,000	2.7%
12	Washington	2,390,000	2.6%
40	West Virginia	484,000	0.5%
13	Wisconsin	2,343,000	2.5%
50	Wyoming	172,000	0.2%

RANK ORDER

RANK	STATE	VOTERS	% of USA
1	California	8,949,000	9.7%
2	Florida	6,220,000	6.7%
3	Texas	5,836,000	6.3%
4	New York	4,680,000	5.1%
5	Pennsylvania	3,803,000	4.1%
6	Illinois	3,734,000	4.0%
7	Michigan	3,416,000	3.7%
8	Ohio	3,378,000	3.7%
9	North Carolina	3,170,000	3.4%
10	Georgia	2,919,000	3.2%
11	Virginia	2,453,000	2.7%
12	Washington	2,390,000	2.6%
13	Wisconsin	2,343,000	2.5%
14	Massachusetts	2,259,000	2.4%
15	Colorado	2,211,000	2.4%
16	New Jersey	2,151,000	2.3%
17	Minnesota	2,047,000	2.2%
18	Maryland	2,028,000	2.2%
19	Arizona	1,785,000	1.9%
20	Tennessee	1,763,000	1.9%
21	Missouri	1,713,000	1.9%
22	Louisiana	1,677,000	1.8%
23	Indiana	1,646,000	1.8%
24	Oregon	1,594,000	1.7%
25	Kentucky	1,525,000	1.7%
26	South Carolina	1,514,000	1.6%
27	Alabama	1,497,000	1.6%
28	Iowa	1,203,000	1.3%
29	Connecticut	1,195,000	1.3%
30	Kansas	962,000	1.0%
31	Oklahoma	920,000	1.0%
32	Mississippi	907,000	1.0%
33	Arkansas	798,000	0.9%
34	Utah	703,000	0.8%
35	Nevada	693,000	0.8%
36	New Mexico	646,000	0.7%
37	Maine	642,000	0.7%
38	Nebraska	579,000	0.6%
39	New Hampshire	509,000	0.6%
40	West Virginia	484,000	0.5%
41	Idaho	462,000	0.5%
42	Hawaii	399,000	0.4%
43	Montana	391,000	0.4%
44	Rhode Island	331,000	0.4%
45	Delaware	299,000	0.3%
46	North Dakota	279,000	0.3%
47	South Dakota	273,000	0.3%
48	Alaska	255,000	0.3%
49	Vermont	205,000	0.2%
50	Wyoming	172,000	0.2%
	District of Columbia	247,000	0.3%

Source: U.S. Bureau of the Census
"Voting and Registration" (Table 4a, http://www.census.gov/hhes/www/socdemo/voting/index.html)

Percent of Eligible Population Reported Voting in 2014

National Percent = 41.9%*

ALPHA ORDER				RANK ORDER		
RANK	STATE	PERCENT		RANK	STATE	PERCENT
27	Alabama	42.5		1	Maine	61.5
8	Alaska	50.7		2	Colorado	59.3
35	Arizona	40.6		3	Oregon	55.5
39	Arkansas	38.8		4	Wisconsin	55.4
42	California	36.6		5	Iowa	52.9
2	Colorado	59.3		6	Minnesota	52.0
18	Connecticut	46.7		7	North Dakota	51.0
21	Delaware	45.2		8	Alaska	50.7
22	Florida	44.8		9	Louisiana	50.2
26	Georgia	43.2		9	New Hampshire	50.2
31	Hawaii	41.8		11	Montana	50.1
31	Idaho	41.8		12	Washington	50.0
33	Illinois	41.7		13	Maryland	48.9
46	Indiana	35.1		14	Kansas	48.3
5	Iowa	52.9		15	Kentucky	47.5
14	Kansas	48.3		16	Michigan	47.1
15	Kentucky	47.5		17	Massachusetts	46.9
9	Louisiana	50.2		18	Connecticut	46.7
1	Maine	61.5		19	North Carolina	46.2
13	Maryland	48.9		20	New Mexico	45.6
17	Massachusetts	46.9		21	Delaware	45.2
16	Michigan	47.1		22	Florida	44.8
6	Minnesota	52.0		23	Nebraska	44.3
30	Mississippi	42.3		24	South Dakota	44.1
40	Missouri	38.7		25	Rhode Island	43.3
11	Montana	50.1		26	Georgia	43.2
23	Nebraska	44.3		27	Alabama	42.5
41	Nevada	37.3		27	Vermont	42.5
9	New Hampshire	50.2		29	South Carolina	42.4
45	New Jersey	36.4		30	Mississippi	42.3
20	New Mexico	45.6		31	Hawaii	41.8
48	New York	34.4		31	Idaho	41.8
19	North Carolina	46.2		33	Illinois	41.7
7	North Dakota	51.0		33	Virginia	41.7
38	Ohio	39.7		35	Arizona	40.6
49	Oklahoma	34.2		36	Wyoming	40.3
3	Oregon	55.5		37	Pennsylvania	40.0
37	Pennsylvania	40.0		38	Ohio	39.7
25	Rhode Island	43.3		39	Arkansas	38.8
29	South Carolina	42.4		40	Missouri	38.7
24	South Dakota	44.1		41	Nevada	37.3
42	Tennessee	36.6		42	California	36.6
47	Texas	34.6		42	Tennessee	36.6
44	Utah	36.5		44	Utah	36.5
27	Vermont	42.5		45	New Jersey	36.4
33	Virginia	41.7		46	Indiana	35.1
12	Washington	50.0		47	Texas	34.6
50	West Virginia	33.6		48	New York	34.4
4	Wisconsin	55.4		49	Oklahoma	34.2
36	Wyoming	40.3		50	West Virginia	33.6
					District of Columbia	51.4

Source: U.S. Bureau of the Census
    "Voting and Registration" (Table 4a, http://www.census.gov/hhes/www/socdemo/voting/index.html)
*As a percent of citizen population 18 and older.

Population   515

Percent of Registered Population Reported Voting in 2014

National Percent = 64.9%*

ALPHA ORDER

RANK	STATE	PERCENT
35	Alabama	63.3
8	Alaska	75.9
31	Arizona	65.2
39	Arkansas	61.8
34	California	63.4
1	Colorado	83.3
13	Connecticut	71.6
25	Delaware	67.6
13	Florida	71.6
23	Georgia	67.8
2	Hawaii	81.4
20	Idaho	68.9
30	Illinois	65.3
48	Indiana	54.0
8	Iowa	75.9
16	Kansas	71.1
26	Kentucky	66.4
18	Louisiana	69.9
3	Maine	80.4
24	Maryland	67.7
19	Massachusetts	69.5
29	Michigan	66.2
12	Minnesota	72.5
46	Mississippi	55.7
50	Missouri	53.6
6	Montana	77.3
27	Nebraska	66.3
33	Nevada	63.7
10	New Hampshire	73.3
47	New Jersey	54.9
17	New Mexico	70.3
43	New York	57.9
27	North Carolina	66.3
7	North Dakota	76.9
41	Ohio	59.7
45	Oklahoma	56.0
4	Oregon	79.4
38	Pennsylvania	62.1
21	Rhode Island	68.1
40	South Carolina	61.6
21	South Dakota	68.1
44	Tennessee	57.1
42	Texas	58.7
32	Utah	63.9
35	Vermont	63.3
37	Virginia	62.5
11	Washington	72.8
48	West Virginia	54.0
5	Wisconsin	78.0
15	Wyoming	71.4

RANK ORDER

RANK	STATE	PERCENT
1	Colorado	83.3
2	Hawaii	81.4
3	Maine	80.4
4	Oregon	79.4
5	Wisconsin	78.0
6	Montana	77.3
7	North Dakota	76.9
8	Alaska	75.9
8	Iowa	75.9
10	New Hampshire	73.3
11	Washington	72.8
12	Minnesota	72.5
13	Connecticut	71.6
13	Florida	71.6
15	Wyoming	71.4
16	Kansas	71.1
17	New Mexico	70.3
18	Louisiana	69.9
19	Massachusetts	69.5
20	Idaho	68.9
21	Rhode Island	68.1
21	South Dakota	68.1
23	Georgia	67.8
24	Maryland	67.7
25	Delaware	67.6
26	Kentucky	66.4
27	Nebraska	66.3
27	North Carolina	66.3
29	Michigan	66.2
30	Illinois	65.3
31	Arizona	65.2
32	Utah	63.9
33	Nevada	63.7
34	California	63.4
35	Alabama	63.3
35	Vermont	63.3
37	Virginia	62.5
38	Pennsylvania	62.1
39	Arkansas	61.8
40	South Carolina	61.6
41	Ohio	59.7
42	Texas	58.7
43	New York	57.9
44	Tennessee	57.1
45	Oklahoma	56.0
46	Mississippi	55.7
47	New Jersey	54.9
48	Indiana	54.0
48	West Virginia	54.0
50	Missouri	53.6
	District of Columbia	70.0

Source: CQ Press using data from U.S. Bureau of the Census
"Voting and Registration" (Table 4a, http://www.census.gov/hhes/www/socdemo/voting/index.html)
*As a percent of citizen population 18 and older registered to vote.

XIV. Social Welfare

Poverty Rate in 2014. 519
Percent of Senior Citizens Living in Poverty in 2014 520
Percent of Children Living in Poverty in 2014. 521
Percent of Families Living in Poverty in 2014. 522
Percent of Female-Headed Families with Children Living
  in Poverty in 2014 523
State and Local Government Expenditures for Public
  Welfare Programs in 2013 524
Per Capita State and Local Government Expenditures for
  Public Welfare Programs in 2013. 525
State and Local Government Spending for Public
  Welfare Programs as a Percent of All State and Local
  Government Expenditures in 2013. 526
Social Security (OASDI) Payments in 2013. 527
Per Capita Social Security (OASDI) Payments in 2013. . . 528
Social Security (OASDI) Monthly Payments in 2013 529
Social Security (OASDI) Beneficiaries in 2013 530
Average Monthly Social Security (OASDI) Payment
  in 2013 531
Social Security Supplemental Security Income
  Beneficiaries in 2013 532
Average Monthly Social Security Supplemental Security
  Income Payment in 2013 533
Medicare Enrollees in 2014 534
Percent of Population Enrolled in Medicare in 2014 535
Medicare Program Payments in 2012. 536
Medicare Program Payments per Enrollee in 2012 537
Medicaid Enrollment in 2013 538
Percent of Population Enrolled in Medicaid in 2013 539

Estimated Medicaid Expenditures in 2015. 540
Percent Change in Medicaid Expenditures: 2014 to
  2015 541
Percent of Population Receiving Public Aid in 2013 542
Recipients of Temporary Assistance to Needy Families
  (TANF) Payments in 2015. 543
Percent Change in TANF Recipients: 2014 to 2015. 544
TANF Work Participation Rates in 2013 545
Average Monthly TANF Assistance per Family in 2013 . . 546
Percent of Households with Food Insecurity in 2014. 547
Supplemental Nutrition Assistance Program Benefits
  in 2015 548
Monthly Supplemental Nutrition Assistance Program
  Recipients in 2015 549
Average Monthly Supplemental Nutrition Assistance
  Program Benefit per Recipient in 2015 550
Percent of Population Receiving Supplemental Nutrition
  Assistance Program Benefits in 2015. 551
Percent of Households Receiving Supplemental Nutrition
  Assistance Program Benefits in 2015. 552
Average Monthly Participants in Women, Infants, and
  Children (WIC) Special Nutrition Program in 2015 . . . 553
Average Monthly Benefit per Participant in Women,
  Infants, and Children (WIC) Special Nutrition Program
  in 2015 554
Percent of Public Elementary and Secondary School
  Students Eligible for Free or Reduced-Price Meals
  in 2014 555
Child Support Collections in 2014 556

Poverty Rate in 2014

National Rate = 15.5% of Population in Poverty*

ALPHA ORDER

RANK	STATE	PERCENT
4	Alabama	19.3
45	Alaska	11.2
10	Arizona	18.2
6	Arkansas	18.9
17	California	16.4
38	Colorado	12.0
48	Connecticut	10.8
34	Delaware	12.5
16	Florida	16.5
7	Georgia	18.3
44	Hawaii	11.4
25	Idaho	14.8
26	Illinois	14.4
23	Indiana	15.2
36	Iowa	12.2
30	Kansas	13.6
5	Kentucky	19.1
3	Louisiana	19.8
29	Maine	14.1
49	Maryland	10.1
41	Massachusetts	11.6
18	Michigan	16.2
42	Minnesota	11.5
1	Mississippi	21.5
21	Missouri	15.5
22	Montana	15.4
35	Nebraska	12.4
23	Nevada	15.2
50	New Hampshire	9.2
47	New Jersey	11.1
2	New Mexico	21.3
19	New York	15.9
12	North Carolina	17.2
42	North Dakota	11.5
20	Ohio	15.8
14	Oklahoma	16.6
14	Oregon	16.6
30	Pennsylvania	13.6
27	Rhode Island	14.3
11	South Carolina	18.0
28	South Dakota	14.2
7	Tennessee	18.3
12	Texas	17.2
40	Utah	11.7
36	Vermont	12.2
39	Virginia	11.8
32	Washington	13.2
7	West Virginia	18.3
32	Wisconsin	13.2
45	Wyoming	11.2

RANK ORDER

RANK	STATE	PERCENT
1	Mississippi	21.5
2	New Mexico	21.3
3	Louisiana	19.8
4	Alabama	19.3
5	Kentucky	19.1
6	Arkansas	18.9
7	Georgia	18.3
7	Tennessee	18.3
7	West Virginia	18.3
10	Arizona	18.2
11	South Carolina	18.0
12	North Carolina	17.2
12	Texas	17.2
14	Oklahoma	16.6
14	Oregon	16.6
16	Florida	16.5
17	California	16.4
18	Michigan	16.2
19	New York	15.9
20	Ohio	15.8
21	Missouri	15.5
22	Montana	15.4
23	Indiana	15.2
23	Nevada	15.2
25	Idaho	14.8
26	Illinois	14.4
27	Rhode Island	14.3
28	South Dakota	14.2
29	Maine	14.1
30	Kansas	13.6
30	Pennsylvania	13.6
32	Washington	13.2
32	Wisconsin	13.2
34	Delaware	12.5
35	Nebraska	12.4
36	Iowa	12.2
36	Vermont	12.2
38	Colorado	12.0
39	Virginia	11.8
40	Utah	11.7
41	Massachusetts	11.6
42	Minnesota	11.5
42	North Dakota	11.5
44	Hawaii	11.4
45	Alaska	11.2
45	Wyoming	11.2
47	New Jersey	11.1
48	Connecticut	10.8
49	Maryland	10.1
50	New Hampshire	9.2
	District of Columbia	17.7

Source: U.S. Bureau of the Census
"2014 American Community Survey-Table GCT1701" (http://www.census.gov/programs-surveys/acs/)
*This is a one-year figure. Census has discontinued three-year averages that had been used previously. The poverty threshold for a family of four (two children) in 2014 was $23,850.

Percent of Senior Citizens Living in Poverty in 2014

National Percent = 9.5%*

ALPHA ORDER

RANK	STATE	PERCENT
6	Alabama	11.2
50	Alaska	4.3
17	Arizona	9.4
8	Arkansas	10.6
8	California	10.6
44	Colorado	7.1
37	Connecticut	7.8
39	Delaware	7.5
11	Florida	10.5
12	Georgia	10.4
31	Hawaii	8.2
16	Idaho	9.5
23	Illinois	8.8
46	Indiana	7.0
41	Iowa	7.4
35	Kansas	7.9
5	Kentucky	11.3
3	Louisiana	12.8
22	Maine	8.9
41	Maryland	7.4
18	Massachusetts	9.3
32	Michigan	8.1
39	Minnesota	7.5
1	Mississippi	13.2
21	Missouri	9.0
29	Montana	8.3
35	Nebraska	7.9
29	Nevada	8.3
49	New Hampshire	5.1
26	New Jersey	8.6
1	New Mexico	13.2
4	New York	11.7
14	North Carolina	9.7
25	North Dakota	8.7
32	Ohio	8.1
27	Oklahoma	8.5
23	Oregon	8.8
32	Pennsylvania	8.1
14	Rhode Island	9.7
18	South Carolina	9.3
8	South Dakota	10.6
13	Tennessee	10.1
7	Texas	10.9
47	Utah	6.7
44	Vermont	7.1
37	Virginia	7.8
28	Washington	8.4
18	West Virginia	9.3
43	Wisconsin	7.2
48	Wyoming	6.2

RANK ORDER

RANK	STATE	PERCENT
1	Mississippi	13.2
1	New Mexico	13.2
3	Louisiana	12.8
4	New York	11.7
5	Kentucky	11.3
6	Alabama	11.2
7	Texas	10.9
8	Arkansas	10.6
8	California	10.6
8	South Dakota	10.6
11	Florida	10.5
12	Georgia	10.4
13	Tennessee	10.1
14	North Carolina	9.7
14	Rhode Island	9.7
16	Idaho	9.5
17	Arizona	9.4
18	Massachusetts	9.3
18	South Carolina	9.3
18	West Virginia	9.3
21	Missouri	9.0
22	Maine	8.9
23	Illinois	8.8
23	Oregon	8.8
25	North Dakota	8.7
26	New Jersey	8.6
27	Oklahoma	8.5
28	Washington	8.4
29	Montana	8.3
29	Nevada	8.3
31	Hawaii	8.2
32	Michigan	8.1
32	Ohio	8.1
32	Pennsylvania	8.1
35	Kansas	7.9
35	Nebraska	7.9
37	Connecticut	7.8
37	Virginia	7.8
39	Delaware	7.5
39	Minnesota	7.5
41	Iowa	7.4
41	Maryland	7.4
43	Wisconsin	7.2
44	Colorado	7.1
44	Vermont	7.1
46	Indiana	7.0
47	Utah	6.7
48	Wyoming	6.2
49	New Hampshire	5.1
50	Alaska	4.3
	District of Columbia	14.5

Source: U.S. Bureau of the Census
"2014 American Community Survey-Table GCT1703" (http://www.census.gov/programs-surveys/acs/)
*People 65 years and older living with incomes below the poverty level.

Percent of Children Living in Poverty in 2014

National Percent = 21.3%*

ALPHA ORDER

RANK	STATE	PERCENT
4	Alabama	27.5
38	Alaska	15.3
10	Arizona	25.2
7	Arkansas	26.0
16	California	22.4
40	Colorado	15.1
44	Connecticut	14.4
32	Delaware	17.5
14	Florida	23.5
6	Georgia	26.1
44	Hawaii	14.4
28	Idaho	18.5
24	Illinois	19.9
21	Indiana	21.2
41	Iowa	14.9
33	Kansas	17.4
9	Kentucky	25.8
3	Louisiana	27.6
27	Maine	18.7
48	Maryland	12.7
41	Massachusetts	14.9
17	Michigan	22.2
43	Minnesota	14.6
2	Mississippi	29.0
23	Missouri	20.7
29	Montana	18.1
35	Nebraska	15.8
20	Nevada	21.7
49	New Hampshire	12.5
36	New Jersey	15.7
1	New Mexico	29.1
17	New York	22.2
13	North Carolina	24.0
46	North Dakota	14.3
15	Ohio	22.5
19	Oklahoma	22.1
22	Oregon	21.1
26	Pennsylvania	19.0
25	Rhode Island	19.5
5	South Carolina	26.7
31	South Dakota	17.7
8	Tennessee	25.9
11	Texas	24.3
47	Utah	13.0
38	Vermont	15.3
37	Virginia	15.5
34	Washington	17.0
11	West Virginia	24.3
29	Wisconsin	18.1
50	Wyoming	12.1

RANK ORDER

RANK	STATE	PERCENT
1	New Mexico	29.1
2	Mississippi	29.0
3	Louisiana	27.6
4	Alabama	27.5
5	South Carolina	26.7
6	Georgia	26.1
7	Arkansas	26.0
8	Tennessee	25.9
9	Kentucky	25.8
10	Arizona	25.2
11	Texas	24.3
11	West Virginia	24.3
13	North Carolina	24.0
14	Florida	23.5
15	Ohio	22.5
16	California	22.4
17	Michigan	22.2
17	New York	22.2
19	Oklahoma	22.1
20	Nevada	21.7
21	Indiana	21.2
22	Oregon	21.1
23	Missouri	20.7
24	Illinois	19.9
25	Rhode Island	19.5
26	Pennsylvania	19.0
27	Maine	18.7
28	Idaho	18.5
29	Montana	18.1
29	Wisconsin	18.1
31	South Dakota	17.7
32	Delaware	17.5
33	Kansas	17.4
34	Washington	17.0
35	Nebraska	15.8
36	New Jersey	15.7
37	Virginia	15.5
38	Alaska	15.3
38	Vermont	15.3
40	Colorado	15.1
41	Iowa	14.9
41	Massachusetts	14.9
43	Minnesota	14.6
44	Connecticut	14.4
44	Hawaii	14.4
46	North Dakota	14.3
47	Utah	13.0
48	Maryland	12.7
49	New Hampshire	12.5
50	Wyoming	12.1
	District of Columbia	25.9

Source: U.S. Bureau of the Census
"2014 American Community Survey-Table GCT1702" (http://www.census.gov/programs-surveys/acs/)
*Children 17 and under living in families with incomes below the poverty level.

Percent of Families Living in Poverty in 2014

National Percent = 11.3%*

ALPHA ORDER

RANK	STATE	PERCENT
3	Alabama	15.0
42	Alaska	7.9
10	Arizona	13.2
7	Arkansas	13.8
14	California	12.2
41	Colorado	8.0
45	Connecticut	7.5
36	Delaware	8.5
17	Florida	12.0
6	Georgia	14.1
44	Hawaii	7.8
25	Idaho	10.2
24	Illinois	10.5
22	Indiana	10.9
42	Iowa	7.9
31	Kansas	9.2
5	Kentucky	14.5
4	Louisiana	14.9
27	Maine	9.7
49	Maryland	7.1
38	Massachusetts	8.3
19	Michigan	11.4
45	Minnesota	7.5
1	Mississippi	16.5
23	Missouri	10.7
28	Montana	9.5
34	Nebraska	8.7
20	Nevada	11.0
50	New Hampshire	6.0
38	New Jersey	8.3
1	New Mexico	16.5
14	New York	12.2
13	North Carolina	12.8
47	North Dakota	7.4
18	Ohio	11.6
14	Oklahoma	12.2
20	Oregon	11.0
29	Pennsylvania	9.4
26	Rhode Island	10.0
10	South Carolina	13.2
29	South Dakota	9.4
8	Tennessee	13.7
9	Texas	13.4
36	Utah	8.5
34	Vermont	8.7
38	Virginia	8.3
33	Washington	8.8
12	West Virginia	13.1
32	Wisconsin	9.0
47	Wyoming	7.4

RANK ORDER

RANK	STATE	PERCENT
1	Mississippi	16.5
1	New Mexico	16.5
3	Alabama	15.0
4	Louisiana	14.9
5	Kentucky	14.5
6	Georgia	14.1
7	Arkansas	13.8
8	Tennessee	13.7
9	Texas	13.4
10	Arizona	13.2
10	South Carolina	13.2
12	West Virginia	13.1
13	North Carolina	12.8
14	California	12.2
14	New York	12.2
14	Oklahoma	12.2
17	Florida	12.0
18	Ohio	11.6
19	Michigan	11.4
20	Nevada	11.0
20	Oregon	11.0
22	Indiana	10.9
23	Missouri	10.7
24	Illinois	10.5
25	Idaho	10.2
26	Rhode Island	10.0
27	Maine	9.7
28	Montana	9.5
29	Pennsylvania	9.4
29	South Dakota	9.4
31	Kansas	9.2
32	Wisconsin	9.0
33	Washington	8.8
34	Nebraska	8.7
34	Vermont	8.7
36	Delaware	8.5
36	Utah	8.5
38	Massachusetts	8.3
38	New Jersey	8.3
38	Virginia	8.3
41	Colorado	8.0
42	Alaska	7.9
42	Iowa	7.9
44	Hawaii	7.8
45	Connecticut	7.5
45	Minnesota	7.5
47	North Dakota	7.4
47	Wyoming	7.4
49	Maryland	7.1
50	New Hampshire	6.0
	District of Columbia	14.2

Source: U.S. Bureau of the Census
"2014 American Community Survey-Table DP03" (http://www.census.gov/programs-surveys/acs/)
*Families living with incomes below the poverty level.

Percent of Female-Headed Families with Children Living in Poverty in 2014

National Percent = 40.6%*

ALPHA ORDER

RANK	STATE	PERCENT
2	Alabama	51.0
48	Alaska	29.0
25	Arizona	40.3
7	Arkansas	46.7
35	California	38.5
45	Colorado	31.7
46	Connecticut	31.3
47	Delaware	30.6
28	Florida	39.7
13	Georgia	43.2
49	Hawaii	26.8
21	Idaho	41.7
23	Illinois	41.0
16	Indiana	42.7
34	Iowa	38.7
31	Kansas	39.2
3	Kentucky	49.1
6	Louisiana	47.6
17	Maine	42.1
50	Maryland	25.4
41	Massachusetts	35.6
12	Michigan	43.7
40	Minnesota	36.1
5	Mississippi	48.0
19	Missouri	41.8
11	Montana	45.1
36	Nebraska	37.7
42	Nevada	34.3
43	New Hampshire	32.7
44	New Jersey	31.8
8	New Mexico	46.6
31	New York	39.2
15	North Carolina	42.9
22	North Dakota	41.5
10	Ohio	45.4
13	Oklahoma	43.2
24	Oregon	40.8
28	Pennsylvania	39.7
26	Rhode Island	40.2
8	South Carolina	46.6
30	South Dakota	39.3
4	Tennessee	48.7
19	Texas	41.8
38	Utah	36.9
27	Vermont	40.0
39	Virginia	36.6
37	Washington	37.1
1	West Virginia	52.3
17	Wisconsin	42.1
33	Wyoming	39.0

RANK ORDER

RANK	STATE	PERCENT
1	West Virginia	52.3
2	Alabama	51.0
3	Kentucky	49.1
4	Tennessee	48.7
5	Mississippi	48.0
6	Louisiana	47.6
7	Arkansas	46.7
8	New Mexico	46.6
8	South Carolina	46.6
10	Ohio	45.4
11	Montana	45.1
12	Michigan	43.7
13	Georgia	43.2
13	Oklahoma	43.2
15	North Carolina	42.9
16	Indiana	42.7
17	Maine	42.1
17	Wisconsin	42.1
19	Missouri	41.8
19	Texas	41.8
21	Idaho	41.7
22	North Dakota	41.5
23	Illinois	41.0
24	Oregon	40.8
25	Arizona	40.3
26	Rhode Island	40.2
27	Vermont	40.0
28	Florida	39.7
28	Pennsylvania	39.7
30	South Dakota	39.3
31	Kansas	39.2
31	New York	39.2
33	Wyoming	39.0
34	Iowa	38.7
35	California	38.5
36	Nebraska	37.7
37	Washington	37.1
38	Utah	36.9
39	Virginia	36.6
40	Minnesota	36.1
41	Massachusetts	35.6
42	Nevada	34.3
43	New Hampshire	32.7
44	New Jersey	31.8
45	Colorado	31.7
46	Connecticut	31.3
47	Delaware	30.6
48	Alaska	29.0
49	Hawaii	26.8
50	Maryland	25.4
	District of Columbia	38.5

Source: U.S. Bureau of the Census
   "2014 American Community Survey-Table DP03" (http://www.census.gov/programs-surveys/acs/)
*Households headed by females with own children under 18 years living with them with incomes below the poverty level as a percent of all such female-headed households.

State and Local Government Expenditures for Public Welfare Programs in 2013

National Total = $516,389,152,000*

ALPHA ORDER

RANK	STATE	EXPENDITURES	% of USA
25	Alabama	$6,326,146,000	1.2%
43	Alaska	2,009,980,000	0.4%
20	Arizona	8,397,182,000	1.6%
32	Arkansas	5,155,738,000	1.0%
1	California	68,771,620,000	13.3%
29	Colorado	5,976,360,000	1.2%
23	Connecticut	7,069,245,000	1.4%
44	Delaware	1,962,263,000	0.4%
5	Florida	23,756,928,000	4.6%
13	Georgia	11,385,261,000	2.2%
42	Hawaii	2,131,666,000	0.4%
41	Idaho	2,230,121,000	0.4%
7	Illinois	19,476,378,000	3.8%
14	Indiana	10,765,595,000	2.1%
31	Iowa	5,228,096,000	1.0%
35	Kansas	3,416,810,000	0.7%
24	Kentucky	7,009,360,000	1.4%
22	Louisiana	7,110,090,000	1.4%
37	Maine	2,912,654,000	0.6%
16	Maryland	10,270,659,000	2.0%
8	Massachusetts	15,365,584,000	3.0%
10	Michigan	13,288,951,000	2.6%
12	Minnesota	12,388,628,000	2.4%
30	Mississippi	5,432,632,000	1.1%
21	Missouri	8,161,781,000	1.6%
47	Montana	1,445,309,000	0.3%
39	Nebraska	2,585,725,000	0.5%
38	Nevada	2,594,799,000	0.5%
45	New Hampshire	1,751,752,000	0.3%
9	New Jersey	14,786,149,000	2.9%
33	New Mexico	4,031,407,000	0.8%
2	New York	59,392,585,000	11.5%
11	North Carolina	13,029,028,000	2.5%
48	North Dakota	995,658,000	0.2%
6	Ohio	20,427,712,000	4.0%
26	Oklahoma	6,239,178,000	1.2%
27	Oregon	6,165,361,000	1.2%
4	Pennsylvania	25,104,191,000	4.9%
40	Rhode Island	2,323,329,000	0.4%
28	South Carolina	5,997,375,000	1.2%
49	South Dakota	982,021,000	0.2%
17	Tennessee	10,269,110,000	2.0%
3	Texas	30,710,282,000	5.9%
36	Utah	3,135,390,000	0.6%
46	Vermont	1,632,174,000	0.3%
15	Virginia	10,726,064,000	2.1%
19	Washington	8,568,413,000	1.7%
34	West Virginia	3,492,943,000	0.7%
18	Wisconsin	10,005,925,000	1.9%
50	Wyoming	805,392,000	0.2%

RANK ORDER

RANK	STATE	EXPENDITURES	% of USA
1	California	$68,771,620,000	13.3%
2	New York	59,392,585,000	11.5%
3	Texas	30,710,282,000	5.9%
4	Pennsylvania	25,104,191,000	4.9%
5	Florida	23,756,928,000	4.6%
6	Ohio	20,427,712,000	4.0%
7	Illinois	19,476,378,000	3.8%
8	Massachusetts	15,365,584,000	3.0%
9	New Jersey	14,786,149,000	2.9%
10	Michigan	13,288,951,000	2.6%
11	North Carolina	13,029,028,000	2.5%
12	Minnesota	12,388,628,000	2.4%
13	Georgia	11,385,261,000	2.2%
14	Indiana	10,765,595,000	2.1%
15	Virginia	10,726,064,000	2.1%
16	Maryland	10,270,659,000	2.0%
17	Tennessee	10,269,110,000	2.0%
18	Wisconsin	10,005,925,000	1.9%
19	Washington	8,568,413,000	1.7%
20	Arizona	8,397,182,000	1.6%
21	Missouri	8,161,781,000	1.6%
22	Louisiana	7,110,090,000	1.4%
23	Connecticut	7,069,245,000	1.4%
24	Kentucky	7,009,360,000	1.4%
25	Alabama	6,326,146,000	1.2%
26	Oklahoma	6,239,178,000	1.2%
27	Oregon	6,165,361,000	1.2%
28	South Carolina	5,997,375,000	1.2%
29	Colorado	5,976,360,000	1.2%
30	Mississippi	5,432,632,000	1.1%
31	Iowa	5,228,096,000	1.0%
32	Arkansas	5,155,738,000	1.0%
33	New Mexico	4,031,407,000	0.8%
34	West Virginia	3,492,943,000	0.7%
35	Kansas	3,416,810,000	0.7%
36	Utah	3,135,390,000	0.6%
37	Maine	2,912,654,000	0.6%
38	Nevada	2,594,799,000	0.5%
39	Nebraska	2,585,725,000	0.5%
40	Rhode Island	2,323,329,000	0.4%
41	Idaho	2,230,121,000	0.4%
42	Hawaii	2,131,666,000	0.4%
43	Alaska	2,009,980,000	0.4%
44	Delaware	1,962,263,000	0.4%
45	New Hampshire	1,751,752,000	0.3%
46	Vermont	1,632,174,000	0.3%
47	Montana	1,445,309,000	0.3%
48	North Dakota	995,658,000	0.2%
49	South Dakota	982,021,000	0.2%
50	Wyoming	805,392,000	0.2%
	District of Columbia	3,192,152,000	0.6%

Source: U.S. Bureau of the Census, Governments Division
"2013 State and Local Government Finances" (http://www.census.gov/govs/local/)
*Direct general expenditures. Includes funds for cash assistance programs, medical and other vendor payments, welfare institutions, and other public welfare programs.

Per Capita State and Local Government Expenditures for Public Welfare Programs in 2013
National Per Capita = $1,632*

ALPHA ORDER

RANK	STATE	PER CAPITA
38	Alabama	$1,310
2	Alaska	2,726
40	Arizona	1,266
16	Arkansas	1,743
14	California	1,790
48	Colorado	1,134
9	Connecticut	1,965
8	Delaware	2,121
43	Florida	1,212
47	Georgia	1,139
27	Hawaii	1,513
30	Idaho	1,383
28	Illinois	1,511
21	Indiana	1,638
19	Iowa	1,691
44	Kansas	1,180
23	Kentucky	1,594
26	Louisiana	1,536
7	Maine	2,192
18	Maryland	1,730
4	Massachusetts	2,290
35	Michigan	1,342
5	Minnesota	2,285
13	Mississippi	1,816
34	Missouri	1,350
29	Montana	1,425
30	Nebraska	1,383
50	Nevada	930
36	New Hampshire	1,324
20	New Jersey	1,660
11	New Mexico	1,932
1	New York	3,016
37	North Carolina	1,323
33	North Dakota	1,376
15	Ohio	1,765
22	Oklahoma	1,619
25	Oregon	1,570
10	Pennsylvania	1,964
6	Rhode Island	2,207
41	South Carolina	1,258
45	South Dakota	1,162
24	Tennessee	1,581
46	Texas	1,159
49	Utah	1,080
3	Vermont	2,603
39	Virginia	1,297
42	Washington	1,229
12	West Virginia	1,885
17	Wisconsin	1,742
32	Wyoming	1,381

RANK ORDER

RANK	STATE	PER CAPITA
1	New York	$3,016
2	Alaska	2,726
3	Vermont	2,603
4	Massachusetts	2,290
5	Minnesota	2,285
6	Rhode Island	2,207
7	Maine	2,192
8	Delaware	2,121
9	Connecticut	1,965
10	Pennsylvania	1,964
11	New Mexico	1,932
12	West Virginia	1,885
13	Mississippi	1,816
14	California	1,790
15	Ohio	1,765
16	Arkansas	1,743
17	Wisconsin	1,742
18	Maryland	1,730
19	Iowa	1,691
20	New Jersey	1,660
21	Indiana	1,638
22	Oklahoma	1,619
23	Kentucky	1,594
24	Tennessee	1,581
25	Oregon	1,570
26	Louisiana	1,536
27	Hawaii	1,513
28	Illinois	1,511
29	Montana	1,425
30	Idaho	1,383
30	Nebraska	1,383
32	Wyoming	1,381
33	North Dakota	1,376
34	Missouri	1,350
35	Michigan	1,342
36	New Hampshire	1,324
37	North Carolina	1,323
38	Alabama	1,310
39	Virginia	1,297
40	Arizona	1,266
41	South Carolina	1,258
42	Washington	1,229
43	Florida	1,212
44	Kansas	1,180
45	South Dakota	1,162
46	Texas	1,159
47	Georgia	1,139
48	Colorado	1,134
49	Utah	1,080
50	Nevada	930
	District of Columbia	4,914

Source: CQ Press using data from U.S. Bureau of the Census, Governments Division
"2013 State and Local Government Finances" (http://www.census.gov/govs/local/)
*Direct general expenditures. Includes funds for cash assistance programs, medical and other vendor payments, welfare institutions, and other public welfare programs.

State and Local Government Spending for Public Welfare Programs as a Percent of All State and Local Government Expenditures in 2013
National Percent = 19.6%*

ALPHA ORDER

RANK	STATE	PERCENT
33	Alabama	17.5
43	Alaska	14.8
20	Arizona	20.3
6	Arkansas	24.1
24	California	19.0
46	Colorado	14.5
20	Connecticut	20.3
19	Delaware	20.9
30	Florida	17.6
35	Georgia	17.4
36	Hawaii	17.3
17	Idaho	21.5
27	Illinois	18.1
10	Indiana	23.0
25	Iowa	18.7
44	Kansas	14.7
16	Kentucky	21.9
38	Louisiana	16.9
1	Maine	26.2
22	Maryland	19.5
9	Massachusetts	23.4
28	Michigan	17.8
2	Minnesota	25.2
13	Mississippi	22.7
25	Missouri	18.7
30	Montana	17.6
39	Nebraska	16.8
48	Nevada	14.3
33	New Hampshire	17.5
30	New Jersey	17.6
14	New Mexico	22.2
5	New York	24.3
28	North Carolina	17.8
49	North Dakota	13.4
15	Ohio	22.0
11	Oklahoma	22.9
23	Oregon	19.1
11	Pennsylvania	22.9
4	Rhode Island	24.6
37	South Carolina	17.1
42	South Dakota	15.8
7	Tennessee	24.0
40	Texas	16.4
44	Utah	14.7
3	Vermont	24.9
40	Virginia	16.4
47	Washington	14.4
8	West Virginia	23.8
18	Wisconsin	21.2
50	Wyoming	10.4

RANK ORDER

RANK	STATE	PERCENT
1	Maine	26.2
2	Minnesota	25.2
3	Vermont	24.9
4	Rhode Island	24.6
5	New York	24.3
6	Arkansas	24.1
7	Tennessee	24.0
8	West Virginia	23.8
9	Massachusetts	23.4
10	Indiana	23.0
11	Oklahoma	22.9
11	Pennsylvania	22.9
13	Mississippi	22.7
14	New Mexico	22.2
15	Ohio	22.0
16	Kentucky	21.9
17	Idaho	21.5
18	Wisconsin	21.2
19	Delaware	20.9
20	Arizona	20.3
20	Connecticut	20.3
22	Maryland	19.5
23	Oregon	19.1
24	California	19.0
25	Iowa	18.7
25	Missouri	18.7
27	Illinois	18.1
28	Michigan	17.8
28	North Carolina	17.8
30	Florida	17.6
30	Montana	17.6
30	New Jersey	17.6
33	Alabama	17.5
33	New Hampshire	17.5
35	Georgia	17.4
36	Hawaii	17.3
37	South Carolina	17.1
38	Louisiana	16.9
39	Nebraska	16.8
40	Texas	16.4
40	Virginia	16.4
42	South Dakota	15.8
43	Alaska	14.8
44	Kansas	14.7
44	Utah	14.7
46	Colorado	14.5
47	Washington	14.4
48	Nevada	14.3
49	North Dakota	13.4
50	Wyoming	10.4
	District of Columbia	27.6

Source: CQ Press using data from U.S. Bureau of the Census, Governments Division
"2013 State and Local Government Finances" (http://www.census.gov/govs/local/)
*As a percent of direct general expenditures. Includes funds for cash assistance programs, medical and other vendor payments, welfare institutions, and other public welfare programs.

Social Security (OASDI) Payments in 2013

National Total = $812,045,000,000*

ALPHA ORDER

RANK	STATE	PAYMENTS	% of USA
20	Alabama	$14,700,000,000	1.8%
50	Alaska	1,157,000,000	0.1%
18	Arizona	16,814,000,000	2.1%
30	Arkansas	8,786,000,000	1.1%
1	California	75,193,000,000	9.3%
27	Colorado	10,826,000,000	1.3%
29	Connecticut	10,046,000,000	1.2%
44	Delaware	2,818,000,000	0.3%
2	Florida	57,664,000,000	7.1%
11	Georgia	22,481,000,000	2.8%
42	Hawaii	3,447,000,000	0.4%
40	Idaho	4,057,000,000	0.5%
8	Illinois	31,067,000,000	3.8%
13	Indiana	18,574,000,000	2.3%
31	Iowa	8,638,000,000	1.1%
33	Kansas	7,441,000,000	0.9%
24	Kentucky	12,579,000,000	1.5%
25	Louisiana	11,042,000,000	1.4%
39	Maine	4,182,000,000	0.5%
23	Maryland	13,451,000,000	1.7%
16	Massachusetts	17,179,000,000	2.1%
7	Michigan	31,425,000,000	3.9%
22	Minnesota	13,672,000,000	1.7%
32	Mississippi	8,247,000,000	1.0%
17	Missouri	17,078,000,000	2.1%
45	Montana	2,796,000,000	0.3%
38	Nebraska	4,515,000,000	0.6%
34	Nevada	6,463,000,000	0.8%
41	New Hampshire	4,050,000,000	0.5%
10	New Jersey	24,204,000,000	3.0%
36	New Mexico	5,122,000,000	0.6%
4	New York	50,463,000,000	6.2%
9	North Carolina	26,608,000,000	3.3%
48	North Dakota	1,663,000,000	0.2%
6	Ohio	31,512,000,000	3.9%
28	Oklahoma	10,100,000,000	1.2%
26	Oregon	11,031,000,000	1.4%
5	Pennsylvania	39,342,000,000	4.8%
43	Rhode Island	3,032,000,000	0.4%
21	South Carolina	14,195,000,000	1.7%
46	South Dakota	2,163,000,000	0.3%
14	Tennessee	18,573,000,000	2.3%
3	Texas	50,946,000,000	6.3%
37	Utah	5,016,000,000	0.6%
47	Vermont	1,922,000,000	0.2%
12	Virginia	19,680,000,000	2.4%
15	Washington	17,457,000,000	2.1%
35	West Virginia	6,392,000,000	0.8%
19	Wisconsin	16,392,000,000	2.0%
49	Wyoming	1,406,000,000	0.2%

RANK ORDER

RANK	STATE	PAYMENTS	% of USA
1	California	$75,193,000,000	9.3%
2	Florida	57,664,000,000	7.1%
3	Texas	50,946,000,000	6.3%
4	New York	50,463,000,000	6.2%
5	Pennsylvania	39,342,000,000	4.8%
6	Ohio	31,512,000,000	3.9%
7	Michigan	31,425,000,000	3.9%
8	Illinois	31,067,000,000	3.8%
9	North Carolina	26,608,000,000	3.3%
10	New Jersey	24,204,000,000	3.0%
11	Georgia	22,481,000,000	2.8%
12	Virginia	19,680,000,000	2.4%
13	Indiana	18,574,000,000	2.3%
14	Tennessee	18,573,000,000	2.3%
15	Washington	17,457,000,000	2.1%
16	Massachusetts	17,179,000,000	2.1%
17	Missouri	17,078,000,000	2.1%
18	Arizona	16,814,000,000	2.1%
19	Wisconsin	16,392,000,000	2.0%
20	Alabama	14,700,000,000	1.8%
21	South Carolina	14,195,000,000	1.7%
22	Minnesota	13,672,000,000	1.7%
23	Maryland	13,451,000,000	1.7%
24	Kentucky	12,579,000,000	1.5%
25	Louisiana	11,042,000,000	1.4%
26	Oregon	11,031,000,000	1.4%
27	Colorado	10,826,000,000	1.3%
28	Oklahoma	10,100,000,000	1.2%
29	Connecticut	10,046,000,000	1.2%
30	Arkansas	8,786,000,000	1.1%
31	Iowa	8,638,000,000	1.1%
32	Mississippi	8,247,000,000	1.0%
33	Kansas	7,441,000,000	0.9%
34	Nevada	6,463,000,000	0.8%
35	West Virginia	6,392,000,000	0.8%
36	New Mexico	5,122,000,000	0.6%
37	Utah	5,016,000,000	0.6%
38	Nebraska	4,515,000,000	0.6%
39	Maine	4,182,000,000	0.5%
40	Idaho	4,057,000,000	0.5%
41	New Hampshire	4,050,000,000	0.5%
42	Hawaii	3,447,000,000	0.4%
43	Rhode Island	3,032,000,000	0.4%
44	Delaware	2,818,000,000	0.3%
45	Montana	2,796,000,000	0.3%
46	South Dakota	2,163,000,000	0.3%
47	Vermont	1,922,000,000	0.2%
48	North Dakota	1,663,000,000	0.2%
49	Wyoming	1,406,000,000	0.2%
50	Alaska	1,157,000,000	0.1%
	District of Columbia	1,012,000,000	0.1%

Source: U.S. Department of Health and Human Services, Social Security Administration
   "Social Security Bulletin, Annual Statistical Supplement 2014" (http://www.ssa.gov/policy/docs/statcomps/supplement/2014/)
*"OASDI" is Old Age, Survivors and Disability Insurance. National total includes $13,426,000,000 in payments to recipients in U.S. territories and foreign countries.

Per Capita Social Security (OASDI) Payments in 2013

National Per Capita = $2,524*

ALPHA ORDER

RANK	STATE	PER CAPITA
8	Alabama	$3,043
50	Alaska	1,569
31	Arizona	2,536
10	Arkansas	2,970
47	California	1,957
46	Colorado	2,054
19	Connecticut	2,793
7	Delaware	3,045
11	Florida	2,943
45	Georgia	2,250
36	Hawaii	2,447
33	Idaho	2,516
39	Illinois	2,410
16	Indiana	2,827
19	Iowa	2,793
27	Kansas	2,571
13	Kentucky	2,860
40	Louisiana	2,386
3	Maine	3,147
44	Maryland	2,266
29	Massachusetts	2,561
2	Michigan	3,174
32	Minnesota	2,522
21	Mississippi	2,757
17	Missouri	2,826
22	Montana	2,756
37	Nebraska	2,415
42	Nevada	2,316
6	New Hampshire	3,062
24	New Jersey	2,717
35	New Mexico	2,454
28	New York	2,563
25	North Carolina	2,703
43	North Dakota	2,298
23	Ohio	2,723
26	Oklahoma	2,621
18	Oregon	2,808
4	Pennsylvania	3,078
12	Rhode Island	2,880
9	South Carolina	2,977
30	South Dakota	2,559
14	Tennessee	2,859
48	Texas	1,922
49	Utah	1,727
5	Vermont	3,065
41	Virginia	2,380
34	Washington	2,503
1	West Virginia	3,450
15	Wisconsin	2,854
38	Wyoming	2,411

RANK ORDER

RANK	STATE	PER CAPITA
1	West Virginia	$3,450
2	Michigan	3,174
3	Maine	3,147
4	Pennsylvania	3,078
5	Vermont	3,065
6	New Hampshire	3,062
7	Delaware	3,045
8	Alabama	3,043
9	South Carolina	2,977
10	Arkansas	2,970
11	Florida	2,943
12	Rhode Island	2,880
13	Kentucky	2,860
14	Tennessee	2,859
15	Wisconsin	2,854
16	Indiana	2,827
17	Missouri	2,826
18	Oregon	2,808
19	Connecticut	2,793
19	Iowa	2,793
21	Mississippi	2,757
22	Montana	2,756
23	Ohio	2,723
24	New Jersey	2,717
25	North Carolina	2,703
26	Oklahoma	2,621
27	Kansas	2,571
28	New York	2,563
29	Massachusetts	2,561
30	South Dakota	2,559
31	Arizona	2,536
32	Minnesota	2,522
33	Idaho	2,516
34	Washington	2,503
35	New Mexico	2,454
36	Hawaii	2,447
37	Nebraska	2,415
38	Wyoming	2,411
39	Illinois	2,410
40	Louisiana	2,386
41	Virginia	2,380
42	Nevada	2,316
43	North Dakota	2,298
44	Maryland	2,266
45	Georgia	2,250
46	Colorado	2,054
47	California	1,957
48	Texas	1,922
49	Utah	1,727
50	Alaska	1,569
	District of Columbia	1,558

Source: CQ Press using data from U.S. Department of Health and Human Services, Social Security Administration
"Social Security Bulletin, Annual Statistical Supplement 2014" (http://www.ssa.gov/policy/docs/statcomps/supplement/2014/)
*"OASDI" is Old Age, Survivors and Disability Insurance. National per capita does not include payments or population in U.S. territories and foreign countries.

Social Security (OASDI) Monthly Payments in 2013

National Total = $68,544,382,000*

ALPHA ORDER

RANK	STATE	PAYMENTS	% of USA
20	Alabama	$1,222,936,000	1.8%
50	Alaska	97,786,000	0.1%
17	Arizona	1,436,771,000	2.1%
30	Arkansas	731,882,000	1.1%
1	California	6,385,417,000	9.3%
26	Colorado	925,092,000	1.3%
28	Connecticut	854,037,000	1.2%
44	Delaware	240,777,000	0.4%
2	Florida	4,924,575,000	7.2%
11	Georgia	1,901,327,000	2.8%
42	Hawaii	296,423,000	0.4%
41	Idaho	346,011,000	0.5%
8	Illinois	2,610,862,000	3.8%
13	Indiana	1,560,900,000	2.3%
31	Iowa	728,571,000	1.1%
33	Kansas	627,902,000	0.9%
24	Kentucky	1,040,087,000	1.5%
27	Louisiana	905,116,000	1.3%
39	Maine	352,605,000	0.5%
23	Maryland	1,144,155,000	1.7%
16	Massachusetts	1,452,820,000	2.1%
6	Michigan	2,637,905,000	3.8%
22	Minnesota	1,165,159,000	1.7%
32	Mississippi	684,993,000	1.0%
18	Missouri	1,432,365,000	2.1%
45	Montana	237,234,000	0.3%
38	Nebraska	381,367,000	0.6%
34	Nevada	554,818,000	0.8%
40	New Hampshire	346,045,000	0.5%
10	New Jersey	2,053,219,000	3.0%
36	New Mexico	432,570,000	0.6%
4	New York	4,262,027,000	6.2%
9	North Carolina	2,260,248,000	3.3%
48	North Dakota	139,058,000	0.2%
7	Ohio	2,626,678,000	3.8%
29	Oklahoma	844,203,000	1.2%
25	Oregon	940,453,000	1.4%
5	Pennsylvania	3,306,501,000	4.8%
43	Rhode Island	256,785,000	0.4%
21	South Carolina	1,204,469,000	1.8%
46	South Dakota	183,482,000	0.3%
14	Tennessee	1,559,929,000	2.3%
3	Texas	4,279,628,000	6.2%
37	Utah	426,372,000	0.6%
47	Vermont	163,301,000	0.2%
12	Virginia	1,669,228,000	2.4%
15	Washington	1,489,035,000	2.2%
35	West Virginia	524,739,000	0.8%
19	Wisconsin	1,392,058,000	2.0%
49	Wyoming	119,807,000	0.2%

RANK ORDER

RANK	STATE	PAYMENTS	% of USA
1	California	$6,385,417,000	9.3%
2	Florida	4,924,575,000	7.2%
3	Texas	4,279,628,000	6.2%
4	New York	4,262,027,000	6.2%
5	Pennsylvania	3,306,501,000	4.8%
6	Michigan	2,637,905,000	3.8%
7	Ohio	2,626,678,000	3.8%
8	Illinois	2,610,862,000	3.8%
9	North Carolina	2,260,248,000	3.3%
10	New Jersey	2,053,219,000	3.0%
11	Georgia	1,901,327,000	2.8%
12	Virginia	1,669,228,000	2.4%
13	Indiana	1,560,900,000	2.3%
14	Tennessee	1,559,929,000	2.3%
15	Washington	1,489,035,000	2.2%
16	Massachusetts	1,452,820,000	2.1%
17	Arizona	1,436,771,000	2.1%
18	Missouri	1,432,365,000	2.1%
19	Wisconsin	1,392,058,000	2.0%
20	Alabama	1,222,936,000	1.8%
21	South Carolina	1,204,469,000	1.8%
22	Minnesota	1,165,159,000	1.7%
23	Maryland	1,144,155,000	1.7%
24	Kentucky	1,040,087,000	1.5%
25	Oregon	940,453,000	1.4%
26	Colorado	925,092,000	1.3%
27	Louisiana	905,116,000	1.3%
28	Connecticut	854,037,000	1.2%
29	Oklahoma	844,203,000	1.2%
30	Arkansas	731,882,000	1.1%
31	Iowa	728,571,000	1.1%
32	Mississippi	684,993,000	1.0%
33	Kansas	627,902,000	0.9%
34	Nevada	554,818,000	0.8%
35	West Virginia	524,739,000	0.8%
36	New Mexico	432,570,000	0.6%
37	Utah	426,372,000	0.6%
38	Nebraska	381,367,000	0.6%
39	Maine	352,605,000	0.5%
40	New Hampshire	346,045,000	0.5%
41	Idaho	346,011,000	0.5%
42	Hawaii	296,423,000	0.4%
43	Rhode Island	256,785,000	0.4%
44	Delaware	240,777,000	0.4%
45	Montana	237,234,000	0.3%
46	South Dakota	183,482,000	0.3%
47	Vermont	163,301,000	0.2%
48	North Dakota	139,058,000	0.2%
49	Wyoming	119,807,000	0.2%
50	Alaska	97,786,000	0.1%
	District of Columbia	85,513,000	0.1%

Source: U.S. Department of Health and Human Services, Social Security Administration
  "Social Security Bulletin, Annual Statistical Supplement 2014" (http://www.ssa.gov/policy/docs/statcomps/supplement/2014/)
*For December 2013. "OASDI" is Old Age, Survivors and Disability Insurance. National total includes $1,099,141,000 in payments to recipients in U.S. territories and foreign countries.

Social Security (OASDI) Beneficiaries in 2013

National Total = 57,978,610*

ALPHA ORDER					RANK ORDER			
RANK	STATE	BENEFICIARIES	% of USA		RANK	STATE	BENEFICIARIES	% of USA
20	Alabama	1,081,046	1.9%		1	California	5,414,499	9.3%
50	Alaska	86,861	0.1%		2	Florida	4,114,745	7.1%
18	Arizona	1,174,944	2.0%		3	Texas	3,756,420	6.5%
29	Arkansas	666,172	1.1%		4	New York	3,444,200	5.9%
1	California	5,414,499	9.3%		5	Pennsylvania	2,697,111	4.7%
27	Colorado	774,056	1.3%		6	Ohio	2,239,797	3.9%
30	Connecticut	648,466	1.1%		7	Illinois	2,133,829	3.7%
45	Delaware	187,246	0.3%		8	Michigan	2,098,078	3.6%
2	Florida	4,114,745	7.1%		9	North Carolina	1,907,394	3.3%
10	Georgia	1,632,953	2.8%		10	Georgia	1,632,953	2.8%
42	Hawaii	246,477	0.4%		11	New Jersey	1,548,525	2.7%
40	Idaho	298,269	0.5%		12	Virginia	1,384,419	2.4%
7	Illinois	2,133,829	3.7%		13	Tennessee	1,348,004	2.3%
14	Indiana	1,267,542	2.2%		14	Indiana	1,267,542	2.2%
32	Iowa	609,067	1.1%		15	Missouri	1,232,526	2.1%
33	Kansas	515,969	0.9%		16	Massachusetts	1,206,184	2.1%
23	Kentucky	944,041	1.6%		17	Washington	1,197,824	2.1%
25	Louisiana	842,160	1.5%		18	Arizona	1,174,944	2.0%
39	Maine	320,482	0.6%		19	Wisconsin	1,134,358	2.0%
24	Maryland	917,497	1.6%		20	Alabama	1,081,046	1.9%
16	Massachusetts	1,206,184	2.1%		21	South Carolina	1,014,683	1.8%
8	Michigan	2,098,078	3.6%		22	Minnesota	948,229	1.6%
22	Minnesota	948,229	1.6%		23	Kentucky	944,041	1.6%
31	Mississippi	632,191	1.1%		24	Maryland	917,497	1.6%
15	Missouri	1,232,526	2.1%		25	Louisiana	842,160	1.5%
44	Montana	208,546	0.4%		26	Oregon	777,832	1.3%
38	Nebraska	321,882	0.6%		27	Colorado	774,056	1.3%
35	Nevada	459,536	0.8%		28	Oklahoma	741,822	1.3%
41	New Hampshire	278,664	0.5%		29	Arkansas	666,172	1.1%
11	New Jersey	1,548,525	2.7%		30	Connecticut	648,466	1.1%
36	New Mexico	392,306	0.7%		31	Mississippi	632,191	1.1%
4	New York	3,444,200	5.9%		32	Iowa	609,067	1.1%
9	North Carolina	1,907,394	3.3%		33	Kansas	515,969	0.9%
48	North Dakota	123,363	0.2%		34	West Virginia	460,494	0.8%
6	Ohio	2,239,797	3.9%		35	Nevada	459,536	0.8%
28	Oklahoma	741,822	1.3%		36	New Mexico	392,306	0.7%
26	Oregon	777,832	1.3%		37	Utah	356,984	0.6%
5	Pennsylvania	2,697,111	4.7%		38	Nebraska	321,882	0.6%
43	Rhode Island	214,095	0.4%		39	Maine	320,482	0.6%
21	South Carolina	1,014,683	1.8%		40	Idaho	298,269	0.5%
46	South Dakota	162,695	0.3%		41	New Hampshire	278,664	0.5%
13	Tennessee	1,348,004	2.3%		42	Hawaii	246,477	0.4%
3	Texas	3,756,420	6.5%		43	Rhode Island	214,095	0.4%
37	Utah	356,984	0.6%		44	Montana	208,546	0.4%
47	Vermont	138,418	0.2%		45	Delaware	187,246	0.3%
12	Virginia	1,384,419	2.4%		46	South Dakota	162,695	0.3%
17	Washington	1,197,824	2.1%		47	Vermont	138,418	0.2%
34	West Virginia	460,494	0.8%		48	North Dakota	123,363	0.2%
19	Wisconsin	1,134,358	2.0%		49	Wyoming	99,134	0.2%
49	Wyoming	99,134	0.2%		50	Alaska	86,861	0.1%
						District of Columbia	78,416	0.1%

Source: U.S. Department of Health and Human Services, Social Security Administration
"Social Security Bulletin, Annual Statistical Supplement 2014" (http://www.ssa.gov/policy/docs/statcomps/supplement/2014/)
*For December 2013. "OASDI" is Old Age, Survivors and Disability Insurance. National total includes 1,498,159 beneficiaries in U.S. territories and foreign countries.

Average Monthly Social Security (OASDI) Payment in 2013

National Average = $1,194 Each Month per Beneficiary*

ALPHA ORDER

RANK	STATE	PER BENEFICIARY
41	Alabama	$1,131
44	Alaska	1,126
14	Arizona	1,223
48	Arkansas	1,099
31	California	1,179
25	Colorado	1,195
2	Connecticut	1,317
3	Delaware	1,286
23	Florida	1,197
33	Georgia	1,164
21	Hawaii	1,203
35	Idaho	1,160
13	Illinois	1,224
9	Indiana	1,231
24	Iowa	1,196
15	Kansas	1,217
46	Kentucky	1,102
50	Louisiana	1,075
47	Maine	1,100
5	Maryland	1,247
20	Massachusetts	1,204
4	Michigan	1,257
10	Minnesota	1,229
49	Mississippi	1,084
34	Missouri	1,162
39	Montana	1,138
28	Nebraska	1,185
18	Nevada	1,207
7	New Hampshire	1,242
1	New Jersey	1,326
45	New Mexico	1,103
8	New York	1,237
28	North Carolina	1,185
43	North Dakota	1,127
32	Ohio	1,173
39	Oklahoma	1,138
16	Oregon	1,209
12	Pennsylvania	1,226
22	Rhode Island	1,199
27	South Carolina	1,187
42	South Dakota	1,128
36	Tennessee	1,157
38	Texas	1,139
26	Utah	1,194
30	Vermont	1,180
19	Virginia	1,206
6	Washington	1,243
37	West Virginia	1,140
11	Wisconsin	1,227
16	Wyoming	1,209

RANK ORDER

RANK	STATE	PER BENEFICIARY
1	New Jersey	$1,326
2	Connecticut	1,317
3	Delaware	1,286
4	Michigan	1,257
5	Maryland	1,247
6	Washington	1,243
7	New Hampshire	1,242
8	New York	1,237
9	Indiana	1,231
10	Minnesota	1,229
11	Wisconsin	1,227
12	Pennsylvania	1,226
13	Illinois	1,224
14	Arizona	1,223
15	Kansas	1,217
16	Oregon	1,209
16	Wyoming	1,209
18	Nevada	1,207
19	Virginia	1,206
20	Massachusetts	1,204
21	Hawaii	1,203
22	Rhode Island	1,199
23	Florida	1,197
24	Iowa	1,196
25	Colorado	1,195
26	Utah	1,194
27	South Carolina	1,187
28	Nebraska	1,185
28	North Carolina	1,185
30	Vermont	1,180
31	California	1,179
32	Ohio	1,173
33	Georgia	1,164
34	Missouri	1,162
35	Idaho	1,160
36	Tennessee	1,157
37	West Virginia	1,140
38	Texas	1,139
39	Montana	1,138
39	Oklahoma	1,138
41	Alabama	1,131
42	South Dakota	1,128
43	North Dakota	1,127
44	Alaska	1,126
45	New Mexico	1,103
46	Kentucky	1,102
47	Maine	1,100
48	Arkansas	1,099
49	Mississippi	1,084
50	Louisiana	1,075
	District of Columbia	1,091

Source: CQ Press using data from U.S. Department of Health and Human Services, Social Security Administration "Social Security Bulletin, Annual Statistical Supplement 2014" (http://www.ssa.gov/policy/docs/statcomps/supplement/2014/)

*As of December 2013. "OASDI" is Old Age, Survivors and Disability Insurance. National average does not include beneficiaries or payments in U.S. territories or foreign countries.

Social Security Supplemental Security Income Beneficiaries in 2013

National Total = 8,363,477 Beneficiaries*

ALPHA ORDER

RANK	STATE	BENEFICIARIES	% of USA
16	Alabama	176,638	2.1%
48	Alaska	12,662	0.2%
23	Arizona	117,961	1.4%
26	Arkansas	112,922	1.4%
1	California	1,305,574	15.6%
31	Colorado	72,005	0.9%
33	Connecticut	62,476	0.7%
45	Delaware	16,630	0.2%
4	Florida	547,594	6.5%
9	Georgia	253,267	3.0%
42	Hawaii	25,314	0.3%
40	Idaho	30,348	0.4%
7	Illinois	278,588	3.3%
20	Indiana	127,225	1.5%
34	Iowa	50,874	0.6%
35	Kansas	49,155	0.6%
11	Kentucky	190,976	2.3%
14	Louisiana	181,647	2.2%
37	Maine	37,484	0.4%
24	Maryland	117,352	1.4%
12	Massachusetts	187,998	2.2%
8	Michigan	277,316	3.3%
28	Minnesota	93,729	1.1%
21	Mississippi	126,311	1.5%
19	Missouri	142,259	1.7%
44	Montana	18,647	0.2%
41	Nebraska	27,496	0.3%
36	Nevada	48,465	0.6%
43	New Hampshire	19,609	0.2%
15	New Jersey	180,543	2.2%
32	New Mexico	64,346	0.8%
2	New York	700,175	8.4%
10	North Carolina	234,257	2.8%
49	North Dakota	8,382	0.1%
6	Ohio	311,021	3.7%
27	Oklahoma	97,647	1.2%
29	Oregon	83,104	1.0%
5	Pennsylvania	378,937	4.5%
38	Rhode Island	33,070	0.4%
22	South Carolina	118,174	1.4%
47	South Dakota	14,858	0.2%
13	Tennessee	183,764	2.2%
3	Texas	665,658	8.0%
39	Utah	31,048	0.4%
46	Vermont	15,775	0.2%
17	Virginia	153,450	1.8%
18	Washington	150,085	1.8%
30	West Virginia	79,048	0.9%
25	Wisconsin	116,703	1.4%
50	Wyoming	6,890	0.1%

RANK ORDER

RANK	STATE	BENEFICIARIES	% of USA
1	California	1,305,574	15.6%
2	New York	700,175	8.4%
3	Texas	665,658	8.0%
4	Florida	547,594	6.5%
5	Pennsylvania	378,937	4.5%
6	Ohio	311,021	3.7%
7	Illinois	278,588	3.3%
8	Michigan	277,316	3.3%
9	Georgia	253,267	3.0%
10	North Carolina	234,257	2.8%
11	Kentucky	190,976	2.3%
12	Massachusetts	187,998	2.2%
13	Tennessee	183,764	2.2%
14	Louisiana	181,647	2.2%
15	New Jersey	180,543	2.2%
16	Alabama	176,638	2.1%
17	Virginia	153,450	1.8%
18	Washington	150,085	1.8%
19	Missouri	142,259	1.7%
20	Indiana	127,225	1.5%
21	Mississippi	126,311	1.5%
22	South Carolina	118,174	1.4%
23	Arizona	117,961	1.4%
24	Maryland	117,352	1.4%
25	Wisconsin	116,703	1.4%
26	Arkansas	112,922	1.4%
27	Oklahoma	97,647	1.2%
28	Minnesota	93,729	1.1%
29	Oregon	83,104	1.0%
30	West Virginia	79,048	0.9%
31	Colorado	72,005	0.9%
32	New Mexico	64,346	0.8%
33	Connecticut	62,476	0.7%
34	Iowa	50,874	0.6%
35	Kansas	49,155	0.6%
36	Nevada	48,465	0.6%
37	Maine	37,484	0.4%
38	Rhode Island	33,070	0.4%
39	Utah	31,048	0.4%
40	Idaho	30,348	0.4%
41	Nebraska	27,496	0.3%
42	Hawaii	25,314	0.3%
43	New Hampshire	19,609	0.2%
44	Montana	18,647	0.2%
45	Delaware	16,630	0.2%
46	Vermont	15,775	0.2%
47	South Dakota	14,858	0.2%
48	Alaska	12,662	0.2%
49	North Dakota	8,382	0.1%
50	Wyoming	6,890	0.1%
	District of Columbia	26,959	0.3%

Source: U.S. Department of Health and Human Services, Social Security Administration
"Social Security Bulletin, Annual Statistical Supplement 2014" (http://www.ssa.gov/policy/docs/statcomps/supplement/2014/)
*For December 2013. National total includes 1,061 beneficiaries in U.S. territories or otherwise not distributed by state. The SSI program provides income support to persons age 65 and older and blind or disabled adults and children.

Average Monthly Social Security Supplemental Security Income Payment in 2013
National Average = $510.21 Each Month per Beneficiary*

ALPHA ORDER

RANK	STATE	AVERAGE BENEFIT
34	Alabama	$497.85
41	Alaska	489.56
10	Arizona	519.12
25	Arkansas	504.94
24	California	504.97
30	Colorado	502.53
13	Connecticut	514.77
11	Delaware	517.19
21	Florida	509.59
28	Georgia	503.61
16	Hawaii	512.97
27	Idaho	503.65
4	Illinois	532.45
8	Indiana	520.60
44	Iowa	485.86
26	Kansas	504.31
22	Kentucky	506.61
18	Louisiana	511.85
47	Maine	480.21
5	Maryland	532.04
20	Massachusetts	509.68
2	Michigan	535.13
7	Minnesota	521.39
38	Mississippi	491.31
31	Missouri	501.93
45	Montana	485.85
42	Nebraska	488.14
12	Nevada	516.27
40	New Hampshire	490.16
36	New Jersey	493.39
43	New Mexico	487.67
9	New York	520.02
39	North Carolina	490.81
50	North Dakota	461.87
6	Ohio	531.25
23	Oklahoma	506.50
15	Oregon	513.98
1	Pennsylvania	537.41
17	Rhode Island	512.41
35	South Carolina	493.52
49	South Dakota	474.44
33	Tennessee	498.40
37	Texas	491.92
29	Utah	503.54
48	Vermont	480.05
32	Virginia	500.39
3	Washington	534.68
19	West Virginia	510.77
14	Wisconsin	514.24
46	Wyoming	482.77

RANK ORDER

RANK	STATE	AVERAGE BENEFIT
1	Pennsylvania	$537.41
2	Michigan	535.13
3	Washington	534.68
4	Illinois	532.45
5	Maryland	532.04
6	Ohio	531.25
7	Minnesota	521.39
8	Indiana	520.60
9	New York	520.02
10	Arizona	519.12
11	Delaware	517.19
12	Nevada	516.27
13	Connecticut	514.77
14	Wisconsin	514.24
15	Oregon	513.98
16	Hawaii	512.97
17	Rhode Island	512.41
18	Louisiana	511.85
19	West Virginia	510.77
20	Massachusetts	509.68
21	Florida	509.59
22	Kentucky	506.61
23	Oklahoma	506.50
24	California	504.97
25	Arkansas	504.94
26	Kansas	504.31
27	Idaho	503.65
28	Georgia	503.61
29	Utah	503.54
30	Colorado	502.53
31	Missouri	501.93
32	Virginia	500.39
33	Tennessee	498.40
34	Alabama	497.85
35	South Carolina	493.52
36	New Jersey	493.39
37	Texas	491.92
38	Mississippi	491.31
39	North Carolina	490.81
40	New Hampshire	490.16
41	Alaska	489.56
42	Nebraska	488.14
43	New Mexico	487.67
44	Iowa	485.86
45	Montana	485.85
46	Wyoming	482.77
47	Maine	480.21
48	Vermont	480.05
49	South Dakota	474.44
50	North Dakota	461.87
	District of Columbia	553.03

Source: CQ Press using data from U.S. Department of Health and Human Services, Social Security Administration "Social Security Bulletin, Annual Statistical Supplement 2014" (http://www.ssa.gov/policy/docs/statcomps/supplement/2014/)

*As of December 2013. National average includes payments to beneficiaries in U.S. territories and foreign countries. The SSI program provides income support to persons age 65 and older and blind or disabled adults and children.

Medicare Enrollees in 2014

National Total = 54,095,565 Enrollees*

ALPHA ORDER

RANK	STATE	ENROLLEES	% of USA
20	Alabama	947,310	1.8%
50	Alaska	80,108	0.1%
18	Arizona	1,092,674	2.0%
30	Arkansas	584,889	1.1%
1	California	5,482,813	10.1%
26	Colorado	755,214	1.4%
29	Connecticut	620,887	1.1%
45	Delaware	174,566	0.3%
2	Florida	3,888,261	7.2%
10	Georgia	1,468,630	2.7%
42	Hawaii	237,336	0.4%
40	Idaho	270,913	0.5%
7	Illinois	2,030,247	3.8%
16	Indiana	1,125,297	2.1%
31	Iowa	561,461	1.0%
33	Kansas	477,520	0.9%
24	Kentucky	846,798	1.6%
25	Louisiana	773,650	1.4%
39	Maine	299,699	0.6%
22	Maryland	906,499	1.7%
14	Massachusetts	1,191,694	2.2%
8	Michigan	1,855,600	3.4%
23	Minnesota	888,371	1.6%
32	Mississippi	549,798	1.0%
17	Missouri	1,114,049	2.1%
44	Montana	194,922	0.4%
38	Nebraska	305,969	0.6%
34	Nevada	433,598	0.8%
41	New Hampshire	259,087	0.5%
11	New Jersey	1,466,034	2.7%
36	New Mexico	361,284	0.7%
4	New York	3,286,882	6.1%
9	North Carolina	1,718,863	3.2%
48	North Dakota	116,858	0.2%
6	Ohio	2,111,104	3.9%
28	Oklahoma	665,825	1.2%
27	Oregon	727,224	1.3%
5	Pennsylvania	2,493,027	4.6%
43	Rhode Island	199,901	0.4%
21	South Carolina	908,531	1.7%
46	South Dakota	151,924	0.3%
13	Tennessee	1,206,356	2.2%
3	Texas	3,516,912	6.5%
37	Utah	332,922	0.6%
47	Vermont	128,074	0.2%
12	Virginia	1,311,884	2.4%
15	Washington	1,146,301	2.1%
35	West Virginia	411,785	0.8%
19	Wisconsin	1,023,781	1.9%
49	Wyoming	92,114	0.2%

RANK ORDER

RANK	STATE	ENROLLEES	% of USA
1	California	5,482,813	10.1%
2	Florida	3,888,261	7.2%
3	Texas	3,516,912	6.5%
4	New York	3,286,882	6.1%
5	Pennsylvania	2,493,027	4.6%
6	Ohio	2,111,104	3.9%
7	Illinois	2,030,247	3.8%
8	Michigan	1,855,600	3.4%
9	North Carolina	1,718,863	3.2%
10	Georgia	1,468,630	2.7%
11	New Jersey	1,466,034	2.7%
12	Virginia	1,311,884	2.4%
13	Tennessee	1,206,356	2.2%
14	Massachusetts	1,191,694	2.2%
15	Washington	1,146,301	2.1%
16	Indiana	1,125,297	2.1%
17	Missouri	1,114,049	2.1%
18	Arizona	1,092,674	2.0%
19	Wisconsin	1,023,781	1.9%
20	Alabama	947,310	1.8%
21	South Carolina	908,531	1.7%
22	Maryland	906,499	1.7%
23	Minnesota	888,371	1.6%
24	Kentucky	846,798	1.6%
25	Louisiana	773,650	1.4%
26	Colorado	755,214	1.4%
27	Oregon	727,224	1.3%
28	Oklahoma	665,825	1.2%
29	Connecticut	620,887	1.1%
30	Arkansas	584,889	1.1%
31	Iowa	561,461	1.0%
32	Mississippi	549,798	1.0%
33	Kansas	477,520	0.9%
34	Nevada	433,598	0.8%
35	West Virginia	411,785	0.8%
36	New Mexico	361,284	0.7%
37	Utah	332,922	0.6%
38	Nebraska	305,969	0.6%
39	Maine	299,699	0.6%
40	Idaho	270,913	0.5%
41	New Hampshire	259,087	0.5%
42	Hawaii	237,336	0.4%
43	Rhode Island	199,901	0.4%
44	Montana	194,922	0.4%
45	Delaware	174,566	0.3%
46	South Dakota	151,924	0.3%
47	Vermont	128,074	0.2%
48	North Dakota	116,858	0.2%
49	Wyoming	92,114	0.2%
50	Alaska	80,108	0.1%
	District of Columbia	86,802	0.2%

Source: U.S. Department of Health and Human Services, Centers for Medicare and Medicaid Services
"Medicare Enrollment Dashboard"
(https://www.cms.gov/Research-Statistics-Data-and-Systems/Statistics-Trends-and-Reports/CMSProgramStatistics/Dashboard.html)
*Includes original Medicare, Medicare Advantage, and other Medicare health plans. Total includes 1,213,320 enrollees in Puerto Rico and other outlying areas, foreign countries, or whose address is unknown.

Percent of Population Enrolled in Medicare in 2014

National Percent = 16.6% of Population*

ALPHA ORDER

RANK	STATE	PERCENT
5	Alabama	19.5
50	Alaska	10.9
36	Arizona	16.2
4	Arkansas	19.7
46	California	14.1
46	Colorado	14.1
24	Connecticut	17.3
13	Delaware	18.7
5	Florida	19.5
45	Georgia	14.5
29	Hawaii	16.7
30	Idaho	16.6
39	Illinois	15.8
28	Indiana	17.1
20	Iowa	18.1
33	Kansas	16.5
9	Kentucky	19.2
30	Louisiana	16.6
1	Maine	22.5
44	Maryland	15.2
23	Massachusetts	17.6
13	Michigan	18.7
35	Minnesota	16.3
15	Mississippi	18.4
15	Missouri	18.4
10	Montana	19.0
36	Nebraska	16.2
43	Nevada	15.3
5	New Hampshire	19.5
34	New Jersey	16.4
24	New Mexico	17.3
30	New York	16.6
24	North Carolina	17.3
39	North Dakota	15.8
19	Ohio	18.2
27	Oklahoma	17.2
18	Oregon	18.3
5	Pennsylvania	19.5
11	Rhode Island	18.9
12	South Carolina	18.8
21	South Dakota	17.8
15	Tennessee	18.4
48	Texas	13.0
49	Utah	11.3
3	Vermont	20.4
39	Virginia	15.8
36	Washington	16.2
2	West Virginia	22.3
21	Wisconsin	17.8
39	Wyoming	15.8

RANK ORDER

RANK	STATE	PERCENT
1	Maine	22.5
2	West Virginia	22.3
3	Vermont	20.4
4	Arkansas	19.7
5	Alabama	19.5
5	Florida	19.5
5	New Hampshire	19.5
5	Pennsylvania	19.5
9	Kentucky	19.2
10	Montana	19.0
11	Rhode Island	18.9
12	South Carolina	18.8
13	Delaware	18.7
13	Michigan	18.7
15	Mississippi	18.4
15	Missouri	18.4
15	Tennessee	18.4
18	Oregon	18.3
19	Ohio	18.2
20	Iowa	18.1
21	South Dakota	17.8
21	Wisconsin	17.8
23	Massachusetts	17.6
24	Connecticut	17.3
24	New Mexico	17.3
24	North Carolina	17.3
27	Oklahoma	17.2
28	Indiana	17.1
29	Hawaii	16.7
30	Idaho	16.6
30	Louisiana	16.6
30	New York	16.6
33	Kansas	16.5
34	New Jersey	16.4
35	Minnesota	16.3
36	Arizona	16.2
36	Nebraska	16.2
36	Washington	16.2
39	Illinois	15.8
39	North Dakota	15.8
39	Virginia	15.8
39	Wyoming	15.8
43	Nevada	15.3
44	Maryland	15.2
45	Georgia	14.5
46	California	14.1
46	Colorado	14.1
48	Texas	13.0
49	Utah	11.3
50	Alaska	10.9
	District of Columbia	13.2

Source: CQ Press using data from U.S. Department of Health and Human Services, Centers for Medicare and Medicaid Services "Medicare Enrollment Dashboard"
(https://www.cms.gov/Research-Statistics-Data-and-Systems/Statistics-Trends-and-Reports/CMSProgramStatistics/Dashboard.html)
*Includes original Medicare, Medicare Advantage, and other Medicare health plans. National rate does not include enrollees or population in Puerto Rico and other outlying areas, foreign countries, or whose address is unknown.

Medicare Program Payments in 2012

National Total = $344,463,000,000*

ALPHA ORDER

RANK	STATE	PAYMENTS	% of USA
18	Alabama	$6,133,000,000	1.8%
50	Alaska	512,000,000	0.1%
23	Arizona	5,576,000,000	1.6%
30	Arkansas	3,737,000,000	1.1%
1	California	31,883,000,000	9.3%
29	Colorado	3,783,000,000	1.1%
25	Connecticut	4,823,000,000	1.4%
41	Delaware	1,459,000,000	0.4%
3	Florida	25,552,000,000	7.4%
12	Georgia	9,047,000,000	2.6%
48	Hawaii	804,000,000	0.2%
42	Idaho	1,285,000,000	0.4%
5	Illinois	16,992,000,000	4.9%
15	Indiana	7,712,000,000	2.2%
31	Iowa	3,667,000,000	1.1%
32	Kansas	3,328,000,000	1.0%
20	Kentucky	5,849,000,000	1.7%
22	Louisiana	5,617,000,000	1.6%
37	Maine	1,853,000,000	0.5%
13	Maryland	8,511,000,000	2.5%
11	Massachusetts	9,462,000,000	2.7%
7	Michigan	13,305,000,000	3.9%
27	Minnesota	4,694,000,000	1.4%
28	Mississippi	4,322,000,000	1.3%
17	Missouri	7,137,000,000	2.1%
43	Montana	1,098,000,000	0.3%
36	Nebraska	2,167,000,000	0.6%
35	Nevada	2,562,000,000	0.7%
38	New Hampshire	1,846,000,000	0.5%
8	New Jersey	12,596,000,000	3.7%
39	New Mexico	1,738,000,000	0.5%
4	New York	21,598,000,000	6.3%
10	North Carolina	11,124,000,000	3.2%
47	North Dakota	805,000,000	0.2%
9	Ohio	12,431,000,000	3.6%
26	Oklahoma	4,785,000,000	1.4%
33	Oregon	2,862,000,000	0.8%
6	Pennsylvania	14,093,000,000	4.1%
44	Rhode Island	1,042,000,000	0.3%
19	South Carolina	6,098,000,000	1.8%
45	South Dakota	996,000,000	0.3%
16	Tennessee	7,181,000,000	2.1%
2	Texas	26,231,000,000	7.6%
40	Utah	1,652,000,000	0.5%
46	Vermont	887,000,000	0.3%
14	Virginia	8,332,000,000	2.4%
21	Washington	5,818,000,000	1.7%
34	West Virginia	2,688,000,000	0.8%
24	Wisconsin	5,392,000,000	1.6%
49	Wyoming	619,000,000	0.2%

RANK ORDER

RANK	STATE	PAYMENTS	% of USA
1	California	$31,883,000,000	9.3%
2	Texas	26,231,000,000	7.6%
3	Florida	25,552,000,000	7.4%
4	New York	21,598,000,000	6.3%
5	Illinois	16,992,000,000	4.9%
6	Pennsylvania	14,093,000,000	4.1%
7	Michigan	13,305,000,000	3.9%
8	New Jersey	12,596,000,000	3.7%
9	Ohio	12,431,000,000	3.6%
10	North Carolina	11,124,000,000	3.2%
11	Massachusetts	9,462,000,000	2.7%
12	Georgia	9,047,000,000	2.6%
13	Maryland	8,511,000,000	2.5%
14	Virginia	8,332,000,000	2.4%
15	Indiana	7,712,000,000	2.2%
16	Tennessee	7,181,000,000	2.1%
17	Missouri	7,137,000,000	2.1%
18	Alabama	6,133,000,000	1.8%
19	South Carolina	6,098,000,000	1.8%
20	Kentucky	5,849,000,000	1.7%
21	Washington	5,818,000,000	1.7%
22	Louisiana	5,617,000,000	1.6%
23	Arizona	5,576,000,000	1.6%
24	Wisconsin	5,392,000,000	1.6%
25	Connecticut	4,823,000,000	1.4%
26	Oklahoma	4,785,000,000	1.4%
27	Minnesota	4,694,000,000	1.4%
28	Mississippi	4,322,000,000	1.3%
29	Colorado	3,783,000,000	1.1%
30	Arkansas	3,737,000,000	1.1%
31	Iowa	3,667,000,000	1.1%
32	Kansas	3,328,000,000	1.0%
33	Oregon	2,862,000,000	0.8%
34	West Virginia	2,688,000,000	0.8%
35	Nevada	2,562,000,000	0.7%
36	Nebraska	2,167,000,000	0.6%
37	Maine	1,853,000,000	0.5%
38	New Hampshire	1,846,000,000	0.5%
39	New Mexico	1,738,000,000	0.5%
40	Utah	1,652,000,000	0.5%
41	Delaware	1,459,000,000	0.4%
42	Idaho	1,285,000,000	0.4%
43	Montana	1,098,000,000	0.3%
44	Rhode Island	1,042,000,000	0.3%
45	South Dakota	996,000,000	0.3%
46	Vermont	887,000,000	0.3%
47	North Dakota	805,000,000	0.2%
48	Hawaii	804,000,000	0.2%
49	Wyoming	619,000,000	0.2%
50	Alaska	512,000,000	0.1%
	District of Columbia	778,000,000	0.2%

Source: U.S. Department of Health and Human Services, Centers for Medicare and Medicaid Services "2013 Medicare and Medicaid Statistical Supplement" (Table 3.5) (www.cms.gov/Research-Statistics-Data-and-Systems/Statistics-Trends-and-Reports/MedicareMedicaidStatSupp/index.html)
*Figures for calendar year 2012. Includes payments to aged and disabled enrollees. Total does not include payments to beneficiaries in Puerto Rico and other outlying areas.

Medicare Program Payments per Enrollee in 2012

National Rate = $9,411*

ALPHA ORDER

RANK	STATE	PER ENROLLEE	% of USA
27	Alabama	8,703	0.0%
48	Alaska	7,163	0.0%
22	Arizona	8,772	0.0%
36	Arkansas	8,144	0.0%
11	California	9,768	0.0%
33	Colorado	8,272	0.0%
7	Connecticut	10,225	0.0%
17	Delaware	9,374	0.0%
2	Florida	10,761	0.0%
21	Georgia	8,778	0.0%
50	Hawaii	6,504	0.0%
45	Idaho	7,310	0.0%
12	Illinois	9,742	0.0%
18	Indiana	9,029	0.0%
40	Iowa	7,896	0.0%
30	Kansas	8,421	0.0%
23	Kentucky	8,768	0.0%
6	Louisiana	10,371	0.0%
42	Maine	7,832	0.0%
1	Maryland	10,958	0.0%
10	Massachusetts	10,188	0.0%
9	Michigan	10,192	0.0%
4	Minnesota	10,507	0.0%
16	Mississippi	9,411	0.0%
26	Missouri	8,708	0.0%
49	Montana	7,109	0.0%
31	Nebraska	8,373	0.0%
15	Nevada	9,518	0.0%
35	New Hampshire	8,236	0.0%
3	New Jersey	10,536	0.0%
46	New Mexico	7,194	0.0%
8	New York	10,197	0.0%
28	North Carolina	8,616	0.0%
39	North Dakota	7,958	0.0%
13	Ohio	9,657	0.0%
19	Oklahoma	9,001	0.0%
47	Oregon	7,172	0.0%
14	Pennsylvania	9,549	0.0%
29	Rhode Island	8,442	0.0%
20	South Carolina	8,876	0.0%
38	South Dakota	8,000	0.0%
25	Tennessee	8,721	0.0%
5	Texas	10,442	0.0%
32	Utah	8,361	0.0%
41	Vermont	7,840	0.0%
37	Virginia	8,014	0.0%
43	Washington	7,702	0.0%
24	West Virginia	8,756	0.0%
34	Wisconsin	8,263	0.0%
44	Wyoming	7,454	0.0%

RANK ORDER

RANK	STATE	PER ENROLLEE	% of USA
1	Maryland	10,958	0.0%
2	Florida	10,761	0.0%
3	New Jersey	10,536	0.0%
4	Minnesota	10,507	0.0%
5	Texas	10,442	0.0%
6	Louisiana	10,371	0.0%
7	Connecticut	10,225	0.0%
8	New York	10,197	0.0%
9	Michigan	10,192	0.0%
10	Massachusetts	10,188	0.0%
11	California	9,768	0.0%
12	Illinois	9,742	0.0%
13	Ohio	9,657	0.0%
14	Pennsylvania	9,549	0.0%
15	Nevada	9,518	0.0%
16	Mississippi	9,411	0.0%
17	Delaware	9,374	0.0%
18	Indiana	9,029	0.0%
19	Oklahoma	9,001	0.0%
20	South Carolina	8,876	0.0%
21	Georgia	8,778	0.0%
22	Arizona	8,772	0.0%
23	Kentucky	8,768	0.0%
24	West Virginia	8,756	0.0%
25	Tennessee	8,721	0.0%
26	Missouri	8,708	0.0%
27	Alabama	8,703	0.0%
28	North Carolina	8,616	0.0%
29	Rhode Island	8,442	0.0%
30	Kansas	8,421	0.0%
31	Nebraska	8,373	0.0%
32	Utah	8,361	0.0%
33	Colorado	8,272	0.0%
34	Wisconsin	8,263	0.0%
35	New Hampshire	8,236	0.0%
36	Arkansas	8,144	0.0%
37	Virginia	8,014	0.0%
38	South Dakota	8,000	0.0%
39	North Dakota	7,958	0.0%
40	Iowa	7,896	0.0%
41	Vermont	7,840	0.0%
42	Maine	7,832	0.0%
43	Washington	7,702	0.0%
44	Wyoming	7,454	0.0%
45	Idaho	7,310	0.0%
46	New Mexico	7,194	0.0%
47	Oregon	7,172	0.0%
48	Alaska	7,163	0.0%
49	Montana	7,109	0.0%
50	Hawaii	6,504	0.0%
	District of Columbia	10,594	0.0%

Source: U.S. Department of Health and Human Services, Centers for Medicare and Medicaid Services
"2013 Medicare and Medicaid Statistical Supplement" (Table 3.5)
(www.cms.gov/Research-Statistics-Data-and-Systems/Statistics-Trends-and-Reports/MedicareMedicaidStatSupp/index.html)
*Figures for calendar year 2012. Includes payments to aged and disabled enrollees. National figure does not include enrollees in managed care plans in the denominator used to calculate average payments. National rate also does not include payments or enrollees in Puerto Rico and other outlying areas.

Medicaid Enrollment in 2013

National Total = 62,151,218 Enrollees*

ALPHA ORDER

RANK	STATE	ENROLLEES	% of USA
21	Alabama	959,607	1.5%
46	Alaska	145,279	0.2%
12	Arizona	1,271,190	2.0%
31	Arkansas	614,466	1.0%
1	California	8,469,015	13.6%
26	Colorado	740,248	1.2%
30	Connecticut	621,770	1.0%
42	Delaware	216,106	0.3%
5	Florida	3,384,173	5.4%
9	Georgia	1,813,771	2.9%
37	Hawaii	307,428	0.5%
40	Idaho	255,295	0.4%
6	Illinois	2,931,023	4.7%
18	Indiana	1,125,683	1.8%
33	Iowa	434,414	0.7%
34	Kansas	398,934	0.6%
25	Kentucky	846,912	1.4%
13	Louisiana	1,256,722	2.0%
39	Maine	262,334	0.4%
19	Maryland	1,089,227	1.8%
11	Massachusetts	1,409,600	2.3%
8	Michigan	1,815,866	2.9%
23	Minnesota	902,415	1.5%
29	Mississippi	689,153	1.1%
24	Missouri	868,226	1.4%
48	Montana	119,086	0.2%
41	Nebraska	244,441	0.4%
36	Nevada	328,748	0.5%
45	New Hampshire	145,982	0.2%
15	New Jersey	1,201,134	1.9%
32	New Mexico	554,620	0.9%
2	New York	5,352,862	8.6%
10	North Carolina	1,589,093	2.6%
49	North Dakota	76,756	0.1%
7	Ohio	2,389,622	3.8%
27	Oklahoma	735,552	1.2%
28	Oregon	694,546	1.1%
4	Pennsylvania	3,446,654	5.5%
43	Rhode Island	197,166	0.3%
20	South Carolina	1,002,319	1.6%
47	South Dakota	121,630	0.2%
14	Tennessee	1,215,624	2.0%
3	Texas	3,878,766	6.2%
38	Utah	265,929	0.4%
44	Vermont	182,096	0.3%
22	Virginia	938,184	1.5%
17	Washington	1,173,312	1.9%
35	West Virginia	330,000	0.5%
16	Wisconsin	1,179,354	1.9%
50	Wyoming	66,321	0.1%

RANK ORDER

RANK	STATE	ENROLLEES	% of USA
1	California	8,469,015	13.6%
2	New York	5,352,862	8.6%
3	Texas	3,878,766	6.2%
4	Pennsylvania	3,446,654	5.5%
5	Florida	3,384,173	5.4%
6	Illinois	2,931,023	4.7%
7	Ohio	2,389,622	3.8%
8	Michigan	1,815,866	2.9%
9	Georgia	1,813,771	2.9%
10	North Carolina	1,589,093	2.6%
11	Massachusetts	1,409,600	2.3%
12	Arizona	1,271,190	2.0%
13	Louisiana	1,256,722	2.0%
14	Tennessee	1,215,624	2.0%
15	New Jersey	1,201,134	1.9%
16	Wisconsin	1,179,354	1.9%
17	Washington	1,173,312	1.9%
18	Indiana	1,125,683	1.8%
19	Maryland	1,089,227	1.8%
20	South Carolina	1,002,319	1.6%
21	Alabama	959,607	1.5%
22	Virginia	938,184	1.5%
23	Minnesota	902,415	1.5%
24	Missouri	868,226	1.4%
25	Kentucky	846,912	1.4%
26	Colorado	740,248	1.2%
27	Oklahoma	735,552	1.2%
28	Oregon	694,546	1.1%
29	Mississippi	689,153	1.1%
30	Connecticut	621,770	1.0%
31	Arkansas	614,466	1.0%
32	New Mexico	554,620	0.9%
33	Iowa	434,414	0.7%
34	Kansas	398,934	0.6%
35	West Virginia	330,000	0.5%
36	Nevada	328,748	0.5%
37	Hawaii	307,428	0.5%
38	Utah	265,929	0.4%
39	Maine	262,334	0.4%
40	Idaho	255,295	0.4%
41	Nebraska	244,441	0.4%
42	Delaware	216,106	0.3%
43	Rhode Island	197,166	0.3%
44	Vermont	182,096	0.3%
45	New Hampshire	145,982	0.2%
46	Alaska	145,279	0.2%
47	South Dakota	121,630	0.2%
48	Montana	119,086	0.2%
49	North Dakota	76,756	0.1%
50	Wyoming	66,321	0.1%
	District of Columbia	252,852	0.4%

Source: U.S. Department of Health and Human Services, Centers for Medicare and Medicaid Services
"2013 Medicaid Managed Care Enrollment Report" (http://www.cms.gov/MedicaidDataSourcesGenInfo/)
*Unduplicated enrollment as of July 1, 2013. National total includes 1,639,712 Medicaid enrollees in U.S. territories.

Percent of Population Enrolled in Medicaid in 2013

National Percent = 19.1% of Population*

ALPHA ORDER

RANK	STATE	PERCENT
16	Alabama	19.9
17	Alaska	19.7
20	Arizona	19.2
13	Arkansas	20.8
9	California	22.0
39	Colorado	14.0
29	Connecticut	17.3
6	Delaware	23.4
29	Florida	17.3
26	Georgia	18.2
10	Hawaii	21.8
35	Idaho	15.8
8	Illinois	22.7
31	Indiana	17.1
39	Iowa	14.0
41	Kansas	13.8
19	Kentucky	19.3
2	Louisiana	27.2
17	Maine	19.7
24	Maryland	18.3
11	Massachusetts	21.0
24	Michigan	18.3
33	Minnesota	16.6
7	Mississippi	23.0
37	Missouri	14.4
45	Montana	11.7
43	Nebraska	13.1
44	Nevada	11.8
48	New Hampshire	11.0
42	New Jersey	13.5
5	New Mexico	26.6
2	New York	27.2
34	North Carolina	16.1
49	North Dakota	10.6
14	Ohio	20.6
21	Oklahoma	19.1
28	Oregon	17.7
4	Pennsylvania	27.0
22	Rhode Island	18.7
11	South Carolina	21.0
37	South Dakota	14.4
22	Tennessee	18.7
36	Texas	14.6
50	Utah	9.2
1	Vermont	29.0
47	Virginia	11.3
32	Washington	16.8
27	West Virginia	17.8
15	Wisconsin	20.5
46	Wyoming	11.4

RANK ORDER

RANK	STATE	PERCENT
1	Vermont	29.0
2	Louisiana	27.2
2	New York	27.2
4	Pennsylvania	27.0
5	New Mexico	26.6
6	Delaware	23.4
7	Mississippi	23.0
8	Illinois	22.7
9	California	22.0
10	Hawaii	21.8
11	Massachusetts	21.0
11	South Carolina	21.0
13	Arkansas	20.8
14	Ohio	20.6
15	Wisconsin	20.5
16	Alabama	19.9
17	Alaska	19.7
17	Maine	19.7
19	Kentucky	19.3
20	Arizona	19.2
21	Oklahoma	19.1
22	Rhode Island	18.7
22	Tennessee	18.7
24	Maryland	18.3
24	Michigan	18.3
26	Georgia	18.2
27	West Virginia	17.8
28	Oregon	17.7
29	Connecticut	17.3
29	Florida	17.3
31	Indiana	17.1
32	Washington	16.8
33	Minnesota	16.6
34	North Carolina	16.1
35	Idaho	15.8
36	Texas	14.6
37	Missouri	14.4
37	South Dakota	14.4
39	Colorado	14.0
39	Iowa	14.0
41	Kansas	13.8
42	New Jersey	13.5
43	Nebraska	13.1
44	Nevada	11.8
45	Montana	11.7
46	Wyoming	11.4
47	Virginia	11.3
48	New Hampshire	11.0
49	North Dakota	10.6
50	Utah	9.2
	District of Columbia	38.9

Source: CQ Press using data from U.S. Department of Health and Human Services, Centers for Medicare and Medicaid Services "2013 Medicaid Managed Care Enrollment Report" (http://www.cms.gov/MedicaidDataSourcesGenInfo/)

*Unduplicated enrollment as of July 1, 2013. National percent does not include recipients or population in U.S. territories.

Estimated Medicaid Expenditures in 2015

National Total = $512,315,000,000*

ALPHA ORDER

RANK	STATE	EXPENDITURES	% of USA
28	Alabama	$6,032,000,000	1.2%
44	Alaska	1,650,000,000	0.3%
12	Arizona	10,921,000,000	2.1%
27	Arkansas	6,059,000,000	1.2%
1	California	74,956,000,000	14.6%
23	Colorado	7,604,000,000	1.5%
26	Connecticut	6,979,000,000	1.4%
42	Delaware	1,875,000,000	0.4%
6	Florida	23,580,000,000	4.6%
17	Georgia	9,324,000,000	1.8%
40	Hawaii	2,048,000,000	0.4%
41	Idaho	2,029,000,000	0.4%
7	Illinois	17,601,000,000	3.4%
18	Indiana	9,162,000,000	1.8%
33	Iowa	4,805,000,000	0.9%
34	Kansas	3,548,000,000	0.7%
16	Kentucky	9,522,000,000	1.9%
25	Louisiana	7,414,000,000	1.4%
38	Maine	2,533,000,000	0.5%
15	Maryland	9,561,000,000	1.9%
9	Massachusetts	13,995,000,000	2.7%
8	Michigan	17,320,000,000	3.4%
13	Minnesota	10,884,000,000	2.1%
32	Mississippi	4,908,000,000	1.0%
20	Missouri	8,708,000,000	1.7%
48	Montana	1,110,000,000	0.2%
43	Nebraska	1,855,000,000	0.4%
36	Nevada	2,903,000,000	0.6%
45	New Hampshire	1,631,000,000	0.3%
10	New Jersey	13,849,000,000	2.7%
30	New Mexico	5,136,000,000	1.0%
2	New York	45,668,000,000	8.9%
11	North Carolina	13,781,000,000	2.7%
47	North Dakota	1,145,000,000	0.2%
4	Ohio	24,327,000,000	4.7%
31	Oklahoma	5,064,000,000	1.0%
21	Oregon	8,671,000,000	1.7%
5	Pennsylvania	24,143,000,000	4.7%
37	Rhode Island	2,579,000,000	0.5%
29	South Carolina	6,022,000,000	1.2%
49	South Dakota	848,000,000	0.2%
14	Tennessee	10,359,000,000	2.0%
3	Texas	37,561,000,000	7.3%
39	Utah	2,481,000,000	0.5%
46	Vermont	1,442,000,000	0.3%
22	Virginia	8,237,000,000	1.6%
24	Washington	7,473,000,000	1.5%
35	West Virginia	3,530,000,000	0.7%
19	Wisconsin	8,878,000,000	1.7%
50	Wyoming	604,000,000	0.1%

RANK ORDER

RANK	STATE	EXPENDITURES	% of USA
1	California	$74,956,000,000	14.6%
2	New York	45,668,000,000	8.9%
3	Texas	37,561,000,000	7.3%
4	Ohio	24,327,000,000	4.7%
5	Pennsylvania	24,143,000,000	4.7%
6	Florida	23,580,000,000	4.6%
7	Illinois	17,601,000,000	3.4%
8	Michigan	17,320,000,000	3.4%
9	Massachusetts	13,995,000,000	2.7%
10	New Jersey	13,849,000,000	2.7%
11	North Carolina	13,781,000,000	2.7%
12	Arizona	10,921,000,000	2.1%
13	Minnesota	10,884,000,000	2.1%
14	Tennessee	10,359,000,000	2.0%
15	Maryland	9,561,000,000	1.9%
16	Kentucky	9,522,000,000	1.9%
17	Georgia	9,324,000,000	1.8%
18	Indiana	9,162,000,000	1.8%
19	Wisconsin	8,878,000,000	1.7%
20	Missouri	8,708,000,000	1.7%
21	Oregon	8,671,000,000	1.7%
22	Virginia	8,237,000,000	1.6%
23	Colorado	7,604,000,000	1.5%
24	Washington	7,473,000,000	1.5%
25	Louisiana	7,414,000,000	1.4%
26	Connecticut	6,979,000,000	1.4%
27	Arkansas	6,059,000,000	1.2%
28	Alabama	6,032,000,000	1.2%
29	South Carolina	6,022,000,000	1.2%
30	New Mexico	5,136,000,000	1.0%
31	Oklahoma	5,064,000,000	1.0%
32	Mississippi	4,908,000,000	1.0%
33	Iowa	4,805,000,000	0.9%
34	Kansas	3,548,000,000	0.7%
35	West Virginia	3,530,000,000	0.7%
36	Nevada	2,903,000,000	0.6%
37	Rhode Island	2,579,000,000	0.5%
38	Maine	2,533,000,000	0.5%
39	Utah	2,481,000,000	0.5%
40	Hawaii	2,048,000,000	0.4%
41	Idaho	2,029,000,000	0.4%
42	Delaware	1,875,000,000	0.4%
43	Nebraska	1,855,000,000	0.4%
44	Alaska	1,650,000,000	0.3%
45	New Hampshire	1,631,000,000	0.3%
46	Vermont	1,442,000,000	0.3%
47	North Dakota	1,145,000,000	0.2%
48	Montana	1,110,000,000	0.2%
49	South Dakota	848,000,000	0.2%
50	Wyoming	604,000,000	0.1%
	District of Columbia**	NA	NA

Source: National Association of State Budget Officers "State Expenditure Report" (http://www.nasbo.org)
*Estimates for fiscal year 2015.
**Not available.

Percent Change in Medicaid Expenditures: 2014 to 2015

National Percent Change = 15.1% Increase*

ALPHA ORDER

RANK	STATE	PERCENT CHANGE
39	Alabama	3.8
5	Alaska	30.7
10	Arizona	21.2
11	Arkansas	20.6
2	California	43.1
31	Colorado	5.4
41	Connecticut	3.1
19	Delaware	12.7
26	Florida	8.2
47	Georgia	(0.5)
36	Hawaii	4.7
30	Idaho	5.7
24	Illinois	10.4
34	Indiana	5.1
18	Iowa	13.0
28	Kansas	7.4
3	Kentucky	37.3
44	Louisiana	1.4
50	Maine	(8.9)
20	Maryland	11.7
13	Massachusetts	16.2
7	Michigan	26.3
21	Minnesota	11.6
28	Mississippi	7.4
35	Missouri	4.9
32	Montana	5.2
45	Nebraska	(0.1)
1	Nevada	43.3
12	New Hampshire	18.1
15	New Jersey	16.1
8	New Mexico	23.1
16	New York	14.2
40	North Carolina	3.6
4	North Dakota	34.9
22	Ohio	10.9
49	Oklahoma	(2.3)
6	Oregon	28.3
32	Pennsylvania	5.2
13	Rhode Island	16.2
22	South Carolina	10.9
43	South Dakota	1.8
25	Tennessee	10.3
17	Texas	13.1
38	Utah	4.2
42	Vermont	2.2
37	Virginia	4.3
9	Washington	22.5
45	West Virginia	(0.1)
27	Wisconsin	7.5
48	Wyoming	(0.7)

RANK ORDER

RANK	STATE	PERCENT CHANGE
1	Nevada	43.3
2	California	43.1
3	Kentucky	37.3
4	North Dakota	34.9
5	Alaska	30.7
6	Oregon	28.3
7	Michigan	26.3
8	New Mexico	23.1
9	Washington	22.5
10	Arizona	21.2
11	Arkansas	20.6
12	New Hampshire	18.1
13	Massachusetts	16.2
13	Rhode Island	16.2
15	New Jersey	16.1
16	New York	14.2
17	Texas	13.1
18	Iowa	13.0
19	Delaware	12.7
20	Maryland	11.7
21	Minnesota	11.6
22	Ohio	10.9
22	South Carolina	10.9
24	Illinois	10.4
25	Tennessee	10.3
26	Florida	8.2
27	Wisconsin	7.5
28	Kansas	7.4
28	Mississippi	7.4
30	Idaho	5.7
31	Colorado	5.4
32	Montana	5.2
32	Pennsylvania	5.2
34	Indiana	5.1
35	Missouri	4.9
36	Hawaii	4.7
37	Virginia	4.3
38	Utah	4.2
39	Alabama	3.8
40	North Carolina	3.6
41	Connecticut	3.1
42	Vermont	2.2
43	South Dakota	1.8
44	Louisiana	1.4
45	Nebraska	(0.1)
45	West Virginia	(0.1)
47	Georgia	(0.5)
48	Wyoming	(0.7)
49	Oklahoma	(2.3)
50	Maine	(8.9)
	District of Columbia**	NA

Source: National Association of State Budget Officers "State Expenditure Report" (http://www.nasbo.org)
*Estimates for fiscal year 2015.
**Not available.

Percent of Population Receiving Public Aid in 2013

National Percent = 3.8% of Population*

ALPHA ORDER

RANK	STATE	PERCENT
8	Alabama	4.6
25	Alaska	3.0
41	Arizona	2.3
10	Arkansas	4.3
1	California	6.7
44	Colorado	2.2
37	Connecticut	2.5
22	Delaware	3.3
22	Florida	3.3
27	Georgia	2.9
16	Hawaii	3.6
45	Idaho	2.1
37	Illinois	2.5
41	Indiana	2.3
30	Iowa	2.8
41	Kansas	2.3
2	Kentucky	5.7
12	Louisiana	4.2
14	Maine	3.8
30	Maryland	2.8
13	Massachusetts	4.0
20	Michigan	3.5
37	Minnesota	2.5
4	Mississippi	4.9
20	Missouri	3.5
35	Montana	2.6
45	Nebraska	2.1
27	Nevada	2.9
47	New Hampshire	2.0
30	New Jersey	2.8
6	New Mexico	4.8
4	New York	4.9
34	North Carolina	2.7
48	North Dakota	1.6
14	Ohio	3.8
27	Oklahoma	2.9
16	Oregon	3.6
10	Pennsylvania	4.3
9	Rhode Island	4.5
25	South Carolina	3.0
37	South Dakota	2.5
7	Tennessee	4.7
30	Texas	2.8
49	Utah	1.4
16	Vermont	3.6
35	Virginia	2.6
16	Washington	3.6
3	West Virginia	5.3
24	Wisconsin	3.2
50	Wyoming	1.3

RANK ORDER

RANK	STATE	PERCENT
1	California	6.7
2	Kentucky	5.7
3	West Virginia	5.3
4	Mississippi	4.9
4	New York	4.9
6	New Mexico	4.8
7	Tennessee	4.7
8	Alabama	4.6
9	Rhode Island	4.5
10	Arkansas	4.3
10	Pennsylvania	4.3
12	Louisiana	4.2
13	Massachusetts	4.0
14	Maine	3.8
14	Ohio	3.8
16	Hawaii	3.6
16	Oregon	3.6
16	Vermont	3.6
16	Washington	3.6
20	Michigan	3.5
20	Missouri	3.5
22	Delaware	3.3
22	Florida	3.3
24	Wisconsin	3.2
25	Alaska	3.0
25	South Carolina	3.0
27	Georgia	2.9
27	Nevada	2.9
27	Oklahoma	2.9
30	Iowa	2.8
30	Maryland	2.8
30	New Jersey	2.8
30	Texas	2.8
34	North Carolina	2.7
35	Montana	2.6
35	Virginia	2.6
37	Connecticut	2.5
37	Illinois	2.5
37	Minnesota	2.5
37	South Dakota	2.5
41	Arizona	2.3
41	Indiana	2.3
41	Kansas	2.3
44	Colorado	2.2
45	Idaho	2.1
45	Nebraska	2.1
47	New Hampshire	2.0
48	North Dakota	1.6
49	Utah	1.4
50	Wyoming	1.3

District of Columbia	6.5

Source: CQ Press using data from U.S. Department of Health and Human Services, Social Security Administration
"Social Security Bulletin, Annual Statistical Supplement 2014" (http://www.ssa.gov/policy/docs/statcomps/supplement/2014/) and
U.S. Department of Health and Human Services, Administration for Children and Families
"TANF Caseload Data" (http://www.acf.hhs.gov/programs/ofa/programs/tanf/data-reports)
*As of December 2013. Includes recipients of Temporary Assistance to Needy Families (TANF) and/or Supplemental Security Income payments.

Recipients of Temporary Assistance to Needy Families (TANF) Payments in 2015
National Total = 2,989,086 Monthly Recipients*

ALPHA ORDER

RANK	STATE	RECIPIENTS	% of USA
21	Alabama	29,536	1.0%
43	Alaska	8,615	0.3%
28	Arizona	22,809	0.8%
39	Arkansas	9,995	0.3%
1	California	1,098,274	36.7%
16	Colorado	43,708	1.5%
25	Connecticut	25,439	0.9%
36	Delaware	12,545	0.4%
6	Florida	82,060	2.7%
26	Georgia	24,943	0.8%
30	Hawaii	20,879	0.7%
49	Idaho	2,639	0.1%
20	Illinois	40,902	1.4%
31	Indiana	16,798	0.6%
23	Iowa	27,033	0.9%
34	Kansas	13,518	0.5%
15	Kentucky	48,444	1.6%
37	Louisiana	11,359	0.4%
40	Maine	9,983	0.3%
19	Maryland	42,186	1.4%
9	Massachusetts	65,400	2.2%
14	Michigan	49,049	1.6%
18	Minnesota	42,459	1.4%
35	Mississippi	12,718	0.4%
10	Missouri	57,279	1.9%
44	Montana	7,007	0.2%
41	Nebraska	9,945	0.3%
24	Nevada	26,591	0.9%
47	New Hampshire	5,542	0.2%
11	New Jersey	53,021	1.8%
22	New Mexico	28,917	1.0%
2	New York	253,932	8.5%
29	North Carolina	21,253	0.7%
48	North Dakota	2,819	0.1%
4	Ohio	110,651	3.7%
32	Oklahoma	15,200	0.5%
17	Oregon	43,342	1.5%
3	Pennsylvania	156,835	5.2%
38	Rhode Island	11,037	0.4%
27	South Carolina	22,967	0.8%
45	South Dakota	5,814	0.2%
5	Tennessee	82,248	2.8%
8	Texas	66,808	2.2%
42	Utah	8,823	0.3%
46	Vermont	5,666	0.2%
13	Virginia	49,571	1.7%
7	Washington	70,639	2.4%
33	West Virginia	15,105	0.5%
12	Wisconsin	50,635	1.7%
50	Wyoming	682	0.0%

RANK ORDER

RANK	STATE	RECIPIENTS	% of USA
1	California	1,098,274	36.7%
2	New York	253,932	8.5%
3	Pennsylvania	156,835	5.2%
4	Ohio	110,651	3.7%
5	Tennessee	82,248	2.8%
6	Florida	82,060	2.7%
7	Washington	70,639	2.4%
8	Texas	66,808	2.2%
9	Massachusetts	65,400	2.2%
10	Missouri	57,279	1.9%
11	New Jersey	53,021	1.8%
12	Wisconsin	50,635	1.7%
13	Virginia	49,571	1.7%
14	Michigan	49,049	1.6%
15	Kentucky	48,444	1.6%
16	Colorado	43,708	1.5%
17	Oregon	43,342	1.5%
18	Minnesota	42,459	1.4%
19	Maryland	42,186	1.4%
20	Illinois	40,902	1.4%
21	Alabama	29,536	1.0%
22	New Mexico	28,917	1.0%
23	Iowa	27,033	0.9%
24	Nevada	26,591	0.9%
25	Connecticut	25,439	0.9%
26	Georgia	24,943	0.8%
27	South Carolina	22,967	0.8%
28	Arizona	22,809	0.8%
29	North Carolina	21,253	0.7%
30	Hawaii	20,879	0.7%
31	Indiana	16,798	0.6%
32	Oklahoma	15,200	0.5%
33	West Virginia	15,105	0.5%
34	Kansas	13,518	0.5%
35	Mississippi	12,718	0.4%
36	Delaware	12,545	0.4%
37	Louisiana	11,359	0.4%
38	Rhode Island	11,037	0.4%
39	Arkansas	9,995	0.3%
40	Maine	9,983	0.3%
41	Nebraska	9,945	0.3%
42	Utah	8,823	0.3%
43	Alaska	8,615	0.3%
44	Montana	7,007	0.2%
45	South Dakota	5,814	0.2%
46	Vermont	5,666	0.2%
47	New Hampshire	5,542	0.2%
48	North Dakota	2,819	0.1%
49	Idaho	2,639	0.1%
50	Wyoming	682	0.0%
	District of Columbia	13,891	0.5%

Source: U.S. Department of Health and Human Services, Administration for Children and Families "TANF Caseload Data" (http://www.acf.hhs.gov/programs/ofa/programs/tanf/data-reports)
*As of June 2015. National total includes 31,575 recipients in U.S. territories (28,205 in Puerto Rico).

Percent Change in TANF Recipients: 2014 to 2015

National Percent Change = 12.9% Decrease*

ALPHA ORDER

RANK	STATE	PERCENT CHANGE
47	Alabama	(22.4)
27	Alaska	(13.0)
38	Arizona	(16.7)
44	Arkansas	(21.2)
33	California	(14.8)
2	Colorado	(1.0)
24	Connecticut	(12.0)
8	Delaware	(3.8)
3	Florida	(2.0)
25	Georgia	(12.2)
22	Hawaii	(11.6)
15	Idaho	(7.6)
18	Illinois	(9.1)
26	Indiana	(12.4)
30	Iowa	(14.1)
31	Kansas	(14.4)
29	Kentucky	(13.4)
12	Louisiana	(5.0)
37	Maine	(16.3)
36	Maryland	(15.3)
35	Massachusetts	(15.2)
31	Michigan	(14.4)
6	Minnesota	(2.5)
49	Mississippi	(25.0)
19	Missouri	(9.3)
11	Montana	(4.9)
7	Nebraska	(3.1)
40	Nevada	(17.5)
27	New Hampshire	(13.0)
41	New Jersey	(17.9)
42	New Mexico	(20.7)
4	New York	(2.4)
50	North Carolina	(26.0)
21	North Dakota	(10.4)
14	Ohio	(6.8)
1	Oklahoma	0.1
43	Oregon	(20.9)
16	Pennsylvania	(8.3)
34	Rhode Island	(14.9)
9	South Carolina	(3.9)
10	South Dakota	(4.7)
48	Tennessee	(23.3)
23	Texas	(11.8)
13	Utah	(5.5)
20	Vermont	(9.9)
17	Virginia	(8.7)
46	Washington	(22.3)
38	West Virginia	(16.7)
45	Wisconsin	(21.4)
4	Wyoming	(2.4)

RANK ORDER

RANK	STATE	PERCENT CHANGE
1	Oklahoma	0.1
2	Colorado	(1.0)
3	Florida	(2.0)
4	New York	(2.4)
4	Wyoming	(2.4)
6	Minnesota	(2.5)
7	Nebraska	(3.1)
8	Delaware	(3.8)
9	South Carolina	(3.9)
10	South Dakota	(4.7)
11	Montana	(4.9)
12	Louisiana	(5.0)
13	Utah	(5.5)
14	Ohio	(6.8)
15	Idaho	(7.6)
16	Pennsylvania	(8.3)
17	Virginia	(8.7)
18	Illinois	(9.1)
19	Missouri	(9.3)
20	Vermont	(9.9)
21	North Dakota	(10.4)
22	Hawaii	(11.6)
23	Texas	(11.8)
24	Connecticut	(12.0)
25	Georgia	(12.2)
26	Indiana	(12.4)
27	Alaska	(13.0)
27	New Hampshire	(13.0)
29	Kentucky	(13.4)
30	Iowa	(14.1)
31	Kansas	(14.4)
31	Michigan	(14.4)
33	California	(14.8)
34	Rhode Island	(14.9)
35	Massachusetts	(15.2)
36	Maryland	(15.3)
37	Maine	(16.3)
38	Arizona	(16.7)
38	West Virginia	(16.7)
40	Nevada	(17.5)
41	New Jersey	(17.9)
42	New Mexico	(20.7)
43	Oregon	(20.9)
44	Arkansas	(21.2)
45	Wisconsin	(21.4)
46	Washington	(22.3)
47	Alabama	(22.4)
48	Tennessee	(23.3)
49	Mississippi	(25.0)
50	North Carolina	(26.0)

District of Columbia (4.2)

Source: CQ Press using data from U.S. Department of Health and Human Services, Administration for Children and Families
"TANF Caseload Data" (http://www.acf.hhs.gov/programs/ofa/programs/tanf/data-reports)
*June 2014 to June 2015. National percent includes recipients in U.S. territories.

TANF Work Participation Rates in 2013

National Rate = 44.9%*

ALPHA ORDER

RANK	STATE	PERCENT
28	Alabama	47.6
40	Alaska	41.7
2	Arizona	77.8
31	Arkansas	46.5
44	California	39.1
45	Colorado	34.8
13	Connecticut	58.2
37	Delaware	43.0
17	Florida	53.9
9	Georgia	61.1
20	Hawaii	53.2
1	Idaho	90.1
28	Illinois	47.6
32	Indiana	45.8
16	Iowa	55.9
48	Kansas	30.1
21	Kentucky	52.8
39	Louisiana	42.0
13	Maine	58.2
24	Maryland	51.8
41	Massachusetts	41.0
22	Michigan	52.5
10	Minnesota	60.3
12	Mississippi	59.4
50	Missouri	21.6
15	Montana	56.3
6	Nebraska	69.5
30	Nevada	46.9
7	New Hampshire	65.5
46	New Jersey	31.9
36	New Mexico	43.7
33	New York	44.8
10	North Carolina	60.3
25	North Dakota	51.3
4	Ohio	73.9
19	Oklahoma	53.3
23	Oregon	52.0
42	Pennsylvania	40.7
49	Rhode Island	29.5
27	South Carolina	48.4
8	South Dakota	64.3
34	Tennessee	44.6
43	Texas	40.2
18	Utah	53.8
35	Vermont	44.3
38	Virginia	42.9
47	Washington	30.7
26	West Virginia	51.1
5	Wisconsin	70.8
3	Wyoming	75.7

RANK ORDER

RANK	STATE	PERCENT
1	Idaho	90.1
2	Arizona	77.8
3	Wyoming	75.7
4	Ohio	73.9
5	Wisconsin	70.8
6	Nebraska	69.5
7	New Hampshire	65.5
8	South Dakota	64.3
9	Georgia	61.1
10	Minnesota	60.3
10	North Carolina	60.3
12	Mississippi	59.4
13	Connecticut	58.2
13	Maine	58.2
15	Montana	56.3
16	Iowa	55.9
17	Florida	53.9
18	Utah	53.8
19	Oklahoma	53.3
20	Hawaii	53.2
21	Kentucky	52.8
22	Michigan	52.5
23	Oregon	52.0
24	Maryland	51.8
25	North Dakota	51.3
26	West Virginia	51.1
27	South Carolina	48.4
28	Alabama	47.6
28	Illinois	47.6
30	Nevada	46.9
31	Arkansas	46.5
32	Indiana	45.8
33	New York	44.8
34	Tennessee	44.6
35	Vermont	44.3
36	New Mexico	43.7
37	Delaware	43.0
38	Virginia	42.9
39	Louisiana	42.0
40	Alaska	41.7
41	Massachusetts	41.0
42	Pennsylvania	40.7
43	Texas	40.2
44	California	39.1
45	Colorado	34.8
46	New Jersey	31.9
47	Washington	30.7
48	Kansas	30.1
49	Rhode Island	29.5
50	Missouri	21.6
	District of Columbia	26.9

Source: U.S. Department of Health and Human Services, Administration for Children and Families
"Work Participation Rates - Fiscal Year 2013" (Table 6C) (http://www.acf.hhs.gov/programs/ofa/resource/wpr2013)
*For fiscal year 2013. Work-eligible individuals with hours of participation in various work and training activities. National average includes recipients in U.S. territories.

Average Monthly TANF Assistance per Family in 2013

National Average = $378*

ALPHA ORDER

RANK	STATE	PER FAMILY
44	Alabama	$195
1	Alaska	595
41	Arizona	218
49	Arkansas	154
7	California	457
17	Colorado	375
10	Connecticut	447
36	Delaware	250
38	Florida	236
42	Georgia	217
3	Hawaii	550
27	Idaho	297
40	Illinois	221
44	Indiana	195
25	Iowa	318
34	Kansas	269
33	Kentucky	273
32	Louisiana	279
19	Maine	360
9	Maryland	452
4	Massachusetts	472
22	Michigan	339
21	Minnesota	352
50	Mississippi	140
39	Missouri	223
14	Montana	417
29	Nebraska	289
23	Nevada	336
5	New Hampshire	470
26	New Jersey	314
30	New Mexico	287
2	New York	579
43	North Carolina	213
28	North Dakota	296
20	Ohio	355
46	Oklahoma	191
13	Oregon	422
24	Pennsylvania	324
12	Rhode Island	427
47	South Carolina	167
16	South Dakota	398
48	Tennessee	164
37	Texas	247
7	Utah	457
6	Vermont	468
35	Virginia	255
18	Washington	366
31	West Virginia	284
11	Wisconsin	430
15	Wyoming	402

RANK ORDER

RANK	STATE	PER FAMILY
1	Alaska	$595
2	New York	579
3	Hawaii	550
4	Massachusetts	472
5	New Hampshire	470
6	Vermont	468
7	California	457
7	Utah	457
9	Maryland	452
10	Connecticut	447
11	Wisconsin	430
12	Rhode Island	427
13	Oregon	422
14	Montana	417
15	Wyoming	402
16	South Dakota	398
17	Colorado	375
18	Washington	366
19	Maine	360
20	Ohio	355
21	Minnesota	352
22	Michigan	339
23	Nevada	336
24	Pennsylvania	324
25	Iowa	318
26	New Jersey	314
27	Idaho	297
28	North Dakota	296
29	Nebraska	289
30	New Mexico	287
31	West Virginia	284
32	Louisiana	279
33	Kentucky	273
34	Kansas	269
35	Virginia	255
36	Delaware	250
37	Texas	247
38	Florida	236
39	Missouri	223
40	Illinois	221
41	Arizona	218
42	Georgia	217
43	North Carolina	213
44	Alabama	195
44	Indiana	195
46	Oklahoma	191
47	South Carolina	167
48	Tennessee	164
49	Arkansas	154
50	Mississippi	140
	District of Columbia	349

Source: U.S. Department of Health and Human Services, Administration for Children and Families "Characteristics and Financial Circumstances of TANF Recipients, Fiscal Year 2013 " (Table 37) (http://www.acf.hhs.gov/programs/ofa/resource/characteristics-and-financial-circumstances-appendix-fy2013)
*For fiscal year 2013. National average includes families in U.S. territories.

Percent of Households with Food Insecurity in 2014

National Percent = 14.3% of Households*

ALPHA ORDER

RANK	STATE	PERCENT
7	Alabama	16.8
38	Alaska	12.0
16	Arizona	15.4
2	Arkansas	19.9
30	California	13.5
29	Colorado	13.6
24	Connecticut	13.9
37	Delaware	12.1
27	Florida	13.8
15	Georgia	15.7
35	Hawaii	12.3
22	Idaho	14.1
40	Illinois	11.7
20	Indiana	14.6
43	Iowa	11.4
14	Kansas	15.9
4	Kentucky	17.5
3	Louisiana	17.6
12	Maine	16.2
34	Maryland	12.5
49	Massachusetts	9.6
19	Michigan	14.7
46	Minnesota	10.4
1	Mississippi	22.0
7	Missouri	16.8
42	Montana	11.5
24	Nebraska	13.9
18	Nevada	15.2
48	New Hampshire	10.0
40	New Jersey	11.7
35	New Mexico	12.3
21	New York	14.4
9	North Carolina	16.7
50	North Dakota	8.4
6	Ohio	16.9
10	Oklahoma	16.5
13	Oregon	16.1
45	Pennsylvania	11.3
32	Rhode Island	12.7
24	South Carolina	13.9
39	South Dakota	11.9
11	Tennessee	16.3
5	Texas	17.2
31	Utah	13.3
33	Vermont	12.6
47	Virginia	10.1
28	Washington	13.7
17	West Virginia	15.3
43	Wisconsin	11.4
23	Wyoming	14.0

RANK ORDER

RANK	STATE	PERCENT
1	Mississippi	22.0
2	Arkansas	19.9
3	Louisiana	17.6
4	Kentucky	17.5
5	Texas	17.2
6	Ohio	16.9
7	Alabama	16.8
7	Missouri	16.8
9	North Carolina	16.7
10	Oklahoma	16.5
11	Tennessee	16.3
12	Maine	16.2
13	Oregon	16.1
14	Kansas	15.9
15	Georgia	15.7
16	Arizona	15.4
17	West Virginia	15.3
18	Nevada	15.2
19	Michigan	14.7
20	Indiana	14.6
21	New York	14.4
22	Idaho	14.1
23	Wyoming	14.0
24	Connecticut	13.9
24	Nebraska	13.9
24	South Carolina	13.9
27	Florida	13.8
28	Washington	13.7
29	Colorado	13.6
30	California	13.5
31	Utah	13.3
32	Rhode Island	12.7
33	Vermont	12.6
34	Maryland	12.5
35	Hawaii	12.3
35	New Mexico	12.3
37	Delaware	12.1
38	Alaska	12.0
39	South Dakota	11.9
40	Illinois	11.7
40	New Jersey	11.7
42	Montana	11.5
43	Iowa	11.4
43	Wisconsin	11.4
45	Pennsylvania	11.3
46	Minnesota	10.4
47	Virginia	10.1
48	New Hampshire	10.0
49	Massachusetts	9.6
50	North Dakota	8.4
	District of Columbia	13.2

Source: U.S. Department of Agriculture, Economic Research Service
"Household Food Security in the United States, 2014" (www.ers.usda.gov/publications/err-economic-research-report/err194.aspx)
*Three-year average for 2012-2014. Refers to households for which access to enough food is limited by a lack of money and other resources. About one-third of food-insecure households have very low food security, meaning that at times the food intake of some household members is reduced and their normal eating patterns are disrupted.

Supplemental Nutrition Assistance Program Benefits in 2015

National Total = $69,655,275,007*

ALPHA ORDER

RANK	STATE	BENEFITS	% of USA
14	Alabama	$1,341,906,577	1.9%
45	Alaska	168,054,411	0.2%
13	Arizona	1,459,584,643	2.1%
31	Arkansas	648,769,562	0.9%
1	California	7,527,764,839	10.8%
28	Colorado	771,959,822	1.1%
29	Connecticut	715,334,947	1.0%
43	Delaware	228,935,464	0.3%
2	Florida	5,688,711,691	8.2%
6	Georgia	2,803,606,880	4.0%
35	Hawaii	505,466,329	0.7%
41	Idaho	273,758,132	0.4%
5	Illinois	3,303,102,831	4.7%
18	Indiana	1,244,188,231	1.8%
34	Iowa	516,608,025	0.7%
37	Kansas	374,432,741	0.5%
24	Kentucky	1,112,381,122	1.6%
15	Louisiana	1,298,445,656	1.9%
40	Maine	282,015,399	0.4%
23	Maryland	1,149,657,588	1.7%
21	Massachusetts	1,202,312,621	1.7%
10	Michigan	2,369,223,448	3.4%
32	Minnesota	627,621,936	0.9%
26	Mississippi	916,551,543	1.3%
17	Missouri	1,258,535,557	1.8%
44	Montana	171,413,823	0.2%
42	Nebraska	242,092,503	0.3%
33	Nevada	605,592,527	0.9%
47	New Hampshire	132,497,777	0.2%
16	New Jersey	1,291,435,885	1.9%
30	New Mexico	685,206,629	1.0%
4	New York	5,046,486,639	7.2%
9	North Carolina	2,395,550,386	3.4%
49	North Dakota	77,912,538	0.1%
8	Ohio	2,528,834,777	3.6%
27	Oklahoma	864,950,565	1.2%
22	Oregon	1,152,975,013	1.7%
7	Pennsylvania	2,699,655,059	3.9%
39	Rhode Island	282,877,635	0.4%
20	South Carolina	1,208,604,782	1.7%
46	South Dakota	148,866,948	0.2%
11	Tennessee	1,884,708,816	2.7%
3	Texas	5,265,414,125	7.6%
38	Utah	313,810,557	0.5%
48	Vermont	124,378,476	0.2%
19	Virginia	1,230,788,073	1.8%
12	Washington	1,527,741,099	2.2%
36	West Virginia	497,268,952	0.7%
25	Wisconsin	1,051,153,941	1.5%
50	Wyoming	46,448,470	0.1%

RANK ORDER

RANK	STATE	BENEFITS	% of USA
1	California	$7,527,764,839	10.8%
2	Florida	5,688,711,691	8.2%
3	Texas	5,265,414,125	7.6%
4	New York	5,046,486,639	7.2%
5	Illinois	3,303,102,831	4.7%
6	Georgia	2,803,606,880	4.0%
7	Pennsylvania	2,699,655,059	3.9%
8	Ohio	2,528,834,777	3.6%
9	North Carolina	2,395,550,386	3.4%
10	Michigan	2,369,223,448	3.4%
11	Tennessee	1,884,708,816	2.7%
12	Washington	1,527,741,099	2.2%
13	Arizona	1,459,584,643	2.1%
14	Alabama	1,341,906,577	1.9%
15	Louisiana	1,298,445,656	1.9%
16	New Jersey	1,291,435,885	1.9%
17	Missouri	1,258,535,557	1.8%
18	Indiana	1,244,188,231	1.8%
19	Virginia	1,230,788,073	1.8%
20	South Carolina	1,208,604,782	1.7%
21	Massachusetts	1,202,312,621	1.7%
22	Oregon	1,152,975,013	1.7%
23	Maryland	1,149,657,588	1.7%
24	Kentucky	1,112,381,122	1.6%
25	Wisconsin	1,051,153,941	1.5%
26	Mississippi	916,551,543	1.3%
27	Oklahoma	864,950,565	1.2%
28	Colorado	771,959,822	1.1%
29	Connecticut	715,334,947	1.0%
30	New Mexico	685,206,629	1.0%
31	Arkansas	648,769,562	0.9%
32	Minnesota	627,621,936	0.9%
33	Nevada	605,592,527	0.9%
34	Iowa	516,608,025	0.7%
35	Hawaii	505,466,329	0.7%
36	West Virginia	497,268,952	0.7%
37	Kansas	374,432,741	0.5%
38	Utah	313,810,557	0.5%
39	Rhode Island	282,877,635	0.4%
40	Maine	282,015,399	0.4%
41	Idaho	273,758,132	0.4%
42	Nebraska	242,092,503	0.3%
43	Delaware	228,935,464	0.3%
44	Montana	171,413,823	0.2%
45	Alaska	168,054,411	0.2%
46	South Dakota	148,866,948	0.2%
47	New Hampshire	132,497,777	0.2%
48	Vermont	124,378,476	0.2%
49	North Dakota	77,912,538	0.1%
50	Wyoming	46,448,470	0.1%
	District of Columbia	224,104,447	0.3%

Source: U.S. Department of Agriculture, Food, Nutrition and Consumer Services "Supplemental Nutrition Assistance Program" (http://www.fns.usda.gov/pd/snapmain.htm)
*Preliminary data for fiscal year 2015. National total includes $165,574,570 to U.S. territories. Costs are for benefits only and exclude administrative expenditures. Program formerly called the Food Stamp Program.

Monthly Supplemental Nutrition Assistance Program Recipients in 2015

National Total = 45,766,672 Recipients*

ALPHA ORDER

RANK	STATE	RECIPIENTS	% of USA
15	Alabama	889,380	1.9%
48	Alaska	81,121	0.2%
13	Arizona	999,401	2.2%
30	Arkansas	468,904	1.0%
1	California	4,417,772	9.7%
29	Colorado	495,134	1.1%
32	Connecticut	442,161	1.0%
43	Delaware	149,981	0.3%
3	Florida	3,656,169	8.0%
7	Georgia	1,800,531	3.9%
40	Hawaii	188,895	0.4%
39	Idaho	196,872	0.4%
5	Illinois	2,042,306	4.5%
19	Indiana	831,740	1.8%
34	Iowa	391,224	0.9%
36	Kansas	273,974	0.6%
25	Kentucky	768,882	1.7%
17	Louisiana	859,738	1.9%
38	Maine	202,579	0.4%
23	Maryland	781,035	1.7%
22	Massachusetts	785,778	1.7%
10	Michigan	1,571,344	3.4%
28	Minnesota	496,023	1.1%
26	Mississippi	636,322	1.4%
18	Missouri	844,597	1.8%
44	Montana	119,082	0.3%
42	Nebraska	174,092	0.4%
33	Nevada	420,413	0.9%
45	New Hampshire	106,296	0.2%
14	New Jersey	905,728	2.0%
31	New Mexico	453,146	1.0%
4	New York	3,039,108	6.6%
9	North Carolina	1,646,202	3.6%
49	North Dakota	53,148	0.1%
8	Ohio	1,676,263	3.7%
27	Oklahoma	598,257	1.3%
24	Oregon	779,749	1.7%
6	Pennsylvania	1,826,667	4.0%
41	Rhode Island	175,025	0.4%
21	South Carolina	804,572	1.8%
46	South Dakota	98,553	0.2%
11	Tennessee	1,229,391	2.7%
2	Texas	3,724,688	8.1%
37	Utah	225,603	0.5%
47	Vermont	84,994	0.2%
16	Virginia	860,375	1.9%
12	Washington	1,070,933	2.3%
35	West Virginia	367,908	0.8%
20	Wisconsin	805,540	1.8%
50	Wyoming	32,606	0.1%

RANK ORDER

RANK	STATE	RECIPIENTS	% of USA
1	California	4,417,772	9.7%
2	Texas	3,724,688	8.1%
3	Florida	3,656,169	8.0%
4	New York	3,039,108	6.6%
5	Illinois	2,042,306	4.5%
6	Pennsylvania	1,826,667	4.0%
7	Georgia	1,800,531	3.9%
8	Ohio	1,676,263	3.7%
9	North Carolina	1,646,202	3.6%
10	Michigan	1,571,344	3.4%
11	Tennessee	1,229,391	2.7%
12	Washington	1,070,933	2.3%
13	Arizona	999,401	2.2%
14	New Jersey	905,728	2.0%
15	Alabama	889,380	1.9%
16	Virginia	860,375	1.9%
17	Louisiana	859,738	1.9%
18	Missouri	844,597	1.8%
19	Indiana	831,740	1.8%
20	Wisconsin	805,540	1.8%
21	South Carolina	804,572	1.8%
22	Massachusetts	785,778	1.7%
23	Maryland	781,035	1.7%
24	Oregon	779,749	1.7%
25	Kentucky	768,882	1.7%
26	Mississippi	636,322	1.4%
27	Oklahoma	598,257	1.3%
28	Minnesota	496,023	1.1%
29	Colorado	495,134	1.1%
30	Arkansas	468,904	1.0%
31	New Mexico	453,146	1.0%
32	Connecticut	442,161	1.0%
33	Nevada	420,413	0.9%
34	Iowa	391,224	0.9%
35	West Virginia	367,908	0.8%
36	Kansas	273,974	0.6%
37	Utah	225,603	0.5%
38	Maine	202,579	0.4%
39	Idaho	196,872	0.4%
40	Hawaii	188,895	0.4%
41	Rhode Island	175,025	0.4%
42	Nebraska	174,092	0.4%
43	Delaware	149,981	0.3%
44	Montana	119,082	0.3%
45	New Hampshire	106,296	0.2%
46	South Dakota	98,553	0.2%
47	Vermont	84,994	0.2%
48	Alaska	81,121	0.2%
49	North Dakota	53,148	0.1%
50	Wyoming	32,606	0.1%
	District of Columbia	141,845	0.3%

Source: U.S. Department of Agriculture, Food, Nutrition and Consumer Services
   "Supplemental Nutrition Assistance Program" (http://www.fns.usda.gov/pd/snapmain.htm)
*Preliminary for fiscal year 2015. National total includes 74,627 recipients in U.S. territories. Program formerly called the Food Stamp Program.

Average Monthly Supplemental Nutrition Assistance Program Benefit per Recipient in 2015
National Average = $126.83 per Recipient*

ALPHA ORDER

RANK	STATE	PER RECIPIENT
17	Alabama	$125.73
2	Alaska	172.64
28	Arizona	121.70
44	Arkansas	115.30
3	California	142.00
8	Colorado	129.92
5	Connecticut	134.82
13	Delaware	127.20
10	Florida	129.66
9	Georgia	129.76
1	Hawaii	222.99
43	Idaho	115.88
6	Illinois	134.78
21	Indiana	124.66
47	Iowa	110.04
45	Kansas	113.89
30	Kentucky	120.56
16	Louisiana	125.86
40	Maine	116.01
25	Maryland	122.66
12	Massachusetts	127.51
19	Michigan	125.65
49	Minnesota	105.44
33	Mississippi	120.03
22	Missouri	124.18
34	Montana	119.96
42	Nebraska	115.88
32	Nevada	120.04
50	New Hampshire	103.87
37	New Jersey	118.82
14	New Mexico	126.01
4	New York	138.38
29	North Carolina	121.27
26	North Dakota	122.16
18	Ohio	125.72
31	Oklahoma	120.48
23	Oregon	123.22
24	Pennsylvania	123.16
7	Rhode Island	134.68
20	South Carolina	125.18
15	South Dakota	125.88
11	Tennessee	127.75
39	Texas	117.80
41	Utah	115.92
27	Vermont	121.95
35	Virginia	119.21
36	Washington	118.88
46	West Virginia	112.63
48	Wisconsin	108.74
38	Wyoming	118.71

RANK ORDER

RANK	STATE	PER RECIPIENT
1	Hawaii	$222.99
2	Alaska	172.64
3	California	142.00
4	New York	138.38
5	Connecticut	134.82
6	Illinois	134.78
7	Rhode Island	134.68
8	Colorado	129.92
9	Georgia	129.76
10	Florida	129.66
11	Tennessee	127.75
12	Massachusetts	127.51
13	Delaware	127.20
14	New Mexico	126.01
15	South Dakota	125.88
16	Louisiana	125.86
17	Alabama	125.73
18	Ohio	125.72
19	Michigan	125.65
20	South Carolina	125.18
21	Indiana	124.66
22	Missouri	124.18
23	Oregon	123.22
24	Pennsylvania	123.16
25	Maryland	122.66
26	North Dakota	122.16
27	Vermont	121.95
28	Arizona	121.70
29	North Carolina	121.27
30	Kentucky	120.56
31	Oklahoma	120.48
32	Nevada	120.04
33	Mississippi	120.03
34	Montana	119.96
35	Virginia	119.21
36	Washington	118.88
37	New Jersey	118.82
38	Wyoming	118.71
39	Texas	117.80
40	Maine	116.01
41	Utah	115.92
42	Nebraska	115.88
43	Idaho	115.88
44	Arkansas	115.30
45	Kansas	113.89
46	West Virginia	112.63
47	Iowa	110.04
48	Wisconsin	108.74
49	Minnesota	105.44
50	New Hampshire	103.87
	District of Columbia	131.66

Source: U.S. Department of Agriculture, Food, Nutrition and Consumer Services "Supplemental Nutrition Assistance Program" (http://www.fns.usda.gov/pd/snapmain.htm)

*Preliminary for fiscal year 2015. National average includes recipients in U.S. territories. Program formerly called the Food Stamp Program.

Percent of Population Receiving Supplemental Nutrition Assistance Program Benefits in 2015
National Percent = 14.2%*

ALPHA ORDER

RANK	STATE	PERCENT
7	Alabama	18.3
40	Alaska	11.0
22	Arizona	14.6
17	Arkansas	15.7
39	California	11.3
45	Colorado	9.1
34	Connecticut	12.3
14	Delaware	15.9
8	Florida	18.0
9	Georgia	17.6
30	Hawaii	13.2
35	Idaho	11.9
14	Illinois	15.9
32	Indiana	12.6
33	Iowa	12.5
43	Kansas	9.4
10	Kentucky	17.4
6	Louisiana	18.4
20	Maine	15.2
31	Maryland	13.0
36	Massachusetts	11.6
16	Michigan	15.8
46	Minnesota	9.0
2	Mississippi	21.3
27	Missouri	13.9
37	Montana	11.5
44	Nebraska	9.2
23	Nevada	14.5
47	New Hampshire	8.0
42	New Jersey	10.1
1	New Mexico	21.7
18	New York	15.4
12	North Carolina	16.4
49	North Dakota	7.0
24	Ohio	14.4
19	Oklahoma	15.3
4	Oregon	19.4
25	Pennsylvania	14.3
11	Rhode Island	16.6
12	South Carolina	16.4
37	South Dakota	11.5
5	Tennessee	18.6
28	Texas	13.6
48	Utah	7.5
28	Vermont	13.6
41	Virginia	10.3
21	Washington	14.9
3	West Virginia	20.0
26	Wisconsin	14.0
50	Wyoming	5.6

RANK ORDER

RANK	STATE	PERCENT
1	New Mexico	21.7
2	Mississippi	21.3
3	West Virginia	20.0
4	Oregon	19.4
5	Tennessee	18.6
6	Louisiana	18.4
7	Alabama	18.3
8	Florida	18.0
9	Georgia	17.6
10	Kentucky	17.4
11	Rhode Island	16.6
12	North Carolina	16.4
12	South Carolina	16.4
14	Delaware	15.9
14	Illinois	15.9
16	Michigan	15.8
17	Arkansas	15.7
18	New York	15.4
19	Oklahoma	15.3
20	Maine	15.2
21	Washington	14.9
22	Arizona	14.6
23	Nevada	14.5
24	Ohio	14.4
25	Pennsylvania	14.3
26	Wisconsin	14.0
27	Missouri	13.9
28	Texas	13.6
28	Vermont	13.6
30	Hawaii	13.2
31	Maryland	13.0
32	Indiana	12.6
33	Iowa	12.5
34	Connecticut	12.3
35	Idaho	11.9
36	Massachusetts	11.6
37	Montana	11.5
37	South Dakota	11.5
39	California	11.3
40	Alaska	11.0
41	Virginia	10.3
42	New Jersey	10.1
43	Kansas	9.4
44	Nebraska	9.2
45	Colorado	9.1
46	Minnesota	9.0
47	New Hampshire	8.0
48	Utah	7.5
49	North Dakota	7.0
50	Wyoming	5.6
	District of Columbia	21.1

Source: CQ Press using data from U.S. Department of Agriculture, Food, Nutrition and Consumer Services
"Supplemental Nutrition Assistance Program" (http://www.fns.usda.gov/pd/snapmain.htm)
*Preliminary data for fiscal year 2015. National rate does not include recipients in U.S. territories. Program formerly called the Food Stamp Program.

Percent of Households Receiving Supplemental Nutrition Assistance Program Benefits in 2015
National Percent = 19.2% of Households*

ALPHA ORDER

RANK	STATE	PERCENT
10	Alabama	22.7
39	Alaska	13.7
27	Arizona	18.1
22	Arkansas	18.9
34	California	16.4
43	Colorado	11.4
26	Connecticut	18.3
19	Delaware	20.5
2	Florida	27.4
8	Georgia	23.4
16	Hawaii	21.2
37	Idaho	14.2
12	Illinois	22.2
35	Indiana	15.2
36	Iowa	14.9
45	Kansas	11.0
13	Kentucky	21.5
10	Louisiana	22.7
21	Maine	19.1
23	Maryland	18.7
29	Massachusetts	17.6
13	Michigan	21.5
44	Minnesota	11.3
3	Mississippi	27.0
32	Missouri	16.9
39	Montana	13.7
46	Nebraska	10.5
19	Nevada	20.5
47	New Hampshire	9.9
37	New Jersey	14.2
3	New Mexico	27.0
9	New York	22.9
16	North Carolina	21.2
49	North Dakota	8.1
28	Ohio	17.8
24	Oklahoma	18.6
1	Oregon	28.8
24	Pennsylvania	18.6
6	Rhode Island	24.6
18	South Carolina	20.8
42	South Dakota	12.9
7	Tennessee	24.4
33	Texas	16.8
48	Utah	9.6
31	Vermont	17.5
41	Virginia	13.1
15	Washington	21.4
5	West Virginia	24.7
29	Wisconsin	17.6
50	Wyoming	6.0

RANK ORDER

RANK	STATE	PERCENT
1	Oregon	28.8
2	Florida	27.4
3	Mississippi	27.0
3	New Mexico	27.0
5	West Virginia	24.7
6	Rhode Island	24.6
7	Tennessee	24.4
8	Georgia	23.4
9	New York	22.9
10	Alabama	22.7
10	Louisiana	22.7
12	Illinois	22.2
13	Kentucky	21.5
13	Michigan	21.5
15	Washington	21.4
16	Hawaii	21.2
16	North Carolina	21.2
18	South Carolina	20.8
19	Delaware	20.5
19	Nevada	20.5
21	Maine	19.1
22	Arkansas	18.9
23	Maryland	18.7
24	Oklahoma	18.6
24	Pennsylvania	18.6
26	Connecticut	18.3
27	Arizona	18.1
28	Ohio	17.8
29	Massachusetts	17.6
29	Wisconsin	17.6
31	Vermont	17.5
32	Missouri	16.9
33	Texas	16.8
34	California	16.4
35	Indiana	15.2
36	Iowa	14.9
37	Idaho	14.2
37	New Jersey	14.2
39	Alaska	13.7
39	Montana	13.7
41	Virginia	13.1
42	South Dakota	12.9
43	Colorado	11.4
44	Minnesota	11.3
45	Kansas	11.0
46	Nebraska	10.5
47	New Hampshire	9.9
48	Utah	9.6
49	North Dakota	8.1
50	Wyoming	6.0
	District of Columbia	28.8

Source: CQ Press using data from U.S. Department of Agriculture, Food, Nutrition and Consumer Services "Supplemental Nutrition Assistance Program" (http://www.fns.usda.gov/pd/snapmain.htm)

*Preliminary data for fiscal year 2015. Percent calculated using 2014 estimated total households. National percent excludes households in U.S. territories. Program formerly called the Food Stamp Program.

Average Monthly Participants in Women, Infants, and Children (WIC) Special Nutrition Program in 2015
National Total = 8,024,083 Participants*

ALPHA ORDER

RANK	STATE	PARTICIPANTS	% of USA
19	Alabama	132,133	1.6%
43	Alaska	19,682	0.2%
12	Arizona	167,072	2.1%
30	Arkansas	84,219	1.0%
1	California	1,265,372	15.8%
28	Colorado	90,954	1.1%
36	Connecticut	51,295	0.6%
45	Delaware	18,963	0.2%
3	Florida	483,811	6.0%
5	Georgia	264,301	3.3%
40	Hawaii	31,616	0.4%
38	Idaho	40,506	0.5%
7	Illinois	247,594	3.1%
14	Indiana	154,484	1.9%
32	Iowa	63,481	0.8%
33	Kansas	62,850	0.8%
22	Kentucky	116,179	1.4%
20	Louisiana	128,935	1.6%
41	Maine	21,777	0.3%
16	Maryland	142,841	1.8%
24	Massachusetts	113,262	1.4%
9	Michigan	244,829	3.1%
21	Minnesota	119,401	1.5%
29	Mississippi	89,449	1.1%
18	Missouri	134,780	1.7%
46	Montana	18,476	0.2%
39	Nebraska	37,601	0.5%
31	Nevada	73,144	0.9%
47	New Hampshire	14,705	0.2%
13	New Jersey	161,664	2.0%
35	New Mexico	55,234	0.7%
4	New York	471,869	5.9%
6	North Carolina	248,890	3.1%
49	North Dakota	12,415	0.2%
10	Ohio	244,200	3.0%
25	Oklahoma	112,883	1.4%
27	Oregon	98,304	1.2%
8	Pennsylvania	245,977	3.1%
42	Rhode Island	20,728	0.3%
23	South Carolina	114,562	1.4%
44	South Dakota	19,474	0.2%
15	Tennessee	150,116	1.9%
2	Texas	886,409	11.0%
34	Utah	58,995	0.7%
48	Vermont	13,733	0.2%
17	Virginia	139,632	1.7%
11	Washington	176,133	2.2%
37	West Virginia	41,698	0.5%
26	Wisconsin	105,504	1.3%
50	Wyoming	10,995	0.1%

RANK ORDER

RANK	STATE	PARTICIPANTS	% of USA
1	California	1,265,372	15.8%
2	Texas	886,409	11.0%
3	Florida	483,811	6.0%
4	New York	471,869	5.9%
5	Georgia	264,301	3.3%
6	North Carolina	248,890	3.1%
7	Illinois	247,594	3.1%
8	Pennsylvania	245,977	3.1%
9	Michigan	244,829	3.1%
10	Ohio	244,200	3.0%
11	Washington	176,133	2.2%
12	Arizona	167,072	2.1%
13	New Jersey	161,664	2.0%
14	Indiana	154,484	1.9%
15	Tennessee	150,116	1.9%
16	Maryland	142,841	1.8%
17	Virginia	139,632	1.7%
18	Missouri	134,780	1.7%
19	Alabama	132,133	1.6%
20	Louisiana	128,935	1.6%
21	Minnesota	119,401	1.5%
22	Kentucky	116,179	1.4%
23	South Carolina	114,562	1.4%
24	Massachusetts	113,262	1.4%
25	Oklahoma	112,883	1.4%
26	Wisconsin	105,504	1.3%
27	Oregon	98,304	1.2%
28	Colorado	90,954	1.1%
29	Mississippi	89,449	1.1%
30	Arkansas	84,219	1.0%
31	Nevada	73,144	0.9%
32	Iowa	63,481	0.8%
33	Kansas	62,850	0.8%
34	Utah	58,995	0.7%
35	New Mexico	55,234	0.7%
36	Connecticut	51,295	0.6%
37	West Virginia	41,698	0.5%
38	Idaho	40,506	0.5%
39	Nebraska	37,601	0.5%
40	Hawaii	31,616	0.4%
41	Maine	21,777	0.3%
42	Rhode Island	20,728	0.3%
43	Alaska	19,682	0.2%
44	South Dakota	19,474	0.2%
45	Delaware	18,963	0.2%
46	Montana	18,476	0.2%
47	New Hampshire	14,705	0.2%
48	Vermont	13,733	0.2%
49	North Dakota	12,415	0.2%
50	Wyoming	10,995	0.1%
	District of Columbia	14,526	0.2%

Source: U.S. Department of Agriculture, Food, Nutrition and Consumer Services
"WIC Program (http://www.fns.usda.gov/pd/wicmain.htm)
*Preliminary data for fiscal year 2015. National total includes 186,433 participants in outlying areas not shown separately (Puerto Rico has 165,042 participants).

Average Monthly Benefit per Participant in Women, Infants, and Children (WIC) Special Nutrition Program in 2015
National Average = $43.56*

ALPHA ORDER

RANK	STATE	AVERAGE BENEFIT
8	Alabama	$48.34
5	Alaska	52.58
16	Arizona	45.30
20	Arkansas	44.81
12	California	47.85
28	Colorado	41.36
10	Connecticut	48.11
29	Delaware	40.72
25	Florida	42.17
32	Georgia	39.97
6	Hawaii	51.40
45	Idaho	35.23
7	Illinois	48.59
34	Indiana	38.67
42	Iowa	36.86
44	Kansas	36.49
27	Kentucky	41.52
11	Louisiana	48.05
21	Maine	44.59
18	Maryland	45.11
38	Massachusetts	38.34
36	Michigan	38.62
26	Minnesota	41.71
1	Mississippi	55.34
39	Missouri	38.19
31	Montana	40.41
17	Nebraska	45.17
40	Nevada	36.93
47	New Hampshire	33.05
3	New Jersey	53.48
41	New Mexico	36.92
2	New York	53.94
24	North Carolina	42.41
14	North Dakota	47.15
46	Ohio	34.85
35	Oklahoma	38.65
30	Oregon	40.69
13	Pennsylvania	47.47
22	Rhode Island	44.23
15	South Carolina	45.84
9	South Dakota	48.25
37	Tennessee	38.40
50	Texas	29.30
43	Utah	36.78
4	Vermont	53.21
49	Virginia	30.78
23	Washington	43.10
33	West Virginia	39.22
19	Wisconsin	44.92
48	Wyoming	32.22

RANK ORDER

RANK	STATE	AVERAGE BENEFIT
1	Mississippi	$55.34
2	New York	53.94
3	New Jersey	53.48
4	Vermont	53.21
5	Alaska	52.58
6	Hawaii	51.40
7	Illinois	48.59
8	Alabama	48.34
9	South Dakota	48.25
10	Connecticut	48.11
11	Louisiana	48.05
12	California	47.85
13	Pennsylvania	47.47
14	North Dakota	47.15
15	South Carolina	45.84
16	Arizona	45.30
17	Nebraska	45.17
18	Maryland	45.11
19	Wisconsin	44.92
20	Arkansas	44.81
21	Maine	44.59
22	Rhode Island	44.23
23	Washington	43.10
24	North Carolina	42.41
25	Florida	42.17
26	Minnesota	41.71
27	Kentucky	41.52
28	Colorado	41.36
29	Delaware	40.72
30	Oregon	40.69
31	Montana	40.41
32	Georgia	39.97
33	West Virginia	39.22
34	Indiana	38.67
35	Oklahoma	38.65
36	Michigan	38.62
37	Tennessee	38.40
38	Massachusetts	38.34
39	Missouri	38.19
40	Nevada	36.93
41	New Mexico	36.92
42	Iowa	36.86
43	Utah	36.78
44	Kansas	36.49
45	Idaho	35.23
46	Ohio	34.85
47	New Hampshire	33.05
48	Wyoming	32.22
49	Virginia	30.78
50	Texas	29.30
	District of Columbia	44.15

Source: U.S. Department of Agriculture, Food, Nutrition and Consumer Services
"WIC Program (http://www.fns.usda.gov/pd/wicmain.htm)
*Preliminary data for fiscal year 2015. National average includes outlying areas and Indian reservations not shown separately.

Percent of Public Elementary and Secondary School Students Eligible for Free or Reduced-Price Meals in 2014
National Percent = 51.7%*

ALPHA ORDER

RANK	STATE	PERCENT
8	Alabama	58.4
32	Alaska	42.8
NA	Arizona**	NA
6	Arkansas	61.2
11	California	58.1
33	Colorado	42.0
45	Connecticut	37.1
38	Delaware	39.5
8	Florida	58.4
4	Georgia	62.1
18	Hawaii	50.5
24	Idaho	47.2
16	Illinois	51.0
21	Indiana	49.2
36	Iowa	40.8
19	Kansas	50.1
13	Kentucky	54.5
3	Louisiana	66.7
27	Maine	45.8
30	Maryland	44.2
42	Massachusetts	38.2
22	Michigan	48.3
41	Minnesota	38.4
1	Mississippi	72.2
20	Missouri	49.4
35	Montana	41.4
28	Nebraska	44.8
15	Nevada	52.9
48	New Hampshire	27.8
43	New Jersey	37.9
2	New Mexico	67.1
23	New York	47.5
14	North Carolina	53.5
47	North Dakota	30.2
29	Ohio	44.3
5	Oklahoma	61.3
17	Oregon	50.8
31	Pennsylvania	43.4
25	Rhode Island	46.7
12	South Carolina	57.4
38	South Dakota	39.5
10	Tennessee	58.2
7	Texas	60.1
46	Utah	37.0
40	Vermont	39.4
37	Virginia	39.6
26	Washington	46.3
NA	West Virginia**	NA
34	Wisconsin	41.9
44	Wyoming	37.7

RANK ORDER

RANK	STATE	PERCENT
1	Mississippi	72.2
2	New Mexico	67.1
3	Louisiana	66.7
4	Georgia	62.1
5	Oklahoma	61.3
6	Arkansas	61.2
7	Texas	60.1
8	Alabama	58.4
8	Florida	58.4
10	Tennessee	58.2
11	California	58.1
12	South Carolina	57.4
13	Kentucky	54.5
14	North Carolina	53.5
15	Nevada	52.9
16	Illinois	51.0
17	Oregon	50.8
18	Hawaii	50.5
19	Kansas	50.1
20	Missouri	49.4
21	Indiana	49.2
22	Michigan	48.3
23	New York	47.5
24	Idaho	47.2
25	Rhode Island	46.7
26	Washington	46.3
27	Maine	45.8
28	Nebraska	44.8
29	Ohio	44.3
30	Maryland	44.2
31	Pennsylvania	43.4
32	Alaska	42.8
33	Colorado	42.0
34	Wisconsin	41.9
35	Montana	41.4
36	Iowa	40.8
37	Virginia	39.6
38	Delaware	39.5
38	South Dakota	39.5
40	Vermont	39.4
41	Minnesota	38.4
42	Massachusetts	38.2
43	New Jersey	37.9
44	Wyoming	37.7
45	Connecticut	37.1
46	Utah	37.0
47	North Dakota	30.2
48	New Hampshire	27.8
NA	Arizona**	NA
NA	West Virginia**	NA
	District of Columbia	99.2

Source: CQ Press using data from U.S. Department of Education, National Center for Education Statistics "Common Core of Data (CCD) Database" (http://nces.ed.gov/ccd/)
*For school year 2013-2014. National percent is based on population of reporting states.
**Not available.

Child Support Collections in 2014

National Total = $27,844,650,133*

ALPHA ORDER

RANK	STATE	COLLECTIONS	% of USA
29	Alabama	$305,979,180	1.1%
42	Alaska	96,470,329	0.3%
25	Arizona	317,199,298	1.1%
32	Arkansas	230,001,139	0.8%
2	California	2,208,197,922	7.9%
27	Colorado	309,678,517	1.1%
31	Connecticut	239,004,703	0.9%
46	Delaware	73,903,748	0.3%
5	Florida	1,450,639,777	5.2%
10	Georgia	658,549,802	2.4%
40	Hawaii	97,700,940	0.4%
38	Idaho	161,391,527	0.6%
9	Illinois	805,081,568	2.9%
19	Indiana	556,624,325	2.0%
28	Iowa	308,319,557	1.1%
36	Kansas	182,077,612	0.7%
22	Kentucky	381,682,114	1.4%
21	Louisiana	394,004,210	1.4%
41	Maine	96,570,225	0.3%
20	Maryland	527,997,612	1.9%
14	Massachusetts	619,591,585	2.2%
6	Michigan	1,314,094,928	4.7%
17	Minnesota	584,663,171	2.1%
26	Mississippi	309,697,386	1.1%
18	Missouri	575,683,350	2.1%
49	Montana	61,057,236	0.2%
33	Nebraska	205,231,434	0.7%
37	Nevada	175,807,832	0.6%
45	New Hampshire	81,882,654	0.3%
8	New Jersey	1,146,736,488	4.1%
39	New Mexico	118,649,455	0.4%
3	New York	1,697,340,934	6.1%
11	North Carolina	655,469,608	2.4%
43	North Dakota	95,110,175	0.3%
4	Ohio	1,680,821,856	6.0%
24	Oklahoma	338,582,208	1.2%
23	Oregon	357,382,407	1.3%
7	Pennsylvania	1,263,370,002	4.5%
47	Rhode Island	71,235,761	0.3%
30	South Carolina	259,070,133	0.9%
44	South Dakota	90,759,898	0.3%
16	Tennessee	593,728,173	2.1%
1	Texas	3,706,766,136	13.3%
34	Utah	205,110,708	0.7%
50	Vermont	45,135,618	0.2%
15	Virginia	611,649,574	2.2%
12	Washington	641,623,544	2.3%
35	West Virginia	195,985,384	0.7%
13	Wisconsin	628,435,812	2.3%
48	Wyoming	65,545,303	0.2%

RANK ORDER

RANK	STATE	COLLECTIONS	% of USA
1	Texas	$3,706,766,136	13.3%
2	California	2,208,197,922	7.9%
3	New York	1,697,340,934	6.1%
4	Ohio	1,680,821,856	6.0%
5	Florida	1,450,639,777	5.2%
6	Michigan	1,314,094,928	4.7%
7	Pennsylvania	1,263,370,002	4.5%
8	New Jersey	1,146,736,488	4.1%
9	Illinois	805,081,568	2.9%
10	Georgia	658,549,802	2.4%
11	North Carolina	655,469,608	2.4%
12	Washington	641,623,544	2.3%
13	Wisconsin	628,435,812	2.3%
14	Massachusetts	619,591,585	2.2%
15	Virginia	611,649,574	2.2%
16	Tennessee	593,728,173	2.1%
17	Minnesota	584,663,171	2.1%
18	Missouri	575,683,350	2.1%
19	Indiana	556,624,325	2.0%
20	Maryland	527,997,612	1.9%
21	Louisiana	394,004,210	1.4%
22	Kentucky	381,682,114	1.4%
23	Oregon	357,382,407	1.3%
24	Oklahoma	338,582,208	1.2%
25	Arizona	317,199,298	1.1%
26	Mississippi	309,697,386	1.1%
27	Colorado	309,678,517	1.1%
28	Iowa	308,319,557	1.1%
29	Alabama	305,979,180	1.1%
30	South Carolina	259,070,133	0.9%
31	Connecticut	239,004,703	0.9%
32	Arkansas	230,001,139	0.8%
33	Nebraska	205,231,434	0.7%
34	Utah	205,110,708	0.7%
35	West Virginia	195,985,384	0.7%
36	Kansas	182,077,612	0.7%
37	Nevada	175,807,832	0.6%
38	Idaho	161,391,527	0.6%
39	New Mexico	118,649,455	0.4%
40	Hawaii	97,700,940	0.4%
41	Maine	96,570,225	0.3%
42	Alaska	96,470,329	0.3%
43	North Dakota	95,110,175	0.3%
44	South Dakota	90,759,898	0.3%
45	New Hampshire	81,882,654	0.3%
46	Delaware	73,903,748	0.3%
47	Rhode Island	71,235,761	0.3%
48	Wyoming	65,545,303	0.2%
49	Montana	61,057,236	0.2%
50	Vermont	45,135,618	0.2%
	District of Columbia	47,357,275	0.2%

Source: U.S. Department of Health and Human Services, Office of Child Support Enforcement
"Child Support Enforcement Preliminary Data Report" (www.acf.hhs.gov/programs/css/resource/fy-2014-preliminary-report)
*Fiscal year 2014. Total does not include $354,405,980 collected in U.S. territories.

XV. Transportation

Federal Highway Funding in 2013 559
Per Capita Federal Highway Funding in 2013 560
Public Road and Street Mileage in 2013. 561
Percent of Public Road and Street Mileage Federally
    Funded in 2013. 562
Interstate Highway Mileage in 2013. 563
Rural Road and Street Mileage in 2013 564
Urban Road and Street Mileage in 2013. 565
Percent of Roadways in Mediocre or Poor Condition
    in 2013 566
Bridges in 2014. 567
Deficient Bridges in 2014 568
Deficient Bridges as a Percent of Total Bridges in 2014 .. 569
Vehicle-Miles of Travel in 2013 570
Highway Fatalities in 2013. 571
Highway Fatality Rate in 2013 572
Percent of Traffic Fatalities That Were Speeding-Related
    in 2013 573
Percent of Vehicles Involved in Fatal Crashes That Were
    Large Trucks in 2013 574
Lives Saved by Child Restraints, Seat Belts, Air Bags,
    and Motorcycle Helmets in 2013. 575
Safety Belt Usage Rate in 2014 576
Percent of Passenger Car Occupant Fatalities Where
    Victim Used a Seat Belt in 2013 577
Fatalities in Alcohol-Related Crashes in 2013 578

Fatalities in Alcohol-Related Crashes as a Percent of
    All Highway Fatalities in 2013 579
Percent of Fatal Traffic Accidents Involving Older
    Drivers in 2013. 580
Percent of Highway Fatalities Who Were Young Drivers
    in 2013 581
Licensed Drivers in 2013 582
Licensed Drivers per 1,000 Driving Age Population
    in 2013 583
Motor Vehicle Registrations in 2013 584
Motor Vehicles per Driving Age Population in 2013 585
Average Travel Time to Work in 2014 586
Percent of Commuters Who Drive to Work Alone
    in 2014 587
Percent of Commuters Who Drive to Work in Carpools
    in 2014 588
Percent of Commuters Who Travel to Work by Public
    Transportation in 2014. 589
Annual Miles per Vehicle in 2013. 590
Average Miles per Gallon in 2013 591
Airports in 2013 592
Inland Waterway Mileage in 2013 593
Percent of Recreational Boating Accidents Involving
    Alcohol in 2014 594
Railroad Accidents and Incidents in 2014 595
Railroad Mileage Operated in 2012 596

Federal Highway Funding in 2013

National Total = $37,798,000,000*

ALPHA ORDER

RANK	STATE	FUNDS	% of USA
16	Alabama	$732,263,000	1.9%
30	Alaska	483,955,000	1.3%
18	Arizona	706,182,000	1.9%
28	Arkansas	499,714,000	1.3%
1	California	3,542,468,000	9.4%
27	Colorado	516,113,000	1.4%
29	Connecticut	484,771,000	1.3%
48	Delaware	163,268,000	0.4%
3	Florida	1,828,689,000	4.8%
8	Georgia	1,246,239,000	3.3%
49	Hawaii	163,244,000	0.4%
41	Idaho	276,061,000	0.7%
6	Illinois	1,372,231,000	3.6%
13	Indiana	919,669,000	2.4%
32	Iowa	474,345,000	1.3%
36	Kansas	364,737,000	1.0%
22	Kentucky	641,292,000	1.7%
19	Louisiana	677,413,000	1.8%
47	Maine	178,166,000	0.5%
26	Maryland	580,007,000	1.5%
25	Massachusetts	586,192,000	1.6%
9	Michigan	1,016,208,000	2.7%
23	Minnesota	629,373,000	1.7%
33	Mississippi	466,804,000	1.2%
14	Missouri	913,720,000	2.4%
35	Montana	396,007,000	1.0%
40	Nebraska	278,977,000	0.7%
38	Nevada	350,473,000	0.9%
50	New Hampshire	159,470,000	0.4%
12	New Jersey	963,683,000	2.5%
37	New Mexico	354,440,000	0.9%
4	New York	1,620,088,000	4.3%
10	North Carolina	1,006,630,000	2.7%
44	North Dakota	239,622,000	0.6%
7	Ohio	1,293,739,000	3.4%
24	Oklahoma	612,128,000	1.6%
31	Oregon	482,423,000	1.3%
5	Pennsylvania	1,583,603,000	4.2%
45	Rhode Island	211,082,000	0.6%
21	South Carolina	646,307,000	1.7%
42	South Dakota	272,191,000	0.7%
15	Tennessee	815,605,000	2.2%
2	Texas	3,331,597,000	8.8%
39	Utah	335,149,000	0.9%
46	Vermont	195,887,000	0.5%
11	Virginia	982,180,000	2.6%
20	Washington	654,305,000	1.7%
34	West Virginia	421,798,000	1.1%
17	Wisconsin	726,227,000	1.9%
43	Wyoming	247,263,000	0.7%

RANK ORDER

RANK	STATE	FUNDS	% of USA
1	California	$3,542,468,000	9.4%
2	Texas	3,331,597,000	8.8%
3	Florida	1,828,689,000	4.8%
4	New York	1,620,088,000	4.3%
5	Pennsylvania	1,583,603,000	4.2%
6	Illinois	1,372,231,000	3.6%
7	Ohio	1,293,739,000	3.4%
8	Georgia	1,246,239,000	3.3%
9	Michigan	1,016,208,000	2.7%
10	North Carolina	1,006,630,000	2.7%
11	Virginia	982,180,000	2.6%
12	New Jersey	963,683,000	2.5%
13	Indiana	919,669,000	2.4%
14	Missouri	913,720,000	2.4%
15	Tennessee	815,605,000	2.2%
16	Alabama	732,263,000	1.9%
17	Wisconsin	726,227,000	1.9%
18	Arizona	706,182,000	1.9%
19	Louisiana	677,413,000	1.8%
20	Washington	654,305,000	1.7%
21	South Carolina	646,307,000	1.7%
22	Kentucky	641,292,000	1.7%
23	Minnesota	629,373,000	1.7%
24	Oklahoma	612,128,000	1.6%
25	Massachusetts	586,192,000	1.6%
26	Maryland	580,007,000	1.5%
27	Colorado	516,113,000	1.4%
28	Arkansas	499,714,000	1.3%
29	Connecticut	484,771,000	1.3%
30	Alaska	483,955,000	1.3%
31	Oregon	482,423,000	1.3%
32	Iowa	474,345,000	1.3%
33	Mississippi	466,804,000	1.2%
34	West Virginia	421,798,000	1.1%
35	Montana	396,007,000	1.0%
36	Kansas	364,737,000	1.0%
37	New Mexico	354,440,000	0.9%
38	Nevada	350,473,000	0.9%
39	Utah	335,149,000	0.9%
40	Nebraska	278,977,000	0.7%
41	Idaho	276,061,000	0.7%
42	South Dakota	272,191,000	0.7%
43	Wyoming	247,263,000	0.7%
44	North Dakota	239,622,000	0.6%
45	Rhode Island	211,082,000	0.6%
46	Vermont	195,887,000	0.5%
47	Maine	178,166,000	0.5%
48	Delaware	163,268,000	0.4%
49	Hawaii	163,244,000	0.4%
50	New Hampshire	159,470,000	0.4%
	District of Columbia	154,003,000	0.4%

Source: U.S. Department of Transportation, Federal Highway Administration
"Federal-aid Highway Fund Apportionments" (Table FA-4, http://www.fhwa.dot.gov/policyinformation/statistics/2013/)
*Fiscal Year 2013. National total does not include federal funds for U.S. territories.

Per Capita Federal Highway Funding in 2013

National Per Capita = $119*

ALPHA ORDER

RANK	STATE	PER CAPITA
16	Alabama	$152
1	Alaska	656
40	Arizona	107
12	Arkansas	169
48	California	92
44	Colorado	98
23	Connecticut	135
9	Delaware	176
47	Florida	93
30	Georgia	125
35	Hawaii	116
10	Idaho	171
41	Illinois	106
21	Indiana	140
15	Iowa	153
25	Kansas	126
19	Kentucky	146
19	Louisiana	146
24	Maine	134
44	Maryland	98
49	Massachusetts	87
42	Michigan	103
35	Minnesota	116
14	Mississippi	156
17	Missouri	151
3	Montana	390
18	Nebraska	149
25	Nevada	126
33	New Hampshire	121
39	New Jersey	108
11	New Mexico	170
50	New York	82
43	North Carolina	102
4	North Dakota	331
38	Ohio	112
13	Oklahoma	159
32	Oregon	123
31	Pennsylvania	124
8	Rhode Island	200
22	South Carolina	136
5	South Dakota	322
25	Tennessee	126
25	Texas	126
37	Utah	115
6	Vermont	312
34	Virginia	119
46	Washington	94
7	West Virginia	228
25	Wisconsin	126
2	Wyoming	424

RANK ORDER

RANK	STATE	PER CAPITA
1	Alaska	$656
2	Wyoming	424
3	Montana	390
4	North Dakota	331
5	South Dakota	322
6	Vermont	312
7	West Virginia	228
8	Rhode Island	200
9	Delaware	176
10	Idaho	171
11	New Mexico	170
12	Arkansas	169
13	Oklahoma	159
14	Mississippi	156
15	Iowa	153
16	Alabama	152
17	Missouri	151
18	Nebraska	149
19	Kentucky	146
19	Louisiana	146
21	Indiana	140
22	South Carolina	136
23	Connecticut	135
24	Maine	134
25	Kansas	126
25	Nevada	126
25	Tennessee	126
25	Texas	126
25	Wisconsin	126
30	Georgia	125
31	Pennsylvania	124
32	Oregon	123
33	New Hampshire	121
34	Virginia	119
35	Hawaii	116
35	Minnesota	116
37	Utah	115
38	Ohio	112
39	New Jersey	108
40	Arizona	107
41	Illinois	106
42	Michigan	103
43	North Carolina	102
44	Colorado	98
44	Maryland	98
46	Washington	94
47	Florida	93
48	California	92
49	Massachusetts	87
50	New York	82
	District of Columbia	237

Source: CQ Press using data from U.S. Department of Transportation, Federal Highway Administration
"Federal-aid Highway Fund Apportionments" (Table FA-4, http://www.fhwa.dot.gov/policyinformation/statistics/2013/)
*Fiscal Year 2013. National per capita does not include population or federal funds for U.S. territories.

Public Road and Street Mileage in 2013

National Total = 4,115,462 Miles*

ALPHA ORDER

RANK	STATE	MILES	% of USA
17	Alabama	101,837	2.5%
46	Alaska	15,680	0.4%
32	Arizona	66,441	1.6%
18	Arkansas	101,656	2.5%
2	California	174,989	4.3%
22	Colorado	88,565	2.2%
44	Connecticut	21,474	0.5%
48	Delaware	6,393	0.2%
10	Florida	122,088	3.0%
7	Georgia	128,620	3.1%
50	Hawaii	4,430	0.1%
35	Idaho	48,082	1.2%
3	Illinois	145,708	3.5%
19	Indiana	97,553	2.4%
14	Iowa	114,429	2.8%
4	Kansas	140,687	3.4%
26	Kentucky	79,598	1.9%
34	Louisiana	61,427	1.5%
43	Maine	22,882	0.6%
41	Maryland	32,422	0.8%
40	Massachusetts	36,370	0.9%
9	Michigan	122,141	3.0%
5	Minnesota	138,767	3.4%
27	Mississippi	75,116	1.8%
6	Missouri	131,900	3.2%
28	Montana	74,933	1.8%
21	Nebraska	93,770	2.3%
37	Nevada	40,139	1.0%
45	New Hampshire	16,098	0.4%
38	New Jersey	39,293	1.0%
31	New Mexico	70,772	1.7%
13	New York	114,728	2.8%
16	North Carolina	106,202	2.6%
23	North Dakota	87,078	2.1%
8	Ohio	123,297	3.0%
15	Oklahoma	112,940	2.7%
30	Oregon	71,228	1.7%
11	Pennsylvania	119,936	2.9%
49	Rhode Island	6,106	0.1%
33	South Carolina	66,232	1.6%
24	South Dakota	82,558	2.0%
20	Tennessee	95,536	2.3%
1	Texas	313,228	7.6%
36	Utah	46,254	1.1%
47	Vermont	14,266	0.3%
29	Virginia	74,748	1.8%
25	Washington	82,448	2.0%
39	West Virginia	38,750	0.9%
12	Wisconsin	115,145	2.8%
42	Wyoming	29,024	0.7%

RANK ORDER

RANK	STATE	MILES	% of USA
1	Texas	313,228	7.6%
2	California	174,989	4.3%
3	Illinois	145,708	3.5%
4	Kansas	140,687	3.4%
5	Minnesota	138,767	3.4%
6	Missouri	131,900	3.2%
7	Georgia	128,620	3.1%
8	Ohio	123,297	3.0%
9	Michigan	122,141	3.0%
10	Florida	122,088	3.0%
11	Pennsylvania	119,936	2.9%
12	Wisconsin	115,145	2.8%
13	New York	114,728	2.8%
14	Iowa	114,429	2.8%
15	Oklahoma	112,940	2.7%
16	North Carolina	106,202	2.6%
17	Alabama	101,837	2.5%
18	Arkansas	101,656	2.5%
19	Indiana	97,553	2.4%
20	Tennessee	95,536	2.3%
21	Nebraska	93,770	2.3%
22	Colorado	88,565	2.2%
23	North Dakota	87,078	2.1%
24	South Dakota	82,558	2.0%
25	Washington	82,448	2.0%
26	Kentucky	79,598	1.9%
27	Mississippi	75,116	1.8%
28	Montana	74,933	1.8%
29	Virginia	74,748	1.8%
30	Oregon	71,228	1.7%
31	New Mexico	70,772	1.7%
32	Arizona	66,441	1.6%
33	South Carolina	66,232	1.6%
34	Louisiana	61,427	1.5%
35	Idaho	48,082	1.2%
36	Utah	46,254	1.1%
37	Nevada	40,139	1.0%
38	New Jersey	39,293	1.0%
39	West Virginia	38,750	0.9%
40	Massachusetts	36,370	0.9%
41	Maryland	32,422	0.8%
42	Wyoming	29,024	0.7%
43	Maine	22,882	0.6%
44	Connecticut	21,474	0.5%
45	New Hampshire	16,098	0.4%
46	Alaska	15,680	0.4%
47	Vermont	14,266	0.3%
48	Delaware	6,393	0.2%
49	Rhode Island	6,106	0.1%
50	Hawaii	4,430	0.1%
	District of Columbia	1,501	0.0%

Source: U.S. Department of Transportation, Federal Highway Administration
"Highway Statistics 2013" (Table HM-20, http://www.fhwa.dot.gov/policyinformation/statistics/2013/)
*Does not include 16,691 miles of roads and streets in Puerto Rico.

Percent of Public Road and Street Mileage Federally Funded in 2013

National Percent = 24.5% of Public Road and Street Mileage*

ALPHA ORDER

RANK	STATE	PERCENT
18	Alabama	26.0
5	Alaska	30.0
43	Arizona	20.3
36	Arkansas	22.0
2	California	32.4
44	Colorado	19.8
9	Connecticut	28.7
27	Delaware	24.0
40	Florida	21.6
22	Georgia	24.7
1	Hawaii	35.1
32	Idaho	23.7
24	Illinois	24.5
26	Indiana	24.1
35	Iowa	22.9
20	Kansas	24.9
49	Kentucky	17.6
39	Louisiana	21.9
13	Maine	27.6
22	Maryland	24.7
4	Massachusetts	31.0
6	Michigan	29.8
30	Minnesota	23.9
7	Mississippi	29.3
34	Missouri	23.3
46	Montana	19.6
36	Nebraska	22.0
48	Nevada	17.8
36	New Hampshire	22.0
12	New Jersey	27.8
50	New Mexico	14.9
27	New York	24.0
42	North Carolina	20.8
41	North Dakota	21.2
31	Ohio	23.8
11	Oklahoma	28.2
19	Oregon	25.7
33	Pennsylvania	23.5
10	Rhode Island	28.6
3	South Carolina	31.7
27	South Dakota	24.0
47	Tennessee	18.8
16	Texas	27.0
45	Utah	19.7
14	Vermont	27.1
8	Virginia	29.2
24	Washington	24.5
16	West Virginia	27.0
21	Wisconsin	24.8
14	Wyoming	27.1

RANK ORDER

RANK	STATE	PERCENT
1	Hawaii	35.1
2	California	32.4
3	South Carolina	31.7
4	Massachusetts	31.0
5	Alaska	30.0
6	Michigan	29.8
7	Mississippi	29.3
8	Virginia	29.2
9	Connecticut	28.7
10	Rhode Island	28.6
11	Oklahoma	28.2
12	New Jersey	27.8
13	Maine	27.6
14	Vermont	27.1
14	Wyoming	27.1
16	Texas	27.0
16	West Virginia	27.0
18	Alabama	26.0
19	Oregon	25.7
20	Kansas	24.9
21	Wisconsin	24.8
22	Georgia	24.7
22	Maryland	24.7
24	Illinois	24.5
24	Washington	24.5
26	Indiana	24.1
27	Delaware	24.0
27	New York	24.0
27	South Dakota	24.0
30	Minnesota	23.9
31	Ohio	23.8
32	Idaho	23.7
33	Pennsylvania	23.5
34	Missouri	23.3
35	Iowa	22.9
36	Arkansas	22.0
36	Nebraska	22.0
36	New Hampshire	22.0
39	Louisiana	21.9
40	Florida	21.6
41	North Dakota	21.2
42	North Carolina	20.8
43	Arizona	20.3
44	Colorado	19.8
45	Utah	19.7
46	Montana	19.6
47	Tennessee	18.8
48	Nevada	17.8
49	Kentucky	17.6
50	New Mexico	14.9
	District of Columbia	30.2

Source: CQ Press using data from U.S. Department of Transportation, Federal Highway Administration "Highway Statistics 2013" (Table HM-15, http://www.fhwa.dot.gov/policyinformation/statistics/2013/)

*National percent does not include federally-funded highway miles in Puerto Rico.

Interstate Highway Mileage in 2013

National Total = 47,575 Miles*

ALPHA ORDER

RANK	STATE	MILES	% of USA
18	Alabama	1,002	2.1%
17	Alaska	1,081	2.3%
14	Arizona	1,168	2.5%
35	Arkansas	656	1.4%
2	California	2,451	5.2%
20	Colorado	952	2.0%
45	Connecticut	346	0.7%
50	Delaware	41	0.1%
7	Florida	1,495	3.1%
10	Georgia	1,247	2.6%
49	Hawaii	55	0.1%
36	Idaho	612	1.3%
3	Illinois	2,185	4.6%
13	Indiana	1,188	2.5%
29	Iowa	782	1.6%
26	Kansas	874	1.8%
28	Kentucky	801	1.7%
23	Louisiana	926	1.9%
44	Maine	367	0.8%
42	Maryland	481	1.0%
38	Massachusetts	575	1.2%
11	Michigan	1,244	2.6%
24	Minnesota	914	1.9%
33	Mississippi	700	1.5%
8	Missouri	1,379	2.9%
12	Montana	1,192	2.5%
41	Nebraska	482	1.0%
37	Nevada	596	1.3%
47	New Hampshire	225	0.5%
43	New Jersey	431	0.9%
19	New Mexico	1,000	2.1%
5	New York	1,724	3.6%
9	North Carolina	1,255	2.6%
39	North Dakota	571	1.2%
6	Ohio	1,574	3.3%
22	Oklahoma	933	2.0%
32	Oregon	730	1.5%
4	Pennsylvania	1,857	3.9%
48	Rhode Island	70	0.1%
27	South Carolina	851	1.8%
34	South Dakota	679	1.4%
16	Tennessee	1,104	2.3%
1	Texas	3,415	7.2%
21	Utah	937	2.0%
46	Vermont	320	0.7%
15	Virginia	1,119	2.4%
30	Washington	764	1.6%
40	West Virginia	555	1.2%
31	Wisconsin	743	1.6%
24	Wyoming	914	1.9%

RANK ORDER

RANK	STATE	MILES	% of USA
1	Texas	3,415	7.2%
2	California	2,451	5.2%
3	Illinois	2,185	4.6%
4	Pennsylvania	1,857	3.9%
5	New York	1,724	3.6%
6	Ohio	1,574	3.3%
7	Florida	1,495	3.1%
8	Missouri	1,379	2.9%
9	North Carolina	1,255	2.6%
10	Georgia	1,247	2.6%
11	Michigan	1,244	2.6%
12	Montana	1,192	2.5%
13	Indiana	1,188	2.5%
14	Arizona	1,168	2.5%
15	Virginia	1,119	2.4%
16	Tennessee	1,104	2.3%
17	Alaska	1,081	2.3%
18	Alabama	1,002	2.1%
19	New Mexico	1,000	2.1%
20	Colorado	952	2.0%
21	Utah	937	2.0%
22	Oklahoma	933	2.0%
23	Louisiana	926	1.9%
24	Minnesota	914	1.9%
24	Wyoming	914	1.9%
26	Kansas	874	1.8%
27	South Carolina	851	1.8%
28	Kentucky	801	1.7%
29	Iowa	782	1.6%
30	Washington	764	1.6%
31	Wisconsin	743	1.6%
32	Oregon	730	1.5%
33	Mississippi	700	1.5%
34	South Dakota	679	1.4%
35	Arkansas	656	1.4%
36	Idaho	612	1.3%
37	Nevada	596	1.3%
38	Massachusetts	575	1.2%
39	North Dakota	571	1.2%
40	West Virginia	555	1.2%
41	Nebraska	482	1.0%
42	Maryland	481	1.0%
43	New Jersey	431	0.9%
44	Maine	367	0.8%
45	Connecticut	346	0.7%
46	Vermont	320	0.7%
47	New Hampshire	225	0.5%
48	Rhode Island	70	0.1%
49	Hawaii	55	0.1%
50	Delaware	41	0.1%
	District of Columbia	12	0.0%

Source: CQ Press using data from U.S. Department of Transportation, Federal Highway Administration "Highway Statistics 2013" (Table HM-15, http://www.fhwa.dot.gov/policyinformation/statistics/2013/)

*Does not include 282 miles of highway in Puerto Rico that are part of the interstate system.

Rural Road and Street Mileage in 2013

National Total = 2,937,476 Rural Miles*

ALPHA ORDER

RANK	STATE	MILES	% of USA
16	Alabama	76,685	2.6%
42	Alaska	13,248	0.5%
34	Arizona	40,129	1.4%
10	Arkansas	85,243	2.9%
13	California	80,801	2.8%
22	Colorado	68,873	2.3%
45	Connecticut	6,261	0.2%
48	Delaware	3,359	0.1%
33	Florida	40,441	1.4%
15	Georgia	77,233	2.6%
49	Hawaii	1,864	0.1%
32	Idaho	42,534	1.4%
6	Illinois	98,094	3.3%
21	Indiana	69,465	2.4%
5	Iowa	101,775	3.5%
2	Kansas	127,048	4.3%
24	Kentucky	66,955	2.3%
31	Louisiana	44,018	1.5%
40	Maine	19,873	0.7%
41	Maryland	13,452	0.5%
46	Massachusetts	6,165	0.2%
12	Michigan	84,255	2.9%
3	Minnesota	116,560	4.0%
26	Mississippi	63,138	2.1%
4	Missouri	107,532	3.7%
19	Montana	70,787	2.4%
9	Nebraska	87,284	3.0%
38	Nevada	31,842	1.1%
44	New Hampshire	11,065	0.4%
47	New Jersey	5,887	0.2%
36	New Mexico	33,640	1.1%
25	New York	66,206	2.3%
23	North Carolina	68,727	2.3%
11	North Dakota	84,925	2.9%
17	Ohio	75,775	2.6%
7	Oklahoma	95,213	3.2%
27	Oregon	58,302	2.0%
18	Pennsylvania	73,870	2.5%
50	Rhode Island	1,364	0.0%
30	South Carolina	49,606	1.7%
14	South Dakota	79,312	2.7%
20	Tennessee	70,015	2.4%
1	Texas	212,918	7.2%
35	Utah	35,020	1.2%
43	Vermont	12,813	0.4%
29	Virginia	50,279	1.7%
28	Washington	56,906	1.9%
37	West Virginia	33,049	1.1%
8	Wisconsin	91,567	3.1%
39	Wyoming	26,104	0.9%

RANK ORDER

RANK	STATE	MILES	% of USA
1	Texas	212,918	7.2%
2	Kansas	127,048	4.3%
3	Minnesota	116,560	4.0%
4	Missouri	107,532	3.7%
5	Iowa	101,775	3.5%
6	Illinois	98,094	3.3%
7	Oklahoma	95,213	3.2%
8	Wisconsin	91,567	3.1%
9	Nebraska	87,284	3.0%
10	Arkansas	85,243	2.9%
11	North Dakota	84,925	2.9%
12	Michigan	84,255	2.9%
13	California	80,801	2.8%
14	South Dakota	79,312	2.7%
15	Georgia	77,233	2.6%
16	Alabama	76,685	2.6%
17	Ohio	75,775	2.6%
18	Pennsylvania	73,870	2.5%
19	Montana	70,787	2.4%
20	Tennessee	70,015	2.4%
21	Indiana	69,465	2.4%
22	Colorado	68,873	2.3%
23	North Carolina	68,727	2.3%
24	Kentucky	66,955	2.3%
25	New York	66,206	2.3%
26	Mississippi	63,138	2.1%
27	Oregon	58,302	2.0%
28	Washington	56,906	1.9%
29	Virginia	50,279	1.7%
30	South Carolina	49,606	1.7%
31	Louisiana	44,018	1.5%
32	Idaho	42,534	1.4%
33	Florida	40,441	1.4%
34	Arizona	40,129	1.4%
35	Utah	35,020	1.2%
36	New Mexico	33,640	1.1%
37	West Virginia	33,049	1.1%
38	Nevada	31,842	1.1%
39	Wyoming	26,104	0.9%
40	Maine	19,873	0.7%
41	Maryland	13,452	0.5%
42	Alaska	13,248	0.5%
43	Vermont	12,813	0.4%
44	New Hampshire	11,065	0.4%
45	Connecticut	6,261	0.2%
46	Massachusetts	6,165	0.2%
47	New Jersey	5,887	0.2%
48	Delaware	3,359	0.1%
49	Hawaii	1,864	0.1%
50	Rhode Island	1,364	0.0%
	District of Columbia	0	0.0%

Source: U.S. Department of Transportation, Federal Highway Administration
"Highway Statistics 2013" (Table HM-20, http://www.fhwa.dot.gov/policyinformation/statistics/2013/)
*Does not include 3,104 miles of rural roads and streets in Puerto Rico.

Urban Road and Street Mileage in 2013

National Total = 1,177,986 Urban Miles*

ALPHA ORDER

RANK	STATE	MILES	% of USA
18	Alabama	25,153	2.1%
48	Alaska	2,432	0.2%
15	Arizona	26,311	2.2%
28	Arkansas	16,413	1.4%
2	California	94,187	8.0%
23	Colorado	19,692	1.7%
29	Connecticut	15,213	1.3%
44	Delaware	3,034	0.3%
3	Florida	81,647	6.9%
4	Georgia	51,387	4.4%
47	Hawaii	2,566	0.2%
39	Idaho	5,548	0.5%
6	Illinois	47,614	4.0%
14	Indiana	28,088	2.4%
32	Iowa	12,654	1.1%
30	Kansas	13,639	1.2%
33	Kentucky	12,643	1.1%
26	Louisiana	17,409	1.5%
45	Maine	3,009	0.3%
24	Maryland	18,970	1.6%
13	Massachusetts	30,205	2.6%
9	Michigan	37,886	3.2%
22	Minnesota	22,208	1.9%
34	Mississippi	11,978	1.0%
20	Missouri	24,367	2.1%
42	Montana	4,146	0.4%
37	Nebraska	6,486	0.6%
36	Nevada	8,297	0.7%
40	New Hampshire	5,032	0.4%
12	New Jersey	33,406	2.8%
11	New Mexico	37,131	3.2%
5	New York	48,522	4.1%
10	North Carolina	37,475	3.2%
49	North Dakota	2,153	0.2%
7	Ohio	47,522	4.0%
25	Oklahoma	17,728	1.5%
31	Oregon	12,926	1.1%
8	Pennsylvania	46,066	3.9%
41	Rhode Island	4,742	0.4%
27	South Carolina	16,626	1.4%
43	South Dakota	3,246	0.3%
17	Tennessee	25,521	2.2%
1	Texas	100,310	8.5%
35	Utah	11,235	1.0%
50	Vermont	1,452	0.1%
19	Virginia	24,469	2.1%
16	Washington	25,542	2.2%
38	West Virginia	5,701	0.5%
21	Wisconsin	23,578	2.0%
46	Wyoming	2,920	0.2%

RANK ORDER

RANK	STATE	MILES	% of USA
1	Texas	100,310	8.5%
2	California	94,187	8.0%
3	Florida	81,647	6.9%
4	Georgia	51,387	4.4%
5	New York	48,522	4.1%
6	Illinois	47,614	4.0%
7	Ohio	47,522	4.0%
8	Pennsylvania	46,066	3.9%
9	Michigan	37,886	3.2%
10	North Carolina	37,475	3.2%
11	New Mexico	37,131	3.2%
12	New Jersey	33,406	2.8%
13	Massachusetts	30,205	2.6%
14	Indiana	28,088	2.4%
15	Arizona	26,311	2.2%
16	Washington	25,542	2.2%
17	Tennessee	25,521	2.2%
18	Alabama	25,153	2.1%
19	Virginia	24,469	2.1%
20	Missouri	24,367	2.1%
21	Wisconsin	23,578	2.0%
22	Minnesota	22,208	1.9%
23	Colorado	19,692	1.7%
24	Maryland	18,970	1.6%
25	Oklahoma	17,728	1.5%
26	Louisiana	17,409	1.5%
27	South Carolina	16,626	1.4%
28	Arkansas	16,413	1.4%
29	Connecticut	15,213	1.3%
30	Kansas	13,639	1.2%
31	Oregon	12,926	1.1%
32	Iowa	12,654	1.1%
33	Kentucky	12,643	1.1%
34	Mississippi	11,978	1.0%
35	Utah	11,235	1.0%
36	Nevada	8,297	0.7%
37	Nebraska	6,486	0.6%
38	West Virginia	5,701	0.5%
39	Idaho	5,548	0.5%
40	New Hampshire	5,032	0.4%
41	Rhode Island	4,742	0.4%
42	Montana	4,146	0.4%
43	South Dakota	3,246	0.3%
44	Delaware	3,034	0.3%
45	Maine	3,009	0.3%
46	Wyoming	2,920	0.2%
47	Hawaii	2,566	0.2%
48	Alaska	2,432	0.2%
49	North Dakota	2,153	0.2%
50	Vermont	1,452	0.1%
	District of Columbia	1,501	0.1%

Source: U.S. Department of Transportation, Federal Highway Administration
"Highway Statistics 2013" (Table HM-20, http://www.fhwa.dot.gov/policyinformation/statistics/2013/)
*Does not include 13,587 miles of urban roads and streets in Puerto Rico.

Percent of Roadways in Mediocre or Poor Condition in 2013

National Percent = 19.9%*

ALPHA ORDER

RANK	STATE	PERCENT
39	Alabama	10.7
14	Alaska	25.4
41	Arizona	9.7
29	Arkansas	16.3
3	California	38.4
21	Colorado	21.2
2	Connecticut	42.3
28	Delaware	16.4
47	Florida	7.0
34	Georgia	12.1
1	Hawaii	43.2
25	Idaho	18.0
22	Illinois	20.6
26	Indiana	17.4
30	Iowa	14.4
36	Kansas	11.0
44	Kentucky	9.0
16	Louisiana	24.9
11	Maine	27.0
19	Maryland	24.2
33	Massachusetts	12.8
6	Michigan	35.8
40	Minnesota	10.3
16	Mississippi	24.9
23	Missouri	20.2
43	Montana	9.1
49	Nebraska	4.7
50	Nevada	3.6
12	New Hampshire	26.1
5	New Jersey	37.8
15	New Mexico	25.3
10	New York	28.3
37	North Carolina	10.9
37	North Dakota	10.9
32	Ohio	13.5
8	Oklahoma	30.2
45	Oregon	8.8
20	Pennsylvania	22.8
4	Rhode Island	38.0
34	South Carolina	12.1
42	South Dakota	9.2
48	Tennessee	6.8
31	Texas	14.2
27	Utah	17.3
18	Vermont	24.4
24	Virginia	19.8
7	Washington	33.0
9	West Virginia	29.7
13	Wisconsin	25.6
46	Wyoming	8.3

RANK ORDER

RANK	STATE	PERCENT
1	Hawaii	43.2
2	Connecticut	42.3
3	California	38.4
4	Rhode Island	38.0
5	New Jersey	37.8
6	Michigan	35.8
7	Washington	33.0
8	Oklahoma	30.2
9	West Virginia	29.7
10	New York	28.3
11	Maine	27.0
12	New Hampshire	26.1
13	Wisconsin	25.6
14	Alaska	25.4
15	New Mexico	25.3
16	Louisiana	24.9
16	Mississippi	24.9
18	Vermont	24.4
19	Maryland	24.2
20	Pennsylvania	22.8
21	Colorado	21.2
22	Illinois	20.6
23	Missouri	20.2
24	Virginia	19.8
25	Idaho	18.0
26	Indiana	17.4
27	Utah	17.3
28	Delaware	16.4
29	Arkansas	16.3
30	Iowa	14.4
31	Texas	14.2
32	Ohio	13.5
33	Massachusetts	12.8
34	Georgia	12.1
34	South Carolina	12.1
36	Kansas	11.0
37	North Carolina	10.9
37	North Dakota	10.9
39	Alabama	10.7
40	Minnesota	10.3
41	Arizona	9.7
42	South Dakota	9.2
43	Montana	9.1
44	Kentucky	9.0
45	Oregon	8.8
46	Wyoming	8.3
47	Florida	7.0
48	Tennessee	6.8
49	Nebraska	4.7
50	Nevada	3.6

District of Columbia	94.5

Source: CQ Press using data from U.S. Department of Transportation, Bureau of Transportation Statistics
"State Transportation Statistics 2015" (Table 1-4, http://www.bts.gov/publications/state_transportation_statistics/)
*Does not include 14,062 miles for which the condition is not reported. Road condition ratings are derived from the International Roughness Index (IRI) and the Present Serviceability Rating (PSR). States are required to report to the Federal Highway Administration (FHWA) IRI data for the Interstate system, other principal arterials, rural minor arterials, and the National Highway System regardless of functional system.

Bridges in 2014

National Total = 608,445 Bridges*

ALPHA ORDER

RANK	STATE	BRIDGES	% of USA
15	Alabama	16,088	2.6%
47	Alaska	1,544	0.3%
30	Arizona	8,035	1.3%
23	Arkansas	12,806	2.1%
4	California	25,406	4.2%
27	Colorado	8,668	1.4%
39	Connecticut	4,218	0.7%
49	Delaware	865	0.1%
24	Florida	12,137	2.0%
17	Georgia	14,795	2.4%
48	Hawaii	1,137	0.2%
37	Idaho	4,431	0.7%
3	Illinois	26,588	4.4%
11	Indiana	19,019	3.1%
7	Iowa	24,300	4.0%
5	Kansas	25,085	4.1%
18	Kentucky	14,194	2.3%
21	Louisiana	12,982	2.1%
45	Maine	2,419	0.4%
34	Maryland	5,305	0.9%
36	Massachusetts	5,141	0.8%
25	Michigan	11,072	1.8%
22	Minnesota	12,961	2.1%
14	Mississippi	17,091	2.8%
6	Missouri	24,385	4.0%
35	Montana	5,251	0.9%
16	Nebraska	15,374	2.5%
46	Nevada	1,898	0.3%
44	New Hampshire	2,467	0.4%
32	New Jersey	6,609	1.1%
40	New Mexico	3,951	0.6%
13	New York	17,456	2.9%
12	North Carolina	18,117	3.0%
38	North Dakota	4,429	0.7%
2	Ohio	26,986	4.4%
8	Oklahoma	23,147	3.8%
29	Oregon	8,052	1.3%
9	Pennsylvania	22,691	3.7%
50	Rhode Island	766	0.1%
26	South Carolina	9,338	1.5%
33	South Dakota	5,872	1.0%
10	Tennessee	20,077	3.3%
1	Texas	52,937	8.7%
42	Utah	3,014	0.5%
43	Vermont	2,745	0.5%
20	Virginia	13,800	2.3%
28	Washington	8,120	1.3%
31	West Virginia	7,187	1.2%
19	Wisconsin	14,109	2.3%
41	Wyoming	3,127	0.5%

RANK ORDER

RANK	STATE	BRIDGES	% of USA
1	Texas	52,937	8.7%
2	Ohio	26,986	4.4%
3	Illinois	26,588	4.4%
4	California	25,406	4.2%
5	Kansas	25,085	4.1%
6	Missouri	24,385	4.0%
7	Iowa	24,300	4.0%
8	Oklahoma	23,147	3.8%
9	Pennsylvania	22,691	3.7%
10	Tennessee	20,077	3.3%
11	Indiana	19,019	3.1%
12	North Carolina	18,117	3.0%
13	New York	17,456	2.9%
14	Mississippi	17,091	2.8%
15	Alabama	16,088	2.6%
16	Nebraska	15,374	2.5%
17	Georgia	14,795	2.4%
18	Kentucky	14,194	2.3%
19	Wisconsin	14,109	2.3%
20	Virginia	13,800	2.3%
21	Louisiana	12,982	2.1%
22	Minnesota	12,961	2.1%
23	Arkansas	12,806	2.1%
24	Florida	12,137	2.0%
25	Michigan	11,072	1.8%
26	South Carolina	9,338	1.5%
27	Colorado	8,668	1.4%
28	Washington	8,120	1.3%
29	Oregon	8,052	1.3%
30	Arizona	8,035	1.3%
31	West Virginia	7,187	1.2%
32	New Jersey	6,609	1.1%
33	South Dakota	5,872	1.0%
34	Maryland	5,305	0.9%
35	Montana	5,251	0.9%
36	Massachusetts	5,141	0.8%
37	Idaho	4,431	0.7%
38	North Dakota	4,429	0.7%
39	Connecticut	4,218	0.7%
40	New Mexico	3,951	0.6%
41	Wyoming	3,127	0.5%
42	Utah	3,014	0.5%
43	Vermont	2,745	0.5%
44	New Hampshire	2,467	0.4%
45	Maine	2,419	0.4%
46	Nevada	1,898	0.3%
47	Alaska	1,544	0.3%
48	Hawaii	1,137	0.2%
49	Delaware	865	0.1%
50	Rhode Island	766	0.1%
	District of Columbia	253	0.0%

Source: U.S. Department of Transportation, Federal Highway Administration
"Deficient Bridges by State and Highway System, 2014" (http://www.fhwa.dot.gov/bridge/deficient.htm)
*As of December 2014. Includes federal-aid and nonfederal-aid system bridges. National total does not include 2,304 bridges in Puerto Rico.

Deficient Bridges in 2014

National Total = 144,621 Deficient Bridges*

ALPHA ORDER

RANK	STATE	BRIDGES	% of USA
19	Alabama	3,532	2.4%
48	Alaska	351	0.2%
37	Arizona	940	0.6%
21	Arkansas	2,855	2.0%
3	California	6,807	4.7%
34	Colorado	1,388	1.0%
31	Connecticut	1,457	1.0%
50	Delaware	171	0.1%
27	Florida	2,003	1.4%
24	Georgia	2,408	1.7%
45	Hawaii	483	0.3%
40	Idaho	877	0.6%
12	Illinois	4,187	2.9%
13	Indiana	4,103	2.8%
7	Iowa	6,205	4.3%
11	Kansas	4,229	2.9%
10	Kentucky	4,444	3.1%
15	Louisiana	3,781	2.6%
41	Maine	796	0.6%
32	Maryland	1,421	1.0%
22	Massachusetts	2,683	1.9%
20	Michigan	3,049	2.1%
35	Minnesota	1,193	0.8%
18	Mississippi	3,565	2.5%
6	Missouri	6,455	4.5%
38	Montana	914	0.6%
16	Nebraska	3,640	2.5%
49	Nevada	249	0.2%
42	New Hampshire	775	0.5%
25	New Jersey	2,343	1.6%
44	New Mexico	643	0.4%
4	New York	6,745	4.7%
9	North Carolina	5,334	3.7%
36	North Dakota	944	0.7%
5	Ohio	6,532	4.5%
8	Oklahoma	5,791	4.0%
30	Oregon	1,858	1.3%
2	Pennsylvania	9,438	6.5%
46	Rhode Island	429	0.3%
29	South Carolina	1,922	1.3%
33	South Dakota	1,412	1.0%
14	Tennessee	3,946	2.7%
1	Texas	9,999	6.9%
47	Utah	419	0.3%
39	Vermont	882	0.6%
17	Virginia	3,574	2.5%
26	Washington	2,093	1.4%
23	West Virginia	2,501	1.7%
28	Wisconsin	1,971	1.4%
43	Wyoming	706	0.5%

RANK ORDER

RANK	STATE	BRIDGES	% of USA
1	Texas	9,999	6.9%
2	Pennsylvania	9,438	6.5%
3	California	6,807	4.7%
4	New York	6,745	4.7%
5	Ohio	6,532	4.5%
6	Missouri	6,455	4.5%
7	Iowa	6,205	4.3%
8	Oklahoma	5,791	4.0%
9	North Carolina	5,334	3.7%
10	Kentucky	4,444	3.1%
11	Kansas	4,229	2.9%
12	Illinois	4,187	2.9%
13	Indiana	4,103	2.8%
14	Tennessee	3,946	2.7%
15	Louisiana	3,781	2.6%
16	Nebraska	3,640	2.5%
17	Virginia	3,574	2.5%
18	Mississippi	3,565	2.5%
19	Alabama	3,532	2.4%
20	Michigan	3,049	2.1%
21	Arkansas	2,855	2.0%
22	Massachusetts	2,683	1.9%
23	West Virginia	2,501	1.7%
24	Georgia	2,408	1.7%
25	New Jersey	2,343	1.6%
26	Washington	2,093	1.4%
27	Florida	2,003	1.4%
28	Wisconsin	1,971	1.4%
29	South Carolina	1,922	1.3%
30	Oregon	1,858	1.3%
31	Connecticut	1,457	1.0%
32	Maryland	1,421	1.0%
33	South Dakota	1,412	1.0%
34	Colorado	1,388	1.0%
35	Minnesota	1,193	0.8%
36	North Dakota	944	0.7%
37	Arizona	940	0.6%
38	Montana	914	0.6%
39	Vermont	882	0.6%
40	Idaho	877	0.6%
41	Maine	796	0.6%
42	New Hampshire	775	0.5%
43	Wyoming	706	0.5%
44	New Mexico	643	0.4%
45	Hawaii	483	0.3%
46	Rhode Island	429	0.3%
47	Utah	419	0.3%
48	Alaska	351	0.2%
49	Nevada	249	0.2%
50	Delaware	171	0.1%
	District of Columbia	178	0.1%

Source: U.S. Department of Transportation, Federal Highway Administration
"Deficient Bridges by State and Highway System, 2014" (http://www.fhwa.dot.gov/bridge/deficient.htm)
*As of December 2014. Includes federal-aid and nonfederal-aid system bridges. National total does not include 1,269 deficient bridges in Puerto Rico. Bridges classified as deficient are either functionally obsolete or structurally deficient and are not necessarily unsafe.

Deficient Bridges as a Percent of Total Bridges in 2014

National Percent = 23.8% of Bridges Are Deficient*

ALPHA ORDER

RANK	STATE	PERCENT
30	Alabama	22.0
27	Alaska	22.7
49	Arizona	11.7
29	Arkansas	22.3
16	California	26.8
44	Colorado	16.0
8	Connecticut	34.5
35	Delaware	19.8
41	Florida	16.5
42	Georgia	16.3
3	Hawaii	42.5
35	Idaho	19.8
45	Illinois	15.7
31	Indiana	21.6
21	Iowa	25.5
40	Kansas	16.9
12	Kentucky	31.3
14	Louisiana	29.1
9	Maine	32.9
16	Maryland	26.8
2	Massachusetts	52.2
15	Michigan	27.5
50	Minnesota	9.2
33	Mississippi	20.9
18	Missouri	26.5
39	Montana	17.4
25	Nebraska	23.7
48	Nevada	13.1
11	New Hampshire	31.4
6	New Jersey	35.5
42	New Mexico	16.3
5	New York	38.6
13	North Carolina	29.4
32	North Dakota	21.3
23	Ohio	24.2
22	Oklahoma	25.0
26	Oregon	23.1
4	Pennsylvania	41.6
1	Rhode Island	56.0
34	South Carolina	20.6
24	South Dakota	24.0
37	Tennessee	19.7
38	Texas	18.9
47	Utah	13.9
10	Vermont	32.1
19	Virginia	25.9
20	Washington	25.8
7	West Virginia	34.8
46	Wisconsin	14.0
28	Wyoming	22.6

RANK ORDER

RANK	STATE	PERCENT
1	Rhode Island	56.0
2	Massachusetts	52.2
3	Hawaii	42.5
4	Pennsylvania	41.6
5	New York	38.6
6	New Jersey	35.5
7	West Virginia	34.8
8	Connecticut	34.5
9	Maine	32.9
10	Vermont	32.1
11	New Hampshire	31.4
12	Kentucky	31.3
13	North Carolina	29.4
14	Louisiana	29.1
15	Michigan	27.5
16	California	26.8
16	Maryland	26.8
18	Missouri	26.5
19	Virginia	25.9
20	Washington	25.8
21	Iowa	25.5
22	Oklahoma	25.0
23	Ohio	24.2
24	South Dakota	24.0
25	Nebraska	23.7
26	Oregon	23.1
27	Alaska	22.7
28	Wyoming	22.6
29	Arkansas	22.3
30	Alabama	22.0
31	Indiana	21.6
32	North Dakota	21.3
33	Mississippi	20.9
34	South Carolina	20.6
35	Delaware	19.8
35	Idaho	19.8
37	Tennessee	19.7
38	Texas	18.9
39	Montana	17.4
40	Kansas	16.9
41	Florida	16.5
42	Georgia	16.3
42	New Mexico	16.3
44	Colorado	16.0
45	Illinois	15.7
46	Wisconsin	14.0
47	Utah	13.9
48	Nevada	13.1
49	Arizona	11.7
50	Minnesota	9.2
	District of Columbia	70.4

Source: CQ Press using data from U.S. Department of Transportation, Federal Highway Administration
"Deficient Bridges by State and Highway System, 2014" (http://www.fhwa.dot.gov/bridge/deficient.htm)
*As of December 2014. Includes federal-aid and nonfederal-aid system bridges. National percent does not include bridges in Puerto Rico. Bridges classified as deficient are either functionally obsolete or structurally deficient and are not necessarily unsafe.

Vehicle-Miles of Travel in 2013

National Total = 2,988,322,739,000 Miles

ALPHA ORDER

RANK	STATE	MILES	% of USA
16	Alabama	65,046,484,000	2.2%
50	Alaska	4,848,455,000	0.2%
17	Arizona	60,586,171,000	2.0%
30	Arkansas	33,493,274,000	1.1%
1	California	329,534,133,000	11.0%
27	Colorado	46,968,085,000	1.6%
32	Connecticut	30,941,186,000	1.0%
46	Delaware	9,307,810,000	0.3%
3	Florida	192,701,816,000	6.4%
6	Georgia	109,354,512,000	3.7%
44	Hawaii	10,099,351,000	0.3%
39	Idaho	15,980,106,000	0.5%
7	Illinois	105,297,104,000	3.5%
12	Indiana	78,311,294,000	2.6%
31	Iowa	31,641,002,000	1.1%
33	Kansas	30,208,284,000	1.0%
26	Kentucky	46,995,997,000	1.6%
25	Louisiana	47,757,967,000	1.6%
40	Maine	14,129,250,000	0.5%
21	Maryland	56,687,640,000	1.9%
22	Massachusetts	56,311,173,000	1.9%
10	Michigan	95,131,565,000	3.2%
20	Minnesota	56,974,045,000	1.9%
28	Mississippi	38,757,693,000	1.3%
15	Missouri	69,458,422,000	2.3%
42	Montana	12,032,727,000	0.4%
37	Nebraska	19,321,561,000	0.6%
36	Nevada	24,649,417,000	0.8%
41	New Hampshire	12,902,815,000	0.4%
13	New Jersey	74,529,792,000	2.5%
35	New Mexico	25,086,111,000	0.8%
4	New York	129,736,747,000	4.3%
8	North Carolina	105,212,558,000	3.5%
43	North Dakota	10,099,649,000	0.3%
5	Ohio	112,766,729,000	3.8%
24	Oklahoma	47,998,608,000	1.6%
29	Oregon	33,705,846,000	1.1%
9	Pennsylvania	98,627,976,000	3.3%
48	Rhode Island	7,775,125,000	0.3%
23	South Carolina	48,986,260,000	1.6%
47	South Dakota	9,121,797,000	0.3%
14	Tennessee	71,067,044,000	2.4%
2	Texas	244,524,883,000	8.2%
34	Utah	27,005,476,000	0.9%
49	Vermont	7,115,877,000	0.2%
11	Virginia	80,767,006,000	2.7%
19	Washington	57,211,211,000	1.9%
38	West Virginia	19,232,347,000	0.6%
18	Wisconsin	59,486,150,000	2.0%
45	Wyoming	9,308,940,000	0.3%

RANK ORDER

RANK	STATE	MILES	% of USA
1	California	329,534,133,000	11.0%
2	Texas	244,524,883,000	8.2%
3	Florida	192,701,816,000	6.4%
4	New York	129,736,747,000	4.3%
5	Ohio	112,766,729,000	3.8%
6	Georgia	109,354,512,000	3.7%
7	Illinois	105,297,104,000	3.5%
8	North Carolina	105,212,558,000	3.5%
9	Pennsylvania	98,627,976,000	3.3%
10	Michigan	95,131,565,000	3.2%
11	Virginia	80,767,006,000	2.7%
12	Indiana	78,311,294,000	2.6%
13	New Jersey	74,529,792,000	2.5%
14	Tennessee	71,067,044,000	2.4%
15	Missouri	69,458,422,000	2.3%
16	Alabama	65,046,484,000	2.2%
17	Arizona	60,586,171,000	2.0%
18	Wisconsin	59,486,150,000	2.0%
19	Washington	57,211,211,000	1.9%
20	Minnesota	56,974,045,000	1.9%
21	Maryland	56,687,640,000	1.9%
22	Massachusetts	56,311,173,000	1.9%
23	South Carolina	48,986,260,000	1.6%
24	Oklahoma	47,998,608,000	1.6%
25	Louisiana	47,757,967,000	1.6%
26	Kentucky	46,995,997,000	1.6%
27	Colorado	46,968,085,000	1.6%
28	Mississippi	38,757,693,000	1.3%
29	Oregon	33,705,846,000	1.1%
30	Arkansas	33,493,274,000	1.1%
31	Iowa	31,641,002,000	1.1%
32	Connecticut	30,941,186,000	1.0%
33	Kansas	30,208,284,000	1.0%
34	Utah	27,005,476,000	0.9%
35	New Mexico	25,086,111,000	0.8%
36	Nevada	24,649,417,000	0.8%
37	Nebraska	19,321,561,000	0.6%
38	West Virginia	19,232,347,000	0.6%
39	Idaho	15,980,106,000	0.5%
40	Maine	14,129,250,000	0.5%
41	New Hampshire	12,902,815,000	0.4%
42	Montana	12,032,727,000	0.4%
43	North Dakota	10,099,649,000	0.3%
44	Hawaii	10,099,351,000	0.3%
45	Wyoming	9,308,940,000	0.3%
46	Delaware	9,307,810,000	0.3%
47	South Dakota	9,121,797,000	0.3%
48	Rhode Island	7,775,125,000	0.3%
49	Vermont	7,115,877,000	0.2%
50	Alaska	4,848,455,000	0.2%
	District of Columbia	3,527,269,000	0.1%

Source: U.S. Department of Transportation, Federal Highway Administration
"Highway Statistics 2013" (Table VM-2, http://www.fhwa.dot.gov/policyinformation/statistics/2013/)

Highway Fatalities in 2013

National Total = 32,719 Fatalities

ALPHA ORDER

RANK	STATE	FATALITIES	% of USA
12	Alabama	852	2.6%
50	Alaska	51	0.2%
13	Arizona	849	2.6%
24	Arkansas	483	1.5%
2	California	3,000	9.2%
25	Colorado	481	1.5%
35	Connecticut	276	0.8%
46	Delaware	99	0.3%
3	Florida	2,407	7.4%
7	Georgia	1,179	3.6%
45	Hawaii	102	0.3%
39	Idaho	214	0.7%
9	Illinois	991	3.0%
14	Indiana	783	2.4%
32	Iowa	317	1.0%
29	Kansas	350	1.1%
20	Kentucky	638	1.9%
18	Louisiana	703	2.1%
42	Maine	145	0.4%
26	Maryland	465	1.4%
31	Massachusetts	326	1.0%
11	Michigan	947	2.9%
28	Minnesota	387	1.2%
21	Mississippi	613	1.9%
16	Missouri	757	2.3%
37	Montana	229	0.7%
40	Nebraska	211	0.6%
36	Nevada	262	0.8%
43	New Hampshire	135	0.4%
23	New Jersey	542	1.7%
34	New Mexico	310	0.9%
6	New York	1,199	3.7%
4	North Carolina	1,289	3.9%
41	North Dakota	148	0.5%
10	Ohio	989	3.0%
19	Oklahoma	678	2.1%
33	Oregon	313	1.0%
5	Pennsylvania	1,208	3.7%
49	Rhode Island	65	0.2%
15	South Carolina	767	2.3%
43	South Dakota	135	0.4%
8	Tennessee	995	3.0%
1	Texas	3,382	10.3%
38	Utah	220	0.7%
48	Vermont	69	0.2%
17	Virginia	740	2.3%
27	Washington	436	1.3%
30	West Virginia	332	1.0%
22	Wisconsin	543	1.7%
47	Wyoming	87	0.3%

RANK ORDER

RANK	STATE	FATALITIES	% of USA
1	Texas	3,382	10.3%
2	California	3,000	9.2%
3	Florida	2,407	7.4%
4	North Carolina	1,289	3.9%
5	Pennsylvania	1,208	3.7%
6	New York	1,199	3.7%
7	Georgia	1,179	3.6%
8	Tennessee	995	3.0%
9	Illinois	991	3.0%
10	Ohio	989	3.0%
11	Michigan	947	2.9%
12	Alabama	852	2.6%
13	Arizona	849	2.6%
14	Indiana	783	2.4%
15	South Carolina	767	2.3%
16	Missouri	757	2.3%
17	Virginia	740	2.3%
18	Louisiana	703	2.1%
19	Oklahoma	678	2.1%
20	Kentucky	638	1.9%
21	Mississippi	613	1.9%
22	Wisconsin	543	1.7%
23	New Jersey	542	1.7%
24	Arkansas	483	1.5%
25	Colorado	481	1.5%
26	Maryland	465	1.4%
27	Washington	436	1.3%
28	Minnesota	387	1.2%
29	Kansas	350	1.1%
30	West Virginia	332	1.0%
31	Massachusetts	326	1.0%
32	Iowa	317	1.0%
33	Oregon	313	1.0%
34	New Mexico	310	0.9%
35	Connecticut	276	0.8%
36	Nevada	262	0.8%
37	Montana	229	0.7%
38	Utah	220	0.7%
39	Idaho	214	0.7%
40	Nebraska	211	0.6%
41	North Dakota	148	0.5%
42	Maine	145	0.4%
43	New Hampshire	135	0.4%
43	South Dakota	135	0.4%
45	Hawaii	102	0.3%
46	Delaware	99	0.3%
47	Wyoming	87	0.3%
48	Vermont	69	0.2%
49	Rhode Island	65	0.2%
50	Alaska	51	0.2%
	District of Columbia	20	0.1%

Source: U.S. Department of Transportation, National Highway Traffic Safety Administration
"Traffic Safety Facts 2013" (http://www-nrd.nhtsa.dot.gov/cats/index.aspx)

Highway Fatality Rate in 2013

National Rate = 1.09 Fatalities per 100 Million Vehicle-Miles of Travel

ALPHA ORDER

RANK	STATE	RATE
15	Alabama	1.31
26	Alaska	1.05
10	Arizona	1.40
8	Arkansas	1.44
40	California	0.91
29	Colorado	1.02
42	Connecticut	0.89
24	Delaware	1.06
16	Florida	1.25
23	Georgia	1.08
30	Hawaii	1.01
14	Idaho	1.34
35	Illinois	0.94
31	Indiana	1.00
31	Iowa	1.00
20	Kansas	1.16
13	Kentucky	1.36
6	Louisiana	1.47
28	Maine	1.03
45	Maryland	0.82
50	Massachusetts	0.58
31	Michigan	1.00
49	Minnesota	0.68
3	Mississippi	1.58
21	Missouri	1.09
1	Montana	1.90
21	Nebraska	1.09
24	Nevada	1.06
26	New Hampshire	1.05
48	New Jersey	0.73
17	New Mexico	1.24
38	New York	0.92
18	North Carolina	1.23
6	North Dakota	1.47
43	Ohio	0.88
9	Oklahoma	1.41
36	Oregon	0.93
19	Pennsylvania	1.22
44	Rhode Island	0.84
4	South Carolina	1.57
5	South Dakota	1.48
10	Tennessee	1.40
12	Texas	1.38
46	Utah	0.81
34	Vermont	0.97
38	Virginia	0.92
47	Washington	0.76
2	West Virginia	1.73
40	Wisconsin	0.91
36	Wyoming	0.93

RANK ORDER

RANK	STATE	RATE
1	Montana	1.90
2	West Virginia	1.73
3	Mississippi	1.58
4	South Carolina	1.57
5	South Dakota	1.48
6	Louisiana	1.47
6	North Dakota	1.47
8	Arkansas	1.44
9	Oklahoma	1.41
10	Arizona	1.40
10	Tennessee	1.40
12	Texas	1.38
13	Kentucky	1.36
14	Idaho	1.34
15	Alabama	1.31
16	Florida	1.25
17	New Mexico	1.24
18	North Carolina	1.23
19	Pennsylvania	1.22
20	Kansas	1.16
21	Missouri	1.09
21	Nebraska	1.09
23	Georgia	1.08
24	Delaware	1.06
24	Nevada	1.06
26	Alaska	1.05
26	New Hampshire	1.05
28	Maine	1.03
29	Colorado	1.02
30	Hawaii	1.01
31	Indiana	1.00
31	Iowa	1.00
31	Michigan	1.00
34	Vermont	0.97
35	Illinois	0.94
36	Oregon	0.93
36	Wyoming	0.93
38	New York	0.92
38	Virginia	0.92
40	California	0.91
40	Wisconsin	0.91
42	Connecticut	0.89
43	Ohio	0.88
44	Rhode Island	0.84
45	Maryland	0.82
46	Utah	0.81
47	Washington	0.76
48	New Jersey	0.73
49	Minnesota	0.68
50	Massachusetts	0.58
	District of Columbia	0.57

Source: U.S. Department of Transportation, National Highway Traffic Safety Administration
"Traffic Safety Facts 2013" (http://www-nrd.nhtsa.dot.gov/cats/index.aspx)

Percent of Traffic Fatalities That Were Speeding-Related in 2013

National Percent = 29.4%*

ALPHA ORDER

RANK	STATE	PERCENT
28	Alabama	29.7
4	Alaska	43.1
16	Arizona	34.2
49	Arkansas	14.9
21	California	32.0
25	Colorado	31.2
40	Connecticut	23.2
13	Delaware	37.4
50	Florida	14.3
47	Georgia	16.7
4	Hawaii	43.1
39	Idaho	23.4
6	Illinois	42.5
30	Indiana	27.7
48	Iowa	16.1
24	Kansas	31.7
43	Kentucky	19.6
32	Louisiana	27.5
15	Maine	34.5
23	Maryland	31.8
33	Massachusetts	27.0
34	Michigan	26.9
42	Minnesota	21.7
45	Mississippi	18.4
8	Missouri	40.7
18	Montana	33.2
44	Nebraska	18.5
18	Nevada	33.2
1	New Hampshire	48.9
41	New Jersey	21.8
11	New Mexico	39.4
27	New York	29.9
21	North Carolina	32.0
9	North Dakota	39.9
31	Ohio	27.6
37	Oklahoma	25.7
26	Oregon	30.4
3	Pennsylvania	45.5
35	Rhode Island	26.2
9	South Carolina	39.9
29	South Dakota	28.1
38	Tennessee	23.7
14	Texas	34.7
17	Utah	34.1
36	Vermont	26.1
46	Virginia	17.8
7	Washington	41.5
12	West Virginia	39.2
20	Wisconsin	32.8
2	Wyoming	46.0

RANK ORDER

RANK	STATE	PERCENT
1	New Hampshire	48.9
2	Wyoming	46.0
3	Pennsylvania	45.5
4	Alaska	43.1
4	Hawaii	43.1
6	Illinois	42.5
7	Washington	41.5
8	Missouri	40.7
9	North Dakota	39.9
9	South Carolina	39.9
11	New Mexico	39.4
12	West Virginia	39.2
13	Delaware	37.4
14	Texas	34.7
15	Maine	34.5
16	Arizona	34.2
17	Utah	34.1
18	Montana	33.2
18	Nevada	33.2
20	Wisconsin	32.8
21	California	32.0
21	North Carolina	32.0
23	Maryland	31.8
24	Kansas	31.7
25	Colorado	31.2
26	Oregon	30.4
27	New York	29.9
28	Alabama	29.7
29	South Dakota	28.1
30	Indiana	27.7
31	Ohio	27.6
32	Louisiana	27.5
33	Massachusetts	27.0
34	Michigan	26.9
35	Rhode Island	26.2
36	Vermont	26.1
37	Oklahoma	25.7
38	Tennessee	23.7
39	Idaho	23.4
40	Connecticut	23.2
41	New Jersey	21.8
42	Minnesota	21.7
43	Kentucky	19.6
44	Nebraska	18.5
45	Mississippi	18.4
46	Virginia	17.8
47	Georgia	16.7
48	Iowa	16.1
49	Arkansas	14.9
50	Florida	14.3
	District of Columbia	45.0

Source: CQ Press using data from U.S. Department of Transportation, National Highway Traffic Safety Administration "Traffic Safety Facts 2013" (http://www-nrd.nhtsa.dot.gov/cats/index.aspx)

*A speeding-related crash is if the driver was charged with a speeding-related offense or if an officer indicated that racing, driving too fast for conditions, or exceeding the posted speed limit was a contributing factor in the crash.

Percent of Vehicles Involved in Fatal Crashes That Were Large Trucks in 2013

National Percent = 8.7%*

ALPHA ORDER

RANK	STATE	PERCENT
20	Alabama	9.6
44	Alaska	6.0
47	Arizona	5.9
6	Arkansas	13.5
44	California	6.0
26	Colorado	8.1
50	Connecticut	5.1
38	Delaware	6.7
49	Florida	5.6
20	Georgia	9.6
48	Hawaii	5.7
9	Idaho	11.6
15	Illinois	10.1
13	Indiana	10.5
5	Iowa	13.6
4	Kansas	14.0
26	Kentucky	8.1
31	Louisiana	7.6
24	Maine	8.5
22	Maryland	9.4
37	Massachusetts	7.0
39	Michigan	6.5
7	Minnesota	13.1
32	Mississippi	7.3
30	Missouri	7.7
35	Montana	7.1
19	Nebraska	9.7
39	Nevada	6.5
39	New Hampshire	6.5
24	New Jersey	8.5
3	New Mexico	14.1
34	New York	7.2
35	North Carolina	7.1
1	North Dakota	29.8
14	Ohio	10.2
8	Oklahoma	11.9
26	Oregon	8.1
16	Pennsylvania	10.0
44	Rhode Island	6.0
39	South Carolina	6.5
18	South Dakota	9.8
23	Tennessee	8.6
11	Texas	10.6
32	Utah	7.3
29	Vermont	7.9
16	Virginia	10.0
43	Washington	6.4
10	West Virginia	11.1
11	Wisconsin	10.6
2	Wyoming	23.6

RANK ORDER

RANK	STATE	PERCENT
1	North Dakota	29.8
2	Wyoming	23.6
3	New Mexico	14.1
4	Kansas	14.0
5	Iowa	13.6
6	Arkansas	13.5
7	Minnesota	13.1
8	Oklahoma	11.9
9	Idaho	11.6
10	West Virginia	11.1
11	Texas	10.6
11	Wisconsin	10.6
13	Indiana	10.5
14	Ohio	10.2
15	Illinois	10.1
16	Pennsylvania	10.0
16	Virginia	10.0
18	South Dakota	9.8
19	Nebraska	9.7
20	Alabama	9.6
20	Georgia	9.6
22	Maryland	9.4
23	Tennessee	8.6
24	Maine	8.5
24	New Jersey	8.5
26	Colorado	8.1
26	Kentucky	8.1
26	Oregon	8.1
29	Vermont	7.9
30	Missouri	7.7
31	Louisiana	7.6
32	Mississippi	7.3
32	Utah	7.3
34	New York	7.2
35	Montana	7.1
35	North Carolina	7.1
37	Massachusetts	7.0
38	Delaware	6.7
39	Michigan	6.5
39	Nevada	6.5
39	New Hampshire	6.5
39	South Carolina	6.5
43	Washington	6.4
44	Alaska	6.0
44	California	6.0
44	Rhode Island	6.0
47	Arizona	5.9
48	Hawaii	5.7
49	Florida	5.6
50	Connecticut	5.1
	District of Columbia	9.7

Source: U.S. Department of Transportation, National Highway Traffic Safety Administration
"Traffic Safety Facts: Large Trucks" (http://www-nrd.nhtsa.dot.gov/cats/Index.aspx)
*Large trucks are those with gross vehicle weight greater than 10,000 pounds. In 2013, 3,906 large trucks were involved in fatal crashes.

Lives Saved by Child Restraints, Seat Belts, Air Bags, and Motorcycle Helmets in 2013
National Total = 16,865 Lives

ALPHA ORDER

RANK	STATE	LIVES	% of USA
12	Alabama	471	2.8%
50	Alaska	23	0.1%
20	Arizona	330	2.0%
26	Arkansas	247	1.5%
2	California	1,588	9.4%
28	Colorado	222	1.3%
33	Connecticut	146	0.9%
45	Delaware	45	0.3%
3	Florida	1,043	6.2%
5	Georgia	627	3.7%
48	Hawaii	33	0.2%
38	Idaho	90	0.5%
10	Illinois	483	2.9%
13	Indiana	459	2.7%
30	Iowa	179	1.1%
31	Kansas	176	1.0%
19	Kentucky	333	2.0%
16	Louisiana	360	2.1%
41	Maine	88	0.5%
25	Maryland	248	1.5%
34	Massachusetts	141	0.8%
7	Michigan	577	3.4%
27	Minnesota	238	1.4%
18	Mississippi	342	2.0%
17	Missouri	358	2.1%
38	Montana	90	0.5%
38	Nebraska	90	0.5%
36	Nevada	119	0.7%
42	New Hampshire	62	0.4%
22	New Jersey	280	1.7%
35	New Mexico	127	0.8%
6	New York	609	3.6%
4	North Carolina	779	4.6%
43	North Dakota	61	0.4%
11	Ohio	479	2.8%
21	Oklahoma	322	1.9%
29	Oregon	217	1.3%
9	Pennsylvania	532	3.2%
49	Rhode Island	26	0.2%
15	South Carolina	370	2.2%
44	South Dakota	60	0.4%
8	Tennessee	546	3.2%
1	Texas	1,938	11.5%
37	Utah	116	0.7%
46	Vermont	42	0.2%
14	Virginia	394	2.3%
23	Washington	274	1.6%
32	West Virginia	171	1.0%
24	Wisconsin	262	1.6%
47	Wyoming	40	0.2%

RANK ORDER

RANK	STATE	LIVES	% of USA
1	Texas	1,938	11.5%
2	California	1,588	9.4%
3	Florida	1,043	6.2%
4	North Carolina	779	4.6%
5	Georgia	627	3.7%
6	New York	609	3.6%
7	Michigan	577	3.4%
8	Tennessee	546	3.2%
9	Pennsylvania	532	3.2%
10	Illinois	483	2.9%
11	Ohio	479	2.8%
12	Alabama	471	2.8%
13	Indiana	459	2.7%
14	Virginia	394	2.3%
15	South Carolina	370	2.2%
16	Louisiana	360	2.1%
17	Missouri	358	2.1%
18	Mississippi	342	2.0%
19	Kentucky	333	2.0%
20	Arizona	330	2.0%
21	Oklahoma	322	1.9%
22	New Jersey	280	1.7%
23	Washington	274	1.6%
24	Wisconsin	262	1.6%
25	Maryland	248	1.5%
26	Arkansas	247	1.5%
27	Minnesota	238	1.4%
28	Colorado	222	1.3%
29	Oregon	217	1.3%
30	Iowa	179	1.1%
31	Kansas	176	1.0%
32	West Virginia	171	1.0%
33	Connecticut	146	0.9%
34	Massachusetts	141	0.8%
35	New Mexico	127	0.8%
36	Nevada	119	0.7%
37	Utah	116	0.7%
38	Idaho	90	0.5%
38	Montana	90	0.5%
38	Nebraska	90	0.5%
41	Maine	88	0.5%
42	New Hampshire	62	0.4%
43	North Dakota	61	0.4%
44	South Dakota	60	0.4%
45	Delaware	45	0.3%
46	Vermont	42	0.2%
47	Wyoming	40	0.2%
48	Hawaii	33	0.2%
49	Rhode Island	26	0.2%
50	Alaska	23	0.1%
	District of Columbia	10	0.1%

Source: CQ Press using data from U.S. Department of Transportation, National Highway Traffic Safety Administration "Traffic Safety Facts: Lives Saved in 2013" (http://www-nrd.nhtsa.dot.gov/cats/Index.aspx)

Safety Belt Usage Rate in 2014

National Rate = 87.0% Use Safety Belts

ALPHA ORDER				RANK ORDER		
RANK	STATE	PERCENT		RANK	STATE	PERCENT
4	Alabama	95.7		1	Oregon	97.8
21	Alaska	88.4		2	Georgia	97.3
26	Arizona	87.2		3	California	97.1
47	Arkansas	74.4		4	Alabama	95.7
3	California	97.1		5	Minnesota	94.7
38	Colorado	82.4		6	Washington	94.5
30	Connecticut	85.1		7	Illinois	94.1
14	Delaware	91.9		8	Nevada	94.0
20	Florida	88.8		9	Hawaii	93.5
2	Georgia	97.3		10	Michigan	93.3
9	Hawaii	93.5		11	Iowa	92.8
40	Idaho	80.2		12	Maryland	92.1
7	Illinois	94.1		12	New Mexico	92.1
18	Indiana	90.2		14	Delaware	91.9
11	Iowa	92.8		15	Texas	90.7
29	Kansas	85.7		16	New York	90.6
28	Kentucky	86.1		16	North Carolina	90.6
34	Louisiana	84.1		18	Indiana	90.2
31	Maine	85.0		19	South Carolina	90.0
12	Maryland	92.1		20	Florida	88.8
46	Massachusetts	76.6		21	Alaska	88.4
10	Michigan	93.3		22	West Virginia	87.8
5	Minnesota	94.7		23	Tennessee	87.7
44	Mississippi	78.3		24	New Jersey	87.6
43	Missouri	78.8		25	Rhode Island	87.4
48	Montana	74.0		26	Arizona	87.2
42	Nebraska	79.0		27	Oklahoma	86.3
8	Nevada	94.0		28	Kentucky	86.1
49	New Hampshire	70.4		29	Kansas	85.7
24	New Jersey	87.6		30	Connecticut	85.1
12	New Mexico	92.1		31	Maine	85.0
16	New York	90.6		31	Ohio	85.0
16	North Carolina	90.6		33	Wisconsin	84.7
39	North Dakota	81.0		34	Louisiana	84.1
31	Ohio	85.0		34	Vermont	84.1
27	Oklahoma	86.3		36	Pennsylvania	83.6
1	Oregon	97.8		37	Utah	83.4
36	Pennsylvania	83.6		38	Colorado	82.4
25	Rhode Island	87.4		39	North Dakota	81.0
19	South Carolina	90.0		40	Idaho	80.2
50	South Dakota	68.9		41	Wyoming	79.2
23	Tennessee	87.7		42	Nebraska	79.0
15	Texas	90.7		43	Missouri	78.8
37	Utah	83.4		44	Mississippi	78.3
34	Vermont	84.1		45	Virginia	77.3
45	Virginia	77.3		46	Massachusetts	76.6
6	Washington	94.5		47	Arkansas	74.4
22	West Virginia	87.8		48	Montana	74.0
33	Wisconsin	84.7		49	New Hampshire	70.4
41	Wyoming	79.2		50	South Dakota	68.9
					District of Columbia	93.2

Source: U.S. Department of Transportation, National Highway Traffic Safety Administration
"Traffic Safety Facts: Seat Belt Use in 2014" (http://www-nrd.nhtsa.dot.gov/cats/Index.aspx)

Percent of Passenger Car Occupant Fatalities Where Victim Used a Seat Belt in 2013
National Percent = 46% of Passenger Car Occupant Fatalities*

ALPHA ORDER

RANK	STATE	PERCENT
29	Alabama	41
17	Alaska	48
35	Arizona	39
34	Arkansas	40
2	California	61
35	Colorado	39
24	Connecticut	44
10	Delaware	52
15	Florida	49
26	Georgia	43
41	Hawaii	36
43	Idaho	34
22	Illinois	45
12	Indiana	51
19	Iowa	46
35	Kansas	39
18	Kentucky	47
29	Louisiana	41
15	Maine	49
5	Maryland	55
48	Massachusetts	29
5	Michigan	55
3	Minnesota	58
29	Mississippi	41
43	Missouri	34
46	Montana	31
49	Nebraska	26
19	Nevada	46
38	New Hampshire	38
9	New Jersey	53
38	New Mexico	38
5	New York	55
10	North Carolina	52
50	North Dakota	25
29	Ohio	41
27	Oklahoma	42
1	Oregon	64
42	Pennsylvania	35
19	Rhode Island	46
24	South Carolina	44
45	South Dakota	32
29	Tennessee	41
13	Texas	50
13	Utah	50
5	Vermont	55
22	Virginia	45
4	Washington	57
38	West Virginia	38
27	Wisconsin	42
47	Wyoming	30

RANK ORDER

RANK	STATE	PERCENT
1	Oregon	64
2	California	61
3	Minnesota	58
4	Washington	57
5	Maryland	55
5	Michigan	55
5	New York	55
5	Vermont	55
9	New Jersey	53
10	Delaware	52
10	North Carolina	52
12	Indiana	51
13	Texas	50
13	Utah	50
15	Florida	49
15	Maine	49
17	Alaska	48
18	Kentucky	47
19	Iowa	46
19	Nevada	46
19	Rhode Island	46
22	Illinois	45
22	Virginia	45
24	Connecticut	44
24	South Carolina	44
26	Georgia	43
27	Oklahoma	42
27	Wisconsin	42
29	Alabama	41
29	Louisiana	41
29	Mississippi	41
29	Ohio	41
29	Tennessee	41
34	Arkansas	40
35	Arizona	39
35	Colorado	39
35	Kansas	39
38	New Hampshire	38
38	New Mexico	38
38	West Virginia	38
41	Hawaii	36
42	Pennsylvania	35
43	Idaho	34
43	Missouri	34
45	South Dakota	32
46	Montana	31
47	Wyoming	30
48	Massachusetts	29
49	Nebraska	26
50	North Dakota	25
	District of Columbia	100

Source: U.S. Department of Transportation, National Highway Traffic Safety Administration "Traffic Safety Facts: Occupant Protection" (http://www-nrd.nhtsa.dot.gov/cats/Index.aspx)
*Only those fatalities where seat belts are known to have been used are counted.

Fatalities in Alcohol-Related Crashes in 2013

National Total = 11,896 Fatalities*

ALPHA ORDER

RANK	STATE	FATALITIES	% of USA
13	Alabama	308	2.6%
50	Alaska	16	0.1%
17	Arizona	262	2.2%
27	Arkansas	156	1.3%
2	California	1,025	8.6%
25	Colorado	170	1.4%
29	Connecticut	132	1.1%
46	Delaware	43	0.4%
3	Florida	790	6.6%
9	Georgia	349	2.9%
44	Hawaii	45	0.4%
38	Idaho	73	0.6%
7	Illinois	389	3.3%
18	Indiana	241	2.0%
34	Iowa	113	0.9%
31	Kansas	119	1.0%
22	Kentucky	193	1.6%
16	Louisiana	272	2.3%
41	Maine	54	0.5%
24	Maryland	175	1.5%
28	Massachusetts	142	1.2%
12	Michigan	309	2.6%
33	Minnesota	115	1.0%
19	Mississippi	240	2.0%
15	Missouri	287	2.4%
36	Montana	104	0.9%
40	Nebraska	70	0.6%
37	Nevada	94	0.8%
42	New Hampshire	52	0.4%
23	New Jersey	184	1.5%
32	New Mexico	118	1.0%
4	New York	442	3.7%
6	North Carolina	428	3.6%
38	North Dakota	73	0.6%
11	Ohio	322	2.7%
21	Oklahoma	206	1.7%
30	Oregon	122	1.0%
5	Pennsylvania	431	3.6%
48	Rhode Island	28	0.2%
8	South Carolina	384	3.2%
43	South Dakota	48	0.4%
10	Tennessee	327	2.7%
1	Texas	1,550	13.0%
45	Utah	44	0.4%
49	Vermont	24	0.2%
14	Virginia	302	2.5%
26	Washington	169	1.4%
35	West Virginia	112	0.9%
20	Wisconsin	210	1.8%
47	Wyoming	29	0.2%

RANK ORDER

RANK	STATE	FATALITIES	% of USA
1	Texas	1,550	13.0%
2	California	1,025	8.6%
3	Florida	790	6.6%
4	New York	442	3.7%
5	Pennsylvania	431	3.6%
6	North Carolina	428	3.6%
7	Illinois	389	3.3%
8	South Carolina	384	3.2%
9	Georgia	349	2.9%
10	Tennessee	327	2.7%
11	Ohio	322	2.7%
12	Michigan	309	2.6%
13	Alabama	308	2.6%
14	Virginia	302	2.5%
15	Missouri	287	2.4%
16	Louisiana	272	2.3%
17	Arizona	262	2.2%
18	Indiana	241	2.0%
19	Mississippi	240	2.0%
20	Wisconsin	210	1.8%
21	Oklahoma	206	1.7%
22	Kentucky	193	1.6%
23	New Jersey	184	1.5%
24	Maryland	175	1.5%
25	Colorado	170	1.4%
26	Washington	169	1.4%
27	Arkansas	156	1.3%
28	Massachusetts	142	1.2%
29	Connecticut	132	1.1%
30	Oregon	122	1.0%
31	Kansas	119	1.0%
32	New Mexico	118	1.0%
33	Minnesota	115	1.0%
34	Iowa	113	0.9%
35	West Virginia	112	0.9%
36	Montana	104	0.9%
37	Nevada	94	0.8%
38	Idaho	73	0.6%
38	North Dakota	73	0.6%
40	Nebraska	70	0.6%
41	Maine	54	0.5%
42	New Hampshire	52	0.4%
43	South Dakota	48	0.4%
44	Hawaii	45	0.4%
45	Utah	44	0.4%
46	Delaware	43	0.4%
47	Wyoming	29	0.2%
48	Rhode Island	28	0.2%
49	Vermont	24	0.2%
50	Alaska	16	0.1%
	District of Columbia	7	0.1%

Source: U.S. Department of Transportation, National Highway Traffic Safety Administration
"Traffic Safety Facts: Alcohol-Impaired Driving" (http://www-nrd.nhtsa.dot.gov/cats/Index.aspx)
*Drivers with Blood Alcohol Content (BAC) of .01 or more. "Legally Drunk" BAC differs from state to state but is often .08 or higher.

Fatalities in Alcohol-Related Crashes as a Percent of All Highway Fatalities in 2013
National Percent = 36% of Highway Fatalities*

ALPHA ORDER

RANK	STATE	PERCENT
23	Alabama	36
42	Alaska	32
44	Arizona	31
42	Arkansas	32
29	California	34
28	Colorado	35
3	Connecticut	48
8	Delaware	43
35	Florida	33
46	Georgia	30
6	Hawaii	44
29	Idaho	34
11	Illinois	39
44	Indiana	31
23	Iowa	36
29	Kansas	34
46	Kentucky	30
11	Louisiana	39
21	Maine	37
18	Maryland	38
6	Massachusetts	44
35	Michigan	33
46	Minnesota	30
11	Mississippi	39
18	Missouri	38
5	Montana	45
35	Nebraska	33
23	Nevada	36
11	New Hampshire	39
29	New Jersey	34
18	New Mexico	38
21	New York	37
35	North Carolina	33
2	North Dakota	49
35	Ohio	33
46	Oklahoma	30
11	Oregon	39
23	Pennsylvania	36
8	Rhode Island	43
1	South Carolina	50
23	South Dakota	36
35	Tennessee	33
4	Texas	46
50	Utah	20
29	Vermont	34
10	Virginia	41
11	Washington	39
29	West Virginia	34
11	Wisconsin	39
35	Wyoming	33

RANK ORDER

RANK	STATE	PERCENT
1	South Carolina	50
2	North Dakota	49
3	Connecticut	48
4	Texas	46
5	Montana	45
6	Hawaii	44
6	Massachusetts	44
8	Delaware	43
8	Rhode Island	43
10	Virginia	41
11	Illinois	39
11	Louisiana	39
11	Mississippi	39
11	New Hampshire	39
11	Oregon	39
11	Washington	39
11	Wisconsin	39
18	Maryland	38
18	Missouri	38
18	New Mexico	38
21	Maine	37
21	New York	37
23	Alabama	36
23	Iowa	36
23	Nevada	36
23	Pennsylvania	36
23	South Dakota	36
28	Colorado	35
29	California	34
29	Idaho	34
29	Kansas	34
29	New Jersey	34
29	Vermont	34
29	West Virginia	34
35	Florida	33
35	Michigan	33
35	Nebraska	33
35	North Carolina	33
35	Ohio	33
35	Tennessee	33
35	Wyoming	33
42	Alaska	32
42	Arkansas	32
44	Arizona	31
44	Indiana	31
46	Georgia	30
46	Kentucky	30
46	Minnesota	30
46	Oklahoma	30
50	Utah	20
	District of Columbia	33

Source: U.S. Department of Transportation, National Highway Traffic Safety Administration
"Traffic Safety Facts: Alcohol-Impaired Driving" (http://www-nrd.nhtsa.dot.gov/cats/Index.aspx)
*Drivers with Blood Alcohol Content (BAC) of .01 or more. "Legally Drunk" BAC differs from state to state but is often .08 or higher.

Percent of Fatal Traffic Accidents Involving Older Drivers in 2013

National Percent = 13.3%*

ALPHA ORDER

RANK	STATE	PERCENT
40	Alabama	11.6
28	Alaska	13.6
22	Arizona	14.7
27	Arkansas	14.1
46	California	10.1
18	Colorado	15.0
41	Connecticut	11.4
43	Delaware	10.7
24	Florida	14.4
35	Georgia	12.2
49	Hawaii	8.9
29	Idaho	13.2
29	Illinois	13.2
31	Indiana	12.9
7	Iowa	17.8
10	Kansas	16.8
21	Kentucky	14.8
48	Louisiana	9.0
1	Maine	20.6
45	Maryland	10.2
11	Massachusetts	16.7
9	Michigan	17.0
14	Minnesota	15.6
42	Mississippi	11.3
17	Missouri	15.1
6	Montana	18.0
33	Nebraska	12.4
36	Nevada	12.1
26	New Hampshire	14.3
2	New Jersey	19.8
36	New Mexico	12.1
14	New York	15.6
23	North Carolina	14.5
50	North Dakota	5.6
32	Ohio	12.7
39	Oklahoma	11.8
16	Oregon	15.5
13	Pennsylvania	16.1
3	Rhode Island	19.3
38	South Carolina	11.9
5	South Dakota	18.1
18	Tennessee	15.0
47	Texas	9.7
8	Utah	17.4
4	Vermont	19.1
12	Virginia	16.3
34	Washington	12.3
24	West Virginia	14.4
20	Wisconsin	14.9
44	Wyoming	10.4

RANK ORDER

RANK	STATE	PERCENT
1	Maine	20.6
2	New Jersey	19.8
3	Rhode Island	19.3
4	Vermont	19.1
5	South Dakota	18.1
6	Montana	18.0
7	Iowa	17.8
8	Utah	17.4
9	Michigan	17.0
10	Kansas	16.8
11	Massachusetts	16.7
12	Virginia	16.3
13	Pennsylvania	16.1
14	Minnesota	15.6
14	New York	15.6
16	Oregon	15.5
17	Missouri	15.1
18	Colorado	15.0
18	Tennessee	15.0
20	Wisconsin	14.9
21	Kentucky	14.8
22	Arizona	14.7
23	North Carolina	14.5
24	Florida	14.4
24	West Virginia	14.4
26	New Hampshire	14.3
27	Arkansas	14.1
28	Alaska	13.6
29	Idaho	13.2
29	Illinois	13.2
31	Indiana	12.9
32	Ohio	12.7
33	Nebraska	12.4
34	Washington	12.3
35	Georgia	12.2
36	Nevada	12.1
36	New Mexico	12.1
38	South Carolina	11.9
39	Oklahoma	11.8
40	Alabama	11.6
41	Connecticut	11.4
42	Mississippi	11.3
43	Delaware	10.7
44	Wyoming	10.4
45	Maryland	10.2
46	California	10.1
47	Texas	9.7
48	Louisiana	9.0
49	Hawaii	8.9
50	North Dakota	5.6
	District of Columbia	9.7

Source: U.S. Department of Transportation, National Highway Traffic Safety Administration
"Traffic Safety Facts: Older Population" (http://www-nrd.nhtsa.dot.gov/cats/Index.aspx)
*Drivers 65 years old and older. People 65 or older make up 14 percent of the total U.S. population.

Percent of Highway Fatalities Who Were Young Drivers in 2013

National Percent = 5.2% of Fatalities*

ALPHA ORDER

RANK	STATE	PERCENT
11	Alabama	6.6
2	Alaska	9.8
38	Arizona	4.8
41	Arkansas	4.3
45	California	3.7
18	Colorado	5.8
7	Connecticut	7.2
50	Delaware	1.0
44	Florida	3.9
27	Georgia	5.3
35	Hawaii	4.9
5	Idaho	7.5
24	Illinois	5.5
20	Indiana	5.7
20	Iowa	5.7
14	Kansas	6.3
35	Kentucky	4.9
24	Louisiana	5.5
4	Maine	8.3
42	Maryland	4.1
43	Massachusetts	4.0
23	Michigan	5.6
29	Minnesota	5.2
12	Mississippi	6.4
6	Missouri	7.4
46	Montana	3.5
3	Nebraska	9.0
32	Nevada	5.0
9	New Hampshire	6.7
48	New Jersey	3.0
49	New Mexico	2.9
29	New York	5.2
39	North Carolina	4.7
16	North Dakota	6.1
15	Ohio	6.2
39	Oklahoma	4.7
31	Oregon	5.1
18	Pennsylvania	5.8
47	Rhode Island	3.1
17	South Carolina	5.9
9	South Dakota	6.7
27	Tennessee	5.3
26	Texas	5.4
32	Utah	5.0
7	Vermont	7.2
35	Virginia	4.9
12	Washington	6.4
20	West Virginia	5.7
32	Wisconsin	5.0
1	Wyoming	10.3

RANK ORDER

RANK	STATE	PERCENT
1	Wyoming	10.3
2	Alaska	9.8
3	Nebraska	9.0
4	Maine	8.3
5	Idaho	7.5
6	Missouri	7.4
7	Connecticut	7.2
7	Vermont	7.2
9	New Hampshire	6.7
9	South Dakota	6.7
11	Alabama	6.6
12	Mississippi	6.4
12	Washington	6.4
14	Kansas	6.3
15	Ohio	6.2
16	North Dakota	6.1
17	South Carolina	5.9
18	Colorado	5.8
18	Pennsylvania	5.8
20	Indiana	5.7
20	Iowa	5.7
20	West Virginia	5.7
23	Michigan	5.6
24	Illinois	5.5
24	Louisiana	5.5
26	Texas	5.4
27	Georgia	5.3
27	Tennessee	5.3
29	Minnesota	5.2
29	New York	5.2
31	Oregon	5.1
32	Nevada	5.0
32	Utah	5.0
32	Wisconsin	5.0
35	Hawaii	4.9
35	Kentucky	4.9
35	Virginia	4.9
38	Arizona	4.8
39	North Carolina	4.7
39	Oklahoma	4.7
41	Arkansas	4.3
42	Maryland	4.1
43	Massachusetts	4.0
44	Florida	3.9
45	California	3.7
46	Montana	3.5
47	Rhode Island	3.1
48	New Jersey	3.0
49	New Mexico	2.9
50	Delaware	1.0
	District of Columbia	0.0

Source: CQ Press using data from U.S. Department of Transportation, National Highway Traffic Safety Administration "Traffic Safety Facts: Young Drivers" (http://www-nrd.nhtsa.dot.gov/cats/Index.aspx)

*Drivers 15 to 20 years old. Based on 1,691 fatalities of young drivers. An additional 2,642 passengers and nonoccupants were killed in crashes involving young drivers. Young drivers accounted for 6 percent of all drivers.

Licensed Drivers in 2013

National Total = 212,159,728 Licensed Drivers

ALPHA ORDER

RANK	STATE	DRIVERS	% of USA
21	Alabama	3,859,403	1.8%
48	Alaska	528,873	0.2%
14	Arizona	4,791,450	2.3%
31	Arkansas	2,097,201	1.0%
1	California	24,390,236	11.5%
22	Colorado	3,837,488	1.8%
28	Connecticut	2,534,090	1.2%
45	Delaware	723,657	0.3%
3	Florida	13,670,441	6.4%
10	Georgia	6,607,016	3.1%
42	Hawaii	915,033	0.4%
39	Idaho	1,111,485	0.5%
6	Illinois	8,261,582	3.9%
17	Indiana	4,500,403	2.1%
30	Iowa	2,143,665	1.0%
32	Kansas	2,017,759	1.0%
26	Kentucky	3,019,283	1.4%
25	Louisiana	3,278,143	1.5%
41	Maine	1,011,385	0.5%
20	Maryland	4,140,105	2.0%
15	Massachusetts	4,765,586	2.2%
8	Michigan	6,986,587	3.3%
24	Minnesota	3,330,725	1.6%
33	Mississippi	1,968,907	0.9%
18	Missouri	4,280,438	2.0%
43	Montana	766,716	0.4%
37	Nebraska	1,374,529	0.6%
34	Nevada	1,756,095	0.8%
40	New Hampshire	1,061,433	0.5%
11	New Jersey	6,081,386	2.9%
36	New Mexico	1,456,500	0.7%
4	New York	11,210,783	5.3%
9	North Carolina	6,822,902	3.2%
49	North Dakota	513,838	0.2%
7	Ohio	8,030,421	3.8%
29	Oklahoma	2,418,307	1.1%
27	Oregon	2,773,373	1.3%
5	Pennsylvania	8,896,590	4.2%
44	Rhode Island	749,232	0.4%
23	South Carolina	3,536,404	1.7%
46	South Dakota	603,643	0.3%
16	Tennessee	4,605,100	2.2%
2	Texas	15,447,273	7.3%
35	Utah	1,661,219	0.8%
47	Vermont	543,057	0.3%
12	Virginia	5,602,765	2.6%
13	Washington	5,301,630	2.5%
38	West Virginia	1,177,136	0.6%
19	Wisconsin	4,171,427	2.0%
50	Wyoming	421,473	0.2%

RANK ORDER

RANK	STATE	DRIVERS	% of USA
1	California	24,390,236	11.5%
2	Texas	15,447,273	7.3%
3	Florida	13,670,441	6.4%
4	New York	11,210,783	5.3%
5	Pennsylvania	8,896,590	4.2%
6	Illinois	8,261,582	3.9%
7	Ohio	8,030,421	3.8%
8	Michigan	6,986,587	3.3%
9	North Carolina	6,822,902	3.2%
10	Georgia	6,607,016	3.1%
11	New Jersey	6,081,386	2.9%
12	Virginia	5,602,765	2.6%
13	Washington	5,301,630	2.5%
14	Arizona	4,791,450	2.3%
15	Massachusetts	4,765,586	2.2%
16	Tennessee	4,605,100	2.2%
17	Indiana	4,500,403	2.1%
18	Missouri	4,280,438	2.0%
19	Wisconsin	4,171,427	2.0%
20	Maryland	4,140,105	2.0%
21	Alabama	3,859,403	1.8%
22	Colorado	3,837,488	1.8%
23	South Carolina	3,536,404	1.7%
24	Minnesota	3,330,725	1.6%
25	Louisiana	3,278,143	1.5%
26	Kentucky	3,019,283	1.4%
27	Oregon	2,773,373	1.3%
28	Connecticut	2,534,090	1.2%
29	Oklahoma	2,418,307	1.1%
30	Iowa	2,143,665	1.0%
31	Arkansas	2,097,201	1.0%
32	Kansas	2,017,759	1.0%
33	Mississippi	1,968,907	0.9%
34	Nevada	1,756,095	0.8%
35	Utah	1,661,219	0.8%
36	New Mexico	1,456,500	0.7%
37	Nebraska	1,374,529	0.6%
38	West Virginia	1,177,136	0.6%
39	Idaho	1,111,485	0.5%
40	New Hampshire	1,061,433	0.5%
41	Maine	1,011,385	0.5%
42	Hawaii	915,033	0.4%
43	Montana	766,716	0.4%
44	Rhode Island	749,232	0.4%
45	Delaware	723,657	0.3%
46	South Dakota	603,643	0.3%
47	Vermont	543,057	0.3%
48	Alaska	528,873	0.2%
49	North Dakota	513,838	0.2%
50	Wyoming	421,473	0.2%
	District of Columbia	405,555	0.2%

Source: U.S. Department of Transportation, Federal Highway Administration "Highway Statistics 2013" (Table DL-22, http://www.fhwa.dot.gov/policyinformation/statistics/2013/)

Licensed Drivers per 1,000 Driving Age Population in 2013

National Ratio = 846 Licensed Drivers

ALPHA ORDER

RANK	STATE	RATIO
2	Alabama	1,003
8	Alaska	932
10	Arizona	923
18	Arkansas	901
43	California	807
11	Colorado	922
30	Connecticut	871
4	Delaware	972
36	Florida	855
38	Georgia	850
41	Hawaii	811
16	Idaho	903
42	Illinois	809
30	Indiana	871
25	Iowa	876
19	Kansas	897
34	Kentucky	864
17	Louisiana	902
12	Maine	920
27	Maryland	874
29	Massachusetts	872
24	Michigan	882
47	Minnesota	778
40	Mississippi	843
21	Missouri	891
7	Montana	939
6	Nebraska	946
45	Nevada	797
3	New Hampshire	976
36	New Jersey	855
20	New Mexico	892
50	New York	705
28	North Carolina	873
23	North Dakota	889
32	Ohio	870
44	Oklahoma	805
26	Oregon	875
35	Pennsylvania	857
33	Rhode Island	867
9	South Carolina	927
14	South Dakota	916
22	Tennessee	890
49	Texas	766
46	Utah	793
1	Vermont	1,046
39	Virginia	849
5	Washington	955
48	West Virginia	776
15	Wisconsin	910
13	Wyoming	917

RANK ORDER

RANK	STATE	RATIO
1	Vermont	1,046
2	Alabama	1,003
3	New Hampshire	976
4	Delaware	972
5	Washington	955
6	Nebraska	946
7	Montana	939
8	Alaska	932
9	South Carolina	927
10	Arizona	923
11	Colorado	922
12	Maine	920
13	Wyoming	917
14	South Dakota	916
15	Wisconsin	910
16	Idaho	903
17	Louisiana	902
18	Arkansas	901
19	Kansas	897
20	New Mexico	892
21	Missouri	891
22	Tennessee	890
23	North Dakota	889
24	Michigan	882
25	Iowa	876
26	Oregon	875
27	Maryland	874
28	North Carolina	873
29	Massachusetts	872
30	Connecticut	871
30	Indiana	871
32	Ohio	870
33	Rhode Island	867
34	Kentucky	864
35	Pennsylvania	857
36	Florida	855
36	New Jersey	855
38	Georgia	850
39	Virginia	849
40	Mississippi	843
41	Hawaii	811
42	Illinois	809
43	California	807
44	Oklahoma	805
45	Nevada	797
46	Utah	793
47	Minnesota	778
48	West Virginia	776
49	Texas	766
50	New York	705
	District of Columbia	744

Source: U.S. Department of Transportation, Federal Highway Administration "Highway Statistics 2013" (Table DL-1C, http://www.fhwa.dot.gov/policyinformation/statistics/2013/)

Motor Vehicle Registrations in 2013

National Total = 255,876,822 Motor Vehicles*

ALPHA ORDER

RANK	STATE	VEHICLES	% of USA
21	Alabama	4,787,219	1.9%
49	Alaska	785,825	0.3%
17	Arizona	5,381,050	2.1%
32	Arkansas	2,417,959	0.9%
1	California	28,074,977	11.0%
22	Colorado	4,683,410	1.8%
30	Connecticut	2,855,538	1.1%
45	Delaware	947,442	0.4%
3	Florida	15,131,735	5.9%
10	Georgia	7,780,346	3.0%
42	Hawaii	1,334,692	0.5%
38	Idaho	1,692,457	0.7%
7	Illinois	10,193,438	4.0%
15	Indiana	5,574,026	2.2%
28	Iowa	3,540,763	1.4%
31	Kansas	2,627,845	1.0%
23	Kentucky	4,031,748	1.6%
25	Louisiana	3,957,174	1.5%
43	Maine	1,199,134	0.5%
26	Maryland	3,833,526	1.5%
20	Massachusetts	4,985,448	1.9%
8	Michigan	8,192,368	3.2%
19	Minnesota	5,219,490	2.0%
34	Mississippi	2,073,535	0.8%
14	Missouri	5,820,656	2.3%
39	Montana	1,539,931	0.6%
36	Nebraska	1,891,253	0.7%
33	Nevada	2,203,096	0.9%
41	New Hampshire	1,408,936	0.6%
11	New Jersey	7,061,343	2.8%
37	New Mexico	1,882,466	0.7%
4	New York	10,674,135	4.2%
9	North Carolina	7,813,854	3.1%
47	North Dakota	845,109	0.3%
6	Ohio	10,360,365	4.0%
29	Oklahoma	3,460,012	1.4%
27	Oregon	3,603,825	1.4%
5	Pennsylvania	10,461,108	4.1%
46	Rhode Island	853,152	0.3%
24	South Carolina	3,986,574	1.6%
44	South Dakota	1,015,173	0.4%
16	Tennessee	5,451,933	2.1%
2	Texas	20,171,135	7.9%
35	Utah	2,060,512	0.8%
50	Vermont	611,789	0.2%
12	Virginia	7,051,016	2.8%
13	Washington	6,392,840	2.5%
40	West Virginia	1,453,395	0.6%
18	Wisconsin	5,338,759	2.1%
48	Wyoming	830,539	0.3%

RANK ORDER

RANK	STATE	VEHICLES	% of USA
1	California	28,074,977	11.0%
2	Texas	20,171,135	7.9%
3	Florida	15,131,735	5.9%
4	New York	10,674,135	4.2%
5	Pennsylvania	10,461,108	4.1%
6	Ohio	10,360,365	4.0%
7	Illinois	10,193,438	4.0%
8	Michigan	8,192,368	3.2%
9	North Carolina	7,813,854	3.1%
10	Georgia	7,780,346	3.0%
11	New Jersey	7,061,343	2.8%
12	Virginia	7,051,016	2.8%
13	Washington	6,392,840	2.5%
14	Missouri	5,820,656	2.3%
15	Indiana	5,574,026	2.2%
16	Tennessee	5,451,933	2.1%
17	Arizona	5,381,050	2.1%
18	Wisconsin	5,338,759	2.1%
19	Minnesota	5,219,490	2.0%
20	Massachusetts	4,985,448	1.9%
21	Alabama	4,787,219	1.9%
22	Colorado	4,683,410	1.8%
23	Kentucky	4,031,748	1.6%
24	South Carolina	3,986,574	1.6%
25	Louisiana	3,957,174	1.5%
26	Maryland	3,833,526	1.5%
27	Oregon	3,603,825	1.4%
28	Iowa	3,540,763	1.4%
29	Oklahoma	3,460,012	1.4%
30	Connecticut	2,855,538	1.1%
31	Kansas	2,627,845	1.0%
32	Arkansas	2,417,959	0.9%
33	Nevada	2,203,096	0.9%
34	Mississippi	2,073,535	0.8%
35	Utah	2,060,512	0.8%
36	Nebraska	1,891,253	0.7%
37	New Mexico	1,882,466	0.7%
38	Idaho	1,692,457	0.7%
39	Montana	1,539,931	0.6%
40	West Virginia	1,453,395	0.6%
41	New Hampshire	1,408,936	0.6%
42	Hawaii	1,334,692	0.5%
43	Maine	1,199,134	0.5%
44	South Dakota	1,015,173	0.4%
45	Delaware	947,442	0.4%
46	Rhode Island	853,152	0.3%
47	North Dakota	845,109	0.3%
48	Wyoming	830,539	0.3%
49	Alaska	785,825	0.3%
50	Vermont	611,789	0.2%
	District of Columbia	332,773	0.1%

Source: U.S. Department of Transportation, Federal Highway Administration
"Highway Statistics 2013" (Table MV-1, http://www.fhwa.dot.gov/policyinformation/statistics/2013/)
*Includes automobiles, trucks and buses and motorcycles.

Motor Vehicles per Driving Age Population in 2013

National Rate = 1.02 Motor Vehicles*

ALPHA ORDER

RANK	STATE	RATE
11	Alabama	1.24
6	Alaska	1.39
31	Arizona	1.04
31	Arkansas	1.04
46	California	0.93
23	Colorado	1.13
42	Connecticut	0.98
10	Delaware	1.27
45	Florida	0.95
35	Georgia	1.00
14	Hawaii	1.18
7	Idaho	1.37
35	Illinois	1.00
27	Indiana	1.08
5	Iowa	1.45
16	Kansas	1.17
18	Kentucky	1.15
25	Louisiana	1.09
25	Maine	1.09
49	Maryland	0.81
47	Massachusetts	0.91
33	Michigan	1.03
12	Minnesota	1.22
48	Mississippi	0.89
13	Missouri	1.21
1	Montana	1.89
8	Nebraska	1.30
35	Nevada	1.00
8	New Hampshire	1.30
40	New Jersey	0.99
18	New Mexico	1.15
50	New York	0.67
35	North Carolina	1.00
4	North Dakota	1.46
24	Ohio	1.12
18	Oklahoma	1.15
22	Oregon	1.14
34	Pennsylvania	1.01
40	Rhode Island	0.99
29	South Carolina	1.05
3	South Dakota	1.54
29	Tennessee	1.05
35	Texas	1.00
42	Utah	0.98
14	Vermont	1.18
28	Virginia	1.07
18	Washington	1.15
44	West Virginia	0.96
17	Wisconsin	1.16
2	Wyoming	1.81

RANK ORDER

RANK	STATE	RATE
1	Montana	1.89
2	Wyoming	1.81
3	South Dakota	1.54
4	North Dakota	1.46
5	Iowa	1.45
6	Alaska	1.39
7	Idaho	1.37
8	Nebraska	1.30
8	New Hampshire	1.30
10	Delaware	1.27
11	Alabama	1.24
12	Minnesota	1.22
13	Missouri	1.21
14	Hawaii	1.18
14	Vermont	1.18
16	Kansas	1.17
17	Wisconsin	1.16
18	Kentucky	1.15
18	New Mexico	1.15
18	Oklahoma	1.15
18	Washington	1.15
22	Oregon	1.14
23	Colorado	1.13
24	Ohio	1.12
25	Louisiana	1.09
25	Maine	1.09
27	Indiana	1.08
28	Virginia	1.07
29	South Carolina	1.05
29	Tennessee	1.05
31	Arizona	1.04
31	Arkansas	1.04
33	Michigan	1.03
34	Pennsylvania	1.01
35	Georgia	1.00
35	Illinois	1.00
35	Nevada	1.00
35	North Carolina	1.00
35	Texas	1.00
40	New Jersey	0.99
40	Rhode Island	0.99
42	Connecticut	0.98
42	Utah	0.98
44	West Virginia	0.96
45	Florida	0.95
46	California	0.93
47	Massachusetts	0.91
48	Mississippi	0.89
49	Maryland	0.81
50	New York	0.67
	District of Columbia	0.61

Source: CQ Press using data from U.S. Department of Transportation, Federal Highway Administration
"Highway Statistics 2013" (Table MV-1, http://www.fhwa.dot.gov/policyinformation/statistics/2013/)
*Persons age 16 and older. Motor Vehicles include automobiles, trucks, buses, and motorcycles.

Average Travel Time to Work in 2014

National Average = 26.0 Minutes*

ALPHA ORDER

RANK	STATE	MINUTES
22	Alabama	24.3
47	Alaska	18.3
20	Arizona	24.5
39	Arkansas	21.7
6	California	28.1
18	Colorado	25.1
16	Connecticut	25.4
19	Delaware	24.6
12	Florida	26.4
9	Georgia	27.6
8	Hawaii	27.9
42	Idaho	20.3
5	Illinois	28.6
31	Indiana	23.3
44	Iowa	18.8
43	Kansas	19.2
35	Kentucky	22.9
16	Louisiana	25.4
29	Maine	23.6
2	Maryland	32.3
4	Massachusetts	28.8
22	Michigan	24.3
30	Minnesota	23.4
24	Mississippi	24.2
33	Missouri	23.1
48	Montana	17.9
46	Nebraska	18.4
28	Nevada	23.8
10	New Hampshire	27.0
3	New Jersey	31.1
38	New Mexico	21.8
1	New York	32.6
27	North Carolina	23.9
49	North Dakota	17.6
32	Ohio	23.2
41	Oklahoma	21.3
33	Oregon	23.1
12	Pennsylvania	26.4
26	Rhode Island	24.0
25	South Carolina	24.1
50	South Dakota	16.7
20	Tennessee	24.5
15	Texas	25.6
40	Utah	21.6
36	Vermont	22.1
6	Virginia	28.1
11	Washington	26.8
14	West Virginia	25.7
37	Wisconsin	21.9
45	Wyoming	18.7

RANK ORDER

RANK	STATE	MINUTES
1	New York	32.6
2	Maryland	32.3
3	New Jersey	31.1
4	Massachusetts	28.8
5	Illinois	28.6
6	California	28.1
6	Virginia	28.1
8	Hawaii	27.9
9	Georgia	27.6
10	New Hampshire	27.0
11	Washington	26.8
12	Florida	26.4
12	Pennsylvania	26.4
14	West Virginia	25.7
15	Texas	25.6
16	Connecticut	25.4
16	Louisiana	25.4
18	Colorado	25.1
19	Delaware	24.6
20	Arizona	24.5
20	Tennessee	24.5
22	Alabama	24.3
22	Michigan	24.3
24	Mississippi	24.2
25	South Carolina	24.1
26	Rhode Island	24.0
27	North Carolina	23.9
28	Nevada	23.8
29	Maine	23.6
30	Minnesota	23.4
31	Indiana	23.3
32	Ohio	23.2
33	Missouri	23.1
33	Oregon	23.1
35	Kentucky	22.9
36	Vermont	22.1
37	Wisconsin	21.9
38	New Mexico	21.8
39	Arkansas	21.7
40	Utah	21.6
41	Oklahoma	21.3
42	Idaho	20.3
43	Kansas	19.2
44	Iowa	18.8
45	Wyoming	18.7
46	Nebraska	18.4
47	Alaska	18.3
48	Montana	17.9
49	North Dakota	17.6
50	South Dakota	16.7
	District of Columbia	29.3

Source: U.S. Bureau of the Census
"2014 American Community Survey-Table R0801" (http://www.census.gov/programs-surveys/acs/)
*Workers 16 and older not working at home.

Percent of Commuters Who Drive to Work Alone in 2014

National Percent = 76.5%*

ALPHA ORDER

RANK	STATE	PERCENT
1	Alabama	85.9
48	Alaska	69.5
34	Arizona	76.9
8	Arkansas	82.5
42	California	73.5
39	Colorado	75.6
29	Connecticut	78.1
16	Delaware	81.5
25	Florida	79.7
26	Georgia	79.6
49	Hawaii	66.4
28	Idaho	78.9
43	Illinois	73.4
5	Indiana	83.2
21	Iowa	80.8
12	Kansas	82.1
13	Kentucky	81.9
11	Louisiana	82.2
33	Maine	77.3
41	Maryland	73.9
46	Massachusetts	71.2
9	Michigan	82.3
30	Minnesota	77.7
2	Mississippi	85.5
14	Missouri	81.8
40	Montana	74.7
15	Nebraska	81.7
32	Nevada	77.6
17	New Hampshire	81.4
45	New Jersey	71.7
23	New Mexico	80.3
50	New York	53.1
17	North Carolina	81.4
19	North Dakota	81.3
3	Ohio	83.6
9	Oklahoma	82.3
47	Oregon	70.5
36	Pennsylvania	76.4
23	Rhode Island	80.3
7	South Carolina	82.7
27	South Dakota	79.2
4	Tennessee	83.4
22	Texas	80.4
38	Utah	76.0
37	Vermont	76.3
30	Virginia	77.7
44	Washington	72.4
6	West Virginia	83.0
20	Wisconsin	80.9
35	Wyoming	76.8

RANK ORDER

RANK	STATE	PERCENT
1	Alabama	85.9
2	Mississippi	85.5
3	Ohio	83.6
4	Tennessee	83.4
5	Indiana	83.2
6	West Virginia	83.0
7	South Carolina	82.7
8	Arkansas	82.5
9	Michigan	82.3
9	Oklahoma	82.3
11	Louisiana	82.2
12	Kansas	82.1
13	Kentucky	81.9
14	Missouri	81.8
15	Nebraska	81.7
16	Delaware	81.5
17	New Hampshire	81.4
17	North Carolina	81.4
19	North Dakota	81.3
20	Wisconsin	80.9
21	Iowa	80.8
22	Texas	80.4
23	New Mexico	80.3
23	Rhode Island	80.3
25	Florida	79.7
26	Georgia	79.6
27	South Dakota	79.2
28	Idaho	78.9
29	Connecticut	78.1
30	Minnesota	77.7
30	Virginia	77.7
32	Nevada	77.6
33	Maine	77.3
34	Arizona	76.9
35	Wyoming	76.8
36	Pennsylvania	76.4
37	Vermont	76.3
38	Utah	76.0
39	Colorado	75.6
40	Montana	74.7
41	Maryland	73.9
42	California	73.5
43	Illinois	73.4
44	Washington	72.4
45	New Jersey	71.7
46	Massachusetts	71.2
47	Oregon	70.5
48	Alaska	69.5
49	Hawaii	66.4
50	New York	53.1
	District of Columbia	35.1

Source: U.S. Bureau of the Census
"2014 American Community Survey-Table R0802" (http://www.census.gov/programs-surveys/acs/)
*Workers 16 and older who traveled to work by car, truck or van.

Percent of Commuters Who Drive to Work in Carpools in 2014

National Percent = 9.2%*

ALPHA ORDER

RANK	STATE	PERCENT
37	Alabama	8.6
2	Alaska	12.0
11	Arizona	10.4
5	Arkansas	10.9
9	California	10.5
21	Colorado	9.6
42	Connecticut	8.1
47	Delaware	7.6
30	Florida	9.1
14	Georgia	10.1
1	Hawaii	13.5
17	Idaho	9.8
43	Illinois	8.0
31	Indiana	9.0
37	Iowa	8.6
22	Kansas	9.5
16	Kentucky	10.0
17	Louisiana	9.8
7	Maine	10.7
25	Maryland	9.3
48	Massachusetts	7.4
32	Michigan	8.9
34	Minnesota	8.8
35	Mississippi	8.7
32	Missouri	8.9
11	Montana	10.4
22	Nebraska	9.5
11	Nevada	10.4
45	New Hampshire	7.8
44	New Jersey	7.9
22	New Mexico	9.5
50	New York	6.5
19	North Carolina	9.7
40	North Dakota	8.3
45	Ohio	7.8
9	Oklahoma	10.5
6	Oregon	10.8
39	Pennsylvania	8.5
48	Rhode Island	7.4
25	South Carolina	9.3
28	South Dakota	9.2
28	Tennessee	9.2
8	Texas	10.6
3	Utah	11.8
35	Vermont	8.7
25	Virginia	9.3
14	Washington	10.1
19	West Virginia	9.7
41	Wisconsin	8.2
4	Wyoming	11.0

RANK ORDER

RANK	STATE	PERCENT
1	Hawaii	13.5
2	Alaska	12.0
3	Utah	11.8
4	Wyoming	11.0
5	Arkansas	10.9
6	Oregon	10.8
7	Maine	10.7
8	Texas	10.6
9	California	10.5
9	Oklahoma	10.5
11	Arizona	10.4
11	Montana	10.4
11	Nevada	10.4
14	Georgia	10.1
14	Washington	10.1
16	Kentucky	10.0
17	Idaho	9.8
17	Louisiana	9.8
19	North Carolina	9.7
19	West Virginia	9.7
21	Colorado	9.6
22	Kansas	9.5
22	Nebraska	9.5
22	New Mexico	9.5
25	Maryland	9.3
25	South Carolina	9.3
25	Virginia	9.3
28	South Dakota	9.2
28	Tennessee	9.2
30	Florida	9.1
31	Indiana	9.0
32	Michigan	8.9
32	Missouri	8.9
34	Minnesota	8.8
35	Mississippi	8.7
35	Vermont	8.7
37	Alabama	8.6
37	Iowa	8.6
39	Pennsylvania	8.5
40	North Dakota	8.3
41	Wisconsin	8.2
42	Connecticut	8.1
43	Illinois	8.0
44	New Jersey	7.9
45	New Hampshire	7.8
45	Ohio	7.8
47	Delaware	7.6
48	Massachusetts	7.4
48	Rhode Island	7.4
50	New York	6.5
	District of Columbia	5.6

Source: U.S. Bureau of the Census
 "2014 American Community Survey-Table R0803" (http://www.census.gov/programs-surveys/acs/)
*Workers 16 and older who traveled to work by car, truck or van.

Percent of Commuters Who Travel to Work by Public Transportation in 2014

National Percent = 5.2%*

ALPHA ORDER

RANK	STATE	PERCENT
47	Alabama	0.4
29	Alaska	1.3
21	Arizona	2.0
49	Arkansas	0.3
9	California	5.3
15	Colorado	3.3
10	Connecticut	4.8
17	Delaware	2.9
19	Florida	2.1
19	Georgia	2.1
6	Hawaii	7.2
38	Idaho	0.8
4	Illinois	9.4
31	Indiana	1.1
36	Iowa	1.0
45	Kansas	0.5
31	Kentucky	1.1
28	Louisiana	1.4
38	Maine	0.8
5	Maryland	9.0
3	Massachusetts	9.8
27	Michigan	1.5
14	Minnesota	3.7
49	Mississippi	0.3
24	Missouri	1.6
31	Montana	1.1
40	Nebraska	0.7
13	Nevada	4.3
40	New Hampshire	0.7
2	New Jersey	11.0
29	New Mexico	1.3
1	New York	28.3
31	North Carolina	1.1
40	North Dakota	0.7
23	Ohio	1.7
47	Oklahoma	0.4
11	Oregon	4.7
8	Pennsylvania	5.7
16	Rhode Island	3.0
40	South Carolina	0.7
45	South Dakota	0.5
37	Tennessee	0.9
24	Texas	1.6
18	Utah	2.5
31	Vermont	1.1
11	Virginia	4.7
7	Washington	6.3
40	West Virginia	0.7
22	Wisconsin	1.9
24	Wyoming	1.6

RANK ORDER

RANK	STATE	PERCENT
1	New York	28.3
2	New Jersey	11.0
3	Massachusetts	9.8
4	Illinois	9.4
5	Maryland	9.0
6	Hawaii	7.2
7	Washington	6.3
8	Pennsylvania	5.7
9	California	5.3
10	Connecticut	4.8
11	Oregon	4.7
11	Virginia	4.7
13	Nevada	4.3
14	Minnesota	3.7
15	Colorado	3.3
16	Rhode Island	3.0
17	Delaware	2.9
18	Utah	2.5
19	Florida	2.1
19	Georgia	2.1
21	Arizona	2.0
22	Wisconsin	1.9
23	Ohio	1.7
24	Missouri	1.6
24	Texas	1.6
24	Wyoming	1.6
27	Michigan	1.5
28	Louisiana	1.4
29	Alaska	1.3
29	New Mexico	1.3
31	Indiana	1.1
31	Kentucky	1.1
31	Montana	1.1
31	North Carolina	1.1
31	Vermont	1.1
36	Iowa	1.0
37	Tennessee	0.9
38	Idaho	0.8
38	Maine	0.8
40	Nebraska	0.7
40	New Hampshire	0.7
40	North Dakota	0.7
40	South Carolina	0.7
40	West Virginia	0.7
45	Kansas	0.5
45	South Dakota	0.5
47	Alabama	0.4
47	Oklahoma	0.4
49	Arkansas	0.3
49	Mississippi	0.3
	District of Columbia	36.1

Source: U.S. Bureau of the Census
 "2014 American Community Survey-Table R0804" (http://www.census.gov/programs-surveys/acs/)
*Workers 16 and older.

Annual Miles per Vehicle in 2013

National Annual Average = 11,679 Miles*

ALPHA ORDER

RANK	STATE	MILES
7	Alabama	13,588
50	Alaska	6,170
28	Arizona	11,259
6	Arkansas	13,852
21	California	11,738
38	Colorado	10,029
34	Connecticut	10,836
39	Delaware	9,824
13	Florida	12,735
3	Georgia	14,055
49	Hawaii	7,567
40	Idaho	9,442
36	Illinois	10,330
4	Indiana	14,049
47	Iowa	8,936
25	Kansas	11,495
22	Kentucky	11,656
17	Louisiana	12,069
20	Maine	11,783
2	Maryland	14,787
27	Massachusetts	11,295
24	Michigan	11,612
32	Minnesota	10,916
1	Mississippi	18,692
19	Missouri	11,933
48	Montana	7,814
37	Nebraska	10,216
30	Nevada	11,189
43	New Hampshire	9,158
35	New Jersey	10,555
9	New Mexico	13,326
15	New York	12,154
8	North Carolina	13,465
18	North Dakota	11,951
33	Ohio	10,884
5	Oklahoma	13,872
42	Oregon	9,353
41	Pennsylvania	9,428
44	Rhode Island	9,113
14	South Carolina	12,288
45	South Dakota	8,985
12	Tennessee	13,035
16	Texas	12,123
11	Utah	13,106
23	Vermont	11,631
26	Virginia	11,455
46	Washington	8,949
10	West Virginia	13,233
31	Wisconsin	11,142
29	Wyoming	11,208

RANK ORDER

RANK	STATE	MILES
1	Mississippi	18,692
2	Maryland	14,787
3	Georgia	14,055
4	Indiana	14,049
5	Oklahoma	13,872
6	Arkansas	13,852
7	Alabama	13,588
8	North Carolina	13,465
9	New Mexico	13,326
10	West Virginia	13,233
11	Utah	13,106
12	Tennessee	13,035
13	Florida	12,735
14	South Carolina	12,288
15	New York	12,154
16	Texas	12,123
17	Louisiana	12,069
18	North Dakota	11,951
19	Missouri	11,933
20	Maine	11,783
21	California	11,738
22	Kentucky	11,656
23	Vermont	11,631
24	Michigan	11,612
25	Kansas	11,495
26	Virginia	11,455
27	Massachusetts	11,295
28	Arizona	11,259
29	Wyoming	11,208
30	Nevada	11,189
31	Wisconsin	11,142
32	Minnesota	10,916
33	Ohio	10,884
34	Connecticut	10,836
35	New Jersey	10,555
36	Illinois	10,330
37	Nebraska	10,216
38	Colorado	10,029
39	Delaware	9,824
40	Idaho	9,442
41	Pennsylvania	9,428
42	Oregon	9,353
43	New Hampshire	9,158
44	Rhode Island	9,113
45	South Dakota	8,985
46	Washington	8,949
47	Iowa	8,936
48	Montana	7,814
49	Hawaii	7,567
50	Alaska	6,170
	District of Columbia	10,600

Source: CQ Press using data from U.S. Department of Transportation, Federal Highway Administration
"Highway Statistics 2013" (Tables MV-1 and VM-2, http://www.fhwa.dot.gov/policyinformation/statistics/2013/)
*Includes automobiles, trucks, buses and motorcycles.

Average Miles per Gallon in 2013

National Average = 17.6 Miles per Gallon*

ALPHA ORDER

RANK	STATE	MILES PER GALLON
4	Alabama	20.0
49	Alaska	12.6
14	Arizona	18.4
32	Arkansas	17.3
7	California	19.3
24	Colorado	17.6
13	Connecticut	18.5
5	Delaware	19.8
1	Florida	20.6
15	Georgia	18.3
1	Hawaii	20.6
34	Idaho	17.2
24	Illinois	17.6
10	Indiana	18.9
44	Iowa	14.6
32	Kansas	17.3
35	Kentucky	16.7
37	Louisiana	16.6
42	Maine	15.4
29	Maryland	17.5
21	Massachusetts	17.7
21	Michigan	17.7
12	Minnesota	18.7
15	Mississippi	18.3
24	Missouri	17.6
39	Montana	15.9
41	Nebraska	15.5
21	Nevada	17.7
37	New Hampshire	16.6
39	New Jersey	15.9
24	New Mexico	17.6
5	New York	19.8
3	North Carolina	20.4
50	North Dakota	12.2
20	Ohio	17.8
18	Oklahoma	18.0
30	Oregon	17.4
42	Pennsylvania	15.4
10	Rhode Island	18.9
44	South Carolina	14.6
47	South Dakota	14.2
19	Tennessee	17.9
46	Texas	14.3
24	Utah	17.6
7	Vermont	19.3
35	Virginia	16.7
30	Washington	17.4
17	West Virginia	18.1
9	Wisconsin	19.2
48	Wyoming	13.2

RANK ORDER

RANK	STATE	MILES PER GALLON
1	Florida	20.6
1	Hawaii	20.6
3	North Carolina	20.4
4	Alabama	20.0
5	Delaware	19.8
5	New York	19.8
7	California	19.3
7	Vermont	19.3
9	Wisconsin	19.2
10	Indiana	18.9
10	Rhode Island	18.9
12	Minnesota	18.7
13	Connecticut	18.5
14	Arizona	18.4
15	Georgia	18.3
15	Mississippi	18.3
17	West Virginia	18.1
18	Oklahoma	18.0
19	Tennessee	17.9
20	Ohio	17.8
21	Massachusetts	17.7
21	Michigan	17.7
21	Nevada	17.7
24	Colorado	17.6
24	Illinois	17.6
24	Missouri	17.6
24	New Mexico	17.6
24	Utah	17.6
29	Maryland	17.5
30	Oregon	17.4
30	Washington	17.4
32	Arkansas	17.3
32	Kansas	17.3
34	Idaho	17.2
35	Kentucky	16.7
35	Virginia	16.7
37	Louisiana	16.6
37	New Hampshire	16.6
39	Montana	15.9
39	New Jersey	15.9
41	Nebraska	15.5
42	Maine	15.4
42	Pennsylvania	15.4
44	Iowa	14.6
44	South Carolina	14.6
46	Texas	14.3
47	South Dakota	14.2
48	Wyoming	13.2
49	Alaska	12.6
50	North Dakota	12.2
	District of Columbia	31.8

Source: CQ Press using data from U.S. Department of Transportation, Federal Highway Administration "Highway Statistics 2013" (Table VM-2, http://www.fhwa.dot.gov/policyinformation/statistics/2013/)

*Total vehicle-miles for 2013 divided by total highway motor-fuel use. Includes gasoline, gasohol, diesel, and other "special fuels."

Airports in 2013

National Total = 13,174 Airports*

ALPHA ORDER

RANK	STATE	AIRPORTS	% of USA
32	Alabama	180	1.4%
2	Alaska	554	4.2%
30	Arizona	189	1.4%
26	Arkansas	215	1.6%
3	California	522	4.0%
21	Colorado	265	2.0%
47	Connecticut	51	0.4%
49	Delaware	31	0.2%
4	Florida	501	3.8%
15	Georgia	336	2.6%
48	Hawaii	32	0.2%
25	Idaho	227	1.7%
5	Illinois	478	3.6%
9	Indiana	405	3.1%
28	Iowa	199	1.5%
16	Kansas	333	2.5%
34	Kentucky	150	1.1%
24	Louisiana	229	1.7%
38	Maine	115	0.9%
35	Maryland	149	1.1%
43	Massachusetts	75	0.6%
13	Michigan	355	2.7%
17	Minnesota	327	2.5%
31	Mississippi	186	1.4%
12	Missouri	363	2.8%
23	Montana	231	1.8%
29	Nebraska	198	1.5%
40	Nevada	97	0.7%
46	New Hampshire	54	0.4%
39	New Jersey	100	0.8%
37	New Mexico	135	1.0%
10	New York	388	2.9%
14	North Carolina	338	2.6%
22	North Dakota	256	1.9%
6	Ohio	450	3.4%
19	Oklahoma	294	2.2%
18	Oregon	325	2.5%
8	Pennsylvania	432	3.3%
50	Rhode Island	9	0.1%
33	South Carolina	158	1.2%
36	South Dakota	143	1.1%
27	Tennessee	212	1.6%
1	Texas	1,466	11.1%
42	Utah	91	0.7%
45	Vermont	61	0.5%
20	Virginia	291	2.2%
11	Washington	370	2.8%
43	West Virginia	75	0.6%
7	Wisconsin	435	3.3%
41	Wyoming	95	0.7%

RANK ORDER

RANK	STATE	AIRPORTS	% of USA
1	Texas	1,466	11.1%
2	Alaska	554	4.2%
3	California	522	4.0%
4	Florida	501	3.8%
5	Illinois	478	3.6%
6	Ohio	450	3.4%
7	Wisconsin	435	3.3%
8	Pennsylvania	432	3.3%
9	Indiana	405	3.1%
10	New York	388	2.9%
11	Washington	370	2.8%
12	Missouri	363	2.8%
13	Michigan	355	2.7%
14	North Carolina	338	2.6%
15	Georgia	336	2.6%
16	Kansas	333	2.5%
17	Minnesota	327	2.5%
18	Oregon	325	2.5%
19	Oklahoma	294	2.2%
20	Virginia	291	2.2%
21	Colorado	265	2.0%
22	North Dakota	256	1.9%
23	Montana	231	1.8%
24	Louisiana	229	1.7%
25	Idaho	227	1.7%
26	Arkansas	215	1.6%
27	Tennessee	212	1.6%
28	Iowa	199	1.5%
29	Nebraska	198	1.5%
30	Arizona	189	1.4%
31	Mississippi	186	1.4%
32	Alabama	180	1.4%
33	South Carolina	158	1.2%
34	Kentucky	150	1.1%
35	Maryland	149	1.1%
36	South Dakota	143	1.1%
37	New Mexico	135	1.0%
38	Maine	115	0.9%
39	New Jersey	100	0.8%
40	Nevada	97	0.7%
41	Wyoming	95	0.7%
42	Utah	91	0.7%
43	Massachusetts	75	0.6%
43	West Virginia	75	0.6%
45	Vermont	61	0.5%
46	New Hampshire	54	0.4%
47	Connecticut	51	0.4%
48	Hawaii	32	0.2%
49	Delaware	31	0.2%
50	Rhode Island	9	0.1%
	District of Columbia	3	0.0%

Source: U.S. Department of Transportation, Bureau of Transportation Statistics
"State Transportation Statistics 2015" (Table 1-10, http://www.bts.gov/publications/state_transportation_statistics/)
*This table comprises all U.S. public use and private use airports. Public use facilities are open to the public with no prior authorization or permission required. Private use facilities are not open to the general public and include medical, law enforcement, corporate, and other such facilities.

Inland Waterway Mileage in 2013

National Total = 29,620 Miles*

ALPHA ORDER

RANK	STATE	MILES	% of USA
6	Alabama	1,270	4.3%
1	Alaska	5,500	18.6%
40	Arizona	0	0.0%
3	Arkansas	1,860	6.3%
26	California	290	1.0%
40	Colorado	0	0.0%
31	Connecticut	120	0.4%
34	Delaware	100	0.3%
5	Florida	1,540	5.2%
14	Georgia	720	2.4%
40	Hawaii	0	0.0%
33	Idaho	110	0.4%
8	Illinois	1,100	3.7%
24	Indiana	350	1.2%
19	Iowa	490	1.7%
31	Kansas	120	0.4%
4	Kentucky	1,590	5.4%
2	Louisiana	2,820	9.5%
37	Maine	70	0.2%
18	Maryland	530	1.8%
35	Massachusetts	90	0.3%
40	Michigan	0	0.0%
27	Minnesota	260	0.9%
12	Mississippi	870	2.9%
10	Missouri	1,030	3.5%
40	Montana	0	0.0%
25	Nebraska	320	1.1%
40	Nevada	0	0.0%
39	New Hampshire	10	0.0%
23	New Jersey	360	1.2%
40	New Mexico	0	0.0%
22	New York	390	1.3%
7	North Carolina	1,150	3.9%
40	North Dakota	0	0.0%
21	Ohio	440	1.5%
30	Oklahoma	150	0.5%
15	Oregon	680	2.3%
27	Pennsylvania	260	0.9%
38	Rhode Island	40	0.1%
20	South Carolina	480	1.6%
36	South Dakota	80	0.3%
11	Tennessee	950	3.2%
13	Texas	830	2.8%
40	Utah	0	0.0%
40	Vermont	0	0.0%
17	Virginia	670	2.3%
9	Washington	1,060	3.6%
15	West Virginia	680	2.3%
29	Wisconsin	230	0.8%
40	Wyoming	0	0.0%

RANK ORDER

RANK	STATE	MILES	% of USA
1	Alaska	5,500	18.6%
2	Louisiana	2,820	9.5%
3	Arkansas	1,860	6.3%
4	Kentucky	1,590	5.4%
5	Florida	1,540	5.2%
6	Alabama	1,270	4.3%
7	North Carolina	1,150	3.9%
8	Illinois	1,100	3.7%
9	Washington	1,060	3.6%
10	Missouri	1,030	3.5%
11	Tennessee	950	3.2%
12	Mississippi	870	2.9%
13	Texas	830	2.8%
14	Georgia	720	2.4%
15	Oregon	680	2.3%
15	West Virginia	680	2.3%
17	Virginia	670	2.3%
18	Maryland	530	1.8%
19	Iowa	490	1.7%
20	South Carolina	480	1.6%
21	Ohio	440	1.5%
22	New York	390	1.3%
23	New Jersey	360	1.2%
24	Indiana	350	1.2%
25	Nebraska	320	1.1%
26	California	290	1.0%
27	Minnesota	260	0.9%
27	Pennsylvania	260	0.9%
29	Wisconsin	230	0.8%
30	Oklahoma	150	0.5%
31	Connecticut	120	0.4%
31	Kansas	120	0.4%
33	Idaho	110	0.4%
34	Delaware	100	0.3%
35	Massachusetts	90	0.3%
36	South Dakota	80	0.3%
37	Maine	70	0.2%
38	Rhode Island	40	0.1%
39	New Hampshire	10	0.0%
40	Arizona	0	0.0%
40	Colorado	0	0.0%
40	Hawaii	0	0.0%
40	Michigan	0	0.0%
40	Montana	0	0.0%
40	Nevada	0	0.0%
40	New Mexico	0	0.0%
40	North Dakota	0	0.0%
40	Utah	0	0.0%
40	Vermont	0	0.0%
40	Wyoming	0	0.0%
	District of Columbia	10	0.0%

Source: U.S. Department of Transportation, Bureau of Transportation Statistics
 "State Transportation Statistics 2015" (Table 1-16, http://www.bts.gov/publications/state_transportation_statistics/)
*Waterway mileage was determined by including the length of channels 1) with a controlling draft of nine feet or greater, 2) with commercial cargo traffic reported for 1998 and 1999, but 3) were not offshore. Channels within major bays are included (e.g., Chesapeake Bay, San Francisco Bay, Puget Sound, Long Island Sound, and major sounds and straits in southeastern Alaska). Channels in the Great Lakes are not included. Approximately 4,600 miles are counted twice as several are state boundaries.

Percent of Recreational Boating Accidents Involving Alcohol in 2014

National Percent = 8.5% of Accidents*

ALPHA ORDER

RANK	STATE	PERCENT
25	Alabama	9.9
12	Alaska	16.7
28	Arizona	8.0
17	Arkansas	13.0
46	California	3.7
47	Colorado	3.5
42	Connecticut	5.0
16	Delaware	13.3
41	Florida	5.2
31	Georgia	7.6
50	Hawaii	0.0
26	Idaho	9.3
7	Illinois	20.2
3	Indiana	25.0
9	Iowa	18.2
37	Kansas	5.9
4	Kentucky	23.9
11	Louisiana	17.7
15	Maine	14.3
39	Maryland	5.4
36	Massachusetts	6.1
27	Michigan	8.2
13	Minnesota	16.0
28	Mississippi	8.0
20	Missouri	11.3
5	Montana	21.4
45	Nebraska	3.8
18	Nevada	12.8
44	New Hampshire	4.5
49	New Jersey	1.8
30	New Mexico	7.7
32	New York	7.4
21	North Carolina	10.5
1	North Dakota	45.5
34	Ohio	7.0
23	Oklahoma	10.0
35	Oregon	6.6
14	Pennsylvania	15.2
42	Rhode Island	5.0
38	South Carolina	5.6
2	South Dakota	37.5
39	Tennessee	5.4
22	Texas	10.2
48	Utah	2.5
8	Vermont	20.0
23	Virginia	10.0
32	Washington	7.4
6	West Virginia	20.8
19	Wisconsin	11.8
9	Wyoming	18.2

RANK ORDER

RANK	STATE	PERCENT
1	North Dakota	45.5
2	South Dakota	37.5
3	Indiana	25.0
4	Kentucky	23.9
5	Montana	21.4
6	West Virginia	20.8
7	Illinois	20.2
8	Vermont	20.0
9	Iowa	18.2
9	Wyoming	18.2
11	Louisiana	17.7
12	Alaska	16.7
13	Minnesota	16.0
14	Pennsylvania	15.2
15	Maine	14.3
16	Delaware	13.3
17	Arkansas	13.0
18	Nevada	12.8
19	Wisconsin	11.8
20	Missouri	11.3
21	North Carolina	10.5
22	Texas	10.2
23	Oklahoma	10.0
23	Virginia	10.0
25	Alabama	9.9
26	Idaho	9.3
27	Michigan	8.2
28	Arizona	8.0
28	Mississippi	8.0
30	New Mexico	7.7
31	Georgia	7.6
32	New York	7.4
32	Washington	7.4
34	Ohio	7.0
35	Oregon	6.6
36	Massachusetts	6.1
37	Kansas	5.9
38	South Carolina	5.6
39	Maryland	5.4
39	Tennessee	5.4
41	Florida	5.2
42	Connecticut	5.0
42	Rhode Island	5.0
44	New Hampshire	4.5
45	Nebraska	3.8
46	California	3.7
47	Colorado	3.5
48	Utah	2.5
49	New Jersey	1.8
50	Hawaii	0.0
	District of Columbia	0.0

Source: CQ Press using data from United States Coast Guard
"Boating Statistics 2014" (http://www.uscgboating.org/statistics/accident_statistics.php)

*Alcohol involvement in a boating accident includes any accident in which alcoholic beverages are consumed in the boat and the investigating official has determined that the operator was impaired or affected while operating the boat.

Railroad Accidents and Incidents in 2014

National Total = 12,007*

ALPHA ORDER

RANK	STATE	ACCIDENTS	% of USA
17	Alabama	206	1.7%
42	Alaska	55	0.5%
38	Arizona	93	0.8%
27	Arkansas	162	1.3%
4	California	790	6.6%
26	Colorado	163	1.4%
29	Connecticut	134	1.1%
39	Delaware	73	0.6%
8	Florida	331	2.8%
10	Georgia	288	2.4%
50	Hawaii	1	0.0%
41	Idaho	57	0.5%
2	Illinois	1,011	8.4%
7	Indiana	345	2.9%
24	Iowa	165	1.4%
19	Kansas	201	1.7%
25	Kentucky	164	1.4%
12	Louisiana	236	2.0%
45	Maine	28	0.2%
28	Maryland	150	1.2%
12	Massachusetts	236	2.0%
20	Michigan	199	1.7%
11	Minnesota	270	2.2%
35	Mississippi	102	0.8%
16	Missouri	213	1.8%
34	Montana	114	0.9%
15	Nebraska	219	1.8%
44	Nevada	37	0.3%
49	New Hampshire	8	0.1%
5	New Jersey	782	6.5%
37	New Mexico	95	0.8%
1	New York	1,387	11.6%
21	North Carolina	197	1.6%
31	North Dakota	121	1.0%
9	Ohio	303	2.5%
31	Oklahoma	121	1.0%
30	Oregon	122	1.0%
6	Pennsylvania	647	5.4%
47	Rhode Island	22	0.2%
33	South Carolina	120	1.0%
48	South Dakota	19	0.2%
23	Tennessee	179	1.5%
3	Texas	874	7.3%
43	Utah	49	0.4%
45	Vermont	28	0.2%
18	Virginia	203	1.7%
14	Washington	220	1.8%
36	West Virginia	97	0.8%
22	Wisconsin	189	1.6%
40	Wyoming	71	0.6%

RANK ORDER

RANK	STATE	ACCIDENTS	% of USA
1	New York	1,387	11.6%
2	Illinois	1,011	8.4%
3	Texas	874	7.3%
4	California	790	6.6%
5	New Jersey	782	6.5%
6	Pennsylvania	647	5.4%
7	Indiana	345	2.9%
8	Florida	331	2.8%
9	Ohio	303	2.5%
10	Georgia	288	2.4%
11	Minnesota	270	2.2%
12	Louisiana	236	2.0%
12	Massachusetts	236	2.0%
14	Washington	220	1.8%
15	Nebraska	219	1.8%
16	Missouri	213	1.8%
17	Alabama	206	1.7%
18	Virginia	203	1.7%
19	Kansas	201	1.7%
20	Michigan	199	1.7%
21	North Carolina	197	1.6%
22	Wisconsin	189	1.6%
23	Tennessee	179	1.5%
24	Iowa	165	1.4%
25	Kentucky	164	1.4%
26	Colorado	163	1.4%
27	Arkansas	162	1.3%
28	Maryland	150	1.2%
29	Connecticut	134	1.1%
30	Oregon	122	1.0%
31	North Dakota	121	1.0%
31	Oklahoma	121	1.0%
33	South Carolina	120	1.0%
34	Montana	114	0.9%
35	Mississippi	102	0.8%
36	West Virginia	97	0.8%
37	New Mexico	95	0.8%
38	Arizona	93	0.8%
39	Delaware	73	0.6%
40	Wyoming	71	0.6%
41	Idaho	57	0.5%
42	Alaska	55	0.5%
43	Utah	49	0.4%
44	Nevada	37	0.3%
45	Maine	28	0.2%
45	Vermont	28	0.2%
47	Rhode Island	22	0.2%
48	South Dakota	19	0.2%
49	New Hampshire	8	0.1%
50	Hawaii	1	0.0%
	District of Columbia	110	0.9%

Source: U.S. Department of Transportation, Federal Railroad Administration, Office of Safety Analysis
"Railroad Accidents and Incidents" (Table 1.11, http://safetydata.fra.dot.gov/OfficeofSafety/Default.aspx)
*Accidents or incidents include all events reportable to the U.S. Department of Transportation. These include train accidents causing damage above an established threshold; highway-rail grade crossing incidents involving impact between railroad equipment and highway users at crossings; and all other reportable incidents that cause a fatality or injury to any person or an occupational illness to a railroad employee. There were 781 fatalities involving railroads.

Railroad Mileage Operated in 2012

National Total = 138,524 Miles of Railroad*

ALPHA ORDER

RANK	STATE	MILES	% of USA
21	Alabama	3,194	2.3%
45	Alaska	506	0.4%
36	Arizona	1,643	1.2%
25	Arkansas	2,698	1.9%
3	California	5,295	3.8%
26	Colorado	2,662	1.9%
46	Connecticut	364	0.3%
48	Delaware	250	0.2%
24	Florida	2,900	2.1%
7	Georgia	4,653	3.4%
50	Hawaii	0	0.0%
37	Idaho	1,623	1.2%
2	Illinois	6,986	5.0%
9	Indiana	4,075	2.9%
11	Iowa	3,869	2.8%
6	Kansas	4,855	3.5%
28	Kentucky	2,608	1.9%
23	Louisiana	2,927	2.1%
40	Maine	1,116	0.8%
43	Maryland	758	0.5%
42	Massachusetts	973	0.7%
12	Michigan	3,542	2.6%
8	Minnesota	4,450	3.2%
29	Mississippi	2,452	1.8%
10	Missouri	3,957	2.9%
20	Montana	3,200	2.3%
15	Nebraska	3,375	2.4%
39	Nevada	1,192	0.9%
47	New Hampshire	344	0.2%
41	New Jersey	981	0.7%
34	New Mexico	1,837	1.3%
14	New York	3,447	2.5%
18	North Carolina	3,258	2.4%
16	North Dakota	3,330	2.4%
4	Ohio	5,288	3.8%
17	Oklahoma	3,273	2.4%
30	Oregon	2,396	1.7%
5	Pennsylvania	5,151	3.7%
49	Rhode Island	19	0.0%
31	South Carolina	2,311	1.7%
35	South Dakota	1,753	1.3%
27	Tennessee	2,649	1.9%
1	Texas	10,469	7.6%
38	Utah	1,343	1.0%
44	Vermont	590	0.4%
19	Virginia	3,215	2.3%
22	Washington	3,192	2.3%
32	West Virginia	2,226	1.6%
13	Wisconsin	3,449	2.5%
33	Wyoming	1,860	1.3%

RANK ORDER

RANK	STATE	MILES	% of USA
1	Texas	10,469	7.6%
2	Illinois	6,986	5.0%
3	California	5,295	3.8%
4	Ohio	5,288	3.8%
5	Pennsylvania	5,151	3.7%
6	Kansas	4,855	3.5%
7	Georgia	4,653	3.4%
8	Minnesota	4,450	3.2%
9	Indiana	4,075	2.9%
10	Missouri	3,957	2.9%
11	Iowa	3,869	2.8%
12	Michigan	3,542	2.6%
13	Wisconsin	3,449	2.5%
14	New York	3,447	2.5%
15	Nebraska	3,375	2.4%
16	North Dakota	3,330	2.4%
17	Oklahoma	3,273	2.4%
18	North Carolina	3,258	2.4%
19	Virginia	3,215	2.3%
20	Montana	3,200	2.3%
21	Alabama	3,194	2.3%
22	Washington	3,192	2.3%
23	Louisiana	2,927	2.1%
24	Florida	2,900	2.1%
25	Arkansas	2,698	1.9%
26	Colorado	2,662	1.9%
27	Tennessee	2,649	1.9%
28	Kentucky	2,608	1.9%
29	Mississippi	2,452	1.8%
30	Oregon	2,396	1.7%
31	South Carolina	2,311	1.7%
32	West Virginia	2,226	1.6%
33	Wyoming	1,860	1.3%
34	New Mexico	1,837	1.3%
35	South Dakota	1,753	1.3%
36	Arizona	1,643	1.2%
37	Idaho	1,623	1.2%
38	Utah	1,343	1.0%
39	Nevada	1,192	0.9%
40	Maine	1,116	0.8%
41	New Jersey	981	0.7%
42	Massachusetts	973	0.7%
43	Maryland	758	0.5%
44	Vermont	590	0.4%
45	Alaska	506	0.4%
46	Connecticut	364	0.3%
47	New Hampshire	344	0.2%
48	Delaware	250	0.2%
49	Rhode Island	19	0.0%
50	Hawaii	0	0.0%
	District of Columbia	20	0.0%

Source: Association of American Railroads
"Railroads and States" (https://www.aar.org/data-center/railroads-states)
*Includes Class I and non-Class I miles. Excludes trackage rights. Synonymous with route-miles, so that a mile of single track is counted the same as a mile of double track.

Sources

ACT, Inc.
500 ACT Drive, P.O. Box 168
Iowa City, IA 52243-0168
319-337-1000
www.act.org

Administration for Children and Families
U.S. Dept. of Health and Human Services
330 C Street, SW
Washington, DC 20201
202-401-9215
www.acf.hhs.gov

American Cancer Society, Inc.
250 Williams Street, NW
Atlanta, GA 30303
800-227-2345
www.cancer.org

American Dental Association
211 E. Chicago Avenue
Chicago, IL 60611-2678
312-440-2500
www.ada.org

American Hospital Association
155 N. Wacker Drive
Chicago, IL 60606
312-422-3000
www.aha.org

American Medical Association
330 N. Wabash Avenue
Chicago, IL 60611-5885
800-621-8335
www.ama-assn.org

Association of American Railroads
425 Third Street, SW, Suite 1000
Washington, DC 20024
202-639-2100
www.aar.org

Bureau of Economic Analysis
U.S. Department of Commerce
1441 L Street, NW
Washington, DC 20005
202-606-9900
www.bea.gov

Bureau of Justice Statistics
U.S. Department of Justice
810 Seventh Street, NW
Washington, DC 20531
202-307-0765
www.bjs.gov

Bureau of Labor Statistics
U.S. Department of Labor
2 Massachusetts Avenue, NE
Washington, DC 20212-0001
202-691-5200
www.bls.gov

Bureau of Transportation Statistics
U.S. Department of Transportation
1200 New Jersey Avenue, SE
Washington, DC 20590
800-853-1351
www.rita.dot.gov

Census Bureau
4600 Silver Hill Road
Washington, DC 20233-0001
800-923-8282
www.census.gov

Centers for Disease Control and Prevention
1600 Clifton Road
Atlanta, GA 30329-4027
800-232-4636
www.cdc.gov

Centers for Medicare and Medicaid Services
7500 Security Boulevard
Baltimore, MD 21244-1850
877-267-2323
www.cms.hhs.gov

College Board
250 Vesey Street
New York, NY 10281
212-713-8000
www.collegeboard.org

Economic Research Service
U.S. Department of Agriculture
1400 Independence Avenue, SW
Mail Stop 1800
Washington, DC 20250-0002
202-694-5139
www.ers.usda.gov

Energy Information Administration
US Department of Energy
1000 Independence Avenue, SW
Washington, DC 20585
202-586-8800
www.eia.doe.gov

Environmental Protection Agency
Ariel Rios Building
1200 Pennsylvania Avenue, NW
Washington, DC 20460
202-272-0167
www.epa.gov

Federal Bureau of Investigation
J Edgar Hoover Building
935 Pennsylvania Avenue, NW
Washington, DC 20535-0001
202-324-3000
www.fbi.gov

Federal Highway Administration
US Department of Transportation
1200 New Jersey Avenue, SE
Washington, DC 20590
202-366-4000
www.fhwa.dot.gov

Federation of Tax Administrators
444 North Capitol Street, NW, Suite 348
Washington, DC 20001
202-624-5890
www.taxadmin.org

Food and Nutrition Service
U.S. Department of Agriculture
3101 Park Center Drive
Alexandria, VA 22302
703-305-2062
www.fns.usda.gov

General Services Administration
1800 F Street, NW
Washington, DC 20450
800-488-3111
www.gsa.gov

Health Resources and Services Administration
Division of Practitioner Data Banks
5600 Fishers Lane
Rockville, MD 20857
301-443-3376
www.hrsa.gov

Institute of Museum and Library Services
1800 M Street, NW, 9th Floor
Washington, DC 20036-5802
202-653-4657
www.imls.gov

Internal Revenue Service
U.S. Department of the Treasury
1111 Constitution Avenue, NW
Washington, DC 20224
202-622-5000
www.irs.gov

Medical Expenditure Panel Survey
Agency for Healthcare Research and Quality
5600 Fishers Lane
Rockville, MD 20857
301-427-1364
www.meps.ahrq.gov

National Agricultural Statistics Service
1400 Independence Avenue, SW
Washington, DC 20250
800-727-9540
www.nass.usda.gov

National Assembly of State Arts Agencies
1200 18th Street, NW, Suite 1100
Washington, DC 20036
202-347-6352
www.nasaa-arts.org

National Center for Education Statistics
U.S. Department of Education
550 12th Street, SW
Washington, DC 20036
202-403-5551
www.nces.ed.gov

National Center for Health Statistics
U.S. Department of Health and Human Services
3311 Toledo Road
Hyattsville, MD 20782
800-232-4636
www.cdc.gov/nchs/

National Conference of State Legislatures
7700 E. First Place
Denver, CO 80230
303-364-7700
www.ncsl.org

National Education Association
1201 16th Street, NW
Washington, DC 20036-3290
202-833-4000
www.nea.org

National Highway Traffic Safety Administration
1200 New Jersey Avenue, SE
Washington, DC 20590
888-327-4236
www.nhtsa.gov

National Institute on Alcohol Abuse and Alcoholism
5635 Fishers Lane, MSC 9304
Bethesda, MD 20892-9304
301-443-3860
www.niaaa.nih.gov

National Oceanic & Atmospheric Administration
U.S. Department of Commerce
1401 Constitution Avenue, NW, Room 5128
Washington, DC 20230
202-482-6090
www.noaa.gov

Office of Management and Budget
725 17th Street, NW
Washington, DC 20503
202-395-3080
www.USAspending.gov

Project on Student Debt
Institute for College Access and Success
405 14th Street, 11th Floor
Oakland, CA 94612
510-318-7900
http://ticas.org/posd/home

Social Security Administration
Windsor Park Building
6401 Security Boulevard
Baltimore, MD 21235
800-772-1213 (information)
www.ssa.gov

Storm Prediction Center
National Weather Service
120 David Boren Boulevard
Norman, OK 73072
405-579-0771
www.spc.noaa.gov

Tax Foundation
1325 G Street, NW, Suite 950
Washington, DC 20005
202-464-6200
www.taxfoundation.org

U.S. Department of Defense
Directorate for Public Inquiry and Analysis
Room 2E565 The Pentagon
1400 Defense Pentagon
Washington, DC 20301-1400
703-571-3343
www.defense.gov

U.S. Department of Veterans Affairs
810 Vermont Avenue, NW
Washington, DC 20420
800-827-1000
www.va.gov

U.S. Geological Survey
12201 Sunrise Valley Drive
Reston, VA 20192
888-275-8747
www.usgs.gov

Index

A

Abortions and rate, 395, 396
Accidents, deaths by, 405, 406
Acres
    harvested, 16–19
    per farm, 5
    planted, 15
ACT test scores, 135
Active duty military personnel, 77
Adjusted Gross Income, federal, 263, 264
Admission, date of states', xix
AFDC program (see TANF program)
Age, median, 477
Aggravated assaults, 44, 45
AGI, 263, 264
Agriculture, 3–26
Aid to Families with Dependent Children program (see TANF program)
AIDS, deaths by, 413, 414
Air bags, lives saved by, 575
Airports, number of, 592
Alcohol consumption, 415
Alcoholic beverage tax revenue, state, 347, 348
American Indian population, 469, 470
Animals, farm, 20, 21, 24, 25
Annual pay, average, 169, 170
Area of states, 241–243
Arts funding, state, 164
Asian population, 467, 468
Assaults, 44, 45

B

Bankruptcy filings, 110–112
Births
    low birthweight, 391
    number, 389
    rates, 390
    to teenage mothers, 392
    to unmarried women, 393
Black population, 463, 464
Boat accidents, 594
Books, library, 160, 161
Bridges, 568, 569
Building permits, 432–434
Buildings and farmland, value of, 6, 7
Burglaries, 49, 50
Business climate, 113

C

Cancer
    cases, 403, 404
    deaths by, 401, 402
Cattle, 20
Cerebrovascular diseases, deaths by, 407, 408
Chickens, 25
Child restraints, lives saved by, 575
Child support collections, 556
Cigarette taxes, 346
Civilian labor force, 182–189
Coal
    mines, 225
    production, of 226
College and universities
    enrollment, 152–155
    number of, 151
    student costs, 147, 148
    student debt, 149, 150
Commodities, income from farm, 11
Community development and housing expenditures, 446–448
Community hospitals, 387, 388
Companies, Fortune 500, 109
Construction employees, 191, 192
Consumption, alcohol, 415
Consumption, energy, 211, 212
Consumption, personal 106–109
Contract awards, federal, 281, 282
Contracts, defense, 73, 74
Correctional population, 59–62
Corrections, expenditures for, 65
Cows, 21–23
Crime
    change in, 31, 34, 48
    number of, 29, 32, 35, 38, 40, 42, 44, 47, 49, 51, 53
    rates of, 30, 33, 36, 39, 41, 43, 45, 47, 48, 50, 52, 54
Crops
    harvest of, 16–19
    income from, 12

D

Death penalty prisoners, 62
Deaths
    by cause, 400, 401, 404–413
    infant, 397, 398
    numbers of, 399
    rates of, 400
Debt
    local government, 370, 371
    state and local government, 317, 318
    state government, 353, 354
    student, 149, 150
Defense
    contracts, 73, 74
    expenditures, 71, 72
    grants, 75, 76
    personnel, 77, 78
Deficient bridges, 568, 569
Disability program, federal, 532, 533
Disposable income, 98, 99
Districts, school, 118
Divorces, 505, 506
Doctors, 383, 384
Drivers, 582, 583
Dropout rate, high school, 134
Drunk driving fatalities, 578, 579

E

Earnings, manufacturing workers, 174–176
Economy, 85–114
Education, 117–166
Education expenditures, 136–145
Educational attainment
    advanced degree, 157
    college, 156
    high school, 131–133
Eggs produced, 26

Elections and voting, 512–516
Electricity
    average monthly bill, 216–218
    from renewable sources, 219, 220
Electronic books, rate of, 161
Elementary/secondary school
    enrollment, 120, 122
    expenditures, 139–141
    schools, 119, 121
Employed civilian labor force, 182
Employment
    construction, 191, 192
    education and health services, 193, 194
    federal government, 291, 292
    finance, 195, 196
    government (all levels), 197, 198
    leisure and hospitality, 199, 200
    local government, 371, 372
    manufacturing, 201, 202
    mining and logging, 203, 204
    nonfarm, 189–208
    number of employees, 181
    professional and business services, 205, 206
    state and local government, 319, 320
    state government, 355, 356
    trade, transportation and public utilities, 207, 208
Energy
    consumption, 211, 212
    expenditures, 214, 215
    prices, 213
English, population speaking language other than, 498, 499
Environment and energy, 211–238
Expenditures, federal government
    assistance, 283, 284, 289, 290
    contract awards, 281, 282
    defense, 71, 72
    homeland security, 69, 70
    grants, 285, 286
    loans, 289, 290
    other financial assistance, 289, 290
Expenditures, personal consumption 106–109
Expenditures, state and local government
    corrections, 65
    education, 136–145
    housing and community development, 446–448
    judicial and legal, 66
    police, 64
    public welfare programs, 524–526
    total, 313, 314
Exports, 90, 91

F

Faculty salaries, 125, 126, 146
Family, average size, 507
Farm
    animals, 20, 21, 24, 25
    income, 8–14
    land in, 4, 5
    number of, 3
    value, 6, 7
Fatalities
    drunk driving, 578, 579
    from hazardous weather, 250, 252
    highway, 571–574, 577–581
    older drivers, 580
    young drivers, 581
Fathers, single, 426
Federal government
    employees, 291, 292
    expenditures, 279–290
    finance, 257–292
    taxes, 259–278
Female population, 459
Finance
    employees in, 195, 196
    federal government, 259–292
    local, 358–371
    state, 322–357
    state and local government, 295–321
Firearms, murders involving, 37
Food insecurity, 547
Food stamp program, 548–552
Fortune 500 companies, 114
Fossil fuel emissions, 230–232

G

Gallon, miles per, 591
Gasoline
    tax rates, 341
    usage, 227, 228
Gay marriage, 428
Geography, 241–256
Government
    employees, all levels, 197, 198
    farm payments, 14
    finance, federal, 259–292
    finance, state and local, 295–375
Graduates
    college, 156, 157
    high school, 131–133
Graduation rate, high school 133
Grain harvested, 17
Gross domestic product, 85–89
Guns, in murders, 37

H

Harvested acres, 16–19
Hawaiian native population, 471, 472
Hazardous waste sites, 236–238
Hazardous weather
    costs of, 253
    fatalities, 250, 252
Head Start program, 165, 166
Health insurance
    coverage, 377–381
    employment-based, 379
    premiums, 377, 378
Heart diseases, deaths by, 409, 410
High school
    dropout rate, 134
    graduates, 131–133
Higher education
    enrollment, 152–155
    expenditures, 143–145
    graduates, 156, 157
    institutions, 151
    salaries, 146
    student costs, 147, 148
    student debt, 149, 150
Highest points of elevation, 244
Highway
    bridges, 567–569
    condition of, 566, 568, 569
    fatalities, 571–574, 577–581
    federal funding, 559, 560
    mileage, 561–565
Hispanic population, 465, 466
Hogs and pigs, 24
Homeland security grants, 69, 70
Homeownership
    percent housing units owner-occupied, 431
    percent housing units renter-occupied, 443
    percent with mortgages, 438
    rate of, 442
Hospitals, 387, 388
Hourly earnings, of manufacturing employees, 174
House of Representatives, seats in U.S., 508, 509
Households
    by head of, 424–426
    income of, 100
    number of, 421
    persons per, 422
    same-sex, 427, 428
    using food stamps, 552
Houses
    median value of, 435
    prices of, 436, 437
Housing and community development expenditures, 446–448
Housing units
    new, 432–434
    per square mile, 430
    total, 429
    value of, 433

I

Imports, 92, 93
Income
    disposable, 98, 99
    farm, 8–14
    household, 100
    personal, 94–98
    real, 102–105
Individual income tax revenue
    federal, 261, 262
    state, 333, 334

Infant mortality, 397, 398
Inland waterways, miles of, 593
Insurance coverage, health, 377, 381
Intergovernmental revenue, 297–299, 324, 325, 360, 361
Internet terminals in public libraries, 162, 163
Interstate highways, 563
Iraq and Afghanistan, U.S. military fatalities in, 81, 82

J
Job growth, 189
Judicial and legal expenditures, 66

L
Labor and employment, 169–208
Labor force
   civilian, 181–188
      women in, 186–188
Land area, 242
Larceny-theft, 51, 52
Legislators, state, 510, 511
Libraries, public, 158–163
Livestock
   income from, 13
   number by type, 20, 21, 24, 25
Loans
   federal government, 287, 288
   student debt, 149, 150
Local government
   debt, 370, 371
   employees, 372–374
   expenditures, 366–369
   revenue, 358–365
Low birthweight births, 391
Lowest points of elevation, 244
Lunch program, school, 555

M
Male population, 458
Male to female ratio, 460
Manufacturing
   employees, 201, 202
   workers hours, 176
   workers pay, 174, 175
Marriages, 500–504
Married couples, households headed by, 424, 428
Mass transit, commuters using, 589
Mean elevation, 246
Medicaid
   enrollment, 538, 539
   expenditures, 540, 541
Medicare
   enrollees, 534, 535
   payments, 536, 537
Migration of population, 495, 496
Mileage
   road, 561–565
   state, 241–243
Military
   contracts, 73, 74
   fatalities in Iraq and Afghanistan, 81, 82

grants, 75, 76
personnel, 77, 78
Milk cows, 21–23
Milk production, 22, 23
Minimum wage rates, 173
Mixed race population (see Multiple race population)
Mortality, infant, 397, 398
Mortgage median payment, 438
Motor fuels tax revenue, state, 339, 340
Motor vehicle
   state tax revenue, 343, 344
   thefts, 53, 54
Multiple race population, 475, 476
Murders, 35–37

N
National Guard and Reserve, 78
National Parks
   land, in 254
   visits to, 255, 256
National School Lunch Program participants, 555
Native Hawaiian population, 471, 472
Natural gas
   consumption, 224
   prices, 221–223
Nonfarm employees, 190–208
Nurses, 385

O
OASDI (Social Security program), 527–531
Oil production, daily, 229

P
Pacific Islander population, 471, 472
Pay, average annual, 169, 170
Permits, building, 432–434
Personal bankruptcy rate, 111, 112
Personal income
   change in, 95, 97, 103
   per capita, 96, 99, 104
   taxes as a percent of, 305, 312, 332
   total, 94, 102
Persons per household, 422
Physicians, 383, 384
Pigs and hogs, 24
Police
   expenditures, for 64
   rate of, 63
Pollution
   air, 234
   total releases, 233
   water, 235
Population
   by age, 477–493
   correctional, 59
   Hispanic, 465, 466
   projected, 456
   by race, 461–464, 467–476
   school-age, 117
   by sex, 458–460

per square mile, 457
total, 450–452
Poverty
   children in, 521
   families in, 522, 523
   female-headed families in, 523
   rate, 519
   senior citizens in, 520
Premiums, health insurance, 377, 378
Prenatal care, lack of, 394
Prices, energy, 213
Prisoners, 59–62
Private elementary/secondary schools, 119
Private school students, elementary/secondary, 120
Property crimes, 46–48
Property tax revenue, state and local, 308–311
Public aid, percent receiving, 542
Public libraries, 158–163
Public utilities, transportation and trade employees, 207, 208
Public welfare expenditures, 524–526
Pupil-teacher ratio, 124

R
Railroad mileage, 596
Rapes, 38–41
Real estate taxes, median, 441
Regional price parities, 101
Registered voters, 512–516
Registrations, vehicle, 584, 585
Rental
   median payment, 444
      percent housing units renter-occupied, 443
      percent renters spending more than 30% of income on rent, 445
Reserve and National Guard personnel, 78
Revenue
   federal government tax, 259–266
   local government, 358–365
   state and local government, 295–312
   state government, 322–349
Road mileage, 561–565
Roadway condition, 566
Robberies, 42, 43

S
Safety belt usage, 576, 577
Salaries
   government, 321, 357, 374
   teachers, 125, 126, 146
Sales tax revenue
   state, 337–348
   state and local, 306, 307
Same-sex households, 427, 428
School
   districts, 118
   enrollment, 120, 122, 152–155
   number of, 119, 121, 151
   population, 117
Seat belt usage, 576, 577
Seat belts, lives saved by, 575

Single fathers, percent of households headed by, 426
Single mothers, percent of households headed by, 425
Single person households, 423
Smokers, 416
Social Security program
    beneficiaries, 530, 532
    payments, 527, 528, 531
Social welfare, 519–556
Soybeans harvested, 18
Spanish, percent speaking, 499
Speeding, fatalities from, 573
SSI program, 532, 533
State and local government
    debt, 317, 318
    employees, 319–321
    finance, 295–374
State government
    debt, 353, 354
    employees, 355–357
    finance, 322–357
    legislators, 510, 511
    taxes, 330–348
State (domestic) product, gross, 85–89
Statehood, year of admission to, xvii
States
    area (square miles) of, xviii
    birds, official, xix
    capitals of, xvii
    flowers, official, xix
    nicknames for, xvii
    songs, official, xix
    trees, official, xix
Street mileage, 561–565
Suicide, deaths by, 411, 412
Sunny days, percent of, 248
Supplemental Security Income program, 532, 533

T
TANF program, 543–546
Tax burden, state and local, 312
Taxes
    climate, 113
    federal, 259–278
    local, 364, 365
    projected vs. actual state, 329
    real estate, 441
    state, 330, 331
    state and local, 302–312
Teachers
    elementary/secondary school, 123
    ratio to pupils, 124
    salaries, 125, 126, 146
Teenage mothers, births to, 392
Temperature, daily mean, 247
Theft and larceny, 51, 53
Thefts, motor vehicle, 53, 54
Tobacco tax revenue, state, 344, 345
Tornadoes, 251, 252
Toxic releases
    air, 234
    fossil fuel, 230–232
    total, 233
    water, 235
Transportation, public utilities and trade employees, 207, 208
Travel
    to work, 587–589
    vehicle miles of, 569
Trucks, in crashes, 574
Tuition, college, 147, 148

U
Unemployment, 184, 185
Unmarried women, births to, 393
Urban roads, 565

V
Vehicle
    miles of travel, 570
    miles per, 590
    registrations, 584, 585
    thefts, 53, 54
Veterans, 79, 80
Violent crime, 32–34
Voting and elections, 512–516

W
Wages
    average annual pay, 169, 170
    manufacturing workers, 174, 175
    state minimum wage rates, 173
Waste, toxic, 233–235
Water area, of states, 243
Waterways, miles of inland, 593
Weather, 247–252
Wheat harvested, 19
White population, 461, 462
White population, non-Hispanic, 473, 474
WIC program, 553, 554
Wind speed, 249
Women, Infants, and Children program, 553, 554
Women in labor force, 186–188
Work week, manufacturing workers, 176
Workers' compensation, 178–180